INGENIX.

ICD-10-CM: Preview of the Structures and Conventions of ICD-10-CM

Latest release of ICD-10-CM

ISBN: 978-1-56337-826-3
Item Number:
Book: 3218
Price: $89.95

Item Number:
CD: 1606
Price: $119.95
Available: Now

Train for the Successful Transition to ICD-10-CM.

ICD-10-CM codes are expected to replace the current ICD-9-CM system for medical documentation and reimbursement pending legislative approval. Preview the lastest draft of this code set now and learn to assign codes for main diagnoses, apply strategies for improving coded data and prepare for coding in a global arena.

← **Prepare for future coding systems**

← **Understand the impact of the conversion to ICD-10-CM**

← **Determine a course of action for implementation**

Key Features and Benefits

The *ICD-10-CM* reference provides the entire pre-release draft of the ICD-10-CM code set as written by the World Health Organization (WHO) and the National Center for Health Statistics (NCHS).

- **Official guidelines.** Learn the official guidance from the National Center for Health Statistics (NCHS) concerning this pre-release draft of ICD-10-CM.

- **ICD-10-CM conventions.** Familiarize yourself with the conventions used in ICD-10-CM.

- **Convenient, official index.** Navigate through the new coding system easily using the index to the tabular section and the index to the external causes.

- **Neoplasm Table and Drugs and Chemicals Table.** Get a first look at these important tables within ICD-10-CM.

- **View the complete set of ICD-10-CM codes.** There are 21 chapters: infectious and parasitic diseases through injuries, including external causes and reasons for visit.

- **Now Available! ICD-10-CM Data File.** Prepare your information systems and data collection processes with this source file that provides the complete list of codes with full descriptions for the very latest draft of ICD-10-CM for diagnoses and conditions affecting health status.

SAVE UP TO 20%

with source code FOBAW9

 Visit **www.shopingenix.com** and enter the source code in the lower right-hand corner and save 20%.

 Call toll-free **1.800.INGENIX** (464.3649), option 1 and save 15%.

Ingenix | Intelligence for Health Care | Call toll-free 1.800.INGENIX (464.3649), option 1.

100% Money Back Guarantee If our merchandise ever fails to meet your expectations, please contact our Customer Service Department toll-free at 1.800.INGENIX (464.3649), option 1, for an immediate response. Software: Credit will be granted for unopened packages only.

Also available from your medical bookstore or distributor.

FOBA09

INGENIX®

Order Form

Information

Customer No. _____ Contact No. _____

Source Code _____

Contact Name _____

Title _____ Specialty _____

Company _____

Street Address _____
NO PO BOXES, PLEASE

City _____ State _____ Zip _____

Telephone ( ) _____ Fax ( ) _____
IN CASE WE HAVE QUESTIONS ABOUT YOUR ORDER

E-mail _____ @ _____
REQUIRED FOR ORDER CONFIRMATION AND SELECT PRODUCT DELIVERY.

Ingenix respects your right to privacy. We will not sell or rent your e-mail address or fax number to anyone outside Ingenix and its business partners. If you would like to remove your name from Ingenix promotion, please call 1.800.ingenix (464.3649), option 1.

Product

Item No.	Qty	Description	Price	Total

Subtotal _____

UT, VA, TN, OH, CT, IA, MD, MN, NC & NJ residents, please add applicable   Sales tax _____

(See chart on the left)   Shipping & handling charges _____
All foreign orders, please call for shipping costs

Total _____

Payment

○ Please bill my credit card   ○ MasterCard   ○ VISA   ○ Amex   ○ Discover

Card No. | | | | | | | | | | | | | | | | Expires | _____
MONTH   YEAR

Signature _____

○ Check enclosed, made payable to: Ingenix, Inc.   ○ Please bill my office

Purchase Order No. _____
ATTACH COPY OF PURCHASE ORDER

FOBA09

March 2009

Dear Ingenix Customer:

This is your 2009 draft for the *ICD-10-PCS: The Complete Official Draft Code Set*.

The Centers for Medicare and Medicaid Services (CMS) is the agency charged with the responsibility of maintaining and updating the International Classification of Diseases 10th Revision Procedure Classification System (ICD-10-PCS). This 2009 draft represents the most current changes to the ICD-10-PCS as released by CMS.

Remember, the codes in ICD-10-PCS are not currently valid for any documentation or reporting of health care services. It is anticipated that several updates and revisions to the draft will be made by CMS prior to implementation of ICD-10-PCS; however, the basic structure will remain the same.

The Department of Health and Human Services (HHS) published the final rule regarding the adoption of both ICD-10-CM and ICD-10-PCS in the January 16, 2009, *Federal Register* (45 CFR part 162 [CMS—0013—F]). The compliance date for implementation of ICD-10-CM and ICD-10-PCS as a replacement for ICD-9-CM is October 1, 2013.

ICD-10-PCS would replace ICD-9-CM Volume 3, including the official coding guidelines, for the following procedures or other actions taken for diseases, injuries, and impairments on **hospital inpatients reported by hospitals**: prevention, diagnosis, treatment, and management.

We appreciate your choosing Ingenix to meet your ICD-10-PCS conversion preparation and coding training needs. If you have any questions or comments concerning your draft *ICD-10-PCS: The Complete Official Draft Code Set*, please do not hesitate to call out customer service department. The toll free number is 1-800-INGENIX (464-3649), option 1.

INGENIX.

ICD-10-PCS
The Complete Official Draft
Code Set

2009

Notice

ICD-10-PCS: The Complete Official Draft Code Set is designed to be an accurate and authoritative source regarding coding and every reasonable effort has been made to ensure accuracy and completeness of the content. However, Ingenix makes no guarantee, warranty, or representation that this publication is accurate, complete, or without errors. It is understood that Ingenix is not rendering any legal or other professional services or advice in this publication and that Ingenix bears no liability for any results or consequences that may arise from the use of this book. Please address all correspondence to:

Ingenix
2525 Lake Park Blvd
Salt Lake City, UT 84120

Our Commitment to Accuracy

Ingenix is committed to producing accurate and reliable materials. To report corrections, please visit www.ingenixonline.com/accuracy or email accuracy@ingenix.com. You can also reach customer service by calling 1.800.INGENIX (464.3649), option 1.

Copyright

Acknowledgments

Anita C. Hart, RHIA, CCS, CCS-P, *Product Manager*
Karen Schmidt, BSN, *Technical Director*
Stacy Perry, *Manager, Desktop Publishing*
Tracy Betzler, *Desktop Publishing Specialist*
Hope M. Dunn, *Desktop Publishing Specialist*
Kate Holden, *Editor*

Anita C. Hart, RHIA, CCS, CCS-P

Ms. Hart's experience includes conducting and publishing research in clinical medicine and human genetics for Yale University, Massachusetts General Hospital, and Massachusetts Institute of Technology. In addition, Ms. Hart has supervised medical records management, health information management, coding and reimbursement, and worker's compensation issues as the office manager for a physical therapy rehabilitation clinic. Ms. Hart is an expert in physician and facility coding, reimbursement systems, and compliance issues. Ms. Hart developed the *ICD-9-CM Changes: An Insider's View*. She has served as technical consultant for numerous other publications for hospital and physician practices. Currrently, Ms. Hart is the Product Manager for the ICD-9-CM and ICD-10-CM/PCS product lines.

Beth Ford, RHIT, CCS

Ms. Ford is a clinical/technical editor for Ingenix. She has extensive background in both physician and facility ICD-9-CM and CPT/HCPCS coding. Ms. Ford has served as a coding specialist, coding manager, coding trainer/ educator, and coding consultant, as well as a health information management director. She is an active member of the American Heath Information Management Association (AHIMA).

Melinda Stegman, MBA, CCS

Ms. Stegman has 28 years of experience in the HIM profession and has been responsible for managing the clinical aspects of the HSS/Ingenix HIM Consulting practice in the Washington, D.C., area office. Her areas of specialization include training on inpatient and DRG coding, outpatient coding, and ambulatory payment classifications (APCs) for HIM professionals, software developers, and other clients; developing an outpatient billing/coding compliance tool for a major accounting firm; and managing HIM consulting practices. Ms. Stegman is a regular contributing author for *Advance for Health Information Management Professionals* and for the *Journal of Health Care Compliance*. She has performed coding assessments and educational sessions throughout the country. Ms. Stegman is credentialed by the American Health Information Management Association (AHIMA) as a certified coding specialist (CCS) and holds a master of business administration degree with a concentration in health care management from the University of New Mexico–Albuquerque.

Contents

Preface

This draft of the International Classification of Diseases, 10th Revision, Procedure Classification System (ICD-10-PCS) has been developed as a replacement for volume 3 of the International Classification of Diseases, Ninth Revision (ICD-9-CM). The development of ICD-10-PCS was funded by the U.S. Centers for Medicare and Medicaid Services under contract nos. 90-138, 91-22300 500-95-0005 and HHSM-550-2004-00011C to 3M Health Information Systems. ICD-10-PCS has a multi-axial, seven-character, alphanumeric code structure that provides a unique code for all substantially different procedures and allows new procedures to be easily incorporated as new codes. The initial draft was formally tested and evaluated by an independent contractor; the final version was released in 1998, with annual updates since the final release.

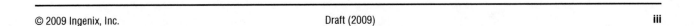

What's New for 2009

The Centers for Medicare and Medicaid Services is the agency charged with maintaining and updating the ICD-10-PCS. The most current changes were released by CMS in January 2009. A summary of the changes may be found on the CMS website at http://www.cms.hhs.gov/ICD10/01m_2009_ICD-10-PCS.asp#TopOfPage. The summary document *2009 Version— What's New* may be accessed directly by this link: http://www.cms.hhs.gov/ICD10/Downloads/PCS_whats_new_2009.pdf. Due to the unique structure of ICD-10-PCS, a change in a character value may affect many individual codes and several Code Tables.

Change Summary Table

2008 Total	New Codes	Revised Codes	Deleted Codes	2009 Total	New Values	Revised Values	Deleted Values
86,916	4,740	4,088	19,067	72,589	37	13	3

ICD-10-PCS Code Changes Summary by Section

Medical/Surgical Section (Section 0):
- New root operation U (*Supplement*) for character 3 for applicable body systems and body parts
- 9 new qualifiers for character 7 (e.g., applies to external heart assist systems, umbilical vein infusion devices, breast reconstruction flap procedures)
- 1 new device value for character 6 (applies to insertion, removal, and revision of external heart assist system)
- 3 new body part values for character 4 (applies to insertion, removal, and revision of applicable devices)
- 9 revised body part values for various body systems
- 2 body part values deleted (applies to ductus arteriosus and neck, left)

Medical and Surgical-related Sections (Section 1–9):
- 1 new qualifier (U—Amniotic fluid, diagnostic) for character 7 under section 1 Obstetrics
- 1 new qualifier (F—Other thoracic) for character 7 under section 4 Measurement and monitoring
- 5 new qualifiers for character 7 under section 5 Extracorporeal assistance and performance:
  - 7—Continuous positive airway pressure
  - 8—Intermittent positive airway pressure
  - 9—Continuous negative airway pressure
  - B—Intermittent negative airway pressure
  - C—Supersaturated
- 4 new qualifiers for body system A, Physiological systems, character 7 under section 6 Extracorporeal therapies:
  - 4—Head and neck vessels
  - 5—Heart
  - 6—Peripheral vessels
  - 7—Other vessels

- 6 new body region values for body system E, character 4 under section 8 Other procedures:
  - 2—Circulatory system
  - 9—Head and neck region
  - K—Musculoskeletal system
  - W—Trunk region
  - X—Upper extremity
  - Y—Lower extremity
- 3 new method values for body system E, character 6 under section 8 Other procedures:
  - B—Computer-assisted procedure
  - C—Robotic-assisted procedure
  - D—Near infrared spectroscopy
- 3 new qualifiers for body system E, character 7, under section 8 Other procedures:
  - F—With fluoroscopy
  - G—With computerized tomography
  - H—With magnetic resonance imaging
- 1 revised qualifier in section 1 (Obstetrics) for amniotic fluid (diagnostic added)
- 3 body region value reassignments in section 8 Other procedures:
  - H—Integumentary system and breast (previously 2)
  - U—Female reproductive system (previously 4)
  - V—Male reproductive system (previously 3)
- 1 deleted body region in section 8 Other procedures (whole body)

The index portion of ICD-10-PCS is derived directly from the PCS tables and is organized in the appropriate hierarchies of main terms and subterms. Although the index revisions were based on the changes in the tables, no new index terms were manually added in this update.

New appendix E, "Body Part Definitions," lists definitions of global body parts and regions and is arranged in two sections: one arranged by anatomical terms in alphabetical order, and one by PCS body part. The body part key definitions are considered "official."

New appendix F, "Physical Rehabilitation and Diagnostic Audiology Type Qualifiers and Definitions," which is arranged in 15 sections by specific treatment, assessment, training, or assistance provided.

Introduction

Volume 3 of the International Classification of Diseases Ninth Revision Clinical Modification (ICD-9-CM) has been used in the United States for reporting inpatient procedures since 1979. The structure of volume 3 of ICD-9-CM has not allowed new procedures associated with rapidly changing technology to be effectively incorporated as new codes. As a result, in 1992 the U.S. Centers for Medicare and Medicaid Services funded a project to design a replacement for volume 3 of ICD-9-CM. In 1995 CMS awarded 3M Health Information Systems a three-year contract to complete development of the replacement system. The new system is the ICD-10 Procedure Coding System (ICD-10-PCS).

History of ICD-10-PCS

The World Health Organization has maintained the International Classification of Diseases (ICD) for recording cause of death since 1893. It has updated the ICD periodically to reflect new discoveries in epidemiology and changes in medical understanding of disease.

The International Classification of Diseases Tenth Revision (ICD-10), published in 1992, is the latest revision of the ICD. The WHO authorized the National Center for Health Statistics (NCHS) to develop a clinical modification of ICD-10 for use in the United States. This version, called ICD-10-CM, is intended to replace the previous U.S. clinical modification, ICD-9-CM, that has been in use since 1979. ICD-9-CM contains a procedure classification; ICD-10-CM does not.

CMS, the agency responsible for maintaining the inpatient procedure code set in the United States, contracted with 3M Health Information Systems in 1993 to design and then develop a procedure classification system to replace volume 3 of ICD-9-CM.

The result, ICD-10-PCS, was initially completed in 1998. The code set has been updated annually since that time to ensure that ICD-10-PCS includes classifications for new procedures, devices, and technologies.

The development of ICD-10-PCS had as its goal the incorporation of four major attributes:

- **Completeness:** There should be a unique code for all substantially different procedures. In volume 3 of ICD-9-CM, procedures on different body parts, with different approaches, or of different types are sometimes assigned to the same code.

- **Expandability:** As new procedures are developed, the structure of ICD-10-PCS should allow them to be easily incorporated as unique codes.

- **Multi-axial codes:** ICD-10-PCS codes should consist of independent characters, with each individual component retaining its meaning across broad ranges of codes to the extent possible.

- **Standardized terminology:** ICD-10-PCS should include definitions of the terminology used. While the meaning of specific words varies in common usage, ICD-10-PCS should not include multiple meanings for the same term, and each term must be assigned a specific meaning. There are no eponyms or common procedure terms in ICD-10-PCS.

In the development of ICD-10-PCS, several general principles were followed:

- **Diagnostic information is not included in procedure description:** When procedures are performed for specific diseases or disorders, the disease or disorder is not contained in the procedure code. The diagnosis codes, not the procedure codes, specify the disease or disorder.

- **Explicit not otherwise specified (NOS) options are not provided:** Explicit "not otherwise specified," (NOS) options are not provided in ICD-10-PCS. A minimal level of specificity is required for each component of the procedure.

- **Limited use of not elsewhere classified (NEC) option:** Because all significant components of a procedure are specified in ICD-10-PCS, there is generally no need for a "not elsewhere classified" (NEC) code option. However, limited NEC options are incorporated into ICD-10-PCS where necessary. For example, new devices are frequently developed, and therefore it is necessary to provide an "other device" option for use until the new device can be explicitly added to the coding system.

- **Level of specificity:** All procedures currently performed can be specified in ICD-10-PCS. The frequency with which a procedure is performed was not a consideration in the development of the system. A unique code is available for variations of a procedure that can be performed.

ICD-10-PCS Code Structure

ICD-10-PCS has a seven-character alphanumeric code structure. Each character contains up to 34 possible values. Each value represents a specific option for the general character definition. The 10 digits 0–9 and the 24 letters A–H, J–N, and P–Z may be used in each character. The letters O and I are not used so as to avoid confusion with the digits 0 and 1. An ICD-10-PCS code is the result of a process rather than as a single fixed set of digits or alphabetic characters. The process consists of combining semi-independent values from among a selection of values, according to the rules governing the construction of codes.

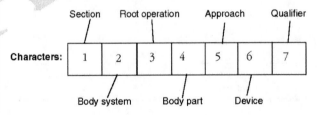

A code is derived by choosing a specific value for each of the seven characters. Based on details about the procedure performed, values for each character specifying the section, body system, root operation, body part, approach, device, and qualifier are assigned. Because the definition of each character is also a function of its physical position in the code, the same letter or number placed in a different position in the code has different meaning.

The seven characters that make up a complete code have specific meanings that vary for each of the 16 sections of the manual. (The resource section of this manual lists character meanings for each section along with body-part definitions.)

Procedures then are divided into sections that identify the general type of procedure (e.g., medical and surgical, obstetrics, imaging). The first character of the procedure code always specifies the section. The second through seventh characters have the same meaning within each section, but may mean different things in other sections. In all sections, the third character specifies the general type of procedure performed (e.g., resection, transfusion, fluoroscopy), while the other characters give additional information such as the body part and approach.

In ICD-10-PCS, the term *procedure* refers to the complete specification of the seven characters.

Number of Codes in ICD-10-PCS

At the time of this publication, there are 72,589 codes in the 2009 ICD-10-PCS. This is a substantial increase over the number of ICD-9-CM procedure codes. However, in 2009, approximately 19,067 codes were eliminated from ICD-10-PCS from the medical and surgical section as part of a planned streamlining and refinement initiated in 2006. This code reduction includes the deletion of certain body system values specified as "other" in order to facilitate more selective body part and system values. For 2009, 4,740 new codes were added to the system, combined with a deletion of 19,067 codes resulting in a total of 72,589 ICD-10-PCS codes.

The table structure of ICD-10-PCS permits the specification of a large number of codes on a single page.

ICD-10-PCS Manual

Index

Codes may be found in the index based on the general type of procedure (e.g., resection, transfusion, fluoroscopy), or a more commonly used term (e.g., appendectomy). For example, the code for percutaneous intraluminal dilation of the coronary arteries with an intraluminal device can be found in the Index under *dilation*, or a synonym of *dilation* (e.g., angioplasty). The Index then specifies the first three or four values of the code or directs the user to see another term.

Example:

> **Dilation**
>   *by* Body Part
>   Artery
>   Coronary, One Site 0270

Based on the first three values of the code provided in the Index, the corresponding table can be located. In the example above, the first three values indicate table 027 is to be referenced for code completion.

The tables and characters are arranged first by number and then by letter for each character (tables for 00-, 01-, 02-, etc., are followed by those for 0A-, 0B-, 0C-, etc., followed by 0B0, 0B1, 0B2, etc., followed by 0BA, 0BC, etc.).

Note: The Tables section must be used to construct a complete and valid code by specifying the last three or four values.

Tables

The Tables section is organized differently from ICD-9-CM. Each page in the section is composed of rows that specify the valid combinations of code values. In most sections of the system, the upper portion of each table contains a description of the first three characters of the procedure code. In the medical and surgical section, for example, the first three characters contain the name of the section, the body system, and the root operation performed.

For instance, the values *027* specify the section *medical and surgical* (0), the body system *heart and great vessels* (2) and the root operation *dilation* (7). As shown in table 027, the root operation (*dilation*) is accompanied by its definition.

The lower portion of the table specifies all the valid combinations of characters 4 through 7. The four columns in the table specify the last four characters. In the medical and surgical section they are labeled body part, approach, device and qualifier, respectively. Each row in the table specifies the valid combination of values for characters 4 through 7.

0 Medical and Surgical
2 Heart and Great Vessels
7 Dilation: Expanding an orifice or the lumen of a tubular body part

Body Part Character 4	Approach Character 5	Device Character 6	Qualifier Character 7
0 Coronary Artery, One Site 1 Coronary Artery, Two Sites 2 Coronary Artery, Three Sites 3 Coronary Artery, Four or More Sites	0 Open 3 Percutaneous 4 Percutaneous Endoscopic	4 Drug-eluting Intraluminal Device D Intraluminal Device Z No Device	6 Bifurcation Z No Qualifier
F Aortic Valve G Mitral Valve H Pulmonary Valve J Tricuspid Valve K Ventricle, Right P Pulmonary Trunk Q Pulmonary Artery, Right S Pulmonary Vein, Right T Pulmonary Vein, Left V Superior Vena Cava W Thoracic Aorta	0 Open 3 Percutaneous 4 Percutaneous Endoscopic	4 Drug-eluting Intraluminal Device D Intraluminal Device Z No Device	Z No Qualifier
R Pulmonary Artery, Left	0 Open 3 Percutaneous 4 Percutaneous Endoscopic	4 Drug-eluting Intraluminal Device D Intraluminal Device Z No Device	T Ductus Arteriosus Z No Qualifier

The rows of this table can be used to construct 204 unique procedure codes. For example, code 02703DZ specifies the procedure for dilation of one coronary artery using an intraluminal device via percutaneous approach (i.e., percutaneous transluminal coronary angioplasty with stent).

Following are examples of the valid combinations of characters 4 through 7 for the medical and surgical procedure dilation of the heart and great vessels (027):

027004Z	Dilation of coronary artery, one site with drug-eluting intraluminal device, open approach
02700DZ	Dilation of coronary artery, one site with intraluminal device, open approach
02700ZZ	Dilation, coronary artery, one site, open approach
027034Z	Dilation, coronary artery, one site with drug-eluting intraluminal device, percutaneous approach
02703DZ	Dilation, coronary artery, one site with intraluminal device, percutaneous approach
02703ZZ	Dilation, coronary artery, one site, percutaneous approach
027044Z	Dilation, coronary artery, one site with drug-eluting intraluminal device, percutaneous endoscopic approach
02704DZ	Dilation, coronary artery, one site with intraluminal device, percutaneous endoscopic approach
02704ZZ	Dilation, coronary artery, one site, percutaneous endoscopic approach

Each table contains only those combinations of values that make up a valid procedure code. In some instances, the tables are split, indicating that there is a restriction in the combination of character choices. In table 027 above, character 7, qualifier 6 Bifurcation can be used only with coronary artery body part characters 0–3 and character 7, qualifier T Ductus arteriosus can be used only with body part character R Pulmonary artery, left. The lower portion of table 001, shown below, is split into two sections; values of characters must be selected from within the same section of the table.

0   Medical and Surgical
0   Central Nervous System
1   Bypass: Altering the route of passage of the contents of a tubular body part

Body Part Character 4	Approach Character 5	Device Character 6	Qualifier Character 7
6 Cerebral Ventricle	**0** Open	**7** Autologous Tissue Substitute **J** Synthetic Substitute **K** Nonautologous Tissue Substitute	**0** Nasopharynx **1** Mastoid Sinus **2** Atrium **3** Blood Vessel **4** Pleural Cavity **5** Intestine **6** Peritoneal Cavity **7** Urinary Tract **8** Bone Marrow **B** Cerebral Cisterns
U Spinal Canal	**0** Open	**7** Autologous Tissue Substitute **J** Synthetic Substitute **K** Nonautologous Tissue Substitute	**4** Pleural Cavity **6** Peritoneal Cavity **7** Urinary Tract **9** Fallopian Tube

Body part value 6 may be in combination with device values 7, J, or K. Body part (character 4) value U may be used only in combination with qualifier (character 7) values of 4, 6, 7, and 9. In other words, code 001U073 is invalid since the qualifier character appears above the line separating the two sections of the table.

Note: In this manual, there are instances in which some tables due to length must be continued on the next page. Each section must be used separately and value selection must be made within the same section of the table.

Character Meanings

In each section each character has a specific meaning. Within a section all character meanings remain constant. The resource section of this manual lists character meanings for each section.

List of Codes

Valid codes can be constructed using each table. Each code has a text description that is complete.

Sections

Procedures are divided into sections that identify the general type of procedure (e.g., medical and surgical, obstetrics, imaging). The first character of the procedure code always specifies the section.

The sections are listed below:

0   Medical and surgical

1   Obstetrics

2   Placement

3   Administration

4   Measurement and monitoring

5   Extracorporeal assistance and performance

6   Extracorporeal therapies

7   Osteopathic

8   Other procedures

9   Chiropractic

B   Imaging

C   Nuclear medicine

D   Radiation oncology

F   Physical rehabilitation and diagnostic audiology

G   Mental health

H   Substance abuse treatment

Medical and Surgical Section (0)

Character Meaning

The seven characters for medical and surgical procedures have the following meaning:

Character	Meaning
1	Section
2	Body System
3	Root Operation
4	Body Part
5	Approach
6	Device
7	Qualifier

The medical and surgical section constitutes the vast majority of procedures reported in an inpatient setting. Medical and surgical procedure codes all have a first-character value of 0. The second character indicates the general body system (e.g., mouth and throat, gastrointestinal). The third character indicates the root operation, or specific objective, of the procedure (e.g., excision). The fourth character indicates the specific body part on which the procedure was performed (e.g., tonsils, duodenum). The fifth character indicates the approach used to reach the procedure site (e.g., open). The sixth character indicates whether a device was used in the procedure (e.g., synthetic substitute). The seventh character is qualifier, which has a specific meaning for each root operation. For example, the qualifier can be used to identify the destination site of a *bypass*. The first through fifth characters are always assigned a specific value, but the device (sixth character) and the qualifier (seventh character) are not applicable to all procedures. The value Z is used for the sixth and seventh characters to indicate that a specific device or qualifier does not apply to the procedure.

Section (Character 1)

Medical and surgical procedure codes all have a first-character value of 0.

Body Systems (Character 2)

Body systems for medical and surgical section codes are specified in the second character.

Body Systems

0   Central nervous system

1   Peripheral nervous system

2   Heart and great vessels

3   Upper arteries

4   Lower arteries

5   Upper veins

6   Lower veins

7   Lymphatic and hemic system

8   Eye

9   Ear, nose, sinus

B   Respiratory system

C   Mouth and throat

D   Gastrointestinal system

F   Hepatobiliary system and pancreas

G   Endocrine system

H   Skin and breast

J   Subcutaneous tissue and fascia

K   Muscles

L   Tendons

M   Bursae and ligaments

N   Head and facial bones

P   Upper bones

Q   Lower bones

R   Upper joints

S   Lower joints

T   Urinary system

U   Female reproductive system

V   Male reproductive system

W   Anatomical regions, general

X   Anatomical regions, upper extremities

Y   Anatomical regions, lower extremities

Root Operations (Character 3)

The root operation is specified in the third character. In the medical and surgical section there are 30 different root operations. The root operation identifies the objective of the procedure. Each root operation has a precise definition.

- *Alteration:* Modifying the natural anatomic structure of a body part without affecting the function of the body part

- *Bypass:* Altering the route of passage of the contents of a tubular body part

- *Change:* Taking out or off a device from a body part and putting back an identical or similar device in or on the same body part without cutting or puncturing the skin or a mucous membrane

- *Control:* Stopping, or attempting to stop, postprocedural bleeding

- *Creation:* Making a new structure that does not take over the place of a body part

- *Destruction:* Physical eradication of all or a portion of a body part by the direct use of energy, force, or a destructive agent

- *Detachment:* Cutting off all or a portion of the upper or lower extremities

- *Dilation:* Expanding an orifice or the lumen of a tubular body part

- *Division:* Cutting into a body part without draining fluids and/or gases from the body part in order to separate or transect a body part

- *Drainage:* Taking or letting out fluids and/or gases from a body part

- *Excision:* Cutting out or off, without replacement, a portion of a body part

- *Extirpation:* Taking or cutting out solid matter from a body part

- *Extraction:* Pulling or stripping out or off all or a portion of a body part by the use of force

- *Fragmentation:* Breaking solid matter in a body part into pieces

- *Fusion:* Joining together portions of an articular body part rendering the articular body part immobile

- *Insertion:* Putting in a nonbiological appliance that monitors, assists, performs, or prevents a physiological function but does not physically take the place of a body part

- *Inspection:* Visually and/or manually exploring a body part

- *Map:* Locating the route of passage of electrical impulses and/or locating functional areas in a body part

- *Occlusion:* Completely closing an orifice or lumen of a tubular body part

- *Reattachment:* Putting back in or on all or a portion of a separated body part to its normal location or other suitable location

- *Release:* Freeing a body part from an abnormal physical constraint

- *Removal:* Taking out or off a device from a body part

- *Repair:* Restoring, to the extent possible, a body part to its normal anatomic structure and function

- *Replacement:* Putting in or on biological or synthetic material that physically takes the place and/or function of all or a portion of a body part

- *Reposition:* Moving to its normal location or other suitable location all or a portion of a body part

- *Resection:* Cutting out or off, without replacement, all of a body part

- *Restriction:* Partially closing an orifice or lumen of a tubular body part

- *Revision:* Correcting, to the extent possible, a malfunctioning or displaced device

- *Supplement:* Putting in or on biological or synthetic material that physically reinforces and/or augments the function of a portion of a body part

- *Transfer:* Moving, without taking out, all or a portion of a body part to another location to take over the function of all or a portion of a body part

- *Transplantation:* Putting in or on all or a portion of a living body part taken from another individual or animal to physically take the place and/or function of all or a portion of a similar body part

The above definitions of root operation illustrate the precision of code values defined in the system. There is a clear distinction between each root operation.

A root operation specifies the objective of the procedure. The term *anastomosis* is not a root operation, because it is a means of joining and is always an integral part of another procedure (e.g., bypass, resection) with a specific objective. Similarly, *incision* is not a root operation, since it is always part of the objective of another procedure (e.g., division, drainage). The root operation *repair* in the medical and surgical section functions as a "not elsewhere classified" option. *Repair* is used when the procedure performed is not one of the other specific root operations.

Appendix A provides additional explanation and representative examples of the medical and surgical root operations. Appendix B groups all root operations in the medical and surgical section into subcategories and provides an example of each root operation.

Body Part (Character 4)

The body part is specified in the fourth character. The body part indicates the specific part of the body system on which the procedure was performed (e.g., duodenum). Tubular body parts are defined in ICD-10-PCS as those hollow body parts that provide a route of passage for solids, liquids, or gases. They include the cardiovascular system and body parts such as those contained in the gastrointestinal tract, genitourinary tract, biliary tract, and respiratory tract.

Approach (Character 5)

The technique used to reach the site of the procedure is specified in the fifth character. There are seven different approaches:

- *Open*: Cutting through the skin or mucous membrane and any other body layers necessary to expose the site of the procedure

- *Percutaneous*: Entry, by puncture or minor incision, of instrumentation through the skin or mucous membrane and any other body layers necessary to reach the site of the procedure

- *Percutaneous endoscopic*: Entry, by puncture or minor incision, of instrumentation through the skin or mucous membrane and any other body layers necessary to reach and visualize the site of the procedure

- *Via natural or artificial opening*: Entry of instrumentation through a natural or artificial external opening to reach the site of the procedure

- *Via natural or artificial opening endoscopic*: Entry of instrumentation through a natural or artificial external opening to reach and visualize the site of the procedure

- *Open with percutaneous endoscopic assistance*: Cutting through the skin or mucous membrane and any other body layers necessary to expose the site of the procedure, and entry, by puncture or minor incision, of instrumentation through the skin or mucous membrane and any other body layers necessary to aid in the performance of the procedure

- *External*: Procedures performed directly on the skin or mucous membrane and procedures performed indirectly by the application of external force through the skin or mucous membrane

The approach comprises three components: the access location, method, and type of instrumentation.

Access location: For procedures performed on an internal body part, the access location specifies the external site through which the site of the procedure is reached. There are two general types of access locations: skin or mucous membranes, and external orifices. Every approach value except external includes one of these two access locations. The skin or mucous membrane can be cut or punctured to reach the procedure site. All open and percutaneous approach values use this access location. The site of a procedure can also be reached through an external opening. External openings can be natural (e.g., mouth) or artificial (e.g., colostomy stoma).

Method: For procedures performed on an internal body part, the method specifies how the external access location is entered. An open method specifies cutting through the skin or mucous membrane and any other intervening body layers necessary to expose the site of the procedure. An instrumental method specifies the entry of instrumentation through the access location to the internal procedure site. Instrumentation can be introduced by puncture or minor incision, or through an external opening. The puncture or minor incision does not constitute an open approach because it does not expose the site of the procedure. An approach can define multiple methods. For example, open with percutaneous endoscopic assistance includes both the open

approach that exposes the body part and the placement of instrumentation into the body part to perform the procedure.

Type of instrumentation: For procedures performed on an internal body part, instrumentation means that specialized equipment is used to perform the procedure. Instrumentation is used in all internal approaches other than the basic open approach. Instrumentation may or may not include the capacity to visualize the procedure site. For example, the instrumentation used to perform a sigmoidoscopy permits the internal site of the procedure to be visualized, while the instrumentation used to perform a needle biopsy of the liver does not. The term "endoscopic" as used in approach values refers to instrumentation that permits a site to be visualized.

Procedures performed directly on the skin or mucous membrane are identified by the external approach (e.g., skin excision). Procedures performed indirectly by the application of external force are also identified by the external approach (e.g., closed reduction of fracture).

Appendix C compares the components (access location, method, and type of instrumentation) of each approach and provides an example of each approach.

Device (Character 6)

The device is specified in the sixth character and is used only to specify devices that remain after the procedure is completed. There are four general types of devices:

- Biological or synthetic material that takes the place of all or a portion of a body part (e.g., skin grafts and joint prosthesis)

- Biological or synthetic material that assists or prevents a physiological function (e.g., IUD)

- Therapeutic material that is not absorbed by, eliminated by, or incorporated into a body part (e.g., radioactive implant)

- Mechanical or electronic appliances used to assist, monitor, take the place of, or prevent a physiological function (e.g., diaphragmatic pacemaker, orthopaedic pins)

While all devices can be removed, some cannot be removed without putting in another nonbiological appliance or body-part substitute. Specific device values may be coded with the root operations *alteration, bypass, creation, dilation, drainage, fusion, occlusion, reposition,* and *restriction*. Specific device values must be coded with the root operations *change, insertion, removal, replacement,* and *revision*. Instruments used to visualize the procedure site are specified in the approach, not the device, value.

If the objective of the procedure is to put in the device, then the root operation is *insertion*. If the device is put in to meet an objective other than *insertion*, then the root operation defining the underlying objective of the procedure is used, with the device specified in the device character. For example, if a procedure to replace the hip joint is performed, the root operation *replacement* is coded, and the prosthetic device is specified in the device character. Materials that are incidental to a procedure such as clips, ligatures, and sutures are not specified in the device character. Because new devices can be developed, the value *other device* is provided as a temporary option for use until a specific device value is added to the system.

Qualifier (Character 7)

The qualifier is specified in the seventh character. The qualifier contains unique values for individual procedures. For example, the qualifier can be used to identify the destination site in a *bypass*.

Medical and Surgical Section Principles

In developing the medical and surgical procedure codes, several specific principles were followed.

Composite Terms Are Not Root Operations

Composite terms such as colonoscopy, sigmoidectomy, or appendectomy do not describe root operations, but they do specify multiple components of a specific root operation. In ICD-10-PCS, the components of a procedure are defined separately by the characters making up the complete code. And the only component of a procedure specified in the root operation is the objective of the procedure. With each complete code the underlying objective of the procedure is specified by the root operation (third character), the precise part is specified by the body part (fourth character), and the method used to reach and visualize the procedure site is specified by the approach (fifth character). While colonoscopy, sigmoidectomy, and appendectomy are included in the Index, they do not constitute root operations in the Tables section. The objective of colonoscopy is the visualization of the colon and the root operation (character 3) is *inspection*. Character 4 specifies the body part, which in this case is part of the colon. These composite terms, like colonoscopy or appendectomy, are included as cross-reference only. The index provides the correct root operation reference. Examples of other types of composite terms not representative of root operations are *partial* sigmoidectomy, *total* hysterectomy, and *partial* hip replacement. Always refer to the correct root operation in the Index and Tables section.

Root Operation Based on Objective of Procedure

The root operation is based on the objective of the procedure, such as *resection* of transverse colon or *dilation* of an artery. The assignment of the root operation is based on the procedure actually performed, which may or may not have been the intended procedure. If the intended procedure is modified or discontinued (e.g., excision instead of resection is performed), the root operation is determined by the procedure actually performed. If the desired result is not attained after completing the procedure (i.e., the artery does not remain expanded after the dilation procedure), the root operation is still determined by procedure actually performed.

Examples:

- Dilating the urethra is coded as *dilation* since the objective of the procedure is to dilate the urethra. If dilation of the urethra includes putting in an intraluminal stent, the root operation remains *dilation* and not *insertion* of the intraluminal device because the underlying objective of the procedure is dilation of the urethra. The stent is identified by the intraluminal device value in the sixth character of the dilation procedure code.

- If the objective is solely to put a radioactive element in the urethra, then the procedure is coded to the root operation *insertion*, with the radioactive element identified in the sixth character of the code.

- If the objective of the procedure is to correct a malfunctioning or displaced device, then the procedure is coded to the root operation *revision*. In the root operation

revision, the original device being revised is identified in the device character. *Revision* is typically performed on mechanical appliances (e.g., diaphragmatic pacemaker) or materials used in replacement procedures (e.g., synthetic substitute). Typical revision procedures include adjustment of pacemaker position and correction of malfunctioning knee prosthesis.

Combination Procedures Are Coded Separately

If multiple procedures as defined by distinct objectives are performed during an operative episode, then multiple codes are used. For example, obtaining the vein graft used for coronary bypass surgery is coded as a separate procedure from the bypass itself.

Redo of Procedures

The complete or partial redo of the original procedure is coded to the root operation that identifies the procedure performed rather than *revision*.

Example:

A complete redo of a hip replacement procedure that requires putting in a new prosthesis is coded to the root operation *replacement* rather than *revision*.

The correction of complications arising from the original procedure, other than device complications, is coded to the procedure performed. Correction of a malfunctioning or displaced device would be coded to the root operation *revision*.

Example:

A procedure to control hemorrhage arising from the original procedure is coded to *control* rather than *revision*.

Examples of Procedures Coded in the Medical Surgical Section

The following are examples of procedures from the medical and surgical section, coded in ICD-10-PCS.

- Suture of skin laceration, left lower arm: 0HQEXZZ

  Medical and surgical section (0), body system *skin and breast* (H), root operation *repair* (Q), body part *skin, left lower arm* (E), *external approach* (X) without device (Z), and without qualifier (Z).

- Laparoscopic appendectomy: 0DTJ4ZZ

  Medical and surgical section (0), body system *gastrointestinal* (D), root operation *resection* (T), body part *appendix* (J), *percutaneous endoscopic* approach (4), without device (Z), and without qualifier (Z).

- Sigmoidoscopy with biopsy: 0DBN8ZX

  Medical and surgical section (0), body system *gastrointestinal* (D), root operation *excision* (B), body part *sigmoid colon* (N), *via natural or artificial opening endoscopic* approach (8), without device (Z), and with qualifier *diagnostic* (X).

- Tracheostomy with tracheostomy tube: 0B110F4

  Medical and surgical section (0), body system *respiratory* (B), root operation *bypass* (1), body part *trachea* (1), *open* approach (0), *with tracheostomy device* (F), and qualifier *cutaneous* (4).

Obstetrics Section

Character Meanings

The seven characters in the obstetrics section have the same meaning as in the medical and surgical section.

Character	Meaning
1	Section
2	Body System
3	Root Operation
4	Body Part
5	Approach
6	Device
7	Qualifier

The obstetrics section includes procedures performed on the products of conception only. Procedures on the pregnant female are coded in the medical and surgical section (e.g., episiotomy). The term "products of conception" refers to all physical components of a pregnancy, including the fetus, amnion, umbilical cord, and placenta. There is no differentiation of the products of conception based on gestational age. Thus, the specification of the products of conception as a zygote, embryo or fetus, or the trimester of the pregnancy is not part of the procedure code but can be found in the diagnosis code.

Section (Character 1)

Obstetrics procedure codes have a first-character value of *1*.

Body System (Character 2)

The second-character value for body system is *pregnancy*.

Root Operation (Character 3)

The root operations *change, drainage, extraction, insertion, inspection, removal, repair, reposition, resection,* and *transplantation* are used in the obstetrics section and have the same meaning as in the medical and surgical section.

The obstetrics section also includes two additional root operations, *abortion* and *delivery*, defined below:

- *Abortion*: Artificially terminating a pregnancy
- *Delivery*: Assisting the passage of the products of conception from the genital canal

A cesarean section is not a separate root operation because the underlying objective is *extraction* (i.e., pulling out all or a portion of a body part).

Body Part (Character 4)

The body-part values in the obstetrics section are:

- *Products of conception*
- *Products of conception, retained*
- *Products of conception, ectopic*

Approach (Character 5)

The fifth character specifies approaches and is defined as are those in the medical and surgical section. In the case of an abortion procedure that uses a laminaria or an abortifacient, the approach is *via natural or artificial opening*.

Device (Character 6)

The sixth character is used for devices such as fetal monitoring electrodes.

Qualifier (Character 7)

Qualifier values are specific to the root operation and are used to specify the type of extraction (e.g., low forceps, high forceps, etc.), the type of cesarean section (e.g., classical, low cervical, etc.), or the type of fluid taken out during a drainage procedure (e.g., amniotic fluid, fetal blood, etc.).

Placement Section

Character Meanings

The seven characters in the placement section have the following meaning:

Character	Meaning
1	Section
2	Body System
3	Root Operation
4	Body Region
5	Approach
6	Device
7	Qualifier

Placement section codes represent procedures for putting a device in or on a body region for the purpose of protection, immobilization, stretching, compression, or packing.

Section (Character 1)

Placement procedure codes have a first-character value of *2*.

Body System (Character 2)

The second character contains two values specifying either *anatomical region* or *body orifice*.

Root Operation (Character 3)

The root operations in the placement section include only those procedures that are performed without making an incision or a puncture. The root operations *change* and *removal* are in the placement section and have the same meaning as in the medical and surgical section.

The placement section also includes five additional root operations, defined as follows:

- *Compression*: Putting pressure on a body region
- *Dressing*: Putting material on a body region for protection
- *Immobilization*: Limiting or preventing motion of a body region
- *Packing*: Putting material in a body region or orifice
- *Traction*: Exerting a pulling force on a body region in a distal direction

Body Region (Character 4)

The fourth-character values are either *body regions* (e.g., upper leg) or *natural orifices* (e.g., ear).

Approach (Character 5)

Since all placement procedures are performed directly on the skin or mucous membrane, or performed indirectly by applying external force through the skin or mucous membrane, the approach value is always *external*.

Device (Character 6)

The device character is always specified (except in the case of manual traction) and indicates the device placed during the procedure (e.g., cast, splint, bandage, etc.). Except for casts for fractures and dislocations, devices in the placement section are off the shelf and do not require any extensive design, fabrication, or fitting. Placement of devices that require extensive design, fabrication, or fitting are coded in the rehabilitation section.

Qualifier (Character 7)

The qualifier character is not specified in the placement section; the qualifier value is always *no qualifier*.

Administration Section

Character Meanings

The seven characters in the administration section have the following meaning:

Character	Meaning
1	Section
2	Body System
3	Root Operation
4	Body System/Region
5	Approach
6	Substance
7	Qualifier

Administration section codes represent procedures for putting in or on a therapeutic, prophylactic, protective, diagnostic, nutritional, or physiological substance. The section includes transfusions, infusions, and injections, along with other similar services such as irrigation and tattooing.

Section (Character 1)

Administration procedure codes have a first-character value of 3.

Body System (Character 2)

The body-system character contains only two values: *physiological systems and anatomical regions,* or *circulatory system*. The circulatory body system is used for transfusion procedures.

Root Operation (Character 3)

There are three root operations in the administration section.

* *Introduction*: Putting in or on a therapeutic, diagnostic, nutritional, physiological, or prophylactic substance except blood or blood products

* *Irrigation*: Putting in or on a cleansing substance

* *Transfusion*: Putting in blood or blood products

Body/System Region (Character 4)

The fourth character specifies the body system/region. The fourth character identifies the site where the substance is administered,

not the site where the substance administered takes effect. Sites include *skin and mucous membrane, subcutaneous tissue* and *muscle*. These differentiate *intradermal, subcutaneous,* and *intramuscular* injections, respectively. Other sites include *eye, respiratory tract, peritoneal cavity,* and *epidural space*.

The body systems/regions for arteries and veins are *peripheral artery, central artery, peripheral vein,* and *central vein*. The *peripheral artery or vein* is typically used when a substance is introduced locally into an artery or vein. For example, chemotherapy is the introduction of an antineoplastic substance into a peripheral artery or vein by a percutaneous approach. In general, the substance introduced into a peripheral artery or vein has a systemic effect.

The *central artery or vein* is typically used when the site where the substance is introduced is distant from the point of entry into the artery or vein. For example, the introduction of a substance directly at the site of a clot within an artery or vein using a catheter is coded as an introduction of a thrombolytic substance into a central artery or vein by a percutaneous approach. In general, the substance introduced into a central artery or vein has a local effect.

Approach (Character 5)

The fifth character specifies approaches as defined in the medical and surgical section. The approach for intradermal, subcutaneous, and intramuscular introductions (i.e., injections) is *percutaneous*. If a catheter is placed to introduce a substance into an internal site within the circulatory system, then the approach is also *percutaneous*. For example, if a catheter is used to introduce contrast directly into the heart for angiography, then the procedure would be coded as a percutaneous introduction of contrast into the heart.

Substance (Character 6)

The sixth character specifies the substance being introduced. Broad categories of substances are defined, such as anesthetic, contrast, dialysate, and blood products such as platelets.

Qualifier (Character 7)

The seventh character is a qualifier and is used to indicate whether the substance is *autologous* or *nonautologous*, or to further specify the substance.

Measurement and Monitoring Section

Character Meanings

The seven characters in the measuring and monitoring section have the following meaning:

Character	Meaning
1	Section
2	Body System
3	Root Operation
4	Body System
5	Approach
6	Function/Device
7	Qualifier

Measurement and monitoring section codes represent procedures for determining the level of a physiological or physical function.

Section (Character 1)

Measurement and monitoring procedure codes have a first-character value of 4.

Body System (Character 2)

The second-character value for body system is A, *physiological systems* or B, *physiological devices.*

Root Operation (Character 3)

There are two root operations in the measurement and monitoring section, as defined below:

- *Measurement*: Determining the level of a physiological or physical function at a point in time
- *Monitoring*: Determining the level of a physiological or physical function repetitively over a period of time

Body System (Character 4)

The fourth character specifies the specific body system measured or monitored.

Approach (Character 5)

The fifth character specifies approaches as defined in the medical and surgical section.

Function/Device (Character 6)

The sixth character specifies the physiological or physical function being measured or monitored. Examples of physiological or physical functions are *conductivity, metabolism, pulse, temperature,* and *volume.* If a device used to perform the measurement or monitoring is inserted and left in, then insertion of the device is coded as a separate procedure.

Qualifier (Character 7)

The seventh-character qualifier contains specific values as needed to further specify the body part (e.g., central, portal, pulmonary) or a variation of the procedure performed (e.g., ambulatory, stress). Examples of typical procedures coded in this section are EKG, EEG, and cardiac catheterization. An EKG is the measurement of cardiac electrical activity, while an EEG is the measurement of electrical activity of the central nervous system. A cardiac catheterization performed to measure the pressure in the heart is coded as the measurement of cardiac pressure by percutaneous approach.

Extracorporeal Assistance and Performance Section

Character Meanings

The seven characters in the extracorporeal assistance and performance section have the following meaning:

Character	Meaning
1	Section
2	Body System
3	Root Operation
4	Body System
5	Duration
6	Function
7	Qualifier

In extracorporeal assistance and performance procedures, equipment outside the body is used to assist or perform a physiological function. The section includes procedures performed in a critical care setting, such as mechanical ventilation and cardioversion; it also includes other services such as hyperbaric oxygen treatment and hemodialysis.

Section (Character 1)

Extracorporeal assistance and performance procedure codes have a first-character value of 5.

Body System (Character 2)

The second-character value for body system is A, *physiological systems.*

Root Operation (Character 3)

There are three root operations in the extracorporeal assistance and performance section, as defined below.

- *Assistance*: Taking over a portion of a physiological function by extracorporeal means
- *Performance*: Completely taking over a physiological function by extracorporeal means
- *Restoration*: Returning, or attempting to return, a physiological function to its original state by extracorporeal means

The root operation *restoration* contains a single procedure code that identifies extracorporeal cardioversion.

Body System (Character 4)

The fourth character specifies the body system (e.g., cardiac, respiratory) to which extracorporeal assistance or performance is applied.

Duration (Character 5)

The fifth character specifies the duration of the procedure—single, intermittent, or continuous. For respiratory ventilation assistance or performance, the duration is specified in hours— < 24 consecutive hours, 24–96 consecutive hours, or > 96 consecutive hours. Value 6 *Multiple* identifies serial procedure treatment.

Function (Character 6)

The sixth character specifies the physiological function assisted or performed (e.g., oxygenation, ventilation) during the procedure.

Qualifier (Character 7)

The seventh-character qualifier specifies the type of equipment used, if any.

Extracorporeal Therapies Section

Character Meanings

The seven characters in the extracorporeal assistance and performance section have the following meaning:

Character	Meaning
1	Section
2	Body System
3	Root Operation
4	Body System
5	Duration
6	Qualifier
7	Qualifier

In extracorporeal therapy, equipment outside the body is used for a therapeutic purpose that does not involve the assistance or performance of a physiological function.

Section (Character 1)

Extracorporeal therapy procedure codes have a first-character value of 6.

Body System (Character 2)

The second-character value for body system is *physiological systems*.

Root Operation (Character 3)

There are 10 root operations in the extracorporeal therapy section, as defined below.

- *Atmospheric control*: Extracorporeal control of atmospheric pressure and composition

- *Decompression*: Extracorporeal elimination of undissolved gas from body fluids

  Coding note: The root operation *decompression* involves only one type of procedure: treatment for decompression sickness (the bends) in a hyperbaric chamber.

- *Electromagnetic therapy*: Extracorporeal treatment by electromagnetic rays

- *Hyperthermia*: Extracorporeal raising of body temperature

  Coding note: The term hyperthermia is used to describe both a temperature imbalance treatment and also as an adjunct radiation treatment for cancer. When treating the temperature imbalance, it is coded to this section; for the cancer treatment, it is coded in section *D Radiation oncology*.

- *Hypothermia*: Extracorporeal lowering of body temperature

- *Pheresis*: Extracorporeal separation of blood products

  Coding note: Pheresis may be used for two main purposes: to treat diseases when too much of a blood component is produced (e.g., leukemia) and to remove a blood product such as platelets from a donor, for transfusion into another patient.

- *Phototherapy*: Extracorporeal treatment by light rays

  Coding note: Phototherapy involves using a machine that exposes the blood to light rays outside the body, recirculates it, and then returns it to the body.

- *Shock wave therapy*: Extracorporeal treatment by shock waves

- *Ultrasound therapy*: Extracorporeal treatment by ultrasound

- *Ultraviolet light therapy*: Extracorporeal treatment by ultraviolet light

Body System (Character 4)

The fourth character specifies the body system on which the extracorporeal therapy is performed (e.g., skin, circulatory).

Duration (Character 5)

The fifth character specifies the duration of the procedure (e.g., single or multiple).

Qualifier (Character 6)

The sixth character is not specified for extracorporeal therapies and always has the value no qualifier.

Qualifier (Character 7)

The seventh-character qualifier is used in the root operation *pheresis* to specify the blood component on which pheresis is performed and in the root operation *ultrasound therapy* to specify site of treatment.

Osteopathic Section

Character Meanings

The seven characters in the osteopathic section have the following meaning:

Character	Meaning
1	Section
2	Body System
3	Root Operation
4	Body Region
5	Approach
6	Method
7	Qualifier

Section (Character 1)

Osteopathic procedure codes have a first-character value of 7.

Body System (Character 2)

The body-system character contains the value *anatomical regions*.

Root Operation (Character 3)

There is only one root operation in the osteopathic section.

- *Treatment*: Manual treatment to eliminate or alleviate somatic dysfunction and related disorders

Body Region (Character 4)

The fourth character specifies the body region on which the osteopathic treatment is performed.

Approach (Character 5)

The approach for osteopathic treatment is always external.

Method (Character 6)

The sixth character specifies the method by which the treatment is accomplished.

Qualifier (Character 7)

The seventh character is not specified in the osteopathic section and always has the value *none*.

Other Procedures Section

Character Meanings

The seven characters in the *other procedures* section have the following meaning:

Character	Meaning
1	Section
2	Body System
3	Root Operation
4	Body Region
5	Approach
6	Method
7	Qualifier

The other procedures section includes acupuncture, suture removal, and in vitro fertilization.

Section (Character 1)

Other procedure section codes have a first-character value of *8*.

Body System (Character 2)

The second-character value for body system is *physiological systems* and *anatomical region*.

Root Operation (Character 3)

The other procedures section has only one root operation, defined as follows:

- *Other procedures*: Methodologies that attempt to remediate or cure a disorder or disease.

Body Region (Character 4)

The fourth character contains specified body-region values, and also the body-region value *none* for extracorporeal procedures.

Approach (Character 5)

The fifth character specifies approaches as defined in the medical and surgical section.

Method (Character 6)

The sixth character specifies the method (e.g., acupuncture, therapeutic massage).

Qualifier (Character 7)

The seventh character is a qualifier and contains specific values as needed.

Chiropractic Section

Character Meanings

The seven characters in the chiropractic section have the following meaning:

Character	Meaning
1	Section
2	Body System
3	Root Operation
4	Body Region
5	Approach
6	Method
7	Qualifier

Section (Character 1)

Chiropractic section procedure codes have a first-character value of *9*.

Body System (Character 2)

The second-character value for body system is *anatomical regions*.

Root Operation (Character 3)

There is only one root operation in the chiropractic section.

- *Manipulation:* Manual procedure that involves a directed thrust to move a joint past the physiological range of motion, without exceeding the anatomical limit.

Body Region (Character 4)

The fourth character specifies the body region on which the chiropractic manipulation is performed.

Approach (Character 5)

The approach for chiropractic manipulation is always *external*.

Method (Character 6)

The sixth character is the method by which the manipulation is accomplished.

Qualifier (Character 7)

The seventh character is not specified in the chiropractic section and always has the value *none*.

Imaging Section

Character Meanings

The seven characters in imaging procedures have the following meaning:

Character	Meaning
1	Section
2	Body System
3	Root Type
4	Body Part
5	Contrast
6	Qualifier
7	Qualifier

Imaging procedures include plain radiography, fluoroscopy, CT, MRI, and ultrasound. Nuclear medicine procedures, including PET, uptakes, and scans, are in the nuclear medicine section. Therapeutic radiation procedure codes are in a separate radiation oncology section.

Section (Character 1)

Imaging procedure codes have a first-character value of *B*.

Body System (Character 2)

In the imaging section, the second character defines the body system

Root Type (Character 3)

The third character defines the type of imaging procedure (e.g., MRI, ultrasound). The following list includes all types in the imaging section with a definition of each type:

- *Computerized tomography (CT scan)* : Computer-reformatted digital display of multiplanar images developed from the capture of multiple exposures of external ionizing radiation.

- *Fluoroscopy*: Single plane or bi-plane real-time display of an image developed from the capture of external ionizing radiation on fluorescent screen. The image may also be stored by either digital or analog means.

- *Magnetic resonance imaging (MRI)* : Computer reformatted digital display of multiplanar images developed from the capture of radiofrequency signals emitted by nuclei in a body site excited within a magnetic field

- *Plain radiography*: Planar display of an image developed from the capture of external ionizing radiation on photographic or photoconductive plate.

- *Ultrasonography*: Real-time display of images of anatomy or flow information developed from the capture of reflected and attenuated high-frequency sound waves

Body Part(Character 4)

The fourth character defines the body part with different values for each body system (character 2) value.

Contrast (Character 5)

The fifth character specifies whether the contrast material used in the imaging procedure is *high* or *low osmolar*, when applicable.

Qualifier (Character 6)

The sixth character qualifier provides further detail as needed, such as *unenhanced and enhanced*.

Qualifier (Character 7)

The seventh character is a qualifier and specifies whether the procedure was performed intraoperatively or using densitometry.

Nuclear Medicine Section

Character Meanings

The seven characters in the nuclear medicine section have the following meaning:

Character	Meaning
1	Section
2	Body System
3	Root Type
4	Body Part
5	Radionuclide
6	Qualifier
7	Qualifier

Nuclear medicine is the introduction of radioactive material into the body to create an image, to diagnose and treat pathologic conditions, or to assess metabolic functions. The nuclear medicine section does not include the introduction of encapsulated radioactive material for the treatment of cancer. These procedures are included in the radiation oncology section.

Section (Character 1)

Nuclear medicine procedure codes have a first-character value of *C*.

Body System (Character 2)

The second character specifies the body system on which the nuclear medicine procedure is performed.

Root Type (Character 3)

The third character indicates the type of nuclear medicine procedure (e.g., planar imaging or nonimaging uptake). The following list includes the types of nuclear medicine procedures with a definition of each type.

- *Nonimaging uptake:* Introduction of radioactive materials into the body for measurements of organ function, from the detection of radioactive emissions

- *Nonimaging probe:* Introduction of radioactive materials into the body for the study of distribution and fate of certain substances by the detection of radioactive emissions from an external source

- *Nonimaging assay:* Introduction of radioactive materials into the body for the study of body fluids and blood elements, by the detection of radioactive emissions

- *Planar imaging:* Introduction of radioactive materials into the body for single-plane display of images developed from the capture of radioactive emissions.

- *Positron emission tomography (PET):* Introduction of radioactive materials into the body for three-dimensional display of images developed from the simultaneous capture, 180 degrees apart, of radioactive emissions

- *Systemic therapy:* Introduction of unsealed radioactive materials into the body for treatment

- *Tomographic (tomo) imaging:* Introduction of radioactive materials into the body for three dimensional display of images developed from the capture of radioactive emissions.

Body Part (Character 4)

The fourth character indicates the body part or body region studied. *Regional* (e.g., lower extremity veins) and *combination* (e.g., liver and spleen) body parts are commonly used in this section.

Radionuclide (Character 5)

The fifth character specifies the radionuclide, the radiation source. The option "other radionuclide" is provided in the nuclear medicine section for newly approved radionuclides until they can be added to the coding system. If more than one radiopharmaceutical is given to perform the procedure, then more than one code is used.

Qualifier (Character 6 and 7)

The sixth and seventh characters are qualifiers but are not specified in the nuclear medicine section; the value is always *none*.

Radiation Oncology Section

Character Meanings

The seven characters in the radiation oncology section have the following meaning:

Character	Meaning
1	Section
2	Body System
3	Root Type
4	Body Part
5	Modality Qualifier
6	Isotope
7	Qualifier

Section (Character 1)

Radiation oncology procedure codes have a first-character value of *D*.

Body System (Character 2)

The second character specifies the body system (e.g., central nervous system, musculoskeletal) irradiated.

Root Type (Character 3)

The third character specifies the general modality used (e.g., beam radiation).

Body Part (Character 4)

The fourth character specifies the body part that is the focus of the radiation therapy.

Modality Qualifier (Character 5)

The fifth character further specifies the radiation modality used (e.g., photons, electrons).

Isotope (Character 6)

The sixth character specifies the isotopes introduced into the body, if applicable.

Qualifier (Character 7)

The seventh character may specify whether the procedure was performed intraoperatively.

Physical Rehabilitation and Diagnostic Audiology Section

Character Meanings

The seven characters in the physical rehabilitation and diagnostic audiology section have the following meaning:

Character	Meaning
1	Section
2	Section Qualifier
3	Root Type
4	Body System & Region
5	Type Qualifier
6	Equipment
7	Qualifier

Physical rehabilitation procedures include physical therapy, occupational therapy, and speech-language pathology. Osteopathic procedures and chiropractic procedures are in separate sections.

Section (Character 1)

Physical rehabilitation and diagnostic audiology procedure codes have a first-character value of *F*.

Section Qualifier (Character 2)

The section qualifier *rehabilitation* or *diagnostic audiology* is specified in the second character.

Root Type (Character 3)

The third character specifies the root type. There are 14 different root type values, which can be classified into four basic types of rehabilitation and diagnostic audiology procedures, defined as follows:

- *Assessment*: Includes a determination of the patient's diagnosis when appropriate, need for treatment, planning for treatment, periodic assessment, and documentation related to these activities

- *Caregiver training*: Educating caregiver with the skills and knowledge used to support the patient's optimal level of function

- *Fitting(s)*: Design, fabrication, modification, selection, and/or application of splint, orthosis, prosthesis, hearing aids, and/or other rehabilitation device

- *Treatment*: Use of specific activities or methods to develop, improve, and/or restore the performance of necessary functions, compensate for dysfunction and/or minimize debilitation

The type of treatment includes training as well as activities that restore function.

Body System & Region (Character 4)

The fourth character specifies the body region and/or system on which the procedure is performed.

Type Qualifier (Character 5)

The fifth character is a type qualifier that further specifies the procedure performed. Examples include therapy to improve the range of motion and training for bathing techniques. Refer to appendix F for definitions of these types of procedures.

Equipment (Character 6)

The sixth character specifies the equipment used. Specific equipment is not defined in the equipment value. Instead, broad categories of equipment are specified (e.g., aerobic endurance and conditioning, assistive/ adaptive/supportive, etc.)

Qualifier (Character 7)

The seventh character is not specified in the physical rehabilitation and diagnostic audiology section and always has the value *none*.

Mental Health Section

Character Meanings

The seven characters in the mental health section have the following meaning:

Character	Meaning
1	Section
2	Body System
3	Root Type
4	Type Qualifier
5	Qualifier
6	Qualifier
7	Qualifier

Section (Character 1)

Mental health procedure codes have a first-character value of *G*.

Body System (Character 2)

The second character is used to identify the body system elsewhere in ICD-10-PCS. In this section it always has the value *none*.

Root Type (Character 3)

The third character specifies the procedure type, such as crisis intervention or counseling. There are 11 types of mental health procedures, each defined below.

Psychological tests:

- Developmental: Age-normed developmental status of cognitive, social, and adaptive behavior skills

- Intellectual and psychoeducational: Intellectual abilities, academic achievement, and learning capabilities (including behavior and emotional factors affecting learning)

- Neurobehavioral and cognitive status: Includes neurobehavioral status exam, interview(s), and observation for the clinical assessment of thinking, reasoning, and judgment, acquired knowledge, attention, memory, visual spatial abilities, language functions, and planning

- Neuropsychological: Thinking, reasoning and judgment, acquired knowledge, attention, memory, visual spatial abilities, language functions, planning

- Personality and behavioral: Mood, emotion, behavior, social functioning, psychopathological conditions, personality traits, and characteristics

Crisis intervention: Includes defusing, debriefing, counseling, psychotherapy, and/or coordination of care with other providers or agencies

Individual psychotherapy:

- Behavior: Primarily to modify behavior. Includes modeling and role playing, positive reinforcement of target behaviors, response cost, and training of self-management skills

- Cognitive/behavioral: Combining cognitive and behavioral treatment strategies to improve functioning. Maladaptive responses are examined to determine how cognitions relate to behavior patterns in response to an event. Uses learning principles and information-processing models

- Cognitive: Primarily to correct cognitive distortions and errors

- Interactive: Uses primarily physical aids and other forms of nonoral interaction with a patient who is physically, psychologically, or developmentally unable to use ordinary language for communication (e.g., the use of toys in symbolic play)

- Interpersonal: Helps an individual make changes in interpersonal behaviors to reduce psychological dysfunction. Includes exploratory techniques, encouragement of affective expression, clarification of patient statements, analysis of communication patterns, use of therapy relationship, and behavior change techniques.

- Psychoanalysis: Methods of obtaining a detailed account of past and present mental and emotional experiences to determine the source and eliminate or diminish the undesirable effects of unconscious conflicts by making the individual aware of their existence, origin, and inappropriate expression in emotions and behavior.

- Psychodynamic: Exploration of past and present emotional experiences to understand motives and drives using insight-oriented techniques (e.g., empathetic listening, clarifying self-defeating behavior patterns, and exploring adaptive alternatives) to reduce the undesirable effects of internal conflicts on emotions and behavior

- Psychophysiological: Monitoring and alternation of physiological processes to help the individual associate physiological reactions combined with cognitive and behavioral strategies to gain improved control of these processes to help the individual cope more effectively

- Supportive: Formation of therapeutic relationship primarily for providing emotional support to prevent further deterioration in functioning during periods of particular stress. Often used in conjunction with other therapeutic approaches

Counseling:

- *Vocational:* Exploration of vocational interest, aptitudes, and required adaptive behavior skills to develop and carry out a plan for achieving a successful vocational placement, enhancing work-related adjustment, and/or pursuing viable options in training education or preparation

- *Family psychotherapy:* Remediation of emotional or behavioral problems presented by one or more family members when psychotherapy with more than one family member is indicated

Electroconvulsive therapy: Includes appropriate sedation and other preparation of the individual

Biofeedback: includes electroencephalogram (EEG), blood pressure, skin temperature or peripheral blood flow, electrocardiogram (ECG), electrooculogram, electromyogram (EMG), respirometry or capnometry, galvanic skin response (GSR) or electrodermal response (EDR), perineometry to monitor and regulate bowel or bladder activity, and electrogastrogram to monitor and regulate gastric motility

Other *mental health* procedures include *hypnosis, narcosynthesis, group psychotherapy,* and *light therapy*; there are no ICD-10-PCS definitions of these procedures at this time.

Type Qualifier (Character 4)
The fourth character is a type qualifier (e.g., to indicate that counseling was educational or vocational).

Qualifier (Character 5, 6 and 7)
The fifth, sixth, and seventh characters are not specified and always have the value *none*.

Substance Abuse Treatment Section

Character Meanings
The seven characters in the substance abuse treatment section have the following meaning:

Character	Meaning
1	Section
2	Body System
3	Root Type
4	Type Qualifier
5	Qualifier
6	Qualifier
7	Qualifier

Section (Character 1)
Substance abuse treatment codes have a first-character value of *H*.

Body System (Character 2)
The second character is used to identify the body system elsewhere in ICD-10-PCS. In this section, it always has the value *none*.

Root Type (Character 3)
The third character specifies the procedure. There are seven root type values classified in this section, as listed below:

- *Detoxification services:* Not a treatment modality but helps the patient stabilize physically and psychologically until the body becomes free of drugs and the effects of alcohol
- *Individual counseling:* Comprising several techniques, which apply various strategies to address drug addiction
- *Group counseling:* Provides structured group counseling sessions and healing power through the connection with others
- *Family counseling:* Provides support and education for family members of addicted individuals. Family member participation seen as critical to substance abuse treatment

- Other root type values in this section include *individual psychotherapy, medication management,* and *pharmacotherapy*; there are no ICD-10-PCS definitions of these procedures at this time.

Type Qualifier (Character 4)
The fourth character further specifies the procedure type. The individual counseling procedure further specified in the fourth character includes the values *cognitive behavioral, 12-step,* and *interpersonal*.

Qualifier (Character 5,6 and 7)
The fifth through seventh characters are designated as qualifiers but are never specified, so they always have the value *none*.

Comparison of ICD-10-PCS and ICD-9-CM

In 1993, the National Committee on Vital and Health Statistics (NCVHS) issued a report specifying recommendations for a new procedure classification system. NCVHS identified the essential characteristics that a procedure classification system should possess. Those characteristics include hierarchical structure, expandability, comprehensive, nonoverlapping, ease of use, setting and provider neutrality, multi-axial structure, and limited to classification of procedures.

ICD-10-PCS meets virtually all NCVHS characteristics, while ICD-9-CM fails to meet many NCVHS characteristics. In addition to the NCVHS characteristics, there are several other attributes of a procedure coding system that should be taken into consideration when comparing systems.

Completeness and Accuracy of Codes
The procedures coded in ICD-10-PCS provided a much more complete and accurate description of the procedure performed. The specification of the procedures performed not only affects payment, but is integral to internal management systems, external performance comparisons, and the assessment of quality of care. The detail and completeness of ICD-10-PCS is essential in today's health care environment.

General Equivalence Mappings
Due to the complexities of ICD-10-PCS and the drastic structural differences between the two coding systems, a direct code crosswalk is not possible. However, a general "mapping" of similar code choices has been developed. This network of relationships between the two code sets may be referred to as general equivalence mappings (GEMs). The purpose of these mappings, from ICD-9-CM to ICD-10-PCS, and vice versa, is to attempt to find corresponding procedure codes in lieu of a direct translation. For example:

- The ICD-9-CM to ICD-10-PCS GEM may help with analyzing or comparing data coded using the ICD-9-CM system to facilitate "forward mapping" to ICD-10-PCS.
- The ICD-10-PCS to ICD-9-CM GEM may help in comparing coded data using the ICD-10-PCS system to facilitate "backward mapping" to ICD-9-CM.

The 2009 ICD-10-PCS update includes data mapping files which are posted on the CMS website at the URL below: http://www.cms.hhs.gov/ICD10/01m_2009_ICD10PCS.asp#TopOfPage.

Communications with Physicians

ICD-9-CM procedure codes often poorly describe the precise procedure performed. Physicians reviewing or analyzing data coded in ICD-9-CM may have difficulty developing clinical pathways, evaluating the coding for possible fraud and abuse, or conducting research. The ICD-10-PCS codes provide more clinically relevant procedure descriptions that can be more readily understood and used by physicians.

Independent evaluation of ICD-10-PCS demonstrated that there is a learning curve associated with ICD-10-PCS. Because of the additional specificity in ICD-10-PCS, it probably takes longer to attain a minimum level of coding proficiency for ICD-10-PCS than for ICD-9-CM. However, it should take less time to become *highly* proficient with ICD-10-PCS than with ICD-9-CM. ICD-9-CM lacks clear definitions, and many substantially different procedures are coded with the same code. Therefore, identifying the correct code requires extensive knowledge of the American Hospital Association's *Coding Clinic for ICD-9-CM* and other coding guidelines. Becoming completely familiar with all the conventions associated with ICD-9-CM requires extensive and continued effort. As a result, becoming highly proficient in ICD-9-CM can take a long time.

Conclusion

ICD-10-PCS has been developed as a replacement for volume 3 of ICD-9-CM. The system has evolved during its development based on extensive input from many segments of the health care industry. The multi-axial structure of the system, combined with its detailed definition of terminology, permits a precise specification of procedures for use in health services research, epidemiology, statistical analysis, and administrative areas. ICD-10-PCS will also allow health information coders to assign accurate procedure codes with minimal effort.

Sources

All material contained in this manual is derived from the ICD-10-PCS Coding System and Training Manual and related files revised and distributed by the Centers for Medicare and Medicaid Services, January 2009.

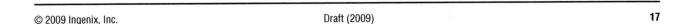

Coding Exercises

Using the ICD-10-PCS tables construct the code that accurately represents the procedure performed. Answers to these coding exercises may be found in appendix F.

Medical Surgical Section

Procedure	Code
Excision of malignant melanoma from skin of right ear	
Laparoscopy with excision of endometrial implant from left ovary	
Percutaneous needle core biopsy of right kidney	
EGD with gastric biopsy	
Open endarterectomy of left common carotid artery	
Excision of basal cell carcinoma of lower lip	
Open excision of tail of pancreas	
Percutaneous biopsy of right gastrocnemius muscle	
Sigmoidoscopy with sigmoid polypectomy	
Open excision of lesion from right Achilles tendon	
Open resection of cecum	
Total excision of pituitary gland, open	
Explantation of left failed kidney, open	
Open left axillary total lymphadenectomy	
Laparoscopic-assisted total vaginal hysterectomy	
Right total mastectomy, open	
Open resection of papillary muscle	
Radical retropubic prostatectomy, open	
Laparoscopic cholecystectomy	
Endoscopic bilateral total maxillary sinusectomy	
Amputation at right elbow level	
Right below-knee amputation, proximal tibia/fibula	
Fifth ray carpometacarpal joint amputation, left hand	
Right leg and hip amputation through ischium	
DIP joint amputation of right thumb	
Right wrist joint amputation	
Trans-metatarsal amputation of foot at left big toe	

Medical Surgical Section *(Continued)*

Procedure	Code
Mid-shaft amputation, right humerus	
Left fourth toe amputation, mid-proximal phalanx	
Right above-knee amputation, distal femur	
Cryotherapy of wart on left hand	
Percutaneous radiofrequency ablation of right vocal cord lesion	
Left heart catheterization with laser destruction of arrhythmogenic focus, A-V node	
Cautery of nosebleed	
Transurethral endoscopic laser ablation of prostate	
Cautery of oozing varicose vein, left calf	
Laparoscopy with destruction of endometriosis, bilateral ovaries	
Laser coagulation of right retinal vessel hemorrhage, percutaneous	
Talc injection pleurodesis, left side	
Sclerotherapy of brachial plexus lesion, alcohol injection	
Forceps total mouth extraction, upper and lower teeth	
Removal of left thumbnail	
Extraction of right intraocular lens without replacement, percutaneous	
Laparoscopy with needle aspiration of ova for in vitro fertilization	
Nonexcisional debridement of skin ulcer, right foot	
Open stripping of abdominal fascia, right side	
Hysteroscopy with D&C, diagnostic	
Liposuction for medical purposes, left upper arm	
Removal of tattered right ear drum fragments with tweezers	
Microincisional phlebectomy of spider veins, right lower leg	
Routine Foley catheter placement	
Incision and drainage of external perianal abscess	
Percutaneous drainage of ascites	

Medical Surgical Section *(Continued)*

Procedure	Code
Laparoscopy with left ovarian cystotomy and drainage	
Laparotomy with hepatotomy and drain placement for liver abscess, right lobe	
Right knee arthrotomy with drain placement	
Thoracentesis of left pleural effusion	
Arterial blood gas sample from right brachial artery line	
Percutaneous chest tube placement for right pneumothorax	
Endoscopic drainage of left ethmoid sinus	
Removal of foreign body, right cornea	
Percutaneous mechanical thrombectomy, left brachial artery	
Esophagogastroscopy with removal of bezoar from stomach	
Foreign body removal, skin of left thumb	
Transurethral cystoscopy with removal of bladder stone	
Forceps removal of foreign body in right nostril	
Laparoscopy with excision of old suture from mesentery	
Incision and removal of right lacrimal duct stone	
Nonincisional removal of intraluminal foreign body from vagina	
Open excision of retained sliver, subcutaneous tissue of left foot	
Extracorporeal shock-wave lithotripsy (ESWL), bilateral ureters	
Endoscopic retrograde cholangiopancreatography (ERCP) with lithotripsy of common bile duct stone	
Thoracotomy with crushing of pericardial calcifications	
Transurethral cystoscopy with fragmentation of bladder calculus	
Hysteroscopy with intraluminal lithotripsy of left fallopian tube calcification	
Division of right foot tendon, percutaneous	
Left heart catheterization with division of bundle of HIS	
Open osteotomy of capitate, left hand	
EGD with esophagotomy of esophagogastric junction	

Medical Surgical Section *(Continued)*

Procedure	Code
Sacral rhizotomy for pain control, percutaneous	
Laparotomy with exploration and adhesiolysis of right ureter	
Incision of scar contracture, right elbow	
Frenulotomy for treatment of tongue-tie syndrome	
Right shoulder arthroscopy with coracoacromial ligament release	
Mitral valvulotomy for release of fused leaflets, open approach	
Percutaneous left Achilles tendon release	
Laparoscopy with lysis of peritoneal adhesions	
Manual rupture of right shoulder joint adhesions under general anesthesia	
Open posterior tarsal tunnel release	
Laparoscopy with freeing of left ovary and fallopian tube	
Liver transplant with donor matched liver	
Orthotopic heart transplant using porcine heart	
Right lung transplant, open, using organ donor match	
Left kidney/pancreas organ bank transplant	
Replantation of avulsed scalp	
Reattachment of severed right ear	
Reattachment of traumatic left gastrocnemius avulsion, open	
Closed replantation of three avulsed teeth, lower jaw	
Reattachment of severed left hand	
Right hand open palmaris longus tendon transfer	
Endoscopic radial to median nerve transfer	
Fasciocutaneous flap closure of left thigh, open	
Transfer left index finger to left thumb position, open	
Percutaneous fascia transfer to fill defect, anterior neck	
Trigeminal to facial nerve transfer, percutaneous endoscopic	
Endoscopic left leg flexor hallucis longus tendon transfer	
Right scalp advancement flap to right temple	

Medical Surgical Section *(Continued)*

Procedure	Code
Bilateral TRAM pedicle flap reconstruction status post mastectomy, muscle only, open	
Skin transfer flap closure of complex open wound, left lower back	
Open fracture reduction, right tibia	
Laparoscopy with gastropexy for malrotation	
Left knee arthroscopy with reposition of anterior cruciate ligament	
Open transposition of ulnar nerve	
Closed reduction with percutaneous internal fixation of right femoral neck fracture	
Trans-vaginal intraluminal cervical cerclage	
Thoracotomy with banding of left pulmonary artery using extraluminal device	
Restriction of thoracic duct with intraluminal stent, percutaneous	
Craniotomy with clipping of cerebral aneurysm	
Nonincisional, transnasal placement of restrictive stent in right lacrimal duct	
Percutaneous ligation of esophageal vein	
Percutaneous embolization of left internal carotid-cavernous fistula	
Laparoscopy with bilateral occlusion of fallopian tubes using Hulka extraluminal clips	
Open suture ligation of failed A-V graft, left brachial artery	
Percutaneous embolization of vascular supply, intracranial meningioma	
ERCP with balloon dilation of common bile duct	
PTCA of two coronary arteries, LAD with stent placement, RCA with no stent	
Cystoscopy with intraluminal dilation of bladder neck stricture	
Open dilation of old anastomosis, left femoral artery	
Dilation of upper esophageal stricture, direct visualization, with Bougie sound	
PTA of right brachial artery stenosis	
Transnasal dilation and stent placement in right lacrimal duct	
Hysteroscopy with balloon dilation of bilateral fallopian tubes	
Tracheoscopy with intraluminal dilation of tracheal stenosis	

Medical Surgical Section *(Continued)*

Procedure	Code
Cystoscopy with dilation of left ureteral stricture, with stent placement	
Open gastric bypass with Roux-en-Y limb to jejunum	
Right temporal artery to intracranial artery bypass using Gore-Tex graft, open	
Tracheostomy formation with tracheostomy tube placement, percutaneous	
PICVA (percutaneous in situ coronary venous arterialization) of single coronary artery	
Open left femoral-popliteal artery bypass using cadaver vein graft	
Shunting of intrathecal cerebrospinal fluid to peritoneal cavity using synthetic shunt	
Colostomy formation, open, transverse colon to abdominal wall	
Open urinary diversion, left ureter, using ileal conduit to skin	
CABG of LAD using left internal mammary artery, open off-bypass	
Open pleuroperitoneal shunt, right pleural cavity, using synthetic device	
Percutaneous insertion of spinal neurostimulator lead, lumbar spinal cord	
Percutaneous placement of pacemaker lead in left atrium	
Open placement of dual chamber pacemaker generator in chest wall	
Percutaneous placement of venous central line in right internal jugular	
Open insertion of multiple channel cochlear implant, left ear	
Percutaneous placement of Swan-Ganz catheter in superior vena cava	
Bronchoscopy with insertion of brachytherapy seeds, right main bronchus	
Placement of intrathecal infusion pump for pain management, percutaneous	
Open insertion of interspinous process device into lumbar vertebral joint	
Open placement of bone growth stimulator, left femoral shaft	
Cystoscopy with placement of brachytherapy seeds in prostate gland	
Full-thickness skin graft to right lower arm, autograft (do not code graft harvest for this exercise)	

                                 Draft (2009)

Medical Surgical Section (Continued)

Procedure	Code
Excision of necrosed left femoral head with bone bank bone graft to fill the defect, open	
Penetrating keratoplasty of right cornea with donor matched cornea, percutaneous approach	
Bilateral mastectomy with concomitant saline breast implants, open	
Excision of abdominal aorta with Gore-Tex graft replacement, open	
Total right knee arthroplasty with insertion of total knee prosthesis	
Bilateral mastectomy with free TRAM flap reconstruction	
Tenonectomy with graft to right ankle using cadaver graft, open	
Mitral valve replacement using porcine valve, open	
Percutaneous phacoemulsification of right eye cataract with prosthetic lens insertion	
Aortic valve annuloplasty using ring, open	
Laparoscopic repair of left inguinal hernia with marlex plug	
Autograft nerve graft to right median nerve, percutaneous endoscopic (do not code graft harvest for this exercise)	
Exchange of liner in femoral component of previous left hip replacement, open approach	
Anterior colporrhaphy with polypropylene mesh reinforcement, open approach	
Implantation of CorCap cardiac support device, open approach	
Abdominal wall herniorrhaphy, open, using synthetic mesh	
Tendon graft to strengthen injured left shoulder using autograft, open (do not code graft harvest for this exercise)	
Onlay lamellar keratoplasty of left cornea using autograft, external approach	
Resurfacing procedure on right femoral head, open approach	
Exchange of drainage tube from right hip joint	
Tracheostomy tube exchange	
Change chest tube for left pneumothorax	
Exchange of cerebral ventriculostomy drainage tube	
Foley urinary catheter exchange	

Medical Surgical Section (Continued)

Procedure	Code
Open removal of lumbar sympathetic neurostimulator	
Nonincisional removal of Swan-Ganz catheter from right pulmonary artery	
Laparotomy with removal of pancreatic drain	
Extubation, endotracheal tube	
Nonincisional PEG tube removal	
Transvaginal removal of extraluminal cervical cerclage	
Incision with removal of K-wire fixation, right first metatarsal	
Cystoscopy with retrieval of left ureteral stent	
Removal of nasogastric drainage tube for decompression	
Removal of external fixator, left radial fracture	
Reposition of Swan-Ganz catheter insertion to superior vena cava	
Open revision of right hip replacement, with readjustment of prosthesis	
Adjustment of position, pacemaker lead in left ventricle, percutaneous	
External repositioning of Foley catheter to bladder	
Revision of VAD reservoir placement in chest wall, causing patient discomfort, open	
Thoracotomy with exploration of right pleural cavity	
Diagnostic laryngoscopy	
Exploratory arthrotomy of left knee	
Colposcopy with diagnostic hysteroscopy	
Digital rectal exam	
Diagnostic arthroscopy of right shoulder	
Endoscopy of bilateral maxillary sinus	
Laparotomy with palpation of liver	
Transurethral diagnostic cystoscopy	
Colonoscopy, abandoned at sigmoid colon	
Percutaneous mapping of basal ganglia	
Heart catheterization with cardiac mapping	
Intraoperative whole brain mapping via craniotomy	
Mapping of left cerebral hemisphere, percutaneous endoscopic	

Medical Surgical Section *(Continued)*

Procedure	Code
Intraoperative cardiac mapping during open heart surgery	
Hysteroscopy with cautery of post-hysterectomy oozing and evacuation of clot	
Open exploration and ligation of post-op arterial bleeder, left forearm	
Control of postoperative retroperitoneal bleeding via laparotomy	
Reopening of thoracotomy site with drainage and control of post-op hemopericardium	
Arthroscopy with drainage of hemarthrosis at previous operative site, right knee	
Radiocarpal fusion of left hand with internal fixation, open	
Posterior spinal fusion at L1–L3 level with BAK cage interbody fusion device, open	
Intercarpal fusion of right hand with bone bank bone graft, open	
Sacrococcygeal fusion with bone graft from same operative site, open	
Interphalangeal fusion of left great toe, percutaneous pin fixation	
Suture repair of left radial nerve laceration	
Laparotomy with suture repair of blunt force duodenal laceration	
Cosmetic face lift, open, no other information available	
Bilateral breast augmentation with silicone implants, open	
Cosmetic rhinoplasty with septal reduction and tip elevation using local tissue graft, open	
Abdominoplasty (tummy tuck), open	
Liposuction of bilateral thighs	
Creation of penis in female patient using tissue bank donor graft	
Creation of vagina in male patient using synthetic material	

Obstetrics

Procedure	Code
Abortion by dilation and evacuation following laminaria insertion	
Manually assisted spontaneous abortion	
Abortion by abortifacient insertion	
Bimanual pregnancy examination	
Extraperitoneal C-section, low transverse incision	
Fetal spinal tap, percutaneous	
Fetal kidney transplant, laparoscopic	
Open in utero repair of congenital diaphragmatic hernia	
Laparoscopy with total excision of tubal pregnancy	
Transvaginal removal of fetal monitoring electrode	

Placement

Procedure	Code
Placement of packing material, right ear	
Mechanical traction of entire left leg	
Removal of splint, right shoulder	
Placement of neck brace	
Change of vaginal packing	
Packing of wound, chest wall	
Sterile dressing placement to left groin region	
Removal of packing material from pharynx	
Placement of intermittent pneumatic compression device, covering entire right arm	
Exchange of pressure dressing to left thigh	

Administration

Procedure	Code
Peritoneal dialysis via indwelling catheter	
Transvaginal artificial insemination	
Infusion of total parenteral nutrition via central venous catheter	
Esophagogastroscopy with Botox injection into esophageal sphincter	
Percutaneous irrigation of knee joint	

Administration *(Continued)*

Procedure	Code
Epidural injection of mixed steroid and local anesthetic for pain control	
Chemical pleurodesis using injection of tetracycline	
Transfusion of antihemophilic factor, (nonautologous) via arterial central line	
Transabdominal in vitro fertilization, implantation of donor ovum	
Autologous bone marrow transplant via central venous line	

Measurement and Monitoring

Procedure	Code
Cardiac stress test, single measurement	
EGD with biliary flow measurement	
Temperature monitoring, rectal	
Peripheral venous pulse, external, single measurement	
Holter monitoring	
Respiratory rate, external, single measurement	
Fetal heart rate monitoring, transvaginal	
Visual mobility test, single measurement	
Pulmonary artery wedge pressure monitoring from Swan-Ganz catheter	
Olfactory acuity test, single measurement	

Extracorporeal Assistance and Performance

Procedure	Code
Mechanical ventilation, 16 hours	
Liver dialysis, single encounter	
Cardiac countershock with successful conversion to sinus rhythm	
IPPB (intermittent positive pressure breathing) for mobilization of secretions, 22 hours	
Measurement and monitoring of intracranial pressure, percutaneous approach	
Renal dialysis, series of encounters	

Extracorporeal Assistance and Performance *(Continued)*

Procedure	Code
IABP (intra-aortic balloon pump) continuous	
Intra-operative cardiac pacing, continuous	
ECMO (extracorporeal membrane oxygenation), continuous	
Controlled mechanical ventilation (CMV), 45 hours	
Pulsatile compression boot with intermittent inflation	

Extracorporeal Therapies

Procedure	Code
Donor thrombocytapheresis, single encounter	
Bili-lite UV phototherapy, series treatment	
Whole body hypothermia, single treatment	
Circulatory phototherapy, single encounter	
Shock wave therapy of plantar fascia, single treatment	
Antigen-free air conditioning, series treatment	
TMS (transcranial magnetic stimulation), series treatment	
Therapeutic ultrasound of peripheral vessels, single treatment	
Plasmapheresis, series treatment	
Extracorporeal electromagnetic stimulation (EMS) for urinary incontinence, single treatment	

Osteopathic

Procedures	Code
Isotonic muscle energy treatment of right leg	
Low velocity-high amplitude osteopathic treatment of head	
Lymphatic pump osteopathic treatment of left axilla	
Indirect osteopathic treatment of sacrum	
Articulatory osteopathic treatment of cervical region	

Other Procedures

Procedure	Code
Near infrared spectroscopy of leg vessels	
CT computer assisted sinus surgery	
Suture removal, abdominal wall	
Isolation after infectious disease exposure	
Robotic assisted open prostatectomy	

Chiropractic

Procedure	Code
Chiropractic treatment of lumbar region using long lever specific contact	
Chiropractic manipulation of abdominal region, indirect visceral	
Chiropractic extra-articular treatment of hip region	
Chiropractic treatment of sacrum using long and short lever specific contact	
Mechanically-assisted chiropractic manipulation of head	

Imaging

Procedure	Code
Noncontrast CT of abdomen and pelvis	
Ultrasound guidance for catheter placement, left subclavian artery	
Chest x-ray, AP/PA and lateral views	
Endoluminal ultrasound of gallbladder and bile ducts	
MRI of thyroid gland, contrast unspecified	
Esophageal videofluoroscopy study with oral barium contrast	
Portable x-ray study of right radius/ulna shaft, standard series	
Routine fetal ultrasound, second trimester twin gestation	
CT scan of bilateral lungs, high osmolar contrast with densitometry	
Fluoroscopic guidance for percutaneous transluminal angioplasty (PTA) of left common femoral artery, low osmolar contrast	

Nuclear Medicine

Procedure	Code
Tomo scan of right and left heart, unspecified radiopharmaceutical, qualitative gated rest	
Technetium pentetate assay of kidneys, ureters, and bladder	
Uniplanar scan of spine using technetium oxidronate, with first-pass study	
Thallous chloride tomographic scan of bilateral breasts	
PET scan of myocardium using rubidium	
Gallium citrate scan of head and neck, single plane imaging	
Xenon gas nonimaging probe of brain	
Upper GI scan, radiopharmaceutical unspecified, for gastric emptying	
Carbon 11 PET scan of brain with quantification	
Iodinated albumin nuclear medicine assay, blood plasma volume study	

Radiation Oncology

Procedure	Code
Plaque radiation of left eye, single port	
8 MeV photon beam radiation to brain	
IORT of colon, 3 ports	
HDR brachytherapy of prostate using palladium-103	
Electron radiation treatment of right breast, with custom device	
Hyperthermia oncology treatment of pelvic region	
Contact radiation of tongue	
Heavy particle radiation treatment of pancreas, four risk sites	
LDR brachytherapy to spinal cord using iodine	
Whole body phosphorus-32 administration with risk to hematopoetic system	

Physical Rehabilitation and Diagnostic Audiology

Procedure	Code
Bekesy assessment using audiometer	
Individual fitting of left eye prosthesis	
Physical therapy for range of motion and mobility, patient right hip, no special equipment	
Bedside swallow assessment using assessment kit	
Caregiver training in airway clearance techniques	
Application of short arm cast in rehabilitation setting	
Verbal assessment of patient's pain level	
Caregiver training in communication skills using manual communication board	
Group musculoskeletal balance training exercises, whole body, no special equipment	
Individual therapy for auditory processing using tape recorder	

Mental Health

Procedure	Code
Cognitive-behavioral psychotherapy, individual	
Narcosynthesis	
Light therapy	
ECT (electroconvulsive therapy), unilateral, multiple seizure	
Crisis intervention	
Neuropsychological testing	
Hypnosis	
Developmental testing	
Vocational counseling	
Family psychotherapy	

Substance Abuse Treatment

Procedure	Code
Naltrexone treatment for drug dependency	
Substance abuse treatment family counseling	
Medication monitoring of patient on methadone maintenance	
Individual interpersonal psychotherapy for drug abuse	
Patient in for alcohol detoxification treatment	
Group motivational counseling	
Individual 12-step psychotherapy for substance abuse	
Post-test infectious disease counseling for IV drug abuser	
Psychodynamic psychotherapy for drug-dependent patient	
Group cognitive-behavioral counseling for substance abuse	

ICD-10-PCS Draft Coding Guidelines

These are the current draft ICD-10-PCS guidelines. They are grouped into categories, including general guidelines and guidelines that apply to a section or sections. Guidelines for the Medical and Surgical section are further grouped by character. The guidelines are numbered sequentially within each category.

A. General

A.1. It is not possible to construct a procedure code from the alphabetic index. The purpose of the alphabetic index is to locate the appropriate table that contains all information necessary to construct a procedure code.

A.2. The ICD-10-PCS tables and the definitions that accompany them, the body part key, and the draft guidelines contain the complete information for correct coding. While the index contains a hierarchical lookup for finding a table and supplemental procedure terms that refer the user to the corresponding root operation options, the index does not contain exclusive coding instruction unavailable elsewhere. The user is not required to consult the index before proceeding to the tables to complete the code. The user may choose a valid code directly from the tables.

A.3. All seven characters must contain valid values to be a valid procedure code. If the documentation is incomplete for coding purposes, the physician should be queried for the necessary information.

A.4. The columns in the Tables contain the values for characters four through seven. The rows delineate the valid combinations of values. Any combination of values not contained in a single row of the Tables is invalid.

A.5. "And," when used in a code description, means "and/or."

Example: Lower Arm and Wrist Muscle means lower arm and/or wrist muscle.

B. Medical and Surgical section (section 0)

Body system guidelines

B2.1. Body systems contain body-part values that include contiguous body parts. These general body-part values are used:

a. When a procedure is performed on the general body part as a whole.

b. When the specific body part cannot be determined.

c. In the root operations *Change, Removal* and *Revision*, when the specific body-part value is not in the table.

    Example: Esophagus is a general body-part value; *Esophagus, Upper* is a specific body-part value.

B2.2. Three body systems contain body-part values that represent general anatomical regions, upper extremity anatomical regions, and lower extremity anatomical regions respectively. These body-part values are used when a procedure is performed on body layers that span more than one body system.

Example: Debridement of skin, muscle, and bone at a procedure site is coded to the anatomical regions body systems.

Exception: Composite tissue transfers are coded to the specific body systems (*Muscles* or *Subcutaneous Tissue* and *Fascia*). In these body systems, qualifiers delineate the body layers involved.

B2.3. Body systems designated as upper or lower contain body parts located above or below the diaphragm respectively.

Example: Upper Veins body parts are above the diaphragm; *Lower Veins* body parts are below the diaphragm.

Root operation guidelines

B3.1. In order to determine the appropriate root operation, the full definition of the root operation as contained in the Tables must be applied.

B3.2. Components of a procedure necessary to complete the objective of the procedure specified in the root operation are considered integral to the procedure and are not coded separately.

Example: Resection of a joint is integral to joint replacement.

Multiple procedures

B3.3. During the same operative episode, multiple procedures are coded if:

a. The same root operation is performed on different body parts as defined by distinct values of the body-part character.

    Example: Diagnostic excision of liver and pancreas are coded separately.

b. The same root operation is repeated at different body sites that are included in the same body-part value.

    Example: Excision of the sartorius muscle and excision of the gracilis muscle are both included in the *Upper Leg Muscle* body-part value, and multiple procedures are coded. Destruction of separate skin body sites on the face are all included in the body-part value *Skin, Face,* and multiple procedures are coded.

c. Multiple root operations with distinct objectives are performed on the same body part.

    Example: Destruction of sigmoid lesion and bypass of sigmoid colon are coded separately.

d. The intended root operation is attempted using one approach, but is converted to a different approach.

    Example: Laparoscopic cholecystectomy converted to an open cholecystectomy is coded as *Endoscopic Inspection* and *Open Resection*.

Discontinued procedures

B3.4. If the intended procedure is discontinued, code the procedure to the root operation performed. If a procedure is discontinued before any other root operation is performed, code the root operation Inspection of the body part or anatomical region inspected.

Example: Ureteroscopy with unsuccessful extirpation of ureteral stone is coded to Inspection of ureter.

Bypass

B3.5. Bypass procedures are coded according to the direction of flow of the contents of a tubular body part: the body-part value identifies the origin of the bypass and the qualifier identifies the destination of the bypass.

Example: Bypass from stomach to jejunum, *Stomach* (origin) is the body part and *Jejunum* (destination) is the qualifier.

Note: Coronary arteries are coded differently. The body-part value identifies the number of coronary artery sites bypassed. The qualifier identifies the origin of the bypass.

B3.6. If multiple coronary artery sites are bypassed, a separate procedure is coded for each coronary artery site that uses a different device and/or qualifier.

Example: Aortocoronary artery bypass and internal mammary coronary artery bypass are coded separately.

Control

B3.7. If an attempt to stop postprocedural bleeding is unsuccessful and requires performing *Bypass, Detachment, Excision, Extraction, Reposition, Replacement,* or *Resection* to stop the bleeding, then that root operation is coded instead of *Control.*

Example: Resection of spleen to stop postprocedural bleeding is coded to *Resection* instead of *Control.*

Diagnostic excision

B3.8. If a diagnostic excision (biopsy) is followed by a therapeutic excision at the same procedure site, or by resection of the body part during the same operative episode, code only the therapeutic excision or resection.

Example: Biopsy of breast followed by partial mastectomy at the same procedure site, only the partial mastectomy procedure is coded.

Excision vs. resection

B3.9. *Resection* is coded whenever "all of a body part" is cut out or off without replacement. "All of a body part" includes any anatomical subdivision that has its own body part value. Therefore, *Resection* of a specific anatomical subdivision body part is coded whenever possible, rather than *Excision* of the less specific body part.

Example: Left upper lung lobectomy is coded to *Resection* of upper lung lobe, left and not to *Excision* of lung, left.

Inspection

B3.10. Inspection of a body part(s) integral to the performance of the procedure is not coded separately.

Example: Fiberoptic bronchoscopy with irrigation of bronchus, only the irrigation procedure is coded.

B3.11. If multiple body parts are inspected, the body-part character is defined as the general body-part value that identifies the entire area inspected. If no general body-part value is provided, the body-part character is defined as the most distal body part inspected.

Example: Laparoscopy of pelvic organs is coded to the *pelvic region* body-part value. Cystoureteroscopy with inspection of bladder and ureters is coded to the *Ureter* body-part value.

B3.12. When both an *Inspection* procedure and another procedure are performed on the same body part during the same episode, if the *Inspection* procedure is performed using a different approach than the other procedure, the *Inspection* procedure is coded separately.

Example: Percutaneous endoscopic inspection of the small intestine during a procedure in which open excision of the duodenum is performed is coded separately.

Division and release

B3.13. If the sole objective of the procedure is separating a nontubular body part, the root operation is *Division.* If the sole objective of the procedure is freeing a body part without cutting the body part, the root operation is *Release.*

B3.14. In the root operation *Release,* the body-part value coded is the body part being freed and not the tissue being manipulated or cut to free the body part.

Example: Lysis of intestinal adhesions is coded to one of the intestine body-part values.

Fusion of vertebral joints

B3.15. If multiple vertebral joints included in the same body-part value are fused, a separate procedure is coded for each joint that uses a different device and/or qualifier. Joints between two areas of the spine (e.g., cervicothoracic vertebral joint) have their own body-part values and are coded separately.

Example: Fusion of C-4/5 with fixation device and C-5/6 with bone graft are coded separately. Fusion of the C-5/6 joint and the C7-T1 joint are coded separately.

Fracture treatment

B3.16. Reduction of a displaced fracture is coded to the root operation *Reposition.* Treatment of a nondisplaced fracture is coded to the procedure performed.

Example: Putting a pin in a nondisplaced fracture is coded to the root operation *Insertion.* Casting of a nondisplaced fracture is coded to the root operation *Immobilization* in the Placement section.

Transplantation

B3.17. Putting in a mature and functioning living body part taken from another individual or animal is coded to the root operation *Transplantation.* Putting in autologous or nonautologous cells is coded to the Administration section.

Example: Putting in autologous or nonautologous bone marrow, pancreatic islet cells or stem cells is coded to the Administration section.

Body part guidelines

B4.1. If a procedure is performed on a portion of a body part that does not have a separate body-part value, code the body-part value corresponding to the whole body part.

Example: A procedure performed on the alveolar process of the mandible is coded to the *Mandible* body part.

B4.2. If the prefix "peri" is used with a body part to identify the site of the procedure, the body-part value is defined as the body part named.

Example: A procedure site identified as perirenal is coded to the *Kidney* body part.

B4.3. If the procedure documentation uses a body part to further specify the site of the procedure, the body-part value is defined as the body part on which the procedure is performed.

Example: A procedure site identified as the prostatic urethra is coded to the *Urethra* body part.

Coronary arteries

B4.4. The coronary arteries are classified as a single body part. They are further specified by number of sites treated, not by name or number of arteries. Separate body-part values are provided to indicate the number of sites treated when the same procedure is performed on multiple sites in the coronary arteries.

Example: Two dilations with stents of a coronary artery are coded as dilation of *Coronary Artery, Two Sites,* with intraluminal device. Two dilations, one with stent and one without, are coded separately as dilation of *Coronary Artery, One Site,* with intraluminal device, and dilation of *Coronary Artery, One Site,* with no device.

Bilateral body-part values

B4.5. Bilateral body-part values are available for a limited number of body parts. They are included in the system on the basis of frequency and common practice. If the identical procedure is performed on contralateral body parts, and a bilateral body-part value exists for that body part, a single procedure is coded using the bilateral body-part value. If no bilateral body-part value exists, code each procedure separately using the appropriate body-part value.

Example: The identical procedure performed on both fallopian tubes is coded once using the body-part value *Fallopian Tube, Bilateral.* The identical procedure performed on both knee joints is coded twice using the body-part values *Knee Joint, Right* and *Knee Joint, Left.*

Body parts near a joint

B4.6. Procedures performed on tendons, ligaments, bursae and fascia supporting a joint are coded to the body part that is the focus of the procedure, in the respective body system. Procedures performed on joint structures are coded to the body part in the joint body systems.

Example: Repair of the anterior cruciate ligament of the knee is coded to the *Knee* body part in the *Bursae and Ligaments* body system. Shoulder arthroscopy with shaving of articular cartilage is coded to the *Shoulder Joint* body part.

B4.7. In body systems containing skin, subcutaneous tissue, muscle, and tendon body-part values, where a specific body-part value does not exist for the area surrounding a joint, the corresponding body part is coded as follows:

- Shoulder is coded to *Upper Arm*
- Elbow is coded to *Lower Arm*
- Wrist is coded to *Lower Arm*
- Hip is coded to *Upper Leg*
- Knee is coded to *Lower Leg*
- Ankle is coded to *Foot*

Fingers and toes

B4.8. If a body system does not contain a separate body-part value for fingers, procedures performed on the fingers are coded to the body-part value for the hand. If a body system does not contain a separate body-part value for toes, procedures performed on the toes are coded to the body-part value for the foot.

Example: Excision of finger muscle is coded to the *Hand Muscle* body-part value.

Humerus

B4.9. Procedures performed on the distal (elbow) end of the humerus are coded to the *Humeral Shaft* body-part value.

Skin glands and ducts

B4.10. Procedures performed on skin and breast glands and ducts are coded to body-part values in the body system *Skin and Breast.*

Forequarter and hindquarter

B4.11. In the anatomical regions body system containing lower extremities body parts, the body-part value *Forequarter* describes the entire upper limb plus the scapula and clavicle, and the body-part value *Hindquarter* describes the entire lower limb including all of the pelvic girdle and the buttock.

Nerves and vessels

B4.12. Nerves and vessels that are not identified by a separate body-part value are coded to the closest proximal branch identified by a body-part value.

Example: A procedure performed on the mandibular branch of the trigeminal nerve is coded to the *Trigeminal Nerve* body-part value.

Approach guidelines

Endoscopic assistance

B5.1. Procedures performed using the open approach with percutaneous endoscopic assistance are coded to approach value 0, *Open.*

Example: Laparoscopic-assisted sigmoidectomy is coded to approach value 0, *Open.*

B5.2. Procedures performed via natural or artificial opening with percutaneous endoscopic assistance are coded to approach value F, *Via Natural or Artificial Opening with Percutaneous Endoscopic Assistance.*

Example: Laparoscopic-assisted vaginal hysterectomy (LAVH) is coded to approach value F, *Via Natural or Artificial Opening with Percutaneous Endoscopic Assistance.*

External approach

B5.3a. Procedures performed within an orifice on structures that are visible without the aid of any instrumentation are coded to approach value X, *External.*

Example: Resection of tonsils is coded to approach value X, *External.*

B5.3b. Procedures performed indirectly by the application of external force through the intervening body layers are coded to approach value X, *External.*

Example: Closed reduction of fracture is coded to approach value X, *External.*

Indwelling device

B5.4a. Procedures performed via indwelling devices are coded to approach value 3, *Percutaneous.*

Example: Fragmentation of kidney stone performed via percutaneous nephrostomy is coded to approach value 3, *Percutaneous.*

B5.4b. Procedures performed on a device, as defined in the root operations *Change, Irrigation, Removal and Revision*, are coded to the procedure performed.

Example: Irrigation of percutaneous nephrostomy tube is coded to the root operation *Irrigation of Indwelling Device* in the Administration section.

Device guidelines

B6.1. A device is coded only if a device remains after the procedure is completed. If no device remains, the device value *No Device* is coded.

B6.2. Materials such as sutures, ligatures, radiological markers and temporary post-operative wound drains are considered integral to the performance of a procedure and are not coded as devices.

B6.3. A separate procedure to put in a drainage device is coded to the root operation *Drainage* with the device value *Drainage Device*.

B6.4. If, as part of a procedure, an autograft is obtained from a different body part, a separate procedure is coded.

Example: Coronary bypass with excision of saphenous vein graft, excision of saphenous vein is coded separately.

C. Other medical and surgical-related sections (sections 1–9)

C.1. The Obstetrics section includes only the procedures performed on the products of conception. Procedures performed on the pregnant female, other than the products of conception, are coded to a root operation in the Medical and Surgical section.

Example: Episiotomy is coded to a root operation in the Medical and Surgical section.

Index

A

Abdominohysterectomy
—*see* Excision, Female Reproductive System 0UB
—*see* Resection, Female Reproductive System 0UT

Abdominoplasty
—*see* Alteration, Anatomical Regions, General 0W0
—*see* Repair, Anatomical Regions, General 0WQ

Ablation—*see* Destruction

Abortion
by Body Part
Products of Conception 10A0

Abrasion—*see* Extraction

Acetabulectomy
—*see* Excision, Lower Bones 0QB
—*see* Resection, Lower Bones 0QT

Acetabuloplasty
—*see* Repair, Lower Bones 0QQ
—*see* Replacement, Lower Bones 0QR

Achillorrhaphy—*see* Repair, Tendons 0LQ

Achillotenotomy
—*see* Division, Tendons 0L8
—*see* Drainage, Tendons 0L9
—*see* Inspection, Tendons 0LJ

Achillotomy
—*see* Division, Tendons 0L8
—*see* Drainage, Tendons 0L9
—*see* Inspection, Tendons 0LJ

Acromionectomy
—*see* Excision, Upper Joints 0RB
—*see* Resection, Upper Joints 0RT

Acromioplasty
—*see* Repair, Upper Joints 0RQ
—*see* Replacement, Upper Joints 0RR

Acupuncture 8E0H

Adenoidectomy
—*see* Excision, Mouth and Throat 0CB
—*see* Resection, Mouth and Throat 0CT

Adenoidotomy
—*see* Drainage, Mouth and Throat 0C9
—*see* Inspection, Mouth and Throat 0CJ

Adhesiolysis—*see* Release

Administration
—*see* Introduction
—*see* Irrigation
—*see* Transfusion

Adrenalectomy
—*see* Excision, Endocrine System 0GB
—*see* Resection, Endocrine System 0GT

Adrenalorrhaphy—*see* Repair, Endocrine System 0GQ

Adrenaloscopy—*see* Inspection, Endocrine System 0GJ

Adrenalotomy
—*see* Drainage, Endocrine System 0G9
—*see* Inspection, Endocrine System 0GJ

Alteration
by Body System
Anatomical Regions, General 0W0
Anatomical Regions, Lower Extremities 0Y0
Anatomical Regions, Upper Extremities 0X0
Ear, Nose, Sinus 090
Eye 080
Mouth and Throat 0C0
Skin and Breast 0H0
Subcutaneous Tissue and Fascia 0J0
by Body Part
Abdominal Wall 0W0F

Alteration—*continued*
by Body Part—*continued*
Ankle Region 0Y0
Axilla 0X0
Back, Lower 0W00
Breast 0H0
Buttock, Left 0Y01
Chest Wall 0W08
Ear, External, Bilateral 0900
Elbow Region 0X0
External Ear
Bilateral 0902
Left 0901
Eyelid, Lower, Left 080N
Face 0W02
Gland, Mammary 0H0
Knee Region 0Y0
Lip, Lower 0C00
Lower Arm 0X0
Lower Back 0W0L
Lower Extremity 0Y0
Lower Eyelid 080
Lower Jaw 0W05
Lower Leg 0Y0
Lower Lip 0C01
Neck 0W06
Nose 090K
Perineum
Female 0W0N
Male 0W0M
Region
Ankle, Left 0Y00
Wrist, Left 0X02
Shoulder Region, Left 0X03
Subcutaneous Tissue and Fascia
Abdomen 0J08
Anterior Neck 0J04
Back 0J07
Buttock 0J09
Chest 0J06
Left Lower Arm 0J0H
Left Lower Leg 0J0P
Left Upper Arm 0J0F
Left Upper Leg 0J0M
Lower Leg, Left 0J01
Posterior Neck 0J05
Right Lower Arm 0J0G
Right Lower Leg 0J0N
Right Upper Arm 0J0D
Right Upper Leg 0J0L
Upper Arm 0X0
Upper Back 0W0K
Upper Extremity 0X0
Upper Eyelid, Left 080P
Upper Jaw 0W04
Upper Leg 0Y0
Wrist Region 0X0

Alveolectomy
—*see* Excision, Head and Facial Bones 0NB
—*see* Resection, Head and Facial Bones 0NT

Alveoloplasty
—*see* Repair, Head and Facial Bones 0NQ
—*see* Replacement, Head and Facial Bones 0NR

Alveolotomy
—*see* Division, Head and Facial Bones 0N8
—*see* Drainage, Head and Facial Bones 0N9
—*see* Inspection, Head and Facial Bones 0NJ

Amniocentesis 1090

Amputate—*see* Detachment

Amputation—*see* Detachment

Analog Radiography—*see* Plain Radiography

Analog Radiology—*see* Plain Radiography

Angiectomy
—*see* Excision, Heart and Great Vessels 02B
—*see* Excision, Lower Arteries 04B
—*see* Excision, Lower Veins 06B
—*see* Excision, Upper Arteries 03B
—*see* Excision, Upper Veins 05B
—*see* Resection, Heart and Great Vessels 02T

Angiography
—*see* Fluoroscopy, Heart B21
—*see* Plain Radiography, Heart B20

Angioplasty
—*see* Dilation, Heart and Great Vessels 027
—*see* Dilation, Lower Arteries 047
—*see* Dilation, Lower Veins 067
—*see* Dilation, Upper Arteries 037
—*see* Dilation, Upper Veins 057
—*see* Repair, Heart and Great Vessels 02Q
—*see* Repair, Lower Arteries 04Q
—*see* Repair, Lower Veins 06Q
—*see* Repair, Upper Arteries 03Q
—*see* Repair, Upper Veins 05Q
—*see* Replacement, Heart and Great Vessels 02R
—*see* Replacement, Lower Arteries 04R
—*see* Replacement, Lower Veins 06R
—*see* Replacement, Upper Arteries 03R
—*see* Replacement, Upper Veins 05R

Angiorrhaphy
—*see* Repair, Heart and Great Vessels 02Q
—*see* Repair, Lower Arteries 04Q
—*see* Repair, Lower Veins 06Q
—*see* Repair, Upper Arteries 03Q
—*see* Repair, Upper Veins 05Q

Angioscopy
—*see* Inspection, Heart and Great Vessels 02J
—*see* Inspection, Lower Arteries 04J
—*see* Inspection, Lower Veins 06J
—*see* Inspection, Upper Arteries 03J
—*see* Inspection, Upper Veins 05J

Angiotomy
—*see* Inspection, Heart and Great Vessels 02J
—*see* Inspection, Lower Arteries 04J
—*see* Inspection, Lower Veins 06J
—*see* Inspection, Upper Arteries 03J
—*see* Inspection, Upper Veins 05J

Angiotripsy
—*see* Occlusion, Heart and Great Vessels 02L
—*see* Occlusion, Lower Arteries 04L
—*see* Occlusion, Lower Veins 06L
—*see* Occlusion, Upper Arteries 03L
—*see* Occlusion, Upper Veins 05L

Annuloplasty
—*see* Repair, Heart and Great Vessels 02Q
—*see* Replacement, Heart and Great Vessels 02R

Anoplasty
—*see* Repair, Gastrointestinal System 0DQ
—*see* Replacement, Gastrointestinal System 0DR

Anoscopy—*see* Inspection, Gastrointestinal System 0DJ

Anosigmoidoscopy—*see* Inspection, Gastrointestinal System 0DJ

Antrostomy—*see* Drainage, Ear, Nose, Sinus 099

Antrotomy
—*see* Drainage, Ear, Nose, Sinus 099
—*see* Inspection, Ear, Nose, Sinus 09J

Aortography
—*see* Fluoroscopy, Lower Arteries B41
—*see* Fluoroscopy, Upper Arteries B31
—*see* Plain Radiography, Lower Arteries B40

Aortography—*continued*
—*see* Plain Radiography, Upper Arteries B30

Aortoplasty
—*see* Repair, Heart and Great Vessels 02Q
—*see* Replacement, Heart and Great Vessels 02R

Aortotomy
—*see* Inspection, Heart and Great Vessels 02J
—*see* Inspection, Lower Arteries 04J

Appendectomy
—*see* Excision, Gastrointestinal System 0DB
—*see* Resection, Gastrointestinal System 0DT

Appendicectomy
—*see* Excision, Gastrointestinal System 0DB
—*see* Resection, Gastrointestinal System 0DT

Appendicolysis—*see* Release, Gastrointestinal System 0DN

Appendicotomy
—*see* Drainage, Gastrointestinal System 0D9
—*see* Inspection, Gastrointestinal System 0DJ

Arterial Pulse Tracing 4A03

Arteriectomy
—*see* Excision, Heart and Great Vessels 02B
—*see* Excision, Lower Arteries 04B
—*see* Excision, Upper Arteries 03B

Arteriography
—*see* Fluoroscopy, Heart B21
—*see* Fluoroscopy, Lower Arteries B41
—*see* Fluoroscopy, Upper Arteries B31
—*see* Plain Radiography, Heart B20
—*see* Plain Radiography, Lower Arteries B40
—*see* Plain Radiography, Upper Arteries B30

Arterioplasty
—*see* Repair, Heart and Great Vessels 02Q
—*see* Repair, Lower Arteries 04Q
—*see* Repair, Upper Arteries 03Q
—*see* Replacement, Heart and Great Vessels 02R
—*see* Replacement, Lower Arteries 04R
—*see* Replacement, Upper Arteries 03R

Arteriorrhaphy
—*see* Repair, Heart and Great Vessels 02Q
—*see* Repair, Lower Arteries 04Q
—*see* Repair, Upper Arteries 03Q

Arterioscopy
—*see* Inspection, Heart and Great Vessels 02J
—*see* Inspection, Lower Arteries 04J
—*see* Inspection, Upper Arteries 03J

Arteriotomy
—*see* Inspection, Heart and Great Vessels 02J
—*see* Inspection, Lower Arteries 04J
—*see* Inspection, Upper Arteries 03J

Arthrectomy
—*see* Excision, Lower Joints 0SB
—*see* Excision, Upper Joints 0RB
—*see* Resection, Lower Joints 0ST
—*see* Resection, Upper Joints 0RT

Arthrocentesis
—*see* Drainage, Lower Joints 0S9
—*see* Drainage, Upper Joints 0R9

Arthrodesis
—*see* Fusion, Lower Joints 0SG
—*see* Fusion, Upper Joints 0RG

Arthroendoscopy
—*see* Inspection, Lower Joints 0SJ
—*see* Inspection, Upper Joints 0RJ

Arthrography
—*see* Plain Radiography, Non-Axial Lower Bones BQ0
—*see* Plain Radiography, Non-Axial Upper Bones BP0
—*see* Plain Radiography, Skull and Facial Bones BN0

Arthrolysis
—*see* Release, Lower Joints 0SN
—*see* Release, Upper Joints 0RN

Arthropexy
—*see* Repair, Lower Joints 0SQ
—*see* Repair, Upper Joints 0RQ
—*see* Reposition, Lower Joints 0SS
—*see* Reposition, Upper Joints 0RS

Arthroplasty
—*see* Repair, Lower Joints 0SQ
—*see* Repair, Upper Joints 0RQ
—*see* Replacement, Lower Joints 0SR
—*see* Replacement, Upper Joints 0RR

Arthroscopy
—*see* Inspection, Lower Joints 0SJ
—*see* Inspection, Upper Joints 0RJ

Arthrotomy
—*see* Drainage, Lower Joints 0S9
—*see* Drainage, Upper Joints 0R9
—*see* Inspection, Lower Joints 0SJ
—*see* Inspection, Upper Joints 0RJ

Arytenoidectomy—*see* Excision, Respiratory System 0BB

Arytenoidopexy
—*see* Repair, Respiratory System 0BQ
—*see* Reposition, Respiratory System 0BS

Aspirate—*see* Drainage
Aspiration—*see* Drainage
Assistance
by Function
Output
Cardiac 5A02
Oxygenation
Circulatory 5A05
Ventilation
Respiratory 5A09

Atmospheric Control
Whole Body 6A0G

Atrioseptoplasty
—*see* Repair, Heart and Great Vessels 02Q
—*see* Replacement, Heart and Great Vessels 02R

Avulsion—*see* Extraction

B

Balanoplasty
—*see* Repair, Male Reproductive System 0VQ
—*see* Replacement, Male Reproductive System 0VR

Band—*see* Restriction
Banding—*see* Restriction
Barium Swallow—*see* Fluoroscopy, Gastrointestinal System BD1
Basal Metabolism Rate 4A0G
Beam Radiation
by Body System
Anatomical Regions DW0
Breast DM0
Central and Peripheral Nervous System D00
Ear, Nose, Mouth and Throat D90
Endocrine System DG0
Eye D80
Female Reproductive System DU0
Gastrointestinal System DD0
Hepatobiliary System and Pancreas DF0
Lymphatic and Hematologic System D70
Male Reproductive System DV0
Musculoskeletal System DP0
Respiratory System DB0
Skin DH0
Urinary System DT0
by Body Part
Abdomen DW03

Beam Radiation—*continued*
by Body Part—*continued*
Adrenal Glands DG02
Bile Ducts DF02
Bladder DT02
Bones, Pelvic DP00
Brain Stem D001
Breast DM0
Bronchus DB01
Cervix DU01
Chest DW02
Chest Wall DB07
Colon DD05
Diaphragm DB08
Ducts, Bile DF00
Duodenum DD02
Esophagus DD00
Eye D800
Femur DP09
Gallbladder DF01
Glands, Parathyroid DG00
Hard Palate D908
Hemibody DW04
Humerus DP06
Hypopharynx D903
Ileum DD04
Jejunum DD03
Kidney DT00
Larynx D90B
Lung DB02
Lymphatics
Abdomen D706
Axillary D704
Inguinal D708
Neck D703
Pelvis D707
Thorax D705
Mandible DP03
Marrow, Bone D700
Maxilla DP02
Mediastinum DB06
Mouth D904
Nasopharynx D90D
Nerve, Peripheral D000
Nose D901
Oropharynx D90F
Other Bone DP0C
Ovary DU00
Palate, Soft D900
Pancreas DF03
Parathyroid Glands DG04
Pelvic Bones DP08
Pelvic Region DW06
Peripheral Nerve D007
Pineal Body DG01
Pleura DB05
Prostate DV00
Radius/Ulna DP07
Rectum DD07
Region, Pelvic DW01
Rib(s) DP05
Salivary Glands D906
Sinuses D907
Skin
Abdomen DH08
Arm DH04
Back DH07
Buttock DH09
Chest DH06
Face DH02
Leg DH0B
Neck DH03
Soft Palate D909
Spinal Cord D006
Spleen D702
Sternum DP04

Beam Radiation—*continued*

  by Body Part—*continued*

    Stomach DD01

    Testis DV01

    Thymus D701

    Thyroid DG05

    Tibia/Fibula DP0B

    Tongue D905

    Ureter DT01

    Urethra DT03

    Uterus DU02

    Wall, Chest DB00

    Whole Body DW05

Biofeedback

  by Type Qualifier

    Other Biofeedback GZC9

Biopsy

  —*see* Drainage

  —*see* Excision

Bisect—*see* Division

Bisection—*see* Division

Blepharectomy

  —*see* Excision, Eye 08B

  —*see* Resection, Eye 08T

Blepharoplasty

  —*see* Repair, Eye 08Q

  —*see* Replacement, Eye 08R

Blepharorrhaphy—*see* Repair, Eye 08Q

Blepharotomy—*see* Drainage, Eye 089

Blood Pressure 4A03

BMR 4A0G

BP 4A03

Brachytherapy

  by Body System

    Anatomical Regions DW1

    Breast DM1

    Central and Peripheral Nervous System D01

    Ear, Nose, Mouth and Throat D91

    Endocrine System DG1

    Eye D81

    Female Reproductive System DU1

    Gastrointestinal System DD1

    Hepatobiliary System and Pancreas DF1

    Lymphatic and Hematologic System D71

    Male Reproductive System DV1

    Respiratory System DB1

    Urinary System DT1

  by Body Part

    Abdomen DW13

    Adrenal Glands DG12

    Bile Ducts DF12

    Bladder DT12

    Brain Stem D011

    Breast DM1

    Bronchus DB11

    Cervix DU11

    Chest DW12

    Chest Wall DB17

    Colon DD15

    Diaphragm DB18

    Ducts, Bile DF10

    Duodenum DD12

    Esophagus DD10

    Eye D810

    Gallbladder DF11

    Glands, Parathyroid DG10

    Hard Palate D918

    Hypopharynx D913

    Ileum DD14

    Jejunum DD13

    Kidney DT10

    Larynx D91B

    Lung DB12

Brachytherapy—*continued*

  by Body Part—*continued*

    Lymphatics

      Abdomen D716

      Axillary D714

      Inguinal D718

      Neck D713

      Pelvis D717

      Thorax D715

    Marrow, Bone D710

    Mediastinum DB16

    Mouth D914

    Nasopharynx D91D

    Nerve, Peripheral D010

    Nose D911

    Oropharynx D91F

    Ovary DU10

    Palate, Soft D910

    Pancreas DF13

    Parathyroid Glands DG14

    Pelvic Region DW16

    Peripheral Nerve D017

    Pineal Body DG11

    Pleura DB15

    Prostate DV10

    Rectum DD17

    Region, Pelvic DW11

    Salivary Glands D916

    Sinuses D917

    Soft Palate D919

    Spinal Cord D016

    Spleen D712

    Stomach DD11

    Testis DV11

    Thymus D711

    Thyroid DG15

    Tongue D915

    Ureter DT11

    Urethra DT13

    Uterus DU12

    Wall, Chest DB10

Bronchography

  —*see* Fluoroscopy, Respiratory System BB1

  —*see* Plain Radiography, Respiratory System BB0

Bronchoplasty—*see* Repair, Respiratory System 0BQ

Bronchorrhaphy—*see* Repair, Respiratory System 0BQ

Bronchoscopy—*see* Inspection, Respiratory System 0BJ

Bronchotomy

  —*see* Drainage, Respiratory System 0B9

  —*see* Inspection, Respiratory System 0BJ

Bunionectomy—*see* Excision, Lower Bones 0QB

Bursectomy

  —*see* Excision, Bursae and Ligaments 0MB

  —*see* Resection, Bursae and Ligaments 0MT

Bursography

  —*see* Plain Radiography, Non-Axial Lower Bones BQ0

  —*see* Plain Radiography, Non-Axial Upper Bones BP0

Bursotomy

  —*see* Division, Bursae and Ligaments 0M8

  —*see* Drainage, Bursae and Ligaments 0M9

  —*see* Inspection, Bursae and Ligaments 0MJ

Bypass

  by Body System

    Anatomical Regions, General 0W1

    Central Nervous System 001

    Ear, Nose, Sinus 091

    Eye 081

    Female Reproductive System 0U1

Bypass—*continued*

  by Body System—*continued*

    Gastrointestinal System 0D1

    Heart and Great Vessels 021

    Hepatobiliary System and Pancreas 0F1

    Lower Arteries 041

    Lower Veins 061

    Male Reproductive System 0V1

    Respiratory System 0B1

    Upper Arteries 031

    Upper Veins 051

    Urinary System 0T1

  by Body Part

    Anterior Chamber, Left 0813

    Artery

      Aorta, Thoracic 021W

      Axillary, Left 0312

      Brachial 031

      Common Iliac, Left 0410

      Coronary, Four or More Sites 0210

      External Carotid, Left 031H

      External Iliac, Left 041E

      Femoral, Left 041K

      Popliteal, Left 041M

      Radial 031

      Splenic 0414

      Subclavian, Left 0313

      Temporal, Left 031G

    Atrium, Right 0216

    Axillary Artery 031

    Axillary Vein 051

    Basilic Vein 051

    Bladder 0T1B

    Brachial Vein 051

    Canal, Spinal 001U

    Cavity

      Cranial 0W11

      Pelvic 0W19

    Cecum 0D1H

    Cephalic Vein 051

    Chamber, Anterior, Left 0812

    Colic Vein 0617

    Colon

      Ascending 0D1K

      Descending 0D1M

      Sigmoid 0D1N

      Transverse 0D1L

    Common Bile Duct 0F19

    Common Carotid Artery, Left 031J

    Common Iliac Artery 041

    Common Iliac Vein 061

    Coronary Artery

      Four or More Sites 0213

      Three Sites 0212

      Two Sites 0211

    Cystic Duct 0F18

    Deferens, Vas, Bilateral 0V1N

    Duct

      Common Bile 0F14

      Lacrimal, Left 081X

      Pancreatic, Accessory 0F1D

    Duodenum 0D19

    Ear, Inner, Left 091D

    Esophageal Vein 0613

    Esophagus 0D15

      Lower 0D13

      Middle 0D12

      Upper 0D11

    External Carotid Artery 031

    External Iliac Artery 041

    External Iliac Vein 061

    External Jugular Vein 051

    Face Vein 051

    Fallopian Tube, Left 0U16

    Femoral Artery, Left 041L

    Femoral Vein 061

Bypass—*continued*
  by Body Part—*continued*
    Foot Vein 061
    Greater Saphenous Vein 061
    Hand Vein 051
    Hemiazygos Vein 0511
    Hepatic Duct 0F1
    Hepatic Vein 0614
    Hypogastric Vein 061
    Ileum 0D1B
    Inferior Mesenteric Vein 0616
    Inner Ear, Left 091E
    Innominate Vein 051
    Internal Carotid Artery 031
    Internal Iliac Artery, Left 041F
    Internal Jugular Vein 051
    Intracranial Vein 051L
    Jejunum 0D1A
    Kidney Pelvis, Left 0T14
    Lacrimal Duct, Left 081Y
    Lesser Saphenous Vein 061
    Pancreas 0F1G
      Body 0F1F
      Head 0F1F
      Tail 0F1F
    Pancreatic Duct, Accessory 0F1F
    Pelvic Cavity 0W1J
    Pelvis, Kidney, Left 0T13
    Peritoneal Cavity 0W1G
    Pleural Cavity, Left 0W1B
    Popliteal Artery, Left 041N
    Radial Artery 031
    Renal Pelvis 0T1
    Renal Vein 061
    Stomach 0D16
      Body 0D16
      Fundus 0D16
    Subclavian Artery, Left 0314
    Subclavian Vein 051
    Superior Mesenteric Vein 0615
    Superior Vena Cava 021V
    Temporal Artery 031
    Trachea 0B11
    Tube, Fallopian, Left 0U15
    Ureter 0T1
    Ureters, Bilateral 0T18
    Vas Deferens
      Bilateral 0V1Q
      Left 0V1P
    Vein
      Face, Left 0510
      Foot, Left 0612
      Portal 0618
      Splenic 0611
      Vena Cava, Inferior 0610
      Vena Cava, Superior 0217
    Ventricle 021
      Cerebral 0016
    Vertebral Vein 051

C

C.A.T. —*see* Computerized Tomography (CT Scan)
Caesarean—*see* Cesarean Section
Caesarean Section—*see* Cesarean Section
Cardiolysis—*see* Release, Heart and Great Vessels 02N
Cardiomyopexy—*see* Repair, Heart and Great Vessels 02Q
Cardiorrhaphy—*see* Repair, Heart and Great Vessels 02Q
Cardioversion—*see* Restoration, Extracorporeal Assistance And Performance 5A2

Carpectomy
  —*see* Excision, Upper Bones 0PB
  —*see* Resection, Upper Bones 0PT
Castration
  —*see* Resection, Female Reproductive System 0UT
  —*see* Resection, Male Reproductive System 0VT
Cauterization—*see* Destruction
Cauterize—*see* Destruction
Cavernography
  —*see* Fluoroscopy, Anatomical Regions BW1
  —*see* Plain Radiography, Anatomical Regions BW0
Cecectomy
  —*see* Excision, Gastrointestinal System 0DB
  —*see* Resection, Gastrointestinal System 0DT
Cecocolopexy
  —*see* Repair, Gastrointestinal System 0DQ
  —*see* Reposition, Gastrointestinal System 0DS
Cecocolostomy—*see* Bypass, Gastrointestinal System 0D1
Cecofixation—*see* Repair, Gastrointestinal System 0DQ
Cecoileostomy—*see* Bypass, Gastrointestinal System 0D1
Cecopexy
  —*see* Repair, Gastrointestinal System 0DQ
  —*see* Reposition, Gastrointestinal System 0DS
Cecoplication—*see* Restriction, Gastrointestinal System 0DV
Cecorrhaphy—*see* Repair, Gastrointestinal System 0DQ
Cecosigmoidostomy—*see* Bypass, Gastrointestinal System 0D1
Cecostomy—*see* Bypass, Gastrointestinal System 0D1
Cecotomy
  —*see* Drainage, Gastrointestinal System 0D9
  —*see* Inspection, Gastrointestinal System 0DJ
Central Venous Pressure 4A04
Cerclage—*see* Restriction
Cervicectomy
  —*see* Excision, Female Reproductive System 0UB
  —*see* Resection, Female Reproductive System 0UT
Cesarean—*see* Cesarean Section
Cesarean Section 10D
Change
  by Body System
    Anatomical Regions, General 0W2
    Anatomical Regions, Lower Extremities 0Y2
    Anatomical Regions, Upper Extremities 0X2
    Bursae and Ligaments 0M2
    Central Nervous System 002
    Ear, Nose, Sinus 092
    Endocrine System 0G2
    Eye 082
    Female Reproductive System 0U2
    Gastrointestinal System 0D2
    Head and Facial Bones 0N2
    Hepatobiliary System and Pancreas 0F2
    Lower Bones 0Q2
    Lower Joints 0S2
    Lymphatic and Hemic Systems 072
    Male Reproductive System 0V2
    Mouth and Throat 0C2
    Muscles 0K2
    Peripheral Nervous System 012
    Respiratory System 0B2

Change—*continued*
  by Body System—*continued*
    Skin and Breast 0H2
    Subcutaneous Tissue and Fascia 0J2
    Tendons 0L2
    Upper Bones 0P2
    Upper Joints 0R2
    Urinary System 0T2
  by Device
    Bandage
      Abdominal Wall 2W03
      Back 2W05
      Chest Wall 2W04
      Face 2W01
      Finger 2W0
      Foot 2W0
      Hand 2W0
      Head 2W00
      Inguinal Region 2W0
      Leg, Lower, Left 2W02
      Lower Arm 2W0
      Lower Extremity 2W0
      Lower Leg 2W0
      Thumb 2W0
      Toe 2W0
      Upper Arm 2W0
      Upper Extremity 2W0
      Upper Leg 2W0
    Brace
      Abdominal Wall 2W03
      Back 2W05
      Chest Wall 2W04
      Face 2W01
      Finger 2W0
      Foot 2W0
      Hand 2W0
      Head 2W00
      Inguinal Region 2W0
      Leg, Lower, Left 2W02
      Lower Arm 2W0
      Lower Extremity 2W0
      Lower Leg 2W0
      Thumb 2W0
      Toe 2W0
      Upper Arm 2W0
      Upper Extremity 2W0
      Upper Leg 2W0
    Cast
      Abdominal Wall 2W03
      Back 2W05
      Chest Wall 2W04
      Face 2W01
      Finger 2W0
      Foot 2W0
      Hand 2W0
      Head 2W00
      Inguinal Region 2W0
      Leg, Lower, Left 2W02
      Lower Arm 2W0
      Lower Extremity 2W0
      Lower Leg 2W0
      Thumb 2W0
      Toe 2W0
      Upper Arm 2W0
      Upper Extremity 2W0
      Upper Leg 2W0
    Contraceptive Device
      Cervix, Uterus and 0U2D
    Drainage Device
      Abdominal Wall 0W2F
      Adenohypophysis 0G20
      Adrenal Gland 0G25
      Back, Lower 0W20
      Bladder 0T2B

Codes provided in the index are incomplete. Refer to tables to determine additional character values.   © 2009 Ingenix, Inc.

Change—*continued*
  by Device—*continued*
    Drainage Device—*continued*
      Bone
        Facial 0N20
        Lower 0Q2Y
        Upper 0P2Y
      Bone Marrow 072T
      Breast 0H2
      Bursa and Ligament, Lower 0M2X
      Canal, Spinal 0020
      Cervix, Uterus and 0U2D
      Chest Wall 0W28
      Cisterna Chyli 072L
      Corpora Arenacea, Pineal 0G21
      Cranial Cavity 0W21
      Cranial Nerve 002E
      Cul-de-sac, Vagina and 0U2H
      Deferens, Vas 0V24
      Diaphragm 0B2T
      Duct, Pancreatic 0F20
      Ear 092
      Endocrine Gland 0G2S
      Epididymis and Spermatic Cord 0V2M
      Extremity
        Lower, Left 0Y29
        Upper, Left 0X26
      Eye 082
      Face 0W22
      Facial Bone 0N2W
      Fallopian Tube 0U28
      Gallbladder 0F24
      Gland
        Endocrine 0G20
        Mammary 0H2
        Pineal 0G21
        Salivary 0C2A
      Hepatobiliary Duct 0F2B
      Hypophysis 0G20
      Joint
        Lower 0S2Y
        Upper 0R2Y
      Kidney 0T25
      Larynx 0C2S
      Lower Back 0W2L
      Lower Bursa and Ligament 0M2Y
      Lower Extremity, Left 0Y2B
      Lower Intestinal Tract 0D2D
      Lower Jaw 0W25
      Lower Muscle 0K2Y
      Lower Tendon 0L2Y
      Lung 0B2
      Lymphatic 072N
      Marrow, Bone 072K
      Mediastinum 0W2C
      Mesentery 0D2V
      Mouth and Throat 0C2Y
      Muscle, Lower 0K2X
      Nasal Bone 0N2B
      Neck 0W26
      Nerve, Peripheral 012Y
      Neurohypophysis 0G20
      Nose 092K
      Omentum 0D2U
      Pancreas 0F2G
      Pancreatic Duct 0F2D
      Parathyroid Gland 0G2R
      Pelvic Cavity 0W2J
      Penis 0V2S
      Pericardial Cavity 0W2D
      Perineum
        Female 0W2N
        Male 0W2M
      Peritoneal Cavity 0W2G
      Peritoneum 0D2W
      Pineal Body 0G21

Change—*continued*
  by Device—*continued*
    Drainage Device—*continued*
      Pleura 0B2Q
      Pleural Cavity 0W2
      Retroperitoneum 0W2H
      Scrotum and Tunica Vaginalis 0V28
      Sinus 092Y
      Skin 0H2P
      Spinal Canal 002U
      Spleen 072P
      Subcutaneous Tissue and Fascia
        Head and Neck 0J2S
        Lower Extremity 0J2W
        Trunk 0J2T
        Upper Extremity 0J2V
      Tendon, Lower 0L2X
      Testis 0V2D
      Thymus 072M
      Thyroid Gland 0G2K
      Trachea 0B21
      Tract, Lower Intestinal 0D20
      Tree, Tracheobronchial 0B20
      Tube, Fallopian 0U23
      Upper Back 0W2K
      Upper Extremity, Left 0X27
      Upper Jaw 0W24
      Ureter 0T29
      Urethra 0T2D
      Vas Deferens 0V2R
      Vulva 0U2M
    Endotracheal Device
      Trachea 0B21
    Feeding Device
      Lower Intestinal Tract 0D2D
      Tract, Lower Intestinal 0D20
    Intermittent Pressure Device
      Abdominal Wall 2W03
      Back 2W05
      Chest Wall 2W04
      Face 2W01
      Finger 2W0
      Foot 2W0
      Hand 2W0
      Head 2W00
      Inguinal Region 2W0
      Leg, Lower, Left 2W02
      Lower Arm 2W0
      Lower Extremity 2W0
      Lower Leg 2W0
      Thumb 2W0
      Toe 2W0
      Upper Arm 2W0
      Upper Extremity 2W0
      Upper Leg 2W0
    Monitoring Electrode
      Products of Conception 1020
    Other Device
      Abdominal Wall 0W2F
      Abdominal Wall 2W03
      Adenohypophysis 0G20
      Adrenal Gland 0G25
      Back 2W05
        Lower 0W20
      Bladder 0T2B
      Bone
        Facial 0N20
        Lower 0Q2Y
        Upper 0P2Y
      Bone Marrow 072T
      Breast 0H2
      Bursa and Ligament, Lower 0M2X
      Canal, Spinal 0020
      Cervix, Uterus and 0U2D
      Chest Wall 0W28
      Chest Wall 2W04

Change—*continued*
  by Device—*continued*
    Other Device—*continued*
      Cisterna Chyli 072L
      Corpora Arenacea, Pineal 0G21
      Cranial Cavity 0W21
      Cranial Nerve 002E
      Cul-de-sac, Vagina and 0U2H
      Deferens, Vas 0V24
      Diaphragm 0B2T
      Duct, Pancreatic 0F20
      Ear 092
      Endocrine Gland 0G2S
      Epididymis and Spermatic Cord
        0V2M
      Extremity
        Lower, Left 0Y29
        Upper, Left 0X26
      Eye 082
      Face 0W22
      Face 2W01
      Facial Bone 0N2W
      Fallopian Tube 0U28
      Finger 2W0
      Foot 2W0
      Gallbladder 0F24
      Gland
        Endocrine 0G20
        Mammary 0H2
        Pineal 0G21
        Salivary 0C2A
      Hand 2W0
      Head 2W00
      Hepatobiliary Duct 0F2B
      Hypophysis 0G20
      Inguinal Region 2W0
      Joint
        Lower 0S2Y
        Upper 0R2Y
      Kidney 0T25
      Larynx 0C2S
      Leg, Lower, Left 2W02
      Lower Arm 2W0
      Lower Back 0W2L
      Lower Bursa and Ligament 0M2Y
      Lower Extremity
        Left 0Y2B
      Lower Extremity 2W0
      Lower Intestinal Tract 0D2D
      Lower Jaw 0W25
      Lower Leg 2W0
      Lower Muscle 0K2Y
      Lower Tendon 0L2Y
      Lung 0B2
      Lymphatic 072N
      Marrow, Bone 072K
      Mediastinum 0W2C
      Mesentery 0D2V
      Mouth and Throat 0C2Y
      Muscle, Lower 0K2X
      Nasal Bone 0N2B
      Neck 0W26
      Nerve, Peripheral 012Y
      Neurohypophysis 0G20
      Nose 092K
      Omentum 0D2U
      Pancreas 0F2G
      Pancreatic Duct 0F2D
      Parathyroid Gland 0G2R
      Pelvic Cavity 0W2J
      Penis 0V2S
      Pericardial Cavity 0W2D
      Perineum
        Female 0W2N
        Male 0W2M
      Peritoneal Cavity 0W2G

Change—*continued*
  by Device—continued
    Other Device—*continued*
      Peritoneum 0D2W
      Pineal Body 0G21
      Pleura 0B2Q
      Pleural Cavity 0W2
      Products of Conception 1020
      Retroperitoneum 0W2H
      Scrotum and Tunica Vaginalis 0V28
      Sinus 092Y
      Skin 0H2P
      Spinal Canal 002U
      Spleen 072P
      Subcutaneous Tissue and Fascia
        Head and Neck 0J2S
        Lower Extremity 0J2W
        Trunk 0J2T
        Upper Extremity 0J2V
      Tendon, Lower 0L2X
      Testis 0V2D
      Thumb 2W0
      Thymus 072M
      Thyroid Gland 0G2K
      Toe 2W0
      Trachea 0B21
      Tract, Lower Intestinal 0D20
      Tree, Tracheobronchial 0B20
      Tube, Fallopian 0U23
      Upper Arm 2W0
      Upper Back 0W2K
      Upper Extremity
        Left 0X27
      Upper Extremity 2W0
      Upper Jaw 0W24
      Upper Leg 2W0
      Ureter 0T29
      Urethra 0T2D
      Vas Deferens 0V2R
      Vulva 0U2M
    Packing Material
      Abdominal Wall 2W03
      Anorectal 2Y03
      Back 2W05
      Chest Wall 2W04
      Ear 2Y02
      Face 2W01
      Female Genital Tract 2Y04
      Finger 2W0
      Foot 2W0
      Genital Tract, Female 2Y00
      Hand 2W0
      Head 2W00
      Inguinal Region 2W0
      Leg, Lower, Left 2W02
      Lower Arm 2W0
      Lower Extremity 2W0
      Lower Leg 2W0
      Nasal 2Y01
      Thumb 2W0
      Toe 2W0
      Upper Arm 2W0
      Upper Extremity 2W0
      Upper Leg 2W0
      Urethra 2Y05
    Pessary
      Cul-de-sac, Vagina and 0U2H
    Pressure Dressing
      Abdominal Wall 2W03
      Back 2W05
      Chest Wall 2W04
      Face 2W01
      Finger 2W0
      Foot 2W0
      Hand 2W0
      Head 2W00

Change—*continued*
  by Device—continued
    Pressure Dressing—*continued*
      Inguinal Region 2W0
      Leg, Lower, Left 2W02
      Lower Arm 2W0
      Lower Extremity 2W0
      Lower Leg 2W0
      Thumb 2W0
      Toe 2W0
      Upper Arm 2W0
      Upper Extremity 2W0
      Upper Leg 2W0
    Splint
      Abdominal Wall 2W03
      Back 2W05
      Chest Wall 2W04
      Face 2W01
      Finger 2W0
      Foot 2W0
      Hand 2W0
      Head 2W00
      Inguinal Region 2W0
      Leg, Lower, Left 2W02
      Lower Arm 2W0
      Lower Extremity 2W0
      Lower Leg 2W0
      Thumb 2W0
      Toe 2W0
      Upper Arm 2W0
      Upper Extremity 2W0
      Upper Leg 2W0
    Stereotactic Apparatus
      Head 2W00
    Tracheostomy Device
      Trachea 0B21
    Traction Apparatus
      Abdominal Wall 2W03
      Back 2W05
      Chest Wall 2W04
      Face 2W01
      Finger 2W0
      Foot 2W0
      Hand 2W0
      Head 2W00
      Inguinal Region 2W0
      Leg, Lower, Left 2W02
      Lower Arm 2W0
      Lower Extremity 2W0
      Lower Leg 2W0
      Thumb 2W0
      Toe 2W0
      Upper Arm 2W0
      Upper Extremity 2W0
      Upper Leg 2W0
    Wire
      Face 2W01
Check—*see* Inspection
Chemothalamectomy—*see* Destruction, Central Nervous System 005
Chiropractic—*see* Manipulation
Cholecystectomy
  —*see* Excision, Hepatobiliary System and Pancreas 0FB
  —*see* Resection, Hepatobiliary System and Pancreas 0FT
Cholecystojejunostomy—*see* Bypass, Hepatobiliary System and Pancreas 0F1
Cholecystopexy
  —*see* Repair, Hepatobiliary System and Pancreas 0FQ
  —*see* Reposition, Hepatobiliary System and Pancreas 0FS
Cholecystoscopy—*see* Inspection, Hepatobiliary System and Pancreas 0FJ

Cholecystostomy—*see* Drainage, Hepatobiliary System and Pancreas 0F9
Cholecystotomy
  —*see* Drainage, Hepatobiliary System and Pancreas 0F9
  —*see* Inspection, Hepatobiliary System and Pancreas 0FJ
Choledochectomy
  —*see* Excision, Hepatobiliary System and Pancreas 0FB
  —*see* Resection, Hepatobiliary System and Pancreas 0FT
Choledochoplasty
  —*see* Repair, Hepatobiliary System and Pancreas 0FQ
  —*see* Replacement, Hepatobiliary System and Pancreas 0FR
Choledochoscopy—*see* Inspection, Hepatobiliary System and Pancreas 0FJ
Choledochotomy
  —*see* Drainage, Hepatobiliary System and Pancreas 0F9
  —*see* Inspection, Hepatobiliary System and Pancreas 0FJ
Cholelithotomy
  —*see* Drainage, Hepatobiliary System and Pancreas 0F9
  —*see* Inspection, Hepatobiliary System and Pancreas 0FJ
Chordotomy—*see* Division, Central Nervous System 008
Choroidectomy
  —*see* Excision, Eye 08B
  —*see* Resection, Eye 08T
Cionectomy
  —*see* Excision, Mouth and Throat 0CB
  —*see* Resection, Mouth and Throat 0CT
Cionorrhaphy—*see* Repair, Mouth and Throat 0CQ
Cionotomy
  —*see* Drainage, Mouth and Throat 0C9
  —*see* Inspection, Mouth and Throat 0CJ
Circumcision
  —*see* Resection, Female Reproductive System 0UT
  —*see* Resection, Male Reproductive System 0VT
Clamp—*see* Occlusion
Claviculectomy
  —*see* Excision, Upper Bones 0PB
  —*see* Resection, Upper Bones 0PT
Claviculotomy
  —*see* Division, Upper Bones 0P8
  —*see* Drainage, Upper Bones 0P9
  —*see* Inspection, Upper Bones 0PJ
Clip
  —*see* Occlusion
  —*see* Restriction
Clipping
  —*see* Occlusion
  —*see* Restriction
Clitorectomy
  —*see* Excision, Female Reproductive System 0UB
  —*see* Resection, Female Reproductive System 0UT
Clitoridectomy
  —*see* Excision, Female Reproductive System 0UB
  —*see* Resection, Female Reproductive System 0UT

Computerized Tomography (CT Scan)—
continued
  by Body Part—continued
    Tracheobronchial Trees, Bilateral BB29
    Transplant, Kidney BT20
    Trees, Tracheobronchial, Bilateral BB24
    Upper Arm BP2
    Upper Extremities, Bilateral BP2V
    Upper Extremity BP2
    Veins, Pulmonary, Bilateral B522
    Vertebral Arteries, Bilateral B32G
    Wrist BP2

Condylectomy
  —*see* Excision, Head and Facial Bones 0NB
  —*see* Excision, Lower Bones 0QB
  —*see* Excision, Upper Bones 0PB

Condylotomy
  —*see* Division, Head and Facial Bones 0N8
  —*see* Division, Lower Bones 0Q8
  —*see* Division, Upper Bones 0P8
  —*see* Drainage, Head and Facial Bones 0N9
  —*see* Drainage, Lower Bones 0Q9
  —*see* Drainage, Upper Bones 0P9
  —*see* Inspection, Head and Facial Bones 0NJ
  —*see* Inspection, Lower Bones 0QJ
  —*see* Inspection, Upper Bones 0PJ

Condylysis
  —*see* Release, Head and Facial Bones 0NN
  —*see* Release, Lower Bones 0QN
  —*see* Release, Upper Bones 0PN

Conization—*see* Excision, Female
  Reproductive System 0UB

Conjunctivoplasty
  —*see* Repair, Eye 08Q
  —*see* Replacement, Eye 08R

Continuous Positive Airway Pressure 5A09

Control
  by Body System
    Anatomical Regions, General 0W3
    Anatomical Regions, Lower Extremities
      0Y3
    Anatomical Regions, Upper Extremities
      0X3
  by Body Part
    Abdominal Wall 0W3F
    Ankle Region 0Y3
    Axilla 0X3
    Back, Lower 0W30
    Buttock, Left 0Y31
    Chest Wall 0W38
    Cranial Cavity 0W31
    Elbow Region 0X3
    Face 0W32
    Femoral Region 0Y3
    Foot 0Y3
    Genitourinary Tract 0W3R
    Hand 0X3
    Inguinal Region 0Y3
    Knee Region 0Y3
    Lower Arm 0X3
    Lower Back 0W3L
    Lower Extremity 0Y3
    Lower Jaw 0W35
    Lower Leg 0Y3
    Mediastinum 0W3C
    Neck 0W36
    Oral Cavity and Throat 0W33
    Pelvic Cavity 0W3J
    Pericardial Cavity 0W3D
    Perineum
      Female 0W3N
      Male 0W3M
    Peritoneal Cavity 0W3G
    Pleural Cavity 0W3

Control—*continued*
  by Body Part—continued
    Region
      Ankle, Left 0Y30
      Wrist, Left 0X32
    Respiratory Tract 0W3Q
    Retroperitoneum 0W3H
    Shoulder Region, Left 0X33
    Tract, Genitourinary 0W3P
    Upper Arm 0X3
    Upper Back 0W3K
    Upper Extremity 0X3
    Upper Jaw 0W34
    Upper Leg 0Y3
    Wrist Region 0X3

Cordotomy—*see* Division, Central Nervous
  System 008

Core Needle Biopsy—*see* Excision

Coronary Arteriography
  —*see* Fluoroscopy, Heart B21
  —*see* Plain Radiography, Heart B20

Correction—*see* Repair

Costatectomy
  —*see* Excision, Upper Bones 0PB
  —*see* Resection, Upper Bones 0PT

Costectomy
  —*see* Excision, Upper Bones 0PB
  —*see* Resection, Upper Bones 0PT

Costochondrectomy
  —*see* Excision, Upper Bones 0PB
  —*see* Resection, Upper Bones 0PT

Costosternoplasty
  —*see* Repair, Upper Bones 0PQ
  —*see* Replacement, Upper Bones 0PR

Costotomy
  —*see* Division, Upper Bones 0P8
  —*see* Drainage, Upper Bones 0P9
  —*see* Inspection, Upper Bones 0PJ

Counseling
  by Type Qualifier
    Educational GZ60
    Other Counseling GZ63
    Vocational GZ61

CPAP 5A09

Craniectomy
  —*see* Excision, Head and Facial Bones 0NB
  —*see* Resection, Head and Facial Bones 0NT

Cranioplasty
  —*see* Repair, Head and Facial Bones 0NQ
  —*see* Replacement, Head and Facial Bones
    0NR

Craniotomy
  —*see* Division, Head and Facial Bones 0N8
  —*see* Drainage, Central Nervous System 009
  —*see* Drainage, Head and Facial Bones 0N9
  —*see* Inspection, Central Nervous System
    00J
  —*see* Inspection, Head and Facial Bones 0NJ

Creation
  by Body System
    Anatomical Regions, General 0W4
  by Body Part
    Penis 0W4N
    Vagina 0W4M

Crisis Intervention GZ2Z

Cryoablation—*see* Destruction

Cryotherapy—*see* Destruction

Cryptorchidectomy
  —*see* Excision, Male Reproductive System
    0VB
  —*see* Resection, Male Reproductive System
    0VT

Cryptorchiectomy
  —*see* Excision, Male Reproductive System
    0VB
  —*see* Resection, Male Reproductive System
    0VT

Cryptotomy
  —*see* Division, Gastrointestinal System 0D8
  —*see* Drainage, Gastrointestinal System 0D9
  —*see* Inspection, Gastrointestinal System
    0DJ

CT Scan—*see* Computerized Tomography (CT
  Scan)

CT Sialogram—*see* Computerized
  Tomography (CT Scan), Ear, Nose,
  Mouth and Throat B92

Culdotomy
  —*see* Drainage, Female Reproductive System
    0U9
  —*see* Inspection, Female Reproductive
    System 0UJ

Curettage
  —*see* Excision
  —*see* Extraction

CVP 4A04

Cystectomy
  —*see* Excision, Urinary System 0TB
  —*see* Resection, Urinary System 0TT

Cystography
  —*see* Fluoroscopy, Urinary System BT1
  —*see* Plain Radiography, Urinary System BT0

Cystolithotomy—*see* Extirpation, Urinary
  System 0TC

Cystopexy
  —*see* Repair, Urinary System 0TQ
  —*see* Reposition, Urinary System 0TS

Cystoplasty
  —*see* Repair, Urinary System 0TQ
  —*see* Replacement, Urinary System 0TR

Cystorrhaphy—*see* Repair, Urinary System
  0TQ

Cystoscopy—*see* Inspection, Urinary System
  0TJ

Cystostomy—*see* Bypass, Urinary System 0T1

Cystotomy
  —*see* Drainage, Urinary System 0T9
  —*see* Inspection, Urinary System 0TJ

Cystourethrography
  —*see* Fluoroscopy, Urinary System BT1
  —*see* Plain Radiography, Urinary System BT0

Cystourethropexy
  —*see* Repair, Urinary System 0TQ
  —*see* Reposition, Urinary System 0TS

Cystourethroplasty
  —*see* Repair, Urinary System 0TQ
  —*see* Replacement, Urinary System 0TR

D

Debridement
  —*see* Excision
  —*see* Extraction

Debridement (excisional)—*see* Excision

Debridement (non-excisional)—*see*
  Extraction

Decompression
  —*see* Release Circulatory 6A15

Delivery
  by Body Part
    Products of Conception 10E0

Destruction
  by Body System
    Bursae and Ligaments 0M5
    Central Nervous System 005
    Ear, Nose, Sinus 095

Destruction—*continued*
  by Body System—*continued*
    Endocrine System 0G5
    Eye 085
    Female Reproductive System 0U5
    Gastrointestinal System 0D5
    Head and Facial Bones 0N5
    Heart and Great Vessels 025
    Hepatobiliary System and Pancreas 0F5
    Lower Arteries 045
    Lower Bones 0Q5
    Lower Joints 0S5
    Lower Veins 065
    Lymphatic and Hemic Systems 075
    Male Reproductive System 0V5
    Mouth and Throat 0C5
    Muscles 0K5
    Peripheral Nervous System 015
    Respiratory System 0B5
    Skin and Breast 0H5
    Subcutaneous Tissue and Fascia 0J5
    Tendons 0L5
    Upper Arteries 035
    Upper Bones 0P5
    Upper Joints 0R5
    Upper Veins 055
    Urinary System 0T5
  by Body Part
    Abdomen Bursa and Ligament 0M5
    Abdomen Muscle 0K5
    Abdomen Tendon 0L5
    Abdominal Sympathetic Nerve 015M
    Abducens Nerve 005L
    Accessory Nerve 005R
    Accessory Sinus 095P
    Acetabulum 0Q5
    Acoustic Nerve 005N
    Acromioclavicular Joint 0R5
    Adenohypophysis 0G50
    Adenoids 0C5Q
    Adrenal Gland 0G5
    Adrenal Glands, Bilateral 0G54
    Ampulla of Vater 0F5C
    Ankle Bursa and Ligament 0M5
    Ankle Joint 0S5
    Ankle Tendon 0L5
    Anterior Chamber, Left 0853
    Anterior Tibial Artery 045
    Anus 0D5Q
    Aortic Body 0G5D
    Aortic Valve 025F
    Appendix 0D5J
    Areola 0H5
    Artery
      Aorta, Thoracic 0254
      Lower 0450
      Upper 0350
    Ascending Colon 0D5K
    Atrial Septum 0255'
    Atrium 025
    Auditory Ossicle 095
    Axillary Artery 035
    Axillary Vein 055
    Basal Ganglia 0058
    Basilic Vein 055
    Bladder 0T5B
    Bladder Neck 0T5C
    Body
      Coccygeal 0G59
      Jugulotympanic 0G5B
    Bone, Hyoid 0N50
    Brachial Artery 035
    Brachial Plexus 0153
    Brachial Vein 055
    Breast 0H5
    Bronchus, Segmental, Lingula 0B59

Destruction—*continued*
  by Body Part—*continued*
    Buccal Mucosa 0C54
    Bursa and Ligament, Lower Extremity, Left 0M50
    Canal, External Auditory, Left 0953
    Carina 0B52
    Carotid Bodies, Bilateral 0G58
    Carotid Body 0G5
    Carpal 0P5
    Carpal Joint 0R5
    Cecum 0D5H
    Celiac Artery 0451
    Cephalic Vein 055
    Cerebellum 005C
    Cerebral Hemisphere 0057
    Cerebral Meninges 0051
    Cerebral Ventricle 0056
    Cervical Nerve 0151
    Cervical Spinal Cord 005W
    Cervical Vertebra 0P53
    Cervical Vertebral Disc 0R53
    Cervical Vertebral Joint 0R51
    Cervicothoracic Vertebral Disc 0R55
    Cervicothoracic Vertebral Joint 0R54
    Cervix 0U5C
    Chordae Tendineae 0259
    Choroid, Left 085B
    Chyli, Cisterna 0750
    Cisterna Chyli 075L
    Clavicle 0P5
    Coccygeal Glomus 0G5B
    Coccygeal Joint 0S56
    Coccyx 0Q5S
    Colic Artery 045
    Colic Vein 0657
    Colon, Sigmoid 0D51
    Common Bile Duct 0F59
    Common Carotid Artery 035
    Common Iliac Artery 045
    Common Iliac Vein 065
    Conduction Mechanism 0258
    Conjunctiva 085
    Cord
      Lumbar Spinal 0050
      Vocal, Left 0C5M
    Cornea 085
    Corpora Arenacea, Pineal 0G51
    Cul-de-sac 0U5F
    Cystic Duct 0F58
    Deferens, Vas, Bilateral 0V51
    Descending Colon 0D5M
    Diaphragm 0B5
    Duct
      Lacrimal, Left 085X
      Pancreatic, Accessory 0F55
    Duodenum 0D59
    Dura Mater 0052
    Ear
      External, Left 0950
      Inner, Left 0955
    Elbow Bursa and Ligament 0M5
    Elbow Joint 0R5
    Endometrium 0U5B
    Epididymis 0V5
    Epiglottis 0C5R
    Esophageal Vein 0653
    Esophagogastric Junction 0D54
    Esophagus 0D55
      Lower 0D53
      Middle 0D52
    Ethmoid Bone 0N5
    Ethmoid Sinus 095
    Eustachian Tube 095
    External Auditory Canal, Left 0954
    External Carotid Artery 035

Destruction—*continued*
  by Body Part—*continued*
    External Ear, Left 0951
    External Iliac Artery 045
    External Iliac Vein 065
    External Jugular Vein 055
    Extraocular Muscle 085
    Eye 085
    Eyelid, Lower, Left 085N
    Face Artery 035R
    Face Vein 055
    Facial Muscle 0K51
    Facial Nerve 005M
    Fallopian Tube, Left 0U56
    Fallopian Tubes, Bilateral 0U57
    Femoral Artery 045
    Femoral Nerve 015D
    Femoral Shaft 0Q5
    Femoral Vein 065
    Fibula 0Q5
    Finger Nail 0H5Q
    Finger Phalangeal Joint 0R5
    Finger Phalanx 0P5
    Foot Artery 045
    Foot Bursa and Ligament 0M5
    Foot Muscle 0K5
    Foot Tendon 0L5
    Foot Vein 065
    Frontal Bone 0N5
    Frontal Sinus 095
    Gallbladder 0F54
    Gastric Artery 0452
    Gastric Vein 0652
    Gingiva, Lower 0C50
    Gland
      Lacrimal, Left 085A
      Lower Parathyroid 0G5
      Mammary 0H5
      Minor Salivary 0C58
      Parathyroid 0G50
      Pineal 0G51
      Upper Parathyroid 0G5
      Vestibular 0U5J
    Glenoid Cavity 0P5
    Glomus Jugulare 0G5C
    Glossopharyngeal Nerve 005P
    Greater Omentum 0D5S
    Greater Saphenous Vein 065
    Hand Artery 035
    Hand Bursa and Ligament 0M5
    Hand Muscle 0K5
    Hand Tendon 0L5
    Hand Vein 055
    Hard Palate 0C52
    Head and Neck Sympathetic Nerve 015K
    Hemiazygos Vein 0551
    Hepatic Artery 0453
    Hepatic Duct, Left 0F56
    hepatic Vein 0654
    Hip Bursa and Ligament 0M5
    Hip Joint 0S5
    Hip Muscle 0K5
    Hip Tendon 0L5
    Humeral Head 0P5
    Humeral Shaft 0P5
    Hymen 0U5K
    Hyoid Bone 0N5X
    Hypogastric Vein 065
    Hypoglossal Nerve 005S
    Hypophysis 0G50
    Hypothalamus 005A
    Ileocecal Valve 0D5C
    Ileum 0D5B
    Inferior Mesenteric Artery 045B
    Inferior Mesenteric Vein 0656
    Inferior Parathyroid Gland 0G5

Destruction—*continued*
 by Body Part—*continued*
  Inner Ear 095
  Innominate Artery 0352
  Innominate Vein 055
  Internal Carotid Artery 035
  Internal Iliac Artery 045
  Internal Jugular Vein 055
  Internal Mammary Artery, Left 0351
  Intracranial Artery 035G
  Intracranial Vein 055L
  Iris 085
  Jejunum 0D5A
  Joint
   Finger Phalangeal, Left 0R50
   Toe Phalangeal, Left 0S50
  Kidney, Left 0T51
  Kidney Pelvis 0T5
  Knee Bursa and Ligament 0M5
  Knee Joint 0S5
  Knee Tendon 0L5
  Lacrimal Bone 0N5
  Lacrimal Duct, Left 085Y
  Lacrimal Gland 085
  Large Intestine 0D5
  Larynx 0C5S
  Lens 085
  Lesser Omentum 0D5T
  Lesser Saphenous Vein 065
  Lingula Bronchus 0B59
  Liver 0F50
   Left Lobe 0F52
   Right Lobe 0F51
  Lobe Segmental Bronchus
   Lower 0B5
   Middle, Right 0B55
   Upper 0B5
  Lower Arm and Wrist Muscle 0K5
  Lower Arm and Wrist Tendon 0L5
  Lower Artery 045Y
  Lower Extremity Bursa and Ligament
    0M5
  Lower Eyelid 085
  Lower Femur 0Q5
  Lower Gingiva 0C56
  Lower Leg Muscle 0K5
  Lower Leg Tendon 0L5
  Lower Lip 0C51
  Lower Lobe Bronchus 0B5
  Lower Lung Lobe 0B5
  Lower Tooth 0C5X
  Lower Vein 065Y
  Lumbar Nerve 015B
  Lumbar Plexus 0159
  Lumbar Spinal Cord 005Y
  Lumbar Sympathetic Nerve 015N
  Lumbar Vertebral Disc 0S52
  Lumbosacral Disc 0S54
  Lumbosacral Joint 0S53
  Lumbosacral Plexus 015A
  Lung 0B5
  Lung Lingula 0B5H
  Lung Lingula Segments 0B5H
  Lung Lobe Segments
   Lower 0B5
   Middle, Right 0B5D
   Upper 0B5
  Lungs, Bilateral 0B5M
  Lymphatic
   Aortic 075D
   Internal Mammary 075
   Left Axillary 0756
   Left Inguinal 075J
   Left Lower Extremity 075G
   Left Neck 0752
   Left Upper Extremity 0754

Destruction—*continued*
 by Body Part—*continued*
  Lymphatic—*continued*
   Mesenteric 075B
   Pelvis 075C
   Right Axillary 0755
   Right Inguinal 075H
   Right Lower Extremity 075F
   Right Neck 0751
   Right Upper Extremity 0753
   Thorax 0757
  Main Bronchus 0B5
  Mandible 0N5
  Mastoid Sinus, Left 095C
  Maxilla 0N5
  Maxillary Sinus 095
  Median Nerve 0155
  Medulla Oblongata 005D
  Mesentery 0D5V
  Metacarpal 0P5
  Metacarpocarpal Joint 0R5
  Metacarpophalangeal Joint 0R5
  Metatarsal 0Q5
  Metatarsal-Phalangeal Joint 0S5
  Metatarsal-Tarsal Joint 0S5
  Middle Ear, Left 0956
  Middle Lobe Bronchus, Right 0B55
  Middle Lung Lobe, Right 0B5D
  Minor Salivary Gland 0C5J
  Mitral Valve 025G
  Muscle, Foot, Left 0K50
  Nail, Toe 0H50
  Nail Bed
   Finger 0H5Q
   Toe 0H5R
  Nasal Bone 0N5B
  Nasal Septum 095M
  Nasal Turbinate 095L
  Nasopharynx 095N
  Neck, Bladder 0T50
  Neck Muscle 0K5
  Nerve, Sacral 0150
  Neurohypophysis 0G50
  Nipple 0H5
  Nose 095K
  Occipital Bone 0N5
  Oculomotor Nerve 005H
  Olfactory Nerve 005F
  Omentum, Lesser 0D5R
  Optic Nerve 005G
  Orbit 0N5
  Ovaries, Bilateral 0U52
  Ovary, Left 0U51
  Palatine Bone 0N5
  Pancreas 0F5G
   Body 0F5F
   Head 0F5F
   Tail 0F5F
  Pancreatic Duct 0F5D
   Accessory 0F5F
  Papillary Muscle 025D
  Para-aortic Body 0G59
  Paraganglion Extremity 0G5F
  Parathyroid Gland 0G5R
  Parathyroid Glands, Multiple 0G5Q
  Parietal Bone 0N5
  Parotid Duct 0C5
  Parotid Gland, Left 0C59
  Patella 0Q5
  Pelvic Bone 0Q5
  Penis 0V5S
  Pericardium 025N
  Perineum Bursa and Ligament 0M5K
  Perineum Muscle 0K5M
  Perineum Tendon 0L5H
  Peritoneum 0D5W

Destruction—*continued*
 by Body Part—*continued*
  Peroneal Artery 045
  Peroneal Nerve 015H
  Phalanx
   Finger, Left 0P50
   Toe, Left 0Q50
  Phrenic Nerve 0152
  Pineal Body 0G51
  Pleura 0B5
   Parietal 0B5
   Visceral 0B5
  Pons 005B
  Popliteal Artery 045
  Portal Vein 0658
  Posterior Tibial Artery 045
  Prepuce 0V5T
  Prostate 0V50
  Pudendal Nerve 015C
  Pulmonary Artery 025
  Pulmonary Lingula 0B5H
  Pulmonary Lobe
   Lower 0B5
   Middle, Right 0B5D
   Upper 0B5
  Pulmonary Trunk 025P
  Pulmonary Valve 025H
  Pulmonary Vein 025
  Radial Artery 035
  Radial Nerve 0156
  Radius 0P5
  Rectum 0D5P
  Renal Artery 045
  Renal Pelvis 0T5
  Renal Vein 065
  Retina 085
  Retinal Vessel 085
  Rib 0P5
  Sacral Nerve 015R
  Sacral Plexus 015Q
  Sacral Sympathetic Nerve 015P
  Sacrococcygeal Joint 0S55
  Sacroiliac Joint 0S5
  Sacrum 0Q51
  Scapula 0P5
  Sciatic Nerve 015F
  Sclera 085
  Scrotum 0V55
  Seminal Vesicle, Left 0V52
  Seminal Vesicles, Bilateral 0V53
  Shoulder Bursa and Ligament 0M5
  Shoulder Joint 0R5
  Shoulder Muscle 0K5
  Shoulder Tendon 0L5
  Sigmoid Colon 0D5N
  Sinus, Sphenoid, Left 095B
  Skin
   Abdomen 0H57
   Back 0H56
   Buttock 0H58
   Chest 0H55
   Face 0H51
   Genitalia 0H5A
   Left Ear 0H53
   Left Foot 0H5N
   Left Hand 0H5G
   Left Lower Arm 0H5E
   Left Lower Leg 0H5L
   Left Upper Arm 0H5C
   Left Upper Leg 0H5J
   Neck 0H54
   Perineum 0H59
   Right Ear 0H52
   Right Foot 0H5M
   Right Hand 0H5F
   Right Lower Arm 0H5D

Codes provided in the index are incomplete. Refer to tables to determine additional character values.   © 2009 Ingenix, Inc.

Destruction—*continued*
  by Body Part—*continued*
    Skin—*continued*
      Right Lower Leg 0H5K
      Right Upper Arm 0H5B
      Right Upper Leg 0H5H
    Small Intestine 0D58
    Soft Palate 0C53
    Spermatic Cord 0V5
    Spermatic Cords, Bilateral 0V5H
    Sphenoid Bone 0N5
    Sphenoid Sinus 095
    Spinal Meninges 005T
    Spleen 075P
    Splenic Artery 0454
    Splenic Vein 0651
    Sternoclavicular Joint 0R5
    Stomach 0D56
      Body 0D56
      Fundus 0D56
      Pylorus 0D57
    Structure, Uterine Supporting 0U50
    Subclavian Artery 035
    Subclavian Vein 055
    Subcutaneous Tissue and Fascia
      Abdomen 0J58
      Anterior Neck 0J54
      Back 0J57
      Buttock 0J59
      Chest 0J56
      Face 0J51
      Foot, Left 0J50
      Genitalia 0J5C
      Left Foot 0J5R
      Left Hand 0J5K
      Left Lower Arm 0J5H
      Left Lower Leg 0J5P
      Left Upper Arm 0J5F
      Left Upper Leg 0J5M
      Perineum 0J5B
      Posterior Neck 0J55
      Right Foot 0J5Q
      Right Hand 0J5J
      Right Lower Arm 0J5G
      Right Lower Leg 0J5N
      Right Upper Arm 0J5D
      Right Upper Leg 0J5L
    Sublingual Gland 0C5
    Submaxillary Gland 0C5
    Superior Mesenteric Artery 0455
    Superior Mesenteric Vein 0655
    Superior Parathyroid Gland 0G5
    Superior Vena Cava 025V
    Tarsal 0Q5
    Tarsal Joint 0S5
    Temporal Artery 035
    Temporal Bone 0N5
    Temporomandibular Joint 0R5
    Tendon, Foot, Left 0L50
    Testes, Bilateral 0V5C
    Testis 0V5
    Thalamus 0059
    Thoracic Aorta 025W
    Thoracic Duct 075K
    Thoracic Nerve 0158
    Thoracic Spinal Cord 005X
    Thoracic Sympathetic Nerve 015L
    Thoracic Vertebra 0P54
    Thoracic Vertebral Disc 0R59
    Thoracic Vertebral Joint 0R56
    Thoracolumbar Vertebral Disc 0R5B
    Thoracolumbar Vertebral Joint 0R5A
    Thorax Bursa and Ligament 0M5
    Thorax Muscle 0K5
    Thorax Tendon 0L5
    Thumb Phalanx 0P5

Destruction—*continued*
  by Body Part—*continued*
    Thymus 075M
    Thyroid Artery 035
    Thyroid Gland 0G5K
    Thyroid Gland Lobe 0G5
    Tibia 0Q5
    Tibial Nerve 015G
    Toe Nail 0H5R
    Toe Phalangeal Joint 0S5
    Toe Phalanx 0Q5
    Tongue 0C57
      Palate, Pharynx Muscle 0K54
    Tonsils 0C5P
    Tooth, Lower 0C5W
    Transverse Colon 0D5L
    Tricuspid Valve 025J
    Trigeminal Nerve 005K
    Trochlear Nerve 005J
    Trunk Bursa and Ligament 0M5
    Trunk Muscle 0K5
    Trunk Tendon 0L5
    Tube, Fallopian, Bilateral 0U55
    Tunica Vaginalis 0V5
    Turbinate, Nasal 0957
    Tympanic Membrane, Left 0958
    Tympanicum, Glomus 0G5B
    Ulna 0P5
    Ulnar Artery 035
    Ulnar Nerve 0154
    Upper Arm Muscle 0K5
    Upper Arm Tendon 0L5
    Upper Artery 035Y
    Upper Extremity Bursa and Ligament 0M5
    Upper Eyelid, Left 085P
    Upper Femur 0Q5
    Upper Gingiva 0C55
    Upper Leg Muscle 0K5
  Upper Leg Tendon 0L5
  Upper Lobe Bronchus 0B5
  Upper Lung Lobe 0B5
  Upper Vein 055Y
    Ureter 0T5
    Urethra 0T5D
    Uterine Supporting Structure 0U54
    Uterus 0U59
    Uvula 0C5N
    Vagina 0U5G
    Vagus Nerve 005Q
    Vas Deferens 0V5
    Vein
      Lower 0650
      Upper 0550
    Ventricle 025
    Ventricular Septum 025M
    Vertebral Artery 035
    Vertebral Vein 055
    Vessel, Retinal, Left 0852
    Vestibular Gland 0U5L
    Vitreous 085
    Vocal Cord 0C5
    Vulva 0U5M
    Wrist Bursa and Ligament 0M5
    Wrist Joint 0R5
    Zygomatic Bone 0N5

Detachment
  by Body System
    Anatomical Regions, Lower Extremities 0Y6
    Anatomical Regions, Upper Extremities 0X6
  by Body Part
    1st Toe, Left 0Y6Q
    2nd Toe 0Y6
    3rd Toe 0Y6

Detachment—*continued*
  by Body Part—*continued*
    4th Toe 0Y6
    5th Toe 0Y6
    Arm, Lower, Left 0X68
    Elbow Region 0X6
    Femoral Region 0Y6
    Finger, Little, Left 0X6L
    Foot 0Y6
    Forequarter, Left 0X61
    Hand 0X6
    Hindquarter
      Bilateral 0Y64
      Left 0Y63
    Index Finger 0X6
    Knee Region 0Y6
    Leg, Lower, Left 0Y6C
    Little Finger 0X6
    Lower Arm 0X6
    Lower Leg 0Y6
    Middle Finger 0X6
    Region
      Elbow, Left 0X60
      Knee, Left 0Y62
    Ring Finger 0X6
    Shoulder Region 0X6
    Thumb, Left 0X6M
    Toe, 5th, Left 0Y6P
    Upper Arm, Left 0X69
    Upper Leg, Left 0Y6D
Detoxification Services HZ2Z
Diagnostic Audiology
  by Type Qualifier
    Acoustic Reflex Decay F13
    Acoustic Reflex Patterns F13
    Acoustic Reflex Threshold F13
    Alternate Binaural or Monaural Loudness Balance F13
    Assistive Listening System/Device Selection F14
    Auditory Evoked Potentials F13
    Auditory Processing F13
    Aural Rehabilitation Status F13
    Bekesy Audiometry F13
    Binaural Electroacoustic Hearing Aid Check F14
    Binaural Hearing Aid F14
    Bithermal, Binaural Caloric Irrigation F15
    Bithermal, Monaural Caloric Irrigation F15
    Cochlear Implant F14
    Computerized Dynamic Posturography F15
    Conditioned Play Audiometry F13
    Dix-Hallpike Dynamic F15
    Ear Canal Probe Microphone F14
    Ear Protector Attentuation F14
    Electrocochleography F13
    Eustachian Tube Function F13
    Evoked Otoacoustic Emissions, Diagnostic F13
    Evoked Otoacoustic Emissions, Screening F13
    Hearing Screening F13
    Monaural Electroacoustic Hearing Aid Check F14
    Monaural Hearing Aid F14
    Oscillating Tracking F15
    Pure Tone Audiometry, Air F13
    Pure Tone Audiometry, Air and Bone F13
    Pure Tone Stenger F13
    Select Picture Audiometry F13
    Sensory Aids F14
    Short Increment Sensitivity Index F13
    Sinusoidal Vertical Axis Rotational F15
    Stenger F13

Diagnostic Audiology—continued
  by Type Qualifier—continued
    Tinnitus Masker F15
    Tone Decay F13
    Tympanometry F13
    Unithermal Binaural Screen F15
    Visual Reinforcement Audiometry F13
Diagnostic Imaging—*see* Imaging
Diagnostic Radiology—*see* Imaging
Dialysis
  Hemodialysis 5A1D
  Peritoneal 3E1M
  Renal 5A1D
Digital Radiography, Plain—*see* Plain
    Radiography
Dilation
  by Body System
    Ear, Nose, Sinus 097
    Eye 087
    Female Reproductive System 0U7
    Gastrointestinal System 0D7
    Heart and Great Vessels 027
    Hepatobiliary System and Pancreas 0F7
    Lower Arteries 047
    Lower Veins 067
    Male Reproductive System 0V7
    Mouth and Throat 0C7
    Respiratory System 0B7
    Upper Arteries 037
    Upper Veins 057
    Urinary System 0T7
  by Body Part
    Ampulla of Vater 0F7C
    Anterior Tibial Artery 047
    Anus 0D7Q
    Artery
      Aorta, Thoracic 027F
      Coronary, Four or More Sites 0270
      Lower 0470
      Pulmonary, Left 027R
      Upper 0370
    Ascending Colon 0D7K
    Axillary Artery 037
    Axillary Vein 057
    Basilic Vein 057
    Bladder 0T7B
    Bladder Neck 0T7C
    Brachial Artery 037
    Brachial Vein 057
    Bronchus
      Lower Lobe, Left 0B71
      Segmental, Lingula 0B79
    Carina 0B72
    Cecum 0D7H
    Celiac Artery 0471
    Cephalic Vein 057
    Cervix 0U7C
    Colic Artery 047
    Colic Vein 0677
    Colon, Sigmoid 0D71
    Common Bile Duct 0F79
    Common Carotid Artery 037
    Common Iliac Artery 047
    Common Iliac Vein 067
    Coronary Artery
      Four or More Sites 0273
      Three Sites 0272
      Two Sites 0271
    Cystic Duct 0F78
    Deferens, Vas, Bilateral 0V7N
    Descending Colon 0D7M
    Duct
      Lacrimal, Left 087X
      Pancreatic, Accessory 0F75
      Parotid, Left 0C7B
    Duodenum 0D79

Digital Radiography, Plain—*continued*
  by Body Part—*continued*
    Esophageal Vein 0673
    Esophagogastric Junction 0D74
    Esophagus 0D75
      Lower 0D73
      Middle 0D72
    Eustachian Tube, Left 097G
    External Carotid Artery 037
    External Iliac Artery 047
    External Iliac Vein 067
    External Jugular Vein 057
    Face Artery 037R
    Face Vein 057
    Fallopian Tube, Left 0U76
    Fallopian Tubes, Bilateral 0U77
    Femoral Artery 047
    Femoral Vein 067
    Foot Artery 047
    Foot Vein 067
    Gastric Artery 0472
    Gastric Vein 0672
    Greater Saphenous Vein 067
    Hand Artery 037
    Hand Vein 057
    Hemiazygos Vein 0571
    Hepatic Artery 0473
    Hepatic Duct, Left 0F76
    Hepatic Vein 0674
    Hymen 0U7K
    Hypogastric Vein 067
    Ileocecal Valve 0D7C
    Ileum 0D7B
    Inferior Mesenteric Artery 047B
    Inferior Mesenteric Vein 0676
    Innominate Artery 0372
    Innominate Vein 057
    Internal Carotid Artery 037
    Internal Iliac Artery 047
    Internal Jugular Vein 057
    Internal Mammary Artery, Left 0371
    Intracranial Artery 037G
    Intracranial Vein 057L
    Jejunum 0D7A
    Kidney Pelvis, Left 0T74
    Lacrimal Duct, Left 087Y
    Large Intestine 0D7
    Larynx 0C7S
    Lesser Saphenous Vein 067
    Lingula Bronchus 0B79
    Lobe Segmental Bronchus
      Lower 0B7
      Middle, Right 0B75
      Upper 0B7
    Lower Artery 047Y
    Lower Lobe Bronchus 0B7
    Lower Vein 067Y
    Main Bronchus 0B7
    Middle Lobe Bronchus, Right 0B75
    Mitral Valve 027G
    Neck, Bladder 0T73
    Pancreas
      Body 0F7F
      Head 0F7F
      Tail 0F7F
    Pancreatic Duct 0F7D
      Accessory 0F7F
    Parotid Duct, Left 0C7C
    Peroneal Artery 047
    Pharynx 0C7M
    Popliteal Artery 047
    Portal Vein 0678
    Posterior Tibial Artery 047
    Pulmonary Artery, Right 027Q
    Pulmonary Trunk 027P
    Pulmonary Valve 027H

Digital Radiography, Plain—*continued*
  by Body Part—*continued*
    Pulmonary Vein 027
    Radial Artery 037
    Rectum 0D7P
    Renal Artery 047
    Renal Pelvis 0T7
    Renal Vein 067
    Sigmoid Colon 0D7N
    Small Intestine 0D78
    Splenic Artery 0474
    Splenic Vein 0671
    Stomach 0D76
      Body 0D76
      Fundus 0D76
      Pylorus 0D77
    Subclavian Artery 037
    Subclavian Vein 057
    Superior Mesenteric Artery 0475
    Superior Mesenteric Vein 0675
    Superior Vena Cava 027V
    Temporal Artery 037
    Thoracic Aorta 027W
    Thyroid Artery 037
    Transverse Colon 0D7L
    Tricuspid Valve 027J
    Tube
      Eustachian, Left 097F
      Fallopian, Bilateral 0U75
    Ulnar Artery 037
    Upper Artery 037Y
    Upper Lobe Bronchus 0B7
    Upper Vein 057Y
    Ureter 0T7
    Ureters, Bilateral 0T78
    Urethra 0T7D
    Uterus 0U79
    Vagina 0U7G
    Vas Deferens
      Bilateral 0V7Q
      Left 0V7P
    Vein
      Lower 0670
      Upper 0570
    Ventricle, Right 027K
    Vertebral Artery 037
    Vertebral Vein 057
Disarticulate—*see* Detachment
Disarticulation—*see* Detachment
Discectomy
  —*see* Excision, Lower Joints 0SB
  —*see* Excision, Upper Joints 0RB
  —*see* Resection, Lower Joints 0ST
  —*see* Resection, Upper Joints 0RT
Discography—*see* Fluoroscopy, Axial Skeleton,
    Except Skull and Facial Bones BR1
Discography—*see* Plain Radiography, Axial
    Skeleton, Except Skull and Facial
    Bones BR0
Diskectomy
  —*see* Excision, Lower Joints 0SB
  —*see* Excision, Upper Joints 0RB
  —*see* Resection, Lower Joints 0ST
  —*see* Resection, Upper Joints 0RT
Diversion—*see* Bypass
Division
  by Body System
    Anatomical Regions, General 0W8
    Bursae and Ligaments 0M8
    Central Nervous System 008
    Ear, Nose, Sinus 098
    Endocrine System 0G8
    Female Reproductive System 0U8
    Gastrointestinal System 0D8
    Head and Facial Bones 0N8
    Heart and Great Vessels 028

Division—*continued*
　by Body System—*continued*
　　Hepatobiliary System and Pancreas 0F8
　　Lower Bones 0Q8
　　Muscles 0K8
　　Peripheral Nervous System 018
　　Skin and Breast 0H8
　　Subcutaneous Tissue and Fascia 0J8
　　Tendons 0L8
　　Upper Bones 0P8
　　Urinary System 0T8
　by Body Part
　　Abdomen Bursa and Ligament 0M8
　　Abdomen Muscle 0K8
　　Abdomen Tendon 0L8
　　Abdominal Sympathetic Nerve 018M
　　Abducens Nerve 008L
　　Accessory Nerve 008R
　　Acetabulum 0Q8
　　Acoustic Nerve 008N
　　Adenohypophysis 0G80
　　Ankle Bursa and Ligament 0M8
　　Ankle Tendon 0L8
　　Basal Ganglia 0088
　　Bladder Neck 0T8C
　　Bone, Hyoid 0N80
　　Brachial Plexus 0183
　　Bursa and Ligament, Lower Extremity,
　　　　Left 0M80
　　Carpal 0P8
　　Cerebral Hemisphere 0087
　　Cervical Nerve 0181
　　Cervical Spinal Cord 008W
　　Cervical Vertebra 0P83
　　Chordae Tendineae 0289
　　Clavicle 0P8
　　Coccyx 0Q8S
　　Cord, Lumbar Spinal 0080
　　Elbow Bursa and Ligament 0M8
　　Ethmoid Bone 0N8
　　Facial Muscle 0K81
　　Facial Nerve 008M
　　Femoral Nerve 018D
　　Femoral Shaft 0Q8
　　Fibula 0Q8
　　Finger Phalanx 0P8
　　Foot Bursa and Ligament 0M8
　　Foot Muscle 0K8
　　Foot Tendon 0L8
　　Frontal Bone 0N8
　　Glenoid Cavity 0P8
　　Glossopharyngeal Nerve 008P
　　Hand Bursa and Ligament 0M8
　　Hand Muscle 0K8
　　Hand Tendon 0L8
　　Head and Neck Sympathetic Nerve 018K
　　Hip Bursa and Ligament 0M8
　　Hip Muscle 0K8
　　Hip Tendon 0L8
　　Humeral Head 0P8
　　Humeral Shaft 0P8
　　Hymen 0U8K
　　Hyoid Bone 0N8X
　　Hypoglossal Nerve 008S
　　Hypophysis 0G80
　　Isthmus, Thyroid Gland 0G80
　　Junction, Esophagogastric 0D84
　　Knee Bursa and Ligament 0M8
　　Knee Tendon 0L8
　　Lacrimal Bone 0N8
　　Lower Arm and Wrist Muscle 0K8
　　Lower Arm and Wrist Tendon 0L8
　　Lower Extremity Bursa and Ligament
　　　　0M8
　　Lower Femur 0Q8
　　Lower Leg Muscle 0K8

Division—*continued*
　by Body Part—*continued*
　　Lower Leg Tendon 0L8
　　Lumbar Nerve 018B
　　Lumbar Plexus 0189
　　Lumbar Spinal Cord 008Y
　　Lumbar Sympathetic Nerve 018N
　　Lumbosacral Plexus 018A
　　Mandible 0N8
　　Maxilla 0N8
　　Median Nerve 0185
　　Metacarpal 0P8
　　Metatarsal 0Q8
　　Muscle
　　　Foot, Left 0K80
　　　Papillary 0288
　　Nasal Bone 0N8B
　　Neck, Bladder 0T82
　　Neck Muscle 0K8
　　Nerve, Sacral 0180
　　Neurohypophysis 0G80
　　Occipital Bone 0N8
　　Oculomotor Nerve 008H
　　Olfactory Nerve 008F
　　Optic Nerve 008G
　　Orbit 0N8
　　Ovaries, Bilateral 0U82
　　Ovary, Left 0U81
　　Palatine Bone 0N8
　　Pancreas 0F8G
　　Papillary Muscle 028D
　　Parietal Bone 0N8
　　Patella 0Q8
　　Pelvic Bone 0Q8
　　Perineum, Female 0W8N
　　Perineum Bursa and Ligament 0M8K
　　Perineum Muscle 0K8M
　　Perineum Tendon 0L8H
　　Peroneal Nerve 018H
　　Phalanx
　　　Finger, Left 0P80
　　　Toe, Left 0Q80
　　Phrenic Nerve 0182
　　Pudendal Nerve 018C
　　Radial Nerve 0186
　　Radius 0P8
　　Rib 0P8
　　Sacral Nerve 018R
　　Sacral Plexus 018Q
　　Sacral Sympathetic Nerve 018P
　　Sacrum 0Q81
　　Scapula 0P8
　　Sciatic Nerve 018F
　　Shoulder Bursa and Ligament 0M8
　　Shoulder Muscle 0K8
　　Shoulder Tendon 0L8
　　Skin
　　　Abdomen 0H87
　　　Back 0H86
　　　Buttock 0H88
　　　Chest 0H85
　　　Face 0H81
　　　Foot, Left 0H80
　　　Genitalia 0H8A
　　　Left Ear 0H83
　　　Left Foot 0H8N
　　　Left Hand 0H8G
　　　Left Lower Arm 0H8E
　　　Left Lower Leg 0H8L
　　　Left Upper Arm 0H8C
　　　Left Upper Leg 0H8J
　　　Neck 0H84
　　　Perineum 0H89
　　　Right Ear 0H82
　　　Right Foot 0H8M
　　　Right Hand 0H8F

Division—*continued*
　by Body Part—*continued*
　　Skin—*continued*
　　　Right Lower Arm 0H8D
　　　Right Lower Leg 0H8K
　　　Right Upper Arm 0H8B
　　　Right Upper Leg 0H8H
　　Sphenoid Bone 0N8
　　Sphincter, Anal 0D8R
　　Structure, Uterine Supporting 0U80
　　Subcutaneous Tissue and Fascia
　　　Abdomen 0J88
　　　Anterior Neck 0J84
　　　Back 0J87
　　　Buttock 0J89
　　　Chest 0J86
　　　Face 0J81
　　　Foot, Left 0J80
　　　Genitalia 0J8C
　　　Head and Neck 0J8S
　　　Left Foot 0J8R
　　　Left Hand 0J8K
　　　Left Lower Arm 0J8H
　　　Left Lower Leg 0J8P
　　　Left Upper Arm 0J8F
　　　Left Upper Leg 0J8M
　　　Lower Extremity 0J8W
　　　Perineum 0J8B
　　　Posterior Neck 0J85
　　　Right Foot 0J8Q
　　　Right Hand 0J8J
　　　Right Lower Arm 0J8G
　　　Right Lower Leg 0J8N
　　　Right Upper Arm 0J8D
　　　Right Upper Leg 0J8L
　　　Trunk 0J8T
　　　Upper Extremity 0J8V
　　Tarsal 0Q8
　　Temporal Bone 0N8
　　Tendon, Foot, Left 0L80
　　Thoracic Nerve 0188
　　Thoracic Spinal Cord 008X
　　Thoracic Sympathetic Nerve 018L
　　Thoracic Vertebra 0P84
　　Thorax Bursa and Ligament 0M8
　　Thorax Muscle 0K8
　　Thorax Tendon 0L8
　　Thumb Phalanx 0P8
　　Thyroid Gland Isthmus 0G8J
　　Tibia 0Q8
　　Tibial Nerve 018G
　　Toe Phalanx 0Q8
　　Tongue, Palate, Pharynx Muscle 0K84
　　Trigeminal Nerve 008K
　　Trochlear Nerve 008J
　　Trunk Bursa and Ligament 0M8
　　Trunk Muscle 0K8
　　Trunk Tendon 0L8
　　Turbinate, Nasal 098L
　　Ulna 0P8
　　Ulnar Nerve 0184
　　Upper Arm Muscle 0K8
　　Upper Arm Tendon 0L8
　　Upper Extremity Bursa and Ligament
　　　　0M8
　　Upper Femur 0Q8
　　Upper Leg Muscle 0K8
　　Upper Leg Tendon 0L8
　　Uterine Supporting Structure 0U84
　　Vagus Nerve 008Q
　　Wrist Bursa and Ligament 0M8
　　Zygomatic Bone 0N8
Doppler Study—*see* Ultrasonography
Drainage
　by Body System
　　Anatomical Regions, General 0W9

Drainage—*continued*
- by Body System—*continued*
  - Anatomical Regions, Lower Extremities 0Y9
  - Anatomical Regions, Upper Extremities 0X9
  - Bursae and Ligaments 0M9
  - Central Nervous System 009
  - Ear, Nose, Sinus 099
  - Endocrine System 0G9
  - Eye 089
  - Female Reproductive System 0U9
  - Gastrointestinal System 0D9
  - Head and Facial Bones 0N9
  - Hepatobiliary System and Pancreas 0F9
  - Lower Arteries 049
  - Lower Bones 0Q9
  - Lower Joints 0S9
  - Lower Veins 069
  - Lymphatic and Hemic Systems 079
  - Male Reproductive System 0V9
  - Mouth and Throat 0C9
  - Muscles 0K9
  - Peripheral Nervous System 019
  - Respiratory System 0B9
  - Skin and Breast 0H9
  - Subcutaneous Tissue and Fascia 0J9
  - Tendons 0L9
  - Upper Arteries 039
  - Upper Bones 0P9
  - Upper Joints 0R9
  - Upper Veins 059
  - Urinary System 0T9
- by Body Part
  - Abdomen Bursa and Ligament 0M9
  - Abdomen Muscle 0K9
  - Abdomen Tendon 0L9
  - Abdominal Sympathetic Nerve 019M
  - Abdominal Wall 0W9F
  - Abducens Nerve 009L
  - Accessory Nerve 009R
  - Accessory Sinus 099P
  - Acetabulum 0Q9
  - Acoustic Nerve 009N
  - Acromioclavicular Joint 0R9
  - Adenohypophysis 0G90
  - Adenoids 0C9Q
  - Adrenal Gland 0G9
  - Adrenal Glands, Bilateral 0G94
  - Ampulla of Vater 0F9C
  - Ankle Bursa and Ligament 0M9
  - Ankle Joint 0S9
  - Ankle Region 0Y9
  - Ankle Tendon 0L9
  - Anterior Chamber, Left 0893
  - Anterior Tibial Artery 049
  - Anus 0D9Q
  - Aortic Body 0G9D
  - Appendix 0D9J
  - Areola 0H9
  - Artery
    - Lower 0490
    - Upper 0390
  - Ascending Colon 0D9K
  - Auditory Ossicle 099
  - Axilla 0X9
  - Axillary Artery 039
  - Axillary Vein 059
  - Back, Lower 0W90
  - Basal Ganglia 0098
  - Basilic Vein 059
  - Bladder 0T9B
  - Bladder Neck 0T9C
  - Body
    - Coccygeal 0G99
    - Jugulotympanic 0G9B
  - Bone, Hyoid 0N90

Drainage—*continued*
- by Body System—*continued*
  - Bone Marrow 079T
  - Brachial Artery 039
  - Brachial Plexus 0193
  - Brachial Vein 059
  - Breast 0H9
  - Bronchus, Segmental, Lingula 0B99
  - Buccal Mucosa 0C94
  - Bursa and Ligament, Lower Extremity, Left 0M90
  - Buttock, Left 0Y91
  - Canal, External Auditory, Left 0993
  - Carina 0B92
  - Carotid Bodies, Bilateral 0G98
  - Carotid Body 0G9
  - Carpal 0P9
  - Carpal Joint 0R9
  - Cecum 0D9H
  - Celiac Artery 0491
  - Cephalic Vein 059
  - Cerebellum 009C
  - Cerebral Hemisphere 0097
  - Cerebral Meninges 0091
  - Cerebral Ventricle 0096
  - Cervical Nerve 0191
  - Cervical Spinal Cord 009W
  - Cervical Vertebra 0P93
  - Cervical Vertebral Disc 0R93
  - Cervical Vertebral Joint 0R91
  - Cervicothoracic Vertebral Disc 0R95
  - Cervicothoracic Vertebral Joint 0R94
  - Cervix 0U9C
  - Chest Wall 0W98
  - Choroid, Left 089B
  - Cisterna Chyli 079L
  - Clavicle 0P9
  - Coccygeal Glomus 0G9B
  - Coccygeal Joint 0S96
  - Coccyx 0Q9S
  - Colic Artery 049
  - Colic Vein 0697
  - Colon, Sigmoid 0D91
  - Common Bile Duct 0F99
  - Common Carotid Artery 039
  - Common Iliac Artery 049
  - Common Iliac Vein 069
  - Conjunctiva 089
  - Cord
    - Lumbar Spinal 0090
  - Cord
    - Vocal, Left 0C9M
  - Cornea 089
  - Corpora Arenacea, Pineal 0G91
  - Cranial Cavity 0W91
  - Cul-de-sac 0U9F
  - Cystic Duct 0F98
  - Deferens, Vas, Bilateral 0V91
  - Descending Colon 0D9M
  - Diaphragm 0B9
  - Duct
    - Lacrimal, Left 089X
    - Pancreatic, Accessory 0F95
  - Duodenum 0D99
  - Dura Mater 0092
  - Ear
    - External, Left 0990
    - Inner, Left 0995
  - Elbow Bursa and Ligament 0M9
  - Elbow Joint 0R9
  - Elbow Region 0X9
  - Epididymis 0V9
  - Epidural Space 0093
  - Epiglottis 0C9R
  - Esophageal Vein 0693
  - Esophagogastric Junction 0D94

Drainage—*continued*
- by Body Part—*continued*
  - Esophagus 0D95
    - Lower 0D93
    - Middle 0D92
  - Ethmoid Bone 0N9
  - Ethmoid Sinus 099
  - Eustachian Tube 099
  - External Auditory Canal, Left 0994
  - External Carotid Artery 039
  - External Ear, Left 0991
  - External Iliac Artery 049
  - External Iliac Vein 069
  - External Jugular Vein 059
  - Extraocular Muscle 089
  - Eye 089
  - Eyelid, Lower, Left 089N
  - Face 0W92
  - Face Artery 039R
  - Face Vein 059
  - Facial Muscle 0K91
  - Facial Nerve 009M
  - Fallopian Tube, Left 0U96
  - Fallopian Tubes, Bilateral 0U97
  - Femoral Artery 049
  - Femoral Nerve 019D
  - Femoral Region 0Y9
  - Femoral Shaft 0Q9
  - Femoral Vein 069
  - Fibula 0Q9
  - Finger Nail 0H9Q
  - Finger Phalangeal Joint 0R9
  - Finger Phalanx 0P9
  - Foot 0Y9
  - Foot Artery 049
  - Foot Bursa and Ligament 0M9
  - Foot Muscle 0K9
  - Foot Tendon 0L9
  - Foot Vein 069
  - Frontal Bone 0N9
  - Frontal Sinus 099
  - Gallbladder 0F94
  - Gastric Artery 0492
  - Gastric Vein 0692
  - Gingiva, Lower 0C90
  - Gland
    - Lacrimal, Left 089A
    - Lower Parathyroid 0G9
    - Mammary 0H9
    - Minor Salivary 0C98
    - Parathyroid 0G90
    - Pineal 0G91
    - Upper Parathyroid 0G9
    - Vestibular 0U9J
  - Glenoid Cavity 0P9
  - Glomus Jugulare 0G9C
  - Glossopharyngeal Nerve 009P
  - Greater Omentum 0D9S
  - Greater Saphenous Vein 069
  - Hand 0X9
  - Hand Artery 039
  - Hand Bursa and Ligament 0M9
  - Hand Muscle 0K9
  - Hand Tendon 0L9
  - Hand Vein 059
  - Hard Palate 0C92
  - Head and Neck Sympathetic Nerve 019K
  - Hemiazygos Vein 0591
  - Hepatic Artery 0493
  - Hepatic Duct, Left 0F96
  - Hepatic Vein 0694
  - Hip Bursa and Ligament 0M9
  - Hip Joint 0S9
  - Hip Muscle 0K9
  - Hip Tendon 0L9
  - Humeral Head 0P9

Drainage—*continued*

  by Body Part—*continued*

Humeral Shaft 0P9
Hymen 0U9K
Hyoid Bone 0N9X
Hypogastric Vein 069
Hypoglossal Nerve 009S
Hypophysis 0G90
Hypothalamus 009A
Ileocecal Valve 0D9C
Ileum 0D9B
Inferior Mesenteric Artery 049B
Inferior Mesenteric Vein 0696
Inferior Parathyroid Gland 0G9
Inguinal Region 0Y9
Inner Ear 099
Innominate Artery 0392
Innominate Vein 059
Internal Carotid Artery 039
Internal Iliac Artery 049
Internal Jugular Vein 059
Internal Mammary Artery, Left 0391
Intracranial Artery 039G
Intracranial Vein 059L
Iris 089
Jejunum 0D9A
Joint
    Finger Phalangeal, Left 0R90
    Toe Phalangeal, Left 0S90
Kidney, Left 0T91
Kidney Pelvis 0T9
Knee Bursa and Ligament 0M9
Knee Joint 0S9
Knee Region 0Y9
Knee Tendon 0L9
Lacrimal Bone 0N9
Lacrimal Duct, Left 089Y
Lacrimal Gland 089
Large Intestine 0D9
Larynx 0C9S
Lens 089
Lesser Omentum 0D9T
Lesser Saphenous Vein 069
Lingula Bronchus 0B99
Liver 0F90
    Left Lobe 0F92
    Right Lobe 0F91
Lobe Segmental Bronchus
    Lower 0B9
    Middle, Right 0B95
    Upper 0B9
Lower Arm 0X9
Lower Arm and Wrist Muscle 0K9
Lower Arm and Wrist Tendon 0L9
Lower Artery 049Y
Lower Back 0W9L
Lower Extremity 0Y9
Lower Extremity Bursa and Ligament
    0M9
Lower Eyelid 089
Lower Femur 0Q9
Lower Gingiva 0C96
Lower Jaw 0W95
Lower Leg 0Y9
Lower Leg Muscle 0K9
Lower Leg Tendon 0L9
Lower Lip 0C91
Lower Lobe Bronchus 0B9
Lower Lung Lobe 0B9
Lower Tooth 0C9X
Lower Vein 069Y
Lumbar Nerve 019B
Lumbar Plexus 0199
Lumbar Spinal Cord 009Y
Lumbar Sympathetic Nerve 019N
Lumbar Vertebral Disc 0S92

Drainage—*continued*

  by Body Part—*continued*

Lumbosacral Disc 0S94
Lumbosacral Joint 0S93
Lumbosacral Plexus 019A
Lung 0B9
Lung Lingula 0B9H
Lung Lingula Segments 0B9H
Lung Lobe Segments
    Lower 0B9
    Middle, Right 0B9D
    Upper 0B9
Lungs, Bilateral 0B9M
Lymphatic
    Aortic 079D
    Internal Mammary 079
    Left Axillary 0796
    Left Inguinal 079J
    Left Lower Extremity 079G
    Left Neck 0792
    Left Upper Extremity 0794
    Mesenteric 079B
    Pelvis 079C
    Right Axillary 0795
    Right Inguinal 079H
    Right Lower Extremity 079F
    Right Neck 0791
    Right Upper Extremity 0793
    Thorax 0797
Main Bronchus 0B9
Mandible 0N9
Marrow, Bone 0790
Mastoid Sinus, Left 099C
Maxilla 0N9
Maxillary Sinus 099
Median Nerve 0195
Mediastinum 0W9C
Medulla Oblongata 009D
Mesentery 0D9V
Metacarpal 0P9
Metacarpocarpal Joint 0R9
Metacarpophalangeal Joint 0R9
Metatarsal 0Q9
Metatarsal-Phalangeal Joint 0S9
Metatarsal-Tarsal Joint 0S9
Middle Ear, Left 0996
Middle Lobe Bronchus, Right 0B95
Middle Lung Lobe, Right 0B9D
Minor Salivary Gland 0C9J
Muscle, Foot, Left 0K90
Nail, Toe 0H90
Nail Bed
    Finger 0H9Q
    Toe 0H9R
Nasal Bone 0N9B
Nasal Septum 099M
Nasal Turbinate 099L
Nasopharynx 099N
Neck 0W96
    Bladder 0T90
Neck Muscle 0K9
Nerve, Sacral 0190
Neurohypophysis 0G90
Nipple 0H9
Nose 099K
Occipital Bone 0N9
Oculomotor Nerve 009H
Olfactory Nerve 009F
Omentum, Lesser 0D9R
Optic Nerve 009G
Oral Cavity and Throat 0W93
Orbit 0N9
Ovaries, Bilateral 0U92
Ovary
    Bilateral 0U90
    Left 0U91

Drainage—*continued*

  by Body Part—*continued*

Palatine Bone 0N9
Pancreas 0F9G
    Body 0F9F
    Head 0F9F
    Tail 0F9F
Pancreatic Duct 0F9D
    Accessory 0F9F
Para-aortic Body 0G99
Paraganglion Extremity 0G9F
Parathyroid Gland 0G9R
Parathyroid Glands, Multiple 0G9Q
Parietal Bone 0N9
Parotid Duct 0C9
Parotid Gland, Left 0C99
Patella 0Q9
Pelvic Bone 0Q9
Pelvic Cavity 0W9J
Penis 0V9S
Pericardial Cavity 0W9D
Perineum
    Female 0W9N
    Male 0W9M
Perineum Bursa and Ligament 0M9K
Perineum Muscle 0K9M
Perineum Tendon 0L9H
Peritoneal Cavity 0W9G
Peritoneum 0D9W
Peroneal Artery 049
Peroneal Nerve 019H
Phalanx
    Finger, Left 0P90
    Toe, Left 0Q90
Phrenic Nerve 0192
Pineal Body 0G91
Pleura 0B9
    Parietal 0B9
    Visceral 0B9
Pleural Cavity 0W9
Pons 009B
Popliteal Artery 049
Portal Vein 0698
Posterior Tibial Artery 049
Prepuce 0V9T
Products of Conception 1090
Prostate 0V90
Pudendal Nerve 019C
Pulmonary Lingula 0B9H
Pulmonary Lobe
    Lower 0B9
    Middle, Right 0B9D
    Upper 0B9
Radial Artery 039
Radial Nerve 0196
Radius 0P9
Rectum 0D9P
Region
    Ankle, Left 0Y90
    Wrist, Left 0X92
Renal Artery 049
Renal Pelvis 0T9
Renal Vein 069
Retina 089
Retinal Vessel 089
Retroperitoneum 0W9H
Rib 0P9
Sacral Nerve 019R
Sacral Plexus 019Q
Sacral Sympathetic Nerve 019P
Sacrococcygeal Joint 0S95
Sacroiliac Joint 0S9
Sacrum 0Q91
Scapula 0P9
Sciatic Nerve 019F
Sclera 089

Duodenotomy
—*see* Drainage, Gastrointestinal System 0D9
—*see* Inspection, Gastrointestinal System 0DJ

E

ECG 4A02
Echocardiography—*see* Ultrasonography
Echography—*see* Ultrasonography
ECMO—*see* Extracorporeal Assistance and Performance
EEG 4A00
EGD—*see* Inspection, Gastrointestinal System 0DJ
EKG 4A02
Electrocardiogram 4A02
Electrocoagulation—*see* Destruction
Electroconvulsive Therapy
by Type Qualifier
Bilateral-Multiple Seizure GZB3
Bilateral-Single Seizure GZB2
Other Electroconvulsive Therapy GZB4
Unilateral-Multiple Seizure GZB1
Unilateral-Single Seizure GZB0
Electroencephalogram 4A00
Electromagnetic Therapy
Central Nervous 6A22
Urinary 6A21
Electromyogram 4A0F
Electroneurogram 4A01
Electrophysiologic Stimulation
—*see* Measurement And Monitoring, Physiological Systems 4A02
Embolization—*see* Occlusion
EMG 4A0F
Endarterectomy
—*see* Excision, Lower Arteries 04B
—*see* Excision, Upper Arteries 03B
Epididymectomy
—*see* Excision, Male Reproductive System 0VB
—*see* Resection, Male Reproductive System 0VT
Epididymoplasty
—*see* Repair, Male Reproductive System 0VQ
—*see* Replacement, Male Reproductive System 0VR
Epididymorrhaphy—*see* Repair, Male Reproductive System 0VQ
Epididymotomy
—*see* Drainage, Male Reproductive System 0V9
—*see* Inspection, Male Reproductive System 0VJ
Epiphysiodesis
—*see* Fusion, Lower Joints 0SG
—*see* Fusion, Upper Joints 0RG
Episioplasty—*see* Repair, Female Reproductive System 0UQ
Episiorrhaphy—*see* Repair, Female Reproductive System 0UQ
Episiotomy—*see* Division, Anatomical Regions, General 0W8
EPS—*see* Measurement And Monitoring, Physiological Systems 4A02
ERCP—*see* Fluoroscopy, Hepatobiliary System and Pancreas BF1
Esophagectomy
—*see* Excision, Gastrointestinal System 0DB
—*see* Resection, Gastrointestinal System 0DT
Esophagocoloplasty
—*see* Repair, Gastrointestinal System 0DQ
—*see* Replacement, Gastrointestinal System 0DR

Esophagoduodenostomy—*see* Bypass, Gastrointestinal System 0D1
Esophagoenterostomy—*see* Bypass, Gastrointestinal System 0D1
Esophagoesophagostomy—*see* Bypass, Gastrointestinal System 0D1
Esophagofundopexy—*see* Repair, Gastrointestinal System 0DQ
Esophagogastrectomy
—*see* Excision, Gastrointestinal System 0DB
—*see* Resection, Gastrointestinal System 0DT
Esophagogastroduodenoscopy—*see* Inspection, Gastrointestinal System 0DJ
Esophagogastroplasty
—*see* Repair, Gastrointestinal System 0DQ
—*see* Replacement, Gastrointestinal System 0DR
Esophagogastroscopy—*see* Inspection, Gastrointestinal System 0DJ
Esophagogastrostomy—*see* Bypass, Gastrointestinal System 0D1
Esophagojejunogastrostomy—*see* Bypass, Gastrointestinal System 0D1
Esophagojejunoplasty
—*see* Repair, Gastrointestinal System 0DQ
—*see* Replacement, Gastrointestinal System 0DR
Esophagojejunostomy—*see* Bypass, Gastrointestinal System 0D1
Esophagoplasty
—*see* Repair, Gastrointestinal System 0DQ
—*see* Replacement, Gastrointestinal System 0DR
Esophagoplication—*see* Restriction, Gastrointestinal System 0DV
Esophagoscopy—*see* Inspection, Gastrointestinal System 0DJ
Esophagostomy—*see* Bypass, Gastrointestinal System 0D1
Esophagotomy
—*see* Drainage, Gastrointestinal System 0D9
—*see* Inspection, Gastrointestinal System 0DJ
ESWL—*see* Fragmentation
Ethmoidectomy
—*see* Excision, Ear, Nose, Sinus 09B
—*see* Excision, Head and Facial Bones 0NB
—*see* Resection, Ear, Nose, Sinus 09T
—*see* Resection, Head and Facial Bones 0NT
Ethmoidotomy
—*see* Drainage, Ear, Nose, Sinus 099
—*see* Inspection, Ear, Nose, Sinus 09J
Evacuate—*see* Drainage
Evacuation—*see* Drainage
Evaluation—*see* Vestibular Treatment
Examination
—*see* Inspection
—*see* Vestibular Treatment
Exchange—*see* Change
Excision
by Body System
Anatomical Regions, General 0WB
Anatomical Regions, Lower Extremities 0YB
Anatomical Regions, Upper Extremities 0XB
Bursae and Ligaments 0MB
Central Nervous System 00B
Ear, Nose, Sinus 09B
Endocrine System 0GB
Eye 08B
Female Reproductive System 0UB
Gastrointestinal System 0DB
Head and Facial Bones 0NB

Excision—*continued*
by Body System—*continued*
Heart and Great Vessels 02B
Hepatobiliary System and Pancreas 0FB
Lower Arteries 04B
Lower Bones 0QB
Lower Joints 0SB
Lower Veins 06B
Lymphatic and Hemic Systems 07B
Male Reproductive System 0VB
Mouth and Throat 0CB
Muscles 0KB
Peripheral Nervous System 01B
Respiratory System 0BB
Skin and Breast 0HB
Subcutaneous Tissue and Fascia 0JB
Tendons 0LB
Upper Arteries 03B
Upper Bones 0PB
Upper Joints 0RB
Upper Veins 05B
Urinary System 0TB
by Body Part
Abdomen Bursa and Ligament 0MB
Abdomen Muscle 0KB
Abdomen Tendon 0LB
Abdominal Sympathetic Nerve 01BM
Abdominal Wall 0WBF
Abducens Nerve 00BL
Accessory Nerve 00BR
Accessory Sinus 09BP
Acetabulum 0QB
Acoustic Nerve 00BN
Acromioclavicular Joint 0RB
Adenohypophysis 0GB0
Adenoids 0CBQ
Adrenal Gland 0GB
Adrenal Glands, Bilateral 0GB4
Ampulla of Vater 0FBC
Ankle Bursa and Ligament 0MB
Ankle Joint 0SB
Ankle Region 0YB
Ankle Tendon 0LB
Anterior Tibial Artery 04B
Anus 0DBQ
Aortic Body 0GBD
Aortic Valve 02BF
Appendix 0DBJ
Areola 0HB
Artery
Aorta, Thoracic 02B4
Lower 04B0
Upper 03B0
Ascending Colon 0DBK
Atrial Septum 02B5
Atrium 02B
Auditory Ossicle 09B
Axilla 0XB
Axillary Artery 03B
Axillary Vein 05B
Back, Lower 0WB0
Basal Ganglia 00B8
Basilic Vein 05B
Bladder 0TBB
Bladder Neck 0TBC
Body
Coccygeal 0GB9
Jugulotympanic 0GBB
Bone, Hyoid 0NB0
Brachial Artery 03B
Brachial Plexus 01B3
Brachial Vein 05B
Breast
Aberrant 0HBY
Bilateral 0HBV
Left 0HBU

Excision—*continued*
  by Body Part—*continued*
    Breast—*continued*
      Supernumerary 0HBT
    Bronchus, Segmental, Lingula 0BB9
    Buccal Mucosa 0CB4
    Bursa and Ligament, Lower Extremity,
      Left 0MB0
    Buttock, Left 0YB1
    Canal, External Auditory, Left 09B3
    Carina 0BB2
    Carotid Bodies, Bilateral 0GB8
    Carotid Body 0GB
    Carpal 0PB
    Carpal Joint 0RB
    Cecum 0DBH
    Celiac Artery 04B1
    Cephalic Vein 05B
    Cerebellum 00BC
    Cerebral Hemisphere 00B7
    Cerebral Meninges 00B1
    Cerebral Ventricle 00B6
    Cervical Nerve 01B1
    Cervical Spinal Cord 00BW
    Cervical Vertebra 0PB3
    Cervical Vertebral Disc 0RB3
    Cervical Vertebral Joint 0RB1
    Cervicothoracic Vertebral Disc 0RB5
    Cervicothoracic Vertebral Joint 0RB4
    Cervix 0UBC
    Chest Wall 0WB8
    Chordae Tendineae 02B9
    Choroid, Left 08BB
    Chyli, Cisterna 07B0
    Cisterna Chyli 07BL
    Clavicle 0PB
    Coccygeal Glomus 0GBB
    Coccygeal Joint 0SB6
    Coccyx 0QBS
    Colic Artery 04B
    Colic Vein 06B7
    Colon, Sigmoid 0DB1
    Common Bile Duct 0FB9
    Common Carotid Artery 03B
    Common Iliac Artery 04B
    Common Iliac Vein 06B
    Conduction Mechanism 02B8
    Conjunctiva 08B
    Cord
      Lumbar Spinal 00B0
      Vocal, Left 0CBM
    Cornea 08B
    Corpora Arenacea, Pineal 0GB1
    Cul-de-sac 0UBF
    Cystic Duct 0FB8
    Deferens, Vas, Bilateral 0VB1
    Descending Colon 0DBM
    Diaphragm 0BB
    Duct
      Lacrimal, Left 08BX
      Pancreatic, Accessory 0FB5
    Duodenum 0DB9
    Dura Mater 00B2
    Ear
      External, Left 09B0
      Inner, Left 09B5
    Elbow Bursa and Ligament 0MB
    Elbow Joint 0RB
    Elbow Region 0XB
    Epididymis 0VB
    Epiglottis 0CBR
    Esophageal Vein 06B3
    Esophagogastric Junction 0DB4
    Esophagus 0DB5
      Lower 0DB3
      Middle 0DB2

    Ethmoid Bone 0NB
    Ethmoid Sinus 09B
    Eustachian Tube 09B
    External Auditory Canal, Left 09B4
    External Carotid Artery 03B
    External Ear, Left 09B1
    External Iliac Artery 04B
    External Iliac Vein 06B
    External Jugular Vein 05B
    Extraocular Muscle 08B
    Eye, Left 08B1
    Eyelid, Lower, Left 08B0
    Face 0WB2
    Face Artery 03BR
    Face Vein 05B
    Facial Muscle 0KB1
    Facial Nerve 00BM
    Fallopian Tube 0UB
    Fallopian Tubes, Bilateral 0UB7
    Femoral Artery 04B
    Femoral Nerve 01BD
    Femoral Region 0YB
    Femoral Shaft 0QB
    Femoral Vein 06B
    Fibula 0QB
    Finger Nail 0HBQ
    Finger Phalangeal Joint 0RB
    Finger Phalanx 0PB
    Foot 0YB
    Foot Artery 04B
    Foot Bursa and Ligament 0MB
    Foot Muscle 0KB
    Foot Tendon 0LB
    Foot Vein 06B
    Frontal Bone 0NB
    Frontal Sinus 09B
    Gallbladder 0FB4
    Gastric Artery 04B2
    Gastric Vein 06B2
    Gingiva, Lower 0CB0
    Gland
      Lacrimal, Left 08BA
      Lower Parathyroid 0GB
      Mammary 0HB
      Minor Salivary 0CB8
      Parathyroid 0GB0
      Pineal 0GB1
      Upper Parathyroid 0GB
      Vestibular 0UBJ
    Glenoid Cavity 0PB
    Glomus Jugulare 0GBC
    Glossopharyngeal Nerve 00BP
    Greater Omentum 0DBS
    Greater Saphenous Vein 06B
    Hand 0XB
    Hand Artery 03B
    Hand Bursa and Ligament 0MB
    Hand Muscle 0KB
    Hand Tendon 0LB
    Hand Vein 05B
    Hard Palate 0CB2
    Head and Neck Sympathetic Nerve 01BK
    Hemiazygos Vein 05B1
    Hepatic Artery 04B3
    Hepatic Duct, Left 0FB6
    Hepatic Vein 06B4
    Hip Bursa and Ligament 0MB
    Hip Joint 0SB
    Hip Muscle 0KB
    Hip Tendon 0LB
    Humeral Head 0PB
    Humeral Shaft 0PB
    Hymen 0UBK
    Hyoid Bone 0NBX

    Hypogastric Vein 06B
    Hypoglossal Nerve 00BS
    Hypophysis 0GB0
    Hypothalamus 00BA
    Ileocecal Valve 0DBC
    Ileum 0DBB
    Inferior Mesenteric Artery 04BB
    Inferior Mesenteric Vein 06B6
    Inferior Parathyroid Gland 0GB
    Inguinal Region 0YB
    Inner Ear 09B
    Innominate Artery 03B2
    Innominate Vein 05B
    Internal Carotid Artery 03B
    Internal Iliac Artery 04B
    Internal Jugular Vein 05B
    Internal Mammary Artery, Left 03B1
    Intracranial Artery 03BG
    Intracranial Vein 05BL
    Iris 08B
    Jejunum 0DBA
    Joint
      Finger Phalangeal, Left 0RB0
      Toe Phalangeal, Left 0SB0
    Kidney, Left 0TB1
    Kidney Pelvis 0TB
    Knee Bursa and Ligament 0MB
    Knee Joint 0SB
    Knee Region 0YB
    Knee Tendon 0LB
    Lacrimal Bone 0NB
    Lacrimal Duct, Left 08BY
    Lacrimal Gland 08B
    Large Intestine 0DB
    Larynx 0CBS
    Lens 08B
    Lesser Omentum 0DBT
    Lesser Saphenous Vein 06B
    Lingula Bronchus 0BB9
    Liver 0FB0
      Left Lobe 0FB2
      Right Lobe 0FB1
    Lobe Segmental Bronchus
      Lower 0BB
      Middle, Right 0BB5
      Upper 0BB
    Lower Arm 0XB
    Lower Arm and Wrist Muscle 0KB
    Lower Arm and Wrist Tendon 0LB
    Lower Artery 04BY
    Lower Back 0WBL
    Lower Extremity 0YB
    Lower Extremity Bursa and Ligament
      0MB
    Lower Eyelid 08B
    Lower Femur 0QB
    Lower Gingiva 0CB6
    Lower Jaw 0WB5
    Lower Leg 0YB
    Lower Leg Muscle 0KB
    Lower Leg Tendon 0LB
    Lower Lip 0CB1
    Lower Lobe Bronchus 0BB
    Lower Lung Lobe 0BB
    Lower Tooth 0CBX
    Lower Vein 06BY
    Lumbar Nerve 01BB
    Lumbar Plexus 01B9
    Lumbar Spinal Cord 00BY
    Lumbar Sympathetic Nerve 01BN
    Lumbar Vertebral Disc 0SB2
    Lumbosacral Disc 0SB4
    Lumbosacral Joint 0SB3
    Lumbosacral Plexus 01BA

Excision—*continued*
  by Body Part—*continued*
    Lung 0BB
    Lung Lingula 0BBH
    Lung Lingula Segments 0BBH
    Lung Lobe Segments
      Lower 0BB
      Middle, Right 0BBD
      Upper 0BB
    Lungs, Bilateral 0BBM
    Lymphatic
      Aortic 07BD
      Internal Mammary 07B
      Left Axillary 07B6
      Left Inguinal 07BJ
      Left Lower Extremity 07BG
      Left Neck 07B2
      Left Upper Extremity 07B4
      Mesenteric 07BB
      Pelvis 07BC
      Right Axillary 07B5
      Right Inguinal 07BH
      Right Lower Extremity 07BF
      Right Neck 07B1
      Right Upper Extremity 07B3
      Thorax 07B7
    Main Bronchus 0BB
    Mandible 0NB
    Mastoid Sinus, Left 09BC
    Maxilla 0NB
    Maxillary Sinus 09B
    Median Nerve 01B5
    Mediastinum 0WBC
    Medulla Oblongata 00BD
    Mesentery 0DBV
    Metacarpal 0PB
    Metacarpocarpal Joint 0RB
    Metacarpophalangeal Joint 0RB
    Metatarsal 0QB
    Metatarsal-Phalangeal Joint 0SB
    Metatarsal-Tarsal Joint 0SB
    Middle Ear, Left 09B6
    Middle Lobe Bronchus, Right 0BB5
    Middle Lung Lobe, Right 0BBD
    Minor Salivary Gland 0CBJ
    Mitral Valve 02BG
    Muscle, Foot, Left 0KB0
    Nail, Toe 0HB0
    Nail Bed
      Finger 0HBQ
      Toe 0HBR
    Nasal Bone 0NBB
    Nasal Septum 09BM
    Nasal Turbinate 09BL
    Nasopharynx 09BN
    Neck, Bladder 0TB0
    Neck Muscle 0KB
    Nerve, Sacral 01B0
    Neurohypophysis 0GB0
    Nipple 0HB
    Nose 09BK
    Occipital Bone 0NB
    Oculomotor Nerve 00BH
    Olfactory Nerve 00BF
    Omentum, Lesser 0DBR
    Optic Nerve 00BG
    Orbit 0NB
    Ovaries, Bilateral 0UB2
    Ovary, Left 0UB1
    Palatine Bone 0NB
    Pancreas 0FBG
      Body 0FBF
      Head 0FBF
      Tail 0FBF
    Pancreatic Duct 0FBD
      Accessory 0FBF

Excision—*continued*
  by Body Part—*continued*
    Papillary Muscle 02BD
    Para-aortic Body 0GB9
    Paraganglion Extremity 0GBF
    Parathyroid Gland 0GBR
    Parathyroid Glands, Multiple 0GBQ
    Parietal Bone 0NB
    Parotid Duct 0CB
    Parotid Gland, Left 0CB9
    Patella 0QB
    Pelvic Bone 0QB
    Penis 0VBS
    Pericardium 02BN
    Perineum
      Female 0WBN
      Male 0WBM
    Perineum Bursa and Ligament 0MBK
    Perineum Muscle 0KBM
    Perineum Tendon 0LBH
    Peritoneum 0DBW
    Peroneal Artery 04B
    Peroneal Nerve 01BH
    Phalanx
      Finger, Left 0PB0
      Toe, Left 0QB0
    Phrenic Nerve 01B2
    Pineal Body 0GB1
    Pleura 0BB
      Parietal 0BB
      Visceral 0BB
    Pons 00BB
    Popliteal Artery 04B
    Portal Vein 06B8
    Posterior Tibial Artery 04B
    Prepuce 0VBT
    Prostate 0VB0
    Pudendal Nerve 01BC
    Pulmonary Artery 02B
    Pulmonary Lingula 0BBH
    Pulmonary Lobe
      Lower 0BB
      Middle, Right 0BBD
      Upper 0BB
    Pulmonary Trunk 02BP
    Pulmonary Valve 02BH
    Pulmonary Vein 02B
    Radial Artery 03B
    Radial Nerve 01B6
    Radius 0PB
    Rectum 0DBP
    Region
      Ankle, Left 0YB0
      Wrist, Left 0XB2
    Renal Artery 04B
    Renal Pelvis 0TB
    Renal Vein 06B
    Retina 08B
    Retroperitoneum 0WBH
    Rib 0PB
    Sacral Nerve 01BR
    Sacral Plexus 01BQ
    Sacral Sympathetic Nerve 01BP
    Sacrococcygeal Joint 0SB5
    Sacroiliac Joint 0SB
    Sacrum 0QB1
    Scapula 0PB
    Sciatic Nerve 01BF
    Sclera 08B
    Scrotum 0VB5
    Seminal Vesicle, Left 0VB2
    Seminal Vesicles, Bilateral 0VB3
    Shoulder Bursa and Ligament 0MB
    Shoulder Joint 0RB
    Shoulder Muscle 0KB
    Shoulder Region, Left 0XB3

Excision—*continued*
  by Body Part—*continued*
    Shoulder Tendon 0LB
    Sigmoid Colon 0DBN
    Sinus, Sphenoid, Left 09BB
    Skin
      Abdomen 0HB7
      Back 0HB6
      Buttock 0HB8
      Chest 0HB5
      Face 0HB1
      Genitalia 0HBA
      Left Ear 0HB3
      Left Foot 0HBN
      Left Hand 0HBG
      Left Lower Arm 0HBE
      Left Lower Leg 0HBL
      Left Upper Arm 0HBC
      Left Upper Leg 0HBJ
      Neck 0HB4
      Perineum 0HB9
      Right Ear 0HB2
      Right Foot 0HBM
      Right Hand 0HBF
      Right Lower Arm 0HBD
      Right Lower Leg 0HBK
      Right Upper Arm 0HBB
      Right Upper Leg 0HBH
    Small Intestine 0DB8
    Soft Palate 0CB3
    Spermatic Cord 0VB
    Spermatic Cords, Bilateral 0VBH
    Sphenoid Bone 0NB
    Sphenoid Sinus 09B
    Spinal Meninges 00BT
    Spleen 07BP
    Splenic Artery 04B4
    Splenic Vein 06B1
    Sternoclavicular Joint 0RB
    Stomach 0DB6
      Body 0DB6
      Fundus 0DB6
      Pylorus 0DB7
    Subclavian Artery 03B
    Subclavian Vein 05B
    Subcutaneous Tissue and Fascia
      Abdomen 0JB8
      Anterior Neck 0JB4
      Back 0JB7
      Buttock 0JB9
      Chest 0JB6
      Face 0JB1
      Foot, Left 0JB0
      Genitalia 0JBC
      Left Foot 0JBR
      Left Hand 0JBK
      Left Lower Arm 0JBH
      Left Lower Leg 0JBP
      Left Upper Arm 0JBF
      Left Upper Leg 0JBM
      Perineum 0JBB
      Posterior Neck 0JB5
      Right Foot 0JBQ
      Right Hand 0JBJ
      Right Lower Arm 0JBG
      Right Lower Leg 0JBN
      Right Upper Arm 0JBD
      Right Upper Leg 0JBL
    Sublingual Gland 0CB
    Submaxillary Gland 0CB
    Superior Mesenteric Artery 04B5
    Superior Mesenteric Vein 06B5
    Superior Parathyroid Gland 0GB
    Superior Vena Cava 02BV
    Supernumerary Breast 0HBY
    Tarsal 0QB

Excision—*continued*
  by Body Part—*continued*
    Tarsal Joint 0SB
    Temporal Artery 03B
    Temporal Bone 0NB
    Temporomandibular Joint 0RB
    Tendon, Foot, Left 0LB0
    Testes, Bilateral 0VBC
    Testis 0VB
    Thalamus 00B9
    Thoracic Aorta 02BW
    Thoracic Duct 07BK
    Thoracic Nerve 01B8
    Thoracic Spinal Cord 00BX
    Thoracic Sympathetic Nerve 01BL
    Thoracic Vertebra 0PB4
    Thoracic Vertebral Disc 0RB9
    Thoracic Vertebral Joint 0RB6
    Thoracolumbar Vertebral Disc 0RBB
    Thoracolumbar Vertebral Joint 0RBA
    Thorax Bursa and Ligament 0MB
    Thorax Muscle 0KB
    Thorax Tendon 0LB
    Thumb Phalanx 0PB
    Thymus 07BM
    Thyroid Artery 03B
    Thyroid Gland Lobe 0GB
    Tibia 0QB
    Tibial Nerve 01BG
    Toe Nail 0HBR
    Toe Phalangeal Joint 0SB
    Toe Phalanx 0QB
    Tongue 0CB7
      Palate, Pharynx Muscle 0KB4
    Tonsils 0CBP
    Tooth, Lower 0CBW
    Transverse Colon 0DBL
    Tricuspid Valve 02BJ
    Trigeminal Nerve 00BK
    Trochlear Nerve 00BJ
    Trunk Bursa and Ligament 0MB
    Trunk Muscle 0KB
    Trunk Tendon 0LB
    Tube, Fallopian, Bilateral 0UB0
    Tunica Vaginalis 0VB
    Turbinate, Nasal 09B7
    Tympanic Membrane, Left 09B8
    Tympanicum, Glomus 0GBB
    Ulna 0PB
    Ulnar Artery 03B
    Ulnar Nerve 01B4
    Upper Arm 0XB
    Upper Arm Muscle 0KB
    Upper Arm Tendon 0LB
    Upper Artery 03BY
    Upper Back 0WBK
    Upper Extremity 0XB
    Upper Extremity Bursa and Ligament
      0MB
    Upper Eyelid 08B
    Upper Femur 0QB
    Upper Gingiva 0CB5
    Upper Jaw 0WB4
    Upper Leg 0YB
    Upper Leg Muscle 0KB
    Upper Leg Tendon 0LB
    Upper Lobe Bronchus 0BB
    Upper Lung Lobe 0BB
    Upper Vein 05BY
    Ureter 0TB
    Urethra 0TBD
    Uterine Supporting Structure 0UB4
    Uterus 0UB9
    Uvula 0CBN
    Vagina 0UBG
    Vagus Nerve 00BQ

Excision—*continued*
  by Body Part—*continued*
    Vas Deferens 0VB
    Vein
      Lower 06B0
      Upper 05B0
    Ventricle 02B
    Ventricular Septum 02BM
    Vertebral Artery 03B
    Vertebral Vein 05B
    Vestibular Gland 0UBL
    Vitreous 08B
    Vocal Cord 0CB
    Vulva 0UBM
    Wall, Abdominal 0WB6
    Wrist Bursa and Ligament 0MB
    Wrist Joint 0RB
    Wrist Region 0XB
    Zygomatic Bone 0NB
Exploration—*see* Inspection
Explore—*see* Inspection
Expose—*see* Inspection
Extirpation
  by Body System
    Anatomical Regions, General 0WC
    Bursae and Ligaments 0MC
    Central Nervous System 00C
    Ear, Nose, Sinus 09C
    Endocrine System 0GC
    Eye 08C
    Female Reproductive System 0UC
    Gastrointestinal System 0DC
    Head and Facial Bones 0NC
    Heart and Great Vessels 02C
    Hepatobiliary System and Pancreas 0FC
    Lower Arteries 04C
    Lower Bones 0QC
    Lower Joints 0SC
    Lower Veins 06C
    Lymphatic and Hemic Systems 07C
    Male Reproductive System 0VC
    Mouth and Throat 0CC
    Muscles 0KC
    Peripheral Nervous System 01C
    Respiratory System 0BC
    Skin and Breast 0HC
    Subcutaneous Tissue and Fascia 0JC
    Tendons 0LC
    Upper Arteries 03C
    Upper Bones 0PC
    Upper Joints 0RC
    Upper Veins 05C
    Urinary System 0TC
  by Body Part
    Abdomen Bursa and Ligament 0MC
    Abdomen Muscle 0KC
    Abdomen Tendon 0LC
    Abdominal Sympathetic Nerve 01CM
    Abducens Nerve 00CL
    Accessory Nerve 00CR
    Accessory Sinus 09CP
    Acetabulum 0QC
    Acoustic Nerve 00CN
    Acromioclavicular Joint 0RC
    Adenohypophysis 0GC0
    Adenoids 0CCQ
    Adrenal Gland 0GC
    Adrenal Glands, Bilateral 0GC4
    Ampulla of Vater 0FCC
    Ankle Bursa and Ligament 0MC
    Ankle Joint 0SC
    Ankle Tendon 0LC
    Anterior Chamber, Left 08C3
    Anterior Tibial Artery 04C
    Anus 0DCQ
    Aortic Body 0GCD

Extirpation—*continued*
  by Body Part—*continued*
    Aortic Valve 02CF
    Appendix 0DCJ
    Areola 0HC
    Artery
      Aorta, Thoracic 02C0
      Lower 04C0
      Upper 03C0
    Ascending Colon 0DCK
    Atrial Septum 02C5
    Atrium 02C
    Auditory Ossicle 09C
    Axillary Artery 03C
    Axillary Vein 05C
    Basal Ganglia 00C8
    Basilic Vein 05C
    Bladder 0TCB
    Bladder Neck 0TCC
    Body
      Coccygeal 0GC9
      Jugulotympanic 0GCB
    Bone, Hyoid 0NC1
    Brachial Artery 03C
    Brachial Plexus 01C3
    Brachial Vein 05C
    Breast 0HC
    Bronchus, Segmental, Lingula 0BC9
    Buccal Mucosa 0CC4
    Bursa and Ligament, Lower Extremity,
      Left 0MC0
    Canal, External Auditory, Left 09C3
    Carina 0BC2
    Carotid Bodies, Bilateral 0GC8
    Carotid Body 0GC
    Carpal 0PC
    Carpal Joint 0RC
    Cavity, Pelvic 0WC1
    Cecum 0DCH
    Celiac Artery 04C1
    Cephalic Vein 05C
    Cerebellum 00CC
    Cerebral Hemisphere 00C7
    Cerebral Meninges 00C1
    Cerebral Ventricle 00C6
    Cervical Nerve 01C1
    Cervical Spinal Cord 00CW
    Cervical Vertebra 0PC3
    Cervical Vertebral Disc 0RC3
    Cervical Vertebral Joint 0RC1
    Cervicothoracic Vertebral Disc 0RC5
    Cervicothoracic Vertebral Joint 0RC4
    Cervix 0UCC
    Chordae Tendineae 02C9
    Choroid, Left 08CB
    Chyli, Cisterna 07C0
    Cisterna Chyli 07CL
    Clavicle 0PC
    Coccygeal Glomus 0GCB
    Coccygeal Joint 0SC6
    Coccyx 0QCS
    Colic Artery 04C
    Colic Vein 06C7
    Colon, Sigmoid 0DC1
    Common Bile Duct 0FC9
    Common Carotid Artery 03C
    Common Iliac Artery 04C
    Common Iliac Vein 06C
    Conduction Mechanism 02C8
    Conjunctiva 08C
    Cord
      Lumbar Spinal 00C0
      Vocal, Left 0CCM
    Cornea 08C

Extirpation—*continued*
  by Body Part—*continued*
    Coronary Artery
      Four or More Sites 02C3
      Three Sites 02C2
      Two Sites 02C1
    Coronary Vein 02C4
    Corpora Arenacea, Pineal 0GC1
    Cul-de-sac 0UCF
    Cystic Duct 0FC8
    Deferens, Vas, Bilateral 0VC1
    Descending Colon 0DCM
    Diaphragm 0BC
    Duct
      Lacrimal, Left 08CX
      Pancreatic, Accessory 0FC5
    Duodenum 0DC9
    Dura Mater 00C2
    Ear
      External, Left 09C0
      Inner, Left 09C5
    Elbow Bursa and Ligament 0MC
    Elbow Joint 0RC
    Endometrium 0UCB
    Epididymis 0VC
    Epidural Space 00C3
    Epiglottis 0CCR
    Esophageal Vein 06C3
    Esophagogastric Junction 0DC4
    Esophagus 0DC5
      Lower 0DC3
      Middle 0DC2
    Ethmoid Bone 0NC
    Ethmoid Sinus 09C
    Eustachian Tube 09C
    External Auditory Canal, Left 09C4
    External Carotid Artery 03C
    External Ear, Left 09C1
    External Iliac Artery 04C
    External Iliac Vein 06C
    External Jugular Vein 05C
    Extraocular Muscle 08C
    Eye 08C
    Face Artery 03CR
    Face Vein 05C
    Facial Muscle 0KC1
    Facial Nerve 00CM
    Fallopian Tube, Left 0UC6
    Fallopian Tubes, Bilateral 0UC7
    Femoral Artery 04C
    Femoral Nerve 01CD
    Femoral Shaft 0QC
    Femoral Vein 06C
    Fibula 0QC
    Finger Nail 0HCQ
    Finger Phalangeal Joint 0RC
    Finger Phalanx 0PC
    Foot Artery 04C
    Foot Bursa and Ligament 0MC
    Foot Muscle 0KC
    Foot Tendon 0LC
    Foot Vein 06C
    Frontal Bone, Left 0NC2
    Frontal Sinus 09C
    Gallbladder 0FC4
    Gastric Artery 04C2
    Gastric Vein 06C2
    Genitourinary Tract 0WCR
    Gingiva, Lower 0CC0
    Gland
      Lacrimal, Left 08CA
      Lower Parathyroid 0GC
      Mammary 0HC
      Minor Salivary 0CC8
      Parathyroid 0GC0
      Pineal 0GC1

Extirpation—*continued*
  by Body Part—*continued*
    Gland—*continued*
      Upper Parathyroid 0GC
      Vestibular 0UCJ
    Glenoid Cavity 0PC
    Glomus Jugulare 0GCC
    Glossopharyngeal Nerve 00CP
    Greater Omentum 0DCS
    Greater Saphenous Vein 06C
    Hand Artery 03C
    Hand Bursa and Ligament 0MC
    Hand Muscle 0KC
    Hand Tendon 0LC
    Hand Vein 05C
    Hard Palate 0CC2
    Head and Neck Sympathetic Nerve 01CK
    Hemiazygos Vein 05C1
    Hepatic Artery 04C3
    Hepatic Duct, Left 0FC6
    Hepatic Vein 06C4
    Hip Bursa and Ligament 0MC
    Hip Joint 0SC
    Hip Muscle 0KC
    Hip Tendon 0LC
    Humeral Head 0PC
    Humeral Shaft 0PC
    Hymen 0UCK
    Hyoid Bone 0NCX
    Hypogastric Vein 06C
    Hypoglossal Nerve 00CS
    Hypophysis 0GC0
    Hypothalamus 00CA
    Ileocecal Valve 0DCC
    Ileum 0DCB
    Inferior Mesenteric Artery 04CB
    Inferior Mesenteric Vein 06C6
    Inferior Parathyroid Gland 0GC
    Inner Ear 09C
    Innominate Artery 03C2
    Innominate Vein 05C
    Internal Carotid Artery 03C
    Internal Iliac Artery 04C
    Internal Jugular Vein 05C
    Internal Mammary Artery, Left 03C1
    Intracranial Artery 03CG
    Intracranial Vein 05CL
    Iris 08C
    Jejunum 0DCA
    Joint
      Finger Phalangeal, Left 0RC0
      Toe Phalangeal, Left 0SC0
    Kidney, Left 0TC1
    Kidney Pelvis 0TC
    Knee Bursa and Ligament 0MC
    Knee Joint 0SC
    Knee Tendon 0LC
    Lacrimal Bone 0NC
    Lacrimal Duct, Left 08CY
    Lacrimal Gland 08C
    Large Intestine 0DC
    Larynx 0CCS
    Lens 08C
    Lesser Omentum 0DCT
    Lesser Saphenous Vein 06C
    Lingula Bronchus 0BC9
    Liver 0FC0
      Left Lobe 0FC2
      Right Lobe 0FC1
    Lobe Segmental Bronchus
      Lower 0BC
      Middle, Right 0BC5
      Upper 0BC
    Lower Arm and Wrist Muscle 0KC
    Lower Arm and Wrist Tendon 0LC
    Lower Artery 04CY

Extirpation—*continued*
  by Body Part—*continued*
    Lower Extremity Bursa and Ligament 0MC
    Lower Eyelid 08C
    Lower Femur 0QC
    Lower Gingiva 0CC6
    Lower Leg Muscle 0KC
    Lower Leg Tendon 0LC
    Lower Lip 0CC1
    Lower Lobe Bronchus 0BC
    Lower Lung Lobe 0BC
    Lower Tooth 0CCX
    Lower Vein 06CY
    Lumbar Nerve 01CB
    Lumbar Plexus 01C9
    Lumbar Spinal Cord 00CY
    Lumbar Sympathetic Nerve 01CN
    Lumbar Vertebral Disc 0SC2
    Lumbosacral Disc 0SC4
    Lumbosacral Joint 0SC3
    Lumbosacral Plexus 01CA
    Lung 0BC
    Lung Lingula 0BCH
    Lung Lingula Segments 0BCH
    Lung Lobe Segments
      Lower 0BC
      Middle, Right 0BCD
      Upper 0BC
    Lungs, Bilateral 0BCM
    Lymphatic
      Aortic 07CD
      Internal Mammary 07C
      Left Axillary 07C6
      Left Inguinal 07CJ
      Left Lower Extremity 07CG
      Left Neck 07C2
      Left Upper Extremity 07C4
      Mesenteric 07CB
      Pelvis 07CC
      Right Axillary 07C5
      Right Inguinal 07CH
      Right Lower Extremity 07CF
      Right Neck 07C1
      Right Upper Extremity 07C3
      Thorax 07C7
    Main Bronchus 0BC
    Mandible 0NC
    Mastoid Sinus, Left 09CC
    Maxilla 0NC
    Maxillary Sinus 09C
    Median Nerve 01C5
    Mediastinum 0WCC
    Medulla Oblongata 00CD
    Mesentery 0DCV
    Metacarpal 0PC
    Metacarpocarpal Joint 0RC
    Metacarpophalangeal Joint 0RC
    Metatarsal 0QC
    Metatarsal-Phalangeal Joint 0SC
    Metatarsal-Tarsal Joint 0SC
    Middle Ear, Left 09C6
    Middle Lobe Bronchus, Right 0BC5
    Middle Lung Lobe, Right 0BCD
    Minor Salivary Gland 0CCJ
    Mitral Valve 02CG
    Muscle, Foot, Left 0KC0
    Nail, Toe 0HC0
    Nail Bed
      Finger 0HCQ
      Toe 0HCR
    Nasal Bone 0NCB
    Nasal Septum 09CM
    Nasal Turbinate 09CL
    Nasopharynx 09CN
    Neck, Bladder 0TC0

Extirpation—*continued*
  by Body Part—*continued*
Neck Muscle 0KC
Nerve, Sacral 01C0
Neurohypophysis 0GC0
Nipple 0HC
Nose 09CK
Occipital Bone 0NC
Oculomotor Nerve 00CH
Olfactory Nerve 00CF
Omentum, Lesser 0DCR
Optic Nerve 00CG
Oral Cavity and Throat 0WC3
Orbit 0NC
Ovaries, Bilateral 0UC2
Ovary, Left 0UC1
Palatine Bone 0NC
Pancreas 0FCG
  Body 0FCF
  Head 0FCF
  Tail 0FCF
Pancreatic Duct 0FCD
  Accessory 0FCF
Papillary Muscle 02CD
Para-aortic Body 0GC9
Paraganglion Extremity 0GCF
Parathyroid Gland 0GCR
Parathyroid Glands, Multiple 0GCQ
Parietal Bone 0NC
Parotid Duct 0CC
Parotid Gland, Left 0CC9
Patella 0QC
Pelvic Bone 0QC
Pelvic Cavity 0WCJ
Penis 0VCS
Pericardial Cavity 0WCD
Pericardium 02CN
Perineum Bursa and Ligament 0MCK
Perineum Muscle 0KCM
Perineum Tendon 0LCH
Peritoneal Cavity 0WCG
Peritoneum 0DCW
Peroneal Artery 04C
Peroneal Nerve 01CH
Phalanx
  Finger, Left 0PC0
  Toe, Left 0QC0
Phrenic Nerve 01C2
Pineal Body 0GC1
Pleura 0BC
  Parietal 0BC
  Visceral 0BC
Pleural Cavity 0WC
Pons 00CB
Popliteal Artery 04C
Portal Vein 06C8
Posterior Tibial Artery 04C
Prepuce 0VCT
Prostate 0VC0
Pudendal Nerve 01CC
Pulmonary Artery 02C
Pulmonary Lingula 0BCH
Pulmonary Lobe
  Lower 0BC
  Middle, Right 0BCD
  Upper 0BC
Pulmonary Trunk 02CP
Pulmonary Valve 02CH
Pulmonary Vein 02C
Radial Artery 03C
Radial Nerve 01C6
Radius 0PC
Rectum 0DCP
Renal Artery 04C
Renal Pelvis 0TC
Renal Vein 06C

Extirpation—*continued*
  by Body Part—*continued*
Respiratory Tract 0WCQ
Retina 08C
Retinal Vessel 08C
Rib 0PC
Sacral Nerve 01CR
Sacral Plexus 01CQ
Sacral Sympathetic Nerve 01CP
Sacrococcygeal Joint 0SC5
Sacroiliac Joint 0SC
Sacrum 0QC1
Scapula 0PC
Sciatic Nerve 01CF
Sclera 08C
Scrotum 0VC5
Seminal Vesicle, Left 0VC2
Seminal Vesicles, Bilateral 0VC3
Shoulder Bursa and Ligament 0MC
Shoulder Joint 0RC
Shoulder Muscle 0KC
Shoulder Tendon 0LC
Sigmoid Colon 0DCN
Sinus, Sphenoid, Left 09CB
Skin
  Abdomen 0HC7
  Back 0HC6
  Buttock 0HC8
  Chest 0HC5
  Face 0HC1
  Genitalia 0HCA
  Left Ear 0HC3
  Left Foot 0HCN
  Left Hand 0HCG
  Left Lower Arm 0HCE
  Left Lower Leg 0HCL
  Left Upper Arm 0HCC
  Left Upper Leg 0HCJ
  Neck 0HC4
  Perineum 0HC9
  Right Ear 0HC2
  Right Foot 0HCM
  Right Hand 0HCF
  Right Lower Arm 0HCD
  Right Lower Leg 0HCK
  Right Upper Arm 0HCB
  Right Upper Leg 0HCH
Small Intestine 0DC8
Soft Palate 0CC3
Spermatic Cord 0VC
Spermatic Cords, Bilateral 0VCH
Sphenoid Bone 0NC
Sphenoid Sinus 09C
Spinal Meninges 00CT
Spleen 07CP
Splenic Artery 04C4
Splenic Vein 06C1
Sternoclavicular Joint 0RC
Stomach 0DC6
  Body 0DC6
  Fundus 0DC6
  Pylorus 0DC7
Structure, Uterine Supporting 0UC0
Subarachnoid Space 00C5
Subclavian Artery 03C
Subclavian Vein 05C
Subcutaneous Tissue and Fascia
  Abdomen 0JC8
  Anterior Neck 0JC4
  Back 0JC7
  Buttock 0JC9
  Chest 0JC6
  Face 0JC1
  Foot, Left 0JC0
  Genitalia 0JCC
  Left Foot 0JCR

Extirpation—*continued*
  by Body Part—*continued*
  Subcutaneous Tissue and Fascia—
    continued
  Left Hand 0JCK
  Left Lower Arm 0JCH
  Left Lower Leg 0JCP
  Left Upper Arm 0JCF
  Left Upper Leg 0JCM
  Perineum 0JCB
  Posterior Neck 0JC5
  Right Foot 0JCQ
  Right Hand 0JCJ
  Right Lower Arm 0JCG
  Right Lower Leg 0JCN
  Right Upper Arm 0JCD
  Right Upper Leg 0JCL
Subdural Space 00C4
Sublingual Gland 0CC
Submaxillary Gland 0CC
Superior Mesenteric Artery 04C5
Superior Mesenteric Vein 06C5
Superior Parathyroid Gland 0GC
Superior Vena Cava 02CV
Tarsal 0QC
Tarsal Joint 0SC
Temporal Artery 03C
Temporal Bone 0NC
Temporomandibular Joint 0RC
Tendon, Foot, Left 0LC0
Testes, Bilateral 0VCC
Testis 0VC
Thalamus 00C9
Thoracic Aorta 02CW
Thoracic Duct 07CK
Thoracic Nerve 01C8
Thoracic Spinal Cord 00CX
Thoracic Sympathetic Nerve 01CL
Thoracic Vertebra 0PC4
Thoracic Vertebral Disc 0RC9
Thoracic Vertebral Joint 0RC6
Thoracolumbar Vertebral Disc 0RCB
Thoracolumbar Vertebral Joint 0RCA
Thorax Bursa and Ligament 0MC
Thorax Muscle 0KC
Thorax Tendon 0LC
Thumb Phalanx 0PC
Thymus 07CM
Thyroid Artery 03C
Thyroid Gland 0GCK
Thyroid Gland Lobe 0GC
Tibia 0QC
Tibial Nerve 01CG
Toe Nail 0HCR
Toe Phalangeal Joint 0SC
Toe Phalanx 0QC
Tongue 0CC7
  Palate, Pharynx Muscle 0KC4
Tonsils 0CCP
Tooth, Lower 0CCW
Tract, Genitourinary 0WCP
Transverse Colon 0DCL
Tricuspid Valve 02CJ
Trigeminal Nerve 00CK
Trochlear Nerve 00CJ
Trunk Bursa and Ligament 0MC
Trunk Muscle 0KC
Trunk Tendon 0LC
Tube, Fallopian, Bilateral 0UC5
Tunica Vaginalis 0VC
Turbinate, Nasal 09C7
Tympanic Membrane, Left 09C8
Tympanicum, Glomus 0GCB
Ulna 0PC
Ulnar Artery 03C
Ulnar Nerve 01C4

   Codes provided in the index are incomplete. Refer to tables to determine additional character values.   © 2009 Ingenix, Inc.

Extirpation—*continued*

  by Body Part—*continued*

    Upper Arm Muscle 0KC

    Upper Arm Tendon 0LC

    Upper Artery 03CY

    Upper Extremity Bursa and Ligament
      0MC

    Upper Eyelid 08C

    Upper Femur 0QC

    Upper Gingiva 0CC5

    Upper Leg Muscle 0KC

    Upper Leg Tendon 0LC

    Upper Lobe Bronchus 0BC

    Upper Lung Lobe 0BC

    Upper Vein 05CY

    Ureter 0TC

    Urethra 0TCD

    Uterine Supporting Structure 0UC4

    Uterus 0UC9

    Uvula 0CCN

    Vagina 0UCG

    Vagus Nerve 00CQ

    Vas Deferens 0VC

    Vein

      Lower 06C0

      Upper 05C0

    Ventricle 02C

    Ventricular Septum 02CM

    Vertebral Artery 03C

    Vertebral Vein 05C

    Vessel, Retinal, Left 08C2

    Vestibular Gland 0UCL

    Vitreous 08C

    Vocal Cord 0CC

    Vulva 0UCM

    Wrist Bursa and Ligament 0MC

    Wrist Joint 0RC

    Zygomatic Bone 0NC

Extracorporeal Assistance and Performance

  —*see* Assistance

  —*see* Performance

  —*see* Restoration

Extracorporeal Shock Wave Lithotripsy—

    see Fragmentation

Extracorporeal Therapies

  —*see* Atmospheric Control

  —*see* Decompression

  —*see* Electromagnetic Therapy

  —*see* Hyperthermia

  —*see* Hypothermia

  —*see* Pheresis

  —*see* Phototherapy

  —*see* Shock Wave Therapy

  —*see* Ultrasound Therapy

  —*see* Ultraviolet Light Therapy

Extract—*see* Extraction

Extraction

  by Body System

    Bursae and Ligaments 0MD

    Central Nervous System 00D

    Ear, Nose, Sinus 09D

    Eye 08D

    Female Reproductive System 0UD

    Lower Veins 06D

    Lymphatic and Hemic Systems 07D

    Mouth and Throat 0CD

    Peripheral Nervous System 01D

    Respiratory System 0BD

    Skin and Breast 0HD

    Subcutaneous Tissue and Fascia 0JD

    Upper Veins 05D

    Urinary System 0TD

  by Body Part

    Abdomen Bursa and Ligament 0MD

    Abdominal Sympathetic Nerve 01DM

    Abducens Nerve 00DL

Extraction—*continued*

  by Body Part—*continued*

    Accessory Nerve 00DR

    Accessory Sinus 09DP

    Acoustic Nerve 00DN

    Ankle Bursa and Ligament 0MD

    Auditory Ossicle, Left 09DA

    Basilic Vein 05D

    Bone Marrow

      Iliac 07DR

      Vertebral 07DS

    Brachial Plexus 01D3

    Brachial Vein, Left 05DA

    Bursa and Ligament, Lower Extremity,
      Left 0MD0

    Cephalic Vein 05D

    Cervical Nerve 01D1

    Cord, Vocal, Left 0CDT

    Cornea 08D

    Dura Mater 00D2

    Elbow Bursa and Ligament 0MD

    Endometrium 0UDB

    Ethmoid Sinus 09D

    Facial Nerve 00DM

    Femoral Nerve 01DD

    Femoral Vein, Left 06DN

    Finger Nail 0HDQ

    Foot Bursa and Ligament 0MD

    Foot Vein 06D

    Frontal Sinus 09D

    Glossopharyngeal Nerve 00DP

    Greater Saphenous Vein 06D

    Hair 0HDS

    Hand Bursa and Ligament 0MD

    Hand Vein 05D

    Head and Neck Sympathetic Nerve 01DK

    Hip Bursa and Ligament 0MD

    Hypoglossal Nerve 00DS

    Kidney 0TD

    Knee Bursa and Ligament 0MD

    Lens 08D

    Lesser Saphenous Vein 06D

    Lower Extremity Bursa and Ligament
      0MD

    Lower Tooth 0CDX

    Lower Vein 06DY

    Lumbar Nerve 01DB

    Lumbar Plexus 01D9

    Lumbar Sympathetic Nerve 01DN

    Lumbosacral Plexus 01DA

    Marrow, Bone, Vertebral 07DQ

    Mastoid Sinus, Left 09DC

    Maxillary Sinus 09D

    Median Nerve 01D5

    Meninges, Spinal 00D1

    Nail, Toe 0HD0

    Nail Bed

      Finger 0HDQ

      Toe 0HDR

    Nasal Septum 09DM

    Nasal Turbinate 09DL

    Nerve, Sacral 01D0

    Oculomotor Nerve 00DH

    Olfactory Nerve 00DF

    Optic Nerve 00DG

    Ossicle, Auditory, Left 09D9

    Ova 0UDN

    Perineum Bursa and Ligament 0MDK

    Peroneal Nerve 01DH

    Phrenic Nerve 01D2

    Pleura 0BD

      Parietal 0BD

      Visceral 0BD

    Products of Conception 10D0

      Ectopic 10D2

      Retained 10D1

Extraction—*continued*

  by Body Part—*continued*

    Pudendal Nerve 01DC

    Pudendum Femininum, Right 0UDN

    Radial Nerve 01D6

    Sacral Nerve 01DR

    Sacral Plexus 01DQ

    Sacral Sympathetic Nerve 01DP

    Sciatic Nerve 01DF

    Shoulder Bursa and Ligament 0MD

    Sinus, Sphenoid, Left 09DB

    Skin

      Abdomen 0HD7

      Back 0HD6

      Buttock 0HD8

      Chest 0HD5

      Face 0HD1

      Genitalia 0HDA

      Left Ear 0HD3

      Left Foot 0HDN

      Left Hand 0HDG

      Left Lower Arm 0HDE

      Left Lower Leg 0HDL

      Left Upper Arm 0HDC

      Left Upper Leg 0HDJ

      Neck 0HD4

      Perineum 0HD9

      Right Ear 0HD2

      Right Foot 0HDM

      Right Hand 0HDF

      Right Lower Arm 0HDD

      Right Lower Leg 0HDK

      Right Upper Arm 0HDB

      Right Upper Leg 0HDH

    Sphenoid Sinus 09D

    Spinal Meninges 00DT

    Subcutaneous Tissue and Fascia

      Abdomen 0JD8

      Anterior Neck 0JD4

      Back 0JD7

      Buttock 0JD9

      Chest 0JD6

      Face 0JD1

      Foot, Left 0JD0

      Genitalia 0JDC

      Left Foot 0JDR

      Left Hand 0JDK

      Left Lower Arm 0JDH

      Left Lower Leg 0JDP

      Left Upper Arm 0JDF

      Left Upper Leg 0JDM

      Perineum 0JDB

      Posterior Neck 0JD5

      Right Foot 0JDQ

      Right Hand 0JDJ

      Right Lower Arm 0JDG

      Right Lower Leg 0JDN

      Right Upper Arm 0JDD

      Right Upper Leg 0JDL

    Thoracic Nerve 01D8

    Thoracic Sympathetic Nerve 01DL

    Thorax Bursa and Ligament 0MD

    Tibial Nerve 01DG

    Toe Nail 0HDR

    Tooth, Lower 0CDW

    Trigeminal Nerve 00DK

    Trochlear Nerve 00DJ

    Trunk Bursa and Ligament 0MD

    Turbinate, Nasal 09D7

    Tympanic Membrane, Left 09D8

    Ulnar Nerve 01D4

    Upper Extremity Bursa and Ligament
      0MD

    Upper Vein 05DY

    Vagus Nerve 00DQ

Extraction—*continued*
  by Body Part—*continued*
    Vein
      Lower 06DM
      Upper 05D9
    Vocal Cord, Left 0CDV
    Wrist Bursa and Ligament 0MD

F

Family Counseling
  by Type Qualifier
Family Psychotherapy
  by Type Qualifier
    Other Family Counseling HZ63
    Other Family Psychotherapy GZ72
Fasciaplasty—*see* Repair, Bursae and
    Ligaments 0MQ
Fasciectomy
  —*see* Excision, Bursae and Ligaments 0MB
  —*see* Resection, Bursae and Ligaments 0MT
Fascioplasty—*see* Repair, Bursae and
    Ligaments 0MQ
Fasciorrhaphy—*see* Repair, Bursae and
    Ligaments 0MQ
Fasciotomy
  —*see* Division, Bursae and Ligaments 0M8
  —*see* Drainage, Bursae and Ligaments 0M9
  —*see* Inspection, Bursae and Ligaments 0MJ
Fimbriectomy
  —*see* Excision, Female Reproductive System
    0UB
  —*see* Resection, Female Reproductive
    System 0UT
Fluoroscopy
  by Body System
    Anatomical Regions BW1
    Axial Skeleton, Except Skull and Facial
      Bones BR1
    Central Nervous System B01
    Ear, Nose, Mouth and Throat B91
    Female Reproductive System BU1
    Gastrointestinal System BD1
    Heart B21
    Hepatobiliary System and Pancreas BF1
    Lower Arteries B41
    Male Reproductive System BV1
    Non-Axial Lower Bones BQ1
    Non-Axial Upper Bones BP1
    Respiratory System BB1
    Skull and Facial Bones BN1
    Upper Arteries B31
    Urinary System BT1
    Veins B51
  by Body Part
    Acromioclavicular Joints, Bilateral BP13
    Airways, Upper BB12
    Ankle BQ1
    Aorta and Bilateral Lower Extremity
      Arteries B41D
    Arm, Upper, Left BP10
    Arteries, Lower, Other B410
    Artery, Pulmonary, Left B310
    Artery Bypass Grafts, Coronary, Multiple
      B210
    Biliary and Pancreatic Ducts BF11
    Bladder BT10
    Bladder and Urethra BT1B
    Brachiocephalic-Subclavian Artery, Right
      B311
    Bypass Graft
      Internal Mammary, Left B214
      Other B21F
    Calcaneus BQ1
    Cerebral and Cerebellar Veins B511

Fluoroscopy—*continued*
  by Body Part—*continued*
    Cervical Disc(s) BR11
    Cervical Facet Joint(s) BR14
    Cervico-Cerebral Arch B31Q
    Clavicle BP1
    Colon BD14
    Common Carotid Arteries, Bilateral B315
    Common Carotid Artery B31
    Cord, Spinal B01B
    Coronary Arteries, Multiple B211
    Coronary Artery Bypass Graft, Single
      B212
    Coronary Artery Bypass Grafts, Multiple
      B213
    Corpora Cavernosa BV10
    Dialysis Shunt/Fistula B51W
    Diaphragm BB16
    Ducts, Pancreatic BF10
    Duodenum BD19
    Elbow BP1
    External Carotid Arteries, Bilateral B31C
    External Carotid Artery B31
    Extremity, Upper BW11
    Fallopian Tube, Left BU11
    Fallopian Tubes, Bilateral BU12
    Femur, Left BQ14
    Finger(s) BP1
    Foot BQ1
    Foot/Toe Joint BQ1
    Forearm BP1
    Gallbladder BF12
      Bile Ducts and Pancreatic Ducts BF14
    Gallbladder and Bile Ducts BF13
    GI, Upper BD11
    Hand BP1
    Hand/Finger Joint BP1
    Head and Neck BW19
    Heart
      Left B215
      Right and Left B216
    Hepatic Artery B412
    Hip BQ1
    Humerus BP1
    Ileal Diversion Loop BT1C
    Ileal Loop, Ureters and Kidneys BT1G
    Inferior Mesenteric Artery B415
    Inferior Vena Cava B519
    Intercostal and Bronchial Arteries B31L
    Internal Carotid Arteries, Bilateral B318
    Internal Carotid Artery B31
    Internal Mammary Bypass Graft B21
    Intra-Abdominal Arteries, Other B41B
    Intracranial Arteries B31R
    Intracranial Sinuses B512
    Joints
      Sacroiliac BR10
      Temporomandibular, Bilateral BN17
    Jugular Veins B51
    Kidney BT1
      Ureter and Bladder BT1
    Kidneys
      Bilateral BT13
      Ureters and Bladder BT14
    Knee BQ1
    Larynx B91J
    Leg, Lower, Left BQ13
    Lower Arteries, Other B41J
    Lower Extremity BW1C
    Lower Extremity Arteries B41
    Lower Extremity Veins B51
    Lower Leg BQ1
    Lumbar Arteries B419
    Lumbar Disc(s) BR13
    Lumbar Facet Joint(s) BR16
    Lumbar Spine BR19

Fluoroscopy—*continued*
  by Body Part—*continued*
    Lumbosacral Joint BR1B
    Lung, Left BB13
    Lungs, Bilateral BB14
    Mediastinum BB1C
    Mouth/Oropharynx BD1B
    Pancreatic Ducts BF18
    Patella BQ1
    Pelvic (Iliac) Veins B51
    Pelvic Arteries B41C
    Pelvis BR1C
    Pharynx and Epiglottis B91G
    Portal and Splanchnic Veins B51T
    Pulmonary Artery B31
    Pulmonary Vein B51
    Pulmonary Veins, Bilateral B51S
    Renal Arteries, Bilateral B418
    Renal Artery B41
    Renal Vein B51
    Renal Veins, Bilateral B51L
    Ribs BP1
    Sacroiliac Joints BR1D
    Sacrum and Coccyx BR1F
    Scapula BP1
    Shoulder BP1
    Small Bowel BD13
    Spinal Arteries B31M
    Splenic Arteries B413
    Sternoclavicular Joint, Left BP11
    Sternoclavicular Joints, Bilateral BP12
    Sternum BR1H
    Stomach BD12
    Subclavian Artery, Left B312
    Subclavian Vein B51
    Superior Mesenteric Artery B414
    Superior Vena Cava B518
    Temporomandibular Joint, Left BN18
    Temporomandibular Joints, Bilateral BN19
    Thoracic Disc(s) BR12
    Thoracic Facet Joint(s) BR15
    Thoracic Spine BR17
    Thoraco-Abdominal Aorta B31P
    Thoracolumbar Joint BR18
    Toe(s) BQ1
    Tracheobronchial Tree, Left BB18
    Tracheobronchial Trees, Bilateral BB19
    Trees, Tracheobronchial, Bilateral BB17
    Tubes, Fallopian, Bilateral BU10
    Upper Airways BB1D
    Upper Arm BP1
    Upper Arteries, Other B31N
    Upper Extremity BW1J
    Upper Extremity Arteries B31
    Upper Extremity Veins B51
    Upper GI BD15
    Upper GI and Small Bowel BD16
    Ureter BT1
    Urethra BT15
    Uterus BU16
    Uterus and Fallopian Tubes BU18
    Vagina BU19
    Vasa Vasorum BV18
    Veins
      Other B51V
      Pulmonary, Bilateral B510
    Vertebral Arteries, Bilateral B31G
    Vertebral Artery B31
    Whole Spine BR1G
    Wrist BP1
Formation
  —*see* Bypass
  —*see* Creation
Fragmentation
  by Body System
    Anatomical Regions, General 0WF

Fragmentation—*continued*
  by Body System—*continued*
    Central Nervous System 00F
    Eye 08F
    Female Reproductive System 0UF
    Gastrointestinal System 0DF
    Heart and Great Vessels 02F
    Hepatobiliary System and Pancreas 0FF
    Mouth and Throat 0CF
    Respiratory System 0BF
    Urinary System 0TF
  by Body Part
    Ampulla of Vater 0FFC
    Anus 0DFQ
    Appendix 0DFJ
    Ascending Colon 0DFK
    Bladder 0TFB
    Bladder Neck 0TFC
    Bronchus
      Lower Lobe, Left 0BF1
      Segmental, Lingula 0BF9
    Canal, Spinal 00F3
    Carina 0BF2
    Cavity, Pelvic 0WF1
    Cecum 0DFH
    Cerebral Ventricle 00F6
    Colon, Sigmoid 0DF5
    Common Bile Duct 0FF9
    Cystic Duct 0FF8
    Descending Colon 0DFM
    Duct
      Pancreatic, Accessory 0FF4
      Parotid, Left 0CFB
    Duodenum 0DF9
    Fallopian Tube, Left 0UF6
    Fallopian Tubes, Bilateral 0UF7
    Genitourinary Tract 0WFR
    Hepatic Duct 0FF
    Ileum 0DFB
    Jejunum 0DFA
    Kidney Pelvis, Left 0TF4
    Large Intestine 0DF
    Lingula Bronchus 0BF9
    Lobe Segmental Bronchus
      Lower 0BF
      Middle, Right 0BF5
      Upper 0BF
    Lower Lobe Bronchus 0BF
    Main Bronchus 0BF
    Mediastinum 0WFC
    Middle Lobe Bronchus, Right 0BF5
    Neck, Bladder 0TF3
    Oral Cavity and Throat 0WF3
    Pancreas
      Body 0FFF
      Head 0FFF
      Tail 0FFF
    Pancreatic Duct 0FFD
      Accessory 0FFF
    Parotid Duct, Left 0CFC
    Pelvic Cavity 0WFJ
    Pericardial Cavity 0WFD
    Pericardium 02FN
    Peritoneal Cavity 0WFG
    Pleural Cavity 0WF
    Rectum 0DFP
    Renal Pelvis 0TF
    Respiratory Tract 0WFQ
    Sigmoid Colon 0DFN
    Small Intestine 0DF8
    Spinal Canal 00FU
    Stomach 0DF6
      Body 0DF6
      Fundus 0DF6
    Subarachnoid Space 00F5
    Subdural Space 00F4

Fragmentation—*continued*
  by Body Part—*continued*
    Tract, Genitourinary 0WFP
    Transverse Colon 0DFL
    Tube, Fallopian, Bilateral 0UF5
    Upper Lobe Bronchus 0BF
    Ureter 0TF
    Urethra 0TFD
    Uterus 0UF9
    Vitreous 08F
Free—*see* Release
Frenectomy
  —*see* Excision, Mouth and Throat 0CB
  —*see* Resection, Mouth and Throat 0CT
Frenoplasty
  —*see* Repair, Mouth and Throat 0CQ
  —*see* Replacement, Mouth and Throat 0CR
Frenotomy
  —*see* Drainage, Mouth and Throat 0C9
  —*see* Inspection, Mouth and Throat 0CJ
  —*see* Release, Mouth and Throat 0CN
Frenuloplasty
  —*see* Repair, Mouth and Throat 0CQ
  —*see* Replacement, Mouth and Throat 0CR
Frenulotomy
  —*see* Drainage, Mouth and Throat 0C9
  —*see* Inspection, Mouth and Throat 0CJ
  —*see* Release, Mouth and Throat 0CN
Frenulumectomy
  —*see* Excision, Mouth and Throat 0CB
  —*see* Resection, Mouth and Throat 0CT
Fulgurate—*see* Destruction
Fulguration—*see* Destruction
Fundoplication
  —*see* Restriction
  —*see* Restriction, Gastrointestinal System
    0DV
Fusion
  by Body System
    Lower Joints 0SG
    Upper Joints 0RG
  by Body Part
    Acromioclavicular Joint 0RG
    Ankle Joint 0SG
    Carpal Joint 0RG
    Cervical Vertebral Joint 0RG1
    Cervical Vertebral Joints, 2 or more 0RG2
    Cervicothoracic Vertebral Joint 0RG4
    Coccygeal Joint 0SG6
    Elbow Joint, Left 0RGM
    Finger Phalangeal Joint 0RG
    Hip Joint, Left 0SGB
    Joint
      Finger Phalangeal, Left 0RGL
      Lumbosacral 0SG0
      Sacroiliac, Left 0SG5
      Shoulder, Left 0RGC
      Thoracolumbar Vertebral 0RG0
      Toe Phalangeal, Left 0SG9
    Knee Joint 0SG
    Lumbar Vertebral Joints, 2 or more 0SG1
    Lumbosacral Joint 0SG3
    Metacarpocarpal Joint 0RG
    Metacarpophalangeal Joint 0RG
    Metatarsal-Phalangeal Joint 0SG
    Metatarsal-Tarsal Joint 0SG
    Sacroiliac Joint 0SG
    Shoulder Joint 0RG
    Sternoclavicular Joint 0RG
    Tarsal Joint 0SG
    Temporomandibular Joint, Left 0RGD
    Thoracic Vertebral Joint 0RG6
    Thoracic Vertebral Joints
      2 to 7 0RG7
      8 or more 0RG8

Fusion—*continued*
  by Body Part—*continued*
    Thoracolumbar Vertebral Joint 0RGA
    Toe Phalangeal Joint 0SG
    Wrist Joint 0RG

G

Gastrectomy
  —*see* Excision, Gastrointestinal System 0DB
  —*see* Resection, Gastrointestinal System 0DT
Gastrocolostomy—*see* Bypass, Gastrointestinal
  System 0D1
Gastroduodenectomy
  —*see* Excision, Gastrointestinal System 0DB
  —*see* Resection, Gastrointestinal System 0DT
Gastroduodenoscopy—*see* Inspection,
  Gastrointestinal System 0DJ
Gastroduodenostomy—*see* Bypass,
  Gastrointestinal System 0D1
Gastroenterocolostomy—*see* Bypass,
  Gastrointestinal System 0D1
Gastroenteroplasty
  —*see* Repair, Gastrointestinal System 0DQ
  —*see* Replacement, Gastrointestinal System
    0DR
Gastroenterostomy—*see* Bypass,
  Gastrointestinal System 0D1
Gastrogastrostomy—*see* Bypass,
  Gastrointestinal System 0D1
Gastroileostomy—*see* Bypass, Gastrointestinal
  System 0D1
Gastrojejunostomy—*see* Bypass,
  Gastrointestinal System 0D1
Gastrolysis—*see* Release, Gastrointestinal
  System 0DN
Gastronesteostomy—*see* Bypass,
  Gastrointestinal System 0D1
Gastropexy
  —*see* Repair, Gastrointestinal System 0DQ
  —*see* Reposition, Gastrointestinal System
    0DS
Gastroplasty
  —*see* Repair, Gastrointestinal System 0DQ
  —*see* Replacement, Gastrointestinal System
    0DR
Gastroplication—*see* Restriction,
  Gastrointestinal System 0DV
Gastropylorectomy—*see* Excision,
  Gastrointestinal System 0DB
Gastrorrhaphy—*see* Repair, Gastrointestinal
  System 0DQ
Gastroscopy—*see* Inspection, Gastrointestinal
  System 0DJ
Gastrostomy—*see* Bypass, Gastrointestinal
  System 0D1
Gastrotomy
  —*see* Drainage, Gastrointestinal System 0D9
  —*see* Inspection, Gastrointestinal System
    0DJ
Genioplasty
  —*see* Repair, Head and Facial Bones 0NQ
  —*see* Replacement, Head and Facial Bones
    0NR
Gingivectomy—*see* Excision, Mouth and
  Throat 0CB
Gingivoplasty
  —*see* Repair, Mouth and Throat 0CQ
  —*see* Replacement, Mouth and Throat 0CR
Glomectomy
  —*see* Excision, Endocrine System 0GB
  —*see* Resection, Endocrine System 0GT

Glossectomy
—*see* Excision, Mouth and Throat 0CB
—*see* Resection, Mouth and Throat 0CT

Glossopexy
—*see* Repair, Mouth and Throat 0CQ
—*see* Reposition, Mouth and Throat 0CS

Glossoplasty
—*see* Repair, Mouth and Throat 0CQ
—*see* Replacement, Mouth and Throat 0CR

Glossorrhaphy—*see* Repair, Mouth and Throat 0CQ

Glossotomy
—see Drainage, Mouth and Throat 0C9
—see Inspection, Mouth and Throat 0CJ

Group Counseling
by Type Qualifier
12-Step HZ43
Behavioral HZ41
Cognitive HZ40
Cognitive-Behavioral HZ42
Confrontational HZ48
Continuing Care HZ49
Interpersonal HZ44
Motivational Enhancement HZ47
Pre/Post-Test Infectious Disease HZ4C
Psychoeducation HZ46
Spiritual HZ4B
Vocational HZ45

Group Psychotherapy GZHZ

H

Hemicolectomy—*see* Resection, Gastrointestinal System 0DT

Hemicystectomy—*see* Excision, Urinary System 0TB

Hemigastrectomy—*see* Excision, Gastrointestinal System 0DB

Hemiglossectomy—*see* Excision, Mouth and Throat 0CB

Hemilaminectomy
—*see* Excision, Lower Bones 0QB
—*see* Excision, Upper Bones 0PB

Hemilaryngectomy—*see* Excision, Mouth and Throat 0CB

Hemimandibulectomy—*see* Excision, Head and Facial Bones 0NB

Hemimaxillectomy—*see* Excision, Head and Facial Bones 0NB

Hemipylorectomy—*see* Excision, Gastrointestinal System 0DB

Hemispherectomy
—*see* Excision, Central Nervous System 00B
—*see* Resection, Central Nervous System 00T

Hemithyroidectomy—*see* Excision, Endocrine System 0GB

Hemodialysis 5A1D

Hepatectomy
—*see* Excision, Hepatobiliary System and Pancreas 0FB
—*see* Resection, Hepatobiliary System and Pancreas 0FT

Hepaticotomy
—*see* Drainage, Hepatobiliary System and Pancreas 0F9
—*see* Inspection, Hepatobiliary System and Pancreas 0FJ

Hepatopexy
—*see* Repair, Hepatobiliary System and Pancreas 0FQ
—*see* Reposition, Hepatobiliary System and Pancreas 0FS

Hepatorrhaphy—*see* Repair, Hepatobiliary System and Pancreas 0FQ

Hepatotomy
—*see* Drainage, Hepatobiliary System and Pancreas 0F9
—*see* Inspection, Hepatobiliary System and Pancreas 0FJ

Herniorrhaphy
—*see* Repair, Anatomical Regions, Lower Extremities 0YQ
—*see* Repair, Respiratory System 0BQ

Holter Monitoring 4A12

Hymenectomy
—*see* Excision, Female Reproductive System 0UB
—*see* Resection, Female Reproductive System 0UT

Hymenoplasty—*see* Repair, Female Reproductive System 0UQ

Hymenorrhaphy—*see* Repair, Female Reproductive System 0UQ

Hymenotomy
—*see* Division, Female Reproductive System 0U8
—*see* Drainage, Female Reproductive System 0U9
—*see* Inspection, Female Reproductive System 0UJ

Hyperthermia
Whole Body 6A3G

Hypnosis GZFZ

Hypophysectomy
—*see* Excision, Endocrine System 0GB
—*see* Resection, Endocrine System 0GT

Hypothalamotomy—*see* Destruction, Central Nervous System 005

Hypothermia
Whole Body 6A4G

Hysterectomy
—*see* Excision, Female Reproductive System 0UB
—*see* Resection, Female Reproductive System 0UT

Hysterolysis—*see* Release, Female Reproductive System 0UN

Hysteropexy
—*see* Repair, Female Reproductive System 0UQ
—*see* Reposition, Female Reproductive System 0US

Hysteroplasty—*see* Repair, Female Reproductive System 0UQ

Hysterorrhaphy—*see* Repair, Female Reproductive System 0UQ

Hysteroscopy—*see* Inspection, Female Reproductive System 0UJ

Hysterotomy
—*see* Division, Female Reproductive System 0U8
—*see* Drainage, Female Reproductive System 0U9
—*see* Inspection, Female Reproductive System 0UJ

Hysterotrachelectomy—*see* Resection, Female Reproductive System 0UT

Hysterotracheloplasty—*see* Repair, Female Reproductive System 0UQ

Hysterotrachelorrhaphy—*see* Repair, Female Reproductive System 0UQ

I

Ileectomy
—*see* Excision, Gastrointestinal System 0DB
—*see* Resection, Gastrointestinal System 0DT

Ileocecostomy—*see* Bypass, Gastrointestinal System 0D1

Ileocolectomy
—*see* Excision, Gastrointestinal System 0DB
—*see* Resection, Gastrointestinal System 0DT

Ileocolostomy—*see* Bypass, Gastrointestinal System 0D1

Ileocolotomy
—*see* Drainage, Gastrointestinal System 0D9
—*see* Inspection, Gastrointestinal System 0DJ

Ileoileostomy—*see* Bypass, Gastrointestinal System 0D1

Ileopexy
—*see* Repair, Gastrointestinal System 0DQ
—*see* Reposition, Gastrointestinal System 0DS

Ileoproctostomy—*see* Bypass, Gastrointestinal System 0D1

Ileorectostomy—*see* Bypass, Gastrointestinal System 0D1

Ileorrhaphy—*see* Repair, Gastrointestinal System 0DQ

Ileoscopy—*see* Inspection, Gastrointestinal System 0DJ

Ileosigmoidostomy—*see* Bypass, Gastrointestinal System 0D1

Ileostomy—*see* Bypass, Gastrointestinal System 0D1

Ileotomy
—*see* Drainage, Gastrointestinal System 0D9
—*see* Inspection, Gastrointestinal System 0DJ

Ileotransversostomy—*see* Bypass, Gastrointestinal System 0D1

Imaging
—*see* Computerized Tomography (CT Scan)
—*see* Fluoroscopy
—*see* Magnetic Resonance Imaging (MRI)
—*see* Plain Radiography
—*see* Ultrasonography

Immobilization
by Body Region
Abdominal Wall 2W33
Back 2W35
Chest Wall 2W34
Face 2W31
Finger 2W3
Foot 2W3
Hand 2W3
Head 2W30
Inguinal Region 2W3
Leg, Lower, Left 2W32
Lower Arm 2W3
Lower Extremity 2W3
Lower Leg 2W3
Thumb 2W3
Toe 2W3
Upper Arm 2W3
Upper Extremity 2W3
Upper Leg 2W3

Implant—*see* Insertion

Implantation—*see* Insertion

IMV 5A09

Incudectomy
—*see* Excision, Ear, Nose, Sinus 09B
—*see* Resection, Ear, Nose, Sinus 09T

Incudopexy
—*see* Repair, Ear, Nose, Sinus 09Q
—*see* Reposition, Ear, Nose, Sinus 09S

Individual Counseling
by Type Qualifier
12-Step HZ33
Behavioral HZ31
Cognitive HZ30
Cognitive-Behavioral HZ32
Confrontational HZ38
Continuing Care HZ39
Interpersonal HZ34

Insertion—*continued*
  by Device—*continued*
    Infusion Device—*continued*
      Cervicothoracic Vertebral Disc 0RH5
      Cervicothoracic Vertebral Joint 0RH4
      Chest Wall 0WH8
      Chyli, Cisterna 07HK
      Cisterna Chyli 07HL
      Coccygeal Joint 0SH6
      Colic Artery 04H
      Colic Vein 06H7
      Common Carotid Artery 03H
      Common Iliac Artery 04H
      Common Iliac Vein 06H
      Cord, Spinal 00H0
      Cranial Cavity 0WH1
      Cranial Nerve 00HE
      Cul-de-sac, Vagina and 0UH8
      Deferens, Vas 0VH4
      Disc
        Lumbosacral 0SH2
        Thoracolumbar Vertebral 0RH3
      Duct, Pancreatic 0FHB
      Duodenum 0DH9
      Elbow Joint, Left 0RHM
      Elbow Region 0XH
      Epididymis and Spermatic Cord 0VHM
      Esophageal Vein 06H3
      Esophagus 0DH5
      External Carotid Artery 03H
      External Iliac Artery 04H
      External Iliac Vein 06H
      External Jugular Vein 05H
      Eye 08H
      Face 0WH2
      Face Artery 03HR
      Face Vein 05H
      Femoral Artery 04H
      Femoral Region 0YH
      Femoral Vein 06H
      Finger Phalangeal Joint 0RH
      Foot 0YH
      Foot Artery 04H
      Foot Vein 06H
      Gallbladder 0FH4
      Gastric Artery 04H2
      Gastric Vein 06H2
      Genitourinary Tract 0WHR
      Gland, Endocrine 0GHS
      Greater Saphenous Vein 06H
      Hand 0XH
      Hand Artery 03H
      Hand Vein 05H
      Hemiazygos Vein 05H1
      Hepatic Artery 04H3
      Hepatic Vein 06H4
      Hip Joint, Left 0SHB
      Hypogastric Vein 06H
      Ileum 0DHB
      Inferior Mesenteric Artery 04HB
      Inferior Mesenteric Vein 06H6
      Inguinal Region 0YH
      Innominate Artery 03H2
      Innominate Vein 05H
      Internal Carotid Artery 03H
      Internal Iliac Artery 04H
      Internal Jugular Vein 05H
      Internal Mammary Artery, Left 03H1
      Intestine, Small 0DH8
      Intracranial Artery 03HG
      Intracranial Vein 05HL
      Jejunum 0DHA
      Joint
        Finger Phalangeal, Left 0RHL
        Lumbosacral 0SH0
        Sacroiliac, Left 0SH5

Insertion—*continued*
  by Device—*continued*
    Infusion Device—*continued*
      Joint—*continued*
        Shoulder, Left 0RHC
        Thoracolumbar Vertebral 0RH0
        Toe Phalangeal, Left 0SH9
      Kidney 0TH5
      Knee Joint 0SH
      Knee Region 0YH
      Lesser Saphenous Vein 06H
      Liver 0FH0
        Left Lobe 0FH2
        Right Lobe 0FH1
      Lower Arm 0XH
      Lower Back 0WHL
      Lower Extremity 0YH
      Lower Jaw 0WH5
      Lower Leg 0YH
      Lumbosacral Disc 0SH4
      Lumbosacral Joint 0SH3
      Lung 0BH
      Lymphatic 07HN
      Mediastinum 0WHC
      Metacarpocarpal Joint 0RH
      Metacarpophalangeal Joint 0RH
      Metatarsal-Phalangeal Joint 0SH
      Metatarsal-Tarsal Joint 0SH
      Neck 0WH6
      Oral Cavity and Throat 0WH3
      Ovary 0UH3
      Pancreas 0FHG
      Pancreatic Duct 0FHD
      Pelvic Cavity 0WHJ
      Penis 0VHS
      Pericardial Cavity 0WHD
      Perineum
        Female 0WHN
        Male 0WHM
      Peritoneal Cavity 0WHG
      Peroneal Artery 04H
      Pleural Cavity 0WH
      Popliteal Artery 04H
      Portal Vein 06H8
      Posterior Tibial Artery 04H
      Pulmonary Artery 02H
      Pulmonary Vein 02H
      Radial Artery 03H
      Region
        Ankle, Left 0YH0
        Wrist, Left 0XH2
      Renal Artery 04H
      Renal Vein 06H
      Respiratory Tract 0WHQ
      Retroperitoneum 0WHH
      Sacroiliac Joint 0SH
      Scrotum and Tunica Vaginalis 0VH8
      Shoulder Joint 0RH
      Shoulder Region, Left 0XH3
      Spinal Canal 00HU
      Spinal Cord 00HV
      Spleen 07HP
      Splenic Artery 04H4
      Sternoclavicular Joint 0RH
      Stomach 0DH6
        Body 0DH6
        Fundus 0DH6
      Subclavian Artery 03H
      Subclavian Vein 05H
      Subcutaneous Tissue and Fascia
        Head and Neck 0JHS
        Lower Extremity 0JHW
        Trunk 0JHT
        Upper Extremity 0JHV
      Superior Mesenteric Artery 04H5
      Superior Mesenteric Vein 06H5

Insertion—*continued*
  by Device—*continued*
    Infusion Device—*continued*
      Superior Vena Cava 02HV
      Tarsal Joint 0SH
      Temporal Artery 03H
      Temporomandibular Joint, Left 0RHD
      Testis 0VHD
      Thoracic Aorta 02HW
      Thoracic Vertebral Disc 0RH9
      Thoracic Vertebral Joint 0RH6
      Thoracolumbar Vertebral Disc 0RHB
      Thoracolumbar Vertebral Joint 0RHA
      Thymus 07HM
      Thyroid Artery 03H
      Toe Phalangeal Joint 0SH
      Tract, Genitourinary 0WHP
      Tree, Tracheobronchial 0BH0
      Ulnar Artery 03H
      Upper Arm 0XH
      Upper Back 0WHK
      Upper Extremity 0XH
      Upper Jaw 0WH4
      Upper Leg 0YH
      Ureter 0TH9
      Urethra 0THD
      Uterus and Cervix 0UHD
      Vagina and Cul-de-sac 0UHH
      Vas Deferens 0VHR
      Vein
        Coronary 02H4
        Face, Left 05H0
        Foot, Left 06H1
        Lower 06HY
        Upper 05HY
        Vena Cava, Inferior 06H0
      Ventricle 02H
      Vertebral Artery 03H
      Vertebral Vein 05H
      Wrist Joint 0RH
      Wrist Region 0XH
    Infusion Pump
      Subcutaneous Tissue and Fascia
        Abdomen 0JH8
        Back 0JH7
        Chest 0JH6
        Left Lower Arm 0JHH
        Left Lower Leg 0JHP
        Left Upper Arm 0JHF
        Left Upper Leg 0JHM
        Lower Leg, Left 0JHD
        Right Lower Arm 0JHG
        Right Lower Leg 0JHN
        Right Upper Leg 0JHL
        Trunk 0JHT
    Internal Fixation Device
      Acetabulum 0QH
      Acromioclavicular Joint 0RH
      Ankle Joint 0SH
      Bone
        Hyoid 0NH1
        Nasal 0NHB
      Bone
        Temporal, Left 0NH5
      Carpal, Left 0PHN
      Carpal Joint 0RH
      Cavity, Glenoid, Left 0PH0
      Cervical Vertebra 0PH3
      Cervical Vertebral Joint 0RH1
      Cervicothoracic Vertebral Joint 0RH4
      Clavicle 0PH
      Coccygeal Joint 0SH6
      Coccyx 0QHS
      Elbow Joint, Left 0RHM
      Ethmoid Bone 0NH
      Femoral Shaft 0QH

Insertion—*continued*
  by Device—*continued*
    Internal Fixation Device—*continued*
      Femur, Lower, Left 0QH6
      Fibula 0QH
      Finger Phalangeal Joint 0RH
      Finger Phalanx 0PH
      Frontal Bone, Left 0NH2
      Glenoid Cavity 0PH
      Hip Joint, Left 0SHB
      Humeral Head, Left 0PHD
      Humeral Shaft 0PH
      Hyoid Bone 0NHX
      Joint
        Finger Phalangeal, Left 0RHL
        Lumbosacral 0SH0
        Sacroiliac, Left 0SH5
        Shoulder, Left 0RHC
        Thoracolumbar Vertebral 0RH0
        Toe Phalangeal, Left 0SH9
      Knee Joint 0SH
      Lacrimal Bone 0NH
      Lower Femur 0QH
      Lumbosacral Joint 0SH3
      Mandible 0NH
      Maxilla 0NH
      Metacarpal 0PH
      Metacarpocarpal Joint 0RH
      Metacarpophalangeal Joint 0RH
      Metatarsal 0QH
      Metatarsal-Phalangeal Joint 0SH
      Metatarsal-Tarsal Joint 0SH
      Occipital Bone 0NH
      Orbit 0NH
      Palatine Bone 0NH
      Parietal Bone 0NH
      Patella 0QH
      Pelvic Bone 0QH
      Phalanx
        Finger, Left 0PHM
        Toe, Left 0QH0
      Radius 0PH
      Rib 0PH
      Sacroiliac Joint 0SH
      Sacrum 0QH1
      Scapula 0PH
      Shaft, Humeral, Left 0PHC
      Shoulder Joint 0RH
      Skull 0NH0
      Sphenoid Bone 0NH
      Sternoclavicular Joint 0RH
      Tarsal 0QH
      Tarsal Joint 0SH
      Temporal Bone, Left 0NH6
      Temporomandibular Joint, Left 0RHD
      Thoracic Vertebra 0PH4
      Thoracic Vertebral Joint 0RH6
      Thoracolumbar Vertebral Joint 0RHA
      Thumb Phalanx 0PH
      Tibia 0QH
      Toe Phalangeal Joint 0SH
      Toe Phalanx 0QH
      Ulna 0PH
      Upper Femur, Left 0QH7
      Wrist Joint 0RH
      Zygomatic Bone 0NH
    Intraluminal Device
      Artery
        Aorta, Abdominal 04H0
        Aorta, Thoracic 02HP
        Atrium 02H
        Axillary Vein 05H
        Basilic Vein 05H
        Brachial Vein 05H
        Cephalic Vein 05H
        Colic Vein 06H7

Insertion—*continued*
  by Device—*continued*
    Intraluminal Device—*continued*
      Common Iliac Vein 06H
      Esophageal Vein 06H3
      External Iliac Vein 06H
      External Jugular Vein 05H
      Face Vein 05H
      Femoral Vein 06H
      Foot Vein 06H
      Gastric Vein 06H2
      Greater Saphenous Vein 06H
      Hand Vein 05H
      Hemiazygos Vein 05H1
      Hepatic Vein 06H4
      Hypogastric Vein 06H
      Inferior Mesenteric Vein 06H6
      Innominate Vein 05H
      Internal Jugular Vein 05H
      Intracranial Vein 05HL
      Lesser Saphenous Vein 06H
      Portal Vein 06H8
      Pulmonary Artery 02H
      Pulmonary Vein 02H
      Renal Vein 06H
      Subclavian Vein 05H
      Superior Mesenteric Vein 06H5
      Superior Vena Cava 02HV
      Thoracic Aorta 02HW
      Vein
        Coronary 02H4
        Face, Left 05H0
        Foot, Left 06H1
        Lower 06HY
        Upper 05HY
        Vena Cava, Inferior 06H0
      Ventricle 02H
      Vertebral Vein 05H
    Intramedullary Fixation Device
      Femoral Shaft 0QH
      Femur, Lower, Left 0QH6
      Fibula 0QH
      Humeral Head, Left 0PHD
      Humeral Shaft 0PH
      Lower Femur 0QH
      Radius 0PH
      Shaft, Humeral, Left 0PHC
      Tibia 0QH
      Ulna 0PH
      Upper Femur, Left 0QH7
    Monitoring Device
      Artery
        Aorta, Abdominal 04H0
        Aorta, Thoracic 02HP
        Lower 04HY
        Upper 03HY
      Atrium 02H
      Bladder 0THB
      Cerebral Ventricle 00H6
      Cord, Spinal 00H0
      Cranial Nerve 00HE
      Diaphragm 0BH
      Duct, Pancreatic 0FHB
      Duodenum 0DH9
      Esophagus 0DH5
      Gallbladder 0FH4
      Gland, Endocrine 0GHS
      Ileum 0DHB
      Intestine, Small 0DH8
      Jejunum 0DHA
      Kidney 0TH5
      Liver 0FH0
        Left Lobe 0FH2
        Right Lobe 0FH1
      Lung 0BH
      Nerve, Peripheral 01HY

Insertion—*continued*
  by Device—*continued*
    Monitoring Device—*continued*
      Pancreas 0FHG
      Pancreatic Duct 0FHD
      Pericardium 02HN
      Pulmonary Artery 02H
      Pulmonary Vein 02H
      Spinal Canal 00HU
      Spinal Cord 00HV
      Stomach 0DH6
        Body 0DH6
        Fundus 0DH6
      Superior Vena Cava 02HV
      Thoracic Aorta 02HW
      Trachea 0BH1
      Tree, Tracheobronchial 0BH0
      Ureter 0TH9
      Urethra 0THD
      Vein
        Coronary 02H4
        Lower 06HY
        Upper 05HY
      Ventricle 02H
    Monitoring Electrode
      Products of Conception 10H0
    Other Device
      Abdominal Wall 0WHF
      Ankle Region 0YH
      Axilla 0XH
      Back, Lower 0WH0
      Buttock, Left 0YH1
      Chest Wall 0WH8
      Cranial Cavity 0WH1
      Elbow Region 0XH
      Face 0WH2
      Femoral Region 0YH
      Foot 0YH
      Genitourinary Tract 0WHR
      Hand 0XH
      Inguinal Region 0YH
      Knee Region 0YH
      Lower Arm 0XH
      Lower Back 0WHL
      Lower Extremity 0YH
      Lower Jaw 0WH5
      Lower Leg 0YH
      Mediastinum 0WHC
      Neck 0WH6
      Oral Cavity and Throat 0WH3
      Pelvic Cavity 0WHJ
      Pericardial Cavity 0WHD
      Perineum
        Female 0WHN
        Male 0WHM
      Peritoneal Cavity 0WHG
      Pleural Cavity 0WH
      Products of Conception 10H0
      Region
        Ankle, Left 0YH0
        Wrist, Left 0XH2
      Respiratory Tract 0WHQ
      Retroperitoneum 0WHH
      Shoulder Region, Left 0XH3
      Tract, Genitourinary 0WHP
      Upper Arm 0XH
      Upper Back 0WHK
      Upper Extremity 0XH
      Upper Jaw 0WH4
      Upper Leg 0YH
      Wrist Region 0XH
    Pacemaker / Defibrillator
      Subcutaneous Tissue and Fascia
        Abdomen 0JH8
        Chest 0JH6

Insertion—*continued*
  by Device—*continued*
    Pessary
      Cul-de-sac 0UHF
      Vagina 0UHG
    Radioactive Element
      Abdominal Wall 0WHF
      Ankle Region 0YH
      Areola 0HH
      Axilla 0XH
      Back, Lower 0WH0
      Breast 0HH
      Buttock, Left 0YH1
      Chest Wall 0WH8
      Cranial Cavity 0WH1
      Duct, Pancreatic 0FHB
      Elbow Region 0XH
      Esophagus 0DH5
      Eye 08H
      Face 0WH2
      Femoral Region 0YH
      Foot 0YH
      Genitourinary Tract 0WHR
      Gland, Mammary 0HH
      Hand 0XH
      Inguinal Region 0YH
      Knee Region 0YH
      Lower Arm 0XH
      Lower Back 0WHL
      Lower Extremity 0YH
      Lower Jaw 0WH5
      Lower Leg 0YH
      Lung 0BH
      Mediastinum 0WHC
      Neck 0WH6
      Nipple 0HH
      Oral Cavity and Throat 0WH3
      Pancreatic Duct 0FHD
      Pelvic Cavity 0WHJ
      Pericardial Cavity 0WHD
      Perineum
        Female 0WHN
        Male 0WHM
      Peritoneal Cavity 0WHG
      Pleural Cavity 0WH
      Prostate 0VH0
      Rectum 0DHP
      Region
        Ankle, Left 0YH0
        Wrist, Left 0XH2
      Respiratory Tract 0WHQ
      Retroperitoneum 0WHH
      Shoulder Region, Left 0XH3
      Subcutaneous Tissue and Fascia
        Head and Neck 0JHS
        Lower Extremity 0JHW
        Trunk 0JHT
        Upper Extremity 0JHV
      Tongue 0CH7
      Tract, Genitourinary 0WHP
      Tree, Tracheobronchial 0BH0
      Upper Arm 0XH
      Upper Back 0WHK
      Upper Extremity 0XH
      Upper Jaw 0WH4
      Upper Leg 0YH
      Vagina 0UHG
      Wrist Region 0XH
    Reservoir
      Subcutaneous Tissue and Fascia
        Abdomen 0JH8
        Chest 0JH6
        Left Lower Arm 0JHH
        Left Lower Leg 0JHP
        Left Upper Arm 0JHF
        Left Upper Leg 0JHM

Insertion—*continued*
  by Device—*continued*
    Reservoir—*continued*
      Subcutaneous Tissue and Fascia—
        continued
        Lower Leg, Left 0JHD
        Right Lower Arm 0JHG
        Right Lower Leg 0JHN
        Right Upper Leg 0JHL
    Spacer
      Acromioclavicular Joint 0RH
      Ankle Joint 0SH
      Carpal Joint 0RH
      Cervical Vertebral Joint 0RH1
      Cervicothoracic Vertebral Joint 0RH4
      Coccygeal Joint 0SH6
      Disc, Lumbosacral 0SH2
      Elbow Joint, Left 0RHM
      Finger Phalangeal Joint 0RH
      Hip Joint, Left 0SHB
      Joint
        Finger Phalangeal, Left 0RHL
        Lumbosacral 0SH0
        Sacroiliac, Left 0SH5
        Shoulder, Left 0RHC
        Thoracolumbar Vertebral 0RH0
        Toe Phalangeal, Left 0SH9
      Knee Joint 0SH
      Lumbosacral Disc 0SH4
      Lumbosacral Joint 0SH3
      Metacarpocarpal Joint 0RH
      Metacarpophalangeal Joint 0RH
      Metatarsal-Phalangeal Joint 0SH
      Metatarsal-Tarsal Joint 0SH
      Sacroiliac Joint 0SH
      Shoulder Joint 0RH
      Sternoclavicular Joint 0RH
      Tarsal Joint 0SH
      Temporomandibular Joint, Left 0RHD
      Thoracic Vertebral Joint 0RH6
      Thoracolumbar Vertebral Joint 0RHA
      Toe Phalangeal Joint 0SH
      Wrist Joint 0RH
    Stimulator Generator
      Subcutaneous Tissue and Fascia
        Abdomen 0JH8
        Anterior Neck 0JH4
        Back 0JH7
        Buttock 0JH9
        Chest 0JH6
        Face 0JH1
        Foot, Left 0JH0
        Genitalia 0JHC
        Left Foot 0JHR
        Left Hand 0JHK
        Left Lower Arm 0JHH
        Left Lower Leg 0JHP
        Left Upper Arm 0JHF
        Left Upper Leg 0JHM
        Lower Leg, Left 0JHD
        Perineum 0JHB
        Posterior Neck 0JH5
        Right Foot 0JHQ
        Right Hand 0JHJ
        Right Lower Arm 0JHG
        Right Lower Leg 0JHN
        Right Upper Leg 0JHL
    Tissue Expander
      Areola 0HH
      Breast 0HH
      Gland, Mammary 0HH
      Nipple 0HH
      Subcutaneous Tissue and Fascia
        Abdomen 0JH8
        Anterior Neck 0JH4
        Back 0JH7

Insertion—*continued*
  by Device—*continued*
    Tissue Expander—*continued*
      Subcutaneous Tissue and Fascia—
        continued
        Buttock 0JH9
        Chest 0JH6
        Face 0JH1
        Foot, Left 0JH0
        Genitalia 0JHC
        Left Foot 0JHR
        Left Hand 0JHK
        Left Lower Arm 0JHH
        Left Lower Leg 0JHP
        Left Upper Arm 0JHF
        Left Upper Leg 0JHM
        Lower Leg, Left 0JHD
        Perineum 0JHB
        Posterior Neck 0JH5
        Right Foot 0JHQ
        Right Hand 0JHJ
        Right Lower Arm 0JHG
        Right Lower Leg 0JHN
        Right Upper Leg 0JHL
    Vascular Access Device
      Subcutaneous Tissue and Fascia
        Abdomen 0JH8
        Chest 0JH6
        Left Lower Arm 0JHH
        Left Lower Leg 0JHP
        Left Upper Arm 0JHF
        Left Upper Leg 0JHM
        Lower Leg, Left 0JHD
        Right Lower Arm 0JHG
        Right Lower Leg 0JHN
        Right Upper Leg 0JHL

Inspection
  by Body System
    Anatomical Regions, General 0WJ
    Anatomical Regions, Lower Extremities 0YJ
    Anatomical Regions, Upper Extremities 0XJ
    Bursae and Ligaments 0MJ
    Central Nervous System 00J
    Ear, Nose, Sinus 09J
    Endocrine System 0GJ
    Eye 08J
    Female Reproductive System 0UJ
    Gastrointestinal System 0DJ
    Head and Facial Bones 0NJ
    Heart and Great Vessels 02J
    Hepatobiliary System and Pancreas 0FJ
    Lower Arteries 04J
    Lower Bones 0QJ
    Lower Joints 0SJ
    Lower Veins 06J
    Lymphatic and Hemic Systems 07J
    Male Reproductive System 0VJ
    Mouth and Throat 0CJ
    Muscles 0KJ
    Peripheral Nervous System 01J
    Respiratory System 0BJ
    Skin and Breast 0HJ
    Subcutaneous Tissue and Fascia 0JJ
    Tendons 0LJ
    Upper Arteries 03J
    Upper Bones 0PJ
    Upper Joints 0RJ
    Upper Veins 05J
    Urinary System 0TJ
  by Body Part
    Abdomen Bursa and Ligament 0MJ
    Abdomen Muscle 0KJ
    Abdomen Tendon 0LJ
    Abdominal Sympathetic Nerve 01JM
    Abdominal Wall 0WJF
    Abducens Nerve 00JL

Inspection—*continued*
  by Body Part—*continued*
    Accessory Nerve 00JR
    Accessory Sinus 09JP
    Acetabulum 0QJ
    Acoustic Nerve 00JN
    Acromioclavicular Joint 0RJ
    Adenohypophysis 0GJ0
    Adenoids 0CJQ
    Adrenal Gland 0GJ
    Adrenal Glands, Bilateral 0GJ4
    Ampulla of Vater 0FJC
    Ankle Bursa and Ligament 0MJ
    Ankle Joint 0SJ
    Ankle Region 0YJ
    Ankle Tendon 0LJ
    Anterior Chamber 08J
    Anterior Tibial Artery 04J
    Anus 0DJQ
    Aortic Body 0GJD
    Aortic Valve 02JF
    Appendix 0DJJ
    Areola 0HJ
    Artery
      Aorta, Thoracic 02J4
      Lower 04J0
      Upper 03J5
      Vertebral, Left 03J0
    Ascending Colon 0DJK
    Atrial Septum 02J5
    Atrium 02J
    Auditory Ossicle 09J
    Axilla 0XJ
    Axillary Artery, Left 03J6
    Axillary Vein, Left 05J8
    Back, Lower 0WJ0
    Basal Ganglia 00J8
    Basilic Vein 05J
    Bladder 0TJB
    Bladder Neck 0TJC
    Body
      Coccygeal 0GJ9
      Jugulotympanic 0GJB
    Bone, Hyoid 0NJ0
    Bone Marrow 07JT
      Iliac 07JR
      Sternum 07JQ
      Vertebral 07JS
    Brachial Artery 03J
    Brachial Plexus 01J3
    Brachial Vein 05J
    Breast
      Aberrant 0HJY
      Bilateral 0HJV
      Left 0HJU
      Supernumerary 0HJT
    Bronchus, Segmental, Lingula 0BJ9
    Buccal Mucosa 0CJ4
    Bursa and Ligament, Lower Extremity,
      Left 0MJ0
    Buttock, Left 0YJ1
    Carina 0BJ2
    Carotid Bodies, Bilateral 0GJ8
    Carotid Body 0GJ
    Carpal 0PJ
    Carpal Joint 0RJ
    Cavity, Pelvic 0WJ1
    Cecum 0DJH
    Celiac Artery 04J1
    Cephalic Vein 05J
    Cerebellum 00JC
    Cerebral Hemisphere 00J7
    Cerebral Meninges 00J1
    Cerebral Ventricle 00J6
    Cervical Nerve 01J1
    Cervical Spinal Cord 00JW

Inspection—*continued*
  by Body Part—*continued*
    Cervical Vertebra 0PJ3
    Cervical Vertebral Disc 0RJ3
    Cervical Vertebral Joint 0RJ1
    Cervicothoracic Vertebral Disc 0RJ5
    Cervicothoracic Vertebral Joint 0RJ4
    Cervix 0UJC
    Chest Wall 0WJ8
    Chordae Tendineae 02J9
    Choroid, Left 08JB
    Cisterna Chyli 07JL
    Clavicle 0PJ
    Coccygeal Glomus 0GJB
    Coccygeal Joint 0SJ6
    Coccyx 0QJS
    Colic Artery 04J
    Colic Vein 06J7
    Colon, Sigmoid 0DJ0
    Common Bile Duct 0FJ9
    Common Carotid Artery 03J
    Common Iliac Artery 04J
    Common Iliac Vein 06J
    Conduction Mechanism 02J8
    Conjunctiva 08J
    Cord
      Cervical Spinal 00JW
      Lumbar Spinal 00JY
      Spermatic 0VJ
      Thoracic Spinal 00JX
      Vocal 0CJ
    Cornea 08J
    Corpora Arenacea, Pineal 0GJ1
    Cul-de-sac 0UJF
    Cystic Duct 0FJ8
    Descending Colon 0DJM
    Diaphragm 0BJ
    Duct
      Lacrimal, Left 08JX
      Pancreatic, Accessory 0FJ5
    Duodenum 0DJ9
    Dura Mater 00J2
    Ear, Inner, Left 09J5
    Elbow Bursa and Ligament 0MJ
    Elbow Joint 0RJ
    Elbow Region 0XJ
    Endometrium 0UJB
    Epididymis 0VJ
    Epidural Space 00J3
    Epiglottis 0CJR
    Esophageal Vein 06J3
    Esophagogastric Junction 0DJ4
    Esophagus 0DJ5
      Lower 0DJ3
      Middle 0DJ2
      Upper 0DJ1
    Ethmoid Bone 0NJ
    Ethmoid Sinus 09J
    Eustachian Tube 09J
    External Auditory Canal, Left 09J4
    External Carotid Artery 03J
    External Ear, Left 09J1
    External Iliac Artery 04J
    External Iliac Vein 06J
    External Jugular Vein 05J
    Extraocular Muscle 08J
    Eye, Left 08J1
    Face 0WJ2
    Face Artery 03JR
    Face Vein 05J
    Facial Muscle 0KJ1
    Facial Nerve 00JM
    Fallopian Tube, Left 0UJ6
    Fallopian Tubes, Bilateral 0UJ7
    Femoral Artery 04J
    Femoral Nerve 01JD

Inspection—*continued*
  by Body Part—*continued*
    Femoral Region 0YJ
    Femoral Shaft 0QJ
    Femoral Vein, Left 06JN
    Fibula 0QJ
    Finger Nail 0HJQ
    Finger Phalangeal Joint 0RJ
    Finger Phalanx 0PJ
    Foot 0YJ
    Foot Artery 04J
    Foot Bursa and Ligament 0MJ
    Foot Muscle 0KJ
    Foot Tendon 0LJ
    Foot Vein 06J
    Frontal Bone 0NJ
    Frontal Sinus 09J
    Gallbladder 0FJ4
    Gastric Artery 04J2
    Gastric Vein 06J2
    Genitalia, Male External 0VJ1
    Gland
      Lacrimal, Left 08JA
      Lower Parathyroid 0GJ
      Mammary 0HJ
      Minor Salivary 0CJ0
      Parathyroid 0GJ0
      Pineal 0GJ1
      Upper Parathyroid 0GJ
      Vestibular 0UJJ
    Glenoid Cavity 0PJ
    Glomus Jugulare 0GJC
    Glossopharyngeal Nerve 00JP
    Greater Omentum 0DJS
    Greater Saphenous Vein 06J
    Hair 0HJS
    Hand 0XJ
    Hand Artery 03J
    Hand Bursa and Ligament 0MJ
    Hand Muscle 0KJ
    Hand Tendon 0LJ
    Hand Vein 05J
    Hard Palate 0CJ2
    Head and Neck Sympathetic Nerve 01JK
    Heart 02J
    Hemiazygos Vein 05J1
    Hepatic Artery 04J3
    Hepatic Duct, Left 0FJ6
    Hepatic Vein 06J4
    Hip Bursa and Ligament 0MJ
    Hip Joint 0SJ
    Hip Muscle 0KJ
    Hip Tendon 0LJ
    Humeral Head 0PJ
    Humeral Shaft 0PJ
    Hymen 0UJK
    Hyoid Bone 0NJX
    Hypogastric Vein 06J
    Hypoglossal Nerve 00JS
    Hypophysis 0GJ0
    Hypothalamus 00JA
    Ileocecal Valve 0DJC
    Ileum 0DJB
    Inferior Mesenteric Artery 04JB
    Inferior Mesenteric Vein 06J6
    Inferior Parathyroid Gland 0GJ
    Inguinal Region 0YJ
    Inner Ear 09J
    Innominate Artery 03J2
    Innominate Vein 05J
    Internal Carotid Artery 03J
    Internal Iliac Artery 04J
    Internal Jugular Vein 05J
    Internal Mammary Artery, Left 03J1
    Intracranial Artery 03JG
    Intracranial Vein 05JL

Inspection—*continued*
  by Body Part—*continued*
    Iris 08J
    Jejunum 0DJA
    Joint
      Finger Phalangeal, Left 0RJ0
      Toe Phalangeal, Left 0SJ0
    Kidney, Left 0TJ1
    Kidney Pelvis 0TJ
    Kidneys, Bilateral 0TJ2
    Knee Bursa and Ligament 0MJ
    Knee Joint 0SJ
    Knee Region 0YJ
    Knee Tendon 0LJ
    Lacrimal Bone 0NJ
    Lacrimal Duct, Left 08JY
    Lacrimal Gland 08J
    Large Intestine 0DJ
    Larynx 0CJS
    Lens 08J
    Lesser Omentum 0DJT
    Lesser Saphenous Vein 06J
    Lingula Bronchus 0BJ9
    Liver 0FJ0
      Left Lobe 0FJ2
      Right Lobe 0FJ1
    Lobe Segmental Bronchus
      Lower 0BJ
      Middle, Right 0BJ5
      Upper 0BJ
    Lower Arm 0XJ
    Lower Arm and Wrist Muscle 0KJ
    Lower Arm and Wrist Tendon 0LJ
    Lower Artery 04JY
    Lower Back 0WJL
    Lower Extremity 0YJ
    Lower Extremity Bursa and Ligament
      0MJ
    Lower Eyelid 08J
    Lower Femur 0QJ
    Lower Gingiva 0CJ6
    Lower Jaw 0WJ5
    Lower Leg 0YJ
    Lower Leg Muscle 0KJ
    Lower Leg Tendon 0LJ
    Lower Lip 0CJ1
    Lower Lobe Bronchus 0BJ
    Lower Lung Lobe 0BJ
    Lower Tooth 0CJX
    Lower Vein 06JY
    Lumbar Nerve 01JB
    Lumbar Plexus 01J9
    Lumbar Spinal Cord 00JY
    Lumbar Sympathetic Nerve 01JN
    Lumbar Vertebral Disc 0SJ2
    Lumbosacral Disc 0SJ4
    Lumbosacral Joint 0SJ3
    Lumbosacral Plexus 01JA
    Lung 0BJ
    Lung Lingula 0BJH
    Lung Lingula Segments 0BJH
    Lung Lobe Segments
      Lower 0BJ
      Middle, Right 0BJD
      Upper 0BJ
    Lungs, Bilateral 0BJM
    Lymphatic
      Aortic 07JD
      Inguinal, Left 07J0
      Internal Mammary 07J
      Left Axillary 07J6
      Left Inguinal 07JJ
      Left Lower Extremity 07JG
      Left Neck 07J2
      Left Upper Extremity 07J4
      Mesenteric 07JB

Inspection—*continued*
  by Body Part—*continued*
    Lymphatic—*continued*
      Pelvis 07JC
      Right Axillary 07J5
      Right Inguinal 07JH
      Right Lower Extremity 07JF
      Right Neck 07J1
      Right Upper Extremity 07J3
    Main Bronchus 0BJ
    Male External Genitalia 0VJV
    Mandible 0NJ
    Marrow, Bone 07J7
    Mastoid Sinus 09J
    Maxilla 0NJ
    Maxillary Sinus 09J
    Median Nerve 01J5
    Mediastinum 0WJC
    Medulla Oblongata 00JD
    Mesentery 0DJV
    Metacarpal 0PJ
    Metacarpocarpal Joint 0RJ
    Metacarpophalangeal Joint 0RJ
    Metatarsal 0QJ
    Metatarsal-Phalangeal Joint 0SJ
    Metatarsal-Tarsal Joint 0SJ
    Middle Ear, Left 09J6
    Middle Lobe Bronchus, Right 0BJ5
    Middle Lung Lobe, Right 0BJD
    Minor Salivary Gland 0CJJ
    Mitral Valve 02JG
    Muscle, Foot, Left 0KJ0
    Nail, Toe 0HJ0
    Nail Bed
      Finger 0HJQ
      Toe 0HJR
    Nasal Bone 0NJB
    Nasal Septum 09JM
    Nasal Turbinate 09JL
    Nasopharynx 09JN
    Neck 0WJ6
      Bladder 0TJ0
    Neck Muscle 0KJ
    Nerve, Sacral 01J0
    Neurohypophysis 0GJ0
    Nipple 0HJ
    Nose 09JK
    Occipital Bone 0NJ
    Oculomotor Nerve 00JH
    Olfactory Nerve 00JF
    Omentum, Lesser 0DJR
    Optic Nerve 00JG
    Oral Cavity and Throat 0WJ3
    Orbit 0NJ
    Ovaries, Bilateral 0UJ2
    Ovary, Left 0UJ1
    Palatine Bone 0NJ
    Pancreas 0FJG
      Body 0FJF
      Head 0FJF
      Tail 0FJF
    Pancreatic Duct 0FJD
      Accessory 0FJF
    Papillary Muscle 02JD
    Para-aortic Body 0GJ9
    Paraganglion Extremity 0GJF
    Parathyroid Gland 0GJR
    Parathyroid Glands, Multiple 0GJQ
    Parietal Bone 0NJ
    Parotid Duct 0CJ
    Parotid Gland 0CJ
    Patella 0QJ
    Pelvic Bone 0QJ
    Pelvic Cavity 0WJJ
    Penis 0VJS
    Pericardial Cavity 0WJD

Inspection—*continued*
  by Body Part—*continued*
    Pericardium 02JN
    Perineum
      Female 0WJN
      Male 0WJM
    Perineum Bursa and Ligament 0MJK
    Perineum Muscle 0KJM
    Perineum Tendon 0LJH
    Peritoneal Cavity 0WJG
    Peritoneum 0DJW
    Peroneal Artery 04J
    Peroneal Nerve 01JH
    Phalanx
      Finger, Left 0PJ0
      Toe, Left 0QJ0
    Phrenic Nerve 01J2
    Pineal Body 0GJ1
    Pleura 0BJ
      Parietal 0BJ
      Visceral 0BJ
    Pleural Cavity 0WJ
    Pons 00JB
    Popliteal Artery 04J
    Portal Vein 06J8
    Posterior Tibial Artery 04J
    Prepuce 0VJT
    Products of Conception 10J0
      Ectopic 10J2
      Retained 10J1
    Prostate 0VJ0
    Pudendal Nerve 01JC
    Pulmonary Artery 02J
    Pulmonary Lingula 0BJH
    Pulmonary Lobe
      Lower 0BJ
      Middle, Right 0BJD
      Upper 0BJ
    Pulmonary Trunk 02JP
    Pulmonary Valve 02JH
    Pulmonary Vein 02J
    Radial Artery 03J
    Radial Nerve 01J6
    Radius 0PJ
    Rectum 0DJP
    Region
      Ankle, Left 0YJ0
      Wrist, Left 0XJ2
    Renal Artery 04J
    Renal Pelvis 0TJ
    Renal Vein 06J
    Retina 08J
    Retinal Vessel 08J
    Retroperitoneum 0WJH
    Rib 0PJ
    Sacral Nerve 01JR
    Sacral Plexus 01JQ
    Sacral Sympathetic Nerve 01JP
    Sacrococcygeal Joint 0SJ5
    Sacroiliac Joint 0SJ
    Sacrum 0QJ1
    Scapula 0PJ
    Sciatic Nerve 01JF
    Sclera 08J
    Scrotum 0VJ5
    Seminal Vesicle, Left 0VJ2
    Seminal Vesicles, Bilateral 0VJ3
    Shoulder Bursa and Ligament 0MJ
    Shoulder Joint 0RJ
    Shoulder Muscle 0KJ
    Shoulder Region, Left 0XJ3
    Shoulder Tendon 0LJ
    Sigmoid Colon 0DJN
    Sinus, Sphenoid, Left 09J0

Irrigation
  by Body System
      Whole Body 3C1Z
  by Body System/Region
      Biliary and Pancreatic Tract 3E1J
      Cavity
          Pericardial 3E1L
          Peritoneal 3E1M
      Cranial Cavity and Brain 3E1Q
      Ear 3E1B
      Epidural Space 3E1S
      Eye 3E1C
      Female Reproductive 3E1P
      Genitourinary Tract 3E1K
      Joints 3E1U
      Lower GI 3E1H
      Male Reproductive 3E1N
      Pericardial Cavity 3E1Y
      Reproductive, Female 3E19
      Respiratory Tract 3E1F
      Skin and Mucous Membranes 3E10
      Spinal Canal 3E1R
      Upper GI 3E1G
Isthmectomy
  —*see* Excision, Endocrine System 0GB
  —*see* Resection, Endocrine System 0GT

J

Jejunectomy
  —*see* Excision, Gastrointestinal System 0DB
  —*see* Resection, Gastrointestinal System 0DT
Jejunocecostomy—*see* Bypass, Gastrointestinal System 0D1
Jejunocolostomy—*see* Bypass, Gastrointestinal System 0D1
Jejunoileostomy—*see* Bypass, Gastrointestinal System 0D1
Jejunopexy
  —*see* Repair, Gastrointestinal System 0DQ
  —*see* Reposition, Gastrointestinal System 0DS
Jejunostomy—*see* Bypass, Gastrointestinal System 0D1
Jejunotomy
  —*see* Drainage, Gastrointestinal System 0D9
  —*see* Inspection, Gastrointestinal System 0DJ

K

Keratectomy
  —*see* Excision, Eye 08B
  —*see* Resection, Eye 08T
Keratocentesis—*see* Drainage, Eye 089
Keratoplasty
  —*see* Repair, Eye 08Q
  —*see* Replacement, Eye 08R
Keratoscopy—*see* Inspection, Eye 08J
Keratotomy
  —*see* Drainage, Eye 089
  —*see* Inspection, Eye 08J
  —*see* Repair, Eye 08Q
Kerectomy
  —*see* Excision, Eye 08B
  —*see* Resection, Eye 08T
KUB X-ray—*see* Plain Radiography, Urinary System BT0

L

Labiectomy
  —*see* Excision, Female Reproductive System 0UB
  —*see* Resection, Female Reproductive System 0UT

Laminectomy
  —*see* Excision, Lower Bones 0QB
  —*see* Excision, Upper Bones 0PB
Laminotomy
  —*see* Division, Lower Bones 0Q8
  —*see* Division, Upper Bones 0P8
  —*see* Drainage, Lower Bones 0Q9
  —*see* Drainage, Upper Bones 0P9
  —*see* Inspection, Lower Bones 0QJ
  —*see* Inspection, Upper Bones 0PJ
Laparoscopy
  —*see* Inspection
Laryngectomy
  —*see* Excision, Mouth and Throat 0CB
  —*see* Resection, Mouth and Throat 0CT
Laryngocentesis—*see* Drainage, Mouth and Throat 0C9
Laryngopexy
  —*see* Repair, Mouth and Throat 0CQ
  —*see* Reposition, Mouth and Throat 0CS
Laryngoplasty
  —*see* Repair, Mouth and Throat 0CQ
  —*see* Replacement, Mouth and Throat 0CR
Laryngorrhaphy—*see* Repair, Mouth and Throat 0CQ
Laryngoscopy—*see* Inspection, Mouth and Throat 0CJ
Laryngotomy
  —*see* Drainage, Mouth and Throat 0C9
  —*see* Inspection, Mouth and Throat 0CJ
Ligate—*see* Occlusion
Ligation—*see* Occlusion
Light Therapy GZJZ
Lingulectomy
  —*see* Excision, Respiratory System 0BB
  —*see* Resection, Respiratory System 0BT
Lithotripsy—*see* Fragmentation
Lobectomy
  —*see* Excision, Central Nervous System 00B
  —*see* Excision, Endocrine System 0GB
  —*see* Excision, Hepatobiliary System and Pancreas 0FB
  —*see* Excision, Respiratory System 0BB
  —*see* Resection, Endocrine System 0GT
  —*see* Resection, Hepatobiliary System and Pancreas 0FT
  —*see* Resection, Respiratory System 0BT
Lobotomy—*see* Division, Central Nervous System 008
Localization—*see* Map
Lower GI Series—*see* Fluoroscopy, Gastrointestinal System BD1
Lumpectomy
  —*see* Excision
  —*see* Resection
Lymphadenectomy
  —*see* Excision, Lymphatic and Hemic Systems 07B
  —*see* Resection, Lymphatic and Hemic Systems 07T
Lymphadenotomy
  —*see* Drainage, Lymphatic and Hemic Systems 079
  —*see* Inspection, Lymphatic and Hemic Systems 07J
Lymphangiectomy
  —*see* Excision, Lymphatic and Hemic Systems 07B
  —*see* Resection, Lymphatic and Hemic Systems 07T
Lymphangiography—*see* Plain Radiography, Lymphatic System B70
Lymphangioplasty—*see* Repair, Lymphatic and Hemic Systems 07Q

Lymphangiorrhaphy—*see* Repair, Lymphatic and Hemic Systems 07Q
Lymphangiotomy
  —*see* Drainage, Lymphatic and Hemic Systems 079
  —*see* Inspection, Lymphatic and Hemic Systems 07J
Lysis—*see* Release

M

Magnetic Resonance Imaging (MRI)
  by Body System
      Anatomical Regions BW3
      Axial Skeleton, Except Skull and Facial Bones BR3
      Central Nervous System B03
      Connective Tissue BL3
      Ear, Nose, Mouth and Throat B93
      Endocrine System BG3
      Eye B83
      Female Reproductive System BU3
      Fetus and Obstetrical BY3
      Heart B23
      Hepatobiliary System and Pancreas BF3
      Lower Arteries B43
      Male Reproductive System BV3
      Non-Axial Lower Bones BQ3
      Non-Axial Upper Bones BP3
      Respiratory System BB3
      Skin, Subcutaneous Tissue and Breast BH3
      Skull and Facial Bones BN3
      Upper Arteries B33
      Urinary System BT3
      Veins B53
  by Body Part
      Acoustic Nerves B03C
      Ankle BQ3
      Apices, Lung BB3G
      Arm, Upper, Left BP38
      Arteries
          Intracranial B330
      Arteries
          Lower Extremity, Bilateral B430
      Artery Bypass Grafts, Coronary, Multiple B231
      Brachial Plexus BW3P
      Breast, Left BH31
      Breasts, Bilateral BH32
      Calcaneus BQ3
      Celiac Artery B431
      Cervical Disc(s) BR31
      Cervico-Cerebral Arch B33Q
      Chest BW33
      Common Carotid Arteries, Bilateral B335
      Connective Tissue
          Lower Extremity BL31
          Upper Extremity BL30
      Coronary Artery Bypass Grafts, Multiple B233
      Corpora Cavernosa BV30
      Elbow BP3
      Eye B83
      Eyes, Bilateral B837
      Femur BQ3
      Fetal Abdomen BY33
      Fetal Extremities BY35
      Fetal Head BY30
      Fetal Heart BY31
      Fetal Spine BY34
      Fetal Thorax BY32
      Foot BQ3
      Forearm BP3
      Gland, Thyroid BG32
      Glands, Salivary, Bilateral B930

Magnetic Resonance Imaging (MRI)—
continued
by Body Part—*continued*
Hand/Finger Joint BP3
Head BW38
Heart, Right and Left B236
Hip, Left BQ31
Inferior Vena Cava B539
Internal Carotid Arteries, Bilateral B338
Intracranial Arteries B33R
Intracranial Sinuses B532
Joints, Temporomandibular, Bilateral
　　BN39
Jugular Veins, Bilateral B535
Kidney BT3
Kidney Transplant BT39
Kidneys, Bilateral BT33
Knee BQ3
Larynx B93J
Leg, Lower, Left BQ30
Liver BF35
Liver and Spleen BF36
Lower Extremity Arteries B43
Lower Extremity Veins B53
Lower Leg BQ3
Lumbar Disc(s) BR33
Lumbar Spine BR39
Nasopharynx/Oropharynx B93F
Neck BW3F
Nerves, Acoustic B030
Ovaries, Bilateral BU35
Ovary BU3
Pancreas BF37
Paranasal Sinuses B932
Parathyroid Glands BG33
Parotid Glands, Bilateral B936
Patella BQ3
Pelvic (Iliac) Veins, Bilateral B53H
Pelvic Arteries B43C
Pelvic Region BW3G
Pelvis BR3C
Plexus, Brachial BW30
Portal and Splanchnic Veins B53T
Pregnant Uterus BU3B
Prostate BV33
Pulmonary Veins, Bilateral B53S
Renal Arteries, Bilateral B438
Renal Veins, Bilateral B53L
Retroperitoneum BW3H
Sacrum and Coccyx BR3F
Salivary Glands, Bilateral B93D
Scrotum BV34
Sella Turcica/Pituitary Gland B039
Shoulder, Left BP39
Spinal Arteries B33M
Spinal Cord B03B
Spine, Lumbar BR30
Subcutaneous Tissue
　　Abdomen and Pelvis BH3H
　　Head/Neck BH3D
　　Lower Extremity BH3J
　　Thorax BH3G
　　Upper Extremity BH3F
Submandibular Glands, Bilateral B939
Superior Mesenteric Artery B434
Superior Vena Cava B538
Tendons
　　Lower Extremity BL33
　　Upper Extremity BL32
Testicle BV3
Testicles, Bilateral BV37
Thoracic Disc(s) BR32
Thoracic Spine BR37
Thyroid Gland BG34
Tissue, Subcutaneous, Lower Extremity
　　BH30

Magnetic Resonance Imaging (MRI)—
continued
by Body Part—*continued*
Toe(s) BQ3
Transplant, Kidney BT30
Upper Arm BP3
Upper Extremity Arteries B33
Upper Extremity Veins B53
Uterus BU36
Uterus and Ovaries BU3C
Vagina BU39
Veins
　　Other B53V
　　Pulmonary, Bilateral B531
Vertebral Arteries, Bilateral B33G
Whole Fetus BY36
Wrist BP3
Malleotomy
　—*see* Drainage, Ear, Nose, Sinus 099
　—*see* Inspection, Ear, Nose, Sinus 09J
Mamilliplasty—*see* Repair, Skin and Breast
　　0HQ
Mammaplasty
　—*see* Alteration, Skin and Breast 0H0
　—*see* Repair, Skin and Breast 0HQ
　—*see* Replacement, Skin and Breast 0HR
Mammectomy
　—*see* Excision, Skin and Breast 0HB
　—*see* Resection, Skin and Breast 0HT
Mammilliplasty
　—*see* Alteration, Skin and Breast 0H0
　—*see* Repair, Skin and Breast 0HQ
　—*see* Replacement, Skin and Breast 0HR
Mammography—*see* Plain Radiography, Skin,
　　Subcutaneous Tissue and Breast BH0
Mammoplasty
　—*see* Alteration, Skin and Breast 0H0
　—*see* Repair, Skin and Breast 0HQ
　—*see* Replacement, Skin and Breast 0HR
Mammotomy
　—*see* Drainage, Skin and Breast 0H9
　—*see* Inspection, Skin and Breast 0HJ
Mandibulectomy
　—*see* Excision, Head and Facial Bones 0NB
　—*see* Resection, Head and Facial Bones 0NT
Manipulation—*see* Cochlear Implant
　　Treatment
Chiropractic
　Abdomen 9WB9
　Cervical 9WB1
　Extremities, Upper 9WB0
　Lower Extremities 9WB6
　Lumbar 9WB3
　Pelvis 9WB5
　Rib Cage 9WB8
　Sacrum 9WB4
　Thoracic 9WB2
　Upper Extremities 9WB7
Map
by Body System
　Central Nervous System 00K
　Heart and Great Vessels 02K
by Body Part
　Basal Ganglia 00K8
　Cerebellum 00KC
　Cerebral Hemisphere 00K7
　Hypothalamus 00KA
　Mechanism, Conduction 02K8
　Medulla Oblongata 00KD
　Oblongata, Medulla 00K0
　Pons 00KB
　Thalamus 00K9
Marsupialization—*see* Drainage
Mastectomy
　—*see* Excision, Skin and Breast 0HB

Mastectomy—*continued*
　—*see* Resection, Skin and Breast 0HT
Mastoidectomy
　—*see* Excision, Ear, Nose, Sinus 09B
　—*see* Resection, Ear, Nose, Sinus 09T
Mastoidotomy
　—*see* Drainage, Ear, Nose, Sinus 099
　—*see* Inspection, Ear, Nose, Sinus 09J
Mastotomy
　—*see* Drainage, Skin and Breast 0H9
　—*see* Inspection, Skin and Breast 0HJ
Measurement
by Function
　Action Currents
　　Cardiac 4A02
　Acuity
　　Olfactory 4A08
　　Visual 4A07
　Capacity
　　Respiratory 4A09
　Conductivity
　　Central Nervous 4A00
　　Peripheral Nervous 4A01
　　Products of Conception, Nervous
　　　4A0J
　Contractility
　　Musculoskeletal 4A0F
　　Urinary 4A0D
　Defibrillator
　　Cardiac 4B02
　Electrical Activity
　　Cardiac 4A02
　　Central Nervous 4A00
　　Products of Conception
　　　Cardiac 4A0H
　　　Nervous 4A0J
　Flow
　　Arterial 4A03
　　Biliary 4A0C
　　Lymphatic 4A06
　　Respiratory 4A09
　　Urinary 4A0D
　　Venous 4A04
　Metabolism
　　Whole Body 4A0G
　Mobility
　　Visual 4A07
　Motility
　　Gastrointestinal 4A0B
　Output
　　Cardiac 4A02
　Pacemaker
　　Cardiac 4B02
　　Respiratory 4B09
　Pressure
　　Arterial 4A03
　　Biliary 4A0C
　　Central Nervous 4A00
　　Gastrointestinal 4A0B
　　Lymphatic 4A06
　　Products of Conception, Nervous
　　　4A0J
　　Urinary 4A0D
　　Venous 4A04
　　Visual 4A07
　Pulse
　　Arterial 4A03
　　Venous 4A04
　Rate
　　Cardiac 4A02
　　Products of Conception, Cardiac
　　　4A0H
　　Respiratory 4A09
　Resistance
　　Respiratory 4A09
　　Urinary 4A0D

Measurement—*continued*
  by Function—*continued*
    Rhythm
      Cardiac 4A02
      Products of Conception, Cardiac 4A0H
    Sampling and Pressure
      Cardiac 4A02
    Saturation
      Arterial 4A03
      Central Nervous 4A00
      Venous 4A04
    Secretion
      Gastrointestinal 4A0B
    Sleep
      Whole Body 4A0G
    Sound
      Arterial 4A03
      Cardiac 4A02
      Products of Conception, Cardiac
        4A0H
    Stimulator
      Central Nervous 4B00
      Musculoskeletal 4B0F
      Peripheral Nervous 4B01
    Temperature
      Central Nervous 4A00
      Whole Body 4A0G
    Total Activity
      Cardiac 4A02
      Respiratory 4A09
    Volume
      Circulatory 4A05
      Respiratory 4A09
      Urinary 4A0D
Measurement—*see* Vestibular Treatment
Measurement and Monitoring
  —*see* Measurement
  —*see* Monitoring
Meatotomy
  —*see* Drainage, Urinary System 0T9
  —*see* Inspection, Urinary System 0TJ
Mechanical Ventilation—*see* Extracorporeal
      Assistance And Performance 5A1
Mediastinectomy—*see* Excision, Anatomical
      Regions, General 0WB
Mediastinoscopy—*see* Inspection, Anatomical
      Regions, General 0WJ
Medical and Surgical
  —*see* Alteration
  —*see* Bypass
  —*see* Change
  —*see* Control
  —*see* Creation
  —*see* Destruction
  —*see* Detachment
  —*see* Dilation
  —*see* Division
  —*see* Drainage
  —*see* Excision
  —*see* Extirpation
  —*see* Extraction
  —*see* Fragmentation
  —*see* Fusion
  —*see* Insertion
  —*see* Inspection
  —*see* Map
  —*see* Occlusion
  —*see* Reattachment
  —*see* Release
  —*see* Removal
  —*see* Repair
  —*see* Replacement
  —*see* Reposition
  —*see* Resection
  —*see* Restriction

Medical and Surgical—*continued*
  —*see* Revision
  —*see* Supplement
  —*see* Transfer
  —*see* Transplantation
Medication Management
  by Type Qualifier
    Antabuse HZ83
    Bupropion HZ87
    Clonidine HZ86
    Levo-alpha-acetyl-methadol (LAAM)
        HZ82
    Methadone Maintenance HZ81
    Naloxone HZ85
    Naltrexone HZ84
    Nicotine Replacement HZ80
    Other Replacement Medication HZ89
    Psychiatric Medication HZ88
  Mental Health GZ3Z
Meningeorrhaphy—*see* Repair, Central
      Nervous System 00Q
Meniscectomy
  —*see* Excision, Lower Joints 0SB
  —*see* Resection, Lower Joints 0ST
Mental Health
  —*see* Biofeedback
  —*see* Counseling
  —*see* Crisis Intervention
  —*see* Electroconvulsive Therapy
  —*see* Family Psychotherapy
  —*see* Group Psychotherapy
  —*see* Hypnosis
  —*see* Individual Psychotherapy
  —*see* Light Therapy
  —*see* Medication Management
  —*see* Narcosynthesis
  —*see* Psychological Tests
Mentoplasty
  —*see* Repair, Head and Facial Bones 0NQ
  —*see* Replacement, Head and Facial Bones
        0NR
Mesenterectomy
  —*see* Excision, Gastrointestinal System 0DB
  —*see* Resection, Gastrointestinal System 0DT
Mesenteriorrhaphy—*see* Repair,
      Gastrointestinal System 0DQ
Mesenteriplication—*see* Restriction,
      Gastrointestinal System 0DV
Mesenterorrhaphy—*see* Repair,
      Gastrointestinal System 0DQ
Metatarsectomy
  —*see* Excision, Lower Bones 0QB
  —*see* Resection, Lower Bones 0QT
Mobilization—*see* Release
Monitoring
  by Function
    Capacity
      Respiratory 4A19
    Conductivity
      Central Nervous 4A10
      Peripheral Nervous 4A11
      Products of Conception, Nervous
        4A1J
    Contractility
      Urinary 4A1D
    Electrical Activity
      Cardiac 4A12
      Central Nervous 4A10
      Products of Conception
        Cardiac 4A1H
        Nervous 4A1J
    Flow
      Arterial 4A13
      Lymphatic 4A16

Monitoring—*continued*
  by Function—*continued*
    Flow—*continued*
      Respiratory 4A19
      Urinary 4A1D
      Venous 4A14
    Motility
      Gastrointestinal 4A1B
    Output
      Cardiac 4A12
    Pressure
      Arterial 4A13
      Central Nervous 4A10
      Gastrointestinal 4A1B
      Lymphatic 4A16
      Products of Conception, Nervous 4A1J
      Urinary 4A1D
      Venous 4A14
    Pulse
      Arterial 4A13
      Venous 4A14
    Rate
      Cardiac 4A12
      Products of Conception, Cardiac
        4A1H
      Respiratory 4A19
    Resistance
      Respiratory 4A19
      Urinary 4A1D
    Rhythm
      Cardiac 4A12
      Products of Conception, Cardiac
        4A1H
    Saturation
      Arterial 4A13
      Central Nervous 4A10
      Venous 4A14
    Secretion
      Gastrointestinal 4A1B
    Sleep
      Whole Body 4A1G
    Sound
      Arterial 4A13
      Cardiac 4A12
      Products of Conception, Cardiac 4A1H
    Temperature
      Central Nervous 4A10
      Whole Body 4A1G
    Total Activity
      Cardiac 4A12
    Volume
      Respiratory 4A19
      Urinary 4A1D
MR Angiography
  —*see* Magnetic Resonance Imaging (MRI),
      Heart B23
  —*see* Magnetic Resonance Imaging (MRI),
      Lower Arteries B43
  —*see* Magnetic Resonance Imaging (MRI),
      Upper Arteries B33
Musculopexy
  —*see* Repair, Muscles 0KQ
  —*see* Reposition, Muscles 0KS
Musculoplasty—*see* Repair, Muscles 0KQ
Musculorrhaphy—*see* Repair, Muscles 0KQ
Myectomy
  —*see* Excision, Muscles 0KB
  —*see* Resection, Muscles 0KT
Myelography—*see* Fluoroscopy, Axial Skeleton,
      Except Skull and Facial Bones BR1
Myelography—*see* Plain Radiography, Axial
      Skeleton, Except Skull and Facial
      Bones BR0
Myomectomy—*see* Excision, Female
      Reproductive System 0UB

Myopexy
—*see* Repair, Muscles 0KQ
—*see* Reposition, Muscles 0KS
Myoplasty—*see* Repair, Muscles 0KQ
Myorrhaphy—*see* Repair, Muscles 0KQ
Myoscopy—*see* Inspection, Muscles 0KJ
Myotomy
—*see* Division, Muscles 0K8
—*see* Drainage, Muscles 0K9
—*see* Inspection, Muscles 0KJ
Myringectomy
—*see* Excision, Ear, Nose, Sinus 09B
—*see* Resection, Ear, Nose, Sinus 09T
Myringoplasty
—*see* Repair, Ear, Nose, Sinus 09Q
—*see* Replacement, Ear, Nose, Sinus 09R
Myringostomy—*see* Drainage, Ear, Nose, Sinus 099
Myringotomy—*see* Drainage, Ear, Nose, Sinus 099

N

Narcosynthesis GZGZ
Near Infrared Spectroscopy 8E02
Nephrectomy
—*see* Excision, Urinary System 0TB
—*see* Resection, Urinary System 0TT
Nephrolithotomy—*see* Extirpation, Urinary System 0TC
Nephrolysis—*see* Release, Urinary System 0TN
Nephropexy
—*see* Repair, Urinary System 0TQ
—*see* Reposition, Urinary System 0TS
Nephroplasty
—*see* Repair, Urinary System 0TQ
—*see* Replacement, Urinary System 0TR
Nephrorrhaphy—*see* Repair, Urinary System 0TQ
Nephroscopy—*see* Inspection, Urinary System 0TJ
Nephrostomy—*see* Bypass, Urinary System 0T1
Nephrotomography
—*see* Fluoroscopy, Urinary System BT1
—*see* Plain Radiography, Urinary System BT0
Nephrotomy
—*see* Drainage, Urinary System 0T9
—*see* Inspection, Urinary System 0TJ
Nerve Conduction Study
by Body Part
Central Nervous 4A00
Peripheral Nervous 4A01
Neurectomy
—*see* Excision, Central Nervous System 00B
—*see* Excision, Peripheral Nervous System 01B
—*see* Resection, Central Nervous System 00T
Neurexeresis
—*see* Extraction, Central Nervous System 00D
—*see* Extraction, Peripheral Nervous System 01D
Neurolysis
—*see* Release, Central Nervous System 00N
—*see* Release, Peripheral Nervous System 01N
Neuroplasty
—*see* Repair, Central Nervous System 00Q
—*see* Repair, Peripheral Nervous System 01Q
Neurorrhaphy—*see* Repair, Central Nervous System 00Q

Neurotomy
—*see* Division, Central Nervous System 008
—*see* Division, Peripheral Nervous System 018
Neurotripsy
—*see* Destruction, Central Nervous System 005
—*see* Destruction, Peripheral Nervous System 015
Nonimaging Nuclear Medicine Assay
by Body System
Lymphatic and Hematologic System C76
Urinary System CT6
by Body Part
Blood C763
Kidneys, Ureters and Bladder CT63
Lymphatic and Hematologic System C76Y
Urinary System CT6Y
Nonimaging Nuclear Medicine Probe
by Body System
Anatomical Regions CW5
Central Nervous System C05
Heart C25
Lymphatic and Hematologic System C75
Musculoskeletal System CP5
by Body Part
Abdomen and Pelvis CW51
Brain C050
Central Nervous System C05Y
Chest CW53
Chest and Abdomen CW54
Chest and Neck CW56
Extremities, Lower CP55
Extremity, Upper CW50
Head and Neck CW5B
Heart C25Y
Right and Left C256
Lower Extremities CP5P
Lower Extremity CW5D
Lymphatic and Hematologic System C75Y
Lymphatics
Head C75J
Head and Neck C755
Lower Extremity C75P
Neck C75K
Pelvic C75D
Trunk C75M
Upper Chest C75L
Upper Extremity C75N
Musculoskeletal System, Other CP5Y
Pelvic Region CW5J
Upper Extremities CP5N
Upper Extremity CW5M
Nonimaging Nuclear Medicine Uptake
by Body System
Endocrine System CG4
by Body Part
Gland, Thyroid CG42
System, Endocrine CG4Y
Nuclear Medicine
—*see* Nonimaging Nuclear Medicine Assay
—*see* Nonimaging Nuclear Medicine Probe
—*see* Nonimaging Nuclear Medicine Uptake
—*see* Planar Nuclear Medicine Imaging
—*see* Positron Emission Tomographic (PET) Imaging
—*see* Systemic Nuclear Medicine Therapy
—*see* Tomographic (Tomo) Nuclear Medicine Imaging
Nuclear Scintigraphy—*see* Nuclear Medicine

O

Obliterate—*see* Destruction
Obliteration—*see* Destruction
Obstetrics
—*see* Abortion
—*see* Change
—*see* Delivery
—*see* Drainage
—*see* Extraction
—*see* Insertion
—*see* Inspection
—*see* Removal
—*see* Repair
—*see* Reposition
—*see* Resection
—*see* Transplantation
Occlusion
by Body System
Eye 08L
Female Reproductive System 0UL
Gastrointestinal System 0DL
Heart and Great Vessels 02L
Hepatobiliary System and Pancreas 0FL
Lower Arteries 04L
Lower Veins 06L
Lymphatic and Hemic Systems 07L
Male Reproductive System 0VL
Mouth and Throat 0CL
Respiratory System 0BL
Upper Arteries 03L
Upper Veins 05L
Urinary System 0TL
by Body Part
Ampulla of Vater 0FLC
Anterior Tibial Artery 04L
Anus 0DLQ
Artery
Lower 04L0
Artery
Pulmonary, Left 02LR
Upper 03L0
Ascending Colon 0DLK
Axillary Artery 03L
Axillary Vein 05L
Basilic Vein 05L
Bladder 0TLB
Bladder Neck 0TLC
Brachial Artery 03L
Brachial Vein 05L
Bronchus
Lower Lobe, Left 0BL1
Segmental, Lingula 0BL9
Carina 0BL2
Cecum 0DLH
Celiac Artery 04L1
Cephalic Vein 05L
Chyli, Cisterna 07L0
Cisterna Chyli 07LL
Colic Artery 04L
Colic Vein 06L7
Colon, Sigmoid 0DL1
Common Bile Duct 0FL9
Common Carotid Artery 03L
Common Iliac Artery 04L
Common Iliac Vein 06L
Cul-de-sac 0ULF
Cystic Duct 0FL8
Deferens, Vas, Bilateral 0VLF
Descending Colon 0DLM
Duct
Lacrimal, Left 08LX
Pancreatic, Accessory 0FL5
Parotid, Left 0CLB
Duodenum 0DL9
Esophageal Vein 06L3

Occlusion—*continued*
  by Body Part—*continued*
    Esophagogastric Junction 0DL4
    Esophagus 0DL5
      Lower 0DL3
      Middle 0DL2
    External Carotid Artery 03L
    External Iliac Artery 04L
    External Iliac Vein 06L
    External Jugular Vein 05L
    Face Artery 03LR
    Face Vein 05L
    Fallopian Tube, Left 0UL6
    Fallopian Tubes, Bilateral 0UL7
    Femoral Artery 04L
    Femoral Vein 06L
    Foot Artery 04L
    Foot Vein 06L
    Gastric Artery 04L2
    Gastric Vein 06L2
    Greater Saphenous Vein 06L
    Hand Artery 03L
    Hand Vein 05L
    Hemiazygos Vein 05L1
    Hepatic Artery 04L3
    Hepatic Duct, Left 0FL6
    Hepatic Vein 06L4
    Hypogastric Vein 06L
    Ileocecal Valve 0DLC
    Ileum 0DLB
    Inferior Mesenteric Artery 04LB
    Inferior Mesenteric Vein 06L6
    Innominate Artery 03L2
    Innominate Vein 05L
    Internal Carotid Artery 03L
    Internal Iliac Artery 04L
    Internal Jugular Vein 05L
    Internal Mammary Artery, Left 03L1
    Intracranial Artery 03LG
    Intracranial Vein 05LL
    Jejunum 0DLA
    Kidney Pelvis, Left 0TL4
    Lacrimal Duct, Left 08LY
    Large Intestine 0DL
    Lesser Saphenous Vein 06L
    Lingula Bronchus 0BL9
    Lobe Segmental Bronchus
      Lower 0BL
      Middle, Right 0BL5
      Upper 0BL
    Lower Artery 04LY
    Lower Lobe Bronchus 0BL
    Lower Vein 06LY
    Lymphatic
      Aortic 07LD
      Internal Mammary 07L
      Left Axillary 07L6
      Left Inguinal 07LJ
      Left Lower Extremity 07LG
      Left Neck 07L2
      Left Upper Extremity 07L4
      Mesenteric 07LB
      Pelvis 07LC
      Right Axillary 07L5
      Right Inguinal 07LH
      Right Lower Extremity 07LF
      Right Neck 07L1
      Right Upper Extremity 07L3
      Thorax 07L7
    Main Bronchus 0BL
    Middle Lobe Bronchus, Right 0BL5
    Neck, Bladder 0TL3
    Pancreas
      Body 0FLF
      Head 0FLF
      Tail 0FLF

Occlusion—*continued*
  by Body Part—*continued*
    Pancreatic Duct 0FLD
      Accessory 0FLF
    Parotid Duct, Left 0CLC
    Peroneal Artery 04L
    Popliteal Artery 04L
    Portal Vein 06L8
    Posterior Tibial Artery 04L
    Pulmonary Vein, Left 02LT
    Radial Artery 03L
    Rectum 0DLP
    Renal Artery 04L
    Renal Pelvis 0TL
    Renal Vein 06L
    Sigmoid Colon 0DLN
    Small Intestine 0DL8
    Spermatic Cord, Left 0VLG
    Spermatic Cords, Bilateral 0VLH
    Splenic Artery 04L4
    Splenic Vein 06L1
    Stomach 0DL6
      Body 0DL6
      Fundus 0DL6
      Pylorus 0DL7
    Subclavian Artery 03L
    Subclavian Vein 05L
    Superior Mesenteric Artery 04L5
    Superior Mesenteric Vein 06L5
    Superior Vena Cava 02LV
    Temporal Artery 03L
    Thoracic Duct 07LK
    Thyroid Artery 03L
    Transverse Colon 0DLL
    Tube, Fallopian, Bilateral 0UL5
    Ulnar Artery 03L
    Upper Artery 03LY
    Upper Lobe Bronchus 0BL
    Upper Vein 05LY
    Ureter 0TL
    Urethra 0TLD
    Vagina 0ULG
    Vas Deferens 0VL
    Vein
      Lower 06L0
      Upper 05L0
    Vein
      Vena Cava, Superior 02LS
    Vertebral Artery 03L
    Vertebral Vein 05L
Occupational Therapy—*see* Physical
    Rehabilitation and Diagnostic
    Audiology
Odentectomy
  —*see* Excision, Mouth and Throat 0CB
  —*see* Resection, Mouth and Throat 0CT
Omentectomy
  —*see* Excision, Gastrointestinal System 0DB
  —*see* Resection, Gastrointestinal System 0DT
Omentofixation—*see* Repair, Gastrointestinal
    System 0DQ
Omentopexy—*see* Repair, Gastrointestinal
    System 0DQ
Omentoplasty
  —*see* Repair, Gastrointestinal System 0DQ
  —*see* Replacement, Gastrointestinal System
    0DR
Omentorrhaphy—*see* Repair, Gastrointestinal
    System 0DQ
Omentosplenopexy—*see* Repair, Hepatobiliary
    System and Pancreas 0FQ
Omentotomy
  —*see* Drainage, Gastrointestinal System 0D9
  —*see* Inspection, Gastrointestinal System
    0DJ

Omentumectomy
  —*see* Excision, Gastrointestinal System 0DB
  —*see* Resection, Gastrointestinal System 0DT
Onychectomy
  —*see* Excision, Skin and Breast 0HB
  —*see* Resection, Skin and Breast 0HT
Onychoplasty
  —*see* Repair, Skin and Breast 0HQ
  —*see* Replacement, Skin and Breast 0HR
Onychotomy
  —*see* Drainage, Skin and Breast 0H9
  —*see* Inspection, Skin and Breast 0HJ
Oophorectomy
  —*see* Excision, Female Reproductive System
    0UB
  —*see* Resection, Female Reproductive
    System 0UT
Oophoropexy
  —*see* Repair, Female Reproductive System
    0UQ
  —*see* Reposition, Female Reproductive
    System 0US
Oophoroplasty—*see* Repair, Female
    Reproductive System 0UQ
Oophorostomy—*see* Drainage, Female
    Reproductive System 0U9
Oophorotomy
  —*see* Drainage, Female Reproductive System
    0U9
  —*see* Inspection, Female Reproductive
    System 0UJ
Oophorrhaphy—*see* Repair, Female
    Reproductive System 0UQ
Orchectomy
  —*see* Excision, Male Reproductive System
    0VB
  —*see* Resection, Male Reproductive System
    0VT
Orchidectomy
  —*see* Excision, Male Reproductive System
    0VB
  —*see* Resection, Male Reproductive System
    0VT
Orchidopexy
  —*see* Repair, Male Reproductive System 0VQ
  —*see* Reposition, Male Reproductive System
    0VS
Orchidoplasty
  —*see* Repair, Male Reproductive System 0VQ
  —*see* Replacement, Male Reproductive
    System 0VR
Orchidorrhaphy—*see* Repair, Male
    Reproductive System 0VQ
Orchidotomy
  —*see* Drainage, Male Reproductive System
    0V9
  —*see* Inspection, Male Reproductive System
    0VJ
Orchiectomy
  —*see* Excision, Male Reproductive System
    0VB
  —*see* Resection, Male Reproductive System
    0VT
Orchiopexy
  —*see* Repair, Male Reproductive System 0VQ
  —*see* Reposition, Male Reproductive System
    0VS
Orchioplasty
  —*see* Repair, Male Reproductive System 0VQ
  —*see* Replacement, Male Reproductive
    System 0VR
Orchiorrhaphy—*see* Repair, Male
    Reproductive System 0VQ

Orchiotomy—see Drainage, Male Reproductive
System 0V9
—see Inspection, Male Reproductive System 0VJ
Orchotomy
—see Drainage, Male Reproductive System
0V9
—see Inspection, Male Reproductive System
0VJ
Ossiculectomy
—see Excision, Ear, Nose, Sinus 09B
—see Resection, Ear, Nose, Sinus 09T
Ossiculotomy
—see Drainage, Ear, Nose, Sinus 099
—see Inspection, Ear, Nose, Sinus 09J
Ostectomy—see Excision, Head and Facial
Bones 0NB
—see Excision, Lower Bones 0QB
—see Excision, Upper Bones 0PB
—see Resection, Head and Facial Bones 0NT
—see Resection, Lower Bones 0QT
—see Resection, Upper Bones 0PT
Osteoclasis—see Division, Head and Facial
Bones 0N8
—see Division, Lower Bones 0Q8
—see Division, Upper Bones 0P8
Osteolysis—see Release, Head and Facial Bones
0NN
—see Release, Lower Bones 0QN
—see Release, Upper Bones 0PN
Osteopathic—see Treatment
Osteopexy
—see Repair, Head and Facial Bones 0NQ
—see Repair, Lower Bones 0QQ
—see Repair, Upper Bones 0PQ
—see Reposition, Head and Facial Bones
0NS
—see Reposition, Lower Bones 0QS
—see Reposition, Upper Bones 0PS
Osteoplasty
—see Repair, Head and Facial Bones 0NQ
—see Repair, Lower Bones 0QQ
—see Repair, Upper Bones 0PQ
—see Replacement, Head and Facial Bones
0NR
—see Replacement, Lower Bones 0QR
Osteoplasty
—see Replacement, Upper Bones 0PR
Osteorrhaphy
—see Repair, Head and Facial Bones 0NQ
—see Repair, Lower Bones 0QQ
—see Repair, Upper Bones 0PQ
Osteotomy
—see Division, Head and Facial Bones 0N8
—see Division, Lower Bones 0Q8
—see Division, Upper Bones 0P8
—see Drainage, Head and Facial Bones 0N9
—see Drainage, Lower Bones 0Q9
—see Drainage, Upper Bones 0P9
—see Inspection, Head and Facial Bones 0NJ
—see Inspection, Lower Bones 0QJ
—see Inspection, Upper Bones 0PJ
Ostotomy
—see Division, Head and Facial Bones 0N8
—see Division, Lower Bones 0Q8
—see Division, Upper Bones 0P8
—see Drainage, Head and Facial Bones 0N9
—see Drainage, Lower Bones 0Q9
—see Drainage, Upper Bones 0P9
—see Inspection, Head and Facial Bones 0NJ
—see Inspection, Lower Bones 0QJ
—see Inspection, Upper Bones 0PJ
Other Method
8E01
8E09
8E0H

Other Method—continued
8E0K
8E0U
8E0W
8E0X
8E0Y
8E0Z
Other Procedures
by Body Region
Circulatory System 8E02
Female Reproductive System 8E0U
Head and Neck Region 8E09
Integumentary System and Breast 8E0H
Lower Extremity 8E0Y
Male Reproductive System 8E0V
Musculoskeletal System 8E0K
Nervous System 8E01
None 8E0Z
Trunk Region 8E0W
Upper Extremity 8E0X
by Method
Acupuncture
Acupuncture 8E0H
Collection
Collection 8E0H
Collection 8E0V
Computer Assisted Procedure
Computer Assisted Procedure 8E09
Computer Assisted Procedure 8E0W
Computer Assisted Procedure 8E0X
Computer Assisted Procedure 8E0Y
Near Infrared Spectroscopy
Near Infrared Spectroscopy 8E02
Other Method
Other Method 8E01
Other Method 8E09
Other Method 8E0H
Other Method 8E0K
Other Method 8E0U
Other Method 8E0W
Other Method 8E0X
Other Method 8E0Y
Other Method 8E0Z
Robotic Assisted Procedure
Robotic Assisted Procedure 8E09
Robotic Assisted Procedure 8E0W
Robotic Assisted Procedure 8E0X
Robotic Assisted Procedure 8E0Y
Therapeutic Massage
Therapeutic Massage 8E0K
Therapeutic Massage 8E0V
Other Procedures—see Other Procedures
Other Radiation
by Body System
Anatomical Regions DWY
Breast DMY
Central and Peripheral Nervous System
D0Y
Ear, Nose, Mouth and Throat D9Y
Endocrine System DGY
Eye D8Y
Female Reproductive System DUY
Gastrointestinal System DDY
Hepatobiliary System and Pancreas DFY
Lymphatic and Hematologic System D7Y
Male Reproductive System DVY
Musculoskeletal System DPY
Respiratory System DBY
Skin DHY
Urinary System DTY
by Body Part
Abdomen DWY3
Adrenal Glands DGY2
Anus DDY8
Bile Ducts DFY2
Bladder DTY2

Other Radiation—continued
by Body Part—continued
Bones, Pelvic DPY0
Brain Stem D0Y1
Breast DMY
Bronchus DBY1
Cervix DUY1
Chest DWY2
Chest Wall DBY7
Colon DDY5
Diaphragm DBY8
Ducts, Bile DFY0
Duodenum DDY2
Esophagus DDY0
Eye D8Y0
Femur DPY9
Gallbladder DFY1
Glands, Parathyroid DGY0
Hard Palate D9Y8
Hemibody DWY4
Humerus DPY6
Hypopharynx D9Y3
Ileum DDY4
Jejunum DDY3
Kidney DTY0
Larynx D9YB
Lung DBY2
Lymphatics
Abdomen D7Y6
Axillary D7Y4
Inguinal D7Y8
Neck D7Y3
Pelvis D7Y7
Thorax D7Y5
Mandible DPY3
Marrow, Bone D7Y0
Maxilla DPY2
Mediastinum DBY6
Mouth D9Y4
Nasopharynx D9YD
Nerve, Peripheral D0Y0
Nose D9Y1
Oropharynx D9YF
Other Bone DPYC
Ovary DUY0
Palate, Soft D9Y0
Pancreas DFY3
Parathyroid Glands DGY4
Pelvic Bones DPY8
Pelvic Region DWY6
Peripheral Nerve D0Y7
Pharynx D9YC
Pineal Body DGY1
Pleura DBY5
Prostate DVY0
Radius/Ulna DPY7
Rectum DDY7
Region, Pelvic DWY1
Rib(s) DPY5
Salivary Glands D9Y6
Sinuses D9Y7
Skin
Abdomen DHY8
Arm DHY4
Back DHY7
Buttock DHY9
Chest DHY6
Face DHY2
Foot DHYC
Hand DHY5
Leg DHYB
Neck DHY3
Soft Palate D9Y9
Spinal Cord D0Y6
Spleen D7Y2
Sternum DPY4

Other Radiation—*continued*

  by Body Part—*continued*

    Stomach DDY1

    Testis DVY1

    Thymus D7Y1

    Thyroid DGY5

    Tibia/Fibula DPYB

    Tongue D9Y5

    Ureter DTY1

    Urethra DTY3

    Uterus DUY2

    Wall, Chest DBY0

    Whole Body DWY5

Otoplasty

  —*see* Repair, Ear, Nose, Sinus 09Q

  —*see* Replacement, Ear, Nose, Sinus 09R

Ovariectomy

  —*see* Excision, Female Reproductive System 0UB

  —*see* Resection, Female Reproductive System 0UT

Ovariocentesis—*see* Drainage, Female Reproductive System 0U9

Ovariopexy

  —*see* Repair, Female Reproductive System 0UQ

  —*see* Reposition, Female Reproductive System 0US

Ovariostomy—*see* Drainage, Female Reproductive System 0U9

Ovariotomy

  —*see* Drainage, Female Reproductive System 0U9

  —*see* Inspection, Female Reproductive System 0UJ

P

P.E.T.—*see* Positron Emission Tomographic (PET) Imaging

Packing

  by Body Region

    Abdominal Wall 2W43

    Anorectal 2Y43

    Back 2W45

    Chest Wall 2W44

    Ear 2Y42

    Face 2W41

    Female Genital Tract 2Y44

    Finger 2W4

    Foot 2W4

    Genital Tract, Female 2Y40

    Hand 2W4

    Inguinal Region 2W4

    Leg, Lower, Left 2W40

    Lower Arm 2W4

    Lower Extremity 2W4

    Lower Leg 2W4

    Nasal 2Y41

    Neck 2W42

    Thumb 2W4

    Toe 2W4

    Upper Arm 2W4

    Upper Extremity 2W4

    Upper Leg 2W4

    Urethra 2Y45

Palatoplasty

  —*see* Repair, Mouth and Throat 0CQ

  —*see* Replacement, Mouth and Throat 0CR

Palatorrhaphy—*see* Repair, Mouth and Throat 0CQ

Pancreatectomy

  —*see* Excision, Hepatobiliary System and Pancreas 0FB

Pancreatectomy—*continued*

  —*see* Resection, Hepatobiliary System and Pancreas 0FT

Pancreaticoduodenostomy—*see* Bypass, Hepatobiliary System and Pancreas 0F1

Pancreatolithotomy—*see* Extirpation, Hepatobiliary System and Pancreas 0FC

Pancreatotomy

  —*see* Drainage, Hepatobiliary System and Pancreas 0F9

  —*see* Inspection, Hepatobiliary System and Pancreas 0FJ

Panniculectomy

  —*see* Alteration, Anatomical Regions, General 0W0

  —*see* Excision, Anatomical Regions, General 0WB

Parathyroidectomy

  —*see* Excision, Endocrine System 0GB

  —*see* Resection, Endocrine System 0GT

Parenteral Nutrition, Total

  —*see* Administration, Physiological Systems And Anatomical Regions 3E0

Parotidectomy

  —*see* Excision, Mouth and Throat 0CB

  —*see* Resection, Mouth and Throat 0CT

Passage—*see* Insertion

Patellapexy

  —*see* Repair, Lower Bones 0QQ

  —*see* Reposition, Lower Bones 0QS

Patellaplasty

  —*see* Repair, Lower Bones 0QQ

  —*see* Replacement, Lower Bones 0QR

Patellectomy

  —*see* Excision, Lower Bones 0QB

  —*see* Resection, Lower Bones 0QT

PEEP 5A19

Penectomy

  —*see* Excision, Male Reproductive System 0VB

  —*see* Resection, Male Reproductive System 0VT

Percutaneous Transluminal Coronary Angioplasty

  —*see* Dilation, Heart and Great Vessels 027

Performance

  by Function

    Filtration

      Biliary 5A1C

      Urinary 5A1D

    Output

      Cardiac 5A12

    Oxygenation

      Circulatory 5A15

    Pacing

      Cardiac 5A12

    Ventilation

      Respiratory 5A19

Pericardiectomy

  —*see* Excision, Heart and Great Vessels 02B

  —*see* Resection, Heart and Great Vessels 02T

Pericardiolysis—*see* Release, Heart and Great Vessels 02N

Pericardioplasty

  —*see* Repair, Heart and Great Vessels 02Q

  —*see* Replacement, Heart and Great Vessels 02R

Pericardiorrhaphy—*see* Repair, Heart and Great Vessels 02Q

Pericardiotomy—*see* Inspection, Heart and Great Vessels 02J

Peripheral Parenteral Nutrition

  —*see* Administration, Physiological Systems And Anatomical Regions 3E0

Peritoneal Dialysis 3E1M

Peritoneocentesis—*see* Drainage, Gastrointestinal System 0D9

Peritoneoplasty

  —*see* Repair, Gastrointestinal System 0DQ

  —*see* Replacement, Gastrointestinal System 0DR

Peritoneoscopy—*see* Inspection, Gastrointestinal System 0DJ

Peritoneotomy

  —*see* Drainage, Gastrointestinal System 0D9

  —*see* Inspection, Gastrointestinal System 0DJ

Peritoneumectomy

  —*see* Excision, Gastrointestinal System 0DB

  —*see* Resection, Gastrointestinal System 0DT

Phacoemulsification-w IOL implant—*see* Replacement, Eye 08R

Phacoemulsification-w.o IOL implant—*see* Extraction, Eye 08D

Phalangectomy

  —*see* Excision, Lower Bones 0QB

  —*see* Excision, Upper Bones 0PB

  —*see* Resection, Lower Bones 0QT

  —*see* Resection, Upper Bones 0PT

Phallectomy

  —*see* Excision, Male Reproductive System 0VB

  —*see* Resection, Male Reproductive System 0VT

Phalloplasty

  —*see* Repair, Male Reproductive System 0VQ

  —*see* Replacement, Male Reproductive System 0VR

Phallotomy

  —*see* Drainage, Male Reproductive System 0V9

  —*see* Inspection, Male Reproductive System 0VJ

Pharmacotherapy

  by Type Qualifier

    Antabuse HZ93

    Bupropion HZ97

    Clonidine HZ96

    Levo-alpha-acetyl-methadol (LAAM) HZ92

    Methadone Maintenance HZ91

    Naloxone HZ95

    Naltrexone HZ94

    Nicotine Replacement HZ90

    Other Replacement Medication HZ99

    Psychiatric Medication HZ98

Pharyngoplasty

  —*see* Repair, Mouth and Throat 0CQ

  —*see* Replacement, Mouth and Throat 0CR

Pharyngorrhaphy—*see* Repair, Mouth and Throat 0CQ

Pharyngotomy

  —*see* Drainage, Mouth and Throat 0C9

  —*see* Inspection, Mouth and Throat 0CJ

Pheresis

  Circulatory 6A55

Phlebectomy

  —*see* Excision, Lower Veins 06B

  —*see* Excision, Upper Veins 05B

  —*see* Extraction, Lower Veins 06D

  —*see* Extraction, Upper Veins 05D

Phleborrhaphy

  —*see* Repair, Lower Veins 06Q

  —*see* Repair, Upper Veins 05Q

Phlebotomy
—*see* Drainage, Lower Veins 069
—*see* Drainage, Upper Veins 059
—*see* Inspection, Lower Veins 06J
—*see* Inspection, Upper Veins 05J

Phonocardiogram 4A02

Phototherapy
Circulatory 6A65
Skin 6A60

Phrenectomy—*see* Excision, Peripheral Nervous System 01B

Phrenemphraxis—*see* Destruction, Peripheral Nervous System 015

Phrenicectomy—*see* Excision, Peripheral Nervous System 01B

Phreniclasis—*see* Destruction, Peripheral Nervous System 015

Phrenicoexeresis—*see* Extraction, Peripheral Nervous System 01D

Phreniconeurectomy—*see* Excision, Peripheral Nervous System 01B

Phrenicotomy —*see* Division, Peripheral Nervous System 018

Phrenicotripsy—*see* Destruction, Peripheral Nervous System 015

Phrenoplasty—*see* Repair, Respiratory System 0BQ

Phrenotomy
—*see* Drainage, Respiratory System 0B9
—*see* Inspection, Respiratory System 0BJ

Physiatry—*see* Physical Rehabilitation and Diagnostic Audiology

Physical Medicine—*see* Physical Rehabilitation and Diagnostic Audiology

Physical Rehabilitation and Diagnostic Audiology
—*see* Diagnostic Audiology
—*see* Rehabilitation

Physical Therapy—*see* Physical Rehabilitation and Diagnostic Audiology

Pinealectomy
—*see* Excision, Endocrine System 0GB
—*see* Resection, Endocrine System 0GT

Pinealoscopy—*see* Inspection, Endocrine System 0GJ

Pinealotomy
—*see* Drainage, Endocrine System 0G9
—*see* Inspection, Endocrine System 0GJ

Pituitectomy
—*see* Excision, Endocrine System 0GB
—*see* Resection, Endocrine System 0GT

Placement
—*see* Change
—*see* Compression
—*see* Dressing
—*see* Immobilization
—*see* Packing
—*see* Removal
—*see* Traction

Plain Film—*see* Plain Radiography

Plain Radiography
by Body System
Anatomical Regions BW0
Axial Skeleton, Except Skull and Facial Bones BR0
Central Nervous System B00
Ear, Nose, Mouth and Throat B90
Eye B80
Female Reproductive System BU0
Heart B20
Hepatobiliary System and Pancreas BF0
Lower Arteries B40
Lymphatic System B70
Male Reproductive System BV0

Plain Radiography—*continued*
by Body System—*continued*
Non-Axial Lower Bones BQ0
Non-Axial Upper Bones BP0
Respiratory System BB0
Skin, Subcutaneous Tissue and Breast BH0
Skull and Facial Bones BN0
Upper Arteries B30
Urinary System BT0
Veins B50
by Body Part
Abdomen and Pelvis BW01
Abdominal/Retroperitoneal Lymphatics, Bilateral B701
Acromioclavicular Joints, Bilateral BP03
Airways, Upper BB0D
Ankle BQ0
Aorta and Bilateral Lower Extremity Arteries B40D
Arches, Zygomatic, Bilateral BN00
Arm, Upper, Left BP00
Artery, Pulmonary, Left B300
Artery Transplant, Renal B400
Bladder BT00
Bladder and Urethra BT0B
Brachiocephalic-Subclavian Artery, Right B301
Breast BH0
Breasts, Bilateral BH02
Bypass Graft
Internal Mammary, Left B200
Other B20F
Calcaneus BQ0
Cerebral and Cerebellar Veins B501
Cervical Facet Joint(s) BR04
Cervico-Cerebral Arch B30Q
Chest BW03
Clavicle BP0
Common Carotid Arteries, Bilateral B305
Common Carotid Artery B30
Cord, Spinal B00B
Coronary Arteries, Multiple B201
Coronary Artery Bypass Graft, Single B202
Coronary Artery Bypass Grafts, Multiple B203
Corpora Cavernosa BV00
Dialysis Shunt/Fistula B50W
Ducts
Lacrimal, Bilateral B800
Mammary, Multiple, Left BH03
Elbow BP0
Epididymis BV0
External Carotid Arteries, Bilateral B30C
External Carotid Artery B30
Extremity, Upper BW00
Eye B80
Eyes, Bilateral B807
Facial Bones BN05
Fallopian Tube, Left BU01
Fallopian Tubes, Bilateral BU02
Femur BQ0
Finger(s) BP0
Foot BQ0
Foot/Toe Joint BQ0
Foramina, Optic, Left B803
Forearm BP0
Gallbladder and Bile Ducts BF03
Glands, Salivary, Bilateral B904
Hand BP0
Hand/Finger Joint BP0
Heart B20
Hepatic Artery B402
Hepatobiliary System, All BF0C
Hip BQ0

Plain Radiography—*continued*
by Body Part—*continued*
Humerus BP0
Ileal Diversion Loop BT0C
Inferior Mesenteric Artery B405
Inferior Vena Cava B509
Intercostal and Bronchial Arteries B30L
Internal Carotid Arteries, Bilateral B308
Internal Carotid Artery B30
Internal Mammary Bypass Graft B20
Intra-Abdominal Arteries, Other B40B
Intracranial Arteries B30R
Intracranial Sinuses B502
Joint, Lumbosacral BR08
Joints
Sacroiliac BR01
Temporomandibular, Bilateral BN07
Jugular Veins B50
Kidney BT0
Kidneys
Bilateral BT03
Ureters and Bladder BT04
Knee BQ0
Lacrimal Duct, Left B801
Lacrimal Ducts, Bilateral B802
Leg, Lower, Left BQ0D
Long Bones, All BW0B
Lower Arteries, Other B40J
Lower Extremity BW0C
Lower Extremity Arteries B40
Lower Extremity Lymphatics B70
Lower Extremity Veins B50
Lower Leg, Left BQ0F
Lumbar Arteries B409
Lumbar Disc(s) BR03
Lumbar Facet Joint(s) BR06
Lumbar Spine BR09
Lumbosacral Joint BR0B
Lymphatics
Head and Neck B704
Lymphatics
Lower Extremity, Bilateral B700
Pelvic B70C
Mandible BN06
Mastoids B90H
Multiple Mammary Ducts BH0
Nasal Bones BN04
Nasopharynx/Oropharynx B90F
Optic Foramina, Left B804
Orbit BN0
Orbits, Bilateral BN03
Paranasal Sinuses B902
Parotid Gland, Left B905
Parotid Glands, Bilateral B906
Patella BQ0
Pelvic (Iliac) Veins B50
Pelvic Arteries B40C
Pelvis BR0C
Portal and Splanchnic Veins B50T
Prostate BV03
Pulmonary Artery B30
Pulmonary Vein B50
Pulmonary Veins, Bilateral B50S
Renal Arteries, Bilateral B408
Renal Artery B40
Renal Artery Transplant B40M
Renal Vein B50
Renal Veins, Bilateral B50L
Ribs BP0
Sacroiliac Joints BR0D
Sacrum and Coccyx BR0F
Salivary Gland B90
Salivary Glands, Bilateral B90D
Scapula BP0
Shoulder BP0

Plain Radiography—*continued*
  by Body Part—*continued*
    Single Mammary Duct, Left BH04
    Spinal Arteries B30M
    Spine, Lumbar BR00
    Splenic Arteries B403
    Sternoclavicular Joint, Left BP01
    Sternoclavicular Joints, Bilateral BP02
    Sternum BR0H
    Subclavian Artery, Left B302
    Subclavian Vein B50
    Submandibular Gland B90
    Submandibular Glands, Bilateral B909
    Superior Mesenteric Artery B404
    Superior Vena Cava B508
    System, Hepatobiliary, All BF00
    Teeth
      All BN0J
      Multiple BN0H
    Temporomandibular Joint, Left BN08
    Temporomandibular Joints, Bilateral BN09
    Testicle BV0
    Thoracic Disc(s) BR02
    Thoracic Facet Joint(s) BR05
    Thoracic Spine BR07
    Thoraco-Abdominal Aorta B30P
    Toe(s) BQ0
    Tooth, Single BN0G
    Tracheobronchial Tree, Left BB08
    Tracheobronchial Trees, Bilateral BB09
    Trees, Tracheobronchial, Bilateral BB07
    Tubes, Fallopian, Bilateral BU00
    Upper Arm BP0
    Upper Arteries, Other B30N
    Upper Extremity BW0J
    Upper Extremity Arteries B30
    Upper Extremity Lymphatics B70
    Upper Extremity Veins B50
    Ureter BT0
    Ureters, Bilateral BT08
    Urethra BT05
    Uterus BU06
    Uterus and Fallopian Tubes BU08
    Vagina BU09
    Vasa Vasorum BV08
    Veins
      Other B50V
      Pulmonary, Bilateral B500
    Vertebral Arteries, Bilateral B30G
    Vertebral Artery B30
    Whole Body BW0K
      Infant BW0M
    Whole Skeleton BW0L
    Whole Spine BR0G
    Wrist BP0
    Zygomatic Arch BN0
    Zygomatic Arches, Bilateral BN0D
Plain Radiology—*see* Plain Radiography
Planar Nuclear Medicine Imaging
  by Body System
    Anatomical Regions CW1
    Central Nervous System C01
    Ear, Nose, Mouth and Throat C91
    Endocrine System CG1
    Eye C81
    Gastrointestinal System CD1
    Heart C21
    Hepatobiliary System and Pancreas CF1
    Lymphatic and Hematologic System C71
    Male Reproductive System CV1
    Musculoskeletal System CP1
    Respiratory System CB1
    Skin, Subcutaneous Tissue and Breast CH1
    Urinary System CT1
    Veins C51

Planar Nuclear Medicine Imaging—
  continued
  by Body Part
    Abdomen and Pelvis CW11
    Anatomical Region, Other CW1Z
    Anatomical Regions, Multiple CW1Y
    Bladder and Ureters CT1H
    Blood C713
    Brain C010
    Breast CH1
    Breasts, Bilateral CH12
    Central Nervous System C01Y
    Central Veins C51R
    Cerebrospinal Fluid C015
    Chest CW13
    Chest and Abdomen CW14
    Chest and Neck CW16
    Digestive System CD1Y
    Ducts, Lacrimal, Bilateral C819
    Ear, Nose, Mouth and Throat C91Y
    Extremities, Lower, Bilateral CP11
    Extremity, Upper CW10
    Eye C81Y
    Gastrointestinal Tract CD17
    Gland, Thyroid CG12
    Glands
      Adrenal, Bilateral CG14
      Parathyroid CG11
      Salivary, Bilateral C91B
    Head and Neck CW1B
    Heart C21Y
      Right and Left C216
    Hepatobiliary System, All CF1C
    Hepatobiliary System and Pancreas CF1Y
    Kidneys, Ureters and Bladder CT13
    Liver CF15
    Liver and Spleen CF16
    Lower Extremities, Bilateral CP1F
    Lower Extremity CP1, CW1D
    Lower Extremity Veins
      Bilateral C51D
      Left C51C
    Lungs and Bronchi CB12
    Lymphatic and Hematologic System C71Y
    Lymphatics
      Head C71J
      Head and Neck C715
      Lower Extremity C71P
      Neck C71K
      Pelvic C71D
      Trunk C71M
      Upper Chest C71L
      Upper Extremity C71N
    Marrow, Bone C710
    Musculoskeletal System
      All CP1Z
      Other CP1Y
    Myocardium C21G
    Pelvic Region CW1J
    Pelvis CP16
    Reproductive System, Male CV1Y
    Skin, Subcutaneous Tissue and Breast
      CH1Y
    Spine CP15
    Spine and Pelvis CP17
    Spleen C712
    System
      Endocrine CG1Y
    System
      Hepatobiliary, All CF14
      Respiratory CB1Y
    Testicles, Bilateral CV19
    Thorax CP14
    Tract, Gastrointestinal CD15
    Upper Extremities, Bilateral CP1B
    Upper Extremity CP1, CW1M

Planar Nuclear Medicine Imaging—
  continued
  by Body Part—*continued*
    Upper Extremity Veins C51
    Urinary System CT1Y
    Veins C51Y
      Upper Extremity, Bilateral C51B
    Whole Body CW1N
Pleurectomy
  —*see* Excision, Respiratory System 0BB
  —*see* Resection, Respiratory System 0BT
Pleurocentesis—*see* Drainage, Anatomical
  Regions, General 0W9
Pleurolysis—*see* Release, Respiratory System
  0BN
Pleuroparietopexy—*see* Repair, Respiratory
  System 0BQ
Pleuropexy—*see* Repair, Respiratory System
  0BQ
Pleuroscopy—*see* Inspection, Respiratory
  System 0BJ
Pleurotomy
  —*see* Drainage, Respiratory System 0B9
  —*see* Inspection, Respiratory System 0BJ
Plicate—*see* Restriction
Plication—*see* Restriction
Pneumectomy
  —*see* Excision, Respiratory System 0BB
  —*see* Resection, Respiratory System 0BT
Pneumocentesis—*see* Drainage, Respiratory
  System 0B9
Pneumolysis—*see* Release, Respiratory System
  0BN
Pneumonectomy—*see* Resection, Respiratory
  System 0BT
Pneumonolysis—*see* Release, Respiratory
  System 0BN
Pneumonopexy
  —*see* Repair, Respiratory System 0BQ
  —*see* Reposition, Respiratory System 0BS
Pneumonorrhaphy —*see* Repair, Respiratory
  System 0BQ
Pneumonotomy—*see* Drainage, Respiratory
  System 0B9
Pneumotomy—*see* Drainage, Respiratory
  System 0B9
Positive End Expiratory Pressure 5A19
Positron Emission Tomographic (PET)
    Imaging
  by Body System
    Anatomical Regions CW3
    Central Nervous System C03
    Heart C23
    Respiratory System CB3
  by Body Part
    Brain C030
    Central Nervous System C03Y
    Heart C23Y
    Lungs and Bronchi CB32
    Myocardium C23G
    System, Respiratory CB3Y
    Whole Body CW3N
Positron Emission Tomography—*see*
    Positron Emission Tomographic (PET)
    Imaging
PPN—*see* Administration, Physiological
    Systems And Anatomical Regions 3E0
Preputiotomy
  —*see* Drainage, Male Reproductive System
    0V9
  —*see* Inspection, Male Reproductive System
    0VJ
Pressure Support Ventilation 5A19

     Codes provided in the index are incomplete. Refer to tables to determine additional character values.   © 2009 Ingenix, Inc.

Proctectomy
—see Excision, Gastrointestinal System 0DB
—see Resection, Gastrointestinal System 0DT
Procteurysis—see Dilation, Gastrointestinal System 0D7
Proctococcypexy—see Repair, Gastrointestinal System 0DQ
Proctocolectomy
—see Excision, Gastrointestinal System 0DB
—see Resection, Gastrointestinal System 0DT
Proctocolpoplasty
—see Repair, Gastrointestinal System 0DQ
—see Replacement, Gastrointestinal System 0DR
Proctoperineoplasty
—see Repair, Gastrointestinal System 0DQ
—see Replacement, Gastrointestinal System 0DR
Proctoperineorrhaphy—see Repair, Gastrointestinal System 0DQ
Proctopexy
—see Repair, Gastrointestinal System 0DQ
—see Reposition, Gastrointestinal System 0DS
Proctoplasty
—see Repair, Gastrointestinal System 0DQ
—see Replacement, Gastrointestinal System 0DR
Proctorrhaphy—see Repair, Gastrointestinal System 0DQ
Proctoscopy—see Inspection, Gastrointestinal System 0DJ
Proctosigmoidectomy
—see Excision, Gastrointestinal System 0DB
—see Resection, Gastrointestinal System 0DT
Proctosigmoidopexy—see Repair, Gastrointestinal System 0DQ
Proctosigmoidoscopy—see Inspection, Gastrointestinal System 0DJ
Proctotomy
—see Drainage, Gastrointestinal System 0D9
—see Inspection, Gastrointestinal System 0DJ
Prostatectomy
—see Excision, Male Reproductive System 0VB
—see Resection, Male Reproductive System 0VT
Prostatomy
—see Drainage, Male Reproductive System 0V9
—see Inspection, Male Reproductive System 0VJ
Prostatotomy
—see Drainage, Male Reproductive System 0V9
Prostatotomy—see Inspection, Male Reproductive System 0VJ
PSV 5A19
Psychological Tests
by Type Qualifier
Developmental GZ10
Intellectual and Psychoeducational GZ12
Neurobehavioral and Cognitive Status GZ14
Neuropsychological GZ13
Personality and Behavioral GZ11
PTCA—see Dilation, Heart and Great Vessels 027
Pull—see Extraction
Pulmonary Artery Wedge Monitoring 4A13
Pulverization—see Fragmentation
Punch—see Excision
Puncture—see Drainage

Pyelography
—see Fluoroscopy, Urinary System BT1
—see Plain Radiography, Urinary System BT0
Pyeloplasty
—see Repair, Urinary System 0TQ
—see Replacement, Urinary System 0TR
Pyelorrhaphy—see Repair, Urinary System 0TQ
Pyeloscopy—see Inspection, Urinary System 0TJ
Pyelotomy
—see Drainage, Urinary System 0T9
—see Inspection, Urinary System 0TJ
Pylorectomy
—see Excision, Gastrointestinal System 0DB
—see Resection, Gastrointestinal System 0DT
Pylorodiosis—see Dilation, Gastrointestinal System 0D7
Pylorogastrectomy
—see Excision, Gastrointestinal System 0DB
—see Resection, Gastrointestinal System 0DT
Pyloromyotomy—see Division, Gastrointestinal System 0D8
Pyloroplasty
—see Repair, Gastrointestinal System 0DQ
—see Replacement, Gastrointestinal System 0DR
Pyloroscopy—see Inspection, Gastrointestinal System 0DJ
Pylorostomy—see Bypass, Gastrointestinal System 0D1
Pylorotomy
—see Drainage, Gastrointestinal System 0D9
—see Inspection, Gastrointestinal System 0DJ

R

Radiation—see Radiation Oncology
Radiation Oncology
—see Beam Radiation
—see Brachytherapy
—see Other Radiation
—see Stereotactic Radiosurgery
Radiation Therapy—see Radiation Oncology
Radiation Treatment—see Radiation Oncology
Radiography—see Imaging
Radiography, Analog—see Plain Radiography
Radiography, Digital, Plain—see Plain Radiography
Radiology—see Imaging
Radiology, Analog—see Plain Radiography
Radiology, Plain—see Plain Radiography
Reattachment
by Body System
Anatomical Regions, General 0WM
Anatomical Regions, Lower Extremities 0YM
Anatomical Regions, Upper Extremities 0XM
Bursae and Ligaments 0MM
Ear, Nose, Sinus 09M
Endocrine System 0GM
Eye 08M
Female Reproductive System 0UM
Gastrointestinal System 0DM
Hepatobiliary System and Pancreas 0FM
Male Reproductive System 0VM
Mouth and Throat 0CM
Muscles 0KM
Respiratory System 0BM
Skin and Breast 0HM
Tendons 0LM
Urinary System 0TM

Reattachment—continued
by Body Part
1st Toe 0YM
2nd Toe 0YM
3rd Toe 0YM
4th Toe 0YM
5th Toe 0YM
Abdomen Bursa and Ligament 0MM
Abdomen Muscle 0KM
Abdomen Tendon 0LM
Abdominal Wall 0WMF
Adrenal Gland, Right 0GM3
Ampulla of Vater 0FMC
Ankle Bursa and Ligament 0MM
Ankle Region 0YM
Ankle Tendon 0LM
Areola 0HM
Ascending Colon 0DMK
Axilla 0XM
Back, Lower 0WM2
Bladder 0TMB
Bladder Neck 0TMC
Breast 0HM
Bronchus, Segmental, Lingula 0BM9
Bursa and Ligament, Lower Extremity, Left 0MM0
Buttock, Left 0YM1
Carina 0BM2
Cecum 0DMH
Cervix 0UMC
Chest Wall 0WM8
Clitoris 0UMJ
Colon, Sigmoid 0DM5
Common Bile Duct 0FM9
Cord, Spermatic, Bilateral 0VM6
Cul-de-sac 0UMF
Cystic Duct 0FM8
Descending Colon 0DMM
Diaphragm 0BM
Duct, Pancreatic, Accessory 0FM0
Duodenum 0DM9
Ear, External, Left 09M0
Elbow Bursa and Ligament 0MM
Elbow Region 0XM
External Ear, Left 09M1
Eyelid, Lower, Left 08MN
Facial Muscle 0KM1
Fallopian Tube 0UM
Fallopian Tubes, Bilateral 0UM7
Femoral Region 0YM
Finger, Little, Left 0XM0
Foot 0YM
Foot Bursa and Ligament 0MM
Foot Muscle 0KM
Foot Tendon 0LM
Forequarter, Left 0XM1
Gallbladder 0FM4
Gland
Lower Parathyroid 0GM
Mammary 0HM
Parathyroid 0GM2
Upper Parathyroid 0GM
Hand 0XM
Hand Bursa and Ligament 0MM
Hand Muscle 0KM
Hand Tendon 0LM
Hepatic Duct 0FM
Hindquarter 0YM
Hip Bursa and Ligament 0MM
Hip Muscle 0KM
Hip Tendon 0LM
Hymen 0UMK
Ileum 0DMB
Index Finger 0XM
Inferior Parathyroid Gland 0GM
Inguinal Region 0YM

Reattachment—*continued*
  by Body Part—*continued*
    Jejunum 0DMA
    Kidney, Left 0TM1
    Kidney Pelvis 0TM
    Kidneys, Bilateral 0TM2
    Knee Bursa and Ligament 0MM
    Knee Region 0YM
    Knee Tendon 0LM
    Large Intestine 0DM
    Lingula Bronchus 0BM9
    Little Finger 0XM
    Liver
        Left Lobe 0FM2
        Right Lobe 0FM1
    Lobe, Lower Lung, Left 0BM1
    Lobe Segmental Bronchus
        Lower 0BM
        Middle, Right 0BM5
        Upper 0BM
    Lower Arm 0XM
    Lower Arm and Wrist Muscle 0KM
    Lower Arm and Wrist Tendon 0LM
    Lower Back 0WML
    Lower Extremity 0YM
    Lower Extremity Bursa and Ligament 0MM
    Lower Eyelid 08M
    Lower Jaw 0WM5
    Lower Leg 0YM
    Lower Leg Muscle 0KM
    Lower Leg Tendon 0LM
    Lower Lip 0CM1
    Lower Lobe Bronchus 0BM
    Lower Lung Lobe 0BM
    Lower Tooth 0CMX
    Lung 0BM
    Lung Lingula 0BMH
    Lung Lingula Segments 0BMH
    Lung Lobe Segments
        Lower 0BM
        Middle, Right 0BMD
        Upper 0BM
    Main Bronchus 0BM
    Middle Finger 0XM
    Middle Lobe Bronchus, Right 0BM5
    Middle Lung Lobe, Right 0BMD
    Muscle, Foot, Left 0KM0
    Neck 0WM6
        Bladder 0TM0
    Neck Muscle 0KM
    Nipple 0HM
    Nose 09MK
    Ovaries, Bilateral 0UM2
    Ovary, Left 0UM1
    Palate, Soft 0CM0
    Pancreas 0FMG
        Body 0FMF
        Head 0FMF
        Tail 0FMF
    Pancreatic Duct 0FMD
        Accessory 0FMF
    Parathyroid Gland 0GMR
    Parathyroid Glands, Multiple 0GMQ
    Penis 0VMS
    Perineum
        Female 0WMN
        Male 0WMM
    Perineum Bursa and Ligament 0MMK
    Perineum Muscle 0KMM
    Perineum Tendon 0LMH
    Pulmonary Lingula 0BMH
    Pulmonary Lobe
        Lower 0BM
        Middle, Right 0BMD
        Upper 0BM
    Rectum 0DMP

Reattachment—*continued*
  by Body Part—*continued*
    Renal Pelvis 0TM
    Ring Finger 0XM
    Scrotum 0VM5
    Shoulder Bursa and Ligament 0MM
    Shoulder Muscle 0KM
    Shoulder Region 0XM
    Shoulder Tendon 0LM
    Sigmoid Colon 0DMN
    Skin
        Abdomen 0HM7
        Back 0HM6
        Buttock 0HM8
        Chest 0HM5
        Face 0HM1
        Foot, Left 0HM0
        Genitalia 0HMA
        Left Ear 0HM3
        Left Foot 0HMN
        Left Hand 0HMG
        Left Lower Arm 0HME
        Left Lower Leg 0HML
        Left Upper Arm 0HMC
        Left Upper Leg 0HMJ
        Neck 0HM4
        Perineum 0HM9
        Right Ear 0HM2
        Right Foot 0HMM
        Right Hand 0HMF
        Right Lower Arm 0HMD
        Right Lower Leg 0HMK
        Right Upper Arm 0HMB
        Right Upper Leg 0HMH
    Small Intestine 0DM8
    Soft Palate 0CM3
    Spermatic Cord 0VM
    Spermatic Cords, Bilateral 0VMH
    Stomach 0DM6
        Body 0DM6
        Fundus 0DM6
    Superior Parathyroid Gland 0GM
    Tendon, Foot, Left 0LM0
    Testes, Bilateral 0VMC
    Testis 0VM
    Thorax Bursa and Ligament 0MM
    Thorax Muscle 0KM
    Thorax Tendon 0LM
    Thumb 0XM
    Thyroid Gland Lobe 0GM
    Toe, 5th, Left 0YM0
    Tongue 0CM7
        Palate, Pharynx Muscle 0KM4
    Tooth, Lower 0CMW
    Transverse Colon 0DML
    Trunk Bursa and Ligament 0MM
    Trunk Muscle 0KM
    Trunk Tendon 0LM
    Tube, Fallopian, Bilateral 0UM0
    Tunica Vaginalis, Left 0VM7
    Upper Arm 0XM
    Upper Arm Muscle 0KM
    Upper Arm Tendon 0LM
    Upper Back 0WMK
    Upper Extremity 0XM
    Upper Extremity Bursa and Ligament 0MM
    Upper Eyelid, Left 08MP
    Upper Jaw 0WM4
    Upper Leg 0YM
    Upper Leg Muscle 0KM
    Upper Leg Tendon 0LM
    Upper Lobe Bronchus 0BM
    Upper Lung Lobe 0BM
    Ureter 0TM
    Ureters, Bilateral 0TM8

Reattachment—*continued*
  by Body Part—*continued*
    Urethra 0TMD
    Uterine Supporting Structure 0UM4
    Uterus 0UM9
    Uvula 0CMN
    Vagina 0UMG
    Vulva 0UMM
    Wrist Bursa and Ligament 0MM
    Wrist Region 0XM
Rectectomy
  —*see* Excision, Gastrointestinal System 0DB
  —*see* Resection, Gastrointestinal System 0DT
Rectococcypexy—*see* Repair, Gastrointestinal System 0DQ
Rectomanoscopy—*see* Inspection, Gastrointestinal System 0DJ
Rectoperineorrhaphy—*see* Repair, Gastrointestinal System 0DQ
Rectopexy
  —*see* Repair, Gastrointestinal System 0DQ
  —*see* Reposition, Gastrointestinal System 0DS
Rectoplasty
  —*see* Repair, Gastrointestinal System 0DQ
  —*see* Replacement, Gastrointestinal System 0DR
Rectorrhaphy—*see* Repair, Gastrointestinal System 0DQ
Rectoscopy—*see* Inspection, Gastrointestinal System 0DJ
Rectosigmoidectomy
  —*see* Excision, Gastrointestinal System 0DB
  —*see* Resection, Gastrointestinal System 0DT
Rectotomy
  —*see* Drainage, Gastrointestinal System 0D9
  —*see* Inspection, Gastrointestinal System 0DJ
Refusion—*see* Fusion
Rehabilitation
  by Type Qualifier
    Aerobic Capacity and Endurance F02
    Airway Clearance Techniques F0F
    Anthropometric Characteristics F02
    Aphasia F00
    Aphasia F06
    Application, Proper Use and Care of Assistive, Adaptive, Supportive or Protective Devices F0F
    Application, Proper Use and Care of Orthoses F0F
    Application, Proper Use and Care of Prosthesis F0F
    Articulation/Phonology F00
    Articulation/Phonology F06
    Assistive, Adaptive, Supportive or Protective Devices F0D
    Assistive Listening Device F0D
    Auditory Processing F09
    Augmentative/Alternative Communication System F00
    Augmentative/Alternative Communication System F0D
    Aural Rehabilitation F06
    Bathing/Showering F02
    Bathing/Showering Technique F0F
    Bathing/Showering Techniques F08
    Bed Mobility F01
    Bed Mobility F07
    Bed Mobility F0F
    Bedside Swallowing and Oral Function F00
    Binaural Hearing Aid F0D
    Brief Tone Stimuli F00
    Cerumen Management F09
    Cochlear Implant Rehabilitation F0B

Codes provided in the index are incomplete. Refer to tables to determine additional character values.   © 2009 Ingenix, Inc.

Rehabilitation—*continued*
  by Type Qualifier—*continued*
    Communication Skills F0F
    Communicative/Cognitive Integration
      Skills F00
    Communicative/Cognitive Integration
      Skills F06
    Coordination/Dexterity F01
    Coordination/Dexterity F07
    Cranial Nerve Integrity F02
    Dichotic Stimuli F00
    Distorted Speech F00
    Dressing F02
    Dressing F0F
    Dressing Techniques F08
    Dynamic Orthosis F0D
    Environmental, Home and Work Barriers
      F02
    Ergonomics and Body Mechanics F02
    Facial Nerve Function F01
    Feeding and Eating F0F
    Feeding/Eating F02
    Feeding/Eating F08
    Filtered Speech F00
    Fluency F00
    Fluency F06
    Gait and/or Balance F01
    Gait Training/Functional Ambulation F07
    Gait Training/Functional Ambulation F0F
    Grooming/Personal Hygiene F02
    Grooming/Personal Hygiene F08
    Grooming/Personal Hygiene F0F
    Hearing and Related Disorders
      Counseling F09
    Hearing and Related Disorders
      Prevention F09
    Home Management F02
    Home Management F08
    Home Management F0F
    Instrumental Swallowing and Oral
      Function F00
    Integumentary Integrity F01
    Manual Therapy Techniques F07
    Masking Patterns F00
    Monaural Hearing Aid F0D
    Motor Function F01
    Motor Function F07
    Motor Speech F00
    Motor Speech F06
    Muscle Performance F01
    Muscle Performance F07
    Neuromotor Development F02
    Neurophysiologic Intraoperative F01
    Non-invasive Instrumental Status F00
    Nonspoken Language F00
    Nonspoken Language F06
    Oral Peripheral Mechanism F00
    Orofacial Myofunctional F00
    Orofacial Myofunctional F06
    Other Specified Central Auditory
      Processing F00
    Pain F02
    Perceptual Processing F02
    Perceptual Processing F0C
    Performance Intensity Phonetically
      Balanced Speech Discrimination
      F00
    Postural Control F0C
    Prosthesis F0D
    Psychosocial Skills F02
    Psychosocial Skills F08
    Range of Motion and Joint Integrity F01
    Range of Motion and Joint Mobility F07
    Receptive/Expressive Language F00
    Receptive/Expressive Language F06
    Reflex Integrity F01

Rehabilitation—*continued*
  by Type Qualifier—*continued*
    Sensorineural Acuity Level F00
    Sensory Awareness/Processing/Integrity
      F01
    Somatosensory Evoked Potentials F01
    Speech and/or Language Screening F00
    Speech Threshold F00
    Speech-Language Pathology and Related
      Disorders Counseling F06
    Speech-Language Pathology and Related
      Disorders Prevention F06
    Speech/Word Recognition F00
    Staggered Spondaic Word F00
    Static Orthosis F0D
    Swallowing Dysfunction F06
    Synthetic Sentence Identification F00
    Temporal Ordering of Stimuli F00
    Therapeutic Exercise F07
    Therapeutic Exercise F0F
    Tinnitus Masker F0D
    Transfer F01
    Transfer F0F
    Transfer Training F07
    Ventilation, Respiration and Circulation
      F02
    Vestibular F0C
    Visual Motor Integration F01
    Visual Motor Integration F0C
    Vocational Activities and Functional
      Community or Work Reintegration
      Skills F02
    Vocational Activities and Functional
      Community or Work Reintegration
      Skills F08
    Vocational Activities and Functional
      Community or Work Reintegration
      Skills F0F
    Voice F00
    Voice F06
    Voice Prosthetic F00
    Voice Prosthetic F0D
    Wheelchair Mobility F01
    Wheelchair Mobility F07
    Wheelchair Mobility F0F
    Wound Management F08
    Wound Management F0F
Reinforcement—*see* Repair
Relaxation—*see* Release
Release
  by Body System
    Bursae and Ligaments 0MN
    Central Nervous System 00N
    Ear, Nose, Sinus 09N
    Endocrine System 0GN
    Eye 08N
    Female Reproductive System 0UN
    Gastrointestinal System 0DN
    Head and Facial Bones 0NN
    Heart and Great Vessels 02N
    Hepatobiliary System and Pancreas 0FN
    Lower Arteries 04N
    Lower Bones 0QN
    Lower Joints 0SN
    Lower Veins 06N
    Lymphatic and Hemic Systems 07N
    Male Reproductive System 0VN
    Mouth and Throat 0CN
    Muscles 0KN
    Peripheral Nervous System 01N
    Respiratory System 0BN
    Skin and Breast 0HN
    Subcutaneous Tissue and Fascia 0JN
    Tendons 0LN
    Upper Arteries 03N
    Upper Bones 0PN

Release—*continued*
  by Body System—*continued*
    Upper Joints 0RN
    Upper Veins 05N
    Urinary System 0TN
  by Body Part
    Abdomen Bursa and Ligament 0MN
    Abdomen Muscle 0KN
    Abdomen Tendon 0LN
    Abdominal Sympathetic Nerve 01NM
    Abducens Nerve 00NL
    Accessory Nerve 00NR
    Accessory Sinus 09NP
    Acetabulum 0QN
    Acoustic Nerve 00NN
    Acromioclavicular Joint 0RN
    Adenohypophysis 0GN0
    Adenoids 0CNQ
    Adrenal Gland 0GN
    Adrenal Glands, Bilateral 0GN4
    Ampulla of Vater 0FNC
    Ankle Bursa and Ligament 0MN
    Ankle Joint 0SN
    Ankle Tendon 0LN
    Anterior Chamber, Left 08N3
    Anterior Tibial Artery 04N
    Anus 0DNQ
    Aortic Body 0GND
    Aortic Valve 02NF
    Appendix 0DNJ
    Areola 0HN
    Artery
      Aorta, Thoracic 02N4
      Lower 04N0
      Upper 03N0
    Ascending Colon 0DNK
    Atrial Septum 02N5
    Atrium 02N
    Auditory Ossicle 09N
    Axillary Artery 03N
    Axillary Vein 05N
    Basal Ganglia 00N8
    Basilic Vein 05N
    Bladder 0TNB
    Bladder Neck 0TNC
    Body
      Coccygeal 0GN9
      Jugulotympanic 0GNB
    Bone, Hyoid 0NN1
    Brachial Artery 03N
    Brachial Plexus 01N3
    Brachial Vein 05N
    Breast 0HN
    Bronchus, Segmental, Lingula 0BN9
    Buccal Mucosa 0CN4
    Bursa and Ligament, Lower Extremity,
      Left 0MN0
    Canal, External Auditory, Left 09N3
    Carina 0BN2
    Carotid Bodies, Bilateral 0GN8
    Carotid Body 0GN
    Carpal 0PN
    Carpal Joint 0RN
    Cecum 0DNH
    Celiac Artery 04N1
    Cephalic Vein 05N
    Cerebellum 00NC
    Cerebral Hemisphere 00N7
    Cerebral Meninges 00N1
    Cerebral Ventricle 00N6
    Cervical Nerve 01N1
    Cervical Spinal Cord 00NW
    Cervical Vertebra 0PN3
    Cervical Vertebral Disc 0RN3
    Cervical Vertebral Joint 0RN1
    Cervicothoracic Vertebral Disc 0RN5

Release—*continued*
by Body Part—*continued*

Cervicothoracic Vertebral Joint 0RN4
Cervix 0UNC
Chordae Tendineae 02N9
Choroid, Left 08NB
Chyli, Cisterna 07N0
Cisterna Chyli 07NL
Clavicle 0PN
Coccygeal Glomus 0GNB
Coccygeal Joint 0SN6
Coccyx 0QNS
Colic Artery 04N
Colic Vein 06N7
Colon, Sigmoid 0DN1
Common Bile Duct 0FN9
Common Carotid Artery 03N
Common Iliac Artery 04N
Common Iliac Vein 06N
Conduction Mechanism 02N8
Conjunctiva 08N
Cord
    Lumbar Spinal 00N0
    Vocal, Left 0CNM
Cornea 08N
Corpora Arenacea, Pineal 0GN1
Cul-de-sac 0UNF
Cystic Duct 0FN8
Deferens, Vas, Bilateral 0VN1
Descending Colon 0DNM
Diaphragm 0BN
Duct
    Lacrimal, Left 08NX
    Pancreatic, Accessory 0FN5
Duodenum 0DN9
Dura Mater 00N2
Ear
    External, Left 09N0
    Inner, Left 09N5
Elbow Bursa and Ligament 0MN
Elbow Joint 0RN
Epididymis 0VN
Epiglottis 0CNR
Esophageal Vein 06N3
Esophagogastric Junction 0DN4
Esophagus 0DN5
    Lower 0DN3
    Middle 0DN2
Ethmoid Bone 0NN
Ethmoid Sinus 09N
Eustachian Tube 09N
External Auditory Canal, Left 09N4
External Carotid Artery 03N
External Ear, Left 09N1
External Iliac Artery 04N
External Iliac Vein 06N
External Jugular Vein 05N
Extraocular Muscle 08N
Eye 08N
Eyelid, Lower, Left 08NN
Face Artery 03NR
Face Vein 05N
Facial Muscle 0KN1
Facial Nerve 00NM
Fallopian Tube, Left 0UN6
Fallopian Tubes, Bilateral 0UN7
Femoral Artery 04N
Femoral Nerve 01ND
Femoral Shaft 0QN
Femoral Vein 06N
Fibula 0QN
Finger Nail 0HNQ
Finger Phalangeal Joint 0RN
Finger Phalanx 0PN
Foot Artery 04N
Foot Bursa and Ligament 0MN

Foot Muscle 0KN
Foot Tendon 0LN
Foot Vein 06N
Frontal Bone, Left 0NN2
Frontal Sinus 09N
Gallbladder 0FN4
Gastric Artery 04N2
Gastric Vein 06N2
Gingiva, Lower 0CN0
Gland
    Lacrimal, Left 08NA
    Lower Parathyroid 0GN
    Mammary 0HN
    Minor Salivary 0CN8
    Parathyroid 0GN0
    Pineal 0GN1
    Upper Parathyroid 0GN
    Vestibular 0UNJ
Glenoid Cavity 0PN
Glomus Jugulare 0GNC
Glossopharyngeal Nerve 00NP
Greater Omentum 0DNS
Greater Saphenous Vein 06N
Hand Artery 03N
Hand Bursa and Ligament 0MN
Hand Muscle 0KN
Hand Tendon 0LN
Hand Vein 05N
Hard Palate 0CN2
Head and Neck Sympathetic Nerve 01NK
Hemiazygos Vein 05N1
Hepatic Artery 04N3
Hepatic Duct, Left 0FN6
Hepatic Vein 06N4
Hip Bursa and Ligament 0MN
Hip Joint 0SN
Hip Muscle 0KN
Hip Tendon 0LN
Humeral Head 0PN
Humeral Shaft 0PN
Hymen 0UNK
Hyoid Bone 0NNX
Hypogastric Vein 06N
Hypoglossal Nerve 00NS
Hypophysis 0GN0
Hypothalamus 00NA
Ileocecal Valve 0DNC
Ileum 0DNB
Inferior Mesenteric Artery 04NB
Inferior Mesenteric Vein 06N6
Inferior Parathyroid Gland 0GN
Inner Ear 09N
Innominate Artery 03N2
Innominate Vein 05N
Internal Carotid Artery 03N
Internal Iliac Artery 04N
Internal Jugular Vein 05N
Internal Mammary Artery, Left 03N1
Intracranial Artery 03NG
Intracranial Vein 05NL
Iris 08N
Jejunum 0DNA
Joint
    Finger Phalangeal, Left 0RN0
    Toe Phalangeal, Left 0SN0
Kidney, Left 0TN1
Kidney Pelvis 0TN
Knee Bursa and Ligament 0MN
Knee Joint 0SN
Knee Tendon 0LN
Lacrimal Bone 0NN
Lacrimal Duct, Left 08NY
Lacrimal Gland 08N
Large Intestine 0DN

Larynx 0CNS
Lens 08N
Lesser Omentum 0DNT
Lesser Saphenous Vein 06N
Lingula Bronchus 0BN9
Liver 0FN0
    Left Lobe 0FN2
    Right Lobe 0FN1
Lobe Segmental Bronchus
    Lower 0BN
    Middle, Right 0BN5
    Upper 0BN
Lower Arm and Wrist Muscle 0KN
Lower Arm and Wrist Tendon 0LN
Lower Artery 04NY
Lower Extremity Bursa and Ligament 0MN
Lower Eyelid 08N
Lower Femur 0QN
Lower Gingiva 0CN6
Lower Leg Muscle 0KN
Lower Leg Tendon 0LN
Lower Lip 0CN1
Lower Lobe Bronchus 0BN
Lower Lung Lobe 0BN
Lower Tooth 0CNX
Lower Vein 06NY
Lumbar Nerve 01NB
Lumbar Plexus 01N9
Lumbar Spinal Cord 00NY
Lumbar Sympathetic Nerve 01NN
Lumbar Vertebral Disc 0SN2
Lumbosacral Disc 0SN4
Lumbosacral Joint 0SN3
Lumbosacral Plexus 01NA
Lung 0BN
Lung Lingula 0BNH
Lung Lingula Segments 0BNH
Lung Lobe Segments
    Lower 0BN
    Middle, Right 0BND
    Upper 0BN
Lungs, Bilateral 0BNM
Lymphatic
    Aortic 07ND
    Internal Mammary 07N
    Left Axillary 07N6
    Left Inguinal 07NJ
    Left Lower Extremity 07NG
    Left Neck 07N2
    Left Upper Extremity 07N4
    Mesenteric 07NB
    Pelvis 07NC
    Right Axillary 07N5
    Right Inguinal 07NH
    Right Lower Extremity 07NF
    Right Neck 07N1
    Right Upper Extremity 07N3
    Thorax 07N7
Main Bronchus 0BN
Mandible 0NN
Mastoid Sinus, Left 09NC
Maxilla 0NN
Maxillary Sinus 09N
Median Nerve 01N5
Medulla Oblongata 00ND
Mesentery 0DNV
Metacarpal 0PN
Metacarpocarpal Joint 0RN
Metacarpophalangeal Joint 0RN
Metatarsal 0QN
Metatarsal-Phalangeal Joint 0SN
Metatarsal-Tarsal Joint 0SN
Middle Ear, Left 09N6
Middle Lobe Bronchus, Right 0BN5

Release—*continued*
  by Body Part—*continued*
    Middle Lung Lobe, Right 0BND
    Minor Salivary Gland 0CNJ
    Mitral Valve 02NG
    Muscle, Foot, Left 0KN0
    Nail, Toe 0HN0
    Nail Bed
      Finger 0HNQ
      Toe 0HNR
    Nasal Bone 0NNB
    Nasal Septum 09NM
    Nasal Turbinate 09NL
    Nasopharynx 09NN
    Neck, Bladder 0TN0
    Neck Muscle 0KN
    Nerve, Sacral 01N0
    Neurohypophysis 0GN0
    Nipple 0HN
    Nose 09NK
    Occipital Bone 0NN
    Oculomotor Nerve 00NH
    Olfactory Nerve 00NF
    Omentum, Lesser 0DNR
    Optic Nerve 00NG
    Orbit 0NN
    Ovaries, Bilateral 0UN2
    Ovary, Left 0UN1
    Palatine Bone 0NN
    Pancreas 0FNG
      Body 0FNF
      Head 0FNF
      Tail 0FNF
    Pancreatic Duct 0FND
      Accessory 0FNF
    Papillary Muscle 02ND
    Para-aortic Body 0GN9
    Paraganglion Extremity 0GNF
    Parathyroid Gland 0GNR
    Parathyroid Glands, Multiple 0GNQ
    Parietal Bone 0NN
    Parotid Duct 0CN
    Parotid Gland, Left 0CN9
    Patella 0QN
    Pelvic Bone 0QN
    Penis 0VNS
    Pericardium 02NN
    Perineum Bursa and Ligament 0MNK
    Perineum Muscle 0KNM
    Perineum Tendon 0LNH
    Peritoneum 0DNW
    Peroneal Artery 04N
    Peroneal Nerve 01NH
    Phalanx
      Finger, Left 0PN0
      Toe, Left 0QN0
    Phrenic Nerve 01N2
    Pineal Body 0GN1
    Pleura 0BN
      Parietal 0BN
      Visceral 0BN
    Pons 00NB
    Popliteal Artery 04N
    Portal Vein 06N8
    Posterior Tibial Artery 04N
    Prepuce 0VNT
    Prostate 0VN0
    Pudendal Nerve 01NC
    Pulmonary Artery 02N
    Pulmonary Lingula 0BNH
    Pulmonary Lobe
      Lower 0BN
    Pulmonary Lobe
      Middle, Right 0BND
      Upper 0BN
    Pulmonary Trunk 02NP

Release—*continued*
  by Body Part—*continued*
    Pulmonary Valve 02NH
    Pulmonary Vein 02N
    Radial Artery 03N
    Radial Nerve 01N6
    Radius 0PN
    Rectum 0DNP
    Renal Artery 04N
    Renal Pelvis 0TN
    Renal Vein 06N
    Retina 08N
    Retinal Vessel 08N
    Rib 0PN
    Sacral Nerve 01NR
    Sacral Plexus 01NQ
    Sacral Sympathetic Nerve 01NP
    Sacrococcygeal Joint 0SN5
    Sacroiliac Joint 0SN
    Sacrum 0QN1
    Scapula 0PN
    Sciatic Nerve 01NF
    Sclera 08N
    Scrotum 0VN5
    Seminal Vesicle, Left 0VN2
    Seminal Vesicles, Bilateral 0VN3
    Shoulder Bursa and Ligament 0MN
    Shoulder Joint 0RN
    Shoulder Muscle 0KN
    Shoulder Tendon 0LN
    Sigmoid Colon 0DNN
    Sinus, Sphenoid, Left 09NB
    Skin
      Abdomen 0HN7
      Back 0HN6
      Buttock 0HN8
      Chest 0HN5
      Face 0HN1
      Genitalia 0HNA
      Left Ear 0HN3
      Left Foot 0HNN
      Left Hand 0HNG
      Left Lower Arm 0HNE
      Left Lower Leg 0HNL
      Left Upper Arm 0HNC
      Left Upper Leg 0HNJ
      Neck 0HN4
      Perineum 0HN9
      Right Ear 0HN2
      Right Foot 0HNM
      Right Hand 0HNF
      Right Lower Arm 0HND
      Right Lower Leg 0HNK
      Right Upper Arm 0HNB
      Right Upper Leg 0HNH
    Small Intestine 0DN8
    Soft Palate 0CN3
    Spermatic Cord 0VN
    Spermatic Cords, Bilateral 0VNH
    Sphenoid Bone 0NN
    Sphenoid Sinus 09N
    Spinal Meninges 00NT
    Spleen 07NP
    Splenic Artery 04N4
    Splenic Vein 06N1
    Sternoclavicular Joint 0RN
    Stomach 0DN6
      Body 0DN6
      Fundus 0DN6
      Pylorus 0DN7
    Structure, Uterine Supporting 0UN0
    Subclavian Artery 03N
    Subclavian Vein 05N
    Subcutaneous Tissue and Fascia
      Abdomen 0JN8
      Anterior Neck 0JN4

Release—*continued*
  by Body Part—*continued*
    Subcutaneous Tissue and Fascia—
      continued
      Back 0JN7
      Buttock 0JN9
      Chest 0JN6
      Face 0JN1
      Foot, Left 0JN0
      Genitalia 0JNC
      Left Foot 0JNR
      Left Hand 0JNK
      Left Lower Arm 0JNH
      Left Lower Leg 0JNP
      Left Upper Arm 0JNF
      Left Upper Leg 0JNM
      Perineum 0JNB
      Posterior Neck 0JN5
      Right Foot 0JNQ
      Right Hand 0JNJ
      Right Lower Arm 0JNG
      Right Lower Leg 0JNN
      Right Upper Arm 0JND
      Right Upper Leg 0JNL
    Sublingual Gland 0CN
    Submaxillary Gland 0CN
    Superior Mesenteric Artery 04N5
    Superior Mesenteric Vein 06N5
    Superior Parathyroid Gland 0GN
    Superior Vena Cava 02NV
    Tarsal 0QN
    Tarsal Joint 0SN
    Temporal Artery 03N
    Temporal Bone 0NN
    Temporomandibular Joint 0RN
    Tendon, Foot, Left 0LN0
    Testes, Bilateral 0VNC
    Testis 0VN
    Thalamus 00N9
    Thoracic Aorta 02NW
    Thoracic Duct 07NK
    Thoracic Nerve 01N8
    Thoracic Spinal Cord 00NX
    Thoracic Sympathetic Nerve 01NL
    Thoracic Vertebra 0PN4
    Thoracic Vertebral Disc 0RN9
    Thoracic Vertebral Joint 0RN6
    Thoracolumbar Vertebral Disc 0RNB
    Thoracolumbar Vertebral Joint 0RNA
    Thorax Bursa and Ligament 0MN
    Thorax Muscle 0KN
    Thorax Tendon 0LN
    Thumb Phalanx 0PN
    Thymus 07NM
    Thyroid Artery 03N
    Thyroid Gland 0GNK
    Thyroid Gland Lobe 0GN
    Tibia 0QN
    Tibial Nerve 01NG
    Toe Nail 0HNR
    Toe Phalangeal Joint 0SN
    Toe Phalanx 0QN
    Tongue 0CN7
      Palate, Pharynx Muscle 0KN4
    Tonsils 0CNP
    Tooth, Lower 0CNW
    Transverse Colon 0DNL
    Tricuspid Valve 02NJ
    Trigeminal Nerve 00NK
    Trochlear Nerve 00NJ
    Trunk Bursa and Ligament 0MN
    Trunk Muscle 0KN
    Trunk Tendon 0LN
    Tube, Fallopian, Bilateral 0UN5
    Tunica Vaginalis 0VN
    Turbinate, Nasal 09N7

Release—*continued*
- *by Body Part*—*continued*
    - Tympanic Membrane, Left 09N8
    - Tympanicum, Glomus 0GNB
    - Ulna 0PN
    - Ulnar Artery 03N
    - Ulnar Nerve 01N4
    - Upper Arm Muscle 0KN
    - Upper Arm Tendon 0LN
    - Upper Artery 03NY
    - Upper Extremity Bursa and Ligament 0MN
    - Upper Eyelid, Left 08NP
    - Upper Femur 0QN
    - Upper Gingiva 0CN5
    - Upper Leg Muscle 0KN
    - Upper Leg Tendon 0LN
    - Upper Lobe Bronchus 0BN
    - Upper Lung Lobe 0BN
    - Upper Vein 05NY
    - Ureter 0TN
    - Urethra 0TND
    - Uterine Supporting Structure 0UN4
    - Uterus 0UN9
    - Uvula 0CNN
    - Vagina 0UNG
    - Vagus Nerve 00NQ
    - Vas Deferens 0VN
    - Vein
        - Lower 06N0
        - Upper 05N0
    - Ventricle 02N
    - Ventricular Septum 02NM
    - Vertebral Artery 03N
    - Vertebral Vein 05N
    - Vessel, Retinal, Left 08N2
    - Vestibular Gland 0UNL
    - Vitreous 08N
    - Vocal Cord 0CN
    - Vulva 0UNM
    - Wrist Bursa and Ligament 0MN
    - Wrist Joint 0RN
    - Zygomatic Bone 0NN

Relief—*see* Release
Relocate—*see* Reposition
Relocation—*see* Reposition
Removal
- *by Body System*
    - Anatomical Regions, General 0WP
    - Anatomical Regions, Lower Extremities 0YP
    - Anatomical Regions, Upper Extremities 0XP
    - Bursae and Ligaments 0MP
    - Central Nervous System 00P
    - Ear, Nose, Sinus 09P
    - Endocrine System 0GP
    - Eye 08P
    - Female Reproductive System 0UP
    - Gastrointestinal System 0DP
    - Head and Facial Bones 0NP
    - Heart and Great Vessels 02P
    - Hepatobiliary System and Pancreas 0FP
    - Lower Arteries 04P
    - Lower Bones 0QP
    - Lower Joints 0SP
    - Lower Veins 06P
    - Lymphatic and Hemic Systems 07P
    - Male Reproductive System 0VP
    - Mouth and Throat 0CP
    - Muscles 0KP
    - Peripheral Nervous System 01P
    - Respiratory System 0BP
    - Skin and Breast 0HP
    - Subcutaneous Tissue and Fascia 0JP
    - Tendons 0LP
    - Upper Arteries 03P

Removal—*continued*
- *by Body System*—*continued*
    - Upper Bones 0PP
    - Upper Joints 0RP
    - Upper Veins 05P
    - Urinary System 0TP
- *by Device*
    - Airway
        - Esophagus 0DP5
        - Nose 09PK
    - Artificial Sphincter
        - Anus 0DPQ
        - Bladder 0TPB
        - Urethra 0TPD
    - Autologous Arterial Tissue
        - Artery
            - Lower 04PY
            - Upper 03PY
        - Heart 02PA
        - Vein
            - Lower 06PY
            - Upper 05PY
        - Vessel, Great 02PY
    - Autologous Tissue Substitute
        - Abdominal Wall 0WPF
        - Acetabulum 0QP
        - Acromioclavicular Joint 0RP
        - Ankle Joint, Left 0SPG
        - Artery
            - Lower 04PY
            - Upper 03PY
        - Back, Lower 0WP0
        - Bladder 0TPB
        - Bone, Facial 0NPB
        - Breast 0HP
        - Bursa and Ligament, Lower 0MPX
        - Carpal, Left 0PPN
        - Carpal Joint 0RP
        - Cavity, Glenoid, Left 0PP0
        - Cervical Vertebra 0PP3
        - Cervical Vertebral Joint 0RP1
        - Cervicothoracic Vertebral Disc 0RP5
        - Cervicothoracic Vertebral Joint 0RP4
        - Cervix, Uterus and 0UPD
        - Chest Wall 0WP8
        - Chyli, Cisterna 07PK
        - Cisterna Chyli 07PL
        - Clavicle 0PP
        - Coccygeal Joint 0SP6
        - Coccyx 0QPS
        - Cord
            - Epididymis and Spermatic 0VPM
            - Spinal 00P0
        - Cul-de-sac, Vagina and 0UPH
        - Deferens, Vas 0VPR
        - Diaphragm 0BPT
        - Disc
            - Lumbosacral 0SP2
            - Thoracolumbar Vertebral 0RP3
        - Duct, Pancreatic 0FPB
        - Ear 09P
        - Elbow Joint, Left 0RPM
        - Extraocular Muscle, Left 08PM
        - Extremity
            - Lower, Left 0YP9
            - Upper, Left 0XP6
        - Eye 08P
        - Face 0WP2
        - Facial Bone 0NPW
        - Femoral Shaft 0QP
        - Femur, Lower, Left 0QP6
        - Fibula 0QP
        - Finger Nail 0HPQ
        - Finger Phalangeal Joint 0RP
        - Finger Phalanx 0PP
        - Gland, Mammary 0HP

Removal—*continued*
- *by Device*—*continued*
    - Autologous Tissue Substitute—*continued*
        - Glenoid Cavity 0PP
        - Hair 0HPS
        - Heart 02PA
        - Hip Joint, Left 0SPB
        - Humeral Head, Left 0PPD
        - Humeral Shaft 0PP
        - Joint
            - Finger Phalangeal, Left 0RPL
            - Hip, Left 0SP9
            - Knee, Left 0SPC
            - Sacroiliac, Left 0SP0
            - Shoulder, Left 0RP0
            - Toe Phalangeal, Left 0SPF
        - Kidney 0TP5
        - Knee Joint, Left 0SPD
        - Larynx 0CPS
        - Lower Back 0WPL
        - Lower Bursa and Ligament 0MPY
        - Lower Extremity, Left 0YPB
        - Lower Femur 0QP
        - Lower Intestinal Tract 0DPD
        - Lower Jaw 0WP5
        - Lower Muscle 0KPY
        - Lower Tendon 0LPY
        - Lumbosacral Disc 0SP4
        - Lumbosacral Joint 0SP3
        - Lymphatic 07PN
        - Mediastinum 0WPC
        - Mesentery 0DPV
        - Metacarpal 0PP
        - Metacarpocarpal Joint 0RP
        - Metacarpophalangeal Joint 0RP
        - Metatarsal 0QP
        - Metatarsal-Phalangeal Joint 0SP
        - Metatarsal-Tarsal Joint 0SP
        - Mouth and Throat 0CPY
        - Muscle
            - Extraocular, Left 08PL
            - Lower 0KPX
        - Nail, Toe 0HPP
        - Nail Bed
            - Finger 0HPQ
            - Toe 0HPR
        - Neck 0WP6
        - Nerve
            - Cranial 00PE
            - Peripheral 01PY
        - Nose 09PK
        - Omentum 0DPU
        - Pancreatic Duct 0FPD
        - Patella 0QP
        - Pelvic Bone, Left 0QP3
        - Penis 0VPS
        - Perineum
            - Female 0WPN
            - Male 0WPM
        - Peritoneum 0DPW
        - Phalanx
            - Finger, Left 0PPM
            - Toe, Left 0QP2
        - Radius 0PP
        - Rib 0PP
        - Sacrococcygeal Joint 0SP5
        - Sacroiliac Joint 0SP
        - Sacrum 0QP1
        - Scapula 0PP
        - Shaft, Humeral, Left 0PPC
        - Shoulder Joint 0RP
        - Skull 0NP0
        - Spinal Cord 00PV
        - Sternoclavicular Joint 0RP

     Codes provided in the index are incomplete. Refer to tables to determine additional character values.

Removal—*continued*
  by Device—*continued*
    Autologous Tissue Substitute—*continued*
      Stomach 0DP6
        Body 0DP6
        Fundus 0DP6
      Subcutaneous Tissue and Fascia
        Head and Neck 0JPS
        Lower Extremity 0JPW
        Trunk 0JPT
        Upper Extremity 0JPV
      Tarsal 0QP
      Tarsal Joint 0SP
      Temporomandibular Joint 0RP
      Tendon, Lower 0LPX
      Testis 0VPD
      Thoracic Vertebra 0PP4
      Thoracic Vertebral Disc 0RP9
      Thoracic Vertebral Joint 0RP6
      Thoracolumbar Vertebral Disc 0RPB
      Thoracolumbar Vertebral Joint 0RPA
      Thumb Phalanx 0PP
      Tibia 0QP
      Toe Nail 0HPR
      Toe Phalangeal Joint 0SP
      Toe Phalanx 0QP
      Trachea 0BP1
      Tract, Lower Intestinal 0DP0
      Tree, Tracheobronchial 0BP0
      Tube, Fallopian 0UP8
      Ulna 0PP
      Upper Back 0WPK
      Upper Extremity, Left 0XP7
      Upper Femur, Left 0QP7
      Upper Jaw 0WP4
      Ureter 0TP9
      Urethra 0TPD
      Vaginalis, Scrotum and Tunica 0VP8
      Vein
        Lower 06PY
        Upper 05PY
      Vertebra, Lumbar 0QP0
      Vesicles, Prostate and Seminal 0VP4
      Vessel, Great 02PY
      Vulva 0UPM
      Wrist Joint 0RP
    Autologous Venous Tissue
      Artery
        Lower 04PY
        Upper 03PY
      Heart 02PA
      Vein
        Lower 06PY
        Upper 05PY
      Vessel, Great 02PY
    Bandage
      Abdominal Wall 2W53
      Back 2W55
      Chest Wall 2W54
      Face 2W51
      Finger 2W5
      Foot 2W5
      Hand 2W5
      Head 2W50
      Inguinal Region 2W5
      Leg, Lower, Left 2W52
      Lower Arm 2W5
      Lower Extremity 2W5
      Lower Leg 2W5
      Thumb 2W5
      Toe 2W5
      Upper Arm 2W5
      Upper Extremity 2W5
      Upper Leg 2W5

Removal—*continued*
  by Device—*continued*
    Brace
      Abdominal Wall 2W53
      Back 2W55
      Chest Wall 2W54
      Face 2W51
      Finger 2W5
      Foot 2W5
      Hand 2W5
      Head 2W50
      Inguinal Region 2W5
      Leg, Lower, Left 2W52
      Lower Arm 2W5
      Lower Extremity 2W5
      Lower Leg 2W5
      Thumb 2W5
      Toe 2W5
      Upper Arm 2W5
      Upper Extremity 2W5
      Upper Leg 2W5
    Cast
      Abdominal Wall 2W53
      Back 2W55
      Chest Wall 2W54
      Face 2W51
      Finger 2W5
      Foot 2W5
      Hand 2W5
      Head 2W50
      Inguinal Region 2W5
      Leg, Lower, Left 2W52
      Lower Arm 2W5
      Lower Extremity 2W5
      Lower Leg 2W5
      Thumb 2W5
      Toe 2W5
      Upper Arm 2W5
      Upper Extremity 2W5
      Upper Leg 2W5
    Contraceptive Device
      Cervix, Uterus and 0UPD
      Subcutaneous Tissue and Fascia
        Lower Extremity 0JPW
        Trunk 0JPT
        Upper Extremity 0JPV
    Drainage Device
      Abdominal Wall 0WPF
      Acromioclavicular Joint 0RP
      Adenohypophysis 0GP0
      Adrenal Gland 0GP5
      Ankle Joint, Left 0SPG
      Artery
        Lower 04PY
        Upper 03PY
      Back, Lower 0WP0
      Bladder 0TPB
      Bone
        Facial 0NPB
        Lower 0QPY
        Upper 0PPY
      Breast 0HP
      Bursa and Ligament, Lower 0MPX
      Canal, Spinal 00P6
      Carpal Joint 0RP
      Cavity
        Pelvic 0WP1
        Pericardial 0WPD
      Cervical Vertebral Joint 0RP1
      Cervicothoracic Vertebral Disc 0RP5
      Cervicothoracic Vertebral Joint 0RP4
      Cervix, Uterus and 0UPD
      Chest Wall 0WP8
      Chyli, Cisterna 07PK
      Cisterna Chyli 07PL
      Coccygeal Joint 0SP6

Removal—*continued*
  by Device—*continued*
    Drainage Device—*continued*
      Cord
        Epididymis and Spermatic 0VPM
        Spinal 00P0
      Corpora Arenacea, Pineal 0GP1
      Cul-de-sac, Vagina and 0UPH
      Deferens, Vas 0VPR
      Diaphragm 0BPT
      Disc
        Lumbosacral 0SP2
        Thoracolumbar Vertebral 0RP3
      Duct, Pancreatic 0FPB
      Ear 09P
      Elbow Joint, Left 0RPM
      Extraocular Muscle, Left 08PM
      Extremity
        Lower, Left 0YP9
        Upper, Left 0XP6
      Eye 08P
      Face 0WP2
      Facial Bone 0NPW
      Finger Nail 0HPQ
      Finger Phalangeal Joint 0RP
      Gallbladder 0FP4
      Gland
        Endocrine 0GPS
        Mammary 0HP
        Parathyroid 0GP0
        Pineal 0GP1
        Salivary 0CPA
      Hip Joint, Left 0SPB
      Hypophysis 0GP0
      Joint
        Finger Phalangeal, Left 0RPL
        Hip, Left 0SP9
        Knee, Left 0SPC
        Sacroiliac, Left 0SP0
        Shoulder, Left 0RP0
        Toe Phalangeal, Left 0SPF
      Kidney 0TP5
      Knee Joint, Left 0SPD
      Larynx 0CPS
      Liver 0FP0
      Lower Back 0WPL
      Lower Bursa and Ligament 0MPY
      Lower Extremity, Left 0YPB
      Lower Intestinal Tract 0DPD
      Lower Jaw 0WP5
      Lower Muscle 0KPY
      Lower Tendon 0LPY
      Lumbosacral Disc 0SP4
      Lumbosacral Joint 0SP3
      Lung 0BP
      Lymphatic 07PN
      Marrow, Bone 07PT
      Mediastinum 0WPC
      Membrane, Tympanic, Left 09P7
      Mesentery 0DPV
      Metacarpocarpal Joint 0RP
      Metacarpophalangeal Joint 0RP
      Metatarsal-Phalangeal Joint 0SP
      Metatarsal-Tarsal Joint 0SP
      Mouth and Throat 0CPY
      Muscle
        Extraocular, Left 08PL
        Lower 0KPX
      Nail, Toe 0HPP
      Nail Bed
        Finger 0HPQ
        Toe 0HPR
      Neck 0WP6
      Nerve
        Cranial 00PE
        Peripheral 01PY

Removal—*continued*
   by Device—*continued*
      Drainage Device—*continued*
         Neurohypophysis 0GP0
         Nose 09PK
         Omentum 0DPU
         Ovary 0UP3
         Pancreas 0FPG
         Pancreatic Duct 0FPD
         Parathyroid Gland 0GPR
         Pelvic Cavity 0WPJ
         Penis 0VPS
         Perineum
            Female 0WPN
            Male 0WPM
         Peritoneal Cavity 0WPG
         Peritoneum 0DPW
         Pineal Body 0GP1
         Pleura 0BPQ
         Pleural Cavity 0WP
         Retroperitoneum 0WPH
         Sacrococcygeal Joint 0SP5
         Sacroiliac Joint 0SP
         Shoulder Joint 0RP
         Sinus 09PY
         Skull 0NP0
         Spinal Canal 00PU
         Spinal Cord 00PV
         Spleen 07PP
         Sternoclavicular Joint 0RP
         Stomach 0DP6
            Body 0DP6
            Fundus 0DP6
         Subcutaneous Tissue and Fascia
            Head and Neck 0JPS
            Lower Extremity 0JPW
            Trunk 0JPT
            Upper Extremity 0JPV
         Tarsal Joint 0SP
         Temporomandibular Joint 0RP
         Tendon, Lower 0LPX
         Testis 0VPD
         Thoracic Vertebral Disc 0RP9
         Thoracic Vertebral Joint 0RP6
         Thoracolumbar Vertebral Disc 0RPB
         Thoracolumbar Vertebral Joint 0RPA
         Thymus 07PM
         Thyroid Gland 0GPK
         Toe Nail 0HPR
         Toe Phalangeal Joint 0SP
         Trachea 0BP1
         Tract, Lower Intestinal 0DP0
         Tree, Tracheobronchial 0BP0
         Tube, Fallopian 0UP8
         Tympanic Membrane, Left 09P8
         Upper Back 0WPK
         Upper Extremity, Left 0XP7
         Upper Jaw 0WP4
         Ureter 0TP9
         Urethra 0TPD
         Vaginalis, Scrotum and Tunica 0VP8
         Vein
            Lower 06PY
            Upper 05PY
         Vesicles, Prostate and Seminal 0VP4
         Vulva 0UPM
         Wrist Joint 0RP
      Drug-eluting Intraluminal Device
         Artery
            Lower 04PY
            Upper 03PY
         Heart 02PA
         Vessel, Great 02PY
      Electrode
         Anus 0DPQ
         Bladder 0TPB

Removal—*continued*
   by Device—*continued*
      Electrode—*continued*
         Bone
            Facial 0NPB
            Lower 0QPY
            Upper 0PPY
         Canal, Spinal 00P6
         Cord, Spinal 00P0
         Diaphragm 0BPT
         Facial Bone 0NPW
         Heart 02PA
         Kidney 0TP5
         Lower Muscle 0KPY
         Muscle, Lower 0KPX
         Nerve
            Cranial 00PE
            Peripheral 01PY
         Skull 0NP0
         Spinal Canal 00PU
         Spinal Cord 00PV
         Stomach 0DP6
            Body 0DP6
            Fundus 0DP6
         Ureter 0TP9
         Urethra 0TPD
      Endobronchial Device
         Tree, Tracheobronchial 0BP0
      Endotracheal Device
         Trachea 0BP1
      External Fixation Device
         Ankle Joint, Left 0SPG
         Carpal, Left 0PPN
         Carpal Joint 0RP
         Elbow Joint, Left 0RPM
         Femoral Shaft 0QP
         Femur, Lower, Left 0QP6
         Fibula 0QP
         Finger Phalangeal Joint 0RP
         Finger Phalanx 0PP
         Hip Joint, Left 0SPB
         Humeral Head, Left 0PPD
         Humeral Shaft 0PP
         Joint
            Finger Phalangeal, Left 0RPL
            Hip, Left 0SP9
            Knee, Left 0SPC
            Toe Phalangeal, Left 0SPF
         Knee Joint, Left 0SPD
         Lower Femur 0QP
         Metacarpal 0PP
         Metacarpocarpal Joint 0RP
         Metacarpophalangeal Joint 0RP
         Metatarsal 0QP
         Metatarsal-Phalangeal Joint 0SP
         Metatarsal-Tarsal Joint 0SP
         Patella 0QP
         Pelvic Bone, Left 0QP3
         Phalanx
            Finger, Left 0PPM
            Toe, Left 0QP2
         Radius 0PP
         Shaft, Humeral, Left 0PPC
         Skull 0NP0
         Tarsal 0QP
         Tarsal Joint 0SP
         Thumb Phalanx 0PP
         Tibia 0QP
         Toe Phalangeal Joint 0SP
         Toe Phalanx 0QP
         Ulna 0PP
         Upper Femur, Left 0QP7
         Wrist Joint 0RP
      External Heart Assist System
         Heart 02PA

Removal—*continued*
   by Device—*continued*
      Extraluminal Device
         Artery
            Lower 04PY
            Upper 03PY
         Bladder 0TPB
         Cervix, Uterus and 0UPD
         Chyli, Cisterna 07PK
         Cisterna Chyli 07PL
         Cord, Epididymis and Spermatic 0VPM
         Deferens, Vas 0VPR
         Duct, Pancreatic 0FPB
         Eye 08P
         Gland, Salivary 0CPA
         Heart 02PA
         Kidney 0TP5
         Lower Intestinal Tract 0DPD
         Lymphatic 07PN
         Pancreatic Duct 0FPD
         Stomach 0DP6
            Body 0DP6
            Fundus 0DP6
         Trachea 0BP1
         Tract, Lower Intestinal 0DP0
         Tree, Tracheobronchial 0BP0
         Tube, Fallopian 0UP8
         Ureter 0TP9
         Urethra 0TPD
         Vein
            Lower 06PY
            Upper 05PY
         Vessel, Great 02PY
      Feeding Device
         Esophagus 0DP5
         Lower Intestinal Tract 0DPD
         Stomach 0DP6
            Body 0DP6
            Fundus 0DP6
         Tract, Lower Intestinal 0DP0
      Hearing Device
         Ear, Inner, Left 09PD
         Inner Ear, Left 09PE
         Skull 0NP0
      Implantable Heart Assist System
         Heart 02PA
      Infusion Device
         Abdominal Wall 0WPF
         Acromioclavicular Joint 0RP
         Ankle Joint, Left 0SPG
         Artery
            Lower 04PY
            Upper 03PY
         Back, Lower 0WP0
         Bladder 0TPB
         Canal, Spinal 00P6
         Carpal Joint 0RP
         Cavity
            Pelvic 0WP1
            Pericardial 0WPD
         Cervical Vertebral Joint 0RP1
         Cervicothoracic Vertebral Disc 0RP5
         Cervicothoracic Vertebral Joint 0RP4
         Cervix, Uterus and 0UPD
         Chest Wall 0WP8
         Chyli, Cisterna 07PK
         Cisterna Chyli 07PL
         Coccygeal Joint 0SP6
         Cord
            Epididymis and Spermatic 0VPM
            Spinal 00P0
         Cul-de-sac, Vagina and 0UPH
         Deferens, Vas 0VPR
         Disc
            Lumbosacral 0SP2
            Thoracolumbar Vertebral 0RP3

Removal—*continued*
  by Device—*continued*
    Infusion Device—*continued*
      Duct, Pancreatic 0FPB
      Elbow Joint, Left 0RPM
      Esophagus 0DP5
      Extremity
        Lower, Left 0YP9
        Upper, Left 0XP6
      Eye 08P
      Face 0WP2
      Finger Phalangeal Joint 0RP
      Gallbladder 0FP4
      Genitourinary Tract 0WPR
      Gland, Endocrine 0GPS
      Heart 02PA
      Hip Joint, Left 0SPB
      Joint
        Finger Phalangeal, Left 0RPL
        Hip, Left 0SP9
        Knee, Left 0SPC
        Sacroiliac, Left 0SP0
        Shoulder, Left 0RP0
        Toe Phalangeal, Left 0SPF
      Kidney 0TP5
      Knee Joint, Left 0SPD
      Liver 0FP0
      Lower Back 0WPL
      Lower Extremity, Left 0YPB
      Lower Intestinal Tract 0DPD
      Lower Jaw 0WP5
      Lumbosacral Disc 0SP4
      Lumbosacral Joint 0SP3
      Lung 0BP
      Lymphatic 07PN
      Mediastinum 0WPC
      Metacarpocarpal Joint 0RP
      Metacarpophalangeal Joint 0RP
      Metatarsal-Phalangeal Joint 0SP
      Metatarsal-Tarsal Joint 0SP
      Neck 0WP6
      Nerve, Cranial 00PE
      Ovary 0UP3
      Pancreas 0FPG
      Pancreatic Duct 0FPD
      Pelvic Cavity 0WPJ
      Penis 0VPS
      Perineum
        Female 0WPN
        Male 0WPM
      Peritoneal Cavity 0WPG
      Pleural Cavity 0WP
      Respiratory Tract 0WPQ
      Retroperitoneum 0WPH
      Sacrococcygeal Joint 0SP5
      Sacroiliac Joint 0SP
      Shoulder Joint 0RP
      Spinal Canal 00PU
      Spinal Cord 00PV
      Spleen 07PP
      Sternoclavicular Joint 0RP
      Stomach 0DP6
        Body 0DP6
        Fundus 0DP6
      Subcutaneous Tissue and Fascia
        Head and Neck 0JPS
        Lower Extremity 0JPW
        Trunk 0JPT
        Upper Extremity 0JPV
      Tarsal Joint 0SP
      Temporomandibular Joint 0RP
      Testis 0VPD
      Thoracic Vertebral Disc 0RP9
      Thoracic Vertebral Joint 0RP6
      Thoracolumbar Vertebral Disc 0RPB
      Thoracolumbar Vertebral Joint 0RPA

Removal—*continued*
  by Device—*continued*
    Infusion Device—*continued*
      Thymus 07PM
      Toe Phalangeal Joint 0SP
      Tract
        Genitourinary 0WPP
        Lower Intestinal 0DP0
      Tree, Tracheobronchial 0BP0
      Tube, Fallopian 0UP8
      Upper Back 0WPK
      Upper Extremity, Left 0XP7
      Upper Jaw 0WP4
      Ureter 0TP9
      Urethra 0TPD
      Vaginalis, Scrotum and Tunica 0VP8
      Vein
        Lower 06PY
        Upper 05PY
      Vesicles, Prostate and Seminal 0VP4
      Vessel, Great 02PY
      Wrist Joint 0RP
    Infusion Pump
      Subcutaneous Tissue and Fascia
        Lower Extremity 0JPW
        Trunk 0JPT
        Upper Extremity 0JPV
    Intermittent Pressure Device
      Abdominal Wall 2W53
      Back 2W55
      Chest Wall 2W54
      Face 2W51
      Finger 2W5
      Foot 2W5
      Hand 2W5
      Head 2W50
      Inguinal Region 2W5
      Leg, Lower, Left 2W52
      Lower Arm 2W5
      Lower Extremity 2W5
      Lower Leg 2W5
      Thumb 2W5
      Toe 2W5
      Upper Arm 2W5
      Upper Extremity 2W5
      Upper Leg 2W5
    Internal Fixation Device
      Acetabulum 0QP
      Acromioclavicular Joint 0RP
      Ankle Joint, Left 0SPG
      Bone, Facial 0NPB
      Carpal, Left 0PPN
      Carpal Joint 0RP
      Cavity, Glenoid, Left 0PP0
      Cervical Vertebra 0PP3
      Cervical Vertebral Joint 0RP1
      Cervicothoracic Vertebral Joint 0RP4
      Clavicle 0PP
      Coccygeal Joint 0SP6
      Coccyx 0QPS
      Elbow Joint, Left 0RPM
      Facial Bone 0NPW
      Femoral Shaft 0QP
      Femur, Lower, Left 0QP6
      Fibula 0QP
      Finger Phalangeal Joint 0RP
      Finger Phalanx 0PP
      Glenoid Cavity 0PP
      Hip Joint, Left 0SPB
      Humeral Head, Left 0PPD
      Humeral Shaft 0PP
      Joint
        Finger Phalangeal, Left 0RPL
        Hip, Left 0SP9
        Knee, Left 0SPC
        Sacroiliac, Left 0SP0

Removal—*continued*
  by Device—*continued*
    Internal Fixation Device—*continued*
      Joint—*continued*
        Shoulder, Left 0RP0
        Toe Phalangeal, Left 0SPF
      Knee Joint, Left 0SPD
      Lower Femur 0QP
      Lumbosacral Joint 0SP3
      Metacarpal 0PP
      Metacarpocarpal Joint 0RP
      Metacarpophalangeal Joint 0RP
      Metatarsal 0QP
      Metatarsal-Phalangeal Joint 0SP
      Metatarsal-Tarsal Joint 0SP
      Patella 0QP
      Pelvic Bone, Left 0QP3
      Phalanx
        Finger, Left 0PPM
        Toe, Left 0QP2
      Radius 0PP
      Rib 0PP
      Sacrococcygeal Joint 0SP5
      Sacroiliac Joint 0SP
      Sacrum 0QP1
      Scapula 0PP
      Shaft, Humeral, Left 0PPC
      Shoulder Joint 0RP
      Skull 0NP0
      Sternoclavicular Joint 0RP
      Tarsal 0QP
      Tarsal Joint 0SP
      Temporomandibular Joint 0RP
      Thoracic Vertebra 0PP4
      Thoracic Vertebral Joint 0RP6
      Thoracolumbar Vertebral Joint 0RPA
      Thumb Phalanx 0PP
      Tibia 0QP
      Toe Phalangeal Joint 0SP
        Toe Phalanx 0QP
        Ulna 0PP
        Upper Femur, Left 0QP7
        Vertebra, Lumbar 0QP0
        Wrist Joint 0RP
    Intraluminal Device
      Artery
        Lower 04PY
        Upper 03PY
      Bladder 0TPB
      Cervix, Uterus and 0UPD
      Chyli, Cisterna 07PK
      Cisterna Chyli 07PL
      Cul-de-sac, Vagina and 0UPH
      Deferens, Vas 0VPR
      Duct, Pancreatic 0FPB
      Ear 09P
      Eye 08P
      Gallbladder 0FP4
      Heart 02PA
      Kidney 0TP5
      Larynx 0CPS
      Lower Intestinal Tract 0DPD
      Lymphatic 07PN
      Mouth and Throat 0CPY
      Pancreas 0FPG
      Pancreatic Duct 0FPD
      Stomach 0DP6
        Body 0DP6
        Fundus 0DP6
      Trachea 0BP1
      Tract, Lower Intestinal 0DP0
      Tree, Tracheobronchial 0BP0
      Tube, Fallopian 0UP8
      Ureter 0TP9
      Urethra 0TPD

Removal—*continued*
  by Device—*continued*
    Intraluminal Device—*continued*
      Vein
        Lower 06PY
        Upper 05PY
      Vessel, Great 02PY
    Intramedullary Fixation Device
      Femoral Shaft 0QP
      Femur, Lower, Left 0QP6
      Fibula 0QP
      Humeral Head, Left 0PPD
      Humeral Shaft 0PP
      Lower Femur 0QP
      Radius 0PP
      Shaft, Humeral, Left 0PPC
      Tibia 0QP
      Ulna 0PP
      Upper Femur, Left 0QP7
    Liner
      Hip Joint, Left 0SPB
      Joint
        Hip, Left 0SP9
        Knee, Left 0SPC
      Knee Joint, Left 0SPD
    Monitoring Device
      Artery
        Lower 04PY
        Upper 03PY
      Bladder 0TPB
      Canal, Spinal 00P6
      Cord, Spinal 00P0
      Diaphragm 0BPT
      Duct, Pancreatic 0FPB
      Esophagus 0DP5
      Gallbladder 0FP4
      Gland, Endocrine 0GPS
      Heart 02PA
      Kidney 0TP5
      Liver 0FP0
      Lower Intestinal Tract 0DPD
      Lung 0BP
      Nerve
        Cranial 00PE
        Peripheral 01PY
      Pancreas 0FPG
      Pancreatic Duct 0FPD
      Pleura 0BPQ
      Spinal Canal 00PU
      Spinal Cord 00PV
      Stomach 0DP6
        Body 0DP6
        Fundus 0DP6
      Trachea 0BP1
      Tract, Lower Intestinal 0DP0
      Tree, Tracheobronchial 0BP0
      Ureter 0TP9
      Urethra 0TPD
      Vein
        Lower 06PY
        Upper 05PY
      Vessel, Great 02PY
    Monitoring Electrode
      Products of Conception 10P0
    Nonautologous Tissue Substitute
      Abdominal Wall 0WPF
      Acetabulum 0QP
      Acromioclavicular Joint 0RP
      Ankle Joint, Left 0SPG
      Artery
        Lower 04PY
        Upper 03PY
      Back, Lower 0WP0
      Bladder 0TPB
      Bone, Facial 0NPB
      Breast 0HP

Removal—*continued*
  by Device—*continued*
    Nonautologous Tissue Substitute—
      continued
      Bursa and Ligament, Lower 0MPX
      Carpal, Left 0PPN
      Carpal Joint 0RP
      Cavity, Glenoid, Left 0PP0
      Cervical Vertebra 0PP3
      Cervical Vertebral Joint 0RP1
      Cervicothoracic Vertebral Disc 0RP5
      Cervicothoracic Vertebral Joint 0RP4
      Cervix, Uterus and 0UPD
      Chest Wall 0WP8
      Chyli, Cisterna 07PK
      Cisterna Chyli 07PL
      Clavicle 0PP
      Coccygeal Joint 0SP6
      Coccyx 0QPS
      Cord
        Epididymis and Spermatic 0VPM
        Spinal 00P0
      Cul-de-sac, Vagina and 0UPH
      Deferens, Vas 0VPR
      Diaphragm 0BPT
      Disc
        Lumbosacral 0SP2
        Thoracolumbar Vertebral 0RP3
      Duct, Pancreatic 0FPB
      Ear 09P
      Elbow Joint, Left 0RPM
      Extraocular Muscle, Left 08PM
      Extremity
        Lower, Left 0YP9
        Upper, Left 0XP6
      Eye 08P
      Face 0WP2
      Facial Bone 0NPW
      Femoral Shaft 0QP
      Femur, Lower, Left 0QP6
      Fibula 0QP
      Finger Nail 0HPQ
      Finger Phalangeal Joint 0RP
      Finger Phalanx 0PP
      Gland, Mammary 0HP
      Glenoid Cavity 0PP
      Hair 0HPS
      Heart 02PA
      Hip Joint, Left 0SPB
      Humeral Head, Left 0PPD
      Humeral Shaft 0PP
      Joint
        Finger Phalangeal, Left 0RPL
        Hip, Left 0SP9
        Knee, Left 0SPC
        Sacroiliac, Left 0SP0
        Shoulder, Left 0RP0
        Toe Phalangeal, Left 0SPF
      Kidney 0TP5
      Knee Joint, Left 0SPD
      Larynx 0CPS
      Lower Back 0WPL
      Lower Bursa and Ligament 0MPY
      Lower Extremity, Left 0YPB
      Lower Femur 0QP
      Lower Intestinal Tract 0DPD
      Lower Jaw 0WP5
      Lower Muscle 0KPY
      Lower Tendon 0LPY
      Lumbosacral Disc 0SP4
      Lumbosacral Joint 0SP3
      Lymphatic 07PN
      Mediastinum 0WPC
      Mesentery 0DPV
      Metacarpal 0PP
      Metacarpocarpal Joint 0RP

Removal—*continued*
  by Device—*continued*
    Nonautologous Tissue Substitute—
      continued
      Metacarpophalangeal Joint 0RP
      Metatarsal 0QP
      Metatarsal-Phalangeal Joint 0SP
      Metatarsal-Tarsal Joint 0SP
      Mouth and Throat 0CPY
      Muscle
        Extraocular, Left 08PL
        Lower 0KPX
      Nail, Toe 0HPP
      Nail Bed
        Finger 0HPQ
        Toe 0HPR
      Neck 0WP6
      Nose 09PK
      Omentum 0DPU
      Pancreatic Duct 0FPD
      Patella 0QP
      Pelvic Bone, Left 0QP3
      Penis 0VPS
      Perineum
        Female 0WPN
        Male 0WPM
      Peritoneum 0DPW
      Phalanx
        Finger, Left 0PPM
        Toe, Left 0QP2
      Radius 0PP
      Rib 0PP
      Sacrococcygeal Joint 0SP5
      Sacroiliac Joint 0SP
      Sacrum 0QP1
      Scapula 0PP
      Shaft, Humeral, Left 0PPC
      Shoulder Joint 0RP
      Skull 0NP0
      Spinal Cord 00PV
      Sternoclavicular Joint 0RP
      Stomach 0DP6
        Body 0DP6
        Fundus 0DP6
      Subcutaneous Tissue and Fascia
        Head and Neck 0JPS
        Lower Extremity 0JPW
        Trunk 0JPT
        Upper Extremity 0JPV
      Tarsal 0QP
      Tarsal Joint 0SP
      Temporomandibular Joint 0RP
      Tendon, Lower 0LPX
      Testis 0VPD
      Thoracic Vertebra 0PP4
      Thoracic Vertebral Disc 0RP9
      Thoracic Vertebral Joint 0RP6
      Thoracolumbar Vertebral Disc 0RPB
      Thoracolumbar Vertebral Joint 0RPA
      Thumb Phalanx 0PP
      Tibia 0QP
      Toe Nail 0HPR
      Toe Phalangeal Joint 0SP
      Toe Phalanx 0QP
      Trachea 0BP1
      Tract, Lower Intestinal 0DP0
      Tree, Tracheobronchial 0BP0
      Tube, Fallopian 0UP8
      Ulna 0PP
      Upper Back 0WPK
      Upper Extremity, Left 0XP7
      Upper Femur, Left 0QP7
      Upper Jaw 0WP4
      Ureter 0TP9
      Urethra 0TPD
      Vaginalis, Scrotum and Tunica 0VP8

Codes provided in the index are incomplete. Refer to tables to determine additional character values.

Removal—*continued*
  by Device—*continued*
    Nonautologous Tissue Substitute—
      continued
      Vein
        Lower 06PY
        Upper 05PY
      Vertebra, Lumbar 0QP0
      Vesicles, Prostate and Seminal 0VP4
      Vessel, Great 02PY
      Vulva 0UPM
      Wrist Joint 0RP
    Other Device
      Abdominal Wall 0WPF
      Abdominal Wall 2W53
      Back 2W55
        Lower 0WP0
      Cavity
        Pelvic 0WP1
        Pericardial 0WPD
      Chest Wall 0WP8
      Chest Wall 2W54
      Extremity
        Lower, Left 0YP9
        Upper, Left 0XP6
      Face 0WP2
      Face 2W51
      Finger 2W5
      Foot 2W5
      Genitourinary Tract 0WPR
      Hand 2W5
      Head 2W50
      Inguinal Region 2W5
      Leg, Lower, Left 2W52
      Lower Arm 2W5
      Lower Back 0WPL
      Lower Extremity
        Left 0YPB
      Lower Extremity 2W5
      Lower Jaw 0WP5
      Lower Leg 2W5
      Mediastinum 0WPC
      Neck 0WP6
      Pelvic Cavity 0WPJ
      Perineum
        Female 0WPN
        Male 0WPM
      Peritoneal Cavity 0WPG
      Pleural Cavity 0WP
      Products of Conception 10P0
      Respiratory Tract 0WPQ
      Retroperitoneum 0WPH
      Thumb 2W5
      Toe 2W5
      Tract, Genitourinary 0WPP
      Upper Arm 2W5
      Upper Back 0WPK
      Upper Extremity
        Left 0XP7
      Upper Extremity 2W5
      Upper Jaw 0WP4
      Upper Leg 2W5
    Pacemaker / Defibrillator
      Subcutaneous Tissue and Fascia,
        Trunk 0JPT
    Packing Material
      Abdominal Wall 2W53
      Anorectal 2Y53
      Back 2W55
      Chest Wall 2W54
      Ear 2Y52
      Face 2W51
      Female Genital Tract 2Y54
      Finger 2W5
      Foot 2W5
      Genital Tract, Female 2Y50

Removal—*continued*
  by Device—*continued*
    Packing Material—*continued*
      Hand 2W5
      Head 2W50
      Inguinal Region 2W5
      Leg, Lower, Left 2W52
      Lower Arm 2W5
      Lower Extremity 2W5
      Lower Leg 2W5
      Nasal 2Y51
      Thumb 2W5
      Toe 2W5
      Upper Arm 2W5
      Upper Extremity 2W5
      Upper Leg 2W5
      Urethra 2Y55
    Pessary
      Cul-de-sac, Vagina and 0UPH
    Pressure Dressing
      Abdominal Wall 2W53
      Back 2W55
      Chest Wall 2W54
      Face 2W51
      Finger 2W5
      Foot 2W5
      Hand 2W5
      Head 2W50
      Inguinal Region 2W5
      Leg, Lower, Left 2W52
      Lower Arm 2W5
      Lower Extremity 2W5
      Lower Leg 2W5
      Thumb 2W5
      Toe 2W5
      Upper Arm 2W5
      Upper Extremity 2W5
      Upper Leg 2W5
    Radioactive Element
      Abdominal Wall 0WPF
      Artery, Lower 04PY
      Back, Lower 0WP0
      Breast 0HP
      Cavity
        Pelvic 0WP1
        Pericardial 0WPD
      Chest Wall 0WP8
      Cul-de-sac, Vagina and 0UPH
      Duct, Pancreatic 0FPB
      Esophagus 0DP5
      Extremity
        Lower, Left 0YP9
        Upper, Left 0XP6
      Eye 08P
      Face 0WP2
      Genitourinary Tract 0WPR
      Gland, Mammary 0HP
      Lower Back 0WPL
      Lower Extremity, Left 0YPB
      Lower Jaw 0WP5
      Lung 0BP
      Mediastinum 0WPC
      Mesentery 0DPV
      Mouth and Throat 0CPY
      Neck 0WP6
      Omentum 0DPU
      Pancreatic Duct 0FPD
      Pelvic Cavity 0WPJ
      Perineum
        Female 0WPN
        Male 0WPM
      Peritoneal Cavity 0WPG
      Peritoneum 0DPW
      Pleura 0BPQ
      Pleural Cavity 0WP
      Rectum 0DPP

Removal—*continued*
  by Device—*continued*
    Radioactive Element—*continued*
      Respiratory Tract 0WPQ
      Retroperitoneum 0WPH
      Subcutaneous Tissue and Fascia
        Head and Neck 0JPS
        Lower Extremity 0JPW
        Trunk 0JPT
        Upper Extremity 0JPV
      Tract, Genitourinary 0WPP
      Tree, Tracheobronchial 0BP0
      Upper Back 0WPK
      Upper Extremity, Left 0XP7
      Upper Jaw 0WP4
      Vesicles, Prostate and Seminal 0VP4
    Reservoir
      Subcutaneous Tissue and Fascia
        Lower Extremity 0JPW
        Trunk 0JPT
        Upper Extremity 0JPV
    Resurfacing Device
      Hip Joint, Left 0SPB
      Joint, Hip, Left 0SP9
    Spacer
      Acromioclavicular Joint 0RP
      Ankle Joint, Left 0SPG
      Carpal Joint 0RP
      Cervical Vertebral Joint 0RP1
      Cervicothoracic Vertebral Joint 0RP4
      Coccygeal Joint 0SP6
      Elbow Joint, Left 0RPM
      Finger Phalangeal Joint 0RP
      Hip Joint, Left 0SPB
      Joint
        Finger Phalangeal, Left 0RPL
        Hip, Left 0SP9
        Knee, Left 0SPC
        Sacroiliac, Left 0SP0
        Shoulder, Left 0RP0
        Toe Phalangeal, Left 0SPF
      Knee Joint, Left 0SPD
      Lumbosacral Joint 0SP3
      Metacarpocarpal Joint 0RP
      Metacarpophalangeal Joint 0RP
      Metatarsal-Phalangeal Joint 0SP
      Metatarsal-Tarsal Joint 0SP
      Sacrococcygeal Joint 0SP5
      Sacroiliac Joint 0SP
      Shoulder Joint 0RP
      Sternoclavicular Joint 0RP
      Tarsal Joint 0SP
      Temporomandibular Joint 0RP
      Thoracic Vertebral Joint 0RP6
      Thoracolumbar Vertebral Joint 0RPA
      Toe Phalangeal Joint 0SP
      Wrist Joint 0RP
    Splint
      Abdominal Wall 2W53
      Back 2W55
      Chest Wall 2W54
      Face 2W51
      Finger 2W5
      Foot 2W5
      Hand 2W5
      Head 2W50
      Inguinal Region 2W5
      Leg, Lower, Left 2W52
      Lower Arm 2W5
      Lower Extremity 2W5
      Lower Leg 2W5
      Thumb 2W5
      Toe 2W5
      Upper Arm 2W5
      Upper Extremity 2W5
      Upper Leg 2W5

Removal—*continued*
  by Device—*continued*
    Stereotactic Apparatus
      Head 2W50
    Stimulator Generator
      Subcutaneous Tissue and Fascia
        Head and Neck 0JPS
        Lower Extremity 0JPW
        Trunk 0JPT
        Upper Extremity 0JPV
    Synthetic Substitute
      Abdominal Wall 0WPF
      Acetabulum 0QP
      Acromioclavicular Joint 0RP
      Ankle Joint, Left 0SPG
      Artery
        Lower 04PY
        Upper 03PY
      Back, Lower 0WP0
      Bladder 0TPB
      Bone, Facial 0NPB
      Breast 0HP
      Bursa and Ligament, Lower 0MPX
      Canal, Spinal 00P6
      Carpal, Left 0PPN
      Carpal Joint 0RP
      Cavity
        Glenoid, Left 0PP0
        Pelvic 0WP1
      Cervical Vertebra 0PP3
      Cervical Vertebral Joint 0RP1
      Cervicothoracic Vertebral Disc 0RP5
      Cervicothoracic Vertebral Joint 0RP4
      Cervix, Uterus and 0UPD
      Chest Wall 0WP8
      Chyli, Cisterna 07PK
      Cisterna Chyli 07PL
      Clavicle 0PP
      Coccygeal Joint 0SP6
      Coccyx 0QPS
      Cord
        Epididymis and Spermatic 0VPM
        Spinal 00P0
      Cul-de-sac, Vagina and 0UPH
      Deferens, Vas 0VPR
      Diaphragm 0BPT
      Disc
        Lumbosacral 0SP2
        Thoracolumbar Vertebral 0RP3
      Duct, Pancreatic 0FPB
      Ear 09P
      Elbow Joint, Left 0RPM
      Extraocular Muscle, Left 08PM
      Extremity
        Lower, Left 0YP9
        Upper, Left 0XP6
      Eye 08P
      Face 0WP2
      Facial Bone 0NPW
      Femoral Shaft 0QP
      Femur, Lower, Left 0QP6
      Fibula 0QP
      Finger Nail 0HPQ
      Finger Phalangeal Joint 0RP
      Finger Phalanx 0PP
      Gland, Mammary 0HP
      Glenoid Cavity 0PP
      Hair 0HPS
      Heart 02PA
      Hip Joint, Left 0SPB
      Humeral Head, Left 0PPD
      Humeral Shaft 0PP
      Joint
        Finger Phalangeal, Left 0RPL
        Hip, Left 0SP9
        Knee, Left 0SPC

Removal—*continued*
  by Device—*continued*
    Synthetic Substitute—*continued*
      Joint—*continued*
        Sacroiliac, Left 0SP0
        Shoulder, Left 0RP0
        Toe Phalangeal, Left 0SPF
      Kidney 0TP5
      Knee Joint, Left 0SPD
      Larynx 0CPS
      Lens 08P
      Lower Back 0WPL
      Lower Bursa and Ligament 0MPY
      Lower Extremity, Left 0YPB
      Lower Femur 0QP
      Lower Intestinal Tract 0DPD
      Lower Jaw 0WP5
      Lower Muscle 0KPY
      Lower Tendon 0LPY
      Lumbosacral Disc 0SP4
      Lumbosacral Joint 0SP3
      Lymphatic 07PN
      Mediastinum 0WPC
      Mesentery 0DPV
      Metacarpal 0PP
      Metacarpocarpal Joint 0RP
      Metacarpophalangeal Joint 0RP
      Metatarsal 0QP
      Metatarsal-Phalangeal Joint 0SP
      Metatarsal-Tarsal Joint 0SP
      Mouth and Throat 0CPY
      Muscle
        Extraocular, Left 08PL
        Lower 0KPX
      Nail, Toe 0HPP
      Nail Bed
        Finger 0HPQ
        Toe 0HPR
      Neck 0WP6
      Nose 09PK
      Omentum 0DPU
      Pancreatic Duct 0FPD
      Patella 0QP
      Pelvic Bone, Left 0QP3
      Pelvic Cavity 0WPJ
      Penis 0VPS
      Perineum
        Female 0WPN
        Male 0WPM
      Peritoneal Cavity 0WPG
      Peritoneum 0DPW
      Phalanx
        Finger, Left 0PPM
        Toe, Left 0QP2
      Pleural Cavity 0WP
      Radius 0PP
      Rib 0PP
      Sacrococcygeal Joint 0SP5
      Sacroiliac Joint 0SP
      Sacrum 0QP1
      Scapula 0PP
      Shaft, Humeral, Left 0PPC
      Shoulder Joint 0RP
      Skull 0NP0
      Spinal Canal 00PU
      Spinal Cord 00PV
      Sternoclavicular Joint 0RP
      Stomach 0DP6
        Body 0DP6
        Fundus 0DP6
      Subcutaneous Tissue and Fascia
        Head and Neck 0JPS
        Lower Extremity 0JPW
        Trunk 0JPT
        Upper Extremity 0JPV
      Tarsal 0QP

Removal—*continued*
  by Device—*continued*
    Synthetic Substitute—*continued*
      Tarsal Joint 0SP
      Temporomandibular Joint 0RP
      Tendon, Lower 0LPX
      Testis 0VPD
      Thoracic Vertebra 0PP4
      Thoracic Vertebral Disc 0RP9
      Thoracic Vertebral Joint 0RP6
      Thoracolumbar Vertebral Disc 0RPB
      Thoracolumbar Vertebral Joint 0RPA
      Thumb Phalanx 0PP
      Tibia 0QP
      Toe Nail 0HPR
      Toe Phalangeal Joint 0SP
      Toe Phalanx 0QP
      Trachea 0BP1
      Tract, Lower Intestinal 0DP0
      Tree, Tracheobronchial 0BP0
      Tube, Fallopian 0UP8
      Ulna 0PP
      Upper Back 0WPK
      Upper Extremity, Left 0XP7
      Upper Femur, Left 0QP7
      Upper Jaw 0WP4
      Ureter 0TP9
      Urethra 0TPD
      Vaginalis, Scrotum and Tunica 0VP8
      Vein
        Lower 06PY
        Upper 05PY
      Vertebra, Lumbar 0QP0
      Vesicles, Prostate and Seminal 0VP4
      Vessel, Great 02PY
      Vulva 0UPM
      Wrist Joint 0RP
    Tissue Expander
      Breast 0HP
      Gland, Mammary 0HP
      Subcutaneous Tissue and Fascia
        Head and Neck 0JPS
        Lower Extremity 0JPW
        Trunk 0JPT
        Upper Extremity 0JPV
    Tracheostomy Device
      Trachea 0BP1
    Traction Apparatus
      Abdominal Wall 2W53
      Back 2W55
      Chest Wall 2W54
      Face 2W51
      Finger 2W5
      Foot 2W5
      Hand 2W5
      Head 2W50
      Inguinal Region 2W5
      Leg, Lower, Left 2W52
      Lower Arm 2W5
      Lower Extremity 2W5
      Lower Leg 2W5
      Thumb 2W5
      Toe 2W5
      Upper Arm 2W5
      Upper Extremity 2W5
      Upper Leg 2W5
    Vascular Access Device
      Subcutaneous Tissue and Fascia
        Lower Extremity 0JPW
        Trunk 0JPT
        Upper Extremity 0JPV
    Wire
      Face 2W51
    Zooplastic Tissue
      Heart 02PA
      Vessel, Great 02PY

Codes provided in the index are incomplete. Refer to tables to determine additional character values.

Renal Dialysis 5A1D

Repair

  by Body System

    Anatomical Regions, General 0WQ

    Anatomical Regions, Lower Extremities 0YQ

    Anatomical Regions, Upper Extremities 0XQ

    Bursae and Ligaments 0MQ

    Central Nervous System 00Q

    Ear, Nose, Sinus 09Q

    Endocrine System 0GQ

    Eye 08Q

    Female Reproductive System 0UQ

    Gastrointestinal System 0DQ

    Head and Facial Bones 0NQ

    Heart and Great Vessels 02Q

    Hepatobiliary System and Pancreas 0FQ

    Lower Arteries 04Q

    Lower Bones 0QQ

    Lower Joints 0SQ

    Lower Veins 06Q

    Lymphatic and Hemic Systems 07Q

    Male Reproductive System 0VQ

    Mouth and Throat 0CQ

    Muscles 0KQ

    Peripheral Nervous System 01Q

    Respiratory System 0BQ

    Skin and Breast 0HQ

    Subcutaneous Tissue and Fascia 0JQ

    Tendons 0LQ

    Upper Arteries 03Q

    Upper Bones 0PQ

    Upper Joints 0RQ

    Upper Veins 05Q

    Urinary System 0TQ

  by Body Part

    1st Toe 0YQ

    2nd Toe 0YQ

    3rd Toe 0YQ

    4th Toe 0YQ

    5th Toe 0YQ

    Abdomen Bursa and Ligament 0MQ

    Abdomen Muscle 0KQ

    Abdomen Tendon 0LQ

    Abdominal Sympathetic Nerve 01QM

    Abdominal Wall 0WQF

    Abducens Nerve 00QL

    Accessory Nerve 00QR

    Accessory Sinus 09QP

    Acetabulum 0QQ

    Acoustic Nerve 00QN

    Acromioclavicular Joint 0RQ

    Adenohypophysis 0GQ0

    Adenoids 0CQQ

    Adrenal Gland 0GQ

    Adrenal Glands, Bilateral 0GQ4

    Ampulla of Vater 0FQC

    Ankle Bursa and Ligament 0MQ

    Ankle Joint 0SQ

    Ankle Region 0YQ

    Ankle Tendon 0LQ

    Anterior Chamber, Left 08Q3

    Anterior Tibial Artery 04Q

    Anus 0DQQ

    Aortic Body 0GQD

    Aortic Valve 02QF

    Appendix 0DQJ

    Areola 0HQ

    Artery

      Aorta, Thoracic 02Q0

      Lower 04Q0

      Upper 03Q0

    Ascending Colon 0DQK

    Atrial Septum 02Q5

    Atrium 02Q

Repair—*continued*

  by Body Part—*continued*

    Auditory Ossicle 09Q

    Axilla 0XQ

    Axillary Artery 03Q

    Axillary Vein 05Q

    Back, Lower 0WQ0

    Basal Ganglia 00Q8

    Basilic Vein 05Q

    Bladder 0TQB

    Bladder Neck 0TQC

    Body

      Coccygeal 0GQ9

      Jugulotympanic 0GQB

    Bone, Hyoid 0NQ0

    Brachial Artery 03Q

    Brachial Plexus 01Q3

    Brachial Vein 05Q

    Breast

      Aberrant 0HQY

      Bilateral 0HQV

      Left 0HQU

      Supernumerary 0HQT

    Bronchus, Segmental, Lingula 0BQ9

    Buccal Mucosa 0CQ4

    Bursa and Ligament, Lower Extremity, Left 0MQ0

    Buttock, Left 0YQ1

    Carina 0BQ2

    Carotid Bodies, Bilateral 0GQ8

    Carotid Body 0GQ

    Carpal 0PQ

    Carpal Joint 0RQ

    Cecum 0DQH

    Celiac Artery 04Q1

    Cephalic Vein 05Q

    Cerebellum 00QC

    Cerebral Hemisphere 00Q7

    Cerebral Meninges 00Q1

    Cerebral Ventricle 00Q6

    Cervical Nerve 01Q1

    Cervical Spinal Cord 00QW

    Cervical Vertebra 0PQ3

    Cervical Vertebral Disc 0RQ3

    Cervical Vertebral Joint 0RQ1

    Cervicothoracic Vertebral Disc 0RQ5

    Cervicothoracic Vertebral Joint 0RQ4

    Cervix 0UQC

    Chest Wall 0WQ8

    Chordae Tendineae 02Q9

    Choroid, Left 08QB

    Chyli, Cisterna 07Q0

    Cisterna Chyli 07QL

    Clavicle 0PQ

    Coccygeal Glomus 0GQB

    Coccygeal Joint 0SQ6

    Coccyx 0QQS

    Colic Artery 04Q

    Colic Vein 06Q7

    Colon, Sigmoid 0DQ1

    Common Bile Duct 0FQ9

    Common Carotid Artery 03Q

    Common Iliac Artery 04Q

    Common Iliac Vein 06Q

    Conduction Mechanism 02Q8

    Conjunctiva 08Q

    Cord

      Lumbar Spinal 00Q0

      Vocal, Left 0CQM

    Cornea 08Q

    Coronary Artery

      Four or More Sites 02Q3

      Three Sites 02Q2

      Two Sites 02Q1

    Coronary Vein 02Q4

    Corpora Arenacea, Pineal 0GQ1

Repair—*continued*

  by Body Part—*continued*

    Cul-de-sac 0UQF

    Cystic Duct 0FQ8

    Deferens, Vas, Bilateral 0VQ1

    Descending Colon 0DQM

    Diaphragm 0BQ

    Duct

      Lacrimal, Left 08QX

      Pancreatic, Accessory 0FQ5

    Duodenum 0DQ9

    Dura Mater 00Q2

    Ear

      External, Bilateral 09Q0

      Inner, Left 09Q5

    Elbow Bursa and Ligament 0MQ

    Elbow Joint 0RQ

    Elbow Region 0XQ

    Epididymis 0VQ

    Epiglottis 0CQR

    Esophageal Vein 06Q3

    Esophagogastric Junction 0DQ4

    Esophagus 0DQ5

      Lower 0DQ3

      Middle 0DQ2

    Ethmoid Bone 0NQ

    Ethmoid Sinus 09Q

    Eustachian Tube 09Q

    External Auditory Canal, Left 09Q4

    External Carotid Artery 03Q

    External Ear

      Bilateral 09Q2

      Left 09Q1

    External Iliac Artery 04Q

    External Iliac Vein 06Q

    External Jugular Vein 05Q

    Extraocular Muscle 08Q

    Eye 08Q

    Eyelid, Lower, Left 08QN

    Face 0WQ2

    Face Artery 03QR

    Face Vein 05Q

    Facial Muscle 0KQ1

    Facial Nerve 00QM

    Fallopian Tube, Left 0UQ6

    Fallopian Tubes, Bilateral 0UQ7

    Femoral Artery 04Q

    Femoral Nerve 01QD

    Femoral Region 0YQ

    Femoral Shaft 0QQ

    Femoral Vein 06Q

    Fibula 0QQ

    Finger, Little, Left 0XQ2

    Finger Nail 0HQQ

    Finger Phalangeal Joint 0RQ

    Finger Phalanx 0PQ

    Foot 0YQ

    Foot Artery 04Q

    Foot Bursa and Ligament 0MQ

    Foot Muscle 0KQ

    Foot Tendon 0LQ

    Foot Vein 06Q

    Frontal Bone 0NQ

    Frontal Sinus 09Q

    Gallbladder 0FQ4

    Gastric Artery 04Q2

    Gastric Vein 06Q2

    Gingiva, Lower 0CQ0

    Gland

      Lacrimal, Left 08QA

      Lower Parathyroid 0GQ

      Mammary 0HQ

      Minor Salivary 0CQ8

      Parathyroid 0GQ0

      Pineal 0GQ1

      Upper Parathyroid 0GQ

      Vestibular 0UQJ

Repair—*continued*
  by Body Part—*continued*
    Glenoid Cavity 0PQ
    Glomus Jugulare 0GQC
    Glossopharyngeal Nerve 00QP
    Greater Omentum 0DQS
    Greater Saphenous Vein 06Q
    Hand 0XQ
    Hand Artery 03Q
    Hand Bursa and Ligament 0MQ
    Hand Muscle 0KQ
    Hand Tendon 0LQ
    Hand Vein 05Q
    Hard Palate 0CQ2
    Head and Neck Sympathetic Nerve 01QK
    Heart 02Q
    Hemiazygos Vein 05Q1
    Hepatic Artery 04Q3
    Hepatic Duct, Left 0FQ6
    Hepatic Vein 06Q4
    Hip Bursa and Ligament 0MQ
    Hip Joint 0SQ
    Hip Muscle 0KQ
    Hip Tendon 0LQ
    Humeral Head 0PQ
    Humeral Shaft 0PQ
    Hymen 0UQK
    Hyoid Bone 0NQX
    Hypogastric Vein 06Q
    Hypoglossal Nerve 00QS
    Hypophysis 0GQ0
    Hypothalamus 00QA
    Ileocecal Valve 0DQC
    Ileum 0DQB
    Index Finger 0XQ
    Inferior Mesenteric Artery 04QB
    Inferior Mesenteric Vein 06Q6
    Inferior Parathyroid Gland 0GQ
    Inguinal Region 0YQ
    Inner Ear 09Q
    Innominate Artery 03Q2
    Innominate Vein 05Q
    Internal Carotid Artery 03Q
    Internal Iliac Artery 04Q
    Internal Jugular Vein 05Q
    Internal Mammary Artery, Left 03Q1
    Intracranial Artery 03QG
    Intracranial Vein 05QL
    Iris 08Q
    Jejunum 0DQA
    Joint
      Finger Phalangeal, Left 0RQ0
      Toe Phalangeal, Left 0SQ0
    Kidney, Left 0TQ1
    Kidney Pelvis 0TQ
    Knee Bursa and Ligament 0MQ
    Knee Joint 0SQ
    Knee Region 0YQ
    Knee Tendon 0LQ
    Lacrimal Bone 0NQ
    Lacrimal Duct, Left 08QY
    Lacrimal Gland 08Q
    Large Intestine 0DQ
    Larynx 0CQS
    Lens 08Q
    Lesser Omentum 0DQT
    Lesser Saphenous Vein 06Q
    Lingula Bronchus 0BQ9
    Little Finger 0XQ
    Liver 0FQ0
      Left Lobe 0FQ2
      Right Lobe 0FQ1
    Lobe Segmental Bronchus
      Lower 0BQ
      Middle, Right 0BQ5
      Upper 0BQ

    Lower Arm 0XQ
    Lower Arm and Wrist Muscle 0KQ
    Lower Arm and Wrist Tendon 0LQ
    Lower Artery 04QY
    Lower Back 0WQL
    Lower Extremity 0YQ
    Lower Extremity Bursa and Ligament 0MQ
    Lower Eyelid 08Q
    Lower Femur 0QQ
    Lower Gingiva 0CQ6
    Lower Jaw 0WQ5
    Lower Leg 0YQ
    Lower Leg Muscle 0KQ
    Lower Leg Tendon 0LQ
    Lower Lip 0CQ1
    Lower Lobe Bronchus 0BQ
    Lower Lung Lobe 0BQ
    Lower Tooth 0CQX
    Lower Vein 06QY
    Lumbar Nerve 01QB
    Lumbar Plexus 01Q9
    Lumbar Spinal Cord 00QY
    Lumbar Sympathetic Nerve 01QN
    Lumbar Vertebral Disc 0SQ2
    Lumbosacral Disc 0SQ4
    Lumbosacral Joint 0SQ3
    Lumbosacral Plexus 01QA
    Lung 0BQ
    Lung Lingula 0BQH
    Lung Lingula Segments 0BQH
    Lung Lobe Segments
      Lower 0BQ
      Middle, Right 0BQD
      Upper 0BQ
    Lungs, Bilateral 0BQM
    Lymphatic
      Aortic 07QD
      Internal Mammary 07Q
      Left Axillary 07Q6
      Left Inguinal 07QJ
      Left Lower Extremity 07QG
      Left Neck 07Q2
      Left Upper Extremity 07Q4
      Mesenteric 07QB
      Pelvis 07QC
      Right Axillary 07Q5
      Right Inguinal 07QH
      Right Lower Extremity 07QF
      Right Neck 07Q1
      Right Upper Extremity 07Q3
      Thorax 07Q7
    Main Bronchus 0BQ
    Mandible 0NQ
    Mastoid Sinus, Left 09QC
    Maxilla 0NQ
    Maxillary Sinus 09Q
    Median Nerve 01Q5
    Mediastinum 0WQC
    Medulla Oblongata 00QD
    Mesentery 0DQV
    Metacarpal 0PQ
    Metacarpocarpal Joint 0RQ
    Metacarpophalangeal Joint 0RQ
    Metatarsal 0QQ
    Metatarsal-Phalangeal Joint 0SQ
    Metatarsal-Tarsal Joint 0SQ
    Middle Ear, Left 09Q6
    Middle Finger 0XQ
    Middle Lobe Bronchus, Right 0BQ5
    Middle Lung Lobe, Right 0BQD
    Minor Salivary Gland 0CQJ
    Mitral Valve 02QG
    Muscle, Foot, Left 0KQ0
    Nail, Toe 0HQ0

    Nail Bed
      Finger 0HQQ
      Toe 0HQR
    Nasal Bone 0NQB
    Nasal Septum 09QM
    Nasal Turbinate 09QL
    Nasopharynx 09QN
    Neck, Bladder 0TQ0
    Neck Muscle 0KQ
    Nerve, Sacral 01Q0
    Neurohypophysis 0GQ0
    Nipple 0HQ
    Nose 09QK
    Occipital Bone 0NQ
    Oculomotor Nerve 00QH
    Olfactory Nerve 00QF
    Omentum, Lesser 0DQR
    Optic Nerve 00QG
    Orbit 0NQ
    Ovaries, Bilateral 0UQ2
    Ovary, Left 0UQ1
    Palatine Bone 0NQ
    Pancreas 0FQG
      Body 0FQF
      Head 0FQF
      Tail 0FQF
    Pancreatic Duct 0FQD
      Accessory 0FQF
    Papillary Muscle 02QD
    Para-aortic Body 0GQ9
    Paraganglion Extremity 0GQF
    Parathyroid Gland 0GQR
    Parathyroid Glands, Multiple 0GQQ
    Parietal Bone 0NQ
    Parotid Duct 0CQ
    Parotid Gland, Left 0CQ9
    Patella 0QQ
    Pelvic Bone 0QQ
    Penis 0VQS
    Pericardium 02QN
    Perineum
      Female 0WQN
      Male 0WQM
    Perineum Bursa and Ligament 0MQK
    Perineum Muscle 0KQM
    Perineum Tendon 0LQH
    Peritoneum 0DQW
    Peroneal Artery 04Q
    Peroneal Nerve 01QH
    Phalanx
      Finger, Left 0PQ0
      Toe, Left 0QQ0
    Phrenic Nerve 01Q2
    Pineal Body 0GQ1
    Pleura 0BQ
      Parietal 0BQ
      Visceral 0BQ
    Pons 00QB
    Popliteal Artery 04Q
    Portal Vein 06Q8
    Posterior Tibial Artery 04Q
    Prepuce 0VQT
    Products of Conception 10Q0
    Prostate 0VQ0
    Pudendal Nerve 01QC
    Pulmonary Artery 02Q
    Pulmonary Lingula 0BQH
    Pulmonary Lobe
      Lower 0BQ
      Middle, Right 0BQD
      Upper 0BQ
    Pulmonary Trunk 02QP
    Pulmonary Valve 02QH
    Pulmonary Vein 02Q

Repair—*continued*
  by Body Part—*continued*
    Radial Artery 03Q
    Radial Nerve 01Q6
    Radius 0PQ
    Rectum 0DQP
    Renal Artery 04Q
    Renal Pelvis 0TQ
    Renal Vein 06Q
    Retina 08Q
    Retinal Vessel 08Q
    Rib 0PQ
    Ring Finger 0XQ
    Sacral Nerve 01QR
    Sacral Plexus 01QQ
    Sacral Sympathetic Nerve 01QP
    Sacrococcygeal Joint 0SQ5
    Sacroiliac Joint 0SQ
    Sacrum 0QQ1
    Scapula 0PQ
    Sciatic Nerve 01QF
    Sclera 08Q
    Scrotum 0VQ5
    Seminal Vesicle, Left 0VQ2
    Seminal Vesicles, Bilateral 0VQ3
    Shoulder Bursa and Ligament 0MQ
    Shoulder Joint 0RQ
    Shoulder Muscle 0KQ
    Shoulder Region, Left 0XQ3
    Shoulder Tendon 0LQ
    Sigmoid Colon 0DQN
    Sinus, Sphenoid, Left 09QB
    Skin
      Abdomen 0HQ7
      Back 0HQ6
      Buttock 0HQ8
      Chest 0HQ5
      Face 0HQ1
      Genitalia 0HQA
      Left Ear 0HQ3
      Left Foot 0HQN
      Left Hand 0HQG
      Left Lower Arm 0HQE
      Left Lower Leg 0HQL
      Left Upper Arm 0HQC
      Left Upper Leg 0HQJ
      Neck 0HQ4
      Perineum 0HQ9
      Right Ear 0HQ2
      Right Foot 0HQM
      Right Hand 0HQF
      Right Lower Arm 0HQD
      Right Lower Leg 0HQK
      Right Upper Arm 0HQB
      Right Upper Leg 0HQH
    Small Intestine 0DQ8
    Soft Palate 0CQ3
    Spermatic Cord 0VQ
    Spermatic Cords, Bilateral 0VQH
    Sphenoid Bone 0NQ
    Sphenoid Sinus 09Q
    Spinal Meninges 00QT
    Spleen 07QP
    Splenic Artery 04Q4
    Splenic Vein 06Q1
    Sternoclavicular Joint 0RQ
    Stomach 0DQ6
      Body 0DQ6
      Fundus 0DQ6
      Pylorus 0DQ7
    Structure, Uterine Supporting 0UQ0
    Subclavian Artery 03Q
    Subclavian Vein 05Q
    Subcutaneous Tissue and Fascia
      Abdomen 0JQ8
      Anterior Neck 0JQ4

Repair—*continued*
  by Body Part—*continued*
    Subcutaneous Tissue and Fascia—
      continued
      Back 0JQ7
      Buttock 0JQ9
      Chest 0JQ6
      Face 0JQ1
      Foot, Left 0JQ0
      Genitalia 0JQC
      Left Foot 0JQR
      Left Hand 0JQK
      Left Lower Arm 0JQH
      Left Lower Leg 0JQP
      Left Upper Arm 0JQF
      Left Upper Leg 0JQM
      Perineum 0JQB
      Posterior Neck 0JQ5
      Right Foot 0JQQ
      Right Hand 0JQJ
      Right Lower Arm 0JQG
      Right Lower Leg 0JQN
      Right Upper Arm 0JQD
      Right Upper Leg 0JQL
    Sublingual Gland 0CQ
    Submaxillary Gland 0CQ
    Superior Mesenteric Artery 04Q5
    Superior Mesenteric Vein 06Q5
    Superior Parathyroid Gland 0GQ
    Superior Vena Cava 02QV
    Supernumerary Breast 0HQY
    Tarsal 0QQ
    Tarsal Joint 0SQ
    Temporal Artery 03Q
    Temporal Bone 0NQ
    Temporomandibular Joint 0RQ
    Tendon, Foot, Left 0LQ0
    Testes, Bilateral 0VQC
    Testis 0VQ
    Thalamus 00Q9
    Thoracic Aorta 02QW
    Thoracic Duct 07QK
    Thoracic Nerve 01Q8
    Thoracic Spinal Cord 00QX
    Thoracic Sympathetic Nerve 01QL
    Thoracic Vertebra 0PQ4
    Thoracic Vertebral Disc 0RQ9
    Thoracic Vertebral Joint 0RQ6
    Thoracolumbar Vertebral Disc 0RQB
    Thoracolumbar Vertebral Joint 0RQA
    Thorax Bursa and Ligament 0MQ
    Thorax Muscle 0KQ
    Thorax Tendon 0LQ
    Thumb 0XQ
    Thumb Phalanx 0PQ
    Thymus 07QM
    Thyroid Artery 03Q
    Thyroid Gland 0GQK
    Thyroid Gland Isthmus 0GQJ
    Thyroid Gland Lobe 0GQ
    Tibia 0QQ
    Tibial Nerve 01QG
    Toe, 5th, Left 0YQ0
    Toe Nail 0HQR
    Toe Phalangeal Joint 0SQ
    Toe Phalanx 0QQ
    Tongue 0CQ7
      Palate, Pharynx Muscle 0KQ4
    Tonsils 0CQP
    Tooth, Lower 0CQW
    Transverse Colon 0DQL
    Tricuspid Valve 02QJ
    Trigeminal Nerve 00QK
    Trochlear Nerve 00QJ
    Trunk Bursa and Ligament 0MQ
    Trunk Muscle 0KQ

Repair—*continued*
  by Body Part—*continued*
    Trunk Tendon 0LQ
    Tube
      Eustachian, Left 09Q3
      Fallopian, Bilateral 0UQ5
    Tunica Vaginalis 0VQ
    Turbinate, Nasal 09Q7
    Tympanic Membrane, Left 09Q8
    Tympanicum, Glomus 0GQB
    Ulna 0PQ
    Ulnar Artery 03Q
    Ulnar Nerve 01Q4
    Upper Arm 0XQ
    Upper Arm Muscle 0KQ
    Upper Arm Tendon 0LQ
    Upper Artery 03QY
    Upper Back 0WQK
    Upper Extremity 0XQ
    Upper Extremity Bursa and Ligament
      0MQ
    Upper Eyelid, Left 08QP
    Upper Femur 0QQ
    Upper Gingiva 0CQ5
    Upper Jaw 0WQ4
    Upper Leg 0YQ
    Upper Leg Muscle 0KQ
    Upper Leg Tendon 0LQ
    Upper Lobe Bronchus 0BQ
    Upper Lung Lobe 0BQ
    Upper Vein 05QY
    Ureter 0TQ
    Urethra 0TQD
    Uterine Supporting Structure 0UQ4
    Uterus 0UQ9
    Uvula 0CQN
    Vagina 0UQG
    Vagus Nerve 00QQ
    Vas Deferens 0VQ
    Vein
      Lower 06Q0
      Upper 05Q0
    Ventricle 02Q
    Ventricular Septum 02QM
    Vertebral Artery 03Q
    Vertebral Vein 05Q
    Vessel, Retinal, Left 08Q2
    Vestibular Gland 0UQL
    Vitreous 08Q
    Vocal Cord 0CQ
    Vulva 0UQM
    Wall, Abdominal 0WQ6
    Wrist Bursa and Ligament 0MQ
    Wrist Joint 0RQ
    Wrist Region 0XQ
    Zygomatic Bone 0NQ

Replacement
  by Body System
    Anatomical Regions, Upper Extremities
      0XR
    Ear, Nose, Sinus 09R
    Eye 08R
    Gastrointestinal System 0DR
    Head and Facial Bones 0NR
    Heart and Great Vessels 02R
    Hepatobiliary System and Pancreas 0FR
    Lower Arteries 04R
    Lower Bones 0QR
    Lower Joints 0SR
    Lower Veins 06R
    Male Reproductive System 0VR
    Mouth and Throat 0CR
    Skin and Breast 0HR
    Subcutaneous Tissue and Fascia 0JR
    Tendons 0LR
    Upper Arteries 03R

Replacement—*continued*
  by Body System—*continued*
    Upper Bones 0PR
    Upper Joints 0RR
    Upper Veins 05R
    Urinary System 0TR
  by Body Part
    Abdomen Tendon 0LR
    Acetabulum 0QR
    Acromioclavicular Joint 0RR
    Ampulla of Vater 0FRC
    Ankle Joint 0SR
    Ankle Tendon 0LR
    Anterior Tibial Artery 04R
    Aortic Valve 02RF
    Areola 0HR
    Artery
      Aorta, Thoracic 02R5
      Lower 04R0
      Upper 03R0
    Atrium 02R
    Auditory Ossicle 09R
    Axillary Artery 03R
    Axillary Vein 05R
    Basilic Vein 05R
    Bladder 0TRB
    Bladder Neck 0TRC
    Bone, Hyoid 0NR0
    Brachial Artery 03R
    Brachial Vein 05R
    Breast 0HR
    Buccal Mucosa 0CR4
    Carpal 0PR
    Carpal Joint 0RR
    Celiac Artery 04R1
    Cephalic Vein 05R
    Cervical Vertebra 0PR3
    Cervical Vertebral Joint 0RR1
    Cervicothoracic Vertebral Disc 0RR5
    Cervicothoracic Vertebral Joint 0RR4
    Chordae Tendineae 02R9
    Choroid 08R
    Clavicle 0PR
    Coccygeal Joint 0SR6
    Coccyx 0QRS
    Colic Artery 04R
    Colic Vein 06R7
    Common Bile Duct 0FR9
    Common Carotid Artery 03R
    Common Iliac Artery 04R
    Common Iliac Vein 06R
    Conjunctiva 08R
    Cord, Vocal, Left 0CRM
    Cornea 08R
    Cystic Duct 0FR8
    Duct
      Lacrimal, Left 08RX
      Pancreatic, Accessory 0FR5
      Parotid, Left 0CRB
    Ear
      External, Bilateral 09R0
      Inner, Left 09R5
    Elbow Joint 0RR
    Epiglottis 0CRR
    Esophageal Vein 06R3
    Esophagus 0DR5
    Ethmoid Bone 0NR
    External Carotid Artery 03R
    External Ear
      Bilateral 09R2
      Left 09R1
    External Iliac Artery 04R
    External Iliac Vein 06R
    External Jugular Vein 05R
    Eye 08R
    Eyelid, Lower, Left 08RN

Replacement—*continued*
  by Body Part—*continued*
    Face Artery 03RR
    Face Vein 05R
    Femoral Artery 04R
    Femoral Shaft 0QR
    Femoral Vein 06R
    Fibula 0QR
    Finger Phalangeal Joint 0RR
    Finger Phalanx 0PR
    Foot Artery 04R
    Foot Tendon 0LR
    Foot Vein 06R
    Frontal Bone 0NR
    Gastric Artery 04R2
    Gastric Vein 06R2
    Gingiva, Lower 0CR0
    Gland, Mammary 0HR
    Glenoid Cavity 0PR
    Greater Omentum 0DRS
    Greater Saphenous Vein 06R
    Hair 0HRS
    Hand Artery 03R
    Hand Tendon 0LR
    Hand Vein 05R
    Hard Palate 0CR2
    Hemiazygos Vein 05R1
    Hepatic Artery 04R3
    Hepatic Duct, Left 0FR6
    Hepatic Vein 06R4
    Hip Joint, Left 0SRB
    Hip Tendon 0LR
    Humeral Head 0PR
    Humeral Shaft 0PR
    Hyoid Bone 0NRX
    Hypogastric Vein 06R
    Inferior Mesenteric Artery 04RB
    Inferior Mesenteric Vein 06R6
    Inner Ear 09R
    Innominate Artery 03R2
    Innominate Vein 05R
    Internal Carotid Artery 03R
    Internal Iliac Artery 04R
    Internal Jugular Vein 05R
    Internal Mammary Artery, Left 03R1
    Intracranial Artery 03RG
    Intracranial Vein 05RL
    Iris 08R
    Joint
      Finger Phalangeal, Left 0RR3
      Hip, Left 0SR9
      Lumbosacral 0SR0
      Thoracolumbar Vertebral 0RR0
      Toe Phalangeal, Left 0SR2
    Kidney Pelvis, Left 0TR4
    Knee Joint 0SR
    Knee Tendon 0LR
    Lacrimal Bone 0NR
    Lacrimal Duct, Left 08RY
    Larynx 0CRS
    Lens 08R
    Lesser Omentum 0DRT
    Lesser Saphenous Vein 06R
    Lower Arm and Wrist Tendon 0LR
    Lower Artery 04RY
    Lower Eyelid 08R
    Lower Femur 0QR
    Lower Gingiva 0CR6
    Lower Leg Tendon 0LR
    Lower Lip 0CR1
    Lower Tooth 0CRX
    Lower Vein 06RY
    Lumbosacral Disc 0SR4
    Lumbosacral Joint 0SR3
    Mandible 0NR
    Maxilla 0NR

Replacement—*continued*
  by Body Part—*continued*
    Membrane, Tympanic, Left 09R7
    Mesentery 0DRV
    Metacarpal 0PR
    Metacarpocarpal Joint 0RR
    Metacarpophalangeal Joint 0RR
    Metatarsal 0QR
    Metatarsal-Phalangeal Joint 0SR
    Metatarsal-Tarsal Joint 0SR
    Middle Ear, Left 09R6
    Mitral Valve 02RG
    Nail, Toe 0HRQ
    Nail Bed
      Finger 0HRQ
      Toe 0HRR
    Nasal Bone 0NRB
    Nasopharynx 09RN
    Neck, Bladder 0TR3
    Nipple 0HR
    Nose 09RK
    Occipital Bone 0NR
    Omentum, Lesser 0DRR
    Orbit 0NR
    Palatine Bone 0NR
    Pancreas
      Body 0FRF
      Head 0FRF
      Tail 0FRF
    Pancreatic Duct 0FRD
      Accessory 0FRF
    Papillary Muscle 02RD
    Parietal Bone 0NR
    Parotid Duct, Left 0CRC
    Patella 0QR
    Pelvic Bone 0QR
    Pericardium 02RN
    Perineum Tendon 0LRH
    Peritoneum 0DRW
    Peroneal Artery 04R
    Phalanx
      Finger, Left 0PR0
      Toe, Left 0QR0
    Popliteal Artery 04R
    Portal Vein 06R8
    Posterior Tibial Artery 04R
    Pulmonary Artery 02R
    Pulmonary Trunk 02RP
    Pulmonary Valve 02RH
    Pulmonary Vein 02R
    Radial Artery 03R
    Radius 0PR
    Renal Artery 04R
    Renal Pelvis 0TR
    Renal Vein 06R
    Retinal Vessel 08R
    Rib 0PR
    Sacrococcygeal Joint 0SR5
    Sacroiliac Joint 0SR
    Sacrum 0QR1
    Scapula 0PR
    Sclera 08R
    Septum, Nasal 09RM
    Shoulder Joint 0RR
    Shoulder Tendon 0LR
    Skin
      Abdomen 0HR7
      Back 0HR6
      Buttock 0HR8
      Chest 0HR5
      Face 0HR1
      Foot, Left 0HR0
      Genitalia 0HRA
      Left Ear 0HR3
      Left Foot 0HRN
      Left Hand 0HRG

Codes provided in the index are incomplete. Refer to tables to determine additional character values.

Replacement—*continued*
  by Body Part—*continued*
    Skin—*continued*
      Left Lower Arm 0HRE
      Left Lower Leg 0HRL
      Left Upper Arm 0HRC
      Left Upper Leg 0HRJ
      Neck 0HR4
      Perineum 0HR9
      Right Ear 0HR2
      Right Foot 0HRM
      Right Hand 0HRF
      Right Lower Arm 0HRD
      Right Lower Leg 0HRK
      Right Upper Arm 0HRB
      Right Upper Leg 0HRH
    Soft Palate 0CR3
    Sphenoid Bone 0NR
    Splenic Artery 04R4
    Splenic Vein 06R1
    Sternoclavicular Joint 0RR
    Subclavian Artery 03R
    Subclavian Vein 05R
    Subcutaneous Tissue and Fascia
      Abdomen 0JR8
      Anterior Neck 0JR4
      Back 0JR7
      Buttock 0JR9
      Chest 0JR6
      Face 0JR1
      Foot, Left 0JR0
      Genitalia 0JRC
      Left Foot 0JRR
      Left Hand 0JRK
      Left Lower Arm 0JRH
      Left Lower Leg 0JRP
      Left Upper Arm 0JRF
      Left Upper Leg 0JRM
      Perineum 0JRB
      Posterior Neck 0JR5
      Right Foot 0JRQ
      Right Hand 0JRJ
      Right Lower Arm 0JRG
      Right Lower Leg 0JRN
      Right Upper Arm 0JRD
      Right Upper Leg 0JRL
    Superior Mesenteric Artery 04R5
    Superior Mesenteric Vein 06R5
    Superior Vena Cava 02RV
    Tarsal 0QR
    Tarsal Joint 0SR
    Temporal Artery 03R
    Temporal Bone 0NR
    Temporomandibular Joint 0RR
    Tendon, Foot, Left 0LR0
    Testes, Bilateral 0VRC
    Testis
      Bilateral 0VR9
      Left 0VRB
    Thoracic Aorta 02RW
    Thoracic Vertebra 0PR4
    Thoracic Vertebral Disc 0RR9
    Thoracic Vertebral Joint 0RR6
    Thoracolumbar Vertebral Disc 0RRB
    Thoracolumbar Vertebral Joint 0RRA
    Thorax Tendon 0LR
    Thumb 0XR
    Thumb Phalanx 0PR
    Thyroid Artery 03R
    Tibia 0QR
    Toe Nail 0HRR
    Toe Phalangeal Joint 0SR
    Toe Phalanx 0QR
    Tongue 0CR7
    Tooth, Lower 0CRW
    Tricuspid Valve 02RJ

Replacement—*continued*
  by Body Part—*continued*
    Trunk Tendon 0LR
    Turbinate, Nasal 09RL
    Tympanic Membrane, Left 09R8
    Ulna 0PR
    Ulnar Artery 03R
    Upper Arm Tendon 0LR
    Upper Artery 03RY
    Upper Eyelid, Left 08RP
    Upper Femur 0QR
    Upper Gingiva 0CR5
    Upper Leg Tendon 0LR
    Upper Vein 05RY
    Ureter 0TR
    Urethra 0TRD
    Uvula 0CRN
    Vein
      Lower 06R0
      Upper 05R0
    Ventricle 02R
    Ventricular Septum 02RM
    Vertebral Artery 03R
    Vertebral Vein 05R
    Vessel, Retinal, Left 08R4
    Vitreous, Left 08R5
    Vocal Cord 0CR
    Wrist Joint 0RR
    Zygomatic Bone 0NR
Replant—*see* Reattachment
Replantation—*see* Reattachment
Reposition
  by Body System
    Bursae and Ligaments 0MS
    Central Nervous System 00S
    Ear, Nose, Sinus 09S
    Endocrine System 0GS
    Eye 08S
    Female Reproductive System 0US
    Gastrointestinal System 0DS
    Head and Facial Bones 0NS
    Heart and Great Vessels 02S
    Hepatobiliary System and Pancreas 0FS
    Lower Arteries 04S
    Lower Bones 0QS
    Lower Joints 0SS
    Lower Veins 06S
    Lymphatic and Hemic Systems 07S
    Male Reproductive System 0VS
    Mouth and Throat 0CS
    Muscles 0KS
    Peripheral Nervous System 01S
    Respiratory System 0BS
    Skin and Breast 0HS
    Tendons 0LS
    Upper Arteries 03S
    Upper Bones 0PS
    Upper Joints 0RS
    Upper Veins 05S
    Urinary System 0TS
  by Body Part
    Abdomen Bursa and Ligament 0MS
    Abdomen Muscle 0KS
    Abdomen Tendon 0LS
    Abducens Nerve 00SL
    Accessory Nerve 00SR
    Acetabulum 0QS
    Acoustic Nerve 00SN
    Acromioclavicular Joint 0RS
    Adrenal Gland, Right 0GS3
    Ampulla of Vater 0FSC
    Ankle Bursa and Ligament 0MS
    Ankle Joint 0SS
    Ankle Tendon 0LS
    Anterior Tibial Artery 04S
    Anus 0DSQ

Reposition—*continued*
  by Body Part—*continued*
    Areola 0HS
    Artery
      Aorta, Thoracic 02SP
      Lower 04S0
      Upper 03S0
    Ascending Colon 0DSK
    Auditory Ossicle, Left 09SA
    Axillary Artery 03S
    Axillary Vein 05S
    Basilic Vein 05S
    Bladder 0TSB
    Bladder Neck 0TSC
    Bone, Hyoid 0NS1
    Brachial Artery 03S
    Brachial Plexus 01S3
    Brachial Vein 05S
    Breast 0HS
    Bronchus, Segmental, Lingula 0BS9
    Bursa and Ligament, Lower Extremity,
      Left 0MS0
    Carina 0BS2
    Carpal, Left 0PSN
    Carpal Joint 0RS
    Cavity, Glenoid, Left 0PS0
    Cecum 0DSH
    Celiac Artery 04S1
    Cephalic Vein 05S
    Cervical Nerve 01S1
    Cervical Spinal Cord 00SW
    Cervical Vertebra 0PS3
    Cervical Vertebral Joint 0RS1
    Cervicothoracic Vertebral Joint 0RS4
    Cervix 0USC
    Clavicle 0PS
    Coccygeal Joint 0SS6
    Coccyx 0QSS
    Colic Artery 04S
    Colic Vein 06S7
    Colon, Sigmoid 0DS5
    Common Bile Duct 0FS9
    Common Carotid Artery 03S
    Common Iliac Artery 04S
    Common Iliac Vein 06S
    Cord
      Lumbar Spinal 00SF
      Spermatic, Bilateral 0VS9
      Vocal, Left 0CSR
    Cul-de-sac 0USF
    Cystic Duct 0FS8
    Descending Colon 0DSM
    Diaphragm 0BS
    Duct
      Lacrimal, Left 08SX
      Pancreatic, Accessory 0FS0
      Parotid, Left 0CSB
    Duodenum 0DS9
    Ear, External, Bilateral 09S0
    Elbow Bursa and Ligament 0MS
    Elbow Joint, Left 0RSM
    Esophageal Vein 06S3
    Ethmoid Bone 0NS
    Eustachian Tube 09S
    External Carotid Artery 03S
    External Ear
      Bilateral 09S2
      Left 09S1
    External Iliac Artery 04S
    External Iliac Vein 06S
    External Jugular Vein 05S
    Extraocular Muscle, Left 08SM
    Face Artery 03SR
    Face Vein 05S
    Facial Muscle 0KS1
    Facial Nerve 00SM

Reposition—*continued*
  by Body Part—*continued*

Fallopian Tube 0US
Fallopian Tubes, Bilateral 0US7
Femoral Artery 04S
Femoral Nerve 01SD
Femoral Shaft 0QS
Femoral Vein 06S
Femur, Lower, Left 0QS6
Fibula 0QS
Finger Phalangeal Joint 0RS
Finger Phalanx 0PS
Foot Artery 04S
Foot Bursa and Ligament 0MS
Foot Muscle 0KS
Foot Tendon 0LS
Foot Vein 06S
Frontal Bone, Left 0NS2
Gallbladder 0FS4
Gastric Artery 04S2
Gastric Vein 06S2
Gland
    Lacrimal, Left 08SL
    Lower Parathyroid 0GS
    Mammary 0HS
    Parathyroid 0GS2
    Upper Parathyroid 0GS
Glenoid Cavity 0PS
Glossopharyngeal Nerve 00SP
Greater Saphenous Vein 06S
Hair 0HSS
Hand Artery 03S
Hand Bursa and Ligament 0MS
Hand Muscle 0KS
Hand Tendon 0LS
Hand Vein 05S
Hard Palate 0CS2
Hemiazygos Vein 05S1
Hepatic Artery 04S3
Hepatic Duct 0FS
Hepatic Vein 06S4
Hip Bursa and Ligament 0MS
Hip Joint, Left 0SSB
Hip Muscle 0KS
Hip Tendon 0LS
Humeral Head, Left 0PSD
Humeral Shaft 0PS
Hyoid Bone 0NSX
Hypogastric Vein 06S
Hypoglossal Nerve 00SS
Ileum 0DSB
Inferior Mesenteric Artery 04SB
Inferior Mesenteric Vein 06S6
Inferior Parathyroid Gland 0GS
Innominate Artery 03S2
Innominate Vein 05S
Internal Carotid Artery 03S
Internal Iliac Artery 04S
Internal Jugular Vein 05S
Internal Mammary Artery, Left 03S1
Intracranial Artery 03SG
Intracranial Vein 05SL
Iris, Left 08SD
Jejunum 0DSA
Joint
    Finger Phalangeal, Left 0RSL
    Sacroiliac, Left 0SS0
    Shoulder, Left 0RS0
    Toe Phalangeal, Left 0SS9
Kidney, Left 0TS1
Kidney Pelvis 0TS
Kidneys, Bilateral 0TS2
Knee Bursa and Ligament 0MS
Knee Joint 0SS
Knee Tendon 0LS
Lacrimal Bone 0NS

Lacrimal Duct, Left 08SY
Lacrimal Gland 08S
Lens 08S
Lesser Saphenous Vein 06S
Lingula Bronchus 0BS9
Lobe, Lower Lung, Left 0BS1
Lobe Segmental Bronchus
    Lower 0BS
    Middle, Right 0BS5
    Upper 0BS
Lower Arm and Wrist Muscle 0KS
Lower Arm and Wrist Tendon 0LS
Lower Artery 04SY
Lower Extremity Bursa and Ligament 0MS
Lower Femur 0QS
Lower Leg Muscle 0KS
Lower Leg Tendon 0LS
Lower Lip 0CS1
Lower Lobe Bronchus 0BS
Lower Lung Lobe 0BS
Lower Tooth 0CSX
Lower Vein 06SY
Lumbar Nerve 01SB
Lumbar Plexus 01S9
Lumbar Spinal Cord 00SY
Lumbosacral Joint 0SS3
Lumbosacral Plexus 01SA
Lung 0BS
Lung Lingula 0BSH
Lung Lingula Segments 0BSH
Lung Lobe Segments
    Lower 0BS
    Middle, Right 0BSD
    Upper 0BS
Main Bronchus 0BS
Mandible 0NS
Maxilla 0NS
Median Nerve 01S5
Metacarpal 0PS
Metacarpocarpal Joint 0RS
Metacarpophalangeal Joint 0RS
Metatarsal 0QS
Metatarsal-Phalangeal Joint 0SS
Metatarsal-Tarsal Joint 0SS
Middle Lobe Bronchus, Right 0BS5
Middle Lung Lobe, Right 0BSD
Muscle, Foot, Left 0KS0
Nasal Bone 0NSB
Nasal Turbinate 09SL
Neck, Bladder 0TS0
Neck Muscle 0KS
Nerve, Sacral 01S0
Nipple 0HS
Nose 09SK
Occipital Bone 0NS
Oculomotor Nerve 00SH
Optic Nerve 00SG
Orbit 0NS
Ossicle, Auditory, Left 09S9
Ovaries, Bilateral 0US2
Ovary, Left 0US1
Palate, Soft 0CS0
Palatine Bone 0NS
Pancreas 0FSG
    Body 0FSF
    Head 0FSF
    Tail 0FSF
Pancreatic Duct 0FSD
    Accessory 0FSF
Parathyroid Gland 0GSR
Parathyroid Glands, Multiple 0GSQ
Parietal Bone 0NS
Parotid Duct, Left 0CSC
Patella 0QS

Pelvic Bone, Left 0QS3
Perineum Bursa and Ligament 0MSK
Perineum Muscle 0KSM
Perineum Tendon 0LSH
Peroneal Artery 04S
Peroneal Nerve 01SH
Phalanx
    Finger, Left 0PSM
    Toe, Left 0QS2
Phrenic Nerve 01S2
Popliteal Artery 04S
Portal Vein 06S8
Posterior Tibial Artery 04S
Products of Conception 10S0
    Ectopic 10S2
Pudendal Nerve 01SC
Pulmonary Artery 02S
Pulmonary Lingula 0BSH
Pulmonary Lobe
    Lower 0BS
    Middle, Right 0BSD
    Upper 0BS
Pulmonary Vein 02S
Radial Artery 03S
Radial Nerve 01S6
Radius 0PS
Rectum 0DSP
Renal Artery 04S
Renal Pelvis 0TS
Renal Vein 06S
Retinal Vessel 08S
Rib 0PS
Sacral Nerve 01SR
Sacral Plexus 01SQ
Sacrococcygeal Joint 0SS5
Sacroiliac Joint 0SS
Sacrum 0QS1
Scapula 0PS
Sciatic Nerve 01SF
Shaft, Humeral, Left 0PSC
Shoulder Bursa and Ligament 0MS
Shoulder Joint 0RS
Shoulder Muscle 0KS
Shoulder Tendon 0LS
Sigmoid Colon 0DSN
Skull 0NS0
Soft Palate 0CS3
Spermatic Cord 0VS
Spermatic Cords, Bilateral 0VSH
Sphenoid Bone 0NS
Spleen 07SP
Splenic Artery 04S4
Splenic Vein 06S1
Sternoclavicular Joint 0RS
Stomach 0DS6
    Body 0DS6
    Fundus 0DS6
Subclavian Artery 03S
Subclavian Vein 05S
Superior Mesenteric Artery 04S5
Superior Mesenteric Vein 06S5
Superior Parathyroid Gland 0GS
Superior Vena Cava 02SV
Tarsal 0QS
Tarsal Joint 0SS
Temporal Artery 03S
Temporal Bone 0NS
Temporomandibular Joint 0RS
Tendon, Foot, Left 0LS0
Testes, Bilateral 0VSC
Testis, Left 0VSB
Thoracic Aorta 02SW
Thoracic Nerve 01S8
Thoracic Spinal Cord 00SX

Reposition—*continued*

by Body Part—continued

Thoracic Vertebra 0PS4
Thoracic Vertebral Joint 0RS6
Thoracolumbar Vertebral Joint 0RSA
Thorax Bursa and Ligament 0MS
Thorax Muscle 0KS
Thorax Tendon 0LS
Thumb Phalanx 0PS
Thymus 07SM
Thyroid Artery 03S
Thyroid Gland Lobe 0GS
Tibia 0QS
Tibial Nerve 01SG
Toe Phalangeal Joint 0SS
Toe Phalanx 0QS
Tongue 0CS7
      Palate, Pharynx Muscle 0KS4
Tooth, Lower 0CSW
Transverse Colon 0DSL
Trigeminal Nerve 00SK
Trochlear Nerve 00SJ
Trunk Bursa and Ligament 0MS
Trunk Muscle 0KS
Trunk Tendon 0LS
Tube, Fallopian, Bilateral 0US0
Turbinate, Nasal 09S7
Tympanic Membrane, Left 09S8
Ulna 0PS
Ulnar Artery 03S
Ulnar Nerve 01S4
Upper Arm Muscle 0KS
Upper Arm Tendon 0LS
Upper Artery 03SY
Upper Extremity Bursa and Ligament 0MS
Upper Femur, Left 0QS7
Upper Leg Muscle 0KS
Upper Leg Tendon 0LS
Upper Lobe Bronchus 0BS
Upper Lung Lobe 0BS
Upper Vein 05SY
Ureter 0TS
Ureters, Bilateral 0TS8
Urethra 0TSD
Uterine Supporting Structure 0US4
Uterus 0US9
Uvula 0CSN
Vagina 0USG
Vagus Nerve 00SQ
Vein
      Lower 06S0
      Upper 05S0
Vertebra, Lumbar 0QS0
Vertebral Artery 03S
Vertebral Vein 05S
Vessel, Retinal, Left 08SC
Vocal Cord 0CS
Wrist Bursa and Ligament 0MS
Wrist Joint 0RS
Zygomatic Bone 0NS

Reroute—*see* Bypass

Resection

by Body System

Bursae and Ligaments 0MT
Central Nervous System 00T
Ear, Nose, Sinus 09T
Endocrine System 0GT
Eye 08T
Female Reproductive System 0UT
Gastrointestinal System 0DT
Head and Facial Bones 0NT
Heart and Great Vessels 02T
Hepatobiliary System and Pancreas 0FT
Lower Bones 0QT
Lower Joints 0ST
Lymphatic and Hemic Systems 07T

Resection—*continued*

by Body System—continued

Male Reproductive System 0VT
Mouth and Throat 0CT
Muscles 0KT
Respiratory System 0BT
Skin and Breast 0HT
Tendons 0LT
Upper Bones 0PT
Upper Joints 0RT
Urinary System 0TT

by Body Part

Abdomen Bursa and Ligament 0MT
Abdomen Muscle 0KT
Abdomen Tendon 0LT
Accessory Sinus 09TP
Acetabulum 0QT
Acromioclavicular Joint 0RT
Adenohypophysis 0GT0
Adenoids 0CTQ
Adrenal Gland 0GT
Adrenal Glands, Bilateral 0GT4
Ampulla of Vater 0FTC
Ankle Bursa and Ligament 0MT
Ankle Joint 0ST
Ankle Tendon 0LT
Anus 0DTQ
Aortic Body 0GTD
Appendix 0DTJ
Areola 0HT
Ascending Colon 0DTK
Auditory Ossicle 09T
Bladder 0TTB
Bladder Neck 0TTC
Body
      Coccygeal 0GT9
      Jugulotympanic 0GTB
Bone, Hyoid 0NT1
Breast
      Aberrant 0HTY
      Bilateral 0HTV
      Left 0HTU
      Supernumerary 0HTT
Bronchus, Segmental, Lingula 0BT9
Bursa and Ligament, Lower Extremity,
      Left 0MT0
Carina 0BT2
Carotid Bodies, Bilateral 0GT8
Carotid Body 0GT
Carpal 0PT
Carpal Joint 0RT
Cecum 0DTH
Cervicothoracic Vertebral Disc 0RT5
Cervicothoracic Vertebral Joint 0RT4
Cervix 0UTC
Chordae Tendineae 02T9
Chyli, Cisterna 07T0
Cisterna Chyli 07TL
Clavicle 0PT
Coccygeal Glomus 0GTB
Coccygeal Joint 0ST6
Coccyx 0QTS
Colon, Sigmoid 0DT1
Common Bile Duct 0FT9
Conduction Mechanism 02T8
Cord, Vocal, Left 0CTM
Cornea 08T
Corpora Arenacea, Pineal 0GT1
Cul-de-sac 0UTF
Cystic Duct 0FT8
Deferens, Vas, Bilateral 0VT1
Descending Colon 0DTM
Diaphragm 0BT
Duct
      Lacrimal, Left 08TX
      Pancreatic, Accessory 0FT5

Resection—*continued*

by Body Part—continued

Duodenum 0DT9
Ear
      External, Left 09T0
      Inner, Left 09T5
Elbow Bursa and Ligament 0MT
Elbow Joint 0RT
Epididymis 0VT
Epiglottis 0CTR
Esophagogastric Junction 0DT4
Esophagus 0DT5
      Lower 0DT3
      Middle 0DT2
Ethmoid Bone 0NT
Ethmoid Sinus 09T
Eustachian Tube 09T
External Ear, Left 09T1
Extraocular Muscle, Left 08TM
Eye 08T
Eyelid, Lower, Left 08TN
Facial Muscle 0KT1
Fallopian Tube 0UT
Fallopian Tubes, Bilateral 0UT7
Femoral Shaft 0QT
Fibula 0QT
Finger Phalangeal Joint 0RT
Finger Phalanx 0PT
Foot Bursa and Ligament 0MT
Foot Muscle 0KT
Foot Tendon 0LT
Frontal Bone, Left 0NT2
Frontal Sinus 09T
Gallbladder 0FT4
Gland
      Lacrimal, Left 08TL
      Lower Parathyroid 0GT
      Mammary 0HT
      Minor Salivary 0CT8
      Parathyroid 0GT0
      Pineal 0GT1
      Upper Parathyroid 0GT
      Vestibular 0UTJ
Glenoid Cavity 0PT
Glomus Jugulare 0GTC
Greater Omentum 0DTS
Hand Bursa and Ligament 0MT
Hand Muscle 0KT
Hand Tendon 0LT
Hard Palate 0CT2
Hemisphere, Cerebral 00T7
Hepatic Duct, Left 0FT6
Hip Bursa and Ligament 0MT
Hip Joint 0ST
Hip Muscle 0KT
Hip Tendon 0LT
Humeral Head 0PT
Humeral Shaft 0PT
Hymen 0UTK
Hyoid Bone 0NTX
Hypophysis 0GT0
Ileocecal Valve 0DTC
Ileum 0DTB
Inferior Parathyroid Gland 0GT
Inner Ear 09T
Iris 08T
Jejunum 0DTA
Joint
      Finger Phalangeal, Left 0RT3
      Toe Phalangeal, Left 0ST2
Kidney 0TT
Kidney Pelvis, Left 0TT4
Kidneys, Bilateral 0TT2
Knee Bursa and Ligament 0MT
Knee Joint 0ST
Knee Tendon 0LT

Restriction—*continued*

by Body System—*continued*
Heart and Great Vessels 02V
Hepatobiliary System and Pancreas 0FV
Lower Arteries 04V
Lower Veins 06V
Lymphatic and Hemic Systems 07V
Mouth and Throat 0CV
Respiratory System 0BV
Upper Arteries 03V
Upper Veins 05V
Urinary System 0TV

by Body Part
Ampulla of Vater 0FVC
Anterior Tibial Artery 04V
Anus 0DVQ
Artery
    Aorta, Thoracic 02VP
    Lower 04V0
    Pulmonary, Left 02VR
    Upper 03V0
Ascending Colon 0DVK
Axillary Artery 03V
Axillary Vein 05V
Basilic Vein 05V
Bladder 0TVB
Bladder Neck 0TVC
Brachial Artery 03V
Brachial Vein 05V
Bronchus
    Lower Lobe, Left 0BV1
    Segmental, Lingula 0BV9
Carina 0BV2
Cecum 0DVH
Celiac Artery 04V1
Cephalic Vein 05V
Cervix 0UVC
Chyli, Cisterna 07V0
Cisterna Chyli 07VL
Colic Artery 04V
Colic Vein 06V7
Colon, Sigmoid 0DV1
Common Bile Duct 0FV9
Common Carotid Artery 03V
Common Iliac Artery 04V
Common Iliac Vein 06V
Cystic Duct 0FV8
Descending Colon 0DVM
Duct
    Lacrimal, Left 08VX
    Pancreatic, Accessory 0FV5
    Parotid, Left 0CVB
Duodenum 0DV9
Esophageal Vein 06V3
Esophagogastric Junction 0DV4
Esophagus 0DV5
    Lower 0DV3
    Middle 0DV2
External Carotid Artery 03V
External Iliac Artery 04V
External Iliac Vein 06V
External Jugular Vein 05V
Face Artery 03VR
Face Vein 05V
Femoral Artery 04V
Femoral Vein 06V
Foot Artery 04V
Foot Vein 06V
Gastric Artery 04V2
Gastric Vein 06V2
Greater Saphenous Vein 06V
Hand Artery 03V
Hand Vein 05V
Heart 02VA
Hemiazygos Vein 05V1
Hepatic Artery 04V3

Restriction—*continued*

by Body Part—*continued*
Hepatic Duct, Left 0FV6
Hepatic Vein 06V4
Hypogastric Vein 06V
Ileocecal Valve 0DVC
Ileum 0DVB
Inferior Mesenteric Artery 04VB
Inferior Mesenteric Vein 06V6
Innominate Artery 03V2
Innominate Vein 05V
Internal Carotid Artery 03V
Internal Iliac Artery 04V
Internal Jugular Vein 05V
Internal Mammary Artery, Left 03V1
Intracranial Artery 03VG
Intracranial Vein 05VL
Jejunum 0DVA
Kidney Pelvis, Left 0TV4
Lacrimal Duct, Left 08VY
Large Intestine 0DV
Lesser Saphenous Vein 06V
Lingula Bronchus 0BV9
Lobe Segmental Bronchus
    Lower 0BV
    Middle, Right 0BV5
    Upper 0BV
Lower Artery 04VY
Lower Lobe Bronchus 0BV
Lower Vein 06VY
Lymphatic
    Aortic 07VD
    Internal Mammary 07V
    Left Axillary 07V6
    Left Inguinal 07VJ
    Left Lower Extremity 07VG
    Left Neck 07V2
    Left Upper Extremity 07V4
    Mesenteric 07VB
    Pelvis 07VC
    Right Axillary 07V5
    Right Inguinal 07VH
    Right Lower Extremity 07VF
    Right Neck 07V1
    Right Upper Extremity 07V3
    Thorax 07V7
Main Bronchus 0BV
Middle Lobe Bronchus, Right 0BV5
Neck, Bladder 0TV3
Pancreas
    Body 0FVF
    Head 0FVF
    Tail 0FVF
Pancreatic Duct 0FVD
    Accessory 0FVF
Parotid Duct, Left 0CVC
Peroneal Artery 04V
Popliteal Artery 04V
Portal Vein 06V8
Posterior Tibial Artery 04V
Pulmonary Artery, Right 02VQ
Pulmonary Vein 02V
Radial Artery 03V
Rectum 0DVP
Renal Artery 04V
Renal Pelvis 0TV
Renal Vein 06V
Sigmoid Colon 0DVN
Small Intestine 0DV8
Splenic Artery 04V4
Splenic Vein 06V1
Stomach 0DV6
    Body 0DV6
    Fundus 0DV6
    Pylorus 0DV7
Subclavian Artery 03V

Restriction—*continued*

by Body Part—*continued*
Subclavian Vein 05V
Superior Mesenteric Artery 04V5
Superior Mesenteric Vein 06V5
Superior Vena Cava 02VV
Temporal Artery 03V
Thoracic Aorta 02VW
Thoracic Duct 07VK
Thyroid Artery 03V
Transverse Colon 0DVL
Ulnar Artery 03V
Upper Artery 03VY
Upper Lobe Bronchus 0BV
Upper Vein 05VY
Ureter 0TV
Urethra 0TVD
Vein
    Lower 06V0
    Upper 05V0
Vertebral Artery 03V
Vertebral Vein 05V

Retrogasserian Rhizotomy—*see* Division, Central Nervous System 008

Revision

by Body System
Anatomical Regions, General 0WW
Anatomical Regions, Lower Extremities 0YW
Anatomical Regions, Upper Extremities 0XW
Bursae and Ligaments 0MW
Central Nervous System 00W
Ear, Nose, Sinus 09W
Endocrine System 0GW
Eye 08W
Female Reproductive System 0UW
Gastrointestinal System 0DW
Head and Facial Bones 0NW
Heart and Great Vessels 02W
Hepatobiliary System and Pancreas 0FW
Lower Arteries 04W
Lower Bones 0QW
Lower Joints 0SW
Lower Veins 06W
Lymphatic and Hemic Systems 07W
Male Reproductive System 0VW
Mouth and Throat 0CW
Muscles 0KW
Peripheral Nervous System 01W
Respiratory System 0BW
Skin and Breast 0HW
Subcutaneous Tissue and Fascia 0JW
Tendons 0LW
Upper Arteries 03W
Upper Bones 0PW
Upper Joints 0RW
Upper Veins 05W
Urinary System 0TW

by Device
Airway
    Esophagus 0DW5
    Nose 09WK
Artificial Sphincter
    Anus 0DWQ
    Bladder 0TWB
    Urethra 0TWD
Autologous Arterial Tissue
    Artery
        Lower 04WY
        Upper 03WY
    Heart 02WA
    Vein
        Lower 06WY
        Upper 05WY
    Vessel, Great 02WY

Revision—*continued*
  by Device—*continued*
    Autologous Tissue Substitute
      Abdominal Wall 0WWF
      Acetabulum 0QW
      Acromioclavicular Joint 0RW
      Ankle Joint, Left 0SWG
      Artery
        Lower 04WY
        Upper 03WY
      Auditory Ossicle 09W
      Back, Lower 0WW0
      Bladder 0TWB
      Bone, Facial 0NWB
      Breast 0HW
      Bursa and Ligament, Lower 0MWX
      Carpal, Left 0PWN
      Carpal Joint 0RW
      Cavity, Glenoid, Left 0PW0
      Cervical Vertebra 0PW3
      Cervical Vertebral Joint 0RW1
      Cervicothoracic Vertebral Disc 0RW5
      Cervicothoracic Vertebral Joint 0RW4
      Cervix, Uterus and 0UWD
      Chest Wall 0WW8
      Chyli, Cisterna 07WK
      Cisterna Chyli 07WL
      Clavicle 0PW
      Coccygeal Joint 0SW6
      Coccyx 0QWS
      Cord
        Epididymis and Spermatic 0VWM
        Spinal 00W0
      Cul-de-sac, Vagina and 0UWH
      Deferens, Vas 0VWR
      Diaphragm 0BWT
      Disc
        Lumbosacral 0SW2
        Thoracolumbar Vertebral 0RW3
      Duct, Pancreatic 0FWB
      Ear 09W
      Elbow Joint, Left 0RWM
      Extraocular Muscle, Left 08WM
      Extremity
        Lower, Left 0YW9
        Upper, Left 0XW6
      Eye 08W
      Face 0WW2
      Facial Bone 0NWW
      Femoral Shaft 0QW
      Femur, Lower, Left 0QW6
      Fibula 0QW
      Finger Nail 0HWQ
      Finger Phalangeal Joint 0RW
      Finger Phalanx 0PW
      Gland, Mammary 0HW
      Glenoid Cavity 0PW
      Hair 0HWS
      Heart 02WA
      Hip Joint, Left 0SWB
      Humeral Head, Left 0PWD
      Humeral Shaft 0PW
      Intestine, Large 0DW8
      Joint
        Finger Phalangeal, Left 0RWL
        Hip, Left 0SW9
        Knee, Left 0SWC
        Sacroiliac, Left 0SW0
        Shoulder, Left 0RW0
        Toe Phalangeal, Left 0SWF
      Kidney 0TW5
      Knee Joint, Left 0SWD
      Large Intestine 0DWE
      Larynx 0CWS
      Lower Back 0WWL
      Lower Bursa and Ligament 0MWY

Revision—*continued*
  by Device—*continued*
    Autologous Tissue Substitute—*continued*
      Lower Extremity, Left 0YWB
      Lower Femur 0QW
      Lower Intestinal Tract 0DWD
      Lower Jaw 0WW5
      Lower Muscle 0KWY
      Lower Tendon 0LWY
      Lumbosacral Disc 0SW4
      Lumbosacral Joint 0SW3
      Lymphatic 07WN
      Mediastinum 0WWC
      Mesentery 0DWV
      Metacarpal 0PW
      Metacarpocarpal Joint 0RW
      Metacarpophalangeal Joint 0RW
      Metatarsal 0QW
      Metatarsal-Phalangeal Joint 0SW
      Metatarsal-Tarsal Joint 0SW
      Mitral Valve 02WG
      Mouth and Throat 0CWY
      Muscle
        Extraocular, Left 08WL
        Lower 0KWX
      Nail, Toe 0HWP
      Nail Bed
        Finger 0HWQ
        Toe 0HWR
      Neck 0WW6
      Nerve
        Cranial 00WE
        Peripheral 01WY
      Nose 09WK
      Omentum 0DWU
      Ossicle, Auditory, Left 09W7
      Pancreatic Duct 0FWD
      Patella 0QW
      Pelvic Bone, Left 0QW3
      Penis 0VWS
      Perineum
        Female 0WWN
        Male 0WWM
      Peritoneum 0DWW
      Phalanx
        Finger, Left 0PWM
        Toe, Left 0QW2
      Pulmonary Valve 02WH
      Radius 0PW
      Rib 0PW
      Sacrococcygeal Joint 0SW5
      Sacroiliac Joint 0SW
      Sacrum 0QW1
      Scapula 0PW
      Scrotum and Tunica Vaginalis 0VW8
      Shaft, Humeral, Left 0PWC
      Shoulder Joint 0RW
      Skull 0NW0
      Spinal Cord 00WV
      Sternoclavicular Joint 0RW
      Stomach 0DW6
        Body 0DW6
        Fundus 0DW6
      Subcutaneous Tissue and Fascia
        Head and Neck 0JWS
        Lower Extremity 0JWW
        Trunk 0JWT
        Upper Extremity 0JWV
      Tarsal 0QW
      Tarsal Joint 0SW
      Temporomandibular Joint 0RW
      Tendon, Lower 0LWX
      Testis 0VWD
      Thoracic Vertebra 0PW4
      Thoracic Vertebral Disc 0RW9
      Thoracic Vertebral Joint 0RW6

Revision—*continued*
  by Device—*continued*
    Autologous Tissue Substitute—*continued*
      Thoracolumbar Vertebral Disc 0RWB
      Thoracolumbar Vertebral Joint 0RWA
      Thumb Phalanx 0PW
      Tibia 0QW
      Toe Nail 0HWR
      Toe Phalangeal Joint 0SW
      Toe Phalanx 0QW
      Trachea 0BW1
      Tract, Lower Intestinal 0DW0
      Tree, Tracheobronchial 0BW0
      Tricuspid Valve 02WJ
      Tube, Fallopian 0UW8
      Tympanic Membrane, Left 09W8
      Ulna 0PW
      Upper Back 0WWK
      Upper Extremity, Left 0XW7
      Upper Femur, Left 0QW7
      Upper Jaw 0WW4
      Ureter 0TW9
      Urethra 0TWD
      Vaginalis, Scrotum and Tunica 0VW4
      Valve, Tricuspid 02WF
      Vein
        Lower 06WY
        Upper 05WY
      Vertebra, Lumbar 0QW0
      Vessel, Great 02WY
      Vulva 0UWM
      Wrist Joint 0RW
    Autologous Venous Tissue
      Artery
        Lower 04WY
        Upper 03WY
      Heart 02WA
      Vein
        Lower 06WY
        Upper 05WY
      Vessel, Great 02WY
    Contraceptive Device
      Cervix, Uterus and 0UWD
      Subcutaneous Tissue and Fascia
        Lower Extremity 0JWW
        Trunk 0JWT
        Upper Extremity 0JWV
    Drainage Device
      Abdominal Wall 0WWF
      Acromioclavicular Joint 0RW
      Adenohypophysis 0GW0
      Adrenal Gland 0GW5
      Ankle Joint, Left 0SWG
      Artery
        Lower 04WY
        Upper 03WY
      Back, Lower 0WW0
      Bladder 0TWB
      Bone
        Facial 0NWB
        Lower 0QWY
        Upper 0PWY
      Breast 0HW
      Bursa and Ligament, Lower 0MWX
      Canal, Spinal 00W6
      Carpal Joint 0RW
      Cavity
        Pelvic 0WW1
        Pericardial 0WWD
      Cervical Vertebral Joint 0RW1
      Cervicothoracic Vertebral Disc 0RW5
      Cervicothoracic Vertebral Joint 0RW4
      Cervix, Uterus and 0UWD
      Chest Wall 0WW8
      Chyli, Cisterna 07WK
      Cisterna Chyli 07WL

Revision—continued
  by Device—continued
    Drainage Device—continued
      Coccygeal Joint 0SW6
      Cord
        Epididymis and Spermatic 0VWM
        Spinal 00W0
      Corpora Arenacea, Pineal 0GW1
      Cul-de-sac, Vagina and 0UWH
      Deferens, Vas 0VWR
      Diaphragm 0BWT
      Disc
        Lumbosacral 0SW2
        Thoracolumbar Vertebral 0RW3
      Duct, Pancreatic 0FWB
      Ear 09W
      Elbow Joint, Left 0RWM
      Extraocular Muscle, Left 08WM
      Extremity
        Lower, Left 0YW9
        Upper, Left 0XW6
      Eye 08W
      Face 0WW2
      Facial Bone 0NWW
      Finger Nail 0HWQ
      Finger Phalangeal Joint 0RW
      Gallbladder 0FW4
      Gland
        Endocrine 0GWS
        Mammary 0HW
        Parathyroid 0GW0
        Pineal 0GW1
        Salivary 0CWA
      Hip Joint, Left 0SWB
      Hypophysis 0GW0
      Joint
        Finger Phalangeal, Left 0RWL
        Hip, Left 0SW9
        Knee, Left 0SWC
        Sacroiliac, Left 0SW0
        Shoulder, Left 0RW0
        Toe Phalangeal, Left 0SWF
      Kidney 0TW5
      Knee Joint, Left 0SWD
      Larynx 0CWS
      Liver 0FW0
      Lower Back 0WWL
      Lower Bursa and Ligament 0MWY
      Lower Extremity, Left 0YWB
      Lower Intestinal Tract 0DWD
      Lower Jaw 0WW5
      Lower Muscle 0KWY
      Lower Tendon 0LWY
      Lumbosacral Disc 0SW4
      Lumbosacral Joint 0SW3
      Lung 0BW
      Lymphatic 07WN
      Marrow, Bone 07WT
      Mediastinum 0WWC
      Mesentery 0DWV
      Metacarpocarpal Joint 0RW
      Metacarpophalangeal Joint 0RW
      Metatarsal-Phalangeal Joint 0SW
      Metatarsal-Tarsal Joint 0SW
      Mouth and Throat 0CWY
      Muscle
        Extraocular, Left 08WL
        Lower 0KWX
      Nail, Toe 0HWP
      Nail Bed
        Finger 0HWQ
        Toe 0HWR
      Neck 0WW6
      Nerve
        Cranial 00WE
        Peripheral 01WY

Revision—continued
  by Device—continued
    Drainage Device—continued
      Neurohypophysis 0GW0
      Nose 09WK
      Omentum 0DWU
      Ovary 0UW3
      Pancreas 0FWG
      Pancreatic Duct 0FWD
      Parathyroid Gland 0GWR
      Pelvic Cavity 0WWJ
      Penis 0VWS
      Perineum
        Female 0WWN
        Male 0WWM
      Peritoneal Cavity 0WWG
      Peritoneum 0DWW
      Pineal Body 0GW1
      Pleura 0BWQ
      Pleural Cavity 0WW
      Retroperitoneum 0WWH
      Sacrococcygeal Joint 0SW5
      Sacroiliac Joint 0SW
      Scrotum and Tunica Vaginalis 0VW8
      Shoulder Joint 0RW
      Sinus 09WY
      Skull 0NW0
      Spinal Canal 00WU
      Spinal Cord 00WV
      Spleen 07WP
      Sternoclavicular Joint 0RW
      Stomach 0DW6
        Body 0DW6
        Fundus 0DW6
      Subcutaneous Tissue and Fascia
        Head and Neck 0JWS
        Lower Extremity 0JWW
        Trunk 0JWT
        Upper Extremity 0JWV
      Tarsal Joint 0SW
      Temporomandibular Joint 0RW
      Tendon, Lower 0LWX
      Testis 0VWD
      Thoracic Vertebral Disc 0RW9
      Thoracic Vertebral Joint 0RW6
      Thoracolumbar Vertebral Disc 0RWB
      Thoracolumbar Vertebral Joint 0RWA
      Thymus 07WM
      Thyroid Gland 0GWK
      Toe Nail 0HWR
      Toe Phalangeal Joint 0SW
      Trachea 0BW1
      Tract, Lower Intestinal 0DW0
      Tree, Tracheobronchial 0BW0
      Tube, Fallopian 0UW8
      Upper Back 0WWK
      Upper Extremity, Left 0XW7
      Upper Jaw 0WW4
      Ureter 0TW9
      Urethra 0TWD
      Vaginalis, Scrotum and Tunica 0VW4
      Vein
        Lower 06WY
        Upper 05WY
      Vulva 0UWM
      Wrist Joint 0RW
    Drug-eluting Intraluminal Device
      Artery
        Lower 04WY
        Upper 03WY
      Heart 02WA
      Vessel, Great 02WY
    Electrode
      Anus 0DWQ
      Bladder 0TWB

Revision—continued
  by Device—continued
    Electrode—continued
      Bone
        Facial 0NWB
        Lower 0QWY
        Upper 0PWY
      Canal, Spinal 00W6
      Cord, Spinal 00W0
      Diaphragm 0BWT
      Facial Bone 0NWW
      Heart 02WA
      Kidney 0TW5
      Lower Muscle 0KWY
      Muscle, Lower 0KWX
      Nerve
        Cranial 00WE
        Peripheral 01WY
      Skull 0NW0
      Spinal Canal 00WU
      Spinal Cord 00WV
      Stomach 0DW6
        Body 0DW6
        Fundus 0DW6
      Ureter 0TW9
      Urethra 0TWD
    Endobronchial Device
      Tree, Tracheobronchial 0BW0
    Endotracheal Device
      Trachea 0BW1
    External Fixation Device
      Ankle Joint, Left 0SWG
      Carpal, Left 0PWN
      Carpal Joint 0RW
      Elbow Joint, Left 0RWM
      Femoral Shaft 0QW
      Femur, Lower, Left 0QW6
      Fibula 0QW
      Finger Phalangeal Joint 0RW
      Finger Phalanx 0PW
      Hip Joint, Left 0SWB
      Humeral Head, Left 0PWD
      Humeral Shaft 0PW
      Joint
        Finger Phalangeal, Left 0RWL
        Hip, Left 0SW9
        Knee, Left 0SWC
        Toe Phalangeal, Left 0SWF
      Knee Joint, Left 0SWD
      Lower Femur 0QW
      Metacarpal 0PW
      Metacarpocarpal Joint 0RW
      Metacarpophalangeal Joint 0RW
      Metatarsal 0QW
      Metatarsal-Phalangeal Joint 0SW
      Metatarsal-Tarsal Joint 0SW
      Patella 0QW
      Pelvic Bone, Left 0QW3
      Phalanx
        Finger, Left 0PWM
        Toe, Left 0QW2
      Radius 0PW
      Shaft, Humeral, Left 0PWC
      Skull 0NW0
      Tarsal 0QW
      Tarsal Joint 0SW
      Thumb Phalanx 0PW
      Tibia 0QW
      Toe Phalangeal Joint 0SW
      Toe Phalanx 0QW
      Ulna 0PW
      Upper Femur, Left 0QW7
      Wrist Joint 0RW
    External Heart Assist System
      Heart 02WA

Revision—*continued*
  by Device—*continued*
    Extraluminal Device
      Artery
        Lower 04WY
        Upper 03WY
      Bladder 0TWB
      Cervix, Uterus and 0UWD
      Chyli, Cisterna 07WK
      Cisterna Chyli 07WL
      Cord, Epididymis and Spermatic
        0VWM
      Deferens, Vas 0VWR
      Duct, Pancreatic 0FWB
      Eye 08W
      Gland, Salivary 0CWA
      Heart 02WA
      Kidney 0TW5
      Lower Intestinal Tract 0DWD
      Lymphatic 07WN
      Pancreatic Duct 0FWD
      Stomach 0DW6
        Body 0DW6
        Fundus 0DW6
      Trachea 0BW1
      Tract, Lower Intestinal 0DW0
      Tree, Tracheobronchial 0BW0
      Tube, Fallopian 0UW8
      Ureter 0TW9
      Urethra 0TWD
      Vein
        Lower 06WY
        Upper 05WY
      Vessel, Great 02WY
    Feeding Device
      Lower Intestinal Tract 0DWD
      Stomach 0DW6
        Body 0DW6
        Fundus 0DW6
      Tract, Lower Intestinal 0DW0
    Hearing Device
      Ear, Inner, Left 09WD
      Inner Ear, Left 09WE
      Skull 0NW0
    Implantable Heart Assist System
      Heart 02WA
    Infusion Device
      Abdominal Wall 0WWF
      Acromioclavicular Joint 0RW
      Ankle Joint, Left 0SWG
      Artery
        Lower 04WY
        Upper 03WY
      Back, Lower 0WW0
      Bladder 0TWB
      Canal, Spinal 00W6
      Carpal Joint 0RW
      Cavity
        Pelvic 0WW1
        Pericardial 0WWD
      Cervical Vertebral Joint 0RW1
      Cervicothoracic Vertebral Disc 0RW5
      Cervicothoracic Vertebral Joint 0RW4
      Cervix, Uterus and 0UWD
      Chest Wall 0WW8
      Chyli, Cisterna 07WK
      Cisterna Chyli 07WL
      Coccygeal Joint 0SW6
      Cord
        Epididymis and Spermatic 0VWM
        Spinal 00W0
      Cul-de-sac, Vagina and 0UWH
      Deferens, Vas 0VWR
      Disc
        Lumbosacral 0SW2
        Thoracolumbar Vertebral 0RW3

Revision—*continued*
  by Device—*continued*
    Infusion Device—*continued*
      Duct, Pancreatic 0FWB
      Elbow Joint, Left 0RWM
      Extremity
        Lower, Left 0YW9
        Upper, Left 0XW6
      Eye 08W
      Face 0WW2
      Finger Phalangeal Joint 0RW
      Gallbladder 0FW4
      Genitourinary Tract 0WWR
      Gland, Endocrine 0GWS
      Heart 02WA
      Hip Joint, Left 0SWB
      Joint
        Finger Phalangeal, Left 0RWL
        Hip, Left 0SW9
        Knee, Left 0SWC
        Sacroiliac, Left 0SW0
        Shoulder, Left 0RW0
        Toe Phalangeal, Left 0SWF
      Kidney 0TW5
      Knee Joint, Left 0SWD
      Liver 0FW0
      Lower Back 0WWL
      Lower Extremity, Left 0YWB
      Lower Intestinal Tract 0DWD
      Lower Jaw 0WW5
      Lumbosacral Disc 0SW4
      Lumbosacral Joint 0SW3
      Lung 0BW
      Lymphatic 07WN
      Mediastinum 0WWC
      Metacarpocarpal Joint 0RW
      Metacarpophalangeal Joint 0RW
      Metatarsal-Phalangeal Joint 0SW
      Metatarsal-Tarsal Joint 0SW
      Neck 0WW6
      Nerve, Cranial 00WE
      Ovary 0UW3
      Pancreas 0FWG
      Pancreatic Duct 0FWD
      Pelvic Cavity 0WWJ
      Penis 0VWS
      Perineum
        Female 0WWN
        Male 0WWM
      Peritoneal Cavity 0WWG
      Pleural Cavity 0WW
      Respiratory Tract 0WWQ
      Retroperitoneum 0WWH
      Sacrococcygeal Joint 0SW5
      Sacroiliac Joint 0SW
      Scrotum and Tunica Vaginalis 0VW8
      Shoulder Joint 0RW
      Spinal Canal 00WU
      Spinal Cord 00WV
      Spleen 07WP
      Sternoclavicular Joint 0RW
      Stomach 0DW6
        Body 0DW6
        Fundus 0DW6
      Subcutaneous Tissue and Fascia
        Head and Neck 0JWS
        Lower Extremity 0JWW
        Trunk 0JWT
        Upper Extremity 0JWV
      Tarsal Joint 0SW
      Temporomandibular Joint 0RW
      Testis 0VWD
      Thoracic Vertebral Disc 0RW9
      Thoracic Vertebral Joint 0RW6
      Thoracolumbar Vertebral Disc 0RWB
      Thoracolumbar Vertebral Joint 0RWA

Revision—*continued*
  by Device—*continued*
    Infusion Device—*continued*
      Thymus 07WM
      Toe Phalangeal Joint 0SW
      Tract
        Genitourinary 0WWP
        Lower Intestinal 0DW0
      Tree, Tracheobronchial 0BW0
      Tube, Fallopian 0UW8
      Upper Back 0WWK
      Upper Extremity, Left 0XW7
      Upper Jaw 0WW4
      Ureter 0TW9
      Urethra 0TWD
      Vaginalis, Scrotum and Tunica 0VW4
      Vein
        Lower 06WY
        Upper 05WY
      Vessel, Great 02WY
      Wrist Joint 0RW
    Infusion Pump
      Subcutaneous Tissue and Fascia
        Lower Extremity 0JWW
        Trunk 0JWT
        Upper Extremity 0JWV
    Internal Fixation Device
      Acetabulum 0QW
      Acromioclavicular Joint 0RW
      Ankle Joint, Left 0SWG
      Bone, Facial 0NWB
      Carpal, Left 0PWN
      Carpal Joint 0RW
      Cavity, Glenoid, Left 0PW0
      Cervical Vertebra 0PW3
      Cervical Vertebral Joint 0RW1
      Cervicothoracic Vertebral Joint 0RW4
      Clavicle 0PW
      Coccygeal Joint 0SW6
      Coccyx 0QWS
      Elbow Joint, Left 0RWM
      Facial Bone 0NWW
      Femoral Shaft 0QW
      Femur, Lower, Left 0QW6
      Fibula 0QW
      Finger Phalangeal Joint 0RW
      Finger Phalanx 0PW
      Glenoid Cavity 0PW
      Hip Joint, Left 0SWB
      Humeral Head, Left 0PWD
      Humeral Shaft 0PW
      Joint
        Finger Phalangeal, Left 0RWL
        Hip, Left 0SW9
        Knee, Left 0SWC
        Sacroiliac, Left 0SW0
        Shoulder, Left 0RW0
        Toe Phalangeal, Left 0SWF
      Knee Joint, Left 0SWD
      Lower Femur 0QW
      Lumbosacral Joint 0SW3
      Metacarpal 0PW
      Metacarpocarpal Joint 0RW
      Metacarpophalangeal Joint 0RW
      Metatarsal 0QW
      Metatarsal-Phalangeal Joint 0SW
      Metatarsal-Tarsal Joint 0SW
      Patella 0QW
      Pelvic Bone, Left 0QW3
      Phalanx
        Finger, Left 0PWM
        Toe, Left 0QW2
      Radius 0PW
      Rib 0PW
      Sacrococcygeal Joint 0SW5
      Sacroiliac Joint 0SW

Revision—*continued*
  by Device—*continued*
    Internal Fixation Device—*continued*
      Sacrum 0QW1
      Scapula 0PW
      Shaft, Humeral, Left 0PWC
      Shoulder Joint 0RW
      Skull 0NW0
      Sternoclavicular Joint 0RW
      Tarsal 0QW
      Tarsal Joint 0SW
      Temporomandibular Joint 0RW
      Thoracic Vertebra 0PW4
      Thoracic Vertebral Joint 0RW6
      Thoracolumbar Vertebral Joint 0RWA
      Thumb Phalanx 0PW
      Tibia 0QW
      Toe Phalangeal Joint 0SW
      Toe Phalanx 0QW
      Ulna 0PW
      Upper Femur, Left 0QW7
      Vertebra, Lumbar 0QW0
      Wrist Joint 0RW
    Intraluminal Device
      Artery
        Lower 04WY
        Upper 03WY
      Bladder 0TWB
      Cervix, Uterus and 0UWD
      Chyli, Cisterna 07WK
      Cisterna Chyli 07WL
      Cul-de-sac, Vagina and 0UWH
      Deferens, Vas 0VWR
      Duct, Pancreatic 0FWB
      Ear 09W
      Eye 08W
      Gallbladder 0FW4
      Heart 02WA
      Kidney 0TW5
      Larynx 0CWS
      Lower Intestinal Tract 0DWD
      Lymphatic 07WN
      Mouth and Throat 0CWY
      Pancreas 0FWG
      Pancreatic Duct 0FWD
      Stomach 0DW6
        Body 0DW6
        Fundus 0DW6
      Trachea 0BW1
      Tract, Lower Intestinal 0DW0
      Tree, Tracheobronchial 0BW0
      Tube, Fallopian 0UW8
      Ureter 0TW9
      Urethra 0TWD
      Vein
        Lower 06WY
        Upper 05WY
      Vessel, Great 02WY
    Intramedullary Fixation Device
      Femoral Shaft 0QW
      Femur, Lower, Left 0QW6
      Fibula 0QW
      Humeral Head, Left 0PWD
      Humeral Shaft 0PW
      Lower Femur 0QW
      Radius 0PW
      Shaft, Humeral, Left 0PWC
      Tibia 0QW
      Ulna 0PW
      Upper Femur, Left 0QW7
    Liner
      Hip Joint, Left 0SWB
      Joint
        Hip, Left 0SW9
        Knee, Left 0SWC
      Knee Joint, Left 0SWD

Revision—*continued*
  by Device—*continued*
    Monitoring Device
      Artery
        Lower 04WY
        Upper 03WY
      Bladder 0TWB
      Canal, Spinal 00W6
      Cord, Spinal 00W0
      Diaphragm 0BWT
      Duct, Pancreatic 0FWB
      Gallbladder 0FW4
      Gland, Endocrine 0GWS
      Heart 02WA
      Kidney 0TW5
      Liver 0FW0
      Lower Intestinal Tract 0DWD
      Lung 0BW
      Nerve
        Cranial 00WE
        Peripheral 01WY
      Pancreas 0FWG
      Pancreatic Duct 0FWD
      Pleura 0BWQ
      Spinal Canal 00WU
      Spinal Cord 00WV
      Stomach 0DW6
        Body 0DW6
        Fundus 0DW6
      Trachea 0BW1
      Tract, Lower Intestinal 0DW0
      Tree, Tracheobronchial 0BW0
      Ureter 0TW9
      Urethra 0TWD
      Vein
        Lower 06WY
        Upper 05WY
      Vessel, Great 02WY
    Nonautologous Tissue Substitute
      Abdominal Wall 0WWF
      Acetabulum 0QW
      Acromioclavicular Joint 0RW
      Ankle Joint, Left 0SWG
      Artery
        Lower 04WY
        Upper 03WY
      Auditory Ossicle 09W
      Back, Lower 0WW0
      Bladder 0TWB
      Bone, Facial 0NWB
      Breast 0HW
      Bursa and Ligament, Lower 0MWX
      Carpal, Left 0PWN
      Carpal Joint 0RW
      Cavity, Glenoid, Left 0PW0
      Cervical Vertebra 0PW3
      Cervical Vertebral Joint 0RW1
      Cervicothoracic Vertebral Disc 0RW5
      Cervicothoracic Vertebral Joint 0RW4
      Cervix, Uterus and 0UWD
      Chest Wall 0WW8
      Chyli, Cisterna 07WK
      Cisterna Chyli 07WL
      Clavicle 0PW
      Coccygeal Joint 0SW6
      Coccyx 0QWS
      Cord
        Epididymis and Spermatic 0VWM
        Spinal 00W0
      Cul-de-sac, Vagina and 0UWH
      Deferens, Vas 0VWR
      Diaphragm 0BWT
      Disc
        Lumbosacral 0SW2
        Thoracolumbar Vertebral 0RW3
      Duct, Pancreatic 0FWB

Revision—*continued*
  by Device—*continued*
    Nonautologous Tissue Substitute—
      continued
      Ear 09W
      Elbow Joint, Left 0RWM
      Extraocular Muscle, Left 08WM
      Extremity
        Lower, Left 0YW9
        Upper, Left 0XW6
      Eye 08W
      Face 0WW2
      Facial Bone 0NWW
      Femoral Shaft 0QW
      Femur, Lower, Left 0QW6
      Fibula 0QW
      Finger Nail 0HWQ
      Finger Phalangeal Joint 0RW
      Finger Phalanx 0PW
      Gland, Mammary 0HW
      Glenoid Cavity 0PW
      Hair 0HWS
      Heart 02WA
      Hip Joint, Left 0SWB
      Humeral Head, Left 0PWD
      Humeral Shaft 0PW
      Intestine, Large 0DW8
      Joint
        Finger Phalangeal, Left 0RWL
        Hip, Left 0SW9
        Knee, Left 0SWC
        Sacroiliac, Left 0SW0
        Shoulder, Left 0RW0
        Toe Phalangeal, Left 0SWF
      Kidney 0TW5
      Knee Joint, Left 0SWD
      Large Intestine 0DWE
      Larynx 0CWS
      Lower Back 0WWL
      Lower Bursa and Ligament 0MWY
      Lower Extremity, Left 0YWB
      Lower Femur 0QW
      Lower Intestinal Tract 0DWD
      Lower Jaw 0WW5
      Lower Muscle 0KWY
      Lower Tendon 0LWY
      Lumbosacral Disc 0SW4
      Lumbosacral Joint 0SW3
      Lymphatic 07WN
      Mediastinum 0WWC
      Mesentery 0DWV
      Metacarpal 0PW
      Metacarpocarpal Joint 0RW
      Metacarpophalangeal Joint 0RW
      Metatarsal 0QW
      Metatarsal-Phalangeal Joint 0SW
      Metatarsal-Tarsal Joint 0SW
      Mitral Valve 02WG
      Mouth and Throat 0CWY
      Muscle
        Extraocular, Left 08WL
        Lower 0KWX
      Nail, Toe 0HWP
      Nail Bed
        Finger 0HWQ
        Toe 0HWR
      Neck 0WW6
      Nose 09WK
      Omentum 0DWU
      Ossicle, Auditory, Left 09W7
      Pancreatic Duct 0FWD
      Patella 0QW
      Pelvic Bone, Left 0QW3
      Penis 0VWS

Revision—*continued*
  by Device—*continued*
    Nonautologous Tissue Substitute—*continued*
      Perineum
        Female 0WWN
        Male 0WWM
      Peritoneum 0DWW
      Phalanx
        Finger, Left 0PWM
        Toe, Left 0QW2
      Pulmonary Valve 02WH
      Radius 0PW
      Rib 0PW
      Sacrococcygeal Joint 0SW5
      Sacroiliac Joint 0SW
      Sacrum 0QW1
      Scapula 0PW
      Scrotum and Tunica Vaginalis 0VW8
      Shaft, Humeral, Left 0PWC
      Shoulder Joint 0RW
      Skull 0NW0
      Spinal Cord 00WV
      Sternoclavicular Joint 0RW
      Stomach 0DW6
        Body 0DW6
        Fundus 0DW6
      Subcutaneous Tissue and Fascia
        Head and Neck 0JWS
        Lower Extremity 0JWW
        Trunk 0JWT
        Upper Extremity 0JWV
      Tarsal 0QW
      Tarsal Joint 0SW
      Temporomandibular Joint 0RW
      Tendon, Lower 0LWX
      Testis 0VWD
      Thoracic Vertebra 0PW4
      Thoracic Vertebral Disc 0RW9
      Thoracic Vertebral Joint 0RW6
      Thoracolumbar Vertebral Disc 0RWB
      Thoracolumbar Vertebral Joint 0RWA
      Thumb Phalanx 0PW
      Tibia 0QW
      Toe Nail 0HWR
      Toe Phalangeal Joint 0SW
      Toe Phalanx 0QW
      Trachea 0BW1
      Tract, Lower Intestinal 0DW0
      Tree, Tracheobronchial 0BW0
      Tricuspid Valve 02WJ
      Tube, Fallopian 0UW8
      Tympanic Membrane, Left 09W8
      Ulna 0PW
      Upper Back 0WWK
      Upper Extremity, Left 0XW7
      Upper Femur, Left 0QW7
      Upper Jaw 0WW4
      Ureter 0TW9
      Urethra 0TWD
      Vaginalis, Scrotum and Tunica 0VW4
      Valve, Tricuspid 02WF
      Vein
        Lower 06WY
        Upper 05WY
      Vertebra, Lumbar 0QW0
      Vessel, Great 02WY
      Vulva 0UWM
      Wrist Joint 0RW
    Other Device
      Abdominal Wall 0WWF
      Back, Lower 0WW0
      Cavity
        Pelvic 0WW1
        Pericardial 0WWD
      Chest Wall 0WW8

Revision—*continued*
  by Device—*continued*
    Other Device—*continued*
      Extremity
        Lower, Left 0YW9
        Upper, Left 0XW6
      Face 0WW2
      Genitourinary Tract 0WWR
      Lower Back 0WWL
      Lower Extremity, Left 0YWB
      Lower Jaw 0WW5
      Mediastinum 0WWC
      Neck 0WW6
      Pelvic Cavity 0WWJ
      Perineum
        Female 0WWN
        Male 0WWM
      Peritoneal Cavity 0WWG
      Pleural Cavity 0WW
      Respiratory Tract 0WWQ
      Retroperitoneum 0WWH
      Tract, Genitourinary 0WWP
      Upper Back 0WWK
      Upper Extremity, Left 0XW7
      Upper Jaw 0WW4
    Pacemaker / Defibrillator
      Subcutaneous Tissue and Fascia, Trunk 0JWT
    Pessary
      Cul-de-sac, Vagina and 0UWH
    Radioactive Element
      Abdominal Wall 0WWF
      Back, Lower 0WW0
      Cavity
        Pelvic 0WW1
        Pericardial 0WWD
      Chest Wall 0WW8
      Face 0WW2
      Genitourinary Tract 0WWR
      Lower Back 0WWL
      Lower Jaw 0WW5
      Mediastinum 0WWC
      Mouth and Throat 0CWY
      Neck 0WW6
      Pelvic Cavity 0WWJ
      Perineum
        Female 0WWN
        Male 0WWM
      Peritoneal Cavity 0WWG
      Pleural Cavity 0WW
      Respiratory Tract 0WWQ
      Retroperitoneum 0WWH
      Tract, Genitourinary 0WWP
      Upper Back 0WWK
      Upper Jaw 0WW4
    Reservoir
      Subcutaneous Tissue and Fascia
        Lower Extremity 0JWW
        Trunk 0JWT
        Upper Extremity 0JWV
    Resurfacing Device
      Hip Joint, Left 0SWB
      Joint, Hip, Left 0SW9
    Spacer
      Acromioclavicular Joint 0RW
      Ankle Joint, Left 0SWG
      Carpal Joint 0RW
      Cervical Vertebral Joint 0RW1
      Cervicothoracic Vertebral Joint 0RW4
      Coccygeal Joint 0SW6
      Elbow Joint, Left 0RWM
      Finger Phalangeal Joint 0RW
      Hip Joint, Left 0SWB
      Joint
        Finger Phalangeal, Left 0RWL
        Hip, Left 0SW9

Revision—*continued*
  by Device—*continued*
    Spacer—*continued*
      Joint—*continued*
        Knee, Left 0SWC
        Sacroiliac, Left 0SW0
        Shoulder, Left 0RW0
        Toe Phalangeal, Left 0SWF
      Knee Joint, Left 0SWD
      Lumbosacral Joint 0SW3
      Metacarpocarpal Joint 0RW
      Metacarpophalangeal Joint 0RW
      Metatarsal-Phalangeal Joint 0SW
      Metatarsal-Tarsal Joint 0SW
      Sacrococcygeal Joint 0SW5
      Sacroiliac Joint 0SW
      Shoulder Joint 0RW
      Sternoclavicular Joint 0RW
      Tarsal Joint 0SW
      Temporomandibular Joint 0RW
      Thoracic Vertebral Joint 0RW6
      Thoracolumbar Vertebral Joint 0RWA
      Toe Phalangeal Joint 0SW
      Wrist Joint 0RW
    Stimulator Generator
      Subcutaneous Tissue and Fascia
        Head and Neck 0JWS
        Lower Extremity 0JWW
        Trunk 0JWT
        Upper Extremity 0JWV
    Synthetic Substitute
      Abdominal Wall 0WWF
      Acetabulum 0QW
      Acromioclavicular Joint 0RW
      Ankle Joint, Left 0SWG
      Artery
        Lower 04WY
        Upper 03WY
      Auditory Ossicle 09W
      Back, Lower 0WW0
      Bladder 0TWB
      Bone, Facial 0NWB
      Breast 0HW
      Bursa and Ligament, Lower 0MWX
      Canal, Spinal 00W6
      Carpal, Left 0PWN
      Carpal Joint 0RW
      Cavity
        Glenoid, Left 0PW0
        Pelvic 0WW1
      Cervical Vertebra 0PW3
      Cervical Vertebral Joint 0RW1
      Cervicothoracic Vertebral Disc 0RW5
      Cervicothoracic Vertebral Joint 0RW4
      Cervix, Uterus and 0UWD
      Chest Wall 0WW8
      Chyli, Cisterna 07WK
      Cisterna Chyli 07WL
      Clavicle 0PW
      Coccygeal Joint 0SW6
      Coccyx 0QWS
      Cord
        Epididymis and Spermatic 0VWM
        Spinal 00W0
      Cul-de-sac, Vagina and 0UWH
      Deferens, Vas 0VWR
      Diaphragm 0BWT
      Disc
        Lumbosacral 0SW2
        Thoracolumbar Vertebral 0RW3
      Duct, Pancreatic 0FWB
      Ear 09W
      Elbow Joint, Left 0RWM
      Extraocular Muscle, Left 08WM
      Extremity
        Lower, Left 0YW9

Revision—*continued*
  by Device—*continued*
    Synthetic Substitute—*continued*
      Extremity—*continued*
        Upper, Left 0XW6
      Eye 08W
      Face 0WW2
      Facial Bone 0NWW
      Femoral Shaft 0QW
      Femur, Lower, Left 0QW6
      Fibula 0QW
      Finger Nail 0HWQ
      Finger Phalangeal Joint 0RW
      Finger Phalanx 0PW
      Gland, Mammary 0HW
      Glenoid Cavity 0PW
      Hair 0HWS
      Heart 02WA
      Hip Joint, Left 0SWB
      Humeral Head, Left 0PWD
      Humeral Shaft 0PW
      Intestine, Large 0DW8
      Joint
        Finger Phalangeal, Left 0RWL
        Hip, Left 0SW9
        Knee, Left 0SWC
        Sacroiliac, Left 0SW0
        Shoulder, Left 0RW0
        Toe Phalangeal, Left 0SWF
      Kidney 0TW5
      Knee Joint, Left 0SWD
      Large Intestine 0DWE
      Larynx 0CWS
      Lens 08W
      Lower Back 0WWL
      Lower Bursa and Ligament 0MWY
      Lower Extremity, Left 0YWB
      Lower Femur 0QW
      Lower Intestinal Tract 0DWD
      Lower Jaw 0WW5
      Lower Muscle 0KWY
      Lower Tendon 0LWY
      Lumbosacral Disc 0SW4
      Lumbosacral Joint 0SW3
      Lymphatic 07WN
      Mediastinum 0WWC
      Mesentery 0DWV
      Metacarpal 0PW
      Metacarpocarpal Joint 0RW
      Metacarpophalangeal Joint 0RW
      Metatarsal 0QW
      Metatarsal-Phalangeal Joint 0SW
      Metatarsal-Tarsal Joint 0SW
      Mitral Valve 02WG
      Mouth and Throat 0CWY
      Muscle
        Extraocular, Left 08WL
        Lower 0KWX
      Nail, Toe 0HWP
      Nail Bed
        Finger 0HWQ
        Toe 0HWR
      Neck 0WW6
      Nose 09WK
      Omentum 0DWU
      Ossicle, Auditory, Left 09W7
      Pancreatic Duct 0FWD
      Patella 0QW
      Pelvic Bone, Left 0QW3
      Pelvic Cavity 0WWJ
      Penis 0VWS
      Perineum
        Female 0WWN
        Male 0WWM
      Peritoneal Cavity 0WWG
      Peritoneum 0DWW

Revision—*continued*
  by Device—*continued*
    Synthetic Substitute—*continued*
      Phalanx
        Finger, Left 0PWM
        Toe, Left 0QW2
      Pleural Cavity 0WW
      Pulmonary Valve 02WH
      Radius 0PW
      Rib 0PW
      Sacrococcygeal Joint 0SW5
      Sacroiliac Joint 0SW
      Sacrum 0QW1
      Scapula 0PW
      Scrotum and Tunica Vaginalis 0VW8
      Septum, Ventricular 02W5
      Shaft, Humeral, Left 0PWC
      Shoulder Joint 0RW
      Skull 0NW0
      Spinal Canal 00WU
      Spinal Cord 00WV
      Sternoclavicular Joint 0RW
      Stomach 0DW6
        Body 0DW6
        Fundus 0DW6
      Subcutaneous Tissue and Fascia
        Head and Neck 0JWS
        Lower Extremity 0JWW
        Trunk 0JWT
        Upper Extremity 0JWV
      Tarsal 0QW
      Tarsal Joint 0SW
      Temporomandibular Joint 0RW
      Tendon, Lower 0LWX
      Testis 0VWD
      Thoracic Vertebra 0PW4
      Thoracic Vertebral Disc 0RW9
      Thoracic Vertebral Joint 0RW6
      Thoracolumbar Vertebral Disc 0RWB
      Thoracolumbar Vertebral Joint 0RWA
      Thumb Phalanx 0PW
      Tibia 0QW
      Toe Nail 0HWR
      Toe Phalangeal Joint 0SW
      Toe Phalanx 0QW
      Trachea 0BW1
      Tract, Lower Intestinal 0DW0
      Tree, Tracheobronchial 0BW0
      Tricuspid Valve 02WJ
      Tube, Fallopian 0UW8
      Tympanic Membrane, Left 09W8
      Ulna 0PW
      Upper Back 0WWK
      Upper Extremity, Left 0XW7
      Upper Femur, Left 0QW7
      Upper Jaw 0WW4
      Ureter 0TW9
      Urethra 0TWD
      Vaginalis, Scrotum and Tunica 0VW4
      Valve, Tricuspid 02WF
      Vein
        Lower 06WY
        Upper 05WY
      Ventricular Septum 02WM
      Vertebra, Lumbar 0QW0
      Vessel, Great 02WY
      Vulva 0UWM
      Wrist Joint 0RW
    Tissue Expander
      Breast 0HW
      Gland, Mammary 0HW
      Subcutaneous Tissue and Fascia
        Head and Neck 0JWS
        Lower Extremity 0JWW
        Trunk 0JWT
        Upper Extremity 0JWV

Revision—*continued*
  by Device—*continued*
    Tracheostomy Device
      Trachea 0BW1
    Vascular Access Device
      Subcutaneous Tissue and Fascia
        Lower Extremity 0JWW
        Trunk 0JWT
        Upper Extremity 0JWV
    Zooplastic Tissue
      Heart 02WA
      Mitral Valve 02WG
      Pulmonary Valve 02WH
      Tricuspid Valve 02WJ
      Valve, Tricuspid 02WF
      Vessel, Great 02WY

Rhinoplasty
  —*see* Alteration, Ear, Nose, Sinus 090
  —*see* Repair, Ear, Nose, Sinus 09Q
  —*see* Replacement, Ear, Nose, Sinus 09R
Rhinorrhaphy—*see* Repair, Ear, Nose, Sinus 09Q
Rhizotomy
  —*see* Division, Central Nervous System 008
  —*see* Division, Peripheral Nervous System 018
Rhythm Electrocardiogram 4A02
Robotic Assisted Procedure
  8E09
  8E0W
  8E0X
  8E0Y
Rupture
  —*see* Drainage
  —*see* Release

S

Sacrectomy—*see* Excision, Lower Bones 0QB
Salpingectomy
  —*see* Excision, Female Reproductive System 0UB
  —*see* Resection, Female Reproductive System 0UT
Salpingolysis—*see* Release, Female Reproductive System 0UN
Salpingopexy
  —*see* Repair, Female Reproductive System 0UQ
  —*see* Reposition, Female Reproductive System 0US
Salpingoplasty—*see* Repair, Female Reproductive System 0UQ
Salpingoscopy—*see* Inspection, Female Reproductive System 0UJ
Salpingotomy
  —*see* Drainage, Female Reproductive System 0U9
  —*see* Inspection, Female Reproductive System 0UJ
Scapulectomy
  —*see* Excision, Upper Bones 0PB
  —*see* Resection, Upper Bones 0PT
Scapulopexy
  —*see* Repair, Upper Bones 0PQ
  —*see* Reposition, Upper Bones 0PS
Sclerectomy
  —*see* Excision, Eye 08B
  —*see* Resection, Eye 08T
Sclerotherapy—*see* Destruction
Sclerotomy
  —*see* Drainage, Eye 089
  —*see* Inspection, Eye 08J

Scrotectomy
—see Excision, Male Reproductive System 0VB
—see Resection, Male Reproductive System 0VT

Scrotoplasty
—see Repair, Male Reproductive System 0VQ
—see Replacement, Male Reproductive System 0VR

Scrotorrhaphy—see Repair, Male Reproductive System 0VQ

Scrototomy
—see Drainage, Male Reproductive System 0V9
—see Inspection, Male Reproductive System 0VJ

Section, Caesarean—see Cesarean Section
Section, Cesarean—see Cesarean Section
Separate—see Division
Separation—see Division
Septectomy
—see Excision, Ear, Nose, Sinus 09B
—see Excision, Heart and Great Vessels 02B
—see Resection, Ear, Nose, Sinus 09T
—see Resection, Heart and Great Vessels 02T

Septoplasty
—see Repair, Ear, Nose, Sinus 09Q
—see Replacement, Ear, Nose, Sinus 09R

Septotomy
—see Drainage, Ear, Nose, Sinus 099
—see Inspection, Ear, Nose, Sinus 09J

Shock Wave Therapy
Musculoskeletal 6A93

Shunt—see Bypass
Sialodochoplasty
—see Repair, Mouth and Throat 0CQ
—see Replacement, Mouth and Throat 0CR

Sialoectomy
—see Excision, Mouth and Throat 0CB
—see Resection, Mouth and Throat 0CT

Sialography—see Plain Radiography, Ear, Nose, Mouth and Throat B90
Sialolithotomy—see Extirpation, Mouth and Throat 0CC
Sigmoidectomy
—see Excision, Gastrointestinal System 0DB
—see Resection, Gastrointestinal System 0DT

Sigmoidorrhaphy—see Repair, Gastrointestinal System 0DQ
Sigmoidoscopy—see Inspection, Gastrointestinal System 0DJ
Sigmoidotomy
—see Drainage, Gastrointestinal System 0D9
—see Inspection, Gastrointestinal System 0DJ

Sinusectomy
—see Excision, Ear, Nose, Sinus 09B
—see Resection, Ear, Nose, Sinus 09T

Sinusoscopy—see Inspection, Ear, Nose, Sinus 09J
Sinusotomy
—see Drainage, Ear, Nose, Sinus 099
—see Inspection, Ear, Nose, Sinus 09J

Small Bowel Series—see Fluoroscopy, Gastrointestinal System BD1
Speech, Language, Hearing—see Physical Rehabilitation and Diagnostic Audiology
Speech Therapy—see Physical Rehabilitation and Diagnostic Audiology

Sphenoidectomy
—see Excision, Ear, Nose, Sinus 09B
—see Excision, Head and Facial Bones 0NB
—see Resection, Ear, Nose, Sinus 09T
—see Resection, Head and Facial Bones 0NT

Sphenoidotomy
—see Drainage, Ear, Nose, Sinus 099
—see Inspection, Ear, Nose, Sinus 09J

Sphincterotomy
—see Drainage
—see Inspection

Splenectomy
—see Excision, Lymphatic and Hemic Systems 07B
—see Resection, Lymphatic and Hemic Systems 07T

Splenolysis—see Release, Lymphatic and Hemic Systems 07N
Splenopexy—see Repair, Lymphatic and Hemic Systems 07Q
Splenoplasty—see Repair, Lymphatic and Hemic Systems 07Q
Splenorrhaphy—see Repair, Lymphatic and Hemic Systems 07Q
Splenotomy
—see Drainage, Lymphatic and Hemic Systems 079
—see Inspection, Lymphatic and Hemic Systems 07J

Stapedectomy
—see Excision, Ear, Nose, Sinus 09B
—see Resection, Ear, Nose, Sinus 09T

Stapediolysis—see Release, Ear, Nose, Sinus 09N
Stapedioplasty
—see Repair, Ear, Nose, Sinus 09Q
—see Replacement, Ear, Nose, Sinus 09R

Stapedotomy
—see Drainage, Ear, Nose, Sinus 099
—see Inspection, Ear, Nose, Sinus 09J

Staphylectomy
—see Excision, Mouth and Throat 0CB
—see Resection, Mouth and Throat 0CT

Staphyloplasty
—see Repair, Mouth and Throat 0CQ
—see Replacement, Mouth and Throat 0CR

Staphylorrhaphy—see Repair, Mouth and Throat 0CQ
Staphylotomy
—see Drainage, Mouth and Throat 0C9
—see Inspection, Mouth and Throat 0CJ

Stereotactic Radiosurgery
by Body System
Anatomical Regions DW2
Breast DM2
Central and Peripheral Nervous System D02
Ear, Nose, Mouth and Throat D92
Endocrine System DG2
Eye D82
Female Reproductive System DU2
Gastrointestinal System DD2
Hepatobiliary System and Pancreas DF2
Lymphatic and Hematologic System D72
Male Reproductive System DV2
Respiratory System DB2
Urinary System DT2
by Body Part
Abdomen DW23
Adrenal Glands DG22
Bile Ducts DF22
Bladder DT22
Brain Stem D021
Breast DM2
Bronchus DB21

Stereotactic Radiosurgery—*continued*
by Body Part—*continued*
Cervix DU21
Chest DW22
Chest Wall DB27
Colon DD25
Diaphragm DB28
Ducts, Bile DF20
Duodenum DD22
Esophagus DD20
Eye D820
Gallbladder DF21
Glands, Parathyroid DG20
Hard Palate D928
Ileum DD24
Jejunum DD23
Kidney DT20
Larynx D92B
Lung DB22
Lymphatics
Abdomen D726
Axillary D724
Inguinal D728
Neck D723
Pelvis D727
Thorax D725
Marrow, Bone D720
Mediastinum DB26
Mouth D924
Nasopharynx D92D
Nerve, Peripheral D020
Nose D921
Ovary DU20
Palate, Soft D920
Pancreas DF23
Parathyroid Glands DG24
Pelvic Region DW26
Peripheral Nerve D027
Pharynx D92C
Pineal Body DG21
Pleura DB25
Prostate DV20
Rectum DD27
Region, Pelvic DW21
Salivary Glands D926
Sinuses D927
Soft Palate D929
Spinal Cord D026
Spleen D722
Stomach DD21
Testis DV21
Thymus D721
Thyroid DG25
Tongue D925
Ureter DT21
Urethra DT23
Uterus DU22
Wall, Chest DB20

Sternotomy
—see Division, Upper Bones 0P8
—see Drainage, Upper Bones 0P9

Stitch—see Repair
Stomatoplasty
—see Repair, Mouth and Throat 0CQ
—see Replacement, Mouth and Throat 0CR

Stomatorrhaphy—see Repair, Mouth and Throat 0CQ
Stress Test
4A02
4A12

Strip—see Extraction
Stripping—see Extraction
Substance Abuse Treatment
—see Detoxification Services
—see Family Counseling

Substance Abuse Treatment—*continued*
—*see* Group Counseling
—*see* Individual Counseling
—*see* Individual Psychotherapy
—*see* Medication Management
—*see* Pharmacotherapy

Suction
—*see* Drainage
—*see* Extraction

Supplement
by Body System
  Anatomical Regions, General 0WU
  Anatomical Regions, Lower Extremities 0YU
  Anatomical Regions, Upper Extremities 0XU
  Bursae and Ligaments 0MU
  Central Nervous System 00U
  Ear, Nose, Sinus 09U
  Eye 08U
  Female Reproductive System 0UU
  Gastrointestinal System 0DU
  Head and Facial Bones 0NU
  Heart and Great Vessels 02U
  Hepatobiliary System and Pancreas 0FU
  Lower Arteries 04U
  Lower Bones 0QU
  Lower Joints 0SU
  Lower Veins 06U
  Lymphatic and Hemic Systems 07U
  Male Reproductive System 0VU
  Mouth and Throat 0CU
  Muscles 0KU
  Peripheral Nervous System 01U
  Respiratory System 0BU
  Skin and Breast 0HU
  Tendons 0LU
  Upper Arteries 03U
  Upper Bones 0PU
  Upper Joints 0RU
  Upper Veins 05U
  Urinary System 0TU
by Body Part
  1st Toe 0YU
  2nd Toe 0YU
  3rd Toe 0YU
  4th Toe 0YU
  5th Toe 0YU
  Abdomen Bursa and Ligament 0MU
  Abdomen Muscle 0KU
  Abdomen Tendon 0LU
  Abdominal Wall 0WUF
  Abducens Nerve 00UL
  Accessory Nerve 00UR
  Acetabulum 0QU
  Acoustic Nerve 00UN
  Acromioclavicular Joint 0RU
  Ampulla of Vater 0FUC
  Ankle Bursa and Ligament 0MU
  Ankle Joint 0SU
  Ankle Region 0YU
  Ankle Tendon 0LU
  Anterior Tibial Artery 04U
  Anus 0DUQ
  Aortic Valve 02UF
  Areola 0HU
  Artery
      Aorta, Thoracic 02U5
      Lower 04U0
      Upper 03U0
  Ascending Colon 0DUK
  Atrium 02U
  Auditory Ossicle 09U
  Axilla 0XU
  Axillary Artery 03U
  Axillary Vein 05U

Supplement—*continued*
by Body Part—*continued*
  Back, Lower 0WU0
  Basilic Vein 05U
  Bladder 0TUB
  Bladder Neck 0TUC
  Bone, Hyoid 0NU0
  Brachial Artery 03U
  Brachial Vein 05U
  Breast 0HU
  Bronchus
      Lower Lobe, Left 0BU1
      Segmental, Lingula 0BU9
  Buccal Mucosa 0CU4
  Bursa and Ligament, Lower Extremity, Left 0MU0
  Buttock, Left 0YU1
  Carina 0BU2
  Carpal 0PU
  Carpal Joint 0RU
  Cecum 0DUH
  Celiac Artery 04U1
  Cephalic Vein 05U
  Cervical Vertebra 0PU3
  Cervical Vertebral Joint 0RU1
  Cervicothoracic Vertebral Disc 0RU5
  Cervicothoracic Vertebral Joint 0RU4
  Chest Wall 0WU8
  Chordae Tendineae 02U9
  Chyli, Cisterna 07U0
  Cisterna Chyli 07UL
  Clavicle 0PU
  Clitoris 0UUJ
  Coccygeal Joint 0SU6
  Coccyx 0QUS
  Colic Artery 04U
  Colic Vein 06U7
  Colon, Sigmoid 0DU1
  Common Bile Duct 0FU9
  Common Carotid Artery 03U
  Common Iliac Artery 04U
  Common Iliac Vein 06U
  Cord, Vocal, Left 0CUM
  Cornea, Left 08U9
  Cul-de-sac 0UUF
  Cystic Duct 0FU8
  Deferens, Vas, Bilateral 0VU1
  Descending Colon 0DUM
  Diaphragm 0BU
  Duct
      Lacrimal, Left 08UX
      Pancreatic, Accessory 0FU5
  Duodenum 0DU9
  Dura Mater 00U2
  Ear
      External, Bilateral 09U0
      Inner, Left 09U5
  Elbow Bursa and Ligament 0MU
  Elbow Joint 0RU
  Elbow Region 0XU
  Epididymis 0VU
  Epiglottis 0CUR
  Esophageal Vein 06U3
  Esophagogastric Junction 0DU4
  Esophagus 0DU5
      Lower 0DU3
      Middle 0DU2
  Ethmoid Bone 0NU
  External Carotid Artery 03U
  External Ear
      Bilateral 09U2
      Left 09U1
  External Iliac Artery 04U
  External Iliac Vein 06U
  External Jugular Vein 05U
  Extraocular Muscle 08U

Supplement—*continued*
by Body Part—*continued*
  Eyelid, Lower, Left 08U8
  Face 0WU2
  Face Artery 03UR
  Face Vein 05U
  Facial Muscle 0KU1
  Facial Nerve 00UM
  Fallopian Tube, Left 0UU6
  Fallopian Tubes, Bilateral 0UU7
  Femoral Artery 04U
  Femoral Nerve 01UD
  Femoral Region 0YU
  Femoral Shaft 0QU
  Femoral Vein 06U
  Fibula 0QU
  Finger, Little, Left 0XU2
  Finger Phalangeal Joint 0RU
  Finger Phalanx 0PU
  Foot 0YU
  Foot Artery 04U
  Foot Bursa and Ligament 0MU
  Foot Muscle 0KU
  Foot Tendon 0LU
  Foot Vein 06U
  Frontal Bone 0NU
  Gastric Artery 04U2
  Gastric Vein 06U2
  Gingiva, Lower 0CU0
  Gland, Mammary 0HU
  Glenoid Cavity 0PU
  Glossopharyngeal Nerve 00UP
  Greater Omentum 0DUS
  Greater Saphenous Vein 06U
  Hand 0XU
  Hand Artery 03U
  Hand Bursa and Ligament 0MU
  Hand Muscle 0KU
  Hand Tendon 0LU
  Hand Vein 05U
  Hard Palate 0CU2
  Heart 02UA
  Hemiazygos Vein 05U1
  Hepatic Artery 04U3
  Hepatic Duct, Left 0FU6
  Hepatic Vein 06U4
  Hip Bursa and Ligament 0MU
  Hip Joint, Left 0SUB
  Hip Muscle 0KU
  Hip Tendon 0LU
  Humeral Head 0PU
  Humeral Shaft 0PU
  Hymen 0UUK
  Hyoid Bone 0NUX
  Hypogastric Vein 06U
  Hypoglossal Nerve 00US
  Ileocecal Valve 0DUC
  Ileum 0DUB
  Index Finger 0XU
  Inferior Mesenteric Artery 04UB
  Inferior Mesenteric Vein 06U6
  Inguinal Region 0YU
  Inner Ear 09U
  Innominate Artery 03U2
  Innominate Vein 05U
  Internal Carotid Artery 03U
  Internal Iliac Artery 04U
  Internal Jugular Vein 05U
  Internal Mammary Artery, Left 03U1
  Intracranial Artery 03UG
  Intracranial Vein 05UL
  Iris, Left 08UD
  Jejunum 0DUA
  Joint
      Finger Phalangeal, Left 0RU3
      Hip, Left 0SU9

Supplement—*continued*
  by Body Part—*continued*
    Joint—*continued*
      Knee, Left 0SUC
      Lumbosacral 0SU0
      Thoracolumbar Vertebral 0RU0
      Toe Phalangeal, Left 0SU2
    Kidney Pelvis, Left 0TU4
    Knee Bursa and Ligament 0MU
    Knee Joint, Left 0SUD
    Knee Region 0YU
    Knee Tendon 0LU
    Lacrimal Bone 0NU
    Lacrimal Duct, Left 08UY
    Large Intestine 0DU
    Larynx 0CUS
    Lesser Omentum 0DUT
    Lesser Saphenous Vein 06U
    Lingula Bronchus 0BU9
    Little Finger 0XU
    Lobe Segmental Bronchus
      Lower 0BU
      Middle, Right 0BU5
      Upper 0BU
    Lower Arm 0XU
    Lower Arm and Wrist Muscle 0KU
    Lower Arm and Wrist Tendon 0LU
    Lower Artery 04UY
    Lower Back 0WUL
    Lower Extremity 0YU
    Lower Extremity Bursa and Ligament
      0MU
    Lower Eyelid 08U
    Lower Femur 0QU
    Lower Gingiva 0CU6
    Lower Jaw 0WU5
    Lower Leg 0YU
    Lower Leg Muscle 0KU
    Lower Leg Tendon 0LU
    Lower Lip 0CU1
    Lower Lobe Bronchus 0BU
    Lower Vein 06UY
    Lumbar Nerve 01UB
    Lumbosacral Disc 0SU4
    Lumbosacral Joint 0SU3
    Lymphatic
      Aortic 07UD
      Internal Mammary 07U
      Left Axillary 07U6
      Left Inguinal 07UJ
      Left Lower Extremity 07UG
      Left Neck 07U2
      Left Upper Extremity 07U4
      Mesenteric 07UB
      Pelvis 07UC
      Right Axillary 07U5
      Right Inguinal 07UH
      Right Lower Extremity 07UF
      Right Neck 07U1
      Right Upper Extremity 07U3
      Thorax 07U7
    Main Bronchus 0BU
    Mandible 0NU
    Maxilla 0NU
    Median Nerve 01U5
    Mediastinum 0WUC
    Membrane, Tympanic, Left 09U7
    Meninges, Spinal 00U1
    Mesentery 0DUV
    Metacarpal 0PU
    Metacarpocarpal Joint 0RU
    Metacarpophalangeal Joint 0RU
    Metatarsal 0QU
    Metatarsal-Phalangeal Joint 0SU
    Metatarsal-Tarsal Joint 0SU
    Middle Ear, Left 09U6

Supplement—*continued*
  by Body Part—*continued*
    Middle Finger 0XU
    Middle Lobe Bronchus, Right 0BU5
    Mitral Valve 02UG
    Muscle
      Extraocular, Left 08UC
      Foot, Left 0KU0
    Nasal Bone 0NUB
    Nasopharynx 09UN
    Neck 0WU6
      Bladder 0TU3
    Neck Muscle 0KU
    Nerve
      Hypoglossal 00UF
      Sacral 01U1
    Nipple 0HU
    Nose 09UK
    Occipital Bone 0NU
    Oculomotor Nerve 00UH
    Omentum, Lesser 0DUR
    Optic Nerve 00UG
    Orbit 0NU
    Palatine Bone 0NU
    Pancreas
      Body 0FUF
      Head 0FUF
      Tail 0FUF
    Pancreatic Duct 0FUD
      Accessory 0FUF
    Papillary Muscle 02UD
    Parietal Bone 0NU
    Patella 0QU
    Pelvic Bone 0QU
    Penis 0VUS
    Pericardium 02UN
    Perineum
      Female 0WUN
      Male 0WUM
    Perineum Bursa and Ligament 0MUK
    Perineum Muscle 0KUM
    Perineum Tendon 0LUH
    Peritoneum 0DUW
    Peroneal Artery 04U
    Peroneal Nerve 01UH
    Phalanx
      Finger, Left 0PU0
      Toe, Left 0QU0
    Phrenic Nerve 01U2
    Popliteal Artery 04U
    Portal Vein 06U8
    Posterior Tibial Artery 04U
    Prepuce 0VUT
    Pudendal Nerve 01UC
    Pulmonary Artery 02U
    Pulmonary Trunk 02UP
    Pulmonary Valve 02UH
    Pulmonary Vein 02U
    Radial Artery 03U
    Radial Nerve 01U6
    Radius 0PU
    Rectum 0DUP
    Renal Artery 04U
    Renal Pelvis 0TU
    Renal Vein 06U
    Retina 08U
    Retinal Vessel 08U
    Rib 0PU
    Ring Finger 0XU
    Sacral Nerve 01UR
    Sacrococcygeal Joint 0SU5
    Sacroiliac Joint 0SU
    Sacrum 0QU1
    Scapula 0PU
    Sciatic Nerve 01UF
    Scrotum 0VU5

Supplement—*continued*
  by Body Part—*continued*
    Seminal Vesicle, Left 0VU2
    Seminal Vesicles, Bilateral 0VU3
    Septum, Nasal 09UM
    Shoulder Bursa and Ligament 0MU
    Shoulder Joint 0RU
    Shoulder Muscle 0KU
    Shoulder Region, Left 0XU3
    Shoulder Tendon 0LU
    Sigmoid Colon 0DUN
    Small Intestine 0DU8
    Soft Palate 0CU3
    Spermatic Cord 0VU
    Spermatic Cords, Bilateral 0VUH
    Sphenoid Bone 0NU
    Spinal Meninges 00UT
    Splenic Artery 04U4
    Splenic Vein 06U1
    Sternoclavicular Joint 0RU
    Stomach 0DU6
      Body 0DU6
      Fundus 0DU6
      Pylorus 0DU7
    Structure, Uterine Supporting 0UU4
    Subclavian Artery 03U
    Subclavian Vein 05U
    Superior Mesenteric Artery 04U5
    Superior Mesenteric Vein 06U5
    Superior Vena Cava 02UV
    Tarsal 0QU
    Tarsal Joint 0SU
    Temporal Artery 03U
    Temporal Bone 0NU
    Temporomandibular Joint 0RU
    Tendon, Foot, Left 0LU0
    Testes, Bilateral 0VUC
    Testis
      Bilateral 0VU9
      Left 0VUB
    Thoracic Aorta 02UW
    Thoracic Duct 07UK
    Thoracic Nerve 01U8
    Thoracic Vertebra 0PU4
    Thoracic Vertebral Disc 0RU9
    Thoracic Vertebral Joint 0RU6
    Thoracolumbar Vertebral Disc 0RUB
    Thoracolumbar Vertebral Joint 0RUA
    Thorax Bursa and Ligament 0MU
    Thorax Muscle 0KU
    Thorax Tendon 0LU
    Thumb 0XU
    Thumb Phalanx 0PU
    Thyroid Artery 03U
    Tibia 0QU
    Tibial Nerve 01UG
    Toe, 5th, Left 0YU0
    Toe Phalangeal Joint 0SU
    Toe Phalanx 0QU
    Tongue 0CU7
      Palate, Pharynx Muscle 0KU4
    Transverse Colon 0DUL
    Tricuspid Valve 02UJ
    Trigeminal Nerve 00UK
    Trochlear Nerve 00UJ
    Trunk Bursa and Ligament 0MU
    Trunk Muscle 0KU
    Trunk Tendon 0LU
    Tube, Fallopian, Bilateral 0UU5
    Tunica Vaginalis 0VU
    Turbinate, Nasal 09UL
    Tympanic Membrane, Left 09U8
    Ulna 0PU
    Ulnar Artery 03U
    Ulnar Nerve 01U4
    Upper Arm 0XU

     Codes provided in the index are incomplete. Refer to tables to determine additional character values.

Supplement—*continued*
  by Body Part—*continued*
    Upper Arm Muscle 0KU
    Upper Arm Tendon 0LU
    Upper Artery 03UY
    Upper Back 0WUK
    Upper Extremity 0XU
    Upper Extremity Bursa and Ligament 0MU
    Upper Eyelid 08U
    Upper Femur 0QU
    Upper Gingiva 0CU5
    Upper Jaw 0WU4
    Upper Leg 0YU
    Upper Leg Muscle 0KU
    Upper Leg Tendon 0LU
    Upper Lobe Bronchus 0BU
    Upper Vein 05UY
    Ureter 0TU
    Urethra 0TUD
    Uvula 0CUN
    Vagina 0UUG
    Vagus Nerve 00UQ
    Vas Deferens 0VU
    Vein
      Lower 06U0
      Upper 05U0
    Ventricle 02U
    Ventricular Septum 02UM
    Vertebral Artery 03U
    Vertebral Vein 05U
    Vocal Cord 0CU
    Vulva 0UUM
    Wrist Bursa and Ligament 0MU
    Wrist Joint 0RU
    Wrist Region 0XU
    Zygomatic Bone 0NU
Suture—*see* Repair
Suture Ligation—*see* Occlusion
Sympathectomy—*see* Excision, Peripheral
    Nervous System 01B
Systemic Nuclear Medicine Therapy
  by Body System
    Anatomical Regions CW7
  by Body Part
    Abdomen CW70
    Anatomical Regions, Multiple CW7Y
    Chest CW73
    Thyroid CW7G
    Whole Body CW7N

T

Take Down—*see* Repair
Tap—*see* Drainage
Tarsectomy
  —*see* Excision, Lower Bones 0QB
  —*see* Resection, Lower Bones 0QT
Tarsorrhaphy—*see* Repair, Eye 08Q
Tattoo 3E00
Tendolysis—*see* Release, Tendons 0LN
Tendonectomy
  —*see* Excision, Tendons 0LB
  —*see* Resection, Tendons 0LT
Tendonoplasty
  —*see* Repair, Tendons 0LQ
  —*see* Replacement, Tendons 0LR
Tendoplasty
  —*see* Repair, Tendons 0LQ
  —*see* Replacement, Tendons 0LR
Tendorrhaphy—*see* Repair, Tendons 0LQ
Tendototomy
  —*see* Division, Tendons 0L8
  —*see* Drainage, Tendons 0L9
  —*see* Inspection, Tendons 0LJ

Tenectomy
  —*see* Excision, Tendons 0LB
  —*see* Resection, Tendons 0LT
Tenolysis—*see* Release, Tendons 0LN
Tenontorrhaphy—*see* Repair, Tendons 0LQ
Tenontotomy
  —*see* Division, Tendons 0L8
  —*see* Drainage, Tendons 0L9
  —*see* Inspection, Tendons 0LJ
Tenoplasty
  —*see* Repair, Tendons 0LQ
  —*see* Replacement, Tendons 0LR
Tenorrhaphy—*see* Repair, Tendons 0LQ
Tenosynovectomy
  —*see* Excision, Tendons 0LB
  —*see* Resection, Tendons 0LT
Tenotomy
  —*see* Division, Tendons 0L8
  —*see* Drainage, Tendons 0L9
  —*see* Inspection, Tendons 0LJ
Testectomy
  —*see* Excision, Male Reproductive System
    0VB
  —*see* Resection, Male Reproductive System
    0VT
Testing—*see* Vestibular Treatment
Thalamectomy—*see* Destruction, Central
    Nervous System 005
Thalamotomy—*see* Destruction, Central
    Nervous System 005
Theleplasty
  —*see* Repair, Skin and Breast 0HQ
  —*see* Replacement, Skin and Breast 0HR
Therapeutic Massage
  8E0K
  8E0V
Therapeutic Radiation—*see* Radiation
    Oncology
Thoracectomy—*see* Excision, Anatomical
    Regions, General 0WB
Thoracentesis
  —*see* Drainage
  —*see* Drainage, Anatomical Regions, General
    0W9
Thoracocentesis—*see* Drainage, Anatomical
    Regions, General 0W9
Thoracoplasty—*see* Repair, Anatomical
    Regions, General 0WQ
Thoracotomy—*see* Drainage, Anatomical
    Regions, General 0W9
Thromboendarterectomy
  —*see* Excision, Heart and Great Vessels
    02B
  —*see* Excision, Lower Arteries 04B
  —*see* Excision, Upper Arteries 03B
Thymectomy
  —*see* Excision, Lymphatic and Hemic
    Systems 07B
  —*see* Resection, Lymphatic and Hemic
    Systems 07T
Thymopexy
  —*see* Repair, Lymphatic and Hemic Systems
    07Q
  —*see* Reposition, Lymphatic and Hemic
    Systems 07S
Thyroidectomy
  —*see* Excision, Endocrine System 0GB
  —*see* Resection, Endocrine System 0GT
Thyroidorrhaphy—*see* Repair, Endocrine
    System 0GQ
Thyroidoscopy—*see* Inspection, Endocrine
    System 0GJ

Thyroidotomy
  —*see* Drainage, Endocrine System 0G9
  —*see* Inspection, Endocrine System 0GJ
Tomographic (Tomo) Nuclear Medicine
    Imaging
  by Body System
    Anatomical Regions CW2
    Central Nervous System C02
    Endocrine System CG2
    Gastrointestinal System CD2
    Heart C22
    Hepatobiliary System and Pancreas CF2
    Lymphatic and Hematologic System C72
    Musculoskeletal System CP2
    Respiratory System CB2
    Skin, Subcutaneous Tissue and Breast
      CH2
    Urinary System CT2
  by Body Part
    Abdomen and Pelvis CW21
    Anatomical Regions, Multiple CW2Y
    Brain C020
    Breast CH2
    Breasts, Bilateral CH22
    Central Nervous System C02Y
    Cerebrospinal Fluid C025
    Cervical Spine CP22
    Chest CW23
    Chest and Abdomen CW24
    Chest and Neck CW26
    Digestive System CD2Y
    Extremity, Upper CW20
    Gallbladder CF24
    Glands, Parathyroid CG21
    Head and Neck CW2B
    Heart C22Y
      Right and Left C226
    Hepatobiliary System and Pancreas CF2Y
    Kidneys, Ureters and Bladder CT23
    Liver CF25
    Liver and Spleen CF26
    Lower Extremities, Bilateral CP2F
    Lower Extremity CP2, CW2D
    Lumbar Spine CP2H
    Lungs and Bronchi CB22
    Lymphatic and Hematologic System
      C72Y
    Musculoskeletal System, Other CP2Y
    Myocardium C22G
    Pelvic Region CW2J
    Pelvis CP26
    Skin, Subcutaneous Tissue and Breast
      CH2Y
    Skull and Cervical Spine CP23
    Spine, Thoracolumbar CP21
    Spine and Pelvis CP27
    Spleen C722
    System
      Endocrine CG2Y
      Respiratory CB2Y
    Thoracic Spine CP2G
    Thoracolumbar Spine CP2J
    Thorax CP24
    Tract, Gastrointestinal CD27
    Upper Extremities, Bilateral CP2B
    Upper Extremity CP2, CW2M
    Urinary System CT2Y
Tomography—*see* Plain Radiography
Tonsillectomy
  —*see* Excision, Mouth and Throat 0CB
  —*see* Resection, Mouth and Throat 0CT
Tonsillotomy
  —*see* Drainage, Mouth and Throat 0C9
  —*see* Inspection, Mouth and Throat 0CJ

Total Parenteral Nutrition—*see*
    Administration, Physiological Systems
    And Anatomical Regions 3E0
TPN—*see* Administration, Physiological
    Systems And Anatomical Regions 3E0
Trachectomy
    —*see* Excision, Respiratory System 0BB
    —*see* Resection, Respiratory System 0BT
Trachelectomy
    —*see* Excision, Female Reproductive System
    0UB
    —*see* Resection, Female Reproductive
    System 0UT
Trachelopexy
    —*see* Repair, Female Reproductive System
    0UQ
    —*see* Reposition, Female Reproductive
    System 0US
Tracheloplasty—*see* Repair, Female
    Reproductive System 0UQ
Trachelorrhaphy—*see* Repair, Female
    Reproductive System 0UQ
Trachelotomy—*see* Drainage, Female
    Reproductive System 0U9
Tracheo-esophageal fistulization 0B11
Tracheolysis—*see* Release, Respiratory System
    0BN
Tracheoplasty—*see* Repair, Respiratory System
    0BQ
Tracheorrhaphy—*see* Repair, Respiratory
    System 0BQ
Tracheoscopy—*see* Inspection, Respiratory
    System 0BJ
Tracheostomy—*see* Bypass, Respiratory
    System 0B1
Tracheotomy
    —*see* Drainage, Respiratory System 0B9
    —*see* Inspection, Respiratory System 0BJ
Traction
    by Body Region
      Abdominal Wall 2W63
      Back 2W65
      Chest Wall 2W64
      Face 2W61
      Finger 2W6
      Foot 2W6
      Hand 2W6
      Inguinal Region 2W6
      Leg, Lower, Left 2W60
      Lower Arm 2W6
      Lower Extremity 2W6
      Lower Leg 2W6
      Neck 2W62
      Thumb 2W6
      Toe 2W6
      Upper Arm 2W6
      Upper Extremity 2W6
      Upper Leg 2W6
Tractotomy—*see* Division, Central Nervous
    System 008
Training—*see* Cochlear Implant Treatment
Transect—*see* Division
Transection—*see* Division
Transfer
    by Body System
      Anatomical Regions, Upper Extremities
      0XX
      Bursae and Ligaments 0MX
      Central Nervous System 00X
      Eye 08X
      Female Reproductive System 0UX
      Gastrointestinal System 0DX
      Mouth and Throat 0CX
      Muscles 0KX
      Peripheral Nervous System 01X

Transfer—*continued*
    by Body System—*continued*
      Skin and Breast 0HX
      Subcutaneous Tissue and Fascia 0JX
      Tendons 0LX
      Urinary System 0TX
    by Body Part
      Abdomen Bursa and Ligament 0MX
      Abdomen Muscle, Left 0KXL
      Abdomen Tendon 0LX
      Abducens Nerve 00XL
      Accessory Nerve 00XR
      Acoustic Nerve 00XN
      Ankle Bursa and Ligament 0MX
      Ankle Tendon 0LX
      Buccal Mucosa 0CX4
      Bursa and Ligament, Lower Extremity,
      Left 0MX0
      Elbow Bursa and Ligament 0MX
      Extraocular Muscle, Left 08XM
      Facial Muscle 0KX1
      Facial Nerve 00XM
      Fallopian Tube 0UX
      Finger, Index 0XX
      Foot Bursa and Ligament 0MX
      Foot Muscle 0KX
      Foot Tendon 0LX
      Gingiva, Lower 0CX0
      Glossopharyngeal Nerve 00XP
      Hand Bursa and Ligament 0MX
      Hand Muscle 0KX
      Hand Tendon 0LX
      Hip Bursa and Ligament 0MX
      Hip Muscle 0KX
      Hip Tendon 0LX
      Hypoglossal Nerve 00XS
      Intestine, Large 0DX6
      Kidney 0TX
      Knee Bursa and Ligament 0MX
      Knee Tendon 0LX
      Large Intestine 0DXE
      Lower Arm and Wrist Muscle 0KX
      Lower Arm and Wrist Tendon 0LX
      Lower Extremity Bursa and Ligament
      0MX
      Lower Gingiva 0CX6
      Lower Leg Muscle 0KX
      Lower Leg Tendon 0LX
      Lower Lip 0CX1
      Median Nerve 01X5
      Muscle
        Abdomen, Left 0KXK
        Extraocular, Left 08XL
        Foot, Left 0KX0
      Neck Muscle 0KX
      Nerve
        Hypoglossal 00XF
        Lumbar 01XB
        Peroneal 01XD
        Phrenic 01X1
        Radial 01X4
        Thoracic 01X8
      Oculomotor Nerve 00XH
      Optic Nerve 00XG
      Ovary, Left 0UX1
      Perineum Bursa and Ligament 0MXK
      Perineum Muscle 0KXM
      Perineum Tendon 0LXH
      Peroneal Nerve 01XH
      Phrenic Nerve 01X2
      Pudendal Nerve 01XC
      Radial Nerve 01X6
      Sciatic Nerve 01XF
      Shoulder Bursa and Ligament 0MX
      Shoulder Muscle 0KX
      Shoulder Tendon 0LX

Transfer—*continued*
    by Body Part—*continued*
      Skin
        Abdomen 0HX7
        Back 0HX6
        Buttock 0HX8
        Chest 0HX5
        Face 0HX1
        Foot, Left 0HX0
        Genitalia 0HXA
        Left Ear 0HX3
        Left Foot 0HXN
        Left Hand 0HXG
        Left Lower Arm 0HXE
        Left Lower Leg 0HXL
        Left Upper Arm 0HXC
        Left Upper Leg 0HXJ
        Neck 0HX4
        Perineum 0HX9
        Right Ear 0HX2
        Right Foot 0HXM
        Right Hand 0HXF
        Right Lower Arm 0HXD
        Right Lower Leg 0HXK
        Right Upper Arm 0HXB
        Right Upper Leg 0HXH
      Small Intestine 0DX8
      Soft Palate 0CX3
      Stomach
        Body 0DX6
        Fundus 0DX6
      Subcutaneous Tissue and Fascia
        Abdomen 0JX8
        Anterior Neck 0JX4
        Back 0JX7
        Buttock 0JX9
        Chest 0JX6
        Face 0JX1
        Foot, Left 0JX0
        Genitalia 0JXC
        Left Foot 0JXR
        Left Hand 0JXK
        Left Lower Arm 0JXH
        Left Lower Leg 0JXP
        Left Upper Arm 0JXF
        Left Upper Leg 0JXM
        Perineum 0JXB
        Posterior Neck 0JX5
        Right Foot 0JXQ
        Right Hand 0JXJ
        Right Lower Arm 0JXG
        Right Lower Leg 0JXN
        Right Upper Arm 0JXD
        Right Upper Leg 0JXL
      Tendon, Foot, Left 0LX0
      Thorax Bursa and Ligament 0MX
      Thorax Muscle 0KX
      Thorax Tendon 0LX
      Tibial Nerve 01XG
      Tongue 0CX7
        Palate, Pharynx Muscle 0KX4
      Trigeminal Nerve 00XK
      Trochlear Nerve 00XJ
      Trunk Bursa and Ligament 0MX
      Trunk Muscle 0KX
      Trunk Tendon 0LX
      Tube, Fallopian, Left 0UX0
      Upper Arm Muscle 0KX
      Upper Arm Tendon 0LX
      Upper Extremity Bursa and Ligament
      0MX
      Upper Gingiva 0CX5
      Upper Leg Muscle 0KX
      Upper Leg Tendon 0LX
      Vagus Nerve 00XQ
      Wrist Bursa and Ligament 0MX

Transfusion

by Body System
  Artery, Peripheral 3025
  Central Artery 3026
  Central Vein 3024
  Products of Conception, Circulatory
    3027
  Vein, Peripheral 3023
by Substance
  Antihemophilic Factors 302
  Bone Marrow 302
  Factor IX 302
  Fibrinogen 302
  Fresh Plasma 302
  Frozen Plasma 302
  Frozen Red Cells 302
  Globulin 302
  Plasma Cryoprecipitate 302
  Platelets 302
  Red Blood Cells 302
  Serum Albumin 302
  Stem Cells
    Cord Blood 302
    Embryonic 302
    Hematopoietic 302
  White Cells 302
  Whole Blood 302

Transplantation

by Body System
  Female Reproductive System 0UY
  Gastrointestinal System 0DY
  Heart and Great Vessels 02Y
  Hepatobiliary System and Pancreas 0FY
  Lymphatic and Hemic Systems 07Y
  Respiratory System 0BY
  Urinary System 0TY
by Body Part
  Heart 02YA
  Intestine, Large 0DY5
  Kidney 0TY
  Large Intestine 0DYE
  Liver 0FY0
  Lower Lung Lobe 0BY
  Lung 0BY
  Lung Lingula 0BYH
  Lung Lingula Segments 0BYH
  Lung Lobe Segments
    Lower 0BY
    Middle, Right 0BYD
    Upper 0BY
  Lungs, Bilateral 0BYM
  Middle Lung Lobe, Right 0BYD
  Ovary 0UY
  Pancreas 0FYG
  Products of Conception 10Y0
  Pulmonary Lingula 0BYH
  Pulmonary Lobe
    Lower 0BY
    Middle, Right 0BYD
    Upper 0BY
  Small Intestine 0DY8
  Spleen 07YP
  Stomach 0DY6
    Body 0DY6
    Fundus 0DY6
  Thymus 07YM
  Upper Lung Lobe, Left 0BYG

Transpose

—*see* Reposition
—*see* Transfer

Transposition

—*see* Reposition
—*see* Transfer

Transurethral Destruction Of Prostate Tissue By Microwave Thermotherapy

—*see* Destruction, Male Reproductive
  System 0V5

Transurethral Microwave Thermotherapy of Prostate—*see* Destruction, Male

Reproductive System 0V5

Transurethral Needle Ablation Of Prostate

—*see* Destruction, Male Reproductive
  System 0V5

Treatment

Osteopathic
  Abdomen 7W09
  Cervical 7W01
  Extremities, Upper 7W00
  Lower Extremities 7W06
  Lumbar 7W03
  Pelvis 7W05
  Rib Cage 7W08
  Sacrum 7W04
  Thoracic 7W02
  Upper Extremities 7W07

Trim—*see* Excision

TUMT—*see* Destruction, Male Reproductive
  System 0V5

TUNA—*see* Destruction, Male Reproductive
  System 0V5

Turbinectomy

—*see* Excision, Ear, Nose, Sinus 09B
—*see* Resection, Ear, Nose, Sinus 09T

Turbinoplasty

—*see* Repair, Ear, Nose, Sinus 09Q
—*see* Replacement, Ear, Nose, Sinus 09R

Turbinotomy

—*see* Drainage, Ear, Nose, Sinus 099
—*see* Inspection, Ear, Nose, Sinus 09J

Tympanoplasty

—*see* Repair, Ear, Nose, Sinus 09Q
—*see* Replacement, Ear, Nose, Sinus 09R

U

Ultrasonography

by Body System
  Anatomical Regions BW4
  Axial Skeleton, Except Skull and Facial
    Bones BR4
  Central Nervous System B04
  Connective Tissue BL4
  Endocrine System BG4
  Eye B84
  Female Reproductive System BU4
  Fetus and Obstetrical BY4
  Gastrointestinal System BD4
  Heart B24
  Hepatobiliary System and Pancreas BF4
  Lower Arteries B44
  Male Reproductive System BV4
  Non-Axial Lower Bones BQ4
  Non-Axial Upper Bones BP4
  Respiratory System BB4
  Skin, Subcutaneous Tissue and Breast BH4
  Upper Arteries B34
  Urinary System BT4
  Veins B54
by Body Part
  Abdomen and Pelvis BW41
  Abdominal Wall BH49
  Adrenal Gland, Left BG41
  Adrenal Glands, Bilateral BG42
  Appendix BD48
  Arteries, Coronary, Multiple B240
  Artery
    Femoral B440
    Pulmonary, Left B340

Ultrasonography—*continued*

by Body Part—*continued*
  Brachiocephalic-Subclavian Artery, Right
    B341
  Breast, Left BH41
  Breasts, Bilateral BH42
  Celiac and Mesenteric Arteries B44K
  Chest Wall BH4B
  Common Carotid Arteries, Bilateral B345
  Common Carotid Artery B34
  Connective Tissue
    Lower Extremity BL41
    Upper Extremity BL40
  Cord, Spinal B040
  Coronary Arteries, Multiple B241
  Duodenum BD49
  Elbow BP4
  Extremity
    Lower BH48
    Upper BH47
  Eye B84
  Eyes, Bilateral B847
  Fallopian Tube, Left BU41
  Fallopian Tubes, Bilateral BU42
  Femoral Artery B44L
  Fetal Umbilical Cord BY47
  First Trimester
    Multiple Gestation BY4B
    Single Fetus BY49
  Gallbladder BF42
  Gallbladder and Bile Ducts BF43
  Gastrointestinal Tract BD47
  Gland, Thyroid BG40
  Hand BP4
  Head and Neck BH4C
  Heart B24
  Heart with Aorta B24B
  Hepatobiliary System, All BF4C
  Hip BQ4
  Hips, Bilateral BQ42
  Inferior Mesenteric Artery B445
  Inferior Vena Cava B549
  Internal Carotid Arteries, Bilateral B348
  Internal Carotid Artery B34
  Intra-Abdominal Arteries, Other B44B
  Intracranial Arteries B34R
  Jugular Veins, Left B544
  Kidney BT4
  Kidney Transplant BT49
  Kidneys, Bilateral BT43
  Kidneys and Bladder BT4J
  Knee BQ4
  Knees, Bilateral BQ49
  Liver BF45
  Liver and Spleen BF46
  Lower Extremity Arteries B44
  Lower Extremity Veins B54
  Lumbar Spine BR49
  Mediastinum BB4C
  Neck BW4F
  Ophthalmic Arteries B34V
  Ovaries, Bilateral BU45
  Ovary BU4
  Pancreas BF47
  Parathyroid Glands BG43
  Pediatric Heart B24D
  Pelvic Region BW4G
  Penile Arteries B44N
  Penis BV4B
  Pericardium B24C
  Placenta BY48
  Pleura BB4B
  Portal and Splanchnic Veins B54T
  Prostate and Seminal Vesicles BV49
  Pulmonary Artery B34
  Rectum BD4C

Ultrasonography—*continued*
  by Body Part—*continued*
    Region, Pelvic BW40
    Renal Arteries, Bilateral B448
    Renal Artery B44
    Renal Vein B54
    Renal Veins, Bilateral B54L
    Sacrum and Coccyx BR4F
    Scrotum BV44
    Second Trimester
      Multiple Gestation BY4D
      Single Fetus BY4C
    Shoulder BP4
    Spinal Cord B04B
    Spine, Lumbar BR40
    Stomach BD42
    Subclavian Artery, Left B342
    Subclavian Vein B54
    Superior Mesenteric Artery B444
    System, Hepatobiliary, All BF40
    Tendons
      Lower Extremity BL43
      Upper Extremity BL42
    Third Trimester
      Multiple Gestation BY4G
      Single Fetus BY4F
    Thoracic Spine BR47
    Thyroid Gland BG44
    Tract, Gastrointestinal BD41
    Transplant, Kidney BT40
    Tubes, Fallopian, Bilateral BU40
    Upper Extremity Arteries B34
    Upper Extremity Veins B54
    Ureter BT4
    Ureters, Bilateral BT48
    Urethra BT45
    Uterus BU46
    Uterus and Ovaries BU4C
    Veins, Upper Extremity, Bilateral B543
    Wall, Chest BH40
    Wrist BP4
Ultrasound Therapy
  Circulatory 6A75
Ultraviolet Light Therapy
  Skin 6A80
Unbridle—*see* Release
Undercut—*see* Release
Upper GI Series—*see* Fluoroscopy,
    Gastrointestinal System BD1
Ureterectomy
  —*see* Excision, Urinary System 0TB
  —*see* Resection, Urinary System 0TT
Ureterocolostomy—*see* Bypass, Urinary
    System 0T1
Ureterocystostomy—*see* Bypass, Urinary
    System 0T1
Ureteroenterostomy—*see* Bypass, Urinary
    System 0T1
Ureteroileostomy—*see* Bypass, Urinary System
    0T1
Ureterolithotomy—*see* Extirpation, Urinary
    System 0TC
Ureterolysis—*see* Release, Urinary System
    0TN
Ureteropexy
  —*see* Repair, Urinary System 0TQ
  —*see* Reposition, Urinary System 0TS
Ureteroplasty
  —*see* Repair, Urinary System 0TQ
  —*see* Replacement, Urinary System 0TR
Ureteroplication—*see* Restriction, Urinary
    System 0TV
Ureterorrhaphy—*see* Repair, Urinary System
    0TQ
Ureteroscopy—*see* Inspection, Urinary System 0TJ

Ureterostomy—*see* Bypass, Urinary System
    0T1
Ureterotomy
  —*see* Drainage, Urinary System 0T9
  —*see* Inspection, Urinary System 0TJ
Ureteroureterostomy—*see* Bypass, Urinary
    System 0T1
Urethrectomy
  —*see* Excision, Urinary System 0TB
  —*see* Resection, Urinary System 0TT
Urethrolithotomy—*see* Extirpation, Urinary
    System 0TC
Urethrolysis—*see* Release, Urinary System
    0TN
Urethropexy
  —*see* Repair, Urinary System 0TQ
  —*see* Reposition, Urinary System 0TS
Urethroplasty
  —*see* Repair, Urinary System 0TQ
  —*see* Replacement, Urinary System 0TR
Urethrorrhaphy—*see* Repair, Urinary System
    0TQ
Urethroscopy—*see* Inspection, Urinary System
    0TJ
Urethrotomy
  —*see* Drainage, Urinary System 0T9
  —*see* Inspection, Urinary System 0TJ
Uvulectomy
  —*see* Excision, Mouth and Throat 0CB
  —*see* Resection, Mouth and Throat 0CT
Uvulorrhaphy—*see* Repair, Mouth and Throat
    0CQ
Uvulotomy
  —*see* Drainage, Mouth and Throat 0C9
  —*see* Inspection, Mouth and Throat 0CJ

V

Vacuum Extraction, Fetal Head—*see*
    Delivery, Obstetrics 10E
Vaginectomy
  —*see* Excision, Female Reproductive System
    0UB
  —*see* Resection, Female Reproductive
    System 0UT
Vaginofixation
  —*see* Repair, Female Reproductive System
    0UQ
  —*see* Reposition, Female Reproductive
    System 0US
Vaginoplasty—*see* Repair, Female
    Reproductive System 0UQ
Vaginorrhaphy—*see* Repair, Female
    Reproductive System 0UQ
Vaginoscopy—*see* Inspection, Female
    Reproductive System 0UJ
Vaginotomy
  —*see* Drainage, Female Reproductive System
    0U9
  —*see* Inspection, Female Reproductive
    System 0UJ
Vagotomy—*see* Division, Central Nervous
    System 008
Valvotomy
  —*see* Division, Heart and Great Vessels 028
  —*see* Release, Heart and Great Vessels 02N
Valvuloplasty
  —*see* Repair, Heart and Great Vessels 02Q
  —*see* Replacement, Heart and Great Vessels
    02R
Valvulotomy
  —*see* Division, Heart and Great Vessels 028
  —*see* Release, Heart and Great Vessels 02N
Vasectomy—*see* Excision, Male Reproductive
    System 0VB

Vasography
  —*see* Fluoroscopy, Anatomical Regions BW1
  —*see* Plain Radiography, Anatomical Regions
    BW0
Vasoligation—*see* Occlusion, Male
    Reproductive System 0VL
Vasorrhaphy—*see* Repair, Male Reproductive
    System 0VQ
Vasostomy—*see* Bypass, Male Reproductive
    System 0V1
Vasotomy
  —*see* Drainage, Male Reproductive System
    0V9
  —*see* Inspection, Male Reproductive System
    0VJ
Vasovasostomy—*see* Repair, Male
    Reproductive System 0VQ
VCG 4A02
Vectorcardiogram 4A02
Venectomy
  —*see* Excision, Lower Veins 06B
  —*see* Excision, Upper Veins 05B
Venography
  —*see* Fluoroscopy, Veins B51
  —*see* Plain Radiography, Veins B50
Venorrhaphy
  —*see* Repair, Lower Veins 06Q
  —*see* Repair, Upper Veins 05Q
Venotripsy
  —*see* Occlusion, Lower Veins 06L
  —*see* Occlusion, Upper Veins 05L
Ventriculoatriostomy—*see* Bypass, Central
    Nervous System 001
Ventriculocisternostomy—*see* Bypass, Central
    Nervous System 001
Ventriculography
  —*see* Fluoroscopy, Heart B21
  —*see* Plain Radiography, Heart B20
Ventriculoscopy—*see* Inspection, Central
    Nervous System 00J
Ventriculostomy—*see* Bypass, Central Nervous
    System 001
Ventriculovenostomy—*see* Bypass, Central
    Nervous System 001
Vesicotomy
  —*see* Drainage, Urinary System 0T9
  —*see* Inspection, Urinary System 0TJ
Vesiculectomy
  —*see* Excision, Male Reproductive System
    0VB
  —*see* Resection, Male Reproductive System
    0VT
Vesiculotomy
  —*see* Drainage, Male Reproductive System
    0V9
  —*see* Inspection, Male Reproductive System
    0VJ
Vitrectomy
  —*see* Excision, Eye 08B
  —*see* Resection, Eye 08T
Vulvectomy
  —*see* Excision, Female Reproductive System
    0UB
  —*see* Resection, Female Reproductive
    System 0UT

W

Wedge—*see* Excision
Window—*see* Drainage

X

X-ray—*see* Imaging

Tables

Central Nervous System 001–00X

0 Medical and Surgical
0 Central Nervous System
1 Bypass: Altering the route of passage of the contents of a tubular body part

Body Part Character 4	Approach Character 5	Device Character 6	Qualifier Character 7
6 Cerebral Ventricle	0 Open	7 Autologous Tissue Substitute J Synthetic Substitute K Nonautologous Tissue Substitute	0 Nasopharynx 1 Mastoid Sinus 2 Atrium 3 Blood Vessel 4 Pleural Cavity 5 Intestine 6 Peritoneal Cavity 7 Urinary Tract 8 Bone Marrow B Cerebral Cisterns
U Spinal Canal	0 Open	7 Autologous Tissue Substitute J Synthetic Substitute K Nonautologous Tissue Substitute	4 Pleural Cavity 6 Peritoneal Cavity 7 Urinary Tract 9 Fallopian Tube

0 Medical and Surgical
0 Central Nervous System
2 Change: Taking out or off a device from a body part and putting back an identical or similar device in or on the same body part without cutting or puncturing the skin or a mucous membrane

Body Part Character 4	Approach Character 5	Device Character 6	Qualifier Character 7
0 Brain E Cranial Nerve U Spinal Canal	X External	0 Drainage Device Y Other Device	Z No Qualifier

0 Medical and Surgical
0 Central Nervous System
5 Destruction: Physical eradication of all or a portion of a body part by the direct use of energy, force, or a destructive agent

Body Part Character 4	Approach Character 5	Device Character 6	Qualifier Character 7
0 Brain 1 Cerebral Meninges 2 Dura Mater 6 Cerebral Ventricle 7 Cerebral Hemisphere 8 Basal Ganglia 9 Thalamus A Hypothalamus B Pons C Cerebellum D Medulla Oblongata F Olfactory Nerve G Optic Nerve H Oculomotor Nerve J Trochlear Nerve K Trigeminal Nerve L Abducens Nerve M Facial Nerve N Acoustic Nerve P Glossopharyngeal Nerve Q Vagus Nerve R Accessory Nerve S Hypoglossal Nerve T Spinal Meninges W Cervical Spinal Cord X Thoracic Spinal Cord Y Lumbar Spinal Cord	0 Open 3 Percutaneous 4 Percutaneous Endoscopic	Z No Device	T Stereotactic U Nonstereotactic

0 **Medical and Surgical**
0 **Central Nervous System**
8 **Division:**   Cutting into a body part without draining fluids and/or gases from the body part in order to separate or transect a body part

Body Part Character 4	Approach Character 5	Device Character 6	Qualifier Character 7
0 Brain **7** Cerebral Hemisphere **8** Basal Ganglia **F** Olfactory Nerve **G** Optic Nerve **H** Oculomotor Nerve **J** Trochlear Nerve **K** Trigeminal Nerve **L** Abducens Nerve **M** Facial Nerve **N** Acoustic Nerve **P** Glossopharyngeal Nerve **Q** Vagus Nerve **R** Accessory Nerve **S** Hypoglossal Nerve **W** Cervical Spinal Cord **X** Thoracic Spinal Cord **Y** Lumbar Spinal Cord	**0** Open **3** Percutaneous **4** Percutaneous Endoscopic	**Z** No Device	**Z** No Qualifier

0 **Medical and Surgical**
0 **Central Nervous System**
9 **Drainage:**   Taking or letting out fluids and/or gases from a body part

Body Part Character 4	Approach Character 5	Device Character 6	Qualifier Character 7
0 Brain **1** Cerebral Meninges **2** Dura Mater **3** Epidural Space **4** Subdural Space **5** Subarachnoid Space **6** Cerebral Ventricle **7** Cerebral Hemisphere **8** Basal Ganglia **9** Thalamus **A** Hypothalamus **B** Pons **C** Cerebellum **D** Medulla Oblongata **F** Olfactory Nerve **G** Optic Nerve **H** Oculomotor Nerve **J** Trochlear Nerve **K** Trigeminal Nerve **L** Abducens Nerve **M** Facial Nerve **N** Acoustic Nerve **P** Glossopharyngeal Nerve **Q** Vagus Nerve **R** Accessory Nerve **S** Hypoglossal Nerve **T** Spinal Meninges **U** Spinal Canal **W** Cervical Spinal Cord **X** Thoracic Spinal Cord **Y** Lumbar Spinal Cord	**0** Open **3** Percutaneous **4** Percutaneous Endoscopic	**0** Drainage Device	**Z** No Qualifier

Continued on next page

0   **Medical and Surgical**   *Continued from previous page*
0   **Central Nervous System**
9   **Drainage:**   Taking or letting out fluids and/or gases from a body part

Body Part Character 4	Approach Character 5	Device Character 6	Qualifier Character 7
0 Brain 1 Cerebral Meninges 2 Dura Mater 3 Epidural Space 4 Subdural Space 5 Subarachnoid Space 6 Cerebral Ventricle 7 Cerebral Hemisphere 8 Basal Ganglia 9 Thalamus A Hypothalamus B Pons C Cerebellum D Medulla Oblongata F Olfactory Nerve G Optic Nerve H Oculomotor Nerve J Trochlear Nerve K Trigeminal Nerve L Abducens Nerve M Facial Nerve N Acoustic Nerve P Glossopharyngeal Nerve Q Vagus Nerve R Accessory Nerve S Hypoglossal Nerve T Spinal Meninges U Spinal Canal W Cervical Spinal Cord X Thoracic Spinal Cord Y Lumbar Spinal Cord	0 Open 3 Percutaneous 4 Percutaneous Endoscopic	Z No Device	X Diagnostic Z No Qualifier

0   **Medical and Surgical**
0   **Central Nervous System**
B   **Excision:**   Cutting out or off, without replacement, a portion of a body part

Body Part Character 4	Approach Character 5	Device Character 6	Qualifier Character 7
0 Brain 1 Cerebral Meninges 2 Dura Mater 6 Cerebral Ventricle 7 Cerebral Hemisphere 8 Basal Ganglia 9 Thalamus A Hypothalamus B Pons C Cerebellum D Medulla Oblongata F Olfactory Nerve G Optic Nerve H Oculomotor Nerve J Trochlear Nerve K Trigeminal Nerve L Abducens Nerve M Facial Nerve N Acoustic Nerve P Glossopharyngeal Nerve Q Vagus Nerve R Accessory Nerve S Hypoglossal Nerve T Spinal Meninges W Cervical Spinal Cord X Thoracic Spinal Cord Y Lumbar Spinal Cord	0 Open 3 Percutaneous 4 Percutaneous Endoscopic	Z No Device	T Stereotactic V Diagnostic Stereotactic X Diagnostic Z No Qualifier

0   **Medical and Surgical**
0   **Central Nervous System**
C   **Extirpation:**   Taking or cutting out solid matter from a body part

Body Part Character 4	Approach Character 5	Device Character 6	Qualifier Character 7
0 Brain **1** Cerebral Meninges **2** Dura Mater **3** Epidural Space **4** Subdural Space **5** Subarachnoid Space **6** Cerebral Ventricle **7** Cerebral Hemisphere **8** Basal Ganglia **9** Thalamus **A** Hypothalamus **B** Pons **C** Cerebellum **D** Medulla Oblongata **F** Olfactory Nerve **G** Optic Nerve **H** Oculomotor Nerve **J** Trochlear Nerve **K** Trigeminal Nerve **L** Abducens Nerve **M** Facial Nerve **N** Acoustic Nerve **P** Glossopharyngeal Nerve **Q** Vagus Nerve **R** Accessory Nerve **S** Hypoglossal Nerve **T** Spinal Meninges **W** Cervical Spinal Cord **X** Thoracic Spinal Cord **Y** Lumbar Spinal Cord	**0** Open **3** Percutaneous **4** Percutaneous Endoscopic	**Z** No Device	**Z** No Qualifier

0   **Medical and Surgical**
0   **Central Nervous System**
D   **Extraction:**   Pulling or stripping out or off all or a portion of a body part by the use of force

Body Part Character 4	Approach Character 5	Device Character 6	Qualifier Character 7
1 Cerebral Meninges **2** Dura Mater **F** Olfactory Nerve **G** Optic Nerve **H** Oculomotor Nerve **J** Trochlear Nerve **K** Trigeminal Nerve **L** Abducens Nerve **M** Facial Nerve **N** Acoustic Nerve **P** Glossopharyngeal Nerve **Q** Vagus Nerve **R** Accessory Nerve **S** Hypoglossal Nerve **T** Spinal Meninges	**0** Open **3** Percutaneous **4** Percutaneous Endoscopic	**Z** No Device	**Z** No Qualifier

0   **Medical and Surgical**
0   **Central Nervous System**
F   **Fragmentation:**   Breaking solid matter in a body part into pieces

Body Part Character 4	Approach Character 5	Device Character 6	Qualifier Character 7
3 Epidural Space **4** Subdural Space **5** Subarachnoid Space **6** Cerebral Ventricle **U** Spinal Canal	**0** Open **3** Percutaneous **4** Percutaneous Endoscopic **X** External	**Z** No Device	**Z** No Qualifier

0   Medical and Surgical
0   Central Nervous System
H   Insertion: Putting in a nonbiological appliance that monitors, assists, performs or prevents a physiological function, but does not physically take the place of a body part

Body Part Character 4	Approach Character 5	Device Character 6	Qualifier Character 7
0 Brain **6** Cerebral Ventricle **E** Cranial Nerve **U** Spinal Canal **V** Spinal Cord	**0** Open **3** Percutaneous **4** Percutaneous Endoscopic	**2** Monitoring Device **3** Infusion Device **M** Electrode	**Z** No Qualifier

0   Medical and Surgical
0   Central Nervous System
J   Inspection: Visually and/or manually exploring a body part

Body Part Character 4	Approach Character 5	Device Character 6	Qualifier Character 7
0 Brain **1** Cerebral Meninges **2** Dura Mater **3** Epidural Space **4** Subdural Space **5** Subarachnoid Space **6** Cerebral Ventricle **7** Cerebral Hemisphere **8** Basal Ganglia **9** Thalamus **A** Hypothalamus **B** Pons **C** Cerebellum **D** Medulla Oblongata **F** Olfactory Nerve **G** Optic Nerve **H** Oculomotor Nerve **J** Trochlear Nerve **K** Trigeminal Nerve **L** Abducens Nerve **M** Facial Nerve **N** Acoustic Nerve **P** Glossopharyngeal Nerve **Q** Vagus Nerve **R** Accessory Nerve **S** Hypoglossal Nerve **T** Spinal Meninges **W** Cervical Spinal Cord **X** Thoracic Spinal Cord **Y** Lumbar Spinal Cord	**0** Open **3** Percutaneous **4** Percutaneous Endoscopic	**Z** No Device	**Z** No Qualifier

0   Medical and Surgical
0   Central Nervous System
K   Map: Locating the route of passage of electrical impulses and/or locating functional areas in a body part

Body Part Character 4	Approach Character 5	Device Character 6	Qualifier Character 7
0 Brain **7** Cerebral Hemisphere **8** Basal Ganglia **9** Thalamus **A** Hypothalamus **B** Pons **C** Cerebellum **D** Medulla Oblongata	**0** Open **3** Percutaneous **4** Percutaneous Endoscopic	**Z** No Device	**Z** No Qualifier

0 Medical and Surgical
0 Central Nervous System
N Release: Freeing a body part from an abnormal physical constraint

Body Part Character 4	Approach Character 5	Device Character 6	Qualifier Character 7
0 Brain 1 Cerebral Meninges 2 Dura Mater 6 Cerebral Ventricle 7 Cerebral Hemisphere 8 Basal Ganglia 9 Thalamus A Hypothalamus B Pons C Cerebellum D Medulla Oblongata F Olfactory Nerve G Optic Nerve H Oculomotor Nerve J Trochlear Nerve K Trigeminal Nerve L Abducens Nerve M Facial Nerve N Acoustic Nerve P Glossopharyngeal Nerve Q Vagus Nerve R Accessory Nerve S Hypoglossal Nerve T Spinal Meninges W Cervical Spinal Cord X Thoracic Spinal Cord Y Lumbar Spinal Cord	0 Open 3 Percutaneous 4 Percutaneous Endoscopic	Z No Device	Z No Qualifier

0 Medical and Surgical
0 Central Nervous System
P Removal: Taking out or off a device from a body part

Body Part Character 4	Approach Character 5	Device Character 6	Qualifier Character 7
0 Brain 6 Cerebral Ventricle E Cranial Nerve U Spinal Canal V Spinal Cord	X External	0 Drainage Device 2 Monitoring Device 3 Infusion Device M Electrode	Z No Qualifier
0 Brain V Spinal Cord	0 Open 3 Percutaneous 4 Percutaneous Endoscopic	0 Drainage Device 2 Monitoring Device 3 Infusion Device 7 Autologous Tissue Substitute J Synthetic Substitute K Nonautologous Tissue Substitute M Electrode	Z No Qualifier
6 Cerebral Ventricle U Spinal Canal	0 Open 3 Percutaneous 4 Percutaneous Endoscopic	0 Drainage Device 2 Monitoring Device 3 Infusion Device J Synthetic Substitute M Electrode	Z No Qualifier
E Cranial Nerve	0 Open 3 Percutaneous 4 Percutaneous Endoscopic	0 Drainage Device 2 Monitoring Device 3 Infusion Device 7 Autologous Tissue Substitute M Electrode	Z No Qualifier

0   **Medical and Surgical**
0   **Central Nervous System**
Q   **Repair:**   Restoring, to the extent possible, a body part to its normal anatomic structure and function

Body Part Character 4	Approach Character 5	Device Character 6	Qualifier Character 7
0 Brain **1** Cerebral Meninges **2** Dura Mater **6** Cerebral Ventricle **7** Cerebral Hemisphere **8** Basal Ganglia **9** Thalamus **A** Hypothalamus **B** Pons **C** Cerebellum **D** Medulla Oblongata **F** Olfactory Nerve **G** Optic Nerve **H** Oculomotor Nerve **J** Trochlear Nerve **K** Trigeminal Nerve **L** Abducens Nerve **M** Facial Nerve **N** Acoustic Nerve **P** Glossopharyngeal Nerve **Q** Vagus Nerve **R** Accessory Nerve **S** Hypoglossal Nerve **T** Spinal Meninges **W** Cervical Spinal Cord **X** Thoracic Spinal Cord **Y** Lumbar Spinal Cord	**0** Open **3** Percutaneous **4** Percutaneous Endoscopic	**Z** No Device	**Z** No Qualifier

0   **Medical and Surgical**
0   **Central Nervous System**
S   **Reposition:**   Moving to its normal location or other suitable location all or a portion of a body part

Body Part Character 4	Approach Character 5	Device Character 6	Qualifier Character 7
F Olfactory Nerve **G** Optic Nerve **H** Oculomotor Nerve **J** Trochlear Nerve **K** Trigeminal Nerve **L** Abducens Nerve **M** Facial Nerve **N** Acoustic Nerve **P** Glossopharyngeal Nerve **Q** Vagus Nerve **R** Accessory Nerve **S** Hypoglossal Nerve **W** Cervical Spinal Cord **X** Thoracic Spinal Cord **Y** Lumbar Spinal Cord	**0** Open **3** Percutaneous **4** Percutaneous Endoscopic	**Z** No Device	**Z** No Qualifier

0   **Medical and Surgical**
0   **Central Nervous System**
T   **Resection:**   Cutting out or off, without replacement, all of a body part

Body Part Character 4	Approach Character 5	Device Character 6	Qualifier Character 7
7 Cerebral Hemisphere	**0** Open **3** Percutaneous **4** Percutaneous Endoscopic	**Z** No Device	**Z** No Qualifier

0   **Medical and Surgical**
0   **Central Nervous System**
U   **Supplement:**   Putting in or on biological or synthetic material that physically reinforces and/or augments the function of a portion of a body part

Body Part Character 4	Approach Character 5	Device Character 6	Qualifier Character 7
1 Cerebral Meninges **2** Dura Mater **T** Spinal Meninges	**0** Open **4** Percutaneous Endoscopic	**7** Autologous Tissue Substitute **J** Synthetic Substitute **K** Nonautologous Tissue Substitute	**Z** No Qualifier

Continued on next page

0   Medical and Surgical
0   Central Nervous System   *Continued from previous page*
U   Supplement: Putting in or on biological or synthetic material that physically reinforces and/or augments the function of a portion of a body part

Body Part Character 4	Approach Character 5	Device Character 6	Qualifier Character 7
F Olfactory Nerve G Optic Nerve H Oculomotor Nerve J Trochlear Nerve K Trigeminal Nerve L Abducens Nerve M Facial Nerve N Acoustic Nerve P Glossopharyngeal Nerve Q Vagus Nerve R Accessory Nerve S Hypoglossal Nerve	0 Open 4 Percutaneous Endoscopic	7 Autologous Tissue Substitute	Z No Qualifier

0   Medical and Surgical
0   Central Nervous System
W   Revision: Correcting, to the extent possible, a malfunctioning or displaced device

Body Part Character 4	Approach Character 5	Device Character 6	Qualifier Character 7
0 Brain V Spinal Cord	0 Open 3 Percutaneous 4 Percutaneous Endoscopic X External	0 Drainage Device 2 Monitoring Device 3 Infusion Device 7 Autologous Tissue Substitute J Synthetic Substitute K Nonautologous Tissue Substitute M Electrode	Z No Qualifier
6 Cerebral Ventricle U Spinal Canal	0 Open 3 Percutaneous 4 Percutaneous Endoscopic X External	0 Drainage Device 2 Monitoring Device 3 Infusion Device J Synthetic Substitute M Electrode	Z No Qualifier
E Cranial Nerve	0 Open 3 Percutaneous 4 Percutaneous Endoscopic X External	0 Drainage Device 2 Monitoring Device 3 Infusion Device 7 Autologous Tissue Substitute M Electrode	Z No Qualifier

0   Medical and Surgical
0   Central Nervous System
X   Transfer: Moving, without taking out, all or a portion of a body part to another location to take over the function of all or a portion of a body part

Body Part Character 4	Approach Character 5	Device Character 6	Qualifier Character 7
F Olfactory Nerve G Optic Nerve H Oculomotor Nerve J Trochlear Nerve K Trigeminal Nerve L Abducens Nerve M Facial Nerve N Acoustic Nerve P Glossopharyngeal Nerve Q Vagus Nerve R Accessory Nerve S Hypoglossal Nerve	0 Open 4 Percutaneous Endoscopic	Z No Device	F Olfactory Nerve G Optic Nerve H Oculomotor Nerve J Trochlear Nerve K Trigeminal Nerve L Abducens Nerve M Facial Nerve N Acoustic Nerve P Glossopharyngeal Nerve Q Vagus Nerve R Accessory Nerve S Hypoglossal Nerve

Peripheral Nervous System 012–01X

0 **Medical and Surgical**
1 **Peripheral Nervous System**
2 **Change:** Taking out or off a device from a body part and putting back an identical or similar device in or on the same body part without cutting or puncturing the skin or a mucous membrane

Body Part Character 4	Approach Character 5	Device Character 6	Qualifier Character 7
Y Peripheral Nerve	X External	0 Drainage Device Y Other Device	Z No Qualifier

0 **Medical and Surgical**
1 **Peripheral Nervous System**
5 **Destruction:** Physical eradication of all or a portion of a body part by the direct use of energy, force, or a destructive agent

Body Part Character 4	Approach Character 5	Device Character 6	Qualifier Character 7
0 Cervical Plexus 1 Cervical Nerve 2 Phrenic Nerve 3 Brachial Plexus 4 Ulnar Nerve 5 Median Nerve 6 Radial Nerve 8 Thoracic Nerve 9 Lumbar Plexus A Lumbosacral Plexus B Lumbar Nerve C Pudendal Nerve D Femoral Nerve F Sciatic Nerve G Tibial Nerve H Peroneal Nerve K Head and Neck Sympathetic Nerve L Thoracic Sympathetic Nerve M Abdominal Sympathetic Nerve N Lumbar Sympathetic Nerve P Sacral Sympathetic Nerve Q Sacral Plexus R Sacral Nerve	0 Open 3 Percutaneous 4 Percutaneous Endoscopic	Z No Device	Z No Qualifier

0 **Medical and Surgical**
1 **Peripheral Nervous System**
8 **Division:** Cutting into a body part without draining fluids and/or gases from the body part in order to separate or transect a body part

Body Part Character 4	Approach Character 5	Device Character 6	Qualifier Character 7
0 Cervical Plexus 1 Cervical Nerve 2 Phrenic Nerve 3 Brachial Plexus 4 Ulnar Nerve 5 Median Nerve 6 Radial Nerve 8 Thoracic Nerve 9 Lumbar Plexus A Lumbosacral Plexus B Lumbar Nerve C Pudendal Nerve D Femoral Nerve F Sciatic Nerve G Tibial Nerve H Peroneal Nerve K Head and Neck Sympathetic Nerve L Thoracic Sympathetic Nerve M Abdominal Sympathetic Nerve N Lumbar Sympathetic Nerve P Sacral Sympathetic Nerve Q Sacral Plexus R Sacral Nerve	0 Open 3 Percutaneous 4 Percutaneous Endoscopic	Z No Device	Z No Qualifier

0   Medical and Surgical
1   Peripheral Nervous System
9   Drainage: Taking or letting out fluids and/or gases from a body part

Body Part Character 4	Approach Character 5	Device Character 6	Qualifier Character 7
0 Cervical Plexus 1 Cervical Nerve 2 Phrenic Nerve 3 Brachial Plexus 4 Ulnar Nerve 5 Median Nerve 6 Radial Nerve 8 Thoracic Nerve 9 Lumbar Plexus A Lumbosacral Plexus B Lumbar Nerve C Pudendal Nerve D Femoral Nerve F Sciatic Nerve G Tibial Nerve H Peroneal Nerve K Head and Neck Sympathetic Nerve L Thoracic Sympathetic Nerve M Abdominal Sympathetic Nerve N Lumbar Sympathetic Nerve P Sacral Sympathetic Nerve Q Sacral Plexus R Sacral Nerve	0 Open 3 Percutaneous 4 Percutaneous Endoscopic	0 Drainage Device	Z No Qualifier
0 Cervical Plexus 1 Cervical Nerve 2 Phrenic Nerve 3 Brachial Plexus 4 Ulnar Nerve 5 Median Nerve 6 Radial Nerve 8 Thoracic Nerve 9 Lumbar Plexus A Lumbosacral Plexus B Lumbar Nerve C Pudendal Nerve D Femoral Nerve F Sciatic Nerve G Tibial Nerve H Peroneal Nerve K Head and Neck Sympathetic Nerve L Thoracic Sympathetic Nerve M Abdominal Sympathetic Nerve N Lumbar Sympathetic Nerve P Sacral Sympathetic Nerve Q Sacral Plexus R Sacral Nerve	0 Open 3 Percutaneous 4 Percutaneous Endoscopic	Z No Device	X Diagnostic Z No Qualifier

0 **Medical and Surgical**
1 **Peripheral Nervous System**
B **Excision:**   Cutting out or off, without replacement, a portion of a body part

Body Part Character 4	Approach Character 5	Device Character 6	Qualifier Character 7
0 Cervical Plexus 1 Cervical Nerve 2 Phrenic Nerve 3 Brachial Plexus 4 Ulnar Nerve 5 Median Nerve 6 Radial Nerve 8 Thoracic Nerve 9 Lumbar Plexus A Lumbosacral Plexus B Lumbar Nerve C Pudendal Nerve D Femoral Nerve F Sciatic Nerve G Tibial Nerve H Peroneal Nerve K Head and Neck Sympathetic Nerve L Thoracic Sympathetic Nerve M Abdominal Sympathetic Nerve N Lumbar Sympathetic Nerve P Sacral Sympathetic Nerve Q Sacral Plexus R Sacral Nerve	0 Open 3 Percutaneous 4 Percutaneous Endoscopic	Z No Device	X Diagnostic Z No Qualifier

0 **Medical and Surgical**
1 **Peripheral Nervous System**
C **Extirpation:**   Taking or cutting out solid matter from a body part

Body Part Character 4	Approach Character 5	Device Character 6	Qualifier Character 7
0 Cervical Plexus 1 Cervical Nerve 2 Phrenic Nerve 3 Brachial Plexus 4 Ulnar Nerve 5 Median Nerve 6 Radial Nerve 8 Thoracic Nerve 9 Lumbar Plexus A Lumbosacral Plexus B Lumbar Nerve C Pudendal Nerve D Femoral Nerve F Sciatic Nerve G Tibial Nerve H Peroneal Nerve K Head and Neck Sympathetic Nerve L Thoracic Sympathetic Nerve M Abdominal Sympathetic Nerve N Lumbar Sympathetic Nerve P Sacral Sympathetic Nerve Q Sacral Plexus R Sacral Nerve	0 Open 3 Percutaneous 4 Percutaneous Endoscopic	Z No Device	Z No Qualifier

0 Medical and Surgical
1 Peripheral Nervous System
D Extraction: Pulling or stripping out or off all or a portion of a body part by the use of force

Body Part Character 4	Approach Character 5	Device Character 6	Qualifier Character 7
0 Cervical Plexus 1 Cervical Nerve 2 Phrenic Nerve 3 Brachial Plexus 4 Ulnar Nerve 5 Median Nerve 6 Radial Nerve 8 Thoracic Nerve 9 Lumbar Plexus A Lumbosacral Plexus B Lumbar Nerve C Pudendal Nerve D Femoral Nerve F Sciatic Nerve G Tibial Nerve H Peroneal Nerve K Head and Neck Sympathetic Nerve L Thoracic Sympathetic Nerve M Abdominal Sympathetic Nerve N Lumbar Sympathetic Nerve P Sacral Sympathetic Nerve Q Sacral Plexus R Sacral Nerve	0 Open 3 Percutaneous 4 Percutaneous Endoscopic	Z No Device	Z No Qualifier

0 Medical and Surgical
1 Peripheral Nervous System
H Insertion: Putting in a nonbiological appliance that monitors, assists, performs or prevents a physiological function, but does not physically take the place of a body part

Body Part Character 4	Approach Character 5	Device Character 6	Qualifier Character 7
Y Peripheral Nerve	0 Open 3 Percutaneous 4 Percutaneous Endoscopic	2 Monitoring Device M Electrode	Z No Qualifier

0 Medical and Surgical
1 Peripheral Nervous System
J Inspection: Visually and/or manually exploring a body part

Body Part Character 4	Approach Character 5	Device Character 6	Qualifier Character 7
0 Cervical Plexus 1 Cervical Nerve 2 Phrenic Nerve 3 Brachial Plexus 4 Ulnar Nerve 5 Median Nerve 6 Radial Nerve 8 Thoracic Nerve 9 Lumbar Plexus A Lumbosacral Plexus B Lumbar Nerve C Pudendal Nerve D Femoral Nerve F Sciatic Nerve G Tibial Nerve H Peroneal Nerve K Head and Neck Sympathetic Nerve L Thoracic Sympathetic Nerve M Abdominal Sympathetic Nerve N Lumbar Sympathetic Nerve P Sacral Sympathetic Nerve Q Sacral Plexus R Sacral Nerve	0 Open 3 Percutaneous 4 Percutaneous Endoscopic	Z No Device	Z No Qualifier

0   Medical and Surgical
1   Peripheral Nervous System
N   Release: Freeing a body part from an abnormal physical constraint

Body Part Character 4	Approach Character 5	Device Character 6	Qualifier Character 7
0 Cervical Plexus 1 Cervical Nerve 2 Phrenic Nerve 3 Brachial Plexus 4 Ulnar Nerve 5 Median Nerve 6 Radial Nerve 8 Thoracic Nerve 9 Lumbar Plexus A Lumbosacral Plexus B Lumbar Nerve C Pudendal Nerve D Femoral Nerve F Sciatic Nerve G Tibial Nerve H Peroneal Nerve K Head and Neck Sympathetic Nerve L Thoracic Sympathetic Nerve M Abdominal Sympathetic Nerve N Lumbar Sympathetic Nerve P Sacral Sympathetic Nerve Q Sacral Plexus R Sacral Nerve	0 Open 3 Percutaneous 4 Percutaneous Endoscopic	Z No Device	Z No Qualifier

0   Medical and Surgical
1   Peripheral Nervous System
P   Removal: Taking out or off a device from a body part

Body Part Character 4	Approach Character 5	Device Character 6	Qualifier Character 7
Y Peripheral Nerve	0 Open 3 Percutaneous 4 Percutaneous Endoscopic	0 Drainage Device 2 Monitoring Device 7 Autologous Tissue Substitute M Electrode	Z No Qualifier
Y Peripheral Nerve	X External	0 Drainage Device 2 Monitoring Device M Electrode	Z No Qualifier

0   Medical and Surgical
1   Peripheral Nervous System
Q   Repair: Restoring, to the extent possible, a body part to its normal anatomic structure and function

Body Part Character 4	Approach Character 5	Device Character 6	Qualifier Character 7
0 Cervical Plexus 1 Cervical Nerve 2 Phrenic Nerve 3 Brachial Plexus 4 Ulnar Nerve 5 Median Nerve 6 Radial Nerve 8 Thoracic Nerve 9 Lumbar Plexus A Lumbosacral Plexus B Lumbar Nerve C Pudendal Nerve D Femoral Nerve F Sciatic Nerve G Tibial Nerve H Peroneal Nerve K Head and Neck Sympathetic Nerve L Thoracic Sympathetic Nerve M Abdominal Sympathetic Nerve N Lumbar Sympathetic Nerve P Sacral Sympathetic Nerve Q Sacral Plexus R Sacral Nerve	0 Open 3 Percutaneous 4 Percutaneous Endoscopic	Z No Device	Z No Qualifier

0   **Medical and Surgical**
1   **Peripheral Nervous System**
S   **Reposition:**   Moving to its normal location or other suitable location all or a portion of a body part

Body Part Character 4	Approach Character 5	Device Character 6	Qualifier Character 7
0 Cervical Plexus 1 Cervical Nerve 2 Phrenic Nerve 3 Brachial Plexus 4 Ulnar Nerve 5 Median Nerve 6 Radial Nerve 8 Thoracic Nerve 9 Lumbar Plexus A Lumbosacral Plexus B Lumbar Nerve C Pudendal Nerve D Femoral Nerve F Sciatic Nerve G Tibial Nerve H Peroneal Nerve Q Sacral Plexus R Sacral Nerve	0 Open 3 Percutaneous 4 Percutaneous Endoscopic	Z No Device	Z No Qualifier

0   **Medical and Surgical**
1   **Peripheral Nervous System**
U   **Supplement:**   Putting in or on biological or synthetic material that physically reinforces and/or augments the function of a portion of a body part

Body Part Character 4	Approach Character 5	Device Character 6	Qualifier Character 7
1 Cervical Nerve 2 Phrenic Nerve 4 Ulnar Nerve 5 Median Nerve 6 Radial Nerve 8 Thoracic Nerve B Lumbar Nerve C Pudendal Nerve D Femoral Nerve F Sciatic Nerve G Tibial Nerve H Peroneal Nerve R Sacral Nerve	0 Open 4 Percutaneous Endoscopic	7 Autologous Tissue Substitute	Z No Qualifier

0   **Medical and Surgical**
1   **Peripheral Nervous System**
W   **Revision:**   Correcting, to the extent possible, a malfunctioning or displaced device

Body Part Character 4	Approach Character 5	Device Character 6	Qualifier Character 7
Y Peripheral Nerve	0 Open 3 Percutaneous 4 Percutaneous Endoscopic X External	0 Drainage Device 2 Monitoring Device 7 Autologous Tissue Substitute M Electrode	Z No Qualifier

0   **Medical and Surgical**
1   **Peripheral Nervous System**
X   **Transfer:**   Moving, without taking out, all or a portion of a body part to another location to take over the function of all or a portion of a body part

Body Part Character 4	Approach Character 5	Device Character 6	Qualifier Character 7
1 Cervical Nerve 2 Phrenic Nerve	0 Open 4 Percutaneous Endoscopic	Z No Device	1 Cervical Nerve 2 Phrenic Nerve
4 Ulnar Nerve 5 Median Nerve 6 Radial Nerve	0 Open 4 Percutaneous Endoscopic	Z No Device	4 Ulnar Nerve 5 Median Nerve 6 Radial Nerve
8 Thoracic Nerve	0 Open 4 Percutaneous Endoscopic	Z No Device	8 Thoracic Nerve
B Lumbar Nerve C Pudendal Nerve	0 Open 4 Percutaneous Endoscopic	Z No Device	B Lumbar Nerve C Perineal Nerve
D Femoral Nerve F Sciatic Nerve G Tibial Nerve H Peroneal Nerve	0 Open 4 Percutaneous Endoscopic	Z No Device	D Femoral Nerve F Sciatic Nerve G Tibial Nerve H Peroneal Nerve

Heart and Great Vessels 021–02Y

0   **Medical and Surgical**
2   **Heart and Great Vessels**
1   **Bypass:**   Altering the route of passage of the contents of a tubular body part

Body Part Character 4	Approach Character 5	Device Character 6	Qualifier Character 7
0 Coronary Artery, One Site 1 Coronary Artery, Two Sites 2 Coronary Artery, Three Sites 3 Coronary Artery, Four or More Sites	0 Open 4 Percutaneous Endoscopic	9 Autologous Venous Tissue A Autologous Arterial Tissue J Synthetic Substitute K Nonautologous Tissue Substitute	3 Coronary Artery 8 Internal Mammary, Right 9 Internal Mammary, Left C Thoracic Artery F Abdominal Artery W Aorta
0 Coronary Artery, One Site 1 Coronary Artery, Two Sites 2 Coronary Artery, Three Sites 3 Coronary Artery, Four or More Sites	0 Open 4 Percutaneous Endoscopic	Z No Device	3 Coronary Artery 8 Internal Mammary, Right 9 Internal Mammary, Left C Thoracic Artery F Abdominal Artery
0 Coronary Artery, One Site 1 Coronary Artery, Two Sites 2 Coronary Artery, Three Sites 3 Coronary Artery, Four or More Sites	3 Percutaneous 4 Percutaneous Endoscopic	4 Drug-eluting Intraluminal Device D Intraluminal Device	4 Coronary Vein
6 Atrium, Right	0 Open 4 Percutaneous Endoscopic	Z No Device	7 Atrium, Left P Pulmonary Trunk Q Pulmonary Artery, Right R Pulmonary Artery, Left
6 Atrium, Right K Ventricle, Right L Ventricle, Left	0 Open 4 Percutaneous Endoscopic	9 Autologous Venous Tissue A Autologous Arterial Tissue J Synthetic Substitute K Nonautologous Tissue Substitute	P Pulmonary Trunk Q Pulmonary Artery, Right R Pulmonary Artery, Left
7 Atrium, Left V Superior Vena Cava	0 Open 4 Percutaneous Endoscopic	9 Autologous Venous Tissue A Autologous Arterial Tissue J Synthetic Substitute K Nonautologous Tissue Substitute Z No Device	P Pulmonary Trunk Q Pulmonary Artery, Right R Pulmonary Artery, Left
K Ventricle, Right L Ventricle, Left	0 Open 4 Percutaneous Endoscopic	Z No Device	5 Coronary Circulation 8 Internal Mammary, Right 9 Internal Mammary, Left C Thoracic Artery F Abdominal Artery P Pulmonary Trunk Q Pulmonary Artery, Right R Pulmonary Artery, Left W Aorta
W Thoracic Aorta	0 Open 4 Percutaneous Endoscopic	9 Autologous Venous Tissue A Autologous Arterial Tissue J Synthetic Substitute K Nonautologous Tissue Substitute Z No Device	B Subclavian D Carotid P Pulmonary Trunk Q Pulmonary Artery, Right R Pulmonary Artery, Left

0 Medical and Surgical
2 Heart and Great Vessels
5 Destruction: Physical eradication of all or a portion of a body part by the direct use of energy, force, or a destructive agent

Body Part Character 4	Approach Character 5	Device Character 6	Qualifier Character 7
4 Coronary Vein 5 Atrial Septum 6 Atrium, Right 7 Atrium, Left 8 Conduction Mechanism 9 Chordae Tendineae D Papillary Muscle F Aortic Valve G Mitral Valve H Pulmonary Valve J Tricuspid Valve K Ventricle, Right L Ventricle, Left M Ventricular Septum N Pericardium P Pulmonary Trunk Q Pulmonary Artery, Right R Pulmonary Artery, Left S Pulmonary Vein, Right T Pulmonary Vein, Left V Superior Vena Cava W Thoracic Aorta	0 Open 3 Percutaneous 4 Percutaneous Endoscopic	Z No Device	Z No Qualifier

0 Medical and Surgical
2 Heart and Great Vessels
7 Dilation: Expanding an orifice or the lumen of a tubular body part

Body Part Character 4	Approach Character 5	Device Character 6	Qualifier Character 7
0 Coronary Artery, One Site 1 Coronary Artery, Two Sites 2 Coronary Artery, Three Sites 3 Coronary Artery, Four or More Sites	0 Open 3 Percutaneous 4 Percutaneous Endoscopic	4 Drug-eluting Intraluminal Device D Intraluminal Device Z No Device	6 Bifurcation Z No Qualifier
F Aortic Valve G Mitral Valve H Pulmonary Valve J Tricuspid Valve K Ventricle, Right P Pulmonary Trunk Q Pulmonary Artery, Right S Pulmonary Vein, Right T Pulmonary Vein, Left V Superior Vena Cava W Thoracic Aorta	0 Open 3 Percutaneous 4 Percutaneous Endoscopic	4 Drug-eluting Intraluminal Device D Intraluminal Device Z No Device	Z No Qualifier
R Pulmonary Artery, Left	0 Open 3 Percutaneous 4 Percutaneous Endoscopic	4 Drug-eluting Intraluminal Device D Intraluminal Device Z No Device	T Ductus Arteriosus Z No Qualifier

0 Medical and Surgical
2 Heart and Great Vessels
8 Division: Cutting into a body part without draining fluids and/or gases from the body part in order to separate or transect a body part

Body Part Character 4	Approach Character 5	Device Character 6	Qualifier Character 7
8 Conduction Mechanism 9 Chordae Tendineae D Papillary Muscle	0 Open 3 Percutaneous 4 Percutaneous Endoscopic	Z No Device	Z No Qualifier

0   Medical and Surgical
2   Heart and Great Vessels
B   Excision: Cutting out or off, without replacement, a portion of a body part

Body Part Character 4	Approach Character 5	Device Character 6	Qualifier Character 7
4 Coronary Vein **5** Atrial Septum **6** Atrium, Right **7** Atrium, Left **8** Conduction Mechanism **9** Chordae Tendineae **D** Papillary Muscle **F** Aortic Valve **G** Mitral Valve **H** Pulmonary Valve **J** Tricuspid Valve **K** Ventricle, Right **L** Ventricle, Left **M** Ventricular Septum **N** Pericardium **P** Pulmonary Trunk **Q** Pulmonary Artery, Right **R** Pulmonary Artery, Left **S** Pulmonary Vein, Right **T** Pulmonary Vein, Left **V** Superior Vena Cava **W** Thoracic Aorta	**0** Open **3** Percutaneous **4** Percutaneous Endoscopic	**Z** No Device	**X** Diagnostic **Z** No Qualifier

0   Medical and Surgical
2   Heart and Great Vessels
C   Extirpation: Taking or cutting out solid matter from a body part

Body Part Character 4	Approach Character 5	Device Character 6	Qualifier Character 7
0 Coronary Artery, One Site **1** Coronary Artery, Two Sites **2** Coronary Artery, Three Sites **3** Coronary Artery, Four or More Sites **4** Coronary Vein **5** Atrial Septum **6** Atrium, Right **7** Atrium, Left **8** Conduction Mechanism **9** Chordae Tendineae **D** Papillary Muscle **F** Aortic Valve **G** Mitral Valve **H** Pulmonary Valve **J** Tricuspid Valve **K** Ventricle, Right **L** Ventricle, Left **M** Ventricular Septum **N** Pericardium **P** Pulmonary Trunk **Q** Pulmonary Artery, Right **R** Pulmonary Artery, Left **S** Pulmonary Vein, Right **T** Pulmonary Vein, Left **V** Superior Vena Cava **W** Thoracic Aorta	**0** Open **3** Percutaneous **4** Percutaneous Endoscopic	**Z** No Device	**Z** No Qualifier

0   Medical and Surgical
2   Heart and Great Vessels
F   Fragmentation: Breaking solid matter in a body part into pieces

Body Part Character 4	Approach Character 5	Device Character 6	Qualifier Character 7
N Pericardium	**0** Open **3** Percutaneous **4** Percutaneous Endoscopic **X** External	**Z** No Device	**Z** No Qualifier

0 **Medical and Surgical**
2 **Heart and Great Vessels**
H **Insertion:** Putting in a nonbiological appliance that monitors, assists, performs or prevents a physiological function, but does not physically take the place of a body part

Body Part Character 4	Approach Character 5	Device Character 6	Qualifier Character 7
4 Coronary Vein 6 Atrium, Right 7 Atrium, Left K Ventricle, Right L Ventricle, Left	0 Open 3 Percutaneous 4 Percutaneous Endoscopic	2 Monitoring Device 3 Infusion Device D Intraluminal Device M Electrode	Z No Qualifier
A Heart	0 Open 3 Percutaneous 4 Percutaneous Endoscopic	Q Implantable Heart Assist System	Z No Qualifier
A Heart	0 Open 3 Percutaneous 4 Percutaneous Endoscopic	R External Heart Assist System	S Biventricular Z No Qualifier
N Pericardium	0 Open 3 Percutaneous 4 Percutaneous Endoscopic	2 Monitoring Device M Electrode	Z No Qualifier
P Pulmonary Trunk Q Pulmonary Artery, Right R Pulmonary Artery, Left S Pulmonary Vein, Right T Pulmonary Vein, Left V Superior Vena Cava W Thoracic Aorta	0 Open 3 Percutaneous 4 Percutaneous Endoscopic	2 Monitoring Device 3 Infusion Device D Intraluminal Device	Z No Qualifier

0 **Medical and Surgical**
2 **Heart and Great Vessels**
J **Inspection:** Visually and/or manually exploring a body part

Body Part Character 4	Approach Character 5	Device Character 6	Qualifier Character 7
4 Coronary Vein 5 Atrial Septum 6 Atrium, Right 7 Atrium, Left 8 Conduction Mechanism 9 Chordae Tendineae A Heart B Heart, Right C Heart, Left D Papillary Muscle F Aortic Valve G Mitral Valve H Pulmonary Valve J Tricuspid Valve K Ventricle, Right L Ventricle, Left M Ventricular Septum N Pericardium P Pulmonary Trunk Q Pulmonary Artery, Right R Pulmonary Artery, Left S Pulmonary Vein, Right T Pulmonary Vein, Left V Superior Vena Cava W Thoracic Aorta	0 Open 3 Percutaneous 4 Percutaneous Endoscopic	Z No Device	Z No Qualifier

0 **Medical and Surgical**
2 **Heart and Great Vessels**
K **Map:** Locating the route of passage of electrical impulses and/or locating functional areas in a body part

Body Part Character 4	Approach Character 5	Device Character 6	Qualifier Character 7
8 Conduction Mechanism	0 Open 3 Percutaneous 4 Percutaneous Endoscopic	Z No Device	Z No Qualifier

0   Medical and Surgical
2   Heart and Great Vessels
L   Occlusion: Completely closing an orifice or lumen of a tubular body part

Body Part Character 4	Approach Character 5	Device Character 6	Qualifier Character 7
R Pulmonary Artery, Left	**0** Open **3** Percutaneous **4** Percutaneous Endoscopic	**C** Extraluminal Device **D** Intraluminal Device **Z** No Device	**T** Ductus Arteriosus
S Pulmonary Vein, Right **T** Pulmonary Vein, Left **V** Superior Vena Cava	**0** Open **3** Percutaneous **4** Percutaneous Endoscopic	**C** Extraluminal Device **D** Intraluminal Device **Z** No Device	**Z** No Qualifier

0   Medical and Surgical
2   Heart and Great Vessels
N   Release: Freeing a body part from an abnormal physical constraint

Body Part Character 4	Approach Character 5	Device Character 6	Qualifier Character 7
4 Coronary Vein **5** Atrial Septum **6** Atrium, Right **7** Atrium, Left **8** Conduction Mechanism **9** Chordae Tendineae **D** Papillary Muscle **F** Aortic Valve **G** Mitral Valve **H** Pulmonary Valve **J** Tricuspid Valve **K** Ventricle, Right **L** Ventricle, Left **M** Ventricular Septum **N** Pericardium **P** Pulmonary Trunk **Q** Pulmonary Artery, Right **R** Pulmonary Artery, Left **S** Pulmonary Vein, Right **T** Pulmonary Vein, Left **V** Superior Vena Cava **W** Thoracic Aorta	**0** Open **3** Percutaneous **4** Percutaneous Endoscopic	**Z** No Device	**Z** No Qualifier

0   Medical and Surgical
2   Heart and Great Vessels
P   Removal: Taking out or off a device from a body part

Body Part Character 4	Approach Character 5	Device Character 6	Qualifier Character 7
A Heart	**0** Open **3** Percutaneous **4** Percutaneous Endoscopic	**2** Monitoring Device **3** Infusion Device **4** Drug-eluting Intraluminal Device **7** Autologous Tissue Substitute **8** Zooplastic Tissue **9** Autologous Venous Tissue **A** Autologous Arterial Tissue **C** Extraluminal Device **D** Intraluminal Device **J** Synthetic Substitute **K** Nonautologous Tissue Substitute **M** Electrode **Q** Implantable Heart Assist System **R** External Heart Assist System	**Z** No Qualifier
A Heart	**X** External	**2** Monitoring Device **3** Infusion Device **4** Drug-eluting Intraluminal Device **D** Intraluminal Device **M** Electrode	**Z** No Qualifier
Y Great Vessel	**0** Open **3** Percutaneous **4** Percutaneous Endoscopic	**2** Monitoring Device **3** Infusion Device **4** Drug-eluting Intraluminal Device **7** Autologous Tissue Substitute **8** Zooplastic Tissue **9** Autologous Venous Tissue **A** Autologous Arterial Tissue **C** Extraluminal Device **D** Intraluminal Device **J** Synthetic Substitute **K** Nonautologous Tissue Substitute	**Z** No Qualifier *Continued on next page*

0 Medical and Surgical
2 Heart and Great Vessels
P Removal:　　　Taking out or off a device from a body part

Continued from previous page

Body Part Character 4	Approach Character 5	Device Character 6	Qualifier Character 7
Y Great Vessel	**X** External	**2** Monitoring Device **3** Infusion Device **4** Drug-eluting Intraluminal Device **D** Intraluminal Device	**Z** No Qualifier

0 Medical and Surgical
2 Heart and Great Vessels
Q Repair:　　　Restoring, to the extent possible, a body part to its normal anatomic structure and function

Body Part Character 4	Approach Character 5	Device Character 6	Qualifier Character 7
0 Coronary Artery, One Site **1** Coronary Artery, Two Sites **2** Coronary Artery, Three Sites **3** Coronary Artery, Four or More Sites **4** Coronary Vein **5** Atrial Septum **6** Atrium, Right **7** Atrium, Left **8** Conduction Mechanism **9** Chordae Tendineae **A** Heart **B** Heart, Right **C** Heart, Left **D** Papillary Muscle **F** Aortic Valve **G** Mitral Valve **H** Pulmonary Valve **J** Tricuspid Valve **K** Ventricle, Right **L** Ventricle, Left **M** Ventricular Septum **N** Pericardium **P** Pulmonary Trunk **Q** Pulmonary Artery, Right **R** Pulmonary Artery, Left **S** Pulmonary Vein, Right **T** Pulmonary Vein, Left **V** Superior Vena Cava **W** Thoracic Aorta	**0** Open **3** Percutaneous **4** Percutaneous Endoscopic	**Z** No Device	**Z** No Qualifier

0 Medical and Surgical
2 Heart and Great Vessels
R Replacement:　　　Putting in or on biological or synthetic material that physically takes the place and/or function of all or a portion of a body part

Body Part Character 4	Approach Character 5	Device Character 6	Qualifier Character 7
5 Atrial Septum **6** Atrium, Right **7** Atrium, Left **9** Chordae Tendineae **D** Papillary Muscle **F** Aortic Valve **G** Mitral Valve **H** Pulmonary Valve **J** Tricuspid Valve **K** Ventricle, Right **L** Ventricle, Left **M** Ventricular Septum **N** Pericardium **P** Pulmonary Trunk **Q** Pulmonary Artery, Right **R** Pulmonary Artery, Left **S** Pulmonary Vein, Right **T** Pulmonary Vein, Left **V** Superior Vena Cava **W** Thoracic Aorta	**0** Open **4** Percutaneous Endoscopic	**7** Autologous Tissue Substitute **8** Zooplastic Tissue **J** Synthetic Substitute **K** Nonautologous Tissue Substitute	**Z** No Qualifier

0 Medical and Surgical
2 Heart and Great Vessels
S Reposition: Moving to its normal location or other suitable location all or a portion of a body part

Body Part Character 4	Approach Character 5	Device Character 6	Qualifier Character 7
P Pulmonary Trunk Q Pulmonary Artery, Right R Pulmonary Artery, Left S Pulmonary Vein, Right T Pulmonary Vein, Left V Superior Vena Cava W Thoracic Aorta	0 Open	Z No Device	Z No Qualifier

0 Medical and Surgical
2 Heart and Great Vessels
T Resection: Cutting out or off, without replacement, all of a body part

Body Part Character 4	Approach Character 5	Device Character 6	Qualifier Character 7
5 Atrial Septum 8 Conduction Mechanism 9 Chordae Tendineae D Papillary Muscle H Pulmonary Valve M Ventricular Septum N Pericardium	0 Open 3 Percutaneous 4 Percutaneous Endoscopic	Z No Device	Z No Qualifier

0 Medical and Surgical
2 Heart and Great Vessels
U Supplement: Putting in or on biological or synthetic material that physically reinforces and/or augments the function of a portion of a body part

Body Part Character 4	Approach Character 5	Device Character 6	Qualifier Character 7
5 Atrial Septum 6 Atrium, Right 7 Atrium, Left 9 Chordae Tendineae A Heart D Papillary Muscle F Aortic Valve G Mitral Valve H Pulmonary Valve J Tricuspid Valve K Ventricle, Right L Ventricle, Left M Ventricular Septum N Pericardium P Pulmonary Trunk Q Pulmonary Artery, Right R Pulmonary Artery, Left S Pulmonary Vein, Right T Pulmonary Vein, Left V Superior Vena Cava W Thoracic Aorta	0 Open 4 Percutaneous Endoscopic	7 Autologous Tissue Substitute 8 Zooplastic Tissue J Synthetic Substitute K Nonautologous Tissue Substitute	Z No Qualifier

0 Medical and Surgical
2 Heart and Great Vessels
V Restriction: Partially closing the orifice or lumen of a tubular body part

Body Part Character 4	Approach Character 5	Device Character 6	Qualifier Character 7
A Heart	0 Open 3 Percutaneous 4 Percutaneous Endoscopic	C Extraluminal Device Z No Device	Z No Qualifier
P Pulmonary Trunk Q Pulmonary Artery, Right S Pulmonary Vein, Right T Pulmonary Vein, Left V Superior Vena Cava W Thoracic Aorta	0 Open 3 Percutaneous 4 Percutaneous Endoscopic	C Extraluminal Device D Intraluminal Device Z No Device	Z No Qualifier
R Pulmonary Artery, Left	0 Open 3 Percutaneous 4 Percutaneous Endoscopic	C Extraluminal Device D Intraluminal Device Z No Device	T Ductus Arteriosus Z No Qualifier

0   Medical and Surgical
2   Heart and Great Vessels
W   Revision: Correcting, to the extent possible, a malfunctioning or displaced device

Body Part Character 4	Approach Character 5	Device Character 6	Qualifier Character 7
5 Atrial Septum **M** Ventricular Septum	**0** Open **4** Percutaneous Endoscopic	**J** Synthetic Substitute	**Z** No Qualifier
A Heart	**0** Open **3** Percutaneous **4** Percutaneous Endoscopic **X** External	**2** Monitoring Device **3** Infusion Device **4** Drug-eluting Intraluminal Device **7** Autologous Tissue Substitute **8** Zooplastic Tissue **9** Autologous Venous Tissue **A** Autologous Arterial Tissue **C** Extraluminal Device **D** Intraluminal Device **J** Synthetic Substitute **K** Nonautologous Tissue Substitute **M** Electrode **Q** Implantable Heart Assist System **R** External Heart Assist System	**Z** No Qualifier
F Aortic Valve **G** Mitral Valve **H** Pulmonary Valve **J** Tricuspid Valve	**0** Open **4** Percutaneous Endoscopic	**7** Autologous Tissue Substitute **8** Zooplastic Tissue **J** Synthetic Substitute **K** Nonautologous Tissue Substitute	**Z** No Qualifier
Y Great Vessel	**0** Open **3** Percutaneous **4** Percutaneous Endoscopic **X** External	**2** Monitoring Device **3** Infusion Device **4** Drug-eluting Intraluminal Device **7** Autologous Tissue Substitute **8** Zooplastic Tissue **9** Autologous Venous Tissue **A** Autologous Arterial Tissue **C** Extraluminal Device **D** Intraluminal Device **J** Synthetic Substitute **K** Nonautologous Tissue Substitute	**Z** No Qualifier

0   Medical and Surgical
2   Heart and Great Vessels
Y   Transplantation: Putting in or on all or a portion of a living body part taken from another individual or animal to
physically take the place and/or function of all or a portion of a similar body part

Body Part Character 4	Approach Character 5	Device Character 6	Qualifier Character 7
A Heart	**0** Open	**Z** No Device	**0** Allogeneic **1** Syngeneic **2** Zooplastic

Upper Arteries 031–03W

0 **Medical and Surgical**
3 **Upper Arteries**
1 **Bypass:**   Altering the route of passage of the contents of a tubular body part

Body Part Character 4	Approach Character 5	Device Character 6	Qualifier Character 7
2 Innominate Artery 5 Axillary Artery, Right 6 Axillary Artery, Left	0 Open	9 Autologous Venous Tissue A Autologous Arterial Tissue J Synthetic Substitute K Nonautologous Tissue Substitute Z No Device	0 Upper Arm Artery, Right 1 Upper Arm Artery, Left 2 Upper Arm Artery, Bilateral 3 Lower Arm Artery, Right 4 Lower Arm Artery, Left 5 Lower Arm Artery, Bilateral 6 Upper Leg Artery, Right 7 Upper Leg Artery, Left 8 Upper Leg Artery, Bilateral 9 Lower Leg Artery, Right B Lower Leg Artery, Left C Lower Leg Artery, Bilateral D Upper Arm Vein F Lower Arm Vein J Extracranial Artery, Right K Extracranial Artery, Left
3 Subclavian Artery, Right 4 Subclavian Artery, Left	0 Open	9 Autologous Venous Tissue A Autologous Arterial Tissue J Synthetic Substitute K Nonautologous Tissue Substitute Z No Device	0 Upper Arm Artery, Right 1 Upper Arm Artery, Left 2 Upper Arm Artery, Bilateral 3 Lower Arm Artery, Right 4 Lower Arm Artery, Left 5 Lower Arm Artery, Bilateral 6 Upper Leg Artery, Right 7 Upper Leg Artery, Left 8 Upper Leg Artery, Bilateral 9 Lower Leg Artery, Right B Lower Leg Artery, Left C Lower Leg Artery, Bilateral D Upper Arm Vein F Lower Arm Vein J Extracranial Artery, Right K Extracranial Artery, Left M Pulmonary Artery, Right N Pulmonary Artery, Left
7 Brachial Artery, Right	0 Open	9 Autologous Venous Tissue A Autologous Arterial Tissue J Synthetic Substitute K Nonautologous Tissue Substitute Z No Device	0 Upper Arm Artery, Right 3 Lower Arm Artery, Right D Upper Arm Vein F Lower Arm Vein
8 Brachial Artery, Left	0 Open	9 Autologous Venous Tissue A Autologous Arterial Tissue J Synthetic Substitute K Nonautologous Tissue Substitute Z No Device	1 Upper Arm Artery, Left 4 Lower Arm Artery, Left D Upper Arm Vein F Lower Arm Vein
9 Ulnar Artery, Right B Radial Artery, Right	0 Open	9 Autologous Venous Tissue A Autologous Arterial Tissue J Synthetic Substitute K Nonautologous Tissue Substitute Z No Device	3 Lower Arm Artery, Right F Lower Arm Vein
A Ulnar Artery, Left C Radial Artery, Left	0 Open	9 Autologous Venous Tissue A Autologous Arterial Tissue J Synthetic Substitute K Nonautologous Tissue Substitute Z No Device	4 Lower Arm Artery, Left F Lower Arm Vein
G Intracranial Artery S Temporal Artery, Right T Temporal Artery, Left	0 Open	9 Autologous Venous Tissue A Autologous Arterial Tissue J Synthetic Substitute K Nonautologous Tissue Substitute Z No Device	G Intracranial Artery
H Common Carotid Artery, Right J Common Carotid Artery, Left K Internal Carotid Artery, Right L Internal Carotid Artery, Left M External Carotid Artery, Right N External Carotid Artery, Left	0 Open	9 Autologous Venous Tissue A Autologous Arterial Tissue J Synthetic Substitute K Nonautologous Tissue Substitute Z No Device	J Extracranial Artery, Right K Extracranial Artery, Left

0 **Medical and Surgical**
3 **Upper Arteries**
5 **Destruction:** Physical eradication of all or a portion of a body part by the direct use of energy, force, or a destructive agent

Body Part Character 4	Approach Character 5	Device Character 6	Qualifier Character 7
0 Internal Mammary Artery, Right **1** Internal Mammary Artery, Left **2** Innominate Artery **3** Subclavian Artery, Right **4** Subclavian Artery, Left **5** Axillary Artery, Right **6** Axillary Artery, Left **7** Brachial Artery, Right **8** Brachial Artery, Left **9** Ulnar Artery, Right **A** Ulnar Artery, Left **B** Radial Artery, Right **C** Radial Artery, Left **D** Hand Artery, Right **F** Hand Artery, Left **G** Intracranial Artery **H** Common Carotid Artery, Right **J** Common Carotid Artery, Left **K** Internal Carotid Artery, Right **L** Internal Carotid Artery, Left **M** External Carotid Artery, Right **N** External Carotid Artery, Left **P** Vertebral Artery, Right **Q** Vertebral Artery, Left **R** Face Artery **S** Temporal Artery, Right **T** Temporal Artery, Left **U** Thyroid Artery, Right **V** Thyroid Artery, Left **Y** Upper Artery	**0** Open **3** Percutaneous **4** Percutaneous Endoscopic	**Z** No Device	**Z** No Qualifier

0 **Medical and Surgical**
3 **Upper Arteries**
7 **Dilation:** Expanding an orifice or the lumen of a tubular body part

Body Part Character 4	Approach Character 5	Device Character 6	Qualifier Character 7
0 Internal Mammary Artery, Right **1** Internal Mammary Artery, Left **2** Innominate Artery **3** Subclavian Artery, Right **4** Subclavian Artery, Left **5** Axillary Artery, Right **6** Axillary Artery, Left **7** Brachial Artery, Right **8** Brachial Artery, Left **9** Ulnar Artery, Right **A** Ulnar Artery, Left **B** Radial Artery, Right **C** Radial Artery, Left **D** Hand Artery, Right **F** Hand Artery, Left **G** Intracranial Artery **H** Common Carotid Artery, Right **J** Common Carotid Artery, Left **K** Internal Carotid Artery, Right **L** Internal Carotid Artery, Left **M** External Carotid Artery, Right **N** External Carotid Artery, Left **P** Vertebral Artery, Right **Q** Vertebral Artery, Left **R** Face Artery **S** Temporal Artery, Right **T** Temporal Artery, Left **U** Thyroid Artery, Right **V** Thyroid Artery, Left **Y** Upper Artery	**0** Open **3** Percutaneous **4** Percutaneous Endoscopic	**4** Drug-eluting Intraluminal Device **D** Intraluminal Device **Z** No Device	**Z** No Qualifier

0   **Medical and Surgical**
3   **Upper Arteries**
9   **Drainage:**   Taking or letting out fluids and/or gases from a body part

Body Part Character 4	Approach Character 5	Device Character 6	Qualifier Character 7
0 Internal Mammary Artery, Right 1 Internal Mammary Artery, Left 2 Innominate Artery 3 Subclavian Artery, Right 4 Subclavian Artery, Left 5 Axillary Artery, Right 6 Axillary Artery, Left 7 Brachial Artery, Right 8 Brachial Artery, Left 9 Ulnar Artery, Right A Ulnar Artery, Left B Radial Artery, Right C Radial Artery, Left D Hand Artery, Right F Hand Artery, Left G Intracranial Artery H Common Carotid Artery, Right J Common Carotid Artery, Left K Internal Carotid Artery, Right L Internal Carotid Artery, Left M External Carotid Artery, Right N External Carotid Artery, Left P Vertebral Artery, Right Q Vertebral Artery, Left R Face Artery S Temporal Artery, Right T Temporal Artery, Left U Thyroid Artery, Right V Thyroid Artery, Left Y Upper Artery	0 Open 3 Percutaneous 4 Percutaneous Endoscopic	0 Drainage Device	Z No Qualifier
0 Internal Mammary Artery, Right 1 Internal Mammary Artery, Left 2 Innominate Artery 3 Subclavian Artery, Right 4 Subclavian Artery, Left 5 Axillary Artery, Right 6 Axillary Artery, Left 7 Brachial Artery, Right 8 Brachial Artery, Left 9 Ulnar Artery, Right A Ulnar Artery, Left B Radial Artery, Right C Radial Artery, Left D Hand Artery, Right F Hand Artery, Left G Intracranial Artery H Common Carotid Artery, Right J Common Carotid Artery, Left K Internal Carotid Artery, Right L Internal Carotid Artery, Left M External Carotid Artery, Right N External Carotid Artery, Left P Vertebral Artery, Right Q Vertebral Artery, Left R Face Artery S Temporal Artery, Right T Temporal Artery, Left U Thyroid Artery, Right V Thyroid Artery, Left Y Upper Artery	0 Open 3 Percutaneous 4 Percutaneous Endoscopic	Z No Device	X Diagnostic Z No Qualifier

0 Medical and Surgical
3 Upper Arteries
B Excision: Cutting out or off, without replacement, a portion of a body part

Body Part Character 4	Approach Character 5	Device Character 6	Qualifier Character 7
0 Internal Mammary Artery, Right **1** Internal Mammary Artery, Left **2** Innominate Artery **3** Subclavian Artery, Right **4** Subclavian Artery, Left **5** Axillary Artery, Right **6** Axillary Artery, Left **7** Brachial Artery, Right **8** Brachial Artery, Left **9** Ulnar Artery, Right **A** Ulnar Artery, Left **B** Radial Artery, Right **C** Radial Artery, Left **D** Hand Artery, Right **F** Hand Artery, Left **G** Intracranial Artery **H** Common Carotid Artery, Right **J** Common Carotid Artery, Left **K** Internal Carotid Artery, Right **L** Internal Carotid Artery, Left **M** External Carotid Artery, Right **N** External Carotid Artery, Left **P** Vertebral Artery, Right **Q** Vertebral Artery, Left **R** Face Artery **S** Temporal Artery, Right **T** Temporal Artery, Left **U** Thyroid Artery, Right **V** Thyroid Artery, Left **Y** Upper Artery	**0** Open **3** Percutaneous **4** Percutaneous Endoscopic	**Z** No Device	**X** Diagnostic **Z** No Qualifier

0 Medical and Surgical
3 Upper Arteries
C Extirpation: Taking or cutting out solid matter from a body part

Body Part Character 4	Approach Character 5	Device Character 6	Qualifier Character 7
0 Internal Mammary Artery, Right **1** Internal Mammary Artery, Left **2** Innominate Artery **3** Subclavian Artery, Right **4** Subclavian Artery, Left **5** Axillary Artery, Right **6** Axillary Artery, Left **7** Brachial Artery, Right **8** Brachial Artery, Left **9** Ulnar Artery, Right **A** Ulnar Artery, Left **B** Radial Artery, Right **C** Radial Artery, Left **D** Hand Artery, Right **F** Hand Artery, Left **G** Intracranial Artery **H** Common Carotid Artery, Right **J** Common Carotid Artery, Left **K** Internal Carotid Artery, Right **L** Internal Carotid Artery, Left **M** External Carotid Artery, Right **N** External Carotid Artery, Left **P** Vertebral Artery, Right **Q** Vertebral Artery, Left **R** Face Artery **S** Temporal Artery, Right **T** Temporal Artery, Left **U** Thyroid Artery, Right **V** Thyroid Artery, Left **Y** Upper Artery	**0** Open **3** Percutaneous **4** Percutaneous Endoscopic	**Z** No Device	**Z** No Qualifier

0   Medical and Surgical
3   Upper Arteries
H   Insertion: Putting in a nonbiological appliance that monitors, assists, performs or prevents a physiological function, but does not physically take the place of a body part

Body Part Character 4	Approach Character 5	Device Character 6	Qualifier Character 7
0 Internal Mammary Artery, Right **1** Internal Mammary Artery, Left **2** Innominate Artery **3** Subclavian Artery, Right **4** Subclavian Artery, Left **5** Axillary Artery, Right **6** Axillary Artery, Left **7** Brachial Artery, Right **8** Brachial Artery, Left **9** Ulnar Artery, Right **A** Ulnar Artery, Left **B** Radial Artery, Right **C** Radial Artery, Left **D** Hand Artery, Right **F** Hand Artery, Left **G** Intracranial Artery **H** Common Carotid Artery, Right **J** Common Carotid Artery, Left **K** Internal Carotid Artery, Right **L** Internal Carotid Artery, Left **M** External Carotid Artery, Right **N** External Carotid Artery, Left **P** Vertebral Artery, Right **Q** Vertebral Artery, Left **R** Face Artery **S** Temporal Artery, Right **T** Temporal Artery, Left **U** Thyroid Artery, Right **V** Thyroid Artery, Left	**0** Open **3** Percutaneous **4** Percutaneous Endoscopic	**3** Infusion Device	**Z** No Qualifier
Y Upper Artery	**0** Open **3** Percutaneous **4** Percutaneous Endoscopic	**2** Monitoring Device **3** Infusion Device	**Z** No Qualifier

0   Medical and Surgical
3   Upper Arteries
J   Inspection: Visually and/or manually exploring a body part

Body Part Character 4	Approach Character 5	Device Character 6	Qualifier Character 7
0 Internal Mammary Artery, Right **1** Internal Mammary Artery, Left **2** Innominate Artery **3** Subclavian Artery, Right **4** Subclavian Artery, Left **G** Intracranial Artery **H** Common Carotid Artery, Right **J** Common Carotid Artery, Left **K** Internal Carotid Artery, Right **L** Internal Carotid Artery, Left **P** Vertebral Artery, Right **Q** Vertebral Artery, Left	**0** Open **3** Percutaneous **4** Percutaneous Endoscopic	**Z** No Device	**Z** No Qualifier
5 Axillary Artery, Right **6** Axillary Artery, Left **7** Brachial Artery, Right **8** Brachial Artery, Left **9** Ulnar Artery, Right **A** Ulnar Artery, Left **B** Radial Artery, Right **C** Radial Artery, Left **D** Hand Artery, Right **F** Hand Artery, Left **M** External Carotid Artery, Right **N** External Carotid Artery, Left **R** Face Artery **S** Temporal Artery, Right **T** Temporal Artery, Left **U** Thyroid Artery, Right **V** Thyroid Artery, Left **Y** Upper Artery	**0** Open **3** Percutaneous **4** Percutaneous Endoscopic **X** External	**Z** No Device	**Z** No Qualifier

0   **Medical and Surgical**
3   **Upper Arteries**
L   **Occlusion:**   Completely closing an orifice or lumen of a tubular body part

Body Part Character 4	Approach Character 5	Device Character 6	Qualifier Character 7
0 Internal Mammary Artery, Right	**0** Open	**C** Extraluminal Device	**Z** No Qualifier
1 Internal Mammary Artery, Left	**3** Percutaneous	**D** Intraluminal Device	
2 Innominate Artery	**4** Percutaneous Endoscopic	**Z** No Device	
3 Subclavian Artery, Right			
4 Subclavian Artery, Left			
5 Axillary Artery, Right			
6 Axillary Artery, Left			
7 Brachial Artery, Right			
8 Brachial Artery, Left			
9 Ulnar Artery, Right			
A Ulnar Artery, Left			
B Radial Artery, Right			
C Radial Artery, Left			
D Hand Artery, Right			
F Hand Artery, Left			
G Intracranial Artery			
H Common Carotid Artery, Right			
J Common Carotid Artery, Left			
K Internal Carotid Artery, Right			
L Internal Carotid Artery, Left			
M External Carotid Artery, Right			
N External Carotid Artery, Left			
P Vertebral Artery, Right			
Q Vertebral Artery, Left			
R Face Artery			
S Temporal Artery, Right			
T Temporal Artery, Left			
U Thyroid Artery, Right			
V Thyroid Artery, Left			
Y Upper Artery			

0   **Medical and Surgical**
3   **Upper Arteries**
N   **Release:**   Freeing a body part from an abnormal physical constraint

Body Part Character 4	Approach Character 5	Device Character 6	Qualifier Character 7
0 Internal Mammary Artery, Right	**0** Open	**Z** No Device	**Z** No Qualifier
1 Internal Mammary Artery, Left	**3** Percutaneous		
2 Innominate Artery	**4** Percutaneous Endoscopic		
3 Subclavian Artery, Right			
4 Subclavian Artery, Left			
5 Axillary Artery, Right			
6 Axillary Artery, Left			
7 Brachial Artery, Right			
8 Brachial Artery, Left			
9 Ulnar Artery, Right			
A Ulnar Artery, Left			
B Radial Artery, Right			
C Radial Artery, Left			
D Hand Artery, Right			
F Hand Artery, Left			
G Intracranial Artery			
H Common Carotid Artery, Right			
J Common Carotid Artery, Left			
K Internal Carotid Artery, Right			
L Internal Carotid Artery, Left			
M External Carotid Artery, Right			
N External Carotid Artery, Left			
P Vertebral Artery, Right			
Q Vertebral Artery, Left			
R Face Artery			
S Temporal Artery, Right			
T Temporal Artery, Left			
U Thyroid Artery, Right			
V Thyroid Artery, Left			
Y Upper Artery			

0   Medical and Surgical
3   Upper Arteries
P   Removal: Taking out or off a device from a body part

Body Part Character 4	Approach Character 5	Device Character 6	Qualifier Character 7
Y Upper Artery	**0** Open **3** Percutaneous **4** Percutaneous Endoscopic	**0** Drainage Device **2** Monitoring Device **3** Infusion Device **4** Drug-eluting Intraluminal Device **7** Autologous Tissue Substitute **9** Autologous Venous Tissue **A** Autologous Arterial Tissue **C** Extraluminal Device **D** Intraluminal Device **J** Synthetic Substitute **K** Nonautologous Tissue Substitute	**Z** No Qualifier
Y Upper Artery	**X** External	**0** Drainage Device **2** Monitoring Device **3** Infusion Device **4** Drug-eluting Intraluminal Device **D** Intraluminal Device	**Z** No Qualifier

0   Medical and Surgical
3   Upper Arteries
Q   Repair: Restoring, to the extent possible, a body part to its normal anatomic structure and function

Body Part Character 4	Approach Character 5	Device Character 6	Qualifier Character 7
0 Internal Mammary Artery, Right **1** Internal Mammary Artery, Left **2** Innominate Artery **3** Subclavian Artery, Right **4** Subclavian Artery, Left **5** Axillary Artery, Right **6** Axillary Artery, Left **7** Brachial Artery, Right **8** Brachial Artery, Left **9** Ulnar Artery, Right **A** Ulnar Artery, Left **B** Radial Artery, Right **C** Radial Artery, Left **D** Hand Artery, Right **F** Hand Artery, Left **G** Intracranial Artery **H** Common Carotid Artery, Right **J** Common Carotid Artery, Left **K** Internal Carotid Artery, Right **L** Internal Carotid Artery, Left **M** External Carotid Artery, Right **N** External Carotid Artery, Left **P** Vertebral Artery, Right **Q** Vertebral Artery, Left **R** Face Artery **S** Temporal Artery, Right **T** Temporal Artery, Left **U** Thyroid Artery, Right **V** Thyroid Artery, Left **Y** Upper Artery	**0** Open **3** Percutaneous **4** Percutaneous Endoscopic	**Z** No Device	**Z** No Qualifier

0   Medical and Surgical
3   Upper Arteries
R   Replacement: Putting in or on biological or synthetic material that physically takes the place and/or function of all or a portion of a body part

Body Part Character 4	Approach Character 5	Device Character 6	Qualifier Character 7
0 Internal Mammary Artery, Right **1** Internal Mammary Artery, Left **2** Innominate Artery **3** Subclavian Artery, Right **4** Subclavian Artery, Left **5** Axillary Artery, Right **6** Axillary Artery, Left **7** Brachial Artery, Right **8** Brachial Artery, Left **9** Ulnar Artery, Right **A** Ulnar Artery, Left **B** Radial Artery, Right **C** Radial Artery, Left **D** Hand Artery, Right **F** Hand Artery, Left **G** Intracranial Artery **H** Common Carotid Artery, Right **J** Common Carotid Artery, Left **K** Internal Carotid Artery, Right **L** Internal Carotid Artery, Left **M** External Carotid Artery, Right **N** External Carotid Artery, Left **P** Vertebral Artery, Right **Q** Vertebral Artery, Left **R** Face Artery **S** Temporal Artery, Right **T** Temporal Artery, Left **U** Thyroid Artery, Right **V** Thyroid Artery, Left **Y** Upper Artery	**0** Open **4** Percutaneous Endoscopic	**7** Autologous Tissue Substitute **J** Synthetic Substitute **K** Nonautologous Tissue Substitute	**Z** No Qualifier

0   Medical and Surgical
3   Upper Arteries
S   Reposition: Moving to its normal location or other suitable location all or a portion of a body part

Body Part Character 4	Approach Character 5	Device Character 6	Qualifier Character 7
0 Internal Mammary Artery, Right **1** Internal Mammary Artery, Left **2** Innominate Artery **3** Subclavian Artery, Right **4** Subclavian Artery, Left **5** Axillary Artery, Right **6** Axillary Artery, Left **7** Brachial Artery, Right **8** Brachial Artery, Left **9** Ulnar Artery, Right **A** Ulnar Artery, Left **B** Radial Artery, Right **C** Radial Artery, Left **D** Hand Artery, Right **F** Hand Artery, Left **G** Intracranial Artery **H** Common Carotid Artery, Right **J** Common Carotid Artery, Left **K** Internal Carotid Artery, Right **L** Internal Carotid Artery, Left **M** External Carotid Artery, Right **N** External Carotid Artery, Left **P** Vertebral Artery, Right **Q** Vertebral Artery, Left **R** Face Artery **S** Temporal Artery, Right **T** Temporal Artery, Left **U** Thyroid Artery, Right **V** Thyroid Artery, Left **Y** Upper Artery	**0** Open **3** Percutaneous **4** Percutaneous Endoscopic	**Z** No Device	**Z** No Qualifier

0 **Medical and Surgical**
3 **Upper Arteries**
U **Supplement:** Putting in or on biological or synthetic material that physically reinforces and/or augments the function of a portion of a body part

Body Part Character 4	Approach Character 5	Device Character 6	Qualifier Character 7
0 Internal Mammary Artery, Right 1 Internal Mammary Artery, Left 2 Innominate Artery 3 Subclavian Artery, Right 4 Subclavian Artery, Left 5 Axillary Artery, Right 6 Axillary Artery, Left 7 Brachial Artery, Right 8 Brachial Artery, Left 9 Ulnar Artery, Right A Ulnar Artery, Left B Radial Artery, Right C Radial Artery, Left D Hand Artery, Right F Hand Artery, Left G Intracranial Artery H Common Carotid Artery, Right J Common Carotid Artery, Left K Internal Carotid Artery, Right L Internal Carotid Artery, Left M External Carotid Artery, Right N External Carotid Artery, Left P Vertebral Artery, Right Q Vertebral Artery, Left R Face Artery S Temporal Artery, Right T Temporal Artery, Left U Thyroid Artery, Right V Thyroid Artery, Left Y Upper Artery	0 Open 4 Percutaneous Endoscopic	7 Autologous Tissue Substitute J Synthetic Substitute K Nonautologous Tissue Substitute	Z No Qualifier

0 **Medical and Surgical**
3 **Upper Arteries**
V **Restriction:** Partially closing the orifice or lumen of a tubular body part

Body Part Character 4	Approach Character 5	Device Character 6	Qualifier Character 7
0 Internal Mammary Artery, Right 1 Internal Mammary Artery, Left 2 Innominate Artery 3 Subclavian Artery, Right 4 Subclavian Artery, Left 5 Axillary Artery, Right 6 Axillary Artery, Left 7 Brachial Artery, Right 8 Brachial Artery, Left 9 Ulnar Artery, Right A Ulnar Artery, Left B Radial Artery, Right C Radial Artery, Left D Hand Artery, Right F Hand Artery, Left G Intracranial Artery H Common Carotid Artery, Right J Common Carotid Artery, Left K Internal Carotid Artery, Right L Internal Carotid Artery, Left M External Carotid Artery, Right N External Carotid Artery, Left P Vertebral Artery, Right Q Vertebral Artery, Left R Face Artery S Temporal Artery, Right T Temporal Artery, Left U Thyroid Artery, Right V Thyroid Artery, Left Y Upper Artery	0 Open 3 Percutaneous 4 Percutaneous Endoscopic	C Extraluminal Device D Intraluminal Device Z No Device	Z No Qualifier

0 **Medical and Surgical**
3 **Upper Arteries**
W **Revision:**   Correcting, to the extent possible, a malfunctioning or displaced device

Body Part Character 4	Approach Character 5	Device Character 6	Qualifier Character 7
Y Upper Artery	**0** Open **3** Percutaneous **4** Percutaneous Endoscopic **X** External	**0** Drainage Device **2** Monitoring Device **3** Infusion Device **4** Drug-eluting Intraluminal Device **7** Autologous Tissue Substitute **9** Autologous Venous Tissue **A** Autologous Arterial Tissue **C** Extraluminal Device **D** Intraluminal Device **J** Synthetic Substitute **K** Nonautologous Tissue Substitute	**Z** No Qualifier

Lower Arteries 041–04W

0 Medical and Surgical
4 Lower Arteries
1 Bypass: Altering the route of passage of the contents of a tubular body part

Body Part Character 4	Approach Character 5	Device Character 6	Qualifier Character 7
0 Abdominal Aorta **C** Common Iliac Artery, Right **D** Common Iliac Artery, Left	**0** Open **4** Percutaneous Endoscopic	**9** Autologous Venous Tissue **A** Autologous Arterial Tissue **J** Synthetic Substitute **K** Nonautologous Tissue Substitute **Z** No Device	**0** Abdominal Aorta **1** Celiac Artery **2** Mesenteric Artery **3** Renal Artery, Right **4** Renal Artery, Left **5** Renal Artery, Bilateral **6** Common Iliac Artery, Right **7** Common Iliac Artery, Left **8** Common Iliac Arteries, Bilateral **9** Internal Iliac Artery, Right **B** Internal Iliac Artery, Left **C** Internal Iliac Arteries, Bilateral **D** External Iliac Artery, Right **F** External Iliac Artery, Left **G** External Iliac Arteries, Bilateral **H** Femoral Artery, Right **J** Femoral Artery, Left **K** Femoral Arteries, Bilateral **Q** Lower Extremity Artery **R** Lower Artery
4 Splenic Artery	**0** Open **4** Percutaneous Endoscopic	**9** Autologous Venous Tissue **A** Autologous Arterial Tissue **J** Synthetic Substitute **K** Nonautologous Tissue Substitute **Z** No Device	**3** Renal Artery, Right **4** Renal Artery, Left **5** Renal Artery, Bilateral
E Internal Iliac Artery, Right **F** Internal Iliac Artery, Left **H** External Iliac Artery, Right **J** External Iliac Artery, Left	**0** Open **4** Percutaneous Endoscopic	**9** Autologous Venous Tissue **A** Autologous Arterial Tissue **J** Synthetic Substitute **K** Nonautologous Tissue Substitute **Z** No Device	**9** Internal Iliac Artery, Right **B** Internal Iliac Artery, Left **C** Internal Iliac Arteries, Bilateral **D** External Iliac Artery, Right **F** External Iliac Artery, Left **G** External Iliac Arteries, Bilateral **H** Femoral Artery, Right **J** Femoral Artery, Left **K** Femoral Arteries, Bilateral **P** Foot Artery **Q** Lower Extremity Artery
K Femoral Artery, Right **L** Femoral Artery, Left	**0** Open **4** Percutaneous Endoscopic	**9** Autologous Venous Tissue **A** Autologous Arterial Tissue **J** Synthetic Substitute **K** Nonautologous Tissue Substitute **Z** No Device	**H** Femoral Artery, Right **J** Femoral Artery, Left **K** Femoral Arteries, Bilateral **L** Popliteal Artery **M** Peroneal Artery **N** Posterior Tibial Artery **P** Foot Artery **Q** Lower Extremity Artery **S** Lower Extremity Vein
M Popliteal Artery, Right **N** Popliteal Artery, Left	**0** Open **4** Percutaneous Endoscopic	**9** Autologous Venous Tissue **A** Autologous Arterial Tissue **J** Synthetic Substitute **K** Nonautologous Tissue Substitute **Z** No Device	**L** Popliteal Artery **M** Peroneal Artery **P** Foot Artery **Q** Lower Extremity Artery **S** Lower Extremity Vein

0 **Medical and Surgical**
4 **Lower Arteries**
5 **Destruction:**   Physical eradication of all or a portion of a body part by the direct use of energy, force, or a destructive agent

Body Part Character 4	Approach Character 5	Device Character 6	Qualifier Character 7
0 Abdominal Aorta	0 Open	Z No Device	Z No Qualifier
1 Celiac Artery	3 Percutaneous		
2 Gastric Artery	4 Percutaneous Endoscopic		
3 Hepatic Artery			
4 Splenic Artery			
5 Superior Mesenteric Artery			
6 Colic Artery, Right			
7 Colic Artery, Left			
8 Colic Artery, Middle			
9 Renal Artery, Right			
A Renal Artery, Left			
B Inferior Mesenteric Artery			
C Common Iliac Artery, Right			
D Common Iliac Artery, Left			
E Internal Iliac Artery, Right			
F Internal Iliac Artery, Left			
H External Iliac Artery, Right			
J External Iliac Artery, Left			
K Femoral Artery, Right			
L Femoral Artery, Left			
M Popliteal Artery, Right			
N Popliteal Artery, Left			
P Anterior Tibial Artery, Right			
Q Anterior Tibial Artery, Left			
R Posterior Tibial Artery, Right			
S Posterior Tibial Artery, Left			
T Peroneal Artery, Right			
U Peroneal Artery, Left			
V Foot Artery, Right			
W Foot Artery, Left			
Y Lower Artery			

0 **Medical and Surgical**
4 **Lower Arteries**
7 **Dilation:**   Expanding an orifice or the lumen of a tubular body part

Body Part Character 4	Approach Character 5	Device Character 6	Qualifier Character 7
0 Abdominal Aorta	0 Open	4 Drug-eluting Intraluminal Device	Z No Qualifier
1 Celiac Artery	3 Percutaneous	D Intraluminal Device	
2 Gastric Artery	4 Percutaneous Endoscopic	Z No Device	
3 Hepatic Artery			
4 Splenic Artery			
5 Superior Mesenteric Artery			
6 Colic Artery, Right			
7 Colic Artery, Left			
8 Colic Artery, Middle			
9 Renal Artery, Right			
A Renal Artery, Left			
B Inferior Mesenteric Artery			
C Common Iliac Artery, Right			
D Common Iliac Artery, Left			
E Internal Iliac Artery, Right			
F Internal Iliac Artery, Left			
H External Iliac Artery, Right			
J External Iliac Artery, Left			
K Femoral Artery, Right			
L Femoral Artery, Left			
M Popliteal Artery, Right			
N Popliteal Artery, Left			
P Anterior Tibial Artery, Right			
Q Anterior Tibial Artery, Left			
R Posterior Tibial Artery, Right			
S Posterior Tibial Artery, Left			
T Peroneal Artery, Right			
U Peroneal Artery, Left			
V Foot Artery, Right			
W Foot Artery, Left			
Y Lower Artery			

0 **Medical and Surgical**
4 **Lower Arteries**
9 **Drainage:** Taking or letting out fluids and/or gases from a body part

Body Part Character 4	Approach Character 5	Device Character 6	Qualifier Character 7
0 Abdominal Aorta **1** Celiac Artery **2** Gastric Artery **3** Hepatic Artery **4** Splenic Artery **5** Superior Mesenteric Artery **6** Colic Artery, Right **7** Colic Artery, Left **8** Colic Artery, Middle **9** Renal Artery, Right **A** Renal Artery, Left **B** Inferior Mesenteric Artery **C** Common Iliac Artery, Right **D** Common Iliac Artery, Left **E** Internal Iliac Artery, Right **F** Internal Iliac Artery, Left **H** External Iliac Artery, Right **J** External Iliac Artery, Left **K** Femoral Artery, Right **L** Femoral Artery, Left **M** Popliteal Artery, Right **N** Popliteal Artery, Left **P** Anterior Tibial Artery, Right **Q** Anterior Tibial Artery, Left **R** Posterior Tibial Artery, Right **S** Posterior Tibial Artery, Left **T** Peroneal Artery, Right **U** Peroneal Artery, Left **V** Foot Artery, Right **W** Foot Artery, Left **Y** Lower Artery	**0** Open **3** Percutaneous **4** Percutaneous Endoscopic	**0** Drainage Device	**Z** No Qualifier
0 Abdominal Aorta **1** Celiac Artery **2** Gastric Artery **3** Hepatic Artery **4** Splenic Artery **5** Superior Mesenteric Artery **6** Colic Artery, Right **7** Colic Artery, Left **8** Colic Artery, Middle **9** Renal Artery, Right **A** Renal Artery, Left **B** Inferior Mesenteric Artery **C** Common Iliac Artery, Right **D** Common Iliac Artery, Left **E** Internal Iliac Artery, Right **F** Internal Iliac Artery, Left **H** External Iliac Artery, Right **J** External Iliac Artery, Left **K** Femoral Artery, Right **L** Femoral Artery, Left **M** Popliteal Artery, Right **N** Popliteal Artery, Left **P** Anterior Tibial Artery, Right **Q** Anterior Tibial Artery, Left **R** Posterior Tibial Artery, Right **S** Posterior Tibial Artery, Left **T** Peroneal Artery, Right **U** Peroneal Artery, Left **V** Foot Artery, Right **W** Foot Artery, Left **Y** Lower Artery	**0** Open **3** Percutaneous **4** Percutaneous Endoscopic	**Z** No Device	**X** Diagnostic **Z** No Qualifier

0 Medical and Surgical
4 Lower Arteries
B Excision: Cutting out or off, without replacement, a portion of a body part

Body Part Character 4	Approach Character 5	Device Character 6	Qualifier Character 7
0 Abdominal Aorta 1 Celiac Artery 2 Gastric Artery 3 Hepatic Artery 4 Splenic Artery 5 Superior Mesenteric Artery 6 Colic Artery, Right 7 Colic Artery, Left 8 Colic Artery, Middle 9 Renal Artery, Right A Renal Artery, Left B Inferior Mesenteric Artery C Common Iliac Artery, Right D Common Iliac Artery, Left E Internal Iliac Artery, Right F Internal Iliac Artery, Left H External Iliac Artery, Right J External Iliac Artery, Left K Femoral Artery, Right L Femoral Artery, Left M Popliteal Artery, Right N Popliteal Artery, Left P Anterior Tibial Artery, Right Q Anterior Tibial Artery, Left R Posterior Tibial Artery, Right S Posterior Tibial Artery, Left T Peroneal Artery, Right U Peroneal Artery, Left V Foot Artery, Right W Foot Artery, Left Y Lower Artery	0 Open 3 Percutaneous 4 Percutaneous Endoscopic	Z No Device	X Diagnostic Z No Qualifier

0 Medical and Surgical
4 Lower Arteries
C Extirpation: Taking or cutting out solid matter from a body part

Body Part Character 4	Approach Character 5	Device Character 6	Qualifier Character 7
0 Abdominal Aorta 1 Celiac Artery 2 Gastric Artery 3 Hepatic Artery 4 Splenic Artery 5 Superior Mesenteric Artery 6 Colic Artery, Right 7 Colic Artery, Left 8 Colic Artery, Middle 9 Renal Artery, Right A Renal Artery, Left B Inferior Mesenteric Artery C Common Iliac Artery, Right D Common Iliac Artery, Left E Internal Iliac Artery, Right F Internal Iliac Artery, Left H External Iliac Artery, Right J External Iliac Artery, Left K Femoral Artery, Right L Femoral Artery, Left M Popliteal Artery, Right N Popliteal Artery, Left P Anterior Tibial Artery, Right Q Anterior Tibial Artery, Left R Posterior Tibial Artery, Right S Posterior Tibial Artery, Left T Peroneal Artery, Right U Peroneal Artery, Left V Foot Artery, Right W Foot Artery, Left Y Lower Artery	0 Open 3 Percutaneous 4 Percutaneous Endoscopic	Z No Device	Z No Qualifier

0 Medical and Surgical
4 Lower Arteries
H Insertion: Putting in a nonbiological appliance that monitors, assists, performs or prevents a physiological function, but does not physically take the place of a body part

Body Part Character 4	Approach Character 5	Device Character 6	Qualifier Character 7
0 Abdominal Aorta	**0** Open **3** Percutaneous **4** Percutaneous Endoscopic	**2** Monitoring Device **3** Infusion Device **D** Intraluminal Device	**Z** No Qualifier
1 Celiac Artery **2** Gastric Artery **3** Hepatic Artery **4** Splenic Artery **5** Superior Mesenteric Artery **6** Colic Artery, Right **7** Colic Artery, Left **8** Colic Artery, Middle **9** Renal Artery, Right **A** Renal Artery, Left **B** Inferior Mesenteric Artery **C** Common Iliac Artery, Right **D** Common Iliac Artery, Left **E** Internal Iliac Artery, Right **F** Internal Iliac Artery, Left **H** External Iliac Artery, Right **J** External Iliac Artery, Left **K** Femoral Artery, Right **L** Femoral Artery, Left **M** Popliteal Artery, Right **N** Popliteal Artery, Left **P** Anterior Tibial Artery, Right **Q** Anterior Tibial Artery, Left **R** Posterior Tibial Artery, Right **S** Posterior Tibial Artery, Left **T** Peroneal Artery, Right **U** Peroneal Artery, Left **V** Foot Artery, Right **W** Foot Artery, Left	**0** Open **3** Percutaneous **4** Percutaneous Endoscopic	**3** Infusion Device	**Z** No Qualifier
Y Lower Artery	**0** Open **3** Percutaneous **4** Percutaneous Endoscopic	**2** Monitoring Device **3** Infusion Device	**Z** No Qualifier

0 Medical and Surgical
4 Lower Arteries
J Inspection: Visually and/or manually exploring a body part

Body Part Character 4	Approach Character 5	Device Character 6	Qualifier Character 7
0 Abdominal Aorta **1** Celiac Artery **2** Gastric Artery **3** Hepatic Artery **4** Splenic Artery **5** Superior Mesenteric Artery **6** Colic Artery, Right **7** Colic Artery, Left **8** Colic Artery, Middle **9** Renal Artery, Right **A** Renal Artery, Left **B** Inferior Mesenteric Artery **C** Common Iliac Artery, Right **D** Common Iliac Artery, Left **E** Internal Iliac Artery, Right **F** Internal Iliac Artery, Left **H** External Iliac Artery, Right **J** External Iliac Artery, Left **K** Femoral Artery, Right **L** Femoral Artery, Left **M** Popliteal Artery, Right **N** Popliteal Artery, Left **P** Anterior Tibial Artery, Right **Q** Anterior Tibial Artery, Left **R** Posterior Tibial Artery, Right **S** Posterior Tibial Artery, Left **T** Peroneal Artery, Right **U** Peroneal Artery, Left **V** Foot Artery, Right **W** Foot Artery, Left **Y** Lower Artery	**0** Open **3** Percutaneous **4** Percutaneous Endoscopic **X** External	**Z** No Device	**Z** No Qualifier

0   **Medical and Surgical**
4   **Lower Arteries**
L   **Occlusion:**   Completely closing an orifice or lumen of a tubular body part

Body Part Character 4	Approach Character 5	Device Character 6	Qualifier Character 7
0 Abdominal Aorta **1** Celiac Artery **2** Gastric Artery **3** Hepatic Artery **4** Splenic Artery **5** Superior Mesenteric Artery **6** Colic Artery, Right **7** Colic Artery, Left **8** Colic Artery, Middle **9** Renal Artery, Right **A** Renal Artery, Left **B** Inferior Mesenteric Artery **C** Common Iliac Artery, Right **D** Common Iliac Artery, Left **E** Internal Iliac Artery, Right **F** Internal Iliac Artery, Left **H** External Iliac Artery, Right **J** External Iliac Artery, Left **K** Femoral Artery, Right **L** Femoral Artery, Left **M** Popliteal Artery, Right **N** Popliteal Artery, Left **P** Anterior Tibial Artery, Right **Q** Anterior Tibial Artery, Left **R** Posterior Tibial Artery, Right **S** Posterior Tibial Artery, Left **T** Peroneal Artery, Right **U** Peroneal Artery, Left **V** Foot Artery, Right **W** Foot Artery, Left **Y** Lower Artery	**0** Open **3** Percutaneous **4** Percutaneous Endoscopic	**C** Extraluminal Device **D** Intraluminal Device **Z** No Device	**Z** No Qualifier

0   **Medical and Surgical**
4   **Lower Arteries**
N   **Release:**   Freeing a body part from an abnormal physical constraint

Body Part Character 4	Approach Character 5	Device Character 6	Qualifier Character 7
0 Abdominal Aorta **1** Celiac Artery **2** Gastric Artery **3** Hepatic Artery **4** Splenic Artery **5** Superior Mesenteric Artery **6** Colic Artery, Right **7** Colic Artery, Left **8** Colic Artery, Middle **9** Renal Artery, Right **A** Renal Artery, Left **B** Inferior Mesenteric Artery **C** Common Iliac Artery, Right **D** Common Iliac Artery, Left **E** Internal Iliac Artery, Right **F** Internal Iliac Artery, Left **H** External Iliac Artery, Right **J** External Iliac Artery, Left **K** Femoral Artery, Right **L** Femoral Artery, Left **M** Popliteal Artery, Right **N** Popliteal Artery, Left **P** Anterior Tibial Artery, Right **Q** Anterior Tibial Artery, Left **R** Posterior Tibial Artery, Right **S** Posterior Tibial Artery, Left **T** Peroneal Artery, Right **U** Peroneal Artery, Left **V** Foot Artery, Right **W** Foot Artery, Left **Y** Lower Artery	**0** Open **3** Percutaneous **4** Percutaneous Endoscopic	**Z** No Device	**Z** No Qualifier

0 Medical and Surgical
4 Lower Arteries
P Removal: Taking out or off a device from a body part

Body Part Character 4	Approach Character 5	Device Character 6	Qualifier Character 7
Y Lower Artery	0 Open 3 Percutaneous 4 Percutaneous Endoscopic	0 Drainage Device 2 Monitoring Device 3 Infusion Device 4 Drug-eluting Intraluminal Device 7 Autologous Tissue Substitute 9 Autologous Venous Tissue A Autologous Arterial Tissue C Extraluminal Device D Intraluminal Device J Synthetic Substitute K Nonautologous Tissue Substitute	Z No Qualifier
Y Lower Artery	X External	0 Drainage Device 1 Radioactive Element 2 Monitoring Device 3 Infusion Device 4 Drug-eluting Intraluminal Device D Intraluminal Device	Z No Qualifier

0 Medical and Surgical
4 Lower Arteries
Q Repair: Restoring, to the extent possible, a body part to its normal anatomic structure and function

Body Part Character 4	Approach Character 5	Device Character 6	Qualifier Character 7
0 Abdominal Aorta 1 Celiac Artery 2 Gastric Artery 3 Hepatic Artery 4 Splenic Artery 5 Superior Mesenteric Artery 6 Colic Artery, Right 7 Colic Artery, Left 8 Colic Artery, Middle 9 Renal Artery, Right A Renal Artery, Left B Inferior Mesenteric Artery C Common Iliac Artery, Right D Common Iliac Artery, Left E Internal Iliac Artery, Right F Internal Iliac Artery, Left H External Iliac Artery, Right J External Iliac Artery, Left K Femoral Artery, Right L Femoral Artery, Left M Popliteal Artery, Right N Popliteal Artery, Left P Anterior Tibial Artery, Right Q Anterior Tibial Artery, Left R Posterior Tibial Artery, Right S Posterior Tibial Artery, Left T Peroneal Artery, Right U Peroneal Artery, Left V Foot Artery, Right W Foot Artery, Left Y Lower Artery	0 Open 3 Percutaneous 4 Percutaneous Endoscopic	Z No Device	Z No Qualifier

0   Medical and Surgical
4   Lower Arteries
R   Replacement: Putting in or on biological or synthetic material that physically takes the place and/or function of all or a portion of a body part

Body Part Character 4	Approach Character 5	Device Character 6	Qualifier Character 7
0 Abdominal Aorta 1 Celiac Artery 2 Gastric Artery 3 Hepatic Artery 4 Splenic Artery 5 Superior Mesenteric Artery 6 Colic Artery, Right 7 Colic Artery, Left 8 Colic Artery, Middle 9 Renal Artery, Right A Renal Artery, Left B Inferior Mesenteric Artery C Common Iliac Artery, Right D Common Iliac Artery, Left E Internal Iliac Artery, Right F Internal Iliac Artery, Left H External Iliac Artery, Right J External Iliac Artery, Left K Femoral Artery, Right L Femoral Artery, Left M Popliteal Artery, Right N Popliteal Artery, Left P Anterior Tibial Artery, Right Q Anterior Tibial Artery, Left R Posterior Tibial Artery, Right S Posterior Tibial Artery, Left T Peroneal Artery, Right U Peroneal Artery, Left V Foot Artery, Right W Foot Artery, Left Y Lower Artery	0 Open 4 Percutaneous Endoscopic	7 Autologous Tissue Substitute J Synthetic Substitute K Nonautologous Tissue Substitute	Z No Qualifier

0   Medical and Surgical
4   Lower Arteries
S   Reposition: Moving to its normal location or other suitable location all or a portion of a body part

Body Part Character 4	Approach Character 5	Device Character 6	Qualifier Character 7
0 Abdominal Aorta 1 Celiac Artery 2 Gastric Artery 3 Hepatic Artery 4 Splenic Artery 5 Superior Mesenteric Artery 6 Colic Artery, Right 7 Colic Artery, Left 8 Colic Artery, Middle 9 Renal Artery, Right A Renal Artery, Left B Inferior Mesenteric Artery C Common Iliac Artery, Right D Common Iliac Artery, Left E Internal Iliac Artery, Right F Internal Iliac Artery, Left H External Iliac Artery, Right J External Iliac Artery, Left K Femoral Artery, Right L Femoral Artery, Left M Popliteal Artery, Right N Popliteal Artery, Left P Anterior Tibial Artery, Right Q Anterior Tibial Artery, Left R Posterior Tibial Artery, Right S Posterior Tibial Artery, Left T Peroneal Artery, Right U Peroneal Artery, Left V Foot Artery, Right W Foot Artery, Left Y Lower Artery	0 Open 3 Percutaneous 4 Percutaneous Endoscopic	Z No Device	Z No Qualifier

0 **Medical and Surgical**
4 **Lower Arteries**
U **Supplement:** Putting in or on biological or synthetic material that physically reinforces and/or augments the function of a portion of a body part

Body Part Character 4	Approach Character 5	Device Character 6	Qualifier Character 7
0 Abdominal Aorta **1** Celiac Artery **2** Gastric Artery **3** Hepatic Artery **4** Splenic Artery **5** Superior Mesenteric Artery **6** Colic Artery, Right **7** Colic Artery, Left **8** Colic Artery, Middle **9** Renal Artery, Right **A** Renal Artery, Left **B** Inferior Mesenteric Artery **C** Common Iliac Artery, Right **D** Common Iliac Artery, Left **E** Internal Iliac Artery, Right **F** Internal Iliac Artery, Left **H** External Iliac Artery, Right **J** External Iliac Artery, Left **K** Femoral Artery, Right **L** Femoral Artery, Left **M** Popliteal Artery, Right **N** Popliteal Artery, Left **P** Anterior Tibial Artery, Right **Q** Anterior Tibial Artery, Left **R** Posterior Tibial Artery, Right **S** Posterior Tibial Artery, Left **T** Peroneal Artery, Right **U** Peroneal Artery, Left **V** Foot Artery, Right **W** Foot Artery, Left **Y** Lower Artery	**0** Open **4** Percutaneous Endoscopic	**7** Autologous Tissue Substitute **J** Synthetic Substitute **K** Nonautologous Tissue Substitute	**Z** No Qualifier

0 **Medical and Surgical**
4 **Lower Arteries**
V **Restriction:** Partially closing the orifice or lumen of a tubular body part

Body Part Character 4	Approach Character 5	Device Character 6	Qualifier Character 7
0 Abdominal Aorta **1** Celiac Artery **2** Gastric Artery **3** Hepatic Artery **4** Splenic Artery **5** Superior Mesenteric Artery **6** Colic Artery, Right **7** Colic Artery, Left **8** Colic Artery, Middle **9** Renal Artery, Right **A** Renal Artery, Left **B** Inferior Mesenteric Artery **C** Common Iliac Artery, Right **D** Common Iliac Artery, Left **E** Internal Iliac Artery, Right **F** Internal Iliac Artery, Left **H** External Iliac Artery, Right **J** External Iliac Artery, Left **K** Femoral Artery, Right **L** Femoral Artery, Left **M** Popliteal Artery, Right **N** Popliteal Artery, Left **P** Anterior Tibial Artery, Right **Q** Anterior Tibial Artery, Left **R** Posterior Tibial Artery, Right **S** Posterior Tibial Artery, Left **T** Peroneal Artery, Right **U** Peroneal Artery, Left **V** Foot Artery, Right **W** Foot Artery, Left **Y** Lower Artery	**0** Open **3** Percutaneous **4** Percutaneous Endoscopic	**C** Extraluminal Device **D** Intraluminal Device **Z** No Device	**Z** No Qualifier

0 Medical and Surgical
4 Lower Arteries
W Revision: Correcting, to the extent possible, a malfunctioning or displaced device

Body Part Character 4	Approach Character 5	Device Character 6	Qualifier Character 7
Y Lower Artery	**0** Open **3** Percutaneous **4** Percutaneous Endoscopic **X** External	**0** Drainage Device **2** Monitoring Device **3** Infusion Device **4** Drug-eluting Intraluminal Device **7** Autologous Tissue Substitute **9** Autologous Venous Tissue **A** Autologous Arterial Tissue **C** Extraluminal Device **D** Intraluminal Device **J** Synthetic Substitute **K** Nonautologous Tissue Substitute	**Z** No Qualifier

Upper Veins 051–05W

0 Medical and Surgical
5 Upper Veins
1 Bypass: Altering the route of passage of the contents of a tubular body part

Body Part Character 4	Approach Character 5	Device Character 6	Qualifier Character 7
0 Azygos Vein 1 Hemiazygos Vein 3 Innominate Vein, Right 4 Innominate Vein, Left 5 Subclavian Vein, Right 6 Subclavian Vein, Left 7 Axillary Vein, Right 8 Axillary Vein, Left 9 Brachial Vein, Right A Brachial Vein, Left B Basilic Vein, Right C Basilic Vein, Left D Cephalic Vein, Right F Cephalic Vein, Left G Hand Vein, Right H Hand Vein, Left L Intracranial Vein M Internal Jugular Vein, Right N Internal Jugular Vein, Left P External Jugular Vein, Right Q External Jugular Vein, Left R Vertebral Vein, Right S Vertebral Vein, Left T Face Vein, Right V Face Vein, Left	0 Open 4 Percutaneous Endoscopic	7 Autologous Tissue Substitute 9 Autologous Venous Tissue A Autologous Arterial Tissue J Synthetic Substitute K Nonautologous Tissue Substitute Z No Device	Y Upper Vein

0 Medical and Surgical
5 Upper Veins
5 Destruction: Physical eradication of all or a portion of a body part by the direct use of energy, force, or a destructive agent

Body Part Character 4	Approach Character 5	Device Character 6	Qualifier Character 7
0 Azygos Vein 1 Hemiazygos Vein 3 Innominate Vein, Right 4 Innominate Vein, Left 5 Subclavian Vein, Right 6 Subclavian Vein, Left 7 Axillary Vein, Right 8 Axillary Vein, Left 9 Brachial Vein, Right A Brachial Vein, Left B Basilic Vein, Right C Basilic Vein, Left D Cephalic Vein, Right F Cephalic Vein, Left G Hand Vein, Right H Hand Vein, Left L Intracranial Vein M Internal Jugular Vein, Right N Internal Jugular Vein, Left P External Jugular Vein, Right Q External Jugular Vein, Left R Vertebral Vein, Right S Vertebral Vein, Left T Face Vein, Right V Face Vein, Left Y Upper Vein	0 Open 3 Percutaneous 4 Percutaneous Endoscopic	Z No Device	Z No Qualifier

0   **Medical and Surgical**
5   **Upper Veins**
7   **Dilation:**   Expanding an orifice or the lumen of a tubular body part

Body Part Character 4	Approach Character 5	Device Character 6	Qualifier Character 7
0 Azygos Vein 1 Hemiazygos Vein 3 Innominate Vein, Right 4 Innominate Vein, Left 5 Subclavian Vein, Right 6 Subclavian Vein, Left 7 Axillary Vein, Right 8 Axillary Vein, Left 9 Brachial Vein, Right A Brachial Vein, Left B Basilic Vein, Right C Basilic Vein, Left D Cephalic Vein, Right F Cephalic Vein, Left G Hand Vein, Right H Hand Vein, Left L Intracranial Vein M Internal Jugular Vein, Right N Internal Jugular Vein, Left P External Jugular Vein, Right Q External Jugular Vein, Left R Vertebral Vein, Right S Vertebral Vein, Left T Face Vein, Right V Face Vein, Left Y Upper Vein	0 Open 3 Percutaneous 4 Percutaneous Endoscopic	D Intraluminal Device Z No Device	Z No Qualifier

0   **Medical and Surgical**
5   **Upper Veins**
9   **Drainage:**   Taking or letting out fluids and/or gases from a body part

Body Part Character 4	Approach Character 5	Device Character 6	Qualifier Character 7
0 Azygos Vein 1 Hemiazygos Vein 3 Innominate Vein, Right 4 Innominate Vein, Left 5 Subclavian Vein, Right 6 Subclavian Vein, Left 7 Axillary Vein, Right 8 Axillary Vein, Left 9 Brachial Vein, Right A Brachial Vein, Left B Basilic Vein, Right C Basilic Vein, Left D Cephalic Vein, Right F Cephalic Vein, Left G Hand Vein, Right H Hand Vein, Left L Intracranial Vein M Internal Jugular Vein, Right N Internal Jugular Vein, Left P External Jugular Vein, Right Q External Jugular Vein, Left R Vertebral Vein, Right S Vertebral Vein, Left T Face Vein, Right V Face Vein, Left Y Upper Vein	0 Open 3 Percutaneous 4 Percutaneous Endoscopic	0 Drainage Device	Z No Qualifier

Continued on next page

0   **Medical and Surgical**   *Continued from previous page*
5   **Upper Veins**
9   **Drainage:**   Taking or letting out fluids and/or gases from a body part

Body Part Character 4	Approach Character 5	Device Character 6	Qualifier Character 7
0 Azygos Vein	0 Open	Z No Device	X Diagnostic
1 Hemiazygos Vein	3 Percutaneous		Z No Qualifier
3 Innominate Vein, Right	4 Percutaneous Endoscopic		
4 Innominate Vein, Left			
5 Subclavian Vein, Right			
6 Subclavian Vein, Left			
7 Axillary Vein, Right			
8 Axillary Vein, Left			
9 Brachial Vein, Right			
A Brachial Vein, Left			
B Basilic Vein, Right			
C Basilic Vein, Left			
D Cephalic Vein, Right			
F Cephalic Vein, Left			
G Hand Vein, Right			
H Hand Vein, Left			
L Intracranial Vein			
M Internal Jugular Vein, Right			
N Internal Jugular Vein, Left			
P External Jugular Vein, Right			
Q External Jugular Vein, Left			
R Vertebral Vein, Right			
S Vertebral Vein, Left			
T Face Vein, Right			
V Face Vein, Left			
Y Upper Vein			

0   **Medical and Surgical**
5   **Upper Veins**
B   **Excision:**   Cutting out or off, without replacement, a portion of a body part

Body Part Character 4	Approach Character 5	Device Character 6	Qualifier Character 7
0 Azygos Vein	0 Open	Z No Device	X Diagnostic
1 Hemiazygos Vein	3 Percutaneous		Z No Qualifier
3 Innominate Vein, Right	4 Percutaneous Endoscopic		
4 Innominate Vein, Left			
5 Subclavian Vein, Right			
6 Subclavian Vein, Left			
7 Axillary Vein, Right			
8 Axillary Vein, Left			
9 Brachial Vein, Right			
A Brachial Vein, Left			
B Basilic Vein, Right			
C Basilic Vein, Left			
D Cephalic Vein, Right			
F Cephalic Vein, Left			
G Hand Vein, Right			
H Hand Vein, Left			
L Intracranial Vein			
M Internal Jugular Vein, Right			
N Internal Jugular Vein, Left			
P External Jugular Vein, Right			
Q External Jugular Vein, Left			
R Vertebral Vein, Right			
S Vertebral Vein, Left			
T Face Vein, Right			
V Face Vein, Left			
Y Upper Vein			

0 **Medical and Surgical**
5 **Upper Veins**
C **Extirpation:**   Taking or cutting out solid matter from a body part

Body Part Character 4	Approach Character 5	Device Character 6	Qualifier Character 7
0 Azygos Vein 1 Hemiazygos Vein 3 Innominate Vein, Right 4 Innominate Vein, Left 5 Subclavian Vein, Right 6 Subclavian Vein, Left 7 Axillary Vein, Right 8 Axillary Vein, Left 9 Brachial Vein, Right A Brachial Vein, Left B Basilic Vein, Right C Basilic Vein, Left D Cephalic Vein, Right F Cephalic Vein, Left G Hand Vein, Right H Hand Vein, Left L Intracranial Vein M Internal Jugular Vein, Right N Internal Jugular Vein, Left P External Jugular Vein, Right Q External Jugular Vein, Left R Vertebral Vein, Right S Vertebral Vein, Left T Face Vein, Right V Face Vein, Left Y Upper Vein	0 Open 3 Percutaneous 4 Percutaneous Endoscopic	Z No Device	Z No Qualifier

0 **Medical and Surgical**
5 **Upper Veins**
D **Extraction:**   Pulling or stripping out or off all or a portion of a body part by the use of force

Body Part Character 4	Approach Character 5	Device Character 6	Qualifier Character 7
9 Brachial Vein, Right A Brachial Vein, Left B Basilic Vein, Right C Basilic Vein, Left D Cephalic Vein, Right F Cephalic Vein, Left G Hand Vein, Right H Hand Vein, Left Y Upper Vein	0 Open 3 Percutaneous	Z No Device	Z No Qualifier

0 **Medical and Surgical**
5 **Upper Veins**
H **Insertion:**   Putting in a nonbiological appliance that monitors, assists, performs or prevents a physiological function, but does not physically take the place of a body part

Body Part Character 4	Approach Character 5	Device Character 6	Qualifier Character 7
0 Azygos Vein 1 Hemiazygos Vein 3 Innominate Vein, Right 4 Innominate Vein, Left 5 Subclavian Vein, Right 6 Subclavian Vein, Left 7 Axillary Vein, Right 8 Axillary Vein, Left 9 Brachial Vein, Right A Brachial Vein, Left B Basilic Vein, Right C Basilic Vein, Left D Cephalic Vein, Right F Cephalic Vein, Left G Hand Vein, Right H Hand Vein, Left L Intracranial Vein M Internal Jugular Vein, Right N Internal Jugular Vein, Left P External Jugular Vein, Right Q External Jugular Vein, Left R Vertebral Vein, Right S Vertebral Vein, Left T Face Vein, Right V Face Vein, Left	0 Open 3 Percutaneous 4 Percutaneous Endoscopic	3 Infusion Device D Intraluminal Device	Z No Qualifier

Continued on next page

0 Medical and Surgical
5 Upper Veins
H Insertion: *Continued from previous page* Putting in a nonbiological appliance that monitors, assists, performs or prevents a physiological function, but does not physically take the place of a body part

Body Part Character 4	Approach Character 5	Device Character 6	Qualifier Character 7
Y Upper Vein	0 Open 3 Percutaneous 4 Percutaneous Endoscopic	2 Monitoring Device 3 Infusion Device D Intraluminal Device	Z No Qualifier

0 Medical and Surgical
5 Upper Veins
J Inspection: Visually and/or manually exploring a body part

Body Part Character 4	Approach Character 5	Device Character 6	Qualifier Character 7
0 Azygos Vein 1 Hemiazygos Vein 3 Innominate Vein, Right 4 Innominate Vein, Left 5 Subclavian Vein, Right 6 Subclavian Vein, Left B Basilic Vein, Right C Basilic Vein, Left D Cephalic Vein, Right F Cephalic Vein, Left L Intracranial Vein M Internal Jugular Vein, Right N Internal Jugular Vein, Left R Vertebral Vein, Right S Vertebral Vein, Left	0 Open 3 Percutaneous 4 Percutaneous Endoscopic	Z No Device	Z No Qualifier
7 Axillary Vein, Right 8 Axillary Vein, Left 9 Brachial Vein, Right A Brachial Vein, Left G Hand Vein, Right H Hand Vein, Left P External Jugular Vein, Right Q External Jugular Vein, Left T Face Vein, Right V Face Vein, Left Y Upper Vein	0 Open 3 Percutaneous 4 Percutaneous Endoscopic X External	Z No Device	Z No Qualifier

0 Medical and Surgical
5 Upper Veins
L Occlusion: Completely closing an orifice or lumen of a tubular body part

Body Part Character 4	Approach Character 5	Device Character 6	Qualifier Character 7
0 Azygos Vein 1 Hemiazygos Vein 3 Innominate Vein, Right 4 Innominate Vein, Left 5 Subclavian Vein, Right 6 Subclavian Vein, Left 7 Axillary Vein, Right 8 Axillary Vein, Left 9 Brachial Vein, Right A Brachial Vein, Left B Basilic Vein, Right C Basilic Vein, Left D Cephalic Vein, Right F Cephalic Vein, Left G Hand Vein, Right H Hand Vein, Left L Intracranial Vein M Internal Jugular Vein, Right N Internal Jugular Vein, Left P External Jugular Vein, Right Q External Jugular Vein, Left R Vertebral Vein, Right S Vertebral Vein, Left T Face Vein, Right V Face Vein, Left Y Upper Vein	0 Open 3 Percutaneous 4 Percutaneous Endoscopic	C Extraluminal Device D Intraluminal Device Z No Device	Z No Qualifier

0   Medical and Surgical
5   Upper Veins
N   Release: Freeing a body part from an abnormal physical constraint

Body Part Character 4	Approach Character 5	Device Character 6	Qualifier Character 7
0 Azygos Vein 1 Hemiazygos Vein 3 Innominate Vein, Right 4 Innominate Vein, Left 5 Subclavian Vein, Right 6 Subclavian Vein, Left 7 Axillary Vein, Right 8 Axillary Vein, Left 9 Brachial Vein, Right A Brachial Vein, Left B Basilic Vein, Right C Basilic Vein, Left D Cephalic Vein, Right F Cephalic Vein, Left G Hand Vein, Right H Hand Vein, Left L Intracranial Vein M Internal Jugular Vein, Right N Internal Jugular Vein, Left P External Jugular Vein, Right Q External Jugular Vein, Left R Vertebral Vein, Right S Vertebral Vein, Left T Face Vein, Right V Face Vein, Left Y Upper Vein	0 Open 3 Percutaneous 4 Percutaneous Endoscopic	Z No Device	Z No Qualifier

0   Medical and Surgical
5   Upper Veins
P   Removal: Taking out or off a device from a body part

Body Part Character 4	Approach Character 5	Device Character 6	Qualifier Character 7
Y Upper Vein	0 Open 3 Percutaneous 4 Percutaneous Endoscopic	0 Drainage Device 2 Monitoring Device 3 Infusion Device 7 Autologous Tissue Substitute 9 Autologous Venous Tissue A Autologous Arterial Tissue C Extraluminal Device D Intraluminal Device J Synthetic Substitute K Nonautologous Tissue Substitute	Z No Qualifier
Y Upper Vein	X External	0 Drainage Device 2 Monitoring Device 3 Infusion Device D Intraluminal Device	Z No Qualifier

0   Medical and Surgical
5   Upper Veins
Q   Repair: Restoring, to the extent possible, a body part to its normal anatomic structure and function

Body Part Character 4	Approach Character 5	Device Character 6	Qualifier Character 7
0 Azygos Vein 1 Hemiazygos Vein 3 Innominate Vein, Right 4 Innominate Vein, Left 5 Subclavian Vein, Right 6 Subclavian Vein, Left 7 Axillary Vein, Right 8 Axillary Vein, Left 9 Brachial Vein, Right A Brachial Vein, Left B Basilic Vein, Right C Basilic Vein, Left D Cephalic Vein, Right F Cephalic Vein, Left G Hand Vein, Right H Hand Vein, Left L Intracranial Vein M Internal Jugular Vein, Right N Internal Jugular Vein, Left P External Jugular Vein, Right Q External Jugular Vein, Left R Vertebral Vein, Right S Vertebral Vein, Left T Face Vein, Right V Face Vein, Left Y Upper Vein	0 Open 3 Percutaneous 4 Percutaneous Endoscopic	Z No Device	Z No Qualifier

0   Medical and Surgical
5   Upper Veins
R   Replacement: Putting in or on biological or synthetic material that physically takes the place and/or function of all or a portion of a body part

Body Part Character 4	Approach Character 5	Device Character 6	Qualifier Character 7
0 Azygos Vein 1 Hemiazygos Vein 3 Innominate Vein, Right 4 Innominate Vein, Left 5 Subclavian Vein, Right 6 Subclavian Vein, Left 7 Axillary Vein, Right 8 Axillary Vein, Left 9 Brachial Vein, Right A Brachial Vein, Left B Basilic Vein, Right C Basilic Vein, Left D Cephalic Vein, Right F Cephalic Vein, Left G Hand Vein, Right H Hand Vein, Left L Intracranial Vein M Internal Jugular Vein, Right N Internal Jugular Vein, Left P External Jugular Vein, Right Q External Jugular Vein, Left R Vertebral Vein, Right S Vertebral Vein, Left T Face Vein, Right V Face Vein, Left Y Upper Vein	0 Open 4 Percutaneous Endoscopic	7 Autologous Tissue Substitute J Synthetic Substitute K Nonautologous Tissue Substitute	Z No Qualifier

0   **Medical and Surgical**
5   **Upper Veins**
S   **Reposition:**   Moving to its normal location or other suitable location all or a portion of a body part

Body Part Character 4	Approach Character 5	Device Character 6	Qualifier Character 7
0 Azygos Vein	0 Open	Z No Device	Z No Qualifier
1 Hemiazygos Vein	3 Percutaneous		
3 Innominate Vein, Right	4 Percutaneous Endoscopic		
4 Innominate Vein, Left			
5 Subclavian Vein, Right			
6 Subclavian Vein, Left			
7 Axillary Vein, Right			
8 Axillary Vein, Left			
9 Brachial Vein, Right			
A Brachial Vein, Left			
B Basilic Vein, Right			
C Basilic Vein, Left			
D Cephalic Vein, Right			
F Cephalic Vein, Left			
G Hand Vein, Right			
H Hand Vein, Left			
L Intracranial Vein			
M Internal Jugular Vein, Right			
N Internal Jugular Vein, Left			
P External Jugular Vein, Right			
Q External Jugular Vein, Left			
R Vertebral Vein, Right			
S Vertebral Vein, Left			
T Face Vein, Right			
V Face Vein, Left			
Y Upper Vein			

0   **Medical and Surgical**
5   **Upper Veins**
U   **Supplement:**   Putting in or on biological or synthetic material that physically reinforces and/or augments the function of a portion of a body part

Body Part Character 4	Approach Character 5	Device Character 6	Qualifier Character 7
0 Azygos Vein	0 Open	7 Autologous Tissue Substitute	Z No Qualifier
1 Hemiazygos Vein	4 Percutaneous Endoscopic	J Synthetic Substitute	
3 Innominate Vein, Right		K Nonautologous Tissue Substitute	
4 Innominate Vein, Left			
5 Subclavian Vein, Right			
6 Subclavian Vein, Left			
7 Axillary Vein, Right			
8 Axillary Vein, Left			
9 Brachial Vein, Right			
A Brachial Vein, Left			
B Basilic Vein, Right			
C Basilic Vein, Left			
D Cephalic Vein, Right			
F Cephalic Vein, Left			
G Hand Vein, Right			
H Hand Vein, Left			
L Intracranial Vein			
M Internal Jugular Vein, Right			
N Internal Jugular Vein, Left			
P External Jugular Vein, Right			
Q External Jugular Vein, Left			
R Vertebral Vein, Right			
S Vertebral Vein, Left			
T Face Vein, Right			
V Face Vein, Left			
Y Upper Vein			

0 **Medical and Surgical**
5 **Upper Veins**
V **Restriction:**   Partially closing the orifice or lumen of a tubular body part

Body Part Character 4	Approach Character 5	Device Character 6	Qualifier Character 7
0 Azygos Vein **1** Hemiazygos Vein **3** Innominate Vein, Right **4** Innominate Vein, Left **5** Subclavian Vein, Right **6** Subclavian Vein, Left **7** Axillary Vein, Right **8** Axillary Vein, Left **9** Brachial Vein, Right **A** Brachial Vein, Left **B** Basilic Vein, Right **C** Basilic Vein, Left **D** Cephalic Vein, Right **F** Cephalic Vein, Left **G** Hand Vein, Right **H** Hand Vein, Left **L** Intracranial Vein **M** Internal Jugular Vein, Right **N** Internal Jugular Vein, Left **P** External Jugular Vein, Right **Q** External Jugular Vein, Left **R** Vertebral Vein, Right **S** Vertebral Vein, Left **T** Face Vein, Right **V** Face Vein, Left **Y** Upper Vein	**0** Open **3** Percutaneous **4** Percutaneous Endoscopic	**C** Extraluminal Device **D** Intraluminal Device **Z** No Device	**Z** No Qualifier

0 **Medical and Surgical**
5 **Upper Veins**
W **Revision:**   Correcting, to the extent possible, a malfunctioning or displaced device

Body Part Character 4	Approach Character 5	Device Character 6	Qualifier Character 7
Y Upper Vein	**0** Open **3** Percutaneous **4** Percutaneous Endoscopic **X** External	**0** Drainage Device **2** Monitoring Device **3** Infusion Device **7** Autologous Tissue Substitute **9** Autologous Venous Tissue **A** Autologous Arterial Tissue **C** Extraluminal Device **D** Intraluminal Device **J** Synthetic Substitute **K** Nonautologous Tissue Substitute	**Z** No Qualifier

Lower Veins 061–06W

0   Medical and Surgical
6   Lower Veins
1   Bypass: Altering the route of passage of the contents of a tubular body part

Body Part Character 4	Approach Character 5	Device Character 6	Qualifier Character 7
0 Inferior Vena Cava	0 Open 4 Percutaneous Endoscopic	7 Autologous Tissue Substitute 9 Autologous Venous Tissue A Autologous Arterial Tissue J Synthetic Substitute K Nonautologous Tissue Substitute Z No Device	5 Superior Mesenteric Vein 6 Inferior Mesenteric Vein Y Lower Vein
1 Splenic Vein 8 Portal Vein	0 Open 4 Percutaneous Endoscopic	7 Autologous Tissue Substitute 9 Autologous Venous Tissue A Autologous Arterial Tissue J Synthetic Substitute K Nonautologous Tissue Substitute Z No Device	9 Renal Vein, Right B Renal Vein, Left Y Lower Vein
2 Gastric Vein 3 Esophageal Vein 4 Hepatic Vein 5 Superior Mesenteric Vein 6 Inferior Mesenteric Vein 7 Colic Vein 9 Renal Vein, Right B Renal Vein, Left C Common Iliac Vein, Right D Common Iliac Vein, Left F External Iliac Vein, Right G External Iliac Vein, Left H Hypogastric Vein, Right J Hypogastric Vein, Left M Femoral Vein, Right N Femoral Vein, Left P Greater Saphenous Vein, Right Q Greater Saphenous Vein, Left R Lesser Saphenous Vein, Right S Lesser Saphenous Vein, Left T Foot Vein, Right V Foot Vein, Left	0 Open 4 Percutaneous Endoscopic	7 Autologous Tissue Substitute 9 Autologous Venous Tissue A Autologous Arterial Tissue J Synthetic Substitute K Nonautologous Tissue Substitute Z No Device	Y Lower Vein
8 Portal Vein	3 Percutaneous 4 Percutaneous Endoscopic	D Intraluminal Device	Y Lower Vein

0   Medical and Surgical
6   Lower Veins
5   Destruction: Physical eradication of all or a portion of a body part by the direct use of energy, force, or a destructive agent

Body Part Character 4	Approach Character 5	Device Character 6	Qualifier Character 7
0 Inferior Vena Cava 1 Splenic Vein 2 Gastric Vein 3 Esophageal Vein 4 Hepatic Vein 5 Superior Mesenteric Vein 6 Inferior Mesenteric Vein 7 Colic Vein 8 Portal Vein 9 Renal Vein, Right B Renal Vein, Left C Common Iliac Vein, Right D Common Iliac Vein, Left F External Iliac Vein, Right G External Iliac Vein, Left H Hypogastric Vein, Right J Hypogastric Vein, Left M Femoral Vein, Right N Femoral Vein, Left P Greater Saphenous Vein, Right Q Greater Saphenous Vein, Left R Lesser Saphenous Vein, Right S Lesser Saphenous Vein, Left T Foot Vein, Right V Foot Vein, Left Y Lower Vein	0 Open 3 Percutaneous 4 Percutaneous Endoscopic	Z No Device	Z No Qualifier

0 Medical and Surgical
6 Lower Veins
7 Dilation: Expanding an orifice or the lumen of a tubular body part

Body Part Character 4	Approach Character 5	Device Character 6	Qualifier Character 7
0 Inferior Vena Cava **1** Splenic Vein **2** Gastric Vein **3** Esophageal Vein **4** Hepatic Vein **5** Superior Mesenteric Vein **6** Inferior Mesenteric Vein **7** Colic Vein **8** Portal Vein **9** Renal Vein, Right **B** Renal Vein, Left **C** Common Iliac Vein, Right **D** Common Iliac Vein, Left **F** External Iliac Vein, Right **G** External Iliac Vein, Left **H** Hypogastric Vein, Right **J** Hypogastric Vein, Left **M** Femoral Vein, Right **N** Femoral Vein, Left **P** Greater Saphenous Vein, Right **Q** Greater Saphenous Vein, Left **R** Lesser Saphenous Vein, Right **S** Lesser Saphenous Vein, Left **T** Foot Vein, Right **V** Foot Vein, Left **Y** Lower Vein	**0** Open **3** Percutaneous **4** Percutaneous Endoscopic	**D** Intraluminal Device **Z** No Device	**Z** No Qualifier

0 Medical and Surgical
6 Lower Veins
9 Drainage: Taking or letting out fluids and/or gases from a body part

Body Part Character 4	Approach Character 5	Device Character 6	Qualifier Character 7
0 Inferior Vena Cava **1** Splenic Vein **2** Gastric Vein **3** Esophageal Vein **4** Hepatic Vein **5** Superior Mesenteric Vein **6** Inferior Mesenteric Vein **7** Colic Vein **8** Portal Vein **9** Renal Vein, Right **B** Renal Vein, Left **C** Common Iliac Vein, Right **D** Common Iliac Vein, Left **F** External Iliac Vein, Right **G** External Iliac Vein, Left **H** Hypogastric Vein, Right **J** Hypogastric Vein, Left **M** Femoral Vein, Right **N** Femoral Vein, Left **P** Greater Saphenous Vein, Right **Q** Greater Saphenous Vein, Left **R** Lesser Saphenous Vein, Right **S** Lesser Saphenous Vein, Left **T** Foot Vein, Right **V** Foot Vein, Left **Y** Lower Vein	**0** Open **3** Percutaneous **4** Percutaneous Endoscopic	**0** Drainage Device	**Z** No Qualifier

Continued on next page

0 **Medical and Surgical** *Continued from previous page*
6 **Lower Veins**
9 **Drainage:** Taking or letting out fluids and/or gases from a body part

Body Part Character 4	Approach Character 5	Device Character 6	Qualifier Character 7
0 Inferior Vena Cava **1** Splenic Vein **2** Gastric Vein **3** Esophageal Vein **4** Hepatic Vein **5** Superior Mesenteric Vein **6** Inferior Mesenteric Vein **7** Colic Vein **8** Portal Vein **9** Renal Vein, Right **B** Renal Vein, Left **C** Common Iliac Vein, Right **D** Common Iliac Vein, Left **F** External Iliac Vein, Right **G** External Iliac Vein, Left **H** Hypogastric Vein, Right **J** Hypogastric Vein, Left **M** Femoral Vein, Right **N** Femoral Vein, Left **P** Greater Saphenous Vein, Right **Q** Greater Saphenous Vein, Left **R** Lesser Saphenous Vein, Right **S** Lesser Saphenous Vein, Left **T** Foot Vein, Right **V** Foot Vein, Left **Y** Lower Vein	**0** Open **3** Percutaneous **4** Percutaneous Endoscopic	**Z** No Device	**X** Diagnostic **Z** No Qualifier

0 **Medical and Surgical**
6 **Lower Veins**
B **Excision:** Cutting out or off, without replacement, a portion of a body part

Body Part Character 4	Approach Character 5	Device Character 6	Qualifier Character 7
0 Inferior Vena Cava **1** Splenic Vein **2** Gastric Vein **3** Esophageal Vein **4** Hepatic Vein **5** Superior Mesenteric Vein **6** Inferior Mesenteric Vein **7** Colic Vein **8** Portal Vein **9** Renal Vein, Right **B** Renal Vein, Left **C** Common Iliac Vein, Right **D** Common Iliac Vein, Left **F** External Iliac Vein, Right **G** External Iliac Vein, Left **H** Hypogastric Vein, Right **J** Hypogastric Vein, Left **M** Femoral Vein, Right **N** Femoral Vein, Left **P** Greater Saphenous Vein, Right **Q** Greater Saphenous Vein, Left **R** Lesser Saphenous Vein, Right **S** Lesser Saphenous Vein, Left **T** Foot Vein, Right **V** Foot Vein, Left **Y** Lower Vein	**0** Open **3** Percutaneous **4** Percutaneous Endoscopic	**Z** No Device	**X** Diagnostic **Z** No Qualifier

0   **Medical and Surgical**
6   **Lower Veins**
C   **Extirpation:**   Taking or cutting out solid matter from a body part

Body Part Character 4	Approach Character 5	Device Character 6	Qualifier Character 7
0 Inferior Vena Cava **1** Splenic Vein **2** Gastric Vein **3** Esophageal Vein **4** Hepatic Vein **5** Superior Mesenteric Vein **6** Inferior Mesenteric Vein **7** Colic Vein **8** Portal Vein **9** Renal Vein, Right **B** Renal Vein, Left **C** Common Iliac Vein, Right **D** Common Iliac Vein, Left **F** External Iliac Vein, Right **G** External Iliac Vein, Left **H** Hypogastric Vein, Right **J** Hypogastric Vein, Left **M** Femoral Vein, Right **N** Femoral Vein, Left **P** Greater Saphenous Vein, Right **Q** Greater Saphenous Vein, Left **R** Lesser Saphenous Vein, Right **S** Lesser Saphenous Vein, Left **T** Foot Vein, Right **V** Foot Vein, Left **Y** Lower Vein	**0** Open **3** Percutaneous **4** Percutaneous Endoscopic	**Z** No Device	**Z** No Qualifier

0   **Medical and Surgical**
6   **Lower Veins**
D   **Extraction:**   Pulling or stripping out or off all or a portion of a body part by the use of force

Body Part Character 4	Approach Character 5	Device Character 6	Qualifier Character 7
M Femoral Vein, Right **N** Femoral Vein, Left **P** Greater Saphenous Vein, Right **Q** Greater Saphenous Vein, Left **R** Lesser Saphenous Vein, Right **S** Lesser Saphenous Vein, Left **T** Foot Vein, Right **V** Foot Vein, Left **Y** Lower Vein	**0** Open **3** Percutaneous **4** Percutaneous Endoscopic	**Z** No Device	**Z** No Qualifier

0   **Medical and Surgical**
6   **Lower Veins**
H   **Insertion:**   Putting in a nonbiological appliance that monitors, assists, performs or prevents a physiological function, but does not physically take the place of a body part

Body Part Character 4	Approach Character 5	Device Character 6	Qualifier Character 7
0 Inferior Vena Cava	**0** Open **3** Percutaneous	**3** Infusion Device	**T** Via Umbilical Vein **Z** No Qualifier
0 Inferior Vena Cava	**0** Open **3** Percutaneous	**D** Intraluminal Device	**Z** No Qualifier
0 Inferior Vena Cava	**4** Percutaneous Endoscopic	**3** Infusion Device **D** Intraluminal Device	**Z** No Qualifier

Continued on next page

0   Medical and Surgical   *Continued from previous page*
6   Lower Veins
H   Insertion: Putting in a nonbiological appliance that monitors, assists, performs or prevents a physiological function, but does not physically take the place of a body part

Body Part Character 4	Approach Character 5	Device Character 6	Qualifier Character 7
1 Splenic Vein 2 Gastric Vein 3 Esophageal Vein 4 Hepatic Vein 5 Superior Mesenteric Vein 6 Inferior Mesenteric Vein 7 Colic Vein 8 Portal Vein 9 Renal Vein, Right B Renal Vein, Left C Common Iliac Vein, Right D Common Iliac Vein, Left F External Iliac Vein, Right G External Iliac Vein, Left H Hypogastric Vein, Right J Hypogastric Vein, Left M Femoral Vein, Right N Femoral Vein, Left P Greater Saphenous Vein, Right Q Greater Saphenous Vein, Left R Lesser Saphenous Vein, Right S Lesser Saphenous Vein, Left T Foot Vein, Right V Foot Vein, Left	0 Open 3 Percutaneous 4 Percutaneous Endoscopic	3 Infusion Device D Intraluminal Device	Z No Qualifier
Y Lower Vein	0 Open 3 Percutaneous 4 Percutaneous Endoscopic	2 Monitoring Device 3 Infusion Device D Intraluminal Device	Z No Qualifier

0   Medical and Surgical
6   Lower Veins
J   Inspection: Visually and/or manually exploring a body part

Body Part Character 4	Approach Character 5	Device Character 6	Qualifier Character 7
0 Inferior Vena Cava 1 Splenic Vein 2 Gastric Vein 3 Esophageal Vein 4 Hepatic Vein 5 Superior Mesenteric Vein 6 Inferior Mesenteric Vein 7 Colic Vein 8 Portal Vein 9 Renal Vein, Right B Renal Vein, Left C Common Iliac Vein, Right D Common Iliac Vein, Left F External Iliac Vein, Right G External Iliac Vein, Left H Hypogastric Vein, Right J Hypogastric Vein, Left	0 Open 3 Percutaneous 4 Percutaneous Endoscopic	Z No Device	Z No Qualifier
M Femoral Vein, Right N Femoral Vein, Left P Greater Saphenous Vein, Right Q Greater Saphenous Vein, Left R Lesser Saphenous Vein, Right S Lesser Saphenous Vein, Left T Foot Vein, Right V Foot Vein, Left Y Lower Vein	0 Open 3 Percutaneous 4 Percutaneous Endoscopic X External	Z No Device	Z No Qualifier

0   Medical and Surgical
6   Lower Veins
L   Occlusion: Completely closing an orifice or lumen of a tubular body part

Body Part Character 4	Approach Character 5	Device Character 6	Qualifier Character 7
0 Inferior Vena Cava 1 Splenic Vein 2 Gastric Vein 3 Esophageal Vein 4 Hepatic Vein 5 Superior Mesenteric Vein 6 Inferior Mesenteric Vein 7 Colic Vein 8 Portal Vein 9 Renal Vein, Right B Renal Vein, Left C Common Iliac Vein, Right D Common Iliac Vein, Left F External Iliac Vein, Right G External Iliac Vein, Left H Hypogastric Vein, Right J Hypogastric Vein, Left M Femoral Vein, Right N Femoral Vein, Left P Greater Saphenous Vein, Right Q Greater Saphenous Vein, Left R Lesser Saphenous Vein, Right S Lesser Saphenous Vein, Left T Foot Vein, Right V Foot Vein, Left Y Lower Vein	0 Open 3 Percutaneous 4 Percutaneous Endoscopic	C Extraluminal Device D Intraluminal Device Z No Device	Z No Qualifier

0   Medical and Surgical
6   Lower Veins
N   Release: Freeing a body part from an abnormal physical constraint

Body Part Character 4	Approach Character 5	Device Character 6	Qualifier Character 7
0 Inferior Vena Cava 1 Splenic Vein 2 Gastric Vein 3 Esophageal Vein 4 Hepatic Vein 5 Superior Mesenteric Vein 6 Inferior Mesenteric Vein 7 Colic Vein 8 Portal Vein 9 Renal Vein, Right B Renal Vein, Left C Common Iliac Vein, Right D Common Iliac Vein, Left F External Iliac Vein, Right G External Iliac Vein, Left H Hypogastric Vein, Right J Hypogastric Vein, Left M Femoral Vein, Right N Femoral Vein, Left P Greater Saphenous Vein, Right Q Greater Saphenous Vein, Left R Lesser Saphenous Vein, Right S Lesser Saphenous Vein, Left T Foot Vein, Right V Foot Vein, Left Y Lower Vein	0 Open 3 Percutaneous 4 Percutaneous Endoscopic	Z No Device	Z No Qualifier

0   Medical and Surgical
6   Lower Veins
P   Removal: Taking out or off a device from a body part

Body Part Character 4	Approach Character 5	Device Character 6	Qualifier Character 7
Y Lower Vein	**0** Open **3** Percutaneous **4** Percutaneous Endoscopic	**0** Drainage Device **2** Monitoring Device **3** Infusion Device **7** Autologous Tissue Substitute **9** Autologous Venous Tissue **A** Autologous Arterial Tissue **C** Extraluminal Device **D** Intraluminal Device **J** Synthetic Substitute **K** Nonautologous Tissue Substitute	**Z** No Qualifier
Y Lower Vein	**X** External	**0** Drainage Device **2** Monitoring Device **3** Infusion Device **D** Intraluminal Device	**Z** No Qualifier

0   Medical and Surgical
6   Lower Veins
Q   Repair: Restoring, to the extent possible, a body part to its normal anatomic structure and function

Body Part Character 4	Approach Character 5	Device Character 6	Qualifier Character 7
0 Inferior Vena Cava **1** Splenic Vein **2** Gastric Vein **3** Esophageal Vein **4** Hepatic Vein **5** Superior Mesenteric Vein **6** Inferior Mesenteric Vein **7** Colic Vein **8** Portal Vein **9** Renal Vein, Right **B** Renal Vein, Left **C** Common Iliac Vein, Right **D** Common Iliac Vein, Left **F** External Iliac Vein, Right **G** External Iliac Vein, Left **H** Hypogastric Vein, Right **J** Hypogastric Vein, Left **M** Femoral Vein, Right **N** Femoral Vein, Left **P** Greater Saphenous Vein, Right **Q** Greater Saphenous Vein, Left **R** Lesser Saphenous Vein, Right **S** Lesser Saphenous Vein, Left **T** Foot Vein, Right **V** Foot Vein, Left **Y** Lower Vein	**0** Open **3** Percutaneous **4** Percutaneous Endoscopic	**Z** No Device	**Z** No Qualifier

0 Medical and Surgical
6 Lower Veins
R Replacement: Putting in or on biological or synthetic material that physically takes the place and/or function of all or a portion of a body part

Body Part Character 4	Approach Character 5	Device Character 6	Qualifier Character 7
0 Inferior Vena Cava 1 Splenic Vein 2 Gastric Vein 3 Esophageal Vein 4 Hepatic Vein 5 Superior Mesenteric Vein 6 Inferior Mesenteric Vein 7 Colic Vein 8 Portal Vein 9 Renal Vein, Right B Renal Vein, Left C Common Iliac Vein, Right D Common Iliac Vein, Left F External Iliac Vein, Right G External Iliac Vein, Left H Hypogastric Vein, Right J Hypogastric Vein, Left M Femoral Vein, Right N Femoral Vein, Left P Greater Saphenous Vein, Right Q Greater Saphenous Vein, Left R Lesser Saphenous Vein, Right S Lesser Saphenous Vein, Left T Foot Vein, Right V Foot Vein, Left Y Lower Vein	0 Open 4 Percutaneous Endoscopic	7 Autologous Tissue Substitute J Synthetic Substitute K Nonautologous Tissue Substitute	Z No Qualifier

0 Medical and Surgical
6 Lower Veins
S Reposition: Moving to its normal location or other suitable location all or a portion of a body part

Body Part Character 4	Approach Character 5	Device Character 6	Qualifier Character 7
0 Inferior Vena Cava 1 Splenic Vein 2 Gastric Vein 3 Esophageal Vein 4 Hepatic Vein 5 Superior Mesenteric Vein 6 Inferior Mesenteric Vein 7 Colic Vein 8 Portal Vein 9 Renal Vein, Right B Renal Vein, Left C Common Iliac Vein, Right D Common Iliac Vein, Left F External Iliac Vein, Right G External Iliac Vein, Left H Hypogastric Vein, Right J Hypogastric Vein, Left M Femoral Vein, Right N Femoral Vein, Left P Greater Saphenous Vein, Right Q Greater Saphenous Vein, Left R Lesser Saphenous Vein, Right S Lesser Saphenous Vein, Left T Foot Vein, Right V Foot Vein, Left Y Lower Vein	0 Open 3 Percutaneous 4 Percutaneous Endoscopic	Z No Device	Z No Qualifier

0 Medical and Surgical
6 Lower Veins
U Supplement: Putting in or on biological or synthetic material that physically reinforces and/or augments the function of a portion of a body part

Body Part Character 4	Approach Character 5	Device Character 6	Qualifier Character 7
0 Inferior Vena Cava 1 Splenic Vein 2 Gastric Vein 3 Esophageal Vein 4 Hepatic Vein 5 Superior Mesenteric Vein 6 Inferior Mesenteric Vein 7 Colic Vein 8 Portal Vein 9 Renal Vein, Right B Renal Vein, Left C Common Iliac Vein, Right D Common Iliac Vein, Left F External Iliac Vein, Right G External Iliac Vein, Left H Hypogastric Vein, Right J Hypogastric Vein, Left M Femoral Vein, Right N Femoral Vein, Left P Greater Saphenous Vein, Right Q Greater Saphenous Vein, Left R Lesser Saphenous Vein, Right S Lesser Saphenous Vein, Left T Foot Vein, Right V Foot Vein, Left Y Lower Vein	0 Open 4 Percutaneous Endoscopic	7 Autologous Tissue Substitute J Synthetic Substitute K Nonautologous Tissue Substitute	Z No Qualifier

0 Medical and Surgical
6 Lower Veins
V Restriction: Partially closing the orifice or lumen of a tubular body part

Body Part Character 4	Approach Character 5	Device Character 6	Qualifier Character 7
0 Inferior Vena Cava 1 Splenic Vein 2 Gastric Vein 3 Esophageal Vein 4 Hepatic Vein 5 Superior Mesenteric Vein 6 Inferior Mesenteric Vein 7 Colic Vein 8 Portal Vein 9 Renal Vein, Right B Renal Vein, Left C Common Iliac Vein, Right D Common Iliac Vein, Left F External Iliac Vein, Right G External Iliac Vein, Left H Hypogastric Vein, Right J Hypogastric Vein, Left M Femoral Vein, Right N Femoral Vein, Left P Greater Saphenous Vein, Right Q Greater Saphenous Vein, Left R Lesser Saphenous Vein, Right S Lesser Saphenous Vein, Left T Foot Vein, Right V Foot Vein, Left Y Lower Vein	0 Open 3 Percutaneous 4 Percutaneous Endoscopic	C Extraluminal Device D Intraluminal Device Z No Device	Z No Qualifier

0 **Medical and Surgical**
6 **Lower Veins**
W **Revision:** Correcting, to the extent possible, a malfunctioning or displaced device

Body Part Character 4	Approach Character 5	Device Character 6	Qualifier Character 7
Y Lower Vein	**0** Open **3** Percutaneous **4** Percutaneous Endoscopic **X** External	**0** Drainage Device **2** Monitoring Device **3** Infusion Device **7** Autologous Tissue Substitute **9** Autologous Venous Tissue **A** Autologous Arterial Tissue **C** Extraluminal Device **D** Intraluminal Device **J** Synthetic Substitute **K** Nonautologous Tissue Substitute	**Z** No Qualifier

Lymphatic and Hemic Systems 072–07Y

0 **Medical and Surgical**
7 **Lymphatic and Hemic Systems**
2 **Change:** Taking out or off a device from a body part and putting back an identical or similar device in or on the same body part without cutting or puncturing the skin or a mucous membrane

Body Part Character 4	Approach Character 5	Device Character 6	Qualifier Character 7
K Thoracic Duct **L** Cisterna Chyli **M** Thymus **N** Lymphatic **P** Spleen **T** Bone Marrow	**X** External	**0** Drainage Device **Y** Other Device	**Z** No Qualifier

0 **Medical and Surgical**
7 **Lymphatic and Hemic Systems**
5 **Destruction:** Physical eradication of all or a portion of a body part by the direct use of energy, force, or a destructive agent

Body Part Character 4	Approach Character 5	Device Character 6	Qualifier Character 7
0 Lymphatic, Head **1** Lymphatic, Right Neck **2** Lymphatic, Left Neck **3** Lymphatic, Right Upper Extremity **4** Lymphatic, Left Upper Extremity **5** Lymphatic, Right Axillary **6** Lymphatic, Left Axillary **7** Lymphatic, Thorax **8** Lymphatic, Internal Mammary, Right **9** Lymphatic, Internal Mammary, Left **B** Lymphatic, Mesenteric **C** Lymphatic, Pelvis **D** Lymphatic, Aortic **F** Lymphatic, Right Lower Extremity **G** Lymphatic, Left Lower Extremity **H** Lymphatic, Right Inguinal **J** Lymphatic, Left Inguinal **K** Thoracic Duct **L** Cisterna Chyli **M** Thymus **P** Spleen	**0** Open **3** Percutaneous **4** Percutaneous Endoscopic	**Z** No Device	**Z** No Qualifier

0 **Medical and Surgical**
7 **Lymphatic and Hemic Systems**
9 **Drainage:** Taking or letting out fluids and/or gases from a body part

Body Part Character 4	Approach Character 5	Device Character 6	Qualifier Character 7
0 Lymphatic, Head **1** Lymphatic, Right Neck **2** Lymphatic, Left Neck **3** Lymphatic, Right Upper Extremity **4** Lymphatic, Left Upper Extremity **5** Lymphatic, Right Axillary **6** Lymphatic, Left Axillary **7** Lymphatic, Thorax **8** Lymphatic, Internal Mammary, Right **9** Lymphatic, Internal Mammary, Left **B** Lymphatic, Mesenteric **C** Lymphatic, Pelvis **D** Lymphatic, Aortic **F** Lymphatic, Right Lower Extremity **G** Lymphatic, Left Lower Extremity **H** Lymphatic, Right Inguinal **J** Lymphatic, Left Inguinal **K** Thoracic Duct **L** Cisterna Chyli **M** Thymus **P** Spleen **T** Bone Marrow	**0** Open **3** Percutaneous **4** Percutaneous Endoscopic	**0** Drainage Device	**Z** No Qualifier

Continued on next page

0 Medical and Surgical
7 Lymphatic and Hemic Systems
9 Drainage: Taking or letting out fluids and/or gases from a body part

Continued from previous page

Body Part Character 4	Approach Character 5	Device Character 6	Qualifier Character 7

0 Lymphatic, Head
1 Lymphatic, Right Neck
2 Lymphatic, Left Neck
3 Lymphatic, Right Upper
   Extremity
4 Lymphatic, Left Upper Extremity
5 Lymphatic, Right Axillary
6 Lymphatic, Left Axillary
7 Lymphatic, Thorax
8 Lymphatic, Internal Mammary,
   Right
9 Lymphatic, Internal Mammary,
   Left
B Lymphatic, Mesenteric
C Lymphatic, Pelvis
D Lymphatic, Aortic
F Lymphatic, Right Lower
   Extremity
G Lymphatic, Left Lower Extremity
H Lymphatic, Right Inguinal
J Lymphatic, Left Inguinal
K Thoracic Duct
L Cisterna Chyli
M Thymus
P Spleen
T Bone Marrow
	0 Open
	3 Percutaneous
	4 Percutaneous Endoscopic
		Z No Device	X Diagnostic
			Z No Qualifier

0 Medical and Surgical
7 Lymphatic and Hemic Systems
B Excision: Cutting out or off, without replacement, a portion of a body part

Body Part Character 4	Approach Character 5	Device Character 6	Qualifier Character 7

0 Lymphatic, Head
1 Lymphatic, Right Neck
2 Lymphatic, Left Neck
3 Lymphatic, Right Upper
   Extremity
4 Lymphatic, Left Upper Extremity
5 Lymphatic, Right Axillary
6 Lymphatic, Left Axillary
7 Lymphatic, Thorax
8 Lymphatic, Internal Mammary,
   Right
9 Lymphatic, Internal Mammary,
   Left
B Lymphatic, Mesenteric
C Lymphatic, Pelvis
D Lymphatic, Aortic
F Lymphatic, Right Lower
   Extremity
G Lymphatic, Left Lower Extremity
H Lymphatic, Right Inguinal
J Lymphatic, Left Inguinal
K Thoracic Duct
L Cisterna Chyli
M Thymus
P Spleen
	0 Open
	3 Percutaneous
	4 Percutaneous Endoscopic
		Z No Device	X Diagnostic
			Z No Qualifier

0   Medical and Surgical
7   Lymphatic and Hemic Systems
C   Extirpation: Taking or cutting out solid matter from a body part

Body Part Character 4	Approach Character 5	Device Character 6	Qualifier Character 7
0 Lymphatic, Head 1 Lymphatic, Right Neck 2 Lymphatic, Left Neck 3 Lymphatic, Right Upper Extremity 4 Lymphatic, Left Upper Extremity 5 Lymphatic, Right Axillary 6 Lymphatic, Left Axillary 7 Lymphatic, Thorax 8 Lymphatic, Internal Mammary, Right 9 Lymphatic, Internal Mammary, Left B Lymphatic, Mesenteric C Lymphatic, Pelvis D Lymphatic, Aortic F Lymphatic, Right Lower Extremity G Lymphatic, Left Lower Extremity H Lymphatic, Right Inguinal J Lymphatic, Left Inguinal K Thoracic Duct L Cisterna Chyli M Thymus P Spleen	0 Open 3 Percutaneous 4 Percutaneous Endoscopic	Z No Device	Z No Qualifier

0   Medical and Surgical
7   Lymphatic and Hemic Systems
D   Extraction: Pulling or stripping out or off all or a portion of a body part by the use of force

Body Part Character 4	Approach Character 5	Device Character 6	Qualifier Character 7
Q Bone Marrow, Sternum R Bone Marrow, Iliac S Bone Marrow, Vertebral	0 Open 3 Percutaneous	Z No Device	X Diagnostic Z No Qualifier

0   Medical and Surgical
7   Lymphatic and Hemic Systems
H   Insertion: Putting in a nonbiological appliance that monitors, assists, performs or prevents a physiological function, but does not physically take the place of a body part

Body Part Character 4	Approach Character 5	Device Character 6	Qualifier Character 7
K Thoracic Duct L Cisterna Chyli M Thymus N Lymphatic P Spleen	0 Open 3 Percutaneous 4 Percutaneous Endoscopic	3 Infusion Device	Z No Qualifier

0   Medical and Surgical
7   Lymphatic and Hemic Systems
J   Inspection: Visually and/or manually exploring a body part

Body Part Character 4	Approach Character 5	Device Character 6	Qualifier Character 7
0 Lymphatic, Head 1 Lymphatic, Right Neck 2 Lymphatic, Left Neck 3 Lymphatic, Right Upper Extremity 4 Lymphatic, Left Upper Extremity 5 Lymphatic, Right Axillary 6 Lymphatic, Left Axillary B Lymphatic, Mesenteric C Lymphatic, Pelvis D Lymphatic, Aortic F Lymphatic, Right Lower Extremity G Lymphatic, Left Lower Extremity H Lymphatic, Right Inguinal J Lymphatic, Left Inguinal P Spleen	0 Open 3 Percutaneous 4 Percutaneous Endoscopic X External	Z No Device	Z No Qualifier

Continued on next page

0   **Medical and Surgical**
7   **Lymphatic and Hemic Systems**
J   **Inspection:**   Visually and/or manually exploring a body part

Continued from previous page

Body Part Character 4	Approach Character 5	Device Character 6	Qualifier Character 7
7 Lymphatic, Thorax **8** Lymphatic, Internal Mammary, Right **9** Lymphatic, Internal Mammary, Left **K** Thoracic Duct **L** Cisterna Chyli **M** Thymus **Q** Bone Marrow, Sternum **R** Bone Marrow, Iliac **S** Bone Marrow, Vertebral **T** Bone Marrow	**0** Open **3** Percutaneous **4** Percutaneous Endoscopic	**Z** No Device	**Z** No Qualifier

0   **Medical and Surgical**
7   **Lymphatic and Hemic Systems**
L   **Occlusion:**   Completely closing an orifice or lumen of a tubular body part

Body Part Character 4	Approach Character 5	Device Character 6	Qualifier Character 7
0 Lymphatic, Head **1** Lymphatic, Right Neck **2** Lymphatic, Left Neck **3** Lymphatic, Right Upper Extremity **4** Lymphatic, Left Upper Extremity **5** Lymphatic, Right Axillary **6** Lymphatic, Left Axillary **7** Lymphatic, Thorax **8** Lymphatic, Internal Mammary, Right **9** Lymphatic, Internal Mammary, Left **B** Lymphatic, Mesenteric **C** Lymphatic, Pelvis **D** Lymphatic, Aortic **F** Lymphatic, Right Lower Extremity **G** Lymphatic, Left Lower Extremity **H** Lymphatic, Right Inguinal **J** Lymphatic, Left Inguinal **K** Thoracic Duct **L** Cisterna Chyli	**0** Open **3** Percutaneous **4** Percutaneous Endoscopic	**C** Extraluminal Device **D** Intraluminal Device **Z** No Device	**Z** No Qualifier

0   **Medical and Surgical**
7   **Lymphatic and Hemic Systems**
N   **Release:**   Freeing a body part from an abnormal physical constraint

Body Part Character 4	Approach Character 5	Device Character 6	Qualifier Character 7
0 Lymphatic, Head **1** Lymphatic, Right Neck **2** Lymphatic, Left Neck **3** Lymphatic, Right Upper Extremity **4** Lymphatic, Left Upper Extremity **5** Lymphatic, Right Axillary **6** Lymphatic, Left Axillary **7** Lymphatic, Thorax **8** Lymphatic, Internal Mammary, Right **9** Lymphatic, Internal Mammary, Left **B** Lymphatic, Mesenteric **C** Lymphatic, Pelvis **D** Lymphatic, Aortic **F** Lymphatic, Right Lower Extremity **G** Lymphatic, Left Lower Extremity **H** Lymphatic, Right Inguinal **J** Lymphatic, Left Inguinal **K** Thoracic Duct **L** Cisterna Chyli **M** Thymus **P** Spleen	**0** Open **3** Percutaneous **4** Percutaneous Endoscopic	**Z** No Device	**Z** No Qualifier

0   Medical and Surgical
7   Lymphatic and Hemic Systems
P   Removal: Taking out or off a device from a body part

Body Part Character 4	Approach Character 5	Device Character 6	Qualifier Character 7
K Thoracic Duct **L** Cisterna Chyli **N** Lymphatic	**0** Open **3** Percutaneous **4** Percutaneous Endoscopic	**0** Drainage Device **3** Infusion Device **7** Autologous Tissue Substitute **C** Extraluminal Device **D** Intraluminal Device **J** Synthetic Substitute **K** Nonautologous Tissue Substitute	**Z** No Qualifier
K Thoracic Duct **L** Cisterna Chyli **N** Lymphatic	**X** External	**0** Drainage Device **3** Infusion Device **D** Intraluminal Device	**Z** No Qualifier
M Thymus **P** Spleen	**0** Open **3** Percutaneous **4** Percutaneous Endoscopic **X** External	**0** Drainage Device **3** Infusion Device	**Z** No Qualifier
T Bone Marrow	**0** Open **3** Percutaneous **4** Percutaneous Endoscopic **X** External	**0** Drainage Device	**Z** No Qualifier

0   Medical and Surgical
7   Lymphatic and Hemic Systems
Q   Repair: Restoring, to the extent possible, a body part to its normal anatomic structure and function

Body Part Character 4	Approach Character 5	Device Character 6	Qualifier Character 7
0 Lymphatic, Head **1** Lymphatic, Right Neck **2** Lymphatic, Left Neck **3** Lymphatic, Right Upper Extremity **4** Lymphatic, Left Upper Extremity **5** Lymphatic, Right Axillary **6** Lymphatic, Left Axillary **7** Lymphatic, Thorax **8** Lymphatic, Internal Mammary, Right **9** Lymphatic, Internal Mammary, Left **B** Lymphatic, Mesenteric **C** Lymphatic, Pelvis **D** Lymphatic, Aortic **F** Lymphatic, Right Lower Extremity **G** Lymphatic, Left Lower Extremity **H** Lymphatic, Right Inguinal **J** Lymphatic, Left Inguinal **K** Thoracic Duct **L** Cisterna Chyli **M** Thymus **P** Spleen	**0** Open **3** Percutaneous **4** Percutaneous Endoscopic	**Z** No Device	**Z** No Qualifier

0   Medical and Surgical
7   Lymphatic and Hemic Systems
S   Reposition: Moving to its normal location or other suitable location all or a portion of a body part

Body Part Character 4	Approach Character 5	Device Character 6	Qualifier Character 7
M Thymus **P** Spleen	**0** Open	**Z** No Device	**Z** No Qualifier

0   **Medical and Surgical**
7   **Lymphatic and Hemic Systems**
T   **Resection:**   Cutting out or off, without replacement, all of a body part

Body Part Character 4	Approach Character 5	Device Character 6	Qualifier Character 7

0 Lymphatic, Head
1 Lymphatic, Right Neck
2 Lymphatic, Left Neck
3 Lymphatic, Right Upper
   Extremity
4 Lymphatic, Left Upper Extremity
5 Lymphatic, Right Axillary
6 Lymphatic, Left Axillary
7 Lymphatic, Thorax
8 Lymphatic, Internal Mammary,
   Right
9 Lymphatic, Internal Mammary,
   Left
B Lymphatic, Mesenteric
C Lymphatic, Pelvis
D Lymphatic, Aortic
F Lymphatic, Right Lower
   Extremity
G Lymphatic, Left Lower Extremity
H Lymphatic, Right Inguinal
J Lymphatic, Left Inguinal
K Thoracic Duct
L Cisterna Chyli
M Thymus
P Spleen
	0 Open
	4 Percutaneous Endoscopic
		Z No Device	**Z** No Qualifier

0   **Medical and Surgical**
7   **Lymphatic and Hemic Systems**
U   **Supplement:**   Putting in or on biological or synthetic material that physically reinforces and/or augments the function of a portion of a body part

Body Part Character 4	Approach Character 5	Device Character 6	Qualifier Character 7

0 Lymphatic, Head
1 Lymphatic, Right Neck
2 Lymphatic, Left Neck
3 Lymphatic, Right Upper
   Extremity
4 Lymphatic, Left Upper Extremity
5 Lymphatic, Right Axillary
6 Lymphatic, Left Axillary
7 Lymphatic, Thorax
8 Lymphatic, Internal Mammary,
   Right
9 Lymphatic, Internal Mammary,
   Left
B Lymphatic, Mesenteric
C Lymphatic, Pelvis
D Lymphatic, Aortic
F Lymphatic, Right Lower
   Extremity
G Lymphatic, Left Lower Extremity
H Lymphatic, Right Inguinal
J Lymphatic, Left Inguinal
K Thoracic Duct
L Cisterna Chyli
	0 Open
	4 Percutaneous Endoscopic
		7 Autologous Tissue Substitute
		J Synthetic Substitute
		K Nonautologous Tissue Substitute
			Z No Qualifier

0   **Medical and Surgical**
7   **Lymphatic and Hemic Systems**
V   **Restriction:**   Partially closing the orifice or lumen of a tubular body part

Body Part Character 4	Approach Character 5	Device Character 6	Qualifier Character 7

0 Lymphatic, Head
1 Lymphatic, Right Neck
2 Lymphatic, Left Neck
3 Lymphatic, Right Upper
   Extremity
4 Lymphatic, Left Upper Extremity
5 Lymphatic, Right Axillary
6 Lymphatic, Left Axillary
7 Lymphatic, Thorax
8 Lymphatic, Internal Mammary,
   Right
9 Lymphatic, Internal Mammary,
   Left
B Lymphatic, Mesenteric
C Lymphatic, Pelvis
D Lymphatic, Aortic
F Lymphatic, Right Lower
   Extremity
G Lymphatic, Left Lower Extremity
H Lymphatic, Right Inguinal
J Lymphatic, Left Inguinal
K Thoracic Duct
L Cisterna Chyli
	0 Open
	3 Percutaneous
	4 Percutaneous Endoscopic
		C Extraluminal Device
		D Intraluminal Device
		Z No Device
			Z No Qualifier

0   **Medical and Surgical**
7   **Lymphatic and Hemic Systems**
W   **Revision:**   Correcting, to the extent possible, a malfunctioning or displaced device

Body Part Character 4	Approach Character 5	Device Character 6	Qualifier Character 7
K Thoracic Duct L Cisterna Chyli N Lymphatic	0 Open 3 Percutaneous 4 Percutaneous Endoscopic X External	0 Drainage Device 3 Infusion Device 7 Autologous Tissue Substitute C Extraluminal Device D Intraluminal Device J Synthetic Substitute K Nonautologous Tissue Substitute	Z No Qualifier
M Thymus P Spleen	0 Open 3 Percutaneous 4 Percutaneous Endoscopic X External	0 Drainage Device 3 Infusion Device	Z No Qualifier
T Bone Marrow	0 Open 3 Percutaneous 4 Percutaneous Endoscopic X External	0 Drainage Device	Z No Qualifier

0   **Medical and Surgical**
7   **Lymphatic and Hemic Systems**
Y   **Transplantation:**   Putting in or on all or a portion of a living body part taken from another individual or animal to physically take the place and/or function of all or a portion of a similar body part

Body Part Character 4	Approach Character 5	Device Character 6	Qualifier Character 7
M Thymus P Spleen	0 Open	Z No Device	0 Allogeneic 1 Syngeneic 2 Zooplastic

Eye 080–08Y

0 Medical and Surgical
8 Eye
0 Alteration: Modifying the anatomic structure of a body part without affecting the function of the body part

Body Part Character 4	Approach Character 5	Device Character 6	Qualifier Character 7
N Upper Eyelid, Right P Upper Eyelid, Left Q Lower Eyelid, Right R Lower Eyelid, Left	0 Open 3 Percutaneous X External	7 Autologous Tissue Substitute J Synthetic Substitute K Nonautologous Tissue Substitute Z No Device	Z No Qualifier

0 Medical and Surgical
8 Eye
1 Bypass: Altering the route of passage of the contents of a tubular body part

Body Part Character 4	Approach Character 5	Device Character 6	Qualifier Character 7
2 Anterior Chamber, Right 3 Anterior Chamber, Left	3 Percutaneous	J Synthetic Substitute K Nonautologous Tissue Substitute Z No Device	4 Sclera
X Lacrimal Duct, Right Y Lacrimal Duct, Left	0 Open 3 Percutaneous	J Synthetic Substitute K Nonautologous Tissue Substitute Z No Device	3 Nasal Cavity

0 Medical and Surgical
8 Eye
2 Change: Taking out or off a device from a body part and putting back an identical or similar device in or on the same body part without cutting or puncturing the skin or a mucous membrane

Body Part Character 4	Approach Character 5	Device Character 6	Qualifier Character 7
0 Eye, Right 1 Eye, Left	X External	0 Drainage Device Y Other Device	Z No Qualifier

0 Medical and Surgical
8 Eye
5 Destruction: Physical eradication of all or a portion of a body part by the direct use of energy, force, or a destructive agent

Body Part Character 4	Approach Character 5	Device Character 6	Qualifier Character 7
0 Eye, Right 1 Eye, Left 6 Sclera, Right 7 Sclera, Left 8 Cornea, Right 9 Cornea, Left S Conjunctiva, Right T Conjunctiva, Left	X External	Z No Device	Z No Qualifier
2 Anterior Chamber, Right 3 Anterior Chamber, Left 4 Vitreous, Right 5 Vitreous, Left C Iris, Right D Iris, Left E Retina, Right F Retina, Left G Retinal Vessel, Right H Retinal Vessel, Left J Lens, Right K Lens, Left	3 Percutaneous	Z No Device	Z No Qualifier
A Choroid, Right B Choroid, Left L Extraocular Muscle, Right M Extraocular Muscle, Left V Lacrimal Gland, Right W Lacrimal Gland, Left	0 Open 3 Percutaneous	Z No Device	Z No Qualifier
N Upper Eyelid, Right P Upper Eyelid, Left Q Lower Eyelid, Right R Lower Eyelid, Left	0 Open 3 Percutaneous X External	Z No Device	Z No Qualifier

Continued on next page

0   Medical and Surgical
8   Eye
5   Destruction: Physical eradication of all or a portion of a body part by the direct use of energy, force, or a destructive agent

Continued from previous page

Body Part Character 4	Approach Character 5	Device Character 6	Qualifier Character 7
X Lacrimal Duct, Right **Y** Lacrimal Duct, Left	**0** Open **3** Percutaneous **7** Via Natural or Artificial Opening **8** Via Natural or Artificial Opening 　Endoscopic	**Z** No Device	**Z** No Qualifier

0   Medical and Surgical
8   Eye
7   Dilation: Expanding an orifice or the lumen of a tubular body part

Body Part Character 4	Approach Character 5	Device Character 6	Qualifier Character 7
X Lacrimal Duct, Right **Y** Lacrimal Duct, Left	**0** Open **3** Percutaneous **7** Via Natural or Artificial Opening **8** Via Natural or Artificial Opening 　Endoscopic	**D** Intraluminal Device **Z** No Device	**Z** No Qualifier

0   Medical and Surgical
8   Eye
9   Drainage: Taking or letting out fluids and/or gases from a body part

Body Part Character 4	Approach Character 5	Device Character 6	Qualifier Character 7
0 Eye, Right **1** Eye, Left **6** Sclera, Right **7** Sclera, Left **8** Cornea, Right **9** Cornea, Left **S** Conjunctiva, Right **T** Conjunctiva, Left	**X** External	**0** Drainage Device	**Z** No Qualifier
0 Eye, Right **1** Eye, Left **6** Sclera, Right **7** Sclera, Left **8** Cornea, Right **9** Cornea, Left **S** Conjunctiva, Right **T** Conjunctiva, Left	**X** External	**Z** No Device	**X** Diagnostic **Z** No Qualifier
2 Anterior Chamber, Right **3** Anterior Chamber, Left **4** Vitreous, Right **5** Vitreous, Left **C** Iris, Right **D** Iris, Left **E** Retina, Right **F** Retina, Left **G** Retinal Vessel, Right **H** Retinal Vessel, Left **J** Lens, Right **K** Lens, Left	**3** Percutaneous	**0** Drainage Device	**Z** No Qualifier
2 Anterior Chamber, Right **3** Anterior Chamber, Left **4** Vitreous, Right **5** Vitreous, Left **C** Iris, Right **D** Iris, Left **E** Retina, Right **F** Retina, Left **G** Retinal Vessel, Right **H** Retinal Vessel, Left **J** Lens, Right **K** Lens, Left	**3** Percutaneous	**Z** No Device	**X** Diagnostic **Z** No Qualifier
A Choroid, Right **B** Choroid, Left **L** Extraocular Muscle, Right **M** Extraocular Muscle, Left **V** Lacrimal Gland, Right **W** Lacrimal Gland, Left	**0** Open **3** Percutaneous	**0** Drainage Device	**Z** No Qualifier

Continued on next page

0 Medical and Surgical
8 Eye
9 Drainage: Taking or letting out fluids and/or gases from a body part

Continued from previous page

Body Part Character 4	Approach Character 5	Device Character 6	Qualifier Character 7
A Choroid, Right **B** Choroid, Left **L** Extraocular Muscle, Right **M** Extraocular Muscle, Left **V** Lacrimal Gland, Right **W** Lacrimal Gland, Left	**0** Open **3** Percutaneous	**Z** No Device	**X** Diagnostic **Z** No Qualifier
N Upper Eyelid, Right **P** Upper Eyelid, Left **Q** Lower Eyelid, Right **R** Lower Eyelid, Left	**0** Open **3** Percutaneous **X** External	**0** Drainage Device	**Z** No Qualifier
N Upper Eyelid, Right **P** Upper Eyelid, Left **Q** Lower Eyelid, Right **R** Lower Eyelid, Left	**0** Open **3** Percutaneous **X** External	**Z** No Device	**X** Diagnostic **Z** No Qualifier
X Lacrimal Duct, Right **Y** Lacrimal Duct, Left	**0** Open **3** Percutaneous **7** Via Natural or Artificial Opening **8** Via Natural or Artificial Opening Endoscopic	**0** Drainage Device	**Z** No Qualifier
X Lacrimal Duct, Right **Y** Lacrimal Duct, Left	**0** Open **3** Percutaneous **7** Via Natural or Artificial Opening **8** Via Natural or Artificial Opening Endoscopic	**Z** No Device	**X** Diagnostic **Z** No Qualifier

0 Medical and Surgical
8 Eye
B Excision: Cutting out or off, without replacement, a portion of a body part

Body Part Character 4	Approach Character 5	Device Character 6	Qualifier Character 7
0 Eye, Right **1** Eye, Left **N** Upper Eyelid, Right **P** Upper Eyelid, Left **Q** Lower Eyelid, Right **R** Lower Eyelid, Left	**0** Open **3** Percutaneous **X** External	**Z** No Device	**X** Diagnostic **Z** No Qualifier
4 Vitreous, Right **5** Vitreous, Left **C** Iris, Right **D** Iris, Left **E** Retina, Right **F** Retina, Left **J** Lens, Right **K** Lens, Left	**3** Percutaneous	**Z** No Device	**X** Diagnostic **Z** No Qualifier
6 Sclera, Right **7** Sclera, Left **8** Cornea, Right **9** Cornea, Left **S** Conjunctiva, Right **T** Conjunctiva, Left	**X** External	**Z** No Device	**X** Diagnostic **Z** No Qualifier
A Choroid, Right **B** Choroid, Left **L** Extraocular Muscle, Right **M** Extraocular Muscle, Left **V** Lacrimal Gland, Right **W** Lacrimal Gland, Left	**0** Open **3** Percutaneous	**Z** No Device	**X** Diagnostic **Z** No Qualifier
X Lacrimal Duct, Right **Y** Lacrimal Duct, Left	**0** Open **3** Percutaneous **7** Via Natural or Artificial Opening **8** Via Natural or Artificial Opening Endoscopic	**Z** No Device	**X** Diagnostic **Z** No Qualifier

0 Medical and Surgical
8 Eye
C Extirpation: Taking or cutting out solid matter from a body part

Body Part Character 4	Approach Character 5	Device Character 6	Qualifier Character 7
0 Eye, Right 1 Eye, Left 6 Sclera, Right 7 Sclera, Left 8 Cornea, Right 9 Cornea, Left S Conjunctiva, Right T Conjunctiva, Left	X External	Z No Device	Z No Qualifier
2 Anterior Chamber, Right 3 Anterior Chamber, Left 4 Vitreous, Right 5 Vitreous, Left C Iris, Right D Iris, Left E Retina, Right F Retina, Left G Retinal Vessel, Right H Retinal Vessel, Left J Lens, Right K Lens, Left	3 Percutaneous X External	Z No Device	Z No Qualifier
A Choroid, Right B Choroid, Left L Extraocular Muscle, Right M Extraocular Muscle, Left N Upper Eyelid, Right P Upper Eyelid, Left Q Lower Eyelid, Right R Lower Eyelid, Left V Lacrimal Gland, Right W Lacrimal Gland, Left	0 Open 3 Percutaneous X External	Z No Device	Z No Qualifier
X Lacrimal Duct, Right Y Lacrimal Duct, Left	0 Open 3 Percutaneous 7 Via Natural or Artificial Opening 8 Via Natural or Artificial Opening Endoscopic	Z No Device	Z No Qualifier

0 Medical and Surgical
8 Eye
D Extraction: Pulling or stripping out or off all or a portion of a body part by the use of force

Body Part Character 4	Approach Character 5	Device Character 6	Qualifier Character 7
8 Cornea, Right 9 Cornea, Left	X External	Z No Device	X Diagnostic Z No Qualifier
J Lens, Right K Lens, Left	3 Percutaneous	Z No Device	Z No Qualifier

0 Medical and Surgical
8 Eye
F Fragmentation: Breaking solid matter in a body part into pieces

Body Part Character 4	Approach Character 5	Device Character 6	Qualifier Character 7
4 Vitreous, Right 5 Vitreous, Left	3 Percutaneous X External	Z No Device	Z No Qualifier

0 Medical and Surgical
8 Eye
H Insertion: Putting in a nonbiological appliance that monitors, assists, performs or prevents a physiological function, but does not physically take the place of a body part

Body Part Character 4	Approach Character 5	Device Character 6	Qualifier Character 7
0 Eye, Right 1 Eye, Left	X External	1 Radioactive Element 3 Infusion Device	Z No Qualifier

0 **Medical and Surgical**
8 **Eye**
J **Inspection:**   Visually and/or manually exploring a body part

Body Part Character 4	Approach Character 5	Device Character 6	Qualifier Character 7
0 Eye, Right 1 Eye, Left 2 Anterior Chamber, Right 3 Anterior Chamber, Left 4 Vitreous, Right 5 Vitreous, Left 6 Sclera, Right 7 Sclera, Left 8 Cornea, Right 9 Cornea, Left C Iris, Right D Iris, Left E Retina, Right F Retina, Left G Retinal Vessel, Right H Retinal Vessel, Left J Lens, Right K Lens, Left S Conjunctiva, Right T Conjunctiva, Left	X External	Z No Device	Z No Qualifier
A Choroid, Right B Choroid, Left L Extraocular Muscle, Right M Extraocular Muscle, Left N Upper Eyelid, Right P Upper Eyelid, Left Q Lower Eyelid, Right R Lower Eyelid, Left V Lacrimal Gland, Right W Lacrimal Gland, Left	0 Open X External	Z No Device	Z No Qualifier
X Lacrimal Duct, Right Y Lacrimal Duct, Left	0 Open 7 Via Natural or Artificial Opening 8 Via Natural or Artificial Opening Endoscopic X External	Z No Device	Z No Qualifier

0 **Medical and Surgical**
8 **Eye**
L **Occlusion:**   Completely closing an orifice or lumen of a tubular body part

Body Part Character 4	Approach Character 5	Device Character 6	Qualifier Character 7
X Lacrimal Duct, Right Y Lacrimal Duct, Left	0 Open 3 Percutaneous	C Extraluminal Device D Intraluminal Device Z No Device	Z No Qualifier
X Lacrimal Duct, Right Y Lacrimal Duct, Left	7 Via Natural or Artificial Opening 8 Via Natural or Artificial Opening Endoscopic	D Intraluminal Device Z No Device	Z No Qualifier

0 **Medical and Surgical**
8 **Eye**
M **Reattachment:**   Putting back in or on all or a portion of a separated body part to its normal location or other suitable location

Body Part Character 4	Approach Character 5	Device Character 6	Qualifier Character 7
N Upper Eyelid, Right P Upper Eyelid, Left Q Lower Eyelid, Right R Lower Eyelid, Left	X External	Z No Device	Z No Qualifier

0   **Medical and Surgical**
8   **Eye**
N   **Release:**   Freeing a body part from an abnormal physical constraint

Body Part Character 4	Approach Character 5	Device Character 6	Qualifier Character 7
0 Eye, Right **1** Eye, Left **6** Sclera, Right **7** Sclera, Left **8** Cornea, Right **9** Cornea, Left **S** Conjunctiva, Right **T** Conjunctiva, Left	**X** External	**Z** No Device	**Z** No Qualifier
2 Anterior Chamber, Right **3** Anterior Chamber, Left **4** Vitreous, Right **5** Vitreous, Left **C** Iris, Right **D** Iris, Left **E** Retina, Right **F** Retina, Left **G** Retinal Vessel, Right **H** Retinal Vessel, Left **J** Lens, Right **K** Lens, Left	**3** Percutaneous	**Z** No Device	**Z** No Qualifier
A Choroid, Right **B** Choroid, Left **L** Extraocular Muscle, Right **M** Extraocular Muscle, Left **V** Lacrimal Gland, Right **W** Lacrimal Gland, Left	**0** Open **3** Percutaneous	**Z** No Device	**Z** No Qualifier
N Upper Eyelid, Right **P** Upper Eyelid, Left **Q** Lower Eyelid, Right **R** Lower Eyelid, Left	**0** Open **3** Percutaneous **X** External	**Z** No Device	**Z** No Qualifier
X Lacrimal Duct, Right **Y** Lacrimal Duct, Left	**0** Open **3** Percutaneous **7** Via Natural or Artificial Opening **8** Via Natural or Artificial Opening Endoscopic	**Z** No Device	**Z** No Qualifier

0   **Medical and Surgical**
8   **Eye**
P   **Removal:**   Taking out or off a device from a body part

Body Part Character 4	Approach Character 5	Device Character 6	Qualifier Character 7
0 Eye, Right **1** Eye, Left	**0** Open **3** Percutaneous **7** Via Natural or Artificial Opening **8** Via Natural or Artificial Opening Endoscopic **X** External	**0** Drainage Device **1** Radioactive Element **3** Infusion Device **7** Autologous Tissue Substitute **C** Extraluminal Device **D** Intraluminal Device **J** Synthetic Substitute **K** Nonautologous Tissue Substitute	**Z** No Qualifier
J Lens, Right **K** Lens, Left	**3** Percutaneous	**J** Synthetic Substitute	**Z** No Qualifier
L Extraocular Muscle, Right **M** Extraocular Muscle, Left	**0** Open **3** Percutaneous	**0** Drainage Device **7** Autologous Tissue Substitute **J** Synthetic Substitute **K** Nonautologous Tissue Substitute	**Z** No Qualifier

0   **Medical and Surgical**
8   **Eye**
Q   **Repair:**   Restoring, to the extent possible, a body part to its normal anatomic structure and function

Body Part Character 4	Approach Character 5	Device Character 6	Qualifier Character 7
0 Eye, Right **1** Eye, Left **6** Sclera, Right **7** Sclera, Left **8** Cornea, Right **9** Cornea, Left **S** Conjunctiva, Right **T** Conjunctiva, Left	**X** External	**Z** No Device	**Z** No Qualifier
2 Anterior Chamber, Right **3** Anterior Chamber, Left **4** Vitreous, Right **5** Vitreous, Left **C** Iris, Right **D** Iris, Left **E** Retina, Right **F** Retina, Left **G** Retinal Vessel, Right **H** Retinal Vessel, Left **J** Lens, Right **K** Lens, Left	**3** Percutaneous	**Z** No Device	**Z** No Qualifier
A Choroid, Right **B** Choroid, Left **L** Extraocular Muscle, Right **M** Extraocular Muscle, Left **V** Lacrimal Gland, Right **W** Lacrimal Gland, Left	**0** Open **3** Percutaneous	**Z** No Device	**Z** No Qualifier
N Upper Eyelid, Right **P** Upper Eyelid, Left **Q** Lower Eyelid, Right **R** Lower Eyelid, Left	**0** Open **3** Percutaneous **X** External	**Z** No Device	**Z** No Qualifier
X Lacrimal Duct, Right **Y** Lacrimal Duct, Left	**0** Open **3** Percutaneous **7** Via Natural or Artificial Opening **8** Via Natural or Artificial Opening Endoscopic	**Z** No Device	**Z** No Qualifier

0   **Medical and Surgical**
8   **Eye**
R   **Replacement:**   Putting in or on biological or synthetic material that physically takes the place and/or function of all or a portion of a body part

Body Part Character 4	Approach Character 5	Device Character 6	Qualifier Character 7
0 Eye, Right **1** Eye, Left **A** Choroid, Right **B** Choroid, Left	**0** Open **3** Percutaneous	**7** Autologous Tissue Substitute **J** Synthetic Substitute **K** Nonautologous Tissue Substitute	**Z** No Qualifier
4 Vitreous, Right **5** Vitreous, Left **C** Iris, Right **D** Iris, Left **G** Retinal Vessel, Right **H** Retinal Vessel, Left	**3** Percutaneous	**7** Autologous Tissue Substitute **J** Synthetic Substitute **K** Nonautologous Tissue Substitute	**Z** No Qualifier
6 Sclera, Right **7** Sclera, Left **S** Conjunctiva, Right **T** Conjunctiva, Left	**X** External	**7** Autologous Tissue Substitute **J** Synthetic Substitute **K** Nonautologous Tissue Substitute	**Z** No Qualifier
8 Cornea, Right **9** Cornea, Left	**3** Percutaneous **X** External	**7** Autologous Tissue Substitute **J** Synthetic Substitute **K** Nonautologous Tissue Substitute	**Z** No Qualifier
J Lens, Right **K** Lens, Left	**3** Percutaneous	**7** Autologous Tissue Substitute **K** Nonautologous Tissue Substitute	**Z** No Qualifier
J Lens, Right **K** Lens, Left	**3** Percutaneous	**J** Synthetic Substitute	**5** Intraocular Telescope **Z** No Qualifier
N Upper Eyelid, Right **P** Upper Eyelid, Left **Q** Lower Eyelid, Right **R** Lower Eyelid, Left	**0** Open **3** Percutaneous **X** External	**7** Autologous Tissue Substitute **J** Synthetic Substitute **K** Nonautologous Tissue Substitute	**Z** No Qualifier

Continued on next page

0 Medical and Surgical
8 Eye
R Replacement: *Continued from previous page*

Putting in or on biological or synthetic material that physically takes the place and/or function of all or a portion of a body part

Body Part Character 4	Approach Character 5	Device Character 6	Qualifier Character 7
X Lacrimal Duct, Right **Y** Lacrimal Duct, Left	**0** Open **3** Percutaneous **7** Via Natural or Artificial Opening **8** Via Natural or Artificial Opening Endoscopic	**7** Autologous Tissue Substitute **J** Synthetic Substitute **K** Nonautologous Tissue Substitute	**Z** No Qualifier

0 Medical and Surgical
8 Eye
S Reposition: Moving to its normal location or other suitable location all or a portion of a body part

Body Part Character 4	Approach Character 5	Device Character 6	Qualifier Character 7
C Iris, Right **D** Iris, Left **G** Retinal Vessel, Right **H** Retinal Vessel, Left **J** Lens, Right **K** Lens, Left	**3** Percutaneous	**Z** No Device	**Z** No Qualifier
L Extraocular Muscle, Right **M** Extraocular Muscle, Left **V** Lacrimal Gland, Right **W** Lacrimal Gland, Left	**0** Open **3** Percutaneous	**Z** No Device	**Z** No Qualifier
X Lacrimal Duct, Right **Y** Lacrimal Duct, Left	**0** Open **3** Percutaneous **7** Via Natural or Artificial Opening **8** Via Natural or Artificial Opening Endoscopic	**Z** No Device	**Z** No Qualifier

0 Medical and Surgical
8 Eye
T Resection: Cutting out or off, without replacement, all of a body part

Body Part Character 4	Approach Character 5	Device Character 6	Qualifier Character 7
0 Eye, Right **1** Eye, Left **8** Cornea, Right **9** Cornea, Left	**X** External	**Z** No Device	**Z** No Qualifier
4 Vitreous, Right **5** Vitreous, Left **C** Iris, Right **D** Iris, Left **J** Lens, Right **K** Lens, Left	**3** Percutaneous	**Z** No Device	**Z** No Qualifier
L Extraocular Muscle, Right **M** Extraocular Muscle, Left **V** Lacrimal Gland, Right **W** Lacrimal Gland, Left	**0** Open **3** Percutaneous	**Z** No Device	**Z** No Qualifier
N Upper Eyelid, Right **P** Upper Eyelid, Left **Q** Lower Eyelid, Right **R** Lower Eyelid, Left	**0** Open **X** External	**Z** No Device	**Z** No Qualifier
X Lacrimal Duct, Right **Y** Lacrimal Duct, Left	**0** Open **3** Percutaneous **7** Via Natural or Artificial Opening **8** Via Natural or Artificial Opening Endoscopic	**Z** No Device	**Z** No Qualifier

0 **Medical and Surgical**
8 **Eye**
U **Supplement:** Putting in or on biological or synthetic material that physically reinforces and/or augments the function of a portion of a body part

Body Part Character 4	Approach Character 5	Device Character 6	Qualifier Character 7
8 Cornea, Right 9 Cornea, Left N Upper Eyelid, Right P Upper Eyelid, Left Q Lower Eyelid, Right R Lower Eyelid, Left	0 Open 3 Percutaneous X External	7 Autologous Tissue Substitute J Synthetic Substitute K Nonautologous Tissue Substitute	Z No Qualifier
C Iris, Right D Iris, Left E Retina, Right F Retina, Left G Retinal Vessel, Right H Retinal Vessel, Left L Extraocular Muscle, Right M Extraocular Muscle, Left	0 Open 3 Percutaneous	7 Autologous Tissue Substitute J Synthetic Substitute K Nonautologous Tissue Substitute	Z No Qualifier
X Lacrimal Duct, Right Y Lacrimal Duct, Left	0 Open 3 Percutaneous 7 Via Natural or Artificial Opening 8 Via Natural or Artificial Opening Endoscopic	7 Autologous Tissue Substitute J Synthetic Substitute K Nonautologous Tissue Substitute	Z No Qualifier

0 **Medical and Surgical**
8 **Eye**
V **Restriction:** Partially closing the orifice or lumen of a tubular body part

Body Part Character 4	Approach Character 5	Device Character 6	Qualifier Character 7
X Lacrimal Duct, Right Y Lacrimal Duct, Left	0 Open 3 Percutaneous	C Extraluminal Device D Intraluminal Device Z No Device	Z No Qualifier
X Lacrimal Duct, Right Y Lacrimal Duct, Left	7 Via Natural or Artificial Opening 8 Via Natural or Artificial Opening Endoscopic	D Intraluminal Device Z No Device	Z No Qualifier

0 **Medical and Surgical**
8 **Eye**
W **Revision:** Connecting to the extent possible a malfunctioning or displaced device

Body Part Character 4	Approach Character 5	Device Character 6	Qualifier Character 7
0 Eye, Right 1 Eye, Left	0 Open 3 Percutaneous 7 Via Natural or Artificial Opening 8 Via Natural or Artificial Opening Endoscopic X External	0 Drainage Device 3 Infusion Device 7 Autologous Tissue Substitute C Extraluminal Device D Intraluminal Device J Synthetic Substitute K Nonautologous Tissue Substitute	Z No Qualifier
J Lens, Right K Lens, Left	3 Percutaneous X External	J Synthetic Substitute	Z No Qualifier
L Extraocular Muscle, Right M Extraocular Muscle, Left	0 Open 3 Percutaneous	0 Drainage Device 7 Autologous Tissue Substitute J Synthetic Substitute K Nonautologous Tissue Substitute	Z No Qualifier

0 **Medical and Surgical**
8 **Eye**
X **Transfer:** Moving, without taking out, all or a portion of a body part to another location to take over the function of all or a portion of a body part

Body Part Character 4	Approach Character 5	Device Character 6	Qualifier Character 7
L Extraocular Muscle, Right M Extraocular Muscle, Left	0 Open 3 Percutaneous	Z No Device	Z No Qualifier

Ear, Nose, Sinus 090–09W

0   **Medical and Surgical**
9   **Ear, Nose, Sinus**
0   **Alteration:**   Modifying the anatomic structure of a body part without affecting the function of the body part

Body Part Character 4	Approach Character 5	Device Character 6	Qualifier Character 7
0 External Ear, Right **1** External Ear, Left **2** External Ear, Bilateral **K** Nose	**0** Open **3** Percutaneous **4** Percutaneous Endoscopic **X** External	**7** Autologous Tissue Substitute **J** Synthetic Substitute **K** Nonautologous Tissue Substitute **Z** No Device	**Z** No Qualifier

0   **Medical and Surgical**
9   **Ear, Nose, Sinus**
1   **Bypass:**   Altering the route of passage of the contents of a tubular body part

Body Part Character 4	Approach Character 5	Device Character 6	Qualifier Character 7
D Inner Ear, Right **E** Inner Ear, Left	**0** Open	**7** Autologous Tissue Substitute **J** Synthetic Substitute **K** Nonautologous Tissue Substitute **Z** No Device	**0** Endolymphatic

0   **Medical and Surgical**
9   **Ear, Nose, Sinus**
2   **Change:**   Taking out or off a device from a body part and putting back an identical or similar device in or on the same body part without cutting or puncturing the skin or a mucous membrane

Body Part Character 4	Approach Character 5	Device Character 6	Qualifier Character 7
H Ear, Right **J** Ear, Left **K** Nose **Y** Sinus	**X** External	**0** Drainage Device **Y** Other Device	**Z** No Qualifier

0   **Medical and Surgical**
9   **Ear, Nose, Sinus**
5   **Destruction:**   Physical eradication of all or a portion of a body part by the direct use of energy, force, or a destructive agent

Body Part Character 4	Approach Character 5	Device Character 6	Qualifier Character 7
0 External Ear, Right **1** External Ear, Left **K** Nose	**0** Open **3** Percutaneous **4** Percutaneous Endoscopic **X** External	**Z** No Device	**Z** No Qualifier
3 External Auditory Canal, Right **4** External Auditory Canal, Left	**0** Open **3** Percutaneous **4** Percutaneous Endoscopic **7** Via Natural or Artificial Opening **8** Via Natural or Artificial Opening Endoscopic **X** External	**Z** No Device	**Z** No Qualifier
5 Middle Ear, Right **6** Middle Ear, Left **9** Auditory Ossicle, Right **A** Auditory Ossicle, Left **D** Inner Ear, Right **E** Inner Ear, Left	**0** Open	**Z** No Device	**Z** No Qualifier
7 Tympanic Membrane, Right **8** Tympanic Membrane, Left **F** Eustachian Tube, Right **G** Eustachian Tube, Left **L** Nasal Turbinate **N** Nasopharynx	**0** Open **3** Percutaneous **4** Percutaneous Endoscopic **7** Via Natural or Artificial Opening **8** Via Natural or Artificial Opening Endoscopic	**Z** No Device	**Z** No Qualifier

Continued on next page

0 **Medical and Surgical**   *Continued from previous page*
9 **Ear, Nose, Sinus**
5 **Destruction:**   Physical eradication of all or a portion of a body part by the direct use of energy, force, or a destructive agent

Body Part Character 4	Approach Character 5	Device Character 6	Qualifier Character 7
B Mastoid Sinus, Right **C** Mastoid Sinus, Left **M** Nasal Septum **P** Accessory Sinus **Q** Maxillary Sinus, Right **R** Maxillary Sinus, Left **S** Frontal Sinus, Right **T** Frontal Sinus, Left **U** Ethmoid Sinus, Right **V** Ethmoid Sinus, Left **W** Sphenoid Sinus, Right **X** Sphenoid Sinus, Left	**0** Open **3** Percutaneous **4** Percutaneous Endoscopic	**Z** No Device	**Z** No Qualifier

0 **Medical and Surgical**
9 **Ear, Nose, Sinus**
7 **Dilation:**   Expanding an orifice or the lumen of a tubular body part

Body Part Character 4	Approach Character 5	Device Character 6	Qualifier Character 7
F Eustachian Tube, Right **G** Eustachian Tube, Left	**0** Open **7** Via Natural or Artificial Opening **8** Via Natural or Artificial Opening Endoscopic	**D** Intraluminal Device **Z** No Device	**Z** No Qualifier
F Eustachian Tube, Right **G** Eustachian Tube, Left	**3** Percutaneous **4** Percutaneous Endoscopic	**Z** No Device	**Z** No Qualifier

0 **Medical and Surgical**
9 **Ear, Nose, Sinus**
8 **Division:**   Cutting into a body part without draining fluids and/or gases from the body part in order to separate or transect a body part

Body Part Character 4	Approach Character 5	Device Character 6	Qualifier Character 7
L Nasal Turbinate	**0** Open **3** Percutaneous **4** Percutaneous Endoscopic **7** Via Natural or Artificial Opening **8** Via Natural or Artificial Opening Endoscopic	**Z** No Device	**Z** No Qualifier

0 **Medical and Surgical**
9 **Ear, Nose, Sinus**
9 **Drainage:**   Taking or letting out fluids and/or gases from a body part

Body Part Character 4	Approach Character 5	Device Character 6	Qualifier Character 7
0 External Ear, Right **1** External Ear, Left **K** Nose	**0** Open **3** Percutaneous **4** Percutaneous Endoscopic **X** External	**0** Drainage Device	**Z** No Qualifier
0 External Ear, Right **1** External Ear, Left **K** Nose	**0** Open **3** Percutaneous **4** Percutaneous Endoscopic **X** External	**Z** No Device	**X** Diagnostic **Z** No Qualifier
3 External Auditory Canal, Right **4** External Auditory Canal, Left	**0** Open **3** Percutaneous **4** Percutaneous Endoscopic **7** Via Natural or Artificial Opening **8** Via Natural or Artificial Opening Endoscopic **X** External	**0** Drainage Device	**Z** No Qualifier
3 External Auditory Canal, Right **4** External Auditory Canal, Left	**0** Open **3** Percutaneous **4** Percutaneous Endoscopic **7** Via Natural or Artificial Opening **8** Via Natural or Artificial Opening Endoscopic **X** External	**Z** No Device	**X** Diagnostic **Z** No Qualifier

Continued on next page

0 Medical and Surgical
9 Ear, Nose, Sinus
9 Drainage: Taking or letting out fluids and/or gases from a body part

Continued from previous page

Body Part Character 4	Approach Character 5	Device Character 6	Qualifier Character 7
5 Middle Ear, Right 6 Middle Ear, Left 9 Auditory Ossicle, Right A Auditory Ossicle, Left D Inner Ear, Right E Inner Ear, Left	0 Open	0 Drainage Device	Z No Qualifier
5 Middle Ear, Right 6 Middle Ear, Left 9 Auditory Ossicle, Right A Auditory Ossicle, Left D Inner Ear, Right E Inner Ear, Left	0 Open	Z No Device	X Diagnostic Z No Qualifier
7 Tympanic Membrane, Right 8 Tympanic Membrane, Left F Eustachian Tube, Right G Eustachian Tube, Left L Nasal Turbinate N Nasopharynx	0 Open 3 Percutaneous 4 Percutaneous Endoscopic 7 Via Natural or Artificial Opening 8 Via Natural or Artificial Opening Endoscopic	0 Drainage Device	Z No Qualifier
7 Tympanic Membrane, Right 8 Tympanic Membrane, Left F Eustachian Tube, Right G Eustachian Tube, Left L Nasal Turbinate N Nasopharynx	0 Open 3 Percutaneous 4 Percutaneous Endoscopic 7 Via Natural or Artificial Opening 8 Via Natural or Artificial Opening Endoscopic	Z No Device	X Diagnostic Z No Qualifier
B Mastoid Sinus, Right C Mastoid Sinus, Left M Nasal Septum P Accessory Sinus Q Maxillary Sinus, Right R Maxillary Sinus, Left S Frontal Sinus, Right T Frontal Sinus, Left U Ethmoid Sinus, Right V Ethmoid Sinus, Left W Sphenoid Sinus, Right X Sphenoid Sinus, Left	0 Open 3 Percutaneous 4 Percutaneous Endoscopic	0 Drainage Device	Z No Qualifier
B Mastoid Sinus, Right C Mastoid Sinus, Left M Nasal Septum P Accessory Sinus Q Maxillary Sinus, Right R Maxillary Sinus, Left S Frontal Sinus, Right T Frontal Sinus, Left U Ethmoid Sinus, Right V Ethmoid Sinus, Left W Sphenoid Sinus, Right X Sphenoid Sinus, Left	0 Open 3 Percutaneous 4 Percutaneous Endoscopic	Z No Device	X Diagnostic Z No Qualifier

0 Medical and Surgical
9 Ear, Nose, Sinus
B Excision: Cutting out or off, without replacement, a portion of a body part

Body Part Character 4	Approach Character 5	Device Character 6	Qualifier Character 7
0 External Ear, Right 1 External Ear, Left K Nose	0 Open 3 Percutaneous 4 Percutaneous Endoscopic X External	Z No Device	X Diagnostic Z No Qualifier
3 External Auditory Canal, Right 4 External Auditory Canal, Left	0 Open 3 Percutaneous 4 Percutaneous Endoscopic 7 Via Natural or Artificial Opening 8 Via Natural or Artificial Opening Endoscopic X External	Z No Device	X Diagnostic Z No Qualifier
5 Middle Ear, Right 6 Middle Ear, Left 9 Auditory Ossicle, Right A Auditory Ossicle, Left D Inner Ear, Right E Inner Ear, Left	0 Open	Z No Device	X Diagnostic Z No Qualifier

Continued on next page

0   **Medical and Surgical**   *Continued from previous page*
9   **Ear, Nose, Sinus**
B   **Excision:**   Cutting out or off, without replacement, a portion of a body part

Body Part Character 4	Approach Character 5	Device Character 6	Qualifier Character 7
7 Tympanic Membrane, Right 8 Tympanic Membrane, Left F Eustachian Tube, Right G Eustachian Tube, Left L Nasal Turbinate N Nasopharynx	0 Open 3 Percutaneous 4 Percutaneous Endoscopic 7 Via Natural or Artificial Opening 8 Via Natural or Artificial Opening Endoscopic	Z No Device	X Diagnostic Z No Qualifier
B Mastoid Sinus, Right C Mastoid Sinus, Left M Nasal Septum P Accessory Sinus Q Maxillary Sinus, Right R Maxillary Sinus, Left S Frontal Sinus, Right T Frontal Sinus, Left U Ethmoid Sinus, Right V Ethmoid Sinus, Left W Sphenoid Sinus, Right X Sphenoid Sinus, Left	0 Open 3 Percutaneous 4 Percutaneous Endoscopic	Z No Device	X Diagnostic Z No Qualifier

0   **Medical and Surgical**
9   **Ear, Nose, Sinus**
C   **Extirpation:**   Taking or cutting out solid matter from a body part

Body Part Character 4	Approach Character 5	Device Character 6	Qualifier Character 7
0 External Ear, Right 1 External Ear, Left K Nose	0 Open 3 Percutaneous 4 Percutaneous Endoscopic X External	Z No Device	Z No Qualifier
3 External Auditory Canal, Right 4 External Auditory Canal, Left	0 Open 3 Percutaneous 4 Percutaneous Endoscopic 7 Via Natural or Artificial Opening 8 Via Natural or Artificial Opening Endoscopic X External	Z No Device	Z No Qualifier
5 Middle Ear, Right 6 Middle Ear, Left 9 Auditory Ossicle, Right A Auditory Ossicle, Left D Inner Ear, Right E Inner Ear, Left	0 Open	Z No Device	Z No Qualifier
7 Tympanic Membrane, Right 8 Tympanic Membrane, Left F Eustachian Tube, Right G Eustachian Tube, Left L Nasal Turbinate N Nasopharynx	0 Open 3 Percutaneous 4 Percutaneous Endoscopic 7 Via Natural or Artificial Opening 8 Via Natural or Artificial Opening Endoscopic	Z No Device	Z No Qualifier
B Mastoid Sinus, Right C Mastoid Sinus, Left M Nasal Septum P Accessory Sinus Q Maxillary Sinus, Right R Maxillary Sinus, Left S Frontal Sinus, Right T Frontal Sinus, Left U Ethmoid Sinus, Right V Ethmoid Sinus, Left W Sphenoid Sinus, Right X Sphenoid Sinus, Left	0 Open 3 Percutaneous 4 Percutaneous Endoscopic	Z No Device	Z No Qualifier

0   **Medical and Surgical**
9   **Ear, Nose, Sinus**
D   **Extraction:**   Pulling or stripping out or off all or a portion of a body part by the use of force

Body Part Character 4	Approach Character 5	Device Character 6	Qualifier Character 7
7 Tympanic Membrane, Right **8** Tympanic Membrane, Left **L** Nasal Turbinate	**0** Open **3** Percutaneous **4** Percutaneous Endoscopic **7** Via Natural or Artificial Opening **8** Via Natural or Artificial Opening Endoscopic	**Z** No Device	**Z** No Qualifier
9 Auditory Ossicle, Right **A** Auditory Ossicle, Left	**0** Open	**Z** No Device	**Z** No Qualifier
B Mastoid Sinus, Right **C** Mastoid Sinus, Left **M** Nasal Septum **P** Accessory Sinus **Q** Maxillary Sinus, Right **R** Maxillary Sinus, Left **S** Frontal Sinus, Right **T** Frontal Sinus, Left **U** Ethmoid Sinus, Right **V** Ethmoid Sinus, Left **W** Sphenoid Sinus, Right **X** Sphenoid Sinus, Left	**0** Open **3** Percutaneous **4** Percutaneous Endoscopic	**Z** No Device	**Z** No Qualifier

0   **Medical and Surgical**
9   **Ear, Nose, Sinus**
H   **Insertion:**   Putting in a nonbiological appliance that monitors, assists, performs or prevents a physiological function, but does not physically take the place of a body part

Body Part Character 4	Approach Character 5	Device Character 6	Qualifier Character 7
D Inner Ear, Right **E** Inner Ear, Left	**0** Open	**S** Hearing Device	**1** Bone Conduction **2** Cochlear Prosthesis, Single Channel **3** Cochlear Prosthesis, Multiple Channel **Y** Other Hearing Device
N Nasopharynx	**7** Via Natural or Artificial Opening **8** Via Natural or Artificial Opening Endoscopic	**B** Airway	**Z** No Qualifier

0   **Medical and Surgical**
9   **Ear, Nose, Sinus**
J   **Inspection:**   Visually and/or manually exploring a body part

Body Part Character 4	Approach Character 5	Device Character 6	Qualifier Character 7
0 External Ear, Right **1** External Ear, Left **B** Mastoid Sinus, Right **C** Mastoid Sinus, Left **K** Nose **M** Nasal Septum **P** Accessory Sinus **Q** Maxillary Sinus, Right **R** Maxillary Sinus, Left **S** Frontal Sinus, Right **T** Frontal Sinus, Left **U** Ethmoid Sinus, Right **V** Ethmoid Sinus, Left **W** Sphenoid Sinus, Right **X** Sphenoid Sinus, Left	**0** Open **3** Percutaneous **4** Percutaneous Endoscopic **X** External	**Z** No Device	**Z** No Qualifier
3 External Auditory Canal, Right **4** External Auditory Canal, Left **7** Tympanic Membrane, Right **8** Tympanic Membrane, Left **F** Eustachian Tube, Right **G** Eustachian Tube, Left **L** Nasal Turbinate **N** Nasopharynx	**0** Open **3** Percutaneous **4** Percutaneous Endoscopic **7** Via Natural or Artificial Opening **8** Via Natural or Artificial Opening Endoscopic **X** External	**Z** No Device	**Z** No Qualifier

Continued on next page

0   **Medical and Surgical**   *Continued from previous page*
9   **Ear, Nose, Sinus**
J   **Inspection:**   Visually and/or manually exploring a body part

Body Part Character 4	Approach Character 5	Device Character 6	Qualifier Character 7
5 Middle Ear, Right 6 Middle Ear, Left 9 Auditory Ossicle, Right A Auditory Ossicle, Left D Inner Ear, Right E Inner Ear, Left	0 Open X External	Z No Device	Z No Qualifier

0   **Medical and Surgical**
9   **Ear, Nose, Sinus**
M   **Reattachment:**   Putting back in or on all or a portion of a separated body part to its normal location or other suitable location

Body Part Character 4	Approach Character 5	Device Character 6	Qualifier Character 7
0 External Ear, Right 1 External Ear, Left K Nose	X External	Z No Device	Z No Qualifier

0   **Medical and Surgical**
9   **Ear, Nose, Sinus**
N   **Release:**   Freeing a body part from an abnormal physical constraint

Body Part Character 4	Approach Character 5	Device Character 6	Qualifier Character 7
0 External Ear, Right 1 External Ear, Left K Nose	0 Open 3 Percutaneous 4 Percutaneous Endoscopic X External	Z No Device	Z No Qualifier
3 External Auditory Canal, Right 4 External Auditory Canal, Left	0 Open 3 Percutaneous 4 Percutaneous Endoscopic 7 Via Natural or Artificial Opening 8 Via Natural or Artificial Opening Endoscopic X External	Z No Device	Z No Qualifier
5 Middle Ear, Right 6 Middle Ear, Left 9 Auditory Ossicle, Right A Auditory Ossicle, Left D Inner Ear, Right E Inner Ear, Left	0 Open	Z No Device	Z No Qualifier
7 Tympanic Membrane, Right 8 Tympanic Membrane, Left F Eustachian Tube, Right G Eustachian Tube, Left L Nasal Turbinate N Nasopharynx	0 Open 3 Percutaneous 4 Percutaneous Endoscopic 7 Via Natural or Artificial Opening 8 Via Natural or Artificial Opening Endoscopic	Z No Device	Z No Qualifier
B Mastoid Sinus, Right C Mastoid Sinus, Left M Nasal Septum P Accessory Sinus Q Maxillary Sinus, Right R Maxillary Sinus, Left S Frontal Sinus, Right T Frontal Sinus, Left U Ethmoid Sinus, Right V Ethmoid Sinus, Left W Sphenoid Sinus, Right X Sphenoid Sinus, Left	0 Open 3 Percutaneous 4 Percutaneous Endoscopic	Z No Device	Z No Qualifier

0 Medical and Surgical
9 Ear, Nose, Sinus
P Removal: Taking out or off a device from a body part

Body Part Character 4	Approach Character 5	Device Character 6	Qualifier Character 7
7 Tympanic Membrane, Right 8 Tympanic Membrane, Left	0 Open 7 Via Natural or Artificial Opening 8 Via Natural or Artificial Opening Endoscopic X External	0 Drainage Device	Z No Qualifier
D Inner Ear, Right E Inner Ear, Left	0 Open 7 Via Natural or Artificial Opening 8 Via Natural or Artificial Opening Endoscopic	S Hearing Device	Z No Qualifier
H Ear, Right J Ear, Left	0 Open 3 Percutaneous 4 Percutaneous Endoscopic 7 Via Natural or Artificial Opening 8 Via Natural or Artificial Opening Endoscopic X External	0 Drainage Device 7 Autologous Tissue Substitute D Intraluminal Device J Synthetic Substitute K Nonautologous Tissue Substitute	Z No Qualifier
K Nose	0 Open 3 Percutaneous 4 Percutaneous Endoscopic 7 Via Natural or Artificial Opening 8 Via Natural or Artificial Opening Endoscopic X External	0 Drainage Device 7 Autologous Tissue Substitute B Airway J Synthetic Substitute K Nonautologous Tissue Substitute	Z No Qualifier
Y Sinus	0 Open 3 Percutaneous 4 Percutaneous Endoscopic X External	0 Drainage Device	Z No Qualifier

0 Medical and Surgical
9 Ear, Nose, Sinus
Q Repair: Restoring, to the extent possible, a body part to its normal anatomic structure and function

Body Part Character 4	Approach Character 5	Device Character 6	Qualifier Character 7
0 External Ear, Right 1 External Ear, Left 2 External Ear, Bilateral K Nose	0 Open 3 Percutaneous 4 Percutaneous Endoscopic X External	Z No Device	Z No Qualifier
3 External Auditory Canal, Right 4 External Auditory Canal, Left F Eustachian Tube, Right G Eustachian Tube, Left	0 Open 3 Percutaneous 4 Percutaneous Endoscopic 7 Via Natural or Artificial Opening 8 Via Natural or Artificial Opening Endoscopic X External	Z No Device	Z No Qualifier
5 Middle Ear, Right 6 Middle Ear, Left 9 Auditory Ossicle, Right A Auditory Ossicle, Left D Inner Ear, Right E Inner Ear, Left	0 Open	Z No Device	Z No Qualifier
7 Tympanic Membrane, Right 8 Tympanic Membrane, Left L Nasal Turbinate N Nasopharynx	0 Open 3 Percutaneous 4 Percutaneous Endoscopic 7 Via Natural or Artificial Opening 8 Via Natural or Artificial Opening Endoscopic	Z No Device	Z No Qualifier
B Mastoid Sinus, Right C Mastoid Sinus, Left M Nasal Septum P Accessory Sinus Q Maxillary Sinus, Right R Maxillary Sinus, Left S Frontal Sinus, Right T Frontal Sinus, Left U Ethmoid Sinus, Right V Ethmoid Sinus, Left W Sphenoid Sinus, Right X Sphenoid Sinus, Left	0 Open 3 Percutaneous 4 Percutaneous Endoscopic	Z No Device	Z No Qualifier

0   Medical and Surgical
9   Ear, Nose, Sinus
R   Replacement: Putting in or on biological or synthetic material that physically takes the place and/or function of all or a portion of a body part

Body Part Character 4	Approach Character 5	Device Character 6	Qualifier Character 7
0 External Ear, Right **1** External Ear, Left **2** External Ear, Bilateral **K** Nose	**0** Open **X** External	**7** Autologous Tissue Substitute **J** Synthetic Substitute **K** Nonautologous Tissue Substitute	**Z** No Qualifier
5 Middle Ear, Right **6** Middle Ear, Left **9** Auditory Ossicle, Right **A** Auditory Ossicle, Left **D** Inner Ear, Right **E** Inner Ear, Left	**0** Open	**7** Autologous Tissue Substitute **J** Synthetic Substitute **K** Nonautologous Tissue Substitute	**Z** No Qualifier
7 Tympanic Membrane, Right **8** Tympanic Membrane, Left **N** Nasopharynx	**0** Open **7** Via Natural or Artificial Opening **8** Via Natural or Artificial Opening Endoscopic	**7** Autologous Tissue Substitute **J** Synthetic Substitute **K** Nonautologous Tissue Substitute	**Z** No Qualifier
L Nasal Turbinate	**0** Open **3** Percutaneous **4** Percutaneous Endoscopic **7** Via Natural or Artificial Opening **8** Via Natural or Artificial Opening Endoscopic	**7** Autologous Tissue Substitute **J** Synthetic Substitute **K** Nonautologous Tissue Substitute	**Z** No Qualifier
M Nasal Septum	**0** Open **3** Percutaneous **4** Percutaneous Endoscopic	**7** Autologous Tissue Substitute **J** Synthetic Substitute **K** Nonautologous Tissue Substitute	**Z** No Qualifier

0   Medical and Surgical
9   Ear, Nose, Sinus
S   Reposition: Moving to its normal location or other suitable location all or a portion of a body part

Body Part Character 4	Approach Character 5	Device Character 6	Qualifier Character 7
0 External Ear, Right **1** External Ear, Left **2** External Ear, Bilateral **K** Nose	**0** Open **4** Percutaneous Endoscopic **X** External	**Z** No Device	**Z** No Qualifier
7 Tympanic Membrane, Right **8** Tympanic Membrane, Left **F** Eustachian Tube, Right **G** Eustachian Tube, Left **L** Nasal Turbinate	**0** Open **4** Percutaneous Endoscopic **7** Via Natural or Artificial Opening **8** Via Natural or Artificial Opening Endoscopic	**Z** No Device	**Z** No Qualifier
9 Auditory Ossicle, Right **A** Auditory Ossicle, Left	**0** Open **4** Percutaneous Endoscopic	**Z** No Device	**Z** No Qualifier

0   Medical and Surgical
9   Ear, Nose, Sinus
T   Resection: Cutting out or off, without replacement, all of a body part

Body Part Character 4	Approach Character 5	Device Character 6	Qualifier Character 7
0 External Ear, Right **1** External Ear, Left **K** Nose	**0** Open **4** Percutaneous Endoscopic **X** External	**Z** No Device	**Z** No Qualifier
5 Middle Ear, Right **6** Middle Ear, Left **9** Auditory Ossicle, Right **A** Auditory Ossicle, Left **D** Inner Ear, Right **E** Inner Ear, Left	**0** Open	**Z** No Device	**Z** No Qualifier
7 Tympanic Membrane, Right **8** Tympanic Membrane, Left **F** Eustachian Tube, Right **G** Eustachian Tube, Left **L** Nasal Turbinate **N** Nasopharynx	**0** Open **4** Percutaneous Endoscopic **7** Via Natural or Artificial Opening **8** Via Natural or Artificial Opening Endoscopic	**Z** No Device	**Z** No Qualifier

Continued on next page

0   **Medical and Surgical**   *Continued from previous page*

9   **Ear, Nose, Sinus**
T   **Resection:**   Cutting out or off, without replacement, all of a body part

Body Part Character 4	Approach Character 5	Device Character 6	Qualifier Character 7
B Mastoid Sinus, Right **C** Mastoid Sinus, Left **M** Nasal Septum **P** Accessory Sinus **Q** Maxillary Sinus, Right **R** Maxillary Sinus, Left **S** Frontal Sinus, Right **T** Frontal Sinus, Left **U** Ethmoid Sinus, Right **V** Ethmoid Sinus, Left **W** Sphenoid Sinus, Right **X** Sphenoid Sinus, Left	**0** Open **4** Percutaneous Endoscopic	**Z** No Device	**Z** No Qualifier

0   **Medical and Surgical**
9   **Ear, Nose, Sinus**
U   **Supplement:**   Putting in or on biological or synthetic material that physically reinforces and/or augments the function of a portion of a body part

Body Part Character 4	Approach Character 5	Device Character 6	Qualifier Character 7
0 External Ear, Right **1** External Ear, Left **2** External Ear, Bilateral **K** Nose	**0** Open **X** External	**7** Autologous Tissue Substitute **J** Synthetic Substitute **K** Nonautologous Tissue Substitute	**Z** No Qualifier
5 Middle Ear, Right **6** Middle Ear, Left **9** Auditory Ossicle, Right **A** Auditory Ossicle, Left **D** Inner Ear, Right **E** Inner Ear, Left	**0** Open	**7** Autologous Tissue Substitute **J** Synthetic Substitute **K** Nonautologous Tissue Substitute	**Z** No Qualifier
7 Tympanic Membrane, Right **8** Tympanic Membrane, Left **N** Nasopharynx	**0** Open **7** Via Natural or Artificial Opening **8** Via Natural or Artificial Opening Endoscopic	**7** Autologous Tissue Substitute **J** Synthetic Substitute **K** Nonautologous Tissue Substitute	**Z** No Qualifier
L Nasal Turbinate	**0** Open **3** Percutaneous **4** Percutaneous Endoscopic **7** Via Natural or Artificial Opening **8** Via Natural or Artificial Opening Endoscopic	**7** Autologous Tissue Substitute **J** Synthetic Substitute **K** Nonautologous Tissue Substitute	**Z** No Qualifier
M Nasal Septum	**0** Open **3** Percutaneous **4** Percutaneous Endoscopic	**7** Autologous Tissue Substitute **J** Synthetic Substitute **K** Nonautologous Tissue Substitute	**Z** No Qualifier

0   **Medical and Surgical**
9   **Ear, Nose, Sinus**
W   **Revision:**   Connecting to the extent possible a malfunctioning or displaced device

Body Part Character 4	Approach Character 5	Device Character 6	Qualifier Character 7
7 Tympanic Membrane, Right **8** Tympanic Membrane, Left **9** Auditory Ossicle, Right **A** Auditory Ossicle, Left	**0** Open **7** Via Natural or Artificial Opening **8** Via Natural or Artificial Opening Endoscopic	**7** Autologous Tissue Substitute **J** Synthetic Substitute **K** Nonautologous Tissue Substitute	**Z** No Qualifier
D Inner Ear, Right **E** Inner Ear, Left	**0** Open **7** Via Natural or Artificial Opening **8** Via Natural or Artificial Opening Endoscopic	**S** Hearing Device	**Z** No Qualifier
H Ear, Right **J** Ear, Left	**0** Open **3** Percutaneous **4** Percutaneous Endoscopic **7** Via Natural or Artificial Opening **8** Via Natural or Artificial Opening Endoscopic **X** External	**0** Drainage Device **7** Autologous Tissue Substitute **D** Intraluminal Device **J** Synthetic Substitute **K** Nonautologous Tissue Substitute	**Z** No Qualifier

Continued on next page

0 **Medical and Surgical**   *Continued from previous page*
9 **Ear, Nose, Sinus**
W **Revision:**   Connecting to the extent possible a malfunctioning or displaced device

Body Part Character 4	Approach Character 5	Device Character 6	Qualifier Character 7
K Nose	**0** Open **3** Percutaneous **4** Percutaneous Endoscopic **7** Via Natural or Artificial Opening **8** Via Natural or Artificial Opening Endoscopic **X** External	**0** Drainage Device **7** Autologous Tissue Substitute **B** Airway **J** Synthetic Substitute **K** Nonautologous Tissue Substitute	**Z** No Qualifier
Y Sinus	**0** Open **3** Percutaneous **4** Percutaneous Endoscopic **X** External	**0** Drainage Device	**Z** No Qualifier

Respiratory System 0B1–0BY

0   Medical and Surgical
B   Respiratory System
1   Bypass: Altering the route of passage of the contents of a tubular body part

Body Part Character 4	Approach Character 5	Device Character 6	Qualifier Character 7
1 Trachea	**0** Open	**D** Intraluminal Device	**6** Esophagus
1 Trachea	**0** Open **3** Percutaneous **4** Percutaneous Endoscopic	**F** Tracheostomy Device **Z** No Device	**4** Cutaneous

0   Medical and Surgical
B   Respiratory System
2   Change: Taking out or off a device from a body part and putting back an identical or similar device in or on the same body part without cutting or puncturing the skin or a mucous membrane

Body Part Character 4	Approach Character 5	Device Character 6	Qualifier Character 7
0 Tracheobronchial Tree **K** Lung, Right **L** Lung, Left **Q** Pleura **T** Diaphragm	**X** External	**0** Drainage Device **Y** Other Device	**Z** No Qualifier
1 Trachea	**X** External	**0** Drainage Device **E** Endotracheal Device **F** Tracheostomy Device **Y** Other Device	**Z** No Qualifier

0   Medical and Surgical
B   Respiratory System
5   Destruction: Physical eradication of all or a portion of a body part by the direct use of energy, force, or a destructive agent

Body Part Character 4	Approach Character 5	Device Character 6	Qualifier Character 7
1 Trachea **2** Carina **3** Main Bronchus, Right **4** Upper Lobe Bronchus, Right **5** Middle Lobe Bronchus, Right **6** Lower Lobe Bronchus, Right **7** Main Bronchus, Left **8** Upper Lobe Bronchus, Left **9** Lingula Bronchus **B** Lower Lobe Bronchus, Left **C** Upper Lung Lobe, Right **D** Middle Lung Lobe, Right **F** Lower Lung Lobe, Right **G** Upper Lung Lobe, Left **H** Lung Lingula **J** Lower Lung Lobe, Left **K** Lung, Right **L** Lung, Left **M** Lungs, Bilateral	**0** Open **3** Percutaneous **4** Percutaneous Endoscopic **7** Via Natural or Artificial Opening **8** Via Natural or Artificial Opening Endoscopic	**Z** No Device	**Z** No Qualifier
N Pleura, Right **P** Pleura, Left **R** Diaphragm, Right **S** Diaphragm, Left	**0** Open **3** Percutaneous **4** Percutaneous Endoscopic	**Z** No Device	**Z** No Qualifier

0 Medical and Surgical
B Respiratory System
7 Dilation: Expanding an orifice or the lumen of a tubular body part

Body Part Character 4	Approach Character 5	Device Character 6	Qualifier Character 7
1 Trachea 2 Carina 3 Main Bronchus, Right 4 Upper Lobe Bronchus, Right 5 Middle Lobe Bronchus, Right 6 Lower Lobe Bronchus, Right 7 Main Bronchus, Left 8 Upper Lobe Bronchus, Left 9 Lingula Bronchus B Lower Lobe Bronchus, Left	0 Open 3 Percutaneous 4 Percutaneous Endoscopic 7 Via Natural or Artificial Opening 8 Via Natural or Artificial Opening Endoscopic	D Intraluminal Device Z No Device	Z No Qualifier

0 Medical and Surgical
B Respiratory System
9 Drainage: Taking or letting out fluids and/or gases from a body part

Body Part Character 4	Approach Character 5	Device Character 6	Qualifier Character 7
1 Trachea 2 Carina 3 Main Bronchus, Right 4 Upper Lobe Bronchus, Right 5 Middle Lobe Bronchus, Right 6 Lower Lobe Bronchus, Right 7 Main Bronchus, Left 8 Upper Lobe Bronchus, Left 9 Lingula Bronchus B Lower Lobe Bronchus, Left C Upper Lung Lobe, Right D Middle Lung Lobe, Right F Lower Lung Lobe, Right G Upper Lung Lobe, Left H Lung Lingula J Lower Lung Lobe, Left K Lung, Right L Lung, Left M Lungs, Bilateral	0 Open 3 Percutaneous 4 Percutaneous Endoscopic 7 Via Natural or Artificial Opening 8 Via Natural or Artificial Opening Endoscopic	0 Drainage Device	Z No Qualifier
1 Trachea 2 Carina 3 Main Bronchus, Right 4 Upper Lobe Bronchus, Right 5 Middle Lobe Bronchus, Right 6 Lower Lobe Bronchus, Right 7 Main Bronchus, Left 8 Upper Lobe Bronchus, Left 9 Lingula Bronchus B Lower Lobe Bronchus, Left C Upper Lung Lobe, Right D Middle Lung Lobe, Right F Lower Lung Lobe, Right G Upper Lung Lobe, Left H Lung Lingula J Lower Lung Lobe, Left K Lung, Right L Lung, Left M Lungs, Bilateral	0 Open 3 Percutaneous 4 Percutaneous Endoscopic 7 Via Natural or Artificial Opening 8 Via Natural or Artificial Opening Endoscopic	Z No Device	X Diagnostic Z No Qualifier
N Pleura, Right P Pleura, Left R Diaphragm, Right S Diaphragm, Left	0 Open 3 Percutaneous 4 Percutaneous Endoscopic	0 Drainage Device	Z No Qualifier
N Pleura, Right P Pleura, Left R Diaphragm, Right S Diaphragm, Left	0 Open 3 Percutaneous 4 Percutaneous Endoscopic	Z No Device	X Diagnostic Z No Qualifier

0   **Medical and Surgical**
B   **Respiratory System**
B   **Excision:**   Cutting out or off, without replacement, a portion of a body part

Body Part Character 4	Approach Character 5	Device Character 6	Qualifier Character 7
1 Trachea 2 Carina 3 Main Bronchus, Right 4 Upper Lobe Bronchus, Right 5 Middle Lobe Bronchus, Right 6 Lower Lobe Bronchus, Right 7 Main Bronchus, Left 8 Upper Lobe Bronchus, Left 9 Lingula Bronchus B Lower Lobe Bronchus, Left C Upper Lung Lobe, Right D Middle Lung Lobe, Right F Lower Lung Lobe, Right G Upper Lung Lobe, Left H Lung Lingula J Lower Lung Lobe, Left K Lung, Right L Lung, Left M Lungs, Bilateral	0 Open 3 Percutaneous 4 Percutaneous Endoscopic 7 Via Natural or Artificial Opening 8 Via Natural or Artificial Opening Endoscopic	Z No Device	X Diagnostic Z No Qualifier
N Pleura, Right P Pleura, Left R Diaphragm, Right S Diaphragm, Left	0 Open 3 Percutaneous 4 Percutaneous Endoscopic	Z No Device	X Diagnostic Z No Qualifier

0   **Medical and Surgical**
B   **Respiratory System**
C   **Extirpation:**   Taking or cutting out solid matter from a body part

Body Part Character 4	Approach Character 5	Device Character 6	Qualifier Character 7
1 Trachea 2 Carina 3 Main Bronchus, Right 4 Upper Lobe Bronchus, Right 5 Middle Lobe Bronchus, Right 6 Lower Lobe Bronchus, Right 7 Main Bronchus, Left 8 Upper Lobe Bronchus, Left 9 Lingula Bronchus B Lower Lobe Bronchus, Left C Upper Lung Lobe, Right D Middle Lung Lobe, Right F Lower Lung Lobe, Right G Upper Lung Lobe, Left H Lung Lingula J Lower Lung Lobe, Left K Lung, Right L Lung, Left M Lungs, Bilateral	0 Open 3 Percutaneous 4 Percutaneous Endoscopic 7 Via Natural or Artificial Opening 8 Via Natural or Artificial Opening Endoscopic	Z No Device	Z No Qualifier
N Pleura, Right P Pleura, Left R Diaphragm, Right S Diaphragm, Left	0 Open 3 Percutaneous 4 Percutaneous Endoscopic	Z No Device	Z No Qualifier

0   **Medical and Surgical**
B   **Respiratory System**
D   **Extraction:**   Pulling or stripping out or off all or a portion of a body part by the use of force

Body Part Character 4	Approach Character 5	Device Character 6	Qualifier Character 7
N Pleura, Right P Pleura, Left	0 Open 3 Percutaneous 4 Percutaneous Endoscopic	Z No Device	X Diagnostic Z No Qualifier

0 Medical and Surgical
B Respiratory System
F Fragmentation: Breaking solid matter in a body part into pieces

Body Part Character 4	Approach Character 5	Device Character 6	Qualifier Character 7
1 Trachea 2 Carina 3 Main Bronchus, Right 4 Upper Lobe Bronchus, Right 5 Middle Lobe Bronchus, Right 6 Lower Lobe Bronchus, Right 7 Main Bronchus, Left 8 Upper Lobe Bronchus, Left 9 Lingula Bronchus B Lower Lobe Bronchus, Left	0 Open 3 Percutaneous 4 Percutaneous Endoscopic 7 Via Natural or Artificial Opening 8 Via Natural or Artificial Opening Endoscopic X External	Z No Device	Z No Qualifier

0 Medical and Surgical
B Respiratory System
H Insertion: Putting in a nonbiological appliance that monitors, assists, performs or prevents a physiological function, but does not physically take the place of a body part

Body Part Character 4	Approach Character 5	Device Character 6	Qualifier Character 7
0 Tracheobronchial Tree K Lung, Right L Lung, Left	0 Open 3 Percutaneous 4 Percutaneous Endoscopic 7 Via Natural or Artificial Opening 8 Via Natural or Artificial Opening Endoscopic	1 Radioactive Element 2 Monitoring Device 3 Infusion Device	Z No Qualifier
1 Trachea	0 Open 7 Via Natural or Artificial Opening 8 Via Natural or Artificial Opening Endoscopic	2 Monitoring Device E Endotracheal Device	Z No Qualifier
3 Main Bronchus, Right 4 Upper Lobe Bronchus, Right 5 Middle Lobe Bronchus, Right 6 Lower Lobe Bronchus, Right 7 Main Bronchus, Left 8 Upper Lobe Bronchus, Left 9 Lingula Bronchus B Lower Lobe Bronchus, Left	0 Open 3 Percutaneous 4 Percutaneous Endoscopic 7 Via Natural or Artificial Opening 8 Via Natural or Artificial Opening Endoscopic	G Endobronchial Device	Z No Qualifier
R Diaphragm, Right S Diaphragm, Left	0 Open 3 Percutaneous 4 Percutaneous Endoscopic	2 Monitoring Device M Electrode	Z No Qualifier

0 Medical and Surgical
B Respiratory System
J Inspection: Visually and/or manually exploring a body part

Body Part Character 4	Approach Character 5	Device Character 6	Qualifier Character 7
0 Tracheobronchial Tree 1 Trachea 2 Carina 3 Main Bronchus, Right 4 Upper Lobe Bronchus, Right 5 Middle Lobe Bronchus, Right 6 Lower Lobe Bronchus, Right 7 Main Bronchus, Left 8 Upper Lobe Bronchus, Left 9 Lingula Bronchus B Lower Lobe Bronchus, Left C Upper Lung Lobe, Right D Middle Lung Lobe, Right F Lower Lung Lobe, Right G Upper Lung Lobe, Left H Lung Lingula J Lower Lung Lobe, Left K Lung, Right L Lung, Left M Lungs, Bilateral	0 Open 3 Percutaneous 4 Percutaneous Endoscopic 7 Via Natural or Artificial Opening 8 Via Natural or Artificial Opening Endoscopic	Z No Device	Z No Qualifier
N Pleura, Right P Pleura, Left R Diaphragm, Right S Diaphragm, Left	0 Open 3 Percutaneous 4 Percutaneous Endoscopic	Z No Device	Z No Qualifier

0　Medical and Surgical
B　Respiratory System
L　Occlusion:　　Completely closing an orifice or lumen of a tubular body part

Body Part Character 4	Approach Character 5	Device Character 6	Qualifier Character 7
1 Trachea 2 Carina 3 Main Bronchus, Right 4 Upper Lobe Bronchus, Right 5 Middle Lobe Bronchus, Right 6 Lower Lobe Bronchus, Right 7 Main Bronchus, Left 8 Upper Lobe Bronchus, Left 9 Lingula Bronchus B Lower Lobe Bronchus, Left	0 Open 3 Percutaneous 4 Percutaneous Endoscopic	C Extraluminal Device D Intraluminal Device Z No Device	Z No Qualifier
1 Trachea 2 Carina 3 Main Bronchus, Right 4 Upper Lobe Bronchus, Right 5 Middle Lobe Bronchus, Right 6 Lower Lobe Bronchus, Right 7 Main Bronchus, Left 8 Upper Lobe Bronchus, Left 9 Lingula Bronchus B Lower Lobe Bronchus, Left	7 Via Natural or Artificial Opening 8 Via Natural or Artificial Opening Endoscopic	D Intraluminal Device Z No Device	Z No Qualifier

0　Medical and Surgical
B　Respiratory System
M　Reattachment:　　Putting back in or on all or a portion of a separated body part to its normal location or other suitable location

Body Part Character 4	Approach Character 5	Device Character 6	Qualifier Character 7
1 Trachea 2 Carina 3 Main Bronchus, Right 4 Upper Lobe Bronchus, Right 5 Middle Lobe Bronchus, Right 6 Lower Lobe Bronchus, Right 7 Main Bronchus, Left 8 Upper Lobe Bronchus, Left 9 Lingula Bronchus B Lower Lobe Bronchus, Left C Upper Lung Lobe, Right D Middle Lung Lobe, Right F Lower Lung Lobe, Right G Upper Lung Lobe, Left H Lung Lingula J Lower Lung Lobe, Left K Lung, Right L Lung, Left R Diaphragm, Right S Diaphragm, Left	0 Open	Z No Device	Z No Qualifier

0　Medical and Surgical
B　Respiratory System
N　Release:　　Freeing a body part from an abnormal physical constraint

Body Part Character 4	Approach Character 5	Device Character 6	Qualifier Character 7
1 Trachea 2 Carina 3 Main Bronchus, Right 4 Upper Lobe Bronchus, Right 5 Middle Lobe Bronchus, Right 6 Lower Lobe Bronchus, Right 7 Main Bronchus, Left 8 Upper Lobe Bronchus, Left 9 Lingula Bronchus B Lower Lobe Bronchus, Left C Upper Lung Lobe, Right D Middle Lung Lobe, Right F Lower Lung Lobe, Right G Upper Lung Lobe, Left H Lung Lingula J Lower Lung Lobe, Left K Lung, Right L Lung, Left M Lungs, Bilateral	0 Open 3 Percutaneous 4 Percutaneous Endoscopic 7 Via Natural or Artificial Opening 8 Via Natural or Artificial Opening Endoscopic	Z No Device	Z No Qualifier

Continued on next page

0 **Medical and Surgical**
B **Respiratory System**
N **Release:** Freeing a body part from an abnormal physical constraint

Continued from previous page

Body Part Character 4	Approach Character 5	Device Character 6	Qualifier Character 7
N Pleura, Right P Pleura, Left R Diaphragm, Right S Diaphragm, Left	0 Open 3 Percutaneous 4 Percutaneous Endoscopic	Z No Device	Z No Qualifier

0 **Medical and Surgical**
B **Respiratory System**
P **Removal:** Taking out or off a device from a body part

Body Part Character 4	Approach Character 5	Device Character 6	Qualifier Character 7
0 Tracheobronchial Tree	0 Open 3 Percutaneous 4 Percutaneous Endoscopic 7 Via Natural or Artificial Opening 8 Via Natural or Artificial Opening Endoscopic	0 Drainage Device 1 Radioactive Element 2 Monitoring Device 3 Infusion Device 7 Autologous Tissue Substitute C Extraluminal Device D Intraluminal Device G Endobronchial Device J Synthetic Substitute K Nonautologous Tissue Substitute	Z No Qualifier
0 Tracheobronchial Tree	X External	0 Drainage Device 1 Radioactive Element 2 Monitoring Device 3 Infusion Device D Intraluminal Device	Z No Qualifier
1 Trachea	0 Open 3 Percutaneous 4 Percutaneous Endoscopic 7 Via Natural or Artificial Opening 8 Via Natural or Artificial Opening Endoscopic	0 Drainage Device 2 Monitoring Device 7 Autologous Tissue Substitute C Extraluminal Device D Intraluminal Device E Endotracheal Device F Tracheostomy Device J Synthetic Substitute K Nonautologous Tissue Substitute	Z No Qualifier
1 Trachea	X External	0 Drainage Device 2 Monitoring Device D Intraluminal Device E Endotracheal Device F Tracheostomy Device	Z No Qualifier
K Lung, Right L Lung, Left	0 Open 3 Percutaneous 4 Percutaneous Endoscopic 7 Via Natural or Artificial Opening 8 Via Natural or Artificial Opening Endoscopic X External	0 Drainage Device 1 Radioactive Element 2 Monitoring Device 3 Infusion Device	Z No Qualifier
Q Pleura	0 Open 3 Percutaneous 4 Percutaneous Endoscopic 7 Via Natural or Artificial Opening 8 Via Natural or Artificial Opening Endoscopic X External	0 Drainage Device 1 Radioactive Element 2 Monitoring Device	Z No Qualifier
T Diaphragm	0 Open 3 Percutaneous 4 Percutaneous Endoscopic 7 Via Natural or Artificial Opening 8 Via Natural or Artificial Opening Endoscopic	0 Drainage Device 2 Monitoring Device 7 Autologous Tissue Substitute J Synthetic Substitute K Nonautologous Tissue Substitute M Electrode	Z No Qualifier
T Diaphragm	X External	0 Drainage Device 2 Monitoring Device M Electrode	Z No Qualifier

0   **Medical and Surgical**
B   **Respiratory System**
Q   **Repair:**   Restoring, to the extent possible, a body part to its normal anatomic structure and function

Body Part Character 4	Approach Character 5	Device Character 6	Qualifier Character 7
1 Trachea 2 Carina 3 Main Bronchus, Right 4 Upper Lobe Bronchus, Right 5 Middle Lobe Bronchus, Right 6 Lower Lobe Bronchus, Right 7 Main Bronchus, Left 8 Upper Lobe Bronchus, Left 9 Lingula Bronchus B Lower Lobe Bronchus, Left C Upper Lung Lobe, Right D Middle Lung Lobe, Right F Lower Lung Lobe, Right G Upper Lung Lobe, Left H Lung Lingula J Lower Lung Lobe, Left K Lung, Right L Lung, Left M Lungs, Bilateral	0 Open 3 Percutaneous 4 Percutaneous Endoscopic 7 Via Natural or Artificial Opening 8 Via Natural or Artificial Opening Endoscopic	Z No Device	Z No Qualifier
N Pleura, Right P Pleura, Left R Diaphragm, Right S Diaphragm, Left	0 Open 3 Percutaneous 4 Percutaneous Endoscopic	Z No Device	Z No Qualifier

0   **Medical and Surgical**
B   **Respiratory System**
S   **Reposition:**   Moving to its normal location or other suitable location all or a portion of a body part

Body Part Character 4	Approach Character 5	Device Character 6	Qualifier Character 7
1 Trachea 2 Carina 3 Main Bronchus, Right 4 Upper Lobe Bronchus, Right 5 Middle Lobe Bronchus, Right 6 Lower Lobe Bronchus, Right 7 Main Bronchus, Left 8 Upper Lobe Bronchus, Left 9 Lingula Bronchus B Lower Lobe Bronchus, Left C Upper Lung Lobe, Right D Middle Lung Lobe, Right F Lower Lung Lobe, Right G Upper Lung Lobe, Left H Lung Lingula J Lower Lung Lobe, Left K Lung, Right L Lung, Left R Diaphragm, Right S Diaphragm, Left	0 Open	Z No Device	Z No Qualifier

0 **Medical and Surgical**
B **Respiratory System**
T **Resection:** Cutting out or off, without replacement, all of a body part

Body Part Character 4	Approach Character 5	Device Character 6	Qualifier Character 7
1 Trachea 2 Carina 3 Main Bronchus, Right 4 Upper Lobe Bronchus, Right 5 Middle Lobe Bronchus, Right 6 Lower Lobe Bronchus, Right 7 Main Bronchus, Left 8 Upper Lobe Bronchus, Left 9 Lingula Bronchus B Lower Lobe Bronchus, Left C Upper Lung Lobe, Right D Middle Lung Lobe, Right F Lower Lung Lobe, Right G Upper Lung Lobe, Left H Lung Lingula J Lower Lung Lobe, Left K Lung, Right L Lung, Left M Lungs, Bilateral R Diaphragm, Right S Diaphragm, Left	0 Open 4 Percutaneous Endoscopic	Z No Device	Z No Qualifier

0 **Medical and Surgical**
B **Respiratory System**
U **Supplement:** Putting in or on biological or synthetic material that physically reinforces and/or augments the function of a portion of a body part

Body Part Character 4	Approach Character 5	Device Character 6	Qualifier Character 7
1 Trachea 2 Carina 3 Main Bronchus, Right 4 Upper Lobe Bronchus, Right 5 Middle Lobe Bronchus, Right 6 Lower Lobe Bronchus, Right 7 Main Bronchus, Left 8 Upper Lobe Bronchus, Left 9 Lingula Bronchus B Lower Lobe Bronchus, Left R Diaphragm, Right S Diaphragm, Left	0 Open 4 Percutaneous Endoscopic	7 Autologous Tissue Substitute J Synthetic Substitute K Nonautologous Tissue Substitute	Z No Qualifier

0 **Medical and Surgical**
B **Respiratory System**
V **Restriction:** Partially closing the orifice or lumen of a tubular body part

Body Part Character 4	Approach Character 5	Device Character 6	Qualifier Character 7
1 Trachea 2 Carina 3 Main Bronchus, Right 4 Upper Lobe Bronchus, Right 5 Middle Lobe Bronchus, Right 6 Lower Lobe Bronchus, Right 7 Main Bronchus, Left 8 Upper Lobe Bronchus, Left 9 Lingula Bronchus B Lower Lobe Bronchus, Left	0 Open 3 Percutaneous 4 Percutaneous Endoscopic	C Extraluminal Device D Intraluminal Device Z No Device	Z No Qualifier
1 Trachea 2 Carina 3 Main Bronchus, Right 4 Upper Lobe Bronchus, Right 5 Middle Lobe Bronchus, Right 6 Lower Lobe Bronchus, Right 7 Main Bronchus, Left 8 Upper Lobe Bronchus, Left 9 Lingula Bronchus B Lower Lobe Bronchus, Left	7 Via Natural or Artificial Opening 8 Via Natural or Artificial Opening Endoscopic	D Intraluminal Device Z No Device	Z No Qualifier

0 Medical and Surgical
B Respiratory System
W Revision: Connecting to the extent possible a malfunctioning or displaced device

Body Part Character 4	Approach Character 5	Device Character 6	Qualifier Character 7
0 Tracheobronchial Tree	**0** Open **3** Percutaneous **4** Percutaneous Endoscopic **7** Via Natural or Artificial Opening **8** Via Natural or Artificial Opening Endoscopic **X** External	**0** Drainage Device **2** Monitoring Device **3** Infusion Device **7** Autologous Tissue Substitute **C** Extraluminal Device **D** Intraluminal Device **G** Endobronchial Device **J** Synthetic Substitute **K** Nonautologous Tissue Substitute	**Z** No Qualifier
1 Trachea	**0** Open **3** Percutaneous **4** Percutaneous Endoscopic **7** Via Natural or Artificial Opening **8** Via Natural or Artificial Opening Endoscopic **X** External	**0** Drainage Device **2** Monitoring Device **7** Autologous Tissue Substitute **C** Extraluminal Device **D** Intraluminal Device **E** Endotracheal Device **F** Tracheostomy Device **J** Synthetic Substitute **K** Nonautologous Tissue Substitute	**Z** No Qualifier
K Lung, Right **L** Lung, Left	**0** Open **3** Percutaneous **4** Percutaneous Endoscopic **7** Via Natural or Artificial Opening **8** Via Natural or Artificial Opening Endoscopic **X** External	**0** Drainage Device **2** Monitoring Device **3** Infusion Device	**Z** No Qualifier
Q Pleura	**0** Open **3** Percutaneous **4** Percutaneous Endoscopic **7** Via Natural or Artificial Opening **8** Via Natural or Artificial Opening Endoscopic **X** External	**0** Drainage Device **2** Monitoring Device	**Z** No Qualifier
T Diaphragm	**0** Open **3** Percutaneous **4** Percutaneous Endoscopic **7** Via Natural or Artificial Opening **8** Via Natural or Artificial Opening Endoscopic **X** External	**0** Drainage Device **2** Monitoring Device **7** Autologous Tissue Substitute **J** Synthetic Substitute **K** Nonautologous Tissue Substitute **M** Electrode	**Z** No Qualifier

0 Medical and Surgical
B Respiratory System
Y Transplantation: Putting in or on all or a portion of a living body part taken from another individual or animal to physically take the place and/or function of all or a portion of a similar body part

Body Part Character 4	Approach Character 5	Device Character 6	Qualifier Character 7
C Upper Lung Lobe, Right **D** Middle Lung Lobe, Right **F** Lower Lung Lobe, Right **G** Upper Lung Lobe, Left **H** Lung Lingula **J** Lower Lung Lobe, Left **K** Lung, Right **L** Lung, Left **M** Lungs, Bilateral	**0** Open	**Z** No Device	**0** Allogeneic **1** Syngeneic **2** Zooplastic

Draft (2009)

Mouth and Throat 0C0–0CX

0 Medical and Surgical
C Mouth and Throat
0 Alteration: Modifying the anatomic structure of a body part without affecting the function of the body part

Body Part Character 4	Approach Character 5	Device Character 6	Qualifier Character 7
0 Upper Lip **1** Lower Lip	**X** External	**7** Autologous Tissue Substitute **J** Synthetic Substitute **K** Nonautologous Tissue Substitute **Z** No Device	**Z** No Qualifier

0 Medical and Surgical
C Mouth and Throat
2 Change: Taking out or off a device from a body part and putting back an identical or similar device in or on the same body part without cutting or puncturing the skin or a mucous membrane

Body Part Character 4	Approach Character 5	Device Character 6	Qualifier Character 7
A Salivary Gland **S** Larynx **Y** Mouth and Throat	**X** External	**0** Drainage Device **Y** Other Device	**Z** No Qualifier

0 Medical and Surgical
C Mouth and Throat
5 Destruction: Physical eradication of all or a portion of a body part by the direct use of energy, force, or a destructive agent

Body Part Character 4	Approach Character 5	Device Character 6	Qualifier Character 7
0 Upper Lip **1** Lower Lip **2** Hard Palate **3** Soft Palate **4** Buccal Mucosa **5** Upper Gingiva **6** Lower Gingiva **7** Tongue **N** Uvula **P** Tonsils **Q** Adenoids	**0** Open **3** Percutaneous **X** External	**Z** No Device	**Z** No Qualifier
8 Parotid Gland, Right **9** Parotid Gland, Left **B** Parotid Duct, Right **C** Parotid Duct, Left **D** Sublingual Gland, Right **F** Sublingual Gland, Left **G** Submaxillary Gland, Right **H** Submaxillary Gland, Left **J** Minor Salivary Gland	**0** Open **3** Percutaneous	**Z** No Device	**Z** No Qualifier
M Pharynx **R** Epiglottis **S** Larynx **T** Vocal Cord, Right **V** Vocal Cord, Left	**0** Open **3** Percutaneous **4** Percutaneous Endoscopic **7** Via Natural or Artificial Opening **8** Via Natural or Artificial Opening Endoscopic	**Z** No Device	**Z** No Qualifier
W Upper Tooth **X** Lower Tooth	**0** Open **X** External	**Z** No Device	**0** Single **1** Multiple **2** All

0 Medical and Surgical
C Mouth and Throat
7 Dilation: Expanding an orifice or the lumen of a tubular body part

Body Part Character 4	Approach Character 5	Device Character 6	Qualifier Character 7
B Parotid Duct, Right **C** Parotid Duct, Left	**0** Open **3** Percutaneous **7** Via Natural or Artificial Opening	**D** Intraluminal Device **Z** No Device	**Z** No Qualifier
M Pharynx	**7** Via Natural or Artificial Opening **8** Via Natural or Artificial Opening Endoscopic	**D** Intraluminal Device **Z** No Device	**Z** No Qualifier

Continued on next page

0   Medical and Surgical
C   Mouth and Throat
7   Dilation: Expanding an orifice or the lumen of a tubular body part

Continued from previous page

Body Part Character 4	Approach Character 5	Device Character 6	Qualifier Character 7
S Larynx	**0** Open **3** Percutaneous **4** Percutaneous Endoscopic **7** Via Natural or Artificial Opening **8** Via Natural or Artificial Opening Endoscopic	**D** Intraluminal Device **Z** No Device	**Z** No Qualifier

0   Medical and Surgical
C   Mouth and Throat
9   Drainage: Taking or letting out fluids and/or gases from a body part

Body Part Character 4	Approach Character 5	Device Character 6	Qualifier Character 7
0 Upper Lip **1** Lower Lip **2** Hard Palate **3** Soft Palate **4** Buccal Mucosa **5** Upper Gingiva **6** Lower Gingiva **7** Tongue **N** Uvula **P** Tonsils **Q** Adenoids	**0** Open **3** Percutaneous **X** External	**0** Drainage Device	**Z** No Qualifier
0 Upper Lip **1** Lower Lip **2** Hard Palate **3** Soft Palate **4** Buccal Mucosa **5** Upper Gingiva **6** Lower Gingiva **7** Tongue **N** Uvula **P** Tonsils **Q** Adenoids	**0** Open **3** Percutaneous **X** External	**Z** No Device	**X** Diagnostic **Z** No Qualifier
8 Parotid Gland, Right **9** Parotid Gland, Left **B** Parotid Duct, Right **C** Parotid Duct, Left **D** Sublingual Gland, Right **F** Sublingual Gland, Left **G** Submaxillary Gland, Right **H** Submaxillary Gland, Left **J** Minor Salivary Gland	**0** Open **3** Percutaneous	**0** Drainage Device	**Z** No Qualifier
8 Parotid Gland, Right **9** Parotid Gland, Left **B** Parotid Duct, Right **C** Parotid Duct, Left **D** Sublingual Gland, Right **F** Sublingual Gland, Left **G** Submaxillary Gland, Right **H** Submaxillary Gland, Left **J** Minor Salivary Gland	**0** Open **3** Percutaneous	**Z** No Device	**X** Diagnostic **Z** No Qualifier
M Pharynx **R** Epiglottis **S** Larynx **T** Vocal Cord, Right **V** Vocal Cord, Left	**0** Open **3** Percutaneous **4** Percutaneous Endoscopic **7** Via Natural or Artificial Opening **8** Via Natural or Artificial Opening Endoscopic	**0** Drainage Device	**Z** No Qualifier
M Pharynx **R** Epiglottis **S** Larynx **T** Vocal Cord, Right **V** Vocal Cord, Left	**0** Open **3** Percutaneous **4** Percutaneous Endoscopic **7** Via Natural or Artificial Opening **8** Via Natural or Artificial Opening Endoscopic	**Z** No Device	**X** Diagnostic **Z** No Qualifier
W Upper Tooth **X** Lower Tooth	**0** Open **X** External	**0** Drainage Device **Z** No Device	**0** Single **1** Multiple **2** All

0 **Medical and Surgical**
C **Mouth and Throat**
B **Excision:** Cutting out or off, without replacement, a portion of a body part

Body Part Character 4	Approach Character 5	Device Character 6	Qualifier Character 7
0 Upper Lip **1** Lower Lip **2** Hard Palate **3** Soft Palate **4** Buccal Mucosa **5** Upper Gingiva **6** Lower Gingiva **7** Tongue **N** Uvula **P** Tonsils **Q** Adenoids	**0** Open **3** Percutaneous **X** External	**Z** No Device	**X** Diagnostic **Z** No Qualifier
8 Parotid Gland, Right **9** Parotid Gland, Left **B** Parotid Duct, Right **C** Parotid Duct, Left **D** Sublingual Gland, Right **F** Sublingual Gland, Left **G** Submaxillary Gland, Right **H** Submaxillary Gland, Left **J** Minor Salivary Gland	**0** Open **3** Percutaneous	**Z** No Device	**X** Diagnostic **Z** No Qualifier
M Pharynx **R** Epiglottis **S** Larynx **T** Vocal Cord, Right **V** Vocal Cord, Left	**0** Open **3** Percutaneous **4** Percutaneous Endoscopic **7** Via Natural or Artificial Opening **8** Via Natural or Artificial Opening Endoscopic	**Z** No Device	**X** Diagnostic **Z** No Qualifier
W Upper Tooth **X** Lower Tooth	**0** Open **X** External	**Z** No Device	**0** Single **1** Multiple **2** All

0 **Medical and Surgical**
C **Mouth and Throat**
C **Extirpation:** Taking or cutting out solid matter from a body part

Body Part Character 4	Approach Character 5	Device Character 6	Qualifier Character 7
0 Upper Lip **1** Lower Lip **2** Hard Palate **3** Soft Palate **4** Buccal Mucosa **5** Upper Gingiva **6** Lower Gingiva **7** Tongue **N** Uvula **P** Tonsils **Q** Adenoids	**0** Open **3** Percutaneous **X** External	**Z** No Device	**Z** No Qualifier
8 Parotid Gland, Right **9** Parotid Gland, Left **B** Parotid Duct, Right **C** Parotid Duct, Left **D** Sublingual Gland, Right **F** Sublingual Gland, Left **G** Submaxillary Gland, Right **H** Submaxillary Gland, Left **J** Minor Salivary Gland	**0** Open **3** Percutaneous	**Z** No Device	**Z** No Qualifier
M Pharynx **R** Epiglottis **S** Larynx **T** Vocal Cord, Right **V** Vocal Cord, Left	**0** Open **3** Percutaneous **4** Percutaneous Endoscopic **7** Via Natural or Artificial Opening **8** Via Natural or Artificial Opening Endoscopic	**Z** No Device	**Z** No Qualifier
W Upper Tooth **X** Lower Tooth	**0** Open **X** External	**Z** No Device	**0** Single **1** Multiple **2** All

0   Medical and Surgical
C   Mouth and Throat
D   Extraction: Pulling or stripping out or off all or a portion of a body part by the use of force

Body Part Character 4	Approach Character 5	Device Character 6	Qualifier Character 7
T Vocal Cord, Right V Vocal Cord, Left	0 Open 3 Percutaneous 4 Percutaneous Endoscopic 7 Via Natural or Artificial Opening 8 Via Natural or Artificial Opening Endoscopic	Z No Device	Z No Qualifier
W Upper Tooth X Lower Tooth	X External	Z No Device	0 Single 1 Multiple 2 All

0   Medical and Surgical
C   Mouth and Throat
F   Fragmentation: Breaking solid matter in a body part into pieces

Body Part Character 4	Approach Character 5	Device Character 6	Qualifier Character 7
B Parotid Duct, Right C Parotid Duct, Left	0 Open 3 Percutaneous 7 Via Natural or Artificial Opening X External	Z No Device	Z No Qualifier

0   Medical and Surgical
C   Mouth and Throat
H   Insertion: Putting in a nonbiological appliance that monitors, assists, performs or prevents a physiological function, but does not physically take the place of a body part

Body Part Character 4	Approach Character 5	Device Character 6	Qualifier Character 7
7 Tongue	0 Open 3 Percutaneous X External	1 Radioactive Element	Z No Qualifier

0   Medical and Surgical
C   Mouth and Throat
J   Inspection: Visually and/or manually exploring a body part

Body Part Character 4	Approach Character 5	Device Character 6	Qualifier Character 7
0 Upper Lip 1 Lower Lip 2 Hard Palate 3 Soft Palate 4 Buccal Mucosa 5 Upper Gingiva 6 Lower Gingiva 7 Tongue 8 Parotid Gland, Right 9 Parotid Gland, Left B Parotid Duct, Right C Parotid Duct, Left D Sublingual Gland, Right F Sublingual Gland, Left G Submaxillary Gland, Right H Submaxillary Gland, Left J Minor Salivary Gland N Uvula P Tonsils Q Adenoids	0 Open 3 Percutaneous X External	Z No Device	Z No Qualifier
M Pharynx R Epiglottis S Larynx T Vocal Cord, Right V Vocal Cord, Left	0 Open 3 Percutaneous 4 Percutaneous Endoscopic 7 Via Natural or Artificial Opening 8 Via Natural or Artificial Opening Endoscopic X External	Z No Device	Z No Qualifier
W Upper Tooth X Lower Tooth	0 Open X External	Z No Device	0 Single 1 Multiple 2 All

0 Medical and Surgical
C Mouth and Throat
L Occlusion: Completely closing an orifice or lumen of a tubular body part

Body Part Character 4	Approach Character 5	Device Character 6	Qualifier Character 7
B Parotid Duct, Right C Parotid Duct, Left	0 Open 3 Percutaneous 4 Percutaneous Endoscopic	C Extraluminal Device D Intraluminal Device Z No Device	Z No Qualifier
B Parotid Duct, Right C Parotid Duct, Left	7 Via Natural or Artificial Opening 8 Via Natural or Artificial Opening Endoscopic	D Intraluminal Device Z No Device	Z No Qualifier

0 Medical and Surgical
C Mouth and Throat
M Reattachment: Putting back in or on all or a portion of a separated body part to its normal location or other suitable location

Body Part Character 4	Approach Character 5	Device Character 6	Qualifier Character 7
0 Upper Lip 1 Lower Lip 3 Soft Palate 7 Tongue N Uvula	0 Open	Z No Device	Z No Qualifier
W Upper Tooth X Lower Tooth	0 Open X External	Z No Device	0 Single 1 Multiple 2 All

0 Medical and Surgical
C Mouth and Throat
N Release: Freeing a body part from an abnormal physical constraint

Body Part Character 4	Approach Character 5	Device Character 6	Qualifier Character 7
0 Upper Lip 1 Lower Lip 2 Hard Palate 3 Soft Palate 4 Buccal Mucosa 5 Upper Gingiva 6 Lower Gingiva 7 Tongue N Uvula P Tonsils Q Adenoids	0 Open 3 Percutaneous X External	Z No Device	Z No Qualifier
8 Parotid Gland, Right 9 Parotid Gland, Left B Parotid Duct, Right C Parotid Duct, Left D Sublingual Gland, Right F Sublingual Gland, Left G Submaxillary Gland, Right H Submaxillary Gland, Left J Minor Salivary Gland	0 Open 3 Percutaneous	Z No Device	Z No Qualifier
M Pharynx R Epiglottis S Larynx T Vocal Cord, Right V Vocal Cord, Left	0 Open 3 Percutaneous 4 Percutaneous Endoscopic 7 Via Natural or Artificial Opening 8 Via Natural or Artificial Opening Endoscopic	Z No Device	Z No Qualifier
W Upper Tooth X Lower Tooth	0 Open X External	Z No Device	0 Single 1 Multiple 2 All

0 Medical and Surgical
C Mouth and Throat
P Removal: Taking out or off a device from a body part

Body Part Character 4	Approach Character 5	Device Character 6	Qualifier Character 7
A Salivary Gland	0 Open 3 Percutaneous	0 Drainage Device C Extraluminal Device	Z No Qualifier
S Larynx	0 Open 3 Percutaneous 7 Via Natural or Artificial Opening 8 Via Natural or Artificial Opening Endoscopic X External	0 Drainage Device 7 Autologous Tissue Substitute D Intraluminal Device J Synthetic Substitute K Nonautologous Tissue Substitute	Z No Qualifier
Y Mouth and Throat	0 Open 3 Percutaneous 7 Via Natural or Artificial Opening 8 Via Natural or Artificial Opening Endoscopic X External	0 Drainage Device 1 Radioactive Element 7 Autologous Tissue Substitute D Intraluminal Device J Synthetic Substitute K Nonautologous Tissue Substitute	Z No Qualifier

0 Medical and Surgical
C Mouth and Throat
Q Repair: Restoring, to the extent possible, a body part to its normal anatomic structure and function

Body Part Character 4	Approach Character 5	Device Character 6	Qualifier Character 7
0 Upper Lip 1 Lower Lip 2 Hard Palate 3 Soft Palate 4 Buccal Mucosa 5 Upper Gingiva 6 Lower Gingiva 7 Tongue N Uvula P Tonsils Q Adenoids	0 Open 3 Percutaneous X External	Z No Device	Z No Qualifier
8 Parotid Gland, Right 9 Parotid Gland, Left B Parotid Duct, Right C Parotid Duct, Left D Sublingual Gland, Right F Sublingual Gland, Left G Submaxillary Gland, Right H Submaxillary Gland, Left J Minor Salivary Gland	0 Open 3 Percutaneous	Z No Device	Z No Qualifier
M Pharynx R Epiglottis S Larynx T Vocal Cord, Right V Vocal Cord, Left	0 Open 3 Percutaneous 4 Percutaneous Endoscopic 7 Via Natural or Artificial Opening 8 Via Natural or Artificial Opening Endoscopic	Z No Device	Z No Qualifier
W Upper Tooth X Lower Tooth	0 Open X External	Z No Device	0 Single 1 Multiple 2 All

0 Medical and Surgical
C Mouth and Throat
R Replacement: Putting in or on biological or synthetic material that physically takes the place and/or function of all or a portion of a body part

Body Part Character 4	Approach Character 5	Device Character 6	Qualifier Character 7
0 Upper Lip 1 Lower Lip 2 Hard Palate 3 Soft Palate 4 Buccal Mucosa 5 Upper Gingiva 6 Lower Gingiva 7 Tongue N Uvula	0 Open 3 Percutaneous X External	7 Autologous Tissue Substitute J Synthetic Substitute K Nonautologous Tissue Substitute	Z No Qualifier
B Parotid Duct, Right C Parotid Duct, Left	0 Open 3 Percutaneous	7 Autologous Tissue Substitute J Synthetic Substitute K Nonautologous Tissue Substitute	Z No Qualifier

Continued on next page

0 Medical and Surgical
C Mouth and Throat
R Replacement: Putting in or on biological or synthetic material that physically takes the place and/or function of all or a portion of a body part

Continued from previous page

Body Part Character 4	Approach Character 5	Device Character 6	Qualifier Character 7
M Pharynx R Epiglottis S Larynx T Vocal Cord, Right V Vocal Cord, Left	0 Open 7 Via Natural or Artificial Opening 8 Via Natural or Artificial Opening Endoscopic	7 Autologous Tissue Substitute J Synthetic Substitute K Nonautologous Tissue Substitute	Z No Qualifier
W Upper Tooth X Lower Tooth	0 Open X External	7 Autologous Tissue Substitute J Synthetic Substitute K Nonautologous Tissue Substitute	0 Single 1 Multiple 2 All

0 Medical and Surgical
C Mouth and Throat
S Reposition: Moving to its normal location or other suitable location all or a portion of a body part

Body Part Character 4	Approach Character 5	Device Character 6	Qualifier Character 7
0 Upper Lip 1 Lower Lip 2 Hard Palate 3 Soft Palate 7 Tongue N Uvula	0 Open X External	Z No Device	Z No Qualifier
B Parotid Duct, Right C Parotid Duct, Left	0 Open 3 Percutaneous	Z No Device	Z No Qualifier
R Epiglottis T Vocal Cord, Right V Vocal Cord, Left	0 Open 7 Via Natural or Artificial Opening 8 Via Natural or Artificial Opening Endoscopic	Z No Device	Z No Qualifier
W Upper Tooth X Lower Tooth	0 Open X External	5 External Fixation Device Z No Device	0 Single 1 Multiple 2 All

0 Medical and Surgical
C Mouth and Throat
T Resection: Cutting out or off, without replacement, all of a body part

Body Part Character 4	Approach Character 5	Device Character 6	Qualifier Character 7
0 Upper Lip 1 Lower Lip 2 Hard Palate 3 Soft Palate 7 Tongue N Uvula P Tonsils Q Adenoids	0 Open X External	Z No Device	Z No Qualifier
8 Parotid Gland, Right 9 Parotid Gland, Left B Parotid Duct, Right C Parotid Duct, Left D Sublingual Gland, Right F Sublingual Gland, Left G Submaxillary Gland, Right H Submaxillary Gland, Left J Minor Salivary Gland	0 Open	Z No Device	Z No Qualifier
M Pharynx R Epiglottis S Larynx T Vocal Cord, Right V Vocal Cord, Left	0 Open 4 Percutaneous Endoscopic 7 Via Natural or Artificial Opening 8 Via Natural or Artificial Opening Endoscopic	Z No Device	Z No Qualifier
W Upper Tooth X Lower Tooth	0 Open	Z No Device	0 Single 1 Multiple 2 All

0   Medical and Surgical
C   Mouth and Throat
U   Supplement: Putting in or on biological or synthetic material that physically reinforces and/or augments the function of a portion of a body part

Body Part Character 4	Approach Character 5	Device Character 6	Qualifier Character 7
0 Upper Lip **1** Lower Lip **2** Hard Palate **3** Soft Palate **4** Buccal Mucosa **5** Upper Gingiva **6** Lower Gingiva **7** Tongue **N** Uvula	**0** Open **3** Percutaneous **X** External	**7** Autologous Tissue Substitute **J** Synthetic Substitute **K** Nonautologous Tissue Substitute	**Z** No Qualifier
M Pharynx **R** Epiglottis **S** Larynx **T** Vocal Cord, Right **V** Vocal Cord, Left	**0** Open **7** Via Natural or Artificial Opening **8** Via Natural or Artificial Opening Endoscopic	**7** Autologous Tissue Substitute **J** Synthetic Substitute **K** Nonautologous Tissue Substitute	**Z** No Qualifier

0   Medical and Surgical
C   Mouth and Throat
V   Restriction: Partially closing the orifice or lumen of a tubular body part

Body Part Character 4	Approach Character 5	Device Character 6	Qualifier Character 7
B Parotid Duct, Right **C** Parotid Duct, Left	**0** Open **3** Percutaneous	**C** Extraluminal Device **D** Intraluminal Device **Z** No Device	**Z** No Qualifier
B Parotid Duct, Right **C** Parotid Duct, Left	**7** Via Natural or Artificial Opening **8** Via Natural or Artificial Opening Endoscopic	**D** Intraluminal Device **Z** No Device	**Z** No Qualifier

0   Medical and Surgical
C   Mouth and Throat
W   Revision: Connecting to the extent possible a malfunctioning or displaced device

Body Part Character 4	Approach Character 5	Device Character 6	Qualifier Character 7
A Salivary Gland	**0** Open **3** Percutaneous **X** External	**0** Drainage Device **C** Extraluminal Device	**Z** No Qualifier
S Larynx	**0** Open **3** Percutaneous **7** Via Natural or Artificial Opening **8** Via Natural or Artificial Opening Endoscopic **X** External	**0** Drainage Device **7** Autologous Tissue Substitute **D** Intraluminal Device **J** Synthetic Substitute **K** Nonautologous Tissue Substitute	**Z** No Qualifier
Y Mouth and Throat	**0** Open **3** Percutaneous **7** Via Natural or Artificial Opening **8** Via Natural or Artificial Opening Endoscopic **X** External	**0** Drainage Device **1** Radioactive Element **7** Autologous Tissue Substitute **D** Intraluminal Device **J** Synthetic Substitute **K** Nonautologous Tissue Substitute	**Z** No Qualifier

0   Medical and Surgical
C   Mouth and Throat
X   Transfer: Moving, without taking out, all or a portion of a body part to another location to take over the function of all or a portion of a body part

Body Part Character 4	Approach Character 5	Device Character 6	Qualifier Character 7
0 Upper Lip **1** Lower Lip **3** Soft Palate **4** Buccal Mucosa **5** Upper Gingiva **6** Lower Gingiva **7** Tongue	**0** Open **X** External	**Z** No Device	**Z** No Qualifier

Gastrointestinal System 0D1–0DY

0   **Medical and Surgical**
D   **Gastrointestinal System**
1   **Bypass:**   Altering the route of passage of the contents of a tubular body part

Body Part Character 4	Approach Character 5	Device Character 6	Qualifier Character 7
1 Esophagus, Upper 2 Esophagus, Middle 3 Esophagus, Lower 5 Esophagus	0 Open 4 Percutaneous Endoscopic 8 Via Natural or Artificial Opening Endoscopic	7 Autologous Tissue Substitute J Synthetic Substitute K Nonautologous Tissue Substitute Z No Device	4 Cutaneous 6 Stomach 9 Duodenum A Jejunum B Ileum
1 Esophagus, Upper 2 Esophagus, Middle 3 Esophagus, Lower 5 Esophagus 6 Stomach 9 Duodenum A Jejunum B Ileum H Cecum K Ascending Colon L Transverse Colon M Descending Colon N Sigmoid Colon	3 Percutaneous	J Synthetic Substitute	4 Cutaneous
6 Stomach 9 Duodenum	0 Open 4 Percutaneous Endoscopic 8 Via Natural or Artificial Opening Endoscopic	7 Autologous Tissue Substitute J Synthetic Substitute K Nonautologous Tissue Substitute Z No Device	4 Cutaneous 9 Duodenum A Jejunum B Ileum L Transverse Colon
A Jejunum	0 Open 4 Percutaneous Endoscopic 8 Via Natural or Artificial Opening Endoscopic	7 Autologous Tissue Substitute J Synthetic Substitute K Nonautologous Tissue Substitute Z No Device	4 Cutaneous A Jejunum B Ileum H Cecum K Ascending Colon L Transverse Colon M Descending Colon N Sigmoid Colon P Rectum Q Anus
B Ileum	0 Open 4 Percutaneous Endoscopic 8 Via Natural or Artificial Opening Endoscopic	7 Autologous Tissue Substitute J Synthetic Substitute K Nonautologous Tissue Substitute Z No Device	4 Cutaneous B Ileum H Cecum K Ascending Colon L Transverse Colon M Descending Colon N Sigmoid Colon P Rectum Q Anus
H Cecum	0 Open 4 Percutaneous Endoscopic 8 Via Natural or Artificial Opening Endoscopic	7 Autologous Tissue Substitute J Synthetic Substitute K Nonautologous Tissue Substitute Z No Device	4 Cutaneous H Cecum K Ascending Colon L Transverse Colon M Descending Colon N Sigmoid Colon P Rectum
K Ascending Colon	0 Open 4 Percutaneous Endoscopic 8 Via Natural or Artificial Opening Endoscopic	7 Autologous Tissue Substitute J Synthetic Substitute K Nonautologous Tissue Substitute Z No Device	4 Cutaneous K Ascending Colon L Transverse Colon M Descending Colon N Sigmoid Colon P Rectum
L Transverse Colon	0 Open 4 Percutaneous Endoscopic 8 Via Natural or Artificial Opening Endoscopic	7 Autologous Tissue Substitute J Synthetic Substitute K Nonautologous Tissue Substitute Z No Device	4 Cutaneous L Transverse Colon M Descending Colon N Sigmoid Colon P Rectum
M Descending Colon	0 Open 4 Percutaneous Endoscopic 8 Via Natural or Artificial Opening Endoscopic	7 Autologous Tissue Substitute J Synthetic Substitute K Nonautologous Tissue Substitute Z No Device	4 Cutaneous M Descending Colon N Sigmoid Colon P Rectum
N Sigmoid Colon	0 Open 4 Percutaneous Endoscopic 8 Via Natural or Artificial Opening Endoscopic	7 Autologous Tissue Substitute J Synthetic Substitute K Nonautologous Tissue Substitute Z No Device	4 Cutaneous N Sigmoid Colon P Rectum

0 Medical and Surgical
D Gastrointestinal System
2 Change: Taking out or off a device from a body part and putting back an identical or similar device in or on the same body part without cutting or puncturing the skin or a mucous membrane

Body Part Character 4	Approach Character 5	Device Character 6	Qualifier Character 7
0 Upper Intestinal Tract **D** Lower Intestinal Tract	**X** External	**0** Drainage Device **U** Feeding Device **Y** Other Device	**Z** No Qualifier
U Omentum **V** Mesentery **W** Peritoneum	**X** External	**0** Drainage Device **Y** Other Device	**Z** No Qualifier

0 Medical and Surgical
D Gastrointestinal System
5 Destruction: Physical eradication of all or a portion of a body part by the direct use of energy, force, or a destructive agent

Body Part Character 4	Approach Character 5	Device Character 6	Qualifier Character 7
1 Esophagus, Upper **2** Esophagus, Middle **3** Esophagus, Lower **4** Esophagogastric Junction **5** Esophagus **6** Stomach **7** Stomach, Pylorus **8** Small Intestine **9** Duodenum **A** Jejunum **B** Ileum **C** Ileocecal Valve **E** Large Intestine **F** Large Intestine, Right **G** Large Intestine, Left **H** Cecum **J** Appendix **K** Ascending Colon **L** Transverse Colon **M** Descending Colon **N** Sigmoid Colon **P** Rectum	**0** Open **3** Percutaneous **4** Percutaneous Endoscopic **7** Via Natural or Artificial Opening **8** Via Natural or Artificial Opening Endoscopic	**Z** No Device	**Z** No Qualifier
Q Anus	**0** Open **3** Percutaneous **4** Percutaneous Endoscopic **7** Via Natural or Artificial Opening **8** Via Natural or Artificial Opening Endoscopic **X** External	**Z** No Device	**Z** No Qualifier
R Anal Sphincter **S** Greater Omentum **T** Lesser Omentum **V** Mesentery **W** Peritoneum	**0** Open **3** Percutaneous **4** Percutaneous Endoscopic	**Z** No Device	**Z** No Qualifier

0 **Medical and Surgical**
D **Gastrointestinal System**
7 **Dilation:** Expanding an orifice or the lumen of a tubular body part

Body Part Character 4	Approach Character 5	Device Character 6	Qualifier Character 7
1 Esophagus, Upper **2** Esophagus, Middle **3** Esophagus, Lower **4** Esophagogastric Junction **5** Esophagus **6** Stomach **7** Stomach, Pylorus **8** Small Intestine **9** Duodenum **A** Jejunum **B** Ileum **C** Ileocecal Valve **E** Large Intestine **F** Large Intestine, Right **G** Large Intestine, Left **H** Cecum **K** Ascending Colon **L** Transverse Colon **M** Descending Colon **N** Sigmoid Colon **P** Rectum **Q** Anus	**0** Open **3** Percutaneous **4** Percutaneous Endoscopic **7** Via Natural or Artificial Opening **8** Via Natural or Artificial Opening Endoscopic	**D** Intraluminal Device **Z** No Device	**Z** No Qualifier

0 **Medical and Surgical**
D **Gastrointestinal System**
8 **Division:** Cutting into a body part without draining fluids and/or gases from the body part in order to separate or transect a body part

Body Part Character 4	Approach Character 5	Device Character 6	Qualifier Character 7
4 Esophagogastric Junction	**0** Open **3** Percutaneous **4** Percutaneous Endoscopic **7** Via Natural or Artificial Opening **8** Via Natural or Artificial Opening Endoscopic	**Z** No Device	**Z** No Qualifier
R Anal Sphincter	**0** Open **3** Percutaneous	**Z** No Device	**Z** No Qualifier

0 **Medical and Surgical**
D **Gastrointestinal System**
9 **Drainage:** Taking or letting out fluids and/or gases from a body part

Body Part Character 4	Approach Character 5	Device Character 6	Qualifier Character 7
1 Esophagus, Upper **2** Esophagus, Middle **3** Esophagus, Lower **4** Esophagogastric Junction **5** Esophagus **6** Stomach **7** Stomach, Pylorus **8** Small Intestine **9** Duodenum **A** Jejunum **B** Ileum **C** Ileocecal Valve **E** Large Intestine **F** Large Intestine, Right **G** Large Intestine, Left **H** Cecum **J** Appendix **K** Ascending Colon **L** Transverse Colon **M** Descending Colon **N** Sigmoid Colon **P** Rectum	**0** Open **3** Percutaneous **4** Percutaneous Endoscopic **7** Via Natural or Artificial Opening **8** Via Natural or Artificial Opening Endoscopic	**0** Drainage Device	**Z** No Qualifier

Continued on next page

Draft (2009)

0 **Medical and Surgical**   *Continued from previous page*
D **Gastrointestinal System**
9 **Drainage:**   Taking or letting out fluids and/or gases from a body part

Body Part Character 4	Approach Character 5	Device Character 6	Qualifier Character 7
1 Esophagus, Upper **2** Esophagus, Middle **3** Esophagus, Lower **4** Esophagogastric Junction **5** Esophagus **6** Stomach **7** Stomach, Pylorus **8** Small Intestine **9** Duodenum **A** Jejunum **B** Ileum **C** Ileocecal Valve **E** Large Intestine **F** Large Intestine, Right **G** Large Intestine, Left **H** Cecum **J** Appendix **K** Ascending Colon **L** Transverse Colon **M** Descending Colon **N** Sigmoid Colon **P** Rectum	**0** Open **3** Percutaneous **4** Percutaneous Endoscopic **7** Via Natural or Artificial Opening **8** Via Natural or Artificial Opening Endoscopic	**Z** No Device	**X** Diagnostic **Z** No Qualifier
Q Anus	**0** Open **3** Percutaneous **4** Percutaneous Endoscopic **7** Via Natural or Artificial Opening **8** Via Natural or Artificial Opening Endoscopic **X** External	**0** Drainage Device	**Z** No Qualifier
Q Anus	**0** Open **3** Percutaneous **4** Percutaneous Endoscopic **7** Via Natural or Artificial Opening **8** Via Natural or Artificial Opening Endoscopic **X** External	**Z** No Device	**X** Diagnostic **Z** No Qualifier
R Anal Sphincter **S** Greater Omentum **T** Lesser Omentum **V** Mesentery **W** Peritoneum	**0** Open **3** Percutaneous **4** Percutaneous Endoscopic	**0** Drainage Device	**Z** No Qualifier
R Anal Sphincter **S** Greater Omentum **T** Lesser Omentum **V** Mesentery **W** Peritoneum	**0** Open **3** Percutaneous **4** Percutaneous Endoscopic	**Z** No Device	**X** Diagnostic **Z** No Qualifier

0 **Medical and Surgical**
D **Gastrointestinal System**
B **Excision:** Cutting out or off, without replacement, a portion of a body part

Body Part Character 4	Approach Character 5	Device Character 6	Qualifier Character 7
1 Esophagus, Upper 2 Esophagus, Middle 3 Esophagus, Lower 4 Esophagogastric Junction 5 Esophagus 6 Stomach 7 Stomach, Pylorus 8 Small Intestine 9 Duodenum A Jejunum B Ileum C Ileocecal Valve E Large Intestine F Large Intestine, Right G Large Intestine, Left H Cecum J Appendix K Ascending Colon L Transverse Colon M Descending Colon N Sigmoid Colon P Rectum	0 Open 3 Percutaneous 4 Percutaneous Endoscopic 7 Via Natural or Artificial Opening 8 Via Natural or Artificial Opening Endoscopic	Z No Device	X Diagnostic Z No Qualifier
Q Anus	0 Open 3 Percutaneous 4 Percutaneous Endoscopic 7 Via Natural or Artificial Opening 8 Via Natural or Artificial Opening Endoscopic X External	Z No Device	X Diagnostic Z No Qualifier
R Anal Sphincter S Greater Omentum T Lesser Omentum V Mesentery W Peritoneum	0 Open 3 Percutaneous 4 Percutaneous Endoscopic	Z No Device	X Diagnostic Z No Qualifier

0 **Medical and Surgical**
D **Gastrointestinal System**
C **Extirpation:** Taking or cutting out solid matter from a body part

Body Part Character 4	Approach Character 5	Device Character 6	Qualifier Character 7
1 Esophagus, Upper 2 Esophagus, Middle 3 Esophagus, Lower 4 Esophagogastric Junction 5 Esophagus 6 Stomach 7 Stomach, Pylorus 8 Small Intestine 9 Duodenum A Jejunum B Ileum C Ileocecal Valve E Large Intestine F Large Intestine, Right G Large Intestine, Left H Cecum J Appendix K Ascending Colon L Transverse Colon M Descending Colon N Sigmoid Colon P Rectum	0 Open 3 Percutaneous 4 Percutaneous Endoscopic 7 Via Natural or Artificial Opening 8 Via Natural or Artificial Opening Endoscopic	Z No Device	Z No Qualifier
Q Anus	0 Open 3 Percutaneous 4 Percutaneous Endoscopic 7 Via Natural or Artificial Opening 8 Via Natural or Artificial Opening Endoscopic X External	Z No Device	Z No Qualifier

Continued on next page

0 Medical and Surgical
D Gastrointestinal System
C Extirpation: Taking or cutting out solid matter from a body part

Continued from previous page

Body Part Character 4	Approach Character 5	Device Character 6	Qualifier Character 7
R Anal Sphincter **S** Greater Omentum **T** Lesser Omentum **V** Mesentery **W** Peritoneum	**0** Open **3** Percutaneous **4** Percutaneous Endoscopic	**Z** No Device	**Z** No Qualifier

0 Medical and Surgical
D Gastrointestinal System
F Fragmentation: Breaking solid matter in a body part into pieces

Body Part Character 4	Approach Character 5	Device Character 6	Qualifier Character 7
5 Esophagus **6** Stomach **8** Small Intestine **9** Duodenum **A** Jejunum **B** Ileum **E** Large Intestine **F** Large Intestine, Right **G** Large Intestine, Left **H** Cecum **J** Appendix **K** Ascending Colon **L** Transverse Colon **M** Descending Colon **N** Sigmoid Colon **P** Rectum **Q** Anus	**0** Open **3** Percutaneous **4** Percutaneous Endoscopic **7** Via Natural or Artificial Opening **8** Via Natural or Artificial Opening Endoscopic **X** External	**Z** No Device	**Z** No Qualifier

0 Medical and Surgical
D Gastrointestinal System
H Insertion: Putting in a nonbiological appliance that monitors, assists, performs or prevents a physiological function, but does not physically take the place of a body part

Body Part Character 4	Approach Character 5	Device Character 6	Qualifier Character 7
5 Esophagus	**0** Open **3** Percutaneous **4** Percutaneous Endoscopic	**1** Radioactive Element **2** Monitoring Device **3** Infusion Device **U** Feeding Device	**Z** No Qualifier
5 Esophagus	**7** Via Natural or Artificial Opening **8** Via Natural or Artificial Opening Endoscopic	**1** Radioactive Element **2** Monitoring Device **3** Infusion Device **B** Airway **U** Feeding Device	**Z** No Qualifier
6 Stomach	**0** Open **3** Percutaneous **4** Percutaneous Endoscopic	**2** Monitoring Device **3** Infusion Device **M** Electrode **U** Feeding Device	**Z** No Qualifier
6 Stomach	**7** Via Natural or Artificial Opening **8** Via Natural or Artificial Opening Endoscopic	**2** Monitoring Device **3** Infusion Device **U** Feeding Device	**Z** No Qualifier
8 Small Intestine **9** Duodenum **A** Jejunum **B** Ileum	**0** Open **3** Percutaneous **4** Percutaneous Endoscopic **7** Via Natural or Artificial Opening **8** Via Natural or Artificial Opening Endoscopic	**2** Monitoring Device **3** Infusion Device **U** Feeding Device	**Z** No Qualifier
P Rectum	**0** Open **3** Percutaneous **4** Percutaneous Endoscopic **7** Via Natural or Artificial Opening **8** Via Natural or Artificial Opening Endoscopic	**1** Radioactive Element	**Z** No Qualifier
Q Anus	**0** Open **3** Percutaneous **4** Percutaneous Endoscopic	**L** Artificial Sphincter **M** Electrode	**Z** No Qualifier

0 **Medical and Surgical**
D **Gastrointestinal System**
J **Inspection:** Visually and/or manually exploring a body part

Body Part Character 4	Approach Character 5	Device Character 6	Qualifier Character 7
0 Upper Intestinal Tract 1 Esophagus, Upper 2 Esophagus, Middle 3 Esophagus, Lower 4 Esophagogastric Junction 5 Esophagus 6 Stomach 7 Stomach, Pylorus 8 Small Intestine 9 Duodenum A Jejunum B Ileum C Ileocecal Valve E Large Intestine F Large Intestine, Right G Large Intestine, Left H Cecum J Appendix K Ascending Colon L Transverse Colon M Descending Colon N Sigmoid Colon P Rectum Q Anus	0 Open 3 Percutaneous 4 Percutaneous Endoscopic 7 Via Natural or Artificial Opening 8 Via Natural or Artificial Opening Endoscopic X External	Z No Device	Z No Qualifier
R Anal Sphincter S Greater Omentum T Lesser Omentum V Mesentery W Peritoneum	0 Open 3 Percutaneous 4 Percutaneous Endoscopic X External	Z No Device	Z No Qualifier

0 **Medical and Surgical**
D **Gastrointestinal System**
L **Occlusion:** Completely closing an orifice or lumen of a tubular body part

Body Part Character 4	Approach Character 5	Device Character 6	Qualifier Character 7
1 Esophagus, Upper 2 Esophagus, Middle 3 Esophagus, Lower 4 Esophagogastric Junction 5 Esophagus 6 Stomach 7 Stomach, Pylorus 8 Small Intestine 9 Duodenum A Jejunum B Ileum C Ileocecal Valve E Large Intestine F Large Intestine, Right G Large Intestine, Left H Cecum K Ascending Colon L Transverse Colon M Descending Colon N Sigmoid Colon P Rectum	0 Open 3 Percutaneous 4 Percutaneous Endoscopic	C Extraluminal Device D Intraluminal Device Z No Device	Z No Qualifier

Continued on next page

0 **Medical and Surgical**   *Continued from previous page*
D **Gastrointestinal System**
L **Occlusion:**   Completely closing an orifice or lumen of a tubular body part

Body Part Character 4	Approach Character 5	Device Character 6	Qualifier Character 7
1 Esophagus, Upper 2 Esophagus, Middle 3 Esophagus, Lower 4 Esophagogastric Junction 5 Esophagus 6 Stomach 7 Stomach, Pylorus 8 Small Intestine 9 Duodenum A Jejunum B Ileum C Ileocecal Valve E Large Intestine F Large Intestine, Right G Large Intestine, Left H Cecum K Ascending Colon L Transverse Colon M Descending Colon N Sigmoid Colon P Rectum Q Anus	7 Via Natural or Artificial Opening 8 Via Natural or Artificial Opening Endoscopic	D Intraluminal Device Z No Device	Z No Qualifier
Q Anus	0 Open 3 Percutaneous 4 Percutaneous Endoscopic X External	C Extraluminal Device D Intraluminal Device Z No Device	Z No Qualifier

0 **Medical and Surgical**
D **Gastrointestinal System**
M **Reattachment:**   Putting back in or on all or a portion of a separated body part to its normal location or other suitable location

Body Part Character 4	Approach Character 5	Device Character 6	Qualifier Character 7
5 Esophagus 6 Stomach 8 Small Intestine 9 Duodenum A Jejunum B Ileum E Large Intestine F Large Intestine, Right G Large Intestine, Left H Cecum K Ascending Colon L Transverse Colon M Descending Colon N Sigmoid Colon P Rectum	0 Open 4 Percutaneous Endoscopic	Z No Device	Z No Qualifier

0 **Medical and Surgical**
D **Gastrointestinal System**
N **Release:** Freeing a body part from an abnormal physical constraint

Body Part Character 4	Approach Character 5	Device Character 6	Qualifier Character 7
1 Esophagus, Upper **2** Esophagus, Middle **3** Esophagus, Lower **4** Esophagogastric Junction **5** Esophagus **6** Stomach **7** Stomach, Pylorus **8** Small Intestine **9** Duodenum **A** Jejunum **B** Ileum **C** Ileocecal Valve **E** Large Intestine **F** Large Intestine, Right **G** Large Intestine, Left **H** Cecum **J** Appendix **K** Ascending Colon **L** Transverse Colon **M** Descending Colon **N** Sigmoid Colon **P** Rectum	**0** Open **3** Percutaneous **4** Percutaneous Endoscopic **7** Via Natural or Artificial Opening **8** Via Natural or Artificial Opening Endoscopic	**Z** No Device	**Z** No Qualifier
Q Anus	**0** Open **3** Percutaneous **4** Percutaneous Endoscopic **7** Via Natural or Artificial Opening **8** Via Natural or Artificial Opening Endoscopic **X** External	**Z** No Device	**Z** No Qualifier
R Anal Sphincter **S** Greater Omentum **T** Lesser Omentum **V** Mesentery **W** Peritoneum	**0** Open **3** Percutaneous **4** Percutaneous Endoscopic	**Z** No Device	**Z** No Qualifier

0 **Medical and Surgical**
D **Gastrointestinal System**
P **Removal:** Taking out or off a device from a body part

Body Part Character 4	Approach Character 5	Device Character 6	Qualifier Character 7
0 Upper Intestinal Tract **6** Stomach **D** Lower Intestinal Tract	**X** External	**0** Drainage Device **2** Monitoring Device **3** Infusion Device **D** Intraluminal Device **U** Feeding Device	**Z** No Qualifier
0 Upper Intestinal Tract **D** Lower Intestinal Tract	**0** Open **3** Percutaneous **4** Percutaneous Endoscopic **7** Via Natural or Artificial Opening **8** Via Natural or Artificial Opening Endoscopic	**0** Drainage Device **2** Monitoring Device **3** Infusion Device **7** Autologous Tissue Substitute **C** Extraluminal Device **D** Intraluminal Device **J** Synthetic Substitute **K** Nonautologous Tissue Substitute **U** Feeding Device	**Z** No Qualifier
5 Esophagus	**0** Open **3** Percutaneous **4** Percutaneous Endoscopic	**1** Radioactive Element **2** Monitoring Device **3** Infusion Device **U** Feeding Device	**Z** No Qualifier
5 Esophagus	**7** Via Natural or Artificial Opening **8** Via Natural or Artificial Opening Endoscopic	**1** Radioactive Element **B** Airway	**Z** No Qualifier
5 Esophagus	**X** External	**1** Radioactive Element **2** Monitoring Device **3** Infusion Device **B** Airway **U** Feeding Device	**Z** No Qualifier

Continued on next page

0   **Medical and Surgical**   *Continued from previous page*
D   **Gastrointestinal System**
P   **Removal:**   Taking out or off a device from a body part

Body Part Character 4	Approach Character 5	Device Character 6	Qualifier Character 7
6 Stomach	**0** Open **3** Percutaneous **4** Percutaneous Endoscopic	**0** Drainage Device **2** Monitoring Device **3** Infusion Device **7** Autologous Tissue Substitute **C** Extraluminal Device **D** Intraluminal Device **J** Synthetic Substitute **K** Nonautologous Tissue Substitute **M** Electrode **U** Feeding Device	**Z** No Qualifier
6 Stomach	**7** Via Natural or Artificial Opening **8** Via Natural or Artificial Opening Endoscopic	**0** Drainage Device **2** Monitoring Device **3** Infusion Device **7** Autologous Tissue Substitute **C** Extraluminal Device **D** Intraluminal Device **J** Synthetic Substitute **K** Nonautologous Tissue Substitute **U** Feeding Device	**Z** No Qualifier
P Rectum	**0** Open **3** Percutaneous **4** Percutaneous Endoscopic **7** Via Natural or Artificial Opening **8** Via Natural or Artificial Opening Endoscopic **X** External	**1** Radioactive Element	**Z** No Qualifier
Q Anus	**0** Open **3** Percutaneous **4** Percutaneous Endoscopic	**L** Artificial Sphincter **M** Electrode	**Z** No Qualifier
Q Anus	**7** Via Natural or Artificial Opening **8** Via Natural or Artificial Opening Endoscopic	**L** Artificial Sphincter	**Z** No Qualifier
U Omentum **V** Mesentery **W** Peritoneum	**0** Open **3** Percutaneous **4** Percutaneous Endoscopic	**0** Drainage Device **1** Radioactive Element **7** Autologous Tissue Substitute **J** Synthetic Substitute **K** Nonautologous Tissue Substitute	**Z** No Qualifier

0   **Medical and Surgical**
D   **Gastrointestinal System**
Q   **Repair:**   Restoring, to the extent possible, a body part to its normal anatomic structure and function

Body Part Character 4	Approach Character 5	Device Character 6	Qualifier Character 7
1 Esophagus, Upper **2** Esophagus, Middle **3** Esophagus, Lower **4** Esophagogastric Junction **5** Esophagus **6** Stomach **7** Stomach, Pylorus **8** Small Intestine **9** Duodenum **A** Jejunum **B** Ileum **C** Ileocecal Valve **E** Large Intestine **F** Large Intestine, Right **G** Large Intestine, Left **H** Cecum **J** Appendix **K** Ascending Colon **L** Transverse Colon **M** Descending Colon **N** Sigmoid Colon **P** Rectum	**0** Open **3** Percutaneous **4** Percutaneous Endoscopic **7** Via Natural or Artificial Opening **8** Via Natural or Artificial Opening Endoscopic	**Z** No Device	**Z** No Qualifier

Continued on next page

0   **Medical and Surgical**   *Continued from previous page*
D   **Gastrointestinal System**
Q   **Repair:**   Restoring, to the extent possible, a body part to its normal anatomic structure and function

Body Part Character 4	Approach Character 5	Device Character 6	Qualifier Character 7
Q Anus	**0** Open **3** Percutaneous **4** Percutaneous Endoscopic **7** Via Natural or Artificial Opening **8** Via Natural or Artificial Opening Endoscopic **X** External	**Z** No Device	**Z** No Qualifier
R Anal Sphincter **S** Greater Omentum **T** Lesser Omentum **V** Mesentery **W** Peritoneum	**0** Open **3** Percutaneous **4** Percutaneous Endoscopic	**Z** No Device	**Z** No Qualifier

0   **Medical and Surgical**
D   **Gastrointestinal System**
R   **Replacement:**   Putting in or on biological or synthetic material that physically takes the place and/or function of all or a portion of a body part

Body Part Character 4	Approach Character 5	Device Character 6	Qualifier Character 7
5 Esophagus	**0** Open **4** Percutaneous Endoscopic **7** Via Natural or Artificial Opening **8** Via Natural or Artificial Opening Endoscopic	**7** Autologous Tissue Substitute **J** Synthetic Substitute **K** Nonautologous Tissue Substitute	**Z** No Qualifier
R Anal Sphincter **S** Greater Omentum **T** Lesser Omentum **V** Mesentery **W** Peritoneum	**0** Open **4** Percutaneous Endoscopic	**7** Autologous Tissue Substitute **J** Synthetic Substitute **K** Nonautologous Tissue Substitute	**Z** No Qualifier

0   **Medical and Surgical**
D   **Gastrointestinal System**
S   **Reposition:**   Moving to its normal location or other suitable location all or a portion of a body part

Body Part Character 4	Approach Character 5	Device Character 6	Qualifier Character 7
5 Esophagus **6** Stomach **9** Duodenum **A** Jejunum **B** Ileum **H** Cecum **K** Ascending Colon **L** Transverse Colon **M** Descending Colon **N** Sigmoid Colon **P** Rectum **Q** Anus	**0** Open **4** Percutaneous Endoscopic **7** Via Natural or Artificial Opening **8** Via Natural or Artificial Opening Endoscopic **X** External	**Z** No Device	**Z** No Qualifier

0 **Medical and Surgical**
D **Gastrointestinal System**
T **Resection:** Cutting out or off, without replacement, all of a body part

Body Part Character 4	Approach Character 5	Device Character 6	Qualifier Character 7
1 Esophagus, Upper 2 Esophagus, Middle 3 Esophagus, Lower 4 Esophagogastric Junction 5 Esophagus 6 Stomach 7 Stomach, Pylorus 8 Small Intestine 9 Duodenum A Jejunum B Ileum C Ileocecal Valve E Large Intestine F Large Intestine, Right G Large Intestine, Left H Cecum J Appendix K Ascending Colon L Transverse Colon M Descending Colon N Sigmoid Colon P Rectum Q Anus	0 Open 4 Percutaneous Endoscopic 7 Via Natural or Artificial Opening 8 Via Natural or Artificial Opening Endoscopic	Z No Device	Z No Qualifier
R Anal Sphincter S Greater Omentum T Lesser Omentum	0 Open 4 Percutaneous Endoscopic	Z No Device	Z No Qualifier

0 **Medical and Surgical**
D **Gastrointestinal System**
U **Supplement:** Putting in or on biological or synthetic material that physically reinforces and/or augments the function of a portion of a body part

Body Part Character 4	Approach Character 5	Device Character 6	Qualifier Character 7
1 Esophagus, Upper 2 Esophagus, Middle 3 Esophagus, Lower 4 Esophagogastric Junction 5 Esophagus 6 Stomach 7 Stomach, Pylorus 8 Small Intestine 9 Duodenum A Jejunum B Ileum C Ileocecal Valve E Large Intestine F Large Intestine, Right G Large Intestine, Left H Cecum K Ascending Colon L Transverse Colon M Descending Colon N Sigmoid Colon P Rectum	0 Open 4 Percutaneous Endoscopic 7 Via Natural or Artificial Opening 8 Via Natural or Artificial Opening Endoscopic	7 Autologous Tissue Substitute J Synthetic Substitute K Nonautologous Tissue Substitute	Z No Qualifier
Q Anus	0 Open 4 Percutaneous Endoscopic 7 Via Natural or Artificial Opening 8 Via Natural or Artificial Opening Endoscopic X External	7 Autologous Tissue Substitute J Synthetic Substitute K Nonautologous Tissue Substitute	Z No Qualifier
R Anal Sphincter S Greater Omentum T Lesser Omentum V Mesentery W Peritoneum	0 Open 4 Percutaneous Endoscopic	7 Autologous Tissue Substitute J Synthetic Substitute K Nonautologous Tissue Substitute	Z No Qualifier

0 Medical and Surgical
D Gastrointestinal System
V Restriction: Partially closing the orifice or lumen of a tubular body part

Body Part Character 4	Approach Character 5	Device Character 6	Qualifier Character 7
1 Esophagus, Upper **2** Esophagus, Middle **3** Esophagus, Lower **4** Esophagogastric Junction **5** Esophagus **6** Stomach **7** Stomach, Pylorus **8** Small Intestine **9** Duodenum **A** Jejunum **B** Ileum **C** Ileocecal Valve **E** Large Intestine **F** Large Intestine, Right **G** Large Intestine, Left **H** Cecum **K** Ascending Colon **L** Transverse Colon **M** Descending Colon **N** Sigmoid Colon **P** Rectum	**0** Open **3** Percutaneous **4** Percutaneous Endoscopic	**C** Extraluminal Device **D** Intraluminal Device **Z** No Device	**Z** No Qualifier
1 Esophagus, Upper **2** Esophagus, Middle **3** Esophagus, Lower **4** Esophagogastric Junction **5** Esophagus **6** Stomach **7** Stomach, Pylorus **8** Small Intestine **9** Duodenum **A** Jejunum **B** Ileum **C** Ileocecal Valve **E** Large Intestine **F** Large Intestine, Right **G** Large Intestine, Left **H** Cecum **K** Ascending Colon **L** Transverse Colon **M** Descending Colon **N** Sigmoid Colon **P** Rectum **Q** Anus	**7** Via Natural or Artificial Opening **8** Via Natural or Artificial Opening Endoscopic	**D** Intraluminal Device **Z** No Device	**Z** No Qualifier
Q Anus	**0** Open **3** Percutaneous **4** Percutaneous Endoscopic **X** External	**C** Extraluminal Device **D** Intraluminal Device **Z** No Device	**Z** No Qualifier

0 Medical and Surgical
D Gastrointestinal System
W Revision: Connecting to the extent possible a malfunctioning or displaced device

Body Part Character 4	Approach Character 5	Device Character 6	Qualifier Character 7
0 Upper Intestinal Tract **D** Lower Intestinal Tract	**0** Open **3** Percutaneous **4** Percutaneous Endoscopic **7** Via Natural or Artificial Opening **8** Via Natural or Artificial Opening Endoscopic **X** External	**0** Drainage Device **2** Monitoring Device **3** Infusion Device **7** Autologous Tissue Substitute **C** Extraluminal Device **D** Intraluminal Device **J** Synthetic Substitute **K** Nonautologous Tissue Substitute **U** Feeding Device	**Z** No Qualifier
5 Esophagus	**7** Via Natural or Artificial Opening **8** Via Natural or Artificial Opening Endoscopic **X** External	**B** Airway	**Z** No Qualifier

Continued on next page

0 **Medical and Surgical**
D **Gastrointestinal System**
W **Revision:** Connecting to the extent possible a malfunctioning or displaced device

Continued from previous page

Body Part Character 4	Approach Character 5	Device Character 6	Qualifier Character 7
6 Stomach	**0** Open **3** Percutaneous **4** Percutaneous Endoscopic	**0** Drainage Device **2** Monitoring Device **3** Infusion Device **7** Autologous Tissue Substitute **C** Extraluminal Device **D** Intraluminal Device **J** Synthetic Substitute **K** Nonautologous Tissue Substitute **M** Electrode **U** Feeding Device	**Z** No Qualifier
6 Stomach	**7** Via Natural or Artificial Opening **8** Via Natural or Artificial Opening Endoscopic **X** External	**0** Drainage Device **2** Monitoring Device **3** Infusion Device **7** Autologous Tissue Substitute **C** Extraluminal Device **D** Intraluminal Device **J** Synthetic Substitute **K** Nonautologous Tissue Substitute **U** Feeding Device	**Z** No Qualifier
8 Small Intestine **E** Large Intestine	**0** Open **4** Percutaneous Endoscopic **7** Via Natural or Artificial Opening **8** Via Natural or Artificial Opening Endoscopic	**7** Autologous Tissue Substitute **J** Synthetic Substitute **K** Nonautologous Tissue Substitute	**Z** No Qualifier
Q Anus	**0** Open **3** Percutaneous **4** Percutaneous Endoscopic	**L** Artificial Sphincter **M** Electrode	**Z** No Qualifier
Q Anus	**7** Via Natural or Artificial Opening **8** Via Natural or Artificial Opening Endoscopic	**L** Artificial Sphincter	**Z** No Qualifier
U Omentum **V** Mesentery **W** Peritoneum	**0** Open **3** Percutaneous **4** Percutaneous Endoscopic	**0** Drainage Device **7** Autologous Tissue Substitute **J** Synthetic Substitute **K** Nonautologous Tissue Substitute	**Z** No Qualifier

0 **Medical and Surgical**
D **Gastrointestinal System**
X **Transfer:** Moving, without taking out, all or a portion of a body part to another location to take over the function of all or a portion of a body part

Body Part Character 4	Approach Character 5	Device Character 6	Qualifier Character 7
6 Stomach **8** Small Intestine **E** Large Intestine	**0** Open **4** Percutaneous Endoscopic	**Z** No Device	**5** Esophagus

0 **Medical and Surgical**
D **Gastrointestinal System**
Y **Transplantation:** Putting in or on all or a portion of a living body part taken from another individual or animal to physically take the place and/or function of all or a portion of a similar body part

Body Part Character 4	Approach Character 5	Device Character 6	Qualifier Character 7
5 Esophagus **6** Stomach **8** Small Intestine **E** Large Intestine	**0** Open	**Z** No Device	**0** Allogeneic **1** Syngeneic **2** Zooplastic

Hepatobiliary System and Pancreas 0F1–0FY

0   Medical and Surgical
F   Hepatobiliary System and Pancreas
1   Bypass: Altering the route of passage of the contents of a tubular body part

Body Part Character 4	Approach Character 5	Device Character 6	Qualifier Character 7
4 Gallbladder 5 Hepatic Duct, Right 6 Hepatic Duct, Left 8 Cystic Duct 9 Common Bile Duct	0 Open 4 Percutaneous Endoscopic	D Intraluminal Device Z No Device	3 Duodenum 4 Stomach 5 Hepatic Duct, Right 6 Hepatic Duct, Left 7 Hepatic Duct, Caudate 8 Cystic Duct 9 Common Bile Duct B Small Intestine
D Pancreatic Duct F Pancreatic Duct, Accessory G Pancreas	0 Open 4 Percutaneous Endoscopic	D Intraluminal Device Z No Device	3 Duodenum B Small Intestine C Large Intestine

0   Medical and Surgical
F   Hepatobiliary System and Pancreas
2   Change: Taking out or off a device from a body part and putting back an identical or similar device in or on the same body part without cutting or puncturing the skin or a mucous membrane

Body Part Character 4	Approach Character 5	Device Character 6	Qualifier Character 7
0 Liver 4 Gallbladder B Hepatobiliary Duct D Pancreatic Duct G Pancreas	X External	0 Drainage Device Y Other Device	Z No Qualifier

0   Medical and Surgical
F   Hepatobiliary System and Pancreas
5   Destruction: Physical eradication of all or a portion of a body part by the direct use of energy, force, or a destructive agent

Body Part Character 4	Approach Character 5	Device Character 6	Qualifier Character 7
0 Liver 1 Liver, Right Lobe 2 Liver, Left Lobe 4 Gallbladder G Pancreas	0 Open 3 Percutaneous 4 Percutaneous Endoscopic	Z No Device	Z No Qualifier
5 Hepatic Duct, Right 6 Hepatic Duct, Left 8 Cystic Duct 9 Common Bile Duct C Ampulla of Vater D Pancreatic Duct F Pancreatic Duct, Accessory	0 Open 3 Percutaneous 4 Percutaneous Endoscopic 7 Via Natural or Artificial Opening 8 Via Natural or Artificial Opening Endoscopic	Z No Device	Z No Qualifier

0   Medical and Surgical
F   Hepatobiliary System and Pancreas
7   Dilation: Expanding an orifice or the lumen of a tubular body part

Body Part Character 4	Approach Character 5	Device Character 6	Qualifier Character 7
5 Hepatic Duct, Right 6 Hepatic Duct, Left 8 Cystic Duct 9 Common Bile Duct C Ampulla of Vater D Pancreatic Duct F Pancreatic Duct, Accessory	0 Open 3 Percutaneous 4 Percutaneous Endoscopic 7 Via Natural or Artificial Opening 8 Via Natural or Artificial Opening Endoscopic	D Intraluminal Device Z No Device	Z No Qualifier

0   Medical and Surgical
F   Hepatobiliary System and Pancreas
8   Division: Cutting into a body part without draining fluids and/or gases from the body part in order to separate or transect a body part

Body Part Character 4	Approach Character 5	Device Character 6	Qualifier Character 7
G Pancreas	**0** Open **3** Percutaneous **4** Percutaneous Endoscopic	**Z** No Device	**Z** No Qualifier

0   Medical and Surgical
F   Hepatobiliary System and Pancreas
9   Drainage: Taking or letting out fluids and/or gases from a body part

Body Part Character 4	Approach Character 5	Device Character 6	Qualifier Character 7
0 Liver **1** Liver, Right Lobe **2** Liver, Left Lobe **4** Gallbladder **G** Pancreas	**0** Open **3** Percutaneous **4** Percutaneous Endoscopic	**0** Drainage Device	**Z** No Qualifier
0 Liver **1** Liver, Right Lobe **2** Liver, Left Lobe **4** Gallbladder **G** Pancreas	**0** Open **3** Percutaneous **4** Percutaneous Endoscopic	**Z** No Device	**X** Diagnostic **Z** No Qualifier
5 Hepatic Duct, Right **6** Hepatic Duct, Left **8** Cystic Duct **9** Common Bile Duct **C** Ampulla of Vater **D** Pancreatic Duct **F** Pancreatic Duct, Accessory	**0** Open **3** Percutaneous **4** Percutaneous Endoscopic **7** Via Natural or Artificial Opening **8** Via Natural or Artificial Opening Endoscopic	**0** Drainage Device	**Z** No Qualifier
5 Hepatic Duct, Right **6** Hepatic Duct, Left **8** Cystic Duct **9** Common Bile Duct **C** Ampulla of Vater **D** Pancreatic Duct **F** Pancreatic Duct, Accessory	**0** Open **3** Percutaneous **4** Percutaneous Endoscopic **7** Via Natural or Artificial Opening **8** Via Natural or Artificial Opening Endoscopic	**Z** No Device	**X** Diagnostic **Z** No Qualifier

0   Medical and Surgical
F   Hepatobiliary System and Pancreas
B   Excision: Cutting out or off, without replacement, a portion of a body part

Body Part Character 4	Approach Character 5	Device Character 6	Qualifier Character 7
0 Liver **1** Liver, Right Lobe **2** Liver, Left Lobe **4** Gallbladder **G** Pancreas	**0** Open **3** Percutaneous **4** Percutaneous Endoscopic	**Z** No Device	**X** Diagnostic **Z** No Qualifier
5 Hepatic Duct, Right **6** Hepatic Duct, Left **8** Cystic Duct **9** Common Bile Duct **C** Ampulla of Vater **D** Pancreatic Duct **F** Pancreatic Duct, Accessory	**0** Open **3** Percutaneous **4** Percutaneous Endoscopic **7** Via Natural or Artificial Opening **8** Via Natural or Artificial Opening Endoscopic	**Z** No Device	**X** Diagnostic **Z** No Qualifier

0   Medical and Surgical
F   Hepatobiliary System and Pancreas
C   Extirpation: Taking or cutting out solid matter from a body part

Body Part Character 4	Approach Character 5	Device Character 6	Qualifier Character 7
0 Liver **1** Liver, Right Lobe **2** Liver, Left Lobe **4** Gallbladder **G** Pancreas	**0** Open **3** Percutaneous **4** Percutaneous Endoscopic	**Z** No Device	**Z** No Qualifier

Continued on next page

0	Medical and Surgical
F	Hepatobiliary System and Pancreas
C	Extirpation: Taking or cutting out solid matter from a body part

Continued from previous page

Body Part Character 4	Approach Character 5	Device Character 6	Qualifier Character 7
5 Hepatic Duct, Right 6 Hepatic Duct, Left 8 Cystic Duct 9 Common Bile Duct C Ampulla of Vater D Pancreatic Duct F Pancreatic Duct, Accessory	0 Open 3 Percutaneous 4 Percutaneous Endoscopic 7 Via Natural or Artificial Opening 8 Via Natural or Artificial Opening Endoscopic	Z No Device	Z No Qualifier

0	Medical and Surgical
F	Hepatobiliary System and Pancreas
F	Fragmentation: Breaking solid matter in a body part into pieces

Body Part Character 4	Approach Character 5	Device Character 6	Qualifier Character 7
4 Gallbladder 5 Hepatic Duct, Right 6 Hepatic Duct, Left 8 Cystic Duct 9 Common Bile Duct C Ampulla of Vater D Pancreatic Duct F Pancreatic Duct, Accessory	0 Open 3 Percutaneous 4 Percutaneous Endoscopic 7 Via Natural or Artificial Opening 8 Via Natural or Artificial Opening Endoscopic X External	Z No Device	Z No Qualifier

0	Medical and Surgical
F	Hepatobiliary System and Pancreas
H	Insertion: Putting in a nonbiological appliance that monitors, assists, performs or prevents a physiological function, but does not physically take the place of a body part

Body Part Character 4	Approach Character 5	Device Character 6	Qualifier Character 7
0 Liver 1 Liver, Right Lobe 2 Liver, Left Lobe 4 Gallbladder G Pancreas	0 Open 3 Percutaneous 4 Percutaneous Endoscopic	2 Monitoring Device 3 Infusion Device	Z No Qualifier
B Hepatobiliary Duct D Pancreatic Duct	0 Open 3 Percutaneous 4 Percutaneous Endoscopic 7 Via Natural or Artificial Opening 8 Via Natural or Artificial Opening Endoscopic	1 Radioactive Element 2 Monitoring Device 3 Infusion Device	Z No Qualifier

0	Medical and Surgical
F	Hepatobiliary System and Pancreas
J	Inspection: Visually and/or manually exploring a body part

Body Part Character 4	Approach Character 5	Device Character 6	Qualifier Character 7
0 Liver 1 Liver, Right Lobe 2 Liver, Left Lobe 4 Gallbladder G Pancreas	0 Open 3 Percutaneous 4 Percutaneous Endoscopic X External	Z No Device	Z No Qualifier
5 Hepatic Duct, Right 6 Hepatic Duct, Left 8 Cystic Duct 9 Common Bile Duct C Ampulla of Vater D Pancreatic Duct F Pancreatic Duct, Accessory	0 Open 3 Percutaneous 4 Percutaneous Endoscopic 7 Via Natural or Artificial Opening 8 Via Natural or Artificial Opening Endoscopic	Z No Device	Z No Qualifier

0   **Medical and Surgical**
F   **Hepatobiliary System and Pancreas**
L   **Occlusion:**   Completely closing an orifice or lumen of a tubular body part

Body Part Character 4	Approach Character 5	Device Character 6	Qualifier Character 7
5 Hepatic Duct, Right **6** Hepatic Duct, Left **8** Cystic Duct **9** Common Bile Duct **C** Ampulla of Vater **D** Pancreatic Duct **F** Pancreatic Duct, Accessory	**0** Open **3** Percutaneous **4** Percutaneous Endoscopic	**C** Extraluminal Device **D** Intraluminal Device **Z** No Device	**Z** No Qualifier
5 Hepatic Duct, Right **6** Hepatic Duct, Left **8** Cystic Duct **9** Common Bile Duct **C** Ampulla of Vater **D** Pancreatic Duct **F** Pancreatic Duct, Accessory	**7** Via Natural or Artificial Opening **8** Via Natural or Artificial Opening Endoscopic	**D** Intraluminal Device **Z** No Device	**Z** No Qualifier

0   **Medical and Surgical**
F   **Hepatobiliary System and Pancreas**
M   **Reattachment:**   Putting back in or on all or a portion of a separated body part to its normal location or other suitable location

Body Part Character 4	Approach Character 5	Device Character 6	Qualifier Character 7
0 Liver **1** Liver, Right Lobe **2** Liver, Left Lobe **4** Gallbladder **5** Hepatic Duct, Right **6** Hepatic Duct, Left **8** Cystic Duct **9** Common Bile Duct **C** Ampulla of Vater **D** Pancreatic Duct **F** Pancreatic Duct, Accessory **G** Pancreas	**0** Open **4** Percutaneous Endoscopic	**Z** No Device	**Z** No Qualifier

0   **Medical and Surgical**
F   **Hepatobiliary System and Pancreas**
N   **Release:**   Freeing a body part from an abnormal physical constraint

Body Part Character 4	Approach Character 5	Device Character 6	Qualifier Character 7
0 Liver **1** Liver, Right Lobe **2** Liver, Left Lobe **4** Gallbladder **G** Pancreas	**0** Open **3** Percutaneous **4** Percutaneous Endoscopic	**Z** No Device	**Z** No Qualifier
5 Hepatic Duct, Right **6** Hepatic Duct, Left **8** Cystic Duct **9** Common Bile Duct **C** Ampulla of Vater **D** Pancreatic Duct **F** Pancreatic Duct, Accessory	**0** Open **3** Percutaneous **4** Percutaneous Endoscopic **7** Via Natural or Artificial Opening **8** Via Natural or Artificial Opening Endoscopic	**Z** No Device	**Z** No Qualifier

0   **Medical and Surgical**
F   **Hepatobiliary System and Pancreas**
P   **Removal:**   Taking out or off a device from a body part

Body Part Character 4	Approach Character 5	Device Character 6	Qualifier Character 7
0 Liver	**0** Open **3** Percutaneous **4** Percutaneous Endoscopic **X** External	**0** Drainage Device **2** Monitoring Device **3** Infusion Device	**Z** No Qualifier
4 Gallbladder **G** Pancreas	**0** Open **3** Percutaneous **4** Percutaneous Endoscopic **X** External	**0** Drainage Device **2** Monitoring Device **3** Infusion Device **D** Intraluminal Device	**Z** No Qualifier

Continued on next page

0   Medical and Surgical
F   Hepatobiliary System and Pancreas
P   Removal: Taking out or off a device from a body part

Continued from previous page

Body Part Character 4	Approach Character 5	Device Character 6	Qualifier Character 7
B Hepatobiliary Duct **D** Pancreatic Duct	**0** Open **3** Percutaneous **4** Percutaneous Endoscopic **7** Via Natural or Artificial Opening **8** Via Natural or Artificial Opening Endoscopic	**0** Drainage Device **1** Radioactive Element **2** Monitoring Device **3** Infusion Device **7** Autologous Tissue Substitute **C** Extraluminal Device **D** Intraluminal Device **J** Synthetic Substitute **K** Nonautologous Tissue Substitute	**Z** No Qualifier
B Hepatobiliary Duct **D** Pancreatic Duct	**X** External	**0** Drainage Device **1** Radioactive Element **2** Monitoring Device **3** Infusion Device **D** Intraluminal Device	**Z** No Qualifier

0   Medical and Surgical
F   Hepatobiliary System and Pancreas
Q   Repair: Restoring, to the extent possible, a body part to its normal anatomic structure and function

Body Part Character 4	Approach Character 5	Device Character 6	Qualifier Character 7
0 Liver **1** Liver, Right Lobe **2** Liver, Left Lobe **4** Gallbladder **G** Pancreas	**0** Open **3** Percutaneous **4** Percutaneous Endoscopic	**Z** No Device	**Z** No Qualifier
5 Hepatic Duct, Right **6** Hepatic Duct, Left **8** Cystic Duct **9** Common Bile Duct **C** Ampulla of Vater **D** Pancreatic Duct **F** Pancreatic Duct, Accessory	**0** Open **3** Percutaneous **4** Percutaneous Endoscopic **7** Via Natural or Artificial Opening **8** Via Natural or Artificial Opening Endoscopic	**Z** No Device	**Z** No Qualifier

0   Medical and Surgical
F   Hepatobiliary System and Pancreas
R   Replacement: Putting in or on biological or synthetic material that physically takes the place and/or function of all or a portion of a body part

Body Part Character 4	Approach Character 5	Device Character 6	Qualifier Character 7
5 Hepatic Duct, Right **6** Hepatic Duct, Left **8** Cystic Duct **9** Common Bile Duct **C** Ampulla of Vater **D** Pancreatic Duct **F** Pancreatic Duct, Accessory	**0** Open **4** Percutaneous Endoscopic	**7** Autologous Tissue Substitute **J** Synthetic Substitute **K** Nonautologous Tissue Substitute	**Z** No Qualifier

0   Medical and Surgical
F   Hepatobiliary System and Pancreas
S   Reposition: Moving to its normal location or other suitable location all or a portion of a body part

Body Part Character 4	Approach Character 5	Device Character 6	Qualifier Character 7
0 Liver **4** Gallbladder **5** Hepatic Duct, Right **6** Hepatic Duct, Left **8** Cystic Duct **9** Common Bile Duct **C** Ampulla of Vater **D** Pancreatic Duct **F** Pancreatic Duct, Accessory **G** Pancreas	**0** Open **4** Percutaneous Endoscopic	**Z** No Device	**Z** No Qualifier

0   Medical and Surgical
F   Hepatobiliary System and Pancreas
T   Resection: Cutting out or off, without replacement, all of a body part

Body Part Character 4	Approach Character 5	Device Character 6	Qualifier Character 7
0 Liver **1** Liver, Right Lobe **2** Liver, Left Lobe **4** Gallbladder **G** Pancreas	**0** Open **4** Percutaneous Endoscopic	**Z** No Device	**Z** No Qualifier
5 Hepatic Duct, Right **6** Hepatic Duct, Left **8** Cystic Duct **9** Common Bile Duct **C** Ampulla of Vater **D** Pancreatic Duct **F** Pancreatic Duct, Accessory	**0** Open **4** Percutaneous Endoscopic **7** Via Natural or Artificial Opening **8** Via Natural or Artificial Opening Endoscopic	**Z** No Device	**Z** No Qualifier

0   Medical and Surgical
F   Hepatobiliary System and Pancreas
U   Supplement: Putting in or on biological or synthetic material that physically reinforces and/or augments the function of a portion of a body part

Body Part Character 4	Approach Character 5	Device Character 6	Qualifier Character 7
5 Hepatic Duct, Right **6** Hepatic Duct, Left **8** Cystic Duct **9** Common Bile Duct **C** Ampulla of Vater **D** Pancreatic Duct **F** Pancreatic Duct, Accessory	**0** Open **4** Percutaneous Endoscopic	**7** Autologous Tissue Substitute **J** Synthetic Substitute **K** Nonautologous Tissue Substitute	**Z** No Qualifier

0   Medical and Surgical
F   Hepatobiliary System and Pancreas
V   Restriction: Partially closing the orifice or lumen of a tubular body part

Body Part Character 4	Approach Character 5	Device Character 6	Qualifier Character 7
5 Hepatic Duct, Right **6** Hepatic Duct, Left **8** Cystic Duct **9** Common Bile Duct **C** Ampulla of Vater **D** Pancreatic Duct **F** Pancreatic Duct, Accessory	**0** Open **3** Percutaneous **4** Percutaneous Endoscopic	**C** Extraluminal Device **D** Intraluminal Device **Z** No Device	**Z** No Qualifier
5 Hepatic Duct, Right **6** Hepatic Duct, Left **8** Cystic Duct **9** Common Bile Duct **C** Ampulla of Vater **D** Pancreatic Duct **F** Pancreatic Duct, Accessory	**7** Via Natural or Artificial Opening **8** Via Natural or Artificial Opening Endoscopic	**D** Intraluminal Device **Z** No Device	**Z** No Qualifier

0 **Medical and Surgical**
F **Hepatobiliary System and Pancreas**
W **Revision:**   Correcting, to the extent possible, a malfunctioning or displaced device

Body Part Character 4	Approach Character 5	Device Character 6	Qualifier Character 7
0 Liver	**0** Open **3** Percutaneous **4** Percutaneous Endoscopic **X** External	**0** Drainage Device **2** Monitoring Device **3** Infusion Device	**Z** No Qualifier
4 Gallbladder **G** Pancreas	**0** Open **3** Percutaneous **4** Percutaneous Endoscopic **X** External	**0** Drainage Device **2** Monitoring Device **3** Infusion Device **D** Intraluminal Device	**Z** No Qualifier
B Hepatobiliary Duct **D** Pancreatic Duct	**0** Open **3** Percutaneous **4** Percutaneous Endoscopic **7** Via Natural or Artificial Opening **8** Via Natural or Artificial Opening Endoscopic **X** External	**0** Drainage Device **2** Monitoring Device **3** Infusion Device **7** Autologous Tissue Substitute **C** Extraluminal Device **D** Intraluminal Device **J** Synthetic Substitute **K** Nonautologous Tissue Substitute	**Z** No Qualifier

0 **Medical and Surgical**
F **Hepatobiliary System and Pancreas**
Y **Transplantation:**   Putting in or on all or a portion of a living body part taken from another individual or animal to physically take the place and/or function of all or a portion of a similar body part

Body Part Character 4	Approach Character 5	Device Character 6	Qualifier Character 7
0 Liver **G** Pancreas	**0** Open	**Z** No Device	**0** Allogeneic **1** Syngeneic **2** Zooplastic

Endocrine System 0G2–0GW

0 Medical and Surgical
G Endocrine System
2 **Change:** Taking out or off a device from a body part and putting back an identical or similar device in or on the same body part without cutting or puncturing the skin or a mucous membrane

Body Part Character 4	Approach Character 5	Device Character 6	Qualifier Character 7
0 Pituitary Gland **1** Pineal Body **5** Adrenal Gland **K** Thyroid Gland **R** Parathyroid Gland **S** Endocrine Gland	**X** External	**0** Drainage Device **Y** Other Device	**Z** No Qualifier

0 Medical and Surgical
G Endocrine System
5 **Destruction:** Physical eradication of all or a portion of a body part by the direct use of energy, force, or a destructive agent

Body Part Character 4	Approach Character 5	Device Character 6	Qualifier Character 7
0 Pituitary Gland **1** Pineal Body **2** Adrenal Gland, Left **3** Adrenal Gland, Right **4** Adrenal Glands, Bilateral **6** Carotid Body, Left **7** Carotid Body, Right **8** Carotid Bodies, Bilateral **9** Para-aortic Body **B** Coccygeal Glomus **C** Glomus Jugulare **D** Aortic Body **F** Paraganglion Extremity **G** Thyroid Gland Lobe, Left **H** Thyroid Gland Lobe, Right **K** Thyroid Gland **L** Superior Parathyroid Gland, Right **M** Superior Parathyroid Gland, Left **N** Inferior Parathyroid Gland, Right **P** Inferior Parathyroid Gland, Left **Q** Parathyroid Glands, Multiple **R** Parathyroid Gland	**0** Open **3** Percutaneous **4** Percutaneous Endoscopic	**Z** No Device	**Z** No Qualifier

0 Medical and Surgical
G Endocrine System
8 **Division:** Cutting into a body part without draining fluids and/or gases from the body part in order to separate or transect a body part

Body Part Character 4	Approach Character 5	Device Character 6	Qualifier Character 7
0 Pituitary Gland **J** Thyroid Gland Isthmus	**0** Open **3** Percutaneous **4** Percutaneous Endoscopic	**Z** No Device	**Z** No Qualifier

0   **Medical and Surgical**
G   **Endocrine System**
9   **Drainage:**   Taking or letting out fluids and/or gases from a body part

Body Part Character 4	Approach Character 5	Device Character 6	Qualifier Character 7
0 Pituitary Gland 1 Pineal Body 2 Adrenal Gland, Left 3 Adrenal Gland, Right 4 Adrenal Glands, Bilateral 6 Carotid Body, Left 7 Carotid Body, Right 8 Carotid Bodies, Bilateral 9 Para-aortic Body B Coccygeal Glomus C Glomus Jugulare D Aortic Body F Paraganglion Extremity G Thyroid Gland Lobe, Left H Thyroid Gland Lobe, Right K Thyroid Gland L Superior Parathyroid Gland, Right M Superior Parathyroid Gland, Left N Inferior Parathyroid Gland, Right P Inferior Parathyroid Gland, Left Q Parathyroid Glands, Multiple R Parathyroid Gland	0 Open 3 Percutaneous 4 Percutaneous Endoscopic	0 Drainage Device	Z No Qualifier
0 Pituitary Gland 1 Pineal Body 2 Adrenal Gland, Left 3 Adrenal Gland, Right 4 Adrenal Glands, Bilateral 6 Carotid Body, Left 7 Carotid Body, Right 8 Carotid Bodies, Bilateral 9 Para-aortic Body B Coccygeal Glomus C Glomus Jugulare D Aortic Body F Paraganglion Extremity G Thyroid Gland Lobe, Left H Thyroid Gland Lobe, Right K Thyroid Gland L Superior Parathyroid Gland, Right M Superior Parathyroid Gland, Left N Inferior Parathyroid Gland, Right P Inferior Parathyroid Gland, Left Q Parathyroid Glands, Multiple R Parathyroid Gland	0 Open 3 Percutaneous 4 Percutaneous Endoscopic	Z No Device	X Diagnostic Z No Qualifier

0   **Medical and Surgical**
G   **Endocrine System**
B   **Excision:**   Cutting out or off, without replacement, a portion of a body part

Body Part Character 4	Approach Character 5	Device Character 6	Qualifier Character 7
0 Pituitary Gland 1 Pineal Body 2 Adrenal Gland, Left 3 Adrenal Gland, Right 4 Adrenal Glands, Bilateral 6 Carotid Body, Left 7 Carotid Body, Right 8 Carotid Bodies, Bilateral 9 Para-aortic Body B Coccygeal Glomus C Glomus Jugulare D Aortic Body F Paraganglion Extremity G Thyroid Gland Lobe, Left H Thyroid Gland Lobe, Right L Superior Parathyroid Gland, Right M Superior Parathyroid Gland, Left N Inferior Parathyroid Gland, Right P Inferior Parathyroid Gland, Left Q Parathyroid Glands, Multiple R Parathyroid Gland	0 Open 3 Percutaneous 4 Percutaneous Endoscopic	Z No Device	X Diagnostic Z No Qualifier

0   **Medical and Surgical**
G   **Endocrine System**
C   **Extirpation:**   Taking or cutting out solid matter from a body part

Body Part Character 4	Approach Character 5	Device Character 6	Qualifier Character 7
0 Pituitary Gland **1** Pineal Body **2** Adrenal Gland, Left **3** Adrenal Gland, Right **4** Adrenal Glands, Bilateral **6** Carotid Body, Left **7** Carotid Body, Right **8** Carotid Bodies, Bilateral **9** Para-aortic Body **B** Coccygeal Glomus **C** Glomus Jugulare **D** Aortic Body **F** Paraganglion Extremity **G** Thyroid Gland Lobe, Left **H** Thyroid Gland Lobe, Right **K** Thyroid Gland **L** Superior Parathyroid Gland, Right **M** Superior Parathyroid Gland, Left **N** Inferior Parathyroid Gland, Right **P** Inferior Parathyroid Gland, Left **Q** Parathyroid Glands, Multiple **R** Parathyroid Gland	**0** Open **3** Percutaneous **4** Percutaneous Endoscopic	**Z** No Device	**Z** No Qualifier

0   **Medical and Surgical**
G   **Endocrine System**
H   **Insertion:**   Putting in a nonbiological appliance that monitors, assists, performs or prevents a physiological function, but does not physically take the place of a body part

Body Part Character 4	Approach Character 5	Device Character 6	Qualifier Character 7
S Endocrine Gland	**0** Open **3** Percutaneous **4** Percutaneous Endoscopic	**2** Monitoring Device **3** Infusion Device	**Z** No Qualifier

0   **Medical and Surgical**
G   **Endocrine System**
J   **Inspection:**   Visually and/or manually exploring a body part

Body Part Character 4	Approach Character 5	Device Character 6	Qualifier Character 7
0 Pituitary Gland **1** Pineal Body **2** Adrenal Gland, Left **3** Adrenal Gland, Right **4** Adrenal Glands, Bilateral **6** Carotid Body, Left **7** Carotid Body, Right **8** Carotid Bodies, Bilateral **9** Para-aortic Body **B** Coccygeal Glomus **C** Glomus Jugulare **D** Aortic Body **F** Paraganglion Extremity **G** Thyroid Gland Lobe, Left **H** Thyroid Gland Lobe, Right **J** Thyroid Gland Isthmus **K** Thyroid Gland **L** Superior Parathyroid Gland, Right **M** Superior Parathyroid Gland, Left **N** Inferior Parathyroid Gland, Right **P** Inferior Parathyroid Gland, Left **Q** Parathyroid Glands, Multiple **R** Parathyroid Gland	**0** Open **3** Percutaneous **4** Percutaneous Endoscopic	**Z** No Device	**Z** No Qualifier

0 Medical and Surgical
G Endocrine System
M Reattachment: Putting back in or on all or a portion of a separated body part to its normal location or other suitable location

Body Part Character 4	Approach Character 5	Device Character 6	Qualifier Character 7
2 Adrenal Gland, Left 3 Adrenal Gland, Right G Thyroid Gland Lobe, Left H Thyroid Gland Lobe, Right L Superior Parathyroid Gland, Right M Superior Parathyroid Gland, Left N Inferior Parathyroid Gland, Right P Inferior Parathyroid Gland, Left Q Parathyroid Glands, Multiple R Parathyroid Gland	0 Open 4 Percutaneous Endoscopic	Z No Device	Z No Qualifier

0 Medical and Surgical
G Endocrine System
N Release: Freeing a body part from an abnormal physical constraint

Body Part Character 4	Approach Character 5	Device Character 6	Qualifier Character 7
0 Pituitary Gland 1 Pineal Body 2 Adrenal Gland, Left 3 Adrenal Gland, Right 4 Adrenal Glands, Bilateral 6 Carotid Body, Left 7 Carotid Body, Right 8 Carotid Bodies, Bilateral 9 Para-aortic Body B Coccygeal Glomus C Glomus Jugulare D Aortic Body F Paraganglion Extremity G Thyroid Gland Lobe, Left H Thyroid Gland Lobe, Right K Thyroid Gland L Superior Parathyroid Gland, Right M Superior Parathyroid Gland, Left N Inferior Parathyroid Gland, Right P Inferior Parathyroid Gland, Left Q Parathyroid Glands, Multiple R Parathyroid Gland	0 Open 3 Percutaneous 4 Percutaneous Endoscopic	Z No Device	Z No Qualifier

0 Medical and Surgical
G Endocrine System
P Removal: Taking out or off a device from a body part

Body Part Character 4	Approach Character 5	Device Character 6	Qualifier Character 7
0 Pituitary Gland 1 Pineal Body 5 Adrenal Gland K Thyroid Gland R Parathyroid Gland	0 Open 3 Percutaneous 4 Percutaneous Endoscopic X External	0 Drainage Device	Z No Qualifier
S Endocrine Gland	0 Open 3 Percutaneous 4 Percutaneous Endoscopic X External	0 Drainage Device 2 Monitoring Device 3 Infusion Device	Z No Qualifier

0   Medical and Surgical
G   Endocrine System
Q   Repair: Restoring, to the extent possible, a body part to its normal anatomic structure and function

Body Part Character 4	Approach Character 5	Device Character 6	Qualifier Character 7
0 Pituitary Gland **1** Pineal Body **2** Adrenal Gland, Left **3** Adrenal Gland, Right **4** Adrenal Glands, Bilateral **6** Carotid Body, Left **7** Carotid Body, Right **8** Carotid Bodies, Bilateral **9** Para-aortic Body **B** Coccygeal Glomus **C** Glomus Jugulare **D** Aortic Body **F** Paraganglion Extremity **G** Thyroid Gland Lobe, Left **H** Thyroid Gland Lobe, Right **J** Thyroid Gland Isthmus **K** Thyroid Gland **L** Superior Parathyroid Gland, Right **M** Superior Parathyroid Gland, Left **N** Inferior Parathyroid Gland, Right **P** Inferior Parathyroid Gland, Left **Q** Parathyroid Glands, Multiple **R** Parathyroid Gland	**0** Open **3** Percutaneous **4** Percutaneous Endoscopic	**Z** No Device	**Z** No Qualifier

0   Medical and Surgical
G   Endocrine System
S   Reposition: Moving to its normal location or other suitable location all or a portion of a body part

Body Part Character 4	Approach Character 5	Device Character 6	Qualifier Character 7
2 Adrenal Gland, Left **3** Adrenal Gland, Right **G** Thyroid Gland Lobe, Left **H** Thyroid Gland Lobe, Right **L** Superior Parathyroid Gland, Right **M** Superior Parathyroid Gland, Left **N** Inferior Parathyroid Gland, Right **P** Inferior Parathyroid Gland, Left **Q** Parathyroid Glands, Multiple **R** Parathyroid Gland	**0** Open **4** Percutaneous Endoscopic	**Z** No Device	**Z** No Qualifier

0   Medical and Surgical
G   Endocrine System
T   Resection: Cutting out or off, without replacement, all of a body part

Body Part Character 4	Approach Character 5	Device Character 6	Qualifier Character 7
0 Pituitary Gland **1** Pineal Body **2** Adrenal Gland, Left **3** Adrenal Gland, Right **4** Adrenal Glands, Bilateral **6** Carotid Body, Left **7** Carotid Body, Right **8** Carotid Bodies, Bilateral **9** Para-aortic Body **B** Coccygeal Glomus **C** Glomus Jugulare **D** Aortic Body **F** Paraganglion Extremity **G** Thyroid Gland Lobe, Left **H** Thyroid Gland Lobe, Right **K** Thyroid Gland **L** Superior Parathyroid Gland, Right **M** Superior Parathyroid Gland, Left **N** Inferior Parathyroid Gland, Right **P** Inferior Parathyroid Gland, Left **Q** Parathyroid Glands, Multiple **R** Parathyroid Gland	**0** Open **4** Percutaneous Endoscopic	**Z** No Device	**Z** No Qualifier

0   **Medical and Surgical**
G   **Endocrine System**
W   **Revision:**   Correcting, to the extent possible, a malfunctioning or displaced device

Body Part Character 4	Approach Character 5	Device Character 6	Qualifier Character 7
0 Pituitary Gland **1** Pineal Body **5** Adrenal Gland **K** Thyroid Gland **R** Parathyroid Gland	**0** Open **3** Percutaneous **4** Percutaneous Endoscopic **X** External	**0** Drainage Device	**Z** No Qualifier
S Endocrine Gland	**0** Open **3** Percutaneous **4** Percutaneous Endoscopic **X** External	**0** Drainage Device **2** Monitoring Device **3** Infusion Device	**Z** No Qualifier

Skin and Breast 0H0–0HY

0   Medical and Surgical
H   Skin and Breast
0   Alteration: Modifying the anatomic structure of a body part without affecting the function of the body part

Body Part Character 4	Approach Character 5	Device Character 6	Qualifier Character 7
T Breast, Right **U** Breast, Left **V** Breast, Bilateral	**0** Open **3** Percutaneous **X** External	**7** Autologous Tissue Substitute **J** Synthetic Substitute **K** Nonautologous Tissue Substitute **Z** No Device	**Z** No Qualifier

0   Medical and Surgical
H   Skin and Breast
2   Change: Taking out or off a device from a body part and putting back an identical or similar device in or on the same body part without cutting or puncturing the skin or a mucous membrane

Body Part Character 4	Approach Character 5	Device Character 6	Qualifier Character 7
P Skin **T** Breast, Right **U** Breast, Left	**X** External	**0** Drainage Device **Y** Other Device	**Z** No Qualifier

0   Medical and Surgical
H   Skin and Breast
5   Destruction: Physical eradication of all or a portion of a body part by the direct use of energy, force, or a destructive agent

Body Part Character 4	Approach Character 5	Device Character 6	Qualifier Character 7
0 Skin, Scalp **1** Skin, Face **2** Skin, Right Ear **3** Skin, Left Ear **4** Skin, Neck **5** Skin, Chest **6** Skin, Back **7** Skin, Abdomen **8** Skin, Buttock **9** Skin, Perineum **A** Skin, Genitalia **B** Skin, Right Upper Arm **C** Skin, Left Upper Arm **D** Skin, Right Lower Arm **E** Skin, Left Lower Arm **F** Skin, Right Hand **G** Skin, Left Hand **H** Skin, Right Upper Leg **J** Skin, Left Upper Leg **K** Skin, Right Lower Leg **L** Skin, Left Lower Leg **M** Skin, Right Foot **N** Skin, Left Foot **Q** Finger Nail **R** Toe Nail	**X** External	**Z** No Device	**Z** No Qualifier
T Breast, Right **U** Breast, Left **V** Breast, Bilateral **W** Nipple, Right **X** Nipple, Left	**0** Open **3** Percutaneous **7** Via Natural or Artificial Opening **8** Via Natural or Artificial Opening Endoscopic **X** External	**Z** No Device	**Z** No Qualifier

0 **Medical and Surgical**
H **Skin and Breast**
8 **Division:**   Cutting into a body part without draining fluids and/or gases from the body part in order to separate or transect a body part

Body Part Character 4	Approach Character 5	Device Character 6	Qualifier Character 7
0 Skin, Scalp 1 Skin, Face 2 Skin, Right Ear 3 Skin, Left Ear 4 Skin, Neck 5 Skin, Chest 6 Skin, Back 7 Skin, Abdomen 8 Skin, Buttock 9 Skin, Perineum A Skin, Genitalia B Skin, Right Upper Arm C Skin, Left Upper Arm D Skin, Right Lower Arm E Skin, Left Lower Arm F Skin, Right Hand G Skin, Left Hand H Skin, Right Upper Leg J Skin, Left Upper Leg K Skin, Right Lower Leg L Skin, Left Lower Leg M Skin, Right Foot N Skin, Left Foot	X External	Z No Device	Z No Qualifier

0 **Medical and Surgical**
H **Skin and Breast**
9 **Drainage:**   Taking or letting out fluids and/or gases from a body part

Body Part Character 4	Approach Character 5	Device Character 6	Qualifier Character 7
0 Skin, Scalp 1 Skin, Face 2 Skin, Right Ear 3 Skin, Left Ear 4 Skin, Neck 5 Skin, Chest 6 Skin, Back 7 Skin, Abdomen 8 Skin, Buttock 9 Skin, Perineum A Skin, Genitalia B Skin, Right Upper Arm C Skin, Left Upper Arm D Skin, Right Lower Arm E Skin, Left Lower Arm F Skin, Right Hand G Skin, Left Hand H Skin, Right Upper Leg J Skin, Left Upper Leg K Skin, Right Lower Leg L Skin, Left Lower Leg M Skin, Right Foot N Skin, Left Foot Q Finger Nail R Toe Nail	X External	0 Drainage Device	Z No Qualifier

Continued on next page

0   Medical and Surgical   *Continued from previous page*
H   Skin and Breast
9   Drainage: Taking or letting out fluids and/or gases from a body part

Body Part Character 4	Approach Character 5	Device Character 6	Qualifier Character 7
0 Skin, Scalp **1** Skin, Face **2** Skin, Right Ear **3** Skin, Left Ear **4** Skin, Neck **5** Skin, Chest **6** Skin, Back **7** Skin, Abdomen **8** Skin, Buttock **9** Skin, Perineum **A** Skin, Genitalia **B** Skin, Right Upper Arm **C** Skin, Left Upper Arm **D** Skin, Right Lower Arm **E** Skin, Left Lower Arm **F** Skin, Right Hand **G** Skin, Left Hand **H** Skin, Right Upper Leg **J** Skin, Left Upper Leg **K** Skin, Right Lower Leg **L** Skin, Left Lower Leg **M** Skin, Right Foot **N** Skin, Left Foot **Q** Finger Nail **R** Toe Nail	**X** External	**Z** No Device	**X** Diagnostic **Z** No Qualifier
T Breast, Right **U** Breast, Left **V** Breast, Bilateral **W** Nipple, Right **X** Nipple, Left	**0** Open **3** Percutaneous **7** Via Natural or Artificial Opening **8** Via Natural or Artificial Opening Endoscopic **X** External	**0** Drainage Device	**Z** No Qualifier
T Breast, Right **U** Breast, Left **V** Breast, Bilateral **W** Nipple, Right **X** Nipple, Left	**0** Open **3** Percutaneous **7** Via Natural or Artificial Opening **8** Via Natural or Artificial Opening Endoscopic **X** External	**Z** No Device	**X** Diagnostic **Z** No Qualifier

0   Medical and Surgical
H   Skin and Breast
B   Excision: Cutting out or off, without replacement, a portion of a body part

Body Part Character 4	Approach Character 5	Device Character 6	Qualifier Character 7
0 Skin, Scalp **1** Skin, Face **2** Skin, Right Ear **3** Skin, Left Ear **4** Skin, Neck **5** Skin, Chest **6** Skin, Back **7** Skin, Abdomen **8** Skin, Buttock **9** Skin, Perineum **A** Skin, Genitalia **B** Skin, Right Upper Arm **C** Skin, Left Upper Arm **D** Skin, Right Lower Arm **E** Skin, Left Lower Arm **F** Skin, Right Hand **G** Skin, Left Hand **H** Skin, Right Upper Leg **J** Skin, Left Upper Leg **K** Skin, Right Lower Leg **L** Skin, Left Lower Leg **M** Skin, Right Foot **N** Skin, Left Foot **Q** Finger Nail **R** Toe Nail	**X** External	**Z** No Device	**X** Diagnostic **Z** No Qualifier

Continued on next page

0 Medical and Surgical
H Skin and Breast
B Excision: Cutting out or off, without replacement, a portion of a body part

Continued from previous page

Body Part Character 4	Approach Character 5	Device Character 6	Qualifier Character 7
T Breast, Right **U** Breast, Left **V** Breast, Bilateral **W** Nipple, Right **X** Nipple, Left **Y** Supernumerary Breast	**0** Open **3** Percutaneous **7** Via Natural or Artificial Opening **8** Via Natural or Artificial Opening Endoscopic **X** External	**Z** No Device	**X** Diagnostic **Z** No Qualifier

0 Medical and Surgical
H Skin and Breast
C Extirpation: Taking or cutting out solid matter from a body part

Body Part Character 4	Approach Character 5	Device Character 6	Qualifier Character 7
0 Skin, Scalp **1** Skin, Face **2** Skin, Right Ear **3** Skin, Left Ear **4** Skin, Neck **5** Skin, Chest **6** Skin, Back **7** Skin, Abdomen **8** Skin, Buttock **9** Skin, Perineum **A** Skin, Genitalia **B** Skin, Right Upper Arm **C** Skin, Left Upper Arm **D** Skin, Right Lower Arm **E** Skin, Left Lower Arm **F** Skin, Right Hand **G** Skin, Left Hand **H** Skin, Right Upper Leg **J** Skin, Left Upper Leg **K** Skin, Right Lower Leg **L** Skin, Left Lower Leg **M** Skin, Right Foot **N** Skin, Left Foot **Q** Finger Nail **R** Toe Nail	**X** External	**Z** No Device	**Z** No Qualifier
T Breast, Right **U** Breast, Left **V** Breast, Bilateral **W** Nipple, Right **X** Nipple, Left	**0** Open **3** Percutaneous **7** Via Natural or Artificial Opening **8** Via Natural or Artificial Opening Endoscopic **X** External	**Z** No Device	**Z** No Qualifier

0 Medical and Surgical
H Skin and Breast
D Extraction: Pulling or stripping out or off all or a portion of a body part by the use of force

Body Part Character 4	Approach Character 5	Device Character 6	Qualifier Character 7
0 Skin, Scalp **1** Skin, Face **2** Skin, Right Ear **3** Skin, Left Ear **4** Skin, Neck **5** Skin, Chest **6** Skin, Back **7** Skin, Abdomen **8** Skin, Buttock **9** Skin, Perineum **A** Skin, Genitalia **B** Skin, Right Upper Arm **C** Skin, Left Upper Arm **D** Skin, Right Lower Arm **E** Skin, Left Lower Arm **F** Skin, Right Hand **G** Skin, Left Hand **H** Skin, Right Upper Leg **J** Skin, Left Upper Leg **K** Skin, Right Lower Leg **L** Skin, Left Lower Leg **M** Skin, Right Foot **N** Skin, Left Foot **Q** Finger Nail **R** Toe Nail **S** Hair	**X** External	**Z** No Device	**Z** No Qualifier

0 Medical and Surgical
H Skin and Breast
H Insertion: Putting in a nonbiological appliance that monitors, assists, performs or prevents a physiological function, but does not physically take the place of a body part

Body Part Character 4	Approach Character 5	Device Character 6	Qualifier Character 7
T Breast, Right **U** Breast, Left **V** Breast, Bilateral **W** Nipple, Right **X** Nipple, Left	**0** Open **3** Percutaneous **7** Via Natural or Artificial Opening **8** Via Natural or Artificial Opening Endoscopic	**1** Radioactive Element **N** Tissue Expander	**Z** No Qualifier
T Breast, Right **U** Breast, Left **V** Breast, Bilateral **W** Nipple, Right **X** Nipple, Left	**X** External	**1** Radioactive Element	**Z** No Qualifier

0 **Medical and Surgical**
H **Skin and Breast**
J **Inspection:**   Visually and/or manually exploring a body part

Body Part Character 4	Approach Character 5	Device Character 6	Qualifier Character 7
0 Skin, Scalp 1 Skin, Face 2 Skin, Right Ear 3 Skin, Left Ear 4 Skin, Neck 5 Skin, Chest 6 Skin, Back 7 Skin, Abdomen 8 Skin, Buttock 9 Skin, Perineum A Skin, Genitalia B Skin, Right Upper Arm C Skin, Left Upper Arm D Skin, Right Lower Arm E Skin, Left Lower Arm F Skin, Right Hand G Skin, Left Hand H Skin, Right Upper Leg J Skin, Left Upper Leg K Skin, Right Lower Leg L Skin, Left Lower Leg M Skin, Right Foot N Skin, Left Foot Q Finger Nail R Toe Nail S Hair	X External	Z No Device	Z No Qualifier
T Breast, Right U Breast, Left V Breast, Bilateral W Nipple, Right X Nipple, Left Y Supernumerary Breast	0 Open 3 Percutaneous 7 Via Natural or Artificial Opening 8 Via Natural or Artificial Opening Endoscopic X External	Z No Device	Z No Qualifier

0 **Medical and Surgical**
H **Skin and Breast**
M **Reattachment:**   Putting back in or on all or a portion of a separated body part to its normal location or other suitable location

Body Part Character 4	Approach Character 5	Device Character 6	Qualifier Character 7
0 Skin, Scalp 1 Skin, Face 2 Skin, Right Ear 3 Skin, Left Ear 4 Skin, Neck 5 Skin, Chest 6 Skin, Back 7 Skin, Abdomen 8 Skin, Buttock 9 Skin, Perineum A Skin, Genitalia B Skin, Right Upper Arm C Skin, Left Upper Arm D Skin, Right Lower Arm E Skin, Left Lower Arm F Skin, Right Hand G Skin, Left Hand H Skin, Right Upper Leg J Skin, Left Upper Leg K Skin, Right Lower Leg L Skin, Left Lower Leg M Skin, Right Foot N Skin, Left Foot T Breast, Right U Breast, Left V Breast, Bilateral W Nipple, Right X Nipple, Left	X External	Z No Device	Z No Qualifier

0 Medical and Surgical
H Skin and Breast
N Release: Freeing a body part from an abnormal physical constraint

Body Part Character 4	Approach Character 5	Device Character 6	Qualifier Character 7
0 Skin, Scalp **1** Skin, Face **2** Skin, Right Ear **3** Skin, Left Ear **4** Skin, Neck **5** Skin, Chest **6** Skin, Back **7** Skin, Abdomen **8** Skin, Buttock **9** Skin, Perineum **A** Skin, Genitalia **B** Skin, Right Upper Arm **C** Skin, Left Upper Arm **D** Skin, Right Lower Arm **E** Skin, Left Lower Arm **F** Skin, Right Hand **G** Skin, Left Hand **H** Skin, Right Upper Leg **J** Skin, Left Upper Leg **K** Skin, Right Lower Leg **L** Skin, Left Lower Leg **M** Skin, Right Foot **N** Skin, Left Foot **Q** Finger Nail **R** Toe Nail	**X** External	**Z** No Device	**Z** No Qualifier
T Breast, Right **U** Breast, Left **V** Breast, Bilateral **W** Nipple, Right **X** Nipple, Left	**0** Open **3** Percutaneous **7** Via Natural or Artificial Opening **8** Via Natural or Artificial Opening Endoscopic **X** External	**Z** No Device	**Z** No Qualifier

0 Medical and Surgical
H Skin and Breast
P Removal: Taking out or off a device from a body part

Body Part Character 4	Approach Character 5	Device Character 6	Qualifier Character 7
P Skin **Q** Finger Nail **R** Toe Nail	**X** External	**0** Drainage Device **7** Autologous Tissue Substitute **J** Synthetic Substitute **K** Nonautologous Tissue Substitute	**Z** No Qualifier
S Hair	**X** External	**7** Autologous Tissue Substitute **J** Synthetic Substitute **K** Nonautologous Tissue Substitute	**Z** No Qualifier
T Breast, Right **U** Breast, Left	**0** Open **3** Percutaneous **7** Via Natural or Artificial Opening **8** Via Natural or Artificial Opening Endoscopic	**0** Drainage Device **1** Radioactive Element **7** Autologous Tissue Substitute **J** Synthetic Substitute **K** Nonautologous Tissue Substitute **N** Tissue Expander	**Z** No Qualifier
T Breast, Right **U** Breast, Left	**X** External	**0** Drainage Device **1** Radioactive Element **7** Autologous Tissue Substitute **J** Synthetic Substitute **K** Nonautologous Tissue Substitute	**Z** No Qualifier

0   **Medical and Surgical**
H   **Skin and Breast**
Q   **Repair:**   Restoring, to the extent possible, a body part to its normal anatomic structure and function

Body Part Character 4	Approach Character 5	Device Character 6	Qualifier Character 7
0 Skin, Scalp 1 Skin, Face 2 Skin, Right Ear 3 Skin, Left Ear 4 Skin, Neck 5 Skin, Chest 6 Skin, Back 7 Skin, Abdomen 8 Skin, Buttock 9 Skin, Perineum A Skin, Genitalia B Skin, Right Upper Arm C Skin, Left Upper Arm D Skin, Right Lower Arm E Skin, Left Lower Arm F Skin, Right Hand G Skin, Left Hand H Skin, Right Upper Leg J Skin, Left Upper Leg K Skin, Right Lower Leg L Skin, Left Lower Leg M Skin, Right Foot N Skin, Left Foot Q Finger Nail R Toe Nail	X External	Z No Device	Z No Qualifier
T Breast, Right U Breast, Left V Breast, Bilateral W Nipple, Right X Nipple, Left Y Supernumerary Breast	0 Open 3 Percutaneous 7 Via Natural or Artificial Opening 8 Via Natural or Artificial Opening Endoscopic X External	Z No Device	Z No Qualifier

0   **Medical and Surgical**
H   **Skin and Breast**
R   **Replacement:**   Putting in or on biological or synthetic material that physically takes the place and/or function of all or a portion of a body part

Body Part Character 4	Approach Character 5	Device Character 6	Qualifier Character 7
0 Skin, Scalp 1 Skin, Face 2 Skin, Right Ear 3 Skin, Left Ear 4 Skin, Neck 5 Skin, Chest 6 Skin, Back 7 Skin, Abdomen 8 Skin, Buttock 9 Skin, Perineum A Skin, Genitalia B Skin, Right Upper Arm C Skin, Left Upper Arm D Skin, Right Lower Arm E Skin, Left Lower Arm F Skin, Right Hand G Skin, Left Hand H Skin, Right Upper Leg J Skin, Left Upper Leg K Skin, Right Lower Leg L Skin, Left Lower Leg M Skin, Right Foot N Skin, Left Foot	X External	7 Autologous Tissue Substitute K Nonautologous Tissue Substitute	3 Full Thickness 4 Partial Thickness

Continued on next page

0   Medical and Surgical   *Continued from previous page*
H   Skin and Breast
R   Replacement: Putting in or on biological or synthetic material that physically takes the place and/or function of all or a portion of a body part

Body Part Character 4	Approach Character 5	Device Character 6	Qualifier Character 7
0 Skin, Scalp 1 Skin, Face 2 Skin, Right Ear 3 Skin, Left Ear 4 Skin, Neck 5 Skin, Chest 6 Skin, Back 7 Skin, Abdomen 8 Skin, Buttock 9 Skin, Perineum A Skin, Genitalia B Skin, Right Upper Arm C Skin, Left Upper Arm D Skin, Right Lower Arm E Skin, Left Lower Arm F Skin, Right Hand G Skin, Left Hand H Skin, Right Upper Leg J Skin, Left Upper Leg K Skin, Right Lower Leg L Skin, Left Lower Leg M Skin, Right Foot N Skin, Left Foot	X External	J Synthetic Substitute	3 Full Thickness 4 Partial Thickness Z No Qualifier
Q Finger Nail R Toe Nail S Hair	X External	7 Autologous Tissue Substitute J Synthetic Substitute K Nonautologous Tissue Substitute	Z No Qualifier
T Breast, Right U Breast, Left V Breast, Bilateral	0 Open	7 Autologous Tissue Substitute	5 Latissimus Dorsi Myocutaneous Flap 6 Transverse Rectus Abdominis Myocutaneous Flap 7 Deep Inferior Epigastric Artery Perforator Flap 8 Superficial Inferior Epigastric Artery Flap 9 Gluteal Artery Perforator Flap Z No Qualifier
T Breast, Right U Breast, Left V Breast, Bilateral	0 Open	J Synthetic Substitute K Nonautologous Tissue Substitute	Z No Qualifier
T Breast, Right U Breast, Left V Breast, Bilateral	3 Percutaneous X External	7 Autologous Tissue Substitute J Synthetic Substitute K Nonautologous Tissue Substitute	Z No Qualifier
W Nipple, Right X Nipple, Left	0 Open 3 Percutaneous X External	7 Autologous Tissue Substitute J Synthetic Substitute K Nonautologous Tissue Substitute	Z No Qualifier

0   Medical and Surgical
H   Skin and Breast
S   Reposition: Moving to its normal location or other suitable location all or a portion of a body part

Body Part Character 4	Approach Character 5	Device Character 6	Qualifier Character 7
S Hair W Nipple, Right X Nipple, Left	X External	Z No Device	Z No Qualifier
T Breast, Right U Breast, Left V Breast, Bilateral	0 Open	Z No Device	Z No Qualifier

0   Medical and Surgical
H   Skin and Breast
T   Resection: Cutting out or off, without replacement, all of a body part

Body Part Character 4	Approach Character 5	Device Character 6	Qualifier Character 7
Q Finger Nail R Toe Nail W Nipple, Right X Nipple, Left	X External	Z No Device	Z No Qualifier

Continued on next page

0   Medical and Surgical   *Continued from previous page*
H   Skin and Breast
T   Resection: Cutting out or off, without replacement, all of a body part

Body Part Character 4	Approach Character 5	Device Character 6	Qualifier Character 7
T Breast, Right **U** Breast, Left **V** Breast, Bilateral **Y** Supernumerary Breast	**0** Open	**Z** No Device	**Z** No Qualifier

0   Medical and Surgical
H   Skin and Breast
U   Supplement: Putting in or on biological or synthetic material that physically reinforces and/or augments the function of a portion of a body part

Body Part Character 4	Approach Character 5	Device Character 6	Qualifier Character 7
T Breast, Right **U** Breast, Left **V** Breast, Bilateral **W** Nipple, Right **X** Nipple, Left	**0** Open **3** Percutaneous **7** Via Natural or Artificial Opening **8** Via Natural or Artificial Opening Endoscopic **X** External	**7** Autologous Tissue Substitute **J** Synthetic Substitute **K** Nonautologous Tissue Substitute	**Z** No Qualifier

0   Medical and Surgical
H   Skin and Breast
W   Revision: Correcting, to the extent possible, a malfunctioning or displaced device

Body Part Character 4	Approach Character 5	Device Character 6	Qualifier Character 7
P Skin **Q** Finger Nail **R** Toe Nail **T** Breast, Right **U** Breast, Left	**X** External	**0** Drainage Device **7** Autologous Tissue Substitute **J** Synthetic Substitute **K** Nonautologous Tissue Substitute	**Z** No Qualifier
S Hair	**X** External	**7** Autologous Tissue Substitute **J** Synthetic Substitute **K** Nonautologous Tissue Substitute	**Z** No Qualifier
T Breast, Right **U** Breast, Left	**0** Open **3** Percutaneous **7** Via Natural or Artificial Opening **8** Via Natural or Artificial Opening Endoscopic	**0** Drainage Device **7** Autologous Tissue Substitute **J** Synthetic Substitute **K** Nonautologous Tissue Substitute **N** Tissue Expander	**Z** No Qualifier

0   Medical and Surgical
H   Skin and Breast
X   Transfer: Moving, without taking out, all or a portion of a body part to another location to take over the function of all or a portion of a body part

Body Part Character 4	Approach Character 5	Device Character 6	Qualifier Character 7
0 Skin, Scalp **1** Skin, Face **2** Skin, Right Ear **3** Skin, Left Ear **4** Skin, Neck **5** Skin, Chest **6** Skin, Back **7** Skin, Abdomen **8** Skin, Buttock **9** Skin, Perineum **A** Skin, Genitalia **B** Skin, Right Upper Arm **C** Skin, Left Upper Arm **D** Skin, Right Lower Arm **E** Skin, Left Lower Arm **F** Skin, Right Hand **G** Skin, Left Hand **H** Skin, Right Upper Leg **J** Skin, Left Upper Leg **K** Skin, Right Lower Leg **L** Skin, Left Lower Leg **M** Skin, Right Foot **N** Skin, Left Foot	**X** External	**Z** No Device	**Z** No Qualifier

Subcutaneous Tissue and Fascia 0J0–0JX

0   Medical and Surgical
J   Subcutaneous Tissue and Fascia
0   Alteration: Modifying the anatomic structure of a body part without affecting the function of the body part

Body Part Character 4	Approach Character 5	Device Character 6	Qualifier Character 7
1 Subcutaneous Tissue and Fascia, Face 4 Subcutaneous Tissue and Fascia, Anterior Neck 5 Subcutaneous Tissue and Fascia, Posterior Neck 6 Subcutaneous Tissue and Fascia, Chest 7 Subcutaneous Tissue and Fascia, Back 8 Subcutaneous Tissue and Fascia, Abdomen 9 Subcutaneous Tissue and Fascia, Buttock D Subcutaneous Tissue and Fascia, Right Upper Arm F Subcutaneous Tissue and Fascia, Left Upper Arm G Subcutaneous Tissue and Fascia, Right Lower Arm H Subcutaneous Tissue and Fascia, Left Lower Arm L Subcutaneous Tissue and Fascia, Right Upper Leg M Subcutaneous Tissue and Fascia, Left Upper Leg N Subcutaneous Tissue and Fascia, Right Lower Leg P Subcutaneous Tissue and Fascia, Left Lower Leg	0 Open 3 Percutaneous	Z No Device	Z No Qualifier

0   Medical and Surgical
J   Subcutaneous Tissue and Fascia
2   Change: Taking out or off a device from a body part and putting back an identical or similar device in or on the same body part without cutting or puncturing the skin or a mucous membrane

Body Part Character 4	Approach Character 5	Device Character 6	Qualifier Character 7
S Subcutaneous Tissue and Fascia, Head and Neck T Subcutaneous Tissue and Fascia, Trunk V Subcutaneous Tissue and Fascia, Upper Extremity W Subcutaneous Tissue and Fascia, Lower Extremity	X External	0 Drainage Device Y Other Device	Z No Qualifier

0   Medical and Surgical
J   Subcutaneous Tissue and Fascia
5   Destruction: Physical eradication of all or a portion of a body part by the direct use of energy, force, or a destructive agent

Body Part Character 4	Approach Character 5	Device Character 6	Qualifier Character 7
0 Subcutaneous Tissue and Fascia, Scalp 1 Subcutaneous Tissue and Fascia, Face 4 Subcutaneous Tissue and Fascia, Anterior Neck 5 Subcutaneous Tissue and Fascia, Posterior Neck 6 Subcutaneous Tissue and Fascia, Chest 7 Subcutaneous Tissue and Fascia, Back 8 Subcutaneous Tissue and Fascia, Abdomen 9 Subcutaneous Tissue and Fascia, Buttock B Subcutaneous Tissue and Fascia, Perineum C Subcutaneous Tissue and Fascia, Genitalia D Subcutaneous Tissue and Fascia, Right Upper Arm F Subcutaneous Tissue and Fascia, Left Upper Arm G Subcutaneous Tissue and Fascia, Right Lower Arm H Subcutaneous Tissue and Fascia, Left Lower Arm J Subcutaneous Tissue and Fascia, Right Hand K Subcutaneous Tissue and Fascia, Left Hand L Subcutaneous Tissue and Fascia, Right Upper Leg M Subcutaneous Tissue and Fascia, Left Upper Leg N Subcutaneous Tissue and Fascia, Right Lower Leg P Subcutaneous Tissue and Fascia, Left Lower Leg Q Subcutaneous Tissue and Fascia, Right Foot R Subcutaneous Tissue and Fascia, Left Foot	0 Open 3 Percutaneous	Z No Device	Z No Qualifier

0 **Medical and Surgical**
J **Subcutaneous Tissue and Fascia**
8 **Division:**   Cutting into a body part without draining fluids and/or gases from the body part in order to separate or transect a body part

Body Part Character 4	Approach Character 5	Device Character 6	Qualifier Character 7
0 Subcutaneous Tissue and Fascia, Scalp 1 Subcutaneous Tissue and Fascia, Face 4 Subcutaneous Tissue and Fascia, Anterior Neck 5 Subcutaneous Tissue and Fascia, Posterior Neck 6 Subcutaneous Tissue and Fascia, Chest 7 Subcutaneous Tissue and Fascia, Back 8 Subcutaneous Tissue and Fascia, Abdomen 9 Subcutaneous Tissue and Fascia, Buttock B Subcutaneous Tissue and Fascia, Perineum C Subcutaneous Tissue and Fascia, Genitalia D Subcutaneous Tissue and Fascia, Right Upper Arm F Subcutaneous Tissue and Fascia, Left Upper Arm G Subcutaneous Tissue and Fascia, Right Lower Arm H Subcutaneous Tissue and Fascia, Left Lower Arm J Subcutaneous Tissue and Fascia, Right Hand K Subcutaneous Tissue and Fascia, Left Hand L Subcutaneous Tissue and Fascia, Right Upper Leg M Subcutaneous Tissue and Fascia, Left Upper Leg N Subcutaneous Tissue and Fascia, Right Lower Leg P Subcutaneous Tissue and Fascia, Left Lower Leg Q Subcutaneous Tissue and Fascia, Right Foot R Subcutaneous Tissue and Fascia, Left Foot S Subcutaneous Tissue and Fascia, Head and Neck T Subcutaneous Tissue and Fascia, Trunk V Subcutaneous Tissue and Fascia, Upper Extremity W Subcutaneous Tissue and Fascia, Lower Extremity	0 Open 3 Percutaneous	Z No Device	Z No Qualifier

0 **Medical and Surgical**
J **Subcutaneous Tissue and Fascia**
9 **Drainage:**   Taking or letting out fluids and/or gases from a body part

Body Part Character 4	Approach Character 5	Device Character 6	Qualifier Character 7
0 Subcutaneous Tissue and Fascia, Scalp 1 Subcutaneous Tissue and Fascia, Face 4 Subcutaneous Tissue and Fascia, Anterior Neck 5 Subcutaneous Tissue and Fascia, Posterior Neck 6 Subcutaneous Tissue and Fascia, Chest 7 Subcutaneous Tissue and Fascia, Back 8 Subcutaneous Tissue and Fascia, Abdomen 9 Subcutaneous Tissue and Fascia, Buttock B Subcutaneous Tissue and Fascia, Perineum C Subcutaneous Tissue and Fascia, Genitalia D Subcutaneous Tissue and Fascia, Right Upper Arm F Subcutaneous Tissue and Fascia, Left Upper Arm G Subcutaneous Tissue and Fascia, Right Lower Arm H Subcutaneous Tissue and Fascia, Left Lower Arm J Subcutaneous Tissue and Fascia, Right Hand K Subcutaneous Tissue and Fascia, Left Hand L Subcutaneous Tissue and Fascia, Right Upper Leg M Subcutaneous Tissue and Fascia, Left Upper Leg N Subcutaneous Tissue and Fascia, Right Lower Leg P Subcutaneous Tissue and Fascia, Left Lower Leg Q Subcutaneous Tissue and Fascia, Right Foot R Subcutaneous Tissue and Fascia, Left Foot	0 Open 3 Percutaneous	0 Drainage Device	Z No Qualifier

Continued on next page

0   **Medical and Surgical**
J   **Subcutaneous Tissue and Fascia**
9   **Drainage:**   Taking or letting out fluids and/or gases from a body part

Continued from previous page

Body Part Character 4	Approach Character 5	Device Character 6	Qualifier Character 7
0 Subcutaneous Tissue and Fascia, Scalp **1** Subcutaneous Tissue and Fascia, Face **4** Subcutaneous Tissue and Fascia, Anterior Neck **5** Subcutaneous Tissue and Fascia, Posterior Neck **6** Subcutaneous Tissue and Fascia, Chest **7** Subcutaneous Tissue and Fascia, Back **8** Subcutaneous Tissue and Fascia, Abdomen **9** Subcutaneous Tissue and Fascia, Buttock **B** Subcutaneous Tissue and Fascia, Perineum **C** Subcutaneous Tissue and Fascia, Genitalia **D** Subcutaneous Tissue and Fascia, Right Upper Arm **F** Subcutaneous Tissue and Fascia, Left Upper Arm **G** Subcutaneous Tissue and Fascia, Right Lower Arm **H** Subcutaneous Tissue and Fascia, Left Lower Arm **J** Subcutaneous Tissue and Fascia, Right Hand **K** Subcutaneous Tissue and Fascia, Left Hand **L** Subcutaneous Tissue and Fascia, Right Upper Leg **M** Subcutaneous Tissue and Fascia, Left Upper Leg **N** Subcutaneous Tissue and Fascia, Right Lower Leg **P** Subcutaneous Tissue and Fascia, Left Lower Leg **Q** Subcutaneous Tissue and Fascia, Right Foot **R** Subcutaneous Tissue and Fascia, Left Foot	**0** Open **3** Percutaneous	**Z** No Device	**X** Diagnostic **Z** No Qualifier

0   **Medical and Surgical**
J   **Subcutaneous Tissue and Fascia**
B   **Excision:**   Cutting out or off, without replacement, a portion of a body part

Body Part Character 4	Approach Character 5	Device Character 6	Qualifier Character 7
0 Subcutaneous Tissue and Fascia, Scalp **1** Subcutaneous Tissue and Fascia, Face **4** Subcutaneous Tissue and Fascia, Anterior Neck **5** Subcutaneous Tissue and Fascia, Posterior Neck **6** Subcutaneous Tissue and Fascia, Chest **7** Subcutaneous Tissue and Fascia, Back **8** Subcutaneous Tissue and Fascia, Abdomen **9** Subcutaneous Tissue and Fascia, Buttock **B** Subcutaneous Tissue and Fascia, Perineum **C** Subcutaneous Tissue and Fascia, Genitalia **D** Subcutaneous Tissue and Fascia, Right Upper Arm **F** Subcutaneous Tissue and Fascia, Left Upper Arm **G** Subcutaneous Tissue and Fascia, Right Lower Arm **H** Subcutaneous Tissue and Fascia, Left Lower Arm **J** Subcutaneous Tissue and Fascia, Right Hand **K** Subcutaneous Tissue and Fascia, Left Hand **L** Subcutaneous Tissue and Fascia, Right Upper Leg **M** Subcutaneous Tissue and Fascia, Left Upper Leg **N** Subcutaneous Tissue and Fascia, Right Lower Leg **P** Subcutaneous Tissue and Fascia, Left Lower Leg **Q** Subcutaneous Tissue and Fascia, Right Foot **R** Subcutaneous Tissue and Fascia, Left Foot	**0** Open **3** Percutaneous	**Z** No Device	**X** Diagnostic **Z** No Qualifier

0   **Medical and Surgical**
J   **Subcutaneous Tissue and Fascia**
C   **Extirpation:**   Taking or cutting out solid matter from a body part

Body Part Character 4	Approach Character 5	Device Character 6	Qualifier Character 7
0 Subcutaneous Tissue and Fascia, Scalp 1 Subcutaneous Tissue and Fascia, Face 4 Subcutaneous Tissue and Fascia, Anterior Neck 5 Subcutaneous Tissue and Fascia, Posterior Neck 6 Subcutaneous Tissue and Fascia, Chest 7 Subcutaneous Tissue and Fascia, Back 8 Subcutaneous Tissue and Fascia, Abdomen 9 Subcutaneous Tissue and Fascia, Buttock B Subcutaneous Tissue and Fascia, Perineum C Subcutaneous Tissue and Fascia, Genitalia D Subcutaneous Tissue and Fascia, Right Upper Arm F Subcutaneous Tissue and Fascia, Left Upper Arm G Subcutaneous Tissue and Fascia, Right Lower Arm H Subcutaneous Tissue and Fascia, Left Lower Arm J Subcutaneous Tissue and Fascia, Right Hand K Subcutaneous Tissue and Fascia, Left Hand L Subcutaneous Tissue and Fascia, Right Upper Leg M Subcutaneous Tissue and Fascia, Left Upper Leg N Subcutaneous Tissue and Fascia, Right Lower Leg P Subcutaneous Tissue and Fascia, Left Lower Leg Q Subcutaneous Tissue and Fascia, Right Foot R Subcutaneous Tissue and Fascia, Left Foot	0 Open 3 Percutaneous	Z No Device	Z No Qualifier

0   **Medical and Surgical**
J   **Subcutaneous Tissue and Fascia**
D   **Extraction:**   Pulling or stripping out or off all or a portion of a body part by the use of force

Body Part Character 4	Approach Character 5	Device Character 6	Qualifier Character 7
0 Subcutaneous Tissue and Fascia, Scalp 1 Subcutaneous Tissue and Fascia, Face 4 Subcutaneous Tissue and Fascia, Anterior Neck 5 Subcutaneous Tissue and Fascia, Posterior Neck 6 Subcutaneous Tissue and Fascia, Chest 7 Subcutaneous Tissue and Fascia, Back 8 Subcutaneous Tissue and Fascia, Abdomen 9 Subcutaneous Tissue and Fascia, Buttock B Subcutaneous Tissue and Fascia, Perineum C Subcutaneous Tissue and Fascia, Genitalia D Subcutaneous Tissue and Fascia, Right Upper Arm F Subcutaneous Tissue and Fascia, Left Upper Arm G Subcutaneous Tissue and Fascia, Right Lower Arm H Subcutaneous Tissue and Fascia, Left Lower Arm J Subcutaneous Tissue and Fascia, Right Hand K Subcutaneous Tissue and Fascia, Left Hand L Subcutaneous Tissue and Fascia, Right Upper Leg M Subcutaneous Tissue and Fascia, Left Upper Leg N Subcutaneous Tissue and Fascia, Right Lower Leg P Subcutaneous Tissue and Fascia, Left Lower Leg Q Subcutaneous Tissue and Fascia, Right Foot R Subcutaneous Tissue and Fascia, Left Foot	0 Open 3 Percutaneous	Z No Device	Z No Qualifier

0 Medical and Surgical
J Subcutaneous Tissue and Fascia
H Insertion: Putting in a nonbiological appliance that monitors, assists, performs or prevents a physiological function, but does not physically take the place of a body part

Body Part Character 4	Approach Character 5	Device Character 6	Qualifier Character 7
0 Subcutaneous Tissue and Fascia, Scalp **1** Subcutaneous Tissue and Fascia, Face **4** Subcutaneous Tissue and Fascia, Anterior Neck **5** Subcutaneous Tissue and Fascia, Posterior Neck **6** Subcutaneous Tissue and Fascia, Chest **7** Subcutaneous Tissue and Fascia, Back **8** Subcutaneous Tissue and Fascia, Abdomen **9** Subcutaneous Tissue and Fascia, Buttock **B** Subcutaneous Tissue and Fascia, Perineum **C** Subcutaneous Tissue and Fascia, Genitalia **D** Subcutaneous Tissue and Fascia, Right Upper Arm **F** Subcutaneous Tissue and Fascia, Left Upper Arm **G** Subcutaneous Tissue and Fascia, Right Lower Arm **H** Subcutaneous Tissue and Fascia, Left Lower Arm **J** Subcutaneous Tissue and Fascia, Right Hand **K** Subcutaneous Tissue and Fascia, Left Hand **L** Subcutaneous Tissue and Fascia, Right Upper Leg **M** Subcutaneous Tissue and Fascia, Left Upper Leg **N** Subcutaneous Tissue and Fascia, Right Lower Leg **P** Subcutaneous Tissue and Fascia, Left Lower Leg **Q** Subcutaneous Tissue and Fascia, Right Foot **R** Subcutaneous Tissue and Fascia, Left Foot	**0** Open **3** Percutaneous	**M** Stimulator Generator	**6** Single Array **7** Dual Array **8** Single Array Rechargeable **9** Dual Array Rechargeable
0 Subcutaneous Tissue and Fascia, Scalp **1** Subcutaneous Tissue and Fascia, Face **4** Subcutaneous Tissue and Fascia, Anterior Neck **5** Subcutaneous Tissue and Fascia, Posterior Neck **9** Subcutaneous Tissue and Fascia, Buttock **B** Subcutaneous Tissue and Fascia, Perineum **C** Subcutaneous Tissue and Fascia, Genitalia **J** Subcutaneous Tissue and Fascia, Right Hand **K** Subcutaneous Tissue and Fascia, Left Hand **Q** Subcutaneous Tissue and Fascia, Right Foot **R** Subcutaneous Tissue and Fascia, Left Foot	**0** Open **3** Percutaneous	**N** Tissue Expander	**Z** No Qualifier
6 Subcutaneous Tissue and Fascia, Chest **8** Subcutaneous Tissue and Fascia, Abdomen	**0** Open **3** Percutaneous	**P** Pacemaker / Defibrillator	**0** Pacemaker, Single Chamber **1** Pacemaker, Single Chamber Rate Responsive **2** Pacemaker, Dual Chamber **3** Cardiac Resynchronization Pacemaker Pulse Generator **4** Defibrillator Generator **5** Cardiac Resynchronization Defibrillator Pulse Generator **Y** Other Cardiac Pacemaker / Defibrillator **Z** No Qualifier
6 Subcutaneous Tissue and Fascia, Chest **8** Subcutaneous Tissue and Fascia, Abdomen **D** Subcutaneous Tissue and Fascia, Right Upper Arm **F** Subcutaneous Tissue and Fascia, Left Upper Arm **G** Subcutaneous Tissue and Fascia, Right Lower Arm **H** Subcutaneous Tissue and Fascia, Left Lower Arm **L** Subcutaneous Tissue and Fascia, Right Upper Leg **M** Subcutaneous Tissue and Fascia, Left Upper Leg **N** Subcutaneous Tissue and Fascia, Right Lower Leg **P** Subcutaneous Tissue and Fascia, Left Lower Leg	**0** Open **3** Percutaneous	**H** Contraceptive Device **N** Tissue Expander **V** Infusion Pump **W** Reservoir **X** Vascular Access Device	**Z** No Qualifier
7 Subcutaneous Tissue and Fascia, Back	**0** Open **3** Percutaneous	**N** Tissue Expander **V** Infusion Pump	**Z** No Qualifier
S Subcutaneous Tissue and Fascia, Head and Neck **V** Subcutaneous Tissue and Fascia, Upper Extremity **W** Subcutaneous Tissue and Fascia, Lower Extremity	**0** Open **3** Percutaneous	**1** Radioactive Element **3** Infusion Device	**Z** No Qualifier
T Subcutaneous Tissue and Fascia, Trunk	**0** Open **3** Percutaneous	**1** Radioactive Element **3** Infusion Device **V** Infusion Pump	**Z** No Qualifier

0   **Medical and Surgical**
J   **Subcutaneous Tissue and Fascia**
J   **Inspection:**   Visually and/or manually exploring a body part

Body Part Character 4	Approach Character 5	Device Character 6	Qualifier Character 7
0 Subcutaneous Tissue and Fascia, Scalp 1 Subcutaneous Tissue and Fascia, Face 4 Subcutaneous Tissue and Fascia, Anterior Neck 5 Subcutaneous Tissue and Fascia, Posterior Neck 6 Subcutaneous Tissue and Fascia, Chest 7 Subcutaneous Tissue and Fascia, Back 8 Subcutaneous Tissue and Fascia, Abdomen 9 Subcutaneous Tissue and Fascia, Buttock B Subcutaneous Tissue and Fascia, Perineum C Subcutaneous Tissue and Fascia, Genitalia D Subcutaneous Tissue and Fascia, Right Upper Arm F Subcutaneous Tissue and Fascia, Left Upper Arm G Subcutaneous Tissue and Fascia, Right Lower Arm H Subcutaneous Tissue and Fascia, Left Lower Arm J Subcutaneous Tissue and Fascia, Right Hand K Subcutaneous Tissue and Fascia, Left Hand L Subcutaneous Tissue and Fascia, Right Upper Leg M Subcutaneous Tissue and Fascia, Left Upper Leg N Subcutaneous Tissue and Fascia, Right Lower Leg P Subcutaneous Tissue and Fascia, Left Lower Leg Q Subcutaneous Tissue and Fascia, Right Foot R Subcutaneous Tissue and Fascia, Left Foot	0 Open 3 Percutaneous X External	Z No Device	Z No Qualifier

0   **Medical and Surgical**
J   **Subcutaneous Tissue and Fascia**
N   **Release:**   Freeing a body part from an abnormal physical constraint

Body Part Character 4	Approach Character 5	Device Character 6	Qualifier Character 7
0 Subcutaneous Tissue and Fascia, Scalp 1 Subcutaneous Tissue and Fascia, Face 4 Subcutaneous Tissue and Fascia, Anterior Neck 5 Subcutaneous Tissue and Fascia, Posterior Neck 6 Subcutaneous Tissue and Fascia, Chest 7 Subcutaneous Tissue and Fascia, Back 8 Subcutaneous Tissue and Fascia, Abdomen 9 Subcutaneous Tissue and Fascia, Buttock B Subcutaneous Tissue and Fascia, Perineum C Subcutaneous Tissue and Fascia, Genitalia D Subcutaneous Tissue and Fascia, Right Upper Arm F Subcutaneous Tissue and Fascia, Left Upper Arm G Subcutaneous Tissue and Fascia, Right Lower Arm H Subcutaneous Tissue and Fascia, Left Lower Arm J Subcutaneous Tissue and Fascia, Right Hand K Subcutaneous Tissue and Fascia, Left Hand L Subcutaneous Tissue and Fascia, Right Upper Leg M Subcutaneous Tissue and Fascia, Left Upper Leg N Subcutaneous Tissue and Fascia, Right Lower Leg P Subcutaneous Tissue and Fascia, Left Lower Leg Q Subcutaneous Tissue and Fascia, Right Foot R Subcutaneous Tissue and Fascia, Left Foot	0 Open 3 Percutaneous X External	Z No Device	Z No Qualifier

0   Medical and Surgical
J   Subcutaneous Tissue and Fascia
P   Removal: Taking out or off a device from a body part

Body Part Character 4	Approach Character 5	Device Character 6	Qualifier Character 7
S Subcutaneous Tissue and Fascia, Head and Neck	**0** Open **3** Percutaneous	**0** Drainage Device **1** Radioactive Element **3** Infusion Device **7** Autologous Tissue Substitute **J** Synthetic Substitute **K** Nonautologous Tissue Substitute **M** Stimulator Generator **N** Tissue Expander	**Z** No Qualifier
S Subcutaneous Tissue and Fascia, Head and Neck	**X** External	**0** Drainage Device **1** Radioactive Element **3** Infusion Device	**Z** No Qualifier
T Subcutaneous Tissue and Fascia, Trunk	**0** Open **3** Percutaneous	**0** Drainage Device **1** Radioactive Element **3** Infusion Device **7** Autologous Tissue Substitute **H** Contraceptive Device **J** Synthetic Substitute **K** Nonautologous Tissue Substitute **M** Stimulator Generator **N** Tissue Expander **P** Pacemaker / Defibrillator **V** Infusion Pump **W** Reservoir **X** Vascular Access Device	**Z** No Qualifier
T Subcutaneous Tissue and Fascia, Trunk **V** Subcutaneous Tissue and Fascia, Upper Extremity **W** Subcutaneous Tissue and Fascia, Lower Extremity	**X** External	**0** Drainage Device **1** Radioactive Element **3** Infusion Device **H** Contraceptive Device **V** Infusion Pump **X** Vascular Access Device	**Z** No Qualifier
V Subcutaneous Tissue and Fascia, Upper Extremity **W** Subcutaneous Tissue and Fascia, Lower Extremity	**0** Open **3** Percutaneous	**0** Drainage Device **1** Radioactive Element **3** Infusion Device **7** Autologous Tissue Substitute **H** Contraceptive Device **J** Synthetic Substitute **K** Nonautologous Tissue Substitute **M** Stimulator Generator **N** Tissue Expander **V** Infusion Pump **W** Reservoir **X** Vascular Access Device	**Z** No Qualifier

0 Medical and Surgical
J Subcutaneous Tissue and Fascia
Q Repair: Restoring, to the extent possible, a body part to its normal anatomic structure and function

Body Part Character 4	Approach Character 5	Device Character 6	Qualifier Character 7
0 Subcutaneous Tissue and Fascia, Scalp 1 Subcutaneous Tissue and Fascia, Face 4 Subcutaneous Tissue and Fascia, Anterior Neck 5 Subcutaneous Tissue and Fascia, Posterior Neck 6 Subcutaneous Tissue and Fascia, Chest 7 Subcutaneous Tissue and Fascia, Back 8 Subcutaneous Tissue and Fascia, Abdomen 9 Subcutaneous Tissue and Fascia, Buttock B Subcutaneous Tissue and Fascia, Perineum C Subcutaneous Tissue and Fascia, Genitalia D Subcutaneous Tissue and Fascia, Right Upper Arm F Subcutaneous Tissue and Fascia, Left Upper Arm G Subcutaneous Tissue and Fascia, Right Lower Arm H Subcutaneous Tissue and Fascia, Left Lower Arm J Subcutaneous Tissue and Fascia, Right Hand K Subcutaneous Tissue and Fascia, Left Hand L Subcutaneous Tissue and Fascia, Right Upper Leg M Subcutaneous Tissue and Fascia, Left Upper Leg N Subcutaneous Tissue and Fascia, Right Lower Leg P Subcutaneous Tissue and Fascia, Left Lower Leg Q Subcutaneous Tissue and Fascia, Right Foot R Subcutaneous Tissue and Fascia, Left Foot	0 Open 3 Percutaneous	Z No Device	Z No Qualifier

0 Medical and Surgical
J Subcutaneous Tissue and Fascia
R Replacement: Putting in or on biological or synthetic material that physically takes the place and/or function of all or a portion of a body part

Body Part Character 4	Approach Character 5	Device Character 6	Qualifier Character 7
0 Subcutaneous Tissue and Fascia, Scalp 1 Subcutaneous Tissue and Fascia, Face 4 Subcutaneous Tissue and Fascia, Anterior Neck 5 Subcutaneous Tissue and Fascia, Posterior Neck 6 Subcutaneous Tissue and Fascia, Chest 7 Subcutaneous Tissue and Fascia, Back 8 Subcutaneous Tissue and Fascia, Abdomen 9 Subcutaneous Tissue and Fascia, Buttock B Subcutaneous Tissue and Fascia, Perineum C Subcutaneous Tissue and Fascia, Genitalia D Subcutaneous Tissue and Fascia, Right Upper Arm F Subcutaneous Tissue and Fascia, Left Upper Arm G Subcutaneous Tissue and Fascia, Right Lower Arm H Subcutaneous Tissue and Fascia, Left Lower Arm J Subcutaneous Tissue and Fascia, Right Hand K Subcutaneous Tissue and Fascia, Left Hand L Subcutaneous Tissue and Fascia, Right Upper Leg M Subcutaneous Tissue and Fascia, Left Upper Leg N Subcutaneous Tissue and Fascia, Right Lower Leg P Subcutaneous Tissue and Fascia, Left Lower Leg Q Subcutaneous Tissue and Fascia, Right Foot R Subcutaneous Tissue and Fascia, Left Foot	0 Open 3 Percutaneous	7 Autologous Tissue Substitute J Synthetic Substitute K Nonautologous Tissue Substitute	Z No Qualifier

0　Medical and Surgical
J　Subcutaneous Tissue and Fascia
W　Revision:　　　Correcting, to the extent possible, a malfunctioning or displaced device

Body Part Character 4	Approach Character 5	Device Character 6	Qualifier Character 7
S Subcutaneous Tissue and Fascia, Head and Neck	**0** Open **3** Percutaneous **X** External	**0** Drainage Device **3** Infusion Device **7** Autologous Tissue Substitute **J** Synthetic Substitute **K** Nonautologous Tissue Substitute **M** Stimulator Generator **N** Tissue Expander	**Z** No Qualifier
T Subcutaneous Tissue and Fascia, Trunk	**0** Open **3** Percutaneous **X** External	**0** Drainage Device **3** Infusion Device **7** Autologous Tissue Substitute **H** Contraceptive Device **J** Synthetic Substitute **K** Nonautologous Tissue Substitute **M** Stimulator Generator **N** Tissue Expander **P** Pacemaker / Defibrillator **V** Infusion Pump **W** Reservoir **X** Vascular Access Device	**Z** No Qualifier
V Subcutaneous Tissue and Fascia, Upper Extremity **W** Subcutaneous Tissue and Fascia, Lower Extremity	**0** Open **3** Percutaneous **X** External	**0** Drainage Device **3** Infusion Device **7** Autologous Tissue Substitute **H** Contraceptive Device **J** Synthetic Substitute **K** Nonautologous Tissue Substitute **M** Stimulator Generator **N** Tissue Expander **V** Infusion Pump **W** Reservoir **X** Vascular Access Device	**Z** No Qualifier

0　Medical and Surgical
J　Subcutaneous Tissue and Fascia
X　Transfer:　　Moving, without taking out, all or a portion of a body part to another location to take over the function of all or a portion of a body part

Body Part Character 4	Approach Character 5	Device Character 6	Qualifier Character 7
0 Subcutaneous Tissue and Fascia, Scalp **1** Subcutaneous Tissue and Fascia, Face **4** Subcutaneous Tissue and Fascia, Anterior Neck **5** Subcutaneous Tissue and Fascia, Posterior Neck **6** Subcutaneous Tissue and Fascia, Chest **7** Subcutaneous Tissue and Fascia, Back **8** Subcutaneous Tissue and Fascia, Abdomen **9** Subcutaneous Tissue and Fascia, Buttock **B** Subcutaneous Tissue and Fascia, Perineum **C** Subcutaneous Tissue and Fascia, Genitalia **D** Subcutaneous Tissue and Fascia, Right Upper Arm **F** Subcutaneous Tissue and Fascia, Left Upper Arm **G** Subcutaneous Tissue and Fascia, Right Lower Arm **H** Subcutaneous Tissue and Fascia, Left Lower Arm **J** Subcutaneous Tissue and Fascia, Right Hand **K** Subcutaneous Tissue and Fascia, Left Hand **L** Subcutaneous Tissue and Fascia, Right Upper Leg **M** Subcutaneous Tissue and Fascia, Left Upper Leg **N** Subcutaneous Tissue and Fascia, Right Lower Leg **P** Subcutaneous Tissue and Fascia, Left Lower Leg **Q** Subcutaneous Tissue and Fascia, Right Foot **R** Subcutaneous Tissue and Fascia, Left Foot	**0** Open **3** Percutaneous	**Z** No Device	**B** Skin and Subcutaneous Tissue **C** Skin, Subcutaneous Tissue and Fascia **Z** No Qualifier

Muscles 0K2–0KX

0   Medical and Surgical
K   Muscles
2   Change: Taking out or off a device from a body part and putting back an identical or similar device in or on the same body part without cutting or puncturing the skin or a mucous membrane

Body Part Character 4	Approach Character 5	Device Character 6	Qualifier Character 7
X Upper Muscle **Y** Lower Muscle	**X** External	**0** Drainage Device **Y** Other Device	**Z** No Qualifier

0   Medical and Surgical
K   Muscles
5   Destruction: Physical eradication of all or a portion of a body part by the direct use of energy, force, or a destructive agent

Body Part Character 4	Approach Character 5	Device Character 6	Qualifier Character 7
0 Head Muscle **1** Facial Muscle **2** Neck Muscle, Right **3** Neck Muscle, Left **4** Tongue, Palate, Pharynx Muscle **5** Shoulder Muscle, Right **6** Shoulder Muscle, Left **7** Upper Arm Muscle, Right **8** Upper Arm Muscle, Left **9** Lower Arm and Wrist Muscle, Right **B** Lower Arm and Wrist Muscle, Left **C** Hand Muscle, Right **D** Hand Muscle, Left **F** Trunk Muscle, Right **G** Trunk Muscle, Left **H** Thorax Muscle, Right **J** Thorax Muscle, Left **K** Abdomen Muscle, Right **L** Abdomen Muscle, Left **M** Perineum Muscle **N** Hip Muscle, Right **P** Hip Muscle, Left **Q** Upper Leg Muscle, Right **R** Upper Leg Muscle, Left **S** Lower Leg Muscle, Right **T** Lower Leg Muscle, Left **V** Foot Muscle, Right **W** Foot Muscle, Left	**0** Open **3** Percutaneous **4** Percutaneous Endoscopic	**Z** No Device	**Z** No Qualifier

0　**Medical and Surgical**
K　**Muscles**
8　**Division:**　　　　　Cutting into a body part without draining fluids and/or gases from the body part in order to separate or transect a body part

Body Part Character 4	Approach Character 5	Device Character 6	Qualifier Character 7
0　Head Muscle 1　Facial Muscle 2　Neck Muscle, Right 3　Neck Muscle, Left 4　Tongue, Palate, Pharynx Muscle 5　Shoulder Muscle, Right 6　Shoulder Muscle, Left 7　Upper Arm Muscle, Right 8　Upper Arm Muscle, Left 9　Lower Arm and Wrist Muscle, Right B　Lower Arm and Wrist Muscle, Left C　Hand Muscle, Right D　Hand Muscle, Left F　Trunk Muscle, Right G　Trunk Muscle, Left H　Thorax Muscle, Right J　Thorax Muscle, Left K　Abdomen Muscle, Right L　Abdomen Muscle, Left M　Perineum Muscle N　Hip Muscle, Right P　Hip Muscle, Left Q　Upper Leg Muscle, Right R　Upper Leg Muscle, Left S　Lower Leg Muscle, Right T　Lower Leg Muscle, Left V　Foot Muscle, Right W　Foot Muscle, Left	0　Open 3　Percutaneous 4　Percutaneous Endoscopic	Z　No Device	Z　No Qualifier

0　**Medical and Surgical**
K　**Muscles**
9　**Drainage:**　　　　　Taking or letting out fluids and/or gases from a body part

Body Part Character 4	Approach Character 5	Device Character 6	Qualifier Character 7
0　Head Muscle 1　Facial Muscle 2　Neck Muscle, Right 3　Neck Muscle, Left 4　Tongue, Palate, Pharynx Muscle 5　Shoulder Muscle, Right 6　Shoulder Muscle, Left 7　Upper Arm Muscle, Right 8　Upper Arm Muscle, Left 9　Lower Arm and Wrist Muscle, Right B　Lower Arm and Wrist Muscle, Left C　Hand Muscle, Right D　Hand Muscle, Left F　Trunk Muscle, Right G　Trunk Muscle, Left H　Thorax Muscle, Right J　Thorax Muscle, Left K　Abdomen Muscle, Right L　Abdomen Muscle, Left M　Perineum Muscle N　Hip Muscle, Right P　Hip Muscle, Left Q　Upper Leg Muscle, Right R　Upper Leg Muscle, Left S　Lower Leg Muscle, Right T　Lower Leg Muscle, Left V　Foot Muscle, Right W　Foot Muscle, Left	0　Open 3　Percutaneous 4　Percutaneous Endoscopic	0　Drainage Device	Z　No Qualifier

Continued on next page

Continued from previous page

0 **Medical and Surgical**
K **Muscles**
9 **Drainage:**   Taking or letting out fluids and/or gases from a body part

Body Part Character 4	Approach Character 5	Device Character 6	Qualifier Character 7
0 Head Muscle 1 Facial Muscle 2 Neck Muscle, Right 3 Neck Muscle, Left 4 Tongue, Palate, Pharynx Muscle 5 Shoulder Muscle, Right 6 Shoulder Muscle, Left 7 Upper Arm Muscle, Right 8 Upper Arm Muscle, Left 9 Lower Arm and Wrist Muscle, Right B Lower Arm and Wrist Muscle, Left C Hand Muscle, Right D Hand Muscle, Left F Trunk Muscle, Right G Trunk Muscle, Left H Thorax Muscle, Right J Thorax Muscle, Left K Abdomen Muscle, Right L Abdomen Muscle, Left M Perineum Muscle N Hip Muscle, Right P Hip Muscle, Left Q Upper Leg Muscle, Right R Upper Leg Muscle, Left S Lower Leg Muscle, Right T Lower Leg Muscle, Left V Foot Muscle, Right W Foot Muscle, Left	0 Open 3 Percutaneous 4 Percutaneous Endoscopic	Z No Device	X Diagnostic Z No Qualifier

0 **Medical and Surgical**
K **Muscles**
B **Excision:**   Cutting out or off, without replacement, a portion of a body part

Body Part Character 4	Approach Character 5	Device Character 6	Qualifier Character 7
0 Head Muscle 1 Facial Muscle 2 Neck Muscle, Right 3 Neck Muscle, Left 4 Tongue, Palate, Pharynx Muscle 5 Shoulder Muscle, Right 6 Shoulder Muscle, Left 7 Upper Arm Muscle, Right 8 Upper Arm Muscle, Left 9 Lower Arm and Wrist Muscle, Right B Lower Arm and Wrist Muscle, Left C Hand Muscle, Right D Hand Muscle, Left F Trunk Muscle, Right G Trunk Muscle, Left H Thorax Muscle, Right J Thorax Muscle, Left K Abdomen Muscle, Right L Abdomen Muscle, Left M Perineum Muscle N Hip Muscle, Right P Hip Muscle, Left Q Upper Leg Muscle, Right R Upper Leg Muscle, Left S Lower Leg Muscle, Right T Lower Leg Muscle, Left V Foot Muscle, Right W Foot Muscle, Left	0 Open 3 Percutaneous 4 Percutaneous Endoscopic	Z No Device	X Diagnostic Z No Qualifier

0   **Medical and Surgical**
K   **Muscles**
C   **Extirpation:**   Taking or cutting out solid matter from a body part

Body Part Character 4	Approach Character 5	Device Character 6	Qualifier Character 7
0 Head Muscle **1** Facial Muscle **2** Neck Muscle, Right **3** Neck Muscle, Left **4** Tongue, Palate, Pharynx Muscle **5** Shoulder Muscle, Right **6** Shoulder Muscle, Left **7** Upper Arm Muscle, Right **8** Upper Arm Muscle, Left **9** Lower Arm and Wrist Muscle, Right **B** Lower Arm and Wrist Muscle, Left **C** Hand Muscle, Right **D** Hand Muscle, Left **F** Trunk Muscle, Right **G** Trunk Muscle, Left **H** Thorax Muscle, Right **J** Thorax Muscle, Left **K** Abdomen Muscle, Right **L** Abdomen Muscle, Left **M** Perineum Muscle **N** Hip Muscle, Right **P** Hip Muscle, Left **Q** Upper Leg Muscle, Right **R** Upper Leg Muscle, Left **S** Lower Leg Muscle, Right **T** Lower Leg Muscle, Left **V** Foot Muscle, Right **W** Foot Muscle, Left	**0** Open **3** Percutaneous **4** Percutaneous Endoscopic	**Z** No Device	**Z** No Qualifier

0   **Medical and Surgical**
K   **Muscles**
H   **Insertion:**   Putting in a nonbiological appliance that monitors, assists, performs or prevents a physiological function, but does not physically take the place of a body part

Body Part Character 4	Approach Character 5	Device Character 6	Qualifier Character 7
X Upper Muscle **Y** Lower Muscle	**0** Open **3** Percutaneous **4** Percutaneous Endoscopic	**M** Electrode	**Z** No Qualifier

0   Medical and Surgical
K   Muscles
J   Inspection: Visually and/or manually exploring a body part

Body Part Character 4	Approach Character 5	Device Character 6	Qualifier Character 7
0 Head Muscle 1 Facial Muscle 2 Neck Muscle, Right 3 Neck Muscle, Left 4 Tongue, Palate, Pharynx Muscle 5 Shoulder Muscle, Right 6 Shoulder Muscle, Left 7 Upper Arm Muscle, Right 8 Upper Arm Muscle, Left 9 Lower Arm and Wrist Muscle, Right B Lower Arm and Wrist Muscle, Left C Hand Muscle, Right D Hand Muscle, Left F Trunk Muscle, Right G Trunk Muscle, Left H Thorax Muscle, Right J Thorax Muscle, Left K Abdomen Muscle, Right L Abdomen Muscle, Left M Perineum Muscle N Hip Muscle, Right P Hip Muscle, Left Q Upper Leg Muscle, Right R Upper Leg Muscle, Left S Lower Leg Muscle, Right T Lower Leg Muscle, Left V Foot Muscle, Right W Foot Muscle, Left	0 Open 3 Percutaneous 4 Percutaneous Endoscopic X External	Z No Device	Z No Qualifier

0   Medical and Surgical
K   Muscles
M   Reattachment: Putting back in or on all or a portion of a separated body part to its normal location or other suitable location

Body Part Character 4	Approach Character 5	Device Character 6	Qualifier Character 7
0 Head Muscle 1 Facial Muscle 2 Neck Muscle, Right 3 Neck Muscle, Left 4 Tongue, Palate, Pharynx Muscle 5 Shoulder Muscle, Right 6 Shoulder Muscle, Left 7 Upper Arm Muscle, Right 8 Upper Arm Muscle, Left 9 Lower Arm and Wrist Muscle, Right B Lower Arm and Wrist Muscle, Left C Hand Muscle, Right D Hand Muscle, Left F Trunk Muscle, Right G Trunk Muscle, Left H Thorax Muscle, Right J Thorax Muscle, Left K Abdomen Muscle, Right L Abdomen Muscle, Left M Perineum Muscle N Hip Muscle, Right P Hip Muscle, Left Q Upper Leg Muscle, Right R Upper Leg Muscle, Left S Lower Leg Muscle, Right T Lower Leg Muscle, Left V Foot Muscle, Right W Foot Muscle, Left	0 Open 4 Percutaneous Endoscopic	Z No Device	Z No Qualifier

0 **Medical and Surgical**
K **Muscles**
N **Release:**   Freeing a body part from an abnormal physical constraint

Body Part Character 4	Approach Character 5	Device Character 6	Qualifier Character 7
0 Head Muscle **1** Facial Muscle **2** Neck Muscle, Right **3** Neck Muscle, Left **4** Tongue, Palate, Pharynx Muscle **5** Shoulder Muscle, Right **6** Shoulder Muscle, Left **7** Upper Arm Muscle, Right **8** Upper Arm Muscle, Left **9** Lower Arm and Wrist Muscle, Right **B** Lower Arm and Wrist Muscle, Left **C** Hand Muscle, Right **D** Hand Muscle, Left **F** Trunk Muscle, Right **G** Trunk Muscle, Left **H** Thorax Muscle, Right **J** Thorax Muscle, Left **K** Abdomen Muscle, Right **L** Abdomen Muscle, Left **M** Perineum Muscle **N** Hip Muscle, Right **P** Hip Muscle, Left **Q** Upper Leg Muscle, Right **R** Upper Leg Muscle, Left **S** Lower Leg Muscle, Right **T** Lower Leg Muscle, Left **V** Foot Muscle, Right **W** Foot Muscle, Left	**0** Open **3** Percutaneous **4** Percutaneous Endoscopic **X** External	**Z** No Device	**Z** No Qualifier

0 **Medical and Surgical**
K **Muscles**
P **Removal:**   Taking out or off a device from a body part

Body Part Character 4	Approach Character 5	Device Character 6	Qualifier Character 7
X Upper Muscle **Y** Lower Muscle	**0** Open **3** Percutaneous **4** Percutaneous Endoscopic	**0** Drainage Device **7** Autologous Tissue Substitute **J** Synthetic Substitute **K** Nonautologous Tissue Substitute **M** Electrode	**Z** No Qualifier
X Upper Muscle **Y** Lower Muscle	**X** External	**0** Drainage Device **M** Electrode	**Z** No Qualifier

0   **Medical and Surgical**
K   **Muscles**
Q   **Repair:**   Restoring, to the extent possible, a body part to its normal anatomic structure and function

Body Part Character 4	Approach Character 5	Device Character 6	Qualifier Character 7

0 Head Muscle
1 Facial Muscle
2 Neck Muscle, Right
3 Neck Muscle, Left
4 Tongue, Palate, Pharynx Muscle
5 Shoulder Muscle, Right
6 Shoulder Muscle, Left
7 Upper Arm Muscle, Right
8 Upper Arm Muscle, Left
9 Lower Arm and Wrist Muscle,
   Right
B Lower Arm and Wrist Muscle,
   Left
C Hand Muscle, Right
D Hand Muscle, Left
F Trunk Muscle, Right
G Trunk Muscle, Left
H Thorax Muscle, Right
J Thorax Muscle, Left
K Abdomen Muscle, Right
L Abdomen Muscle, Left
M Perineum Muscle
N Hip Muscle, Right
P Hip Muscle, Left
Q Upper Leg Muscle, Right
R Upper Leg Muscle, Left
S Lower Leg Muscle, Right
T Lower Leg Muscle, Left
V Foot Muscle, Right
W Foot Muscle, Left
	0 Open
	3 Percutaneous
	4 Percutaneous Endoscopic
		Z No Device	Z No Qualifier

0   **Medical and Surgical**
K   **Muscles**
S   **Reposition:**   Moving to its normal location or other suitable location all or a portion of a body part

Body Part Character 4	Approach Character 5	Device Character 6	Qualifier Character 7

0 Head Muscle
1 Facial Muscle
2 Neck Muscle, Right
3 Neck Muscle, Left
4 Tongue, Palate, Pharynx Muscle
5 Shoulder Muscle, Right
6 Shoulder Muscle, Left
7 Upper Arm Muscle, Right
8 Upper Arm Muscle, Left
9 Lower Arm and Wrist Muscle,
   Right
B Lower Arm and Wrist Muscle,
   Left
C Hand Muscle, Right
D Hand Muscle, Left
F Trunk Muscle, Right
G Trunk Muscle, Left
H Thorax Muscle, Right
J Thorax Muscle, Left
K Abdomen Muscle, Right
L Abdomen Muscle, Left
M Perineum Muscle
N Hip Muscle, Right
P Hip Muscle, Left
Q Upper Leg Muscle, Right
R Upper Leg Muscle, Left
S Lower Leg Muscle, Right
T Lower Leg Muscle, Left
V Foot Muscle, Right
W Foot Muscle, Left
	0 Open
	4 Percutaneous Endoscopic
		Z No Device	Z No Qualifier

0   **Medical and Surgical**
K   **Muscles**
T   **Resection:**   Cutting out or off, without replacement, all of a body part

Body Part Character 4	Approach Character 5	Device Character 6	Qualifier Character 7
0 Head Muscle 1 Facial Muscle 2 Neck Muscle, Right 3 Neck Muscle, Left 4 Tongue, Palate, Pharynx Muscle 5 Shoulder Muscle, Right 6 Shoulder Muscle, Left 7 Upper Arm Muscle, Right 8 Upper Arm Muscle, Left 9 Lower Arm and Wrist Muscle, Right B Lower Arm and Wrist Muscle, Left C Hand Muscle, Right D Hand Muscle, Left F Trunk Muscle, Right G Trunk Muscle, Left H Thorax Muscle, Right J Thorax Muscle, Left K Abdomen Muscle, Right L Abdomen Muscle, Left M Perineum Muscle N Hip Muscle, Right P Hip Muscle, Left Q Upper Leg Muscle, Right R Upper Leg Muscle, Left S Lower Leg Muscle, Right T Lower Leg Muscle, Left V Foot Muscle, Right W Foot Muscle, Left	0 Open 4 Percutaneous Endoscopic	Z No Device	Z No Qualifier

0   **Medical and Surgical**
K   **Muscles**
U   **Supplement:**   Putting in or on biological or synthetic material that physically reinforces and/or augments the function of a portion of a body part

Body Part Character 4	Approach Character 5	Device Character 6	Qualifier Character 7
0 Head Muscle 1 Facial Muscle 2 Neck Muscle, Right 3 Neck Muscle, Left 4 Tongue, Palate, Pharynx Muscle 5 Shoulder Muscle, Right 6 Shoulder Muscle, Left 7 Upper Arm Muscle, Right 8 Upper Arm Muscle, Left 9 Lower Arm and Wrist Muscle, Right B Lower Arm and Wrist Muscle, Left C Hand Muscle, Right D Hand Muscle, Left F Trunk Muscle, Right G Trunk Muscle, Left H Thorax Muscle, Right J Thorax Muscle, Left K Abdomen Muscle, Right L Abdomen Muscle, Left M Perineum Muscle N Hip Muscle, Right P Hip Muscle, Left Q Upper Leg Muscle, Right R Upper Leg Muscle, Left S Lower Leg Muscle, Right T Lower Leg Muscle, Left V Foot Muscle, Right W Foot Muscle, Left	0 Open 4 Percutaneous Endoscopic	7 Autologous Tissue Substitute J Synthetic Substitute K Nonautologous Tissue Substitute	Z No Qualifier

0   **Medical and Surgical**
K   **Muscles**
W   **Revision:**   Correcting, to the extent possible, a malfunctioning or displaced device

Body Part Character 4	Approach Character 5	Device Character 6	Qualifier Character 7
X Upper Muscle Y Lower Muscle	0 Open 3 Percutaneous 4 Percutaneous Endoscopic X External	0 Drainage Device 7 Autologous Tissue Substitute J Synthetic Substitute K Nonautologous Tissue Substitute M Electrode	Z No Qualifier

0   **Medical and Surgical**
K   **Muscles**
X   **Transfer:**   Moving, without taking out, all or a portion of a body part to another location to take over the function of all or a portion of a body part

Body Part Character 4	Approach Character 5	Device Character 6	Qualifier Character 7
0 Head Muscle 1 Facial Muscle 2 Neck Muscle, Right 3 Neck Muscle, Left 4 Tongue, Palate, Pharynx Muscle 5 Shoulder Muscle, Right 6 Shoulder Muscle, Left 7 Upper Arm Muscle, Right 8 Upper Arm Muscle, Left 9 Lower Arm and Wrist Muscle, Right B Lower Arm and Wrist Muscle, Left C Hand Muscle, Right D Hand Muscle, Left F Trunk Muscle, Right G Trunk Muscle, Left H Thorax Muscle, Right J Thorax Muscle, Left M Perineum Muscle N Hip Muscle, Right P Hip Muscle, Left Q Upper Leg Muscle, Right R Upper Leg Muscle, Left S Lower Leg Muscle, Right T Lower Leg Muscle, Left V Foot Muscle, Right W Foot Muscle, Left	0 Open 4 Percutaneous Endoscopic	Z No Device	0 Skin 1 Subcutaneous Tissue 2 Skin and Subcutaneous Tissue Z No Qualifier
K Abdomen Muscle, Right L Abdomen Muscle, Left	0 Open 4 Percutaneous Endoscopic	Z No Device	0 Skin 1 Subcutaneous Tissue 2 Skin and Subcutaneous Tissue 6 Transverse Rectus Abdominis Myocutaneous Flap Z No Qualifier

Tendons 0L2–0LX

0 Medical and Surgical
L Tendons
2 Change: Taking out or off a device from a body part and putting back an identical or similar device in or on the same body part without cutting or puncturing the skin or a mucous membrane

Body Part Character 4	Approach Character 5	Device Character 6	Qualifier Character 7
X Upper Tendon **Y** Lower Tendon	**X** External	**0** Drainage Device **Y** Other Device	**Z** No Qualifier

0 Medical and Surgical
L Tendons
5 Destruction: Physical eradication of all or a portion of a body part by the direct use of energy, force, or a destructive agent

Body Part Character 4	Approach Character 5	Device Character 6	Qualifier Character 7
0 Head and Neck Tendon **1** Shoulder Tendon, Right **2** Shoulder Tendon, Left **3** Upper Arm Tendon, Right **4** Upper Arm Tendon, Left **5** Lower Arm and Wrist Tendon, Right **6** Lower Arm and Wrist Tendon, Left **7** Hand Tendon, Right **8** Hand Tendon, Left **9** Trunk Tendon, Right **B** Trunk Tendon, Left **C** Thorax Tendon, Right **D** Thorax Tendon, Left **F** Abdomen Tendon, Right **G** Abdomen Tendon, Left **H** Perineum Tendon **J** Hip Tendon, Right **K** Hip Tendon, Left **L** Upper Leg Tendon, Right **M** Upper Leg Tendon, Left **N** Lower Leg Tendon, Right **P** Lower Leg Tendon, Left **Q** Knee Tendon, Right **R** Knee Tendon, Left **S** Ankle Tendon, Right **T** Ankle Tendon, Left **V** Foot Tendon, Right **W** Foot Tendon, Left	**0** Open **3** Percutaneous **4** Percutaneous Endoscopic	**Z** No Device	**Z** No Qualifier

0   **Medical and Surgical**
L   **Tendons**
8   **Division:**   Cutting into a body part without draining fluids and/or gases from the body part in order to separate or transect a body part

Body Part Character 4	Approach Character 5	Device Character 6	Qualifier Character 7
0 Head and Neck Tendon 1 Shoulder Tendon, Right 2 Shoulder Tendon, Left 3 Upper Arm Tendon, Right 4 Upper Arm Tendon, Left 5 Lower Arm and Wrist Tendon, Right 6 Lower Arm and Wrist Tendon, Left 7 Hand Tendon, Right 8 Hand Tendon, Left 9 Trunk Tendon, Right B Trunk Tendon, Left C Thorax Tendon, Right D Thorax Tendon, Left F Abdomen Tendon, Right G Abdomen Tendon, Left H Perineum Tendon J Hip Tendon, Right K Hip Tendon, Left L Upper Leg Tendon, Right M Upper Leg Tendon, Left N Lower Leg Tendon, Right P Lower Leg Tendon, Left Q Knee Tendon, Right R Knee Tendon, Left S Ankle Tendon, Right T Ankle Tendon, Left V Foot Tendon, Right W Foot Tendon, Left	0 Open 3 Percutaneous 4 Percutaneous Endoscopic	Z No Device	Z No Qualifier

0   **Medical and Surgical**
L   **Tendons**
9   **Drainage:**   Taking or letting out fluids and/or gases from a body part

Body Part Character 4	Approach Character 5	Device Character 6	Qualifier Character 7
0 Head and Neck Tendon 1 Shoulder Tendon, Right 2 Shoulder Tendon, Left 3 Upper Arm Tendon, Right 4 Upper Arm Tendon, Left 5 Lower Arm and Wrist Tendon, Right 6 Lower Arm and Wrist Tendon, Left 7 Hand Tendon, Right 8 Hand Tendon, Left 9 Trunk Tendon, Right B Trunk Tendon, Left C Thorax Tendon, Right D Thorax Tendon, Left F Abdomen Tendon, Right G Abdomen Tendon, Left H Perineum Tendon J Hip Tendon, Right K Hip Tendon, Left L Upper Leg Tendon, Right M Upper Leg Tendon, Left N Lower Leg Tendon, Right P Lower Leg Tendon, Left Q Knee Tendon, Right R Knee Tendon, Left S Ankle Tendon, Right T Ankle Tendon, Left V Foot Tendon, Right W Foot Tendon, Left	0 Open 3 Percutaneous 4 Percutaneous Endoscopic	0 Drainage Device	Z No Qualifier

Continued on next page

0 **Medical and Surgical**
Continued from previous page
L **Tendons**
9 **Drainage:** Taking or letting out fluids and/or gases from a body part

Body Part Character 4	Approach Character 5	Device Character 6	Qualifier Character 7

0 Head and Neck Tendon
1 Shoulder Tendon, Right
2 Shoulder Tendon, Left
3 Upper Arm Tendon, Right
4 Upper Arm Tendon, Left
5 Lower Arm and Wrist Tendon,
    Right
6 Lower Arm and Wrist Tendon,
    Left
7 Hand Tendon, Right
8 Hand Tendon, Left
9 Trunk Tendon, Right
B Trunk Tendon, Left
C Thorax Tendon, Right
D Thorax Tendon, Left
F Abdomen Tendon, Right
G Abdomen Tendon, Left
H Perineum Tendon
J Hip Tendon, Right
K Hip Tendon, Left
L Upper Leg Tendon, Right
M Upper Leg Tendon, Left
N Lower Leg Tendon, Right
P Lower Leg Tendon, Left
Q Knee Tendon, Right
R Knee Tendon, Left
S Ankle Tendon, Right
T Ankle Tendon, Left
V Foot Tendon, Right
W Foot Tendon, Left
	0 Open
	3 Percutaneous
	4 Percutaneous Endoscopic
		Z No Device	**X** Diagnostic
			Z No Qualifier

0 **Medical and Surgical**
L **Tendons**
B **Excision:** Cutting out or off, without replacement, a portion of a body part

Body Part Character 4	Approach Character 5	Device Character 6	Qualifier Character 7

0 Head and Neck Tendon
1 Shoulder Tendon, Right
2 Shoulder Tendon, Left
3 Upper Arm Tendon, Right
4 Upper Arm Tendon, Left
5 Lower Arm and Wrist Tendon,
    Right
6 Lower Arm and Wrist Tendon,
    Left
7 Hand Tendon, Right
8 Hand Tendon, Left
9 Trunk Tendon, Right
B Trunk Tendon, Left
C Thorax Tendon, Right
D Thorax Tendon, Left
F Abdomen Tendon, Right
G Abdomen Tendon, Left
H Perineum Tendon
J Hip Tendon, Right
K Hip Tendon, Left
L Upper Leg Tendon, Right
M Upper Leg Tendon, Left
N Lower Leg Tendon, Right
P Lower Leg Tendon, Left
Q Knee Tendon, Right
R Knee Tendon, Left
S Ankle Tendon, Right
T Ankle Tendon, Left
V Foot Tendon, Right
W Foot Tendon, Left
	0 Open
	3 Percutaneous
	4 Percutaneous Endoscopic
		Z No Device	**X** Diagnostic
			Z No Qualifier

0 **Medical and Surgical**
L **Tendons**
C **Extirpation:** Taking or cutting out solid matter from a body part

Body Part Character 4	Approach Character 5	Device Character 6	Qualifier Character 7
0 Head and Neck Tendon 1 Shoulder Tendon, Right 2 Shoulder Tendon, Left 3 Upper Arm Tendon, Right 4 Upper Arm Tendon, Left 5 Lower Arm and Wrist Tendon, Right 6 Lower Arm and Wrist Tendon, Left 7 Hand Tendon, Right 8 Hand Tendon, Left 9 Trunk Tendon, Right B Trunk Tendon, Left C Thorax Tendon, Right D Thorax Tendon, Left F Abdomen Tendon, Right G Abdomen Tendon, Left H Perineum Tendon J Hip Tendon, Right K Hip Tendon, Left L Upper Leg Tendon, Right M Upper Leg Tendon, Left N Lower Leg Tendon, Right P Lower Leg Tendon, Left Q Knee Tendon, Right R Knee Tendon, Left S Ankle Tendon, Right T Ankle Tendon, Left V Foot Tendon, Right W Foot Tendon, Left	0 Open 3 Percutaneous 4 Percutaneous Endoscopic	Z No Device	Z No Qualifier

0 **Medical and Surgical**
L **Tendons**
J **Inspection:** Visually and/or manually exploring a body part

Body Part Character 4	Approach Character 5	Device Character 6	Qualifier Character 7
0 Head and Neck Tendon 1 Shoulder Tendon, Right 2 Shoulder Tendon, Left 3 Upper Arm Tendon, Right 4 Upper Arm Tendon, Left 5 Lower Arm and Wrist Tendon, Right 6 Lower Arm and Wrist Tendon, Left 7 Hand Tendon, Right 8 Hand Tendon, Left 9 Trunk Tendon, Right B Trunk Tendon, Left C Thorax Tendon, Right D Thorax Tendon, Left F Abdomen Tendon, Right G Abdomen Tendon, Left H Perineum Tendon J Hip Tendon, Right K Hip Tendon, Left L Upper Leg Tendon, Right M Upper Leg Tendon, Left N Lower Leg Tendon, Right P Lower Leg Tendon, Left Q Knee Tendon, Right R Knee Tendon, Left S Ankle Tendon, Right T Ankle Tendon, Left V Foot Tendon, Right W Foot Tendon, Left	0 Open 3 Percutaneous 4 Percutaneous Endoscopic X External	Z No Device	Z No Qualifier

0   **Medical and Surgical**
L   **Tendons**
M   **Reattachment:**   Putting back in or on all or a portion of a separated body part to its normal location or other suitable location

Body Part Character 4	Approach Character 5	Device Character 6	Qualifier Character 7
0 Head and Neck Tendon 1 Shoulder Tendon, Right 2 Shoulder Tendon, Left 3 Upper Arm Tendon, Right 4 Upper Arm Tendon, Left 5 Lower Arm and Wrist Tendon, Right 6 Lower Arm and Wrist Tendon, Left 7 Hand Tendon, Right 8 Hand Tendon, Left 9 Trunk Tendon, Right B Trunk Tendon, Left C Thorax Tendon, Right D Thorax Tendon, Left F Abdomen Tendon, Right G Abdomen Tendon, Left H Perineum Tendon J Hip Tendon, Right K Hip Tendon, Left L Upper Leg Tendon, Right M Upper Leg Tendon, Left N Lower Leg Tendon, Right P Lower Leg Tendon, Left Q Knee Tendon, Right R Knee Tendon, Left S Ankle Tendon, Right T Ankle Tendon, Left V Foot Tendon, Right W Foot Tendon, Left	0 Open 4 Percutaneous Endoscopic	Z No Device	Z No Qualifier

0   **Medical and Surgical**
L   **Tendons**
N   **Release:**   Freeing a body part from an abnormal physical constraint

Body Part Character 4	Approach Character 5	Device Character 6	Qualifier Character 7
0 Head and Neck Tendon 1 Shoulder Tendon, Right 2 Shoulder Tendon, Left 3 Upper Arm Tendon, Right 4 Upper Arm Tendon, Left 5 Lower Arm and Wrist Tendon, Right 6 Lower Arm and Wrist Tendon, Left 7 Hand Tendon, Right 8 Hand Tendon, Left 9 Trunk Tendon, Right B Trunk Tendon, Left C Thorax Tendon, Right D Thorax Tendon, Left F Abdomen Tendon, Right G Abdomen Tendon, Left H Perineum Tendon J Hip Tendon, Right K Hip Tendon, Left L Upper Leg Tendon, Right M Upper Leg Tendon, Left N Lower Leg Tendon, Right P Lower Leg Tendon, Left Q Knee Tendon, Right R Knee Tendon, Left S Ankle Tendon, Right T Ankle Tendon, Left V Foot Tendon, Right W Foot Tendon, Left	0 Open 3 Percutaneous 4 Percutaneous Endoscopic X External	Z No Device	Z No Qualifier

0 Medical and Surgical
L Tendons
P Removal: Taking out or off a device from a body part

Body Part Character 4	Approach Character 5	Device Character 6	Qualifier Character 7
X Upper Tendon Y Lower Tendon	0 Open 3 Percutaneous 4 Percutaneous Endoscopic	0 Drainage Device 7 Autologous Tissue Substitute J Synthetic Substitute K Nonautologous Tissue Substitute	Z No Qualifier
X Upper Tendon Y Lower Tendon	X External	0 Drainage Device	Z No Qualifier

0 Medical and Surgical
L Tendons
Q Repair: Restoring, to the extent possible, a body part to its normal anatomic structure and function

Body Part Character 4	Approach Character 5	Device Character 6	Qualifier Character 7
0 Head and Neck Tendon 1 Shoulder Tendon, Right 2 Shoulder Tendon, Left 3 Upper Arm Tendon, Right 4 Upper Arm Tendon, Left 5 Lower Arm and Wrist Tendon, Right 6 Lower Arm and Wrist Tendon, Left 7 Hand Tendon, Right 8 Hand Tendon, Left 9 Trunk Tendon, Right B Trunk Tendon, Left C Thorax Tendon, Right D Thorax Tendon, Left F Abdomen Tendon, Right G Abdomen Tendon, Left H Perineum Tendon J Hip Tendon, Right K Hip Tendon, Left L Upper Leg Tendon, Right M Upper Leg Tendon, Left N Lower Leg Tendon, Right P Lower Leg Tendon, Left Q Knee Tendon, Right R Knee Tendon, Left S Ankle Tendon, Right T Ankle Tendon, Left V Foot Tendon, Right W Foot Tendon, Left	0 Open 3 Percutaneous 4 Percutaneous Endoscopic	Z No Device	Z No Qualifier

0   Medical and Surgical
L   Tendons
R   Replacement: Putting in or on biological or synthetic material that physically takes the place and/or function of all or a portion of a body part

Body Part Character 4	Approach Character 5	Device Character 6	Qualifier Character 7
0 Head and Neck Tendon **1** Shoulder Tendon, Right **2** Shoulder Tendon, Left **3** Upper Arm Tendon, Right **4** Upper Arm Tendon, Left **5** Lower Arm and Wrist Tendon, Right **6** Lower Arm and Wrist Tendon, Left **7** Hand Tendon, Right **8** Hand Tendon, Left **9** Trunk Tendon, Right **B** Trunk Tendon, Left **C** Thorax Tendon, Right **D** Thorax Tendon, Left **F** Abdomen Tendon, Right **G** Abdomen Tendon, Left **H** Perineum Tendon **J** Hip Tendon, Right **K** Hip Tendon, Left **L** Upper Leg Tendon, Right **M** Upper Leg Tendon, Left **N** Lower Leg Tendon, Right **P** Lower Leg Tendon, Left **Q** Knee Tendon, Right **R** Knee Tendon, Left **S** Ankle Tendon, Right **T** Ankle Tendon, Left **V** Foot Tendon, Right **W** Foot Tendon, Left	**0** Open **4** Percutaneous Endoscopic	**7** Autologous Tissue Substitute **J** Synthetic Substitute **K** Nonautologous Tissue Substitute	**Z** No Qualifier

0   Medical and Surgical
L   Tendons
S   Reposition: Moving to its normal location or other suitable location all or a portion of a body part

Body Part Character 4	Approach Character 5	Device Character 6	Qualifier Character 7
0 Head and Neck Tendon **1** Shoulder Tendon, Right **2** Shoulder Tendon, Left **3** Upper Arm Tendon, Right **4** Upper Arm Tendon, Left **5** Lower Arm and Wrist Tendon, Right **6** Lower Arm and Wrist Tendon, Left **7** Hand Tendon, Right **8** Hand Tendon, Left **9** Trunk Tendon, Right **B** Trunk Tendon, Left **C** Thorax Tendon, Right **D** Thorax Tendon, Left **F** Abdomen Tendon, Right **G** Abdomen Tendon, Left **H** Perineum Tendon **J** Hip Tendon, Right **K** Hip Tendon, Left **L** Upper Leg Tendon, Right **M** Upper Leg Tendon, Left **N** Lower Leg Tendon, Right **P** Lower Leg Tendon, Left **Q** Knee Tendon, Right **R** Knee Tendon, Left **S** Ankle Tendon, Right **T** Ankle Tendon, Left **V** Foot Tendon, Right **W** Foot Tendon, Left	**0** Open **4** Percutaneous Endoscopic	**Z** No Device	**Z** No Qualifier

0   **Medical and Surgical**
L   **Tendons**
T   **Resection:**   Cutting out or off, without replacement, all of a body part

Body Part Character 4	Approach Character 5	Device Character 6	Qualifier Character 7
0 Head and Neck Tendon 1 Shoulder Tendon, Right 2 Shoulder Tendon, Left 3 Upper Arm Tendon, Right 4 Upper Arm Tendon, Left 5 Lower Arm and Wrist Tendon, Right 6 Lower Arm and Wrist Tendon, Left 7 Hand Tendon, Right 8 Hand Tendon, Left 9 Trunk Tendon, Right B Trunk Tendon, Left C Thorax Tendon, Right D Thorax Tendon, Left F Abdomen Tendon, Right G Abdomen Tendon, Left H Perineum Tendon J Hip Tendon, Right K Hip Tendon, Left L Upper Leg Tendon, Right M Upper Leg Tendon, Left N Lower Leg Tendon, Right P Lower Leg Tendon, Left Q Knee Tendon, Right R Knee Tendon, Left S Ankle Tendon, Right T Ankle Tendon, Left V Foot Tendon, Right W Foot Tendon, Left	0 Open 4 Percutaneous Endoscopic	Z No Device	Z No Qualifier

0   **Medical and Surgical**
L   **Tendons**
U   **Supplement:**   Putting in or on biological or synthetic material that physically reinforces and/or augments the function of a portion of a body part

Body Part Character 4	Approach Character 5	Device Character 6	Qualifier Character 7
0 Head and Neck Tendon 1 Shoulder Tendon, Right 2 Shoulder Tendon, Left 3 Upper Arm Tendon, Right 4 Upper Arm Tendon, Left 5 Lower Arm and Wrist Tendon, Right 6 Lower Arm and Wrist Tendon, Left 7 Hand Tendon, Right 8 Hand Tendon, Left 9 Trunk Tendon, Right B Trunk Tendon, Left C Thorax Tendon, Right D Thorax Tendon, Left F Abdomen Tendon, Right G Abdomen Tendon, Left H Perineum Tendon J Hip Tendon, Right K Hip Tendon, Left L Upper Leg Tendon, Right M Upper Leg Tendon, Left N Lower Leg Tendon, Right P Lower Leg Tendon, Left Q Knee Tendon, Right R Knee Tendon, Left S Ankle Tendon, Right T Ankle Tendon, Left V Foot Tendon, Right W Foot Tendon, Left	0 Open 4 Percutaneous Endoscopic	7 Autologous Tissue Substitute J Synthetic Substitute K Nonautologous Tissue Substitute	Z No Qualifier

0   **Medical and Surgical**
L   **Tendons**
W   **Revision:**   Correcting, to the extent possible, a malfunctioning or displaced device

Body Part Character 4	Approach Character 5	Device Character 6	Qualifier Character 7
X Upper Tendon **Y** Lower Tendon	**0** Open **3** Percutaneous **4** Percutaneous Endoscopic **X** External	**0** Drainage Device **7** Autologous Tissue Substitute **J** Synthetic Substitute **K** Nonautologous Tissue Substitute	**Z** No Qualifier

0   **Medical and Surgical**
L   **Tendons**
X   **Transfer:**   Moving, without taking out, all or a portion of a body part to another location to take over the function of all or a portion of a body part

Body Part Character 4	Approach Character 5	Device Character 6	Qualifier Character 7
0 Head and Neck Tendon **1** Shoulder Tendon, Right **2** Shoulder Tendon, Left **3** Upper Arm Tendon, Right **4** Upper Arm Tendon, Left **5** Lower Arm and Wrist Tendon, Right **6** Lower Arm and Wrist Tendon, Left **7** Hand Tendon, Right **8** Hand Tendon, Left **9** Trunk Tendon, Right **B** Trunk Tendon, Left **C** Thorax Tendon, Right **D** Thorax Tendon, Left **F** Abdomen Tendon, Right **G** Abdomen Tendon, Left **H** Perineum Tendon **J** Hip Tendon, Right **K** Hip Tendon, Left **L** Upper Leg Tendon, Right **M** Upper Leg Tendon, Left **N** Lower Leg Tendon, Right **P** Lower Leg Tendon, Left **Q** Knee Tendon, Right **R** Knee Tendon, Left **S** Ankle Tendon, Right **T** Ankle Tendon, Left **V** Foot Tendon, Right **W** Foot Tendon, Left	**0** Open **4** Percutaneous Endoscopic	**Z** No Device	**Z** No Qualifier

Bursae and Ligaments 0M2–0MX

0   **Medical and Surgical**
M   **Bursae and Ligaments**
2   **Change:**   Taking out or off a device from a body part and putting back an identical or similar device in or on the same body part without cutting or puncturing the skin or a mucous membrane

Body Part Character 4	Approach Character 5	Device Character 6	Qualifier Character 7
X Upper Bursa and Ligament **Y** Lower Bursa and Ligament	**X** External	**0** Drainage Device **Y** Other Device	**Z** No Qualifier

0   **Medical and Surgical**
M   **Bursae and Ligaments**
5   **Destruction:**   Physical eradication of all or a portion of a body part by the direct use of energy, force, or a destructive agent

Body Part Character 4	Approach Character 5	Device Character 6	Qualifier Character 7
0 Head and Neck Bursa and Ligament **1** Shoulder Bursa and Ligament, Right **2** Shoulder Bursa and Ligament, Left **3** Elbow Bursa and Ligament, Right **4** Elbow Bursa and Ligament, Left **5** Wrist Bursa and Ligament, Right **6** Wrist Bursa and Ligament, Left **7** Hand Bursa and Ligament, Right **8** Hand Bursa and Ligament, Left **9** Upper Extremity Bursa and Ligament, Right **B** Upper Extremity Bursa and Ligament, Left **C** Trunk Bursa and Ligament, Right **D** Trunk Bursa and Ligament, Left **F** Thorax Bursa and Ligament, Right **G** Thorax Bursa and Ligament, Left **H** Abdomen Bursa and Ligament, Right **J** Abdomen Bursa and Ligament, Left **K** Perineum Bursa and Ligament **L** Hip Bursa and Ligament, Right **M** Hip Bursa and Ligament, Left **N** Knee Bursa and Ligament, Right **P** Knee Bursa and Ligament, Left **Q** Ankle Bursa and Ligament, Right **R** Ankle Bursa and Ligament, Left **S** Foot Bursa and Ligament, Right **T** Foot Bursa and Ligament, Left **V** Lower Extremity Bursa and Ligament, Right **W** Lower Extremity Bursa and Ligament, Left	**0** Open **3** Percutaneous **4** Percutaneous Endoscopic	**Z** No Device	**Z** No Qualifier

0   **Medical and Surgical**
M   **Bursae and Ligaments**
8   **Division:**   Cutting into a body part without draining fluids and/or gases from the body part in order to separate or transect a body part

Body Part Character 4	Approach Character 5	Device Character 6	Qualifier Character 7
0 Head and Neck Bursa and Ligament **1** Shoulder Bursa and Ligament, Right **2** Shoulder Bursa and Ligament, Left **3** Elbow Bursa and Ligament, Right **4** Elbow Bursa and Ligament, Left **5** Wrist Bursa and Ligament, Right **6** Wrist Bursa and Ligament, Left **7** Hand Bursa and Ligament, Right **8** Hand Bursa and Ligament, Left **9** Upper Extremity Bursa and Ligament, Right **B** Upper Extremity Bursa and Ligament, Left **C** Trunk Bursa and Ligament, Right **D** Trunk Bursa and Ligament, Left **F** Thorax Bursa and Ligament, Right **G** Thorax Bursa and Ligament, Left **H** Abdomen Bursa and Ligament, Right **J** Abdomen Bursa and Ligament, Left **K** Perineum Bursa and Ligament **L** Hip Bursa and Ligament, Right **M** Hip Bursa and Ligament, Left **N** Knee Bursa and Ligament, Right **P** Knee Bursa and Ligament, Left **Q** Ankle Bursa and Ligament, Right **R** Ankle Bursa and Ligament, Left **S** Foot Bursa and Ligament, Right **T** Foot Bursa and Ligament, Left **V** Lower Extremity Bursa and Ligament, Right **W** Lower Extremity Bursa and Ligament, Left	**0** Open **3** Percutaneous **4** Percutaneous Endoscopic	**Z** No Device	**Z** No Qualifier

0   **Medical and Surgical**
M   **Bursae and Ligaments**
9   **Drainage:**   Taking or letting out fluids and/or gases from a body part

Body Part Character 4	Approach Character 5	Device Character 6	Qualifier Character 7
0 Head and Neck Bursa and Ligament **1** Shoulder Bursa and Ligament, Right **2** Shoulder Bursa and Ligament, Left **3** Elbow Bursa and Ligament, Right **4** Elbow Bursa and Ligament, Left **5** Wrist Bursa and Ligament, Right **6** Wrist Bursa and Ligament, Left **7** Hand Bursa and Ligament, Right **8** Hand Bursa and Ligament, Left **9** Upper Extremity Bursa and Ligament, Right **B** Upper Extremity Bursa and Ligament, Left **C** Trunk Bursa and Ligament, Right **D** Trunk Bursa and Ligament, Left **F** Thorax Bursa and Ligament, Right **G** Thorax Bursa and Ligament, Left **H** Abdomen Bursa and Ligament, Right **J** Abdomen Bursa and Ligament, Left **K** Perineum Bursa and Ligament **L** Hip Bursa and Ligament, Right **M** Hip Bursa and Ligament, Left **N** Knee Bursa and Ligament, Right **P** Knee Bursa and Ligament, Left **Q** Ankle Bursa and Ligament, Right **R** Ankle Bursa and Ligament, Left **S** Foot Bursa and Ligament, Right **T** Foot Bursa and Ligament, Left **V** Lower Extremity Bursa and Ligament, Right **W** Lower Extremity Bursa and Ligament, Left	**0** Open **3** Percutaneous **4** Percutaneous Endoscopic	**0** Drainage Device	**Z** No Qualifier

Continued on next page

0 Medical and Surgical
M Bursae and Ligaments
9 Drainage: Taking or letting out fluids and/or gases from a body part   *Continued from previous page*

Body Part Character 4	Approach Character 5	Device Character 6	Qualifier Character 7
0 Head and Neck Bursa and Ligament 1 Shoulder Bursa and Ligament, Right 2 Shoulder Bursa and Ligament, Left 3 Elbow Bursa and Ligament, Right 4 Elbow Bursa and Ligament, Left 5 Wrist Bursa and Ligament, Right 6 Wrist Bursa and Ligament, Left 7 Hand Bursa and Ligament, Right 8 Hand Bursa and Ligament, Left 9 Upper Extremity Bursa and Ligament, Right B Upper Extremity Bursa and Ligament, Left C Trunk Bursa and Ligament, Right D Trunk Bursa and Ligament, Left F Thorax Bursa and Ligament, Right G Thorax Bursa and Ligament, Left H Abdomen Bursa and Ligament, Right J Abdomen Bursa and Ligament, Left K Perineum Bursa and Ligament L Hip Bursa and Ligament, Right M Hip Bursa and Ligament, Left N Knee Bursa and Ligament, Right P Knee Bursa and Ligament, Left Q Ankle Bursa and Ligament, Right R Ankle Bursa and Ligament, Left S Foot Bursa and Ligament, Right T Foot Bursa and Ligament, Left V Lower Extremity Bursa and Ligament, Right W Lower Extremity Bursa and Ligament, Left	0 Open 3 Percutaneous 4 Percutaneous Endoscopic	Z No Device	X Diagnostic Z No Qualifier

0 Medical and Surgical
M Bursae and Ligaments
B Excision: Cutting out or off, without replacement, a portion of a body part

Body Part Character 4	Approach Character 5	Device Character 6	Qualifier Character 7
0 Head and Neck Bursa and Ligament 1 Shoulder Bursa and Ligament, Right 2 Shoulder Bursa and Ligament, Left 3 Elbow Bursa and Ligament, Right 4 Elbow Bursa and Ligament, Left 5 Wrist Bursa and Ligament, Right 6 Wrist Bursa and Ligament, Left 7 Hand Bursa and Ligament, Right 8 Hand Bursa and Ligament, Left 9 Upper Extremity Bursa and Ligament, Right B Upper Extremity Bursa and Ligament, Left C Trunk Bursa and Ligament, Right D Trunk Bursa and Ligament, Left F Thorax Bursa and Ligament, Right G Thorax Bursa and Ligament, Left H Abdomen Bursa and Ligament, Right J Abdomen Bursa and Ligament, Left K Perineum Bursa and Ligament L Hip Bursa and Ligament, Right M Hip Bursa and Ligament, Left N Knee Bursa and Ligament, Right P Knee Bursa and Ligament, Left Q Ankle Bursa and Ligament, Right R Ankle Bursa and Ligament, Left S Foot Bursa and Ligament, Right T Foot Bursa and Ligament, Left V Lower Extremity Bursa and Ligament, Right W Lower Extremity Bursa and Ligament, Left	0 Open 3 Percutaneous 4 Percutaneous Endoscopic	Z No Device	X Diagnostic Z No Qualifier

0   **Medical and Surgical**
M   **Bursae and Ligaments**
C   **Extirpation:**   Taking or cutting out solid matter from a body part

Body Part Character 4	Approach Character 5	Device Character 6	Qualifier Character 7
0 Head and Neck Bursa and Ligament 1 Shoulder Bursa and Ligament, Right 2 Shoulder Bursa and Ligament, Left 3 Elbow Bursa and Ligament, Right 4 Elbow Bursa and Ligament, Left 5 Wrist Bursa and Ligament, Right 6 Wrist Bursa and Ligament, Left 7 Hand Bursa and Ligament, Right 8 Hand Bursa and Ligament, Left 9 Upper Extremity Bursa and Ligament, Right B Upper Extremity Bursa and Ligament, Left C Trunk Bursa and Ligament, Right D Trunk Bursa and Ligament, Left F Thorax Bursa and Ligament, Right G Thorax Bursa and Ligament, Left H Abdomen Bursa and Ligament, Right J Abdomen Bursa and Ligament, Left K Perineum Bursa and Ligament L Hip Bursa and Ligament, Right M Hip Bursa and Ligament, Left N Knee Bursa and Ligament, Right P Knee Bursa and Ligament, Left Q Ankle Bursa and Ligament, Right R Ankle Bursa and Ligament, Left S Foot Bursa and Ligament, Right T Foot Bursa and Ligament, Left V Lower Extremity Bursa and Ligament, Right W Lower Extremity Bursa and Ligament, Left	0 Open 3 Percutaneous 4 Percutaneous Endoscopic	Z No Device	Z No Qualifier

0   **Medical and Surgical**
M   **Bursae and Ligaments**
D   **Extraction:**   Pulling or stripping out or off all or a portion of a body part by the use of force

Body Part Character 4	Approach Character 5	Device Character 6	Qualifier Character 7
0 Head and Neck Bursa and Ligament 1 Shoulder Bursa and Ligament, Right 2 Shoulder Bursa and Ligament, Left 3 Elbow Bursa and Ligament, Right 4 Elbow Bursa and Ligament, Left 5 Wrist Bursa and Ligament, Right 6 Wrist Bursa and Ligament, Left 7 Hand Bursa and Ligament, Right 8 Hand Bursa and Ligament, Left 9 Upper Extremity Bursa and Ligament, Right B Upper Extremity Bursa and Ligament, Left C Trunk Bursa and Ligament, Right D Trunk Bursa and Ligament, Left F Thorax Bursa and Ligament, Right G Thorax Bursa and Ligament, Left H Abdomen Bursa and Ligament, Right J Abdomen Bursa and Ligament, Left K Perineum Bursa and Ligament L Hip Bursa and Ligament, Right M Hip Bursa and Ligament, Left N Knee Bursa and Ligament, Right P Knee Bursa and Ligament, Left Q Ankle Bursa and Ligament, Right R Ankle Bursa and Ligament, Left S Foot Bursa and Ligament, Right T Foot Bursa and Ligament, Left V Lower Extremity Bursa and Ligament, Right W Lower Extremity Bursa and Ligament, Left	0 Open 3 Percutaneous 4 Percutaneous Endoscopic	Z No Device	Z No Qualifier

0 **Medical and Surgical**
M **Bursae and Ligaments**
J **Inspection:**   Visually and/or manually exploring a body part

Body Part Character 4	Approach Character 5	Device Character 6	Qualifier Character 7
0 Head and Neck Bursa and Ligament **1** Shoulder Bursa and Ligament, Right **2** Shoulder Bursa and Ligament, Left **3** Elbow Bursa and Ligament, Right **4** Elbow Bursa and Ligament, Left **5** Wrist Bursa and Ligament, Right **6** Wrist Bursa and Ligament, Left **7** Hand Bursa and Ligament, Right **8** Hand Bursa and Ligament, Left **9** Upper Extremity Bursa and Ligament, Right **B** Upper Extremity Bursa and Ligament, Left **C** Trunk Bursa and Ligament, Right **D** Trunk Bursa and Ligament, Left **F** Thorax Bursa and Ligament, Right **G** Thorax Bursa and Ligament, Left **H** Abdomen Bursa and Ligament, Right **J** Abdomen Bursa and Ligament, Left **K** Perineum Bursa and Ligament **L** Hip Bursa and Ligament, Right **M** Hip Bursa and Ligament, Left **N** Knee Bursa and Ligament, Right **P** Knee Bursa and Ligament, Left **Q** Ankle Bursa and Ligament, Right **R** Ankle Bursa and Ligament, Left **S** Foot Bursa and Ligament, Right **T** Foot Bursa and Ligament, Left **V** Lower Extremity Bursa and Ligament, Right **W** Lower Extremity Bursa and Ligament, Left	**0** Open **3** Percutaneous **4** Percutaneous Endoscopic **X** External	**Z** No Device	**Z** No Qualifier

0 **Medical and Surgical**
M **Bursae and Ligaments**
M **Reattachment:**   Putting back in or on all or a portion of a separated body part to its normal location or other suitable location

Body Part Character 4	Approach Character 5	Device Character 6	Qualifier Character 7
0 Head and Neck Bursa and Ligament **1** Shoulder Bursa and Ligament, Right **2** Shoulder Bursa and Ligament, Left **3** Elbow Bursa and Ligament, Right **4** Elbow Bursa and Ligament, Left **5** Wrist Bursa and Ligament, Right **6** Wrist Bursa and Ligament, Left **7** Hand Bursa and Ligament, Right **8** Hand Bursa and Ligament, Left **9** Upper Extremity Bursa and Ligament, Right **B** Upper Extremity Bursa and Ligament, Left **C** Trunk Bursa and Ligament, Right **D** Trunk Bursa and Ligament, Left **F** Thorax Bursa and Ligament, Right **G** Thorax Bursa and Ligament, Left **H** Abdomen Bursa and Ligament, Right **J** Abdomen Bursa and Ligament, Left **K** Perineum Bursa and Ligament **L** Hip Bursa and Ligament, Right **M** Hip Bursa and Ligament, Left **N** Knee Bursa and Ligament, Right **P** Knee Bursa and Ligament, Left **Q** Ankle Bursa and Ligament, Right **R** Ankle Bursa and Ligament, Left **S** Foot Bursa and Ligament, Right **T** Foot Bursa and Ligament, Left **V** Lower Extremity Bursa and Ligament, Right **W** Lower Extremity Bursa and Ligament, Left	**0** Open **4** Percutaneous Endoscopic	**Z** No Device	**Z** No Qualifier

0   Medical and Surgical
M   Bursae and Ligaments
N   Release: Freeing a body part from an abnormal physical constraint

Body Part Character 4	Approach Character 5	Device Character 6	Qualifier Character 7
0 Head and Neck Bursa and Ligament 1 Shoulder Bursa and Ligament, Right 2 Shoulder Bursa and Ligament, Left 3 Elbow Bursa and Ligament, Right 4 Elbow Bursa and Ligament, Left 5 Wrist Bursa and Ligament, Right 6 Wrist Bursa and Ligament, Left 7 Hand Bursa and Ligament, Right 8 Hand Bursa and Ligament, Left 9 Upper Extremity Bursa and Ligament, Right B Upper Extremity Bursa and Ligament, Left C Trunk Bursa and Ligament, Right D Trunk Bursa and Ligament, Left F Thorax Bursa and Ligament, Right G Thorax Bursa and Ligament, Left H Abdomen Bursa and Ligament, Right J Abdomen Bursa and Ligament, Left K Perineum Bursa and Ligament L Hip Bursa and Ligament, Right M Hip Bursa and Ligament, Left N Knee Bursa and Ligament, Right P Knee Bursa and Ligament, Left Q Ankle Bursa and Ligament, Right R Ankle Bursa and Ligament, Left S Foot Bursa and Ligament, Right T Foot Bursa and Ligament, Left V Lower Extremity Bursa and Ligament, Right W Lower Extremity Bursa and Ligament, Left	0 Open 3 Percutaneous 4 Percutaneous Endoscopic X External	Z No Device	Z No Qualifier

0   Medical and Surgical
M   Bursae and Ligaments
P   Removal: Taking out or off a device from a body part

Body Part Character 4	Approach Character 5	Device Character 6	Qualifier Character 7
X Upper Bursa and Ligament Y Lower Bursa and Ligament	0 Open 3 Percutaneous 4 Percutaneous Endoscopic	0 Drainage Device 7 Autologous Tissue Substitute J Synthetic Substitute K Nonautologous Tissue Substitute	Z No Qualifier
X Upper Bursa and Ligament Y Lower Bursa and Ligament	X External	0 Drainage Device	Z No Qualifier

0   **Medical and Surgical**
M   **Bursae and Ligaments**
Q   **Repair:**   Restoring, to the extent possible, a body part to its normal anatomic structure and function

Body Part Character 4	Approach Character 5	Device Character 6	Qualifier Character 7
0 Head and Neck Bursa and Ligament 1 Shoulder Bursa and Ligament, Right 2 Shoulder Bursa and Ligament, Left 3 Elbow Bursa and Ligament, Right 4 Elbow Bursa and Ligament, Left 5 Wrist Bursa and Ligament, Right 6 Wrist Bursa and Ligament, Left 7 Hand Bursa and Ligament, Right 8 Hand Bursa and Ligament, Left 9 Upper Extremity Bursa and Ligament, Right B Upper Extremity Bursa and Ligament, Left C Trunk Bursa and Ligament, Right D Trunk Bursa and Ligament, Left F Thorax Bursa and Ligament, Right G Thorax Bursa and Ligament, Left H Abdomen Bursa and Ligament, Right J Abdomen Bursa and Ligament, Left K Perineum Bursa and Ligament L Hip Bursa and Ligament, Right M Hip Bursa and Ligament, Left N Knee Bursa and Ligament, Right P Knee Bursa and Ligament, Left Q Ankle Bursa and Ligament, Right R Ankle Bursa and Ligament, Left S Foot Bursa and Ligament, Right T Foot Bursa and Ligament, Left V Lower Extremity Bursa and Ligament, Right W Lower Extremity Bursa and Ligament, Left	0 Open 3 Percutaneous 4 Percutaneous Endoscopic	Z No Device	Z No Qualifier

0   **Medical and Surgical**
M   **Bursae and Ligaments**
S   **Reposition:**   Moving to its normal location or other suitable location all or a portion of a body part

Body Part Character 4	Approach Character 5	Device Character 6	Qualifier Character 7
0 Head and Neck Bursa and Ligament 1 Shoulder Bursa and Ligament, Right 2 Shoulder Bursa and Ligament, Left 3 Elbow Bursa and Ligament, Right 4 Elbow Bursa and Ligament, Left 5 Wrist Bursa and Ligament, Right 6 Wrist Bursa and Ligament, Left 7 Hand Bursa and Ligament, Right 8 Hand Bursa and Ligament, Left 9 Upper Extremity Bursa and Ligament, Right B Upper Extremity Bursa and Ligament, Left C Trunk Bursa and Ligament, Right D Trunk Bursa and Ligament, Left F Thorax Bursa and Ligament, Right G Thorax Bursa and Ligament, Left H Abdomen Bursa and Ligament, Right J Abdomen Bursa and Ligament, Left K Perineum Bursa and Ligament L Hip Bursa and Ligament, Right M Hip Bursa and Ligament, Left N Knee Bursa and Ligament, Right P Knee Bursa and Ligament, Left Q Ankle Bursa and Ligament, Right R Ankle Bursa and Ligament, Left S Foot Bursa and Ligament, Right T Foot Bursa and Ligament, Left V Lower Extremity Bursa and Ligament, Right W Lower Extremity Bursa and Ligament, Left	0 Open 4 Percutaneous Endoscopic	Z No Device	Z No Qualifier

0   **Medical and Surgical**
M   **Bursae and Ligaments**
T   **Resection:**   Cutting out or off, without replacement, all of a body part

Body Part Character 4	Approach Character 5	Device Character 6	Qualifier Character 7
0 Head and Neck Bursa and Ligament **1** Shoulder Bursa and Ligament, Right **2** Shoulder Bursa and Ligament, Left **3** Elbow Bursa and Ligament, Right **4** Elbow Bursa and Ligament, Left **5** Wrist Bursa and Ligament, Right **6** Wrist Bursa and Ligament, Left **7** Hand Bursa and Ligament, Right **8** Hand Bursa and Ligament, Left **9** Upper Extremity Bursa and Ligament, Right **B** Upper Extremity Bursa and Ligament, Left **C** Trunk Bursa and Ligament, Right **D** Trunk Bursa and Ligament, Left **F** Thorax Bursa and Ligament, Right **G** Thorax Bursa and Ligament, Left **H** Abdomen Bursa and Ligament, Right **J** Abdomen Bursa and Ligament, Left **K** Perineum Bursa and Ligament **L** Hip Bursa and Ligament, Right **M** Hip Bursa and Ligament, Left **N** Knee Bursa and Ligament, Right **P** Knee Bursa and Ligament, Left **Q** Ankle Bursa and Ligament, Right **R** Ankle Bursa and Ligament, Left **S** Foot Bursa and Ligament, Right **T** Foot Bursa and Ligament, Left **V** Lower Extremity Bursa and Ligament, Right **W** Lower Extremity Bursa and Ligament, Left	**0** Open **4** Percutaneous Endoscopic	**Z** No Device	**Z** No Qualifier

0   **Medical and Surgical**
M   **Bursae and Ligaments**
U   **Supplement:**   Putting in or on biological or synthetic material that physically reinforces and/or augments the function of a portion of a body part

Body Part Character 4	Approach Character 5	Device Character 6	Qualifier Character 7
0 Head and Neck Bursa and Ligament **1** Shoulder Bursa and Ligament, Right **2** Shoulder Bursa and Ligament, Left **3** Elbow Bursa and Ligament, Right **4** Elbow Bursa and Ligament, Left **5** Wrist Bursa and Ligament, Right **6** Wrist Bursa and Ligament, Left **7** Hand Bursa and Ligament, Right **8** Hand Bursa and Ligament, Left **9** Upper Extremity Bursa and Ligament, Right **B** Upper Extremity Bursa and Ligament, Left **C** Trunk Bursa and Ligament, Right **D** Trunk Bursa and Ligament, Left **F** Thorax Bursa and Ligament, Right **G** Thorax Bursa and Ligament, Left **H** Abdomen Bursa and Ligament, Right **J** Abdomen Bursa and Ligament, Left **K** Perineum Bursa and Ligament **L** Hip Bursa and Ligament, Right **M** Hip Bursa and Ligament, Left **N** Knee Bursa and Ligament, Right **P** Knee Bursa and Ligament, Left **Q** Ankle Bursa and Ligament, Right **R** Ankle Bursa and Ligament, Left **S** Foot Bursa and Ligament, Right **T** Foot Bursa and Ligament, Left **V** Lower Extremity Bursa and Ligament, Right **W** Lower Extremity Bursa and Ligament, Left	**0** Open **4** Percutaneous Endoscopic	**7** Autologous Tissue Substitute **J** Synthetic Substitute **K** Nonautologous Tissue Substitute	**Z** No Qualifier

0   **Medical and Surgical**
M   **Bursae and Ligaments**
W   **Revision:**   Correcting, to the extent possible, a malfunctioning or displaced device

Body Part Character 4	Approach Character 5	Device Character 6	Qualifier Character 7
X Upper Bursa and Ligament **Y** Lower Bursa and Ligament	**0** Open **3** Percutaneous **4** Percutaneous Endoscopic **X** External	**0** Drainage Device **7** Autologous Tissue Substitute **J** Synthetic Substitute **K** Nonautologous Tissue Substitute	**Z** No Qualifier

0   **Medical and Surgical**
M   **Bursae and Ligaments**
X   **Transfer:**   Moving, without taking out, all or a portion of a body part to another location to take over the function of all or a portion of a body part

Body Part Character 4	Approach Character 5	Device Character 6	Qualifier Character 7
0 Head and Neck Bursa and Ligament **1** Shoulder Bursa and Ligament, Right **2** Shoulder Bursa and Ligament, Left **3** Elbow Bursa and Ligament, Right **4** Elbow Bursa and Ligament, Left **5** Wrist Bursa and Ligament, Right **6** Wrist Bursa and Ligament, Left **7** Hand Bursa and Ligament, Right **8** Hand Bursa and Ligament, Left **9** Upper Extremity Bursa and Ligament, Right **B** Upper Extremity Bursa and Ligament, Left **C** Trunk Bursa and Ligament, Right **D** Trunk Bursa and Ligament, Left **F** Thorax Bursa and Ligament, Right **G** Thorax Bursa and Ligament, Left **H** Abdomen Bursa and Ligament, Right **J** Abdomen Bursa and Ligament, Left **K** Perineum Bursa and Ligament **L** Hip Bursa and Ligament, Right **M** Hip Bursa and Ligament, Left **N** Knee Bursa and Ligament, Right **P** Knee Bursa and Ligament, Left **Q** Ankle Bursa and Ligament, Right **R** Ankle Bursa and Ligament, Left **S** Foot Bursa and Ligament, Right **T** Foot Bursa and Ligament, Left **V** Lower Extremity Bursa and Ligament, Right **W** Lower Extremity Bursa and Ligament, Left	**0** Open **4** Percutaneous Endoscopic	**Z** No Device	**Z** No Qualifier

Head and Facial Bones 0N2–0NW

0 **Medical and Surgical**
N **Head and Facial Bones**
2 **Change:** Taking out or off a device from a body part and putting back an identical or similar device in or on the same body part without cutting or puncturing the skin or a mucous membrane

Body Part Character 4	Approach Character 5	Device Character 6	Qualifier Character 7
0 Skull B Nasal Bone W Facial Bone	X External	0 Drainage Device Y Other Device	Z No Qualifier

0 **Medical and Surgical**
N **Head and Facial Bones**
5 **Destruction:** Physical eradication of all or a portion of a body part by the direct use of energy, force, or a destructive agent

Body Part Character 4	Approach Character 5	Device Character 6	Qualifier Character 7
0 Skull 1 Frontal Bone, Right 2 Frontal Bone, Left 3 Parietal Bone, Right 4 Parietal Bone, Left 5 Temporal Bone, Right 6 Temporal Bone, Left 7 Occipital Bone, Right 8 Occipital Bone, Left B Nasal Bone C Sphenoid Bone, Right D Sphenoid Bone, Left F Ethmoid Bone, Right G Ethmoid Bone, Left H Lacrimal Bone, Right J Lacrimal Bone, Left K Palatine Bone, Right L Palatine Bone, Left M Zygomatic Bone, Right N Zygomatic Bone, Left P Orbit, Right Q Orbit, Left R Maxilla, Right S Maxilla, Left T Mandible, Right V Mandible, Left X Hyoid Bone	0 Open 3 Percutaneous 4 Percutaneous Endoscopic	Z No Device	Z No Qualifier

0   **Medical and Surgical**
N   **Head and Facial Bones**
8   **Division:**   Cutting into a body part without draining fluids and/or gases from the body part in order to separate or transect a body part

Body Part Character 4	Approach Character 5	Device Character 6	Qualifier Character 7
0 Skull 1 Frontal Bone, Right 2 Frontal Bone, Left 3 Parietal Bone, Right 4 Parietal Bone, Left 5 Temporal Bone, Right 6 Temporal Bone, Left 7 Occipital Bone, Right 8 Occipital Bone, Left B Nasal Bone C Sphenoid Bone, Right D Sphenoid Bone, Left F Ethmoid Bone, Right G Ethmoid Bone, Left H Lacrimal Bone, Right J Lacrimal Bone, Left K Palatine Bone, Right L Palatine Bone, Left M Zygomatic Bone, Right N Zygomatic Bone, Left P Orbit, Right Q Orbit, Left R Maxilla, Right S Maxilla, Left T Mandible, Right V Mandible, Left X Hyoid Bone	0 Open 3 Percutaneous 4 Percutaneous Endoscopic	Z No Device	Z No Qualifier

0   **Medical and Surgical**
N   **Head and Facial Bones**
9   **Drainage:**   Taking or letting out fluids and/or gases from a body part

Body Part Character 4	Approach Character 5	Device Character 6	Qualifier Character 7
0 Skull 1 Frontal Bone, Right 2 Frontal Bone, Left 3 Parietal Bone, Right 4 Parietal Bone, Left 5 Temporal Bone, Right 6 Temporal Bone, Left 7 Occipital Bone, Right 8 Occipital Bone, Left B Nasal Bone C Sphenoid Bone, Right D Sphenoid Bone, Left F Ethmoid Bone, Right G Ethmoid Bone, Left H Lacrimal Bone, Right J Lacrimal Bone, Left K Palatine Bone, Right L Palatine Bone, Left M Zygomatic Bone, Right N Zygomatic Bone, Left P Orbit, Right Q Orbit, Left R Maxilla, Right S Maxilla, Left T Mandible, Right V Mandible, Left X Hyoid Bone	0 Open 3 Percutaneous 4 Percutaneous Endoscopic	0 Drainage Device	Z No Qualifier

Continued on next page

0 **Medical and Surgical**
N **Head and Facial Bones**
9 **Drainage:**   Taking or letting out fluids and/or gases from a body part

Continued from previous page

Body Part Character 4	Approach Character 5	Device Character 6	Qualifier Character 7
0 Skull **1** Frontal Bone, Right **2** Frontal Bone, Left **3** Parietal Bone, Right **4** Parietal Bone, Left **5** Temporal Bone, Right **6** Temporal Bone, Left **7** Occipital Bone, Right **8** Occipital Bone, Left **B** Nasal Bone **C** Sphenoid Bone, Right **D** Sphenoid Bone, Left **F** Ethmoid Bone, Right **G** Ethmoid Bone, Left **H** Lacrimal Bone, Right **J** Lacrimal Bone, Left **K** Palatine Bone, Right **L** Palatine Bone, Left **M** Zygomatic Bone, Right **N** Zygomatic Bone, Left **P** Orbit, Right **Q** Orbit, Left **R** Maxilla, Right **S** Maxilla, Left **T** Mandible, Right **V** Mandible, Left **X** Hyoid Bone	**0** Open **3** Percutaneous **4** Percutaneous Endoscopic	**Z** No Device	**X** Diagnostic **Z** No Qualifier

0 **Medical and Surgical**
N **Head and Facial Bones**
B **Excision:**   Cutting out or off, without replacement, a portion of a body part

Body Part Character 4	Approach Character 5	Device Character 6	Qualifier Character 7
0 Skull **1** Frontal Bone, Right **2** Frontal Bone, Left **3** Parietal Bone, Right **4** Parietal Bone, Left **5** Temporal Bone, Right **6** Temporal Bone, Left **7** Occipital Bone, Right **8** Occipital Bone, Left **B** Nasal Bone **C** Sphenoid Bone, Right **D** Sphenoid Bone, Left **F** Ethmoid Bone, Right **G** Ethmoid Bone, Left **H** Lacrimal Bone, Right **J** Lacrimal Bone, Left **K** Palatine Bone, Right **L** Palatine Bone, Left **M** Zygomatic Bone, Right **N** Zygomatic Bone, Left **P** Orbit, Right **Q** Orbit, Left **R** Maxilla, Right **S** Maxilla, Left **T** Mandible, Right **V** Mandible, Left **X** Hyoid Bone	**0** Open **3** Percutaneous **4** Percutaneous Endoscopic	**Z** No Device	**X** Diagnostic **Z** No Qualifier

0   **Medical and Surgical**
N   **Head and Facial Bones**
C   **Extirpation:**   Taking or cutting out solid matter from a body part

Body Part Character 4	Approach Character 5	Device Character 6	Qualifier Character 7
1 Frontal Bone, Right 2 Frontal Bone, Left 3 Parietal Bone, Right 4 Parietal Bone, Left 5 Temporal Bone, Right 6 Temporal Bone, Left 7 Occipital Bone, Right 8 Occipital Bone, Left B Nasal Bone C Sphenoid Bone, Right D Sphenoid Bone, Left F Ethmoid Bone, Right G Ethmoid Bone, Left H Lacrimal Bone, Right J Lacrimal Bone, Left K Palatine Bone, Right L Palatine Bone, Left M Zygomatic Bone, Right N Zygomatic Bone, Left P Orbit, Right Q Orbit, Left R Maxilla, Right S Maxilla, Left T Mandible, Right V Mandible, Left X Hyoid Bone	0 Open 3 Percutaneous 4 Percutaneous Endoscopic	Z No Device	Z No Qualifier

0   **Medical and Surgical**
N   **Head and Facial Bones**
H   **Insertion:**   Putting in a nonbiological appliance that monitors, assists, performs or prevents a physiological function, but does not physically take the place of a body part

Body Part Character 4	Approach Character 5	Device Character 6	Qualifier Character 7
0 Skull	0 Open 3 Percutaneous 4 Percutaneous Endoscopic	4 Internal Fixation Device 5 External Fixation Device M Electrode	Z No Qualifier
1 Frontal Bone, Right 2 Frontal Bone, Left 3 Parietal Bone, Right 4 Parietal Bone, Left 7 Occipital Bone, Right 8 Occipital Bone, Left C Sphenoid Bone, Right D Sphenoid Bone, Left F Ethmoid Bone, Right G Ethmoid Bone, Left H Lacrimal Bone, Right J Lacrimal Bone, Left K Palatine Bone, Right L Palatine Bone, Left M Zygomatic Bone, Right N Zygomatic Bone, Left P Orbit, Right Q Orbit, Left X Hyoid Bone	0 Open 3 Percutaneous 4 Percutaneous Endoscopic	4 Internal Fixation Device	Z No Qualifier
5 Temporal Bone, Right 6 Temporal Bone, Left	0 Open 3 Percutaneous 4 Percutaneous Endoscopic	4 Internal Fixation Device S Hearing Device	Z No Qualifier
B Nasal Bone	0 Open 3 Percutaneous 4 Percutaneous Endoscopic	4 Internal Fixation Device M Electrode	Z No Qualifier
R Maxilla, Right S Maxilla, Left T Mandible, Right V Mandible, Left	0 Open 3 Percutaneous 4 Percutaneous Endoscopic	4 Internal Fixation Device 5 External Fixation Device	Z No Qualifier
W Facial Bone	0 Open 3 Percutaneous 4 Percutaneous Endoscopic	M Electrode	Z No Qualifier

0   Medical and Surgical
N   Head and Facial Bones
J   Inspection: Visually and/or manually exploring a body part

Body Part Character 4	Approach Character 5	Device Character 6	Qualifier Character 7
0 Skull	0 Open	Z No Device	Z No Qualifier
1 Frontal Bone, Right	3 Percutaneous		
2 Frontal Bone, Left	4 Percutaneous Endoscopic		
3 Parietal Bone, Right	X External		
4 Parietal Bone, Left			
5 Temporal Bone, Right			
6 Temporal Bone, Left			
7 Occipital Bone, Right			
8 Occipital Bone, Left			
B Nasal Bone			
C Sphenoid Bone, Right			
D Sphenoid Bone, Left			
F Ethmoid Bone, Right			
G Ethmoid Bone, Left			
H Lacrimal Bone, Right			
J Lacrimal Bone, Left			
K Palatine Bone, Right			
L Palatine Bone, Left			
M Zygomatic Bone, Right			
N Zygomatic Bone, Left			
P Orbit, Right			
Q Orbit, Left			
R Maxilla, Right			
S Maxilla, Left			
T Mandible, Right			
V Mandible, Left			
X Hyoid Bone			

0   Medical and Surgical
N   Head and Facial Bones
N   Release: Freeing a body part from an abnormal physical constraint

Body Part Character 4	Approach Character 5	Device Character 6	Qualifier Character 7
1 Frontal Bone, Right	0 Open	Z No Device	Z No Qualifier
2 Frontal Bone, Left	3 Percutaneous		
3 Parietal Bone, Right	4 Percutaneous Endoscopic		
4 Parietal Bone, Left			
5 Temporal Bone, Right			
6 Temporal Bone, Left			
7 Occipital Bone, Right			
8 Occipital Bone, Left			
B Nasal Bone			
C Sphenoid Bone, Right			
D Sphenoid Bone, Left			
F Ethmoid Bone, Right			
G Ethmoid Bone, Left			
H Lacrimal Bone, Right			
J Lacrimal Bone, Left			
K Palatine Bone, Right			
L Palatine Bone, Left			
M Zygomatic Bone, Right			
N Zygomatic Bone, Left			
P Orbit, Right			
Q Orbit, Left			
R Maxilla, Right			
S Maxilla, Left			
T Mandible, Right			
V Mandible, Left			
X Hyoid Bone			

0   **Medical and Surgical**
N   **Head and Facial Bones**
P   **Removal:**   Taking out or off a device from a body part

Body Part Character 4	Approach Character 5	Device Character 6	Qualifier Character 7
0 Skull	**0** Open **3** Percutaneous **4** Percutaneous Endoscopic	**0** Drainage Device **4** Internal Fixation Device **5** External Fixation Device **7** Autologous Tissue Substitute **J** Synthetic Substitute **K** Nonautologous Tissue Substitute **M** Electrode **S** Hearing Device	**Z** No Qualifier
0 Skull	**X** External	**0** Drainage Device **4** Internal Fixation Device **5** External Fixation Device **M** Electrode **S** Hearing Device	**Z** No Qualifier
B Nasal Bone **W** Facial Bone	**0** Open **3** Percutaneous **4** Percutaneous Endoscopic	**0** Drainage Device **4** Internal Fixation Device **7** Autologous Tissue Substitute **J** Synthetic Substitute **K** Nonautologous Tissue Substitute **M** Electrode	**Z** No Qualifier
B Nasal Bone **W** Facial Bone	**X** External	**0** Drainage Device **4** Internal Fixation Device **M** Electrode	**Z** No Qualifier

0   **Medical and Surgical**
N   **Head and Facial Bones**
Q   **Repair:**   Restoring, to the extent possible, a body part to its normal anatomic structure and function

Body Part Character 4	Approach Character 5	Device Character 6	Qualifier Character 7
0 Skull **1** Frontal Bone, Right **2** Frontal Bone, Left **3** Parietal Bone, Right **4** Parietal Bone, Left **5** Temporal Bone, Right **6** Temporal Bone, Left **7** Occipital Bone, Right **8** Occipital Bone, Left **B** Nasal Bone **C** Sphenoid Bone, Right **D** Sphenoid Bone, Left **F** Ethmoid Bone, Right **G** Ethmoid Bone, Left **H** Lacrimal Bone, Right **J** Lacrimal Bone, Left **K** Palatine Bone, Right **L** Palatine Bone, Left **M** Zygomatic Bone, Right **N** Zygomatic Bone, Left **P** Orbit, Right **Q** Orbit, Left **R** Maxilla, Right **S** Maxilla, Left **T** Mandible, Right **V** Mandible, Left **X** Hyoid Bone	**0** Open **3** Percutaneous **4** Percutaneous Endoscopic **X** External	**Z** No Device	**Z** No Qualifier

0 **Medical and Surgical**
N **Head and Facial Bones**
R **Replacement:** Putting in or on biological or synthetic material that physically takes the place and/or function of all or a portion of a body part

Body Part Character 4	Approach Character 5	Device Character 6	Qualifier Character 7
0 Skull 1 Frontal Bone, Right 2 Frontal Bone, Left 3 Parietal Bone, Right 4 Parietal Bone, Left 5 Temporal Bone, Right 6 Temporal Bone, Left 7 Occipital Bone, Right 8 Occipital Bone, Left B Nasal Bone C Sphenoid Bone, Right D Sphenoid Bone, Left F Ethmoid Bone, Right G Ethmoid Bone, Left H Lacrimal Bone, Right J Lacrimal Bone, Left K Palatine Bone, Right L Palatine Bone, Left M Zygomatic Bone, Right N Zygomatic Bone, Left P Orbit, Right Q Orbit, Left R Maxilla, Right S Maxilla, Left T Mandible, Right V Mandible, Left X Hyoid Bone	0 Open 3 Percutaneous 4 Percutaneous Endoscopic	7 Autologous Tissue Substitute J Synthetic Substitute K Nonautologous Tissue Substitute	Z No Qualifier

0 **Medical and Surgical**
N **Head and Facial Bones**
S **Reposition:** Moving to its normal location or other suitable location all or a portion of a body part

Body Part Character 4	Approach Character 5	Device Character 6	Qualifier Character 7
0 Skull 1 Frontal Bone, Right 2 Frontal Bone, Left 3 Parietal Bone, Right 4 Parietal Bone, Left 5 Temporal Bone, Right 6 Temporal Bone, Left 7 Occipital Bone, Right 8 Occipital Bone, Left B Nasal Bone C Sphenoid Bone, Right D Sphenoid Bone, Left F Ethmoid Bone, Right G Ethmoid Bone, Left H Lacrimal Bone, Right J Lacrimal Bone, Left K Palatine Bone, Right L Palatine Bone, Left M Zygomatic Bone, Right N Zygomatic Bone, Left P Orbit, Right Q Orbit, Left R Maxilla, Right S Maxilla, Left T Mandible, Right V Mandible, Left X Hyoid Bone	X External	Z No Device	Z No Qualifier
0 Skull R Maxilla, Right S Maxilla, Left T Mandible, Right V Mandible, Left	0 Open 3 Percutaneous 4 Percutaneous Endoscopic	4 Internal Fixation Device 5 External Fixation Device Z No Device	Z No Qualifier

Continued on next page

0   **Medical and Surgical**
N   **Head and Facial Bones**
S   **Reposition:**   Moving to its normal location or other suitable location all or a portion of a body part

Continued from previous page

Body Part Character 4	Approach Character 5	Device Character 6	Qualifier Character 7
1 Frontal Bone, Right 2 Frontal Bone, Left 3 Parietal Bone, Right 4 Parietal Bone, Left 5 Temporal Bone, Right 6 Temporal Bone, Left 7 Occipital Bone, Right 8 Occipital Bone, Left B Nasal Bone C Sphenoid Bone, Right D Sphenoid Bone, Left F Ethmoid Bone, Right G Ethmoid Bone, Left H Lacrimal Bone, Right J Lacrimal Bone, Left K Palatine Bone, Right L Palatine Bone, Left M Zygomatic Bone, Right N Zygomatic Bone, Left P Orbit, Right Q Orbit, Left X Hyoid Bone	0 Open 3 Percutaneous 4 Percutaneous Endoscopic	4 Internal Fixation Device Z No Device	Z No Qualifier

0   **Medical and Surgical**
N   **Head and Facial Bones**
T   **Resection:**   Cutting out or off, without replacement, all of a body part

Body Part Character 4	Approach Character 5	Device Character 6	Qualifier Character 7
1 Frontal Bone, Right 2 Frontal Bone, Left 3 Parietal Bone, Right 4 Parietal Bone, Left 5 Temporal Bone, Right 6 Temporal Bone, Left 7 Occipital Bone, Right 8 Occipital Bone, Left B Nasal Bone C Sphenoid Bone, Right D Sphenoid Bone, Left F Ethmoid Bone, Right G Ethmoid Bone, Left H Lacrimal Bone, Right J Lacrimal Bone, Left K Palatine Bone, Right L Palatine Bone, Left M Zygomatic Bone, Right N Zygomatic Bone, Left P Orbit, Right Q Orbit, Left R Maxilla, Right S Maxilla, Left T Mandible, Right V Mandible, Left X Hyoid Bone	0 Open	Z No Device	Z No Qualifier

0   Medical and Surgical
N   Head and Facial Bones
U   Supplement: Putting in or on biological or synthetic material that physically reinforces and/or augments the function of a portion of a body part

Body Part Character 4	Approach Character 5	Device Character 6	Qualifier Character 7
0 Skull **1** Frontal Bone, Right **2** Frontal Bone, Left **3** Parietal Bone, Right **4** Parietal Bone, Left **5** Temporal Bone, Right **6** Temporal Bone, Left **7** Occipital Bone, Right **8** Occipital Bone, Left **B** Nasal Bone **C** Sphenoid Bone, Right **D** Sphenoid Bone, Left **F** Ethmoid Bone, Right **G** Ethmoid Bone, Left **H** Lacrimal Bone, Right **J** Lacrimal Bone, Left **K** Palatine Bone, Right **L** Palatine Bone, Left **M** Zygomatic Bone, Right **N** Zygomatic Bone, Left **P** Orbit, Right **Q** Orbit, Left **R** Maxilla, Right **S** Maxilla, Left **T** Mandible, Right **V** Mandible, Left **X** Hyoid Bone	**0** Open **3** Percutaneous **4** Percutaneous Endoscopic	**7** Autologous Tissue Substitute **J** Synthetic Substitute **K** Nonautologous Tissue Substitute	**Z** No Qualifier

0   Medical and Surgical
N   Head and Facial Bones
W   Revision: Correcting, to the extent possible, a malfunctioning or displaced device

Body Part Character 4	Approach Character 5	Device Character 6	Qualifier Character 7
0 Skull	**0** Open **3** Percutaneous **4** Percutaneous Endoscopic **X** External	**0** Drainage Device **4** Internal Fixation Device **5** External Fixation Device **7** Autologous Tissue Substitute **J** Synthetic Substitute **K** Nonautologous Tissue Substitute **M** Electrode **S** Hearing Device	**Z** No Qualifier
B Nasal Bone **W** Facial Bone	**0** Open **3** Percutaneous **4** Percutaneous Endoscopic **X** External	**0** Drainage Device **4** Internal Fixation Device **7** Autologous Tissue Substitute **J** Synthetic Substitute **K** Nonautologous Tissue Substitute **M** Electrode	**Z** No Qualifier

Upper Bones 0P2–0PW

0	Medical and Surgical
P	Upper Bones
2	Change:

Taking out or off a device from a body part and putting back an identical or similar device in or on the same body part without cutting or puncturing the skin or a mucous membrane

Body Part Character 4	Approach Character 5	Device Character 6	Qualifier Character 7
Y Upper Bone	**X** External	**0** Drainage Device **Y** Other Device	**Z** No Qualifier

0	Medical and Surgical
P	Upper Bones
5	Destruction:

Physical eradication of all or a portion of a body part by the direct use of energy, force, or a destructive agent

Body Part Character 4	Approach Character 5	Device Character 6	Qualifier Character 7
0 Sternum **1** Rib, Right **2** Rib, Left **3** Cervical Vertebra **4** Thoracic Vertebra **5** Scapula, Right **6** Scapula, Left **7** Glenoid Cavity, Right **8** Glenoid Cavity, Left **9** Clavicle, Right **B** Clavicle, Left **C** Humeral Head, Right **D** Humeral Head, Left **F** Humeral Shaft, Right **G** Humeral Shaft, Left **H** Radius, Right **J** Radius, Left **K** Ulna, Right **L** Ulna, Left **M** Carpal, Right **N** Carpal, Left **P** Metacarpal, Right **Q** Metacarpal, Left **R** Thumb Phalanx, Right **S** Thumb Phalanx, Left **T** Finger Phalanx, Right **V** Finger Phalanx, Left	**0** Open **3** Percutaneous **4** Percutaneous Endoscopic	**Z** No Device	**Z** No Qualifier

0 Medical and Surgical
P Upper Bones
8 Division: Cutting into a body part without draining fluids and/or gases from the body part in order to separate or transect a body part

Body Part Character 4	Approach Character 5	Device Character 6	Qualifier Character 7
0 Sternum **1** Rib, Right **2** Rib, Left **3** Cervical Vertebra **4** Thoracic Vertebra **5** Scapula, Right **6** Scapula, Left **7** Glenoid Cavity, Right **8** Glenoid Cavity, Left **9** Clavicle, Right **B** Clavicle, Left **C** Humeral Head, Right **D** Humeral Head, Left **F** Humeral Shaft, Right **G** Humeral Shaft, Left **H** Radius, Right **J** Radius, Left **K** Ulna, Right **L** Ulna, Left **M** Carpal, Right **N** Carpal, Left **P** Metacarpal, Right **Q** Metacarpal, Left **R** Thumb Phalanx, Right **S** Thumb Phalanx, Left **T** Finger Phalanx, Right **V** Finger Phalanx, Left	**0** Open **3** Percutaneous **4** Percutaneous Endoscopic	**Z** No Device	**Z** No Qualifier

0 Medical and Surgical
P Upper Bones
9 Drainage: Taking or letting out fluids and/or gases from a body part

Body Part Character 4	Approach Character 5	Device Character 6	Qualifier Character 7
0 Sternum **1** Rib, Right **2** Rib, Left **3** Cervical Vertebra **4** Thoracic Vertebra **5** Scapula, Right **6** Scapula, Left **7** Glenoid Cavity, Right **8** Glenoid Cavity, Left **9** Clavicle, Right **B** Clavicle, Left **C** Humeral Head, Right **D** Humeral Head, Left **F** Humeral Shaft, Right **G** Humeral Shaft, Left **H** Radius, Right **J** Radius, Left **K** Ulna, Right **L** Ulna, Left **M** Carpal, Right **N** Carpal, Left **P** Metacarpal, Right **Q** Metacarpal, Left **R** Thumb Phalanx, Right **S** Thumb Phalanx, Left **T** Finger Phalanx, Right **V** Finger Phalanx, Left	**0** Open **3** Percutaneous **4** Percutaneous Endoscopic	**0** Drainage Device	**Z** No Qualifier

Continued on next page

Continued from previous page

0 **Medical and Surgical**
P **Upper Bones**
9 **Drainage:** Taking or letting out fluids and/or gases from a body part

Body Part Character 4	Approach Character 5	Device Character 6	Qualifier Character 7
0 Sternum **1** Rib, Right **2** Rib, Left **3** Cervical Vertebra **4** Thoracic Vertebra **5** Scapula, Right **6** Scapula, Left **7** Glenoid Cavity, Right **8** Glenoid Cavity, Left **9** Clavicle, Right **B** Clavicle, Left **C** Humeral Head, Right **D** Humeral Head, Left **F** Humeral Shaft, Right **G** Humeral Shaft, Left **H** Radius, Right **J** Radius, Left **K** Ulna, Right **L** Ulna, Left **M** Carpal, Right **N** Carpal, Left **P** Metacarpal, Right **Q** Metacarpal, Left **R** Thumb Phalanx, Right **S** Thumb Phalanx, Left **T** Finger Phalanx, Right **V** Finger Phalanx, Left	**0** Open **3** Percutaneous **4** Percutaneous Endoscopic	**Z** No Device	**X** Diagnostic **Z** No Qualifier

0 **Medical and Surgical**
P **Upper Bones**
B **Excision:** Cutting out or off, without replacement, a portion of a body part

Body Part Character 4	Approach Character 5	Device Character 6	Qualifier Character 7
0 Sternum **1** Rib, Right **2** Rib, Left **3** Cervical Vertebra **4** Thoracic Vertebra **5** Scapula, Right **6** Scapula, Left **7** Glenoid Cavity, Right **8** Glenoid Cavity, Left **9** Clavicle, Right **B** Clavicle, Left **C** Humeral Head, Right **D** Humeral Head, Left **F** Humeral Shaft, Right **G** Humeral Shaft, Left **H** Radius, Right **J** Radius, Left **K** Ulna, Right **L** Ulna, Left **M** Carpal, Right **N** Carpal, Left **P** Metacarpal, Right **Q** Metacarpal, Left **R** Thumb Phalanx, Right **S** Thumb Phalanx, Left **T** Finger Phalanx, Right **V** Finger Phalanx, Left	**0** Open **3** Percutaneous **4** Percutaneous Endoscopic	**Z** No Device	**X** Diagnostic **Z** No Qualifier

0   **Medical and Surgical**
P   **Upper Bones**
C   **Extirpation:**   Taking or cutting out solid matter from a body part

Body Part Character 4	Approach Character 5	Device Character 6	Qualifier Character 7
0 Sternum **1** Rib, Right **2** Rib, Left **3** Cervical Vertebra **4** Thoracic Vertebra **5** Scapula, Right **6** Scapula, Left **7** Glenoid Cavity, Right **8** Glenoid Cavity, Left **9** Clavicle, Right **B** Clavicle, Left **C** Humeral Head, Right **D** Humeral Head, Left **F** Humeral Shaft, Right **G** Humeral Shaft, Left **H** Radius, Right **J** Radius, Left **K** Ulna, Right **L** Ulna, Left **M** Carpal, Right **N** Carpal, Left **P** Metacarpal, Right **Q** Metacarpal, Left **R** Thumb Phalanx, Right **S** Thumb Phalanx, Left **T** Finger Phalanx, Right **V** Finger Phalanx, Left	**0** Open **3** Percutaneous **4** Percutaneous Endoscopic	**Z** No Device	**Z** No Qualifier

0   **Medical and Surgical**
P   **Upper Bones**
H   **Insertion:**   Putting in a nonbiological appliance that monitors, assists, performs or prevents a physiological function, but does not physically take the place of a body part

Body Part Character 4	Approach Character 5	Device Character 6	Qualifier Character 7
0 Sternum **1** Rib, Right **2** Rib, Left **3** Cervical Vertebra **4** Thoracic Vertebra **5** Scapula, Right **6** Scapula, Left **7** Glenoid Cavity, Right **8** Glenoid Cavity, Left **9** Clavicle, Right **B** Clavicle, Left	**0** Open **3** Percutaneous **4** Percutaneous Endoscopic	**4** Internal Fixation Device	**Z** No Qualifier
C Humeral Head, Right **D** Humeral Head, Left **F** Humeral Shaft, Right **G** Humeral Shaft, Left **H** Radius, Right **J** Radius, Left **K** Ulna, Right **L** Ulna, Left	**0** Open **3** Percutaneous **4** Percutaneous Endoscopic	**4** Internal Fixation Device **6** Intramedullary Fixation Device	**Z** No Qualifier
C Humeral Head, Right **D** Humeral Head, Left **F** Humeral Shaft, Right **G** Humeral Shaft, Left **H** Radius, Right **J** Radius, Left **K** Ulna, Right **L** Ulna, Left	**0** Open **3** Percutaneous **4** Percutaneous Endoscopic	**5** External Fixation Device	**3** Monoplanar **4** Ring **5** Hybrid **9** Limb Lengthening Device **Z** No Qualifier
M Carpal, Right **N** Carpal, Left **P** Metacarpal, Right **Q** Metacarpal, Left **R** Thumb Phalanx, Right **S** Thumb Phalanx, Left **T** Finger Phalanx, Right **V** Finger Phalanx, Left	**0** Open **3** Percutaneous **4** Percutaneous Endoscopic	**4** Internal Fixation Device **5** External Fixation Device	**Z** No Qualifier
Y Upper Bone	**0** Open **3** Percutaneous **4** Percutaneous Endoscopic	**M** Electrode	**Z** No Qualifier

0 **Medical and Surgical**
P **Upper Bones**
J **Inspection:**   Visually and/or manually exploring a body part

Body Part Character 4	Approach Character 5	Device Character 6	Qualifier Character 7
0 Sternum 1 Rib, Right 2 Rib, Left 3 Cervical Vertebra 4 Thoracic Vertebra 5 Scapula, Right 6 Scapula, Left 7 Glenoid Cavity, Right 8 Glenoid Cavity, Left 9 Clavicle, Right B Clavicle, Left C Humeral Head, Right D Humeral Head, Left F Humeral Shaft, Right G Humeral Shaft, Left H Radius, Right J Radius, Left K Ulna, Right L Ulna, Left M Carpal, Right N Carpal, Left P Metacarpal, Right Q Metacarpal, Left R Thumb Phalanx, Right S Thumb Phalanx, Left T Finger Phalanx, Right V Finger Phalanx, Left	0 Open 3 Percutaneous 4 Percutaneous Endoscopic X External	Z No Device	Z No Qualifier

0 **Medical and Surgical**
P **Upper Bones**
N **Release:**   Freeing a body part from an abnormal physical constraint

Body Part Character 4	Approach Character 5	Device Character 6	Qualifier Character 7
0 Sternum 1 Rib, Right 2 Rib, Left 3 Cervical Vertebra 4 Thoracic Vertebra 5 Scapula, Right 6 Scapula, Left 7 Glenoid Cavity, Right 8 Glenoid Cavity, Left 9 Clavicle, Right B Clavicle, Left C Humeral Head, Right D Humeral Head, Left F Humeral Shaft, Right G Humeral Shaft, Left H Radius, Right J Radius, Left K Ulna, Right L Ulna, Left M Carpal, Right N Carpal, Left P Metacarpal, Right Q Metacarpal, Left R Thumb Phalanx, Right S Thumb Phalanx, Left T Finger Phalanx, Right V Finger Phalanx, Left	0 Open 3 Percutaneous 4 Percutaneous Endoscopic	Z No Device	Z No Qualifier

0   Medical and Surgical
P   Upper Bones
P   Removal: Taking out or off a device from a body part

Body Part Character 4	Approach Character 5	Device Character 6	Qualifier Character 7
0 Sternum 1 Rib, Right 2 Rib, Left 3 Cervical Vertebra 4 Thoracic Vertebra 5 Scapula, Right 6 Scapula, Left 7 Glenoid Cavity, Right 8 Glenoid Cavity, Left 9 Clavicle, Right B Clavicle, Left	0 Open 3 Percutaneous 4 Percutaneous Endoscopic	4 Internal Fixation Device 7 Autologous Tissue Substitute J Synthetic Substitute K Nonautologous Tissue Substitute	Z No Qualifier
0 Sternum 1 Rib, Right 2 Rib, Left 3 Cervical Vertebra 4 Thoracic Vertebra 5 Scapula, Right 6 Scapula, Left 7 Glenoid Cavity, Right 8 Glenoid Cavity, Left 9 Clavicle, Right B Clavicle, Left	X External	4 Internal Fixation Device	Z No Qualifier
C Humeral Head, Right D Humeral Head, Left F Humeral Shaft, Right G Humeral Shaft, Left H Radius, Right J Radius, Left K Ulna, Right L Ulna, Left	0 Open 3 Percutaneous 4 Percutaneous Endoscopic	4 Internal Fixation Device 5 External Fixation Device 6 Intramedullary Fixation Device 7 Autologous Tissue Substitute J Synthetic Substitute K Nonautologous Tissue Substitute	Z No Qualifier
C Humeral Head, Right D Humeral Head, Left F Humeral Shaft, Right G Humeral Shaft, Left H Radius, Right J Radius, Left K Ulna, Right L Ulna, Left M Carpal, Right N Carpal, Left P Metacarpal, Right Q Metacarpal, Left R Thumb Phalanx, Right S Thumb Phalanx, Left T Finger Phalanx, Right V Finger Phalanx, Left	X External	4 Internal Fixation Device 5 External Fixation Device	Z No Qualifier
M Carpal, Right N Carpal, Left P Metacarpal, Right Q Metacarpal, Left R Thumb Phalanx, Right S Thumb Phalanx, Left T Finger Phalanx, Right V Finger Phalanx, Left	0 Open 3 Percutaneous 4 Percutaneous Endoscopic	4 Internal Fixation Device 5 External Fixation Device 7 Autologous Tissue Substitute J Synthetic Substitute K Nonautologous Tissue Substitute	Z No Qualifier
Y Upper Bone	0 Open 3 Percutaneous 4 Percutaneous Endoscopic X External	0 Drainage Device M Electrode	Z No Qualifier

0 **Medical and Surgical**
P **Upper Bones**
Q **Repair:** Restoring, to the extent possible, a body part to its normal anatomic structure and function

Body Part Character 4	Approach Character 5	Device Character 6	Qualifier Character 7
0 Sternum	0 Open	Z No Device	Z No Qualifier
1 Rib, Right	3 Percutaneous		
2 Rib, Left	4 Percutaneous Endoscopic		
3 Cervical Vertebra	X External		
4 Thoracic Vertebra			
5 Scapula, Right			
6 Scapula, Left			
7 Glenoid Cavity, Right			
8 Glenoid Cavity, Left			
9 Clavicle, Right			
B Clavicle, Left			
C Humeral Head, Right			
D Humeral Head, Left			
F Humeral Shaft, Right			
G Humeral Shaft, Left			
H Radius, Right			
J Radius, Left			
K Ulna, Right			
L Ulna, Left			
M Carpal, Right			
N Carpal, Left			
P Metacarpal, Right			
Q Metacarpal, Left			
R Thumb Phalanx, Right			
S Thumb Phalanx, Left			
T Finger Phalanx, Right			
V Finger Phalanx, Left			

0 **Medical and Surgical**
P **Upper Bones**
R **Replacement:** Putting in or on biological or synthetic material that physically takes the place and/or function of all or a portion of a body part

Body Part Character 4	Approach Character 5	Device Character 6	Qualifier Character 7
0 Sternum	0 Open	7 Autologous Tissue Substitute	Z No Qualifier
1 Rib, Right	3 Percutaneous	J Synthetic Substitute	
2 Rib, Left	4 Percutaneous Endoscopic	K Nonautologous Tissue Substitute	
3 Cervical Vertebra			
4 Thoracic Vertebra			
5 Scapula, Right			
6 Scapula, Left			
7 Glenoid Cavity, Right			
8 Glenoid Cavity, Left			
9 Clavicle, Right			
B Clavicle, Left			
C Humeral Head, Right			
D Humeral Head, Left			
F Humeral Shaft, Right			
G Humeral Shaft, Left			
H Radius, Right			
J Radius, Left			
K Ulna, Right			
L Ulna, Left			
M Carpal, Right			
N Carpal, Left			
P Metacarpal, Right			
Q Metacarpal, Left			
R Thumb Phalanx, Right			
S Thumb Phalanx, Left			
T Finger Phalanx, Right			
V Finger Phalanx, Left			

0   Medical and Surgical
P   Upper Bones
S   Reposition: Moving to its normal location or other suitable location all or a portion of a body part

Body Part Character 4	Approach Character 5	Device Character 6	Qualifier Character 7
0 Sternum **1** Rib, Right **2** Rib, Left **3** Cervical Vertebra **4** Thoracic Vertebra **5** Scapula, Right **6** Scapula, Left **7** Glenoid Cavity, Right **8** Glenoid Cavity, Left **9** Clavicle, Right **B** Clavicle, Left **C** Humeral Head, Right **D** Humeral Head, Left **F** Humeral Shaft, Right **G** Humeral Shaft, Left **H** Radius, Right **J** Radius, Left **K** Ulna, Right **L** Ulna, Left **M** Carpal, Right **N** Carpal, Left **P** Metacarpal, Right **Q** Metacarpal, Left **R** Thumb Phalanx, Right **S** Thumb Phalanx, Left **T** Finger Phalanx, Right **V** Finger Phalanx, Left	**X** External	**Z** No Device	**Z** No Qualifier
0 Sternum **1** Rib, Right **2** Rib, Left **3** Cervical Vertebra **4** Thoracic Vertebra **5** Scapula, Right **6** Scapula, Left **7** Glenoid Cavity, Right **8** Glenoid Cavity, Left **9** Clavicle, Right **B** Clavicle, Left **M** Carpal, Right **N** Carpal, Left **P** Metacarpal, Right **Q** Metacarpal, Left **R** Thumb Phalanx, Right **S** Thumb Phalanx, Left **T** Finger Phalanx, Right **V** Finger Phalanx, Left	**0** Open **3** Percutaneous **4** Percutaneous Endoscopic	**4** Internal Fixation Device **Z** No Device	**Z** No Qualifier
C Humeral Head, Right **D** Humeral Head, Left **F** Humeral Shaft, Right **G** Humeral Shaft, Left **H** Radius, Right **J** Radius, Left **K** Ulna, Right **L** Ulna, Left	**0** Open **3** Percutaneous **4** Percutaneous Endoscopic	**4** Internal Fixation Device **6** Intramedullary Fixation Device **Z** No Device	**Z** No Qualifier
C Humeral Head, Right **D** Humeral Head, Left **F** Humeral Shaft, Right **G** Humeral Shaft, Left **H** Radius, Right **J** Radius, Left **K** Ulna, Right **L** Ulna, Left **M** Carpal, Right **N** Carpal, Left **P** Metacarpal, Right **Q** Metacarpal, Left **R** Thumb Phalanx, Right **S** Thumb Phalanx, Left **T** Finger Phalanx, Right **V** Finger Phalanx, Left	**0** Open **3** Percutaneous **4** Percutaneous Endoscopic	**5** External Fixation Device	**3** Monoplanar **4** Ring **5** Hybrid **Z** No Qualifier

0   **Medical and Surgical**
P   **Upper Bones**
T   **Resection:**   Cutting out or off, without replacement, all of a body part

Body Part Character 4	Approach Character 5	Device Character 6	Qualifier Character 7
0 Sternum 1 Rib, Right 2 Rib, Left 5 Scapula, Right 6 Scapula, Left 7 Glenoid Cavity, Right 8 Glenoid Cavity, Left 9 Clavicle, Right B Clavicle, Left C Humeral Head, Right D Humeral Head, Left F Humeral Shaft, Right G Humeral Shaft, Left H Radius, Right J Radius, Left K Ulna, Right L Ulna, Left M Carpal, Right N Carpal, Left P Metacarpal, Right Q Metacarpal, Left R Thumb Phalanx, Right S Thumb Phalanx, Left T Finger Phalanx, Right V Finger Phalanx, Left	0 Open	Z No Device	Z No Qualifier

0   **Medical and Surgical**
P   **Upper Bones**
U   **Supplement:**   Putting in or on biological or synthetic material that physically reinforces and/or augments the function of a portion of a body part

Body Part Character 4	Approach Character 5	Device Character 6	Qualifier Character 7
0 Sternum 1 Rib, Right 2 Rib, Left 3 Cervical Vertebra 4 Thoracic Vertebra 5 Scapula, Right 6 Scapula, Left 7 Glenoid Cavity, Right 8 Glenoid Cavity, Left 9 Clavicle, Right B Clavicle, Left C Humeral Head, Right D Humeral Head, Left F Humeral Shaft, Right G Humeral Shaft, Left H Radius, Right J Radius, Left K Ulna, Right L Ulna, Left M Carpal, Right N Carpal, Left P Metacarpal, Right Q Metacarpal, Left R Thumb Phalanx, Right S Thumb Phalanx, Left T Finger Phalanx, Right V Finger Phalanx, Left	0 Open 3 Percutaneous 4 Percutaneous Endoscopic	7 Autologous Tissue Substitute J Synthetic Substitute K Nonautologous Tissue Substitute	Z No Qualifier

0   **Medical and Surgical**
P   **Upper Bones**
W   **Revision:** Correcting, to the extent possible, a malfunctioning or displaced device

Body Part Character 4	Approach Character 5	Device Character 6	Qualifier Character 7
0 Sternum 1 Rib, Right 2 Rib, Left 3 Cervical Vertebra 4 Thoracic Vertebra 5 Scapula, Right 6 Scapula, Left 7 Glenoid Cavity, Right 8 Glenoid Cavity, Left 9 Clavicle, Right B Clavicle, Left	0 Open 3 Percutaneous 4 Percutaneous Endoscopic X External	4 Internal Fixation Device 7 Autologous Tissue Substitute J Synthetic Substitute K Nonautologous Tissue Substitute	Z No Qualifier
C Humeral Head, Right D Humeral Head, Left F Humeral Shaft, Right G Humeral Shaft, Left H Radius, Right J Radius, Left K Ulna, Right L Ulna, Left	0 Open 3 Percutaneous 4 Percutaneous Endoscopic X External	4 Internal Fixation Device 5 External Fixation Device 6 Intramedullary Fixation Device 7 Autologous Tissue Substitute J Synthetic Substitute K Nonautologous Tissue Substitute	Z No Qualifier
M Carpal, Right N Carpal, Left P Metacarpal, Right Q Metacarpal, Left R Thumb Phalanx, Right S Thumb Phalanx, Left T Finger Phalanx, Right V Finger Phalanx, Left	0 Open 3 Percutaneous 4 Percutaneous Endoscopic X External	4 Internal Fixation Device 5 External Fixation Device 7 Autologous Tissue Substitute J Synthetic Substitute K Nonautologous Tissue Substitute	Z No Qualifier
Y Upper Bone	0 Open 3 Percutaneous 4 Percutaneous Endoscopic X External	0 Drainage Device M Electrode	Z No Qualifier

Lower Bones 0Q2–0QW

0 **Medical and Surgical**
Q **Lower Bones**
2 **Change:** Taking out or off a device from a body part and putting back an identical or similar device in or on the same body part without cutting or puncturing the skin or a mucous membrane

Body Part Character 4	Approach Character 5	Device Character 6	Qualifier Character 7
Y Lower Bone	**X** External	**0** Drainage Device **Y** Other Device	**Z** No Qualifier

0 **Medical and Surgical**
Q **Lower Bones**
5 **Destruction:** Physical eradication of all or a portion of a body part by the direct use of energy, force, or a destructive agent

Body Part Character 4	Approach Character 5	Device Character 6	Qualifier Character 7
0 Lumbar Vertebra **1** Sacrum **2** Pelvic Bone, Right **3** Pelvic Bone, Left **4** Acetabulum, Right **5** Acetabulum, Left **6** Upper Femur, Right **7** Upper Femur, Left **8** Femoral Shaft, Right **9** Femoral Shaft, Left **B** Lower Femur, Right **C** Lower Femur, Left **D** Patella, Right **F** Patella, Left **G** Tibia, Right **H** Tibia, Left **J** Fibula, Right **K** Fibula, Left **L** Tarsal, Right **M** Tarsal, Left **N** Metatarsal, Right **P** Metatarsal, Left **Q** Toe Phalanx, Right **R** Toe Phalanx, Left **S** Coccyx	**0** Open **3** Percutaneous **4** Percutaneous Endoscopic	**Z** No Device	**Z** No Qualifier

0 **Medical and Surgical**
Q **Lower Bones**
8 **Division:** Cutting into a body part without draining fluids and/or gases from the body part in order to separate or transect a body part

Body Part Character 4	Approach Character 5	Device Character 6	Qualifier Character 7
0 Lumbar Vertebra **1** Sacrum **2** Pelvic Bone, Right **3** Pelvic Bone, Left **4** Acetabulum, Right **5** Acetabulum, Left **6** Upper Femur, Right **7** Upper Femur, Left **8** Femoral Shaft, Right **9** Femoral Shaft, Left **B** Lower Femur, Right **C** Lower Femur, Left **D** Patella, Right **F** Patella, Left **G** Tibia, Right **H** Tibia, Left **J** Fibula, Right **K** Fibula, Left **L** Tarsal, Right **M** Tarsal, Left **N** Metatarsal, Right **P** Metatarsal, Left **Q** Toe Phalanx, Right **R** Toe Phalanx, Left **S** Coccyx	**0** Open **3** Percutaneous **4** Percutaneous Endoscopic	**Z** No Device	**Z** No Qualifier

0   Medical and Surgical
Q   Lower Bones
9   Drainage: Taking or letting out fluids and/or gases from a body part

Body Part Character 4	Approach Character 5	Device Character 6	Qualifier Character 7
0 Lumbar Vertebra **1** Sacrum **2** Pelvic Bone, Right **3** Pelvic Bone, Left **4** Acetabulum, Right **5** Acetabulum, Left **6** Upper Femur, Right **7** Upper Femur, Left **8** Femoral Shaft, Right **9** Femoral Shaft, Left **B** Lower Femur, Right **C** Lower Femur, Left **D** Patella, Right **F** Patella, Left **G** Tibia, Right **H** Tibia, Left **J** Fibula, Right **K** Fibula, Left **L** Tarsal, Right **M** Tarsal, Left **N** Metatarsal, Right **P** Metatarsal, Left **Q** Toe Phalanx, Right **R** Toe Phalanx, Left **S** Coccyx	**0** Open **3** Percutaneous **4** Percutaneous Endoscopic	**0** Drainage Device	**Z** No Qualifier
0 Lumbar Vertebra **1** Sacrum **2** Pelvic Bone, Right **3** Pelvic Bone, Left **4** Acetabulum, Right **5** Acetabulum, Left **6** Upper Femur, Right **7** Upper Femur, Left **8** Femoral Shaft, Right **9** Femoral Shaft, Left **B** Lower Femur, Right **C** Lower Femur, Left **D** Patella, Right **F** Patella, Left **G** Tibia, Right **H** Tibia, Left **J** Fibula, Right **K** Fibula, Left **L** Tarsal, Right **M** Tarsal, Left **N** Metatarsal, Right **P** Metatarsal, Left **Q** Toe Phalanx, Right **R** Toe Phalanx, Left **S** Coccyx	**0** Open **3** Percutaneous **4** Percutaneous Endoscopic	**Z** No Device	**X** Diagnostic **Z** No Qualifier

0   **Medical and Surgical**
Q   **Lower Bones**
B   **Excision:**   Cutting out or off, without replacement, a portion of a body part

Body Part Character 4	Approach Character 5	Device Character 6	Qualifier Character 7
0 Lumbar Vertebra 1 Sacrum 2 Pelvic Bone, Right 3 Pelvic Bone, Left 4 Acetabulum, Right 5 Acetabulum, Left 6 Upper Femur, Right 7 Upper Femur, Left 8 Femoral Shaft, Right 9 Femoral Shaft, Left B Lower Femur, Right C Lower Femur, Left D Patella, Right F Patella, Left G Tibia, Right H Tibia, Left J Fibula, Right K Fibula, Left L Tarsal, Right M Tarsal, Left N Metatarsal, Right P Metatarsal, Left Q Toe Phalanx, Right R Toe Phalanx, Left S Coccyx	0 Open 3 Percutaneous 4 Percutaneous Endoscopic	Z No Device	X Diagnostic Z No Qualifier

0   **Medical and Surgical**
Q   **Lower Bones**
C   **Extirpation:**   Taking or cutting out solid matter from a body part

Body Part Character 4	Approach Character 5	Device Character 6	Qualifier Character 7
0 Lumbar Vertebra 1 Sacrum 2 Pelvic Bone, Right 3 Pelvic Bone, Left 4 Acetabulum, Right 5 Acetabulum, Left 6 Upper Femur, Right 7 Upper Femur, Left 8 Femoral Shaft, Right 9 Femoral Shaft, Left B Lower Femur, Right C Lower Femur, Left D Patella, Right F Patella, Left G Tibia, Right H Tibia, Left J Fibula, Right K Fibula, Left L Tarsal, Right M Tarsal, Left N Metatarsal, Right P Metatarsal, Left Q Toe Phalanx, Right R Toe Phalanx, Left S Coccyx	0 Open 3 Percutaneous 4 Percutaneous Endoscopic	Z No Device	Z No Qualifier

0 **Medical and Surgical**
Q **Lower Bones**
H **Insertion:** Putting in a nonbiological appliance that monitors, assists, performs or prevents a physiological function, but does not physically take the place of a body part

Body Part Character 4	Approach Character 5	Device Character 6	Qualifier Character 7
0 Lumbar Vertebra 1 Sacrum 2 Pelvic Bone, Right 3 Pelvic Bone, Left 4 Acetabulum, Right 5 Acetabulum, Left D Patella, Right F Patella, Left L Tarsal, Right M Tarsal, Left N Metatarsal, Right P Metatarsal, Left Q Toe Phalanx, Right R Toe Phalanx, Left S Coccyx	0 Open 3 Percutaneous 4 Percutaneous Endoscopic	4 Internal Fixation Device 5 External Fixation Device	Z No Qualifier
6 Upper Femur, Right 7 Upper Femur, Left 8 Femoral Shaft, Right 9 Femoral Shaft, Left B Lower Femur, Right C Lower Femur, Left G Tibia, Right H Tibia, Left J Fibula, Right K Fibula, Left	0 Open 3 Percutaneous 4 Percutaneous Endoscopic	4 Internal Fixation Device 6 Intramedullary Fixation Device	Z No Qualifier
6 Upper Femur, Right 7 Upper Femur, Left 8 Femoral Shaft, Right 9 Femoral Shaft, Left B Lower Femur, Right C Lower Femur, Left G Tibia, Right H Tibia, Left J Fibula, Right K Fibula, Left	0 Open 3 Percutaneous 4 Percutaneous Endoscopic	5 External Fixation Device	3 Monoplanar 4 Ring 5 Hybrid 9 Limb Lengthening Device Z No Qualifier
Y Lower Bone	0 Open 3 Percutaneous 4 Percutaneous Endoscopic	M Electrode	Z No Qualifier

0 **Medical and Surgical**
Q **Lower Bones**
J **Inspection:** Visually and/or manually exploring a body part

Body Part Character 4	Approach Character 5	Device Character 6	Qualifier Character 7
0 Lumbar Vertebra 1 Sacrum 2 Pelvic Bone, Right 3 Pelvic Bone, Left 4 Acetabulum, Right 5 Acetabulum, Left 6 Upper Femur, Right 7 Upper Femur, Left 8 Femoral Shaft, Right 9 Femoral Shaft, Left B Lower Femur, Right C Lower Femur, Left D Patella, Right F Patella, Left G Tibia, Right H Tibia, Left J Fibula, Right K Fibula, Left L Tarsal, Right M Tarsal, Left N Metatarsal, Right P Metatarsal, Left Q Toe Phalanx, Right R Toe Phalanx, Left S Coccyx	0 Open 3 Percutaneous 4 Percutaneous Endoscopic X External	Z No Device	Z No Qualifier

0 **Medical and Surgical**
Q **Lower Bones**
N **Release:** Freeing a body part from an abnormal physical constraint

Body Part Character 4	Approach Character 5	Device Character 6	Qualifier Character 7
0 Lumbar Vertebra 1 Sacrum 2 Pelvic Bone, Right 3 Pelvic Bone, Left 4 Acetabulum, Right 5 Acetabulum, Left 6 Upper Femur, Right 7 Upper Femur, Left 8 Femoral Shaft, Right 9 Femoral Shaft, Left B Lower Femur, Right C Lower Femur, Left D Patella, Right F Patella, Left G Tibia, Right H Tibia, Left J Fibula, Right K Fibula, Left L Tarsal, Right M Tarsal, Left N Metatarsal, Right P Metatarsal, Left Q Toe Phalanx, Right R Toe Phalanx, Left S Coccyx	0 Open 3 Percutaneous 4 Percutaneous Endoscopic	Z No Device	Z No Qualifier

0 **Medical and Surgical**
Q **Lower Bones**
P **Removal:** Taking out or off a device from a body part

Body Part Character 4	Approach Character 5	Device Character 6	Qualifier Character 7
0 Lumbar Vertebra 1 Sacrum 4 Acetabulum, Right 5 Acetabulum, Left S Coccyx	0 Open 3 Percutaneous 4 Percutaneous Endoscopic	4 Internal Fixation Device 7 Autologous Tissue Substitute J Synthetic Substitute K Nonautologous Tissue Substitute	Z No Qualifier
0 Lumbar Vertebra 1 Sacrum 4 Acetabulum, Right 5 Acetabulum, Left S Coccyx	X External	4 Internal Fixation Device	Z No Qualifier
2 Pelvic Bone, Right 3 Pelvic Bone, Left 6 Upper Femur, Right 7 Upper Femur, Left 8 Femoral Shaft, Right 9 Femoral Shaft, Left B Lower Femur, Right C Lower Femur, Left D Patella, Right F Patella, Left G Tibia, Right H Tibia, Left J Fibula, Right K Fibula, Left L Tarsal, Right M Tarsal, Left N Metatarsal, Right P Metatarsal, Left Q Toe Phalanx, Right R Toe Phalanx, Left	X External	4 Internal Fixation Device 5 External Fixation Device	Z No Qualifier
2 Pelvic Bone, Right 3 Pelvic Bone, Left D Patella, Right F Patella, Left L Tarsal, Right M Tarsal, Left N Metatarsal, Right P Metatarsal, Left Q Toe Phalanx, Right R Toe Phalanx, Left	0 Open 3 Percutaneous 4 Percutaneous Endoscopic	4 Internal Fixation Device 5 External Fixation Device 7 Autologous Tissue Substitute J Synthetic Substitute K Nonautologous Tissue Substitute	Z No Qualifier

Continued on next page

0   **Medical and Surgical**   *Continued from previous page*
Q   **Lower Bones**
P   **Removal:**   Taking out or off a device from a body part

Body Part Character 4	Approach Character 5	Device Character 6	Qualifier Character 7
6 Upper Femur, Right **7** Upper Femur, Left **8** Femoral Shaft, Right **9** Femoral Shaft, Left **B** Lower Femur, Right **C** Lower Femur, Left **G** Tibia, Right **H** Tibia, Left **J** Fibula, Right **K** Fibula, Left	**0** Open **3** Percutaneous **4** Percutaneous Endoscopic	**4** Internal Fixation Device **5** External Fixation Device **6** Intramedullary Fixation Device **7** Autologous Tissue Substitute **J** Synthetic Substitute **K** Nonautologous Tissue Substitute	**Z** No Qualifier
Y Lower Bone	**0** Open **3** Percutaneous **4** Percutaneous Endoscopic **X** External	**0** Drainage Device **M** Electrode	**Z** No Qualifier

0   **Medical and Surgical**
Q   **Lower Bones**
Q   **Repair:**   Restoring, to the extent possible, a body part to its normal anatomic structure and function

Body Part Character 4	Approach Character 5	Device Character 6	Qualifier Character 7
0 Lumbar Vertebra **1** Sacrum **2** Pelvic Bone, Right **3** Pelvic Bone, Left **4** Acetabulum, Right **5** Acetabulum, Left **6** Upper Femur, Right **7** Upper Femur, Left **8** Femoral Shaft, Right **9** Femoral Shaft, Left **B** Lower Femur, Right **C** Lower Femur, Left **D** Patella, Right **F** Patella, Left **G** Tibia, Right **H** Tibia, Left **J** Fibula, Right **K** Fibula, Left **L** Tarsal, Right **M** Tarsal, Left **N** Metatarsal, Right **P** Metatarsal, Left **Q** Toe Phalanx, Right **R** Toe Phalanx, Left **S** Coccyx	**0** Open **3** Percutaneous **4** Percutaneous Endoscopic **X** External	**Z** No Device	**Z** No Qualifier

0   **Medical and Surgical**
Q   **Lower Bones**
R   **Replacement:**   Putting in or on biological or synthetic material that physically takes the place and/or function of all or a portion of a body part

Body Part Character 4	Approach Character 5	Device Character 6	Qualifier Character 7
0 Lumbar Vertebra 1 Sacrum 2 Pelvic Bone, Right 3 Pelvic Bone, Left 4 Acetabulum, Right 5 Acetabulum, Left 6 Upper Femur, Right 7 Upper Femur, Left 8 Femoral Shaft, Right 9 Femoral Shaft, Left B Lower Femur, Right C Lower Femur, Left D Patella, Right F Patella, Left G Tibia, Right H Tibia, Left J Fibula, Right K Fibula, Left L Tarsal, Right M Tarsal, Left N Metatarsal, Right P Metatarsal, Left Q Toe Phalanx, Right R Toe Phalanx, Left S Coccyx	0 Open 3 Percutaneous 4 Percutaneous Endoscopic	7 Autologous Tissue Substitute J Synthetic Substitute K Nonautologous Tissue Substitute	Z No Qualifier

0   **Medical and Surgical**
Q   **Lower Bones**
S   **Reposition:**   Moving to its normal location or other suitable location all or a portion of a body part

Body Part Character 4	Approach Character 5	Device Character 6	Qualifier Character 7
0 Lumbar Vertebra 1 Sacrum 2 Pelvic Bone, Right 3 Pelvic Bone, Left 4 Acetabulum, Right 5 Acetabulum, Left 6 Upper Femur, Right 7 Upper Femur, Left 8 Femoral Shaft, Right 9 Femoral Shaft, Left B Lower Femur, Right C Lower Femur, Left D Patella, Right F Patella, Left G Tibia, Right H Tibia, Left J Fibula, Right K Fibula, Left L Tarsal, Right M Tarsal, Left N Metatarsal, Right P Metatarsal, Left Q Toe Phalanx, Right R Toe Phalanx, Left S Coccyx	X External	Z No Device	Z No Qualifier
0 Lumbar Vertebra 1 Sacrum 2 Pelvic Bone, Right 3 Pelvic Bone, Left 4 Acetabulum, Right 5 Acetabulum, Left D Patella, Right F Patella, Left L Tarsal, Right M Tarsal, Left N Metatarsal, Right P Metatarsal, Left Q Toe Phalanx, Right R Toe Phalanx, Left S Coccyx	0 Open 3 Percutaneous 4 Percutaneous Endoscopic	4 Internal Fixation Device Z No Device	Z No Qualifier

Continued on next page

0   **Medical and Surgical**   *Continued from previous page*
Q   **Lower Bones**
S   **Reposition:**   Moving to its normal location or other suitable location all or a portion of a body part

Body Part Character 4	Approach Character 5	Device Character 6	Qualifier Character 7
2 Pelvic Bone, Right **3** Pelvic Bone, Left **6** Upper Femur, Right **7** Upper Femur, Left **8** Femoral Shaft, Right **9** Femoral Shaft, Left **B** Lower Femur, Right **C** Lower Femur, Left **D** Patella, Right **F** Patella, Left **G** Tibia, Right **H** Tibia, Left **J** Fibula, Right **K** Fibula, Left **L** Tarsal, Right **M** Tarsal, Left **N** Metatarsal, Right **P** Metatarsal, Left **Q** Toe Phalanx, Right **R** Toe Phalanx, Left	**0** Open **3** Percutaneous **4** Percutaneous Endoscopic	**5** External Fixation Device	**3** Monoplanar **4** Ring **5** Hybrid **Z** No Qualifier
6 Upper Femur, Right **7** Upper Femur, Left **8** Femoral Shaft, Right **9** Femoral Shaft, Left **B** Lower Femur, Right **C** Lower Femur, Left **G** Tibia, Right **H** Tibia, Left **J** Fibula, Right **K** Fibula, Left	**0** Open **3** Percutaneous **4** Percutaneous Endoscopic	**4** Internal Fixation Device **6** Intramedullary Fixation Device **Z** No Device	**Z** No Qualifier

0   **Medical and Surgical**
Q   **Lower Bones**
T   **Resection:**   Cutting out or off, without replacement, all of a body part

Body Part Character 4	Approach Character 5	Device Character 6	Qualifier Character 7
2 Pelvic Bone, Right **3** Pelvic Bone, Left **4** Acetabulum, Right **5** Acetabulum, Left **6** Upper Femur, Right **7** Upper Femur, Left **8** Femoral Shaft, Right **9** Femoral Shaft, Left **B** Lower Femur, Right **C** Lower Femur, Left **D** Patella, Right **F** Patella, Left **G** Tibia, Right **H** Tibia, Left **J** Fibula, Right **K** Fibula, Left **L** Tarsal, Right **M** Tarsal, Left **N** Metatarsal, Right **P** Metatarsal, Left **Q** Toe Phalanx, Right **R** Toe Phalanx, Left **S** Coccyx	**0** Open	**Z** No Device	**Z** No Qualifier

0   **Medical and Surgical**
Q   **Lower Bones**
U   **Supplement:**   Putting in or on biological or synthetic material that physically reinforces and/or augments the function of a portion of a body part

Body Part Character 4	Approach Character 5	Device Character 6	Qualifier Character 7
0 Lumbar Vertebra **1** Sacrum **2** Pelvic Bone, Right **3** Pelvic Bone, Left **4** Acetabulum, Right **5** Acetabulum, Left **6** Upper Femur, Right **7** Upper Femur, Left **8** Femoral Shaft, Right **9** Femoral Shaft, Left **B** Lower Femur, Right **C** Lower Femur, Left **D** Patella, Right **F** Patella, Left **G** Tibia, Right **H** Tibia, Left **J** Fibula, Right **K** Fibula, Left **L** Tarsal, Right **M** Tarsal, Left **N** Metatarsal, Right **P** Metatarsal, Left **Q** Toe Phalanx, Right **R** Toe Phalanx, Left **S** Coccyx	**0** Open **3** Percutaneous **4** Percutaneous Endoscopic	**7** Autologous Tissue Substitute **J** Synthetic Substitute **K** Nonautologous Tissue Substitute	**Z** No Qualifier

0   **Medical and Surgical**
Q   **Lower Bones**
W   **Revision:**   Correcting, to the extent possible, a malfunctioning or displaced device

Body Part Character 4	Approach Character 5	Device Character 6	Qualifier Character 7
0 Lumbar Vertebra **1** Sacrum **4** Acetabulum, Right **5** Acetabulum, Left **S** Coccyx	**0** Open **3** Percutaneous **4** Percutaneous Endoscopic **X** External	**4** Internal Fixation Device **7** Autologous Tissue Substitute **J** Synthetic Substitute **K** Nonautologous Tissue Substitute	**Z** No Qualifier
2 Pelvic Bone, Right **3** Pelvic Bone, Left **D** Patella, Right **F** Patella, Left **L** Tarsal, Right **M** Tarsal, Left **N** Metatarsal, Right **P** Metatarsal, Left **Q** Toe Phalanx, Right **R** Toe Phalanx, Left	**0** Open **3** Percutaneous **4** Percutaneous Endoscopic **X** External	**4** Internal Fixation Device **5** External Fixation Device **7** Autologous Tissue Substitute **J** Synthetic Substitute **K** Nonautologous Tissue Substitute	**Z** No Qualifier
6 Upper Femur, Right **7** Upper Femur, Left **8** Femoral Shaft, Right **9** Femoral Shaft, Left **B** Lower Femur, Right **C** Lower Femur, Left **G** Tibia, Right **H** Tibia, Left **J** Fibula, Right **K** Fibula, Left	**0** Open **3** Percutaneous **4** Percutaneous Endoscopic **X** External	**4** Internal Fixation Device **5** External Fixation Device **6** Intramedullary Fixation Device **7** Autologous Tissue Substitute **J** Synthetic Substitute **K** Nonautologous Tissue Substitute	**Z** No Qualifier
Y Lower Bone	**0** Open **3** Percutaneous **4** Percutaneous Endoscopic **X** External	**0** Drainage Device **M** Electrode	**Z** No Qualifier

Upper Joints 0R2–0RW

0 Medical and Surgical
R Upper Joints
2 Change: Taking out or off a device from a body part and putting back an identical or similar device in or on the same body part without cutting or puncturing the skin or a mucous membrane

Body Part Character 4	Approach Character 5	Device Character 6	Qualifier Character 7
Y Upper Joint	**X** External	**0** Drainage Device **Y** Other Device	**Z** No Qualifier

0 Medical and Surgical
R Upper Joints
5 Destruction: Physical eradication of all or a portion of a body part by the direct use of energy, force, or a destructive agent

Body Part Character 4	Approach Character 5	Device Character 6	Qualifier Character 7
0 Occipital-cervical Joint **1** Cervical Vertebral Joint **3** Cervical Vertebral Disc **4** Cervicothoracic Vertebral Joint **5** Cervicothoracic Vertebral Disc **6** Thoracic Vertebral Joint **9** Thoracic Vertebral Disc **A** Thoracolumbar Vertebral Joint **B** Thoracolumbar Vertebral Disc **C** Temporomandibular Joint, Right **D** Temporomandibular Joint, Left **E** Sternoclavicular Joint, Right **F** Sternoclavicular Joint, Left **G** Acromioclavicular Joint, Right **H** Acromioclavicular Joint, Left **J** Shoulder Joint, Right **K** Shoulder Joint, Left **L** Elbow Joint, Right **M** Elbow Joint, Left **N** Wrist Joint, Right **P** Wrist Joint, Left **Q** Carpal Joint, Right **R** Carpal Joint, Left **S** Metacarpocarpal Joint, Right **T** Metacarpocarpal Joint, Left **U** Metacarpophalangeal Joint, Right **V** Metacarpophalangeal Joint, Left **W** Finger Phalangeal Joint, Right **X** Finger Phalangeal Joint, Left	**0** Open **3** Percutaneous **4** Percutaneous Endoscopic	**Z** No Device	**Z** No Qualifier

Draft (2009)

0   Medical and Surgical
R   Upper Joints
9   Drainage: Taking or letting out fluids and/or gases from a body part

Body Part Character 4	Approach Character 5	Device Character 6	Qualifier Character 7
0 Occipital-cervical Joint 1 Cervical Vertebral Joint 3 Cervical Vertebral Disc 4 Cervicothoracic Vertebral Joint 5 Cervicothoracic Vertebral Disc 6 Thoracic Vertebral Joint 9 Thoracic Vertebral Disc A Thoracolumbar Vertebral Joint B Thoracolumbar Vertebral Disc C Temporomandibular Joint, Right D Temporomandibular Joint, Left E Sternoclavicular Joint, Right F Sternoclavicular Joint, Left G Acromioclavicular Joint, Right H Acromioclavicular Joint, Left J Shoulder Joint, Right K Shoulder Joint, Left L Elbow Joint, Right M Elbow Joint, Left N Wrist Joint, Right P Wrist Joint, Left Q Carpal Joint, Right R Carpal Joint, Left S Metacarpocarpal Joint, Right T Metacarpocarpal Joint, Left U Metacarpophalangeal Joint, Right V Metacarpophalangeal Joint, Left W Finger Phalangeal Joint, Right X Finger Phalangeal Joint, Left	0 Open 3 Percutaneous 4 Percutaneous Endoscopic	0 Drainage Device	Z No Qualifier
0 Occipital-cervical Joint 1 Cervical Vertebral Joint 3 Cervical Vertebral Disc 4 Cervicothoracic Vertebral Joint 5 Cervicothoracic Vertebral Disc 6 Thoracic Vertebral Joint 9 Thoracic Vertebral Disc A Thoracolumbar Vertebral Joint B Thoracolumbar Vertebral Disc C Temporomandibular Joint, Right D Temporomandibular Joint, Left E Sternoclavicular Joint, Right F Sternoclavicular Joint, Left G Acromioclavicular Joint, Right H Acromioclavicular Joint, Left J Shoulder Joint, Right K Shoulder Joint, Left L Elbow Joint, Right M Elbow Joint, Left N Wrist Joint, Right P Wrist Joint, Left Q Carpal Joint, Right R Carpal Joint, Left S Metacarpocarpal Joint, Right T Metacarpocarpal Joint, Left U Metacarpophalangeal Joint, Right V Metacarpophalangeal Joint, Left W Finger Phalangeal Joint, Right X Finger Phalangeal Joint, Left	0 Open 3 Percutaneous 4 Percutaneous Endoscopic	Z No Device	X Diagnostic Z No Qualifier

0   Medical and Surgical
R   Upper Joints
B   Excision: Cutting out or off, without replacement, a portion of a body part

Body Part Character 4	Approach Character 5	Device Character 6	Qualifier Character 7
0 Occipital-cervical Joint 1 Cervical Vertebral Joint 3 Cervical Vertebral Disc 4 Cervicothoracic Vertebral Joint 5 Cervicothoracic Vertebral Disc 6 Thoracic Vertebral Joint 9 Thoracic Vertebral Disc A Thoracolumbar Vertebral Joint B Thoracolumbar Vertebral Disc C Temporomandibular Joint, Right D Temporomandibular Joint, Left E Sternoclavicular Joint, Right F Sternoclavicular Joint, Left G Acromioclavicular Joint, Right H Acromioclavicular Joint, Left J Shoulder Joint, Right K Shoulder Joint, Left L Elbow Joint, Right M Elbow Joint, Left N Wrist Joint, Right P Wrist Joint, Left Q Carpal Joint, Right R Carpal Joint, Left S Metacarpocarpal Joint, Right T Metacarpocarpal Joint, Left U Metacarpophalangeal Joint, Right V Metacarpophalangeal Joint, Left W Finger Phalangeal Joint, Right X Finger Phalangeal Joint, Left	0 Open 3 Percutaneous 4 Percutaneous Endoscopic	Z No Device	X Diagnostic Z No Qualifier

0   Medical and Surgical
R   Upper Joints
C   Extirpation: Taking or cutting out solid matter from a body part

Body Part Character 4	Approach Character 5	Device Character 6	Qualifier Character 7
0 Occipital-cervical Joint 1 Cervical Vertebral Joint 3 Cervical Vertebral Disc 4 Cervicothoracic Vertebral Joint 5 Cervicothoracic Vertebral Disc 6 Thoracic Vertebral Joint 9 Thoracic Vertebral Disc A Thoracolumbar Vertebral Joint B Thoracolumbar Vertebral Disc C Temporomandibular Joint, Right D Temporomandibular Joint, Left E Sternoclavicular Joint, Right F Sternoclavicular Joint, Left G Acromioclavicular Joint, Right H Acromioclavicular Joint, Left J Shoulder Joint, Right K Shoulder Joint, Left L Elbow Joint, Right M Elbow Joint, Left N Wrist Joint, Right P Wrist Joint, Left Q Carpal Joint, Right R Carpal Joint, Left S Metacarpocarpal Joint, Right T Metacarpocarpal Joint, Left U Metacarpophalangeal Joint, Right V Metacarpophalangeal Joint, Left W Finger Phalangeal Joint, Right X Finger Phalangeal Joint, Left	0 Open 3 Percutaneous 4 Percutaneous Endoscopic	Z No Device	Z No Qualifier

0   Medical and Surgical
R   Upper Joints
G   Fusion: Joining together portions of an articular body part rendering the articular body part immobile

Body Part Character 4	Approach Character 5	Device Character 6	Qualifier Character 7

0 Occipital-cervical Joint
1 Cervical Vertebral Joint
2 Cervical Vertebral Joints, 2 or
   more
4 Cervicothoracic Vertebral Joint
6 Thoracic Vertebral Joint
7 Thoracic Vertebral Joints, 2 to 7
8 Thoracic Vertebral Joints, 8 or
   more
A Thoracolumbar Vertebral Joint
	0 Open
	3 Percutaneous
	4 Percutaneous Endoscopic
		4 Internal Fixation Device
		7 Autologous Tissue Substitute
		J Synthetic Substitute
		K Nonautologous Tissue Substitute
		Z No Device
			0 Anterior
			1 Posterior

C Temporomandibular Joint, Right D Temporomandibular Joint, Left E Sternoclavicular Joint, Right F Sternoclavicular Joint, Left G Acromioclavicular Joint, Right H Acromioclavicular Joint, Left J Shoulder Joint, Right K Shoulder Joint, Left	0 Open 3 Percutaneous 4 Percutaneous Endoscopic	4 Internal Fixation Device 7 Autologous Tissue Substitute J Synthetic Substitute K Nonautologous Tissue Substitute Z No Device	Z No Qualifier
L Elbow Joint, Right M Elbow Joint, Left N Wrist Joint, Right P Wrist Joint, Left Q Carpal Joint, Right R Carpal Joint, Left S Metacarpocarpal Joint, Right T Metacarpocarpal Joint, Left U Metacarpophalangeal Joint, Right V Metacarpophalangeal Joint, Left W Finger Phalangeal Joint, Right X Finger Phalangeal Joint, Left	0 Open 3 Percutaneous 4 Percutaneous Endoscopic	4 Internal Fixation Device 5 External Fixation Device 7 Autologous Tissue Substitute J Synthetic Substitute K Nonautologous Tissue Substitute Z No Device	Z No Qualifier

0   Medical and Surgical
R   Upper Joints
H   Insertion: Putting in a nonbiological appliance that monitors, assists, performs or prevents a physiological function, but does not
physically take the place of a body part

Body Part Character 4	Approach Character 5	Device Character 6	Qualifier Character 7
0 Occipital-cervical Joint 1 Cervical Vertebral Joint 4 Cervicothoracic Vertebral Joint 6 Thoracic Vertebral Joint A Thoracolumbar Vertebral Joint	0 Open 3 Percutaneous 4 Percutaneous Endoscopic	3 Infusion Device 8 Spacer	Z No Qualifier
0 Occipital-cervical Joint 1 Cervical Vertebral Joint 4 Cervicothoracic Vertebral Joint 6 Thoracic Vertebral Joint A Thoracolumbar Vertebral Joint	0 Open 3 Percutaneous 4 Percutaneous Endoscopic	4 Internal Fixation Device	2 Interspinous Process 3 Pedicle-based Dynamic Stabilization Z No Qualifier
3 Cervical Vertebral Disc 5 Cervicothoracic Vertebral Disc 9 Thoracic Vertebral Disc B Thoracolumbar Vertebral Disc	0 Open 3 Percutaneous 4 Percutaneous Endoscopic	3 Infusion Device	Z No Qualifier
C Temporomandibular Joint, Right D Temporomandibular Joint, Left E Sternoclavicular Joint, Right F Sternoclavicular Joint, Left G Acromioclavicular Joint, Right H Acromioclavicular Joint, Left J Shoulder Joint, Right K Shoulder Joint, Left	0 Open 3 Percutaneous 4 Percutaneous Endoscopic	3 Infusion Device 4 Internal Fixation Device 8 Spacer	Z No Qualifier
L Elbow Joint, Right M Elbow Joint, Left N Wrist Joint, Right P Wrist Joint, Left Q Carpal Joint, Right R Carpal Joint, Left S Metacarpocarpal Joint, Right T Metacarpocarpal Joint, Left U Metacarpophalangeal Joint, Right V Metacarpophalangeal Joint, Left W Finger Phalangeal Joint, Right X Finger Phalangeal Joint, Left	0 Open 3 Percutaneous 4 Percutaneous Endoscopic	3 Infusion Device 4 Internal Fixation Device 5 External Fixation Device 8 Spacer	Z No Qualifier

0   **Medical and Surgical**
R   **Upper Joints**
J   **Inspection:**   Visually and/or manually exploring a body part

Body Part Character 4	Approach Character 5	Device Character 6	Qualifier Character 7
0 Occipital-cervical Joint	0 Open	Z No Device	Z No Qualifier
1 Cervical Vertebral Joint	3 Percutaneous		
3 Cervical Vertebral Disc	4 Percutaneous Endoscopic		
4 Cervicothoracic Vertebral Joint	X External		
5 Cervicothoracic Vertebral Disc			
6 Thoracic Vertebral Joint			
9 Thoracic Vertebral Disc			
A Thoracolumbar Vertebral Joint			
B Thoracolumbar Vertebral Disc			
C Temporomandibular Joint, Right			
D Temporomandibular Joint, Left			
E Sternoclavicular Joint, Right			
F Sternoclavicular Joint, Left			
G Acromioclavicular Joint, Right			
H Acromioclavicular Joint, Left			
J Shoulder Joint, Right			
K Shoulder Joint, Left			
L Elbow Joint, Right			
M Elbow Joint, Left			
N Wrist Joint, Right			
P Wrist Joint, Left			
Q Carpal Joint, Right			
R Carpal Joint, Left			
S Metacarpocarpal Joint, Right			
T Metacarpocarpal Joint, Left			
U Metacarpophalangeal Joint, Right			
V Metacarpophalangeal Joint, Left			
W Finger Phalangeal Joint, Right			
X Finger Phalangeal Joint, Left			

0   **Medical and Surgical**
R   **Upper Joints**
N   **Release:**   Freeing a body part from an abnormal physical constraint

Body Part Character 4	Approach Character 5	Device Character 6	Qualifier Character 7
0 Occipital-cervical Joint	0 Open	Z No Device	Z No Qualifier
1 Cervical Vertebral Joint	3 Percutaneous		
3 Cervical Vertebral Disc	4 Percutaneous Endoscopic		
4 Cervicothoracic Vertebral Joint	X External		
5 Cervicothoracic Vertebral Disc			
6 Thoracic Vertebral Joint			
9 Thoracic Vertebral Disc			
A Thoracolumbar Vertebral Joint			
B Thoracolumbar Vertebral Disc			
C Temporomandibular Joint, Right			
D Temporomandibular Joint, Left			
E Sternoclavicular Joint, Right			
F Sternoclavicular Joint, Left			
G Acromioclavicular Joint, Right			
H Acromioclavicular Joint, Left			
J Shoulder Joint, Right			
K Shoulder Joint, Left			
L Elbow Joint, Right			
M Elbow Joint, Left			
N Wrist Joint, Right			
P Wrist Joint, Left			
Q Carpal Joint, Right			
R Carpal Joint, Left			
S Metacarpocarpal Joint, Right			
T Metacarpocarpal Joint, Left			
U Metacarpophalangeal Joint, Right			
V Metacarpophalangeal Joint, Left			
W Finger Phalangeal Joint, Right			
X Finger Phalangeal Joint, Left			

0   **Medical and Surgical**
R   **Upper Joints**
P   **Removal:**   Taking out or off a device from a body part

Body Part Character 4	Approach Character 5	Device Character 6	Qualifier Character 7
0 Occipital-cervical Joint 1 Cervical Vertebral Joint 4 Cervicothoracic Vertebral Joint 6 Thoracic Vertebral Joint A Thoracolumbar Vertebral Joint C Temporomandibular Joint, Right D Temporomandibular Joint, Left E Sternoclavicular Joint, Right F Sternoclavicular Joint, Left G Acromioclavicular Joint, Right H Acromioclavicular Joint, Left J Shoulder Joint, Right K Shoulder Joint, Left	0 Open 3 Percutaneous 4 Percutaneous Endoscopic	0 Drainage Device 3 Infusion Device 4 Internal Fixation Device 7 Autologous Tissue Substitute 8 Spacer J Synthetic Substitute K Nonautologous Tissue Substitute	Z No Qualifier
0 Occipital-cervical Joint 1 Cervical Vertebral Joint 4 Cervicothoracic Vertebral Joint 6 Thoracic Vertebral Joint A Thoracolumbar Vertebral Joint C Temporomandibular Joint, Right D Temporomandibular Joint, Left E Sternoclavicular Joint, Right F Sternoclavicular Joint, Left G Acromioclavicular Joint, Right H Acromioclavicular Joint, Left J Shoulder Joint, Right K Shoulder Joint, Left	X External	0 Drainage Device 3 Infusion Device 4 Internal Fixation Device	Z No Qualifier
3 Cervical Vertebral Disc 5 Cervicothoracic Vertebral Disc 9 Thoracic Vertebral Disc B Thoracolumbar Vertebral Disc	0 Open 3 Percutaneous 4 Percutaneous Endoscopic	0 Drainage Device 3 Infusion Device 7 Autologous Tissue Substitute J Synthetic Substitute K Nonautologous Tissue Substitute	Z No Qualifier
3 Cervical Vertebral Disc 5 Cervicothoracic Vertebral Disc 9 Thoracic Vertebral Disc B Thoracolumbar Vertebral Disc	X External	0 Drainage Device 3 Infusion Device	Z No Qualifier
L Elbow Joint, Right M Elbow Joint, Left N Wrist Joint, Right P Wrist Joint, Left Q Carpal Joint, Right R Carpal Joint, Left S Metacarpocarpal Joint, Right T Metacarpocarpal Joint, Left U Metacarpophalangeal Joint, Right V Metacarpophalangeal Joint, Left W Finger Phalangeal Joint, Right X Finger Phalangeal Joint, Left	0 Open 3 Percutaneous 4 Percutaneous Endoscopic	0 Drainage Device 3 Infusion Device 4 Internal Fixation Device 5 External Fixation Device 7 Autologous Tissue Substitute 8 Spacer J Synthetic Substitute K Nonautologous Tissue Substitute	Z No Qualifier
L Elbow Joint, Right M Elbow Joint, Left N Wrist Joint, Right P Wrist Joint, Left Q Carpal Joint, Right R Carpal Joint, Left S Metacarpocarpal Joint, Right T Metacarpocarpal Joint, Left U Metacarpophalangeal Joint, Right V Metacarpophalangeal Joint, Left W Finger Phalangeal Joint, Right X Finger Phalangeal Joint, Left	X External	0 Drainage Device 3 Infusion Device 4 Internal Fixation Device 5 External Fixation Device	Z No Qualifier

0   Medical and Surgical
R   Upper Joints
Q   Repair: Restoring, to the extent possible, a body part to its normal anatomic structure and function

Body Part Character 4	Approach Character 5	Device Character 6	Qualifier Character 7
0 Occipital-cervical Joint **1** Cervical Vertebral Joint **3** Cervical Vertebral Disc **4** Cervicothoracic Vertebral Joint **5** Cervicothoracic Vertebral Disc **6** Thoracic Vertebral Joint **9** Thoracic Vertebral Disc **A** Thoracolumbar Vertebral Joint **B** Thoracolumbar Vertebral Disc **C** Temporomandibular Joint, Right **D** Temporomandibular Joint, Left **E** Sternoclavicular Joint, Right **F** Sternoclavicular Joint, Left **G** Acromioclavicular Joint, Right **H** Acromioclavicular Joint, Left **J** Shoulder Joint, Right **K** Shoulder Joint, Left **L** Elbow Joint, Right **M** Elbow Joint, Left **N** Wrist Joint, Right **P** Wrist Joint, Left **Q** Carpal Joint, Right **R** Carpal Joint, Left **S** Metacarpocarpal Joint, Right **T** Metacarpocarpal Joint, Left **U** Metacarpophalangeal Joint, Right **V** Metacarpophalangeal Joint, Left **W** Finger Phalangeal Joint, Right **X** Finger Phalangeal Joint, Left	**0** Open **3** Percutaneous **4** Percutaneous Endoscopic **X** External	**Z** No Device	**Z** No Qualifier

0   Medical and Surgical
R   Upper Joints
R   Replacement: Putting in or on biological or synthetic material that physically takes the place and/or function of all or a portion of a body part

Body Part Character 4	Approach Character 5	Device Character 6	Qualifier Character 7
0 Occipital-cervical Joint **1** Cervical Vertebral Joint **4** Cervicothoracic Vertebral Joint **6** Thoracic Vertebral Joint **A** Thoracolumbar Vertebral Joint	**0** Open	**7** Autologous Tissue Substitute **K** Nonautologous Tissue Substitute	**Z** No Qualifier
0 Occipital-cervical Joint **1** Cervical Vertebral Joint **4** Cervicothoracic Vertebral Joint **6** Thoracic Vertebral Joint **A** Thoracolumbar Vertebral Joint	**0** Open	**J** Synthetic Substitute	**4** Facet **Z** No Qualifier
3 Cervical Vertebral Disc **5** Cervicothoracic Vertebral Disc **9** Thoracic Vertebral Disc **B** Thoracolumbar Vertebral Disc **C** Temporomandibular Joint, Right **D** Temporomandibular Joint, Left **E** Sternoclavicular Joint, Right **F** Sternoclavicular Joint, Left **G** Acromioclavicular Joint, Right **H** Acromioclavicular Joint, Left **J** Shoulder Joint, Right **K** Shoulder Joint, Left **L** Elbow Joint, Right **M** Elbow Joint, Left **N** Wrist Joint, Right **P** Wrist Joint, Left **Q** Carpal Joint, Right **R** Carpal Joint, Left **S** Metacarpocarpal Joint, Right **T** Metacarpocarpal Joint, Left **U** Metacarpophalangeal Joint, Right **V** Metacarpophalangeal Joint, Left **W** Finger Phalangeal Joint, Right **X** Finger Phalangeal Joint, Left	**0** Open	**7** Autologous Tissue Substitute **J** Synthetic Substitute **K** Nonautologous Tissue Substitute	**Z** No Qualifier

0   **Medical and Surgical**
R   **Upper Joints**
S   **Reposition:**   Moving to its normal location or other suitable location all or a portion of a body part

Body Part Character 4	Approach Character 5	Device Character 6	Qualifier Character 7
0 Occipital-cervical Joint 1 Cervical Vertebral Joint 4 Cervicothoracic Vertebral Joint 6 Thoracic Vertebral Joint A Thoracolumbar Vertebral Joint C Temporomandibular Joint, Right D Temporomandibular Joint, Left E Sternoclavicular Joint, Right F Sternoclavicular Joint, Left G Acromioclavicular Joint, Right H Acromioclavicular Joint, Left J Shoulder Joint, Right K Shoulder Joint, Left	0 Open 3 Percutaneous 4 Percutaneous Endoscopic X External	4 Internal Fixation Device Z No Device	Z No Qualifier
L Elbow Joint, Right M Elbow Joint, Left N Wrist Joint, Right P Wrist Joint, Left Q Carpal Joint, Right R Carpal Joint, Left S Metacarpocarpal Joint, Right T Metacarpocarpal Joint, Left U Metacarpophalangeal Joint, Right V Metacarpophalangeal Joint, Left W Finger Phalangeal Joint, Right X Finger Phalangeal Joint, Left	0 Open 3 Percutaneous 4 Percutaneous Endoscopic X External	4 Internal Fixation Device 5 External Fixation Device Z No Device	Z No Qualifier

0   **Medical and Surgical**
R   **Upper Joints**
T   **Resection:**   Cutting out or off, without replacement, all of a body part

Body Part Character 4	Approach Character 5	Device Character 6	Qualifier Character 7
3 Cervical Vertebral Disc 4 Cervicothoracic Vertebral Joint 5 Cervicothoracic Vertebral Disc 9 Thoracic Vertebral Disc B Thoracolumbar Vertebral Disc C Temporomandibular Joint, Right D Temporomandibular Joint, Left E Sternoclavicular Joint, Right F Sternoclavicular Joint, Left G Acromioclavicular Joint, Right H Acromioclavicular Joint, Left J Shoulder Joint, Right K Shoulder Joint, Left L Elbow Joint, Right M Elbow Joint, Left N Wrist Joint, Right P Wrist Joint, Left Q Carpal Joint, Right R Carpal Joint, Left S Metacarpocarpal Joint, Right T Metacarpocarpal Joint, Left U Metacarpophalangeal Joint, Right V Metacarpophalangeal Joint, Left W Finger Phalangeal Joint, Right X Finger Phalangeal Joint, Left	0 Open	Z No Device	Z No Qualifier

0   **Medical and Surgical**
R   **Upper Joints**
U   **Supplement:**   Putting in or on biological or synthetic material that physically reinforces and/or augments the function of a portion of a body part

Body Part Character 4	Approach Character 5	Device Character 6	Qualifier Character 7
0 Occipital-cervical Joint 1 Cervical Vertebral Joint 4 Cervicothoracic Vertebral Joint 6 Thoracic Vertebral Joint A Thoracolumbar Vertebral Joint	0 Open	7 Autologous Tissue Substitute K Nonautologous Tissue Substitute	Z No Qualifier

Continued on next page

0   Medical and Surgical
R   Upper Joints
U   Supplement: Putting in or on biological or synthetic material that physically reinforces and/or augments the function of a portion of a body part

Continued from previous page

Body Part Character 4	Approach Character 5	Device Character 6	Qualifier Character 7
0 Occipital-cervical Joint 1 Cervical Vertebral Joint 4 Cervicothoracic Vertebral Joint 6 Thoracic Vertebral Joint A Thoracolumbar Vertebral Joint	0 Open	J Synthetic Substitute	4 Facet Z No Qualifier
3 Cervical Vertebral Disc 5 Cervicothoracic Vertebral Disc 9 Thoracic Vertebral Disc B Thoracolumbar Vertebral Disc C Temporomandibular Joint, Right D Temporomandibular Joint, Left E Sternoclavicular Joint, Right F Sternoclavicular Joint, Left G Acromioclavicular Joint, Right H Acromioclavicular Joint, Left J Shoulder Joint, Right K Shoulder Joint, Left L Elbow Joint, Right M Elbow Joint, Left N Wrist Joint, Right P Wrist Joint, Left Q Carpal Joint, Right R Carpal Joint, Left S Metacarpocarpal Joint, Right T Metacarpocarpal Joint, Left U Metacarpophalangeal Joint, Right V Metacarpophalangeal Joint, Left W Finger Phalangeal Joint, Right X Finger Phalangeal Joint, Left	0 Open	7 Autologous Tissue Substitute J Synthetic Substitute K Nonautologous Tissue Substitute	Z No Qualifier

0   Medical and Surgical
R   Upper Joints
W   Revision: Correcting, to the extent possible, a malfunctioning or displaced device

Body Part Character 4	Approach Character 5	Device Character 6	Qualifier Character 7
0 Occipital-cervical Joint 1 Cervical Vertebral Joint 4 Cervicothoracic Vertebral Joint 6 Thoracic Vertebral Joint A Thoracolumbar Vertebral Joint C Temporomandibular Joint, Right D Temporomandibular Joint, Left E Sternoclavicular Joint, Right F Sternoclavicular Joint, Left G Acromioclavicular Joint, Right H Acromioclavicular Joint, Left J Shoulder Joint, Right K Shoulder Joint, Left	0 Open 3 Percutaneous 4 Percutaneous Endoscopic X External	0 Drainage Device 3 Infusion Device 4 Internal Fixation Device 7 Autologous Tissue Substitute 8 Spacer J Synthetic Substitute K Nonautologous Tissue Substitute	Z No Qualifier
3 Cervical Vertebral Disc 5 Cervicothoracic Vertebral Disc 9 Thoracic Vertebral Disc B Thoracolumbar Vertebral Disc	0 Open 3 Percutaneous 4 Percutaneous Endoscopic X External	0 Drainage Device 3 Infusion Device 7 Autologous Tissue Substitute J Synthetic Substitute K Nonautologous Tissue Substitute	Z No Qualifier
L Elbow Joint, Right M Elbow Joint, Left N Wrist Joint, Right P Wrist Joint, Left Q Carpal Joint, Right R Carpal Joint, Left S Metacarpocarpal Joint, Right T Metacarpocarpal Joint, Left U Metacarpophalangeal Joint, Right V Metacarpophalangeal Joint, Left W Finger Phalangeal Joint, Right X Finger Phalangeal Joint, Left	0 Open 3 Percutaneous 4 Percutaneous Endoscopic X External	0 Drainage Device 3 Infusion Device 4 Internal Fixation Device 5 External Fixation Device 7 Autologous Tissue Substitute 8 Spacer J Synthetic Substitute K Nonautologous Tissue Substitute	Z No Qualifier

Draft (2009)

Lower Joints 0S2–0SW

0   **Medical and Surgical**
S   **Lower Joints**
2   **Change:**   Taking out or off a device from a body part and putting back an identical or similar device in or on the same body part without cutting or puncturing the skin or a mucous membrane

Body Part Character 4	Approach Character 5	Device Character 6	Qualifier Character 7
Y Lower Joint	X External	0 Drainage Device Y Other Device	Z No Qualifier

0   **Medical and Surgical**
S   **Lower Joints**
5   **Destruction:**   Physical eradication of all or a portion of a body part by the direct use of energy, force, or a destructive agent

Body Part Character 4	Approach Character 5	Device Character 6	Qualifier Character 7
0 Lumbar Vertebral Joint 2 Lumbar Vertebral Disc 3 Lumbosacral Joint 4 Lumbosacral Disc 5 Sacrococcygeal Joint 6 Coccygeal Joint 7 Sacroiliac Joint, Right 8 Sacroiliac Joint, Left 9 Hip Joint, Right B Hip Joint, Left C Knee Joint, Right D Knee Joint, Left F Ankle Joint, Right G Ankle Joint, Left H Tarsal Joint, Right J Tarsal Joint, Left K Metatarsal-Tarsal Joint, Right L Metatarsal-Tarsal Joint, Left M Metatarsal-Phalangeal Joint, Right N Metatarsal-Phalangeal Joint, Left P Toe Phalangeal Joint, Right Q Toe Phalangeal Joint, Left	0 Open 3 Percutaneous 4 Percutaneous Endoscopic	Z No Device	Z No Qualifier

0   **Medical and Surgical**
S   **Lower Joints**
9   **Drainage:**   Taking or letting out fluids and/or gases from a body part

Body Part Character 4	Approach Character 5	Device Character 6	Qualifier Character 7
0 Lumbar Vertebral Joint 2 Lumbar Vertebral Disc 3 Lumbosacral Joint 4 Lumbosacral Disc 5 Sacrococcygeal Joint 6 Coccygeal Joint 7 Sacroiliac Joint, Right 8 Sacroiliac Joint, Left 9 Hip Joint, Right B Hip Joint, Left C Knee Joint, Right D Knee Joint, Left F Ankle Joint, Right G Ankle Joint, Left H Tarsal Joint, Right J Tarsal Joint, Left K Metatarsal-Tarsal Joint, Right L Metatarsal-Tarsal Joint, Left M Metatarsal-Phalangeal Joint, Right N Metatarsal-Phalangeal Joint, Left P Toe Phalangeal Joint, Right Q Toe Phalangeal Joint, Left	0 Open 3 Percutaneous 4 Percutaneous Endoscopic	0 Drainage Device	Z No Qualifier

Continued on next page

0   Medical and Surgical
S   Lower Joints
9   Drainage: Taking or letting out fluids and/or gases from a body part

Continued from previous page

Body Part Character 4	Approach Character 5	Device Character 6	Qualifier Character 7
0 Lumbar Vertebral Joint 2 Lumbar Vertebral Disc 3 Lumbosacral Joint 4 Lumbosacral Disc 5 Sacrococcygeal Joint 6 Coccygeal Joint 7 Sacroiliac Joint, Right 8 Sacroiliac Joint, Left 9 Hip Joint, Right B Hip Joint, Left C Knee Joint, Right D Knee Joint, Left F Ankle Joint, Right G Ankle Joint, Left H Tarsal Joint, Right J Tarsal Joint, Left K Metatarsal-Tarsal Joint, Right L Metatarsal-Tarsal Joint, Left M Metatarsal-Phalangeal Joint, Right N Metatarsal-Phalangeal Joint, Left P Toe Phalangeal Joint, Right Q Toe Phalangeal Joint, Left	0 Open 3 Percutaneous 4 Percutaneous Endoscopic	Z No Device	X Diagnostic Z No Qualifier

0   Medical and Surgical
S   Lower Joints
B   Excision: Cutting out or off, without replacement, a portion of a body part

Body Part Character 4	Approach Character 5	Device Character 6	Qualifier Character 7
0 Lumbar Vertebral Joint 2 Lumbar Vertebral Disc 3 Lumbosacral Joint 4 Lumbosacral Disc 5 Sacrococcygeal Joint 6 Coccygeal Joint 7 Sacroiliac Joint, Right 8 Sacroiliac Joint, Left 9 Hip Joint, Right B Hip Joint, Left C Knee Joint, Right D Knee Joint, Left F Ankle Joint, Right G Ankle Joint, Left H Tarsal Joint, Right J Tarsal Joint, Left K Metatarsal-Tarsal Joint, Right L Metatarsal-Tarsal Joint, Left M Metatarsal-Phalangeal Joint, Right N Metatarsal-Phalangeal Joint, Left P Toe Phalangeal Joint, Right Q Toe Phalangeal Joint, Left	0 Open 3 Percutaneous 4 Percutaneous Endoscopic	Z No Device	X Diagnostic Z No Qualifier

0   Medical and Surgical
S   Lower Joints
C   Extirpation: Taking or cutting out solid matter from a body part

Body Part Character 4	Approach Character 5	Device Character 6	Qualifier Character 7
0 Lumbar Vertebral Joint **2** Lumbar Vertebral Disc **3** Lumbosacral Joint **4** Lumbosacral Disc **5** Sacrococcygeal Joint **6** Coccygeal Joint **7** Sacroiliac Joint, Right **8** Sacroiliac Joint, Left **9** Hip Joint, Right **B** Hip Joint, Left **C** Knee Joint, Right **D** Knee Joint, Left **F** Ankle Joint, Right **G** Ankle Joint, Left **H** Tarsal Joint, Right **J** Tarsal Joint, Left **K** Metatarsal-Tarsal Joint, Right **L** Metatarsal-Tarsal Joint, Left **M** Metatarsal-Phalangeal Joint, Right **N** Metatarsal-Phalangeal Joint, Left **P** Toe Phalangeal Joint, Right **Q** Toe Phalangeal Joint, Left	**0** Open **3** Percutaneous **4** Percutaneous Endoscopic	**Z** No Device	**Z** No Qualifier

0   Medical and Surgical
S   Lower Joints
G   Fusion: Joining together portions of an articular body part rendering the articular body part immobile

Body Part Character 4	Approach Character 5	Device Character 6	Qualifier Character 7
0 Lumbar Vertebral Joint **1** Lumbar Vertebral Joints, 2 or more **3** Lumbosacral Joint	**0** Open **3** Percutaneous **4** Percutaneous Endoscopic	**4** Internal Fixation Device **7** Autologous Tissue Substitute **J** Synthetic Substitute **K** Nonautologous Tissue Substitute **Z** No Device	**0** Anterior **1** Posterior
5 Sacrococcygeal Joint **6** Coccygeal Joint **7** Sacroiliac Joint, Right **8** Sacroiliac Joint, Left	**0** Open **3** Percutaneous **4** Percutaneous Endoscopic	**4** Internal Fixation Device **7** Autologous Tissue Substitute **J** Synthetic Substitute **K** Nonautologous Tissue Substitute **Z** No Device	**Z** No Qualifier
9 Hip Joint, Right **B** Hip Joint, Left **C** Knee Joint, Right **D** Knee Joint, Left **F** Ankle Joint, Right **G** Ankle Joint, Left **H** Tarsal Joint, Right **J** Tarsal Joint, Left **K** Metatarsal-Tarsal Joint, Right **L** Metatarsal-Tarsal Joint, Left **M** Metatarsal-Phalangeal Joint, Right **N** Metatarsal-Phalangeal Joint, Left **P** Toe Phalangeal Joint, Right **Q** Toe Phalangeal Joint, Left	**0** Open **3** Percutaneous **4** Percutaneous Endoscopic	**4** Internal Fixation Device **5** External Fixation Device **7** Autologous Tissue Substitute **J** Synthetic Substitute **K** Nonautologous Tissue Substitute **Z** No Device	**Z** No Qualifier

0   Medical and Surgical
S   Lower Joints
H   Insertion: Putting in a nonbiological appliance that monitors, assists, performs or prevents a physiological function, but does not physically take the place of a body part

Body Part Character 4	Approach Character 5	Device Character 6	Qualifier Character 7
0 Lumbar Vertebral Joint **2** Lumbar Vertebral Disc **3** Lumbosacral Joint **4** Lumbosacral Disc	**0** Open **3** Percutaneous **4** Percutaneous Endoscopic	**3** Infusion Device **8** Spacer	**Z** No Qualifier
0 Lumbar Vertebral Joint **3** Lumbosacral Joint	**0** Open **3** Percutaneous **4** Percutaneous Endoscopic	**4** Internal Fixation Device	**2** Interspinous Process **3** Pedicle-based Dynamic Stabilization **Z** No Qualifier

Continued on next page

0 **Medical and Surgical**
S **Lower Joints**
H **Insertion:** Putting in a nonbiological appliance that monitors, assists, performs or prevents a physiological function, but does not physically take the place of a body part

Continued from previous page

Body Part Character 4	Approach Character 5	Device Character 6	Qualifier Character 7
5 Sacrococcygeal Joint **6** Coccygeal Joint **7** Sacroiliac Joint, Right **8** Sacroiliac Joint, Left	**0** Open **3** Percutaneous **4** Percutaneous Endoscopic	**3** Infusion Device **4** Internal Fixation Device **8** Spacer	**Z** No Qualifier
9 Hip Joint, Right **B** Hip Joint, Left **C** Knee Joint, Right **D** Knee Joint, Left **F** Ankle Joint, Right **G** Ankle Joint, Left **H** Tarsal Joint, Right **J** Tarsal Joint, Left **K** Metatarsal-Tarsal Joint, Right **L** Metatarsal-Tarsal Joint, Left **M** Metatarsal-Phalangeal Joint, Right **N** Metatarsal-Phalangeal Joint, Left **P** Toe Phalangeal Joint, Right **Q** Toe Phalangeal Joint, Left	**0** Open **3** Percutaneous **4** Percutaneous Endoscopic	**3** Infusion Device **4** Internal Fixation Device **5** External Fixation Device **8** Spacer	**Z** No Qualifier

0 **Medical and Surgical**
S **Lower Joints**
J **Inspection:** Visually and/or manually exploring a body part

Body Part Character 4	Approach Character 5	Device Character 6	Qualifier Character 7
0 Lumbar Vertebral Joint **2** Lumbar Vertebral Disc **3** Lumbosacral Joint **4** Lumbosacral Disc **5** Sacrococcygeal Joint **6** Coccygeal Joint **7** Sacroiliac Joint, Right **8** Sacroiliac Joint, Left **9** Hip Joint, Right **B** Hip Joint, Left **C** Knee Joint, Right **D** Knee Joint, Left **F** Ankle Joint, Right **G** Ankle Joint, Left **H** Tarsal Joint, Right **J** Tarsal Joint, Left **K** Metatarsal-Tarsal Joint, Right **L** Metatarsal-Tarsal Joint, Left **M** Metatarsal-Phalangeal Joint, Right **N** Metatarsal-Phalangeal Joint, Left **P** Toe Phalangeal Joint, Right **Q** Toe Phalangeal Joint, Left	**0** Open **3** Percutaneous **4** Percutaneous Endoscopic **X** External	**Z** No Device	**Z** No Qualifier

0 Medical and Surgical
S Lower Joints
N Release: Freeing a body part from an abnormal physical constraint

Body Part Character 4	Approach Character 5	Device Character 6	Qualifier Character 7
0 Lumbar Vertebral Joint **2** Lumbar Vertebral Disc **3** Lumbosacral Joint **4** Lumbosacral Disc **5** Sacrococcygeal Joint **6** Coccygeal Joint **7** Sacroiliac Joint, Right **8** Sacroiliac Joint, Left **9** Hip Joint, Right **B** Hip Joint, Left **C** Knee Joint, Right **D** Knee Joint, Left **F** Ankle Joint, Right **G** Ankle Joint, Left **H** Tarsal Joint, Right **J** Tarsal Joint, Left **K** Metatarsal-Tarsal Joint, Right **L** Metatarsal-Tarsal Joint, Left **M** Metatarsal-Phalangeal Joint, Right **N** Metatarsal-Phalangeal Joint, Left **P** Toe Phalangeal Joint, Right **Q** Toe Phalangeal Joint, Left	**0** Open **3** Percutaneous **4** Percutaneous Endoscopic **X** External	**Z** No Device	**Z** No Qualifier

0 Medical and Surgical
S Lower Joints
P Removal: Taking out or off a device from a body part

Body Part Character 4	Approach Character 5	Device Character 6	Qualifier Character 7
0 Lumbar Vertebral Joint **3** Lumbosacral Joint **5** Sacrococcygeal Joint **6** Coccygeal Joint **7** Sacroiliac Joint, Right **8** Sacroiliac Joint, Left	**0** Open **3** Percutaneous **4** Percutaneous Endoscopic	**0** Drainage Device **3** Infusion Device **4** Internal Fixation Device **7** Autologous Tissue Substitute **8** Spacer **J** Synthetic Substitute **K** Nonautologous Tissue Substitute	**Z** No Qualifier
0 Lumbar Vertebral Joint **3** Lumbosacral Joint **5** Sacrococcygeal Joint **6** Coccygeal Joint **7** Sacroiliac Joint, Right **8** Sacroiliac Joint, Left	**X** External	**0** Drainage Device **3** Infusion Device **4** Internal Fixation Device	**Z** No Qualifier
2 Lumbar Vertebral Disc **4** Lumbosacral Disc	**0** Open **3** Percutaneous **4** Percutaneous Endoscopic	**0** Drainage Device **3** Infusion Device **7** Autologous Tissue Substitute **J** Synthetic Substitute **K** Nonautologous Tissue Substitute	**Z** No Qualifier
2 Lumbar Vertebral Disc **4** Lumbosacral Disc	**X** External	**0** Drainage Device **3** Infusion Device	**Z** No Qualifier
9 Hip Joint, Right **B** Hip Joint, Left	**0** Open	**0** Drainage Device **3** Infusion Device **4** Internal Fixation Device **5** External Fixation Device **7** Autologous Tissue Substitute **8** Spacer **9** Liner **B** Resurfacing Device **J** Synthetic Substitute **K** Nonautologous Tissue Substitute	**Z** No Qualifier
9 Hip Joint, Right **B** Hip Joint, Left **C** Knee Joint, Right **D** Knee Joint, Left	**3** Percutaneous **4** Percutaneous Endoscopic	**0** Drainage Device **3** Infusion Device **4** Internal Fixation Device **5** External Fixation Device **7** Autologous Tissue Substitute **8** Spacer **J** Synthetic Substitute **K** Nonautologous Tissue Substitute	**Z** No Qualifier

Continued on next page

0   Medical and Surgical
S   Lower Joints
P   Removal: Taking out or off a device from a body part

Continued from previous page

Body Part Character 4	Approach Character 5	Device Character 6	Qualifier Character 7
9 Hip Joint, Right B Hip Joint, Left C Knee Joint, Right D Knee Joint, Left F Ankle Joint, Right G Ankle Joint, Left H Tarsal Joint, Right J Tarsal Joint, Left K Metatarsal-Tarsal Joint, Right L Metatarsal-Tarsal Joint, Left M Metatarsal-Phalangeal Joint, Right N Metatarsal-Phalangeal Joint, Left P Toe Phalangeal Joint, Right Q Toe Phalangeal Joint, Left	X External	0 Drainage Device 3 Infusion Device 4 Internal Fixation Device 5 External Fixation Device	Z No Qualifier
C Knee Joint, Right D Knee Joint, Left	0 Open	0 Drainage Device 3 Infusion Device 4 Internal Fixation Device 5 External Fixation Device 7 Autologous Tissue Substitute 8 Spacer 9 Liner J Synthetic Substitute K Nonautologous Tissue Substitute	Z No Qualifier
F Ankle Joint, Right G Ankle Joint, Left H Tarsal Joint, Right J Tarsal Joint, Left K Metatarsal-Tarsal Joint, Right L Metatarsal-Tarsal Joint, Left M Metatarsal-Phalangeal Joint, Right N Metatarsal-Phalangeal Joint, Left P Toe Phalangeal Joint, Right Q Toe Phalangeal Joint, Left	0 Open 3 Percutaneous 4 Percutaneous Endoscopic	0 Drainage Device 3 Infusion Device 4 Internal Fixation Device 5 External Fixation Device 7 Autologous Tissue Substitute 8 Spacer J Synthetic Substitute K Nonautologous Tissue Substitute	Z No Qualifier

0   Medical and Surgical
S   Lower Joints
Q   Repair: Restoring, to the extent possible, a body part to its normal anatomic structure and function

Body Part Character 4	Approach Character 5	Device Character 6	Qualifier Character 7
0 Lumbar Vertebral Joint 2 Lumbar Vertebral Disc 3 Lumbosacral Joint 4 Lumbosacral Disc 5 Sacrococcygeal Joint 6 Coccygeal Joint 7 Sacroiliac Joint, Right 8 Sacroiliac Joint, Left 9 Hip Joint, Right B Hip Joint, Left C Knee Joint, Right D Knee Joint, Left F Ankle Joint, Right G Ankle Joint, Left H Tarsal Joint, Right J Tarsal Joint, Left K Metatarsal-Tarsal Joint, Right L Metatarsal-Tarsal Joint, Left M Metatarsal-Phalangeal Joint, Right N Metatarsal-Phalangeal Joint, Left P Toe Phalangeal Joint, Right Q Toe Phalangeal Joint, Left	0 Open 3 Percutaneous 4 Percutaneous Endoscopic X External	Z No Device	Z No Qualifier

0 Medical and Surgical
S Lower Joints
R Replacement: Putting in or on biological or synthetic material that physically takes the place and/or function of all or a portion of a body part

Body Part Character 4	Approach Character 5	Device Character 6	Qualifier Character 7
0 Lumbar Vertebral Joint 3 Lumbosacral Joint	0 Open	J Synthetic Substitute	4 Facet Z No Qualifier
0 Lumbar Vertebral Joint 3 Lumbosacral Joint 9 Hip Joint, Right B Hip Joint, Left	0 Open	7 Autologous Tissue Substitute K Nonautologous Tissue Substitute	Z No Qualifier
2 Lumbar Vertebral Disc 4 Lumbosacral Disc 5 Sacrococcygeal Joint 6 Coccygeal Joint 7 Sacroiliac Joint, Right 8 Sacroiliac Joint, Left C Knee Joint, Right D Knee Joint, Left F Ankle Joint, Right G Ankle Joint, Left H Tarsal Joint, Right J Tarsal Joint, Left K Metatarsal-Tarsal Joint, Right L Metatarsal-Tarsal Joint, Left M Metatarsal-Phalangeal Joint, Right N Metatarsal-Phalangeal Joint, Left P Toe Phalangeal Joint, Right Q Toe Phalangeal Joint, Left	0 Open	7 Autologous Tissue Substitute J Synthetic Substitute K Nonautologous Tissue Substitute	Z No Qualifier
9 Hip Joint, Right B Hip Joint, Left	0 Open	J Synthetic Substitute	5 Metal on Polyethylene 6 Metal on Metal 7 Ceramic on Ceramic 8 Ceramic on Polyethylene Z No Qualifier

0 Medical and Surgical
S Lower Joints
S Reposition: Moving to its normal location or other suitable location all or a portion of a body part

Body Part Character 4	Approach Character 5	Device Character 6	Qualifier Character 7
0 Lumbar Vertebral Joint 3 Lumbosacral Joint 5 Sacrococcygeal Joint 6 Coccygeal Joint 7 Sacroiliac Joint, Right 8 Sacroiliac Joint, Left	0 Open 3 Percutaneous 4 Percutaneous Endoscopic X External	4 Internal Fixation Device Z No Device	Z No Qualifier
9 Hip Joint, Right B Hip Joint, Left C Knee Joint, Right D Knee Joint, Left F Ankle Joint, Right G Ankle Joint, Left H Tarsal Joint, Right J Tarsal Joint, Left K Metatarsal-Tarsal Joint, Right L Metatarsal-Tarsal Joint, Left M Metatarsal-Phalangeal Joint, Right N Metatarsal-Phalangeal Joint, Left P Toe Phalangeal Joint, Right Q Toe Phalangeal Joint, Left	0 Open 3 Percutaneous 4 Percutaneous Endoscopic X External	4 Internal Fixation Device 5 External Fixation Device Z No Device	Z No Qualifier

0   **Medical and Surgical**
S   **Lower Joints**
T   **Resection:**   Cutting out or off, without replacement, all of a body part

Body Part Character 4	Approach Character 5	Device Character 6	Qualifier Character 7
2 Lumbar Vertebral Disc **4** Lumbosacral Disc **5** Sacrococcygeal Joint **6** Coccygeal Joint **7** Sacroiliac Joint, Right **8** Sacroiliac Joint, Left **9** Hip Joint, Right **B** Hip Joint, Left **C** Knee Joint, Right **D** Knee Joint, Left **F** Ankle Joint, Right **G** Ankle Joint, Left **H** Tarsal Joint, Right **J** Tarsal Joint, Left **K** Metatarsal-Tarsal Joint, Right **L** Metatarsal-Tarsal Joint, Left **M** Metatarsal-Phalangeal Joint, Right **N** Metatarsal-Phalangeal Joint, Left **P** Toe Phalangeal Joint, Right **Q** Toe Phalangeal Joint, Left	**0** Open	**Z** No Device	**Z** No Qualifier

0   **Medical and Surgical**
S   **Lower Joints**
U   **Supplement:**   Putting in or on biological or synthetic material that physically reinforces and/or augments the function of a portion of a body part

Body Part Character 4	Approach Character 5	Device Character 6	Qualifier Character 7
0 Lumbar Vertebral Joint **3** Lumbosacral Joint	**0** Open	**7** Autologous Tissue Substitute **K** Nonautologous Tissue Substitute	**Z** No Qualifier
0 Lumbar Vertebral Joint **3** Lumbosacral Joint	**0** Open	**J** Synthetic Substitute	**4** Facet **Z** No Qualifier
2 Lumbar Vertebral Disc **4** Lumbosacral Disc **5** Sacrococcygeal Joint **6** Coccygeal Joint **7** Sacroiliac Joint, Right **8** Sacroiliac Joint, Left **9** Hip Joint, Right **B** Hip Joint, Left **C** Knee Joint, Right **D** Knee Joint, Left **F** Ankle Joint, Right **G** Ankle Joint, Left **H** Tarsal Joint, Right **J** Tarsal Joint, Left **K** Metatarsal-Tarsal Joint, Right **L** Metatarsal-Tarsal Joint, Left **M** Metatarsal-Phalangeal Joint, Right **N** Metatarsal-Phalangeal Joint, Left **P** Toe Phalangeal Joint, Right **Q** Toe Phalangeal Joint, Left	**0** Open	**7** Autologous Tissue Substitute **J** Synthetic Substitute **K** Nonautologous Tissue Substitute	**Z** No Qualifier
9 Hip Joint, Right **B** Hip Joint, Left	**0** Open	**9** Liner **B** Resurfacing Device	**9** Acetabular Surface **B** Femoral Surface **Z** No Qualifier
C Knee Joint, Right **D** Knee Joint, Left	**0** Open	**9** Liner	**C** Patellar Surface **D** Tibial Surface **Z** No Qualifier

0 **Medical and Surgical**
S **Lower Joints**
W **Revision:**   Correcting, to the extent possible, a malfunctioning or displaced device

Body Part Character 4	Approach Character 5	Device Character 6	Qualifier Character 7
0 Lumbar Vertebral Joint 3 Lumbosacral Joint 5 Sacrococcygeal Joint 6 Coccygeal Joint 7 Sacroiliac Joint, Right 8 Sacroiliac Joint, Left	0 Open 3 Percutaneous 4 Percutaneous Endoscopic X External	0 Drainage Device 3 Infusion Device 4 Internal Fixation Device 7 Autologous Tissue Substitute 8 Spacer J Synthetic Substitute K Nonautologous Tissue Substitute	Z No Qualifier
2 Lumbar Vertebral Disc 4 Lumbosacral Disc	0 Open 3 Percutaneous 4 Percutaneous Endoscopic X External	0 Drainage Device 3 Infusion Device 7 Autologous Tissue Substitute J Synthetic Substitute K Nonautologous Tissue Substitute	Z No Qualifier
9 Hip Joint, Right B Hip Joint, Left	0 Open	0 Drainage Device 3 Infusion Device 4 Internal Fixation Device 5 External Fixation Device 7 Autologous Tissue Substitute 8 Spacer 9 Liner B Resurfacing Device J Synthetic Substitute K Nonautologous Tissue Substitute	Z No Qualifier
9 Hip Joint, Right B Hip Joint, Left C Knee Joint, Right D Knee Joint, Left	3 Percutaneous 4 Percutaneous Endoscopic X External	0 Drainage Device 3 Infusion Device 4 Internal Fixation Device 5 External Fixation Device 7 Autologous Tissue Substitute 8 Spacer J Synthetic Substitute K Nonautologous Tissue Substitute	Z No Qualifier
C Knee Joint, Right D Knee Joint, Left	0 Open	0 Drainage Device 3 Infusion Device 4 Internal Fixation Device 5 External Fixation Device 7 Autologous Tissue Substitute 8 Spacer 9 Liner J Synthetic Substitute K Nonautologous Tissue Substitute	Z No Qualifier
F Ankle Joint, Right G Ankle Joint, Left H Tarsal Joint, Right J Tarsal Joint, Left K Metatarsal-Tarsal Joint, Right L Metatarsal-Tarsal Joint, Left M Metatarsal-Phalangeal Joint, Right N Metatarsal-Phalangeal Joint, Left P Toe Phalangeal Joint, Right Q Toe Phalangeal Joint, Left	0 Open 3 Percutaneous 4 Percutaneous Endoscopic X External	0 Drainage Device 3 Infusion Device 4 Internal Fixation Device 5 External Fixation Device 7 Autologous Tissue Substitute 8 Spacer J Synthetic Substitute K Nonautologous Tissue Substitute	Z No Qualifier

Urinary System 0T1–0TY

0   **Medical and Surgical**
T   **Urinary System**
1   **Bypass:**   Altering the route of passage of the contents of a tubular body part

Body Part Character 4	Approach Character 5	Device Character 6	Qualifier Character 7
3 Kidney Pelvis, Right 4 Kidney Pelvis, Left	0 Open 4 Percutaneous Endoscopic	7 Autologous Tissue Substitute J Synthetic Substitute K Nonautologous Tissue Substitute Z No Device	3 Kidney Pelvis, Right 4 Kidney Pelvis, Left 6 Ureter, Right 7 Ureter, Left 8 Colon 9 Colocutaneous A Ileum B Bladder C Ileocutaneous D Cutaneous
3 Kidney Pelvis, Right 4 Kidney Pelvis, Left 6 Ureter, Right 7 Ureter, Left 8 Ureters, Bilateral B Bladder	3 Percutaneous	J Synthetic Substitute	D Cutaneous
6 Ureter, Right 7 Ureter, Left 8 Ureters, Bilateral	0 Open 4 Percutaneous Endoscopic	7 Autologous Tissue Substitute J Synthetic Substitute K Nonautologous Tissue Substitute Z No Device	6 Ureter, Right 7 Ureter, Left 8 Colon 9 Colocutaneous A Ileum B Bladder C Ileocutaneous D Cutaneous
B Bladder	0 Open 4 Percutaneous Endoscopic	7 Autologous Tissue Substitute J Synthetic Substitute K Nonautologous Tissue Substitute Z No Device	9 Colocutaneous C Ileocutaneous D Cutaneous

0   **Medical and Surgical**
T   **Urinary System**
2   **Change:**   Taking out or off a device from a body part and putting back an identical or similar device in or on the same body part without cutting or puncturing the skin or a mucous membrane

Body Part Character 4	Approach Character 5	Device Character 6	Qualifier Character 7
5 Kidney 9 Ureter B Bladder D Urethra	X External	0 Drainage Device Y Other Device	Z No Qualifier

0   **Medical and Surgical**
T   **Urinary System**
5   **Destruction:**   Physical eradication of all or a portion of a body part by the direct use of energy, force, or a destructive agent

Body Part Character 4	Approach Character 5	Device Character 6	Qualifier Character 7
0 Kidney, Right 1 Kidney, Left 3 Kidney Pelvis, Right 4 Kidney Pelvis, Left 6 Ureter, Right 7 Ureter, Left B Bladder C Bladder Neck	0 Open 3 Percutaneous 4 Percutaneous Endoscopic 7 Via Natural or Artificial Opening 8 Via Natural or Artificial Opening Endoscopic	Z No Device	Z No Qualifier
D Urethra	0 Open 3 Percutaneous 4 Percutaneous Endoscopic 7 Via Natural or Artificial Opening 8 Via Natural or Artificial Opening Endoscopic X External	Z No Device	Z No Qualifier

0 Medical and Surgical
T Urinary System
7 Dilation: Expanding an orifice or the lumen of a tubular body part

Body Part Character 4	Approach Character 5	Device Character 6	Qualifier Character 7
3 Kidney Pelvis, Right 4 Kidney Pelvis, Left 6 Ureter, Right 7 Ureter, Left 8 Ureters, Bilateral B Bladder C Bladder Neck D Urethra	0 Open 3 Percutaneous 4 Percutaneous Endoscopic 7 Via Natural or Artificial Opening 8 Via Natural or Artificial Opening Endoscopic	D Intraluminal Device Z No Device	Z No Qualifier

0 Medical and Surgical
T Urinary System
8 Division: Cutting into a body part without draining fluids and/or gases from the body part in order to separate or transect a body part

Body Part Character 4	Approach Character 5	Device Character 6	Qualifier Character 7
2 Kidneys, Bilateral C Bladder Neck	0 Open 3 Percutaneous 4 Percutaneous Endoscopic	Z No Device	Z No Qualifier

0 Medical and Surgical
T Urinary System
9 Drainage: Taking or letting out fluids and/or gases from a body part

Body Part Character 4	Approach Character 5	Device Character 6	Qualifier Character 7
0 Kidney, Right 1 Kidney, Left 3 Kidney Pelvis, Right 4 Kidney Pelvis, Left 6 Ureter, Right 7 Ureter, Left 8 Ureters, Bilateral B Bladder C Bladder Neck	0 Open 3 Percutaneous 4 Percutaneous Endoscopic 7 Via Natural or Artificial Opening 8 Via Natural or Artificial Opening Endoscopic	0 Drainage Device	Z No Qualifier
0 Kidney, Right 1 Kidney, Left 3 Kidney Pelvis, Right 4 Kidney Pelvis, Left 6 Ureter, Right 7 Ureter, Left 8 Ureters, Bilateral B Bladder C Bladder Neck	0 Open 3 Percutaneous 4 Percutaneous Endoscopic 7 Via Natural or Artificial Opening 8 Via Natural or Artificial Opening Endoscopic	Z No Device	X Diagnostic Z No Qualifier
D Urethra	0 Open 3 Percutaneous 4 Percutaneous Endoscopic 7 Via Natural or Artificial Opening 8 Via Natural or Artificial Opening Endoscopic X External	0 Drainage Device	Z No Qualifier
D Urethra	0 Open 3 Percutaneous 4 Percutaneous Endoscopic 7 Via Natural or Artificial Opening 8 Via Natural or Artificial Opening Endoscopic X External	Z No Device	X Diagnostic Z No Qualifier

0 Medical and Surgical
T Urinary System
B Excision: Cutting out or off, without replacement, a portion of a body part

Body Part Character 4	Approach Character 5	Device Character 6	Qualifier Character 7
0 Kidney, Right 1 Kidney, Left 3 Kidney Pelvis, Right 4 Kidney Pelvis, Left 6 Ureter, Right 7 Ureter, Left B Bladder C Bladder Neck	0 Open 3 Percutaneous 4 Percutaneous Endoscopic 7 Via Natural or Artificial Opening 8 Via Natural or Artificial Opening Endoscopic	Z No Device	X Diagnostic Z No Qualifier
D Urethra	0 Open 3 Percutaneous 4 Percutaneous Endoscopic 7 Via Natural or Artificial Opening 8 Via Natural or Artificial Opening Endoscopic X External	Z No Device	X Diagnostic Z No Qualifier

0 Medical and Surgical
T Urinary System
C Extirpation: Taking or cutting out solid matter from a body part

Body Part Character 4	Approach Character 5	Device Character 6	Qualifier Character 7
0 Kidney, Right 1 Kidney, Left 3 Kidney Pelvis, Right 4 Kidney Pelvis, Left 6 Ureter, Right 7 Ureter, Left B Bladder C Bladder Neck	0 Open 3 Percutaneous 4 Percutaneous Endoscopic 7 Via Natural or Artificial Opening 8 Via Natural or Artificial Opening Endoscopic	Z No Device	Z No Qualifier
D Urethra	0 Open 3 Percutaneous 4 Percutaneous Endoscopic 7 Via Natural or Artificial Opening 8 Via Natural or Artificial Opening Endoscopic X External	Z No Device	Z No Qualifier

0 Medical and Surgical
T Urinary System
D Extraction: Pulling or stripping out or off all or a portion of a body part by the use of force

Body Part Character 4	Approach Character 5	Device Character 6	Qualifier Character 7
0 Kidney, Right 1 Kidney, Left	0 Open 3 Percutaneous 4 Percutaneous Endoscopic	Z No Device	Z No Qualifier

0 Medical and Surgical
T Urinary System
F Fragmentation: Breaking solid matter in a body part into pieces

Body Part Character 4	Approach Character 5	Device Character 6	Qualifier Character 7
3 Kidney Pelvis, Right 4 Kidney Pelvis, Left 6 Ureter, Right 7 Ureter, Left B Bladder C Bladder Neck D Urethra	0 Open 3 Percutaneous 4 Percutaneous Endoscopic 7 Via Natural or Artificial Opening 8 Via Natural or Artificial Opening Endoscopic X External	Z No Device	Z No Qualifier

     Draft (2009)

0   **Medical and Surgical**
T   **Urinary System**
H   **Insertion:**   Putting in a nonbiological appliance that monitors, assists, performs or prevents a physiological function, but does not physically take the place of a body part

Body Part Character 4	Approach Character 5	Device Character 6	Qualifier Character 7
5 Kidney 9 Ureter	0 Open 3 Percutaneous 4 Percutaneous Endoscopic 7 Via Natural or Artificial Opening 8 Via Natural or Artificial Opening Endoscopic	2 Monitoring Device 3 Infusion Device M Electrode	Z No Qualifier
B Bladder	0 Open 3 Percutaneous 4 Percutaneous Endoscopic 7 Via Natural or Artificial Opening 8 Via Natural or Artificial Opening Endoscopic	2 Monitoring Device 3 Infusion Device L Artificial Sphincter M Electrode	Z No Qualifier
C Bladder Neck	0 Open 3 Percutaneous 4 Percutaneous Endoscopic 7 Via Natural or Artificial Opening 8 Via Natural or Artificial Opening Endoscopic	L Artificial Sphincter	Z No Qualifier
D Urethra	0 Open 3 Percutaneous 4 Percutaneous Endoscopic 7 Via Natural or Artificial Opening 8 Via Natural or Artificial Opening Endoscopic X External	2 Monitoring Device 3 Infusion Device L Artificial Sphincter M Electrode	Z No Qualifier

0   **Medical and Surgical**
T   **Urinary System**
J   **Inspection:**   Visually and/or manually exploring a body part

Body Part Character 4	Approach Character 5	Device Character 6	Qualifier Character 7
0 Kidney, Right 1 Kidney, Left 2 Kidneys, Bilateral 3 Kidney Pelvis, Right 4 Kidney Pelvis, Left 6 Ureter, Right 7 Ureter, Left 8 Ureters, Bilateral B Bladder C Bladder Neck D Urethra	0 Open 3 Percutaneous 4 Percutaneous Endoscopic 7 Via Natural or Artificial Opening 8 Via Natural or Artificial Opening Endoscopic X External	Z No Device	Z No Qualifier

0   **Medical and Surgical**
T   **Urinary System**
L   **Occlusion:**   Completely closing an orifice or lumen of a tubular body part

Body Part Character 4	Approach Character 5	Device Character 6	Qualifier Character 7
3 Kidney Pelvis, Right 4 Kidney Pelvis, Left 6 Ureter, Right 7 Ureter, Left B Bladder C Bladder Neck	0 Open 3 Percutaneous 4 Percutaneous Endoscopic	C Extraluminal Device D Intraluminal Device Z No Device	Z No Qualifier
3 Kidney Pelvis, Right 4 Kidney Pelvis, Left 6 Ureter, Right 7 Ureter, Left B Bladder C Bladder Neck D Urethra	7 Via Natural or Artificial Opening 8 Via Natural or Artificial Opening Endoscopic	D Intraluminal Device Z No Device	Z No Qualifier
D Urethra	0 Open 3 Percutaneous 4 Percutaneous Endoscopic X External	C Extraluminal Device D Intraluminal Device Z No Device	Z No Qualifier

0 Medical and Surgical
T Urinary System
M Reattachment: Putting back in or on all or a portion of a separated body part to its normal location or other suitable location

Body Part Character 4	Approach Character 5	Device Character 6	Qualifier Character 7
0 Kidney, Right **1** Kidney, Left **2** Kidneys, Bilateral **3** Kidney Pelvis, Right **4** Kidney Pelvis, Left **6** Ureter, Right **7** Ureter, Left **8** Ureters, Bilateral **B** Bladder **C** Bladder Neck **D** Urethra	**0** Open **4** Percutaneous Endoscopic	**Z** No Device	**Z** No Qualifier

0 Medical and Surgical
T Urinary System
N Release: Freeing a body part from an abnormal physical constraint

Body Part Character 4	Approach Character 5	Device Character 6	Qualifier Character 7
0 Kidney, Right **1** Kidney, Left **3** Kidney Pelvis, Right **4** Kidney Pelvis, Left **6** Ureter, Right **7** Ureter, Left **B** Bladder **C** Bladder Neck	**0** Open **3** Percutaneous **4** Percutaneous Endoscopic **7** Via Natural or Artificial Opening **8** Via Natural or Artificial Opening Endoscopic	**Z** No Device	**Z** No Qualifier
D Urethra	**0** Open **3** Percutaneous **4** Percutaneous Endoscopic **7** Via Natural or Artificial Opening **8** Via Natural or Artificial Opening Endoscopic **X** External	**Z** No Device	**Z** No Qualifier

0 Medical and Surgical
T Urinary System
P Removal: Taking out or off a device from a body part

Body Part Character 4	Approach Character 5	Device Character 6	Qualifier Character 7
5 Kidney **9** Ureter	**0** Open **3** Percutaneous **4** Percutaneous Endoscopic **7** Via Natural or Artificial Opening **8** Via Natural or Artificial Opening Endoscopic	**0** Drainage Device **2** Monitoring Device **3** Infusion Device **7** Autologous Tissue Substitute **C** Extraluminal Device **D** Intraluminal Device **J** Synthetic Substitute **K** Nonautologous Tissue Substitute **M** Electrode	**Z** No Qualifier
5 Kidney **9** Ureter	**X** External	**0** Drainage Device **2** Monitoring Device **3** Infusion Device **D** Intraluminal Device **M** Electrode	**Z** No Qualifier
B Bladder **D** Urethra	**0** Open **3** Percutaneous **4** Percutaneous Endoscopic **7** Via Natural or Artificial Opening **8** Via Natural or Artificial Opening Endoscopic	**0** Drainage Device **2** Monitoring Device **3** Infusion Device **7** Autologous Tissue Substitute **C** Extraluminal Device **D** Intraluminal Device **J** Synthetic Substitute **K** Nonautologous Tissue Substitute **L** Artificial Sphincter **M** Electrode	**Z** No Qualifier
B Bladder **D** Urethra	**X** External	**0** Drainage Device **2** Monitoring Device **3** Infusion Device **D** Intraluminal Device **L** Artificial Sphincter **M** Electrode	**Z** No Qualifier

0   Medical and Surgical
T   Urinary System
Q   Repair: Restoring, to the extent possible, a body part to its normal anatomic structure and function

Body Part Character 4	Approach Character 5	Device Character 6	Qualifier Character 7
0 Kidney, Right 1 Kidney, Left 3 Kidney Pelvis, Right 4 Kidney Pelvis, Left 6 Ureter, Right 7 Ureter, Left B Bladder C Bladder Neck	0 Open 3 Percutaneous 4 Percutaneous Endoscopic 7 Via Natural or Artificial Opening 8 Via Natural or Artificial Opening Endoscopic	Z No Device	Z No Qualifier
D Urethra	0 Open 3 Percutaneous 4 Percutaneous Endoscopic 7 Via Natural or Artificial Opening 8 Via Natural or Artificial Opening Endoscopic X External	Z No Device	Z No Qualifier

0   Medical and Surgical
T   Urinary System
R   Replacement: Putting in or on biological or synthetic material that physically takes the place and/or function of all or a portion of a body part

Body Part Character 4	Approach Character 5	Device Character 6	Qualifier Character 7
3 Kidney Pelvis, Right 4 Kidney Pelvis, Left 6 Ureter, Right 7 Ureter, Left B Bladder C Bladder Neck	0 Open 4 Percutaneous Endoscopic 7 Via Natural or Artificial Opening 8 Via Natural or Artificial Opening Endoscopic	7 Autologous Tissue Substitute J Synthetic Substitute K Nonautologous Tissue Substitute	Z No Qualifier
D Urethra	0 Open 4 Percutaneous Endoscopic 7 Via Natural or Artificial Opening 8 Via Natural or Artificial Opening Endoscopic X External	7 Autologous Tissue Substitute J Synthetic Substitute K Nonautologous Tissue Substitute	Z No Qualifier

0   Medical and Surgical
T   Urinary System
S   Reposition: Moving to its normal location or other suitable location all or a portion of a body part

Body Part Character 4	Approach Character 5	Device Character 6	Qualifier Character 7
0 Kidney, Right 1 Kidney, Left 2 Kidneys, Bilateral 3 Kidney Pelvis, Right 4 Kidney Pelvis, Left 6 Ureter, Right 7 Ureter, Left 8 Ureters, Bilateral B Bladder C Bladder Neck D Urethra	0 Open 4 Percutaneous Endoscopic	Z No Device	Z No Qualifier

0   Medical and Surgical
T   Urinary System
T   Resection: Cutting out or off, without replacement, all of a body part

Body Part Character 4	Approach Character 5	Device Character 6	Qualifier Character 7
0 Kidney, Right 1 Kidney, Left 2 Kidneys, Bilateral	0 Open 4 Percutaneous Endoscopic	Z No Device	Z No Qualifier
3 Kidney Pelvis, Right 4 Kidney Pelvis, Left 6 Ureter, Right 7 Ureter, Left B Bladder C Bladder Neck D Urethra	0 Open 4 Percutaneous Endoscopic 7 Via Natural or Artificial Opening 8 Via Natural or Artificial Opening Endoscopic	Z No Device	Z No Qualifier

0   Medical and Surgical
T   Urinary System
U   Supplement: Putting in or on biological or synthetic material that physically reinforces and/or augments the function of a portion of a body part

Body Part Character 4	Approach Character 5	Device Character 6	Qualifier Character 7
3 Kidney Pelvis, Right **4** Kidney Pelvis, Left **6** Ureter, Right **7** Ureter, Left **B** Bladder **C** Bladder Neck	**0** Open **4** Percutaneous Endoscopic **7** Via Natural or Artificial Opening **8** Via Natural or Artificial Opening Endoscopic	**7** Autologous Tissue Substitute **J** Synthetic Substitute **K** Nonautologous Tissue Substitute	**Z** No Qualifier
D Urethra	**0** Open **4** Percutaneous Endoscopic **7** Via Natural or Artificial Opening **8** Via Natural or Artificial Opening Endoscopic **X** External	**7** Autologous Tissue Substitute **J** Synthetic Substitute **K** Nonautologous Tissue Substitute	**Z** No Qualifier

0   Medical and Surgical
T   Urinary System
V   Restriction: Partially closing the orifice or lumen of a tubular body part

Body Part Character 4	Approach Character 5	Device Character 6	Qualifier Character 7
3 Kidney Pelvis, Right **4** Kidney Pelvis, Left **6** Ureter, Right **7** Ureter, Left **B** Bladder **C** Bladder Neck **D** Urethra	**0** Open **3** Percutaneous **4** Percutaneous Endoscopic	**C** Extraluminal Device **D** Intraluminal Device **Z** No Device	**Z** No Qualifier
3 Kidney Pelvis, Right **4** Kidney Pelvis, Left **6** Ureter, Right **7** Ureter, Left **B** Bladder **C** Bladder Neck **D** Urethra	**7** Via Natural or Artificial Opening **8** Via Natural or Artificial Opening Endoscopic	**D** Intraluminal Device **Z** No Device	**Z** No Qualifier
D Urethra	**X** External	**Z** No Device	**Z** No Qualifier

0   Medical and Surgical
T   Urinary System
W   Revision: Correcting, to the extent possible, a malfunctioning or displaced device

Body Part Character 4	Approach Character 5	Device Character 6	Qualifier Character 7
5 Kidney **9** Ureter	**0** Open **3** Percutaneous **4** Percutaneous Endoscopic **7** Via Natural or Artificial Opening **8** Via Natural or Artificial Opening Endoscopic **X** External	**0** Drainage Device **2** Monitoring Device **3** Infusion Device **7** Autologous Tissue Substitute **C** Extraluminal Device **D** Intraluminal Device **J** Synthetic Substitute **K** Nonautologous Tissue Substitute **M** Electrode	**Z** No Qualifier
B Bladder **D** Urethra	**0** Open **3** Percutaneous **4** Percutaneous Endoscopic **7** Via Natural or Artificial Opening **8** Via Natural or Artificial Opening Endoscopic **X** External	**0** Drainage Device **2** Monitoring Device **3** Infusion Device **7** Autologous Tissue Substitute **C** Extraluminal Device **D** Intraluminal Device **J** Synthetic Substitute **K** Nonautologous Tissue Substitute **L** Artificial Sphincter **M** Electrode	**Z** No Qualifier

0   Medical and Surgical
T   Urinary System
X   Transfer: Moving, without taking out, all or a portion of a body part to another location to take over the function of all or a portion of a body part

Body Part Character 4	Approach Character 5	Device Character 6	Qualifier Character 7
0 Kidney, Right **1** Kidney, Left	**0** Open	**Z** No Device	**Z** No Qualifier

0   Medical and Surgical
T   Urinary System
Y   Transplantation: Putting in or on all or a portion of a living body part taken from another individual or animal to
physically take the place and/or function of all or a portion of a similar body part

Body Part Character 4	Approach Character 5	Device Character 6	Qualifier Character 7
0 Kidney, Right **1** Kidney, Left	**0** Open	**Z** No Device	**0** Allogeneic **1** Syngeneic **2** Zooplastic

Female Reproductive System 0U1–0UY

0 Medical and Surgical
U Female Reproductive System
1 Bypass: Altering the route of passage of the contents of a tubular body part

Body Part Character 4	Approach Character 5	Device Character 6	Qualifier Character 7
5 Fallopian Tube, Right 6 Fallopian Tube, Left	0 Open 4 Percutaneous Endoscopic	7 Autologous Tissue Substitute J Synthetic Substitute K Nonautologous Tissue Substitute Z No Device	5 Fallopian Tube, Right 6 Fallopian Tube, Left 9 Uterus

0 Medical and Surgical
U Female Reproductive System
2 Change: Taking out or off a device from a body part and putting back an identical or similar device in or on the same body part without cutting or puncturing the skin or a mucous membrane

Body Part Character 4	Approach Character 5	Device Character 6	Qualifier Character 7
3 Ovary 8 Fallopian Tube M Vulva	X External	0 Drainage Device Y Other Device	Z No Qualifier
D Uterus and Cervix	X External	0 Drainage Device H Contraceptive Device Y Other Device	Z No Qualifier
H Vagina and Cul-de-sac	X External	0 Drainage Device G Pessary Y Other Device	Z No Qualifier

0 Medical and Surgical
U Female Reproductive System
5 Destruction: Physical eradication of all or a portion of a body part by the direct use of energy, force, or a destructive agent

Body Part Character 4	Approach Character 5	Device Character 6	Qualifier Character 7
0 Ovary, Right 1 Ovary, Left 2 Ovaries, Bilateral 4 Uterine Supporting Structure	0 Open 3 Percutaneous 4 Percutaneous Endoscopic	Z No Device	Z No Qualifier
5 Fallopian Tube, Right 6 Fallopian Tube, Left 7 Fallopian Tubes, Bilateral 9 Uterus B Endometrium C Cervix F Cul-de-sac K Hymen	0 Open 3 Percutaneous 4 Percutaneous Endoscopic 7 Via Natural or Artificial Opening 8 Via Natural or Artificial Opening Endoscopic	Z No Device	Z No Qualifier
G Vagina	0 Open 3 Percutaneous 4 Percutaneous Endoscopic 7 Via Natural or Artificial Opening 8 Via Natural or Artificial Opening Endoscopic X External	Z No Device	Z No Qualifier
J Clitoris L Vestibular Gland M Vulva	0 Open X External	Z No Device	Z No Qualifier

0 Medical and Surgical
U Female Reproductive System
7 Dilation: Expanding an orifice or the lumen of a tubular body part

Body Part Character 4	Approach Character 5	Device Character 6	Qualifier Character 7
5 Fallopian Tube, Right 6 Fallopian Tube, Left 7 Fallopian Tubes, Bilateral 9 Uterus C Cervix G Vagina K Hymen	0 Open 3 Percutaneous 4 Percutaneous Endoscopic 7 Via Natural or Artificial Opening 8 Via Natural or Artificial Opening Endoscopic	D Intraluminal Device Z No Device	Z No Qualifier

0 **Medical and Surgical**
U **Female Reproductive System**
8 **Division:** Cutting into a body part without draining fluids and/or gases from the body part in order to separate or transect a body part

Body Part Character 4	Approach Character 5	Device Character 6	Qualifier Character 7
0 Ovary, Right **1** Ovary, Left **2** Ovaries, Bilateral **4** Uterine Supporting Structure	**0** Open **3** Percutaneous **4** Percutaneous Endoscopic	**Z** No Device	**Z** No Qualifier
K Hymen	**7** Via Natural or Artificial Opening **8** Via Natural or Artificial Opening Endoscopic	**Z** No Device	**Z** No Qualifier

0 **Medical and Surgical**
U **Female Reproductive System**
9 **Drainage:** Taking or letting out fluids and/or gases from a body part

Body Part Character 4	Approach Character 5	Device Character 6	Qualifier Character 7
0 Ovary, Right **1** Ovary, Left **2** Ovaries, Bilateral	**X** External	**Z** No Device	**Z** No Qualifier
0 Ovary, Right **1** Ovary, Left **2** Ovaries, Bilateral **4** Uterine Supporting Structure	**0** Open **3** Percutaneous **4** Percutaneous Endoscopic	**0** Drainage Device	**Z** No Qualifier
0 Ovary, Right **1** Ovary, Left **2** Ovaries, Bilateral **4** Uterine Supporting Structure	**0** Open **3** Percutaneous **4** Percutaneous Endoscopic	**Z** No Device	**X** Diagnostic **Z** No Qualifier
5 Fallopian Tube, Right **6** Fallopian Tube, Left **7** Fallopian Tubes, Bilateral **9** Uterus **C** Cervix **F** Cul-de-sac **K** Hymen	**0** Open **3** Percutaneous **4** Percutaneous Endoscopic **7** Via Natural or Artificial Opening **8** Via Natural or Artificial Opening Endoscopic	**0** Drainage Device	**Z** No Qualifier
5 Fallopian Tube, Right **6** Fallopian Tube, Left **7** Fallopian Tubes, Bilateral **9** Uterus **C** Cervix **F** Cul-de-sac **K** Hymen	**0** Open **3** Percutaneous **4** Percutaneous Endoscopic **7** Via Natural or Artificial Opening **8** Via Natural or Artificial Opening Endoscopic	**Z** No Device	**X** Diagnostic **Z** No Qualifier
G Vagina	**0** Open **3** Percutaneous **4** Percutaneous Endoscopic **7** Via Natural or Artificial Opening **8** Via Natural or Artificial Opening Endoscopic **X** External	**0** Drainage Device	**Z** No Qualifier
G Vagina	**0** Open **3** Percutaneous **4** Percutaneous Endoscopic **7** Via Natural or Artificial Opening **8** Via Natural or Artificial Opening Endoscopic **X** External	**Z** No Device	**X** Diagnostic **Z** No Qualifier
J Clitoris **L** Vestibular Gland **M** Vulva	**0** Open **X** External	**0** Drainage Device	**Z** No Qualifier
J Clitoris **L** Vestibular Gland **M** Vulva	**0** Open **X** External	**Z** No Device	**X** Diagnostic **Z** No Qualifier

0 Medical and Surgical
U Female Reproductive System
B Excision: Cutting out or off, without replacement, a portion of a body part

Body Part Character 4	Approach Character 5	Device Character 6	Qualifier Character 7
0 Ovary, Right 1 Ovary, Left 2 Ovaries, Bilateral 4 Uterine Supporting Structure 5 Fallopian Tube, Right 6 Fallopian Tube, Left 7 Fallopian Tubes, Bilateral 9 Uterus C Cervix F Cul-de-sac K Hymen	0 Open 3 Percutaneous 4 Percutaneous Endoscopic 7 Via Natural or Artificial Opening 8 Via Natural or Artificial Opening Endoscopic	Z No Device	X Diagnostic Z No Qualifier
G Vagina	0 Open 3 Percutaneous 4 Percutaneous Endoscopic 7 Via Natural or Artificial Opening 8 Via Natural or Artificial Opening Endoscopic X External	Z No Device	X Diagnostic Z No Qualifier
J Clitoris L Vestibular Gland M Vulva	0 Open X External	Z No Device	X Diagnostic Z No Qualifier

0 Medical and Surgical
U Female Reproductive System
C Extirpation: Taking or cutting out solid matter from a body part

Body Part Character 4	Approach Character 5	Device Character 6	Qualifier Character 7
0 Ovary, Right 1 Ovary, Left 2 Ovaries, Bilateral 4 Uterine Supporting Structure	0 Open 3 Percutaneous 4 Percutaneous Endoscopic	Z No Device	Z No Qualifier
5 Fallopian Tube, Right 6 Fallopian Tube, Left 7 Fallopian Tubes, Bilateral 9 Uterus B Endometrium C Cervix F Cul-de-sac K Hymen	0 Open 3 Percutaneous 4 Percutaneous Endoscopic 7 Via Natural or Artificial Opening 8 Via Natural or Artificial Opening Endoscopic	Z No Device	Z No Qualifier
G Vagina	0 Open 3 Percutaneous 4 Percutaneous Endoscopic 7 Via Natural or Artificial Opening 8 Via Natural or Artificial Opening Endoscopic X External	Z No Device	Z No Qualifier
J Clitoris L Vestibular Gland M Vulva	0 Open X External	Z No Device	Z No Qualifier

0 Medical and Surgical
U Female Reproductive System
D Extraction: Pulling or stripping out or off all or a portion of a body part by the use of force

Body Part Character 4	Approach Character 5	Device Character 6	Qualifier Character 7
B Endometrium	7 Via Natural or Artificial Opening 8 Via Natural or Artificial Opening Endoscopic	Z No Device	X Diagnostic Z No Qualifier
N Ova	0 Open 3 Percutaneous 4 Percutaneous Endoscopic	Z No Device	Z No Qualifier

0   Medical and Surgical
U   Female Reproductive System
F   Fragmentation: Breaking solid matter in a body part into pieces

Body Part Character 4	Approach Character 5	Device Character 6	Qualifier Character 7
5 Fallopian Tube, Right 6 Fallopian Tube, Left 7 Fallopian Tubes, Bilateral 9 Uterus	0 Open 3 Percutaneous 4 Percutaneous Endoscopic 7 Via Natural or Artificial Opening 8 Via Natural or Artificial Opening Endoscopic X External	Z No Device	Z No Qualifier

0   Medical and Surgical
U   Female Reproductive System
H   Insertion: Putting in a nonbiological appliance that monitors, assists, performs or prevents a physiological function, but does not physically take the place of a body part

Body Part Character 4	Approach Character 5	Device Character 6	Qualifier Character 7
3 Ovary	0 Open 3 Percutaneous 4 Percutaneous Endoscopic	3 Infusion Device	Z No Qualifier
8 Fallopian Tube D Uterus and Cervix H Vagina and Cul-de-sac	0 Open 3 Percutaneous 4 Percutaneous Endoscopic 7 Via Natural or Artificial Opening 8 Via Natural or Artificial Opening Endoscopic	3 Infusion Device	Z No Qualifier
9 Uterus C Cervix	7 Via Natural or Artificial Opening 8 Via Natural or Artificial Opening Endoscopic	H Contraceptive Device	Z No Qualifier
F Cul-de-sac	7 Via Natural or Artificial Opening 8 Via Natural or Artificial Opening Endoscopic	G Pessary	Z No Qualifier
G Vagina	0 Open 3 Percutaneous 4 Percutaneous Endoscopic X External	1 Radioactive Element	Z No Qualifier
G Vagina	7 Via Natural or Artificial Opening 8 Via Natural or Artificial Opening Endoscopic	1 Radioactive Element G Pessary	Z No Qualifier

0   Medical and Surgical
U   Female Reproductive System
J   Inspection: Visually and/or manually exploring a body part

Body Part Character 4	Approach Character 5	Device Character 6	Qualifier Character 7
0 Ovary, Right 1 Ovary, Left 2 Ovaries, Bilateral 4 Uterine Supporting Structure	0 Open 3 Percutaneous 4 Percutaneous Endoscopic X External	Z No Device	Z No Qualifier
5 Fallopian Tube, Right 6 Fallopian Tube, Left 7 Fallopian Tubes, Bilateral 9 Uterus B Endometrium C Cervix F Cul-de-sac G Vagina K Hymen	0 Open 3 Percutaneous 4 Percutaneous Endoscopic 7 Via Natural or Artificial Opening 8 Via Natural or Artificial Opening Endoscopic X External	Z No Device	Z No Qualifier
J Clitoris L Vestibular Gland M Vulva	0 Open X External	Z No Device	Z No Qualifier

0   **Medical and Surgical**
U   **Female Reproductive System**
L   **Occlusion:**   Completely closing an orifice or lumen of a tubular body part

Body Part Character 4	Approach Character 5	Device Character 6	Qualifier Character 7
5 Fallopian Tube, Right **6** Fallopian Tube, Left **7** Fallopian Tubes, Bilateral	**0** Open **3** Percutaneous **4** Percutaneous Endoscopic	**C** Extraluminal Device **D** Intraluminal Device **Z** No Device	**Z** No Qualifier
5 Fallopian Tube, Right **6** Fallopian Tube, Left **7** Fallopian Tubes, Bilateral **F** Cul-de-sac **G** Vagina	**7** Via Natural or Artificial Opening **8** Via Natural or Artificial Opening Endoscopic	**D** Intraluminal Device **Z** No Device	**Z** No Qualifier

0   **Medical and Surgical**
U   **Female Reproductive System**
M   **Reattachment:**   Putting back in or on all or a portion of a separated body part to its normal location or other suitable location

Body Part Character 4	Approach Character 5	Device Character 6	Qualifier Character 7
0 Ovary, Right **1** Ovary, Left **2** Ovaries, Bilateral **4** Uterine Supporting Structure **5** Fallopian Tube, Right **6** Fallopian Tube, Left **7** Fallopian Tubes, Bilateral **9** Uterus **C** Cervix **F** Cul-de-sac **G** Vagina **K** Hymen	**0** Open **4** Percutaneous Endoscopic	**Z** No Device	**Z** No Qualifier
J Clitoris **M** Vulva	**X** External	**Z** No Device	**Z** No Qualifier

0   **Medical and Surgical**
U   **Female Reproductive System**
N   **Release:**   Freeing a body part from an abnormal physical constraint

Body Part Character 4	Approach Character 5	Device Character 6	Qualifier Character 7
0 Ovary, Right **1** Ovary, Left **2** Ovaries, Bilateral **4** Uterine Supporting Structure	**0** Open **3** Percutaneous **4** Percutaneous Endoscopic	**Z** No Device	**Z** No Qualifier
5 Fallopian Tube, Right **6** Fallopian Tube, Left **7** Fallopian Tubes, Bilateral **9** Uterus **C** Cervix **F** Cul-de-sac **K** Hymen	**0** Open **3** Percutaneous **4** Percutaneous Endoscopic **7** Via Natural or Artificial Opening **8** Via Natural or Artificial Opening Endoscopic	**Z** No Device	**Z** No Qualifier
G Vagina	**0** Open **3** Percutaneous **4** Percutaneous Endoscopic **7** Via Natural or Artificial Opening **8** Via Natural or Artificial Opening Endoscopic **X** External	**Z** No Device	**Z** No Qualifier
J Clitoris **L** Vestibular Gland **M** Vulva	**0** Open **X** External	**Z** No Device	**Z** No Qualifier

0   **Medical and Surgical**
U   **Female Reproductive System**
P   **Removal:**   Taking out or off a device from a body part

Body Part Character 4	Approach Character 5	Device Character 6	Qualifier Character 7
3 Ovary	**0** Open **3** Percutaneous **4** Percutaneous Endoscopic **X** External	**0** Drainage Device **3** Infusion Device	**Z** No Qualifier

Continued on next page

0   **Medical and Surgical**   *Continued from previous page*
U   **Female Reproductive System**
P   **Removal:**   Taking out or off a device from a body part

Body Part Character 4	Approach Character 5	Device Character 6	Qualifier Character 7
8 Fallopian Tube	0 Open 3 Percutaneous 4 Percutaneous Endoscopic 7 Via Natural or Artificial Opening 8 Via Natural or Artificial Opening Endoscopic	0 Drainage Device 3 Infusion Device 7 Autologous Tissue Substitute C Extraluminal Device D Intraluminal Device J Synthetic Substitute K Nonautologous Tissue Substitute	Z No Qualifier
8 Fallopian Tube	X External	0 Drainage Device 3 Infusion Device D Intraluminal Device	Z No Qualifier
D Uterus and Cervix	0 Open 3 Percutaneous 4 Percutaneous Endoscopic 7 Via Natural or Artificial Opening 8 Via Natural or Artificial Opening Endoscopic	0 Drainage Device 3 Infusion Device 7 Autologous Tissue Substitute C Extraluminal Device D Intraluminal Device H Contraceptive Device J Synthetic Substitute K Nonautologous Tissue Substitute	Z No Qualifier
D Uterus and Cervix	X External	0 Drainage Device 3 Infusion Device D Intraluminal Device H Contraceptive Device	Z No Qualifier
H Vagina and Cul-de-sac	0 Open 3 Percutaneous 4 Percutaneous Endoscopic 7 Via Natural or Artificial Opening 8 Via Natural or Artificial Opening Endoscopic	0 Drainage Device 3 Infusion Device 7 Autologous Tissue Substitute D Intraluminal Device G Pessary J Synthetic Substitute K Nonautologous Tissue Substitute	Z No Qualifier
H Vagina and Cul-de-sac	X External	0 Drainage Device 1 Radioactive Element 3 Infusion Device D Intraluminal Device G Pessary	Z No Qualifier
M Vulva	0 Open	0 Drainage Device 7 Autologous Tissue Substitute J Synthetic Substitute K Nonautologous Tissue Substitute	Z No Qualifier
M Vulva	X External	0 Drainage Device	Z No Qualifier

0   **Medical and Surgical**
U   **Female Reproductive System**
Q   **Repair:**   Restoring, to the extent possible, a body part to its normal anatomic structure and function

Body Part Character 4	Approach Character 5	Device Character 6	Qualifier Character 7
0 Ovary, Right 1 Ovary, Left 2 Ovaries, Bilateral 4 Uterine Supporting Structure	0 Open 3 Percutaneous 4 Percutaneous Endoscopic	Z No Device	Z No Qualifier
5 Fallopian Tube, Right 6 Fallopian Tube, Left 7 Fallopian Tubes, Bilateral 9 Uterus C Cervix F Cul-de-sac K Hymen	0 Open 3 Percutaneous 4 Percutaneous Endoscopic 7 Via Natural or Artificial Opening 8 Via Natural or Artificial Opening Endoscopic	Z No Device	Z No Qualifier
G Vagina	0 Open 3 Percutaneous 4 Percutaneous Endoscopic 7 Via Natural or Artificial Opening 8 Via Natural or Artificial Opening Endoscopic X External	Z No Device	Z No Qualifier
J Clitoris L Vestibular Gland M Vulva	0 Open X External	Z No Device	Z No Qualifier

0 Medical and Surgical
U Female Reproductive System
S Reposition: Moving to its normal location or other suitable location all or a portion of a body part

Body Part Character 4	Approach Character 5	Device Character 6	Qualifier Character 7
0 Ovary, Right **1** Ovary, Left **2** Ovaries, Bilateral **4** Uterine Supporting Structure **5** Fallopian Tube, Right **6** Fallopian Tube, Left **7** Fallopian Tubes, Bilateral **C** Cervix **F** Cul-de-sac	**0** Open **4** Percutaneous Endoscopic	**Z** No Device	**Z** No Qualifier
9 Uterus **G** Vagina	**0** Open **4** Percutaneous Endoscopic **X** External	**Z** No Device	**Z** No Qualifier

0 Medical and Surgical
U Female Reproductive System
T Resection: Cutting out or off, without replacement, all of a body part

Body Part Character 4	Approach Character 5	Device Character 6	Qualifier Character 7
0 Ovary, Right **1** Ovary, Left **2** Ovaries, Bilateral **5** Fallopian Tube, Right **6** Fallopian Tube, Left **7** Fallopian Tubes, Bilateral **9** Uterus	**0** Open **4** Percutaneous Endoscopic **7** Via Natural or Artificial Opening **8** Via Natural or Artificial Opening Endoscopic **F** Via Natural or Artificial Opening With Percutaneous Endoscopic Assistance	**Z** No Device	**Z** No Qualifier
4 Uterine Supporting Structure **C** Cervix **F** Cul-de-sac **G** Vagina **K** Hymen	**0** Open **4** Percutaneous Endoscopic **7** Via Natural or Artificial Opening **8** Via Natural or Artificial Opening Endoscopic	**Z** No Device	**Z** No Qualifier
J Clitoris **L** Vestibular Gland **M** Vulva	**0** Open **X** External	**Z** No Device	**Z** No Qualifier

0 Medical and Surgical
U Female Reproductive System
U Supplement: Putting in or on biological or synthetic material that physically reinforces and/or augments the function of a portion of a body part

Body Part Character 4	Approach Character 5	Device Character 6	Qualifier Character 7
4 Uterine Supporting Structure	**0** Open **4** Percutaneous Endoscopic	**7** Autologous Tissue Substitute **J** Synthetic Substitute **K** Nonautologous Tissue Substitute	**Z** No Qualifier
5 Fallopian Tube, Right **6** Fallopian Tube, Left **7** Fallopian Tubes, Bilateral **F** Cul-de-sac **K** Hymen	**0** Open **4** Percutaneous Endoscopic **7** Via Natural or Artificial Opening **8** Via Natural or Artificial Opening Endoscopic	**7** Autologous Tissue Substitute **J** Synthetic Substitute **K** Nonautologous Tissue Substitute	**Z** No Qualifier
G Vagina	**0** Open **4** Percutaneous Endoscopic **7** Via Natural or Artificial Opening **8** Via Natural or Artificial Opening Endoscopic **X** External	**7** Autologous Tissue Substitute **J** Synthetic Substitute **K** Nonautologous Tissue Substitute	**Z** No Qualifier
J Clitoris **M** Vulva	**0** Open **X** External	**7** Autologous Tissue Substitute **J** Synthetic Substitute **K** Nonautologous Tissue Substitute	**Z** No Qualifier

0   **Medical and Surgical**
U   **Female Reproductive System**
V   **Restriction:**   Partially closing the orifice or lumen of a tubular body part

Body Part Character 4	Approach Character 5	Device Character 6	Qualifier Character 7
C Cervix	**0** Open **3** Percutaneous **4** Percutaneous Endoscopic	**C** Extraluminal Device **D** Intraluminal Device **Z** No Device	**Z** No Qualifier
C Cervix	**7** Via Natural or Artificial Opening **8** Via Natural or Artificial Opening Endoscopic	**D** Intraluminal Device **Z** No Device	**Z** No Qualifier

0   **Medical and Surgical**
U   **Female Reproductive System**
W   **Revision:**   Correcting, to the extent possible, a malfunctioning or displaced device

Body Part Character 4	Approach Character 5	Device Character 6	Qualifier Character 7
3 Ovary	**0** Open **3** Percutaneous **4** Percutaneous Endoscopic **X** External	**0** Drainage Device **3** Infusion Device	**Z** No Qualifier
8 Fallopian Tube	**0** Open **3** Percutaneous **4** Percutaneous Endoscopic **7** Via Natural or Artificial Opening **8** Via Natural or Artificial Opening Endoscopic **X** External	**0** Drainage Device **3** Infusion Device **7** Autologous Tissue Substitute **C** Extraluminal Device **D** Intraluminal Device **J** Synthetic Substitute **K** Nonautologous Tissue Substitute	**Z** No Qualifier
D Uterus and Cervix	**0** Open **3** Percutaneous **4** Percutaneous Endoscopic **7** Via Natural or Artificial Opening **8** Via Natural or Artificial Opening Endoscopic **X** External	**0** Drainage Device **3** Infusion Device **7** Autologous Tissue Substitute **C** Extraluminal Device **D** Intraluminal Device **H** Contraceptive Device **J** Synthetic Substitute **K** Nonautologous Tissue Substitute	**Z** No Qualifier
H Vagina and Cul-de-sac	**0** Open **3** Percutaneous **4** Percutaneous Endoscopic **7** Via Natural or Artificial Opening **8** Via Natural or Artificial Opening Endoscopic **X** External	**0** Drainage Device **3** Infusion Device **7** Autologous Tissue Substitute **D** Intraluminal Device **G** Pessary **J** Synthetic Substitute **K** Nonautologous Tissue Substitute	**Z** No Qualifier
M Vulva	**0** Open **X** External	**0** Drainage Device **7** Autologous Tissue Substitute **J** Synthetic Substitute **K** Nonautologous Tissue Substitute	**Z** No Qualifier

0   **Medical and Surgical**
U   **Female Reproductive System**
X   **Transfer:**   Moving, without taking out, all or a portion of a body part to another location to take over the function of all or a portion of a body part

Body Part Character 4	Approach Character 5	Device Character 6	Qualifier Character 7
0 Ovary, Right **1** Ovary, Left **5** Fallopian Tube, Right **6** Fallopian Tube, Left	**0** Open **4** Percutaneous Endoscopic	**Z** No Device	**Z** No Qualifier

0   **Medical and Surgical**
U   **Female Reproductive System**
Y   **Transplantation:**   Putting in or on all or a portion of a living body part taken from another individual or animal to physically take the place and/or function of all or a portion of a similar body part

Body Part Character 4	Approach Character 5	Device Character 6	Qualifier Character 7
0 Ovary, Right **1** Ovary, Left	**0** Open	**Z** No Device	**1** Allogeneic **2** Syngeneic **3** Zooplastic

Male Reproductive System 0V1–0VW

0 **Medical and Surgical**
V **Male Reproductive System**
1 **Bypass:** Altering the route of passage of the contents of a tubular body part

Body Part Character 4	Approach Character 5	Device Character 6	Qualifier Character 7
N Vas Deferens, Right **P** Vas Deferens, Left **Q** Vas Deferens, Bilateral	**0** Open **4** Percutaneous Endoscopic	**7** Autologous Tissue Substitute **J** Synthetic Substitute **K** Nonautologous Tissue Substitute **Z** No Device	**J** Epididymis, Right **K** Epididymis, Left **N** Vas Deferens, Right **P** Vas Deferens, Left

0 **Medical and Surgical**
V **Male Reproductive System**
2 **Change:** Taking out or off a device from a body part and putting back an identical or similar device in or on the same body part without cutting or puncturing the skin or a mucous membrane

Body Part Character 4	Approach Character 5	Device Character 6	Qualifier Character 7
4 Prostate and Seminal Vesicles **8** Scrotum and Tunica Vaginalis **D** Testis **M** Epididymis and Spermatic Cord **R** Vas Deferens **S** Penis	**X** External	**0** Drainage Device **Y** Other Device	**Z** No Qualifier

0 **Medical and Surgical**
V **Male Reproductive System**
5 **Destruction:** Physical eradication of all or a portion of a body part by the direct use of energy, force, or a destructive agent

Body Part Character 4	Approach Character 5	Device Character 6	Qualifier Character 7
0 Prostate	**0** Open **3** Percutaneous **4** Percutaneous Endoscopic **7** Via Natural or Artificial Opening **8** Via Natural or Artificial Opening Endoscopic	**Z** No Device	**Z** No Qualifier
1 Seminal Vesicle, Right **2** Seminal Vesicle, Left **3** Seminal Vesicles, Bilateral **6** Tunica Vaginalis, Right **7** Tunica Vaginalis, Left **9** Testis, Right **B** Testis, Left **C** Testes, Bilateral **F** Spermatic Cord, Right **G** Spermatic Cord, Left **H** Spermatic Cords, Bilateral **J** Epididymis, Right **K** Epididymis, Left **L** Epididymis, Bilateral **N** Vas Deferens, Right **P** Vas Deferens, Left **Q** Vas Deferens, Bilateral	**0** Open **3** Percutaneous **4** Percutaneous Endoscopic	**Z** No Device	**Z** No Qualifier
5 Scrotum **S** Penis **T** Prepuce	**0** Open **3** Percutaneous **4** Percutaneous Endoscopic **X** External	**Z** No Device	**Z** No Qualifier

0 **Medical and Surgical**
V **Male Reproductive System**
7 **Dilation:** Expanding an orifice or the lumen of a tubular body part

Body Part Character 4	Approach Character 5	Device Character 6	Qualifier Character 7
N Vas Deferens, Right **P** Vas Deferens, Left **Q** Vas Deferens, Bilateral	**0** Open **3** Percutaneous **4** Percutaneous Endoscopic	**D** Intraluminal Device **Z** No Device	**Z** No Qualifier

0 **Medical and Surgical**
V **Male Reproductive System**
9 **Drainage:**   Taking or letting out fluids and/or gases from a body part

Body Part Character 4	Approach Character 5	Device Character 6	Qualifier Character 7
0 Prostate	**0** Open **3** Percutaneous **4** Percutaneous Endoscopic **7** Via Natural or Artificial Opening **8** Via Natural or Artificial Opening Endoscopic	**0** Drainage Device	**Z** No Qualifier
0 Prostate	**0** Open **3** Percutaneous **4** Percutaneous Endoscopic **7** Via Natural or Artificial Opening **8** Via Natural or Artificial Opening Endoscopic	**Z** No Device	**X** Diagnostic **Z** No Qualifier
1 Seminal Vesicle, Right **2** Seminal Vesicle, Left **3** Seminal Vesicles, Bilateral **6** Tunica Vaginalis, Right **7** Tunica Vaginalis, Left **9** Testis, Right **B** Testis, Left **C** Testes, Bilateral **F** Spermatic Cord, Right **G** Spermatic Cord, Left **H** Spermatic Cords, Bilateral **J** Epididymis, Right **K** Epididymis, Left **L** Epididymis, Bilateral **N** Vas Deferens, Right **P** Vas Deferens, Left **Q** Vas Deferens, Bilateral	**0** Open **3** Percutaneous **4** Percutaneous Endoscopic	**0** Drainage Device	**Z** No Qualifier
1 Seminal Vesicle, Right **2** Seminal Vesicle, Left **3** Seminal Vesicles, Bilateral **6** Tunica Vaginalis, Right **7** Tunica Vaginalis, Left **9** Testis, Right **B** Testis, Left **C** Testes, Bilateral **F** Spermatic Cord, Right **G** Spermatic Cord, Left **H** Spermatic Cords, Bilateral **J** Epididymis, Right **K** Epididymis, Left **L** Epididymis, Bilateral **N** Vas Deferens, Right **P** Vas Deferens, Left **Q** Vas Deferens, Bilateral	**0** Open **3** Percutaneous **4** Percutaneous Endoscopic	**Z** No Device	**X** Diagnostic **Z** No Qualifier
5 Scrotum **S** Penis **T** Prepuce	**0** Open **3** Percutaneous **4** Percutaneous Endoscopic **X** External	**0** Drainage Device	**Z** No Qualifier
5 Scrotum **S** Penis **T** Prepuce	**0** Open **3** Percutaneous **4** Percutaneous Endoscopic **X** External	**Z** No Device	**X** Diagnostic **Z** No Qualifier

0 **Medical and Surgical**
V **Male Reproductive System**
B **Excision:**   Cutting out or off, without replacement, a portion of a body part

Body Part Character 4	Approach Character 5	Device Character 6	Qualifier Character 7
0 Prostate	**0** Open **3** Percutaneous **4** Percutaneous Endoscopic **7** Via Natural or Artificial Opening **8** Via Natural or Artificial Opening Endoscopic	**Z** No Device	**X** Diagnostic **Z** No Qualifier

Continued on next page

0   Medical and Surgical   *Continued from previous page*
V   Male Reproductive System
B   Excision: Cutting out or off, without replacement, a portion of a body part

Body Part Character 4	Approach Character 5	Device Character 6	Qualifier Character 7
1 Seminal Vesicle, Right **2** Seminal Vesicle, Left **3** Seminal Vesicles, Bilateral **6** Tunica Vaginalis, Right **7** Tunica Vaginalis, Left **9** Testis, Right **B** Testis, Left **C** Testes, Bilateral **F** Spermatic Cord, Right **G** Spermatic Cord, Left **H** Spermatic Cords, Bilateral **J** Epididymis, Right **K** Epididymis, Left **L** Epididymis, Bilateral **N** Vas Deferens, Right **P** Vas Deferens, Left **Q** Vas Deferens, Bilateral	**0** Open **3** Percutaneous **4** Percutaneous Endoscopic	**Z** No Device	**X** Diagnostic **Z** No Qualifier
5 Scrotum **S** Penis **T** Prepuce	**0** Open **3** Percutaneous **4** Percutaneous Endoscopic **X** External	**Z** No Device	**X** Diagnostic **Z** No Qualifier

0   Medical and Surgical
V   Male Reproductive System
C   Extirpation: Taking or cutting out solid matter from a body part

Body Part Character 4	Approach Character 5	Device Character 6	Qualifier Character 7
0 Prostate	**0** Open **3** Percutaneous **4** Percutaneous Endoscopic **7** Via Natural or Artificial Opening **8** Via Natural or Artificial Opening Endoscopic	**Z** No Device	**Z** No Qualifier
1 Seminal Vesicle, Right **2** Seminal Vesicle, Left **3** Seminal Vesicles, Bilateral **6** Tunica Vaginalis, Right **7** Tunica Vaginalis, Left **9** Testis, Right **B** Testis, Left **C** Testes, Bilateral **F** Spermatic Cord, Right **G** Spermatic Cord, Left **H** Spermatic Cords, Bilateral **J** Epididymis, Right **K** Epididymis, Left **L** Epididymis, Bilateral **N** Vas Deferens, Right **P** Vas Deferens, Left **Q** Vas Deferens, Bilateral	**0** Open **3** Percutaneous **4** Percutaneous Endoscopic	**Z** No Device	**Z** No Qualifier
5 Scrotum **S** Penis **T** Prepuce	**0** Open **3** Percutaneous **4** Percutaneous Endoscopic **X** External	**Z** No Device	**Z** No Qualifier

0   Medical and Surgical
V   Male Reproductive System
H   Insertion: Putting in a nonbiological appliance that monitors, assists, performs or prevents a physiological function, but does not
physically take the place of a body part

Body Part Character 4	Approach Character 5	Device Character 6	Qualifier Character 7
0 Prostate	**0** Open **3** Percutaneous **4** Percutaneous Endoscopic **7** Via Natural or Artificial Opening **8** Via Natural or Artificial Opening Endoscopic	**1** Radioactive Element	**Z** No Qualifier

Continued on next page

0 Medical and Surgical
V Male Reproductive System
H Insertion: Putting in a nonbiological appliance that monitors, assists, performs or prevents a physiological function, but does not physically take the place of a body part

Continued from previous page

Body Part Character 4	Approach Character 5	Device Character 6	Qualifier Character 7
4 Prostate and Seminal Vesicles 8 Scrotum and Tunica Vaginalis D Testis M Epididymis and Spermatic Cord R Vas Deferens	0 Open 3 Percutaneous 4 Percutaneous Endoscopic 7 Via Natural or Artificial Opening 8 Via Natural or Artificial Opening Endoscopic	3 Infusion Device	Z No Qualifier
S Penis	0 Open 3 Percutaneous 4 Percutaneous Endoscopic X External	3 Infusion Device	Z No Qualifier

0 Medical and Surgical
V Male Reproductive System
J Inspection: Visually and/or manually exploring a body part

Body Part Character 4	Approach Character 5	Device Character 6	Qualifier Character 7
0 Prostate	0 Open 3 Percutaneous 4 Percutaneous Endoscopic 7 Via Natural or Artificial Opening 8 Via Natural or Artificial Opening Endoscopic X External	Z No Device	Z No Qualifier
1 Seminal Vesicle, Right 2 Seminal Vesicle, Left 3 Seminal Vesicles, Bilateral 5 Scrotum 6 Tunica Vaginalis, Right 7 Tunica Vaginalis, Left 9 Testis, Right B Testis, Left C Testes, Bilateral F Spermatic Cord, Right G Spermatic Cord, Left H Spermatic Cords, Bilateral J Epididymis, Right K Epididymis, Left L Epididymis, Bilateral N Vas Deferens, Right P Vas Deferens, Left Q Vas Deferens, Bilateral S Penis T Prepuce V Male External Genitalia	0 Open 3 Percutaneous 4 Percutaneous Endoscopic X External	Z No Device	Z No Qualifier

0 Medical and Surgical
V Male Reproductive System
L Occlusion: Completely closing an orifice or lumen of a tubular body part

Body Part Character 4	Approach Character 5	Device Character 6	Qualifier Character 7
F Spermatic Cord, Right G Spermatic Cord, Left H Spermatic Cords, Bilateral N Vas Deferens, Right P Vas Deferens, Left Q Vas Deferens, Bilateral	0 Open 3 Percutaneous 4 Percutaneous Endoscopic	C Extraluminal Device D Intraluminal Device Z No Device	Z No Qualifier

0 Medical and Surgical
V Male Reproductive System
M Reattachment: Putting back in or on all or a portion of a separated body part to its normal location or other suitable location

Body Part Character 4	Approach Character 5	Device Character 6	Qualifier Character 7
5 Scrotum S Penis	X External	Z No Device	Z No Qualifier

Continued on next page

0   Medical and Surgical   *Continued from previous page*
V   Male Reproductive System
M   Reattachment: Putting back in or on all or a portion of a separated body part to its normal location or other suitable location

Body Part Character 4	Approach Character 5	Device Character 6	Qualifier Character 7
6 Tunica Vaginalis, Right **7** Tunica Vaginalis, Left **9** Testis, Right **B** Testis, Left **C** Testes, Bilateral **F** Spermatic Cord, Right **G** Spermatic Cord, Left **H** Spermatic Cords, Bilateral	**0** Open **4** Percutaneous Endoscopic	**Z** No Device	**Z** No Qualifier

0   Medical and Surgical
V   Male Reproductive System
N   Release: Freeing a body part from an abnormal physical constraint

Body Part Character 4	Approach Character 5	Device Character 6	Qualifier Character 7
0 Prostate	**0** Open **3** Percutaneous **4** Percutaneous Endoscopic **7** Via Natural or Artificial Opening **8** Via Natural or Artificial Opening Endoscopic	**Z** No Device	**Z** No Qualifier
1 Seminal Vesicle, Right **2** Seminal Vesicle, Left **3** Seminal Vesicles, Bilateral **6** Tunica Vaginalis, Right **7** Tunica Vaginalis, Left **9** Testis, Right **B** Testis, Left **C** Testes, Bilateral **F** Spermatic Cord, Right **G** Spermatic Cord, Left **H** Spermatic Cords, Bilateral **J** Epididymis, Right **K** Epididymis, Left **L** Epididymis, Bilateral **N** Vas Deferens, Right **P** Vas Deferens, Left **Q** Vas Deferens, Bilateral	**0** Open **3** Percutaneous **4** Percutaneous Endoscopic	**Z** No Device	**Z** No Qualifier
5 Scrotum **S** Penis **T** Prepuce	**0** Open **3** Percutaneous **4** Percutaneous Endoscopic **X** External	**Z** No Device	**Z** No Qualifier

0   Medical and Surgical
V   Male Reproductive System
P   Removal: Taking out or off a device from a body part

Body Part Character 4	Approach Character 5	Device Character 6	Qualifier Character 7
4 Prostate and Seminal Vesicles	**0** Open **3** Percutaneous **4** Percutaneous Endoscopic **7** Via Natural or Artificial Opening **8** Via Natural or Artificial Opening Endoscopic	**0** Drainage Device **1** Radioactive Element **3** Infusion Device **7** Autologous Tissue Substitute **J** Synthetic Substitute **K** Nonautologous Tissue Substitute	**Z** No Qualifier
4 Prostate and Seminal Vesicles	**X** External	**0** Drainage Device **1** Radioactive Element **3** Infusion Device	**Z** No Qualifier
8 Scrotum and Tunica Vaginalis **D** Testis **M** Epididymis and Spermatic Cord **S** Penis	**X** External	**0** Drainage Device **3** Infusion Device	**Z** No Qualifier
8 Scrotum and Tunica Vaginalis **D** Testis **S** Penis	**0** Open **3** Percutaneous **4** Percutaneous Endoscopic **7** Via Natural or Artificial Opening **8** Via Natural or Artificial Opening Endoscopic	**0** Drainage Device **3** Infusion Device **7** Autologous Tissue Substitute **J** Synthetic Substitute **K** Nonautologous Tissue Substitute	**Z** No Qualifier

Continued on next page

Continued from previous page

0 Medical and Surgical
V Male Reproductive System
P Removal: Taking out or off a device from a body part

Body Part Character 4	Approach Character 5	Device Character 6	Qualifier Character 7
M Epididymis and Spermatic Cord	**0** Open **3** Percutaneous **4** Percutaneous Endoscopic **7** Via Natural or Artificial Opening **8** Via Natural or Artificial Opening Endoscopic	**0** Drainage Device **3** Infusion Device **7** Autologous Tissue Substitute **C** Extraluminal Device **J** Synthetic Substitute **K** Nonautologous Tissue Substitute	**Z** No Qualifier
R Vas Deferens	**0** Open **3** Percutaneous **4** Percutaneous Endoscopic **7** Via Natural or Artificial Opening **8** Via Natural or Artificial Opening Endoscopic	**0** Drainage Device **3** Infusion Device **7** Autologous Tissue Substitute **C** Extraluminal Device **D** Intraluminal Device **J** Synthetic Substitute **K** Nonautologous Tissue Substitute	**Z** No Qualifier
R Vas Deferens	**X** External	**0** Drainage Device **3** Infusion Device **D** Intraluminal Device	**Z** No Qualifier

0 Medical and Surgical
V Male Reproductive System
Q Repair: Restoring, to the extent possible, a body part to its normal anatomic structure and function

Body Part Character 4	Approach Character 5	Device Character 6	Qualifier Character 7
0 Prostate	**0** Open **3** Percutaneous **4** Percutaneous Endoscopic **7** Via Natural or Artificial Opening **8** Via Natural or Artificial Opening Endoscopic	**Z** No Device	**Z** No Qualifier
1 Seminal Vesicle, Right **2** Seminal Vesicle, Left **3** Seminal Vesicles, Bilateral **6** Tunica Vaginalis, Right **7** Tunica Vaginalis, Left **9** Testis, Right **B** Testis, Left **C** Testes, Bilateral **F** Spermatic Cord, Right **G** Spermatic Cord, Left **H** Spermatic Cords, Bilateral **J** Epididymis, Right **K** Epididymis, Left **L** Epididymis, Bilateral **N** Vas Deferens, Right **P** Vas Deferens, Left **Q** Vas Deferens, Bilateral	**0** Open **3** Percutaneous **4** Percutaneous Endoscopic	**Z** No Device	**Z** No Qualifier
5 Scrotum **S** Penis **T** Prepuce	**0** Open **3** Percutaneous **4** Percutaneous Endoscopic **X** External	**Z** No Device	**Z** No Qualifier

0 Medical and Surgical
V Male Reproductive System
R Replacement: Putting in or on biological or synthetic material that physically takes the place and/or function of all or a portion of a body part

Body Part Character 4	Approach Character 5	Device Character 6	Qualifier Character 7
9 Testis, Right **B** Testis, Left **C** Testes, Bilateral	**0** Open	**J** Synthetic Substitute	**Z** No Qualifier

0 Medical and Surgical
V Male Reproductive System
S Reposition: Moving to its normal location or other suitable location all or a portion of a body part

Body Part Character 4	Approach Character 5	Device Character 6	Qualifier Character 7
9 Testis, Right **B** Testis, Left **C** Testes, Bilateral **F** Spermatic Cord, Right **G** Spermatic Cord, Left **H** Spermatic Cords, Bilateral	**0** Open **3** Percutaneous **4** Percutaneous Endoscopic	**Z** No Device	**Z** No Qualifier

0 Medical and Surgical
V Male Reproductive System
T Resection: Cutting out or off, without replacement, all of a body part

Body Part Character 4	Approach Character 5	Device Character 6	Qualifier Character 7
0 Prostate	**0** Open **4** Percutaneous Endoscopic **7** Via Natural or Artificial Opening **8** Via Natural or Artificial Opening Endoscopic	**Z** No Device	**Z** No Qualifier
1 Seminal Vesicle, Right **2** Seminal Vesicle, Left **3** Seminal Vesicles, Bilateral **6** Tunica Vaginalis, Right **7** Tunica Vaginalis, Left **9** Testis, Right **B** Testis, Left **C** Testes, Bilateral **F** Spermatic Cord, Right **G** Spermatic Cord, Left **H** Spermatic Cords, Bilateral **J** Epididymis, Right **K** Epididymis, Left **L** Epididymis, Bilateral **N** Vas Deferens, Right **P** Vas Deferens, Left **Q** Vas Deferens, Bilateral	**0** Open **4** Percutaneous Endoscopic	**Z** No Device	**Z** No Qualifier
5 Scrotum **S** Penis **T** Prepuce	**0** Open **4** Percutaneous Endoscopic **X** External	**Z** No Device	**Z** No Qualifier

0 Medical and Surgical
V Male Reproductive System
U Supplement: Putting in or on biological or synthetic material that physically reinforces and/or augments the function of a portion of a body part

Body Part Character 4	Approach Character 5	Device Character 6	Qualifier Character 7
1 Seminal Vesicle, Right **2** Seminal Vesicle, Left **3** Seminal Vesicles, Bilateral **6** Tunica Vaginalis, Right **7** Tunica Vaginalis, Left **F** Spermatic Cord, Right **G** Spermatic Cord, Left **H** Spermatic Cords, Bilateral **J** Epididymis, Right **K** Epididymis, Left **L** Epididymis, Bilateral **N** Vas Deferens, Right **P** Vas Deferens, Left **Q** Vas Deferens, Bilateral	**0** Open **4** Percutaneous Endoscopic	**7** Autologous Tissue Substitute **J** Synthetic Substitute **K** Nonautologous Tissue Substitute	**Z** No Qualifier
5 Scrotum **S** Penis **T** Prepuce	**0** Open **4** Percutaneous Endoscopic **X** External	**7** Autologous Tissue Substitute **J** Synthetic Substitute **K** Nonautologous Tissue Substitute	**Z** No Qualifier
9 Testis, Right **B** Testis, Left **C** Testes, Bilateral	**0** Open	**7** Autologous Tissue Substitute **J** Synthetic Substitute **K** Nonautologous Tissue Substitute	**Z** No Qualifier

0   **Medical and Surgical**
V   **Male Reproductive System**
W   **Revision:**   Correcting, to the extent possible, a malfunctioning or displaced device

Body Part Character 4	Approach Character 5	Device Character 6	Qualifier Character 7
4 Prostate and Seminal Vesicles **8** Scrotum and Tunica Vaginalis **D** Testis **S** Penis	**0** Open **3** Percutaneous **4** Percutaneous Endoscopic **7** Via Natural or Artificial Opening **8** Via Natural or Artificial Opening Endoscopic **X** External	**0** Drainage Device **3** Infusion Device **7** Autologous Tissue Substitute **J** Synthetic Substitute **K** Nonautologous Tissue Substitute	**Z** No Qualifier
M Epididymis and Spermatic Cord	**0** Open **3** Percutaneous **4** Percutaneous Endoscopic **7** Via Natural or Artificial Opening **8** Via Natural or Artificial Opening Endoscopic **X** External	**0** Drainage Device **3** Infusion Device **7** Autologous Tissue Substitute **C** Extraluminal Device **J** Synthetic Substitute **K** Nonautologous Tissue Substitute	**Z** No Qualifier
R Vas Deferens	**0** Open **3** Percutaneous **4** Percutaneous Endoscopic **7** Via Natural or Artificial Opening **8** Via Natural or Artificial Opening Endoscopic **X** External	**0** Drainage Device **3** Infusion Device **7** Autologous Tissue Substitute **C** Extraluminal Device **D** Intraluminal Device **J** Synthetic Substitute **K** Nonautologous Tissue Substitute	**Z** No Qualifier

Anatomical Regions, General 0W0–0WW

0 Medical and Surgical
W Anatomical Regions, General
0 Alteration:　　　　Modifying the anatomic structure of a body part without affecting the function of the body part

Body Part Character 4	Approach Character 5	Device Character 6	Qualifier Character 7
0 Head **2** Face **4** Upper Jaw **5** Lower Jaw **6** Neck **8** Chest Wall **F** Abdominal Wall **K** Upper Back **L** Lower Back **M** Perineum, Male **N** Perineum, Female	**0** Open **3** Percutaneous **4** Percutaneous Endoscopic	**7** Autologous Tissue Substitute **J** Synthetic Substitute **K** Nonautologous Tissue Substitute **Z** No Device	**Z** No Qualifier

0 Medical and Surgical
W Anatomical Regions, General
1 Bypass:　　　　Altering the route of passage of the contents of a tubular body part

Body Part Character 4	Approach Character 5	Device Character 6	Qualifier Character 7
1 Cranial Cavity	**0** Open	**J** Synthetic Substitute	**9** Pleural Cavity, Right **B** Pleural Cavity, Left **G** Peritoneal Cavity **J** Pelvic Cavity
9 Pleural Cavity, Right **B** Pleural Cavity, Left **G** Peritoneal Cavity **J** Pelvic Cavity	**0** Open **4** Percutaneous Endoscopic	**J** Synthetic Substitute	**4** Cutaneous **9** Pleural Cavity, Right **B** Pleural Cavity, Left **G** Peritoneal Cavity **J** Pelvic Cavity **Y** Lower Vein
9 Pleural Cavity, Right **B** Pleural Cavity, Left **G** Peritoneal Cavity **J** Pelvic Cavity	**3** Percutaneous	**J** Synthetic Substitute	**4** Cutaneous

0 Medical and Surgical
W Anatomical Regions, General
2 Change:　　　　Taking out or off a device from a body part and putting back an identical or similar device in or on the same body part without cutting or puncturing the skin or a mucous membrane

Body Part Character 4	Approach Character 5	Device Character 6	Qualifier Character 7
0 Head **1** Cranial Cavity **2** Face **4** Upper Jaw **5** Lower Jaw **6** Neck **8** Chest Wall **9** Pleural Cavity, Right **B** Pleural Cavity, Left **C** Mediastinum **D** Pericardial Cavity **F** Abdominal Wall **G** Peritoneal Cavity **H** Retroperitoneum **J** Pelvic Cavity **K** Upper Back **L** Lower Back **M** Perineum, Male **N** Perineum, Female	**X** External	**0** Drainage Device **Y** Other Device	**Z** No Qualifier

0 Medical and Surgical
W Anatomical Regions, General
3 Control: Stopping, or attempting to stop, postprocedural bleeding

Body Part Character 4	Approach Character 5	Device Character 6	Qualifier Character 7
0 Head 1 Cranial Cavity 2 Face 3 Oral Cavity and Throat 4 Upper Jaw 5 Lower Jaw 6 Neck 8 Chest Wall 9 Pleural Cavity, Right B Pleural Cavity, Left C Mediastinum D Pericardial Cavity F Abdominal Wall G Peritoneal Cavity H Retroperitoneum J Pelvic Cavity K Upper Back L Lower Back M Perineum, Male N Perineum, Female	0 Open 3 Percutaneous 4 Percutaneous Endoscopic	Z No Device	Z No Qualifier
P Gastrointestinal Tract Q Respiratory Tract R Genitourinary Tract	0 Open 3 Percutaneous 4 Percutaneous Endoscopic 7 Via Natural or Artificial Opening 8 Via Natural or Artificial Opening Endoscopic	Z No Device	Z No Qualifier

0 Medical and Surgical
W Anatomical Regions, General
4 Creation: Making a new genital structure that does not take over the function of a body part

Body Part Character 4	Approach Character 5	Device Character 6	Qualifier Character 7
M Perineum, Male	0 Open	7 Autologous Tissue Substitute J Synthetic Substitute K Nonautologous Tissue Substitute Z No Device	0 Vagina
N Perineum, Female	0 Open	7 Autologous Tissue Substitute J Synthetic Substitute K Nonautologous Tissue Substitute Z No Device	1 Penis

0 Medical and Surgical
W Anatomical Regions, General
8 Division: Cutting into a body part without draining fluids and/or gases from the body part in order to separate or transect a body part

Body Part Character 4	Approach Character 5	Device Character 6	Qualifier Character 7
N Perineum, Female	X External	Z No Device	Z No Qualifier

0 Medical and Surgical
W Anatomical Regions, General
9 Drainage: Taking or letting out fluids and/or gases from a body part

Body Part Character 4	Approach Character 5	Device Character 6	Qualifier Character 7
0 Head 1 Cranial Cavity 2 Face 3 Oral Cavity and Throat 4 Upper Jaw 5 Lower Jaw 6 Neck 8 Chest Wall 9 Pleural Cavity, Right B Pleural Cavity, Left C Mediastinum D Pericardial Cavity F Abdominal Wall G Peritoneal Cavity H Retroperitoneum J Pelvic Cavity K Upper Back L Lower Back M Perineum, Male N Perineum, Female	0 Open 3 Percutaneous 4 Percutaneous Endoscopic	0 Drainage Device	Z No Qualifier
0 Head 1 Cranial Cavity 2 Face 3 Oral Cavity and Throat 4 Upper Jaw 5 Lower Jaw 6 Neck 8 Chest Wall 9 Pleural Cavity, Right B Pleural Cavity, Left C Mediastinum D Pericardial Cavity F Abdominal Wall G Peritoneal Cavity H Retroperitoneum J Pelvic Cavity K Upper Back L Lower Back M Perineum, Male N Perineum, Female	0 Open 3 Percutaneous 4 Percutaneous Endoscopic	Z No Device	X Diagnostic Z No Qualifier

0 Medical and Surgical
W Anatomical Regions, General
B Excision: Cutting out or off, without replacement, a portion of a body part

Body Part Character 4	Approach Character 5	Device Character 6	Qualifier Character 7
0 Head 2 Face 4 Upper Jaw 5 Lower Jaw 8 Chest Wall K Upper Back L Lower Back M Perineum, Male N Perineum, Female	0 Open 3 Percutaneous 4 Percutaneous Endoscopic X External	Z No Device	X Diagnostic Z No Qualifier
6 Neck C Mediastinum F Abdominal Wall H Retroperitoneum	0 Open 3 Percutaneous 4 Percutaneous Endoscopic	Z No Device	X Diagnostic Z No Qualifier
6 Neck F Abdominal Wall	X External	Z No Device	2 Stoma X Diagnostic Z No Qualifier

Draft (2009)

0 Medical and Surgical
W Anatomical Regions, General
C Extirpation: Taking or cutting out solid matter from a body part

Body Part Character 4	Approach Character 5	Device Character 6	Qualifier Character 7
1 Cranial Cavity **3** Oral Cavity and Throat **9** Pleural Cavity, Right **B** Pleural Cavity, Left **C** Mediastinum **D** Pericardial Cavity **G** Peritoneal Cavity **J** Pelvic Cavity	**0** Open **3** Percutaneous **4** Percutaneous Endoscopic **X** External	**Z** No Device	**Z** No Qualifier
P Gastrointestinal Tract **Q** Respiratory Tract **R** Genitourinary Tract	**0** Open **3** Percutaneous **4** Percutaneous Endoscopic **7** Via Natural or Artificial Opening **8** Via Natural or Artificial Opening Endoscopic **X** External	**Z** No Device	**Z** No Qualifier

0 Medical and Surgical
W Anatomical Regions, General
F Fragmentation: Breaking solid matter in a body part into pieces

Body Part Character 4	Approach Character 5	Device Character 6	Qualifier Character 7
1 Cranial Cavity **3** Oral Cavity and Throat **9** Pleural Cavity, Right **B** Pleural Cavity, Left **C** Mediastinum **D** Pericardial Cavity **G** Peritoneal Cavity **J** Pelvic Cavity	**0** Open **3** Percutaneous **4** Percutaneous Endoscopic **X** External	**Z** No Device	**Z** No Qualifier
P Gastrointestinal Tract **Q** Respiratory Tract **R** Genitourinary Tract	**0** Open **3** Percutaneous **4** Percutaneous Endoscopic **7** Via Natural or Artificial Opening **8** Via Natural or Artificial Opening Endoscopic **X** External	**Z** No Device	**Z** No Qualifier

0 Medical and Surgical
W Anatomical Regions, General
H Insertion: Putting in a nonbiological appliance that monitors, assists, performs or prevents a physiological function, but does not physically take the place of a body part

Body Part Character 4	Approach Character 5	Device Character 6	Qualifier Character 7
0 Head **1** Cranial Cavity **2** Face **3** Oral Cavity and Throat **4** Upper Jaw **5** Lower Jaw **6** Neck **8** Chest Wall **9** Pleural Cavity, Right **B** Pleural Cavity, Left **C** Mediastinum **D** Pericardial Cavity **F** Abdominal Wall **G** Peritoneal Cavity **H** Retroperitoneum **J** Pelvic Cavity **K** Upper Back **L** Lower Back **M** Perineum, Male **N** Perineum, Female	**0** Open **3** Percutaneous **4** Percutaneous Endoscopic	**1** Radioactive Element **3** Infusion Device **Y** Other Device	**Z** No Qualifier
P Gastrointestinal Tract **Q** Respiratory Tract **R** Genitourinary Tract	**0** Open **3** Percutaneous **4** Percutaneous Endoscopic **7** Via Natural or Artificial Opening **8** Via Natural or Artificial Opening Endoscopic	**1** Radioactive Element **3** Infusion Device **Y** Other Device	**Z** No Qualifier

0   Medical and Surgical
W   Anatomical Regions, General
J   Inspection: Visually and/or manually exploring a body part

Body Part Character 4	Approach Character 5	Device Character 6	Qualifier Character 7
0 Head 2 Face 3 Oral Cavity and Throat 4 Upper Jaw 5 Lower Jaw 6 Neck 8 Chest Wall F Abdominal Wall K Upper Back L Lower Back M Perineum, Male N Perineum, Female	0 Open 3 Percutaneous 4 Percutaneous Endoscopic X External	Z No Device	Z No Qualifier
1 Cranial Cavity 9 Pleural Cavity, Right B Pleural Cavity, Left C Mediastinum D Pericardial Cavity G Peritoneal Cavity H Retroperitoneum J Pelvic Cavity	0 Open 3 Percutaneous 4 Percutaneous Endoscopic	Z No Device	Z No Qualifier

0   Medical and Surgical
W   Anatomical Regions, General
M   Reattachment: Putting back in or on all or a portion of a separated body part to its normal location or other suitable location

Body Part Character 4	Approach Character 5	Device Character 6	Qualifier Character 7
2 Face 4 Upper Jaw 5 Lower Jaw 6 Neck 8 Chest Wall F Abdominal Wall K Upper Back L Lower Back M Perineum, Male N Perineum, Female	0 Open	Z No Device	Z No Qualifier

0   Medical and Surgical
W   Anatomical Regions, General
P   Removal: Taking out or off a device from a body part

Body Part Character 4	Approach Character 5	Device Character 6	Qualifier Character 7
0 Head 2 Face 4 Upper Jaw 5 Lower Jaw 6 Neck 8 Chest Wall C Mediastinum F Abdominal Wall K Upper Back L Lower Back M Perineum, Male N Perineum, Female	0 Open 3 Percutaneous 4 Percutaneous Endoscopic X External	0 Drainage Device 1 Radioactive Element 3 Infusion Device 7 Autologous Tissue Substitute J Synthetic Substitute K Nonautologous Tissue Substitute Y Other Device	Z No Qualifier
1 Cranial Cavity 9 Pleural Cavity, Right B Pleural Cavity, Left D Pericardial Cavity G Peritoneal Cavity H Retroperitoneum J Pelvic Cavity	X External	0 Drainage Device 1 Radioactive Element 3 Infusion Device	Z No Qualifier
1 Cranial Cavity 9 Pleural Cavity, Right B Pleural Cavity, Left G Peritoneal Cavity J Pelvic Cavity	0 Open 3 Percutaneous 4 Percutaneous Endoscopic	0 Drainage Device 1 Radioactive Element 3 Infusion Device J Synthetic Substitute Y Other Device	Z No Qualifier

Continued on next page

0   **Medical and Surgical**   *Continued from previous page*
W   **Anatomical Regions, General**
P   **Removal:**   Taking out or off a device from a body part

Body Part Character 4	Approach Character 5	Device Character 6	Qualifier Character 7
D Pericardial Cavity **H** Retroperitoneum	**0** Open **3** Percutaneous **4** Percutaneous Endoscopic	**0** Drainage Device **1** Radioactive Element **3** Infusion Device **Y** Other Device	**Z** No Qualifier
P Gastrointestinal Tract **Q** Respiratory Tract **R** Genitourinary Tract	**0** Open **3** Percutaneous **4** Percutaneous Endoscopic **7** Via Natural or Artificial Opening **8** Via Natural or Artificial Opening Endoscopic **X** External	**1** Radioactive Element **3** Infusion Device **Y** Other Device	**Z** No Qualifier

0   **Medical and Surgical**
W   **Anatomical Regions, General**
Q   **Repair:**   Restoring, to the extent possible, a body part to its normal anatomic structure and function

Body Part Character 4	Approach Character 5	Device Character 6	Qualifier Character 7
0 Head **2** Face **4** Upper Jaw **5** Lower Jaw **8** Chest Wall **K** Upper Back **L** Lower Back **M** Perineum, Male **N** Perineum, Female	**0** Open **3** Percutaneous **4** Percutaneous Endoscopic **X** External	**Z** No Device	**Z** No Qualifier
6 Neck **C** Mediastinum **F** Abdominal Wall	**0** Open **3** Percutaneous **4** Percutaneous Endoscopic	**Z** No Device	**Z** No Qualifier
6 Neck **F** Abdominal Wall	**X** External	**Z** No Device	**2** Stoma **Z** No Qualifier

0   **Medical and Surgical**
W   **Anatomical Regions, General**
U   **Supplement:**   Putting in or on biological or synthetic material that physically reinforces and/or augments the function of a portion of a body part

Body Part Character 4	Approach Character 5	Device Character 6	Qualifier Character 7
0 Head **2** Face **4** Upper Jaw **5** Lower Jaw **6** Neck **8** Chest Wall **C** Mediastinum **F** Abdominal Wall **K** Upper Back **L** Lower Back **M** Perineum, Male **N** Perineum, Female	**0** Open **4** Percutaneous Endoscopic	**7** Autologous Tissue Substitute **J** Synthetic Substitute **K** Nonautologous Tissue Substitute	**Z** No Qualifier

0   Medical and Surgical
W   Anatomical Regions, General
W   Revision: Correcting, to the extent possible, a malfunctioning or displaced device

Body Part Character 4	Approach Character 5	Device Character 6	Qualifier Character 7
0 Head **2** Face **4** Upper Jaw **5** Lower Jaw **6** Neck **8** Chest Wall **C** Mediastinum **F** Abdominal Wall **K** Upper Back **L** Lower Back **M** Perineum, Male **N** Perineum, Female	**0** Open **3** Percutaneous **4** Percutaneous Endoscopic **X** External	**0** Drainage Device **1** Radioactive Element **3** Infusion Device **7** Autologous Tissue Substitute **J** Synthetic Substitute **K** Nonautologous Tissue Substitute **Y** Other Device	**Z** No Qualifier
1 Cranial Cavity **9** Pleural Cavity, Right **B** Pleural Cavity, Left **G** Peritoneal Cavity **J** Pelvic Cavity	**0** Open **3** Percutaneous **4** Percutaneous Endoscopic **X** External	**0** Drainage Device **1** Radioactive Element **3** Infusion Device **J** Synthetic Substitute **Y** Other Device	**Z** No Qualifier
D Pericardial Cavity **H** Retroperitoneum	**0** Open **3** Percutaneous **4** Percutaneous Endoscopic **X** External	**0** Drainage Device **1** Radioactive Element **3** Infusion Device **Y** Other Device	**Z** No Qualifier
P Gastrointestinal Tract **Q** Respiratory Tract **R** Genitourinary Tract	**0** Open **3** Percutaneous **4** Percutaneous Endoscopic **7** Via Natural or Artificial Opening **8** Via Natural or Artificial Opening Endoscopic **X** External	**1** Radioactive Element **3** Infusion Device **Y** Other Device	**Z** No Qualifier

Anatomical Regions, Upper Extremities 0X0–0XX

0 Medical and Surgical
X Anatomical Regions, Upper Extremities
0 Alteration: Modifying the anatomic structure of a body part without affecting the function of the body part

Body Part Character 4	Approach Character 5	Device Character 6	Qualifier Character 7
2 Shoulder Region, Right 3 Shoulder Region, Left 4 Axilla, Right 5 Axilla, Left 6 Upper Extremity, Right 7 Upper Extremity, Left 8 Upper Arm, Right 9 Upper Arm, Left B Elbow Region, Right C Elbow Region, Left D Lower Arm, Right F Lower Arm, Left G Wrist Region, Right H Wrist Region, Left	0 Open 3 Percutaneous 4 Percutaneous Endoscopic	7 Autologous Tissue Substitute J Synthetic Substitute K Nonautologous Tissue Substitute Z No Device	Z No Qualifier

0 Medical and Surgical
X Anatomical Regions, Upper Extremities
2 Change: Taking out or off a device from a body part and putting back an identical or similar device in or on the same body part without cutting or puncturing the skin or a mucous membrane

Body Part Character 4	Approach Character 5	Device Character 6	Qualifier Character 7
6 Upper Extremity, Right 7 Upper Extremity, Left	X External	0 Drainage Device Y Other Device	Z No Qualifier

0 Medical and Surgical
X Anatomical Regions, Upper Extremities
3 Control: Stopping, or attempting to stop, postprocedural bleeding

Body Part Character 4	Approach Character 5	Device Character 6	Qualifier Character 7
2 Shoulder Region, Right 3 Shoulder Region, Left 4 Axilla, Right 5 Axilla, Left 6 Upper Extremity, Right 7 Upper Extremity, Left 8 Upper Arm, Right 9 Upper Arm, Left B Elbow Region, Right C Elbow Region, Left D Lower Arm, Right F Lower Arm, Left G Wrist Region, Right H Wrist Region, Left J Hand, Right K Hand, Left	0 Open 3 Percutaneous 4 Percutaneous Endoscopic	Z No Device	Z No Qualifier

0 Medical and Surgical
X Anatomical Regions, Upper Extremities
6 Detachment: Cutting off all or a portion of an extremity

Body Part Character 4	Approach Character 5	Device Character 6	Qualifier Character 7
0 Forequarter, Right 1 Forequarter, Left 2 Shoulder Region, Right 3 Shoulder Region, Left B Elbow Region, Right C Elbow Region, Left	0 Open	Z No Device	Z No Qualifier
8 Upper Arm, Right 9 Upper Arm, Left D Lower Arm, Right F Lower Arm, Left	0 Open	Z No Device	1 High 2 Mid 3 Low

Continued on next page

0 Medical and Surgical
X Anatomical Regions, Upper Extremities
6 Detachment: Cutting off all or a portion of an extremity

Continued from previous page

Body Part Character 4	Approach Character 5	Device Character 6	Qualifier Character 7
J Hand, Right K Hand, Left	0 Open	Z No Device	0 Complete 4 Complete 1st Ray 5 Complete 2nd Ray 6 Complete 3rd Ray 7 Complete 4th Ray 8 Complete 5th Ray 9 Partial 1st Ray B Partial 2nd Ray C Partial 3rd Ray D Partial 4th Ray F Partial 5th Ray
L Thumb, Right M Thumb, Left N Index Finger, Right P Index Finger, Left Q Middle Finger, Right R Middle Finger, Left S Ring Finger, Right T Ring Finger, Left V Little Finger, Right W Little Finger, Left	0 Open	Z No Device	0 Complete 1 High 2 Mid 3 Low

0 Medical and Surgical
X Anatomical Regions, Upper Extremities
9 Drainage: Taking or letting out fluids and/or gases from a body part

Body Part Character 4	Approach Character 5	Device Character 6	Qualifier Character 7
2 Shoulder Region, Right 3 Shoulder Region, Left 4 Axilla, Right 5 Axilla, Left 6 Upper Extremity, Right 7 Upper Extremity, Left 8 Upper Arm, Right 9 Upper Arm, Left B Elbow Region, Right C Elbow Region, Left D Lower Arm, Right F Lower Arm, Left G Wrist Region, Right H Wrist Region, Left J Hand, Right K Hand, Left	0 Open 3 Percutaneous 4 Percutaneous Endoscopic	0 Drainage Device	Z No Qualifier
2 Shoulder Region, Right 3 Shoulder Region, Left 4 Axilla, Right 5 Axilla, Left 6 Upper Extremity, Right 7 Upper Extremity, Left 8 Upper Arm, Right 9 Upper Arm, Left B Elbow Region, Right C Elbow Region, Left D Lower Arm, Right F Lower Arm, Left G Wrist Region, Right H Wrist Region, Left J Hand, Right K Hand, Left	0 Open 3 Percutaneous 4 Percutaneous Endoscopic	Z No Device	X Diagnostic Z No Qualifier

0   Medical and Surgical
X   Anatomical Regions, Upper Extremities
B   Excision: Cutting out or off, without replacement, a portion of a body part

Body Part Character 4	Approach Character 5	Device Character 6	Qualifier Character 7
2 Shoulder Region, Right **3** Shoulder Region, Left **4** Axilla, Right **5** Axilla, Left **6** Upper Extremity, Right **7** Upper Extremity, Left **8** Upper Arm, Right **9** Upper Arm, Left **B** Elbow Region, Right **C** Elbow Region, Left **D** Lower Arm, Right **F** Lower Arm, Left **G** Wrist Region, Right **H** Wrist Region, Left **J** Hand, Right **K** Hand, Left	**0** Open **3** Percutaneous **4** Percutaneous Endoscopic	**Z** No Device	**X** Diagnostic **Z** No Qualifier

0   Medical and Surgical
X   Anatomical Regions, Upper Extremities
H   Insertion: Putting in a nonbiological appliance that monitors, assists, performs or prevents a physiological function, but does not physically take the place of a body part

Body Part Character 4	Approach Character 5	Device Character 6	Qualifier Character 7
2 Shoulder Region, Right **3** Shoulder Region, Left **4** Axilla, Right **5** Axilla, Left **6** Upper Extremity, Right **7** Upper Extremity, Left **8** Upper Arm, Right **9** Upper Arm, Left **B** Elbow Region, Right **C** Elbow Region, Left **D** Lower Arm, Right **F** Lower Arm, Left **G** Wrist Region, Right **H** Wrist Region, Left **J** Hand, Right **K** Hand, Left	**0** Open **3** Percutaneous **4** Percutaneous Endoscopic	**1** Radioactive Element **3** Infusion Device **Y** Other Device	**Z** No Qualifier

0   Medical and Surgical
X   Anatomical Regions, Upper Extremities
J   Inspection: Visually and/or manually exploring a body part

Body Part Character 4	Approach Character 5	Device Character 6	Qualifier Character 7
2 Shoulder Region, Right **3** Shoulder Region, Left **4** Axilla, Right **5** Axilla, Left **6** Upper Extremity, Right **7** Upper Extremity, Left **8** Upper Arm, Right **9** Upper Arm, Left **B** Elbow Region, Right **C** Elbow Region, Left **D** Lower Arm, Right **F** Lower Arm, Left **G** Wrist Region, Right **H** Wrist Region, Left **J** Hand, Right **K** Hand, Left	**0** Open **3** Percutaneous **4** Percutaneous Endoscopic **X** External	**Z** No Device	**Z** No Qualifier

0   Medical and Surgical
X   Anatomical Regions, Upper Extremities
M   Reattachment: Putting back in or on all or a portion of a separated body part to its normal location or other suitable location

Body Part Character 4	Approach Character 5	Device Character 6	Qualifier Character 7
0 Forequarter, Right **1** Forequarter, Left **2** Shoulder Region, Right **3** Shoulder Region, Left **4** Axilla, Right **5** Axilla, Left **6** Upper Extremity, Right **7** Upper Extremity, Left **8** Upper Arm, Right **9** Upper Arm, Left **B** Elbow Region, Right **C** Elbow Region, Left **D** Lower Arm, Right **F** Lower Arm, Left **G** Wrist Region, Right **H** Wrist Region, Left **J** Hand, Right **K** Hand, Left **L** Thumb, Right **M** Thumb, Left **N** Index Finger, Right **P** Index Finger, Left **Q** Middle Finger, Right **R** Middle Finger, Left **S** Ring Finger, Right **T** Ring Finger, Left **V** Little Finger, Right **W** Little Finger, Left	**0** Open	**Z** No Device	**Z** No Qualifier

0   Medical and Surgical
X   Anatomical Regions, Upper Extremities
P   Removal: Taking out or off a device from a body part

Body Part Character 4	Approach Character 5	Device Character 6	Qualifier Character 7
6 Upper Extremity, Right **7** Upper Extremity, Left	**0** Open **3** Percutaneous **4** Percutaneous Endoscopic **X** External	**0** Drainage Device **1** Radioactive Element **3** Infusion Device **7** Autologous Tissue Substitute **J** Synthetic Substitute **K** Nonautologous Tissue Substitute **Y** Other Device	**Z** No Qualifier

0 Medical and Surgical
X Anatomical Regions, Upper Extremities
Q Repair: Restoring, to the extent possible, a body part to its normal anatomic structure and function

Body Part Character 4	Approach Character 5	Device Character 6	Qualifier Character 7
2 Shoulder Region, Right **3** Shoulder Region, Left **4** Axilla, Right **5** Axilla, Left **6** Upper Extremity, Right **7** Upper Extremity, Left **8** Upper Arm, Right **9** Upper Arm, Left **B** Elbow Region, Right **C** Elbow Region, Left **D** Lower Arm, Right **F** Lower Arm, Left **G** Wrist Region, Right **H** Wrist Region, Left **J** Hand, Right **K** Hand, Left **L** Thumb, Right **M** Thumb, Left **N** Index Finger, Right **P** Index Finger, Left **Q** Middle Finger, Right **R** Middle Finger, Left **S** Ring Finger, Right **T** Ring Finger, Left **V** Little Finger, Right **W** Little Finger, Left	**0** Open **3** Percutaneous **4** Percutaneous Endoscopic **X** External	**Z** No Device	**Z** No Qualifier

0 Medical and Surgical
X Anatomical Regions, Upper Extremities
R Replacement: Putting in or on biological or synthetic material that physically takes the place and/or function of all or a portion of a body part

Body Part Character 4	Approach Character 5	Device Character 6	Qualifier Character 7
L Thumb, Right **M** Thumb, Left	**0** Open **4** Percutaneous Endoscopic	**7** Autologous Tissue Substitute	**N** Toe, Right **P** Toe, Left

0 Medical and Surgical
X Anatomical Regions, Upper Extremities
U Supplement: Putting in or on biological or synthetic material that physically reinforces and/or augments the function of a portion of a body part

Body Part Character 4	Approach Character 5	Device Character 6	Qualifier Character 7
2 Shoulder Region, Right **3** Shoulder Region, Left **4** Axilla, Right **5** Axilla, Left **6** Upper Extremity, Right **7** Upper Extremity, Left **8** Upper Arm, Right **9** Upper Arm, Left **B** Elbow Region, Right **C** Elbow Region, Left **D** Lower Arm, Right **F** Lower Arm, Left **G** Wrist Region, Right **H** Wrist Region, Left **J** Hand, Right **K** Hand, Left **L** Thumb, Right **M** Thumb, Left **N** Index Finger, Right **P** Index Finger, Left **Q** Middle Finger, Right **R** Middle Finger, Left **S** Ring Finger, Right **T** Ring Finger, Left **V** Little Finger, Right **W** Little Finger, Left	**0** Open **4** Percutaneous Endoscopic	**7** Autologous Tissue Substitute **J** Synthetic Substitute **K** Nonautologous Tissue Substitute	**Z** No Qualifier

0   Medical and Surgical
X   Anatomical Regions, Upper Extremities
W   Revision: Correcting, to the extent possible, a malfunctioning or displaced device

Body Part Character 4	Approach Character 5	Device Character 6	Qualifier Character 7
6 Upper Extremity, Right **7** Upper Extremity, Left	**0** Open **3** Percutaneous **4** Percutaneous Endoscopic **X** External	**0** Drainage Device **3** Infusion Device **7** Autologous Tissue Substitute **J** Synthetic Substitute **K** Nonautologous Tissue Substitute **Y** Other Device	**Z** No Qualifier

0   Medical and Surgical
X   Anatomical Regions, Upper Extremities
X   Transfer: Moving, without taking out, all or a portion of a body part to another location to take over the function of all or a portion of a body part

Body Part Character 4	Approach Character 5	Device Character 6	Qualifier Character 7
N Index Finger, Right	**0** Open	**Z** No Device	**L** Thumb, Right
P Index Finger, Left	**0** Open	**Z** No Device	**M** Thumb, Left

Anatomical Regions, Lower Extremities 0Y0–0YR

0   Medical and Surgical
Y   Anatomical Regions, Lower Extremities
0   Alteration: Modifying the anatomic structure of a body part without affecting the function of the body part

Body Part Character 4	Approach Character 5	Device Character 6	Qualifier Character 7
0 Buttock, Right 1 Buttock, Left 9 Lower Extremity, Right B Lower Extremity, Left C Upper Leg, Right D Upper Leg, Left F Knee Region, Right G Knee Region, Left H Lower Leg, Right J Lower Leg, Left K Ankle Region, Right L Ankle Region, Left	0 Open 3 Percutaneous 4 Percutaneous Endoscopic	7 Autologous Tissue Substitute J Synthetic Substitute K Nonautologous Tissue Substitute Z No Device	Z No Qualifier

0   Medical and Surgical
Y   Anatomical Regions, Lower Extremities
2   Change: Taking out or off a device from a body part and putting back an identical or similar device in or on the same body part without cutting or puncturing the skin or a mucous membrane

Body Part Character 4	Approach Character 5	Device Character 6	Qualifier Character 7
9 Lower Extremity, Right B Lower Extremity, Left	X External	0 Drainage Device Y Other Device	Z No Qualifier

0   Medical and Surgical
Y   Anatomical Regions, Lower Extremities
3   Control: Stopping, or attempting to stop, postprocedural bleeding

Body Part Character 4	Approach Character 5	Device Character 6	Qualifier Character 7
0 Buttock, Right 1 Buttock, Left 5 Inguinal Region, Right 6 Inguinal Region, Left 7 Femoral Region, Right 8 Femoral Region, Left 9 Lower Extremity, Right B Lower Extremity, Left C Upper Leg, Right D Upper Leg, Left F Knee Region, Right G Knee Region, Left H Lower Leg, Right J Lower Leg, Left K Ankle Region, Right L Ankle Region, Left M Foot, Right N Foot, Left	0 Open 3 Percutaneous 4 Percutaneous Endoscopic	Z No Device	Z No Qualifier

0   Medical and Surgical
Y   Anatomical Regions, Lower Extremities
6   Detachment: Cutting off all or a portion of an extremity

Body Part Character 4	Approach Character 5	Device Character 6	Qualifier Character 7
2 Hindquarter, Right 3 Hindquarter, Left 4 Hindquarter, Bilateral 7 Femoral Region, Right 8 Femoral Region, Left F Knee Region, Right G Knee Region, Left	0 Open	Z No Device	Z No Qualifier
C Upper Leg, Right D Upper Leg, Left H Lower Leg, Right J Lower Leg, Left	0 Open	Z No Device	1 High 2 Mid 3 Low

Continued on next page

0   Medical and Surgical
Y   Anatomical Regions, Lower Extremities
6   Detachment: Cutting off all or a portion of an extremity

Continued from previous page

Body Part Character 4	Approach Character 5	Device Character 6	Qualifier Character 7
M Foot, Right N Foot, Left	0 Open	Z No Device	0 Complete 4 Complete 1st Ray 5 Complete 2nd Ray 6 Complete 3rd Ray 7 Complete 4th Ray 8 Complete 5th Ray 9 Partial 1st Ray B Partial 2nd Ray C Partial 3rd Ray D Partial 4th Ray F Partial 5th Ray
P 1st Toe, Right Q 1st Toe, Left R 2nd Toe, Right S 2nd Toe, Left T 3rd Toe, Right U 3rd Toe, Left V 4th Toe, Right W 4th Toe, Left X 5th Toe, Right Y 5th Toe, Left	0 Open	Z No Device	0 Complete 1 High 2 Mid 3 Low

0   Medical and Surgical
Y   Anatomical Regions, Lower Extremities
9   Drainage: Taking or letting out fluids and/or gases from a body part

Body Part Character 4	Approach Character 5	Device Character 6	Qualifier Character 7
0 Buttock, Right 1 Buttock, Left 5 Inguinal Region, Right 6 Inguinal Region, Left 7 Femoral Region, Right 8 Femoral Region, Left 9 Lower Extremity, Right B Lower Extremity, Left C Upper Leg, Right D Upper Leg, Left F Knee Region, Right G Knee Region, Left H Lower Leg, Right J Lower Leg, Left K Ankle Region, Right L Ankle Region, Left M Foot, Right N Foot, Left	0 Open 3 Percutaneous 4 Percutaneous Endoscopic	0 Drainage Device	Z No Qualifier
0 Buttock, Right 1 Buttock, Left 5 Inguinal Region, Right 6 Inguinal Region, Left 7 Femoral Region, Right 8 Femoral Region, Left 9 Lower Extremity, Right B Lower Extremity, Left C Upper Leg, Right D Upper Leg, Left F Knee Region, Right G Knee Region, Left H Lower Leg, Right J Lower Leg, Left K Ankle Region, Right L Ankle Region, Left M Foot, Right N Foot, Left	0 Open 3 Percutaneous 4 Percutaneous Endoscopic	Z No Device	X Diagnostic Z No Qualifier

0   **Medical and Surgical**
Y   **Anatomical Regions, Lower Extremities**
B   **Excision:**   Cutting out or off, without replacement, a portion of a body part

Body Part Character 4	Approach Character 5	Device Character 6	Qualifier Character 7
0 Buttock, Right 1 Buttock, Left 5 Inguinal Region, Right 6 Inguinal Region, Left 7 Femoral Region, Right 8 Femoral Region, Left 9 Lower Extremity, Right B Lower Extremity, Left C Upper Leg, Right D Upper Leg, Left F Knee Region, Right G Knee Region, Left H Lower Leg, Right J Lower Leg, Left K Ankle Region, Right L Ankle Region, Left M Foot, Right N Foot, Left	0 Open 3 Percutaneous 4 Percutaneous Endoscopic	Z No Device	X Diagnostic Z No Qualifier

0   **Medical and Surgical**
Y   **Anatomical Regions, Lower Extremities**
H   **Insertion:**   Putting in a nonbiological appliance that monitors, assists, performs or prevents a physiological function, but does not physically take the place of a body part

Body Part Character 4	Approach Character 5	Device Character 6	Qualifier Character 7
0 Buttock, Right 1 Buttock, Left 5 Inguinal Region, Right 6 Inguinal Region, Left 7 Femoral Region, Right 8 Femoral Region, Left 9 Lower Extremity, Right B Lower Extremity, Left C Upper Leg, Right D Upper Leg, Left F Knee Region, Right G Knee Region, Left H Lower Leg, Right J Lower Leg, Left K Ankle Region, Right L Ankle Region, Left M Foot, Right N Foot, Left	0 Open 3 Percutaneous 4 Percutaneous Endoscopic	1 Radioactive Element 3 Infusion Device Y Other Device	Z No Qualifier

0   **Medical and Surgical**
Y   **Anatomical Regions, Lower Extremities**
J   **Inspection:**   Visually and/or manually exploring a body part

Body Part Character 4	Approach Character 5	Device Character 6	Qualifier Character 7
0 Buttock, Right 1 Buttock, Left 5 Inguinal Region, Right 6 Inguinal Region, Left 7 Femoral Region, Right 8 Femoral Region, Left 9 Lower Extremity, Right A Inguinal Region, Bilateral B Lower Extremity, Left C Upper Leg, Right D Upper Leg, Left E Femoral Region, Bilateral F Knee Region, Right G Knee Region, Left H Lower Leg, Right J Lower Leg, Left K Ankle Region, Right L Ankle Region, Left M Foot, Right N Foot, Left	0 Open 3 Percutaneous 4 Percutaneous Endoscopic X External	Z No Device	Z No Qualifier

                        Draft (2009)

0   Medical and Surgical
Y   Anatomical Regions, Lower Extremities
M   Reattachment: Putting back in or on all or a portion of a separated body part to its normal location or other suitable location

Body Part Character 4	Approach Character 5	Device Character 6	Qualifier Character 7
0 Buttock, Right **1** Buttock, Left **2** Hindquarter, Right **3** Hindquarter, Left **4** Hindquarter, Bilateral **5** Inguinal Region, Right **6** Inguinal Region, Left **7** Femoral Region, Right **8** Femoral Region, Left **9** Lower Extremity, Right **B** Lower Extremity, Left **C** Upper Leg, Right **D** Upper Leg, Left **F** Knee Region, Right **G** Knee Region, Left **H** Lower Leg, Right **J** Lower Leg, Left **K** Ankle Region, Right **L** Ankle Region, Left **M** Foot, Right **N** Foot, Left **P** 1st Toe, Right **Q** 1st Toe, Left **R** 2nd Toe, Right **S** 2nd Toe, Left **T** 3rd Toe, Right **U** 3rd Toe, Left **V** 4th Toe, Right **W** 4th Toe, Left **X** 5th Toe, Right **Y** 5th Toe, Left	**0** Open	**Z** No Device	**Z** No Qualifier

0   Medical and Surgical
Y   Anatomical Regions, Lower Extremities
P   Removal: Taking out or off a device from a body part

Body Part Character 4	Approach Character 5	Device Character 6	Qualifier Character 7
9 Lower Extremity, Right **B** Lower Extremity, Left	**0** Open **3** Percutaneous **4** Percutaneous Endoscopic **X** External	**0** Drainage Device **1** Radioactive Element **3** Infusion Device **7** Autologous Tissue Substitute **J** Synthetic Substitute **K** Nonautologous Tissue Substitute **Y** Other Device	**Z** No Qualifier

0   Medical and Surgical
Y   Anatomical Regions, Lower Extremities
Q   Repair: Restoring, to the extent possible, a body part to its normal anatomic structure and function

Body Part Character 4	Approach Character 5	Device Character 6	Qualifier Character 7
0 Buttock, Right **1** Buttock, Left **5** Inguinal Region, Right **6** Inguinal Region, Left **7** Femoral Region, Right **8** Femoral Region, Left **9** Lower Extremity, Right **A** Inguinal Region, Bilateral **B** Lower Extremity, Left **C** Upper Leg, Right **D** Upper Leg, Left **E** Femoral Region, Bilateral **F** Knee Region, Right **G** Knee Region, Left **H** Lower Leg, Right **J** Lower Leg, Left **K** Ankle Region, Right **L** Ankle Region, Left **M** Foot, Right **N** Foot, Left **P** 1st Toe, Right **Q** 1st Toe, Left **R** 2nd Toe, Right **S** 2nd Toe, Left **T** 3rd Toe, Right **U** 3rd Toe, Left **V** 4th Toe, Right **W** 4th Toe, Left **X** 5th Toe, Right **Y** 5th Toe, Left	**0** Open **3** Percutaneous **4** Percutaneous Endoscopic **X** External	**Z** No Device	**Z** No Qualifier

0   Medical and Surgical
Y   Anatomical Regions, Lower Extremities
U   Supplement: Putting in or on biological or synthetic material that physically reinforces and/or augments the function of a portion of a body part

Body Part Character 4	Approach Character 5	Device Character 6	Qualifier Character 7
0 Buttock, Right **1** Buttock, Left **5** Inguinal Region, Right **6** Inguinal Region, Left **7** Femoral Region, Right **8** Femoral Region, Left **9** Lower Extremity, Right **A** Inguinal Region, Bilateral **B** Lower Extremity, Left **C** Upper Leg, Right **D** Upper Leg, Left **E** Femoral Region, Bilateral **F** Knee Region, Right **G** Knee Region, Left **H** Lower Leg, Right **J** Lower Leg, Left **K** Ankle Region, Right **L** Ankle Region, Left **M** Foot, Right **N** Foot, Left **P** 1st Toe, Right **Q** 1st Toe, Left **R** 2nd Toe, Right **S** 2nd Toe, Left **T** 3rd Toe, Right **U** 3rd Toe, Left **V** 4th Toe, Right **W** 4th Toe, Left **X** 5th Toe, Right **Y** 5th Toe, Left	**0** Open **4** Percutaneous Endoscopic	**7** Autologous Tissue Substitute **J** Synthetic Substitute **K** Nonautologous Tissue Substitute	**Z** No Qualifier

0 **Medical and Surgical**
Y **Anatomical Regions, Lower Extremities**
W **Revision:**　　　　Correcting, to the extent possible, a malfunctioning or displaced device

Body Part Character 4	Approach Character 5	Device Character 6	Qualifier Character 7
9 Lower Extremity, Right **B** Lower Extremity, Left	**0** Open **3** Percutaneous **4** Percutaneous Endoscopic **X** External	**0** Drainage Device **3** Infusion Device **7** Autologous Tissue Substitute **J** Synthetic Substitute **K** Nonautologous Tissue Substitute **Y** Other Device	**Z** No Qualifier

Obstetrics 102–10Y

1	Obstetrics
0	Pregnancy
2	Change:

Taking out or off a device from a body part and putting back an identical or similar device in or on the same body part without cutting or puncturing the skin or a mucous membrane

Body Part Character 4	Approach Character 5	Device Character 6	Qualifier Character 7
0 Products of Conception	7 Via Natural or Artificial Opening	3 Monitoring Electrode Y Other Device	Z No Qualifier

1	Obstetrics
0	Pregnancy
9	Drainage:

Taking or letting out fluids and/or gases from a body part

Body Part Character 4	Approach Character 5	Device Character 6	Qualifier Character 7
0 Products of Conception	0 Open 3 Percutaneous 4 Percutaneous Endoscopic 7 Via Natural or Artificial Opening 8 Via Natural or Artificial Opening Endoscopic	Z No Device	9 Fetal Blood A Fetal Cerebrospinal Fluid B Fetal Fluid, Other C Amniotic Fluid, Therapeutic D Fluid, Other U Amniotic Fluid, Diagnostic

1	Obstetrics
0	Pregnancy
A	Abortion:

Artificially terminating a pregnancy

Body Part Character 4	Approach Character 5	Device Character 6	Qualifier Character 7
0 Products of Conception	0 Open 2 Open Endoscopic 3 Percutaneous 4 Percutaneous Endoscopic 8 Via Natural or Artificial Opening Endoscopic	Z No Device	Z No Qualifier
0 Products of Conception	7 Via Natural or Artificial Opening	Z No Device	W Laminaria X Abortifacient Z No Qualifier

1	Obstetrics
0	Pregnancy
D	Extraction:

Pulling or stripping out or off all or a portion of a body part by the use of force

Body Part Character 4	Approach Character 5	Device Character 6	Qualifier Character 7
0 Products of Conception	0 Open	Z No Device	0 Classical 1 Low Cervical 2 Extraperitoneal
0 Products of Conception	7 Via Natural or Artificial Opening	Z No Device	3 Low Forceps 4 Mid Forceps 5 High Forceps 6 Vacuum 7 Internal Version 8 Other
1 Products of Conception, Retained 2 Products of Conception, Ectopic	7 Via Natural or Artificial Opening 8 Via Natural or Artificial Opening Endoscopic	Z No Device	Z No Qualifier

1	Obstetrics
0	Pregnancy
E	Delivery:

Assisting the passage of the products of conception from the genital cavity

Body Part Character 4	Approach Character 5	Device Character 6	Qualifier Character 7
0 Products of Conception	X External	Z No Device	Z No Qualifier

1 Obstetrics
0 Pregnancy
H Insertion: Putting in a nonbiological appliance that monitors, assists, performs or prevents a physiological function, but does not physically take the place of a body part

Body Part Character 4	Approach Character 5	Device Character 6	Qualifier Character 7
0 Products of Conception	0 Open 7 Via Natural or Artificial Opening	3 Monitoring Electrode Y Other Device	Z No Qualifier

1 Obstetrics
0 Pregnancy
J Inspection: Visually and/or manually exploring a body part

Body Part Character 4	Approach Character 5	Device Character 6	Qualifier Character 7
0 Products of Conception 1 Products of Conception, Retained 2 Products of Conception, Ectopic	0 Open 2 Open Endoscopic 3 Percutaneous 4 Percutaneous Endoscopic 7 Via Natural or Artificial Opening 8 Via Natural or Artificial Opening Endoscopic X External	Z No Device	Z No Qualifier

1 Obstetrics
0 Pregnancy
P Removal: Taking out or off a device from a body part, region or orifice

Body Part Character 4	Approach Character 5	Device Character 6	Qualifier Character 7
0 Products of Conception	0 Open 7 Via Natural or Artificial Opening	3 Monitoring Electrode Y Other Device	Z No Qualifier

1 Obstetrics
0 Pregnancy
Q Repair: Restoring, to the extent possible, a body part to its normal anatomic structure and function

Body Part Character 4	Approach Character 5	Device Character 6	Qualifier Character 7
0 Products of Conception	0 Open 2 Open Endoscopic 3 Percutaneous 4 Percutaneous Endoscopic 7 Via Natural or Artificial Opening 8 Via Natural or Artificial Opening Endoscopic	Y Other Device Z No Device	E Nervous System F Cardiovascular System G Lymphatics and Hemic H Eye J Ear, Nose and Sinus K Respiratory System L Mouth and Throat M Gastrointestinal System N Hepatobiliary and Pancreas P Endocrine System Q Skin R Musculoskeletal System S Urinary System T Female Reproductive System V Male Reproductive System Y Other Body System

1 Obstetrics
0 Pregnancy
S Reposition: Moving to its normal location or other suitable location all or a portion of a body part

Body Part Character 4	Approach Character 5	Device Character 6	Qualifier Character 7
0 Products of Conception	7 Via Natural or Artificial Opening X External	Z No Device	Z No Qualifier
2 Products of Conception, Ectopic	0 Open 2 Open Endoscopic 3 Percutaneous 4 Percutaneous Endoscopic 7 Via Natural or Artificial Opening 8 Via Natural or Artificial Opening Endoscopic	Z No Device	Z No Qualifier

1   **Obstetrics**
0   **Pregnancy**
T   **Resection:**   Cutting out or off, without replacement, all of a body part

Body Part Character 4	Approach Character 5	Device Character 6	Qualifier Character 7
2 Products of Conception, Ectopic	**0** Open **2** Open Endoscopic **3** Percutaneous **4** Percutaneous Endoscopic **7** Via Natural or Artificial Opening **8** Via Natural or Artificial Opening Endoscopic	**Z** No Device	**Z** No Qualifier

1   **Obstetrics**
0   **Pregnancy**
Y   **Transplantation:**   Putting in or on all or a portion of a living body part taken from another individual or animal to physically take the place and/or function of all or a portion of a similar body part

Body Part Character 4	Approach Character 5	Device Character 6	Qualifier Character 7
0 Products of Conception	**3** Percutaneous **4** Percutaneous Endoscopic **7** Via Natural or Artificial Opening	**Z** No Device	**E** Nervous System **F** Cardiovascular System **G** Lymphatics and Hemic **H** Eye **J** Ear, Nose and Sinus **K** Respiratory System **L** Mouth and Throat **M** Gastrointestinal System **N** Hepatobiliary and Pancreas **P** Endocrine System **Q** Skin **R** Musculoskeletal System **S** Urinary System **T** Female Reproductive System **V** Male Reproductive System **Y** Other Body System

Placement—Anatomical Regions 2W0–2W6

2   Placement
W   Anatomical Regions
0   Change: Taking out or off a device from a body part and putting back an identical or similar device in or on the same body part without cutting or puncturing the skin or a mucous membrane

Body Part Character 4	Approach Character 5	Device Character 6	Qualifier Character 7
0 Head	**X** External	**0** Traction Apparatus **1** Splint **2** Cast **3** Brace **4** Bandage **5** Packing Material **6** Pressure Dressing **7** Intermittent Pressure Device **8** Stereotactic Apparatus **Y** Other Device	**Z** No Qualifier
1 Face	**X** External	**0** Traction Apparatus **1** Splint **2** Cast **3** Brace **4** Bandage **5** Packing Material **6** Pressure Dressing **7** Intermittent Pressure Device **9** Wire **Y** Other Device	**Z** No Qualifier
2 Neck **3** Abdominal Wall **4** Chest Wall **5** Back **6** Inguinal Region, Right **7** Inguinal Region, Left **8** Upper Extremity, Right **9** Upper Extremity, Left **A** Upper Arm, Right **B** Upper Arm, Left **C** Lower Arm, Right **D** Lower Arm, Left **E** Hand, Right **F** Hand, Left **G** Thumb, Right **H** Thumb, Left **J** Finger, Right **K** Finger, Left **L** Lower Extremity, Right **M** Lower Extremity, Left **N** Upper Leg, Right **P** Upper Leg, Left **Q** Lower Leg, Right **R** Lower Leg, Left **S** Foot, Right **T** Foot, Left **U** Toe, Right **V** Toe, Left	**X** External	**0** Traction Apparatus **1** Splint **2** Cast **3** Brace **4** Bandage **5** Packing Material **6** Pressure Dressing **7** Intermittent Pressure Device **Y** Other Device	**Z** No Qualifier

2 Placement
W Anatomical Regions
1 Compression: Putting pressure on a body region

Body Part Character 4	Approach Character 5	Device Character 6	Qualifier Character 7
0 Head 1 Face 2 Neck 3 Abdominal Wall 4 Chest Wall 5 Back 6 Inguinal Region, Right 7 Inguinal Region, Left 8 Upper Extremity, Right 9 Upper Extremity, Left A Upper Arm, Right B Upper Arm, Left C Lower Arm, Right D Lower Arm, Left E Hand, Right F Hand, Left G Thumb, Right H Thumb, Left J Finger, Right K Finger, Left L Lower Extremity, Right M Lower Extremity, Left N Upper Leg, Right P Upper Leg, Left Q Lower Leg, Right R Lower Leg, Left S Foot, Right T Foot, Left U Toe, Right V Toe, Left	X External	6 Pressure Dressing 7 Intermittent Pressure Device	Z No Qualifier

2 Placement
W Anatomical Regions
2 Dressing: Putting material on a body region for protection

Body Part Character 4	Approach Character 5	Device Character 6	Qualifier Character 7
0 Head 1 Face 2 Neck 3 Abdominal Wall 4 Chest Wall 5 Back 6 Inguinal Region, Right 7 Inguinal Region, Left 8 Upper Extremity, Right 9 Upper Extremity, Left A Upper Arm, Right B Upper Arm, Left C Lower Arm, Right D Lower Arm, Left E Hand, Right F Hand, Left G Thumb, Right H Thumb, Left J Finger, Right K Finger, Left L Lower Extremity, Right M Lower Extremity, Left N Upper Leg, Right P Upper Leg, Left Q Lower Leg, Right R Lower Leg, Left S Foot, Right T Foot, Left U Toe, Right V Toe, Left	X External	4 Bandage	Z No Qualifier

2　Placement
W　Anatomical Regions
3　Immobilization:　　Limiting or preventing motion of a body region

Body Part Character 4	Approach Character 5	Device Character 6	Qualifier Character 7
0 Head	**X** External	**1** Splint **2** Cast **3** Brace **8** Stereotactic Apparatus **Y** Other Device	**Z** No Qualifier
1 Face	**X** External	**1** Splint **2** Cast **3** Brace **9** Wire **Y** Other Device	**Z** No Qualifier
2 Neck **3** Abdominal Wall **4** Chest Wall **5** Back **6** Inguinal Region, Right **7** Inguinal Region, Left **8** Upper Extremity, Right **9** Upper Extremity, Left **A** Upper Arm, Right **B** Upper Arm, Left **C** Lower Arm, Right **D** Lower Arm, Left **E** Hand, Right **F** Hand, Left **G** Thumb, Right **H** Thumb, Left **J** Finger, Right **K** Finger, Left **L** Lower Extremity, Right **M** Lower Extremity, Left **N** Upper Leg, Right **P** Upper Leg, Left **Q** Lower Leg, Right **R** Lower Leg, Left **S** Foot, Right **T** Foot, Left **U** Toe, Right **V** Toe, Left	**X** External	**1** Splint **2** Cast **3** Brace **Y** Other Device	**Z** No Qualifier

2　Placement
W　Anatomical Regions
4　Packing:　　Putting material in a body region or orifice

Body Part Character 4	Approach Character 5	Device Character 6	Qualifier Character 7
0 Head **1** Face **2** Neck **3** Abdominal Wall **4** Chest Wall **5** Back **6** Inguinal Region, Right **7** Inguinal Region, Left **8** Upper Extremity, Right **9** Upper Extremity, Left **A** Upper Arm, Right **B** Upper Arm, Left **C** Lower Arm, Right **D** Lower Arm, Left **E** Hand, Right **F** Hand, Left **G** Thumb, Right **H** Thumb, Left **J** Finger, Right **K** Finger, Left **L** Lower Extremity, Right **M** Lower Extremity, Left **N** Upper Leg, Right **P** Upper Leg, Left **Q** Lower Leg, Right **R** Lower Leg, Left **S** Foot, Right **T** Foot, Left **U** Toe, Right **V** Toe, Left	**X** External	**5** Packing Material	**Z** No Qualifier

2 **Placement**
W **Anatomical Regions**
5 **Removal:**   Taking out or off a device from a body part

Body Part Character 4	Approach Character 5	Device Character 6	Qualifier Character 7
0 Head	**X** External	**0** Traction Apparatus **1** Splint **2** Cast **3** Brace **4** Bandage **5** Packing Material **6** Pressure Dressing **7** Intermittent Pressure Device **8** Stereotactic Apparatus **Y** Other Device	**Z** No Qualifier
1 Face	**X** External	**0** Traction Apparatus **1** Splint **2** Cast **3** Brace **4** Bandage **5** Packing Material **6** Pressure Dressing **7** Intermittent Pressure Device **9** Wire **Y** Other Device	**Z** No Qualifier
2 Neck **3** Abdominal Wall **4** Chest Wall **5** Back **6** Inguinal Region, Right **7** Inguinal Region, Left **8** Upper Extremity, Right **9** Upper Extremity, Left **A** Upper Arm, Right **B** Upper Arm, Left **C** Lower Arm, Right **D** Lower Arm, Left **E** Hand, Right **F** Hand, Left **G** Thumb, Right **H** Thumb, Left **J** Finger, Right **K** Finger, Left **L** Lower Extremity, Right **M** Lower Extremity, Left **N** Upper Leg, Right **P** Upper Leg, Left **Q** Lower Leg, Right **R** Lower Leg, Left **S** Foot, Right **T** Foot, Left **U** Toe, Right **V** Toe, Left	**X** External	**0** Traction Apparatus **1** Splint **2** Cast **3** Brace **4** Bandage **5** Packing Material **6** Pressure Dressing **7** Intermittent Pressure Device **Y** Other Device	**Z** No Qualifier

2   Placement
W   Anatomical Regions
6   Traction: Exerting a pulling force on a body region in a distal direction

Body Part Character 4	Approach Character 5	Device Character 6	Qualifier Character 7
0 Head **1** Face **2** Neck **3** Abdominal Wall **4** Chest Wall **5** Back **6** Inguinal Region, Right **7** Inguinal Region, Left **8** Upper Extremity, Right **9** Upper Extremity, Left **A** Upper Arm, Right **B** Upper Arm, Left **C** Lower Arm, Right **D** Lower Arm, Left **E** Hand, Right **F** Hand, Left **G** Thumb, Right **H** Thumb, Left **J** Finger, Right **K** Finger, Left **L** Lower Extremity, Right **M** Lower Extremity, Left **N** Upper Leg, Right **P** Upper Leg, Left **Q** Lower Leg, Right **R** Lower Leg, Left **S** Foot, Right **T** Foot, Left **U** Toe, Right **V** Toe, Left	**X** External	**0** Traction Apparatus **Z** No Device	**Z** No Qualifier

Placement—Anatomical Orifices 2Y0–2Y5

2   **Placement**
Y   **Anatomical Orifices**
0   **Change:**   Taking out or off a device from a body part and putting back an identical or similar device in or on the same body part without cutting or puncturing the skin or a mucous membrane

Body Part Character 4	Approach Character 5	Device Character 6	Qualifier Character 7
0 Mouth and Pharynx **1** Nasal **2** Ear **3** Anorectal **4** Female Genital Tract **5** Urethra	**X** External	**5** Packing Material	**Z** No Qualifier

2   **Placement**
Y   **Anatomical Orifices**
4   **Packing:**   Putting material in a body region or orifice

Body Part Character 4	Approach Character 5	Device Character 6	Qualifier Character 7
0 Mouth and Pharynx **1** Nasal **2** Ear **3** Anorectal **4** Female Genital Tract **5** Urethra	**X** External	**5** Packing Material	**Z** No Qualifier

2   **Placement**
Y   **Anatomical Orifices**
5   **Removal:**   Taking our or off a device from a body region or orifice

Body Part Character 4	Approach Character 5	Device Character 6	Qualifier Character 7
0 Mouth and Pharynx **1** Nasal **2** Ear **3** Anorectal **4** Female Genital Tract **5** Urethra	**X** External	**5** Packing Material	**Z** No Qualifier

Administration 302–3E1

3   **Administration**
0   **Circulatory**
2   **Transfusion:**   Putting in blood or blood products

Body System/Region Character 4	Approach Character 5	Substance Character 6	Qualifier Character 7
3 Peripheral Vein 4 Central Vein	0 Open 3 Percutaneous	A Stem Cells, Embryonic	Z No Qualifier
3 Peripheral Vein 4 Central Vein	0 Open 3 Percutaneous	G Bone Marrow H Whole Blood J Serum Albumin K Frozen Plasma L Fresh Plasma M Plasma Cryoprecipitate N Red Blood Cells P Frozen Red Cells Q White Cells R Platelets S Globulin T Fibrinogen V Antihemophilic Factors W Factor IX X Stem Cells, Cord Blood Y Stem Cells, Hematopoietic	0 Autologous 1 Nonautologous
5 Peripheral Artery 6 Central Artery	0 Open 3 Percutaneous	H Whole Blood J Serum Albumin K Frozen Plasma L Fresh Plasma M Plasma Cryoprecipitate N Red Blood Cells P Frozen Red Cells Q White Cells R Platelets S Globulin T Fibrinogen V Antihemophilic Factors W Factor IX	0 Autologous 1 Nonautologous
7 Products of Conception, Circulatory	3 Percutaneous 7 Via Natural or Artificial Opening	H Whole Blood J Serum Albumin K Frozen Plasma L Fresh Plasma M Plasma Cryoprecipitate N Red Blood Cells P Frozen Red Cells Q White Cells R Platelets S Globulin T Fibrinogen V Antihemophilic Factors W Factor IX	1 Nonautologous

3   **Administration**
C   **Indwelling Device**
1   **Irrigation:**   Putting in or on a cleansing substance

Body System/Region Character 4	Approach Character 5	Substance Character 6	Qualifier Character 7
Z Whole Body	X External	8 Irrigating Substance	Z No Qualifier

3   **Administration**
E   **Physiological Systems and Anatomical Regions**
0   **Introduction:**   Putting in or on a therapeutic diagnostic, nutritional, physiological, or prophylactic substance except blood or blood products

Body System/Region Character 4	Approach Character 5	Substance Character 6	Qualifier Character 7
0 Skin and Mucous Membranes	X External	0 Antineoplastic	5 Other Antineoplastic M Monoclonal Antibody
0 Skin and Mucous Membranes	X External	2 Anti-infective	8 Oxazolidinones 9 Other Anti-infective

Continued on next page

3   Administration   *Continued from previous page*
E   Physiological Systems and Anatomical Regions
0   Introduction: Putting in or on a therapeutic diagnostic, nutritional, physiological, or prophylactic substance except blood or blood products

Body System/Region Character 4	Approach Character 5	Substance Character 6	Qualifier Character 7
0 Skin and Mucous Membranes	**X** External	**3** Anti-inflammatory **4** Serum, Toxoid and Vaccine **B** Local Anesthetic **K** Other Diagnostic Substance **M** Pigment **N** Analgesics, Hypnotics, Sedatives **T** Destructive Agent	**Z** No Qualifier
0 Skin and Mucous Membranes	**X** External	**G** Other Therapeutic Substance	**C** Other Substance
1 Subcutaneous Tissue	**3** Percutaneous	**V** Hormone	**G** Insulin **J** Other Hormone
1 Subcutaneous Tissue **2** Muscle	**3** Percutaneous	**3** Anti-inflammatory **4** Serum, Toxoid and Vaccine **6** Nutritional Substance **7** Electrolytic and Water Balance Substance **B** Local Anesthetic **H** Radioactive Substance **J** Contrast Agent **K** Other Diagnostic Substance **N** Analgesics, Hypnotics, Sedatives **T** Destructive Agent	**Z** No Qualifier
1 Subcutaneous Tissue **2** Muscle **A** Bone Marrow **L** Pleural Cavity **M** Peritoneal Cavity **Q** Cranial Cavity and Brain **R** Spinal Canal **S** Epidural Space **T** Peripheral Nerves and Plexi **U** Joints **W** Lymphatics **X** Cranial Nerves **Y** Pericardial Cavity	**3** Percutaneous	**G** Other Therapeutic Substance	**C** Other Substance
1 Subcutaneous Tissue **2** Muscle **A** Bone Marrow **V** Bones **W** Lymphatics	**3** Percutaneous	**0** Antineoplastic	**5** Other Antineoplastic **M** Monoclonal Antibody
1 Subcutaneous Tissue **2** Muscle **L** Pleural Cavity **M** Peritoneal Cavity **Q** Cranial Cavity and Brain **R** Spinal Canal **S** Epidural Space **U** Joints **V** Bones **W** Lymphatics **Y** Pericardial Cavity	**3** Percutaneous	**2** Anti-infective	**8** Oxazolidinones **9** Other Anti-infective
3 Peripheral Vein	**0** Open **3** Percutaneous	**U** Pancreatic Islet Cells	**0** Autologous **1** Nonautologous
3 Peripheral Vein **4** Central Vein **5** Peripheral Artery **6** Central Artery	**0** Open **3** Percutaneous	**0** Antineoplastic	**2** High-dose Interleukin-2 **3** Low-dose Interleukin-2 **5** Other Antineoplastic **M** Monoclonal Antibody
3 Peripheral Vein **4** Central Vein **5** Peripheral Artery **6** Central Artery	**0** Open **3** Percutaneous	**2** Anti-infective	**8** Oxazolidinones **9** Other Anti-infective
3 Peripheral Vein **4** Central Vein **5** Peripheral Artery **6** Central Artery	**0** Open **3** Percutaneous	**3** Anti-inflammatory **4** Serum, Toxoid and Vaccine **6** Nutritional Substance **7** Electrolytic and Water Balance Substance **F** Intracirculatory Anesthetic **H** Radioactive Substance **J** Contrast Agent **K** Other Diagnostic Substance **N** Analgesics, Hypnotics, Sedatives **P** Platelet Inhibitor **R** Antiarrhythmic **T** Destructive Agent **X** Vasopressor	**Z** No Qualifier

Continued on next page

3 **Administration**
E **Physiological Systems and Anatomical Regions**
0 **Introduction:** Putting in or on a therapeutic diagnostic, nutritional, physiological, or prophylactic substance except blood or blood products

Continued from previous page

Body System/Region Character 4	Approach Character 5	Substance Character 6	Qualifier Character 7
3 Peripheral Vein **4** Central Vein **5** Peripheral Artery **6** Central Artery	**0** Open **3** Percutaneous	**G** Other Therapeutic Substance	**C** Other Substance **N** Blood Brain Barrier Disruption
3 Peripheral Vein **4** Central Vein **5** Peripheral Artery **6** Central Artery	**0** Open **3** Percutaneous	**V** Hormone	**G** Insulin **H** Human B-type Natriuretic Peptide **J** Other Hormone
3 Peripheral Vein **4** Central Vein **5** Peripheral Artery **6** Central Artery	**0** Open **3** Percutaneous	**W** Immunotherapeutic	**K** Immunostimulator **L** Immunosuppressive
3 Peripheral Vein **4** Central Vein **5** Peripheral Artery **6** Central Artery **7** Coronary Artery **8** Heart	**0** Open **3** Percutaneous	**1** Thrombolytic	**6** Recombinant Human-activated Protein C **7** Other Thrombolytic
7 Coronary Artery **8** Heart	**0** Open **3** Percutaneous	**G** Other Therapeutic Substance	**C** Other Substance
7 Coronary Artery **8** Heart	**0** Open **3** Percutaneous	**J** Contrast Agent **K** Other Diagnostic Substance **P** Platelet Inhibitor	**Z** No Qualifier
9 Nose	**3** Percutaneous **7** Via Natural or Artificial Opening **X** External	**0** Antineoplastic	**5** Other Antineoplastic **M** Monoclonal Antibody
9 Nose	**3** Percutaneous **7** Via Natural or Artificial Opening **X** External	**3** Anti-inflammatory **4** Serum, Toxoid and Vaccine **B** Local Anesthetic **H** Radioactive Substance **J** Contrast Agent **K** Other Diagnostic Substance **N** Analgesics, Hypnotics, Sedatives **T** Destructive Agent	**Z** No Qualifier
9 Nose **B** Ear **C** Eye **D** Mouth and Pharynx	**3** Percutaneous **7** Via Natural or Artificial Opening **X** External	**2** Anti-infective	**8** Oxazolidinones **9** Other Anti-infective
9 Nose **B** Ear **C** Eye **D** Mouth and Pharynx	**3** Percutaneous **7** Via Natural or Artificial Opening **X** External	**G** Other Therapeutic Substance	**C** Other Substance
B Ear	**3** Percutaneous **7** Via Natural or Artificial Opening **X** External	**3** Anti-inflammatory **B** Local Anesthetic **H** Radioactive Substance **J** Contrast Agent **K** Other Diagnostic Substance **N** Analgesics, Hypnotics, Sedatives **T** Destructive Agent	**Z** No Qualifier
B Ear **C** Eye **D** Mouth and Pharynx	**3** Percutaneous **7** Via Natural or Artificial Opening **X** External	**0** Antineoplastic	**4** Liquid Brachytherapy Radioisotope **5** Other Antineoplastic **M** Monoclonal Antibody
C Eye	**3** Percutaneous **7** Via Natural or Artificial Opening **X** External	**3** Anti-inflammatory **B** Local Anesthetic **H** Radioactive Substance **K** Other Diagnostic Substance **M** Pigment **N** Analgesics, Hypnotics, Sedatives **T** Destructive Agent	**Z** No Qualifier
C Eye	**3** Percutaneous **7** Via Natural or Artificial Opening **X** External	**S** Gas	**F** Other Gas

Continued on next page

3   Administration   *Continued from previous page*
E   Physiological Systems and Anatomical Regions
0   Introduction: Putting in or on a therapeutic diagnostic, nutritional, physiological, or prophylactic substance except blood or blood products

Body System/Region Character 4	Approach Character 5	Substance Character 6	Qualifier Character 7
D Mouth and Pharynx	**3** Percutaneous **7** Via Natural or Artificial Opening **X** External	**3** Anti-inflammatory **4** Serum, Toxoid and Vaccine **6** Nutritional Substance **7** Electrolytic and Water Balance Substance **B** Local Anesthetic **H** Radioactive Substance **J** Contrast Agent **K** Other Diagnostic Substance **N** Analgesics, Hypnotics, Sedatives **R** Antiarrhythmic **T** Destructive Agent	**Z** No Qualifier
E Products of Conception	**3** Percutaneous **7** Via Natural or Artificial Opening **8** Via Natural or Artificial Opening Endoscopic	**0** Antineoplastic	**2** High-dose Interleukin-2 **3** Low-dose Interleukin-2 **4** Liquid Brachytherapy Radioisotope **5** Other Antineoplastic **M** Monoclonal Antibody
E Products of Conception **F** Respiratory Tract **G** Upper GI **H** Lower GI **J** Biliary and Pancreatic Tract **K** Genitourinary Tract **N** Male Reproductive **P** Female Reproductive	**3** Percutaneous **7** Via Natural or Artificial Opening **8** Via Natural or Artificial Opening Endoscopic	**2** Anti-infective	**8** Oxazolidinones **9** Other Anti-infective
E Products of Conception **F** Respiratory Tract **G** Upper GI **H** Lower GI **J** Biliary and Pancreatic Tract **K** Genitourinary Tract **N** Male Reproductive **P** Female Reproductive	**3** Percutaneous **7** Via Natural or Artificial Opening **8** Via Natural or Artificial Opening Endoscopic	**G** Other Therapeutic Substance	**C** Other Substance
E Products of Conception **G** Upper GI **H** Lower GI **J** Biliary and Pancreatic Tract **K** Genitourinary Tract **N** Male Reproductive	**3** Percutaneous **7** Via Natural or Artificial Opening **8** Via Natural or Artificial Opening Endoscopic	**3** Anti-inflammatory **6** Nutritional Substance **7** Electrolytic and Water Balance Substance **B** Local Anesthetic **H** Radioactive Substance **J** Contrast Agent **K** Other Diagnostic Substance **N** Analgesics, Hypnotics, Sedatives **T** Destructive Agent	**Z** No Qualifier
E Products of Conception **G** Upper GI **H** Lower GI **J** Biliary and Pancreatic Tract **K** Genitourinary Tract **N** Male Reproductive **P** Female Reproductive	**3** Percutaneous **7** Via Natural or Artificial Opening **8** Via Natural or Artificial Opening Endoscopic	**S** Gas	**F** Other Gas
F Respiratory Tract	**3** Percutaneous **7** Via Natural or Artificial Opening **8** Via Natural or Artificial Opening Endoscopic	**S** Gas	**D** Nitric Oxide **F** Other Gas
F Respiratory Tract	**7** Via Natural or Artificial Opening **8** Via Natural or Artificial Opening Endoscopic	**3** Anti-inflammatory **6** Nutritional Substance **7** Electrolytic and Water Balance Substance **B** Local Anesthetic **D** Inhalation Anesthetic **H** Radioactive Substance **J** Contrast Agent **K** Other Diagnostic Substance **N** Analgesics, Hypnotics, Sedatives **T** Destructive Agent	**Z** No Qualifier
F Respiratory Tract **G** Upper GI **H** Lower GI **J** Biliary and Pancreatic Tract **K** Genitourinary Tract **N** Male Reproductive **P** Female Reproductive	**3** Percutaneous **7** Via Natural or Artificial Opening **8** Via Natural or Artificial Opening Endoscopic	**0** Antineoplastic	**4** Liquid Brachytherapy Radioisotope **5** Other Antineoplastic **M** Monoclonal Antibody

Continued on next page

3   Administration
E   Physiological Systems and Anatomical Regions   *Continued from previous page*
0   Introduction: Putting in or on a therapeutic diagnostic, nutritional, physiological, or prophylactic substance except blood or blood products

Body System/Region Character 4	Approach Character 5	Substance Character 6	Qualifier Character 7
F Respiratory Tract **L** Pleural Cavity **M** Peritoneal Cavity **U** Joints **V** Bones **W** Lymphatics **Y** Pericardial Cavity	**3** Percutaneous	**3** Anti-inflammatory **6** Nutritional Substance **7** Electrolytic and Water Balance Substance **B** Local Anesthetic **H** Radioactive Substance **J** Contrast Agent **K** Other Diagnostic Substance **N** Analgesics, Hypnotics, Sedatives **T** Destructive Agent	**Z** No Qualifier
J Biliary and Pancreatic Tract	**3** Percutaneous **7** Via Natural or Artificial Opening **8** Via Natural or Artificial Opening Endoscopic	**U** Pancreatic Islet Cells	**0** Autologous **1** Nonautologous
L Pleural Cavity **M** Peritoneal Cavity **P** Female Reproductive	**0** Open	**5** Adhesion Barrier	**Z** No Qualifier
L Pleural Cavity **M** Peritoneal Cavity **Q** Cranial Cavity and Brain **R** Spinal Canal **S** Epidural Space **U** Joints **Y** Pericardial Cavity	**3** Percutaneous **7** Via Natural or Artificial Opening	**S** Gas	**F** Other Gas
L Pleural Cavity **M** Peritoneal Cavity **Q** Cranial Cavity and Brain **U** Joints **Y** Pericardial Cavity	**3** Percutaneous **7** Via Natural or Artificial Opening	**0** Antineoplastic	**4** Liquid Brachytherapy Radioisotope **5** Other Antineoplastic **M** Monoclonal Antibody
P Female Reproductive	**3** Percutaneous **7** Via Natural or Artificial Opening	**3** Anti-inflammatory **6** Nutritional Substance **7** Electrolytic and Water Balance Substance **B** Local Anesthetic **H** Radioactive Substance **J** Contrast Agent **K** Other Diagnostic Substance **L** Sperm **N** Analgesics, Hypnotics, Sedatives **T** Destructive Agent	**Z** No Qualifier
P Female Reproductive	**3** Percutaneous **7** Via Natural or Artificial Opening	**Q** Fertilized Ovum	**0** Autologous **1** Nonautologous

P Female Reproductive	**8** Via Natural or Artificial Opening
	    Endoscopic
		3 Anti-inflammatory
		6 Nutritional Substance
		7 Electrolytic and Water Balance
		    Substance
		B Local Anesthetic
		H Radioactive Substance
		J Contrast Agent
		K Other Diagnostic Substance
		N Analgesics, Hypnotics, Sedatives
		T Destructive Agent
			Z No Qualifier

Q Cranial Cavity and Brain	**3** Percutaneous	**3** Anti-inflammatory **6** Nutritional Substance **7** Electrolytic and Water Balance Substance **A** Stem Cells, Embryonic **B** Local Anesthetic **H** Radioactive Substance **J** Contrast Agent **K** Other Diagnostic Substance **N** Analgesics, Hypnotics, Sedatives **T** Destructive Agent	**Z** No Qualifier
Q Cranial Cavity and Brain **R** Spinal Canal	**0** Open	**A** Stem Cells, Embryonic	**Z** No Qualifier
Q Cranial Cavity and Brain **R** Spinal Canal	**0** Open **3** Percutaneous	**E** Stem Cells, Somatic	**0** Autologous **1** Nonautologous

Continued on next page

3 Administration
E Physiological Systems and Anatomical Regions
0 Introduction: Putting in or on a therapeutic diagnostic, nutritional, physiological, or prophylactic substance except blood or blood products

Continued from previous page

Body System/Region Character 4	Approach Character 5	Substance Character 6	Qualifier Character 7
R Spinal Canal	**3** Percutaneous	**3** Anti-inflammatory **6** Nutritional Substance **7** Electrolytic and Water Balance Substance **A** Stem Cells, Embryonic **B** Local Anesthetic **C** Regional Anesthetic **H** Radioactive Substance **J** Contrast Agent **K** Other Diagnostic Substance **N** Analgesics, Hypnotics, Sedatives **T** Destructive Agent	**Z** No Qualifier
R Spinal Canal **S** Epidural Space	**3** Percutaneous	**0** Antineoplastic	**2** High-dose Interleukin-2 **3** Low-dose Interleukin-2 **4** Liquid Brachytherapy Radioisotope **5** Other Antineoplastic **M** Monoclonal Antibody
S Epidural Space	**3** Percutaneous	**3** Anti-inflammatory **6** Nutritional Substance **7** Electrolytic and Water Balance Substance **B** Local Anesthetic **C** Regional Anesthetic **H** Radioactive Substance **J** Contrast Agent **K** Other Diagnostic Substance **N** Analgesics, Hypnotics, Sedatives **T** Destructive Agent	**Z** No Qualifier
T Peripheral Nerves and Plexi **X** Cranial Nerves	**3** Percutaneous	**3** Anti-inflammatory **C** Regional Anesthetic **T** Destructive Agent	**Z** No Qualifier
V Bones	**3** Percutaneous	**G** Other Therapeutic Substance	**B** Recombinant Bone Morphogenetic Protein **C** Other Substance

3 Administration
E Physiological Systems and Anatomical Regions
1 Irrigation: Putting in or on a cleansing substance

Body System/Region Character 4	Approach Character 5	Substance Character 6	Qualifier Character 7
0 Skin and Mucous Membranes **C** Eye	**3** Percutaneous **X** External	**8** Irrigating Substance	**X** Diagnostic **Z** No Qualifier
9 Nose **B** Ear **F** Respiratory Tract **G** Upper GI **H** Lower GI **J** Biliary and Pancreatic Tract **K** Genitourinary Tract **N** Male Reproductive **P** Female Reproductive	**3** Percutaneous **7** Via Natural or Artificial Opening **8** Via Natural or Artificial Opening Endoscopic	**8** Irrigating Substance	**X** Diagnostic **Z** No Qualifier
L Pleural Cavity **M** Peritoneal Cavity **Q** Cranial Cavity and Brain **R** Spinal Canal **S** Epidural Space **U** Joints **Y** Pericardial Cavity	**3** Percutaneous	**8** Irrigating Substance	**X** Diagnostic **Z** No Qualifier
M Peritoneal Cavity	**3** Percutaneous	**9** Dialysate	**Z** No Qualifier

Measurement and Monitoring 4A0–4B0

4 Measurement and Monitoring
A Physiological Systems
0 Measurement: Determining the level of a physiological or physical function at a point in time

Body System Character 4	Approach Character 5	Function/Device Character 6	Qualifier Character 7
0 Central Nervous	**0** Open	**2** Conductivity **4** Electrical Activity **B** Pressure	**Z** No Qualifier
0 Central Nervous	**3** Percutaneous **7** Via Natural or Artificial Opening	**B** Pressure **K** Temperature **R** Saturation	**D** Intracranial
0 Central Nervous	**X** External	**2** Conductivity **4** Electrical Activity	**Z** No Qualifier
1 Peripheral Nervous	**0** Open **3** Percutaneous **X** External	**2** Conductivity	**9** Sensory **B** Motor
2 Cardiac	**0** Open **3** Percutaneous	**N** Sampling and Pressure	**6** Right Heart **7** Left Heart **8** Bilateral
2 Cardiac	**0** Open **3** Percutaneous **X** External	**4** Electrical Activity **9** Output **C** Rate **F** Rhythm **H** Sound **P** Action Currents	**Z** No Qualifier
2 Cardiac	**X** External	**M** Total Activity	**4** Stress
3 Arterial	**0** Open **3** Percutaneous	**5** Flow **J** Pulse	**1** Peripheral **3** Pulmonary **C** Coronary
3 Arterial	**0** Open **3** Percutaneous	**B** Pressure	**1** Peripheral **3** Pulmonary **C** Coronary **F** Other Thoracic
3 Arterial	**0** Open **3** Percutaneous	**H** Sound **R** Saturation	**1** Peripheral
3 Arterial	**X** External	**5** Flow **B** Pressure **H** Sound **J** Pulse **R** Saturation	**1** Peripheral
4 Venous	**0** Open **3** Percutaneous	**5** Flow **B** Pressure **J** Pulse	**0** Central **1** Peripheral **2** Portal **3** Pulmonary
4 Venous	**0** Open **3** Percutaneous	**R** Saturation	**1** Peripheral
4 Venous	**X** External	**5** Flow **B** Pressure **J** Pulse **R** Saturation	**1** Peripheral
5 Circulatory	**X** External	**L** Volume	**Z** No Qualifier
6 Lymphatic	**0** Open **3** Percutaneous	**5** Flow **B** Pressure	**Z** No Qualifier
7 Visual	**X** External	**0** Acuity **7** Mobility **B** Pressure	**Z** No Qualifier
8 Olfactory	**X** External	**0** Acuity	**Z** No Qualifier
9 Respiratory	**7** Via Natural or Artificial Opening **8** Via Natural or Artificial Opening Endoscopic **X** External	**1** Capacity **5** Flow **C** Rate **D** Resistance **L** Volume **M** Total Activity	**Z** No Qualifier
B Gastrointestinal	**7** Via Natural or Artificial Opening **8** Via Natural or Artificial Opening Endoscopic	**8** Motility **B** Pressure **G** Secretion	**Z** No Qualifier

Continued on next page

4   Measurement and Monitoring
A   Physiological Systems
0   Measurement: Determining the level of a physiological or physical function at a point in time

Continued from previous page

Body System Character 4	Approach Character 5	Function/Device Character 6	Qualifier Character 7
C Biliary	**3** Percutaneous **4** Percutaneous Endoscopic **7** Via Natural or Artificial Opening **8** Via Natural or Artificial Opening Endoscopic	**5** Flow **B** Pressure	**Z** No Qualifier
D Urinary	**7** Via Natural or Artificial Opening	**3** Contractility **5** Flow **B** Pressure **D** Resistance **L** Volume	**Z** No Qualifier
F Musculoskeletal	**3** Percutaneous **X** External	**3** Contractility	**Z** No Qualifier
G Whole Body	**7** Via Natural or Artificial Opening	**6** Metabolism **K** Temperature	**Z** No Qualifier
G Whole Body	**X** External	**6** Metabolism **K** Temperature **Q** Sleep	**Z** No Qualifier
H Products of Conception, Cardiac	**7** Via Natural or Artificial Opening **8** Via Natural or Artificial Opening Endoscopic	**4** Electrical Activity **C** Rate **F** Rhythm **H** Sound	**Z** No Qualifier
J Products of Conception, Nervous	**7** Via Natural or Artificial Opening **8** Via Natural or Artificial Opening Endoscopic	**2** Conductivity **4** Electrical Activity **B** Pressure	**Z** No Qualifier

4   Measurement and Monitoring
A   Physiological Systems
1   Monitoring: Determining the level of a physiological or physical function repetively over a period of time

Body System Character 4	Approach Character 5	Function/Device Character 6	Qualifier Character 7
0 Central Nervous	**0** Open	**2** Conductivity **4** Electrical Activity **B** Pressure	**Z** No Qualifier
0 Central Nervous	**3** Percutaneous **7** Via Natural or Artificial Opening	**B** Pressure **K** Temperature **R** Saturation	**D** Intracranial
0 Central Nervous	**X** External	**2** Conductivity **4** Electrical Activity	**Z** No Qualifier
1 Peripheral Nervous	**0** Open **3** Percutaneous **X** External	**2** Conductivity	**9** Sensory **B** Motor
2 Cardiac	**0** Open **3** Percutaneous	**4** Electrical Activity **9** Output **C** Rate **F** Rhythm **H** Sound	**Z** No Qualifier
2 Cardiac	**X** External	**4** Electrical Activity	**5** Ambulatory **Z** No Qualifier
2 Cardiac	**X** External	**9** Output **C** Rate **F** Rhythm **H** Sound	**Z** No Qualifier
2 Cardiac	**X** External	**M** Total Activity	**4** Stress
3 Arterial	**0** Open **3** Percutaneous	**5** Flow **B** Pressure **J** Pulse	**1** Peripheral **3** Pulmonary **C** Coronary
3 Arterial	**0** Open **3** Percutaneous	**H** Sound **R** Saturation	**1** Peripheral
3 Arterial	**X** External	**5** Flow **B** Pressure **H** Sound **J** Pulse **R** Saturation	**1** Peripheral

Continued on next page

4   Measurement and Monitoring
A   Physiological Systems
1   Monitoring: Determining the level of a physiological or physical function repetively over a period of time

Continued from previous page

Body System Character 4	Approach Character 5	Function/Device Character 6	Qualifier Character 7
4 Venous	**0** Open **3** Percutaneous	**5** Flow **B** Pressure **J** Pulse	**0** Central **1** Peripheral **2** Portal **3** Pulmonary
4 Venous	**0** Open **3** Percutaneous	**R** Saturation	**0** Central **2** Portal **3** Pulmonary
4 Venous	**X** External	**5** Flow **B** Pressure **J** Pulse	**1** Peripheral
6 Lymphatic	**0** Open **3** Percutaneous	**5** Flow **B** Pressure	**Z** No Qualifier
9 Respiratory	**7** Via Natural or Artificial Opening **X** External	**1** Capacity **5** Flow **C** Rate **D** Resistance **L** Volume	**Z** No Qualifier
B Gastrointestinal	**7** Via Natural or Artificial Opening **8** Via Natural or Artificial Opening Endoscopic	**8** Motility **B** Pressure **G** Secretion	**Z** No Qualifier
D Urinary	**7** Via Natural or Artificial Opening	**3** Contractility **5** Flow **B** Pressure **D** Resistance **L** Volume	**Z** No Qualifier
G Whole Body	**7** Via Natural or Artificial Opening	**K** Temperature	**Z** No Qualifier
G Whole Body	**X** External	**K** Temperature **Q** Sleep	**Z** No Qualifier
H Products of Conception, Cardiac	**7** Via Natural or Artificial Opening **8** Via Natural or Artificial Opening Endoscopic	**4** Electrical Activity **C** Rate **F** Rhythm **H** Sound	**Z** No Qualifier
J Products of Conception, Nervous	**7** Via Natural or Artificial Opening **8** Via Natural or Artificial Opening Endoscopic	**2** Conductivity **4** Electrical Activity **B** Pressure	**Z** No Qualifier

4   Measurement and Monitoring
B   Physiological Devices
0   Measurement: Determining the level of a physiological or physical function at a point in time

Body System Character 4	Approach Character 5	Function/Device Character 6	Qualifier Character 7
0 Central Nervous **1** Peripheral Nervous **F** Musculoskeletal	**X** External	**V** Stimulator	**Z** No Qualifier
2 Cardiac	**X** External	**S** Pacemaker **T** Defibrillator	**Z** No Qualifier
9 Respiratory	**X** External	**S** Pacemaker	**Z** No Qualifier

Extracorporeal Assistance and Performance 5A0–5A2

5   Extracorporeal Assistance and Performance
A   Physiological Systems
0   Assistance: Taking over a portion of a physiological function by extracorporeal means

Body System Character 4	Duration Character 5	Function Character 6	Qualifier Character 7
2 Cardiac	**1** Intermittent **2** Continuous	**1** Output	**0** Balloon Pump **5** Pulsatile Compression **6** Pump
5 Circulatory	**1** Intermittent **2** Continuous	**2** Oxygenation	**1** Hyperbaric **3** Membrane **C** Supersaturated
9 Respiratory	**3** Less than 24 Consecutive Hours **4** 24-96 Consecutive Hours **5** Greater than 96 Consecutive Hours	**5** Ventilation	**7** Continuous Positive Airway Pressure **8** Intermittent Positive Airway Pressure **9** Continuous Negative Airway Pressure **B** Intermittent Negative Airway Pressure **Z** No Qualifier

5   Extracorporeal Assistance and Performance
A   Physiological Systems
1   Performance: Completely taking over a physiological function by extracorporal means

Body System Character 4	Duration Character 5	Function Character 6	Qualifier Character 7
2 Cardiac	**0** Single	**1** Output	**2** Manual
2 Cardiac	**1** Intermittent	**3** Pacing	**Z** No Qualifier
2 Cardiac	**2** Continuous	**1** Output **3** Pacing	**Z** No Qualifier
5 Circulatory	**2** Continuous	**2** Oxygenation	**3** Membrane
9 Respiratory	**0** Single	**5** Ventilation	**4** Nonmechanical
9 Respiratory	**3** Less than 24 Consecutive Hours **4** 24-96 Consecutive Hours **5** Greater than 96 Consecutive Hours	**5** Ventilation	**Z** No Qualifier
C Biliary **D** Urinary	**0** Single **6** Multiple	**0** Filtration	**Z** No Qualifier

5   Extracorporeal Assistance and Performance
A   Physiological Systems
2   Restoration: Returning, or attempting to return, a physiological function to its original state by extracorporeal means

Body System Character 4	Duration Character 5	Function Character 6	Qualifier Character 7
2 Cardiac	**0** Single	**4** Rhythm	**Z** No Qualifier

Extracorporeal Therapies 6A0–6A9

6   Extracorporeal Therapies
A   Physiological Systems
0   Atmospheric Control: Extracorporeal control of atmospheric pressure and composition

Body System Character 4	Duration Character 5	Qualifier Character 6	Qualifier Character 7
G Whole Body	**0** Single **1** Multiple	**Z** No Qualifier	**Z** No Qualifier

6   Extracorporeal Therapies
A   Physiological Systems
1   Decompression: Extracorporal elimination of undissolved gas from body fluids

Body System Character 4	Duration Character 5	Qualifier Character 6	Qualifier Character 7
5 Circulatory	**0** Single **1** Multiple	**Z** No Qualifier	**Z** No Qualifier

6   Extracorporeal Therapies
A   Physiological Systems
2   Electromagnetic Therapy: Extracorporeal treatment by electromagnetic rays

Body System Character 4	Duration Character 5	Qualifier Character 6	Qualifier Character 7
1 Urinary **2** Central Nervous	**0** Single **1** Multiple	**Z** No Qualifier	**Z** No Qualifier

6   Extracorporeal Therapies
A   Physiological Systems
3   Hyperthermia: Extracorporeal raising of body temperature

Body System Character 4	Duration Character 5	Qualifier Character 6	Qualifier Character 7
G Whole Body	**0** Single **1** Multiple	**Z** No Qualifier	**Z** No Qualifier

6   Extracorporeal Therapies
A   Physiological Systems
4   Hypothermia: Extracorporeal lowering of body temperature

Body System Character 4	Duration Character 5	Qualifier Character 6	Qualifier Character 7
G Whole Body	**0** Single **1** Multiple	**Z** No Qualifier	**Z** No Qualifier

6   Extracorporeal Therapies
A   Physiological Systems
5   Pheresis: Extracorporeal separation of blood products

Body System Character 4	Duration Character 5	Qualifier Character 6	Qualifier Character 7
5 Circulatory	**0** Single **1** Multiple	**Z** No Qualifier	**0** Erythrocytes **1** Leukocytes **2** Platelets **3** Plasma **T** Stem Cells, Cord Blood **V** Stem Cells, Hematopoietic

6 Extracorporeal Therapies
A Physiological Systems
6 Phototherapy: Extracorporeal treatment by light rays

Body System Character 4	Duration Character 5	Qualifier Character 6	Qualifier Character 7
0 Skin 5 Circulatory	0 Single 1 Multiple	Z No Qualifier	Z No Qualifier

6 Extracorporeal Therapies
A Physiological Systems
7 Ultrasound Therapy: Extracorporeal treatment by ultrasound

Body System Character 4	Duration Character 5	Qualifier Character 6	Qualifier Character 7
5 Circulatory	0 Single 1 Multiple	Z No Qualifier	4 Head and Neck Vessels 5 Heart 6 Peripheral Vessels 7 Other Vessels Z No Qualifier

6 Extracorporeal Therapies
A Physiological Systems
8 Ultraviolet Light Therapy: Extracorporeal treatment by ultraviolet light

Body System Character 4	Duration Character 5	Qualifier Character 6	Qualifier Character 7
0 Skin	0 Single 1 Multiple	Z No Qualifier	Z No Qualifier

6 Extracorporeal Therapies
A Physiological Systems
9 Shock Wave Therapy: Extracorporeal treatment by shock waves

Body System Character 4	Duration Character 5	Qualifier Character 6	Qualifier Character 7
3 Musculoskeletal	0 Single 1 Multiple	Z No Qualifier	Z No Qualifier

Osteopathic 7W0

7 Osteopathic
W Anatomical Regions
0 Treatment: Manual treatment to eliminate or alleviate somatic dysfunction and related disorders

Body Region Character 4	Approach Character 5	Method Character 6	Qualifier Character 7
0 Head 1 Cervical 2 Thoracic 3 Lumbar 4 Sacrum 5 Pelvis 6 Lower Extremities 7 Upper Extremities 8 Rib Cage 9 Abdomen	X External	0 Articulatory-Raising 1 Fascial Release 2 General Mobilization 3 High Velocity-Low Amplitude 4 Indirect 5 Low Velocity-High Amplitude 6 Lymphatic Pump 7 Muscle Energy-Isometric 8 Muscle Energy-Isotonic 9 Other Method	Z None

Other Procedures 8E0

8   Other Procedures
E   Physiological Systems and Anatomical Regions
0   Other Procedures: Methodologies which attempt to remediate or cure a disorder or disease

Body Region Character 4	Approach Character 5	Method Character 6	Qualifier Character 7
1 Nervous System K Musculoskeletal System U Female Reproductive System	X External	Y Other Method	7 Examination
2 Circulatory System	3 Percutaneous	D Near Infrared Spectroscopy	Z No Qualifier
9 Head and Neck Region W Trunk Region	0 Open 3 Percutaneous 4 Percutaneous Endoscopic 7 Via Natural or Artificial Opening 8 Via Natural or Artificial Opening Endoscopic X External	C Robotic Assisted Procedure	Z No Qualifier
9 Head and Neck Region W Trunk Region X Upper Extremity Y Lower Extremity	X External	B Computer Assisted Procedure	F With Fluoroscopy G With Computerized Tomography H With Magnetic Resonance Imaging Z No Qualifier
9 Head and Neck Region W Trunk Region X Upper Extremity Y Lower Extremity	X External	Y Other Method	8 Suture Removal
H Integumentary System and Breast	3 Percutaneous	0 Acupuncture	0 Anesthesia Z No Qualifier
H Integumentary System and Breast	X External	6 Collection	2 Breast Milk
H Integumentary System and Breast	X External	Y Other Method	9 Piercing
K Musculoskeletal System	X External	1 Therapeutic Massage	Z No Qualifier
V Male Reproductive System	X External	1 Therapeutic Massage	C Prostate D Rectum
V Male Reproductive System	X External	6 Collection	3 Sperm
X Upper Extremity Y Lower Extremity	0 Open 3 Percutaneous 4 Percutaneous Endoscopic X External	C Robotic Assisted Procedure	Z No Qualifier
Z None	X External	Y Other Method	1 In Vitro Fertilization 4 Yoga Therapy 5 Meditation 6 Isolation

Chiropractic 9WB

9   Chiropractic
W   Anatomical Regions
B   Manipulation: Manual procedure that involves a directed thrust to move a joint past the physiological range of motion, without exceeding the anatomical limit

Body Region Character 4	Approach Character 5	Method Character 6	Qualifier Character 7
0 Head 1 Cervical 2 Thoracic 3 Lumbar 4 Sacrum 5 Pelvis 6 Lower Extremities 7 Upper Extremities 8 Rib Cage 9 Abdomen	X External	B Non-Manual C Indirect Visceral D Extra-Articular F Direct Visceral G Long Lever Specific Contact H Short Lever Specific Contact J Long and Short Lever Specific Contact K Mechanically Assisted L Other Method	Z None

Imaging B00–BY4

B **Imaging**
0 **Central Nervous System**
0 **Plain Radiography:** Planar display of an image developed from the capture of external ionizing radiation on photographic or photoconductive plate

Body Part Character 4	Contrast Character 5	Qualifier Character 6	Qualifier Character 7
B Spinal Cord	**0** High Osmolar **1** Low Osmolar **Y** Other Contrast **Z** None	**Z** None	**Z** None

B **Imaging**
0 **Central Nervous System**
1 **Fluoroscopy:** Single plane or bi-plane real-time display of an image developed from the capture of external ionizing radiation on a fluorescent screen. The image may also be stored by either digital or analog means

Body Part Character 4	Contrast Character 5	Qualifier Character 6	Qualifier Character 7
B Spinal Cord	**0** High Osmolar **1** Low Osmolar **Y** Other Contrast **Z** None	**Z** None	**Z** None

B **Imaging**
0 **Central Nervous System**
2 **Computerized Tomography (CT Scan):** Computer reformatted digital display of multiplanar images developed from the capture of multiple exposures of external ionizing radiation

Body Part Character 4	Contrast Character 5	Qualifier Character 6	Qualifier Character 7
0 Brain **7** Cisterna **8** Cerebral Ventricle(s) **9** Sella Turcica/Pituitary Gland **B** Spinal Cord	**0** High Osmolar **1** Low Osmolar **Y** Other Contrast	**0** Unenhanced and Enhanced **Z** None	**Z** None
0 Brain **7** Cisterna **8** Cerebral Ventricle(s) **9** Sella Turcica/Pituitary Gland **B** Spinal Cord	**Z** None	**Z** None	**Z** None

B **Imaging**
0 **Central Nervous System**
3 **Magnetic Resonance Imaging (MRI):** Computer reformatted digital display of multiplanar images developed from the capture of radio-frequency signals emitted by nuclei in a body site excited within a magnetic field

Body Part Character 4	Contrast Character 5	Qualifier Character 6	Qualifier Character 7
0 Brain **9** Sella Turcica/Pituitary Gland **B** Spinal Cord **C** Acoustic Nerves	**Y** Other Contrast	**0** Unenhanced and Enhanced **Z** None	**Z** None
0 Brain **9** Sella Turcica/Pituitary Gland **B** Spinal Cord **C** Acoustic Nerves	**Z** None	**Z** None	**Z** None

B **Imaging**
0 **Central Nervous System**
4 **Ultrasonography:** Real time dispaly of images of anatomy or flow information developed from the capture of relected and attenuated high frequency sound waves

Body Part Character 4	Contrast Character 5	Qualifier Character 6	Qualifier Character 7
0 Brain **B** Spinal Cord	**Z** None	**Z** None	**Z** None

B Imaging
2 Heart
0 **Plain Radiography:** Planar display of an image developed from the capture of external ionizing radiation on photographic or photoconductive plate

Body Part Character 4	Contrast Character 5	Qualifier Character 6	Qualifier Character 7
0 Coronary Artery, Single 1 Coronary Arteries, Multiple 2 Coronary Artery Bypass Graft, Single 3 Coronary Artery Bypass Grafts, Multiple 4 Heart, Right 5 Heart, Left 6 Heart, Right and Left 7 Internal Mammary Bypass Graft, Right 8 Internal Mammary Bypass Graft, Left F Bypass Graft, Other	0 High Osmolar 1 Low Osmolar Y Other Contrast	Z None	Z None

B Imaging
2 Heart
1 **Fluoroscopy:** Single plane or bi-plane real time display of an image developed from the capture of external ionizing radioation on a fluorescent screen. The image may also be stored by either digital or analog means

Body Part Character 4	Contrast Character 5	Qualifier Character 6	Qualifier Character 7
0 Coronary Artery, Single 1 Coronary Arteries, Multiple 2 Coronary Artery Bypass Graft, Single 3 Coronary Artery Bypass Grafts, Multiple	0 High Osmolar 1 Low Osmolar Y Other Contrast	1 Laser	0 Intraoperative
0 Coronary Artery, Single 1 Coronary Arteries, Multiple 2 Coronary Artery Bypass Graft, Single 3 Coronary Artery Bypass Grafts, Multiple 4 Heart, Right 5 Heart, Left 6 Heart, Right and Left 7 Internal Mammary Bypass Graft, Right 8 Internal Mammary Bypass Graft, Left F Bypass Graft, Other	0 High Osmolar 1 Low Osmolar Y Other Contrast	Z None	Z None

B Imaging
2 Heart
2 **Computerized Tomography (CT Scan):** Computer reformatted digital display of multiplanar images developed from the capture of multiple exposures of external ionizing radiation

Body Part Character 4	Contrast Character 5	Qualifier Character 6	Qualifier Character 7
1 Coronary Arteries, Multiple 3 Coronary Artery Bypass Grafts, Multiple 6 Heart, Right and Left	0 High Osmolar 1 Low Osmolar Y Other Contrast	0 Unenhanced and Enhanced Z None	Z None
1 Coronary Arteries, Multiple 3 Coronary Artery Bypass Grafts, Multiple 6 Heart, Right and Left	Z None	Z None	Z None

B Imaging
2 Heart
3 **Magnetic Resonance Imaging (MRI):** Computer reformatted digital display of multiplanar images developed from the capture of radio-frequency signals emitted by nuclei in a body site excited within a magnetic field

Body Part Character 4	Contrast Character 5	Qualifier Character 6	Qualifier Character 7
1 Coronary Arteries, Multiple 3 Coronary Artery Bypass Grafts, Multiple 6 Heart, Right and Left	Y Other Contrast	0 Unenhanced and Enhanced Z None	Z None
1 Coronary Arteries, Multiple 3 Coronary Artery Bypass Grafts, Multiple 6 Heart, Right and Left	Z None	Z None	Z None

B   Imaging
2   Heart
4   Ultrasonography: Real time dispaly of images of anatomy or flow information developed from the capture of relected and attenuated high
          frequency sound waves

Body Part Character 4	Contrast Character 5	Qualifier Character 6	Qualifier Character 7
0 Coronary Artery, Single **1** Coronary Arteries, Multiple **4** Heart, Right **5** Heart, Left **6** Heart, Right and Left **B** Heart with Aorta **C** Pericardium **D** Pediatric Heart	**Y** Other Contrast **Z** None	**Z** None	**Z** None

B   Imaging
3   Upper Arteries
0   Plain Radiography: Planar display of an image developed from the capture of external ionizing radiation on photographic or photoconductive
          plate

Body Part Character 4	Contrast Character 5	Qualifier Character 6	Qualifier Character 7

0 Thoracic Aorta
1 Brachiocephalic-Subclavian
      Artery, Right
2 Subclavian Artery, Left
3 Common Carotid Artery, Right
4 Common Carotid Artery, Left
5 Common Carotid Arteries,
      Bilateral
6 Internal Carotid Artery, Right
7 Internal Carotid Artery, Left
8 Internal Carotid Arteries,
      Bilateral
9 External Carotid Artery, Right
B External Carotid Artery, Left
C External Carotid Arteries,
      Bilateral
D Vertebral Artery, Right
F Vertebral Artery, Left
G Vertebral Arteries, Bilateral
H Upper Extremity Arteries, Right
J Upper Extremity Arteries, Left
K Upper Extremity Arteries,
      Bilateral
L Intercostal and Bronchial Arteries
M Spinal Arteries
N Upper Arteries, Other
P Thoraco-Abdominal Aorta
Q Cervico-Cerebral Arch
R Intracranial Arteries
S Pulmonary Artery, Right
T Pulmonary Artery, Left
	0 High Osmolar
	1 Low Osmolar
	Y Other Contrast
	Z None
		Z None	**Z** None

B   **Imaging**
3   **Upper Arteries**
1   **Fluoroscopy:**   Single plane or bi-plane real time display of an image developed from the c apture of external ionizing radioation on a fluorescent screen. The image may also be stored by either digital or analog means

Body Part Character 4	Contrast Character 5	Qualifier Character 6	Qualifier Character 7
0 Thoracic Aorta 1 Brachiocephalic-Subclavian Artery, Right 2 Subclavian Artery, Left 3 Common Carotid Artery, Right 4 Common Carotid Artery, Left 5 Common Carotid Arteries, Bilateral 6 Internal Carotid Artery, Right 7 Internal Carotid Artery, Left 8 Internal Carotid Arteries, Bilateral 9 External Carotid Artery, Right B External Carotid Artery, Left C External Carotid Arteries, Bilateral D Vertebral Artery, Right F Vertebral Artery, Left G Vertebral Arteries, Bilateral H Upper Extremity Arteries, Right J Upper Extremity Arteries, Left K Upper Extremity Arteries, Bilateral L Intercostal and Bronchial Arteries M Spinal Arteries N Upper Arteries, Other P Thoraco-Abdominal Aorta Q Cervico-Cerebral Arch R Intracranial Arteries S Pulmonary Artery, Right T Pulmonary Artery, Left	0 High Osmolar 1 Low Osmolar Y Other Contrast Z None	Z None	Z None

B   **Imaging**
3   **Upper Arteries**
2   **Computerized Tomography (CT Scan):**   Computer reformatted digital display of multiplanar images developed from the capture of multiple exposures of external ionizing radiation

Body Part Character 4	Contrast Character 5	Qualifier Character 6	Qualifier Character 7
0 Thoracic Aorta 5 Common Carotid Arteries, Bilateral 8 Internal Carotid Arteries, Bilateral G Vertebral Arteries, Bilateral R Intracranial Arteries S Pulmonary Artery, Right T Pulmonary Artery, Left	0 High Osmolar 1 Low Osmolar Y Other Contrast Z None	Z None	Z None

B   **Imaging**
3   **Upper Arteries**
3   **Magnetic Resonance Imaging (MRI):** Computer reformatted digital display of multiplanar images developed from the capture of radio-frequency signals emitted by nuclei in a body site excited within a magnetic field

Body Part Character 4	Contrast Character 5	Qualifier Character 6	Qualifier Character 7
0 Thoracic Aorta 5 Common Carotid Arteries, Bilateral 8 Internal Carotid Arteries, Bilateral G Vertebral Arteries, Bilateral H Upper Extremity Arteries, Right J Upper Extremity Arteries, Left K Upper Extremity Arteries, Bilateral M Spinal Arteries Q Cervico-Cerebral Arch R Intracranial Arteries	Y Other Contrast	0 Unenhanced and Enhanced Z None	Z None

Continued on next page

Continued from previous page

B **Imaging**
3 **Upper Arteries**
3 **Magnetic Resonance Imaging (MRI):** Computer reformatted digital display of multiplanar images developed from the capture of radio-frequency signals emitted by nuclei in a body site excited within a magnetic field

Body Part Character 4	Contrast Character 5	Qualifier Character 6	Qualifier Character 7
0 Thoracic Aorta **5** Common Carotid Arteries, Bilateral **8** Internal Carotid Arteries, Bilateral **G** Vertebral Arteries, Bilateral **H** Upper Extremity Arteries, Right **J** Upper Extremity Arteries, Left **K** Upper Extremity Arteries, Bilateral **M** Spinal Arteries **Q** Cervico-Cerebral Arch **R** Intracranial Arteries	**Z** None	**Z** None	**Z** None

B **Imaging**
3 **Upper Arteries**
4 **Ultrasonography:** Real time display of images of anatomy or flow information developed from the capture of reflected and attenuated high frequency sound waves

Body Part Character 4	Contrast Character 5	Qualifier Character 6	Qualifier Character 7
0 Thoracic Aorta **1** Brachiocephalic-Subclavian Artery, Right **2** Subclavian Artery, Left **3** Common Carotid Artery, Right **4** Common Carotid Artery, Left **5** Common Carotid Arteries, Bilateral **6** Internal Carotid Artery, Right **7** Internal Carotid Artery, Left **8** Internal Carotid Arteries, Bilateral **H** Upper Extremity Arteries, Right **J** Upper Extremity Arteries, Left **K** Upper Extremity Arteries, Bilateral **R** Intracranial Arteries **S** Pulmonary Artery, Right **T** Pulmonary Artery, Left **V** Ophthalmic Arteries	**Z** None	**Z** None	**Z** None

B **Imaging**
4 **Lower Arteries**
0 **Plain Radiography:** Planar display of an image developed from the capture of external ionizing radiation on photographic or photoconductive plate

Body Part Character 4	Contrast Character 5	Qualifier Character 6	Qualifier Character 7
0 Abdominal Aorta **2** Hepatic Artery **3** Splenic Arteries **4** Superior Mesenteric Artery **5** Inferior Mesenteric Artery **6** Renal Artery, Right **7** Renal Artery, Left **8** Renal Arteries, Bilateral **9** Lumbar Arteries **B** Intra-Abdominal Arteries, Other **C** Pelvic Arteries **D** Aorta and Bilateral Lower Extremity Arteries **F** Lower Extremity Arteries, Right **G** Lower Extremity Arteries, Left **J** Lower Arteries, Other **M** Renal Artery Transplant	**0** High Osmolar **1** Low Osmolar **Y** Other Contrast	**Z** None	**Z** None

B   Imaging
4   Lower Arteries
1   Fluoroscopy: Single plane or bi-plane real time display of an image developed from the capture of external ionizing radioation on a fluorescent screen. The image may also be stored by either digital or analog means

Body Part Character 4	Contrast Character 5	Qualifier Character 6	Qualifier Character 7
0 Abdominal Aorta **2** Hepatic Artery **3** Splenic Arteries **4** Superior Mesenteric Artery **5** Inferior Mesenteric Artery **6** Renal Artery, Right **7** Renal Artery, Left **8** Renal Arteries, Bilateral **9** Lumbar Arteries **B** Intra-Abdominal Arteries, Other **C** Pelvic Arteries **D** Aorta and Bilateral Lower Extremity Arteries **F** Lower Extremity Arteries, Right **G** Lower Extremity Arteries, Left **J** Lower Arteries, Other	**0** High Osmolar **1** Low Osmolar **Y** Other Contrast **Z** None	**Z** None	**Z** None

B   Imaging
4   Lower Arteries
2   Computerized Tomography (CT Scan):   Computer reformatted digital display of multiplanar images developed from the capture of multiple exposures of external ionizing radiation

Body Part Character 4	Contrast Character 5	Qualifier Character 6	Qualifier Character 7
0 Abdominal Aorta **1** Celiac Artery **4** Superior Mesenteric Artery **8** Renal Arteries, Bilateral **C** Pelvic Arteries **F** Lower Extremity Arteries, Right **G** Lower Extremity Arteries, Left **H** Lower Extremity Arteries, Bilateral **M** Renal Artery Transplant	**0** High Osmolar **1** Low Osmolar **Y** Other Contrast **Z** None	**Z** None	**Z** None

B   Imaging
4   Lower Arteries
3   Magnetic Resonance Imaging (MRI): Computer reformatted digital display of multiplanar images developed from the capture of radio-frequency signals emitted by nuclei in a body site excited within a magnetic field

Body Part Character 4	Contrast Character 5	Qualifier Character 6	Qualifier Character 7
0 Abdominal Aorta **1** Celiac Artery **4** Superior Mesenteric Artery **8** Renal Arteries, Bilateral **C** Pelvic Arteries **F** Lower Extremity Arteries, Right **G** Lower Extremity Arteries, Left **H** Lower Extremity Arteries, Bilateral	**Y** Other Contrast	**0** Unenhanced and Enhanced **Z** None	**Z** None
0 Abdominal Aorta **1** Celiac Artery **4** Superior Mesenteric Artery **8** Renal Arteries, Bilateral **C** Pelvic Arteries **F** Lower Extremity Arteries, Right **G** Lower Extremity Arteries, Left **H** Lower Extremity Arteries, Bilateral	**Z** None	**Z** None	**Z** None

B   Imaging
4   Lower Arteries
4   Ultrasonography: Real time dispaly of images of anatomy or flow information developed from the capture of relected and attenuated high frequency sound waves

Body Part Character 4	Contrast Character 5	Qualifier Character 6	Qualifier Character 7
0 Abdominal Aorta **4** Superior Mesenteric Artery **5** Inferior Mesenteric Artery **6** Renal Artery, Right **7** Renal Artery, Left **8** Renal Arteries, Bilateral **B** Intra-Abdominal Arteries, Other **F** Lower Extremity Arteries, Right **G** Lower Extremity Arteries, Left **H** Lower Extremity Arteries, Bilateral **K** Celiac and Mesenteric Arteries **L** Femoral Artery **N** Penile Arteries	**Z** None	**Z** None	**Z** None

B   Imaging
5   Veins
0   Plain Radiography: Planar display of an image developed from the capture of external ionizing radiation on photographic or photoconductive plate

Body Part Character 4	Contrast Character 5	Qualifier Character 6	Qualifier Character 7
0 Epidural Veins **1** Cerebral and Cerebellar Veins **2** Intracranial Sinuses **3** Jugular Veins, Right **4** Jugular Veins, Left **5** Jugular Veins, Bilateral **6** Subclavian Vein, Right **7** Subclavian Vein, Left **8** Superior Vena Cava **9** Inferior Vena Cava **B** Lower Extremity Veins, Right **C** Lower Extremity Veins, Left **D** Lower Extremity Veins, Bilateral **F** Pelvic (Iliac) Veins, Right **G** Pelvic (Iliac) Veins, Left **H** Pelvic (Iliac) Veins, Bilateral **J** Renal Vein, Right **K** Renal Vein, Left **L** Renal Veins, Bilateral **M** Upper Extremity Veins, Right **N** Upper Extremity Veins, Left **P** Upper Extremity Veins, Bilateral **Q** Pulmonary Vein, Right **R** Pulmonary Vein, Left **S** Pulmonary Veins, Bilateral **T** Portal and Splanchnic Veins **V** Veins, Other **W** Dialysis Shunt/Fistula	**0** High Osmolar **1** Low Osmolar **Y** Other Contrast	**Z** None	**Z** None

B Imaging
5 Veins
1 Fluoroscopy: Single plane or bi-plane real time display of an image developed from the capture of external ionizing radioation on a fluorescent screen. The image may also be stored by either digital or analog means

Body Part Character 4	Contrast Character 5	Qualifier Character 6	Qualifier Character 7
0 Epidural Veins 1 Cerebral and Cerebellar Veins 2 Intracranial Sinuses 3 Jugular Veins, Right 4 Jugular Veins, Left 5 Jugular Veins, Bilateral 6 Subclavian Vein, Right 7 Subclavian Vein, Left 8 Superior Vena Cava 9 Inferior Vena Cava B Lower Extremity Veins, Right C Lower Extremity Veins, Left D Lower Extremity Veins, Bilateral F Pelvic (Iliac) Veins, Right G Pelvic (Iliac) Veins, Left H Pelvic (Iliac) Veins, Bilateral J Renal Vein, Right K Renal Vein, Left L Renal Veins, Bilateral M Upper Extremity Veins, Right N Upper Extremity Veins, Left P Upper Extremity Veins, Bilateral Q Pulmonary Vein, Right R Pulmonary Vein, Left S Pulmonary Veins, Bilateral T Portal and Splanchnic Veins V Veins, Other W Dialysis Shunt/Fistula	0 High Osmolar 1 Low Osmolar Y Other Contrast Z None	Z None	Z None

B Imaging
5 Veins
2 Computerized Tomography (CT Scan): Computer reformatted digital display of multiplanar images developed from the capture of multiple exposures of external ionizing radiation

Body Part Character 4	Contrast Character 5	Qualifier Character 6	Qualifier Character 7
2 Intracranial Sinuses 8 Superior Vena Cava 9 Inferior Vena Cava F Pelvic (Iliac) Veins, Right G Pelvic (Iliac) Veins, Left H Pelvic (Iliac) Veins, Bilateral J Renal Vein, Right K Renal Vein, Left L Renal Veins, Bilateral Q Pulmonary Vein, Right R Pulmonary Vein, Left S Pulmonary Veins, Bilateral T Portal and Splanchnic Veins	0 High Osmolar 1 Low Osmolar Y Other Contrast	0 Unenhanced and Enhanced Z None	Z None
2 Intracranial Sinuses 8 Superior Vena Cava 9 Inferior Vena Cava F Pelvic (Iliac) Veins, Right G Pelvic (Iliac) Veins, Left H Pelvic (Iliac) Veins, Bilateral J Renal Vein, Right K Renal Vein, Left L Renal Veins, Bilateral Q Pulmonary Vein, Right R Pulmonary Vein, Left S Pulmonary Veins, Bilateral T Portal and Splanchnic Veins	Z None	Z None	Z None

B **Imaging**
5 **Veins**
3 **Magnetic Resonance Imaging (MRI):** Computer reformatted digital display of multiplanar images developed from the capture of radio-frequency signals emitted by nuclei in a body site excited within a magnetic field

Body Part Character 4	Contrast Character 5	Qualifier Character 6	Qualifier Character 7
1 Cerebral and Cerebellar Veins **2** Intracranial Sinuses **5** Jugular Veins, Bilateral **8** Superior Vena Cava **9** Inferior Vena Cava **B** Lower Extremity Veins, Right **C** Lower Extremity Veins, Left **D** Lower Extremity Veins, Bilateral **H** Pelvic (Iliac) Veins, Bilateral **L** Renal Veins, Bilateral **M** Upper Extremity Veins, Right **N** Upper Extremity Veins, Left **P** Upper Extremity Veins, Bilateral **S** Pulmonary Veins, Bilateral **T** Portal and Splanchnic Veins **V** Veins, Other	**Y** Other Contrast	**0** Unenhanced and Enhanced **Z** None	**Z** None
1 Cerebral and Cerebellar Veins **2** Intracranial Sinuses **5** Jugular Veins, Bilateral **8** Superior Vena Cava **9** Inferior Vena Cava **B** Lower Extremity Veins, Right **C** Lower Extremity Veins, Left **D** Lower Extremity Veins, Bilateral **H** Pelvic (Iliac) Veins, Bilateral **L** Renal Veins, Bilateral **M** Upper Extremity Veins, Right **N** Upper Extremity Veins, Left **P** Upper Extremity Veins, Bilateral **S** Pulmonary Veins, Bilateral **T** Portal and Splanchnic Veins **V** Veins, Other	**Z** None	**Z** None	**Z** None

B **Imaging**
5 **Veins**
4 **Ultrasonography:** Real time dispaly of images of anatomy or flow information developed from the capture of relected and attenuated high frequency sound waves

Body Part Character 4	Contrast Character 5	Qualifier Character 6	Qualifier Character 7
3 Jugular Veins, Right **4** Jugular Veins, Left **6** Subclavian Vein, Right **7** Subclavian Vein, Left **9** Inferior Vena Cava **B** Lower Extremity Veins, Right **C** Lower Extremity Veins, Left **D** Lower Extremity Veins, Bilateral **J** Renal Vein, Right **K** Renal Vein, Left **L** Renal Veins, Bilateral **M** Upper Extremity Veins, Right **N** Upper Extremity Veins, Left **P** Upper Extremity Veins, Bilateral **T** Portal and Splanchnic Veins	**Z** None	**Z** None	**Z** None

B Imaging
7 **Lymphatic System**
0 **Plain Radiography:** Planar display of an image developed from the capture of external ionizing radiation on photographic or photoconductive plate

Body Part Character 4	Contrast Character 5	Qualifier Character 6	Qualifier Character 7
0 Abdominal/Retroperitoneal Lymphatics, Unilateral **1** Abdominal/Retroperitoneal Lymphatics, Bilateral **4** Lymphatics, Head and Neck **5** Upper Extremity Lymphatics, Right **6** Upper Extremity Lymphatics, Left **7** Upper Extremity Lymphatics, Bilateral **8** Lower Extremity Lymphatics, Right **9** Lower Extremity Lymphatics, Left **B** Lower Extremity Lymphatics, Bilateral **C** Lymphatics, Pelvic	**0** High Osmolar **1** Low Osmolar **Y** Other Contrast	**Z** None	**Z** None

B Imaging
8 **Eye**
0 **Plain Radiography:** Planar display of an image developed from the capture of external ionizing radiation on photographic or photoconductive plate

Body Part Character 4	Contrast Character 5	Qualifier Character 6	Qualifier Character 7
0 Lacrimal Duct, Right **1** Lacrimal Duct, Left **2** Lacrimal Ducts, Bilateral	**0** High Osmolar **1** Low Osmolar **Y** Other Contrast	**Z** None	**Z** None
3 Optic Foramina, Right **4** Optic Foramina, Left **5** Eye, Right **6** Eye, Left **7** Eyes, Bilateral	**Z** None	**Z** None	**Z** None

B Imaging
8 **Eye**
2 **Computerized Tomography (CT Scan):** Computer reformatted digital display of multiplanar images developed from the capture of multiple exposures of external ionizing radiation

Body Part Character 4	Contrast Character 5	Qualifier Character 6	Qualifier Character 7
5 Eye, Right **6** Eye, Left **7** Eyes, Bilateral	**0** High Osmolar **1** Low Osmolar **Y** Other Contrast	**0** Unenhanced and Enhanced **Z** None	**Z** None
5 Eye, Right **6** Eye, Left **7** Eyes, Bilateral	**Z** None	**Z** None	**Z** None

B Imaging
8 **Eye**
3 **Magnetic Resonance Imaging (MRI):** Computer reformatted digital display of multiplanar images developed from the capture of radio-frequency signals emitted by nuclei in a body site excited within a magnetic field

Body Part Character 4	Contrast Character 5	Qualifier Character 6	Qualifier Character 7
5 Eye, Right **6** Eye, Left **7** Eyes, Bilateral	**Y** Other Contrast	**0** Unenhanced and Enhanced **Z** None	**Z** None
5 Eye, Right **6** Eye, Left **7** Eyes, Bilateral	**Z** None	**Z** None	**Z** None

B **Imaging**
8 **Eye**
4 **Ultrasonography:** Real time dispaly of images of anatomy or flow information developed from the capture of relected and attenuated high frequency sound waves

Body Part Character 4	Contrast Character 5	Qualifier Character 6	Qualifier Character 7
5 Eye, Right 6 Eye, Left 7 Eyes, Bilateral	Z None	Z None	Z None

B **Imaging**
9 **Ear, Nose, Mouth and Throat**
0 **Plain Radiography:** Planar display of an image developed from the capture of external ionizing radiation on photographic or photoconductive plate

Body Part Character 4	Contrast Character 5	Qualifier Character 6	Qualifier Character 7
2 Paranasal Sinuses F Nasopharynx/Oropharynx H Mastoids	Z None	Z None	Z None
4 Parotid Gland, Right 5 Parotid Gland, Left 6 Parotid Glands, Bilateral 7 Submandibular Gland, Right 8 Submandibular Gland, Left 9 Submandibular Glands, Bilateral B Salivary Gland, Right C Salivary Gland, Left D Salivary Glands, Bilateral	0 High Osmolar 1 Low Osmolar Y Other Contrast	Z None	Z None

B **Imaging**
9 **Ear, Nose, Mouth and Throat**
1 **Fluoroscopy:** Single plane or bi-plane real time display of an image developed from the capture of external ionizing radioation on a fluorescent screen. The image may also be stored by either digital or analog means

Body Part Character 4	Contrast Character 5	Qualifier Character 6	Qualifier Character 7
G Pharynx and Epiglottis J Larynx	Y Other Contrast Z None	Z None	Z None

B **Imaging**
9 **Ear, Nose, Mouth and Throat**
2 **Computerized Tomography (CT Scan):** Computer reformatted digital display of multiplanar images developed from the capture of multiple exposures of external ionizing radiation

Body Part Character 4	Contrast Character 5	Qualifier Character 6	Qualifier Character 7
0 Ear 2 Paranasal Sinuses 6 Parotid Glands, Bilateral 9 Submandibular Glands, Bilateral D Salivary Glands, Bilateral F Nasopharynx/Oropharynx J Larynx	0 High Osmolar 1 Low Osmolar Y Other Contrast	0 Unenhanced and Enhanced Z None	Z None
0 Ear 2 Paranasal Sinuses 6 Parotid Glands, Bilateral 9 Submandibular Glands, Bilateral D Salivary Glands, Bilateral F Nasopharynx/Oropharynx J Larynx	Z None	Z None	Z None

B Imaging
9 Ear, Nose, Mouth and Throat
3 Magnetic Resonance Imaging (MRI): Computer reformatted digital display of multiplanar images developed from the capture of radio-frequency signals emitted by nuclei in a body site excited within a magnetic field

Body Part Character 4	Contrast Character 5	Qualifier Character 6	Qualifier Character 7
0 Ear **2** Paranasal Sinuses **6** Parotid Glands, Bilateral **9** Submandibular Glands, Bilateral **D** Salivary Glands, Bilateral **F** Nasopharynx/Oropharynx **J** Larynx	**Y** Other Contrast	**0** Unenhanced and Enhanced **Z** None	**Z** None
0 Ear **2** Paranasal Sinuses **6** Parotid Glands, Bilateral **9** Submandibular Glands, Bilateral **D** Salivary Glands, Bilateral **F** Nasopharynx/Oropharynx **J** Larynx	**Z** None	**Z** None	**Z** None

B Imaging
B Respiratory System
0 Plain Radiography: Planar display of an image developed from the capture of external ionizing radiation on photographic or photoconductive plate

Body Part Character 4	Contrast Character 5	Qualifier Character 6	Qualifier Character 7
7 Tracheobronchial Tree, Right **8** Tracheobronchial Tree, Left **9** Tracheobronchial Trees, Bilateral	**Y** Other Contrast	**Z** None	**Z** None
D Upper Airways	**Z** None	**Z** None	**Z** None

B Imaging
B Respiratory System
1 Fluoroscopy: Single plane or bi-plane real time display of an image developed from the capture of external ionizing radioation on a fluorescent screen. The image may also be stored by either digital or analog means

Body Part Character 4	Contrast Character 5	Qualifier Character 6	Qualifier Character 7
2 Lung, Right **3** Lung, Left **4** Lungs, Bilateral **6** Diaphragm **C** Mediastinum **D** Upper Airways	**Z** None	**Z** None	**Z** None
7 Tracheobronchial Tree, Right **8** Tracheobronchial Tree, Left **9** Tracheobronchial Trees, Bilateral	**Y** Other Contrast	**Z** None	**Z** None

B Imaging
B Respiratory System
2 Computerized Tomography (CT Scan): Computer reformatted digital display of multiplanar images developed from the capture of multiple exposures of external ionizing radiation

Body Part Character 4	Contrast Character 5	Qualifier Character 6	Qualifier Character 7
4 Lungs, Bilateral **7** Tracheobronchial Tree, Right **8** Tracheobronchial Tree, Left **9** Tracheobronchial Trees, Bilateral **F** Trachea/Airways	**0** High Osmolar **1** Low Osmolar **Y** Other Contrast	**0** Unenhanced and Enhanced **Z** None	**Z** None
4 Lungs, Bilateral **7** Tracheobronchial Tree, Right **8** Tracheobronchial Tree, Left **9** Tracheobronchial Trees, Bilateral **F** Trachea/Airways	**Z** None	**Z** None	**Z** None

B   **Imaging**
B   **Respiratory System**
3   **Magnetic Resonance Imaging (MRI):** Computer reformatted digital display of multiplanar images developed from the capture of radio-frequency signals emitted by nuclei in a body site excited within a magnetic field

Body Part Character 4	Contrast Character 5	Qualifier Character 6	Qualifier Character 7
G Lung Apices	**Y** Other Contrast	**0** Unenhanced and Enhanced **Z** None	**Z** None
G Lung Apices	**Z** None	**Z** None	**Z** None

B   **Imaging**
B   **Respiratory System**
4   **Ultrasonography:** Real time dispaly of images of anatomy or flow information developed from the capture of relected and attenuated high frequency sound waves

Body Part Character 4	Contrast Character 5	Qualifier Character 6	Qualifier Character 7
B Pleura **C** Mediastinum	**Z** None	**Z** None	**Z** None

B   **Imaging**
D   **Gastrointestinal System**
1   **Fluoroscopy:** Single plane or bi-plane real time display of an image developed from the capture of external ionizing radioation on a fluorescent screen. The image may also be stored by either digital or analog means

Body Part Character 4	Contrast Character 5	Qualifier Character 6	Qualifier Character 7
1 Esophagus **2** Stomach **3** Small Bowel **4** Colon **5** Upper GI **6** Upper GI and Small Bowel **9** Duodenum **B** Mouth/Oropharynx	**Y** Other Contrast **Z** None	**Z** None	**Z** None

B   **Imaging**
D   **Gastrointestinal System**
2   **Computerized Tomography (CT Scan):** Computer reformatted digital display of multiplanar images developed from the capture of multiple exposures of external ionizing radiation

Body Part Character 4	Contrast Character 5	Qualifier Character 6	Qualifier Character 7
4 Colon	**0** High Osmolar **1** Low Osmolar **Y** Other Contrast	**0** Unenhanced and Enhanced **Z** None	**Z** None
4 Colon	**Z** None	**Z** None	**Z** None

B   **Imaging**
D   **Gastrointestinal System**
4   **Ultrasonography:** Real time dispaly of images of anatomy or flow information developed from the capture of relected and attenuated high frequency sound waves

Body Part Character 4	Contrast Character 5	Qualifier Character 6	Qualifier Character 7
1 Esophagus **2** Stomach **7** Gastrointestinal Tract **8** Appendix **9** Duodenum **C** Rectum	**Z** None	**Z** None	**Z** None

B   **Imaging**
F   **Hepatobiliary System and Pancreas**
0   **Plain Radiography:** Planar display of an image developed from the capture of external ionizing radiation on photographic or photoconductive plate

Body Part Character 4	Contrast Character 5	Qualifier Character 6	Qualifier Character 7
0 Bile Ducts 3 Gallbladder and Bile Ducts C Hepatobiliary System, All	0 High Osmolar 1 Low Osmolar Y Other Contrast	Z None	Z None

B   **Imaging**
F   **Hepatobiliary System and Pancreas**
1   **Fluoroscopy:** Single plane or bi-plane real time display of an image developed from the capture of external ionizing radioation on a fluorescent screen. The image may also be stored by either digital or analog means

Body Part Character 4	Contrast Character 5	Qualifier Character 6	Qualifier Character 7
0 Bile Ducts 1 Biliary and Pancreatic Ducts 2 Gallbladder 3 Gallbladder and Bile Ducts 4 Gallbladder, Bile Ducts and Pancreatic Ducts 8 Pancreatic Ducts	0 High Osmolar 1 Low Osmolar Y Other Contrast	Z None	Z None

B   **Imaging**
F   **Hepatobiliary System and Pancreas**
2   **Computerized Tomography (CT Scan):** Computer reformatted digital display of multiplanar images developed from the capture of multiple exposures of external ionizing radiation

Body Part Character 4	Contrast Character 5	Qualifier Character 6	Qualifier Character 7
5 Liver 6 Liver and Spleen 7 Pancreas C Hepatobiliary System, All	0 High Osmolar 1 Low Osmolar Y Other Contrast	0 Unenhanced and Enhanced Z None	Z None
5 Liver 6 Liver and Spleen 7 Pancreas C Hepatobiliary System, All	Z None	Z None	Z None

B   **Imaging**
F   **Hepatobiliary System and Pancreas**
3   **Magnetic Resonance Imaging (MRI):** Computer reformatted digital display of multiplanar images developed from the capture of radio-frequency signals emitted by nuclei in a body site excited within a magnetic field

Body Part Character 4	Contrast Character 5	Qualifier Character 6	Qualifier Character 7
5 Liver 6 Liver and Spleen 7 Pancreas	Y Other Contrast	0 Unenhanced and Enhanced Z None	Z None
5 Liver 6 Liver and Spleen 7 Pancreas	Z None	Z None	Z None

B   **Imaging**
F   **Hepatobiliary System and Pancreas**
4   **Ultrasonography:** Real time dispaly of images of anatomy or flow information developed from the capture of relected and attenuated high frequency sound waves

Body Part Character 4	Contrast Character 5	Qualifier Character 6	Qualifier Character 7
0 Bile Ducts 2 Gallbladder 3 Gallbladder and Bile Ducts 5 Liver 6 Liver and Spleen 7 Pancreas C Hepatobiliary System, All	Z None	Z None	Z None

   Draft (2009)

B   Imaging
G   Endocrine System
2   Computerized Tomography (CT Scan):   Computer reformatted digital display of multiplanar images developed from the capture of multiple exposures of external ionizing radiation

Body Part Character 4	Contrast Character 5	Qualifier Character 6	Qualifier Character 7
2 Adrenal Glands, Bilateral 3 Parathyroid Glands 4 Thyroid Gland	0 High Osmolar 1 Low Osmolar Y Other Contrast	0 Unenhanced and Enhanced Z None	Z None
2 Adrenal Glands, Bilateral 3 Parathyroid Glands 4 Thyroid Gland	Z None	Z None	Z None

B   Imaging
G   Endocrine System
3   Magnetic Resonance Imaging (MRI):   Computer reformatted digital display of multiplanar images developed from the capture of radio-frequency signals emitted by nuclei in a body site excited within a magnetic field

Body Part Character 4	Contrast Character 5	Qualifier Character 6	Qualifier Character 7
2 Adrenal Glands, Bilateral 3 Parathyroid Glands 4 Thyroid Gland	Y Other Contrast	0 Unenhanced and Enhanced Z None	Z None
2 Adrenal Glands, Bilateral 3 Parathyroid Glands 4 Thyroid Gland	Z None	Z None	Z None

B   Imaging
G   Endocrine System
4   Ultrasonography: Real time dispaly of images of anatomy or flow information developed from the capture of relected and attenuated high frequency sound waves

Body Part Character 4	Contrast Character 5	Qualifier Character 6	Qualifier Character 7
0 Adrenal Gland, Right 1 Adrenal Gland, Left 2 Adrenal Glands, Bilateral 3 Parathyroid Glands 4 Thyroid Gland	Z None	Z None	Z None

B   Imaging
H   Skin, Subcutaneous Tissue and Breast
0   Plain Radiography: Planar display of an image developed from the capture of external ionizing radiation on photographic or photoconductive plate

Body Part Character 4	Contrast Character 5	Qualifier Character 6	Qualifier Character 7
0 Breast, Right 1 Breast, Left 2 Breasts, Bilateral	Z None	Z None	Z None
3 Single Mammary Duct, Right 4 Single Mammary Duct, Left 5 Multiple Mammary Ducts, Right 6 Multiple Mammary Ducts, Left	0 High Osmolar 1 Low Osmolar Y Other Contrast Z None	Z None	Z None

B   Imaging
H   Skin, Subcutaneous Tissue and Breast
3   **Magnetic Resonance Imaging (MRI):** Computer reformatted digital display of multiplanar images developed from the capture of radio-frequency signals emitted by nuclei in a body site excited within a magnetic field

Body Part Character 4	Contrast Character 5	Qualifier Character 6	Qualifier Character 7
0 Breast, Right **1** Breast, Left **2** Breasts, Bilateral **D** Subcutaneous Tissue, Head/Neck **F** Subcutaneous Tissue, Upper Extremity **G** Subcutaneous Tissue, Thorax **H** Subcutaneous Tissue, Abdomen and Pelvis **J** Subcutaneous Tissue, Lower Extremity	**Y** Other Contrast	**0** Unenhanced and Enhanced **Z** None	**Z** None
0 Breast, Right **1** Breast, Left **2** Breasts, Bilateral **D** Subcutaneous Tissue, Head/Neck **F** Subcutaneous Tissue, Upper Extremity **G** Subcutaneous Tissue, Thorax **H** Subcutaneous Tissue, Abdomen and Pelvis **J** Subcutaneous Tissue, Lower Extremity	**Z** None	**Z** None	**Z** None

B   Imaging
H   Skin, Subcutaneous Tissue and Breast
4   **Ultrasonography:** Real time dispaly of images of anatomy or flow information developed from the capture of relected and attenuated high frequency sound waves

Body Part Character 4	Contrast Character 5	Qualifier Character 6	Qualifier Character 7
0 Breast, Right **1** Breast, Left **2** Breasts, Bilateral **7** Extremity, Upper **8** Extremity, Lower **9** Abdominal Wall **B** Chest Wall **C** Head and Neck	**Z** None	**Z** None	**Z** None

B   Imaging
L   Connective Tissue
3   **Magnetic Resonance Imaging (MRI):** Computer reformatted digital display of multiplanar images developed from the capture of radio-frequency signals emitted by nuclei in a body site excited within a magnetic field

Body Part Character 4	Contrast Character 5	Qualifier Character 6	Qualifier Character 7
0 Connective Tissue, Upper Extremity **1** Connective Tissue, Lower Extremity **2** Tendons, Upper Extremity **3** Tendons, Lower Extremity	**Y** Other Contrast	**0** Unenhanced and Enhanced **Z** None	**Z** None
0 Connective Tissue, Upper Extremity **1** Connective Tissue, Lower Extremity **2** Tendons, Upper Extremity **3** Tendons, Lower Extremity	**Z** None	**Z** None	**Z** None

B Imaging
L Connective Tissue
4 Ultrasonography: Real time dispaly of images of anatomy or flow information developed from the capture of relected and attenuated high frequency sound waves

Body Part Character 4	Contrast Character 5	Qualifier Character 6	Qualifier Character 7
0 Connective Tissue, Upper Extremity **1** Connective Tissue, Lower Extremity **2** Tendons, Upper Extremity **3** Tendons, Lower Extremity	**Z** None	**Z** None	**Z** None

B Imaging
N Skull and Facial Bones
0 Plain Radiography: Planar display of an image developed from the capture of external ionizing radiation on photographic or photoconductive plate

Body Part Character 4	Contrast Character 5	Qualifier Character 6	Qualifier Character 7
0 Skull **1** Orbit, Right **2** Orbit, Left **3** Orbits, Bilateral **4** Nasal Bones **5** Facial Bones **6** Mandible **B** Zygomatic Arch, Right **C** Zygomatic Arch, Left **D** Zygomatic Arches, Bilateral **G** Tooth, Single **H** Teeth, Multiple **J** Teeth, All	**Z** None	**Z** None	**Z** None
7 Temporomandibular Joint, Right **8** Temporomandibular Joint, Left **9** Temporomandibular Joints, Bilateral	**0** High Osmolar **1** Low Osmolar **Y** Other Contrast **Z** None	**Z** None	**Z** None

B Imaging
N Skull and Facial Bones
1 Fluoroscopy: Single plane or bi-plane real time display of an image developed from the capture of external ionizing radioation on a fluorescent screen. The image may also be stored by either digital or analog means

Body Part Character 4	Contrast Character 5	Qualifier Character 6	Qualifier Character 7
7 Temporomandibular Joint, Right **8** Temporomandibular Joint, Left **9** Temporomandibular Joints, Bilateral	**0** High Osmolar **1** Low Osmolar **Y** Other Contrast **Z** None	**Z** None	**Z** None

B Imaging
N Skull and Facial Bones
2 Computerized Tomography (CT Scan): Computer reformatted digital display of multiplanar images developed from the capture of multiple exposures of external ionizing radiation

Body Part Character 4	Contrast Character 5	Qualifier Character 6	Qualifier Character 7
0 Skull **3** Orbits, Bilateral **5** Facial Bones **6** Mandible **9** Temporomandibular Joints, Bilateral **F** Temporal Bones	**0** High Osmolar **1** Low Osmolar **Y** Other Contrast **Z** None	**Z** None	**Z** None

B Imaging
N Skull and Facial Bones
3 Magnetic Resonance Imaging (MRI): Computer reformatted digital display of multiplanar images developed from the capture of radio-frequency signals emitted by nuclei in a body site excited within a magnetic field

Body Part Character 4	Contrast Character 5	Qualifier Character 6	Qualifier Character 7
9 Temporomandibular Joints, Bilateral	**Y** Other Contrast **Z** None	**Z** None	**Z** None

B   **Imaging**
P   **Non-Axial Upper Bones**
0   **Plain Radiography:** Planar display of an image developed from the capture of external ionizing radiation on photographic or photoconductive plate

Body Part Character 4	Contrast Character 5	Qualifier Character 6	Qualifier Character 7
0 Sternoclavicular Joint, Right **1** Sternoclavicular Joint, Left **2** Sternoclavicular Joints, Bilateral **3** Acromioclavicular Joints, Bilateral **4** Clavicle, Right **5** Clavicle, Left **6** Scapula, Right **7** Scapula, Left **A** Humerus, Right **B** Humerus, Left **E** Upper Arm, Right **F** Upper Arm, Left **J** Forearm, Right **K** Forearm, Left **N** Hand, Right **P** Hand, Left **R** Finger(s), Right **S** Finger(s), Left **X** Ribs, Right **Y** Ribs, Left	**Z** None	**Z** None	**Z** None
8 Shoulder, Right **9** Shoulder, Left **C** Hand/Finger Joint, Right **D** Hand/Finger Joint, Left **G** Elbow, Right **H** Elbow, Left **L** Wrist, Right **M** Wrist, Left	**0** High Osmolar **1** Low Osmolar **Y** Other Contrast **Z** None	**Z** None	**Z** None

B   **Imaging**
P   **Non-Axial Upper Bones**
1   **Fluoroscopy:**   Single plane or bi-plane real time display of an image developed from the capture of external ionizing radioation on a fluorescent screen. The image may also be stored by either digital or analog means

Body Part Character 4	Contrast Character 5	Qualifier Character 6	Qualifier Character 7
0 Sternoclavicular Joint, Right **1** Sternoclavicular Joint, Left **2** Sternoclavicular Joints, Bilateral **3** Acromioclavicular Joints, Bilateral **4** Clavicle, Right **5** Clavicle, Left **6** Scapula, Right **7** Scapula, Left **A** Humerus, Right **B** Humerus, Left **E** Upper Arm, Right **F** Upper Arm, Left **J** Forearm, Right **K** Forearm, Left **N** Hand, Right **P** Hand, Left **R** Finger(s), Right **S** Finger(s), Left **X** Ribs, Right **Y** Ribs, Left	**Z** None	**Z** None	**Z** None
8 Shoulder, Right **9** Shoulder, Left **L** Wrist, Right **M** Wrist, Left	**0** High Osmolar **1** Low Osmolar **Y** Other Contrast **Z** None	**Z** None	**Z** None
C Hand/Finger Joint, Right **D** Hand/Finger Joint, Left **G** Elbow, Right **H** Elbow, Left	**0** High Osmolar **1** Low Osmolar **Y** Other Contrast	**Z** None	**Z** None

B   Imaging
P   Non-Axial Upper Bones
2   Computerized Tomography (CT Scan):   Computer reformatted digital display of multiplanar images developed from the capture of multiple exposures of external ionizing radiation

Body Part Character 4	Contrast Character 5	Qualifier Character 6	Qualifier Character 7
0 Sternoclavicular Joint, Right **1** Sternoclavicular Joint, Left **W** Thorax	**0** High Osmolar **1** Low Osmolar **Y** Other Contrast	**Z** None	**Z** None
2 Sternoclavicular Joints, Bilateral **3** Acromioclavicular Joints, Bilateral **4** Clavicle, Right **5** Clavicle, Left **6** Scapula, Right **7** Scapula, Left **8** Shoulder, Right **9** Shoulder, Left **A** Humerus, Right **B** Humerus, Left **E** Upper Arm, Right **F** Upper Arm, Left **G** Elbow, Right **H** Elbow, Left **J** Forearm, Right **K** Forearm, Left **L** Wrist, Right **M** Wrist, Left **N** Hand, Right **P** Hand, Left **Q** Hands and Wrists, Bilateral **R** Finger(s), Right **S** Finger(s), Left **T** Upper Extremity, Right **U** Upper Extremity, Left **V** Upper Extremities, Bilateral **X** Ribs, Right **Y** Ribs, Left	**0** High Osmolar **1** Low Osmolar **Y** Other Contrast **Z** None	**Z** None	**Z** None
C Hand/Finger Joint, Right **D** Hand/Finger Joint, Left	**Z** None	**Z** None	**Z** None

B   Imaging
P   Non-Axial Upper Bones
3   Magnetic Resonance Imaging (MRI):   Computer reformatted digital display of multiplanar images developed from the capture of radio-frequency signals emitted by nuclei in a body site excited within a magnetic field

Body Part Character 4	Contrast Character 5	Qualifier Character 6	Qualifier Character 7
8 Shoulder, Right **9** Shoulder, Left **C** Hand/Finger Joint, Right **D** Hand/Finger Joint, Left **E** Upper Arm, Right **F** Upper Arm, Left **G** Elbow, Right **H** Elbow, Left **J** Forearm, Right **K** Forearm, Left **L** Wrist, Right **M** Wrist, Left	**Y** Other Contrast	**0** Unenhanced and Enhanced **Z** None	**Z** None
8 Shoulder, Right **9** Shoulder, Left **C** Hand/Finger Joint, Right **D** Hand/Finger Joint, Left **E** Upper Arm, Right **F** Upper Arm, Left **G** Elbow, Right **H** Elbow, Left **J** Forearm, Right **K** Forearm, Left **L** Wrist, Right **M** Wrist, Left	**Z** None	**Z** None	**Z** None

B   Imaging
P   Non-Axial Upper Bones
4   Ultrasonography: Real time dispaly of images of anatomy or flow information developed from the capture of relected and attenuated high frequency sound waves

Body Part Character 4	Contrast Character 5	Qualifier Character 6	Qualifier Character 7
8 Shoulder, Right 9 Shoulder, Left G Elbow, Right H Elbow, Left L Wrist, Right M Wrist, Left N Hand, Right P Hand, Left	Z None	Z None	1 Densitometry Z None

B   Imaging
Q   Non-Axial Lower Bones
0   Plain Radiography: Planar display of an image developed from the capture of external ionizing radiation on photographic or photoconductive plate

Body Part Character 4	Contrast Character 5	Qualifier Character 6	Qualifier Character 7
0 Hip, Right 1 Hip, Left 3 Femur, Right 4 Femur, Left	Z None	Z None	1 Densitometry Z None
0 Hip, Right 1 Hip, Left X Foot/Toe Joint, Right Y Foot/Toe Joint, Left	0 High Osmolar 1 Low Osmolar Y Other Contrast	Z None	Z None
7 Knee, Right 8 Knee, Left G Ankle, Right H Ankle, Left	0 High Osmolar 1 Low Osmolar Y Other Contrast Z None	Z None	Z None
D Lower Leg, Right F Lower Leg, Left J Calcaneus, Right K Calcaneus, Left L Foot, Right M Foot, Left P Toe(s), Right Q Toe(s), Left V Patella, Right W Patella, Left	Z None	Z None	Z None

B   Imaging
Q   Non-Axial Lower Bones
1   Fluoroscopy: Single plane or bi-plane real time display of an image developed from the capture of external ionizing radioation on a fluorescent screen. The image may also be stored by either digital or analog means

Body Part Character 4	Contrast Character 5	Qualifier Character 6	Qualifier Character 7
0 Hip, Right 1 Hip, Left 7 Knee, Right 8 Knee, Left G Ankle, Right H Ankle, Left X Foot/Toe Joint, Right Y Foot/Toe Joint, Left	0 High Osmolar 1 Low Osmolar Y Other Contrast Z None	Z None	Z None
3 Femur, Right 4 Femur, Left D Lower Leg, Right F Lower Leg, Left J Calcaneus, Right K Calcaneus, Left L Foot, Right M Foot, Left P Toe(s), Right Q Toe(s), Left V Patella, Right W Patella, Left	Z None	Z None	Z None

B   Imaging
Q   Non-Axial Lower Bones
2   Computerized Tomography (CT Scan):   Computer reformatted digital display of multiplanar images developed from the capture of multiple exposures of external ionizing radiation

Body Part Character 4	Contrast Character 5	Qualifier Character 6	Qualifier Character 7
0 Hip, Right **1** Hip, Left **3** Femur, Right **4** Femur, Left **7** Knee, Right **8** Knee, Left **D** Lower Leg, Right **F** Lower Leg, Left **G** Ankle, Right **H** Ankle, Left **J** Calcaneus, Right **K** Calcaneus, Left **L** Foot, Right **M** Foot, Left **P** Toe(s), Right **Q** Toe(s), Left **R** Lower Extremity, Right **S** Lower Extremity, Left **V** Patella, Right **W** Patella, Left **X** Foot/Toe Joint, Right **Y** Foot/Toe Joint, Left	**0** High Osmolar **1** Low Osmolar **Y** Other Contrast **Z** None	**Z** None	**Z** None
B Tibia/Fibula, Right **C** Tibia/Fibula, Left	**0** High Osmolar **1** Low Osmolar **Y** Other Contrast	**Z** None	**Z** None

B   Imaging
Q   Non-Axial Lower Bones
3   Magnetic Resonance Imaging (MRI): Computer reformatted digital display of multiplanar images developed from the capture of radio-frequency signals emitted by nuclei in a body site excited within a magnetic field

Body Part Character 4	Contrast Character 5	Qualifier Character 6	Qualifier Character 7
0 Hip, Right **1** Hip, Left **3** Femur, Right **4** Femur, Left **7** Knee, Right **8** Knee, Left **D** Lower Leg, Right **F** Lower Leg, Left **G** Ankle, Right **H** Ankle, Left **J** Calcaneus, Right **K** Calcaneus, Left **L** Foot, Right **M** Foot, Left **P** Toe(s), Right **Q** Toe(s), Left **V** Patella, Right **W** Patella, Left	**Y** Other Contrast	**0** Unenhanced and Enhanced **Z** None	**Z** None
0 Hip, Right **1** Hip, Left **3** Femur, Right **4** Femur, Left **7** Knee, Right **8** Knee, Left **D** Lower Leg, Right **F** Lower Leg, Left **G** Ankle, Right **H** Ankle, Left **J** Calcaneus, Right **K** Calcaneus, Left **L** Foot, Right **M** Foot, Left **P** Toe(s), Right **Q** Toe(s), Left **V** Patella, Right **W** Patella, Left	**Z** None	**Z** None	**Z** None

B **Imaging**
Q **Non-Axial Lower Bones**
4 **Ultrasonography:** Real time dispaly of images of anatomy or flow information developed from the capture of relected and attenuated high frequency sound waves

Body Part Character 4	Contrast Character 5	Qualifier Character 6	Qualifier Character 7
0 Hip, Right **1** Hip, Left **2** Hips, Bilateral **7** Knee, Right **8** Knee, Left **9** Knees, Bilateral	**Z** None	**Z** None	**Z** None

B **Imaging**
R **Axial Skeleton, Except Skull and Facial Bones**
0 **Plain Radiography:** Planar display of an image developed from the capture of external ionizing radiation on photographic or photoconductive plate

Body Part Character 4	Contrast Character 5	Qualifier Character 6	Qualifier Character 7
0 Cervical Spine **7** Thoracic Spine **9** Lumbar Spine **G** Whole Spine	**Z** None	**Z** None	**1** Densitometry **Z** None
1 Cervical Disc(s) **2** Thoracic Disc(s) **3** Lumbar Disc(s) **4** Cervical Facet Joint(s) **5** Thoracic Facet Joint(s) **6** Lumbar Facet Joint(s) **D** Sacroiliac Joints	**0** High Osmolar **1** Low Osmolar **Y** Other Contrast **Z** None	**Z** None	**Z** None
8 Thoracolumbar Joint **B** Lumbosacral Joint **C** Pelvis **F** Sacrum and Coccyx **H** Sternum	**Z** None	**Z** None	**Z** None

B **Imaging**
R **Axial Skeleton, Except Skull and Facial Bones**
1 **Fluoroscopy:** Single plane or bi-plane real time display of an image developed from the capture of external ionizing radioation on a fluorescent screen. The image may also be stored by either digital or analog means

Body Part Character 4	Contrast Character 5	Qualifier Character 6	Qualifier Character 7
0 Cervical Spine **1** Cervical Disc(s) **2** Thoracic Disc(s) **3** Lumbar Disc(s) **4** Cervical Facet Joint(s) **5** Thoracic Facet Joint(s) **6** Lumbar Facet Joint(s) **7** Thoracic Spine **8** Thoracolumbar Joint **9** Lumbar Spine **B** Lumbosacral Joint **C** Pelvis **D** Sacroiliac Joints **F** Sacrum and Coccyx **G** Whole Spine **H** Sternum	**0** High Osmolar **1** Low Osmolar **Y** Other Contrast **Z** None	**Z** None	**Z** None

B **Imaging**
R **Axial Skeleton, Except Skull and Facial Bones**
2 **Computerized Tomography (CT Scan):** Computer reformatted digital display of multiplanar images developed from the capture of multiple exposures of external ionizing radiation

Body Part Character 4	Contrast Character 5	Qualifier Character 6	Qualifier Character 7
0 Cervical Spine **7** Thoracic Spine **9** Lumbar Spine **C** Pelvis **D** Sacroiliac Joints **F** Sacrum and Coccyx	**0** High Osmolar **1** Low Osmolar **Y** Other Contrast **Z** None	**Z** None	**Z** None

B Imaging
R Axial Skeleton, Except Skull and Facial Bones
3 Magnetic Resonance Imaging (MRI): Computer reformatted digital display of multiplanar images developed from the capture of radio-frequency signals emitted by nuclei in a body site excited within a magnetic field

Body Part Character 4	Contrast Character 5	Qualifier Character 6	Qualifier Character 7
0 Cervical Spine 1 Cervical Disc(s) 2 Thoracic Disc(s) 3 Lumbar Disc(s) 7 Thoracic Spine 9 Lumbar Spine C Pelvis F Sacrum and Coccyx	Y Other Contrast	0 Unenhanced and Enhanced Z None	Z None
0 Cervical Spine 1 Cervical Disc(s) 2 Thoracic Disc(s) 3 Lumbar Disc(s) 7 Thoracic Spine 9 Lumbar Spine C Pelvis F Sacrum and Coccyx	Z None	Z None	Z None

B Imaging
R Axial Skeleton, Except Skull and Facial Bones
4 Ultrasonography: Real time dispaly of images of anatomy or flow information developed from the capture of relected and attenuated high frequency sound waves

Body Part Character 4	Contrast Character 5	Qualifier Character 6	Qualifier Character 7
0 Cervical Spine 7 Thoracic Spine 9 Lumbar Spine F Sacrum and Coccyx	Z None	Z None	Z None

B Imaging
T Urinary System
0 Plain Radiography: Planar display of an image developed from the capture of external ionizing radiation on photographic or photoconductive plate

Body Part Character 4	Contrast Character 5	Qualifier Character 6	Qualifier Character 7
0 Bladder 1 Kidney, Right 2 Kidney, Left 3 Kidneys, Bilateral 4 Kidneys, Ureters and Bladder 5 Urethra 6 Ureter, Right 7 Ureter, Left 8 Ureters, Bilateral B Bladder and Urethra C Ileal Diversion Loop	0 High Osmolar 1 Low Osmolar Y Other Contrast Z None	Z None	Z None

B Imaging
T Urinary System
1 Fluoroscopy: Single plane or bi-plane real time display of an image developed from the capture of external ionizing radioation on a fluorescent screen. The image may also be stored by either digital or analog means

Body Part Character 4	Contrast Character 5	Qualifier Character 6	Qualifier Character 7
0 Bladder 1 Kidney, Right 2 Kidney, Left 3 Kidneys, Bilateral 4 Kidneys, Ureters and Bladder 5 Urethra 6 Ureter, Right 7 Ureter, Left B Bladder and Urethra C Ileal Diversion Loop D Kidney, Ureter and Bladder, Right F Kidney, Ureter and Bladder, Left G Ileal Loop, Ureters and Kidneys	0 High Osmolar 1 Low Osmolar Y Other Contrast Z None	Z None	Z None

B **Imaging**
T **Urinary System**
2 **Computerized Tomography (CT Scan):** Computer reformatted digital display of multiplanar images developed from the capture of multiple exposures of external ionizing radiation

Body Part Character 4	Contrast Character 5	Qualifier Character 6	Qualifier Character 7
0 Bladder 1 Kidney, Right 2 Kidney, Left 3 Kidneys, Bilateral 9 Kidney Transplant	0 High Osmolar 1 Low Osmolar Y Other Contrast	0 Unenhanced and Enhanced Z None	Z None
0 Bladder 1 Kidney, Right 2 Kidney, Left 3 Kidneys, Bilateral 9 Kidney Transplant	Z None	Z None	Z None

B **Imaging**
T **Urinary System**
3 **Magnetic Resonance Imaging (MRI):** Computer reformatted digital display of multiplanar images developed from the capture of radio-frequency signals emitted by nuclei in a body site excited within a magnetic field

Body Part Character 4	Contrast Character 5	Qualifier Character 6	Qualifier Character 7
0 Bladder 1 Kidney, Right 2 Kidney, Left 3 Kidneys, Bilateral 9 Kidney Transplant	Y Other Contrast	0 Unenhanced and Enhanced Z None	Z None
0 Bladder 1 Kidney, Right 2 Kidney, Left 3 Kidneys, Bilateral 9 Kidney Transplant	Z None	Z None	Z None

B **Imaging**
T **Urinary System**
4 **Ultrasonography:** Real time dispaly of images of anatomy or flow information developed from the capture of relected and attenuated high frequency sound waves

Body Part Character 4	Contrast Character 5	Qualifier Character 6	Qualifier Character 7
0 Bladder 1 Kidney, Right 2 Kidney, Left 3 Kidneys, Bilateral 5 Urethra 6 Ureter, Right 7 Ureter, Left 8 Ureters, Bilateral 9 Kidney Transplant J Kidneys and Bladder	Z None	Z None	Z None

B **Imaging**
U **Female Reproductive System**
0 **Plain Radiography:** Planar display of an image developed from the capture of external ionizing radiation on photographic or photoconductive plate

Body Part Character 4	Contrast Character 5	Qualifier Character 6	Qualifier Character 7
0 Fallopian Tube, Right 1 Fallopian Tube, Left 2 Fallopian Tubes, Bilateral 6 Uterus 8 Uterus and Fallopian Tubes 9 Vagina	0 High Osmolar 1 Low Osmolar Y Other Contrast	Z None	Z None

B   Imaging
U   Female Reproductive System
1   Fluoroscopy: Single plane or bi-plane real time display of an image developed from the capture of external ionizing radioation on a fluorescent screen. The image may also be stored by either digital or analog means

Body Part Character 4	Contrast Character 5	Qualifier Character 6	Qualifier Character 7
0 Fallopian Tube, Right 1 Fallopian Tube, Left 2 Fallopian Tubes, Bilateral 6 Uterus 8 Uterus and Fallopian Tubes 9 Vagina	0 High Osmolar 1 Low Osmolar Y Other Contrast Z None	Z None	Z None

B   Imaging
U   Female Reproductive System
3   Magnetic Resonance Imaging (MRI): Computer reformatted digital display of multiplanar images developed from the capture of radio-frequency signals emitted by nuclei in a body site excited within a magnetic field

Body Part Character 4	Contrast Character 5	Qualifier Character 6	Qualifier Character 7
3 Ovary, Right 4 Ovary, Left 5 Ovaries, Bilateral 6 Uterus 9 Vagina B Pregnant Uterus C Uterus and Ovaries	Y Other Contrast	0 Unenhanced and Enhanced Z None	Z None
3 Ovary, Right 4 Ovary, Left 5 Ovaries, Bilateral 6 Uterus 9 Vagina B Pregnant Uterus C Uterus and Ovaries	Z None	Z None	Z None

B   Imaging
U   Female Reproductive System
4   Ultrasonography: Real time dispaly of images of anatomy or flow information developed from the capture of relected and attenuated high frequency sound waves

Body Part Character 4	Contrast Character 5	Qualifier Character 6	Qualifier Character 7
0 Fallopian Tube, Right 1 Fallopian Tube, Left 2 Fallopian Tubes, Bilateral 3 Ovary, Right 4 Ovary, Left 5 Ovaries, Bilateral 6 Uterus C Uterus and Ovaries	Y Other Contrast Z None	Z None	Z None

B   Imaging
V   Male Reproductive System
0   Plain Radiography: Planar display of an image developed from the capture of external ionizing radiation on photographic or photoconductive plate

Body Part Character 4	Contrast Character 5	Qualifier Character 6	Qualifier Character 7
0 Corpora Cavernosa 1 Epididymis, Right 2 Epididymis, Left 3 Prostate 5 Testicle, Right 6 Testicle, Left 8 Vasa Vasorum	0 High Osmolar 1 Low Osmolar Y Other Contrast	Z None	Z None

B **Imaging**
V **Male Reproductive System**
1 **Fluoroscopy:** Single plane or bi-plane real time display of an image developed from the capture of external ionizing radioation on a fluorescent screen. The image may also be stored by either digital or analog means

Body Part Character 4	Contrast Character 5	Qualifier Character 6	Qualifier Character 7
0 Corpora Cavernosa **8** Vasa Vasorum	**0** High Osmolar **1** Low Osmolar **Y** Other Contrast **Z** None	**Z** None	**Z** None

B **Imaging**
V **Male Reproductive System**
2 **Computerized Tomography (CT Scan):** Computer reformatted digital display of multiplanar images developed from the capture of multiple exposures of external ionizing radiation

Body Part Character 4	Contrast Character 5	Qualifier Character 6	Qualifier Character 7
3 Prostate	**0** High Osmolar **1** Low Osmolar **Y** Other Contrast	**0** Unenhanced and Enhanced **Z** None	**Z** None
3 Prostate	**Z** None	**Z** None	**Z** None

B **Imaging**
V **Male Reproductive System**
3 **Magnetic Resonance Imaging (MRI):** Computer reformatted digital display of multiplanar images developed from the capture of radio-frequency signals emitted by nuclei in a body site excited within a magnetic field

Body Part Character 4	Contrast Character 5	Qualifier Character 6	Qualifier Character 7
0 Corpora Cavernosa **3** Prostate **4** Scrotum **5** Testicle, Right **6** Testicle, Left **7** Testicles, Bilateral	**Y** Other Contrast	**0** Unenhanced and Enhanced **Z** None	**Z** None
0 Corpora Cavernosa **3** Prostate **4** Scrotum **5** Testicle, Right **6** Testicle, Left **7** Testicles, Bilateral	**Z** None	**Z** None	**Z** None

B **Imaging**
V **Male Reproductive System**
4 **Ultrasonography:** Real time dispaly of images of anatomy or flow information developed from the capture of relected and attenuated high frequency sound waves

Body Part Character 4	Contrast Character 5	Qualifier Character 6	Qualifier Character 7
4 Scrotum **9** Prostate and Seminal Vesicles **B** Penis	**Z** None	**Z** None	**Z** None

B **Imaging**
W **Anatomical Regions**
0 **Plain Radiography:** Planar display of an image developed from the capture of external ionizing radiation on photographic or photoconductive plate

Body Part Character 4	Contrast Character 5	Qualifier Character 6	Qualifier Character 7
0 Abdomen **1** Abdomen and Pelvis **3** Chest **B** Long Bones, All **C** Lower Extremity **J** Upper Extremity **K** Whole Body **L** Whole Skeleton **M** Whole Body, Infant	**Z** None	**Z** None	**Z** None

B Imaging
W Anatomical Regions
1 Fluoroscopy: Single plane or bi-plane real time display of an image developed from the capture of external ionizing radioation on a fluorescent screen. The image may also be stored by either digital or analog means

Body Part Character 4	Contrast Character 5	Qualifier Character 6	Qualifier Character 7
1 Abdomen and Pelvis **9** Head and Neck **C** Lower Extremity **J** Upper Extremity	**0** High Osmolar **1** Low Osmolar **Y** Other Contrast **Z** None	**Z** None	**Z** None

B Imaging
W Anatomical Regions
2 Computerized Tomography (CT Scan): Computer reformatted digital display of multiplanar images developed from the capture of multiple exposures of external ionizing radiation

Body Part Character 4	Contrast Character 5	Qualifier Character 6	Qualifier Character 7
0 Abdomen **1** Abdomen and Pelvis **4** Chest and Abdomen **5** Chest, Abdomen and Pelvis **8** Head **9** Head and Neck **F** Neck **G** Pelvic Region	**0** High Osmolar **1** Low Osmolar **Y** Other Contrast	**0** Unenhanced and Enhanced **Z** None	**Z** None
0 Abdomen **1** Abdomen and Pelvis **4** Chest and Abdomen **5** Chest, Abdomen and Pelvis **8** Head **9** Head and Neck **F** Neck **G** Pelvic Region	**Z** None	**Z** None	**Z** None

B Imaging
W Anatomical Regions
3 Magnetic Resonance Imaging (MRI): Computer reformatted digital display of multiplanar images developed from the capture of radio-frequency signals emitted by nuclei in a body site excited within a magnetic field

Body Part Character 4	Contrast Character 5	Qualifier Character 6	Qualifier Character 7
0 Abdomen **3** Chest **8** Head **F** Neck **G** Pelvic Region **H** Retroperitoneum **P** Brachial Plexus	**Y** Other Contrast	**0** Unenhanced and Enhanced **Z** None	**Z** None
0 Abdomen **8** Head **F** Neck **G** Pelvic Region **H** Retroperitoneum **P** Brachial Plexus	**Z** None	**Z** None	**Z** None

B Imaging
W Anatomical Regions
4 Ultrasonography: Real time dispaly of images of anatomy or flow information developed from the capture of relected and attenuated high frequency sound waves

Body Part Character 4	Contrast Character 5	Qualifier Character 6	Qualifier Character 7
0 Abdomen **1** Abdomen and Pelvis **F** Neck **G** Pelvic Region	**Z** None	**Z** None	**Z** None

B   **Imaging**
Y   **Fetus and Obstetrical**
3   **Magnetic Resonance Imaging (MRI):** Computer reformatted digital display of multiplanar images developed from the capture of radio-frequency signals emitted by nuclei in a body site excited within a magnetic field

Body Part Character 4	Contrast Character 5	Qualifier Character 6	Qualifier Character 7
0 Fetal Head **1** Fetal Heart **2** Fetal Thorax **3** Fetal Abdomen **4** Fetal Spine **5** Fetal Extremities **6** Whole Fetus	**Y** Other Contrast	**0** Unenhanced and Enhanced **Z** None	**Z** None
0 Fetal Head **1** Fetal Heart **2** Fetal Thorax **3** Fetal Abdomen **4** Fetal Spine **5** Fetal Extremities **6** Whole Fetus	**Z** None	**Z** None	**Z** None

B   **Imaging**
Y   **Fetus and Obstetrical**
4   **Ultrasonography:** Real time dispaly of images of anatomy or flow information developed from the capture of relected and attenuated high frequency sound waves

Body Part Character 4	Contrast Character 5	Qualifier Character 6	Qualifier Character 7
7 Fetal Umbilical Cord **8** Placenta **9** First Trimester, Single Fetus **B** First Trimester, Multiple Gestation **C** Second Trimester, Single Fetus **D** Second Trimester, Multiple Gestation **F** Third Trimester, Single Fetus **G** Third Trimester, Multiple Gestation	**Z** None	**Z** None	**Z** None

Nuclear Medicine C01–CW7

C **Nuclear Medicine**
0 **Central Nervous System**
1 **Planar Nuclear Medicine Imaging:** Introduction of radioactive materials into the body for single plane display of images developed from the capture of radioactive emissions

Body Part Character 4	Radionuclide Character 5	Qualifier Character 6	Qualifier Character 7
0 Brain	**1** Technetium 99m (Tc-99m) **Y** Other Radionuclide	**Z** None	**Z** None
5 Cerebrospinal Fluid	**D** Indium 111 (In-111) **Y** Other Radionuclide	**Z** None	**Z** None
Y Central Nervous System	**Y** Other Radionuclide	**Z** None	**Z** None

C **Nuclear Medicine**
0 **Central Nervous System**
2 **Tomographic (Tomo) Nuclear Medicine Imaging:** Introduction of radioactive materials into the body for three dimensional display of images developed from the capture of radioactive emissions

Body Part Character 4	Radionuclide Character 5	Qualifier Character 6	Qualifier Character 7
0 Brain	**1** Technetium 99m (Tc-99m) **F** Iodine 123 (I-123) **S** Thallium 201 (Tl-201) **Y** Other Radionuclide	**Z** None	**Z** None
5 Cerebrospinal Fluid	**D** Indium 111 (In-111) **Y** Other Radionuclide	**Z** None	**Z** None
Y Central Nervous System	**Y** Other Radionuclide	**Z** None	**Z** None

C **Nuclear Medicine**
0 **Central Nervous System**
3 **Positron Emission Tomographic (PET) Imaging:** Introduction of radioactive materials into the body for three dimensional display of images developed from the simultaneous capture, 180 degrees apart, of radioactive emissions

Body Part Character 4	Radionuclide Character 5	Qualifier Character 6	Qualifier Character 7
0 Brain	**B** Carbon 11 (C-11) **K** Fluorine 18 (F-18) **M** Oxygen 15 (O-15) **Y** Other Radionuclide	**Z** None	**Z** None
Y Central Nervous System	**Y** Other Radionuclide	**Z** None	**Z** None

C **Nuclear Medicine**
0 **Central Nervous System**
5 **Nonimaging Nuclear Medicine Probe:** Introduction of radioactive materials into the body for the study of distribution and fate of certain substances by the detection of radioactive emissions; or, alternatively, measurement of absorption of radioactive emissions from an external source

Body Part Character 4	Radionuclide Character 5	Qualifier Character 6	Qualifier Character 7
0 Brain	**V** Xenon 133 (Xe-133) **Y** Other Radionuclide	**Z** None	**Z** None
Y Central Nervous System	**Y** Other Radionuclide	**Z** None	**Z** None

C **Nuclear Medicine**
2 **Heart**
1 **Planar Nuclear Medicine Imaging:** Introduction of radioactive materials into the body for single plane display of images developed from the capture of radioactive emissions

Body Part Character 4	Radionuclide Character 5	Qualifier Character 6	Qualifier Character 7
6 Heart, Right and Left	**1** Technetium 99m (Tc-99m) **Y** Other Radionuclide	**Z** None	**Z** None
G Myocardium	**1** Technetium 99m (Tc-99m) **D** Indium 111 (In-111) **S** Thallium 201 (Tl-201) **Y** Other Radionuclide **Z** None	**Z** None	**Z** None
Y Heart	**Y** Other Radionuclide	**Z** None	**Z** None

C Nuclear Medicine
2 Heart
2 Tomographic (Tomo) Nuclear Medicine Imaging: Introduction of radioactive materials into the body for three dimensional display of images developed from the capture of radioactive emissions

Body Part Character 4	Radionuclide Character 5	Qualifier Character 6	Qualifier Character 7
6 Heart, Right and Left	**1** Technetium 99m (Tc-99m) **Y** Other Radionuclide	**Z** None	**Z** None
G Myocardium	**1** Technetium 99m (Tc-99m) **D** Indium 111 (In-111) **K** Fluorine 18 (F-18) **S** Thallium 201 (Tl-201) **Y** Other Radionuclide **Z** None	**Z** None	**Z** None
Y Heart	**Y** Other Radionuclide	**Z** None	**Z** None

C Nuclear Medicine
2 Heart
3 Positron Emission Tomographic (PET) Imaging: Introduction of radioactive materials into the body for three dimensional display of images developed from the simultaneous capture, 180 degrees apart, of radioactive emissions

Body Part Character 4	Radionuclide Character 5	Qualifier Character 6	Qualifier Character 7
G Myocardium	**K** Fluorine 18 (F-18) **M** Oxygen 15 (O-15) **Q** Rubidium 82 (Rb-82) **R** Nitrogen 13 (N-13) **Y** Other Radionuclide	**Z** None	**Z** None
Y Heart	**Y** Other Radionuclide	**Z** None	**Z** None

C Nuclear Medicine
2 Heart
5 Nonimaging Nuclear Medicine Probe: Introduction of radioactive materials into the body for the study of distribution and fate of certain substances by the detection of radioactive emissions; or, alternatively, measurement of absorption of radioactive emissions from an external source

Body Part Character 4	Radionuclide Character 5	Qualifier Character 6	Qualifier Character 7
6 Heart, Right and Left	**1** Technetium 99m (Tc-99m) **Y** Other Radionuclide	**Z** None	**Z** None
Y Heart	**Y** Other Radionuclide	**Z** None	**Z** None

C Nuclear Medicine
5 Veins
1 Planar Nuclear Medicine Imaging: Introduction of radioactive materials into the body for single plane display of images developed from the capture of radioactive emissions

Body Part Character 4	Radionuclide Character 5	Qualifier Character 6	Qualifier Character 7
B Lower Extremity Veins, Right **C** Lower Extremity Veins, Left **D** Lower Extremity Veins, Bilateral **N** Upper Extremity Veins, Right **P** Upper Extremity Veins, Left **Q** Upper Extremity Veins, Bilateral **R** Central Veins	**1** Technetium 99m (Tc-99m) **Y** Other Radionuclide	**Z** None	**Z** None
Y Veins	**Y** Other Radionuclide	**Z** None	**Z** None

C Nuclear Medicine
7 Lymphatic and Hematologic System
1 Planar Nuclear Medicine Imaging: Introduction of radioactive materials into the body for single plane display of images developed from the capture of radioactive emissions

Body Part Character 4	Radionuclide Character 5	Qualifier Character 6	Qualifier Character 7
0 Bone Marrow	**1** Technetium 99m (Tc-99m) **D** Indium 111 (In-111) **Y** Other Radionuclide	**Z** None	**Z** None
2 Spleen **5** Lymphatics, Head and Neck **D** Lymphatics, Pelvic **J** Lymphatics, Head **K** Lymphatics, Neck **L** Lymphatics, Upper Chest **M** Lymphatics, Trunk **N** Lymphatics, Upper Extremity **P** Lymphatics, Lower Extremity	**1** Technetium 99m (Tc-99m) **Y** Other Radionuclide	**Z** None	**Z** None
3 Blood	**D** Indium 111 (In-111) **Y** Other Radionuclide	**Z** None	**Z** None
Y Lymphatic and Hematologic System	**Y** Other Radionuclide	**Z** None	**Z** None

C Nuclear Medicine
7 Lymphatic and Hematologic System
2 Tomographic (Tomo) Nuclear Medicine Imaging: Introduction of radioactive materials into the body for three dimensional display of images developed from the capture of radioactive emissions

Body Part Character 4	Radionuclide Character 5	Qualifier Character 6	Qualifier Character 7
2 Spleen	**1** Technetium 99m (Tc-99m) **Y** Other Radionuclide	**Z** None	**Z** None
Y Lymphatic and Hematologic System	**Y** Other Radionuclide	**Z** None	**Z** None

C Nuclear Medicine
7 Lymphatic and Hematologic System
5 Nonimaging Nuclear Medicine Probe: Introduction of radioactive materials into the body for the study of distribution and fate of certain substances by the detection of radioactive emissions; or, alternatively, measurement of absorption of radioactive emissions from an external source

Body Part Character 4	Radionuclide Character 5	Qualifier Character 6	Qualifier Character 7
5 Lymphatics, Head and Neck **D** Lymphatics, Pelvic **J** Lymphatics, Head **K** Lymphatics, Neck **L** Lymphatics, Upper Chest **M** Lymphatics, Trunk **N** Lymphatics, Upper Extremity **P** Lymphatics, Lower Extremity	**1** Technetium 99m (Tc-99m) **Y** Other Radionuclide	**Z** None	**Z** None
Y Lymphatic and Hematologic System	**Y** Other Radionuclide	**Z** None	**Z** None

C Nuclear Medicine
7 Lymphatic and Hematologic System
6 Nonimaging Nuclear Medicine Assay: Introduction of radioactive materials into the body for the study of body fluids and blood elements, by the detection of radioactive emissions

Body Part Character 4	Radionuclide Character 5	Qualifier Character 6	Qualifier Character 7
3 Blood	**1** Technetium 99m (Tc-99m) **7** Cobalt 58 (Co-58) **C** Cobalt 57 (Co-57) **D** Indium 111 (In-111) **H** Iodine 125 (I-125) **W** Chromium (Cr-51) **Y** Other Radionuclide	**Z** None	**Z** None
Y Lymphatic and Hematologic System	**Y** Other Radionuclide	**Z** None	**Z** None

C   **Nuclear Medicine**
8   **Eye**
1   **Planar Nuclear Medicine Imaging:** Introduction of radioactive materials into the body for single plane display of images developed from the capture of radioactive emissions

Body Part Character 4	Radionuclide Character 5	Qualifier Character 6	Qualifier Character 7
9 Lacrimal Ducts, Bilateral	**1** Technetium 99m (Tc-99m) **Y** Other Radionuclide	**Z** None	**Z** None
Y Eye	**Y** Other Radionuclide	**Z** None	**Z** None

C   **Nuclear Medicine**
9   **Ear, Nose, Mouth and Throat**
1   **Planar Nuclear Medicine Imaging:** Introduction of radioactive materials into the body for single plane display of images developed from the capture of radioactive emissions

Body Part Character 4	Radionuclide Character 5	Qualifier Character 6	Qualifier Character 7
B Salivary Glands, Bilateral	**1** Technetium 99m (Tc-99m) **Y** Other Radionuclide	**Z** None	**Z** None
Y Ear, Nose, Mouth and Throat	**Y** Other Radionuclide	**Z** None	**Z** None

C   **Nuclear Medicine**
B   **Respiratory System**
1   **Planar Nuclear Medicine Imaging:** Introduction of radioactive materials into the body for single plane display of images developed from the capture of radioactive emissions

Body Part Character 4	Radionuclide Character 5	Qualifier Character 6	Qualifier Character 7
2 Lungs and Bronchi	**1** Technetium 99m (Tc-99m) **9** Krypton (Kr-81m) **T** Xenon 127 (Xe-127) **V** Xenon 133 (Xe-133) **Y** Other Radionuclide	**Z** None	**Z** None
Y Respiratory System	**Y** Other Radionuclide	**Z** None	**Z** None

C   **Nuclear Medicine**
B   **Respiratory System**
2   **Tomographic (Tomo) Nuclear Medicine Imaging:** Introduction of radioactive materials into the body for three dimensional display of images developed from the capture of radioactive emissions

Body Part Character 4	Radionuclide Character 5	Qualifier Character 6	Qualifier Character 7
2 Lungs and Bronchi	**1** Technetium 99m (Tc-99m) **9** Krypton (Kr-81m) **Y** Other Radionuclide	**Z** None	**Z** None
Y Respiratory System	**Y** Other Radionuclide	**Z** None	**Z** None

C   **Nuclear Medicine**
B   **Respiratory System**
3   **Positron Emission Tomographic (PET) Imaging:** Introduction of radioactive materials into the body for three dimensional display of images developed from the simultaneous capture, 180 degrees apart, of radioactive emissions

Body Part Character 4	Radionuclide Character 5	Qualifier Character 6	Qualifier Character 7
2 Lungs and Bronchi	**K** Fluorine 18 (F-18) **Y** Other Radionuclide	**Z** None	**Z** None
Y Respiratory System	**Y** Other Radionuclide	**Z** None	**Z** None

C   **Nuclear Medicine**
D   **Gastrointestinal System**
1   **Planar Nuclear Medicine Imaging:** Introduction of radioactive materials into the body for single plane display of images developed from the capture of radioactive emissions

Body Part Character 4	Radionuclide Character 5	Qualifier Character 6	Qualifier Character 7
5 Upper Gastrointestinal Tract **7** Gastrointestinal Tract	**1** Technetium 99m (Tc-99m) **D** Indium 111 (In-111) **Y** Other Radionuclide	**Z** None	**Z** None *Continued on next page*

C   **Nuclear Medicine**   *Continued from previous page*
D   **Gastrointestinal System**
1   **Planar Nuclear Medicine Imaging:** Introduction of radioactive materials into the body for single plane display of images developed from the capture of radioactive emissions

Body Part Character 4	Radionuclide Character 5	Qualifier Character 6	Qualifier Character 7
Y Digestive System	**Y** Other Radionuclide	**Z** None	**Z** None

C   **Nuclear Medicine**
D   **Gastrointestinal System**
2   **Tomographic (Tomo) Nuclear Medicine Imaging:** Introduction of radioactive materials into the body for three dimensional display of images developed from the capture of radioactive emissions

Body Part Character 4	Radionuclide Character 5	Qualifier Character 6	Qualifier Character 7
7 Gastrointestinal Tract	**1** Technetium 99m (Tc-99m) **D** Indium 111 (In-111) **Y** Other Radionuclide	**Z** None	**Z** None
Y Digestive System	**Y** Other Radionuclide	**Z** None	**Z** None

C   **Nuclear Medicine**
F   **Hepatobiliary System and Pancreas**
1   **Planar Nuclear Medicine Imaging:** Introduction of radioactive materials into the body for single plane display of images developed from the capture of radioactive emissions

Body Part Character 4	Radionuclide Character 5	Qualifier Character 6	Qualifier Character 7
4 Gallbladder **5** Liver **6** Liver and Spleen **C** Hepatobiliary System, All	**1** Technetium 99m (Tc-99m) **Y** Other Radionuclide	**Z** None	**Z** None
Y Hepatobiliary System and Pancreas	**Y** Other Radionuclide	**Z** None	**Z** None

C   **Nuclear Medicine**
F   **Hepatobiliary System and Pancreas**
2   **Tomographic (Tomo) Nuclear Medicine Imaging:** Introduction of radioactive materials into the body for three dimensional display of images developed from the capture of radioactive emissions

Body Part Character 4	Radionuclide Character 5	Qualifier Character 6	Qualifier Character 7
4 Gallbladder **5** Liver **6** Liver and Spleen	**1** Technetium 99m (Tc-99m) **Y** Other Radionuclide	**Z** None	**Z** None
Y Hepatobiliary System and Pancreas	**Y** Other Radionuclide	**Z** None	**Z** None

C   **Nuclear Medicine**
G   **Endocrine System**
1   **Planar Nuclear Medicine Imaging:** Introduction of radioactive materials into the body for single plane display of images developed from the capture of radioactive emissions

Body Part Character 4	Radionuclide Character 5	Qualifier Character 6	Qualifier Character 7
1 Parathyroid Glands	**1** Technetium 99m (Tc-99m) **S** Thallium 201 (Tl-201) **Y** Other Radionuclide	**Z** None	**Z** None
2 Thyroid Gland	**1** Technetium 99m (Tc-99m) **F** Iodine 123 (I-123) **G** Iodine 131 (I-131) **Y** Other Radionuclide	**Z** None	**Z** None
4 Adrenal Glands, Bilateral	**G** Iodine 131 (I-131) **Y** Other Radionuclide	**Z** None	**Z** None
Y Endocrine System	**Y** Other Radionuclide	**Z** None	**Z** None

C **Nuclear Medicine**
G **Endocrine System**
2 **Tomographic (Tomo) Nuclear Medicine Imaging:** Introduction of radioactive materials into the body for three dimensional display of images developed from the capture of radioactive emissions

Body Part Character 4	Radionuclide Character 5	Qualifier Character 6	Qualifier Character 7
1 Parathyroid Glands	**1** Technetium 99m (Tc-99m) **S** Thallium 201 (Tl-201) **Y** Other Radionuclide	**Z** None	**Z** None
Y Endocrine System	**Y** Other Radionuclide	**Z** None	**Z** None

C **Nuclear Medicine**
G **Endocrine System**
4 **Nonimaging Nuclear Medicine Uptake:** Introduction of radioactive materials into the body for measurements of organ function, from the detection of radioactive emmissions

Body Part Character 4	Radionuclide Character 5	Qualifier Character 6	Qualifier Character 7
2 Thyroid Gland	**1** Technetium 99m (Tc-99m) **F** Iodine 123 (I-123) **G** Iodine 131 (I-131) **Y** Other Radionuclide	**Z** None	**Z** None
Y Endocrine System	**Y** Other Radionuclide	**Z** None	**Z** None

C **Nuclear Medicine**
H **Skin, Subcutaneous Tissue and Breast**
1 **Planar Nuclear Medicine Imaging:** Introduction of radioactive materials into the body for single plane display of images developed from the capture of radioactive emissions

Body Part Character 4	Radionuclide Character 5	Qualifier Character 6	Qualifier Character 7
0 Breast, Right **1** Breast, Left **2** Breasts, Bilateral	**1** Technetium 99m (Tc-99m) **S** Thallium 201 (Tl-201) **Y** Other Radionuclide	**Z** None	**Z** None
Y Skin, Subcutaneous Tissue and Breast	**Y** Other Radionuclide	**Z** None	**Z** None

C **Nuclear Medicine**
H **Skin, Subcutaneous Tissue and Breast**
2 **Tomographic (Tomo) Nuclear Medicine Imaging:** Introduction of radioactive materials into the body for three dimensional display of images developed from the capture of radioactive emissions

Body Part Character 4	Radionuclide Character 5	Qualifier Character 6	Qualifier Character 7
0 Breast, Right **1** Breast, Left **2** Breasts, Bilateral	**1** Technetium 99m (Tc-99m) **S** Thallium 201 (Tl-201) **Y** Other Radionuclide	**Z** None	**Z** None
Y Skin, Subcutaneous Tissue and Breast	**Y** Other Radionuclide	**Z** None	**Z** None

C **Nuclear Medicine**
P **Musculoskeletal System**
1 **Planar Nuclear Medicine Imaging:** Introduction of radioactive materials into the body for single plane display of images developed from the capture of radioactive emissions

Body Part Character 4	Radionuclide Character 5	Qualifier Character 6	Qualifier Character 7
1 Skull **4** Thorax **5** Spine **6** Pelvis **7** Spine and Pelvis **8** Upper Extremity, Right **9** Upper Extremity, Left **B** Upper Extremities, Bilateral **C** Lower Extremity, Right **D** Lower Extremity, Left **F** Lower Extremities, Bilateral **Z** Musculoskeletal System, All	**1** Technetium 99m (Tc-99m) **Y** Other Radionuclide	**Z** None	**Z** None
Y Musculoskeletal System, Other	**Y** Other Radionuclide	**Z** None	**Z** None

C   **Nuclear Medicine**
P   **Musculoskeletal System**
2   **Tomographic (Tomo) Nuclear Medicine Imaging:**   Introduction of radioactive materials into the body for three dimensional display of images developed from the capture of radioactive emissions

Body Part Character 4	Radionuclide Character 5	Qualifier Character 6	Qualifier Character 7
1 Skull **2** Cervical Spine **3** Skull and Cervical Spine **4** Thorax **6** Pelvis **7** Spine and Pelvis **8** Upper Extremity, Right **9** Upper Extremity, Left **B** Upper Extremities, Bilateral **C** Lower Extremity, Right **D** Lower Extremity, Left **F** Lower Extremities, Bilateral **G** Thoracic Spine **H** Lumbar Spine **J** Thoracolumbar Spine	**1** Technetium 99m (Tc-99m) **Y** Other Radionuclide	**Z** None	**Z** None
Y Musculoskeletal System, Other	**Y** Other Radionuclide	**Z** None	**Z** None

C   **Nuclear Medicine**
P   **Musculoskeletal System**
5   **Nonimaging Nuclear Medicine Probe:**   Introduction of radioactive materials into the body for the study of distribution and fate of certain substances by the detection of radioactive emissions; or, alternatively, measurement of absorption of radioactive emissions from an external source

Body Part Character 4	Radionuclide Character 5	Qualifier Character 6	Qualifier Character 7
5 Spine **N** Upper Extremities **P** Lower Extremities	**Z** None	**Z** None	**Z** None
Y Musculoskeletal System, Other	**Y** Other Radionuclide	**Z** None	**Z** None

C   **Nuclear Medicine**
T   **Urinary System**
1   **Planar Nuclear Medicine Imaging:**   Introduction of radioactive materials into the body for single plane display of images developed from the capture of radioactive emissions

Body Part Character 4	Radionuclide Character 5	Qualifier Character 6	Qualifier Character 7
3 Kidneys, Ureters and Bladder	**1** Technetium 99m (Tc-99m) **F** Iodine 123 (I-123) **G** Iodine 131 (I-131) **Y** Other Radionuclide	**Z** None	**Z** None
H Bladder and Ureters	**1** Technetium 99m (Tc-99m) **Y** Other Radionuclide	**Z** None	**Z** None
Y Urinary System	**Y** Other Radionuclide	**Z** None	**Z** None

C   **Nuclear Medicine**
T   **Urinary System**
2   **Tomographic (Tomo) Nuclear Medicine Imaging:**   Introduction of radioactive materials into the body for three dimensional display of images developed from the capture of radioactive emissions

Body Part Character 4	Radionuclide Character 5	Qualifier Character 6	Qualifier Character 7
3 Kidneys, Ureters and Bladder	**1** Technetium 99m (Tc-99m) **Y** Other Radionuclide	**Z** None	**Z** None
Y Urinary System	**Y** Other Radionuclide	**Z** None	**Z** None

C **Nuclear Medicine**
T **Urinary System**
6 **Nonimaging Nuclear Medicine Assay:**   Introduction of radioactive materials into the body for the study of body fluids and blood elements, by the detection of radioactive emissions

Body Part Character 4	Radionuclide Character 5	Qualifier Character 6	Qualifier Character 7
3 Kidneys, Ureters and Bladder	**1** Technetium 99m (Tc-99m) **F** Iodine 123 (I-123) **G** Iodine 131 (I-131) **H** Iodine 125 (I-125) **Y** Other Radionuclide	**Z** None	**Z** None
Y Urinary System	**Y** Other Radionuclide	**Z** None	**Z** None

C **Nuclear Medicine**
V **Male Reproductive System**
1 **Planar Nuclear Medicine Imaging:**   Introduction of radioactive materials into the body for single plane display of images developed from the capture of radioactive emissions

Body Part Character 4	Radionuclide Character 5	Qualifier Character 6	Qualifier Character 7
9 Testicles, Bilateral	**1** Technetium 99m (Tc-99m) **Y** Other Radionuclide	**Z** None	**Z** None
Y Male Reproductive System	**Y** Other Radionuclide	**Z** None	**Z** None

C **Nuclear Medicine**
W **Anatomical Regions**
1 **Planar Nuclear Medicine Imaging:**   Introduction of radioactive materials into the body for single plane display of images developed from the capture of radioactive emissions

Body Part Character 4	Radionuclide Character 5	Qualifier Character 6	Qualifier Character 7
0 Abdomen **1** Abdomen and Pelvis **4** Chest and Abdomen **6** Chest and Neck **B** Head and Neck **D** Lower Extremity **J** Pelvic Region **M** Upper Extremity **N** Whole Body	**1** Technetium 99m (Tc-99m) **D** Indium 111 (In-111) **F** Iodine 123 (I-123) **G** Iodine 131 (I-131) **L** Gallium 67 (Ga-67) **S** Thallium 201 (Tl-201) **Y** Other Radionuclide	**Z** None	**Z** None
3 Chest	**1** Technetium 99m (Tc-99m) **D** Indium 111 (In-111) **F** Iodine 123 (I-123) **G** Iodine 131 (I-131) **K** Fluorine 18 (F-18) **L** Gallium 67 (Ga-67) **S** Thallium 201 (Tl-201) **Y** Other Radionuclide	**Z** None	**Z** None
Y Anatomical Regions, Multiple	**Y** Other Radionuclide	**Z** None	**Z** None
Z Anatomical Region, Other	**Z** None	**Z** None	**Z** None

C **Nuclear Medicine**
W **Anatomical Regions**
2 **Tomographic (Tomo) Nuclear Medicine Imaging:**   Introduction of radioactive materials into the body for three dimensional display of images developed from the capture of radioactive emissions

Body Part Character 4	Radionuclide Character 5	Qualifier Character 6	Qualifier Character 7
0 Abdomen **1** Abdomen and Pelvis **3** Chest **4** Chest and Abdomen **6** Chest and Neck **B** Head and Neck **D** Lower Extremity **J** Pelvic Region **M** Upper Extremity	**1** Technetium 99m (Tc-99m) **D** Indium 111 (In-111) **F** Iodine 123 (I-123) **G** Iodine 131 (I-131) **K** Fluorine 18 (F-18) **L** Gallium 67 (Ga-67) **S** Thallium 201 (Tl-201) **Y** Other Radionuclide	**Z** None	**Z** None
Y Anatomical Regions, Multiple	**Y** Other Radionuclide	**Z** None	**Z** None

C   **Nuclear Medicine**
W **Anatomical Regions**
3   **Positron Emission Tomographic (PET) Imaging:**   Introduction of radioactive materials into the body for three dimensional display of images developed from the simultaneous capture, 180 degrees apart, of radioactive emissions

Body Part Character 4	Radionuclide Character 5	Qualifier Character 6	Qualifier Character 7
N Whole Body	**Y** Other Radionuclide	**Z** None	**Z** None

C   **Nuclear Medicine**
W **Anatomical Regions**
5   **Nonimaging Nuclear Medicine Probe:**   Introduction of radioactive materials into the body for the study of distribution and fate of certain substances by the detection of radioactive emissions; or, alternatively, measurement of absorption of radioactive emissions from an external source

Body Part Character 4	Radionuclide Character 5	Qualifier Character 6	Qualifier Character 7
0 Abdomen **1** Abdomen and Pelvis **3** Chest **4** Chest and Abdomen **6** Chest and Neck **B** Head and Neck **D** Lower Extremity **J** Pelvic Region **M** Upper Extremity	**1** Technetium 99m (Tc-99m) **D** Indium 111 (In-111) **Y** Other Radionuclide	**Z** None	**Z** None

C   **Nuclear Medicine**
W **Anatomical Regions**
7   **Systemic Nuclear Medicine Therapy:**   Introduction of radioactive materials into the body for treatment

Body Part Character 4	Radionuclide Character 5	Qualifier Character 6	Qualifier Character 7
0 Abdomen **3** Chest	**N** Phosphorus 32 (P-32) **Y** Other Radionuclide	**Z** None	**Z** None
G Thyroid	**G** Iodine 131 (I-131) **Y** Other Radionuclide	**Z** None	**Z** None
N Whole Body	**8** Samarium 153 (Sm-153) **G** Iodine 131 (I-131) **N** Phosphorus 32 (P-32) **P** Strontium 89 (Sr-89) **Y** Other Radionuclide	**Z** None	**Z** None
Y Anatomical Regions, Multiple	**Y** Other Radionuclide	**Z** None	**Z** None

Radiation Oncology D00–DWY

D Radiation Oncology
0 Central and Peripheral Nervous System
0 Beam Radiation

Treatment Site Character 4	Modality Qualifier Character 5	Isotope Character 6	Qualifier Character 7
0 Brain **1** Brain Stem **6** Spinal Cord **7** Peripheral Nerve	**0** Photons <1 MeV **1** Photons 1-10 MeV **2** Photons >10 MeV **4** Heavy Particles (Protons,Ions) **5** Neutrons **6** Neutron Capture	**Z** None	**Z** None
0 Brain **1** Brain Stem **6** Spinal Cord **7** Peripheral Nerve	**3** Electrons	**Z** None	**0** Intraoperative **Z** None

D Radiation Oncology
0 Central and Peripheral Nervous System
1 Brachytherapy

Treatment Site Character 4	Modality Qualifier Character 5	Isotope Character 6	Qualifier Character 7
0 Brain **1** Brain Stem **6** Spinal Cord **7** Peripheral Nerve	**9** High Dose Rate (HDR) **B** Low Dose Rate (LDR)	**7** Cesium 137 (Cs-137) **8** Iridium 192 (Ir-192) **9** Iodine 125 (I-125) **B** Palladium 103 (Pd-103) **C** Californium 252 (Cf-252) **Y** Other Isotope	**Z** None

D Radiation Oncology
0 Central and Peripheral Nervous System
2 Stereotactic Radiosurgery

Treatment Site Character 4	Modality Qualifier Character 5	Isotope Character 6	Qualifier Character 7
0 Brain **1** Brain Stem **6** Spinal Cord **7** Peripheral Nerve	**D** Stereotactic Other Photon Radiosurgery **H** Stereotactic Particulate Radiosurgery **J** Stereotactic Gamma Beam Radiosurgery	**Z** None	**Z** None

D Radiation Oncology
0 Central and Peripheral Nervous System
Y Other Radiation

Treatment Site Character 4	Modality Qualifier Character 5	Isotope Character 6	Qualifier Character 7
0 Brain **1** Brain Stem **6** Spinal Cord **7** Peripheral Nerve	**7** Contact Radiation **8** Hyperthermia **F** Plaque Radiation	**Z** None	**Z** None

D Radiation Oncology
7 Lymphatic and Hematologic System
0 Beam Radiation

Treatment Site Character 4	Modality Qualifier Character 5	Isotope Character 6	Qualifier Character 7
0 Bone Marrow **1** Thymus **2** Spleen **3** Lymphatics, Neck **4** Lymphatics, Axillary **5** Lymphatics, Thorax **6** Lymphatics, Abdomen **7** Lymphatics, Pelvis **8** Lymphatics, Inguinal	**0** Photons <1MeV **1** Photons 1- 10MeV **2** Photons >10MeV **4** Heavy Particles (Protons,Ions) **5** Neutrons **6** Neutron Capture	**Z** None	**Z** None *Continued on next page*

D   Radiation Oncology
7   Lymphatic and Hematologic System
0   Beam Radiation

Continued from previous page

Treatment Site Character 4	Modality Qualifier Character 5	Isotope Character 6	Qualifier Character 7
0 Bone Marrow 1 Thymus 2 Spleen 3 Lymphatics, Neck 4 Lymphatics, Axillary 5 Lymphatics, Thorax 6 Lymphatics, Abdomen 7 Lymphatics, Pelvis 8 Lymphatics, Inguinal	3 Electrons	Z None	0 Intraoperative Z None

D   Radiation Oncology
7   Lymphatic and Hematologic System
1   Brachytherapy

Treatment Site Character 4	Modality Qualifier Character 5	Isotope Character 6	Qualifier Character 7
0 Bone Marrow 1 Thymus 2 Spleen 3 Lymphatics, Neck 4 Lymphatics, Axillary 5 Lymphatics, Thorax 6 Lymphatics, Abdomen 7 Lymphatics, Pelvis 8 Lymphatics, Inguinal	9 High Dose Rate (HDR) B Low Dose Rate (LDR)	7 Cesium 137 (Cs-137) 8 Iridium 192 (Ir-192) 9 Iodine 125 (I-125) B Palladium 103 (Pd-103) C Californium 252 (Cf-252) Y Other Isotope	Z None

D   Radiation Oncology
7   Lymphatic and Hematologic System
2   Stereotactic Radiosurgery

Treatment Site Character 4	Modality Qualifier Character 5	Isotope Character 6	Qualifier Character 7

0 Bone Marrow
1 Thymus
2 Spleen
3 Lymphatics, Neck
4 Lymphatics, Axillary
5 Lymphatics, Thorax
6 Lymphatics, Abdomen
7 Lymphatics, Pelvis
8 Lymphatics, Inguinal
	D Stereotactic Other Photon
	    Radiosurgery
	H Stereotactic Particulate
	    Radiosurgery
	J Stereotactic Gamma Beam
	    Radiosurgery
		Z None	Z None

D   Radiation Oncology
7   Lymphatic and Hematologic System
Y   Other Radiation

Treatment Site Character 4	Modality Qualifier Character 5	Isotope Character 6	Qualifier Character 7
0 Bone Marrow 1 Thymus 2 Spleen 3 Lymphatics, Neck 4 Lymphatics, Axillary 5 Lymphatics, Thorax 6 Lymphatics, Abdomen 7 Lymphatics, Pelvis 8 Lymphatics, Inguinal	8 Hyperthermia F Plaque Radiation	Z None	Z None

D Radiation Oncology
8 Eye
0 Beam Radiation

Treatment Site Character 4	Modality Qualifier Character 5	Isotope Character 6	Qualifier Character 7
0 Eye	**0** Photons <1 MeV **1** Photons 1-10 MeV **2** Photons >10 MeV **4** Heavy Particles (Protons,Ions) **5** Neutrons **6** Neutron Capture	**Z** None	**Z** None
0 Eye	**3** Electrons	**Z** None	**0** Intraoperative **Z** None

D Radiation Oncology
8 Eye
1 Brachytherapy

Treatment Site Character 4	Modality Qualifier Character 5	Isotope Character 6	Qualifier Character 7
0 Eye	**9** High Dose Rate (HDR) **B** Low Dose Rate (LDR)	**7** Cesium 137 (Cs-137) **8** Iridium 192 (Ir-192) **9** Iodine 125 (I-125) **B** Palladium 103 (Pd-103) **C** Californium 252 (Cf-252) **Y** Other Isotope	**Z** None

D Radiation Oncology
8 Eye
2 Stereotactic Radiosurgery

Treatment Site Character 4	Modality Qualifier Character 5	Isotope Character 6	Qualifier Character 7
0 Eye	**D** Stereotactic Other Photon Radiosurgery **H** Stereotactic Particulate Radiosurgery **J** Stereotactic Gamma Beam Radiosurgery	**Z** None	**Z** None

D Radiation Oncology
8 Eye
Y Other Radiation

Treatment Site Character 4	Modality Qualifier Character 5	Isotope Character 6	Qualifier Character 7
0 Eye	**7** Contact Radiation **8** Hyperthermia **F** Plaque Radiation	**Z** None	**Z** None

D Radiation Oncology
9 Ear, Nose, Mouth and Throat
0 Beam Radiation

Treatment Site Character 4	Modality Qualifier Character 5	Isotope Character 6	Qualifier Character 7
0 Ear **1** Nose **3** Hypopharynx **4** Mouth **5** Tongue **6** Salivary Glands **7** Sinuses **8** Hard Palate **9** Soft Palate **B** Larynx **D** Nasopharynx **F** Oropharynx	**0** Photons < 1 MeV **1** Photons 1-10 MeV **2** Photons >10 MeV **4** Heavy Particles (Protons,Ions) **5** Neutrons **6** Neutron Capture	**Z** None	**Z** None

Continued on next page

D Radiation Oncology
9 Ear, Nose, Mouth and Throat
0 Beam Radiation

Continued from previous page

Treatment Site Character 4	Modality Qualifier Character 5	Isotope Character 6	Qualifier Character 7
0 Ear 1 Nose 3 Hypopharynx 4 Mouth 5 Tongue 6 Salivary Glands 7 Sinuses 8 Hard Palate 9 Soft Palate B Larynx D Nasopharynx F Oropharynx	3 Electrons	Z None	0 Intraoperative Z None

D Radiation Oncology
9 Ear, Nose, Mouth and Throat
1 Brachytherapy

Treatment Site Character 4	Modality Qualifier Character 5	Isotope Character 6	Qualifier Character 7
0 Ear 1 Nose 3 Hypopharynx 4 Mouth 5 Tongue 6 Salivary Glands 7 Sinuses 8 Hard Palate 9 Soft Palate B Larynx D Nasopharynx F Oropharynx	9 High Dose Rate (HDR) B Low Dose Rate (LDR)	7 Cesium 137 (Cs-137) 8 Iridium 192 (Ir-192) 9 Iodine 125 (I-125) B Palladium 103 (Pd-103) C Californium 252 (Cf-252) Y Other Isotope	Z None

D Radiation Oncology
9 Ear, Nose, Mouth and Throat
2 Stereotactic Radiosurgery

Treatment Site Character 4	Modality Qualifier Character 5	Isotope Character 6	Qualifier Character 7

0 Ear
1 Nose
4 Mouth
5 Tongue
6 Salivary Glands
7 Sinuses
8 Hard Palate
9 Soft Palate
B Larynx
C Pharynx
D Nasopharynx
	D Stereotactic Other Photon
	   Radiosurgery
	H Stereotactic Particulate
	   Radiosurgery
	J Stereotactic Gamma Beam
	   Radiosurgery
		Z None	Z None

D Radiation Oncology
9 Ear, Nose, Mouth and Throat
Y Other Radiation

Treatment Site Character 4	Modality Qualifier Character 5	Isotope Character 6	Qualifier Character 7
0 Ear 1 Nose 5 Tongue 6 Salivary Glands 7 Sinuses 8 Hard Palate 9 Soft Palate	7 Contact Radiation 8 Hyperthermia F Plaque Radiation	Z None	Z None
3 Hypopharynx F Oropharynx	7 Contact Radiation 8 Hyperthermia	Z None	Z None

Continued on next page

D **Radiation Oncology**
9 **Ear, Nose, Mouth and Throat**
Y **Other Radiation**

Continued from previous page

Treatment Site Character 4	Modality Qualifier Character 5	Isotope Character 6	Qualifier Character 7
4 Mouth **B** Larynx **D** Nasopharynx	**7** Contact Radiation **8** Hyperthermia **C** Intraoperative Radiation Therapy (IORT) **F** Plaque Radiation	**Z** None	**Z** None
C Pharynx	**C** Intraoperative Radiation Therapy (IORT) **F** Plaque Radiation	**Z** None	**Z** None

D **Radiation Oncology**
B **Respiratory System**
0 **Beam Radiation**

Treatment Site Character 4	Modality Qualifier Character 5	Isotope Character 6	Qualifier Character 7
0 Trachea **1** Bronchus **2** Lung **5** Pleura **6** Mediastinum **7** Chest Wall **8** Diaphragm	**0** Photons <1 MeV **1** Photons 1- 10 MeV **2** Photons >10 MeV **4** Heavy Particles (Protons,Ions) **5** Neutrons **6** Neutron Capture	**Z** None	**Z** None
0 Trachea **1** Bronchus **2** Lung **5** Pleura **6** Mediastinum **7** Chest Wall **8** Diaphragm	**3** Electrons	**Z** None	**0** Intraoperative **Z** None

D **Radiation Oncology**
B **Respiratory System**
1 **Brachytherapy**

Treatment Site Character 4	Modality Qualifier Character 5	Isotope Character 6	Qualifier Character 7
0 Trachea **1** Bronchus **2** Lung **5** Pleura **6** Mediastinum **7** Chest Wall **8** Diaphragm	**9** High Dose Rate (HDR) **B** Low Dose Rate (LDR)	**7** Cesium 137 (Cs-137) **8** Iridium 192 (Ir-192) **9** Iodine 125 (I-125) **B** Palladium 103 (Pd-103) **C** Californium 252 (Cf-252) **Y** Other Isotope	**Z** None

D **Radiation Oncology**
B **Respiratory System**
2 **Stereotactic Radiosurgery**

Treatment Site Character 4	Modality Qualifier Character 5	Isotope Character 6	Qualifier Character 7
0 Trachea **1** Bronchus **2** Lung **5** Pleura **6** Mediastinum **7** Chest Wall **8** Diaphragm	**D** Stereotactic Other Photon Radiosurgery **H** Stereotactic Particulate Radiosurgery **J** Stereotactic Gamma Beam Radiosurgery	**Z** None	**Z** None

D **Radiation Oncology**
B **Respiratory System**
Y **Other Radiation**

Treatment Site Character 4	Modality Qualifier Character 5	Isotope Character 6	Qualifier Character 7
0 Trachea **1** Bronchus **2** Lung **5** Pleura **6** Mediastinum **7** Chest Wall **8** Diaphragm	**7** Contact Radiation **8** Hyperthermia **F** Plaque Radiation	**Z** None	**Z** None

D Radiation Oncology
D Gastrointestinal System
0 Beam Radiation

Treatment Site Character 4	Modality Qualifier Character 5	Isotope Character 6	Qualifier Character 7
0 Esophagus 1 Stomach 2 Duodenum 3 Jejunum 4 Ileum 5 Colon 7 Rectum	0 Photons <1 MeV 1 Photons 1-10 MeV 2 Photons >10 MeV 4 Heavy Particles (Protons,Ions) 5 Neutrons 6 Neutron Capture	Z None	Z None
0 Esophagus 1 Stomach 2 Duodenum 3 Jejunum 4 Ileum 5 Colon 7 Rectum	3 Electrons	Z None	0 Intraoperative Z None

D Radiation Oncology
D Gastrointestinal System
1 Brachytherapy

Treatment Site Character 4	Modality Qualifier Character 5	Isotope Character 6	Qualifier Character 7
0 Esophagus 1 Stomach 2 Duodenum 3 Jejunum 4 Ileum 5 Colon 7 Rectum	9 High Dose Rate (HDR) B Low Dose Rate (LDR)	7 Cesium 137 (Cs-137) 8 Iridium 192 (Ir-192) 9 Iodine 125 (I-125) B Palladium 103 (Pd-103) C Californium 252 (Cf-252) Y Other Isotope	Z None

D Radiation Oncology
D Gastrointestinal System
2 Stereotactic Radiosurgery

Treatment Site Character 4	Modality Qualifier Character 5	Isotope Character 6	Qualifier Character 7
0 Esophagus 1 Stomach 2 Duodenum 3 Jejunum 4 Ileum 5 Colon 7 Rectum	D Stereotactic Other Photon Radiosurgery H Stereotactic Particulate Radiosurgery J Stereotactic Gamma Beam Radiosurgery	Z None	Z None

D Radiation Oncology
D Gastrointestinal System
Y Other Radiation

Treatment Site Character 4	Modality Qualifier Character 5	Isotope Character 6	Qualifier Character 7
0 Esophagus	7 Contact Radiation 8 Hyperthermia F Plaque Radiation	Z None	Z None
1 Stomach 2 Duodenum 3 Jejunum 4 Ileum 5 Colon 7 Rectum	7 Contact Radiation 8 Hyperthermia C Intraoperative Radiation Therapy (IORT) F Plaque Radiation	Z None	Z None
8 Anus	C Intraoperative Radiation Therapy (IORT) F Plaque Radiation	Z None	Z None

D   Radiation Oncology
F   Hepatobiliary System and Pancreas
0   Beam Radiation

Treatment Site Character 4	Modality Qualifier Character 5	Isotope Character 6	Qualifier Character 7
0 Liver **1** Gallbladderv **2** Bile Ducts **3** Pancreas	**0** Photons <1 MeV **1** Photons 1-10 MeV **2** Photons >10 MeV **4** Heavy Particles (Protons,Ions) **5** Neutrons **6** Neutron Capture	**Z** None	**Z** None
0 Liver **1** Gallbladder **2** Bile Ducts **3** Pancreas	**3** Electrons	**Z** None	**0** Intraoperative **Z** None

D   Radiation Oncology
F   Hepatobiliary System and Pancreas
1   Brachytherapy

Treatment Site Character 4	Modality Qualifier Character 5	Isotope Character 6	Qualifier Character 7
0 Liver **1** Gallbladder **2** Bile Ducts **3** Pancreas	**9** High Dose Rate (HDR) **B** Low Dose Rate (LDR)	**7** Cesium 137 (Cs-137) **8** Iridium 192 (Ir-192) **9** Iodine 125 (I-125) **B** Palladium 103 (Pd-103) **C** Californium 252 (Cf-252) **Y** Other Isotope	**Z** None

D   Radiation Oncology
F   Hepatobiliary System and Pancreas
2   Stereotactic Radiosurgery

Treatment Site Character 4	Modality Qualifier Character 5	Isotope Character 6	Qualifier Character 7

0 Liver
1 Gallbladder
2 Bile Ducts
3 Pancreas
	D Stereotactic Other Photon
	    Radiosurgery
	H Stereotactic Particulate
	    Radiosurgery
	J Stereotactic Gamma Beam
	    Radiosurgery
		Z None	**Z** None

D   Radiation Oncology
F   Hepatobiliary System and Pancreas
Y   Other Radiation

Treatment Site Character 4	Modality Qualifier Character 5	Isotope Character 6	Qualifier Character 7
0 Liver **1** Gallbladder **2** Bile Ducts **3** Pancreas	**7** Contact Radiation **8** Hyperthermia **C** Intraoperative Radiation Therapy (IORT) **F** Plaque Radiation	**Z** None	**Z** None

D   Radiation Oncology
G   Endocrine System
0   Beam Radiation

Treatment Site Character 4	Modality Qualifier Character 5	Isotope Character 6	Qualifier Character 7
0 Pituitary Gland **1** Pineal Body **2** Adrenal Glands **4** Parathyroid Glands **5** Thyroid	**0** Photons <1 MeV **1** Photons 1-10 MeV **2** Photons >10 MeV **5** Neutrons **6** Neutron Capture	**Z** None	**Z** None
0 Pituitary Gland **1** Pineal Body **2** Adrenal Glands **4** Parathyroid Glands **5** Thyroid	**3** Electrons	**Z** None	**0** Intraoperative **Z** None

D   Radiation Oncology
G   Endocrine System
1   Brachytherapy

Treatment Site Character 4	Modality Qualifier Character 5	Isotope Character 6	Qualifier Character 7
0 Pituitary Gland 1 Pineal Body 2 Adrenal Glands 4 Parathyroid Glands 5 Thyroid	9 High Dose Rate (HDR) B Low Dose Rate (LDR)	7 Cesium 137 (Cs-137) 8 Iridium 192 (Ir-192) 9 Iodine 125 (I-125) B Palladium 103 (Pd-103) C Californium 252 (Cf-252) Y Other Isotope	Z None

D   Radiation Oncology
G   Endocrine System
2   Stereotactic Radiosurgery

Treatment Site Character 4	Modality Qualifier Character 5	Isotope Character 6	Qualifier Character 7

0 Pituitary Gland
1 Pineal Body
2 Adrenal Glands
4 Parathyroid Glands
5 Thyroid
	D Stereotactic Other Photon
	   Radiosurgery
	H Stereotactic Particulate
	   Radiosurgery
	J Stereotactic Gamma Beam
	   Radiosurgery
		Z None	Z None

D   Radiation Oncology
G   Endocrine System
Y   Other Radiation

Treatment Site Character 4	Modality Qualifier Character 5	Isotope Character 6	Qualifier Character 7
0 Pituitary Gland 1 Pineal Body 2 Adrenal Glands 4 Parathyroid Glands 5 Thyroid	7 Contact Radiation 8 Hyperthermia F Plaque Radiation	Z None	Z None

D   Radiation Oncology
H   Skin
0   Beam Radiation

Treatment Site Character 4	Modality Qualifier Character 5	Isotope Character 6	Qualifier Character 7
2 Skin, Face 3 Skin, Neck 4 Skin, Arm 6 Skin, Chest 7 Skin, Back 8 Skin, Abdomen 9 Skin, Buttock B Skin, Leg	0 Photons <1 MeV 1 Photons 1-10 MeV 2 Photons >10 MeV 4 Heavy Particles (Protons,Ions) 5 Neutrons 6 Neutron Capture	Z None	Z None
2 Skin, Face 3 Skin, Neck 4 Skin, Arm 6 Skin, Chest 7 Skin, Back 8 Skin, Abdomen 9 Skin, Buttock B Skin, Leg	3 Electrons	Z None	0 Intraoperative Z None

D Radiation Oncology
H Skin
Y Other Radiation

Treatment Site Character 4	Modality Qualifier Character 5	Isotope Character 6	Qualifier Character 7
2 Skin, Face 3 Skin, Neck 4 Skin, Arm 6 Skin, Chest 7 Skin, Back 8 Skin, Abdomen 9 Skin, Buttock B Skin, Leg	7 Contact Radiation 8 Hyperthermia F Plaque Radiation	Z None	Z None
5 Skin, Hand C Skin, Foot	F Plaque Radiation	Z None	Z None

D Radiation Oncology
M Breast
0 Beam Radiation

Treatment Site Character 4	Modality Qualifier Character 5	Isotope Character 6	Qualifier Character 7
0 Breast, Left 1 Breast, Right	0 Photons <1 MeV 1 Photons 1-10 MeV 2 Photons >10 MeV 4 Heavy Particles (Protons,Ions) 5 Neutrons 6 Neutron Capture	Z None	Z None
0 Breast, Left 1 Breast, Right	3 Electrons	Z None	0 Intraoperative Z None

D Radiation Oncology
M Breast
1 Brachytherapy

Treatment Site Character 4	Modality Qualifier Character 5	Isotope Character 6	Qualifier Character 7
0 Breast, Left 1 Breast, Right	9 High Dose Rate (HDR) B Low Dose Rate (LDR)	7 Cesium 137 (Cs-137) 8 Iridium 192 (Ir-192) 9 Iodine 125 (I-125) B Palladium 103 (Pd-103) C Californium 252 (Cf-252) Y Other Isotope	Z None

D Radiation Oncology
M Breast
2 Stereotactic Radiosurgery

Treatment Site Character 4	Modality Qualifier Character 5	Isotope Character 6	Qualifier Character 7

0 Breast, Left
1 Breast, Right
	D Stereotactic Other Photon
	    Radiosurgery
	H Stereotactic Particulate
	    Radiosurgery
	J Stereotactic Gamma Beam
	    Radiosurgery
		Z None	Z None

D Radiation Oncology
M Breast
Y Other Radiation

Treatment Site Character 4	Modality Qualifier Character 5	Isotope Character 6	Qualifier Character 7
0 Breast, Left 1 Breast, Right	7 Contact Radiation 8 Hyperthermia F Plaque Radiation	Z None	Z None

D   Radiation Oncology
P   Musculoskeletal System
0   Beam Radiation

Treatment Site Character 4	Modality Qualifier Character 5	Isotope Character 6	Qualifier Character 7
0 Skull 2 Maxilla 3 Mandible 4 Sternum 5 Rib(s) 6 Humerus 7 Radius/Ulna 8 Pelvic Bones 9 Femur B Tibia/Fibula C Other Bone	0 Photons <1 MeV 1 Photons 1-10 MeV 2 Photons >10 MeV 4 Heavy Particles (Protons,Ions) 5 Neutrons 6 Neutron Capture	Z None	Z None
0 Skull 2 Maxilla 3 Mandible 4 Sternum 5 Rib(s) 6 Humerus 7 Radius/Ulna 8 Pelvic Bones 9 Femur B Tibia/Fibula C Other Bone	3 Electrons	Z None	0 Intraoperative Z None

D   Radiation Oncology
P   Musculoskeletal System
Y   Other Radiation

Treatment Site Character 4	Modality Qualifier Character 5	Isotope Character 6	Qualifier Character 7
0 Skull 2 Maxilla 3 Mandible 4 Sternum 5 Rib(s) 6 Humerus 7 Radius/Ulna 8 Pelvic Bones 9 Femur B Tibia/Fibula C Other Bone	7 Contact Radiation 8 Hyperthermia F Plaque Radiation	Z None	Z None

D   Radiation Oncology
T   Urinary System
0   Beam Radiation

Treatment Site Character 4	Modality Qualifier Character 5	Isotope Character 6	Qualifier Character 7
0 Kidney 1 Ureter 2 Bladder 3 Urethra	0 Photons <1 MeV 1 Photons 1-10 MeV 2 Photons >10 MeV 4 Heavy Particles (Protons,Ions) 5 Neutrons 6 Neutron Capture	Z None	Z None
0 Kidney 1 Ureter 2 Bladder 3 Urethra	3 Electrons	Z None	0 Intraoperative Z None

D   Radiation Oncology
T   Urinary System
1   Brachytherapy

Treatment Site Character 4	Modality Qualifier Character 5	Isotope Character 6	Qualifier Character 7
0 Kidney 1 Ureter 2 Bladder 3 Urethra	9 High Dose Rate (HDR) B Low Dose Rate (LDR)	7 Cesium 137 (Cs-137) 8 Iridium 192 (Ir-192) 9 Iodine 125 (I-125) B Palladium 103 (Pd-103) C Californium 252 (Cf-252) Y Other Isotope	Z None

D Radiation Oncology
T Urinary System
2 Stereotactic Radiosurgery

Treatment Site Character 4	Modality Qualifier Character 5	Isotope Character 6	Qualifier Character 7

0 Kidney
1 Ureter
2 Bladder
3 Urethra
	D Stereotactic Other Photon
	   Radiosurgery
	H Stereotactic Particulate
	   Radiosurgery
	J Stereotactic Gamma Beam
	   Radiosurgery
		Z None	Z None

D Radiation Oncology
T Urinary System
Y Other Radiation

Treatment Site Character 4	Modality Qualifier Character 5	Isotope Character 6	Qualifier Character 7
0 Kidney 1 Ureter 2 Bladder 3 Urethra	7 Contact Radiation 8 Hyperthermia C Intraoperative Radiation Therapy (IORT) F Plaque Radiation	Z None	Z None

D Radiation Oncology
U Female Reproductive System
0 Beam Radiation

Treatment Site Character 4	Modality Qualifier Character 5	Isotope Character 6	Qualifier Character 7
0 Ovary 1 Cervix 2 Uterus	0 Photons <1 MeV 1 Photons 1-10 MeV 2 Photons >10 MeV 4 Heavy Particles (Protons,Ions) 5 Neutrons 6 Neutron Capture	Z None	Z None
0 Ovary 1 Cervix 2 Uterus	3 Electrons	Z None	0 Intraoperative Z None

D Radiation Oncology
U Female Reproductive System
1 Brachytherapy

Treatment Site Character 4	Modality Qualifier Character 5	Isotope Character 6	Qualifier Character 7
0 Ovary 1 Cervix 2 Uterus	9 High Dose Rate (HDR) B Low Dose Rate (LDR)	7 Cesium 137 (Cs-137) 8 Iridium 192 (Ir-192) 9 Iodine 125 (I-125) B Palladium 103 (Pd-103) C Californium 252 (Cf-252) Y Other Isotope	Z None

D Radiation Oncology
U Female Reproductive System
2 Stereotactic Radiosurgery

Treatment Site Character 4	Modality Qualifier Character 5	Isotope Character 6	Qualifier Character 7

0 Ovary
1 Cervix
2 Uterus
	D Stereotactic Other Photon
	   Radiosurgery
	H Stereotactic Particulate
	   Radiosurgery
	J Stereotactic Gamma Beam
	   Radiosurgery
		Z None	Z None

D   Radiation Oncology
U   Female Reproductive System
Y   Other Radiation

Treatment Site Character 4	Modality Qualifier Character 5	Isotope Character 6	Qualifier Character 7
0 Ovary **1** Cervix **2** Uterus	**7** Contact Radiation **8** Hyperthermia **C** Intraoperative Radiation Therapy (IORT) **F** Plaque Radiation	**Z** None	**Z** None

D   Radiation Oncology
V   Male Reproductive System
0   Beam Radiation

Treatment Site Character 4	Modality Qualifier Character 5	Isotope Character 6	Qualifier Character 7
0 Prostate **1** Testis	**0** Photons <1 MeV **1** Photons 1-10 MeV **2** Photons >10 MeV **4** Heavy Particles (Protons,Ions) **5** Neutrons **6** Neutron Capture	**Z** None	**Z** None
0 Prostate **1** Testis	**3** Electrons	**Z** None	**0** Intraoperative **Z** None

D   Radiation Oncology
V   Male Reproductive System
1   Brachytherapy

Treatment Site Character 4	Modality Qualifier Character 5	Isotope Character 6	Qualifier Character 7
0 Prostate **1** Testis	**9** High Dose Rate (HDR) **B** Low Dose Rate (LDR)	**7** Cesium 137 (Cs-137) **8** Iridium 192 (Ir-192) **9** Iodine 125 (I-125) **B** Palladium 103 (Pd-103) **C** Californium 252 (Cf-252) **Y** Other Isotope	**Z** None

D   Radiation Oncology
V   Male Reproductive System
2   Stereotactic Radiosurgery

Treatment Site Character 4	Modality Qualifier Character 5	Isotope Character 6	Qualifier Character 7
0 Prostate **1** Testis	**D** Stereotactic Other Photon Radiosurgery **H** Stereotactic Particulate Radiosurgery **J** Stereotactic Gamma Beam Radiosurgery	**Z** None	**Z** None

D   Radiation Oncology
V   Male Reproductive System
Y   Other Radiation

Treatment Site Character 4	Modality Qualifier Character 5	Isotope Character 6	Qualifier Character 7
0 Prostate	**7** Contact Radiation **8** Hyperthermia **C** Intraoperative Radiation Therapy (IORT) **F** Plaque Radiation	**Z** None	**Z** None
1 Testis	**7** Contact Radiation **8** Hyperthermia **F** Plaque Radiation	**Z** None	**Z** None

D   Radiation Oncology
W   Anatomical Regions
0   Beam Radiation

Treatment Site Character 4	Modality Qualifier Character 5	Isotope Character 6	Qualifier Character 7
1 Head and Neck 2 Chest 3 Abdomen 4 Hemibody 5 Whole Body 6 Pelvic Region	0 Photons <1 MeV 1 Photons 1-10 MeV 2 Photons >10 MeV 4 Heavy Particles (Protons,Ions) 5 Neutrons 6 Neutron Capture	Z None	Z None
1 Head and Neck 2 Chest 3 Abdomen 4 Hemibody 5 Whole Body 6 Pelvic Region	3 Electrons	Z None	0 Intraoperative Z None

D   Radiation Oncology
W   Anatomical Regions
1   Brachytherapy

Treatment Site Character 4	Modality Qualifier Character 5	Isotope Character 6	Qualifier Character 7
1 Head and Neck 2 Chest 3 Abdomen 6 Pelvic Region	9 High Dose Rate (HDR) B Low Dose Rate (LDR)	7 Cesium 137 (Cs-137) 8 Iridium 192 (Ir-192) 9 Iodine 125 (I-125) B Palladium 103 (Pd-103) C Californium 252 (Cf-252) Y Other Isotope	Z None

D   Radiation Oncology
W   Anatomical Regions
2   Stereotactic Radiosurgery

Treatment Site Character 4	Modality Qualifier Character 5	Isotope Character 6	Qualifier Character 7
1 Head and Neck 2 Chest 3 Abdomen 6 Pelvic Region	D Stereotactic Other Photon Radiosurgery H Stereotactic Particulate Radiosurgery J Stereotactic Gamma Beam Radiosurgery	Z None	Z None

D   Radiation Oncology
W   Anatomical Regions
Y   Other Radiation

Treatment Site Character 4	Modality Qualifier Character 5	Isotope Character 6	Qualifier Character 7
1 Head and Neck 2 Chest 3 Abdomen 4 Hemibody 5 Whole Body 6 Pelvic Region	7 Contact Radiation 8 Hyperthermia F Plaque Radiation	Z None	Z None
5 Whole Body	G Isotope Administration	D Iodine 131 (I-131) F Phosphorus 32 (P-32) G Strontium 89 (Sr-89) H Strontium 90 (Sr-90) Y Other Isotope	Z None

Physical Rehabilitation and Diagnostic Audiology F00–F15

F   **Physical Rehabilitation and Diagnostic Audiology**
0   **Rehabilitation**
0   **Speech Assessment:** Measurement of speech and related functions

Body System and Region Character 4	Type Qualifier Character 5	Equipment Character 6	Qualifier Character 7
3 Neurological System - Whole Body	**G** Communicative/Cognitive Integration Skills	**K** Audiovisual **M** Augmentative / Alternative Communication **P** Computer **Y** Other Equipment **Z** None	**Z** None
Z None	**0** Filtered Speech **3** Staggered Spondaic Word **Q** Performance Intensity Phonetically Balanced Speech Discrimination **R** Brief Tone Stimuli **S** Distorted Speech **T** Dichotic Stimuli **V** Temporal Ordering of Stimuli **W** Masking Patterns	**1** Audiometer **2** Sound Field / Booth **K** Audiovisual **Z** None	**Z** None
Z None	**1** Speech Threshold **2** Speech/Word Recognition	**1** Audiometer **2** Sound Field / Booth **9** Cochlear Implant **K** Audiovisual **Z** None	**Z** None
Z None	**4** Sensorineural Acuity Level	**1** Audiometer **2** Sound Field / Booth **Z** None	**Z** None
Z None	**5** Synthetic Sentence Identification	**1** Audiometer **2** Sound Field / Booth **9** Cochlear Implant **K** Audiovisual	**Z** None
Z None	**6** Speech and/or Language Screening **7** Nonspoken Language **8** Receptive/Expressive Language **C** Aphasia **G** Communicative/Cognitive Integration Skills **L** Augmentative/Alternative Communication System	**K** Audiovisual **M** Augmentative / Alternative Communication **P** Computer **Y** Other Equipment **Z** None	**Z** None
Z None	**9** Articulation/Phonology	**K** Audiovisual **P** Computer **Q** Speech Analysis **Y** Other Equipment **Z** None	**Z** None
Z None	**B** Motor Speech	**K** Audiovisual **N** Biosensory Feedback **P** Computer **Q** Speech Analysis **T** Aerodynamic Function **Y** Other Equipment **Z** None	**Z** None
Z None	**D** Fluency	**K** Audiovisual **N** Biosensory Feedback **P** Computer **Q** Speech Analysis **S** Voice Analysis **T** Aerodynamic Function **Y** Other Equipment **Z** None	**Z** None
Z None	**F** Voice	**K** Audiovisual **N** Biosensory Feedback **P** Computer **S** Voice Analysis **T** Aerodynamic Function **Y** Other Equipment **Z** None	**Z** None
Z None	**H** Bedside Swallowing and Oral Function **P** Oral Peripheral Mechanism	**Y** Other Equipment **Z** None	**Z** None

Continued on next page

F Physical Rehabilitation and Diagnostic Audiology   *Continued from previous page*
0 Rehabilitation
0 Speech Assessment: Measurement of speech and related functions

Body System and Region Character 4	Type Qualifier Character 5	Equipment Character 6	Qualifier Character 7
Z None	**J** Instrumental Swallowing and Oral Function	**T** Aerodynamic Function **W** Swallowing **Y** Other Equipment	**Z** None
Z None	**K** Orofacial Myofunctional	**K** Audiovisual **P** Computer **Y** Other Equipment **Z** None	**Z** None
Z None	**M** Voice Prosthetic	**K** Audiovisual **P** Computer **S** Voice Analysis **V** Speech Prosthesis **Y** Other Equipment **Z** None	**Z** None
Z None	**N** Non-invasive Instrumental Status	**N** Biosensory Feedback **P** Computer **Q** Speech Analysis **S** Voice Analysis **T** Aerodynamic Function **Y** Other Equipment	**Z** None
Z None	**X** Other Specified Central Auditory Processing	**Z** None	**Z** None

F Physical Rehabilitation and Diagnostic Audiology
0 Rehabilitation
1 Motor and/or Nerve Function Assessment: Measurement of motor, nerve, and related functions

Body System and Region Character 4	Type Qualifier Character 5	Equipment Character 6	Qualifier Character 7
0 Neurological System - Head and Neck **1** Neurological System - Upper Back / Upper Extremity **2** Neurological System - Lower Back / Lower Extremity **3** Neurological System - Whole Body	**1** Integumentary Integrity **3** Coordination/Dexterity **4** Motor Function **G** Reflex Integrity	**Z** None	**Z** None
0 Neurological System - Head and Neck **1** Neurological System - Upper Back / Upper Extremity **2** Neurological System - Lower Back / Lower Extremity **3** Neurological System - Whole Body **D** Integumentary System - Head and Neck **F** Integumentary System - Upper Back / Upper Extremity **G** Integumentary System - Lower Back / Lower Extremity **H** Integumentary System - Whole Body **J** Musculoskeletal System - Head and Neck **K** Musculoskeletal System - Upper Back / Upper Extremity **L** Musculoskeletal System - Lower Back / Lower Extremity **M** Musculoskeletal System - Whole Body	**5** Range of Motion and Joint Integrity **6** Sensory Awareness/Processing/ Integrity	**Y** Other Equipment **Z** None	**Z** None

Continued on next page

F   Physical Rehabilitation and Diagnostic Audiology   *Continued from previous page*
0   Rehabilitation
1   Motor and/or Nerve Function Assessment: Measurement of motor, nerve, and related functions

Body System and Region Character 4	Type Qualifier Character 5	Equipment Character 6	Qualifier Character 7
0 Neurological System - Head and Neck **1** Neurological System - Upper Back / Upper Extremity **2** Neurological System - Lower Back / Lower Extremity **3** Neurological System - Whole Body **D** Integumentary System - Head and Neck **F** Integumentary System - Upper Back / Upper Extremity **G** Integumentary System - Lower Back / Lower Extremity **H** Integumentary System - Whole Body **J** Musculoskeletal System - Head and Neck **K** Musculoskeletal System - Upper Back / Upper Extremity **L** Musculoskeletal System - Lower Back / Lower Extremity **M** Musculoskeletal System - Whole Body **N** Genitourinary System	**0** Muscle Performance	**E** Orthosis **F** Assistive, Adaptive, Supportive or Protective **U** Prosthesis **Y** Other Equipment **Z** None	**Z** None
D Integumentary System - Head and Neck **F** Integumentary System - Upper Back / Upper Extremity **G** Integumentary System - Lower Back / Lower Extremity **H** Integumentary System - Whole Body **J** Musculoskeletal System - Head and Neck **K** Musculoskeletal System - Upper Back / Upper Extremity **L** Musculoskeletal System - Lower Back / Lower Extremity **M** Musculoskeletal System - Whole Body	**1** Integumentary Integrity	**Z** None	**Z** None
Z None	**2** Visual Motor Integration	**K** Audiovisual **M** Augmentative / Alternative Communication **N** Biosensory Feedback **P** Computer **Q** Speech Analysis **S** Voice Analysis **Y** Other Equipment **Z** None	**Z** None
Z None	**7** Facial Nerve Function	**7** Electrophysiologic	**Z** None
Z None	**8** Neurophysiologic Intraoperative	**7** Electrophysiologic **J** Somatosensory	**Z** None
Z None	**9** Somatosensory Evoked Potentials	**J** Somatosensory	**Z** None
Z None	**B** Bed Mobility **C** Transfer **F** Wheelchair Mobility	**E** Orthosis **F** Assistive, Adaptive, Supportive or Protective **U** Prosthesis **Z** None	**Z** None
Z None	**D** Gait and/or Balance	**E** Orthosis **F** Assistive, Adaptive, Supportive or Protective **U** Prosthesis **Y** Other Equipment **Z** None	**Z** None

F　Physical Rehabilitation and Diagnostic Audiology
0　Rehabilitation
2　**Activities of Daily Living Assessment:**　Measurement of functional level for activities of daily living

Body System and Region Character 4	Type Qualifier Character 5	Equipment Character 6	Qualifier Character 7
0 Neurological System - Head and Neck	**9** Cranial Nerve Integrity **D** Neuromotor Development	**Y** Other Equipment **Z** None	**Z** None
1 Neurological System - Upper Back / Upper Extremity **2** Neurological System - Lower Back / Lower Extremity **3** Neurological System - Whole Body	**D** Neuromotor Development	**Y** Other Equipment **Z** None	**Z** None
4 Circulatory System - Head and Neck **5** Circulatory System - Upper Back / Upper Extremity **6** Circulatory System - Lower Back / Lower Extremity **7** Circulatory System - Whole Body **8** Respiratory System - Head and Neck **9** Respiratory System - Upper Back / Upper Extremity **B** Respiratory System - Lower Back / Lower Extremity **C** Respiratory System - Whole Body	**G** Ventilation, Respiration and Circulation	**C** Mechanical **G** Aerobic Endurance and Conditioning **Y** Other Equipment **Z** None	**Z** None
7 Circulatory System - Whole Body **C** Respiratory System - Whole Body	**7** Aerobic Capacity and Endurance	**E** Orthosis **G** Aerobic Endurance and Conditioning **U** Prosthesis **Y** Other Equipment **Z** None	**Z** None
Z None	**0** Bathing/Showering **1** Dressing **3** Grooming/Personal Hygiene **4** Home Management	**E** Orthosis **F** Assistive, Adaptive, Supportive or Protective **U** Prosthesis **Z** None	**Z** None
Z None	**2** Feeding/Eating **8** Anthropometric Characteristics **F** Pain	**Y** Other Equipment **Z** None	**Z** None
Z None	**5** Perceptual Processing	**K** Audiovisual **M** Augmentative / Alternative Communication **N** Biosensory Feedback **P** Computer **Q** Speech Analysis **S** Voice Analysis **Y** Other Equipment **Z** None	**Z** None
Z None	**6** Psychosocial Skills	**Z** None	**Z** None
Z None	**B** Environmental, Home and Work Barriers **C** Ergonomics and Body Mechanics	**E** Orthosis **F** Assistive, Adaptive, Supportive or Protective **U** Prosthesis **Y** Other Equipment **Z** None	**Z** None
Z None	**H** Vocational Activities and Functional Community or Work Reintegration Skills	**E** Orthosis **F** Assistive, Adaptive, Supportive or Protective **G** Aerobic Endurance and Conditioning **U** Prosthesis **Y** Other Equipment **Z** None	**Z** None

F   Physical Rehabilitation and Diagnostic Audiology
0   Rehabilitation
6   Speech Treatment: Application of techniques to improve, augment, or compensate for speech and related functional impairment

Body System and Region Character 4	Type Qualifier Character 5	Equipment Character 6	Qualifier Character 7
3 Neurological System - Whole Body	**6** Communicative/Cognitive Integration Skills	**K** Audiovisual **M** Augmentative / Alternative Communication **P** Computer **Y** Other Equipment **Z** None	**Z** None
Z None	**0** Nonspoken Language **3** Aphasia **6** Communicative/Cognitive Integration Skills	**K** Audiovisual **M** Augmentative / Alternative Communication **P** Computer **Y** Other Equipment **Z** None	**Z** None
Z None	**1** Speech-Language Pathology and Related Disorders Counseling **2** Speech-Language Pathology and Related Disorders Prevention	**K** Audiovisual **Z** None	**Z** None
Z None	**4** Articulation/Phonology	**K** Audiovisual **P** Computer **Q** Speech Analysis **T** Aerodynamic Function **Y** Other Equipment **Z** None	**Z** None
Z None	**5** Aural Rehabilitation	**K** Audiovisual **L** Assistive Listening **M** Augmentative / Alternative Communication **N** Biosensory Feedback **P** Computer **Q** Speech Analysis **S** Voice Analysis **Y** Other Equipment **Z** None	**Z** None
Z None	**7** Fluency	**4** Electroacoustic Immitance / Acoustic Reflex **K** Audiovisual **N** Biosensory Feedback **Q** Speech Analysis **S** Voice Analysis **T** Aerodynamic Function **Y** Other Equipment **Z** None	**Z** None
Z None	**8** Motor Speech	**K** Audiovisual **N** Biosensory Feedback **P** Computer **Q** Speech Analysis **S** Voice Analysis **T** Aerodynamic Function **Y** Other Equipment **Z** None	**Z** None
Z None	**9** Orofacial Myofunctional	**K** Audiovisual **P** Computer **Y** Other Equipment **Z** None	**Z** None
Z None	**B** Receptive/Expressive Language	**K** Audiovisual **L** Assistive Listening **M** Augmentative / Alternative Communication **P** Computer **Y** Other Equipment **Z** None	**Z** None
Z None	**C** Voice	**K** Audiovisual **N** Biosensory Feedback **P** Computer **S** Voice Analysis **T** Aerodynamic Function **V** Speech Prosthesis **Y** Other Equipment **Z** None	**Z** None
Z None	**D** Swallowing Dysfunction	**M** Augmentative / Alternative Communication **T** Aerodynamic Function **V** Speech Prosthesis **Y** Other Equipment **Z** None	**Z** None

F Physical Rehabilitation and Diagnostic Audiology
0 Rehabilitation
7 Motor Treatment: Exercise or activities to increase or facilitate motor function

Body System and Region Character 4	Type Qualifier Character 5	Equipment Character 6	Qualifier Character 7
0 Neurological System - Head and Neck 1 Neurological System - Upper Back / Upper Extremity 2 Neurological System - Lower Back / Lower Extremity 3 Neurological System - Whole Body 4 Circulatory System - Head and Neck 5 Circulatory System - Upper Back / Upper Extremity 6 Circulatory System - Lower Back / Lower Extremity 7 Circulatory System - Whole Body 8 Respiratory System - Head and Neck 9 Respiratory System - Upper Back / Upper Extremity B Respiratory System - Lower Back / Lower Extremity C Respiratory System - Whole Body D Integumentary System - Head and Neck F Integumentary System - Upper Back / Upper Extremity G Integumentary System - Lower Back / Lower Extremity H Integumentary System - Whole Body J Musculoskeletal System - Head and Neck K Musculoskeletal System - Upper Back / Upper Extremity L Musculoskeletal System - Lower Back / Lower Extremity M Musculoskeletal System - Whole Body N Genitourinary System	6 Therapeutic Exercise	B Physical Agents C Mechanical D Electrotherapeutic E Orthosis F Assistive, Adaptive, Supportive or Protective G Aerobic Endurance and Conditioning H Mechanical or Electromechanical U Prosthesis Y Other Equipment Z None	Z None
0 Neurological System - Head and Neck 1 Neurological System - Upper Back / Upper Extremity 2 Neurological System - Lower Back / Lower Extremity 3 Neurological System - Whole Body D Integumentary System - Head and Neck F Integumentary System - Upper Back / Upper Extremity G Integumentary System - Lower Back / Lower Extremity H Integumentary System - Whole Body J Musculoskeletal System - Head and Neck K Musculoskeletal System - Upper Back / Upper Extremity L Musculoskeletal System - Lower Back / Lower Extremity M Musculoskeletal System - Whole Body	0 Range of Motion and Joint Mobility 1 Muscle Performance 2 Coordination/Dexterity 3 Motor Function	E Orthosis F Assistive, Adaptive, Supportive or Protective U Prosthesis Y Other Equipment Z None	Z None
0 Neurological System - Head and Neck 1 Neurological System - Upper Back / Upper Extremity 2 Neurological System - Lower Back / Lower Extremity 3 Neurological System - Whole Body D Integumentary System - Head and Neck F Integumentary System - Upper Back / Upper Extremity G Integumentary System - Lower Back / Lower Extremity H Integumentary System - Whole Body J Musculoskeletal System - Head and Neck K Musculoskeletal System - Upper Back / Upper Extremity L Musculoskeletal System - Lower Back / Lower Extremity M Musculoskeletal System - Whole Body	7 Manual Therapy Techniques	Z None	Z None

Continued on next page

F   **Physical Rehabilitation and Diagnostic Audiology**   *Continued from previous page*
0   **Rehabilitation**
7   **Motor Treatment:**   Exercise or activities to increase or facilitate motor function

Body System and Region Character 4	Type Qualifier Character 5	Equipment Character 6	Qualifier Character 7
N Genitourinary System	**1** Muscle Performance	**E** Orthosis **F** Assistive, Adaptive, Supportive or Protective **U** Prosthesis **Y** Other Equipment **Z** None	**Z** None
Z None	**4** Wheelchair Mobility	**D** Electrotherapeutic **E** Orthosis **F** Assistive, Adaptive, Supportive or Protective **U** Prosthesis **Y** Other Equipment **Z** None	**Z** None
Z None	**5** Bed Mobility	**C** Mechanical **E** Orthosis **F** Assistive, Adaptive, Supportive or Protective **U** Prosthesis **Y** Other Equipment **Z** None	**Z** None
Z None	**8** Transfer Training	**C** Mechanical **D** Electrotherapeutic **E** Orthosis **F** Assistive, Adaptive, Supportive or Protective **U** Prosthesis **Y** Other Equipment **Z** None	**Z** None
Z None	**9** Gait Training/Functional Ambulation	**C** Mechanical **D** Electrotherapeutic **E** Orthosis **F** Assistive, Adaptive, Supportive or Protective **G** Aerobic Endurance and Conditioning **U** Prosthesis **Y** Other Equipment **Z** None	**Z** None

F   **Physical Rehabilitation and Diagnostic Audiology**
0   **Rehabilitation**
8   **Activities of Daily Living Treatment:** Exercise or activities to facilitate functional competence for activities of daily living

Body System and Region Character 4	Type Qualifier Character 5	Equipment Character 6	Qualifier Character 7
D Integumentary System - Head and Neck **F** Integumentary System - Upper Back / Upper Extremity **G** Integumentary System - Lower Back / Lower Extremity **H** Integumentary System - Whole Body **J** Musculoskeletal System - Head and Neck **K** Musculoskeletal System - Upper Back / Upper Extremity **L** Musculoskeletal System - Lower Back / Lower Extremity **M** Musculoskeletal System - Whole Body	**5** Wound Management	**B** Physical Agents **C** Mechanical **D** Electrotherapeutic **E** Orthosis **F** Assistive, Adaptive, Supportive or Protective **U** Prosthesis **Y** Other Equipment **Z** None	**Z** None
Z None	**0** Bathing/Showering Techniques **1** Dressing Techniques **2** Grooming/Personal Hygiene	**E** Orthosis **F** Assistive, Adaptive, Supportive or Protective **U** Prosthesis **Y** Other Equipment **Z** None	**Z** None

Continued on next page

F **Physical Rehabilitation and Diagnostic Audiology**　　　　　　　　　*Continued from previous page*
0 **Rehabilitation**
8 **Activities of Daily Living Treatment:** Exercise or activities to facilitate functional competence for activities of daily living

Body System and Region Character 4	Type Qualifier Character 5	Equipment Character 6	Qualifier Character 7
Z None	**3** Feeding/Eating	**C** Mechanical **D** Electrotherapeutic **E** Orthosis **F** Assistive, Adaptive, Supportive or Protective **U** Prosthesis **Y** Other Equipment **Z** None	**Z** None
Z None	**4** Home Management	**D** Electrotherapeutic **E** Orthosis **F** Assistive, Adaptive, Supportive or Protective **U** Prosthesis **Y** Other Equipment **Z** None	**Z** None
Z None	**6** Psychosocial Skills	**Z** None	**Z** None
Z None	**7** Vocational Activities and Functional Community or Work Reintegration Skills	**B** Physical Agents **C** Mechanical **D** Electrotherapeutic **E** Orthosis **F** Assistive, Adaptive, Supportive or Protective **G** Aerobic Endurance and Conditioning **U** Prosthesis **Y** Other Equipment **Z** None	**Z** None

F **Physical Rehabilitation and Diagnostic Audiology**
0 **Rehabilitation**
9 **Hearing Treatment:** Application of techniques to improve, augment, or compensate for hearing and related functional impairment

Body System and Region Character 4	Type Qualifier Character 5	Equipment Character 6	Qualifier Character 7
Z None	**0** Hearing and Related Disorders Counseling **1** Hearing and Related Disorders Prevention	**K** Audiovisual **Z** None	**Z** None
Z None	**2** Auditory Processing	**K** Audiovisual **L** Assistive Listening **P** Computer **Y** Other Equipment **Z** None	**Z** None
Z None	**3** Cerumen Management	**X** Cerumen Management **Z** None	**Z** None

F **Physical Rehabilitation and Diagnostic Audiology**
0 **Rehabilitation**
B **Cochlear Implant Treatment:** Application of techniques to improve the communication abilities of individuals with cochlear implant

Body System and Region Character 4	Type Qualifier Character 5	Equipment Character 6	Qualifier Character 7
Z None	**0** Cochlear Implant Rehabilitation	**1** Audiometer **2** Sound Field / Booth **9** Cochlear Implant **K** Audiovisual **P** Computer **Y** Other Equipment	**Z** None

F   **Physical Rehabilitation and Diagnostic Audiology**
0   **Rehabilitation**
C   **Vestibular Treatment:**   Application of techniques to improve, augment, or compensate for vestibular and related functional impairment

Body System and Region Character 4	Type Qualifier Character 5	Equipment Character 6	Qualifier Character 7
3 Neurological System - Whole Body **H** Integumentary System - Whole Body **M** Musculoskeletal System - Whole Body	**3** Postural Control	**E** Orthosis **F** Assistive, Adaptive, Supportive or Protective **U** Prosthesis **Y** Other Equipment **Z** None	**Z** None
Z None	**0** Vestibular	**8** Vestibular / Balance **Z** None	**Z** None
Z None	**1** Perceptual Processing **2** Visual Motor Integration	**K** Audiovisual **L** Assistive Listening **N** Biosensory Feedback **P** Computer **Q** Speech Analysis **S** Voice Analysis **T** Aerodynamic Function **Y** Other Equipment **Z** None	**Z** None

F   **Physical Rehabilitation and Diagnostic Audiology**
0   **Rehabilitation**
D   **Device Fitting:**   Fitting of a device designed to facilitate or support achievement of a higher level of function

Body System and Region Character 4	Type Qualifier Character 5	Equipment Character 6	Qualifier Character 7
Z None	**0** Tinnitus Masker	**5** Hearing Aid Selection / Fitting / Test **Z** None	**Z** None
Z None	**1** Monaural Hearing Aid **2** Binaural Hearing Aid **5** Assistive Listening Device	**1** Audiometer **2** Sound Field / Booth **5** Hearing Aid Selection / Fitting / Test **K** Audiovisual **L** Assistive Listening **Z** None	**Z** None
Z None	**3** Augmentative/Alternative Communication System	**M** Augmentative / Alternative Communication	**Z** None
Z None	**4** Voice Prosthetic	**S** Voice Analysis **V** Speech Prosthesis	**Z** None
Z None	**6** Dynamic Orthosis **7** Static Orthosis **8** Prosthesis **9** Assistive, Adaptive, Supportive or Protective Devices	**E** Orthosis **F** Assistive, Adaptive, Supportive or Protective **U** Prosthesis **Z** None	**Z** None

F   Physical Rehabilitation and Diagnostic Audiology
0   Rehabilitation
F   Caregiver Training: Training in activities to support patient's optimal level of function

Body System and Region Character 4	Type Qualifier Character 5	Equipment Character 6	Qualifier Character 7
Z None	**0** Bathing/Showering Technique **1** Dressing **2** Feeding and Eating **3** Grooming/Personal Hygiene **4** Bed Mobility **5** Transfer **6** Wheelchair Mobility **7** Therapeutic Exercise **8** Airway Clearance Techniques **9** Wound Management **B** Vocational Activities and Functional Community or Work Reintegration Skills **C** Gait Training/Functional Ambulation **D** Application, Proper Use and Care of Assistive, Adaptive, Supportive or Protective Devices **F** Application, Proper Use and Care of Orthoses **G** Application, Proper Use and Care of Prosthesis **H** Home Management	**E** Orthosis **F** Assistive, Adaptive, Supportive or Protective **U** Prosthesis **Z** None	**Z** None
Z None	**J** Communication Skills	**K** Audiovisual **L** Assistive Listening **M** Augmentative / Alternative Communication **P** Computer **Z** None	**Z** None

F   Physical Rehabilitation and Diagnostic Audiology
1   Diagnostic Audiology
3   Hearing Assessment: Measurement of hearing and related functions

Body System and Region Character 4	Type Qualifier Character 5	Equipment Character 6	Qualifier Character 7
Z None	**0** Hearing Screening	**0** Occupational Hearing **1** Audiometer **2** Sound Field / Booth **3** Tympanometer **8** Vestibular / Balance **9** Cochlear Implant **Z** None	**Z** None
Z None	**1** Pure Tone Audiometry, Air **2** Pure Tone Audiometry, Air and Bone	**0** Occupational Hearing **1** Audiometer **2** Sound Field / Booth **Z** None	**Z** None

Z None	**3** Bekesy Audiometry
	6 Visual Reinforcement
	   Audiometry
	9 Short Increment Sensitivity
	   Index
	B Stenger
	C Pure Tone Stenger
		1 Audiometer
		2 Sound Field / Booth
		Z None
			Z None

Z None	**4** Conditioned Play Audiometry **5** Select Picture Audiometry	**1** Audiometer **2** Sound Field / Booth **K** Audiovisual **Z** None	**Z** None
Z None	**7** Alternate Binaural or Monaural Loudness Balance	**1** Audiometer **K** Audiovisual **Z** None	**Z** None
Z None	**8** Tone Decay **D** Tympanometry **F** Eustachian Tube Function **G** Acoustic Reflex Patterns **H** Acoustic Reflex Threshold **J** Acoustic Reflex Decay	**3** Tympanometer **4** Electroacoustic Immitance / Acoustic Reflex **Z** None	**Z** None
Z None	**K** Electrocochleography **L** Auditory Evoked Potentials	**7** Electrophysiologic **Z** None	**Z** None

Z None	**M** Evoked Otoacoustic Emissions,
	   Screening
	N Evoked Otoacoustic Emissions,
	   Diagnostic
		6 Otoacoustic Emission (OAE)
		Z None
			Z None

Z None	**P** Aural Rehabilitation Status	**1** Audiometer **2** Sound Field / Booth **4** Electroacoustic Immitance / Acoustic Reflex **9** Cochlear Implant **K** Audiovisual **L** Assistive Listening **P** Computer **Z** None	**Z** None
Z None	**Q** Auditory Processing	**K** Audiovisual **P** Computer **Y** Other Equipment **Z** None	**Z** None

F　Physical Rehabilitation and Diagnostic Audiology
1　Diagnostic Audiology
4　Hearing Aid Assessment:　Measurement of the appropriateness and/or effectiveness of a hearing device

Body System and Region Character 4	Type Qualifier Character 5	Equipment Character 6	Qualifier Character 7
Z None	0 Cochlear Implant	1 Audiometer 2 Sound Field / Booth 3 Tympanometer 4 Electroacoustic Immitance / Acoustic Reflex 5 Hearing Aid Selection / Fitting / Test 7 Electrophysiologic 9 Cochlear Implant K Audiovisual L Assistive Listening P Computer Y Other Equipment Z None	Z None
Z None	1 Ear Canal Probe Microphone 6 Binaural Electroacoustic Hearing Aid Check 8 Monaural Electroacoustic Hearing Aid Check	5 Hearing Aid Selection / Fitting / Test Z None	Z None
Z None	2 Monaural Hearing Aid 3 Binaural Hearing Aid	1 Audiometer 2 Sound Field / Booth 3 Tympanometer 4 Electroacoustic Immitance / Acoustic Reflex 5 Hearing Aid Selection / Fitting / Test K Audiovisual L Assistive Listening P Computer Z None	Z None
Z None	4 Assistive Listening System/ Device Selection	1 Audiometer 2 Sound Field / Booth 3 Tympanometer 4 Electroacoustic Immitance / Acoustic Reflex K Audiovisual L Assistive Listening Z None	Z None
Z None	5 Sensory Aids	1 Audiometer 2 Sound Field / Booth 3 Tympanometer 4 Electroacoustic Immitance / Acoustic Reflex 5 Hearing Aid Selection / Fitting / Test K Audiovisual L Assistive Listening Z None	Z None
Z None	7 Ear Protector Attentuation	0 Occupational Hearing Z None	Z None

F　Physical Rehabilitation and Diagnostic Audiology
1　Diagnostic Audiology
5　Vestibular Assessment:　Measurement of the vestibular system and related functions

Body System and Region Character 4	Type Qualifier Character 5	Equipment Character 6	Qualifier Character 7
Z None	0 Bithermal, Binaural Caloric Irrigation 1 Bithermal, Monaural Caloric Irrigation 2 Unithermal Binaural Screen 3 Oscillating Tracking 4 Sinusoidal Vertical Axis Rotational 5 Dix-Hallpike Dynamic 6 Computerized Dynamic Posturography	8 Vestibular / Balance Z None	Z None
Z None	7 Tinnitus Masker	5 Hearing Aid Selection / Fitting / Test Z None	Z None

Mental Health GZ1–GZJ

G Mental Health
Z None
1 **Psychological Tests:** The administration and interpretation of standardized psychological tests and measurement instruments for the assessment of psychological function

Qualifier Character 4	Qualifier Character 5	Qualifier Character 6	Qualifier Character 7
0 Developmental **1** Personality and Behavioral **2** Intellectual and Psychoeducational **3** Neuropsychological **4** Neurobehavioral and Cognitive Status	**Z** None	**Z** None	**Z** None

G Mental Health
Z None
2 **Crisis Intervention:** Treatment of a traumatized, acutely disturbed or distressed individual for the purpose of short-term stabilization

Qualifier Character 4	Qualifier Character 5	Qualifier Character 6	Qualifier Character 7
Z None	**Z** None	**Z** None	**Z** None

G Mental Health
Z None
3 **Medication Management:** Monitoring and adjusting the use of medications for the treatment of a mental health disorder

Qualifier Character 4	Qualifier Character 5	Qualifier Character 6	Qualifier Character 7
Z None	**Z** None	**Z** None	**Z** None

G Mental Health
Z None
5 **Individual Psychotherapy:** Treatment of an individual with a mental health disorder by behavioral, cognitive, psychoanalytic, psychodynamic or psychophysiological means to improve functioning or well-being

Qualifier Character 4	Qualifier Character 5	Qualifier Character 6	Qualifier Character 7
0 Interactive **1** Behavioral **2** Cognitive **3** Interpersonal **4** Psychoanalysis **5** Psychodynamic **6** Supportive **8** Cognitive-Behavioral **9** Psychophysiological	**Z** None	**Z** None	**Z** None

G Mental Health
Z None
6 **Counseling:** The application of psychological methods to treat an individual with normal developmental issues and psychological problems in order to increase function, improve well-being, alleviate distress, maladjustment or resolve crises

Qualifier Character 4	Qualifier Character 5	Qualifier Character 6	Qualifier Character 7
0 Educational **1** Vocational **3** Other Counseling	**Z** None	**Z** None	**Z** None

G Mental Health
Z None
7 **Family Psychotherapy:** Treatment that includes one or more family members of an individual with a mental health disorder by behavioral, cognitive, psychoanalytic, psychodynamic or psychophysiological means to improve functioning or well-being

Qualifier Character 4	Qualifier Character 5	Qualifier Character 6	Qualifier Character 7
2 Other Family Psychotherapy	**Z** None	**Z** None	**Z** None

G Mental Health
Z None
B Electroconvulsive Therapy: The application of controlled electrical voltages to treat a mental health disorder

Qualifier Character 4	Qualifier Character 5	Qualifier Character 6	Qualifier Character 7
0 Unilateral-Single Seizure 1 Unilateral-Multiple Seizure 2 Bilateral-Single Seizure 3 Bilateral-Multiple Seizure 4 Other Electroconvulsive Therapy	Z None	Z None	Z None

G Mental Health
Z None
C Biofeedback: Provision of information from the monitoring and regulating of physiological processes in conjunction with cognitive-behavioral techniques to improve patient functioning or well-being

Qualifier Character 4	Qualifier Character 5	Qualifier Character 6	Qualifier Character 7
9 Other Biofeedback	Z None	Z None	Z None

G Mental Health
Z None
F Hypnosis: Induction of a state of heightened suggestibility by auditory, visual and tactile techniques to elicit an emotional or behavioral response

Qualifier Character 4	Qualifier Character 5	Qualifier Character 6	Qualifier Character 7
Z None	Z None	Z None	Z None

G Mental Health
Z None
G Narcosynthesis: Administration of intravenous barbiturates in order to release suppressed or repressed thoughts

Qualifier Character 4	Qualifier Character 5	Qualifier Character 6	Qualifier Character 7
Z None	Z None	Z None	Z None

G Mental Health
Z None
H Group Psychotherapy: Treatment of two or more individuals with a mental health disorder by behavioral, cognitive, psychoanalytic, psychodynamic or psychophysiological means to improve functioning or well-being

Qualifier Character 4	Qualifier Character 5	Qualifier Character 6	Qualifier Character 7
Z None	Z None	Z None	Z None

G Mental Health
Z None
J Light Therapy: Application of specialized light treatments to improve functioning or well-being

Qualifier Character 4	Qualifier Character 5	Qualifier Character 6	Qualifier Character 7
Z None	Z None	Z None	Z None

Substance Abuse HZ2–HZ9

H **Substance Abuse**
Z **None**
2 **Detoxification Services:**   Detoxification from alcohol and/or drugs

Qualifier Character 4	Qualifier Character 5	Qualifier Character 6	Qualifier Character 7
Z None	**Z** None	**Z** None	**Z** None

H **Substance Abuse**
Z **None**
3 **Individual Counseling:**   The application of psychological methods to treat an individual with addictive behavior

Qualifier Character 4	Qualifier Character 5	Qualifier Character 6	Qualifier Character 7
0 Cognitive **1** Behavioral **2** Cognitive-Behavioral **3** 12-Step **4** Interpersonal **5** Vocational **6** Psychoeducation **7** Motivational Enhancement **8** Confrontational **9** Continuing Care **B** Spiritual **C** Pre/Post-Test Infectious Disease	**Z** None	**Z** None	**Z** None

H **Substance Abuse**
Z **None**
4 **Group Counseling:**   The application of psychological methods to treat two or more individuals with addictive behavior

Qualifier Character 4	Qualifier Character 5	Qualifier Character 6	Qualifier Character 7
0 Cognitive **1** Behavioral **2** Cognitive-Behavioral **3** 12-Step **4** Interpersonal **5** Vocational **6** Psychoeducation **7** Motivational Enhancement **8** Confrontational **9** Continuing Care **B** Spiritual **C** Pre/Post-Test Infectious Disease	**Z** None	**Z** None	**Z** None

H **Substance Abuse**
Z **None**
5 **Individual Psychotherapy:**   Treatment of an individual with addictive behavior by behavioral, cognitive, psychoanalytic, psychodynamic or psychophysiological means

Qualifier Character 4	Qualifier Character 5	Qualifier Character 6	Qualifier Character 7
0 Cognitive **1** Behavioral **2** Cognitive-Behavioral **3** 12-Step **4** Interpersonal **5** Interactive **6** Psychoeducation **7** Motivational Enhancement **8** Confrontational **9** Supportive **B** Psychoanalysis **C** Psychodynamic **D** Psychophysiological	**Z** None	**Z** None	**Z** None

H   Substance Abuse
Z   None
6   Family Counseling: The application of psychological methods that includes one or more family members to treat an individual with addictive behavior

Qualifier Character 4	Qualifier Character 5	Qualifier Character 6	Qualifier Character 7
3 Other Family Counseling	Z None	Z None	Z None

H   Substance Abuse
Z   None
8   Medication Management: Monitoring or adjusting the use of replacment medications for the treatment of addiction

Qualifier Character 4	Qualifier Character 5	Qualifier Character 6	Qualifier Character 7
0 Nicotine Replacement 1 Methadone Maintenance 2 Levo-alpha-acetyl-methadol (LAAM) 3 Antabuse 4 Naltrexone 5 Naloxone 6 Clonidine 7 Bupropion 8 Psychiatric Medication 9 Other Replacement Medication	Z None	Z None	Z None

H   Substance Abuse
Z   None
9   Pharmacotherapy: The use of replacement medications for the treatment of addiction

Qualifier Character 4	Qualifier Character 5	Qualifier Character 6	Qualifier Character 7
0 Nicotine Replacement 1 Methadone Maintenance 2 Levo-alpha-acetyl-methadol (LAAM) 3 Antabuse 4 Naltrexone 5 Naloxone 6 Clonidine 7 Bupropion 8 Psychiatric Medication 9 Other Replacement Medication	Z None	Z None	Z None

Appendix A: Root Operations Definitions

0   Medical and Surgical

0	Alteration	Definition:	Modifying the natural anatomic structure of a body part without affecting the function of the body part
		Explanation:	Principal purpose is to improve appearance
		Examples:	Face lift, breast augmentation
1	Bypass	Definition:	Altering the route of passage of the contents of a tubular body part
		Explanation:	Rerouting contents around an area of a body part to another distal (downstream) area in the normal route; rerouting the contents to another different but similar route and body part; or to an abnormal route and another dissimilar body part. It includes one or more concurrent anastomoses with or without the use of a device such as autografts, tissue substitutes, and synthetic substitutes.
		Examples:	Coronary artery bypass, colostomy formation
2	Change	Definition:	Taking out or off a device from a body part and putting back an identical or similar device in or on the same body part without cutting or puncturing the skin or a mucous membrane
		Explanation:	None
		Example:	Urinary catheter change, gastrostomy tube change
3	Control	Definition:	Stopping, or attempting to stop, postprocedural bleeding
		Explanation:	The site of the bleeding is coded as an anatomical region and not to a specific body part.
		Examples:	Control of post-prostatectomy hemorrhage, control of post-tonsillectomy hemorrhage
4	Creation	Definition:	Making a new genital structure that does not take over the function of a body part
		Explanation:	Used only for sex change operations where genitalia are made
		Examples:	Creation of vagina in a male, creation of penis in a female
5	Destruction	Definition:	Eradicating all or a portion of a body part by the direct use of energy, force, or a destructive agent
		Explanation:	Used for the actual physical destruction of all or a portion of a body part by the direct use of energy, force or a destructive agent. None of the body part is taken out.
		Examples:	Fulguration of rectal polyp, cautery of skin lesion
6	Detachment	Definition:	Cutting off all or a portion of an extremity
		Explanation:	Cutting off all or part of the upper or lower extremities
		Examples:	Below knee amputation, disarticulation of shoulder
7	Dilation	Definition:	Expanding an orifice or the lumen of a tubular body part
		Explanation:	The orifice can be a natural orifice or an artificially created orifice. Dilation involves stretching a tubular body part using intraluminal pressure or by cutting part or all of wall of the tubular body part.
		Examples:	Percutaneous transluminal angioplasty, pyloromyotomy
8	Division	Definition:	Separating, without taking out or draining fluids or gases from a body part
		Explanation:	All or a portion of the body part is separated into two or more portions.
		Examples:	Spinal cordotomy, osteotomy
9	Drainage	Definition:	Taking or letting out fluids and/or gases from a body part
		Explanation:	The qualifier *diagnostic* is used to identify drainage procedures that are biopsies.
		Examples:	Thoracentesis, incision and drainage
B	Excision	Definition:	Cutting out or off, without replacement, a portion of a body part
		Explanation:	The qualifier *diagnostic* is used to identify excision procedures that are biopsies.
		Examples:	Partial nephrectomy, liver biopsy
C	Extirpation	Definition:	Taking or cutting out solid matter from a body part
		Explanation:	The solid matter may be an abnormal byproduct of a biological function or a foreign body. The solid matter is imbedded in a body part or is in the lumen of a tubular body part. The solid matter may or may not have been previously broken into pieces. No appreciable amount of the body part is taken out.
		Examples:	Thrombectomy, choledocholithotomy

Continued on next page

0　Medical and Surgical　　　　　　　　　　　　　　　　　　*Continued from previous page*

D	Extraction	Definition:	Pulling or stripping out or off all or a portion of a body part
		Explanation:	The body part is pulled or stripped from its location by the use of force (e.g., manual, suction). The qualifier *diagnostic* is used to identify extractions that are biopsies.
		Examples:	Dilation and curettage, vein stripping
F	Fragmentation	Definition:	Breaking solid matter in a body part into pieces
		Explanation:	The solid matter may be an abnormal byproduct of a biological function or a foreign body. Physical force (e.g., manual, ultrasonic) applied directly or indirectly through intervening body parts are used to break the solid matter into pieces. The pieces of solid matter are not taken out, but are eliminated or absorbed through normal biological functions.
		Examples:	Extracorporeal shockwave lithotripsy, transurethral lithotripsy
G	Fusion	Definition:	Joining together portions of an articular body part, rendering the articular body part immobile
		Explanation:	The body part is joined together by fixation device, bone graft, or other means.
		Examples:	Spinal fusion, ankle arthrodesis
H	Insertion	Definition:	Putting in a nonbiological appliance that monitors, assists, performs, or prevents a physiological function but does not physically take the place of a body part
		Explanation:	None
		Examples:	Insertion of radioactive implant, insertion of central venous catheter
J	Inspection	Definition:	Visually and/or manually exploring a body part
		Explanation:	Visual exploration may be performed with or without optical instrumentation. Manual exploration may be performed directly or through intervening body layers.
		Examples:	Diagnostic arthroscopy, exploratory laparotomy
K	Map	Definition:	Locating the route of passage of electrical impulses and/or locating functional areas in a body part
		Explanation:	Applicable only to the cardiac conduction mechanism and the central nervous system
		Examples:	Cardiac mapping, cortical mapping
L	Occlusion	Definition:	Completely closing an orifice or lumen of a tubular body part
		Explanation:	The orifice can be a natural orifice or an artificially created orifice.
		Examples:	Fallopian tube ligation, ligation of inferior vena cava
M	Reattachment	Definition:	Putting back in or on all or a portion of a separated body part to its normal location or other suitable location
		Explanation:	Vascular circulation and nervous pathways may or may not be reestablished.
		Examples:	Reattachment of hand, reattachment of avulsed kidney
N	Release	Definition:	Freeing a body part
		Explanation:	Eliminating an abnormal constraint of a body part by cutting or by use of force. Some of the restraining tissue may be taken out but none of the body part is taken out.
		Examples:	Adhesiolysis, carpal tunnel release
P	Removal	Definition:	Taking out or off a device from a body part
		Explanation:	If taking out a device and putting in a similar device is performed with an external approach, the procedure is coded to the root operation *change*. Otherwise, the procedure for taking out the device is coded to the root operation *removal*, and the procedure for putting in the new device is coded to the root operation performed.
		Examples:	Drainage tube removal, cardiac pacemaker removal
Q	Repair	Definition:	Restoring, to the extent possible, a body part to its normal anatomic structure and function
		Explanation:	Used only when the method to accomplish the repair is not one of the other root operations
		Examples:	Herniorrhaphy, suture of laceration

Continued on next page

0	**Medical and Surgical**		*Continued from previous page*
R	Replacement	Definition:	Putting in or on a biological or synthetic material that physically takes the place of all or a portion of a body part
		Explanation:	The biological material is nonliving, or the biological material is living and from the same individual. The body part may have been previously taken out, previously replaced, or may be taken out concomitantly with the replacement procedure. If the body part has been previously replaced, a separate removal procedure is coded for taking out the device used in the previous replacement.
		Examples:	Total hip replacement, free skin graft
S	Reposition	Definition:	Moving to its normal location or other suitable location all or a portion of a body part
		Explanation:	The body part is moved to a new location from an aberrant location, or from a normal location where it is not functioning correctly. The body part may or may not be cut out or off to be moved to the new location.
		Examples:	Reposition of undescended testicle, fracture reduction
T	Resection	Definition:	Cutting out or off, without replacement, all of a body part
		Explanation:	None
		Examples:	Total nephrectomy, total lobectomy of lung
V	Restriction	Definition:	Partially closing the orifice or lumen of a tubular body part
		Explanation:	The orifice can be a natural orifice or an artificially created orifice.
		Examples:	Esophagogastric fundoplication, cervical cerclage
W	Revision	Definition:	Correcting, to the extent possible, a malfunctioning or displaced device
		Explanation:	Revision can include correcting a malfunctioning or displaced device by taking out or putting in components of the device such as a screw or pin.
		Examples:	Adjustment of pacemaker lead, adjustment of hip prosthesis
U	Supplement	Definition:	Putting in or on material that physically reinforces and/or augments the function of a portion of a body part
		Explanation:	Material may be biological or synthetic
		Examples:	Herniorrhaphy using mesh, heart valve annuloplasty
X	Transfer	Definition:	Moving, without taking out, all or a portion of a body part to another location to take over the function of all or a portion of a body part
		Explanation:	The body part transferred remains connected to its vascular and nervous supply.
		Examples:	Tendon transfer, skin pedicle flap transfer
Y	Transplantation	Definition:	Putting in or on all or a portion of a living body part taken from another individual or animal to physically take the place and/or function of all or a portion of a similar body part
		Explanation:	The native body part may or may not be taken out, and the transplanted body part may take over all or a portion of its function.
		Examples:	Kidney transplant, heart transplant

Root Operation Definitions for Other Sections

1   Obstetrics

A	Abortion	Definition:	Artificially terminating a pregnancy
		Explanation:	Subdivided according to whether an additional device such as a laminaria or abortifacient is used, or whether the abortion was performed by mechanical means
		Examples:	Transvaginal abortion using vacuum aspiration technique
E	Delivery	Definition:	Assisting the passage of the products of conception from the genital canal
		Explanation:	Applies only to manually-assisted, vaginal delivery
		Examples:	Manually-assisted delivery

2   Placement

0	Change	Definition:	Taking out or off a device from a body region and putting back an identical or similar device in or on the same body region without cutting or puncturing the skin or a mucous membrane
		Explanation:	Procedures performed without making an incision or a puncture.
		Examples:	Change of vaginal packing
1	Compression	Definition:	Putting pressure on a body region
		Explanation:	Procedures performed without making an incision or a puncture
		Examples:	Placement of pressure dressing on abdominal wall
2	Dressing	Definition:	Putting material on a body region for protection
		Explanation:	Procedures performed without making an incision or a puncture
		Examples:	Application of sterile dressing to head wound
3	Immobilization	Definition:	Limiting or preventing motion of a body region
		Explanation:	Procedures to fit a device, such as splints and braces, as described in F0DZ6EZ and F0DZ7EZ, apply only to the rehabilitation setting.
		Examples:	Placement of splint on left finger
4	Packing	Definition:	Putting material in a body region or orifice
		Explanation:	Procedures performed without making an incision or a puncture
		Examples:	Placement of nasal packing
5	Removal	Definition:	Taking out or off a device from a body region
		Explanation:	Procedures performed without making an incision or a puncture
		Examples:	Removal of stereotactic head frame
6	Traction	Definition:	Exerting a pulling force on a body region in a distal direction
		Explanation:	Traction in this section includes only the task performed using a mechanical traction apparatus.
		Examples:	Lumbar traction using motorized split-traction table

3   Administration

0	Introduction	Definition:	Putting in or on a therapeutic, diagnostic, nutritional, physiological, or prophylactic substance except blood or blood products
		Explanation:	All other substances administered, such as antineoplastic substance
		Examples:	Nerve block injection to median nerve
1	Irrigation	Definition:	Putting in or on a cleansing substance
		Explanation:	Substance given is a cleansing substance or dialysate
		Examples:	Flushing of eye
2	Transfusion	Definition:	Putting in blood or blood products
		Explanation:	Substance given is a blood product or a stem cell substance
		Examples:	Transfusion of cell saver red cells into central venous line

4   Measurement and Monitoring

0	Measurement	Definition:	Determining the level of a physiological or physical function at a point in time
		Explanation:	A single temperature reading is considered measurement.
		Examples:	External electrocardiogram(EKG), single reading
1	Monitoring	Definition:	Determining the level of a physiological or physical function repetitively over a period of time
		Explanation:	Temperature taken every half hour for 8 hours is considered monitoring
		Examples:	Urinary pressure monitoring

5   Extracorporeal Assistance and Performance

0	Assistance	Definition:	Taking over a portion of a physiological function by extracorporeal means
		Explanation:	Procedures that support a physiological function but do not take complete control of it, such as intra-aortic balloon pump to support cardiac output and hyperbaric oxygen treatment
		Examples:	Hyperbaric oxygenation of wound
1	Performance	Definition:	Completely taking over a physiological function by extracorporeal means
		Explanation:	Procedures in which complete control is exercised over a physiological function, such as total mechanical ventilation, cardiac pacing, and cardiopulmonary bypass
		Examples:	Cardiopulmonary bypass in conjunction with CABG
2	Restoration	Definition:	Returning, or attempting to return, a physiological function to its original state by extracorporeal means
		Explanation:	Only external cardioversion and defibrillation procedures. Failed cardioversion procedures are also included in the definition of restoration, and are coded the same as successful procedures
		Examples:	Attempted cardiac defibrillation, unsuccessful

6   Extracorporeal Therapies

0	Atmospheric Control	Definition:	Extracorporeal control of atmospheric pressure and composition
		Explanation:	None
		Examples:	Antigen-free air conditioning, series treatment
1	Decompression	Definition:	Extracorporeal elimination of undissolved gas from body fluids
		Explanation:	A single type of procedure—treatment for decompression sickness (the bends) in a hyperbaric chamber
		Examples:	Hyperbaric decompression treatment, single
2	Electromagnetic Therapy	Definition:	Extracorporeal treatment by electromagnetic rays
		Explanation:	None
		Examples:	TMS (transcranial magnetic stimulation), series treatment
3	Hyperthermia	Definition:	Extracorporeal raising of body temperature
		Explanation:	To treat temperature imbalance, and as an adjunct radiation treatment for cancer. When performed to treat temperature imbalance, the procedure is coded to this section. When performed for cancer treatment, whole-body hyperthermia is classified as a modality in section D, "Radiation Oncology."
		Examples:	None
4	Hypothermia	Definition:	Extracorporeal lowering of body temperature
		Explanation:	None
		Examples:	Whole body hypothermia treatment, series
5	Pheresis	Definition:	Extracorporeal separation of blood products
		Explanation:	Used in medical practice for two main purposes: to treat diseases where too much of a blood component is produced, such as leukemia, or to remove a blood product such as platelets from a donor, for transfusion into a patient who needs them
		Examples:	Therapeutic leukapheresis, single treatment

Continued on next page

6   Extracorporeal Therapies

Continued from previous page

6	Phototherapy	Definition:	Extracorporeal treatment by light rays
		Explanation:	Phototherapy to the circulatory system means exposing the blood to light rays outside the body, using a machine that recirculates the blood and returns it to the body after phototherapy.
		Examples:	Phototherapy of circulatory system, series treatment
7	Ultrasound Therapy	Definition:	Extracorporeal treatment by ultrasound
		Explanation:	None
		Examples:	Therapeutic ultrasound of peripheral vessels, single treatment
8	Ultraviolet Light Therapy	Definition:	Extracorporeal treatment by ultraviolet light
		Explanation:	None
		Examples:	Ultraviolet light phototherapy, series treatment
9	Shock Wave Therapy	Definition:	Extracorporeal treatment by shockwaves
		Explanation:	None
		Examples:	Shockwave therapy of plantar fascia, single treatment

7   Osteopathic

0	Treatment	Definition:	Manual treatment to eliminate or alleviate somatic dysfunction and related disorders
		Explanation:	None
		Examples:	Fascial release of abdomen, osteopathic treatment

8   Other Procedures

0	Other Procedures	Definition:	Methodologies that attempt to remediate or cure a disorder or disease
		Explanation:	For nontraditional, whole-body therapies including acupuncture and meditation
		Examples:	Acupuncture

9   Chiropractic

B	Manipulation	Definition:	Manual procedure that involves a directed thrust to move a joint past the physiological range of motion, without exceeding the anatomical limit
		Explanation:	None
		Examples:	Chiropractic treatment of cervical spine, short lever specific contact

Note: Sections B-H (Imaging through Substance Abuse Treatment) do not include root operations. Character 3 position represents type of procedure, therefore those definitions are not included in this appendix.

Appendix B: Comparison of Medical and Surgical Root Operations

Procedures That Take Out Some or All of a Body Part

Operation	Action	Target	Clarification	Example
Excision	Cutting out or off	Portion of a body part	Without replacing body part	Sigmoid polypectomy
Resection	Cutting out or off	All of a body part	Without replacing body part	Total nephrectomy
Extraction	Pulling out or off	All or a portion of a body part	Without replacing body part	Suction D&C
Destruction	Eradicating	All or a portion of a body part	Without taking out or replacing body part	Rectal polyp fulguration
Detachment	Cutting off	All or a portion of an extremity	Without replacing extremity	Below knee amputation

Procedures That Involve Putting In or On, Putting Back, or Moving Living Body Parts

Operation	Action	Target	Clarification	Example
Transplantation	Putting in or on	All or a portion of a living body part from other individual or animal	Physically takes the place and/or function of all or a portion of a body part	Heart transplant
Reattachment	Putting back in or on	All or a portion of a separated body part	Put in its normal or other suitable location.	Finger reattachment
Reposition	Moving	All or a portion of a body part	Put in its normal or other suitable location. Body part may or may not be cut out or off	Reposition undescended testicle
Transfer	Moving	All or a portion of a body part	Without taking out body part; assumes function of similar body part and remains connected to its vascular and nervous supply	Tendon transfer

Procedures That Take Out or Eliminate Solid Matter, Fluids, or Gases From a Body Part

Operation	Action	Target	Clarification	Example
Drainage	Taking or letting out	Fluids and/or gases from a body part	Without taking out any of the body part	Incision and drainage
Extirpation	Taking or cutting out	Solid matter in a body part	Without taking out any of the body part	Thrombectomy
Fragmentation	Breaking down	Solid matter in a body part	Without taking out any of the body part or any solid matter	Lithotripsy of gallstones

Procedures That Involve Only Examination of Body Parts and Regions

Operation	Action	Target	Clarification	Example
Inspection	Visual and/or manual exploration	A body part	Performed with or without optical instrumentation, directly or through body layers	Diagnostic arthroscopy
Map	Locating	Route of passage of electrical impulses or functional areas in a body part	Applicable only to cardiac conduction mechanism and central nervous system	Cardiac mapping

Procedures That Alter the Diameter/Route of a Tubular Body Part

Operation	Action	Target	Clarification	Example
Bypass	Altering the route of passage	Contents of tubular body part	May include use of living tissue, nonliving biological material or synthetic material which does not take the place of the body part	Gastrojejunal bypass
Dilation	Expanding	Orifice or lumen of tubular body part	By application of intraluminal pressure or by cutting the wall or orifice	Percutaneous transluminal angioplasty
Occlusion	Completely closing	Orifice or lumen of tubular body part	Orifice may be natural or artificially created	Fallopian tube ligation
Restriction	Partially closing	Orifice or lumen of tubular body part	Orifice may be natural or artificially created	Cervical cerclage

Procedures That Always Involve Devices

Operation	Action	Target	Clarification	Example
Insertion	Putting in	Device in or on a body part	Does not physically take the place of a body part	Pacemaker insertion
Replacement	Putting in or on	Biological or synthetic material; living tissue taken from same individual	Physically takes the place of all or a portion of a body part	Total hip replacement
Supplement	Putting in or on	Device that reinforces or augments a body part	Biological material is nonliving or living and from the same individual	Herniorrhaphy using mesh
Removal	Taking out or off	Device from a body part	If a new device is inserted via an incision or puncture, that procedure is coded separately	Cardiac pacemaker removal
Change	Taking out or off and putting back	Identical or similar device in or on a body part	Without cutting or puncturing skin or mucous membrane; all *change* procedures are coded using the *External* approach	Drainage tube change
Revision	Correcting	Malfunctioning or displaced device in or on a body part	To the extent possible	Hip prosthesis adjustment

Procedures Involving Cutting or Separation Only

Operation	Action	Target	Clarification	Example
Division	Separating	A body part	Without taking out any of the body part	Osteotomy
Release	Freeing	A body part	Eliminating abnormal constraint without taking out any of the body part	Peritoneal adhesiolysis

Procedures Involving Other Repairs

Operation	Action	Target	Clarification	Example
Control	Stopping or attempting to stop	Postprocedural bleeding	Limited to anatomic regions and extremities	Control of postprostatectomy bleeding
Repair	Restoring	A body part to its natural anatomic structure	To the extent possible	Hernia repair

Procedures with Other Objectives

Operation	Action	Target	Clarification	Example
Alteration	Modifying	Natural anatomical structure of a body part	Without affecting function of body part, performed for cosmetic purposes	Face lift
Creation	Making	New genital structure	Does not physically take the place of a body part, used for sex change operations	Artificial vagina creation
Fusion	Unification and immobilization	Joint	Stabilization of damaged joints by graft and/or fixation	Spinal fusion

Appendix C: Components of the Medical and Surgical Approach Definitions

Access Location	Method	Type of Instrumentation	Approach	Example
Skin or mucous membrane	Open	N/A	Open	Abdominal hysterectomy
Skin or mucous membrane	Instrumental	Without visualization	Percutaneous	Needle biopsy of liver
Skin or mucous membrane	Instrumental	With visualization	Percutaneous endoscopic	Arthroscopy
Orifice	Instrumental	Without visualization	Via natural or artificial opening	Endotracheal tube insertion
Orifice	Instrumental	With visualization	Via natural or artificial opening endoscopic	Sigmoidoscopy
Skin or mucous membrane	Open	With visualization	Open with percutaneous endoscopic assistance	Laparoscopic-assisted vaginal hysterectomy
Skin or mucous membrane	N/A	N/A	External	Closed fracture reduction

Appendix D: Character Meanings

0: Medical and Surgical

0: Central Nervous System

Operation–Character 3	Body Part–Character 4	Approach–Character 5	Device–Character 6	Qualifier–Character 7
1 Bypass	0 Brain	0 Open	0 Drainage Device	0 Nasopharynx
2 Change	1 Cerebral Meninges	3 Percutaneous	2 Monitoring Device	1 Mastoid Sinus
5 Destruction	2 Dura Mater	4 Percutaneous Endoscopic	3 Infusion Device	2 Atrium
8 Division	3 Epidural Space	X External	7 Autologous Tissue Substitute	3 Blood Vessel
9 Drainage	4 Subdural Space		J Synthetic Substitute	4 Pleural Cavity
B Excision	5 Subarachnoid Space		K Nonautologous Tissue Substitute	5 Intestine
C Extirpation	6 Cerebral Ventricle		M Electrode	6 Peritoneal Cavity
D Extraction	7 Cerebral Hemisphere		Y Other Device	7 Urinary Tract
F Fragmentation	8 Basal Ganglia		Z No Device	8 Bone Marrow
H Insertion	9 Thalamus			9 Fallopian Tube
J Inspection	A Hypothalamus			B Cerebral Cisterns
K Map	B Pons			F Olfactory Nerve
N Release	C Cerebellum			G Optic Nerve
P Removal	D Medulla Oblongata			H Oculomotor Nerve
Q Repair	E Cranial Nerve			J Trochlear Nerve
S Reposition	F Olfactory Nerve			K Trigeminal Nerve
T Resection	G Optic Nerve			L Abducens Nerve
U Supplement	H Oculomotor Nerve			M Facial Nerve
W Revision	J Trochlear Nerve			N Acoustic Nerve
X Transfer	K Trigeminal Nerve			P Glossopharyngeal Nerve
	L Abducens Nerve			Q Vagus Nerve
	M Facial Nerve			R Accessory Nerve
	N Acoustic Nerve			S Hypoglossal Nerve
	P Glossopharyngeal Nerve			T Stereotactic
	Q Vagus Nerve			U Nonstereotactic
	R Accessory Nerve			V Diagnostic Stereotactic
	S Hypoglossal Nerve			X Diagnostic
	T Spinal Meninges			Z No Qualifier
	U Spinal Canal			
	V Spinal Cord			
	W Cervical Spinal Cord			
	X Thoracic Spinal Cord			
	Y Lumbar Spinal Cord			

0: Medical and Surgical

1: Peripheral Nervous System

Operation–Character 3	Body Part–Character 4	Approach–Character 5	Device–Character 6	Qualifier–Character 7
2 Change	0 Cervical Plexus	0 Open	0 Drainage Device	1 Cervical Nerve
5 Destruction	1 Cervical Nerve	3 Percutaneous	2 Monitoring Device	2 Phrenic Nerve
8 Division	2 Phrenic Nerve	4 Percutaneous Endoscopic	7 Autologous Tissue Substitute	4 Ulnar Nerve
9 Drainage	3 Brachial Plexus	X External	M Electrode	5 Median Nerve
B Excision	4 Ulnar Nerve		Y Other Device	6 Radial Nerve
C Extirpation	5 Median Nerve		Z No Device	8 Thoracic Nerve
D Extraction	6 Radial Nerve			B Lumbar Nerve
H Insertion	8 Thoracic Nerve			C Perineal Nerve
J Inspection	9 Lumbar Plexus			D Femoral Nerve
N Release	A Lumbosacral Plexus			F Sciatic Nerve
P Removal	B Lumbar Nerve			G Tibial Nerve
Q Repair	C Pudendal Nerve			H Peroneal Nerve
S Reposition	D Femoral Nerve			X Diagnostic
U Supplement	F Sciatic Nerve			Z No Qualifier
W Revision	G Tibial Nerve			
X Transfer	H Peroneal Nerve			
	K Head and Neck Sympathetic Nerve			
	L Thoracic Sympathetic Nerve			
	M Abdominal Sympathetic Nerve			
	N Lumbar Sympathetic Nerve			
	P Sacral Sympathetic Nerve			
	Q Sacral Plexus			
	R Sacral Nerve			
	Y Peripheral Nerve			

0: Medical and Surgical

2: Heart and Great Vessels

Operation–Character 3	Body Part–Character 4	Approach–Character 5	Device–Character 6	Qualifier–Character 7
1 Bypass	0 Coronary Artery, One Site	0 Open	2 Monitoring Device	0 Allogeneic
5 Destruction	1 Coronary Artery, Two Sites	3 Percutaneous	3 Infusion Device	1 Syngeneic
7 Dilation	2 Coronary Artery, Three Sites	4 Percutaneous Endoscopic	4 Drug-eluting Intraluminal Device	2 Zooplastic
8 Division	3 Coronary Artery, Four or More Sites	X External	7 Autologous Tissue Substitute	3 Coronary Artery
B Excision	4 Coronary Vein		8 Zooplastic Tissue	4 Coronary Vein
C Extirpation	5 Atrial Septum		9 Autologous Venous Tissue	5 Coronary Circulation
F Fragmentation	6 Atrium, Right		A Autologous Arterial Tissue	6 Bifurcation
H Insertion	7 Atrium, Left		C Extraluminal Device	7 Atrium, Left
J Inspection	8 Conduction Mechanism		D Intraluminal Device	8 Internal Mammary, Right
K Map	9 Chordae Tendineae		J Synthetic Substitute	9 Internal Mammary, Left
L Occlusion	A Heart		K Nonautologous Tissue Substitute	B Subclavian
N Release	B Heart, Right		M Electrode	C Thoracic Artery
P Removal	C Heart, Left		Q Implantable Heart Assist System	D Carotid
Q Repair	D Papillary Muscle		R External Heart Assist System	F Abdominal Artery
R Replacement	F Aortic Valve		Z No Device	P Pulmonary Trunk
S Reposition	G Mitral Valve			Q Pulmonary Artery, Right
T Resection	H Pulmonary Valve			R Pulmonary Artery, Left
U Supplement	J Tricuspid Valve			S Biventricular
V Restriction	K Ventricle, Right			T Ductus Arteriosus
W Revision	L Ventricle, Left			W Aorta
Y Transplantation	M Ventricular Septum			X Diagnostic
	N Pericardium			Z No Qualifier
	P Pulmonary Trunk			
	Q Pulmonary Artery, Right			
	R Pulmonary Artery, Left			
	S Pulmonary Vein, Right			
	T Pulmonary Vein, Left			
	V Superior Vena Cava			
	W Thoracic Aorta			
	Y Great Vessel			

0: Medical and Surgical

3: Upper Arteries

Operation–Character 3	Body Part–Character 4	Approach–Character 5	Device–Character 6	Qualifier–Character 7
1 Bypass	0 Internal Mammary Artery, Right	0 Open	0 Drainage Device	0 Upper Arm Artery, Right
5 Destruction	1 Internal Mammary Artery, Left	3 Percutaneous	2 Monitoring Device	1 Upper Arm Artery, Left
7 Dilation	2 Innominate Artery	4 Percutaneous Endoscopic	3 Infusion Device	2 Upper Arm Artery, Bilateral
9 Drainage	3 Subclavian Artery, Right	X External	4 Drug-eluting Intraluminal Device	3 Lower Arm Artery, Right
B Excision	4 Subclavian Artery, Left		7 Autologous Tissue Substitute	4 Lower Arm Artery, Left
C Extirpation	5 Axillary Artery, Right		9 Autologous Venous Tissue	5 Lower Arm Artery, Bilateral
H Insertion	6 Axillary Artery, Left		A Autologous Arterial Tissue	6 Upper Leg Artery, Right
J Inspection	7 Brachial Artery, Right		C Extraluminal Device	7 Upper Leg Artery, Left
L Occlusion	8 Brachial Artery, Left		D Intraluminal Device	8 Upper Leg Artery, Bilateral
N Release	9 Ulnar Artery, Right		J Synthetic Substitute	9 Lower Leg Artery, Right
P Removal	A Ulnar Artery, Left		K Nonautologous Tissue Substitute	B Lower Leg Artery, Left
Q Repair	B Radial Artery, Right		Z No Device	C Lower Leg Artery, Bilateral
R Replacement	C Radial Artery, Left			D Upper Arm Vein
S Reposition	D Hand Artery, Right			F Lower Arm Vein
U Supplement	F Hand Artery, Left			G Intracranial Artery
V Restriction	G Intracranial Artery			J Extracranial Artery, Right
W Revision	H Common Carotid Artery, Right			K Extracranial Artery, Left
	J Common Carotid Artery, Left			M Pulmonary Artery, Right
	K Internal Carotid Artery, Right			N Pulmonary Artery, Left
	L Internal Carotid Artery, Left			X Diagnostic
	M External Carotid Artery, Right			Z No Qualifier
	N External Carotid Artery, Left			
	P Vertebral Artery, Right			
	Q Vertebral Artery, Left			
	R Face Artery			
	S Temporal Artery, Right			
	T Temporal Artery, Left			
	U Thyroid Artery, Right			
	V Thyroid Artery, Left			
	Y Upper Artery			

   Draft (2009)

0: Medical and Surgical

4: Lower Arteries

Operation–Character 3	Body Part–Character 4	Approach–Character 5	Device–Character 6	Qualifier–Character 7
1 Bypass	0 Abdominal Aorta	0 Open	0 Drainage Device	0 Abdominal Aorta
5 Destruction	1 Celiac Artery	3 Percutaneous	1 Radioactive Element	1 Celiac Artery
7 Dilation	2 Gastric Artery	4 Percutaneous Endoscopic	2 Monitoring Device	2 Mesenteric Artery
9 Drainage	3 Hepatic Artery	X External	3 Infusion Device	3 Renal Artery, Right
B Excision	4 Splenic Artery		4 Drug-eluting Intraluminal Device	4 Renal Artery, Left
C Extirpation	5 Superior Mesenteric Artery		7 Autologous Tissue Substitute	5 Renal Artery, Bilateral
H Insertion	6 Colic Artery, Right		9 Autologous Venous Tissue	6 Common Iliac Artery, Right
J Inspection	7 Colic Artery, Left		A Autologous Arterial Tissue	7 Common Iliac Artery, Left
L Occlusion	8 Colic Artery, Middle		C Extraluminal Device	8 Common Iliac Arteries, Bilateral
N Release	9 Renal Artery, Right		D Intraluminal Device	9 Internal Iliac Artery, Right
P Removal	A Renal Artery, Left		J Synthetic Substitute	B Internal Iliac Artery, Left
Q Repair	B Inferior Mesenteric Artery		K Nonautologous Tissue Substitute	C Internal Iliac Arteries, Bilateral
R Replacement	C Common Iliac Artery, Right		Z No Device	D External Iliac Artery, Right
S Reposition	D Common Iliac Artery, Left			F External Iliac Artery, Left
U Supplement	E Internal Iliac Artery, Right			G External Iliac Arteries, Bilateral
V Restriction	F Internal Iliac Artery, Left			H Femoral Artery, Right
W Revision	H External Iliac Artery, Right			J Femoral Artery, Left
	J External Iliac Artery, Left			K Femoral Arteries, Bilateral
	K Femoral Artery, Right			L Popliteal Artery
	L Femoral Artery, Left			M Peroneal Artery
	M Popliteal Artery, Right			N Posterior Tibial Artery
	N Popliteal Artery, Left			P Foot Artery
	P Anterior Tibial Artery, Right			Q Lower Extremity Artery
	Q Anterior Tibial Artery, Left			R Lower Artery
	R Posterior Tibial Artery, Right			S Lower Extremity Vein
	S Posterior Tibial Artery, Left			X Diagnostic
	T Peroneal Artery, Right			Z No Qualifier
	U Peroneal Artery, Left			
	V Foot Artery, Right			
	W Foot Artery, Left			
	Y Lower Artery			

0: Medical and Surgical

5: Upper Veins

Operation–Character 3	Body Part–Character 4	Approach–Character 5	Device–Character 6	Qualifier–Character 7
1 Bypass	0 Azygos Vein	0 Open	0 Drainage Device	X Diagnostic
5 Destruction	1 Hemiazygos Vein	3 Percutaneous	2 Monitoring Device	Y Upper Vein
7 Dilation	3 Innominate Vein, Right	4 Percutaneous Endoscopic	3 Infusion Device	Z No Qualifier
9 Drainage	4 Innominate Vein, Left	X External	7 Autologous Tissue Substitute	
B Excision	5 Subclavian Vein, Right		9 Autologous Venous Tissue	
C Extirpation	6 Subclavian Vein, Left		A Autologous Arterial Tissue	
D Extraction	7 Axillary Vein, Right		C Extraluminal Device	
H Insertion	8 Axillary Vein, Left		D Intraluminal Device	
J Inspection	9 Brachial Vein, Right		J Synthetic Substitute	
L Occlusion	A Brachial Vein, Left		K Nonautologous Tissue Substitute	
N Release	B Basilic Vein, Right		Z No Device	
P Removal	C Basilic Vein, Left			
Q Repair	D Cephalic Vein, Right			
R Replacement	F Cephalic Vein, Left			
S Reposition	G Hand Vein, Right			
U Supplement	H Hand Vein, Left			
V Restriction	L Intracranial Vein			
W Revision	M Internal Jugular Vein, Right			
	N Internal Jugular Vein, Left			
	P External Jugular Vein, Right			
	Q External Jugular Vein, Left			
	R Vertebral Vein, Right			
	S Vertebral Vein, Left			
	T Face Vein, Right			
	V Face Vein, Left			
	Y Upper Vein			

0: Medical and Surgical

6: Lower Veins

Operation–Character 3	Body Part–Character 4	Approach–Character 5	Device–Character 6	Qualifier–Character 7
1 Bypass	0 Inferior Vena Cava	0 Open	0 Drainage Device	5 Superior Mesenteric Vein
5 Destruction	1 Splenic Vein	3 Percutaneous	2 Monitoring Device	6 Inferior Mesenteric Vein
7 Dilation	2 Gastric Vein	4 Percutaneous Endoscopic	3 Infusion Device	9 Renal Vein, Right
9 Drainage	3 Esophageal Vein	X External	7 Autologous Tissue Substitute	B Renal Vein, Left
B Excision	4 Hepatic Vein		9 Autologous Venous Tissue	T Via Umbilical Vein
C Extirpation	5 Superior Mesenteric Vein		A Autologous Arterial Tissue	X Diagnostic
D Extraction	6 Inferior Mesenteric Vein		C Extraluminal Device	Y Lower Vein
H Insertion	7 Colic Vein		D Intraluminal Device	Z No Qualifier
J Inspection	8 Portal Vein		J Synthetic Substitute	
L Occlusion	9 Renal Vein, Right		K Nonautologous Tissue Substitute	
N Release	B Renal Vein, Left		Z No Device	
P Removal	C Common Iliac Vein, Right			
Q Repair	D Common Iliac Vein, Left			
R Replacement	F External Iliac Vein, Right			
S Reposition	G External Iliac Vein, Left			
U Supplement	H Hypogastric Vein, Right			
V Restriction	J Hypogastric Vein, Left			
W Revision	M Femoral Vein, Right			
	N Femoral Vein, Left			
	P Greater Saphenous Vein, Right			
	Q Greater Saphenous Vein, Left			
	R Lesser Saphenous Vein, Right			
	S Lesser Saphenous Vein, Left			
	T Foot Vein, Right			
	V Foot Vein, Left			
	Y Lower Vein			

0: Medical and Surgical

7: Lymphatic and Hemic Systems

Operation–Character 3	Body Part–Character 4	Approach–Character 5	Device–Character 6	Qualifier–Character 7
2 Change	0 Lymphatic, Head	0 Open	0 Drainage Device	0 Allogeneic
5 Destruction	1 Lymphatic, Right Neck	3 Percutaneous	3 Infusion Device	1 Syngeneic
9 Drainage	2 Lymphatic, Left Neck	4 Percutaneous Endoscopic	7 Autologous Tissue Substitute	2 Zooplastic
B Excision	3 Lymphatic, Right Upper Extremity	X External	C Extraluminal Device	X Diagnostic
C Extirpation	4 Lymphatic, Left Upper Extremity		D Intraluminal Device	Z No Qualifier
D Extraction	5 Lymphatic, Right Axillary		J Synthetic Substitute	
H Insertion	6 Lymphatic, Left Axillary		K Nonautologous Tissue Substitute	
J Inspection	7 Lymphatic, Thorax		Y Other Device	
L Occlusion	8 Lymphatic, Internal Mammary, Right		Z No Device	
N Release	9 Lymphatic, Internal Mammary, Left			
P Removal	B Lymphatic, Mesenteric			
Q Repair	C Lymphatic, Pelvis			
S Reposition	D Lymphatic, Aortic			
T Resection	F Lymphatic, Right Lower Extremity			
U Supplement	G Lymphatic, Left Lower Extremity			
V Restriction	H Lymphatic, Right Inguinal			
W Revision	J Lymphatic, Left Inguinal			
Y Transplantation	K Thoracic Duct			
	L Cisterna Chyli			
	M Thymus			
	N Lymphatic			
	P Spleen			
	Q Bone Marrow, Sternum			
	R Bone Marrow, Iliac			
	S Bone Marrow, Vertebral			
	T Bone Marrow			

* Includes lymph vessels and lymph nodes.

0: Medical and Surgical

8: Eye

Operation–Character 3	Body Part–Character 4	Approach–Character 5	Device–Character 6	Qualifier–Character 7
0 Alteration	0 Eye, Right	0 Open	0 Drainage Device	3 Nasal Cavity
1 Bypass	1 Eye, Left	3 Percutaneous	1 Radioactive Element	4 Sclera
2 Change	2 Anterior Chamber, Right	7 Via Natural or Artificial Opening	3 Infusion Device	5 Intraocular Telescope
5 Destruction	3 Anterior Chamber, Left	8 Via Natural or Artificial Opening Endoscopic	7 Autologous Tissue Substitute	X Diagnostic
7 Dilation	4 Vitreous, Right	X External	C Extraluminal Device	Z No Qualifier
9 Drainage	5 Vitreous, Left		D Intraluminal Device	
B Excision	6 Sclera, Right		J Synthetic Substitute	
C Extirpation	7 Sclera, Left		K Nonautologous Tissue Substitute	
D Extraction	8 Cornea, Right		Y Other Device	
F Fragmentation	9 Cornea, Left		Z No Device	
H Insertion	A Choroid, Right			
J Inspection	B Choroid, Left			
L Occlusion	C Iris, Right			
M Reattachment	D Iris, Left			
N Release	E Retina, Right			
P Removal	F Retina, Left			
Q Repair	G Retinal Vessel, Right			
R Replacement	H Retinal Vessel, Left			
S Reposition	J Lens, Right			
T Resection	K Lens, Left			
U Supplement	L Extraocular Muscle, Right			
V Restriction	M Extraocular Muscle, Left			
W Revision	N Upper Eyelid, Right			
X Transfer	P Upper Eyelid, Left			
	Q Lower Eyelid, Right			
	R Lower Eyelid, Left			
	S Conjunctiva, Right			
	T Conjunctiva, Left			
	V Lacrimal Gland, Right			
	W Lacrimal Gland, Left			
	X Lacrimal Duct, Right			
	Y Lacrimal Duct, Left			

0: Medical and Surgical

9: Ear, Nose, Sinus

Operation–Character 3	Body Part–Character 4	Approach–Character 5	Device–Character 6	Qualifier–Character 7
0　Alteration	0　External Ear, Right	0　Open	0　Drainage Device	0　Endolymphatic
1　Bypass	1　External Ear, Left	3　Percutaneous	7　Autologous Tissue Substitute	1　Bone Conduction
2　Change	2　External Ear, Bilateral	4　Percutaneous Endoscopic	B　Airway	2　Cochlear Prosthesis, Single Channel
5　Destruction	3　External Auditory Canal, Right	7　Via Natural or Artificial Opening	D　Intraluminal Device	3　Cochlear Prosthesis, Multiple Channel
7　Dilation	4　External Auditory Canal, Left	8　Via Natural or Artificial Opening Endoscopic	J　Synthetic Substitute	X　Diagnostic
8　Division	5　Middle Ear, Right	X　External	K　Nonautologous Tissue Substitute	Y　Other Hearing Device
9　Drainage	6　Middle Ear, Left		S　Hearing Device	Z　No Qualifier
B　Excision	7　Tympanic Membrane, Right		Y　Other Device	
C　Extirpation	8　Tympanic Membrane, Left		Z　No Device	
D　Extraction	9　Auditory Ossicle, Right			
H　Insertion	A　Auditory Ossicle, Left			
J　Inspection	B　Mastoid Sinus, Right			
M　Reattachment	C　Mastoid Sinus, Left			
N　Release	D　Inner Ear, Right			
P　Removal	E　Inner Ear, Left			
Q　Repair	F　Eustachian Tube, Right			
R　Replacement	G　Eustachian Tube, Left			
S　Reposition	H　Ear, Right			
T　Resection	J　Ear, Left			
U　Supplement	K　Nose			
W　Revision	L　Nasal Turbinate			
	M　Nasal Septum			
	N　Nasopharynx			
	P　Accessory Sinus			
	Q　Maxillary Sinus, Right			
	R　Maxillary Sinus, Left			
	S　Frontal Sinus, Right			
	T　Frontal Sinus, Left			
	U　Ethmoid Sinus, Right			
	V　Ethmoid Sinus, Left			
	W　Sphenoid Sinus, Right			
	X　Sphenoid Sinus, Left			
	Y　Sinus			

* Includes sinus ducts.

0: Medical and Surgical

B: Respiratory System

Operation–Character 3	Body Part–Character 4	Approach–Character 5	Device–Character 6	Qualifier–Character 7
1 Bypass	0 Tracheobronchial Tree	0 Open	0 Drainage Device	0 Allogeneic
2 Change	1 Trachea	3 Percutaneous	1 Radioactive Element	1 Syngeneic
5 Destruction	2 Carina	4 Percutaneous Endoscopic	2 Monitoring Device	2 Zooplastic
7 Dilation	3 Main Bronchus, Right	7 Via Natural or Artificial Opening	3 Infusion Device	4 Cutaneous
9 Drainage	4 Upper Lobe Bronchus, Right	8 Via Natural or Artificial Opening Endoscopic	7 Autologous Tissue Substitute	6 Esophagus
B Excision	5 Middle Lobe Bronchus, Right	X External	C Extraluminal Device	X Diagnostic
C Extirpation	6 Lower Lobe Bronchus, Right		D Intraluminal Device	Z No Qualifier
D Extraction	7 Main Bronchus, Left		E Endotracheal Device	
F Fragmentation	8 Upper Lobe Bronchus, Left		F Tracheostomy Device	
H Insertion	9 Lingula Bronchus		G Endobronchial Device	
J Inspection	B Lower Lobe Bronchus, Left		J Synthetic Substitute	
L Occlusion	C Upper Lung Lobe, Right		K Nonautologous Tissue Substitute	
M Reattachment	D Middle Lung Lobe, Right		M Electrode	
N Release	F Lower Lung Lobe, Right		Y Other Device	
P Removal	G Upper Lung Lobe, Left		Z No Device	
Q Repair	H Lung Lingula			
S Reposition	J Lower Lung Lobe, Left			
T Resection	K Lung, Right			
U Supplement	L Lung, Left			
V Restriction	M Lungs, Bilateral			
W Revision	N Pleura, Right			
Y Transplantation	P Pleura, Left			
	Q Pleura			
	R Diaphragm, Right			
	S Diaphragm, Left			
	T Diaphragm			

0: Medical and Surgical

C: Mouth and Throat

Operation–Character 3	Body Part–Character 4	Approach–Character 5	Device–Character 6	Qualifier–Character 7
0 Alteration	0 Upper Lip	0 Open	0 Drainage Device	0 Single
2 Change	1 Lower Lip	3 Percutaneous	1 Radioactive Element	1 Multiple
5 Destruction	2 Hard Palate	4 Percutaneous Endoscopic	5 External Fixation Device	2 All
7 Dilation	3 Soft Palate	7 Via Natural or Artificial Opening	7 Autologous Tissue Substitute	X Diagnostic
9 Drainage	4 Buccal Mucosa	8 Via Natural or Artificial Opening Endoscopic	C Extraluminal Device	Z No Qualifier
B Excision	5 Upper Gingiva	X External	D Intraluminal Device	
C Extirpation	6 Lower Gingiva		J Synthetic Substitute	
D Extraction	7 Tongue		K Nonautologous Tissue Substitute	
F Fragmentation	8 Parotid Gland, Right		Y Other Device	
H Insertion	9 Parotid Gland, Left		Z No Device	
J Inspection	A Salivary Gland			
L Occlusion	B Parotid Duct, Right			
M Reattachment	C Parotid Duct, Left			
N Release	D Sublingual Gland, Right			
P Removal	F Sublingual Gland, Left			
Q Repair	G Submaxillary Gland, Right			
R Replacement	H Submaxillary Gland, Left			
S Reposition	J Minor Salivary Gland			
T Resection	M Pharynx			
U Supplement	N Uvula			
V Restriction	P Tonsils			
W Revision	Q Adenoids			
X Transfer	R Epiglottis			
	S Larynx			
	T Vocal Cord, Right			
	V Vocal Cord, Left			
	W Upper Tooth			
	X Lower Tooth			
	Y Mouth and Throat			

0: Medical and Surgical

D: Gastrointestinal System

Operation–Character 3	Body Part–Character 4	Approach–Character 5	Device–Character 6	Qualifier–Character 7
1 Bypass	0 Upper Intestinal Tract	0 Open	0 Drainage Device	0 Allogeneic
2 Change	1 Esophagus, Upper	3 Percutaneous	1 Radioactive Element	1 Syngeneic
5 Destruction	2 Esophagus, Middle	4 Percutaneous Endoscopic	2 Monitoring Device	2 Zooplastic
7 Dilation	3 Esophagus, Lower	7 Via Natural or Artificial Opening	3 Infusion Device	4 Cutaneous
8 Division	4 Esophagogastric Junction	8 Via Natural or Artificial Opening Endoscopic	7 Autologous Tissue Substitute	5 Esophagus
9 Drainage	5 Esophagus	X External	B Airway	6 Stomach
B Excision	6 Stomach		C Extraluminal Device	9 Duodenum
C Extirpation	7 Stomach, Pylorus		D Intraluminal Device	A Jejunum
F Fragmentation	8 Small Intestine		J Synthetic Substitute	B Ileum
H Insertion	9 Duodenum		K Nonautologous Tissue Substitute	H Cecum
J Inspection	A Jejunum		L Artificial Sphincter	K Ascending Colon
L Occlusion	B Ileum		M Electrode	L Transverse Colon
M Reattachment	C Ileocecal Valve		U Feeding Device	M Descending Colon
N Release	D Lower Intestinal Tract		Y Other Device	N Sigmoid Colon
P Removal	E Large Intestine		Z No Device	P Rectum
Q Repair	F Large Intestine, Right			Q Anus
R Replacement	G Large Intestine, Left			X Diagnostic
S Reposition	H Cecum			Z No Qualifier
T Resection	J Appendix			
U Supplement	K Ascending Colon			
V Restriction	L Transverse Colon			
W Revision	M Descending Colon			
X Transfer	N Sigmoid Colon			
Y Transplantation	P Rectum			
	Q Anus			
	R Anal Sphincter			
	S Greater Omentum			
	T Lesser Omentum			
	U Omentum			
	V Mesentery			
	Peritoneum			

0: Medical and Surgical

F: Hepatobiliary System and Pancreas

Operation–Character 3	Body Part–Character 4	Approach–Character 5	Device–Character 6	Qualifier–Character 7
1　Bypass	0　Liver	0　Open	0　Drainage Device	0　Allogeneic
2　Change	1　Liver, Right Lobe	3　Percutaneous	1　Radioactive Element	1　Syngeneic
5　Destruction	2　Liver, Left Lobe	4　Percutaneous Endoscopic	2　Monitoring Device	2　Zooplastic
7　Dilation	4　Gallbladder	7　Via Natural or Artificial Opening	3　Infusion Device	3　Duodenum
8　Division	5　Hepatic Duct, Right	8　Via Natural or Artificial Opening Endoscopic	7　Autologous Tissue Substitute	4　Stomach
9　Drainage	6　Hepatic Duct, Left	X　External	C　Extraluminal Device	5　Hepatic Duct, Right
B　Excision	8　Cystic Duct		D　Intraluminal Device	6　Hepatic Duct, Left
C　Extirpation	9　Common Bile Duct		J　Synthetic Substitute	7　Hepatic Duct, Caudate
F　Fragmentation	B　Hepatobiliary Duct		K　Nonautologous Tissue Substitute	8　Cystic Duct
H　Insertion	C　Ampulla of Vater		Y　Other Device	9　Common Bile Duct
J　Inspection	D　Pancreatic Duct		Z　No Device	B　Small Intestine
L　Occlusion	F　Pancreatic Duct, Accessory			C　Large Intestine
M　Reattachment	G　Pancreas			X　Diagnostic
N　Release				Z　No Qualifier
P　Removal				
Q　Repair				
R　Replacement				
S　Reposition				
T　Resection				
U　Supplement				
V　Restriction				
W　Revision				
Y　Transplantation				

0: Medical and Surgical

G: Endocrine System

Operation–Character 3	Body Part–Character 4	Approach–Character 5	Device–Character 6	Qualifier–Character 7
2 Change	0 Pituitary Gland	0 Open	0 Drainage Device	X Diagnostic
5 Destruction	1 Pineal Body	3 Percutaneous	2 Monitoring Device	Z No Qualifier
8 Division	2 Adrenal Gland, Left	4 Percutaneous Endoscopic	3 Infusion Device	
9 Drainage	3 Adrenal Gland, Right	X External	Y Other Device	
B Excision	4 Adrenal Glands, Bilateral		Z No Device	
C Extirpation	5 Adrenal Gland			
H Insertion	6 Carotid Body, Left			
J Inspection	7 Carotid Body, Right			
M Reattachment	8 Carotid Bodies, Bilateral			
N Release	9 Para-aortic Body			
P Removal	B Coccygeal Glomus			
Q Repair	C Glomus Jugulare			
S Reposition	D Aortic Body			
T Resection	F Paraganglion Extremity			
W Revision	G Thyroid Gland Lobe, Left			
	H Thyroid Gland Lobe, Right			
	J Thyroid Gland Isthmus			
	K Thyroid Gland			
	L Superior Parathyroid Gland, Right			
	M Superior Parathyroid Gland, Left			
	N Inferior Parathyroid Gland, Right			
	P Inferior Parathyroid Gland, Left			
	Q Parathyroid Glands, Multiple			
	R Parathyroid Gland			
	S Endocrine Gland			

0: Medical and Surgical

H: Skin and Breast

Operation–Character 3	Body Part–Character 4	Approach–Character 5	Device–Character 6	Qualifier–Character 7
0 Alteration	0 Skin, Scalp	0 Open	0 Drainage Device	3 Full Thickness
2 Change	1 Skin, Face	3 Percutaneous	1 Radioactive Element	4 Partial Thickness
5 Destruction	2 Skin, Right Ear	7 Via Natural or Artificial Opening	7 Autologous Tissue Substitute	5 Latissimus Dorsi Myocutaneous Flap
8 Division	3 Skin, Left Ear	8 Via Natural or Artificial Opening Endoscopic	J Synthetic Substitute	6 Transverse Rectus Abdominis Myocutaneous Flap
9 Drainage	4 Skin, Neck	X External	K Nonautologous Tissue Substitute	7 Deep Inferior Epigastric Artery Perforator Flap
B Excision	5 Skin, Chest		N Tissue Expander	8 Superficial Inferior Epigastric Artery Flap
C Extirpation	6 Skin, Back		Y Other Device	9 Gluteal Artery Perforator Flap
D Extraction	7 Skin, Abdomen		Z No Device	X Diagnostic
H Insertion	8 Skin, Buttock			Z No Qualifier
J Inspection	9 Skin, Perineum			
M Reattachment	A Skin, Genitalia			
N Release	B Skin, Right Upper Arm			
P Removal	C Skin, Left Upper Arm			
Q Repair	D Skin, Right Lower Arm			
R Replacement	E Skin, Left Lower Arm			
S Reposition	F Skin, Right Hand			
T Resection	G Skin, Left Hand			
U Supplement	H Skin, Right Upper Leg			
W Revision	J Skin, Left Upper Leg			
X Transfer	K Skin, Right Lower Leg			
	L Skin, Left Lower Leg			
	M Skin, Right Foot			
	N Skin, Left Foot			
	P Skin			
	Q Finger Nail			
	R Toe Nail			
	S Hair			
	T Breast, Right			
	U Breast, Left			
	V Breast, Bilateral			
	W Nipple, Right			
	X Nipple, Left			
	Y Supernumerary Breast			

* Includes skin and breast glands and ducts.

0: Medical and Surgical

J: Subcutaneous Tissue and Fascia

Operation–Character 3	Body Part–Character 4	Approach–Character 5	Device–Character 6	Qualifier–Character 7
0 Alteration	0 Subcutaneous Tissue and Fascia, Scalp	0 Open	0 Drainage Device	0 Pacemaker, Single Chamber
2 Change	1 Subcutaneous Tissue and Fascia, Face	3 Percutaneous	1 Radioactive Element	1 Pacemaker, Single Chamber Rate Responsive
5 Destruction	4 Subcutaneous Tissue and Fascia, Anterior Neck	X External	3 Infusion Device	2 Pacemaker, Dual Chamber
8 Division	5 Subcutaneous Tissue and Fascia, Posterior Neck		7 Autologous Tissue Substitute	3 Cardiac Resynchronization Pacemaker Pulse Generator
9 Drainage	6 Subcutaneous Tissue and Fascia, Chest		H Contraceptive Device	4 Defibrillator Generator
B Excision	7 Subcutaneous Tissue and Fascia, Back		J Synthetic Substitute	5 Cardiac Resynchronization Defibrillator Pulse Generator
C Extirpation	8 Subcutaneous Tissue and Fascia, Abdomen		K Nonautologous Tissue Substitute	6 Single Array
D Extraction	9 Subcutaneous Tissue and Fascia, Buttock		M Stimulator Generator	7 Dual Array
H Insertion	B Subcutaneous Tissue and Fascia, Perineum		N Tissue Expander	8 Single Array Rechargeable
J Inspection	C Subcutaneous Tissue and Fascia, Genitalia		P Pacemaker / Defibrillator	9 Dual Array Rechargeable
N Release	D Subcutaneous Tissue and Fascia, Right Upper Arm		V Infusion Pump	B Skin and Subcutaneous Tissue
P Removal	F Subcutaneous Tissue and Fascia, Left Upper Arm		W Reservoir	C Skin, Subcutaneous Tissue and Fascia
Q Repair	G Subcutaneous Tissue and Fascia, Right Lower Arm		X Vascular Access Device	X Diagnostic
R Replacement	H Subcutaneous Tissue and Fascia, Left Lower Arm		Y Other Device	Y Other Cardiac Pacemaker / Defibrillator
W Revision	J Subcutaneous Tissue and Fascia, Right Hand		Z No Device	Z No Qualifier
X Transfer	K Subcutaneous Tissue and Fascia, Left Hand			
	L Subcutaneous Tissue and Fascia, Right Upper Leg			
	M Subcutaneous Tissue and Fascia, Left Upper Leg			
	N Subcutaneous Tissue and Fascia, Right Lower Leg			
	P Subcutaneous Tissue and Fascia, Left Lower Leg			
	Q Subcutaneous Tissue and Fascia, Right Foot			
	R Subcutaneous Tissue and Fascia, Left Foot			
	S Subcutaneous Tissue and Fascia, Head and Neck			
	T Subcutaneous Tissue and Fascia, Trunk			
	V Subcutaneous Tissue and Fascia, Upper Extremity			
	W Subcutaneous Tissue and Fascia, Lower Extremity			

0: Medical and Surgical

K: Muscles

Operation–Character 3	Body Part–Character 4	Approach–Character 5	Device–Character 6	Qualifier–Character 7
2 Change	0 Head Muscle	0 Open	0 Drainage Device	0 Skin
5 Destruction	1 Facial Muscle	3 Percutaneous	7 Autologous Tissue Substitute	1 Subcutaneous Tissue
8 Division	2 Neck Muscle, Right	4 Percutaneous Endoscopic	J Synthetic Substitute	2 Skin and Subcutaneous Tissue
9 Drainage	3 Neck Muscle, Left	X External	K Nonautologous Tissue Substitute	6 Transverse Rectus Abdominis Myocutaneous Flap
B Excision	4 Tongue, Palate, Pharynx Muscle		M Electrode	X Diagnostic
C Extirpation	5 Shoulder Muscle, Right		Y Other Device	Z No Qualifier
H Insertion	6 Shoulder Muscle, Left		Z No Device	
J Inspection	7 Upper Arm Muscle, Right			
M Reattachment	8 Upper Arm Muscle, Left			
N Release	9 Lower Arm and Wrist Muscle, Right			
P Removal	B Lower Arm and Wrist Muscle, Left			
Q Repair	C Hand Muscle, Right			
S Reposition	D Hand Muscle, Left			
T Resection	F Trunk Muscle, Right			
U Supplement	G Trunk Muscle, Left			
W Revision	H Thorax Muscle, Right			
X Transfer	J Thorax Muscle, Left			
	K Abdomen Muscle, Right			
	L Abdomen Muscle, Left			
	M Perineum Muscle			
	N Hip Muscle, Right			
	P Hip Muscle, Left			
	Q Upper Leg Muscle, Right			
	R Upper Leg Muscle, Left			
	S Lower Leg Muscle, Right			
	T Lower Leg Muscle, Left			
	V Foot Muscle, Right			
	W Foot Muscle, Left			
	X Upper Muscle			
	Y Lower Muscle			

0: Medical and Surgical

L: Tendons

Operation–Character 3	Body Part–Character 4	Approach–Character 5	Device–Character 6	Qualifier–Character 7
2 Change	0 Head and Neck Tendon	0 Open	0 Drainage Device	X Diagnostic
5 Destruction	1 Shoulder Tendon, Right	3 Percutaneous	7 Autologous Tissue Substitute	Z No Qualifier
8 Division	2 Shoulder Tendon, Left	4 Percutaneous Endoscopic	J Synthetic Substitute	
9 Drainage	3 Upper Arm Tendon, Right	X External	K Nonautologous Tissue Substitute	
B Excision	4 Upper Arm Tendon, Left		Y Other Device	
C Extirpation	5 Lower Arm and Wrist Tendon, Right		Z No Device	
J Inspection	6 Lower Arm and Wrist Tendon, Left			
M Reattachment	7 Hand Tendon, Right			
N Release	8 Hand Tendon, Left			
P Removal	9 Trunk Tendon, Right			
Q Repair	B Trunk Tendon, Left			
R Replacement	C Thorax Tendon, Right			
S Reposition	D Thorax Tendon, Left			
T Resection	F Abdomen Tendon, Right			
U Supplement	G Abdomen Tendon, Left			
W Revision	H Perineum Tendon			
X Transfer	J Hip Tendon, Right			
	K Hip Tendon, Left			
	L Upper Leg Tendon, Right			
	M Upper Leg Tendon, Left			
	N Lower Leg Tendon, Right			
	P Lower Leg Tendon, Left			
	Q Knee Tendon, Right			
	R Knee Tendon, Left			
	S Ankle Tendon, Right			
	T Ankle Tendon, Left			
	V Foot Tendon, Right			
	W Foot Tendon, Left			
	X Upper Tendon			
	Y Lower Tendon			

* Includes synovial membrane.

0: Medical and Surgical

M: Bursae and Ligaments

Operation–Character 3	Body Part–Character 4	Approach–Character 5	Device–Character 6	Qualifier–Character 7
2 Change	0 Head and Neck Bursa and Ligament	0 Open	0 Drainage Device	X Diagnostic
5 Destruction	1 Shoulder Bursa and Ligament, Right	3 Percutaneous	7 Autologous Tissue Substitute	Z No Qualifier
8 Division	2 Shoulder Bursa and Ligament, Left	4 Percutaneous Endoscopic	J Synthetic Substitute	
9 Drainage	3 Elbow Bursa and Ligament, Right	X External	K Nonautologous Tissue Substitute	
B Excision	4 Elbow Bursa and Ligament, Left		Y Other Device	
C Extirpation	5 Wrist Bursa and Ligament, Right		Z No Device	
D Extraction	6 Wrist Bursa and Ligament, Left			
J Inspection	7 Hand Bursa and Ligament, Right			
M Reattachment	8 Hand Bursa and Ligament, Left			
N Release	9 Upper Extremity Bursa and Ligament, Right			
P Removal	B Upper Extremity Bursa and Ligament, Left			
Q Repair	C Trunk Bursa and Ligament, Right			
S Reposition	D Trunk Bursa and Ligament, Left			
T Resection	F Thorax Bursa and Ligament, Right			
U Supplement	G Thorax Bursa and Ligament, Left			
W Revision	H Abdomen Bursa and Ligament, Right			
X Transfer	J Abdomen Bursa and Ligament, Left			
	K Perineum Bursa and Ligament			
	L Hip Bursa and Ligament, Right			
	M Hip Bursa and Ligament, Left			
	N Knee Bursa and Ligament, Right			
	P Knee Bursa and Ligament, Left			
	Q Ankle Bursa and Ligament, Right			
	R Ankle Bursa and Ligament, Left			
	S Foot Bursa and Ligament, Right			
	T Foot Bursa and Ligament, Left			
	V Lower Extremity Bursa and Ligament, Right			
	W Lower Extremity Bursa and Ligament, Left			
	X Upper Bursa and Ligament			
	Y Lower Bursa and Ligament			

* Includes synovial membrane.

0: Medical and Surgical

N: Head and Facial Bones

Operation–Character 3	Body Part–Character 4	Approach–Character 5	Device–Character 6	Qualifier–Character 7
2 Change	0 Skull	0 Open	0 Drainage Device	X Diagnostic
5 Destruction	1 Frontal Bone, Right	3 Percutaneous	4 Internal Fixation Device	Z No Qualifier
8 Division	2 Frontal Bone, Left	4 Percutaneous Endoscopic	5 External Fixation Device	
9 Drainage	3 Parietal Bone, Right	X External	7 Autologous Tissue Substitute	
B Excision	4 Parietal Bone, Left		J Synthetic Substitute	
C Extirpation	5 Temporal Bone, Right		K Nonautologous Tissue Substitute	
H Insertion	6 Temporal Bone, Left		M Electrode	
J Inspection	7 Occipital Bone, Right		S Hearing Device	
N Release	8 Occipital Bone, Left		Y Other Device	
P Removal	B Nasal Bone		Z No Device	
Q Repair	C Sphenoid Bone, Right			
R Replacement	D Sphenoid Bone, Left			
S Reposition	F Ethmoid Bone, Right			
T Resection	G Ethmoid Bone, Left			
U Supplement	H Lacrimal Bone, Right			
W Revision	J Lacrimal Bone, Left			
	K Palatine Bone, Right			
	L Palatine Bone, Left			
	M Zygomatic Bone, Right			
	N Zygomatic Bone, Left			
	P Orbit, Right			
	Q Orbit, Left			
	R Maxilla, Right			
	S Maxilla, Left			
	T Mandible, Right			
	V Mandible, Left			
	W Facial Bone			
	X Hyoid Bone			

0: Medical and Surgical

P: Upper Bones

Operation–Character 3	Body Part–Character 4	Approach–Character 5	Device–Character 6	Qualifier–Character 7
2 Change	0 Sternum	0 Open	0 Drainage Device	3 Monoplanar
5 Destruction	1 Rib, Right	3 Percutaneous	4 Internal Fixation Device	4 Ring
8 Division	2 Rib, Left	4 Percutaneous Endoscopic	5 External Fixation Device	5 Hybrid
9 Drainage	3 Cervical Vertebra	X External	6 Intramedullary Fixation Device	9 Limb Lengthening Device
B Excision	4 Thoracic Vertebra		7 Autologous Tissue Substitute	X Diagnostic
C Extirpation	5 Scapula, Right		J Synthetic Substitute	Z No Qualifier
H Insertion	6 Scapula, Left		K Nonautologous Tissue Substitute	
J Inspection	7 Glenoid Cavity, Right		M Electrode	
N Release	8 Glenoid Cavity, Left		Y Other Device	
P Removal	9 Clavicle, Right		Z No Device	
Q Repair	B Clavicle, Left			
R Replacement	C Humeral Head, Right			
S Reposition	D Humeral Head, Left			
T Resection	F Humeral Shaft, Right			
U Supplement	G Humeral Shaft, Left			
W Revision	H Radius, Right			
	J Radius, Left			
	K Ulna, Right			
	L Ulna, Left			
	M Carpal, Right			
	N Carpal, Left			
	P Metacarpal, Right			
	Q Metacarpal, Left			
	R Thumb Phalanx, Right			
	S Thumb Phalanx, Left			
	T Finger Phalanx, Right			
	V Finger Phalanx, Left			
	Y Upper Bone			

0: Medical and Surgical

Q: Lower Bones

Operation–Character 3	Body Part–Character 4	Approach–Character 5	Device–Character 6	Qualifier–Character 7
2 Change	0 Lumbar Vertebra	0 Open	0 Drainage Device	3 Monoplanar
5 Destruction	1 Sacrum	3 Percutaneous	4 Internal Fixation Device	4 Ring
8 Division	2 Pelvic Bone, Right	4 Percutaneous Endoscopic	5 External Fixation Device	5 Hybrid
9 Drainage	3 Pelvic Bone, Left	X External	6 Intramedullary Fixation Device	9 Limb Lengthening Device
B Excision	4 Acetabulum, Right		7 Autologous Tissue Substitute	X Diagnostic
C Extirpation	5 Acetabulum, Left		J Synthetic Substitute	Z No Qualifier
H Insertion	6 Upper Femur, Right		K Nonautologous Tissue Substitute	
J Inspection	7 Upper Femur, Left		M Electrode	
N Release	8 Femoral Shaft, Right		Y Other Device	
P Removal	9 Femoral Shaft, Left		Z No Device	
Q Repair	B Lower Femur, Right			
R Replacement	C Lower Femur, Left			
S Reposition	D Patella, Right			
T Resection	F Patella, Left			
U Supplement	G Tibia, Right			
W Revision	H Tibia, Left			
	J Fibula, Right			
	K Fibula, Left			
	L Tarsal, Right			
	M Tarsal, Left			
	N Metatarsal, Right			
	P Metatarsal, Left			
	Q Toe Phalanx, Right			
	R Toe Phalanx, Left			
	S Coccyx			
	Y Lower Bone			

0: Medical and Surgical

R: Upper Joints

Operation–Character 3	Body Part–Character 4	Approach–Character 5	Device–Character 6	Qualifier–Character 7
2 Change	0 Occipital-cervical Joint	0 Open	0 Drainage Device	0 Anterior
5 Destruction	1 Cervical Vertebral Joint	3 Percutaneous	3 Infusion Device	1 Posterior
9 Drainage	2 Cervical Vertebral Joint, 2 or more	4 Percutaneous Endoscopic	4 Internal Fixation Device	2 Interspinous Process
B Excision	3 Cervical Vertebral Disc	X External	5 External Fixation Device	3 Pedicle-based Dynamic Stabilization
C Extirpation	4 Cervicothoracic Vertebral Joint		7 Autologous Tissue Substitute	4 Facet
G Fusion	5 Cervicothoracic Vertebral Disc		8 Spacer	X Diagnostic
H Insertion	6 Thoracic Vertebral Joint		J Synthetic Substitute	Z No Qualifier
J Inspection	7 Thoracic Vertebral Joint, 2 to 7		K Nonautologous Tissue Substitute	
N Release	8 Thoracic Vertebral Joint, 8 or more		Y Other Device	
P Removal	9 Thoracic Vertebral Disc		Z No Device	
Q Repair	A Thoracolumbar Vertebral Joint			
R Replacement	B Thoracolumbar Vertebral Disc			
S Reposition	C Temporomandibular Joint, Right			
T Resection	D Temporomandibular Joint, Left			
U Supplement	E Sternoclavicular Joint, Right			
W Revision	F Sternoclavicular Joint, Left			
	G Acromioclavicular Joint, Right			
	H Acromioclavicular Joint, Left			
	J Shoulder Joint, Right			
	K Shoulder Joint, Left			
	L Elbow Joint, Right			
	M Elbow Joint, Left			
	N Wrist Joint, Right			
	P Wrist Joint, Left			
	Q Carpal Joint, Right			
	R Carpal Joint, Left			
	S Metacarpocarpal Joint, Right			
	T Metacarpocarpal Joint, Left			
	U Metacarpophalangeal Joint, Right			
	V Metacarpophalangeal Joint, Left			
	W Finger Phalangeal Joint, Right			
	X Finger Phalangeal Joint, Left			
	Y Upper Joint			

* Includes synovial membrane.

0: Medical and Surgical

S: Lower Joints

Operation–Character 3	Body Part–Character 4	Approach–Character 5	Device–Character 6	Qualifier–Character 7
2 Change	0 Lumbar Vertebral Joint	0 Open	0 Drainage Device	0 Anterior
5 Destruction	1 Lumbar Vertebral Joint, 2 or more	3 Percutaneous	3 Infusion Device	1 Posterior
9 Drainage	2 Lumbar Vertebral Disc	4 Percutaneous Endoscopic	4 Internal Fixation Device	2 Interspinous Process
B Excision	3 Lumbosacral Joint	X External	5 External Fixation Device	3 Pedicle-based Dynamic Stabilization
C Extirpation	4 Lumbosacral Disc		7 Autologous Tissue Substitute	4 Facet
G Fusion	5 Sacrococcygeal Joint		8 Spacer	5 Metal on Polyethylene
H Insertion	6 Coccygeal Joint		9 Liner	6 Metal on Metal
J Inspection	7 Sacroiliac Joint, Right		B Resurfacing Device	7 Ceramic on Ceramic
N Release	8 Sacroiliac Joint, Left		J Synthetic Substitute	8 Ceramic on Polyethylene
P Removal	9 Hip Joint, Right		K Nonautologous Tissue Substitute	9 Acetabular Surface
Q Repair	B Hip Joint, Left		Y Other Device	B Femoral Surface
R Replacement	C Knee Joint, Right		Z No Device	C Patellar Surface
S Reposition	D Knee Joint, Left			D Tibial Surface
T Resection	F Ankle Joint, Right			X Diagnostic
U Supplement	G Ankle Joint, Left			Z No Qualifier
W Revision	H Tarsal Joint, Right			
	J Tarsal Joint, Left			
	K Metatarsal-Tarsal Joint, Right			
	L Metatarsal-Tarsal Joint, Left			
	M Metatarsal-Phalangeal Joint, Right			
	N Metatarsal-Phalangeal Joint, Left			
	P Toe Phalangeal Joint, Right			
	Q Toe Phalangeal Joint, Left			
	Y Lower Joint			

* Includes synovial membrane.

0: Medical and Surgical

T: Urinary System

Operation–Character 3	Body Part–Character 4	Approach–Character 5	Device–Character 6	Qualifier–Character 7
1 Bypass	0 Kidney, Right	0 Open	0 Drainage Device	0 Allogeneic
2 Change	1 Kidney, Left	3 Percutaneous	2 Monitoring Device	1 Syngeneic
5 Destruction	2 Kidneys, Bilateral	4 Percutaneous Endoscopic	3 Infusion Device	2 Zooplastic
7 Dilation	3 Kidney Pelvis, Right	7 Via Natural or Artificial Opening	7 Autologous Tissue Substitute	3 Kidney Pelvis, Right
8 Division	4 Kidney Pelvis, Left	8 Via Natural or Artificial Opening Endoscopic	C Extraluminal Device	4 Kidney Pelvis, Left
9 Drainage	5 Kidney	X External	D Intraluminal Device	6 Ureter, Right
B Excision	6 Ureter, Right		J Synthetic Substitute	7 Ureter, Left
C Extirpation	7 Ureter, Left		K Nonautologous Tissue Substitute	8 Colon
D Extraction	8 Ureters, Bilateral		L Artificial Sphincter	9 Colocutaneous
F Fragmentation	9 Ureter		M Electrode	A Ileum
H Insertion	B Bladder		Y Other Device	B Bladder
J Inspection	C Bladder Neck		Z No Device	C Ileocutaneous
L Occlusion				D Cutaneous
M Reattachment				X Diagnostic
N Release				Z No Qualifier
P Removal				
Q Repair				
R Replacement				
S Reposition				
T Resection				
U Supplement				
V Restriction				
W Revision				
X Transfer				
Y Transplantation				

0: Medical and Surgical

U: Female Reproductive System

Operation–Character 3	Body Part–Character 4	Approach–Character 5	Device–Character 6	Qualifier–Character 7
1 Bypass	0 Ovary, Right	0 Open	0 Drainage Device	1 Allogeneic
2 Change	1 Ovary, Left	3 Percutaneous	1 Radioactive Element	2 Syngeneic
5 Destruction	2 Ovaries, Bilateral	4 Percutaneous Endoscopic	3 Infusion Device	3 Zooplastic
7 Dilation	3 Ovary	7 Via Natural or Artificial Opening	7 Autologous Tissue Substitute	5 Fallopian Tube, Right
8 Division	4 Uterine Supporting Structure	8 Via Natural or Artificial Opening Endoscopic	C Extraluminal Device	6 Fallopian Tube, Left
9 Drainage	5 Fallopian Tube, Right	F Via Natural or Artificial Opening With Percutaneous Endoscopic Assistance	D Intraluminal Device	9 Uterus
B Excision	6 Fallopian Tube, Left	X External	G Pessary	X Diagnostic
C Extirpation	7 Fallopian Tubes, Bilateral		H Contraceptive Device	Z No Qualifier
D Extraction	8 Fallopian Tube		J Synthetic Substitute	
F Fragmentation	9 Uterus		K Nonautologous Tissue Substitute	
H Insertion	B Endometrium		Y Other Device	
J Inspection	C Cervix		Z No Device	
L Occlusion	D Uterus and Cervix			
M Reattachment	F Cul-de-sac			
N Release	G Vagina			
P Removal	H Vagina and Cul-de-sac			
Q Repair	J Clitoris			
S Reposition	K Hymen			
T Resection	L Vestibular Gland			
U Supplement	M Vulva			
V Restriction	N Ova			
W Revision				
X Transfer				
Y Transplantation				

0: Medical and Surgical

V: Male Reproductive System

Operation–Character 3	Body Part–Character 4	Approach–Character 5	Device–Character 6	Qualifier–Character 7
1 Bypass	0 Prostate	0 Open	0 Drainage Device	J Epididymis, Right
2 Change	1 Seminal Vesicle, Right	3 Percutaneous	1 Radioactive Element	K Epididymis, Left
5 Destruction	2 Seminal Vesicle, Left	4 Percutaneous Endoscopic	3 Infusion Device	N Vas Deferens, Right
7 Dilation	3 Seminal Vesicles, Bilateral	7 Via Natural or Artificial Opening	7 Autologous Tissue Substitute	P Vas Deferens, Left
9 Drainage	4 Prostate and Seminal Vesicles	8 Via Natural or Artificial Opening Endoscopic	C Extraluminal Device	X Diagnostic
B Excision	5 Scrotum	X External	D Intraluminal Device	Z No Qualifier
C Extirpation	6 Tunica Vaginalis, Right		J Synthetic Substitute	
H Insertion	7 Tunica Vaginalis, Left		K Nonautologous Tissue Substitute	
J Inspection	8 Scrotum and Tunica Vaginalis		Y Other Device	
L Occlusion	9 Testis, Right		Z No Device	
M Reattachment	B Testis, Left			
N Release	C Testes, Bilateral			
P Removal	D Testis			
Q Repair	F Spermatic Cord, Right			
R Replacement	G Spermatic Cord, Left			
S Reposition	H Spermatic Cords, Bilateral			
T Resection	J Epididymis, Right			
U Supplement	K Epididymis, Left			
W Revision	L Epididymis, Bilateral			
	M Epididymis and Spermatic Cord			
	N Vas Deferens, Right			
	P Vas Deferens, Left			
	Q Vas Deferens, Bilateral			
	R Vas Deferens			
	S Penis			
	T Prepuce			
	V Male External Genitalia			

0: Medical and Surgical

W: Anatomical Regions, General

Operation–Character 3	Body Region–Character 4	Approach–Character 5	Device–Character 6	Qualifier–Character 7
0 Alteration	0 Head	0 Open	0 Drainage Device	0 Vagina
1 Bypass	1 Cranial Cavity	3 Percutaneous	1 Radioactive Element	1 Penis
2 Change	2 Face	4 Percutaneous Endoscopic	3 Infusion Device	2 Stoma
3 Control	3 Oral Cavity and Throat	7 Via Natural or Artificial Opening	7 Autologous Tissue Substitute	4 Cutaneous
4 Creation	4 Upper Jaw	8 Via Natural or Artificial Opening Endoscopic	J Synthetic Substitute	9 Pleural Cavity, Right
8 Division	5 Lower Jaw	X External	K Nonautologous Tissue Substitute	B Pleural Cavity, Left
9 Drainage	6 Neck		Y Other Device	G Peritoneal Cavity
B Excision	8 Chest Wall		Z No Device	J Pelvic Cavity
C Extirpation	9 Pleural Cavity, Right			X Diagnostic
F Fragmentation	B Pleural Cavity, Left			Y Lower Vein
H Insertion	C Mediastinum			Z No Qualifier
J Inspection	D Pericardial Cavity			
M Reattachment	F Abdominal Wall			
P Removal	G Peritoneal Cavity			
Q Repair	H Retroperitoneum			
U Supplement	J Pelvic Cavity			
W Revision	K Upper Back			
	L Lower Back			
	M Perineum, Male			
	N Perineum, Female			
	P Gastrointestinal Tract			
	Q Respiratory Tract			
	R Genitourinary Tract			

0: Medical and Surgical

X: Anatomical Regions, Upper Extremities

Operation–Character 3	Body Part–Character 4	Approach–Character 5	Device–Character 6	Qualifier–Character 7
0 Alteration	0 Forequarter, Right	0 Open	0 Drainage Device	0 Complete
2 Change	1 Forequarter, Left	3 Percutaneous	1 Radioactive Element	1 High
3 Control	2 Shoulder Region, Right	4 Percutaneous Endoscopic	3 Infusion Device	2 Mid
6 Detachment	3 Shoulder Region, Left	X External	7 Autologous Tissue Substitute	3 Low
9 Drainage	4 Axilla, Right		J Synthetic Substitute	4 Complete 1st Ray
B Excision	5 Axilla, Left		K Nonautologous Tissue Substitute	5 Complete 2nd Ray
H Insertion	6 Upper Extremity, Right		Y Other Device	6 Complete 3rd Ray
J Inspection	7 Upper Extremity, Left		Z No Device	7 Complete 4th Ray
M Reattachment	8 Upper Arm, Right			8 Complete 5th Ray
P Removal	9 Upper Arm, Left			9 Partial 1st Ray
Q Repair	B Elbow Region, Right			B Partial 2nd Ray
R Replacement	C Elbow Region, Left			C Partial 3rd Ray
U Supplement	D Lower Arm, Right			D Partial 4th Ray
W Revision	F Lower Arm, Left			F Partial 5th Ray
X Transfer	G Wrist Region, Right			L Thumb, Right
	H Wrist Region, Left			M Thumb, Left
	J Hand, Right			N Toe, Right
	K Hand, Left			P Toe, Left
	L Thumb, Right			X Diagnostic
	M Thumb, Left			Z No Qualifier
	N Index Finger, Right			
	P Index Finger, Left			
	Q Middle Finger, Right			
	R Middle Finger, Left			
	S Ring Finger, Right			
	T Ring Finger, Left			
	V Little Finger, Right			
	W Little Finger, Left			

0: Medical and Surgical

Y: Anatomical Regions, Lower Extremities

Operation–Character 3	Body Part–Character 4	Approach–Character 5	Device–Character 6	Qualifier–Character 7
0 Alteration	0 Buttock, Right	0 Open	0 Drainage Device	0 Complete
2 Change	1 Buttock, Left	3 Percutaneous	1 Radioactive Element	1 High
3 Control	2 Hindquarter, Right	4 Percutaneous Endoscopic	3 Infusion Device	2 Mid
6 Detachment	3 Hindquarter, Left	X External	7 Autologous Tissue Substitute	3 Low
9 Drainage	4 Hindquarter, Bilateral		J Synthetic Substitute	4 Complete 1st Ray
B Excision	5 Inguinal Region, Right		K Nonautologous Tissue Substitute	5 Complete 2nd Ray
H Insertion	6 Inguinal Region, Left		Y Other Device	6 Complete 3rd Ray
J Inspection	7 Femoral Region, Right		Z No Device	7 Complete 4th Ray
M Reattachment	8 Femoral Region, Left			8 Complete 5th Ray
P Removal	9 Lower Extremity, Right			9 Partial 1st Ray
Q Repair	A Inguinal Region, Bilateral			B Partial 2nd Ray
U Supplement	B Lower Extremity, Left			
W Revision	C Upper Leg, Right			C Partial 3rd Ray
	D Upper Leg, Left			D Partial 4th Ray
	E Femoral Region, Bilateral			F Partial 5th Ray
	F Knee Region, Right			X Diagnostic
	G Knee Region, Left			Z No Qualifier
	H Lower Leg, Right			
	J Lower Leg, Left			
	K Ankle Region, Right			
	L Ankle Region, Left			
	M Foot, Right			
	N Foot, Left			
	P 1st Toe, Right			
	Q 1st Toe, Left			
	R 2nd Toe, Right			
	S 2nd Toe, Left			
	T 3rd Toe, Right			
	U 3rd Toe, Left			
	V 4th Toe, Right			
	W 4th Toe, Left			
	X 5th Toe, Right			
	Y 5th Toe, Left			

1: Obstetrics

0: Pregnancy

Operation–Character 3	Body Part–Character 4	Approach–Character 5	Device–Character 6	Qualifier–Character 7
2 Change	0 Products of Conception	0 Open	3 Monitoring Electrode	0 Classical
9 Drainage	1 Products of Conception, Retained	2 Open Endoscopic	Y Other Device	1 Low Cervical
A Abortion	2 Products of Conception, Ectopic	3 Percutaneous	Z No Device	2 Extraperitoneal
D Extraction		4 Percutaneous Endoscopic		3 Low Forceps
E Delivery		7 Via Natural or Artificial Opening		4 Mid Forceps
H Insertion		8 Via Natural or Artificial Opening Endoscopic		5 High Forceps
J Inspection		X External		6 Vacuum
P Removal				7 Internal Version
Q Repair				8 Other
S Reposition				9 Fetal Blood
T Resection				A Fetal Cerebrospinal Fluid
Y Transplantation				B Fetal Fluid, Other
				C Amniotic Fluid, Therapeutic
				D Fluid, Other
				E Nervous System
				F Cardiovascular System
				G Lymphatics & Hemic
				H Eye
				J Ear, Nose & Sinus
				K Respiratory System
				L Mouth & Throat
				M Gastrointestinal System
				N Hepatobiliary & Pancreas
				P Endocrine System
				Q Skin
				R Musculoskeletal System
				S Urinary System
				T Female Reproductive System
				U Amniotic Fluid, Diagnostic
				V Male Reproductive System
				W Laminaria
				X Abortifacient
				Y Other Body Systems
				Z No Qualifier

2: Placement

W: Anatomical Regions

Operation–Character 3	Body Region Character 4	Approach–Character 5	Device–Character 6	Qualifier–Character 7
0 Change	0 Head	X External	0 Traction Apparatus	Z No Qualifier
1 Compression	1 Face		1 Splint	
2 Dressing	2 Neck		2 Cast	
3 Immobilization	3 Abdominal Wall		3 Brace	
4 Packing	4 Chest Wall		4 Bandage	
5 Removal	5 Back		5 Packing Material	
6 Traction	6 Inguinal Region, Right		6 Pressure Dressing	
	7 Inguinal Region, Left		7 Intermittent Pressure Device	
	8 Upper Extremity, Right		8 Stereotatic Apparatus	
	9 Upper Extremity, Left		9 Wire	
	A Upper Arm, Right		Y Other Device	
	B Upper Arm, Left		Z No Device	
	C Lower Arm, Right			
	D Lower Arm, Left			
	E Hand, Right			
	F Hand, Left			
	G Thumb, Right			
	H Thumb, Left			
	J Finger, Right			
	K Finger, Left			
	L Lower Extremity, Right			
	M Lower Extremity, Left			
	N Upper Leg, Right			
	P Upper Leg, Left			
	Q Lower Leg, Right			
	R Lower Leg, Left			
	S Foot, Right			
	T Foot, Left			
	U Toe, Right			
	V Toe, Left			

2: Placement

Y: Anatomical Orifices

Operation–Character 3	Body Orifice–Character 4	Approach Character–5	Device Character–6	Qualifier Character–7
0 Change	0 Mouth and Pharynx	X External	5 Packing Material	Z No Qualifier
4 Packing	1 Nasal			
5 Removal	2 Ear			
	3 Anorectal			
	4 Female Genital Tract			
	5 Urethra			

3: Administration

0: Circulatory

Operation–Character 3	Body System Character 4	Approach–Character 5	Substance–Character 6	Qualifier–Character 7
2 Transfusion	3 Peripheral Vein	0 Open	A Stem Cells, Embryonic	0 Autologous
	4 Central Vein	3 Percutaneous	G Bone Marrow	1 Nonautologous
	5 Peripheral Artery	7 Via Natural or Artificial Opening	H Whole Blood	Z No Qualifier
	6 Central Artery		J Serum Albumin	
	7 Products of Conception, Circulatory		K Frozen Plasma	
			L Fresh Plasma	
			M Plasma Cryoprecipitate	
			N Red Blood Cells	
			P Frozen Red Cells	
			Q White Cells	
			R Platelets	
			S Globulin	
			T Fibrinogen	
			V Antihemophilic Factors	
			W Factor IX	
			X Stem Cells, Cord Blood	
			Y Stem Cells, Hematopoietic	

3: Administration

C: Indwelling Device

Operation–Character 3	Body System Character 4	Approach–Character 5	Substance–Character 6	Quali?er–Character 7
1 Irrigation	Z Whole Body	X External	8 Irrigating Substance	Z No Qualifier

3: Administration

E: Physiological Systems and Anatomical Regions

Operation Character 3	Body System/ Region Character 4	Approach–Character 5	Substance–Character 6	Qualifier–Character 7
0 Introduction	0 Skin and Mucous Membranes	0 Open	0 Antineoplastic	0 Autologous
1 Irrigation	1 Subcutaneous Tissue	3 Percutaneous	1 Thrombolytic	1 Nonautologous
	2 Muscle	7 Via Natural or Artificial Opening	2 Anti-infective	2 High-dose Interleukin-2
	3 Peripheral Vein	8 Via Natural or Artificial Opening Endoscopic	3 Anti-inflammatory	3 Low-dose Interleukin-2
	4 Central Vein	X External	4 Serum, Toxoid and Vaccine	4 Liquid Brachytherapy Radioisotope
	5 Peripheral Artery		5 Adhesion Barrier	5 Other Antineoplastic
	6 Central Artery		6 Nutritional Substance	6 Recombinant Human-activated Protein C
	7 Coronary Artery		7 Electrolytic and Water Balance Substance	7 Other Thrombolytic
	8 Heart		8 Irrigating Substance	8 Oxazolidinones
	9 Nose		9 Dialysate	9 Other Anti-infective
	A Bone Marrow		A Stem Cells, Embryonic	B Recombinant Bone Morphogenetic Protein
	B Ear		B Local Anesthetic	C Other Substance
	C Eye		C Regional Anesthetic	D Nitric Oxide
	D Mouth and Pharynx		D Inhalation Anesthetic	F Other Gas
	E Products of Conception		E Stem Cells, Somatic	G Insulin
	F Respiratory Tract		F Intracirculatory Anesthetic	H Human B-type Natriuretic Peptide
	G Upper GI		G Other Therapeutic Substance	J Other Hormone
	H Lower GI		H Radioactive Substance	K Immunostimulator
	J Biliary and Pancreatic Tract		J Contrast Agent	L Immunosuppressive
	K Genitourinary Tract		K Other Diagnostic Substance	M Monoclonal Antibody
	L Pleural Cavity		L Sperm	N Blood Brain Barrier Disruption
	M Peritoneal Cavity		M Pigment	X Diagnostic
	N Male Reproductive		N Analgesics, Hypnotics, Sedatives	Z No Qualifier
	P Female Reproductive		P Platelet Inhibitor	
	Q Cranial Cavity and Brain		Q Fertilized Ovum	
	R Spinal Canal		R Antiarrhythmic	
	S Epidural Space		S Gas	
	T Peripheral Nerves and Plexi		T Destructive Agent	
	U Joints		U Pancreatic Islet Cells	
	V Bones		V Hormone	
	W Lymphatics		W Immunotherapeutic	
	X Cranial Nerves		X Vasopressor	
	Y Pericardial Cavity			

4: Measurement and Monitoring

A: Physiological Systems

Operation–Character 3	Body System–Character 4	Approach–Character 5	Function/Device–Character 6	Qualifier–Character 7
0 Measurement	0 Central Nervous	0 Open	0 Acuity	0 Central
1 Monitoring	1 Peripheral Nervous	3 Percutaneous	1 Capacity	1 Peripheral
	2 Cardiac	4 Percutaneous Endoscopic	2 Conductivity	2 Portal
	3 Arterial	7 Via Natural or Artificial Opening	3 Contractility	3 Pulmonary
	4 Venous	8 Via Natural or Artificial Opening Endoscopic	4 Electrical Activity	4 Stress
	5 Circulatory	X External	5 Flow	5 Ambulatory
	6 Lymphatic		6 Metabolism	6 Right Heart
	7 Visual		7 Mobility	7 Left Heart
	8 Olfactory		8 Motility	8 Bilateral
	9 Respiratory		9 Output	9 Sensory
	B Gastrointestinal		B Pressure	B Motor
	C Biliary		C Rate	C Coronary
	D Urinary		D Resistance	D Intracranial
	F Musculoskeletal		F Rhythm	F Other Thoracic
	G Whole Body		G Secretion	Z No Qualifier
	H Products of Conception, Cardiac		H Sound	
	J Products of Conception, Nervous		J Pulse	
			K Temperature	
			L Volume	
			M Total Activity	
			N Sampling and Pressure	
			P Action Currents	
			Q Sleep	
			R Saturation	

4: Measurement and Monitoring

B: Physiological Devices

Operation–Character 3	Body System–Character 4	Approach–Character 5	Function/Device–Character 6	Qualifier–Character 7
0 Measurement	0 Central Nervous	X External	S Pacemaker	Z No Qualifier
	1 Peripheral Nervous		T Defibrillator	
	2 Cardiac		V Stimulator	
	9 Respiratory			
	F Musculoskeletal			

5: Extracorporeal Assistance and Performance

A: Physiological Systems

Operation–Character 3	Body System–Character 4	Duration–Character 5	Function–Character 6	Qualifier–Character 7
0 Assistance	2 Cardiac	0 Single	0 Filtration	0 Balloon Pump
1 Performance	5 Circulatory	1 Intermittent	1 Output	1 Hyperbaric
2 Restoration	9 Respiratory	2 Continuous	2 Oxygenation	2 Manual
	C Biliary	3 Less than 24 Consecutive Hours	3 Pacing	3 Membrane
	D Urinary	4 24-96 Consecutive Hours	4 Rhythm	4 Nonmechanical
		5 Greater than 96 Consecutive Hours	5 Ventilation	5 Pulsatile Compression
		6 Multiple		6 Pump
				7 Continuous Positive Airway Pressure
				8 Intermittent Positive Airway Pressure
				9 Continuous Negative Airway Pressure
				B Intermittent Negative Airway Pressure
				C Supersaturated
				Z No Qualifier

6: Extracorporeal Therapies

A: Physiological Systems

Operation–Character 3	Body System–Character 4	Duration–Character 5	Qualifier–Character 6	Qualifier–Character 7
0 Atmospheric Control	0 Skin	0 Single	Z No Qualifier	0 Erythrocytes
1 Decompression	1 Urinary	1 Multiple		1 Leukocytes
2 Electromagnetic Therapy	2 Central Nervous			2 Platelets
3 Hyperthermia	3 Musculoskeletal			3 Plasma
4 Hypothermia	5 Circulatory			4 Head and Neck Vessels
5 Pheresis	G Whole Body			5 Heart
6 Phototherapy				6 Peripheral Vessels
7 Ultrasound Therapy				7 Other Vessels
8 Ultraviolet Light Therapy				T Stem Cells, Cord Blood
9 Shock Wave Therapy				V Stem Cells, Hematopoietic
				Z No Qualifier

7: Osteopathic

W: Anatomical Regions

Operation–Character 3	Body Region–Character 4	Approach–Character 5	Method–Character 6	Qualifier–Character 7
0 Treatment	0 Head	X External	0 Articulatory-Raising	Z None
	1 Cervical		1 Fascial Release	
	2 Thoracic		2 General Mobilization	
	3 Lumbar		3 High Velocity-Low Amplitude	
	4 Sacrum		4 Indirect	
	5 Pelvis		5 Low Velocity-High Amplitude	
	6 Lower Extremities		6 Lymphatic Pump	
	7 Upper Extremities		7 Muscle Energy-Isometric	
	8 Rib Cage		8 Muscle Energy-Isotonic	
	9 Abdomen		9 Other Method	

8: Other Procedures

E: Physiological Systems and Anatomical Regions

Operation–Character 3	Body Region–Character 4	Approach–Character 5	Method–Character 6	Qualifier–Character 7
0 Other Procedures	1 Nervous System	0 Open	0 Acupuncture	0 Anesthesia
	2 Circulatory System	3 Percutaneous	1 Therapeutic Massage	1 In Vitro Fertilization
	9 Head and Neck Region	4 Percutaneous Endoscopic	6 Collection	2 Breast Milk
	H Integumentary System and Breast	7 Via Natural or Artificial Opening	B Computer Assisted Procedure	3 Sperm
	K Musculoskeletal System	8 Via Natural or Artificial Opening Endoscopic	C Robotic Assisted Procedure	4 Yoga Therapy
	U Female Reproductive System	X External	D Near Infrared Spectroscopy	5 Meditation
	V Male Reproductive System		Y Other Method	6 Isolation
	W Trunk Region			7 Examination
	X Upper Extremity			8 Suture Removal
	Y Lower Extremity			9 Piercing
	Z None			C Prostate
				D Rectum
				F With Fluoroscopy
				G With Computerized Tomography
				H With Magnetic Resonance Imaging
				Z No Qualifier

9: Chiropractic

W: Anatomical Regions

Operation–Character 3	Body Region–Character 4	Approach–Character 5	Method–Character 6	Qualifier–Character 7
B Manipulation	0 Head	X External	B Non-Manual	Z None
	1 Cervical		C Indirect Visceral	
	2 Thoracic		D Extra-Articular	
	3 Lumbar		F Direct Visceral	
	4 Sacrum		G Long Lever Specific Contact	
	5 Pelvis		H Short Lever Specific Contact	
	6 Lower Extremities		J Long and Short Lever Specific Contact	
	7 Upper Extremities		K Mechanically Assisted	
	8 Rib Cage		L Other Method	
	9 Abdomen			

B: Imaging

Body System–Character 2	Type–Character 3	Contrast–Character 5	Qualifier–Character 6	Qualifier–Character 7
0 Central Nervous System	0 Plain Radiography	0 High Osmolar	0 Unenhanced and Enhanced	0 Intraoperative
2 Heart	1 Fluoroscopy	1 Low Osmolar	1 Laser	1 Densitometry
3 Upper Arteries	2 Computerized Tomography (CT Scan)	Y Other Contrast	Z None	Z None
4 Lower Arteries	3 Magnetic Resonance Imaging (MRI)	Z None		
5 Veins	4 Ultrasonography			
7 Lymphatic System				
8 Eye				
9 Ear, Nose, Mouth and Throat				
B Respiratory System				
D Gastrointestinal System				
F Hepatobiliary System and Pancreas				
G Endocrine System				
H Skin, Subcutaneous Tissue and Breast				
L Connective Tissue				
N Skull and Facial Bones				
P Non-Axial Upper Bones				
Q Non-Axial Lower Bones				
R Axial Skeleton, Except Skull and Facial Bones				
T Urinary System				
U Female Reproductive System				
V Male Reproductive System				
W Anatomical Regions				
Y Fetus and Obstetrical				

B: Imaging

Body Part—Character 4 Meanings

Body System–Character 2		Body Part–Character 4	
0	Central Nervous System	0	Brain
		7	Cisterna
		8	Cerebral Ventricle(s)
		9	Sella Turcica/Pituitary Gland
		B	Spinal Cord
		C	Acoustic Nerves
2	Heart	0	Coronary Artery, Single
		1	Coronary Arteries, Multiple
		2	Coronary Artery Bypass Graft, Single
		3	Coronary Artery Bypass Grafts, Multiple
		4	Heart, Right
		5	Heart, Left
		6	Heart, Right and Left
		7	Internal Mammary Bypass Graft, Right
		8	Internal Mammary Bypass Graft, Left
		B	Heart with Aorta
		C	Pericardium
		D	Pediatric Heart
		F	Bypass Graft, Other
3	Upper Arteries	0	Thoracic Aorta
		1	Brachiocephalic-Subclavian Artery, Right
		2	Subclavian Artery, Left
		3	Common Carotid Artery, Right
		4	Common Carotid Artery, Left
		5	Common Carotid Arteries, Bilateral
		6	Internal Carotid Artery, Right
		7	Internal Carotid Artery, Left
		8	Internal Carotid Arteries, Bilateral
		9	External Carotid Artery, Right
		B	External Carotid Artery, Left
		C	External Carotid Arteries, Bilateral
		D	Vertebral Artery, Right
		F	Vertebral Artery, Left
		G	Vertebral Arteries, Bilateral
		H	Upper Extremity Arteries, Right
		J	Upper Extremity Arteries, Left
		K	Upper Extremity Arteries, Bilateral
		L	Intercostal and Bronchial Arteries
		M	Spinal Arteries
		N	Upper Arteries, Other
		P	Thoraco-Abdominal Aorta
		Q	Cervico-Cerebral Arch
		R	Intracranial Arteries
		S	Pulmonary Artery, Right
		T	Pulmonary Artery, Left
		V	Ophthalmic Arteries

Continued on next page

B: Imaging

Body Part—Character 4 Meanings

Continued from previous page

Body System–Character 2	Body Part–Character 4	
4 Lower Arteries	0	Abdominal Aorta
	1	Celiac Artery
	2	Hepatic Artery
	3	Splenic Arteries
	4	Superior Mesenteric Artery
	5	Inferior Mesenteric Artery
	6	Renal Artery, Right
	7	Renal Artery, Left
	8	Renal Arteries, Bilateral
	9	Lumbar Arteries
	B	Intra-Abdominal Arteries, Other
	C	Pelvic Arteries
	D	Aorta and Bilateral Lower Extremity Arteries
	F	Lower Extremity Arteries, Right
	G	Lower Extremity Arteries, Left
	H	Lower Extremity Arteries, Bilateral
	J	Lower Arteries, Other
	K	Celiac and Mesenteric Arteries
	L	Femoral Artery
	M	Renal Artery Transplant
	N	Penile Arteries
5 Veins	0	Epidural Veins
	1	Cerebral and Cerebellar Veins
	2	Intracranial Sinuses
	3	Jugular Veins, Right
	4	Jugular Veins, Left
	5	Jugular Veins, Bilateral
	6	Subclavian Vein, Right
	7	Subclavian Vein, Left
	8	Superior Vena Cava
	9	Inferior Vena Cava
	B	Lower Extremity Veins, Right
	C	Lower Extremity Veins, Left
	D	Lower Extremity Veins, Bilateral
	F	Pelvic (Iliac) Veins, Right
	G	Pelvic (Iliac) Veins, Left
	H	Pelvic (Iliac) Veins, Bilateral
	J	Renal Vein, Right
	K	Renal Vein, Left
	L	Renal Veins, Bilateral
	M	Upper Extremity Veins, Right
	N	Upper Extremity Veins, Left
	P	Upper Extremity Veins, Bilateral
	Q	Pulmonary Vein, Right
	R	Pulmonary Vein, Left
	S	Pulmonary Veins, Bilateral
	T	Portal and Splanchnic Veins
	V	Veins, Other
	W	Dialysis Shunt/Fistula

Continued on next page

B: Imaging

Body Part—Character 4 Meanings

Continued from previous page

Body System–Character 2		Body Part–Character 4	
7	Lymphatic System	0	Abdominal/Retroperitoneal Lymphatics, Unilateral
		1	Abdominal/Retroperitoneal Lymphatics, Bilateral
		4	Lymphatics, Head and Neck
		5	Upper Extremity Lymphatics, Right
		6	Upper Extremity Lymphatics, Left
		7	Upper Extremity Lymphatics, Bilateral
		8	Lower Extremity Lymphatics, Right
		9	Lower Extremity Lymphatics, Left
		B	Lower Extremity Lymphatics, Bilateral
		C	Lymphatics, Pelvic
8	Eye	0	Lacrimal Duct, Right
		1	Lacrimal Duct, Left
		2	Lacrimal Ducts, Bilateral
		3	Optic Foramina, Right
		4	Optic Foramina, Left
		5	Eye, Right
		6	Eye, Left
		7	Eyes, Bilateral
9	Ear, Nose, Mouth and Throat	0	Ear
		2	Paranasal Sinuses
		4	Parotid Gland, Right
		5	Parotid Gland, Left
		6	Parotid Glands, Bilateral
		7	Submandibular Gland, Right
		8	Submandibular Gland, Left
		9	Submandibular Glands, Bilateral
		B	Salivary Gland, Right
		C	Salivary Gland, Left
		D	Salivary Glands, Bilateral
		F	Nasopharynx/Oropharynx
		G	Pharynx and Epiglottis
		H	Mastoids
		J	Larynx
B	Respiratory System	2	Lung, Right
		3	Lung, Left
		4	Lungs, Bilateral
		6	Diaphragm
		7	Tracheobronchial Tree, Right
		8	Tracheobronchial Tree, Left
		9	Tracheobronchial Trees, Bilateral
		B	Pleura
		C	Mediastinum
		D	Upper Airways
		F	Trachea/Airways
		G	Lung Apices

Continued on next page

Draft (2009)

B: Imaging
Body Part—Character 4 Meanings

Continued from previous page

Body System–Character 2	Body Part–Character 4	
D Gastrointestinal System	1	Esophagus
	2	Stomach
	3	Small Bowel
	4	Colon
	5	Upper GI
	6	Upper GI and Small Bowel
	7	Gastrointestinal Tract
	8	Appendix
	9	Duodenum
	B	Mouth/Oropharynx
	C	Rectum
F Hepatobiliary System and Pancreas	0	Bile Ducts
	1	Biliary and Pancreatic Ducts
	2	Gallbladder
	3	Gallbladder and Bile Ducts
	4	Gallbladder, Bile Ducts and Pancreatic Ducts
	5	Liver
	6	Liver and Spleen
	7	Pancreas
	8	Pancreatic Ducts
	C	Hepatobiliary System, All
G Endocrine System	0	Adrenal Gland, Right
	1	Adrenal Gland, Left
	2	Adrenal Glands, Bilateral
	3	Parathyroid Glands
	4	Thyroid Gland
H Skin, Subcutaneous Tissue and Breast	0	Breast, Right
	1	Breast, Left
	2	Breasts, Bilateral
	3	Single Mammary Duct, Right
	4	Single Mammary Duct, Left
	5	Multiple Mammary Ducts, Right
	6	Multiple Mammary Ducts, Left
	7	Extremity, Upper
	8	Extremity, Lower
	9	Abdominal Wall
	B	Chest Wall
	C	Head and Neck
	D	Subcutaneous Tissue, Head/Neck
	F	Subcutaneous Tissue, Upper Extremity
	G	Subcutaneous Tissue, Thorax
	H	Subcutaneous Tissue, Abdomen and Pelvis
	J	Subcutaneous Tissue, Lower Extremity
L Connective Tissue	0	Connective Tissue, Upper Extremity
	1	Connective Tissue, Lower Extremity
	2	Tendons, Upper Extremity
	3	Tendons, Lower Extremity

Continued on next page

—Character 4 Meanings

Continued from previous page

	Character 2	Body Part–Character 4	
	d Facial Bones	0	Skull
		1	Orbit, Right
		2	Orbit, Left
		3	Orbits, Bilateral
		4	Nasal Bones
		5	Facial Bones
		6	Mandible
		7	Temporomandibular Joint, Right
		8	Temporomandibular Joint, Left
		9	Temporomandibular Joints, Bilateral
		B	Zygomatic Arch, Right
		C	Zygomatic Arch, Left
		D	Zygomatic Arches, Bilateral
		F	Temporal Bones
		G	Tooth, Single
		H	Teeth, Multiple
		J	Teeth, All
P	Non-Axial Upper Bones	0	Sternoclavicular Joint, Right
		1	Sternoclavicular Joint, Left
		2	Sternoclavicular Joints, Bilateral
		3	Acromioclavicular Joints, Bilateral
		4	Clavicle, Right
		5	Clavicle, Left
		6	Scapula, Right
		7	Scapula, Left
		8	Shoulder, Right
		9	Shoulder, Left
		A	Humerus, Right
		B	Humerus, Left
		C	Hand/Finger Joint, Right
		D	Hand/Finger Joint, Left
		E	Upper Arm, Right
		F	Upper Arm, Left
		G	Elbow, Right
		H	Elbow, Left
		J	Forearm, Right
		K	Forearm, Left
		L	Wrist, Right
		M	Wrist, Left
		N	Hand, Right
		P	Hand, Left
		Q	Hands and Wrists, Bilateral
		R	Finger(s), Right
		S	Finger(s), Left
		T	Upper Extremity, Right
		U	Upper Extremity, Left
		V	Upper Extremities, Bilateral
		W	Thorax
		X	Ribs, Right
		Y	Ribs, Left

appendicular

B: Imaging
Body Part—Character 4 Meanings

Continued from previous page

Body System–Character 2	Body Part–Character 4	
Q Non-Axial Lower Bones *(appendicular)*	0	Hip, Right
	1	Hip, Left
	2	Hips, Bilateral
	3	Femur, Right
	4	Femur, Left
	7	Knee, Right
	8	Knee, Left
	9	Knees, Bilateral
	B	Tibia/Fibula, Right
	C	Tibia/Fibula, Left
	D	Lower Leg, Right
	F	Lower Leg, Left
	G	Ankle, Right
	H	Ankle, Left
	J	Calcaneus, Right
	K	Calcaneus, Left
	L	Foot, Right
	M	Foot, Left
	P	Toe(s), Right
	Q	Toe(s), Left
	R	Lower Extremity, Right
	S	Lower Extremity, Left
	V	Patella, Right
	W	Patella, Left
	X	Foot/Toe Joint, Right
	Y	Foot/Toe Joint, Left
R Axial Skeleton, Except Skull and Facial Bones *(central axis)*	0	Cervical Spine
	1	Cervical Disc(s)
	2	Thoracic Disc(s)
	3	Lumbar Disc(s)
	4	Cervical Facet Joint(s)
	5	Thoracic Facet Joint(s)
	6	Lumbar Facet Joint(s)
	7	Thoracic Spine
	8	Thoracolumbar Joint
	9	Lumbar Spine
	B	Lumbosacral Joint
	C	Pelvis
	D	Sacroiliac Joints
	F	Sacrum and Coccyx
	G	Whole Spine
	H	Sternum

Continued on next page

B: Imaging

Body Part—Character 4 Meanings

Continued from previous page

Body System–Character 2	Body Part–Character 4	
T Urinary System	0	Bladder
	1	Kidney, Right
	2	Kidney, Left
	3	Kidneys, Bilateral
	4	Kidneys, Ureters and Bladder
	5	Urethra
	6	Ureter, Right
	7	Ureter, Left
	8	Ureters, Bilateral
	9	Kidney Transplant
	B	Bladder and Urethra
	C	Ileal Diversion Loop
	D	Kidney, Ureter and Bladder, Right
	F	Kidney, Ureter and Bladder, Left
	G	Ileal Loop, Ureters and Kidneys
	J	Kidneys and Bladder
U Female Reproductive System	0	Fallopian Tube, Right
	1	Fallopian Tube, Left
	2	Fallopian Tubes, Bilateral
	3	Ovary, Right
	4	Ovary, Left
	5	Ovaries, Bilateral
	6	Uterus
	8	Uterus and Fallopian Tubes
	9	Vagina
	B	Pregnant Uterus
	C	Uterus and Ovaries
V Male Reproductive System	0	Corpora Cavernosa
	1	Epididymis, Right
	2	Epididymis, Left
	3	Prostate
	4	Scrotum
	5	Testicle, Right
	6	Testicle, Left
	7	Testicles, Bilateral
	8	Vasa Vasorum
	9	Prostate and Seminal Vesicles
	B	Penis

Continued on next page

B: Imaging

Body Part—Character 4 Meanings

Continued from previous page

Body System–Character 2	Body Part–Character 4	
W Anatomical Regions	0	Abdomen
	1	Abdomen and Pelvis
	3	Chest
	4	Chest and Abdomen
	5	Chest, Abdomen and Pelvis
	8	Head
	9	Head and Neck
	B	Long Bones, All
	C	Lower Extremity
	F	Neck
	G	Pelvic Region
	H	Retroperitoneum
	J	Upper Extremity
	K	Whole Body
	L	Whole Skeleton
	M	Whole Body, Infant
	P	Brachial Plexus
Y Fetus and Obstetrical	0	Fetal Head
	1	Fetal Heart
	2	Fetal Thorax
	3	Fetal Abdomen
	4	Fetal Spine
	5	Fetal Extremities
	6	Whole Fetus
	7	Fetal Umbilical Cord
	8	Placenta
	9	First Trimester, Single Fetus
	B	First Trimester, Multiple Gestation
	C	Second Trimester, Single Fetus
	D	Second Trimester, Multiple Gestation
	F	Third Trimester, Single Fetus
	G	Third Trimester, Multiple Gestation

C: Nuclear Medicine

See next page for Character 4 Meanings

Body System–Character 2	Type–Character 3	Radionuclide–Character 5	Qualifier–Character 6	Qualifier–Character 7
0 Central Nervous System	1 Planar Nuclear Medicine Imaging	1 Technetium 99m (Tc-99m)	Z None	Z None
2 Heart	2 Tomographic (Tomo) Nuclear Medicine Imaging	7 Cobalt 58 (Co-58)		
5 Veins	3 Positron Emission Tomographic (PET) Imaging	8 Samarium 153 (Sm-153)		
7 Lymphatic and Hematologic System	4 Nonimaging Nuclear Medicine Uptake	9 Krypton (Kr-81m)		
8 Eye	5 Nonimaging Nuclear Medicine Probe	B Carbon 11 (C-11)		
9 Ear, Nose, Mouth and Throat	6 Nonimaging Nuclear Medicine Assay	C Cobalt 57 (Co-57)		
B Respiratory System	7 Systemic Nuclear Medicine Therapy	D Indium 111 (In-111)		
D Gastrointestinal System		F Iodine 123 (I-123)		
F Hepatobiliary System and Pancreas		G Iodine 131 (I-131)		
G Endocrine System		H Iodine 125 (I-125)		
H Skin, Subcutaneous Tissue and Breast		K Fluorine 18 (F-18)		
P Musculoskeletal System		L Gallium 67 (Ga-67)		
T Urinary System		M Oxygen 15 (O-15)		
V Male Reproductive System		N Phosphorus 32 (P-32)		
W Anatomical Regions		P Strontium 89 (Sr-89)		
		Q Rubidium 82 (Rb-82)		
		R Nitrogen 13 (N-13)		
		S Thallium 201 (Tl-201)		
		T Xenon 127 (Xe-127)		
		V Xenon 133 (Xe-133)		
		W Chromium (Cr-51)		
		Y Other Radionuclide		
		Z None		

C: Nuclear Medicine

Body Part—Character 4 Meanings

Body System–Character 2		Body Part–Character 4	
0	Central Nervous System	0	Brain
		5	Cerebrospinal Fluid
		Y	Central Nervous System
2	Heart	6	Heart, Right and Left
		G	Myocardium
		Y	Heart
5	Veins	B	Lower Extremity Veins, Right
		C	Lower Extremity Veins, Left
		D	Lower Extremity Veins, Bilateral
		N	Upper Extremity Veins, Right
		P	Upper Extremity Veins, Left
		Q	Upper Extremity Veins, Bilateral
		R	Central Veins
		Y	Veins
7	Lymphatic and Hematologic System	0	Bone Marrow
		2	Spleen
		3	Blood
		5	Lymphatics, Head and Neck
		D	Lymphatics, Pelvic
		J	Lymphatics, Head
		K	Lymphatics, Neck
		L	Lymphatics, Upper Chest
		M	Lymphatics, Trunk
		N	Lymphatics, Upper Extremity
		P	Lymphatics, Lower Extremity
		Y	Lymphatic and Hematologic System
8	Eye	9	Lacrimal Ducts, Bilateral
		Y	Eye
9	Ear, Nose, Mouth and Throat	B	Salivary Glands, Bilateral
		Y	Ear, Nose, Mouth and Throat
B	Respiratory System	2	Lungs and Bronchi
		Y	Respiratory System
D	Gastrointestinal System	5	Upper Gastrointestinal Tract
		7	Gastrointestinal Tract
		Y	Digestive System
F	Hepatobiliary System and Pancreas	4	Gallbladder
		5	Liver
		6	Liver and Spleen
		C	Hepatobiliary System, All
		Y	Hepatobiliary System and Pancreas
G	Endocrine System	1	Parathyroid Glands
		2	Thyroid Gland
		4	Adrenal Glands, Bilateral
		Y	Endocrine System
H	Skin, Subcutaneous Tissue and Breast	0	Breast, Right
		1	Breast, Left
		2	Breasts, Bilateral
		Y	Skin, Subcutaneous Tissue and Breast

C: Nuclear Medicine
Body Part—Character 4 Meanings

Continued from previous page

Body System–Character 2		Body Part–Character 4	
P	Musculoskeletal System	1	Skull
		2	Cervical Spine
		3	Skull and Cervical Spine
		4	Thorax
		5	Spine
		6	Pelvis
		7	Spine and Pelvis
		8	Upper Extremity, Right
		9	Upper Extremity, Left
		B	Upper Extremities, Bilateral
		C	Lower Extremity, Right
		D	Lower Extremity, Left
		F	Lower Extremities, Bilateral
		G	Thoracic Spine
		H	Lumbar Spine
		J	Thoracolumbar Spine
		N	Upper Extremities
		P	Lower Extremities
		Y	Musculoskeletal System, Other
		Z	Musculoskeletal System, All
T	Urinary System	3	Kidneys, Ureters and Bladder
		H	Bladder and Ureters
		Y	Urinary System
V	Male Reproductive System	9	Testicles, Bilateral
		Y	Male Reproductive System
W	Anatomical Regions	0	Abdomen
		1	Abdomen and Pelvis
		3	Chest
		4	Chest and Abdomen
		6	Chest and Neck
		B	Head and Neck
		D	Lower Extremity
		G	Thyroid
		J	Pelvic Region
		M	Upper Extremity
		N	Whole Body
		Y	Anatomical Regions, Multiple
		Z	Anatomical Region, Other

D: Radiation Oncology

See next page for Character 4 Meanings

Body System–Character 2	Modality–Character 3	Modality–Qualifier Character 5	Isotope–Character 6	Qualifier–Character 7
0 Central and Peripheral Nervous System	0 Beam Radiation	0 Photons <1 MeV	7 Cesium 137 (Cs-137)	O Intraoperative
7 Lymphatic and Hematologic System	1 Brachytherapy	1 Photons 1 - 10 MeV	8 Iridium 192 (Ir-192)	Z None
8 Eye	2 Stereotactic Radiosurgery	2 Photons >10 MeV	9 Iodine 125 (I-125)	
9 Ear, Nose, Mouth and Throat	Y Other Radiation	3 Electrons	B Palladium 103 (Pd-103)	
B Respiratory System		4 Heavy Particles (Protons,Ions)	C Californium 252 (Cf-252)	
D Gastrointestinal System		5 Neutrons	D Iodine 131 (I-131)	
F Hepatobiliary System and Pancreas		6 Neutron Capture	F Phosphorus 32 (P-32)	
G Endocrine System		7 Contact Radiation	G Strontium 89 (Sr-89)	
H Skin		8 Hyperthermia	H Strontium 90 (Sr-90)	
M Breast		9 High Dose Rate (HDR)	Y Other Isotope	
P Musculoskeletal System		B Low Dose Rate (LDR)	Z None	
T Urinary System		C Intraoperative Radiation Therapy (IORT)		
U Female Reproductive System		D Stereotactic Other Photon Radiosurgery		
V Male Reproductive System		F Plaque Radiation		
W Anatomical Regions		G Isotope Administration		
		H Stereotactic Particulate Radiosurgery		
		J Stereotactic Gamma Beam Radiosurgery		

D. Radiation Oncology

Treatment Site—Character 4 Meanings

Body System–Character 2		Treatment Site–Character 4	
0	Central and Peripheral Nervous System	0	Brain
		1	Brain Stem
		6	Spinal Cord
		7	Peripheral Nerve
7	Lymphatic and Hematologic System	0	Bone Marrow
		1	Thymus
		2	Spleen
		3	Lymphatics, Neck
		4	Lymphatics, Axillary
		5	Lymphatics, Thorax
		6	Lymphatics, Abdomen
		7	Lymphatics, Pelvis
		8	Lymphatics, Inguinal
8	Eye	0	Eye
9	Ear, Nose, Mouth and Throat	0	Ear
		1	Nose
		3	Hypopharynx
		4	Mouth
		5	Tongue
		6	Salivary Glands
		7	Sinuses
		8	Hard Palate
		9	Soft Palate
		B	Larynx
		C	Pharynx
		D	Nasopharynx
		F	Oropharynx
B	Respiratory System	0	Trachea
		1	Bronchus
		2	Lung
		5	Pleura
		6	Mediastinum
		7	Chest Wall
		8	Diaphragm
D	Gastrointestinal System	0	Esophagus
		1	Stomach
		2	Duodenum
		3	Jejunum
		4	Ileum
		5	Colon
		7	Rectum
		8	Anus
F	Hepatobiliary System and Pancreas	0	Liver
		1	Gallbladder
		2	Bile Ducts
		3	Pancreas

Continued on next page

D. Radiation Oncology

Treatment Site—Character 4 Meanings

Continued from previous page

Body System–Character 2	Treatment Site–Character 4	
G	Endocrine System	0	Pituitary Gland
		1	Pineal Body
		2	Adrenal Glands
		4	Parathyroid Glands
		5	Thyroid
H	Skin	2	Skin, Face
		3	Skin, Neck
		4	Skin, Arm
		5	Skin, Hand
		6	Skin, Chest
		7	Skin, Back
		8	Skin, Abdomen
		9	Skin, Buttock
		B	Skin, Leg
		C	Skin, Foot
M	Breast	0	Breast, Left
		1	Breast, Right
P	Musculoskeletal System	0	Skull
		2	Maxilla
		3	Mandible
		4	Sternum
		5	Rib(s)
		6	Humerus
		7	Radius/Ulna
		8	Pelvic Bones
		9	Femur
		B	Tibia/Fibula
		C	Other Bone
T	Urinary System	0	Kidney
		1	Ureter
		2	Bladder
		3	Urethra
U	Female Reproductive System	0	Ovary
		1	Cervix
		2	Uterus
V	Male Reproductive System	0	Prostate
		1	Testis
W	Anatomical Regions	1	Head and Neck
		2	Chest
		3	Abdomen
		4	Hemibody
		5	Whole Body
		6	Pelvic Region

F: Physical Rehabilitation and Diagnostic Audiology

0: Rehabilitation
See next page for Character 5 Meanings

Type–Character 3		Body System–Body Region–Character 4		Equipment Character–6		Qualifier–Character 7	
0	Speech Assessment	0	Neurological System - Head and Neck	1	Audiometer	Z	None
1	Motor and/or Nerve Function Assessment	1	Neurological System - Upper Back / Upper Extremity	2	Sound Field / Booth		
2	Activities of Daily Living Assessment	2	Neurological System - Lower Back / Lower Extremity	4	Electroacoustic Immitance / Acoustic Reflex		
6	Speech Treatment	3	Neurological System - Whole Body	5	Hearing Aid Selection / Fitting / Test		
7	Motor Treatment	4	Circulatory System - Head and Neck	7	Electrophysiologic		
8	Activities of Daily Living Treatment	5	Circulatory System - Upper Back / Upper Extremity	8	Vestibular / Balance		
9	Hearing Treatment	6	Circulatory System - Lower Back / Lower Extremity	9	Cochlear Implant		
B	Cochlear Implant Treatment	7	Circulatory System - Whole Body	B	Physical Agents		
C	Vestibular Treatment	8	Respiratory System - Head and Neck	C	Mechanical		
D	Device Fitting	9	Respiratory System - Upper Back / Upper Extremity	D	Electrotherapeutic		
F	Caregiver Training	B	Respiratory System - Lower Back / Lower Extremity	E	Orthosis		
		C	Respiratory System - Whole Body	F	Assistive, Adaptive, Supportive or Protective		
		D	Integumentary System - Head and Neck	G	Aerobic Endurance and Conditioning		
		F	Integumentary System - Upper Back / Upper Extremity	H	Mechanical or Electromechanical		
		G	Integumentary System - Lower Back / Lower Extremity	J	Somatosensory		
		H	Integumentary System - Whole Body	K	Audiovisual		
		J	Musculoskeletal System - Head and Neck	L	Assistive Listening		
		K	Musculoskeletal System - Upper Back / Upper Extremity	M	Augmentative / Alternative Communication		
		L	Musculoskeletal System - Lower Back / Lower Extremity	N	Biosensory Feedback		
		M	Musculoskeletal System - Whole Body	P	Computer		
		N	Genitourinary System	Q	Speech Analysis		
		Z	None	S	Voice Analysis		
				T	Aerodynamic Function		
				U	Prosthesis		
				V	Speech Prosthesis		
				W	Swallowing		
				X	Cerumen Management		
				Y	Other Equipment		
				Z	None		

F: Physical Rehabilitation and Diagnostic Audiology

0: Rehabilitation

Type Qualifier—Character 5 Meanings

Type–Character 3	Type Qualifier–Character 5
0 Speech Assessment	0 Filtered Speech
	1 Speech Threshold
	2 Speech/Word Recognition
	3 Staggered Spondaic Word
	4 Sensorineural Acuity Level
	5 Synthetic Sentence Identification
	6 Speech and/or Language Screening
	7 Nonspoken Language
	8 Receptive/Expressive Language
	9 Articulation/Phonology
	B Motor Speech
	C Aphasia
	D Fluency
	F Voice
	G Communicative/Cognitive Integration Skills
	H Bedside Swallowing and Oral Function
	J Instrumental Swallowing and Oral Function
	K Orofacial Myofunctional
	L Augmentative/Alternative Communication System
	M Voice Prosthetic
	N Non-invasive Instrumental Status
	P Oral Peripheral Mechanism
	Q Performance Intensity Phonetically Balanced Speech Discrimination
	R Brief Tone Stimuli
	S Distorted Speech
	T Dichotic Stimuli
	V Temporal Ordering of Stimuli
	W Masking Patterns
	X Other Specified Central Auditory Processing
1 Motor and/or Nerve Function Assessment	0 Muscle Performance
	1 Integumentary Integrity
	2 Visual Motor Integration
	3 Coordination/Dexterity
	4 Motor Function
	5 Range of Motion and Joint Integrity
	6 Sensory Awareness/Processing/Integrity
	7 Facial Nerve Function
	8 Neurophysiologic Intraoperative
	9 Somatosensory Evoked Potentials
	B Bed Mobility
	C Transfer
	D Gait and/or Balance
	F Wheelchair Mobility
	G Reflex Integrity

Continued on next page

F: Physical Rehabilitation and Diagnostic Audiology
0: Rehabilitation
Type Qualifier—Character 5 Meanings

Continued from previous page

Type–Character 3	Type Qualifier–Character 5	
2 Activities of Daily Living Assessment	0	Bathing/Showering
	1	Dressing
	2	Feeding/Eating
	3	Grooming/Personal Hygiene
	4	Home Management
	5	Perceptual Processing
	6	Psychosocial Skills
	7	Aerobic Capacity and Endurance
	8	Anthropometric Characteristics
	9	Cranial Nerve Integrity
	B	Environmental, Home and Work Barriers
	C	Ergonomics and Body Mechanics
	D	Neuromotor Development
	F	Pain
	G	Ventilation, Respiration and Circulation
	H	Vocational Activities and Functional Community or Work Reintegration Skills
6 Speech Treatment	0	Nonspoken Language
	1	Speech-Language Pathology and Related Disorders Counseling
	2	Speech-Language Pathology and Related Disorders Prevention
	3	Aphasia
	4	Articulation/Phonology
	5	Aural Rehabilitation
	6	Communicative/Cognitive Integration Skills
	7	Fluency
	8	Motor Speech
	9	Orofacial Myofunctional
	B	Receptive/Expressive Language
	C	Voice
	D	Swallowing Dysfunction
7 Motor Treatment	0	Range of Motion and Joint Mobility
	1	Muscle Performance
	2	Coordination/Dexterity
	3	Motor Function
	4	Wheelchair Mobility
	5	Bed Mobility
	6	Therapeutic Exercise
	7	Manual Therapy Techniques
	8	Transfer Training
	9	Gait Training/Functional Ambulation
8 Activities of Daily Living Treatment	0	Bathing/Showering Techniques
	1	Dressing Techniques
	2	Grooming/Personal Hygiene
	3	Feeding/Eating
	4	Home Management
	5	Wound Management
	6	Psychosocial Skills
	7	Vocational Activities and Functional Community or Work Reintegration Skills

Continued on next page

F: Physical Rehabilitation and Diagnostic Audiology

0: Rehabilitation

Type Qualifier—Character 5 Meanings

Continued from previous page

Type–Character 3		Type Qualifier–Character 5	
9	Hearing Treatment	0	Hearing and Related Disorders Counseling
		1	Hearing and Related Disorders Prevention
		2	Auditory Processing
		3	Cerumen Management
B	Cochlear Implant Treatment	0	Cochlear Implant Rehabilitation
C	Vestibular Treatment	0	Vestibular
		1	Perceptual Processing
		2	Visual Motor Integration
		3	Postural Control
D	Device Fitting	0	Tinnitus Masker
		1	Monaural Hearing Aid
		2	Binaural Hearing Aid
		3	Augmentative/Alternative Communication System
		4	Voice Prosthetic
		5	Assistive Listening Device
		6	Dynamic Orthosis
		7	Static Orthosis
		8	Prosthesis
		9	Assistive, Adaptive, Supportive or Protective Devices
F	Caregiver Training	0	Bathing/Showering Technique
		1	Dressing
		2	Feeding and Eating
		3	Grooming/Personal Hygiene
		4	Bed Mobility
		5	Transfer
		6	Wheelchair Mobility
		7	Therapeutic Exercise
		8	Airway Clearance Techniques
		9	Wound Management
		B	Vocational Activities and Functional Community or Work Reintegration Skills
		C	Gait Training/Functional Ambulation
		D	Application, Proper Use and Care of Assistive, Adaptive, Supportive or Protective Devices
		F	Application, Proper Use and Care of Orthoses
		G	Application, Proper Use and Care of Prosthesis
		H	Home Management
		J	Communication Skills

F: Physical Rehabilitation and Diagnostic Audiology

1: Diagnostic Audiology
See next page for Character 5 Meanings

Type–Character 3	Body System–Body Region–Character 4	Equipment–Character 6	Qualifer–Character 7
3 Hearing Assessment	Z None	0 Occupational Hearing	Z None
4 Hearing Aid Assessment		1 Audiometer	
5 Vestibular Assessment		2 Sound Field / Booth	
		3 Tympanometer	
		4 Electroacoustic Immitance / Acoustic Reflex	
		5 Hearing Aid Selection / Fitting / Test	
		6 Otoacoustic Emission (OAE)	
		7 Electrophysiologic	
		8 Vestibular / Balance	
		9 Cochlear Implant	
		K Audiovisual	
		L Assistive Listening	
		P Computer	
		Y Other Equipment	
		Z None	

Draft (2009)

F: Physical Rehabilitation and Diagnostic Audiology

1: Diagnostic Audiology

Type Qualifier—Character 5 Meanings

Type–Character 3	Type Qualifier–Character 5
3 Hearing Assessment	0 Hearing Screening
	1 Pure Tone Audiometry, Air
	2 Pure Tone Audiometry, Air and Bone
	3 Bekesy Audiometry
	4 Conditioned Play Audiometry
	5 Select Picture Audiometry
	6 Visual Reinforcement Audiometry
	7 Alternate Binaural or Monaural Loudness Balance
	8 Tone Decay
	9 Short Increment Sensitivity Index
	B Stenger
	C Pure Tone Stenger
	D Tympanometry
	F Eustachian Tube Function
	G Acoustic Reflex Patterns
	H Acoustic Reflex Threshold
	J Acoustic Reflex Decay
	K Electrocochleography
	L Auditory Evoked Potentials
	M Evoked Otoacoustic Emissions, Screening
	N Evoked Otoacoustic Emissions, Diagnostic
	P Aural Rehabilitation Status
	Q Auditory Processing
4 Hearing Aid Assessment	0 Cochlear Implant
	1 Ear Canal Probe Microphone
	2 Monaural Hearing Aid
	3 Binaural Hearing Aid
	4 Assistive Listening System/Device Selection
	5 Sensory Aids
	6 Binaural Electroacoustic Hearing Aid Check
	7 Ear Protector Attentuation
	8 Monaural Electroacoustic Hearing Aid Check
5 Vestibular Assessment	0 Bithermal, Bionaural Caloric Irrigation
	1 Bithermal, Monaural Caloric Irrigation
	2 Unithermal Binaural Screen
	3 Oscillating Tracking
	4 Sinusoidal Vertical Axis Rotational
	5 Dix-Hallpike Dynamic
	6 Computerized Dynamic Posturography
	7 Tinnitus Masker

G: Mental Health

Z: Body System—none

Type–Character 3	Type Qualifier – Character 4	Qualifier–Character 5	Qualifier–Character 6	Qualifier–Character 7
1 Psychological Tests	0 Developmental	Z None	Z None	Z None
	1 Personality and Behavioral			
	2 Intellectual and Psychoeducational			
	3 Neuropsychological			
	4 Neurobehavioral and Cognitive Status			
2 Crisis Intervention	Z None			
3 Medication Management	Z None			
5 Individual Psychotherapy	0 Interactive			
	1 Behavioral			
	2 Cognitive			
	3 Interpersonal			
	4 Psychoanalysis			
	5 Psychodynamic			
	6 Supportive			
	8 Cognitive-Behavioral			
	9 Psychophysiological			
6 Counseling	0 Educational			
	1 Vocational			
	3 Other Counseling			
7 Family Psychotherapy	2 Other Family Psychotherapy			
B Electroconvulsive Therapy	0 Unilateral-Single Seizure			
	1 Unilateral-Multiple Seizure			
	2 Bilateral-Single Seizure			
	3 Bilateral-Multiple Seizure			
	4 Other Electroconvulsive Therapy			
C Biofeedback	9 Other Biofeedback			
F Hypnosis	Z None			
G Narcosynthesis	Z None			
H Group Psychotherapy	Z None			
J Light Therapy	Z None			

H: Substance Abuse Treatment

Z: Body System—none

Type–Character 3	Type Qualifier–Character 4	Qualifier–Character 5	Qualifier–Character 6	Qualifier–Character 7
2 Detoxification Services	Z None	Z None	Z None	Z None
3 Individual Counseling	0 Cognitive			
	1 Behavioral			
	2 Cognitive-Behavioral			
	3 12-Step			
	4 Interpersonal			
	5 Vocational			
	6 Psychoeducation			
	7 Motivational Enhancement			
	8 Confrontational			
	9 Continuing Care			
	B Spiritual			
	C Pre/Post-Test Infectious Disease			
4 Group Counseling	0 Cognitive			
	1 Behavioral			
	2 Cognitive-Behavioral			
	3 12-Step			
	4 Interpersonal			
	5 Vocational			
	6 Psychoeducation			
	7 Motivational Enhancement			
	8 Confrontational			
	9 Continuing Care			
	B Spiritual			
	C Pre/Post-Test Infectious Disease			
5 Individual Psychotherapy	0 Cognitive			
	1 Behavioral			
	2 Cognitive-Behavioral			
	3 12-Step			
	4 Interpersonal			
	5 Interactive			
	6 Psychoeducation			
	7 Motivational Enhancement			
	8 Confrontational			
	9 Supportive			
	B Psychoanalysis			
	C Psychodynamic			
	D Psychophysiological			
6 Family Counseling	3 Other Family Counseling			

Z: Body System—none

Type–Character 3	Type Qualifier–Character 4	Qualifier–Character 5	Qualifier–Character 6	Qualifier–Character 7
8 Medication Management	0 Nicotine Replacement			
	1 Methadone Maintenance			
	2 Levo-alpha-acetyl-methadol (LAAM)			
	3 Antabuse			
	4 Naltrexone			
	5 Naloxone			
	6 Clonidine			
	7 Bupropion			
	8 Psychiatric Medication			
	9 Other Replacement Medication			
9 Pharmacotherapy	0 Nicotine Replacement			
	1 Methadone Maintenance			
	2 Levo-alpha-acetyl-methadol (LAAM)			
	3 Antabuse			
	4 Naltrexone			
	5 Naloxone			
	6 Clonidine			
	7 Bupropion			
	8 Psychiatric Medication			
	9 Other Replacement Medication			

Appendix E: Physical Rehabilitation and Diagnostic Audiology Type Qualifier Definitions

F: PHYSICAL REHABILITATION AND DIAGNOSTIC AUDIOLOGY
0: REHABILITATION
0: SPEECH ASSESSMENT

Type Qualifier - Character 5	Includes
0 Filtered Speech	Uses high or low pass filtered speech stimuli to assess central auditory processing disorders, site of lesion testing
1 Speech Threshold	Measures minimal intensity needed to repeat spondaic words
2 Speech/Word Recognition	Measures ability to repeat/identify single syllable words; scores given as a percentage; includes word recognition/speech discrimination
3 Staggered Spondaic Word	Measures central auditory processing site of lesion based upon dichotic presentation of spondaic words
4 Sensorineural Acuity Level	Measures sensorineural acuity masking presented via bone conduction
5 Synthetic Sentence Identification	Measures central auditory dysfunction using identification of third order approximations of sentences and competing messages
6 Speech and/or Language Screening	Identifies need for further speech and/or language evaluation
7 Nonspoken Language	Measures nonspoken language (print, sign, symbols) for communication
8 Receptive/Expressive Language	Measures receptive and expressive language
9 Articulation/Phonology	Measures speech production
B Motor Speech	Measures neurological motor aspects of speech production
C Aphasia	Measures expressive and receptive speech and language function including reading and writing
D Fluency	Measures speech fluency or stuttering
F Voice	Measures vocal structure, function and production
G Communicative/Cognitive Integration Skills	Measures ability to use higher cortical functions. Includes level of arousal, orientation, recognition, attention span, initiation of activity, termination of activity, memory, sequencing, categorizing, concept formation, spatial operations, judgment, problem solving, learning, generalization, and pragmatic communication
H Bedside Swallowing and Oral Function	Bedside swallowing includes assessment of sucking, masticating, coughing, and swallowing. Oral function includes assessment of oropharyngeal musculature for coordinated, controlled movements, aerodigestive structures and functions to determine oral/pharyngeal/respiratory coordination, and oral function for phonation.
J Instrumental Swallowing and Oral Function	Measures swallowing function using instrumental diagnostic procedures (videofluoroscopy, ultrasound, manometry, endoscopy)
K Orofacial Myofunctional	Measures orofacial myofunctional patterns for speech and related functions
L Augmentative/Alternative Communication System	Determines the appropriateness of aids, techniques, symbols, and/or strategies to augment or replace speech and enhance communication. Includes the use of telephones, writing equipment, emergency equipment, and TDD
M Voice Prosthetic	Determines the appropriateness of voice prosthetic/adaptive device to enhance or facilitate communication
N Non-invasive Instrumental Status	Instrumental measures of oral, nasal, vocal, and velopharyngeal functions as they pertain to speech production
P Oral Peripheral Mechanism	Structural measures of face, jaw, lips, tongue, teeth, hard and soft palate, pharynx as related to speech production

Continued on next page

F: PHYSICAL REHABILITATION AND DIAGNOSTIC AUDIOLOGY
0: REHABILITATION
0: SPEECH ASSESSMENT

Continued from previous page

Type Qualifier - Character 5	Includes
R Brief Tone Stimuli	Measures specific central auditory process
S Distorted Speech	Measures specific central auditory process
T Dichotic Stimuli	Measures specific central auditory process
V Temporal Ordering of Stimuli	Measures specific central auditory process
W Masking Patterns	Measures central auditory processing status
X Other Specified Central Auditory Processing	None

F: PHYSICAL REHABILITATION AND DIAGNOSTIC AUDIOLOGY
0: REHABILITATION
1: MOTOR AND/OR NERVE FUNCTION ASSESSMENT

Type Qualifier - Character 5	Includes
0 Muscle Performance	Measures muscle strength, power and endurance using manual testing, dynamometry or computer-assisted electromechanical muscle test; functional muscle strength, power and endurance; muscle pain, tone, or soreness; or pelvic-floor musculature. Muscle endurance refers to the ability to contract a muscle repeatedly over time. (NOTE: EMG coding appears under the Measurement and Monitoring section)
1 Integumentary Integrity	Includes burns, skin conditions, ecchymosis, bleeding, blisters, scar tissue, wounds and other traumas, tissue mobility, turgor and texture
2 Visual Motor Integration	Coordinating the interaction of information from the eyes with body movement during activity
3 Coordination/Dexterity	Measures large and small muscle groups for controlled goal- directed movements. Dexterity includes object manipulation
4 Motor Function	Measures the body's functional and versatile movement patterns. Includes motor assessment scales, analysis of head, trunk and limb movement, and assessment of motor learning
5 Range of Motion and Joint Integrity	Range of Motion is the space, distance or angle through which movement occurs at a joint or series of joints. Joint integrity is the conformance of joints to expected anatomic, biomechanical and kinematic norms. Measures quantity, quality, grade, and classification of joint movement and/or mobility
6 Sensory Awareness/Processing/ Integrity	Includes light touch, pressure, temperature, pain, sharp/dull, proprioception, vestibular, visual, auditory, gustatory, and olfactory
7 Facial Nerve Function	Measures electrical activity of the VIIth cranial nerve (facial nerve)
8 Neurophysiologic Intraoperative	Monitors neural status during surgery
9 Somatosensory Evoked Potentials	Measures neural activity from sites throughout the body
B Bed Mobility	Transitional movement within bed
C Transfer	Transitional movement from one surface to another
D Gait and/or Balance	Measures biomechanical, arthrokinematic and other spatial and temporal characteristics of gait and balance
F Wheelchair Mobility	Measures fit and functional abilities within wheelchair in a variety of environments
G Reflex Integrity	Measures the presence, absence, or exaggeration of developmentally appropriate, pathologic or normal reflexes

F: PHYSICAL REHABILITATION AND DIAGNOSTIC AUDIOLOGY
0: REHABILITATION
2: ACTIVITIES OF DAILY LIVING ASSESSMENT

Type Qualifier - Character 5	Includes
0 Bathing/Showering	Includes obtaining and using supplies; soaping, rinsing, and drying body parts; maintaining bathing position; and transferring to and from bathing positions
1 Dressing	Includes selecting clothing and accessories appropriate to time of day, weather, and occasion; obtaining clothing from storage area; dressing and undressing in a sequential fashion; fastening and adjusting clothing and shoes; and applying and removing personal devices, prosthesis, or orthoses
2 Feeding/Eating	Includes a) Setting up food; selecting and using appropriate utensils and tableware; b) Bringing food or drink to mouth; cleaning face, hands, and clothing; c) Sucking, masticating, coughing and swallowing; assessing the swallowing mechanism in coordination with respiratory function; and management of alternative methods of nourishment
3 Grooming/Personal Hygiene	Includes ability to obtain and use supplies in a sequential fashion: general grooming (removing body hair; applying and removing cosmetics; washing, drying, combing, styling and brushing hair; caring for nails, skin, ears and eyes; and applying deodorant); oral hygiene (obtaining and using supplies; cleaning and reinserting dental orthotics and prosthetics); toilet hygiene (obtaining and using supplies; clothing management; maintaining toilet position; transferring to and from toileting position; cleaning body; and caring for menstrual and continence needs); personal care devices, including care for artificial airways
4 Home Management	Obtaining and maintaining personal and household possessions and environment. Includes clothing care, cleaning, meal preparation and cleanup, shopping, money management, household maintenance, safety procedures, and childcare/parenting
5 Perceptual Processing	Measures stereognosis, kinesthesia, body schema, right-left discrimination, form constancy, position in space, visual closure, figure-ground, depth perception, spatial relations and topographical orientation
6 Psychosocial Skills	The ability to interact in society and to process emotions. Includes psychological (values, interests, self-concept); social (role performance, social conduct, interpersonal skills, self expression); self-management (coping skills, time management, self-control)
7 Aerobic Capacity and Endurance	Measures autonomic responses to positional changes; perceived exertion, dyspnea or angina during activity; performance during exercise protocols; standard vital signs; and blood gas analysis or oxygen consumption
8 Anthropometric Characteristics	Measures edema, body fat composition, height, weight, length and girth
9 Cranial Nerve Integrity	Measures cranial nerve sensory and motor functions, including tastes, smell and facial expression
B Environmental, Home and Work Barriers	Measures current and potential barriers to optimal function, including safety hazards, access problems and home or office design
C Ergonomics and Body Mechanics	Ergonomic measurement of job tasks, work hardening or work conditioning needs; functional capacity; and body mechanics
D Neuromotor Development	Measures motor development, righting and equilibrium reactions, and reflex and equilibrium reactions
F Pain	Measures muscle soreness, pain and soreness with joint movement, and pain perception; includes questionnaires, graphs, symptom magnification scales or visual analog scales
G Ventilation, Respiration and Circulation	Measures adequacy of the ventilatory pump and oxygen uptake and delivery system through thoracoabdominal movements and breathing patterns; ability to clear airway; activities that aggravate or relieve edema, pain, dyspnea or other symptoms; chest wall mobility, expansion and excursion; cardiopulmonary response to performance of ADL and IADL; cough and sputum; standard vital signs; ventilatory muscle strength, power and endurance; pulmonary function and ventilatory mechanics
H Vocational Activities and Functional Community or Work Reintegration Skills	Measures environmental, home, work (job/school/play) barriers that keep patients from functioning optimally in their environment. Includes assessment of vocational skill, abilities and interests; body mechanics; environment of work (job/school/play); injury potential and the need for injury prevention or injury reduction; ergonomic stressors; need for job coaching; need for job simulation, work hardening, or work conditioning; work (job/school/play) performance; public and private transportation skills (including driving ability), and ability to access and use community resources

F: PHYSICAL REHABILITATION AND DIAGNOSTIC AUDIOLOGY
0: REHABILITATION
6: SPEECH TREATMENT

Type Qualifier - Character 5	Includes
0 Nonspoken Language	Applying techniques that improve, augment, or compensate spoken communication
1 Speech-Language Pathology and Related Disorders Counseling	Provides patients/families with information, support, referrals to facilitate recovery from a communication disorder
2 Speech-Language Pathology and Related Disorders Prevention	Applying techniques to avoid or minimize onset and/or development of a communication disorder
3 Aphasia	Applying techniques to improve, augment, or compensate for receptive/ expressive language impairments
4 Articulation/Phonology	Applying techniques to correct, improve, or compensate for speech productive impairment
5 Aural Rehabilitation	Applying techniques to improve the communication abilities associated with hearing loss
6 Communicative/Cognitive Integration Skills	Activities to facilitate the use of higher cortical functions. Includes level of arousal orientation, recognition, attention span, initiation of activity, termination of activity, memory sequencing, categorization, concept formation, spatial operations, judgement and problem solving, learning and generalization, and pragmatic communication
7 Fluency	Applying techniques to improve and augment fluent speech
8 Motor Speech	Applying techniques to improve and augment the impaired neurological motor aspects of speech production
9 Orofacial Myofunctional	Applying techniques to improve, alter, or augment impaired orofacial myofunctional patterns and related speech production errors
B Receptive/Expressive Language	Applying techniques tot improve and augment receptive/expressive language
C Voice	Applying techniques to improve voice and vocal function
D Swallowing Dysfunction	Activities to improve swallowing function in coordination with respiratory function (e.g., sucking, mastication, coughing, swallowing)

F: PHYSICAL REHABILITATION AND DIAGNOSTIC AUDIOLOGY
0: REHABILITATION
7: MOTOR TREATMENT

Type Qualifier - Character 5	Includes
0 Range of Motion and Joint Mobility	Exercise or activities to increase muscle length and joint mobility
1 Muscle Performance	Exercise or activities to increase the capacity of a muscle to do work in terms of strength (the force exerted to overcome resistance in one maximal effort), power (work produced per unit of time, or the product of strength and speed), and/or endurance (the ability to contract a muscle repeatedly over time)
2 Coordination/Dexterity	Exercise or activities to facilitate gross coordination and fine coordination
3 Motor Function	Exercise or activities to facilitate crossing midline, laterality, bilateral integration, praxis, neuromuscular relaxation, inhibition, facilitation, motor function and motor learning
4 Wheelchair Mobility	Parts management, maintenance and controlled operation of a wheelchair, scooter or other device, in and on a variety of surfaces and environments
5 Bed Mobility	Exercise or activities to facilitate transitional movements within bed
6 Therapeutic Exercise	Exercise or activities to facilitate sensory awareness, sensory processing, sensory integration, balance training, conditioning, reconditioning; includes developmental activities, breathing exercises, aerobic endurance activities, aquatic exercises, stretching and ventilatory muscle training
7 Manual Therapy Techniques	Techniques in which the therapist uses his/her hands to administer skilled movements, including connective tissue massage, joint mobilization and manipulation, manual lymph drainage, manual traction, soft tissue mobilization and manipulation and other therapeutic massage
8 Transfer Training	Exercise or activities to facilitate movement from one surface to another
9 Gait Training/Functional Ambulation	Exercise or activities to facilitate ambulation on a variety of surfaces and in a variety of environments

F: PHYSICAL REHABILITATION AND DIAGNOSTIC AUDIOLOGY
0: REHABILITATION
8: ACTIVITIES OF DAILY LIVING TREATMENT

Type Qualifier - Character 5	Includes
0 Bathing/Showering Techniques	Activities to facilitate obtaining and using supplies; soaping, rinsing and drying body parts; maintaining bathing position; and transferring to and from bathing positions
1 Dressing Techniques	Activities to facilitate selecting clothing and accessories appropriate to time of day, weather and occasion; obtaining clothing from storage area; dressing and undressing in a sequential fashion; fastening and adjusting clothing and shoes; applying and removing personal devices, prostheses or orthoses
2 Grooming/Personal Hygiene	Activities to facilitate obtaining and using supplies in a sequential fashion: general grooming (removing body hair; applying and removing cosmetics; washing, drying, combing, styling, and brushing hair; caring for nails, skin, ears and eyes; applying deodorant); oral hygiene (obtaining and using supplies; cleaning mouth; brushing and flossing teeth; or removing, cleaning and reinserting dental orthotics and prosthetics); toilet hygiene (obtaining and using supplies; clothing management; maintaining toileting position; transferring to and from toileting position; cleaning body; and caring for menstrual and other needs); and personal care devices, including care of artificial airways
3 Feeding/Eating	a) Exercise or activities to facilitate setting up food, selecting and using appropriate utensils and tableware b) Bringing food or drink to mouth, cleaning face, hands and clothing c) Sucking, masticating, coughing and swallowing; using swallowing mechanisms in coordination with respiratory function; and management of alternative methods of nourishment
4 Home Management	Activities to facilitate obtaining and maintaining personal household possessions and environment, including clothing care, cleaning, meal preparation and clean-up, shopping, money management, household maintenance, safety procedures, childcare/parenting
5 Wound Management	Includes non-selective and selective debridement (enzymes, autolysis, sharp debridement), dressings (wound coverings, hydrogel, vacuum-assisted closure), topical agents, etc.
6 Psychosocial Skills	The ability to interact in society and to process emotions. Includes psychological (values, interests, self-concept); social (role performance, social conduct, interpersonal skills, self expression); self-management (coping skills, time management, self-control)
7 Vocational Activities and Functional Community or Work Reintegration Skills	Activities to facilitate vocational exploration, body mechanics training, job acquisition, environmental or work (job/school/play) task adaptation, injury prevention, injury reduction, ergonomic stressor reduction, job coaching, job simulation, work hardening, work conditioning, driving training, work (job/school/play) performance, public transportation skills, private transportation skills, and use of community resources

F: PHYSICAL REHABILITATION AND DIAGNOSTIC AUDIOLOGY
0: REHABILITATION
9: HEARING TREATMENT

Type Qualifier - Character 5	Includes
0 Hearing and Related Disorders Counseling	Provides patients/families/caregivers with information, support, referrals to facilitate recovery from a communication disorder; strategies for psychosocial adjustment to hearing loss for clients and families/caregivers
1 Hearing and Related Disorders Prevention	Provides patients/families/caregivers with information and support to prevent communication disorders
2 Auditory Processing	Applying techniques to improve the receiving and processing of auditory information and comprehension of spoken language
3 Cerumen Management	Includes examination of external auditory canal and tympanic membrane and removal of cerumen from external ear canal

F: PHYSICAL REHABILITATION AND DIAGNOSTIC AUDIOLOGY
0: REHABILITATION
B: COCHLEAR IMPLANT TREATMENT

Type Qualifier - Character 5	Includes
0 Cochlear Implant Rehabilitation	Applying techniques to improve the communication abilities of individuals with cochlear implant; includes programming the device, providing patients/families with information

F: PHYSICAL REHABILITATION AND DIAGNOSTIC AUDIOLOGY
0: REHABILITATION
C: VESTIBULAR TREATMENT

Type Qualifier - Character 5	Includes
0 Vestibular	Applying techniques to compensate for balance disorders; includes habituation, exercise therapy, and balance retraining
1 Perceptual Processing	Exercise and activities to facilitate stereognosis, kinesthesia, body schema, right-left discrimination, form constancy, position in space, visual closure, figure-ground, depth perception, spatial relations, and topographical orientation
2 Visual Motor Integration	Exercise or activities to facilitate coordinating the interaction of information from eyes with body movement during activity
3 Postural Control	Exercise or activities to increase postural alignment and control

F: PHYSICAL REHABILITATION AND DIAGNOSTIC AUDIOLOGY
0: REHABILITATION
D: DEVICE FITTING

Type Qualifier - Character 5	Includes
0 Tinnitus Masker	Used to verify physical fit, acoustic appropriateness, and benefit; assists in achieving maximum benefit
1 Monaural Hearing Aid	Assists in achieving maximum understanding and performance
2 Binaural Hearing Aid	Assists in achieving maximum understanding and performance
3 Augmentative/Alternative Communication System	Includes augmentative communication devices and aids
4 Voice Prosthetic	Includes electrolarynx, and other assistive, adaptive, supportive devices
5 Assistive Listening Device	Assists in use of effective and appropriate assistive listening device/system
6 Dynamic Orthosis	Includes customized and prefabricated splints, inhibitory casts, spinal and other braces, and protective devices; allows motion through transfer of movement from other body parts or by use of outside forces
7 Static Orthosis	Includes customized and prefabricated splints, inhibitory casts, spinal and other braces, and protective devices; has no moving parts, maintains joint(s) in desired position
8 Prosthesis	Artificial substitutes for missing body parts, that augment performance or function
9 Assistive, Adaptive, Supportive or Protective Devices	Devices to facilitate or support achievement of a higher level of function in wheelchair mobility; bed mobility; transfer or ambulation ability; bath and showering ability; dressing; grooming; personal hygiene; play or leisure

F: PHYSICAL REHABILITATION AND DIAGNOSTIC AUDIOLOGY
0: REHABILITATION
F: CAREGIVER TRAINING

Type Qualifier - Character 5	Includes
0 Bathing/Showering Technique	None
1 Dressing	None
2 Feeding and Eating	None
3 Grooming/Personal Hygiene	None
4 Bed Mobility	None
5 Transfer	None
6 Wheelchair Mobility	None
7 Therapeutic Exercise	None
8 Airway Clearance Techniques	None
9 Wound Management	None
B Vocational Activities and Functional Community or Work Reintegration Skills	None
C Gait Training/Functional Ambulation	None
D Application, Proper Use and Care of Assistive, Adaptive, Supportive or Protective Devices	None
F Application, Proper Use and Care of Orthoses	None
G Application, Proper Use and Care of Prosthesis	None
H Home Management	None
J Communication Skills	None

F: PHYSICAL REHABILITATION AND DIAGNOSTIC AUDIOLOGY
1: DIAGNOSTIC AUDIOLOGY
3: HEARING ASSESSMENT

Type Qualifier - Character 5	Includes
0 Hearing Screening	Pass/refer measures designed to identify need for further audiologic assessment
1 Pure Tone Audiometry, Air	Air-conduction pure tone threshold measures with appropriate masking
2 Pure Tone Audiometry, Air and Bone	Air-conduction and bone-conduction pure tone threshold measures with appropriate masking
3 Bekesy Audiometry	Uses an instrument that provides a choice of discrete or continuously varying pure tones; choice of pulsed or continuous signal
4 Conditioned Play Audiometry	Behavioral measures using nonspeech and speech stimuli to obtain frequency-specific and ear-specific information on auditory status from the patient; obtains speech reception threshold by having patient point to pictures of spondaic words
5 Select Picture Audiometry	Establishes hearing threshold levels for speech using pictures
6 Visual Reinforcement Audiometry	Behavioral measures using nonspeech and speech stimuli to obtain frequency/ear-specific information on auditory status; includes a conditioned response of looking toward a visual reinforcer (e.g., lights, animated toy) every time auditory stimuli are heard
7 Alternate Binaural or Monaural Loudness Balance	Determines auditory stimulus parameter that yields the same objective sensation; (i.e., intensities that yield same loudness perception)
8 Tone Decay	Measures decrease in hearing sensitivity to a tone; site of lesion test requiring a behavioral response
9 Short Increment Sensitivity Index	Measures the ear's ability to detect small intensity changes; site of lesion test requiring a behavioral response
B Stenger	Measures unilateral nonorganic hearing loss based on simultaneous presentation of signals of differing volume
C Pure Tone Stenger	Measures unilateral nonorganic hearing loss based on simultaneous presentation of pure tones of differing volume
D Tympanometry	Measures the integrity of the middle ear; measures ease at which sound flows through the tympanic membrane while air pressure against the membrane is varied
F Eustachian Tube Function	Measures eustachian tube function and patency of eustachian tube
G Acoustic Reflex Patterns	Defines site of lesion based upon presence/absence of acoustic reflexes with ipsilateral vs. contralateral stimulation
H Acoustic Reflex Threshold	Determines minimal intensity that acoustic reflex occurs with ipsilateral and/or contralateral stimulation
J Acoustic Reflex Decay	Measures reduction in size/strength of acoustic reflex over time. Site of lesion test
K Electrocochleography	Measures the VIIIth cranial nerve action potential
L Auditory Evoked Potentials	Measures electric responses produced by the VIIIth cranial nerve and brainstem following auditory stimulation

F: PHYSICAL REHABILITATION AND DIAGNOSTIC AUDIOLOGY
1: DIAGNOSTIC AUDIOLOGY
3: HEARING ASSESSMENT

Type Qualifier - Character 5	Includes
M Evoked Otoacoustic Emissions, Screening	Measures auditory evoked potentials in a screening format
N Evoked Otoacoustic Emissions, Diagnostic	Measures auditory evoked potentials in a diagnostic format
P Aural Rehabilitation Status	Measures impact of a hearing loss including evaluation of receptive and expressive communication skills
Q Auditory Processing	Evaluates ability to receive and process auditory information and comprehension of spoken language

F: PHYSICAL REHABILITATION AND DIAGNOSTIC AUDIOLOGY
1: DIAGNOSTIC AUDIOLOGY
4: HEARING AID ASSESSMENT

Type Qualifier - Character 5		Includes
0	Cochlear Implant	Measures candidacy for cochlear implant
1	Ear Canal Probe Microphone	Real ear measures
2	Monaural Hearing Aid	Measures the candidacy, effectiveness, and appropriateness of a hearing aid; unilateral fit
3	Binaural Hearing Aid	Measures the candidacy, effectiveness, and appropriateness of a hearing aids; bilateral fit
4	Assistive Listening System/ Device Selection	Measures the effectiveness and appropriateness of assistive listening systems/devices
5	Sensory Aids	Determines the appropriateness of a sensory prosthetic device, other than a hearing aid or assistive listening system/device
6	Binaural Electroacoustic Hearing Aid Check	Determines mechanical and electroacoustic function of bilateral hearing aids using hearing aid test box
7	Ear Protector Attentuation	Measures ear protector fit and effectiveness
8	Monaural Electroacoustic Hearing Aid Check	Determines mechanical and electroacoustic function of one hearing aid using hearing aid test box

F: PHYSICAL REHABILITATION AND DIAGNOSTIC AUDIOLOGY
1: DIAGNOSTIC AUDIOLOGY
5: VESTIBULAR ASSESSMENT

Type Qualifier - Character 5		Includes
0	Bithermal, Binaural Caloric Irrigation	Measures the rhythmic eye movements stimulated by changing the temperature of the vestibular system
1	Bithermal, Monaural Caloric Irrigation	Measures the rhythmic eye movements stimulated by changing the temperature of the vestibular system in one ear
2	Unithermal Binaural Screen	Measures the rhythmic eye movements stimulated by changing the temperature of the vestibular system in both ears using warm water; screening format
3	Oscillating Tracking	Measures ability to visually track
4	Sinusoidal Vertical Axis Rotational	Measures nystagmus following rotation
5	Dix-Hallpike Dynamic	Measures nystagmus following Dix-Hallpike maneuver
6	Computerized Dynamic Posturography	Measures the status of the peripheral and central vestibular system and the sensory/motor component of balance; evaluates the efficacy of vestibular rehabilitation
7	Tinnitus Masker	Determines candidacy for tinnitus masker

Appendix F: Answers to Coding Exercises

Medical Surgical Section

Procedure	Code
Excision of malignant melanoma from skin of right ear	0HB2XZZ
Laparoscopy with excision of endometrial implant from left ovary	0UB14ZZ
Percutaneous needle core biopsy of right kidney	0TB03ZX
EGD with gastric biopsy	0DB68ZX
Open endarterectomy of left common carotid artery	03BJ0ZZ
Excision of basal cell carcinoma of lower lip	0CB1XZZ
Open excision of tail of pancreas	0FBG0ZZ
Percutaneous biopsy of right gastrocnemius muscle	0KBS3ZX
Sigmoidoscopy with sigmoid polypectomy	0DBN8ZZ
Open excision of lesion from right Achilles tendon	0LBN0ZZ
Open resection of cecum	0DTH0ZZ
Total excision of pituitary gland, open	0GT00ZZ
Explantation of left failed kidney, open	0TT10ZZ
Open left axillary total lymphadenectomy	07T60ZZ (*Resection* is coded for cutting out a chain of lymph nodes.)
Laparoscopic-assisted total vaginal hysterectomy	0UT9FZZ
Right total mastectomy, open	0HTT0ZZ
Open resection of papillary muscle	02TD0ZZ (The papillary muscle refers to the heart and is found in the *heart and great vessels* body system.)
Radical retropubic prostatectomy, open	0VT00ZZ
Laparoscopic cholecystectomy	0FT44ZZ
Endoscopic bilateral total maxillary sinusectomy	09TQ4ZZ, 09TR4ZZ
Amputation at right elbow level	0X6B0ZZ
Right below-knee amputation, proximal tibia/fibula	0Y6H0Z1 (The qualifier *high* here means the portion of the tib/fib closest to the knee.)
Fifth ray carpometacarpal joint amputation, left hand	0X6K0Z8 (A *complete* ray amputation is through the carpometacarpal joint.)

Procedure	Code
Right leg and hip amputation through ischium	0Y620ZZ (The *hindquarter* body part includes amputation along any part of the hip bone.)
DIP joint amputation of right thumb	0X6L0Z3 (The qualifier *low* here means through the distal interphalangeal joint.)
Right wrist joint amputation	0X6J0Z0 (Amputation at the wrist joint is actually complete amputation of the hand.)
Trans-metatarsal amputation of foot at left big toe	0Y6N0Z9 (A *partial* amputation is through the shaft of the metatarsal bone.)
Mid-shaft amputation, right humerus	0X680Z2
Left fourth toe amputation, mid-proximal phalanx	0Y6W0Z1 (The qualifier *high* here means anywhere along the proximal phalanx.)
Right above-knee amputation, distal femur	0Y6C0Z3
Cryotherapy of wart on left hand	0H5GXZZ
Percutaneous radiofrequency ablation of right vocal cord lesion	0C5T3ZZ
Left heart catheterization with laser destruction of arrhythmogenic focus, A-V node	02583ZZ
Cautery of nosebleed	095KXZZ
Transurethral endoscopic laser ablation of prostate	0V508ZZ
Cautery of oozing varicose vein, left calf	065Y3ZZ (The approach is coded *percutaneous* because that is the normal route to a vein. No mention is made of approach, because likely the skin has eroded at that spot.)
Laparoscopy with destruction of endometriosis, bilateral ovaries	0U524ZZ
Laser coagulation of right retinal vessel hemorrhage, percutaneous	085G3ZZ (The *retinal vessel* body-part values are in the *eye* body system.)

Procedure	Code
Talc injection pleurodesis, left side	0B5P3ZZ (See section 3, Administration, for applicable injection code.)
Sclerotherapy of brachial plexus lesion, alcohol injection	01533ZZ (See section 3, Administration, for applicable injection code.)
Forceps total mouth extraction, upper and lower teeth	0CDWXZ2, 0CDXXZ2
Removal of left thumbnail	0HDQXZZ (No separate body-part value is given for thumbnail, so this is coded to *fingernail*.)
Extraction of right intraocular lens without replacement, percutaneous	08DJ3ZZ
Laparoscopy with needle aspiration of ova for in vitro fertilization	0UDN4ZZ
Nonexcisional debridement of skin ulcer, right foot	0HDMXZZ
Open stripping of abdominal fascia, right side	0JD80ZZ
Hysteroscopy with D&C, diagnostic	0UDB8ZX
Liposuction for medical purposes, left upper arm	0JDF3ZZ (The *percutaneous* approach is inherent in the liposuction technique.)
Removal of tattered right ear drum fragments with tweezers	09D77ZZ
Microincisional phlebectomy of spider veins, right lower leg	06DY3ZZ
Routine Foley catheter placement	0T9B70Z
Incision and drainage of external perianal abscess	0D9QXZZ
Percutaneous drainage of ascites	0W9G3ZZ (This is drainage of the cavity and not the peritoneal membrane itself.)
Laparoscopy with left ovarian cystotomy and drainage	0U914ZZ
Laparotomy with hepatotomy and drain placement for liver abscess, right lobe	0F9100Z
Right knee arthrotomy with drain placement	0S9C00Z
Removal of foreign body, right cornea	08C8XZZ
Percutaneous mechanical thrombectomy, left brachial artery	03C83ZZ
Esophagogastroscopy with removal of bezoar from stomach	0DC68ZZ

Procedure	Code
Foreign body removal, skin of left thumb	0HCGXZZ (There is no specific value for thumb skin, so the procedure is coded to *hand*.)
Transurethral cystoscopy with removal of bladder stone	0TCB8ZZ
Forceps removal of foreign body in right nostril	09CKXZZ (Nostril is coded to the *nose* body-part value.)
Laparoscopy with excision of old suture from mesentery	0DCV4ZZ
Incision and removal of right lacrimal duct stone	08CX0ZZ
Nonincisional removal of intraluminal foreign body from vagina	0UCG7ZZ (The approach *external* is also a possibility. It is assumed here that since the patient went to the doctor to have the object removed, that it was not in the vaginal orifice.)
Open excision of retained sliver, subcutaneous tissue of left foot	0JCR0ZZ
Extracorporeal shockwave lithotripsy (ESWL), bilateral ureters	0TF6XZZ, 0TF7XZZ (The bilateral ureter body-part value is not available for the root operation *fragmentation,* so the procedures are coded separately.)
Endoscopic Retrograde Cholangiopancreatography (ERCP) with lithotripsy of common bile duct stone	0FF98ZZ (ERCP is performed through the mouth to the biliary system via the duodenum, so the approach value is *via natural or artificial opening endoscopic*.)
Thoracotomy with crushing of pericardial calcifications	02FN0ZZ
Transurethral cystoscopy with fragmentation of bladder calculus	0TFB8ZZ
Hysteroscopy with intraluminal lithotripsy of left fallopian tube calcification	0UF68ZZ
Division of right foot tendon, percutaneous	0L8V3ZZ
Left heart catheterization with division of bundle of HIS	02883ZZ
Open osteotomy of capitate, left hand	0P8N0ZZ (The capitate is one of the carpal bones of the hand.)
EGD with esophagotomy of esophagogastric junction	0D848ZZ

Procedure	Code
Sacral rhizotomy for pain control, percutaneous	018R3ZZ
Laparotomy with exploration and adhesiolysis of right ureter	0TN60ZZ
Incision of scar contracture, right elbow	0HNDXZZ (The skin of the elbow region is coded to *lower arm*.)
Frenulotomy for treatment of tongue-tie syndrome	0CN7XZZ (The frenulum is coded to the body-part value *tongue*.)
Right shoulder arthroscopy with coracoacromial ligament release	0MN14ZZ
Mitral valvulotomy for release of fused leaflets, open approach	02NG0ZZ
Percutaneous left Achilles tendon release	0LNP3ZZ
Laparoscopy with lysis of peritoneal adhesions	0DNW4ZZ
Manual rupture of right shoulder joint adhesions under general anesthesia	0RNJXZZ
Open posterior tarsal tunnel release	01NG0ZZ (The nerve released in the posterior tarsal tunnel is the tibial nerve.)
Laparoscopy with freeing of left ovary and fallopian tube	0UN14ZZ, 0UN64ZZ
Liver transplant with donor matched liver	0FY00Z0
Orthotopic heart transplant using porcine heart	02YA0Z2 (The donor heart comes from an animal [pig], so the qualifier value is *zooplastic.*)
Right lung transplant, open, using organ donor match	0BYK0Z0
Left kidney/pancreas organ bank transplant	0FYG0Z0, 0TY10Z0
Replantation of avulsed scalp	0HM0XZZ
Reattachment of severed right ear	09M0XZZ
Reattachment of traumatic left gastrocnemius avulsion, open	0KMT0ZZ
Closed replantation of three avulsed teeth, lower jaw	0CMXXZ1
Reattachment of severed left hand	0XMK0ZZ
Right hand open palmaris longus tendon transfer	0LX70ZZ
Endoscopic radial to median nerve transfer	01X64Z5
Fasciocutaneous flap closure of left thigh, open	0JXM0ZC (The qualifier identifies the body layers in addition to fascia included in the procedure.)
Transfer left index finger to left thumb position, open	0XXP0ZM

Procedure	Code
Percutaneous fascia transfer to fill defect, anterior neck	0JX43ZZ
Trigeminal to facial nerve transfer, percutaneous endoscopic	00XK4ZM
Endoscopic left leg flexor hallucis longus tendon transfer	0LXP4ZZ
Right scalp advancement flap to right temple	0HX0XZZ
Bilateral TRAM pedicle flap reconstruction status post mastectomy, muscle only, open	0KXK0Z6, 0KXL0Z6 (The transverse rectus abdominus muscle (TRAM) flap is coded for each flap developed.)
Skin transfer flap closure of complex open wound, left lower back	0HX6XZZ
Open fracture reduction, right tibia	0QSG0ZZ
Laparoscopy with gastropexy for malrotation	0DS64ZZ
Left knee arthroscopy with reposition of anterior cruciate ligament	0MSP4ZZ
Open transposition of ulnar nerve	01S40ZZ
Closed reduction with percutaneous internal fixation of right femoral neck fracture	0QS634Z
Trans-vaginal intraluminal cervical cerclage	0UVC7DZ
Thoracotomy with banding of left pulmonary artery using extraluminal device	02VR0CZ
Restriction of thoracic duct with intraluminal stent, percutaneous	07VK3DZ
Craniotomy with clipping of cerebral aneurysm	03VG0CZ (The clip is placed lengthwise on the outside wall of the widened portion of the vessel.)
Nonincisional, trans-nasal placement of restrictive stent in right lacrimal duct	08VX7DZ
Percutaneous ligation of esophageal vein	06L33ZZ
Percutaneous embolization of left internal carotid-cavernous fistula	03LL3DZ
Laparoscopy with bilateral occlusion of fallopian tubes using Hulka extraluminal clips	0UL74CZ
Open suture ligation of failed AV graft, left brachial artery	03L80ZZ
Percutaneous embolization of vascular supply, intracranial meningioma	03LG3DZ
ERCP with balloon dilation of common bile duct	0F798ZZ

Procedure	Code	Procedure	Code
PTCA of two coronary arteries, LAD with stent placement, RCA with no stent	02703DZ, 02703ZZ (A separate procedure is coded for each artery dilated, since the device value differs for each artery.)	Percutaneous placement of Swan-Ganz catheter in superior vena cava	02HV32Z (The Swan-Ganz catheter is coded to the device value *monitoring device* because it monitors pulmonary artery output.)
Cystoscopy with intraluminal dilation of bladder neck stricture	0T7C8ZZ	Bronchoscopy with insertion of brachytherapy seeds, right main bronchus	0BH081Z
Open dilation of old anastomosis, left femoral artery	047L0ZZ	Placement of intrathecal infusion pump for pain management, percutaneous	0JH73VZ (The device resides principally in the subcutaneous tissue of the back, so it is coded to body system J.)
Dilation of upper esophageal stricture, direct visualization, with Bougie sound	0D717ZZ		
PTA of right brachial artery stenosis	03773ZZ		
Transnasal dilation and stent placement in right lacrimal duct	087X7DZ		
Hysteroscopy with balloon dilation of bilateral fallopian tubes	0U778ZZ	Open placement of bone growth stimulator, left femoral shaft	0QHY0MZ
Tracheoscopy with intraluminal dilation of tracheal stenosis	0B718ZZ	Cystoscopy with placement of brachytherapy seeds in prostate gland	0VH081Z
Cystoscopy with dilation of left ureteral stricture, with stent placement	0T778DZ	Full-thickness skin graft to right lower arm, autograft (do not code graft harvest for this exercise)	0HRDX73
Open gastric bypass with Roux-en-Y limb to jejunum	0D160ZA	Excision of necrosed left femoral head with bone bank bone graft to fill the defect, open	0QR70KZ
Right temporal artery to intracranial artery bypass using Gore-Tex graft, open	031S0JG	Penetrating keratoplasty of right cornea with donor matched cornea, percutaneous approach	08R83KZ
Tracheostomy formation with tracheostomy tube placement, percutaneous	0B113F4	Bilateral mastectomy with concomitant saline breast implants, open	0HRV0JZ
PICVA (percutaneous in situ coronary venous arterialization) of single coronary artery	02103D4	Excision of abdominal aorta with Gore-Tex graft replacement, open	04R00JZ
Open left femoral-popliteal artery bypass using cadaver vein graft	041L0KL	Total right knee arthroplasty with insertion of total knee prosthesis	0SRC0JZ
Shunting of intrathecal cerebrospinal fluid to peritoneal cavity using synthetic shunt	00160J6	Bilateral mastectomy with free TRAM flap reconstruction	0HRV076
Colostomy formation, open, transverse colon to abdominal wall	0D1L0Z4	Tenonectomy with graft to right ankle using cadaver graft, open	0LRS0KZ
Open urinary diversion, left ureter, using ileal conduit to skin	0T170ZC	Mitral valve replacement using porcine valve, open	02RG08Z
CABG of LAD using left internal mammary artery, open off-bypass	02100Z9	Percutaneous phacoemulsification of right eye cataract with prosthetic lens insertion	08RJ3JZ
Open pleuroperitoneal shunt, right pleural cavity, using synthetic device	0W190JG	Aortic valve annuloplasty using ring, open	02UF07Z
Percutaneous insertion of spinal neurostimulator lead, lumbar spinal cord	00HY3MZ	Laparoscopic repair of left inguinal hernia with marlex plug	0YU64JZ
Percutaneous placement of pacemaker lead in left atrium	02H73MZ	Autograft nerve graft to right median nerve, percutaneous endoscopic (do not code graft harvest for this exercise)	01U547Z
Open placement of dual chamber pacemaker generator in chest wall	0JH60P2	Exchange of liner in femoral component of previous left hip replacement, open approach	0SUB09B
Percutaneous placement of venous central line in right internal jugular	05HM33Z	Anterior colporrhaphy with polypropylene mesh reinforcement, open approach	0UUG0JZ
Open insertion of multiple channel cochlear implant, left ear	09HE0S3		

Procedure	Code
Implantation of CorCap cardiac support device, open approach	02UA0JZ
Abdominal wall herniorrhaphy, open, using synthetic mesh	0WUF0JZ
Tendon graft to strengthen injured left shoulder using autograft, open (do not code graft harvest for this exercise)	0LU207Z
Onlay lamellar keratoplasty of left cornea using autograft, external approach	08U9X7Z
Resurfacing procedure on right femoral head, open approach	0SU90BB
Exchange of drainage tube from right hip joint	0S2YX0Z
Tracheostomy tube exchange	0B21XFZ
Change chest tube for left pneumothorax	0W2BX0Z
Exchange of cerebral ventriculostomy drainage tube	0020X0Z
Foley urinary catheter exchange	0T2BX0Z (This is coded to *drainage device* because urine is being drained.)
Open removal of lumbar sympathetic neurostimulator	01PY0MZ
Nonincisional removal of Swan-Ganz catheter from right pulmonary artery	02PYX2Z
Laparotomy with removal of pancreatic drain	0FPG00Z
Extubation, endotracheal tube	0BP1XEZ
Nonincisional PEG tube removal	0DP6XUZ
Transvaginal removal of extraluminal cervical cerclage	0UPD7CZ
Incision with removal of K-wire fixation, right first metatarsal	0QPN04Z
Cystoscopy with retrieval of left ureteral stent	0TP98DZ
Removal of nasogastric drainage tube for decompression	0DP6X0Z
Removal of external fixator, left radial fracture	0PPJX5Z
Reposition of Swan-Ganz catheter insertion in superior vena cava	02WYX2Z
Open revision of right hip replacement, with readjustment of prosthesis	0SW90JZ
Adjustment of position, pacemaker lead in left ventricle, percutaneous	02WA3MZ
External repositioning of Foley catheter to bladder	0TWBX0Z
Revision of VAD reservoir placement in chest wall, causing patient discomfort, open	0JWT0WZ
Thoracotomy with exploration of right pleural cavity	0WJ90ZZ
Diagnostic laryngoscopy	0CJS8ZZ
Exploratory arthrotomy of left knee	0SJD0ZZ
Colposcopy with diagnostic hysteroscopy	0UJ98ZZ
Digital rectal exam	0DJP7ZZ

Procedure	Code
Diagnostic arthroscopy of right shoulder	0RJJ4ZZ
Endoscopy of bilateral maxillary sinus	09JQ4ZZ, 09JR4ZZ
Laparotomy with palpation of liver	0FJ00ZZ
Transurethral diagnostic cystoscopy	0TJB8ZZ
Colonoscopy, abandoned at sigmoid colon	0DJN8ZZ
Percutaneous mapping of basal ganglia	00K83ZZ
Heart catheterization with cardiac mapping	02K83ZZ
Intraoperative whole brain mapping via craniotomy	00K00ZZ
Mapping of left cerebral hemisphere, percutaneous endoscopic	00K74ZZ
Intraoperative cardiac mapping during open heart surgery	02K80ZZ
Hysteroscopy with cautery of post-hysterectomy oozing and evacuation of clot	0W3R8ZZ
Open exploration and ligation of post-op arterial bleeder, left forearm	0X3F0ZZ
Control of post-operative retroperitoneal bleeding via laparotomy	0W3H0ZZ
Reopening of thoracotomy site with drainage and control of post-op hemopericardium	0W3C0ZZ
Arthroscopy with drainage of hemarthrosis at previous operative site, right knee	0Y3F4ZZ
Radiocarpal fusion of left hand with internal fixation, open	0RGP04Z
Posterior spinal fusion at L1-L3 level with BAK cage interbody fusion device, open	0SG1041
Intercarpal fusion of right hand with bone bank bone graft, open	0RGQ0KZ
Sacrococcygeal fusion with bone graft from same operative site, open	0SG507Z
Interphalangeal fusion of left great toe, percutaneous pin fixation	0SGQ34Z
Suture repair of left radial nerve laceration	01Q60ZZ (The approach value is *open*, though the surgical exposure may have been created by the wound itself.)
Laparotomy with suture repair of blunt force duodenal laceration	0DQ90ZZ
Perineoplasty with repair of old obstetric laceration, open	0WQN0ZZ
Suture repair of right biceps tendon laceration, open	0LQ30ZZ
Closure of abdominal wall stab wound	0WQF0ZZ
Cosmetic face lift, open, no other information available	0W020ZZ

Procedure	Code
Bilateral breast augmentation with silicone implants, open	0H0V0JZ
Cosmetic rhinoplasty with septal reduction and tip elevation using local tissue graft, open	090K07Z
Abdominoplasty (tummy tuck), open	0W0F0ZZ
Liposuction of bilateral thighs	0J0L3ZZ, 0J0M3ZZ
Creation of penis in female patient using tissue bank donor graft	0W4N0K1
Creation of vagina in male patient using synthetic material	0W4M0J0

Obstetrics

Procedure	Code
Abortion by dilation and evacuation following laminaria insertion	10A07ZW
Manually assisted spontaneous abortion	10E0XZZ (Since the pregnancy was not artificially terminated, this is coded to *delivery* because it captures the procedure objective. The fact that it was an abortion will be identified in the diagnosis coding.)
Abortion by abortifacient insertion	10A07ZX
Bimanual pregnancy examination	10J07ZZ
Extraperitoneal C-section, low transverse incision	10D00Z2
Fetal spinal tap, percutaneous	10903ZA
Fetal kidney transplant, laparoscopic	10Y04ZS
Open in utero repair of congenital diaphragmatic hernia	10Q00ZK (Diaphragm is classified to the *respiratory* body system in the "Medical and Surgical" section.)
Laparoscopy with total excision of tubal pregnancy	10T24ZZ
Transvaginal removal of fetal monitoring electrode	10P073Z

Placement

Procedure	Code
Placement of packing material, right ear	2Y42X5Z
Mechanical traction of entire left leg	2W6MX0Z
Removal of splint, right shoulder	2W5AX1Z
Placement of neck brace	2W32X3Z
Change of vaginal packing	2Y04X5Z
Packing of wound, chest wall	2W44X5Z
Sterile dressing placement to left groin region	2W27X4Z
Removal of packing material from pharynx	2Y50X5Z
Placement of intermittent pneumatic compression device, covering entire right arm	2W18X7Z
Exchange of pressure dressing to left thigh	2W0PX6Z

Administration

Procedure	Code
Peritoneal dialysis via indwelling catheter	3E1M39Z
Transvaginal artificial insemination	3E0P7LZ
Infusion of total parenteral nutrition via central venous catheter	3E0436Z
Esophagogastroscopy with Botox injection into esophageal sphincter	3E0G8GC (Botulinum toxin is a paralyzing agent with temporary effects; it does not sclerose or destroy the nerve.)
Percutaneous irrigation of knee joint	3E1U38Z
Epidural injection of mixed steroid and local anesthetic for pain control	3E0S33Z (This is coded to the substance value *anti-inflammatory*. The anesthetic is added only to lessen the pain of the injection.)
Chemical pleurodesis using injection of tetracycline	3E0L3TZ
Transfusion of antihemophilic factor, (nonautologous) via arterial central line	30263V1
Transabdominal in vitro fertilization, implantation of donor ovum	3E0P3Q1
Autologous bone marrow transplant via central venous line	30243G0

Measurement and Monitoring

Procedure	Code
Cardiac stress test, single measurement	4A02XM4
EGD with biliary flow measurement	4A0C85Z
Temperature monitoring, rectal	4A1G7KZ
Peripheral venous pulse, external, single measurement	4A04XJ1
Holter monitoring	4A12X45
Respiratory rate, external, single measurement	4A09XCZ
Fetal heart rate monitoring, transvaginal	4A1H7CZ
Visual mobility test, single measurement	4A07X7Z
Pulmonary artery wedge pressure monitoring from Swan-Ganz catheter	4A133B3
Olfactory acuity test, single measurement	4A08X0Z

Extracorporeal Assistance and Performance

Procedure	Code
Mechanical ventilation, 16 hours	5A1935Z
Liver dialysis, single encounter	5A1C00Z
Cardiac countershock with successful conversion to sinus rhythm	5A2204Z
IPPB (intermittent positive pressure breathing) for mobilization of secretions, 22 hours	5A09358
Renal dialysis, series of encounters	5A1D60Z
IABP (intra-aortic balloon pump) continuous	5A02210
Intra-operative cardiac pacing, continuous	5A1223Z
ECMO (extracorporeal membrane oxygenation), continuous	5A15223
Controlled mechanical ventilation (CMV), 45 hours	5A1945Z
Pulsatile compression boot with intermittent inflation	5A02115 (This is coded to the function value *cardiac output*, because the purpose of such compression devices is to return blood to the heart faster.)

Extracorporeal Therapies

Procedure	Code
Donor thrombocytapheresis, single encounter	6A550Z2
Bili-lite UV phototherapy, series treatment	6A801ZZ
Whole body hypothermia, single treatment	6A4G0ZZ
Circulatory phototherapy, single encounter	6A650ZZ
Shock wave therapy of plantar fascia, single treatment	6A930ZZ
Antigen-free air conditioning, series treatment	6A0G1ZZ
TMS (transcranial magnetic stimulation), series treatment	6A221ZZ
Therapeutic ultrasound of peripheral vessels, single treatment	6A750ZZ
Plasmapheresis, series treatment	6A551Z3
Extracorporeal electromagnetic stimulation (EMS) for urinary incontinence, single treatment	6A210ZZ

Osteopathic

Procedures	Code
Isotonic muscle energy treatment of right leg	7W06X8Z
Low velocity-high amplitude osteopathic treatment of head	7W00X5Z
Lymphatic pump osteopathic treatment of left axilla	7W07X6Z
Indirect osteopathic treatment of sacrum	7W04X4Z
Articulatory osteopathic treatment of cervical region	7W01X0Z

Other Procedures

Procedure	Code
Near infrared spectroscopy of leg vessels	8E023DZ
CT computer assisted sinus surgery	8E09XBG
Suture removal, abdominal wall	8E0WXY8
Isolation after infectious disease exposure	8E0ZXY6
Robotic assisted open prostatectomy	8E0W0CZ

Chiropractic

Procedure	Code
Chiropractic treatment of lumbar region using long lever specific contact	9WB3XGZ
Chiropractic manipulation of abdominal region, indirect visceral	9WB9XCZ
Chiropractic extra-articular treatment of hip region	9WB6XDZ
Chiropractic treatment of sacrum using long and short lever specific contact	9WB4XJZ
Mechanically-assisted chiropractic manipulation of head	9WB0XKZ

Imaging

Procedure	Code
Noncontrast CT of abdomen and pelvis	BW21ZZZ
Ultrasound guidance for catheter placement, left subclavian artery	B342ZZZ
Chest x-ray, AP/PA and lateral views	BW03ZZZ
Endoluminal ultrasound of gallbladder and bile ducts	BF43ZZZ
MRI of thyroid gland, contrast unspecified	BG34YZZ
Esophageal videofluoroscopy study with oral barium contrast	BD11YZZ
Portable x-ray study of right radius/ulna shaft, standard series	BP0JZZZ
Routine fetal ultrasound, second trimester twin gestation	BY4DZZZ
CT scan of bilateral lungs, high osmolar contrast with densitometry	BB240ZZ
Fluoroscopic guidance for percutaneous transluminal angioplasty (PTA) of left common femoral artery, low osmolar contrast	B41G1ZZ

Nuclear Medicine

Procedure	Code
Tomo scan of right and left heart, unspecified radiopharmaceutical, qualitative gated rest	C226YZZ
Technetium pentetate assay of kidneys, ureters, and bladder	CT631ZZ
Uniplanar scan of spine using technetium oxidronate, with first-pass study	CP151ZZ
Thallous chloride tomographic scan of bilateral breasts	CH22SZZ
PET scan of myocardium using rubidium	C23GQZZ
Gallium citrate scan of head and neck, single plane imaging	CW1BLZZ
Xenon gas nonimaging probe of brain	C050VZZ
Upper GI scan, radiopharmaceutical unspecified, for gastric emptying	CD15YZZ
Carbon 11 PET scan of brain with quantification	C030BZZ
Iodinated albumin nuclear medicine assay, blood plasma volume study	C763HZZ

Radiation Oncology

Procedure	Code
Plaque radiation of left eye, single port	D8Y0FZZ
8 MeV photon beam radiation to brain	D0011ZZ
IORT of colon, 3 ports	DDY5CZZ
HDR brachytherapy of prostate using palladium-103	DV109BZ
Electron radiation treatment of right breast, with custom device	DM013ZZ
Hyperthermia oncology treatment of pelvic region	DWY68ZZ
Contact radiation of tongue	D9Y57ZZ
Heavy particle radiation treatment of pancreas, four risk sites	DF034ZZ
LDR brachytherapy to spinal cord using iodine	D016B9Z
Whole body Phosphorus 32 administration with risk to hematopoetic system	DWY5GFZ

Physical Rehabilitation and Diagnostic Audiology

Procedure	Code
Bekesy assessment using audiometer	F13Z31Z
Individual fitting of left eye prosthesis	F0DZ8UZ
Physical therapy for range of motion and mobility, patient right hip, no special equipment	F07L0ZZ
Bedside swallow assessment using assessment kit	F00ZHYZ
Caregiver training in airway clearance techniques	F0FZ8ZZ
Application of short arm cast in rehabilitation setting	F0DZ7EZ (Inhibitory cast is listed in the equipment reference table under E, *orthosis*.)
Verbal assessment of patient's pain level	F02ZFZZ
Caregiver training in communication skills using manual communication board	F0FZJMZ (Manual communication board is listed in the equipment reference table under M, *augmentative/ alternative communication.*)
Group musculoskeletal balance training exercises, whole body, no special equipment	F07M6ZZ (Balance training is included in the motor treatment reference table under *therapeutic exercise.*)
Individual therapy for auditory processing using tape recorder	F09Z2KZ (Tape recorder is listed in the equipment reference table under *audiovisual equipment.*)

Mental Health

Procedure	Code
Cognitive-behavioral psychotherapy, individual	GZ58ZZZ
Narcosynthesis	GZGZZZZ
Light therapy	GZJZZZZ
ECT (electroconvulsive therapy), unilateral, multiple seizure	GZB1ZZZ
Crisis intervention	GZ2ZZZZ
Neuropsychological testing	GZ13ZZZ
Hypnosis	GZFZZZZ
Developmental testing	GZ10ZZZ
Vocational counseling	GZ61ZZZ
Family psychotherapy	GZ72ZZZ

Substance Abuse Treatment

Procedure	Code
Naltrexone treatment for drug dependency	HZ94ZZZ
Substance abuse treatment family counseling	HZ63ZZZ
Medication monitoring of patient on methadone maintenance	HZ81ZZZ
Individual interpersonal psychotherapy for drug abuse	HZ54ZZZ
Patient in for alcohol detoxification treatment	HZ2ZZZZ
Group motivational counseling	HZ47ZZZ
Individual 12-step psychotherapy for substance abuse	HZ53ZZZ
Post-test infectious disease counseling for IV drug abuser	HZ3CZZZ
Psychodynamic psychotherapy for drug dependent patient	HZ5CZZZ
Group cognitive-behavioral counseling for substance abuse	HZ42ZZZ